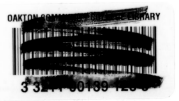

THE BEAT GENERATION

A Gale Critical Companion

THE BEAT GENERATION

GENERATION

A Gale Critical Companion

Volume 3: Authors I-Z

Foreword by **Anne Waldman**
Distinguished Professor of Poetics
The Jack Kerouac School of Disembodied Poetics, Naropa University

Lynn M. Zott, Project Editor

GALE®

THOMSON

GALE

Detroit • New York • San Diego • San Francisco • Cleveland • New Haven, Conn. • Waterville, Maine • London • Munich

The Beat Generation, Vol. 3

Project Editor
Lynn M. Zott

Editorial
Jessica Bomarito, Tom Burns, Jenny Cromie, Elisabeth Gellert, Edna M. Hedblad, Jeffrey W. Hunter, Justin Karr, Michelle Kazensky, Jelena Krstović, Michelle Lee, Allison McClintic Marion, Ellen McGeagh, Linda Pavlovski, Thomas J. Schoenberg, Russel Whitaker

Research
Nicodemus Ford, Sarah Genik, Barbara McNeil, Tamara C. Nott, Gary Oudersluys, Tracie A. Richardson

Editorial Support Services
Mark Hefner

Permissions
Edna Hedblad, Lori Hines

Imaging and Multimedia
Lezlie Light, Kelly A. Quin, Luke Rademacher

Product Design
Pamela Galbreath, Michael Logusz

Composition and Electronic Capture
Carolyn Roney

Manufacturing
Stacy L. Melson

LIBRARY OF CONGRESS CATALOGING-IN-PUBLICATION DATA

Zott, Lynn M. (Lynn Marie), 1969-
    The beat generation : a Gale critical companion / Lynn M. Zott.
       p. cm. -- (Gale critical companion collection)
    Includes bibliographical references and index.
    ISBN 0-7876-7569-5 (hardcover set) -- ISBN 0-7876-7570-9 (v. 1) --
    ISBN 0-7876-7571-7 (v. 2) -- ISBN 0-7876-7572-5 (v. 3)
    1. American literature--20th century--History and criticism. 2. Beat
generation. I. Title. II. Series.
    PS228.B6Z68 2003
    810.9'0054--dc21
                                                    2002155786

Printed in the United States of America
10 9 8 7 6 5 4 3 2 1

CONTENTS

VOLUME 1

VOLUME 2

VOLUME 3

In a recent class I taught at the Jack Kerouac School of Disembodied Poetics entitled "Liberation Now!," students fretted over the cultural imperialism and condescension of various "moderns"—Ezra Pound, William Carlos Williams, and the mad Antonin Artaud as well as the privileged lifestyle of independently "wealthy" Gertrude Stein and H. D. who could afford a "room of one's own" in Virginia Woolf's apt phrase. There was the sense of the white male gaze toward the Balinese and Tarahumara cultures, in the case of Artaud, and of Pound's dabbling with the Noh theatre of Japan and the troubadour tradition, not to mention his problematic anti-semitism. Was "orientalism" the problem here, exoticizing the problematic "other?" I tried to give some historical context and expressed my own gratitude as a writer to the investigative nature, in particular, of Pound's passionate magpie scholarship and how he had championed James Joyce (another sexist?) and T. S. Eliot and opened the floodgates for contemporary poets back into the beauties and exquisite lineaments of the past. Reinventing Chinese poetry, just one example, for our time. William Carlos Williams's "Beautiful Thing" had also been called into question in its objectification of women.

Was there an "internalized repression" going on in Stein's own anti-semitism? Or H. D.'s artistocratic classicism? Was there a reach for the heights of Olympus? A rejection of American democratic values? My advice was: Read the work, use your heads, don't respond with knee-jerk superficial assumptions or clichéd political correctness. It's a complicated world, it's a complicated time. Be investigative, go deeper, see the subtlety of the work, understand "influence," lineage, and also the radical departure from Victorian "official"—and mostly stultifying— "verse."

But I shuddered to think of the discourse we would have around certain so-called Beat writers, known superficially for macho views presented in particular writings: the sexism of Jack Kerouac in *On The Road*; the misogyny of William S. Burroughs in *The Wild Boys*. Was it up to me to contextualize, apologize, get defensive? I had personally seen "beyond" these mindsets in the work and in my own personal experience of these writers. And I had benefited from the liberating quality of the thinking, the imagination, the radical moves of their language and grammar. Just as Marcel Proust and James Joyce and Gertrude Stein had provoked a serious probe and delight in consciousness, pursued a grammar of thinking, as it were, Burroughs and Kerouac and others were raising the ante on what was possible in language. Their writing strove to capture the passing moment, the nuances of speech, the eidolons of history and philosophy and emotion. And I was also aware of the un-mined—in some cases un-voiced—richness of the work of the women writers associated with that community and working in the 1950s—that was immensely conditioning. In those times, the struggle for female individuality, for roles not defined by the Patriarchy, was immense. To fight against the tide of post-war materialism, conformity, the anathemas of "difference" (if one was lesbian, for example, or if one was in a bi-racial relationship, or if one got pregnant out of wedlock) was a constant struggle.

I myself, although a generation younger in most cases, was also being included in the Beat canon, and I felt the resonance of these same issues in my own work which is, in some cases, staunchly feminist. But I had benefited by the previous struggle of my comrades. And there were major differences in the backgrounds and lives and aesthetics and imagination of so many of these Beat writers, compared to the Moderns and compared with one another. Comparisons are odious! It is hard to generalize a generation, a literary movement. And then there was the enormity of influence and all the art, music, and performance that was spawned out of the maelstrom. Go to the work! That is my rallying cry. There is so much there to mine, to probe, to enjoy, that will enlighten you in a spiritual sense. I think I was able, as my class's discussion took shape, to manifest the huge debt I felt to these writers who blazed the way, who turned the establishment on its head!

The Beat literary movement conjures the rhizome as a metaphor or paradigm for its incredibly rich and enduring presence in the worlds of poetry, literature, performance, politics, culture. As such, it is a social phenomenon, a movement that extended and continues to extend beyond the usual parameters of literature and art. Rhizome refers to a living tuber system, literally "an elongate stem or branch of a plant that is often thickened or tuber shaped as a result of deposits of reserves (food) and is usually horizontal and underground, producing shoots above and roots below in which persistent growth and nourishment occurs, moving horizontally rather than vertically." This rhizome pattern might also be compared to Indra's Net or the Buddhist sense of "pratitya samutpada" which translates as interconnectedness. In their book *Rhizome: Introduction* (Minuit, 1976), the critical theorists Gilles Deleuze and Félix Guattari invoke the rhizome as creative paradigm: "Form rhizomes and not roots, never plant! Don't sow, forage! Be neither a One nor a Many, but multiplicities! A rhizome doesn't begin

and doesn't end, but is always in the middle, between things, interbeing, intermezzo."

It is a useful perspective in examining the multi-layered writings and the lives of a very exceptional community of writers which, in mid-20th-Century America, began to change all of our lives. It was propitious that such a conjunction of minds (and hearts) should occur and stimulate each other. That such a conjunction should root and flower in such remarkable and unique ways, having a ripple effect that moved into other realms of pop culture—fashion, film, music, theatre—and now, also, has staying power in the "academy" of officialdom; the Beat influence has been felt all over the world. It has spawned communities of writers and artists the world over. From the Jack Kerouac School of Disembodied Poetics at Naropa University in Boulder, Colorado, to the Schule für Dichtung in Vienna to the City Lights bookstore and publishing house in Florence, Italy. When Allen Ginsberg died, there were memorials in Britain, France, Italy, India, the Czech Republic, and across the United States. The writings of Beat authors are some of the most translated works in the annals of contemporary literature. The Beat movement holds and inculcates promise, fuels new generations of writers and scholarship. Beat writings demand readership, exploration, and scrutiny; their subtexts of gender, sexuality, queerness, race, and addiction beg to be deciphered. Also, importantly, the influence of jazz and negritude on Beat culture. For these writers were not operating in a vacuum: One could look at the political implications and the concern for the desecration of planet earth and notions of ecology in the work of Gary Snyder and Michael McClure. One could examine notions of spirituality (particularly the philosophy and psychology of Buddhism) and vision and the use of entheogens (Yage, mushrooms, peyote, marijuana).

Beats also felt themselves in a lineage with the antinomian William Blake, who referred to imagination as "Big Vision." Ginsberg had an audio-hallucination, imagining he heard Blake speak. This sensory experience fueled Allen's own identity as a mystic and prophet. Ginsberg taught classes in William Blake at Naropa University for years. Gregory Corso invoked the radical Percy Byshe Shelley on many occasions in his "socratic poetry raps." Eliot's "The Wasteland" was one of William Burroughs's favorite poems. Joanne Kyger has led workshops that stake out "location" and sites of activity and their literary histories, herself being the guardian of the coastal town of Bolinas for many years. Diane di Prima taught classes on light in John Keats. Keats' "negative capability" is the epigrammatic slogan of the Kerouac School and also serves as a description of the quality of mind of the Beat Generation. "Subterranean," "radical," "liberating," "subversive"; these are the adjectives that arise frequently in the discourse. One could add: "learned," "visionary," "empathetic."

This three-volume set, *The Beat Generation: A Gale Critical Companion*, covers a vibrant span of the literary movement. It gives ample space to key figures as well as others who were simpatico and shared the belletristic moments "in Eternity" and in community, and who also lived an alternative (and bohemian) lifestyle. Paul Blackburn—one example—fine poet and translator of the troubadours, affiliated with the praxis of Black Mountain, was a progenitor of the Poetry Project in New York, hosting the open and taping readings with his old Wollensack recorder. Chandler Brossard, a subterranean, almost noirish prose master. Neal Cassady, flamboyant muse and hero of Kerouac's novels, fabulous talker, although less prolific on the page. Robert Duncan and Jack Spicer, more associated with their own San Francisco Renaissance—and at times a more mystical poetics (Spicer speaks of receiving dictation from Mars)—shared a mutual "composition by field" approach with the Beats. Bill Everson, printer and former priest, as well as poet, shared an oppositional pacifism and confessionalism. Barbara Guest, historically placed as key among the New York School innovators (with Frank O'Hara, John Ashbery, Kenneth Koch, and James Schuyler), is possibly the most opaque and experimentally obtuse of the writers here and has always been considered a maverick. Other writers covered in this set's biographical entries are official progenitors of the scene and need less justification for inclusion. The topic entries (volume 1) in this collection are apt, up-to-date, expansive, and extremely useful for scholarship into the future. Entries pertaining to performing and visual arts make this collection particularly salient and useful as a full-bodied rhizomic chart of the ever-layered and expanded notion of a Beat Renaissance.

And this compendium also foregrounds the sites, the presses, and further disseminations of influence. It is a living, palpable transmission that continues because in many ways the Beat movement was a radically spiritual one and, as such,

continues a utopian transforming cultural intervention that is so desperately needed now, as it was in 1950s "art." The writing of poetry and fiction for many of these writers was viewed as a "sacred practice, with sacramental approach to each other as characters," as Ginsberg wrote. There's more power in a sacred approach than in a careerist one, which is why the work and activity of these writers resonates for a new audience— vital to these times, as society needs to re-examine its materialistic, conformist, and, in the case of the U.S., its Pax Americana New World Order modus operandi.

We had an ad for the creative writing program at Naropa: "Come to a school where your teachers have been jailed for their work and beliefs!" One feels that these writers and innovators had no choice in their paths. It was a calling that exacted a life commitment, demanding full attention to art and life and its concommitant camaraderie and vow of friendship. The combination of time and place with the intersection of so many prodigious "best minds" was indeed an auspicious and powerful one that is rare in literary annals. Ginsberg spoke of the establishment response to the threat of power in this movement in his introduction to *The Beat Book* (Shambhala), which I edited in 1999:

> This "beat generation" or "sixties" tolerant worldview provoked an intoxicated right wing to go into "Denial" (as in AA terminology) of reality, and reinforced its codependency with repressive laws, incipient police state, death-penalty demagoguery, sex demagoguery, art censorship, fundamentalist monotheistic televangelist quasi-fascist wrath, racism and homophobia. This counter-reaction seems a by-product of the further gulf between the rich and poor classes, growth of a massive abused underclass, increased power and luxury for the rich who control politics and their minions in the media.

These words seem ever more relevant as I write this in the shadow of war, in the aftermath of a highly publicized fracas over a planned (ultimately scuttled) literary event at the White House. First Lady Bush wanted, ironically—perhaps this is a call for help on Laura Bush's part!—to honor radical poets Emily Dickinson, Walt Whitman, and Langston Hughes (who themselves thought and wrote subtly about the horrors and implications of war). The First Lady made the mistake (at least from the perspective of the administration) of inviting Buddhist poet and editor Sam Hamill of

Copper Canyon Press. He responded by inviting poets all over the country to send protest poems opposing a war with Iraq to the White House. The situation prompted the White House to "delay" the First Lady's event. Despite this, over 5,000 poets have responded to Hamill's invitation. These writings can be seen on the poetsforpeace website, www.poets4peace.com. Lawrence Ferlinghetti, poet laureate of San Francisco, weighed in with the timely "Speak Out," first published in the San Francisco *Chronicle* (14 February 2003). In the poem he speaks to the dangers of war, the threats that confront civil liberties. He concludes with the warning lines:

> All you lovers of Liberty . . .
> Now is the time for you to speak
> O silent majority
> Before they come for you

As I sit here pondering the future of the planet, which has suffered so much war and degradation already in the last century, and I contemplate how to best teach new "best minds" in the face of a war that threatens the stability the whole world over, I realize it behooves one to speak with passion and conviction in the spirit of the Beat Generation that tried to save America from itself. Read this historic canon as one might a sacred text, as unfettered imagination that inspires, guides, and reactivates human thought and emotion towards candor, delight, and compassion.

—Anne Waldman
Distinguished Professor of Poetics
Chair, Summer Writing Program
The Jack Kerouac School of Disembodied Poetics
Naropa University, Boulder, Colorado
and
Co-founder
Poetry is News Coalition, New York City

The Gale Critical Companion Collection

In response to a growing demand for relevant criticism and interpretation of perennial topics and important literary movements throughout history, the Gale Critical Companion Collection (GCCC) was designed to meet the research needs of upper high school and undergraduate students. Each edition of GCCC focuses on a different literary movement or topic of broad interest to students of literature, history, multicultural studies, humanities, foreign language studies, and other subject areas. Topics covered are based on feedback from a standing advisory board consisting of reference librarians and subject specialists from public, academic, and school library systems.

The GCCC is designed to complement Gale's existing Literary Criticism Series (LCS) , which includes such award-winning and distinguished titles as *Nineteenth-Century Literature Criticism* (NCLC), *Twentieth-Century Literary Criticism* (TCLC), and *Contemporary Literary Criticism* (CLC). Like the LCS titles, the GCCC editions provide selected reprinted essays that offer an inclusive range of critical and scholarly response to authors and topics widely studied in high school and undergraduate classes; however, the GCCC also includes primary source documents, chronologies, sidebars, supplemental photographs, and other material not included in the LCS products. The graphic and supplemental material is designed to

extend the usefulness of the critical essays and provide students with historical and cultural context on a topic or author's work. GCCC titles will benefit larger institutions with ongoing subscriptions to Gale's LCS products as well as smaller libraries and school systems with less extensive reference collections. Each edition of the GCCC is created as a stand-alone set providing a wealth of information on the topic or movement. Importantly, 15% or less of the critical essays included in GCCC titles have appeared in LCS, ensuring that LCS subscribers who purchase GCCC titles will not duplicate resources in their collection.

Editions within the GCCC are either single-volume or multi-volume sets, depending on the nature and scope of the topic being covered. Topic entries and author entries are treated separately, with entries on related topics appearing first, followed by author entries in an A-Z arrangement. Each volume is approximately 500 pages in length and includes approximately 50 images and sidebar graphics. These sidebars include summaries of important historical events, newspaper clippings, brief biographies of important non-literary figures, complete poems or passages of fiction written by the author, descriptions of events in the related arts (music, visual arts, and dance), and so on.

The reprinted essays in each GCCC edition explicate the major themes and literary techniques of the authors and literary works. It is important to note that approximately 85% of the essays reprinted in GCCC editions are full-text, meaning that they are reprinted in their entirety, including footnotes and lists of abbreviations. Essays are selected based on their coverage of the seminal works and themes of an author, and based on the importance of those essays to an appreciation of the author's contribution to the movement and to literature in general. Gale's editors select those essays of most value to upper high school and undergraduate students, avoiding narrow and highly pedantic interpretations of individual works or of an author's canon.

Scope of The Beat Generation

The Beat Generation, the second set in the Gale Critical Companion Collection, consists of three volumes. Each volume includes a detailed table of contents, a foreword on the Beat Generation written by noted Beat scholar Anne Waldman, and a descriptive chronology of key events of the movement. The main body of volume 1 consists of entries on five topics relevant to the Beat Generation, including 1) The Beat Generation: An Overview; 2) The Beat "Scene": East and West; 3) Beat Generation Publishing: Periodicals, Small Presses, and Censorship; 4) Performing Arts and the Beat Generation; and 5) Visual Arts and the Beat Generation. Volumes 2 and 3 include entries on twenty-nine authors and literary figures associated with the movement, including such notables as William S. Burroughs, Gregory Corso, Lawrence Ferlinghetti, Allen Ginsberg, Jack Kerouac, and Kenneth Rexroth, as well as entries on individuals who have garnered less attention, but whose contributions to the Beat Generation are noteworthy, such as Diane di Prima, William Everson, Bob Kaufman, Ed Sanders, Gary Snyder, Lew Welch, and Philip Whalen.

Organization of The Beat Generation

A *Beat Generation* topic entry consists of the following elements:

- The **Introduction** defines the subject of the entry and provides social and historical information important to understanding the criticism.
- The list of **Representative Works** identifies writings and works by authors and figures associated with the subject. The list is divided into alphabetical sections by name; works listed under each name appear in chronological order. The genre and publication date of each work is given. Unless otherwise indicated, dramas are dated by first performance, not first publication.

- Entries generally begin with a section of **Primary Sources**, which includes essays, speeches, social history, newspaper accounts and other materials that were produced during the time of the Beat Generation.
- Reprinted **Criticism** in topic entries is arranged thematically. Topic entries commonly begin with primary sources, followed by general surveys of the subject or essays providing historical or background information, followed by essays that develop particular aspects of the topic. For example, the Publishing topic entry in volume 1 of *Beat Generation* begins with a section providing primary source material on publishing during the Beat Generation. This is followed by a section providing an overview essay on the topic, and three other sections: Beat Periodicals: "Little Magazines"; Beat Publishing: Small Presses; and Beat Battles with Censorship. Each section has a separate title heading and is identified with a page number in the table of contents. The critic's name and the date of composition or publication of the critical work are given at the beginning of each piece of criticism. Unsigned criticism is preceded by the title of the source in which it appeared. Footnotes are reprinted at the end of each essay or excerpt. In the case of excerpted criticism, only those footnotes that pertain to the excerpted texts are included.
- A complete **Bibliographical Citation** of the original essay or book precedes each piece of criticism.
- Critical essays are prefaced by brief **Annotations** explicating each piece. Unless the descriptor "excerpt" is used in the annotation, the essay is being reprinted in its entirety.
- An annotated bibliography of **Further Reading** appears at the end of each entry and suggests resources for additional study. In some cases, significant essays for which the editors could not obtain reprint rights are included here.

A *Beat Generation* author entry consists of the following elements:

- The **Author Heading** cites the name under which the author most commonly wrote, followed by birth and death dates. Also located here are any name variations under which an author wrote. If the author wrote consistently under a pseudonym, the pseudonym will be listed in the author heading and the author's actual name given in parentheses on the first line of the biographical and critical information. Uncertain birth or death dates are indicated by question marks.

- A **Portrait of the Author** is included when available.

- The **Introduction** contains background information that introduces the reader to the author that is the subject of the entry.

- The list of **Principal Works** is ordered chronologically by date of first publication and lists the most important works by the author. The genre and publication date of each work is given. Unless otherwise indicated, dramas are dated by first performance, not first publication.

- Author entries are arranged into three sections: **Primary Sources, General Commentary,** and **Title Commentary.** The Primary Sources section generally includes letters, poems, short stories, journal entries, novel excerpts, and essays written by the featured author, and sometimes commentary written about the author by the author's contemporaries. General Commentary includes overviews of the author's career and general studies; Title Commentary includes in-depth analyses of seminal works by the author. Within the Title Commentary section, the reprinted criticism is further organized by title, then by date of publication. The critic's name and the date of composition or publication of the critical work are given at the beginning of each piece of criticism. Unsigned criticism is preceded by the title of the source in which it appeared All titles by the author featured in the text are printed in boldface type. However, not all boldfaced titles are included in the author and subject indexes; only substantial discussions of works are indexed. Footnotes are reprinted at the end of each essay or excerpt. In the case of excerpted criticism, only those footnotes that pertain to the excerpted texts are included.

- A complete **Bibliographical Citation** of the original essay or book precedes each piece of criticism.

- Critical essays are prefaced by brief **Annotations** explicating each piece. Unless the descriptor "excerpt" is used in the annotation, the essay is being reprinted in its entirety.

- An annotated bibliography of **Further Reading** appears at the end of each entry and suggests resources for additional study. In some cases, significant essays for which the editors could not obtain reprint rights are included

here. A list of **Other Sources from Gale** follows the further reading section and provides references to other biographical and critical sources on the author in series published by Gale.

Indexes

The **Author Index** lists all of the authors featured in the *Beat Generation* set, with references to the main author entries in volumes 2 and 3 as well as commentary on the featured author in other author entries and in the topic volume. Page references to substantial discussions of the authors appear in boldface. The Author Index also includes birth and death dates and cross references between pseudonyms and actual names, and cross references to other Gale series in which the authors have appeared. A complete list of these sources is found facing the first page of the Author Index.

The **Title Index** alphabetically lists the titles of works written by the authors featured in volumes 2 and 3 and provides page numbers or page ranges where commentary on these titles can be found. Page references to substantial discussions of the titles appear in boldface. English translations of foreign titles and variations of titles are cross-referenced to the title under which a work was originally published. Titles of novels, dramas, nonfiction books, and poetry, short story, or essay collections are printed in italics, while individual poems, short stories, and essays are printed in roman type within quotation marks.

The **Subject Index** includes the authors and titles that appear in the Author Index and the Title Index as well as the names of other authors and figures that are discussed in the set. The Subject Index also lists titles and authors of the critical essays that appear in the set, as well as hundreds of literary terms and topics covered in the criticism. The index provides page numbers or page ranges where subjects are discussed and is fully cross-referenced.

Citing The Beat Generation

When writing papers, students who quote directly from the *BG* set may use the following general format to footnote reprinted criticism. The first example pertains to material drawn from periodicals, the second to material reprinted from books.

Podhoretz, Norman, "The Know-Nothing Bohemians," *Partisan Review* 25, no. 2 (spring 1958): 305-11, 313-16, 318; reprinted in *The Beat Generation: A Gale Critical Companion*, vol. 1, ed. Lynn M. Zott (Farmington Hills, Mich.: The Gale Group, 2003), 13-19.

Rexroth, Kenneth, "Disengagement: The Art of the Beat Generation." in *A Casebook on the Beat,* edited by Thomas Parkinson (New York: Thomas Y. Crowell Company, 1961), 179-93; reprinted in *The Beat Generation: A Gale Critical Companion,* vol. 1, ed. Lynn M. Zott (Farmington Hills, Mich.: The Gale Group, 2003), 6-13.

The Beat Generation *Advisory Board*

The members of the *Beat Generation* Advisory Board—reference librarians and subject specialists from public, academic, and school library systems—offered a variety of informed perspectives on both the presentation and content of the *Beat Generation* set. Advisory board members assessed and defined such quality issues as the relevance, currency, and usefulness of the author coverage, critical content, and topics included in our product; evaluated the layout, presentation, and general quality of our product; provided feedback on the criteria used for selecting authors and topics covered in our product; identified any gaps in our coverage of authors or topics, recommending authors or topics for inclusion; and analyzed the appropriateness of our content and presentation for various user audiences, such as high school students, undergraduates, graduate students, librarians, and educators. We wish to thank the advisors for their advice during the development of the *Beat Generation.*

Suggestions are Welcome

Readers who wish to suggest new features, topics, or authors to appear in future volumes of the Gale Critical Companion Collection, or who have other suggestions or comments are cordially invited to call, write, or fax the Project Editor:

Project Editor, Gale Critical Companion
    Collection
The Gale Group
27500 Drake Road
Farmington Hills, MI 48331-3535
1-800-347-4253 (GALE)
Fax: 248-699-8054

The editors wish to thank the copyright holders of the excerpted criticism included in this volume and the permissions managers of many book and magazine publishing companies for assisting us in securing reproduction rights. We are also grateful to the staffs of the Detroit Public Library, the Library of Congress, the University of Detroit Mercy Library, Wayne State University Purdy/Kresge Library Complex, Oakland University Library, and the University of Michigan Libraries for making their resources available to us. Following is a list of the copyright holders who have granted us permission to reproduce material in this edition of *The Beat Generation*. Every effort has been made to trace copyright, but if omissions have been made, please let us know.

Copyrighted material in The Beat Generation *was reproduced from the following periodicals:*

American Book Review, v. 3, May-June 1981. Reproduced by permission.—*American Literature*, v. 65, No. 1, pp. 117-130, March 1993. Copyright, 1993, Duke University Press. All rights reserved. Used by permission of the publisher. —*American Poetry Review*, v. 23, November-December 1994. Reproduced by permission of the author—*American Studies*, v. 32, 1987; v. 29: 1, Spring 1988. Copyright © Mid America American Studies Association, 2002. Reproduced by permission from American Studies.—*American Studies*, v. 43, 1998. Reproduced by permission of the author.—*The Antioch Review*, v. 31, Fall 1971. Reproduced by permission.—*The Ark*, v. 14, 1980. Reproduced by permission.—*Arshile*, v. 5, 1996. Reproduced by permission of the author. —*Atlantic Monthly*, v. 221, March 1968. Reproduced by permission of Sterling Lord Literistic, Inc.—*Beat Scene*, Autumn, 1993. Reproduced by permission.—*The Cambridge Quarterly*, v. 22, 1993. Copyright © 1993 by the Editors. Reproduced by permission of Oxford University Press. —*Chicago Review*, v. 26, 1974. Reproduced by permission.—*College Literature*, v. 27, Winter 2000. Reproduced by permission.—*Commentary*, v. 49, January 1970. All rights reserved. Reproduced by permission.—*Concerning Poetry*, v. 2, Spring 1969; v. 20, 1987. Reproduced by permission.—*Contemporary Literature*, v. 31, n. 3, Fall 1990; v. 38, n. 2, Summer 1997; v. 42, n. 3, Fall 2001. Copyright © 1990, 1997, 2001 The Board of Regents of the University of Wisconsin System. All rights reserved. Reproduced by permission. —*The Critical Quarterly*, v. 8, Autumn 1966. Reproduced by permission of Blackwell Publishing Ltd.—*ENclitic*, v. 11, Spring 1989. Reproduced by permission of the author.—*Exquisite Corpse: A Journal of Letters and Life*, 2002. Reproduced by permission.—*Extrapolation*, v. 20, Winter 1979. Reproduced by permission.—*Film Quarterly*, v. 45, Spring 1992. Copyright © 1992 by The Regents of the University of California, www.ucpress.edu. Reproduced by permission.—*The Gazette*, September 9, 2000. Reproduced by permission of the author.—*Geographical Review*, v. 86, January 1996. Reproduced by permission of the American Geographical Society.—*Harvard Theological*, v. 84, April 1991. Reproduced by permission. —*Ironwood*, 1983. Reproduced by permission of the author.—*Journal of Modern Literature*, v. 2, 1971-72, for "Theory and Practice of Gary Snyder, by Thomas Parkinson. Reproduced by permission of Indiana University Press.—*Kenyon Review*, v. 14, Winter 1992. Reproduced by permission of the author.—*Literary Review*, v. 33, Spring 1990. Reproduced by permission of the author.—*MELUS*, v. 14, Fall-Winter 1987; v. 19, Fall 1994. Reproduced by permission.—*Midwest Quarterly*, v. 14, July 1973. Copyright © 1973 by The Midwest Quarterly, Pittsburgh State University. Reproduced by permission.—*Modern Drama*, v. 22, March 1979. Copyright © 1979 University of Toronto, Graduate Centre for Study of Drama. Reproduced by permission.—*Moody Street Irregulars*, Summer 1986. Reproduced by permission.—*The Nation*, v. 185, November 9, 1957; v. 186, March, 1958; v. 187, October 11, 1958. © 1957, 1958 The Nation magazine/The Nation Company, Inc. Reproduced by permission.—*New Orleans Review*, v. 19, Spring 1992. Copyright © 1992 by Loyola University. Reproduced by permission.—*New York Times*, August 9, 1996. Copyright © 1996 by The New York Times Company. Reproduced by permission.—*New York Times Book Review*, November 25, 1984. Copyright © 1984 by The New York Times Company. Reproduced by permission. —*New York Times Magazine*, November 16, 1952. Copyright © by Estate of John Clellon Holmes. Reproduced by permission of Sterling Lord Literistic, Inc.—*Newsweek*, November 22, 1971, Newsweek, Inc. All rights reserved. Reproduced by permission.—*North Dakota Quarterly*, Fall 1987. Copyright 1987 by The University of North Dakota. Reproduced by permission.—*Parnassus*, v. 1, 1973; v. 3, Fall-Winter 1974. Copyright © 1973, 1974 Poetry in Review Foundation, NY. Reproduced by permission of authors.—*Partisan Review*, v. 25, Summer 1958, for "The Know-Nothing Bohemians," by Norman Podhoretz. Copyright © 1958 by Norman Podhoretz; v. 25, Summer 1958, for a letter to the editor, by LeRoi Jones; v. 26, Spring 1959, for "The Other Night at Columbia: A Report from the Academy," by Diana Trilling. Copyright © 1959 by Partisan Review, renewed 1987 by Diana Trilling. Reproduced by permission of the author, publisher, and Wylie Agency respectively.—*Playboy Magazine*, v. 6, June 1959, "The Origins of the Beat Generation," by Jack Kerouac. Reproduced by permission of the publisher and Sterling Lord Literistic, Inc.—*Poetry*, v. 90, April 1957, for "Two New Books by Kenneth Rexroth," by William Carlos Williams. Copyright © 1957 by Paul H. Williams and the Estate of William Eric Williams. Reproduced by permission of New Directions Publishing Corp., agents.—*Publishers Weekly*, v. 248, May 7, 2001. Copyright 2001 by Reed Publishing USA. Reproduced from Publishers Weekly, published by the Bowker Magazine Group of Cahners Publishing Co., a division of Reed Publishing USA. Reproduced by permission.—*Religion and the Arts*, v. 2, 1998. Reproduced by permission.—*Review of Contemporary Fiction*, v. 3, Summer 1983; v. 7, Spring 1987; v. 19, Spring 1999. Copyright 1983, 1987, 1999 by John O'Brien. Reproduced by permission.—*Sagetrieb*, v. 2, Spring 1983. Copyright © 1983 by the author. Reproduced by permission of the author.—*The San Francisco Chronicle—Sunday Review Section*, April 22, 2001. Republished with permission of The San Francisco Chronicle, conveyed through Copyright Clearance Center, Inc.—*Sixties*, Spring 1962. Reproduced by permission of the Eighties Press.—*Small Press: The Magazine and Book Review of Independent Publishing*, August 1990. Reproduced by permission.—*Social Research*, v. 68, Fall 2001. Copyright 2001 by New School for Social Research. Reproduced by permission.—*Southern Humanities Review*, v. VI, Fall 1972. Reproduced by permission.—*Southern Review*, v. 21, January 1985. Reproduced by permission.—*Texas Studies in Literature and Language*, v. 44, n. 2, Summer 2002, pp. 211-28. "'The Brake of Time' Corso's Bomb as Postmodern God(dess)," by Christine Hoff Kraemer. Copyright © 2002 by the University of Texas Press. All rights reserved. Reproduced by permission.—*Third Rail*, v. 8, 1987. Reproduced by permission of Mr. Uri Hertz, Editor of Third Rail and the author.—*Times Literary Supplement*, June 3, 1983, pp. 586-7, for "Camp Follower," by James Campbell. © The Times Supplements Limited 1983; March 22, 1991, p. 21, for "The Steinberg Case," by Brian Masters. Reproduced by permission.—*TriQuarterly*, v. 43, Fall 1978. Reproduced by permission of author.—*Western American Literature*, v. 3, Fall 1968. Copyright 1968, by the Western American Literature Association. Reproduced by permission.—*Whole Earth*, v. 98, Fall 1999. Reproduced by permission. —*Women's Studies*, v. 30, 2001. © Gordon and Breach Science Publishers. Reproduced by permission.—*Woodstock Journal*, v. 7, February 2- 16, 2001; v. 7, May 11-25, 2001. Reproduced by permission.—*The Wordsworth Circle*, v. 22, Summer 1991. © 1991 Marilyn Gaull. Reproduced by permission of the editor.

Copyrighted material in The Beat
Generation *was reproduced from the
following books:*

Amram, David. From "This Song's For You, Jack:
Collaborating With Kerouac," in **Beat Culture:
The 1950s and Beyond**. Edited by Cornelis A.
Minnen, Jaap van der Bent, and Mel van Elteren.
VU University Press, 1999. Copyright © 1999 by
Amerika Instituut, Amsterdam. All rights reserved.
Reproduced by permission.—Berger, Maurice.
From "Libraries Full of Tears: The Beats and the
Law," in **Beat Culture and the New America:
1950-1965**, by Lisa Phillips et al. Whitney Mu-
seum of American Art, 1995. Copyright © 1995
by Whitney Museum of American Art. All rights
reserved. Reproduced by permission.—Blaser,
Robin. From "The Practice of Outside," in **The Collected Books of Jack Spicer**, by Jack Spicer. Edited
by Robin Blaser. Black Sparrow Press, 1975. Copyright © 1975 by the Estate of Jack Spicer. All rights
reserved. Reproduced by permission.—Burroughs,
William S. From Introductory Essay to **Mindfield**.
Thunder's Mouth Press, 1989. Copyright © 1989
by William Burroughs. Reproduced by permission
of The Wylie Agency, Inc.—Burroughs, William S.
From **Naked Lunch**. Grove Press Inc., 1959.
Copyright © 1959 by William S. Burroughs. All
rights reserved. Reproduced by permission.—Bur-
roughs, William S. From **The Yage Letters**. City
Lights Books 1963. Copyright © 1963, 1975 by
William S. Burroughs and Allen Ginsberg. All
rights reserved. Reproduced by permission.
—Bush, Clive. From "'Why Do We Always Say
Angel?': Herbert Huncke and Neal Cassady," in
The Beat Generation Writers. Edited by A. Robert
Lee. Pluto Press, 1996. Copyright © 1996 by Lum-
iere (Cooperative) Press Ltd. and Pluto Press. All
rights reserved. Reproduced by permission.
—Campbell, James. From "Behind the Beat: Neu-
rotica," and "The Muses: Huncke-Junkie and Neo-
Cassady," in **This Is the Beat Generation: New
York—San Francisco—Paris**. Secker and Warburg,
1999 and the University of California Press.
Copyright © 1999 by James Campbell. Reproduced by permission of The Random House Group Limited and by the Regents of
the University of California and the University of
California Press.—Carpenter, David. From "Introduction: She That Looketh Forth as the Morning,"
in **The Integral Years: Poems 1966-1994**, by William Everson. Black Sparrow Press, 2000. Copyright © 2000 by David A. Carpenter. All rights
reserved. Reproduced by permission.—Carroll,
Paul. From "I Lift My Voice Aloud/Make Mantra
of American Language Now.../I Here Declare the
End of the War!" in **The Poem in Its Skin**. Follett
Publishing Company, 1968. Copyright © 1968 by
Paul Carroll. All rights reserved. Reproduced by

permission.—Cassady, Carolyn. From "Afterword," in **The First Third and Other Writings**.
Edited by Lawrence Ferlinghetti and Nancy J.
Peters. City Lights Books, 1981. Copyright © 1981
by City Lights Books. All rights reserved. Reproduced by permission.—Cassady, Neal. From Letter
to Jack Kerouac (Kansas City, MO, March 7, 1947),
in **The First Third & Other Writings**. City Lights
Books, 1971. Copyright © 1971 by City Lights
Books. All rights reserved. Reproduced by permission.—Cherkovski, Neeli. From "Bob Kaufman,"
and "The Memory of Love: John Wieners," in
**Whitman's Wild Children: Portraits of Twelve
Poets**. Steerforth Press 1999. Copyright © 1999 by
Neeli Cherkovski (a.k.a. Neeli Cherry). All rights
reserved. Reproduced by permission.—Chris-
tensen, Paul. From Introduction to **Two Novels:
You Didn't Even Try: Imaginary Speeches for a
Brazen Head**. Zephyr Press, 1989. Copyright ©
1989 by Paul Christensen. All rights reserved.
Reproduced by permission.—Christian, Barbara.
From "Whatever Happened to Bob Kaufman," in
The Beats: Essays in Criticism. Edited by Lee Bar-
tlett. McFarland, 1981. Copyright © 1981 by Lee
Bartlett. All rights reserved. Reproduced by permis-
sion.—Clark, Walter Houston. From "Historical
Notes: The Harvard Incident," in **Chemical Ec-
stasy: Psychedelic Drugs and Religion**. Sheed and
Ward, 1969. Copyright © by Sheed and Ward, Inc.
All rights reserved. Reproduced by permission.
—Clay, Steven, and Rodney Phillips. From "A
Little History of the Mimeograph Revolution," in
**A Secret Location on the Lower East Side: Adven-
tures in Writing 1960-1980**. The New York Public
Library and Granary Book, 1998. Copyright ©
1998 by The New York Public Library, Astor, Le-
nox and Tilden Foundations and Granary Books.
All rights reserved. Reproduced by permission.
—Cohen, Ronald D. From "Singing Subversion:
Folk Music and the Counterculture in the 1950s,"
in **Beat Culture: The 1950s and Beyond**. Edited
by Cornelis A. Minnen, Jaap van der Bent, and
Mel van Elteren. VU University Press, 1999.
Copyright © 1999 by Amerika Instituut, Amster-
dam. All rights reserved. Reproduced by permis-
sion.—Corso, Gregory. From "Marriage," in **The
Happy Birthday of Death**. Copyright © 1960 by
New Directions Publishing Corp. Reprinted by
permission of New Directions Publishing Corp.
—Creeley, Robert. From Introduction to **Black
Mountain Review: Volume 1, 1954**. AMS Press,
1969. Copyright © 1969 by AMS Press Inc. All
rights reserved. Reproduced by permission.—Cree-
ley, Robert. From Preface to **Cultural Affairs in
Boston: Poetry and Prose, 1956-1985**, by John
Wieners. Edited by Raymond Foye. Black Sparrow
Press, 1988. Copyright © 1988 by Robert Creeley.
All rights reserved. Reproduced by permission.

—Davidson, Michael. From "'Spotting That Design': Incarnation and Interpretation in Gary Snyder and Philip Whalen," and From "'The City Redefined': Community and Dialogue in Jack Spicer," in *The San Francisco Renaissance: Poetics and Community at Mid-Century*. Cambridge University Press, 1989. Copyright © 1989 by Cambridge University Press. All rights reserved. Reproduced by permission of Cambridge University Press and the author.—Dickey, James. From "Kenneth Patchen," in *Babel to Byzantium Poets and Poetry Now*, by James Dickey. Copyright © 1968 by James Dickey. Reproduced by permission of Farrar, Straus, and Giroux, LLC.—Douglas, Ann. From "'Punching a Hole in the Big Lie': The Achievement of William S. Burroughs," in *Word Virus: The William S. Burroughs Reader*. Edited by James Grauerholz and Ira Silverberg. Grove Press, 1998. Copyright © 1998 by Grove Press. All rights reserved. Reproduced by permission.—Duncan, Robert. From "Often I am Permitted to Return to a Meadow," in *The Opening of the Field*. Copyright © 1960 by Robert Duncan. Reprinted by permission of New Directions Publishing Corp. —Dylan, Bob. From "Blowin in the Wind," in *The Free Wheeling Bob Dylan*. Copyright © 1962 by Warner Bros. Inc. Copyright renewed 1990 Special Rider Music. All rights reserved. International copyright secured. Reproduced by permission. —Dylan, Bob. From "The Times They are a Changin'," in *The Times They are A-Changin'*. Copyright © 1963 by Warner Bros. Inc. Copyright renewed 1991 Special Rider Music. All rights reserved. International copyright secured. Reproduced by permission.—Edmiston, Susan, and Linda D. Cirino. From "The East Village," in *Literary New York*. Houghton Mifflin Company, 1976. Copyright © 1976 by Susan Edmiston and Linda D. Cirino. All rights reserved. Reproduced by permission of the authors.—Ferlinghetti, Lawrence, and Nancy J. Peters. In *Literary San Francisco: A Pictorial from Its Beginning to the Present Day*. City Lights Books and Harper & Row, 1980. Copyright © 1980 by Lawrence Ferlinghetti and Nancy J. Peters. All rights reserved. Reproduced by permission of HarperCollins Publishers Inc., and the author.—Ferlinghetti, Lawrence, and Robert Dana. From "Lawrence Ferlinghetti," in *Against the Grain: Interview with Maverick American Publishers*. Edited by Robert Dana. University of Iowa Press, 1986. All rights reserved. Reproduced by permission of the author.—Ferlinghetti, Lawrence. From "Horn on Howl," in *On the Poetry of Allen Ginsberg*. Edited by Lewis Hyde. University of Michigan Press, 1984. Copyright © 1984 by University of Michigan Press. All rights reserved. Reproduced by permission of the author.—Ferlinghetti, Lawrence. From "I am Waiting," in *A Coney Island of the Mind*. Copyright © 1958 by Lawrence Ferlinghetti. Reprinted by permission of New Directions Publishing Corp. —Ferlinghetti, Lawrence. From "Number 13: It Was a Face Which Darkness Could Kill," in *Pictures of the Gone World*. City Lights, 1955. Copyright © 1955 by Lawrence Ferlinghetti. All rights reserved. Reproduced by permission of the author.—Foster, Edward Halsey. From "Corso," and "Hipsters, Beats, and the True Frontier," in *Understanding the Beats*. University of South Carolina Press, 1992. Copyright © 1992 by University of South Carolina Press. All rights reserved. Reproduced by permission.—Foye, Raymond. From Introduction to *The Herbert Huncke Reader*. Edited by Benjamin G. Schafer. William Morrow, 1997. Copyright © 1997 by the Estate of Herbert E. Hencke, Jerome Poynton, Executor. All rights reserved. Reproduced by permission.—Foye, Raymond, and John Wieners. From Introduction to *Cultural Affairs in Boston: Poetry and Prose, 1956-1985,* by John Wieners. Black Sparrow Press, 1988. Copyright © 1988 by Raymond Foye and John Wieners. All rights reserved. Reproduced by permission.—French, Warren. From "On the Road: Work in Progress," in *Jack Kerouac*. Twayne Publishers, 1986. Copyright © 1986 by G.K. Hall & Co. All rights reserved. Reproduced by permission.—Fuller, Robert C. From "Psychedelics and Metaphysical Illumination," in *Stairways to Heaven: Drugs in American Religious History*. Copyright © 2000 by Westview Press. Reproduced by permission of Westview Press, a member of the Perseus Books, L.L.C.—Gelpi, Albert. From "Introduction: Everson/Antonius: Contending with the Shadow," in *The Veritable Years: Poems 1949-1966,* by William Everson. Black Sparrow Press, 1998. Copyright © 1998 by Albert Gelpi. All rights reserved. Reproduced by permission.—George, Paul S., and Jerold M. Starr. From "Beat Politics: New Left and Hippie Beginnings in the Postwar Counterculture," in *Cultural Politics: Radical Movements in Modern History*. Edited by Jerold M. Starr. Praeger, 1985. Copyright © 1985 by Praeger Publishers. All rights reserved. Reproduced by permission.—Ginsberg, Allen, "Early Journal Entries," found at *http://www.allenginsberg.org*. Copyright © 2000 by the Allen Ginsberg Trust. Reprinted with permission of The Wylie Agency, Inc.—Ginsberg, Allen. From An interview in *Jack's Book*, by Barry Gifford and Lawrence Lee. St. Martin's Press, 1978. Copyright © 1994 by Barry Gifford and Lawrence Lee. Reproduced by permission of St. Martin's Press, LLC.—Ginsberg, Allen. From Foreword to "Out of the World," *Deliberate Prose: Selected Essays 1952-1995*. Edited by Anne Waldman. Crown Publishers, 1991. Copyright © 1999 by Allen Ginsberg Trust. All rights reserved.

Reproduced by permission of HarperCollins Publishers Inc.—Ginsberg, Allen. From Foreword to *Selected Poems, 1958- 1984*, by John Wieners. Edited by Raymond Foye. Black Sparrow Press, 1986. Copyright © 1986 by Allen Ginsberg. All rights reserved. Reproduced by permission. —Ginsberg, Allen. From "Howl," in *Howl and Other Poems*. Copyright © 1956 by the Allen Ginsberg Trust. Reproduced by permission of The Wylie Agency, Inc.—Ginsberg, Allen. From "On Corso's Virtues," in *Mindfield*. Thunder's Mouth Press, 1989. Copyright © 1989 by The Allen Ginsberg Trust and © 2000 by the Allen Ginsberg Trust. Reproduced by permission of The Wylie Agency, Inc.—Ginsberg, Allen. From "Sunflower Sutra," in *Collected Poems: 1947-1980*. Harper Collins, 1984. Copyright © 1955, 1984, 1988 by Allen Ginsberg. All rights reserved. Reproduced by permission of HarperCollins Publishers Inc. —Gold, Herbert. From "When North Beach Made an Offer, Old Bohemia Couldn't Refuse," in *Bohemia: Where Art, Angst, Love, and Strong Coffee Meet*. Reproduced with the permission of Simon & Schuster Adult Publishing Group. Copyright © 1993 by Herbert Gold.—Hassan, Ihab. From "William Burroughs: The Subtracting Machine," in *Rumors of Change: Essays of Five Decades*. University of Alabama Press, 1995. Copyright © 1995 by University of Alabama Press. All rights reserved. Reproduced by permission.—Hicks, Jack. From "Poetic Composting in Gary Snyder's Left Out in the Rain," in *Critical Essays on Gary Snyder*. Edited by Patrick D. Murphy. G.K. Hall, 1991. Copyright © 1991 by Patrick D. Murphy. All rights reserved. Reproduced by permission.—Holmes, John Clellon. From "Crazy Days and Numinous Nights, 1948-1950," in *The Beat Vision: A Primary Sourcebook*. Copyright © by Estate of John Clellon Holmes. Reproduced by permission of Sterling Lord Literistic, Inc.—Holmes, John Clellon, Letter to Jim White (On Writing a Novel: Three Letters from John Clellon Holmes), found at *http://www.americanartists.org/Articles/ Holmes/ on_writing_a_novel.htm*. Published by American Center for Artists, (1999). Copyright by Estate of John Clellon Holmes. Reprinted by permission of Sterling Lord Literistic, Inc. —Howard, Richard. From "Gregory Corso: 'Surely There'll Be Another Table…,'" in *Alone with America: Essays on the Art of Poetry in the United States Since 1950*, Enlarged Edition. Reproduced with the permission of Scribner, an imprint of Simon & Schuster Adult Publishing Group. Original edition copyright © 1969 Richard Howard. This Enlarged Edition copyright © 1980 Richard Howard.—Huncke, Herbert. From "Elsie John," in *Elsie John and Joey Martinez*. Pequod Press, 1979. Copyright © 1979 by Pequod Press.

All rights reserved. Reproduced by permission. —Hunt, Tim. From "An Interview with John Clellon Holmes," in *The Unspeakable Visions of the Individual, Volume 8: The Beat Journey*. A. and K. Knight, 1978. Copyright © 1978 by Arthur & Kit Knight. All rights reserved. Reproduced by permission.—In Introduction and "The Decision," in *Howl of the Censor*. Edited by J.W. Ehrlich. Nourse Publishing, 1961. Introduction copyright © 1961 by J.W. Ehrlich. All rights reserved. Reproduced by permission.—Jarolim, Edith. From Introduction to *The Collected Poems of Paul Blackburn*. Edited by Edith Jarolim. Copyright © 1985 by Edith Jarolim. Reproduced by permission of Persea Books, Inc. (New York).—Johnson, Joyce. From "Beat Women: A Transitional Generation," in *Beat Culture: The 1950s and Beyond*. Edited by Cornelis A. van Minnen, Jaap van der Bent, and Mel van Elteren. VU University Press, 1999. Copyright © 1999 by VU University Press. All rights reserved. Reproduced by permission. —Johnson, Joyce. From "On Women in the Beat Generation," in *The Rolling Stone Book of the Beats: The Beat Generation and American Culture*. Edited by Holly George-Warren. Copyright © 1999 Holly George-Warren. Reprinted by permission of Hyperion.—Johnson, Ronna C. "'An then she went': Beat Departures and Feminine Transgressions in Joyce Johnson's Come and Join the Dance," in *Girls Who Wore Black: Women Writing the Beat Generation*. Edited by Ronna C. Johnson and Nancy Grace. Copyright © 2002 by Ronna C. Johnson. Reproduced by permission of Rutgers University Press.—Kaprow, Allan. From "The Legacy of Jackson Pollock," in *Jackson Pollock: Interviews, Articles, and Reviews*. Edited by Pepe Karmel. Copyright © 1958, ARTnews LLC. All rights reserved. Reproduced by permission. —Kaufman, Bob. From "Jazz Chick," "O, Jazz, O," "On," and "Round about Midnight," in *The Golden Sardine*. City Lights Books, 1967. Copyright © 1967 by City Lights Publishing Company. All rights reserved. Reproduced by permission of Coffee House Press, Minneapolis, Minnesota.—Kerouac, Jack. From "Belief & Technique for Modern Prose," in *Portable Beat Reader*. Edited by Ann Charters. Penguin Books, 1992. Copyright by Jack Kerouac. Reproduced by permission of Sterling Lord Literistic, Inc.—Kerouac, Jack. From "Chapter 2," in *On the Road*. Viking Penguin, 1997. Copyright © 1955, 1957 by Jack Kerouac; © renewed 1983 by Stella Kerouac, renewed © 1985 by Stella Kerouac and Jan Kerouac. Used by permission of Viking Penguin, a division of Penguin Putnam Inc.—Kerouac, Jack. From "Essentials of Spontaneous Prose," in *Portable Beat Reader*. Edited by Ann Charters. Penguin Books, 1992. Copyright by Jack Kerouac. Reproduced by permission of Sterling Lord Literistic, Inc.—Kerouac, Jack. From "Scripture of the Golden Eternity," in *Scripture of the Golden Eternity*. Totem Press, 1960. Copyright © 1960.by Jack Kerouac. All rights reserved. Reproduced by permission of Sterling Lord Literistic, Inc.—Kerouac, Jack. In *The Dharma Bums*. Copyright © 1958 by Jack Kerouac, © renewed 1986 by Stella Kerouac and Jan Kerouac. Used by permission of Viking Penguin, a division of Penguin Putnam, Inc. and Sterling Lord Literistic, Inc.—Kesey, Ken. From "Flowers for Tim," foreword to *On the Bus*, by Paul Perry. Thunder's Mouth Press, 1996. Copyright © 1964 by The Estate of Ken Kesey. All rights reserved. Reproduced by permission of Sterling Lord Literistic, Inc.—Kesey, Ken. From "The Day after Superman Died," in *Demon Box*. Copyright © 1979 by Ken Kesey. Used by permission of Viking Penguin, a division of Penguin Putnam Inc. and Sterling Lord Literistic, Inc.—Knabb, Kenneth, "The Relevance of Rexroth: Magnanimity and Mysticism," at *http://www.bopsecrets.org/PS/rexroth2.htm*. Published by Public Secrets, Bureau of Public Secrets, (1997). Reprinted with permission. —Knight, Brenda. Excepted from "Joan Vollmer Adams Burroughs: Calypso Stranded (1924- 1951)," "Anne Waldman: Fast Speaking Woman," "Eileen Kaufman: Keeper of the Flame (1922-)," "Joanne Kyger, Dharma Sister," "Joyce Johnson: A True Good Heart," and "ruth weiss: The Survivor (1928-)," in *Women of the Beat Generation: The Writers, Artists and Muses at the Heart of a Revolution*. Conari Press, 1996. Copyright © 1996 by Brenda Knight. All rights reserved. Reproduced by permission of Conari Press, an imprint of Red Wheel/ Weiser. Ordering information: Red Wheel/Weiser 1-800-423-7087 Website: Conari.com. —Kowalewski, Michael. From "Jack Kerouac and the Beats in San Francisco," in *San Francisco in Fiction: Essays in a Regional Literature*. Edited by David Fine and Paul Skenazy. University of New Mexico Press, 1995. Copyright © 1995 by University of New Mexico Press. All rights reserved. Reproduced by permission.—Kupferberg, Tuli, and Theresa Stern, An interview with Tuli Kupferberg, *www.furious.com/perfect/tuli.html*. Published by Furious, (1997). Reprinted with permission.—Lauridsen, Inger Thorup, and Per Dalgard. From An Interview with Gary Snyder, in *The Beat Generation and the Russian New Wave*. Ardis, 1990. Copyright © 1990 by Ardis Publishers. All rights reserved. Reproduced by permission of Overlook Press, Inc.—Leavitt, Craig. From "On the Road: Cassady, Kerouac, and Images of Late Western Masculinity," in *Across the Great Divide: Cultures of Manhood in the American West*. Edited by Matthew Basso, Laura McCall, and Dee Garceau. Routledge, 2001. Copyright © 2001 by Routledge.

All rights reserved. Reproduced by permission of Routledge, Inc., part of the Taylor & Francis Group.—Levy, Peter B. From "Beating the Censor: The 'Howl' Trial Revisited," in *Beat Culture: The 1950s and Beyond*. Edited by Cornelis A. Minnen, Jaap van der Bent, and Mel van Elteren. VU University Press, 1999. Copyright © 1999 by Amerika Instituut, Amsterdam. All rights reserved. Reproduced by permission.—Maynard, John Arthur. From Introduction to *Venice West: The Beat Generation in Southern California*. Copyright © 1991 by John Arthur Maynard. Reproduced by permission of Rutgers University Press. —McCarthy, Mary. From "Burroughs' Naked Lunch," in *William S. Burroughs at the Front: Critical Reception, 1959- 1989*. Edited by Jennie Skerl and Robin Lydenberg. Southern Illinois University Press, 1991. Copyright © 1991 by Southern Illinois University Press, reprinted by permission of Harcourt, Inc.—McClure, Michael, and Eduardo Lipschutz-Villa. From "Wallace Berman and Semina," in *Lighting the Corners: On Art, Nature, and the Visionary, Essays and Interviews*. University of New Mexico College of Arts and Sciences, 1993. Copyright © 1993 by Michael McClure. All rights reserved. Reproduced by permission.—McClure, Michael. From "A Mammal Gallery," in *Scratching the Beat Surface*. North Point Press, 1982. Copyright © 1982 by Michael McClure. All rights reserved. Reproduced by permission of the author.—McClure, Michael. From "Bob Dylan: The Poet's Poet," and "Sixty-six Things About the California Assemblage Movement," in *Lighting the Corners: On Art, Nature, and the Visionary, Essays and Interviews*. University of New Mexico College of Arts and Sciences, 1993. Copyright © 1993 by Michael McClure. All rights reserved. Reproduced by permission.—McClure, Michael. From "Point Lobos: Animism," in *Hymns to St. Geryon and Other Poems*. Auerhahn Press, 1959. Copyright © 1959. by Michael McClure. All rights reserved. Reproduced by permission of the author.—Meltzer, David. From "Diane di Prima (1999)," and "Lew Welch (1969)," in *San Francisco Beat: Talking with the Poets*. City Lights Books, 2001. Copyright © 2001 by David Meltzer. All rights reserved. Reproduced by permission.—Meltzer, David, and Jack Shoemaker. From "Lawrence Ferlinghetti I (1969)," in *San Francisco Beat: Talking with the Poets*. Edited by David Meltzer. City Lights Books, 2001. Copyright © 2001 by David Meltzer. All rights reserved. Reproduced by permission.—Meltzer, David, and Jack Shoemaker with Michael McClure. From "Michael McClure I (1969)," in *San Francisco Beat: Talking with the Poets*. Edited by David Meltzer. City Lights Books, 2001. Copyright © 2001 by David Meltzer. All rights reserved. Repro-

by Lee Bartlett. McFarland, 1981. Copyright © by 1981 Lee Bartlett. All rights reserved. Reproduced by permission.—Tytell, John. From "Allen Ginsberg and the Messianic Tradition," and "The Black Beauty of William Burroughs," in *Naked Angels: The Lives and Literature of the Beat Generation*. McGraw-Hill Book Company, 1976. Copyright © 1976 by John Tytell. All rights reserved. Reproduced by permission of the author.—Tytell, John. From "The Frozen Fifties," in *Paradise Outlaws: Remembering the Beats, with Photographs by Mellon*. William Morrow and Company, Inc., 1999. Copyright © 1999 by John Tytell and Mellon. All rights reserved. Reproduced by permission of the author.—Waldman, Anne, "Angel Hair Feature," *http://jacketmagazine.com/16/ah1-wald.html*. Published by Jacket 16, (March 2002). Reprinted with permission of the author.—Waldman, Anne. From Foreword to *Strange Big Moon, The Japan and Indian Journals: 1960-1964*, by Joanne Kyger, published by North Atlantic Books. Copyright © 2000 by Joanne Kyger. Reproduced by permission of the publisher.—Waldman, Anne. From "Our Past," in *Blue Mosque*. United Artists Books, 1988. Copyright © 1988 by United Artist Books. All rights reserved. Reproduced by permission of United Artists Books and author.—Waldman, Anne, "The Weight of the World is Love," *www.naropa.edu/ginstributes8.html*. Published by Naropa Institute, (2002). Reproduced with permission of the author and Coffee House Press, Minneapolis, Minnesota.—Weinreich, Regina. From "The Sound of Despair: A Perfected Nonlinearity," in *The Spontaneous Poetics of Jack Kerouac: A Study of the Fiction*. Southern Illinois University Press, 1987. Copyright © 1987 by The Board of Trustees, Southern Illinois University. All rights reserved. Reproduced by permission of the author.—Whitmer, Peter O. with Bruce Van Wyngarden. From "The Beat Begins," in *Aquarius Revisited: Seven Who Created the Sixties Counterculture that Changed America*, William Burroughs, Allen Ginsberg, Ken Kesey, Timothy Leary, Norman Mailer, Tom Robbins, Hunter S. Thompson. Copyright © 1987 by Peter O. Whitmer. Reproduced by permission of Scribner, an imprint of Simon & Schuster Adult Publishing Group.—Widmer, Kingsley. From "The Beat in the Rise of the Populist Culture," in *The Fifties: Fiction, Poetry, Drama*. Edited by Warren French. Everett/Edwards, Inc., 1970. Copyright © 1970 by Warren French, reassigned 1985 to Kingsley Widmer. All rights reserved. Reproduced by permission.—Wilentz, Elias. From Introduction to *The Beat Scene*. Edited by Elias Wilentz. Corinth Books, 1960. Copyright © 1960 by Fred McDarrah and Elias Wilentz. All rights reserved. Reproduced by permission of the author.—Williams, Mary Elizabeth with Chuck Workman, "The Beats Go On: Filmmaker Chuck Workman on The Source, His Fawning Tribute to the Beat Generation," at *http:www.salon.com*. Published by Salon, (June 1, 1999). Reprinted with permission.—Williams, William Carlos. From "A Counsel of Madness: A Review of The Journal of Albion Moonlight," in *Kenneth Patchen: A Collection of Essays*. Edited by Richard G. Morgan. AMS Press, Inc., 1977. Copyright © 1977 by Richard G. Morgan. All rights reserved. Reproduced by permission. —Wisker, Alistair. From "An Anarchist among the Floorwalkers: The Poetry of Lawrence Ferlinghetti," in *The Beat Generation Writers*. Edited by A Robert Lee. Pluto Press, 1996. Copyright © 1996 by Lumiere (Cooperative) Press Ltd. and Pluto Press. All rights reserved. Reproduced by permission.—Zurbrugg, Nicholas. From "Will Hollywood Never Learn? David Cronenberg's Naked Lunch," in *Adaptations: From Text to Screen, Screen to Text*. Edited by Deborah Cartmell and Imelda Whelehan. Routledge, 1999. Copyright © 1999 by Nicholas Zurbrugg. Selection and editorial matter © Deborah Cartmell and Imelda Whelehan. All rights reserved. Reproduced by permission. —Zweig, Paul. From "A Music of Angels," in *On the Poetry of Allen Ginsberg*. Edited by Lewis Hyde. University of Michigan Press, 1984. © *The Nation* magazine/The Nation Company, Inc. Reproduced by permission of *The Nation* Magazine.

Photographs and illustrations in The Beat Generation *were received from the following sources:*

Beatniks, San Francisco, California, photograph. © Bettmann/Corbis. Reproduced by permission. —Berman, Wallace. *Semina*, assemblage of various photographs. Wallace Berman Estate, Courtesy of LA Louver Gallery. Reproduced by permission. —Blackburn, Paul, photograph. © by Fred W. McDarrah. All rights reserved. Reproduced by permission.—Bremser, Ray, photograph. Original caption: "Ray Bremser, Jazz-ear sound-Poetry genius, syncopating wow-sound word walloper, original N.Y. late-1950s coffee shop bard with Kerouac & Leroi Jones, his long-ago jail songs were noted by Bob Dylan in 'The Times They are a Changin,' at kitchen table, March 15, 1987, he stayed over to read poetry and teach my 'Literary History of Beat Generation' class Brooklyn College, come down from A.A. halfway house in Utica, N.Y., rare trip to the Apple for survivor with big fine beard." Allen Ginsberg/Corbis. Reproduced by permission.—Brown, Joan. *Fur Rat*, sculpture consisting of wood, chicken wire, and raccoon fur, photograph. Berkeley Art Museum, University of California. Reproduced by permission.—Burroughs, William S. (left), and Jack Kerouac in an apartment in New York City, photograph. © Corbis. Reproduced by permission. —Burroughs, William S., sitting in front of a typewriter, at his home in Paris, France, photograph. © Bettmann/Corbis. Reproduced by permission.— Burroughs, William S. (left to right), Lucien Carr, and Allen Ginsberg, sitting together in an apartment in New York City, photograph. © Allen Ginsberg/Corbis. Reproduced by permission. —Campus of Black Mountain College in North Carolina. Courtesy of the North Carolina Offices of Archives and History, Raleigh, North Carolina. Reproduced by permission.—Cassady, Neal, San Francisco, California, 1966, photograph by Ted Streshinsky. Corbis/Ted Streshinsky. Reproduced by permission.—Chase, Hale (left to right), Jack Kerouac, Allen Ginsberg, and William Burroughs, in Morningside Heights near Columbia University campus, New York, c. 1944-1945, photograph. © Allen Ginsberg/Corbis. Reproduced by permission.—City Lights Bookstore, San Francisco, photograph. City Lights Books, Inc. Reproduced by permission.—Corso, Gregory, photograph. © Christopher Felver/Corbis. Reproduced by permission.—Cover of the Black Mountain College publicity booklet, 1936-1938, photograph. Courtesy of the North Carolina Offices of Archives and History, Raleigh, North Carolina. Reproduced by permission.—Cover of "The Black Mountain Review," photograph. Courtesy of the North Carolina Offices of Archives and History, Raleigh, North Carolina. Reproduced by permission.—Defeo, Jay. *After Image*, artwork consisting of graphite, gouache, and transparent acrylic on paper with cut and torn tracing paper, photograph. The Henil Collection, Houston. Reproduced by permission. —di Prima, Diane, photograph. © Chris Felver. Reproduced by permission.—di Prima, Diane, sitting on top of piano, reading selections from her first published book of poetry "This Kind of Bird Flies Backward," to an assembled crowd at the Gas Light Cafe in New York City, photograph. © by Fred W. McDarrah. All rights reserved. Reproduced by permission.—Donlin, Bob, Neal Cassady, Allen Ginsberg, Robert LaVinge, and Lawrence Ferlinghetti (left to right) standing outside Ferlinghetti's City Lights Bookstore, photograph. © Allen Ginsberg/Corbis. Reproduced by permission.— Duncan, Robert, photograph by Nata Piaskowski. Courtesy of New Directions. Reproduced by permission. —Dylan, Bob, photograph. AP/Wide World Photos. Reproduced by permission.—Everson, William, photograph. © Chris Felver. Reproduced by permission.—Ferlinghetti, Lawrence, photograph. AP/Wide World Photos. Reproduced by permission. —Ginsberg, Allen, reading his poem "Howl," outside the U.S. Court of Appeals in Washington, D.C., photograph. AP/Wide World Photos. Reproduced by permission.—Ginsberg, Allen, with fellow poets, original caption: "Philip Whalen, Jerry Heiserman (Hassan later as Sufi) & poet Thomas Jackerell who drove us Vancouver to San Francisco returning from poetry assemblage, we stopped to sightsee Portland where Philip had gone to Reed College with Gary Snyder & Lew Welch. End of July 1963. Vancouver," photograph. © Allen Ginsberg/Corbis. Reproduced by permission. —Ginsberg, Allen, speaking into microphone, 1969, photograph. AP/Wide World Photos. Reproduced by permission.—Guest, Barbara, photograph by Chris Felver. Reproduced by permission.—Guest, Barbara, standing and holding paper in hands while reading poetry at the Living Theatre, photograph. © by Fred W. McDarrah. All rights reserved. Reproduced by permission. —Gysin, Brion, portrait by Carl Van Vechten. The Library of Congress. Reproduced by permission. —Gysin, Brion, portrait by Carl Van Vechten. The Library of Congress. Reproduced by permission. —Holmes, John Clellon, photograph by Chris Felver. Reproduced by permission.—Huncke, Herbert, photograph by Chris Felver. Archive Photos. Reproduced by permission.—Johnson, Joyce, photograph. © Jerry Bauer. Reproduced by permission.—Kandel, Lenore, photograph. The Library of Congress.—Kaufman, Bob, reading his poems at Living Theatre, photograph. © by Fred W. McDarrah. All rights reserved. Reproduced by permission.—Kerouac, Jack, photograph. © Jerry Bauer. Reproduced by permission.—Kerouac, Jack (clockwise from top left), Allen Ginsberg, Gregory Corso, Peter Orlovsky and his brother Lafcadio on vacation in Mexico City, 1956, photograph. © Allen Ginsberg/Corbis. Reproduced by permission. —Kerouac, Jan, photograph. AP/Wide World Photos. Reproduced by permission.—Kesey, Ken, 1990, photograph. AP/Wide World Photos. Reproduced by permission.—Kyger Bolinas, JoAnne, photograph. © Chris Felver. Reproduced by permission.—Landesman, Fran, in a still from the documentary film "Gaslight Square—The Forgotten Landmark" by Bruce Marren. © 2002 Bruce Marren. Reproduced by permission.—Landesman, Jay Irving, in a still from the documentary film "Gaslight Square—The Forgotten Landmark" by Bruce Marren. © 2002 Bruce Marren. Reproduced by permission.—The Merry Pranksters' Bus, preparing it for its drive to the Acid Test Graduation, San Francisco, California, October, 1966, photograph. © Ted Streshinsky/Corbis. Reproduced by permission.—McClure, Michael, photograph. © Roger Ressmeyer/Corbis. Reproduced by permission.—Mingus, Charles (center), playing bass with other musicians during a live performance at the Five Spot Cafe in San Francisco, California, photograph. © by Fred W. McDarrah. All rights reserved. Reproduced by permission.—Mingus, Charles (center), playing bass with his ensemble, while Kenneth Patchen (right) reads poetry during a live performance at the Living Theatre, photograph. © by Fred W. McDarrah. All rights reserved. Reproduced by permission.—Monk, Thelonius, photograph by Jack Vartoogian. Reproduced by permission.—Nicholson, Jack (seated at table), and Vincent Schiavelli standing at left, in the 1975 movie version of "One Flew Over the Cuckoo's Nest," written by Ken Kesey, directed by Milos Forman, movie still. The Kobal Collection/United Artists/Fantasy Films. Reproduced by permission.—Orlovsky, Peter, photograph. AP/Wide World Photos. Reproduced by permission. —Patchen, Kenneth, photograph. Archive Photos, Inc. Reproduced by permission.—Rick Allmen's Cafe Bizarre on West Third Street in Greenwich Village, photograph. © Bettmann/Corbis. Reproduced by permission.—Rexroth, Kenneth, 1952, photograph. AP/Wide World Photos. Reproduced by permission.—St. Mark's-in-the-Bowery, an Episcopal Church built in 1799, photograph. © Lee Snider; Lee Snider/Corbis. Reproduced by permission.—Sanders, Ed, photograph by Chris Felver. Reproduced by permission of Chris Felver.—Snyder, Gary, photograph. AP/Wide World Photos. Reproduced by permission.—Solomon, Carl, photograph. © Allen Ginsberg/ Corbis. Reproduced by permission.—Students sitting under a tree at Columbia University, original caption: "Outdoor Class, Outdoor Class on Columbia University Campus is shown, as class was taken outside on this warm summer day," New York, May 7, 1959, photograph. © Bettmann/ Corbis. Reproduced by permission.—Village Vanguard nightclub, Greenwich Village, New York, January 1, 1967, photograph. © Bettmann/Corbis. Reproduced by permission.—Waldman, Anne, photograph. © Allen Ginsberg/Corbis. Reproduced by permission.—Waldman, Anne, reading a poem in tribute to the late Allen Ginsberg at the Wadsworth Theater in Los Angeles, California, photograph. AP/Wide World Photos. Reproduced by permission.—Washington Square in Greenwich Village and an arch, photograph. © Bettmann/ Corbis. Reproduced by permission.—weiss, ruth, photograph by Daniel Nicoletta. © 2002 Daniel Nicoletta. Reproduced by permission.—Welch, Lew, photograph. © by Fred W. McDarrah. All rights reserved. Reproduced by permission. —Weller, Peter, as Bill Lee in the 1992 film "Naked Lunch," based on the book written by William Burroughs, directed by David Cronenberg, movie still. The Kobal Collection/Recorded Picture Co/ First Independent. Reproduced by permission. —Whalen, Philip, 1984, photograph. © Allen Ginsberg/Corbis. Reproduced by permission. —Wieners, John, photograph. © Allen Ginsberg/ Corbis. Reproduced by permission.

● = historical event

▓ = literary event

1914

● William Seward Burroughs is born on 5 February in St. Louis, Missouri. He is the heir to the Burroughs Adding Machine Corporation.

1915

● Herbert Edwin Huncke is born on 9 January in Greenfield, Massachusetts.

1919

● Lawrence Ferlinghetti is born 24 March in Yonkers, New York.

1922

● Jean-Louis (Jack) Kerouac is born on 12 March in Lowell, Massachusetts.

1926

● Neal Cassady is born 18 February in Salt Lake City, Utah, as his parents travel from Iowa to California.

● Irwin Allen Ginsberg is born on 3 June in Paterson, New Jersey.

1930

● Gregory Nunzio Corso is born on 26 March in Greenwich Village, New York.

1932

● Burroughs enters Harvard University as an English major.

1939

● Huncke arrives in New York City.

● Kerouac attends preparatory school before entering Columbia University on a football scholarship.

1941

● The U.S. Naval base at Pearl Harbor, Hawaii, is attacked by Japanese forces; the event spurs America's entry into World War II.

1942

● Kerouac enlists in the merchant marines, serving on the *S.S. Dorchester*.

● Burroughs finds work in Chicago as a pest exterminator.

1943

● Burroughs arrives in New York City.

■ Kerouac works on the novel "The Sea Is My Brother," which remains unfinished and unpublished.

● Ginsberg meets Lucien Carr while attending Columbia. Carr introduces Ginsberg to Kerouac and Burroughs.

1944

■ Ginsberg, Kerouac, and Carr formulate and discuss "The New Vision" or "New Consciousness," a literary manifesto inspired by the work of such authors as Franz Kafka, Albert Camus, and W. H. Auden. "The New Vision" provides a framework for the Beat aesthetic.

● Carr is arrested for the murder of David Kammerer; Kerouac is detained as a material witness. Kerouac marries Edie Parker as a means of raising money for Carr's defense. Carr is convicted and serves two years in prison.

● Burroughs meets Huncke.

■ Kenneth Rexroth, Philip Lamantia, William Everson, and Robert Creeley orchestrate the Berkeley Renaissance.

1945

● Ginsberg is suspended from Columbia. He moves to a communal apartment occupied by, among others, Kerouac and Joan Vollmer, who will become Burroughs's common-law wife.

● World War II ends.

1946

■ Kerouac begins writing his first published novel, *The Town and the City*.

● Huncke introduces Burroughs to heroin.

● Cassady arrives in New York and begins a friendship with Ginsberg and Kerouac.

● Corso begins a three-year prison sentence for grand theft; he begins writing poetry while incarcerated.

1947

● Burroughs and Vollmer move to Texas, where their son, William Seward, Jr., is born.

● Cassady meets Carolyn Robinson, who will become his second wife.

■ Kerouac travels to Denver, a trip that will inform *On the Road*.

● The House Un-American Activities Committee (HUAAC) begins congressional hearings on suspected American communists.

1948

● Burroughs moves his family to Louisiana.

■ Kerouac completes *The Town and the City*. He coins the phrase "Beat Generation." In the winter, he and Cassady travel the U.S., excursions which will be recounted in *On the Road*.

● John Clellon Holmes meets Kerouac and Ginsberg in New York City.

● Ginsberg has a series of visions involving William Blake.

1949

● Ginsberg is arrested for allowing Huncke to keep stolen goods in his apartment.

■ Kerouac receives a $1000 advance from Harcourt, Brace for *The Town and the City*.

● Burroughs's legal troubles force him to move his family to Mexico.

● Trumpeter Miles Davis's album *The Birth of the Cool* marks the onset of the "Cool Jazz" movement and marks a period of renewed popularity for jazz music; the medium will have a great influence on Beat writers in the next decade.

1950

■ Kerouac's *The Town and the City* is published.

■ Burroughs starts work on *Junkie*.

● Kerouac marries Joan Haverty.

● Ginsberg meets Corso in Greenwich Village.

● Ferlinghetti moves from New York to San Francisco.

1951

■ John Clellon Holmes completes *Go*, the novel is generally credited as the first to chronicle the Beat Generation.

■ Burroughs begins writing *Queer*.

■ Fueled by stimulants, Kerouac composes the scroll version of *On the Road* in one long writing session; the event is an early example of the nascent technique he has dubbed "spontaneous prose."

- In Mexico, Burroughs accidentally shoots and kills Vollmer; he credits her death as his motivation to seriously pursue a writing career.

- American forces join in the Korean War.

1952

- Kerouac visits the Cassadys in San Francisco, where he composes part of *Visions of Cody*. He has an affair with Carolyn Cassady. Later in the year, Kerouac will visit Burroughs in Mexico, where he writes *Doctor Sax*.

- Holmes's *Go* is published by Scribners; he writes the seminal article "This is the Beat Generation" for the *New York Times Magazine*.

1953

- Burroughs's *Junkie: Confessions of an Unredeemed Drug Addict* is published under the pseudonym William Lee by Ace Books.

- Ferlinghetti and Peter Martin open City Lights, the first paperback bookstore in the U.S.

- Burroughs and Ginsberg have a brief affair. At its end, Burroughs moves to Tangiers, where he will live for the next five years. While in Tangiers, he begins work on *Naked Lunch*.

- Kerouac writes *Maggie Cassidy* and *The Subterraneans*.

1954

- Attracted to the tenets of the religion, Kerouac begins studying Buddhism. He begins writing *San Francisco Blues* and *Some of the Dharma*, his unpublished musings on Buddhism.

- Ginsberg moves to San Francisco to work in market research and meets Peter Orlovsky; the two will become lifelong partners.

- In California, the North Beach bohemian scene, comprised of writers such as Jack Spicer, Richard Brautigan, Bob Kaufman, and John Weiners, finds expression in cafés, bars, and jazz clubs.

1955

- Corso publishes his first poetry collection, *The Vestal Lady on Brattle and Other Poems*.

- While in San Francisco, Ginsberg completes the majority of "Howl."

- Ferlinghetti founds City Lights Press; the first book on the imprint is his own *Pictures of the Gone World*; publication of works by Kenneth Patchen, Ginsberg, Corso, and Kerouac soon follow.

- Kerouac writes *Mexico City Blues* and starts work on *Tristessa*. Excerpts from *On the Road* are published in *New World Writing* and *Paris Review*.

- Kenneth Rexroth hosts the landmark poetry reading (organized by Ginsberg) at Six Gallery in San Francisco on 7 October; performers include Ginsberg, who performs a breakthrough reading of "Howl," as well as Philip Lamantia, Gary Snyder, Michael McClure, and Philip Whalen.

1956

- Kerouac completes *Tristessa* and begins work on *Visions of Gerard* and *Desolation Angels*.

- Ginsberg reads the complete "Howl" in Berkeley, California. City Lights publishes the poem in the collection *Howl and Other Poems* with an introduction by William Carlos Williams.

- Ginsberg's mother, Naomi dies; the event has a profound effect on the poet and will influence his later work, notably the poem "Kaddish."

1957

- Kerouac meets up with Ginsberg and Orlovsky in Tangiers where they assist Burroughs in the assembly of *Naked Lunch*.

- In March, copies of *Howl and Other Poems* are confiscated and later released by U. S. Customs officials. Ferlinghetti is subsequently arrested for selling the book, which is alleged to be a work of obscenity. In October, following the famous obscenity trial, Ginsberg's work is found to be "not obscene."

- Rexroth and Ferlinghetti perform their poetry accompanied by a jazz band in a San Francisco bar.

- Kerouac's *On the Road* is published by Viking. Reviews are favorable and the book and its author gain widespread popularity.

- Ginsberg begins writing "Kaddish" in memory of his mother.

The *Evergreen Review* publishes "San Francisco Poets" by Barney Rossett and Donald Allen; the piece is a special focus on the West Coast Beats.

1958

- Ginsberg, Orlovsky, Corso, and Burroughs move into the "Beat Hotel" in Paris.

- Corso's poem "Bomb" is published as a broadside; his collection *Gasoline* is published by City Lights.

- Grove Press publishes Kerouac's *The Subterraneans*; Viking publishes *The Dharma Bums*.

- Kerouac makes an appearance on *The Steve Allen Show*.

- An excerpt from Burroughs's *Naked Lunch* is published in the fall issue of the *Chicago Review*; the work's appearance results in controversy over censorship.

- Cassady begins a two-year prison sentence for possession of marijuana.

- Ferlinghetti's *A Coney Island of the Mind* is published by New Directions.

- Random House publishes Holmes's *The Horn*.

- LeRoi and Hettie Jones found Totem Press as well as the journal *Yugen*.

1959

- Burroughs's *The Naked Lunch* is published in Paris by Olympia Press; Grove will publish the book in the U.S. as *Naked Lunch* in 1962.

- Kerouac publishes several works this year, including *Doctor Sax, Maggie Cassidy, Mexico City Blues,* and *Excerpts from Visions of Cody*.

- Gary Snyder's *Rip Rap* is published in Japan by Origin Press.

- *Pull My Daisy* is produced; the Beat-themed film features appearances by Ginsberg, Corso, and Peter Orlovsky, and Kerouac serves as the narrator.

- Ginsberg records a version of "Howl" to be released on Fantasy Records, a major jazz label.

- Beat literature and lifestyle receives significant attention in publications such as *Time* and *Life,* as well as in the highly critical publication by Lawrence Lipton, *The Holy Barbarians*.

- 29 September debut of television series *The Many Loves of Dobie Gillis*, which features a Beatnik character, Maynard G. Krebbs.

1960

- Kerouac publishes *Tristessa, The Scripture of the Golden Eternity,* and *Lonesome Traveler*.

- Corso's *The Happy Birthday of Death* is published by New Directions.

- Totem Press publishes Snyder's *Myths and Texts*.

- *The New American Poetry* is published by Grove Press; the volume is edited by Donald Allen and presents the work of several Beat poets.

- The film adaptation of Kerouac's *The Subterraneans* is produced by Metro-Goldwyn-Mayer.

- Inspired by interaction with Brion Gysin, Burroughs begins to experiment with the "Cutup" literary technique for *Minutes to Go* and *Exterminator*.

- Seymour Krim's landmark chronicle, *The Beats,* is published by Gold Medal.

- The 7 October debut of the television series *Route 66*, which chronicles the cross-country travels of two young men; the show grew out of plans to create a television series based upon *On the Road*; the concept was rejected by Kerouac and re-tooled as *Route 66*.

1961

- Burroughs's *The Soft Machine* is published by Olympia.

- Corso publishes his only novel, *The American Express*.

- Kerouac begins writing *Big Sur* and completes *Desolations Angels*; he publishes *Book of Dreams* and *Pull My Daisy*.

- City Lights publishes Ginsberg's *Kaddish and Other Poems: 1958-1960*; Ginsberg travels to the Near and Far East.

1962

- Burroughs's *The Ticket That Exploded* is published in Japan; *Naked Lunch* is published in the U.S.

- Kerouac's *Big Sur* is published by Grove.

- Burroughs receives international notice when Norman Mailer and others hail his work at the International Writer's Conference in Edinburgh.

1963

- Kerouac's *Visions of Gerard* is published by Farrar, Strauss.

- Correspondence between Ginsberg and Burroughs is published as *The Yage Letters* by City Lights.
- City Lights publishes Ginsberg's *Reality Sandwiches*.
- Ginsberg is awarded a Guggenheim Fellowship.

1964

- Diane di Prima founds Poets Press.
- Kerouac moves to Tampa, Florida, where he resides with his mother; he and Cassady see each other for the last time.

1965

- Following his travels in France, Kerouac begins writing *Satori in Paris*; *Desolation Angels* is published by Coward-McCann.
- Poets Press publishes *Huncke's Journal*.

1966

- Burroughs moves to London and his novel *The Soft Machine* is published by Grove.
- Kerouac and his mother move to Hyannis on Cape Cod, Massachusetts, where she suffers a stroke. Kerouac marries Stella Sampas, his third wife, and the three move back to his hometown of Lowell.
- A decision is reached in the *Naked Lunch* obscenity trial, with the Massachusetts Supreme Court ruling that while the work is "grossly offensive," it is not obscene.

1967

- Kerouac begins work on *The Valley of Duluoz*.
- *The Ticket That Exploded* is published in America by Grove.
- *Nothing More to Declare* by John Clellon Holmes is published.

1968

- Kerouac's *The Valley of Duluoz* is published by Coward-McCann.
- After a night of heavy drinking, Neal Cassady wanders into the Mexican desert and dies of exposure.

- Ginsberg organizes a protest of the Vietnam War to coincide with the Democratic National Convention in Chicago, Illinois; rioting ensues and the National Guard is called out.

1969

- Kerouac completes his final work, *Pic*; his alcoholism is chronic by this point; on 21 October, a vein in his stomach bursts, and Kerouac dies in St. Petersburg, Florida; he is later buried in Lowell.
- Ginsberg is awarded a poetry grant from the National Institute of Arts and Letters.

1970

- Burroughs's *The Last Words of Dutch Schultz* is published in London; U.S. publication in an enlarged and revised format in 1975 by Viking.

1971

- Burroughs's *The Wild Boys: A Book of the Dead* is published by Grove.

1973

- Viking publishes Burroughs's *Exterminator!*.

1974

- Burroughs returns to America and takes a teaching post at the City College of New York.
- Ginsberg's *Fall of America* wins the National Book Award, and he is inducted into the American Academy of Arts and Letters.
- The Jack Kerouac School of Disembodied Poetics, Naropa Institute, is founded by Ginsberg and Anne Waldman in Boulder, Colorado.

1978

- Ginsberg's *Mindbreaths: Poems 1972-1977* is published by City Lights.
- *As Ever: The Collected Correspondence of Allen Ginsberg & Neal Cassady* is published by Creative Arts.

1981

- Burroughs moves to Lawrence, Kansas.

1982

- The Naropa Institute holds a twenty-fifth anniversary celebration of Kerouac's *On the Road*. In attendance are, among others, Ginsberg, Burroughs, Corso, Ferlinghetti, Michael McClure, Ken Kesey, Abbie Hoffman, Anne Waldman, Timothy Leary, and Herbert Huncke.

1985

- Viking publishes *Queer* by Burroughs.

1989

- Burroughs appears as the Tom, the Junky Priest, in director Gus Van Sant's film *Drugstore Cowboy*.

1990

- Burroughs releases the album *Dead City Radio,* which features readings of unpublished material.

- Director David Cronenberg's loose film adaptation of Burroughs's *Naked Lunch* is released; Peter Weller plays Bill Lee and Judy Davis plays Joan Vollmer.

- Burroughs has triple bypass heart surgery.

1992

- Burroughs and Kurt Cobain of the rock group Nirvana collaborate on the album *The Priest They Called Him.*

1993

- Burroughs collaborates with musician Tom Waits and director Robert Wilson on the musical play and album (released under Waits's name) *The Black Rider.*

1994

- Burroughs appears in Nike television advertisements.

- "The Beat Legacy and Celebration" is held on 18-21 May; sponsored by New York University, the event is chaired by Ginsberg and Ann Charters; speakers include Carolyn Cassady, Corso, Ferlinghetti, Hettie Jones, Ed Sanders, Hunter S. Thompson, and Anne Waldman, among others.

1995

- New York University sponsors "The Writing of Jack Kerouac Conference" on 4-6 June.

1996

- Huncke dies on 8 August from congestive heart failure in NewYork City.

1997

- Ginsberg dies on 5 April from complications of liver cancer in New York City.

- Burroughs dies on 2 August following a heart attack in Lawrence, Kansas.

2001

- Corso dies on 17 January from prostate cancer in Minnesota.

JOYCE JOHNSON

(1935 -)

(Born Joyce Glassman) American novelist, autobiographer, and nonfiction writer.

Johnson was Jack Kerouac's lover during the period when he wrote *On the Road,* and in her memoir *Minor Characters* (1983) she recounts her life as a member of Kerouac's social circle. Her autobiography earned a National Book Critics Circle Award and was hailed as a compelling remembrance of the Beat Generation. During her time with Kerouac, Johnson worked as a secretary while writing her first novel, although her literary aspirations were greatly overshadowed by the notoriety of her famous lover. Since the 1960s she has worked as an editor, written a number of well-received works of fiction and nonfiction, and published a collection of her correspondence with Kerouac in *Door Wide Open* (2000).

BIOGRAPHICAL INFORMATION

Johnson was born in New York City in 1935 to Daniel and Rosalind Glassman. Her family was middle class and conservative, and Johnson led a relatively sheltered life. As a teenager, however, she developed a fascination with artists and radicals, and would sneak away from home to spend time in New York's Greenwich Village. This interest continued during her four years at Colum-

bia University, and she soon became involved with a group of former students from the university who were at the center of the Beat movement. When she was twenty-one, Johnson met and began an affair with Kerouac, who was fifteen years her senior. Because of her involvement with Kerouac, Johnson associated with some of the most influential people of the Beat scene. She and Kerouac lived together in a New York apartment during the time that Kerouac wrote and published *On the Road.* Their troubled relationship ended by 1958, after Kerouac began having affairs with other women. In 1962 Johnson married painter James Johnson, who died the following year; two years later she married Peter Pinchbeck, whom she divorced in 1971. In the 1960s Johnson worked as a secretary in a publishing house to support herself, and by the 1980s she had established herself as a successful editor and author, publishing fiction and nonfiction books as well as articles and stories in magazines and literary journals. She has received a National Endowment for the Arts fellowship, has taught in graduate writing programs at several universities, and continues to work as a book publishing editor.

MAJOR WORKS

Johnson published her first novel, *Come and Join the Dance* (1962), under the name Joyce Glassman. This little-known work, regarded by some as the first female Beat novel, records a week in the life of Susan Leavitt as she searches for "real" life after graduation from college in New York City. For many years after their relationship was over, Johnson was known primarily as Kerouac's former lover, but the publication of *Minor Characters* in 1983 demonstrated her significant literary talents. *Minor Characters* offers a unique, female insider's perspective on the Beat generation and discusses other women writers of the era such as Elise Cowen and Hettie Jones. Johnson's other works include a 1978 novel *Bad Connections*, which examines the feminism of the 1970s; *In the Night Café* (1989), a novel about an aspiring New York actress and her romance with a self-destructive artist that highlights the Beat era of Greenwich Village; and *What Lisa Knew: The Truths and Lies of the Steinberg Case* (1990), a real-life account of the murder of six-year-old Lisa Steinberg by her adoptive parents Joel Steinberg and Hedda Nussbaum. In 2000 she published a collection of her correspondence with Kerouac in *Door Wide Open*.

CRITICAL RECEPTION

During the Beat era, Johnson's work was critically ignored, eclipsed by the charisma and sudden rise to stardom of her famous lover. Since the 1960s, however, critics have found Johnson to be a skilled writer in her own right and an able chronicler of Bohemian Manhattan in the late 1950s and 1960s. *Minor Characters* won the 1984 National Book Critics Circle Award for best autobiography, and reviewers praised it as a compelling look at a turbulent time in American literary history. Her other works have received warm praise, although some commentators have complained that her writing is often too self-consciously lyrical. Reviewers of her correspondence with Kerouac have noted that those letters show Johnson to be a better writer—calmer, more honest, and more astute—than her lover. Critics have also argued that the fact that Kerouac became such an icon while Johnson remained relatively unknown speaks a great deal about the male-dominated Beat society and American writing and literary reception in general.

PRINCIPAL WORKS

Come and Join the Dance [as Joyce Glassman] (novel) 1962

Bad Connections (novel) 1978

Minor Characters: A Young Woman's Coming-of-Age in the Beat Orbit of Jack Kerouac (autobiography) 1983

In the Night Café (novel) 1989

What Lisa Knew: The Truths and Lies of the Steinberg Case (nonfiction) 1990

Door Wide Open: A Beat Love Affair in Letters, 1957-58 (letters) 2000

PRIMARY SOURCES

JOYCE JOHNSON (ESSAY DATE 1999)

SOURCE: Johnson, Joyce. "Beat Queens: Women in Flux." In *The Rolling Stone Book of the Beats: The Beat Generation and American Culture,* edited by Holly George-Warren, pp. 40-50. New York: Hyperion, 1999.

In the following excerpt, Johnson recounts her experiences as a woman among the New York Beats.

What did "real life" mean to a middle-class adolescent girl in 1950. I yearned for it and thought I'd recognize it when I saw it, but I could not quite define it. I was sure real life was sexual, though my ignorance of sex was profound. . . . Until I entered Barnard College in 1951 and took a freshman course called Modern Living, I did not have a very clear idea of how babies were born, nor did many of my classmates. I would meet Jack Kerouac only six years later. . . .

The neighborhood around Columbia University and Barnard College was the birthplace of the Beat Generation, the meeting ground of Allen Ginsberg, Jack Kerouac, William Burroughs, and Lucien Carr. The group included two unusually adventurous young women as well—Edie Parker, Kerouac's first wife, and Joan Vollmer Adams, who had a common-law marriage with Burroughs. As I would be in the next decade, both were drawn to charismatic men who lived the larger lives denied to women, and offered them little in the way of security or protection. . . . Like Carolyn Cassady, who later married Kerouac's friend Neal, these Forties women seemed content to define themselves as wives of geniuses. . . .

The Beats have often been accused of having no respect for creative women. But in truth this lack of respect was so pervasive in American culture in the postwar years that women did not even question it. . . .

[Barnard teacher John Kouwenhoven] told a roomful of girls that if they really wanted to be writers, they wouldn't be enrolled in his class— they'd be out in American hopping freight trains.

Since it was inconceivable in 1953 that a young woman would open herself up to such experience, and since all we had to write about was what Kouwenhoven called our "boring little lives," there was obviously no hope for us. . . .

For some doctrinaire feminists in our own time, *On the Road* has been a deceptively easy target. . . . Reading Kerouac now, they find nothing in his work that speaks to female readers. Yet, in 1957 when *On the Road* was published, thousands of Fifties women experienced a powerful response to what they read. *On the Road* was prophecy, bringing news of the oncoming, unstoppable sexual revolution—the revolution that would precede and ultimately pave the way for women's liberation. . . .

In our downtown scene in the East Village there was an interesting role reversal going on—women were often the breadwinners so the men would be free to pursue their creative work. I had a taste of this the first night I met Kerouac, when I bought him frankfurters and beans at Howard Johnson's because he was absolutely broke. I had never done such a thing before. Interestingly enough, it did not make me feel exploited, but strangely grown up. . . .

Most of us never got the chance to literally go on the road. Our road instead became the strange lives we were leading. We had actually chosen these difficult lives for good reasons; we hadn't fallen into them by default, or been kidnapped into fifth-floor walkups in the East Village. We couldn't take on the task of transforming relationships between men and women because it took such an overwhelming amount of effort to come as far as we had; our most consuming struggle was the break with the mores of our parents' generation. We experienced the thrill of being part of a movement that changed life in America, and we endured the hard times that came with making something new. Many of us discovered we were tougher and more resilient than we'd imagined we could be. . . .

GENERAL COMMENTARY

BRENDA KNIGHT (ESSAY DATE 1996)

SOURCE: Knight, Brenda. "Joyce Johnson: A True Good Heart." In *Women of the Beat Generation: The Writers, Artists, and Muses at the Heart of a Revolution*, pp. 167-81. Berkeley, Calif.: Conari Press, 1996.

In the following essay, Knight discusses Johnson's involvement with the Beats and includes excerpts from Minor Characters, *in which Johnson writes about her relationship with Jack Kerouac.*

"Joyce was a city girl, bookish, the closely watched only child of more ambitious Upper West Side parents. . . . But she was writing—a novel, already under contract—and that was her good fortune, I thought. We shared what was most important to us: common assumptions about our uncommon lives. We lived outside, as if. As if we were men? As if we were new, freer versions of ourselves? There have always been women like us."

—Hettie Jones

Joyce Johnson's ironically titled **Minor Characters** was the first book to focus specifically upon Beat women. Joyce was Jack Kerouac's lover during 1957 and 1958, the two crucial years that brought the Beat Generation into public awareness. In her 1983 memoir, which received a National Book Critics Circle award, she recreates her time in the Beat inner circle during that period, writing not only about herself but about two other women in their early twenties who became her close friends: the doomed Elise Cowen and the stalwart Hettie Jones. Johnson gives an eyewitness account of Kerouac's catastrophic encounter with fame when *On the Road* became a cause célèbre in 1957 and inspired many young people around the world to identify themselves as Beatniks. We see how the members of the Beat Generation, such as Allen Ginsberg and LeRoi Jones, managed to thrive while others like Kerouac and Cowen were unable to survive the seismic shift in sensibility.

But **Minor Characters** is first and foremost Joyce's own story, showing us what it was like to be a young woman coming of age in the tumultuous and transitional fifties, as the youth of postwar America chafed against the constraints of a buttoned-up, conservative society. Joyce, Elise Cowen and most of their contemporaries were expected to marry a wage-earning male as soon as possible and settle down to raise a family. Parental pressure to conform to this ideal was high as Hettie Jones also testifies in *How I Became Hettie Jones*.

Strangely enough, Johnson grew up on West 116th street on Manhattan just around the corner from the apartment salon of William and Joan Vollmer Adams Burroughs where Ginsberg and Kerouac were frequent visitors during the late forties; her parents, Daniel and Rosalind Glassman had moved there from Queens when she was eight years old. The Glassmans, a quiet, hardworking Jewish couple, placed their hopes on Joyce, their precocious only child, and her potential as a librettist and composer of musical comedies; they certainly did not expect her to hook up with a hard-drinking, vagabond writer like Jack Kerouac. At the age of thirteen Joyce began rebelling against their attempts to control her life and started making illicit trips to Washington Square. Over-whelmed by a love affair with an instructor during her last year at Barnard College, she fell short of getting her B.A., and she abandoned music, refusing to be the surrogate for her mother's frustrated ambitions. There was a rift with her family, when she left home following her non-graduation.

In 1955 at the age of twenty, she began her first novel **Come and Join the Dance,** and supported herself by working for literary agents. One of her employers, Phyllis Jackson, turned out to be the agent who had rejected three manuscripts of Jack Kerouac's, including *On the Road* (Kerouac's staunch advocate Allen Ginsberg had once made a memorable trip to the agency to retrieve Jack's work).

Joyce found her way to the heart of the Beat scene through her Barnard classmate Elise Cowen, who had begun a relationship with Allen Ginsberg in 1952, two years before Ginsberg fell in love with Peter Orlovsky. In January, 1957, Ginsberg arranged a blind date for Joyce with Jack Kerouac; the 21-year-old Johnson and the 34-year-old road-weary Kerouac met at a Howard Johnson's in the Village.

As photos of the period attest, the two were a study in contrasts: Joyce all wistful, delicate features and demure blond freshness; Kerouac darkly handsome with striking blue eyes and a rugged, wild air. Joyce was with him the day he went from unknown writer to Beat icon. On September 5, 1957, *On the Road,* the novel he had typed on a long scroll of drawing paper during two feverish weeks in 1949, received an over-whelmingly laudatory review in the *New York Times.* The prescient critic Gilbert Millstein, cited its publication as "a historic occasion . . . the testament . . . of the Beat Generation." After that the phone in Johnson's apartment, where Kerouac was living never stopped ringing. Kerouac had become famous overnight.

To read about Joyce's two-year love affair with Kerouac in **Minor Characters** is to hope against hope that somehow Joyce will be able to save Jack from crushing, unwanted notoriety, from his crippling emotional dependence upon his mother, Mémère, and from alcohol. It was not meant to be.

It was not an easy time for either of them; but for Kerouac it proved disastrous. Joyce writes:

> As of 1982, there is the Jack Kerouac Society for Disembodied Poetics, founded in Boulder, Colorado, in 1976. There is *Jack's Book,* as well as

Desolation Angel: Jack Kerouac, the Beat Generation and America and *Jack Kerouac: A Biography* and—the one I like best—*Kerouac: A Chicken Essay,* by a French-Canadian surrealist poet; as well as proliferating pamphlets, theses, articles, chapters in books. A journal published annually celebrates the Beats and the "Unspeakable Visions of the Individual." It's hagiography in the making. Jack, now delivered into the Void, would be amazed to know there's even a literary fan magazine devoted entirely to him, called *Moody Street Irregulars* (after the street in Lowell where he lived as a child). For a back issue, a graduate student somewhere put together a rather randomly chosen chronology of Jack Kerouac's life. In a column labeled 1957, there's a cryptic entry: *Meets Joyce Glassman.*

"Hello. I'm Jack. Allen tells me you're very nice. Would you like to come down to Howard Johnson's on Eighth Street? I'll be sitting at the counter. I have black hair and I'll be wearing a red and black checked shirt."

I'm standing in Elise's kitchen, holding the phone Allen has just handed me. It's a Saturday night shortly after New Year's.

"Sure," I say. I put on a lot of eye shadow and my coat and take the subway down to Astor Place and begin walking westward, cross-town, passing under the bridge between the two buildings of Wanamaker's Department Store and the eye of the giant illuminated clock. It's a dark, bitter January night with ice all over the pavements, so you have to be careful, but I'm flying along, it's an adventure as opposed to a misadventure—under which category so far I've had to put most of the risky occurrences in my life.

The windows of Howard Johnson's are running with steam so you can't see in. I push open the heavy glass door, and there is, sure enough, a black-haired man at the counter in a flannel lumberjack shirt slightly the worse for wear. He looks up and stares at me hard with blue eyes, amazingly blue. And the skin of his face is so brown. He's the only person in Howard Johnson's in color. I feel a little scared as I walk up to him. "Jack?" I say.

There's an empty stool next to his. I sit down on it and he asks me whether I want anything. "Just coffee." He's awfully quiet. We both lack conversation, but then we don't know each other, so what can we say? He asks after Allen, Lafcadio, that kind of thing. I'd like to tell him I've read his book, if that wouldn't sound gauche, obvious and uncool.

When the coffee arrives, Jack looks glum. He can't pay for it. He has no money, none at all. That morning he'd handed his last ten dollars to a cashier on a grocery store and received change for five. He's waiting for a check from a publisher, he says angrily.

I say, "Look, that's all right. I have money. Do you want me to buy you something to eat?"

"Yeah," he says. "Frankfurters. I'll pay you back. I always pay people back, you know."

I've never bought a man dinner before. It makes me feel very competent and womanly.

He has frankfurters, home fries, and baked beans with Heinz ketchup on them. I keep stealing looks at him because he's beautiful. You're not supposed to say a man is beautiful, but he is. He catches me at it and grins, then mugs it up, putting on one goofy face after another; a whole succession of old-time ridiculous movie-comedian faces flashes before me until I'm laughing too at the absurdity of this blind date Allen has arranged. (The notion of Allen Ginsberg arranging blind dates will crack people up years later when they ask me how on earth I met Kerouac.)

As for what he saw in me that night, I'm not sure at all. A very young woman in a red coat, round-faced and blonde. "An interesting young person," he wrote in *Desolation Angels.* "A Jewess, elegant middleclass sad and looking for something—she looked Polish as hell . . ." Where am I in all those funny categories?

As our paths converge on Howard Johnson's, we're looking for different things. At thirty-four, Jack's worn down, the energy that had moved him to so many different places gone. He's suddenly waited too long. The check for *The Subterraneans* will never arrive, *On the Road* will never be published. Why not let Allen rescue him? He can't go back to the two Virginias.

I see the blue, bruised eye of Kerouac and construe his melancholy as the look of a man needing love because I'm, among other things, twenty-one years old. I believe in the curative powers of love as the English believe in tea or Catholics believe in the Miracle of Lourdes.

He tells me he's spent sixty-three days on a mountaintop without anyone. He made pea soup and wrote in his journal and sang Sinatra songs to keep himself company.

Some warning to me in all this. "You really liked being alone like that?" I ask.

"I wish I was there now. I should've stayed up there."

He could somehow cancel you out and make you feel sad for him at the same time. But I'm sure any mountaintop would be preferable to where he's staying—the Marlton Hotel on Eighth Street, with the dirty shades over the windows and the winos lounging on the steps.

"And where do you live?" Jack asks. He likes it that it's up near Columbia and the West End Bar where he used to hang out. Was Johnny the bartender still there? Johnny the bartender would remember him from the days he was a football hero at Columbia but he broke his leg in his sophomore year and stayed in his room reading Céline, and Shakespeare and never went back to football again—thus losing his scholarship at Columbia, but he's always had affection for the neighborhood, "Why don't you let me stay at your place?" he says.

"If you wish," I say in *Desolation Angels,* deciding fast. And I know how I said it, too. As if it was of no great moment, as if I had no wishes of my own—in keeping with my current philosophy of nothing-to-lose, try anything.

We stood up and put on our coats, we went down into the subway. And there on the IRT, on a signboard I'd never seen before that night, was an ad for an airline with a brand-new slogan: FLY NOW. PAY LATER.

"That's good title for a novel," I said and finally told Jack I was writing one, I wasn't just a secretary. He said Pay Me the Penny After would be a better title, "You should call your novel that." He asked me who my favorite writer was. I said Henry James, and he made a face, and said he figured I had all the wrong models, but maybe I could be a great writer anyway. He asked me if I rewrote a lot, and said you should never revise, never change anything, not even a word. He regretted all the rewriting he'd done on *The Town and the City.* No one could make him do that again, which was why he always got nowhere with publishers. He was going to look at my work and show me that what you wrote first was always best. I said okay, feeling guilty for all that I'd rewritten, but I still loved Henry James.

All though this literary conversation, Jack stood swaying above me on the subway. Hanging on to the strap. Just before we got off, he leaned down. Our foreheads scraped, our eyeballs loomed up on each other—a funny game where I knew you weren't supposed to blink, no matter what.

That was the start of *Meets Joyce Glassman.*

The apartment I lived in at the time was dark and cavernous, on the first floor of a brownstone halfway down the block from the Yorkshire Hotel. Two furnished rooms—the furnishings being the uselessly massive, weak-jointed kind found in the lobbies of antediluvian apartment buildings. A small refrigerator and a two-burner stove stood behind a screen in one corner of the living room, but you had to wash your dishes in the bathroom sink. The windows looked out on a rank back yard where a large tree of heaven battened on bedsprings and broken bottles. I always felt very small in that apartment. One night outside the house a huge grey tomcat with a chewed ear had rubbed against my legs. I'd hauled him inside under the impression I was rescuing him, but he spent his days on the windowsill longing for the street, trying to pry the window open with his paw, or he lurked in the closet vengefully spraying shoes. Jack was the only person I'd brought home so far who saw the beauty of this animal, whom I'd unimaginatively named Smoke. He said he was going to call it Ti Gris, after a cat he once had in Lowell. He seemed to like to rename things. On the walk from the subway I'd become Joycey, which no one had called me since I was little, and he'd put his arm around me, leaning on me playfully and letting his hand angle down over my breast—that was how men walked with their women in

Mexico, he said. "Someday when you go there, you'll see that for yourself."

When we got in the door, he didn't ask to see my manuscript. He pulled me against him and kissed me before I even turned on the light. I kissed him back, and he acted surprised. He said I was even quieter than he was, he had no idea quiet girls liked kissing so much, and undid the buttons of my coat and put both his hands up my back under my sweater. "The trouble is," Jack said with his voice against my ear, "I don't . . . like . . . blondes."

I remember laughing and saying, "Well, in that case I'll just dye my hair"—wondering all the same if it was true.

In the morning Jack left to get his stuff out of the Marlton. He returned with a sleeping bag and a knapsack in which there were jeans and a few old shirts like the one he was already wearing and some notebooks he'd bought in Mexico City. That was all he owned. Not even a typewriter—he'd been borrowing other people's typewriters, he said. I'd never seen such foreign-looking notebooks, long and narrow with shiny black covers and thin, bluish paper on which Jack's slanted penciled printing sped across page after page, interrupted here and there by little sketches. One notebook was just for dreams. He wrote in it every morning.

There was something heartbreakingly attractive in these few essentials to which Jack had reduced his needs. He reminded me of a sailor—not that I knew any sailors—something too about the way he looked coming out of the shower, gleaming and vigorous and ruddy with a white towel around his neck.

Very quickly it didn't seem strange to have him with me, we were somehow like very old friends— "buddies," Jack said, squeezing me affectionately, making me feel both proud and a little disappointed. Crazy as it was, I sometimes really wished I was dark—like this Virginia I felt jealous of for making him so wild. Or the girl named Esmeralda who lived in Mexico City and whom he'd loved tragically for a long time and written an entire novel about in one of his notebooks, calling her Tristessa. But he'd slept with her only once, She was a whore and saint, so beautiful and lost—one of his mysterious fellaheen women, primeval and of the earth.

I was inprimeval and distinctly of the city. I was everydayness, bacon and eggs in the morning or the middle of the night, which I learned to cook just the way he liked—sunny-side up in the black iron frying pan. I'd buy slab bacon in the grocery store, like he'd always had in Lowell—not the skinny kind in packages—and add canned applesauce (a refinement I'd learned from Bickford's Cafeteria), which Jack had never thought of as anything that might enhance eggs. He took extraordinary pleasure in small things like that.

As a lover he wasn't fierce but oddly brotherly and somewhat reticent. I'd listen in amazement to his stories of Berkeley parties where everyone was naked and men and women engaged in some exotic Japanese practice called yabyum (but Jack, fully clothed, had sat apart brooding over his bottle of port, something he didn't tell me). In my memories of Jack in the good times we had together, I'm lying with my head on his chest, his heart pulsing against my ear. His smooth hard powerful arms are around me and I'm burying my face into them because I like them so much, making him laugh, "What are you doing there, Joycey?" And there's always music on the radio, Symphony Sid, whom he taught me to find on the dial, who always comes on at the stroke of midnight, bringing you the sounds of Charlie Parker, Lester Young, Miles Davis, and Stan Getz, and who, according to Jack, is a subterranean himself—you can hear it in his gravel voice smoked down to rasp by innumerable weird cigarettes. "And now—after a few words about that fan-tastic Mo-gen David wine—the great Lady Day . . ." In the darkness of the room we drift together as Billie Holiday bewails lost love . . .

But then Jack leaves me. He goes into a small back bedroom where I never sleep because there's no radiator there. He pulls the window all the way up, closes the door, and lies down on the floor in his sleeping bag alone. This is the cure for the cough he brought with him from Mexico City. In the morning he'll do headstands with his feet against the wall, to reverse the flow of blood in his body. He tells me a frightening thing about himself. He's known for eight years that a blood clot could finish him off at any minute.

How can you bear living, I wonder, knowing death could be so close? Little by little I'm letting go of what I learned on the abortionist's table in the white upstairs room in Canarsie.

I'm good for him, Jack tells me. I don't mind anything he does, I don't mind about the sleeping bag, do I?

I didn't really mind, that was the strange part. Everything seemed so odd, so charmed, so transformed. At night when the cold air came with a rush into the little room where Jack was sleeping, and seeped under the edges of the closed door, I could imagine myself on a place without walls, an immense campground where, lying wrapped in blankets, I could feel in my own warmth absolute proof of my existence.

I'm a regular fool in pale houses enslaved to lust for women who hate me, they lay their bartering flesh all over the divans, it's one fleshpot—insanity all of it, I should forswear and chew em all out and go hit the clean rail—I wake up glad to find myself saved in the wilderness mountains—For that lumpy roll flesh with the juicy hole I'd sit through eternities of horror in gray rooms illuminated by a gray sun, with cops and alimoners at the door and the jail beyond?—It's a bleeding comedy—The Great Wise Stages of pathetic understanding elude me when it comes to harems— Harem-scarem, it's all in heaven now—bless their all their bleating-hearts—Some lambs are female, some angels have womanwings, it's all mothers in the end and forgive me for my sardony—excuse me for my rut.

(Hor hor hor)

Not for Joyce Glassman to read, this bleak passage later written in *Desolation Angels,* this awful metaphysical linking of sex, birth, the grave. I hate Jack's woman-hatred, hate it, mourn it, understand, and finally forgive.

Working as a publishing secretary by day, writing her first novel at night (a Random House editor had bought it after reading only 50 pages), and hanging out at the Five Spot and the Cedar Tavern with "regulars" such as Willem DeKooning, Franz Kline and Frank O'Hara, Joycey, as Kerouac fondly dubbed her, became a full-fledged artist and bohemian herself. She would never turn back.

Come and Join the Dance was published when Johnson was twenty-six, four years after she and Kerouac parted company. Soon afterwards she married James Johnson, a young abstract expressionist painter, who was killed in a motorcycle accident a week before their first anniversary.

Johnson went on to become a respected writer and editor in the New York publishing world, with five books to her credit and numerous articles. She became married to another painter briefly and raised a son as a single mother. She is now on the faculty of the graduate writing program at Columbia University and is working on a new novel.

TITLE COMMENTARY

Minor Characters

JAMES CAMPBELL (REVIEW DATE 3 JUNE 1983)

SOURCE: Campbell, James. "Camp Follower." *Times Literary Supplement* (3 June 1983): 586-7.

In the following review, Campbell offers a mixed assessment of Minor Characters.

Joyce Johnson climbed into bed one night in 1957 with a likeable, immature, heavy-drinking hobo, and woke up with a celebrity. What happened in between was the publication in the *New York Times* of a review of *On the Road,* the first novel by Jack Kerouac (as opposed to "John", who had published one six years earlier). Agents and reporters started knocking on his door at breakfast, and by lunchtime it was, in a sense, all over: Jack was smashed and answering questions, with the drunken incoherence which was to become a trade mark, about the meaning of "beat" and the significance of "the road":

> "What was it really like, Jack? When did you first become aware of this generation? And how many people are involved in it? Is America going to go Beat? Are you telling us now to turn our backs on our families and look for kicks?"

> "Hey," Jack said. "Have some champagne."

They were investigating the birth of the Beat Generation, unaware that it was, for literary purposes at least, already dead. For Jack, there were to be few more kicks and no more "road"— aeroplanes only, from now on—until he died in front of the television set, under his mother's hawkish eye, in 1969. He had continued to write, but most of the books which followed *On the Road* were written before that morning's impromptu publication party.

While the first glasses were being filled, "Joycey", Kerouac's occasional girlfriend, the one who always understood and always forgave, was in the kitchen making coffee and having doubts about her own role in the coming drama of the Beat Generation. She was right, of course, as past experience told her. It was a boys' game: Kerouac and Cassady, Ginsberg and Orlovsky, Burroughs and his Tangier boys. . . . The myth of the freedom-seeking hero and his outcast sidekick is one of the most persistent in American fiction, from Fenimore Cooper's Leatherstocking and Chingagook, to Huck Finn and Jim, right up to the Lone Ranger and Tonto. By living it as well as writing it, Kerouac and friends became a legend.

Minor Characters is an attempt to tell the story from the side of the girl who makes the coffee and stays at home when the boys ride the range. Joyce Johnson cites, with a laconic bitterness, recent efforts by the novelist John Clellon Holmes to match the male characters in his novel, *Go,* with their originals, while admitting that the "centreless young women" were mere amalgams. Ms Johnson's purpose is to reveal the centre of at least one of them.

The Kerouac-Ginsberg-Burroughs legend has been the making of many books. Under her own name of Glassman, Joyce Johnson was one of the contributors to a compilation of interviews with friends of Kerouac, which was published four years ago. She was one of the few who retained a sense of reality in an otherwise indulgent exercise "His mother made this big meal that everybody ate", she told the idolatrous interviewers, "except Jack. He ended up with his head in his plate." ***Minor Characters*** is better written than Carolyn Cassady's *Heartbeat,* although in places it is self-consciously lyrical, and also apt to rely on jargon: "hipster-angel Herbert Huncke"; "*naked,* that angelic word".

The book is composed, in effect, of two parts: there is the story of Joyce Glassman growing up in a polite New York suburb, struggling against her parents, coming to terms with nature's surprises (periods, sex), selling her first novel at the age of twenty-one; and, in counterpoint, the tale of Jack and Allen; eventually, Allen arranges a blind date—and Joyce meets Jack.

Whatever else it is, then, this is not a memoir in the mode of "Jack Kerouac as I knew him . . .". In the end, however, one's suspicions that "the boys" are its *raison d'être* are unallayed. Perhaps this is only because the stories of her own upbringing, though charming at first, are at length tiresome and contrived. Joyce Johnson has not the literary power to transform the mundane details of fussy mothers, severe fathers, discouraging teachers and fat friends into anecdotes with universal appeal. Naturally, then, one's ears prick up—as her publishers' must have done—when Kerouac enters. What was he really like? Did he always need to be free? How was he in bed?

In the act of filling in the centre, Joyce Johnson has also given the legend a bit of extra mileage. "As a lover he wasn't fierce but oddly brotherly and somewhat reticent." He told her about sex orgies, however, omitting to mention that he was the only one who had kept his clothes on. At bedtime, he sometimes went with his sleeping bag to another room. A good deal of the time, he is moving pointlessly from place to place; Joyce thinks of joining him sometimes, but he has already left. Had he had the courage to turn his back on America's desperate appetite for media stars (one which we've caught) Kerouac might have written other books as good as *On the Road*. Instead, there was champagne, and all the holy-rolling phantoms he set in motion gradually coming home to roost. We could do with a book about that: a closer look at the delusions of these hipster-angels.

What Lisa Knew

BRIAN MASTERS (REVIEW DATE 22 MARCH 1991)

SOURCE: Masters, Brian. "The Steinberg Case." *Times Literary Supplement* (22 March 1991): 21.

In the following review of What Lisa Knew, *Masters faults Johnson's "contrived," theatrical prose but says she offers several insights into Hedda Nussbaum's relationship with her adopted daughter, Lisa, and raises important questions about the case.*

Joyce Johnson has set herself two complementary tasks in this detailed and angry book. First, to explain how people from decent, apparently stable

backgrounds could allow their lives to generate to a state of incredible brutishness. Second, to show the lamentable frivolity of American courtroom drama.

Hedda Nussbaum was, apparently, a fairly ordinary young woman. Her childhood had been untroubled, her career from university to teaching to publishing unremarkable. She had intelligence, talent, good looks, was fastidious and vain, although, according to Johnson, she showed little emotion and craved sexual enjoyment for its own sake. In common with many young urban women during the 1970s, she indulged in various kinds of therapy as a hobby. Though Miss Johnson does not say as much, it is clear that she sees Hedda as a typical schizophrenic without moral perception.

Joel was successful and impressive as a criminal lawyer. He was in fact also a pretentious liar, but that apparently passed unnoticed by a woman who needed to worship a dominant healer. He taught her effective ways of releasing spontaneity, and she responded with slavish adoration. She called him "the giver of love", and they seem to have lived what amounts to a sado-masochistic nightmare. As their behaviour grew less and less reliable, she parted company with Random House and he received fewer briefs.

Joel "acquired" the infant Lisa apparently to bolster his self-image as a father-figure. (Joyce Johnson suggests, without providing evidence, that he may well have been party to the sale of other unwanted babies in order to supplement his already substantial capital.) Lisa evidently adored her new father, but the fretful Hedda grew jealous of her and seems to have succeeded in undermining Joel's affection for her. Johnson has interviewed people who saw Steinberg refuse the child permission to eat for long periods, finally to throw her a sandwich as if to a dog. This viciousness seems to have escalated gradually. Lisa's teachers began to notice that she appeared scruffy and listless; one spotted a suspicious bruise but preferred not to interfere. A neighbour had complained repeatedly to the police about loud quarrelling and other suspect noises in the Steinbergs' apartment, but this had been ascribed to normal marital bickering and the child was not thought to be in danger. Finally, though, she was beaten to death.

All this Johnson describes with mounting disquiet and, it must be said, some imaginative padding. But it is the indignant polemic of her final chapters which lifts **What Lisa Knew** above the merely voyeuristic. Hedda Nussbaum's lawyer, Barry Scheck, made a deal with the prosecution that all charges which Nussbaum faced would be dropped if she agreed to testify against Steinberg. Scheck then portrayed her as a victim, a woman so battered that she dare not break free from her tormentor, and it was this picture which the jury accepted. According to Johnson, Nussbaum was rehearsed for two hundred hours in the art of avoiding self-incrimination while appearing numb, vague and suffering. The newspapers accepted this interpretation, but Johnson was, and remains, unconvinced. She details instances of Nussbaum's cruelty to Lisa; points out that she was alone with her for four hours while Steinberg was out at dinner on the night before the child died; that, while Lisa lay unconscious and dying, before telephoning for help she prepared cocaine for Steinberg; she seemed to have felt no affection for the girl and ought, Johnson believes, had natural justice prevailed, to have borne some of the blame.

The contrived theatricality of Johnson's prose—"Perhaps her tragedy was that she lacked the capacity to have one" etc—often diminishes the force of her arguments. But she does raise important questions, such as why the social services, despite repeated warnings from neighbours, did not properly investigate the Steinberg "family". How had Joel Steinberg been able to assume parenthood without legal authority? And why was Nussbaum's tale not subjected to more energetic scrutiny? Johnson's tentative answer is that the notions of family and motherhood are so sacrosanct in the United States that they cannot be questioned; Hedda Nussbaum had to be seen as a victim because it was inconceivable that any woman could be so wicked as to collude in the destruction of a child.

Joel Steinberg is now in prison. Hedda Nussbaum lives in seclusion in a country cottage in upstate New York. . . . Lisa was buried by her natural mother, who had not seen her since she handed her to Steinberg on the day of her birth.

Door Wide Open

IAN MCGILLIS (ESSAY DATE 9 SEPTEMBER 2000)

SOURCE: McGillis, Ian. "A Slice of Kerouac From His Girlfriend." *The Gazette* (9 September 2000): J5.

In the following essay, McGillis discusses Door Wide Open *and includes comments from a phone interview with Johnson in which she discusses her career as a writer and her affair with Jack Kerouac.*

In New York in 1957, poet Allen Ginsberg set up a blind date between 21-year-old aspiring writer Joyce Johnson (née Glassman) and the soon to be notorious Beat Generation avatar Jack Kerouac, 13 years her senior.

It was, in Johnson's words, a "bland and sinister" time in American life; the daughter of aspiring middle-class Jewish parents shouldn't have been in Greenwich Village, let alone dating writer types. But romance (of a sort) blossomed anyway. *Door Wide Open: A Beat Love Affair in Letters* documents with a touching lack of guile a relationship that took place in the trenches of an incipient revolution in American culture.

It was a pivotal time for both parties, in very different ways. Kerouac, after years in the literary wilderness that had left him irreversibly embittered, saw his novel *On the Road* catapult him to a stardom for which he was thoroughly unsuited. Johnson, thrown into a spotlight she could never have anticipated, struggled with the demands of involvement with a peripatetic, hard-drinking, mother-fixated artist, in addition to all the usual confusing stuff that comes with being young, in love, and wanting to write. And write she did—as well as eventually editing, teaching at Columbia, and raising a son as a single mother. Her best known work, the 1983 memoir *Minor Characters*, added a valuable perspective to a subject— the Beat movement—that had, until then, been seen as essentially a boys' club. In its preparation, though, she'd been hamstrung by the lack of access to her own letters written to Kerouac.

"At that time the executor of Jack's estate was his widow, Stella Kerouac, who had a policy of not letting anyone use anything more of Jack's," said Johnson on the phone from her summer home in Woodbury, Vt. (Johnson, a film buff, had planned to come to Montreal for the World Film Festival, but was struck with a virus at the 11th hour.) "I think it was out of a desire to protect Jack posthumously. So many awful things had been written about him."

On Stella's death, control was passed to her brother John Sampas, who sent Johnson her old letters (Johnson's Vermont home was paid for, with supreme irony, with the proceeds from her eventual sale of the same letters) and mooted the idea of a book.

"I was struck by how the letters played off each other in very lively ways, so I decided to do it. Considering all the bullshit that's been written about Jack, I wanted to present a slice of life as it was. It was a terrible time if you were a young woman and wanted to be a writer. The culture assumed that anything you did wouldn't really be worth reading. But Jack, whom I respected enormously, took me very seriously. It added to the relationship. It was a novelty for him. On that level, we were really friends, apart from the love part."

Was there any hesitation about airing some of the more personal (sexual and otherwise) matters described in the letters?

"As a writer, I'm fairly ruthless about revealing private things. I write to find out who I am, why I behaved a certain way. Writing is an act of self discovery. So no, no qualms."

The doctrinaire crusaders who held sway on college campuses in the eighties often dismissed the Beats, and especially their women partners, as hopelessly backward in their sexual politics.

"The problem with that politically correct crowd is that they have no sense of historical context. They judge people in the '50s for not having the attitudes that they deemed proper for the '80s or '90s. In fact, when *On the Road* was published its message had a very strong appeal for thousands of young women as well as young men. It did not exclude women at all.

"You've got to remember that at that time misogyny was so widespread that you didn't even question it, it was like the air that you breathed, but the Beats were a little bit ahead of that. If you were married to a really straight guy in the '50s, you'd be totally squashed and boxed in. The Beats at least gave a woman some freedom. There may not have been a lot in the way of responsibility, but at least you were your own person."

It's been suggested that the Beats paved the way for the current craze for confessional memoir. This is a credit or a curse depending on where one stands on the tell-all phenomenon.

"All the Beats tended to write in an open, confessional mode. Jack's novels were on that borderline between fiction and memoir. Writers have always used their lives as source material. But much more important than giving the facts is the voice, what you do with the material. A lot of good, bad, and indifferent memoirs are being written, but I think it's a form that has given us some of the best books of the 20th century. Think of Nabokov's *Speak, Memory*."

Interest in the Beats has ebbed and flowed over the decades. It's at high tide now, with sales of *On the Road* at 100,000 annually in the U.S. alone. How does Johnson account for this?

"This is a time when young people feel their options are very limited. They're supposed to go to school, then go right into a good job. There's no room in there for self-exploration, for just trying things out. So the spirit of freedom in a book like *On the Road* is very appealing."

Does she see any Beat inheritors on the current scene?

"I've just read that book by Dave Eggers, *A Heartbreaking Work of Staggering Genius*. I feel that he's a descendent of Kerouac's in a way, literarily speaking, with the openness that he shows."

He's a lot more ironic than Kerouac ever was. "Sure, but you don't want writers exactly copying each other."

Has Johnson ever felt that her association with the King of the Beats has distracted people from her own quite distinctive writing? The 1989 novel **In the Night Cafe** is especially fine.

"Well, I was never in competition with Jack. Naturally, I'd like more recognition. Who wouldn't? My greatest wish is that my earlier books might come back into print."

Living about an hour from the border, Johnson makes occasional forays into Quebec. In the course of our talk she asks about the level of interest in Kerouac among young francophones (it's high, as far as I can tell) and praises Victor-Levy Beaulieu's *Jack Kerouac: A Chicken Essay (Essai-Poulet)*, a book that claims Kerouac as a pure product of Catholic Quebec, as "one of my favourite things ever written about Jack."

"I know that the French Canadian side of Jack's life was constantly in his mind. He often spoke his version of French, and was always quoting his family motto, which was Travailler, Souffrir, Mourir."

Though not one to indulge in what-might-have-beens, Johnson can't help but wonder about whether Kerouac's terrified reaction to fame, and his subsequent precipitous decline, would have been softened by the presence of Allen Ginsberg at a crucial juncture.

"I still really miss Allen. It's hard to believe that he's not still around. I knew him from the time I was 16. He could do what Jack couldn't do, in that he could play the role of the public figure quite brilliantly. Instead of letting the press ride all over him, he could play upon the press. I've always thought that things might have been a lot better for Jack if Allen had been around at the time *On the Road* was published. He could have interpreted the situation for Jack, taken some of the heat and shared some of the spotlight. But by then he was in Paris."

As for what life as Mrs. Jack Kerouac might have held, there are no illusions.

"I understood on a deep level that this was a relationship that had no real future. The situation with his mother would have been impossible. There was no getting between them. Also, I could not have dealt for very long with Jack's alcoholism. Nonetheless, I think if Jack had asked me to marry him, I would have done it. Of course, that would have been a real disaster!"

A very creative disaster, no doubt.

Come and Join the Dance

RONNA C. JOHNSON (ESSAY DATE 2002)

SOURCE: Johnson, Ronna C. "'And then she went': Beat Departures and Feminine Transgressions in Joyce Johnson's *Come and Join the Dance*." In *Girls Who Wore Black: Women Writing the Beat Generation*, edited by Ronna C. Johnson and Nancy M. Grace, pp. 69-95. New Brunswick, N.J.: Rutgers University Press, 2002.

In the following essay, Johnson discusses Come and Join the Dance, *and asserts that the novel challenges and revises discourses and assumptions about gender in Beat culture and literature, simultaneously adopting and refuting Beat conventions.*

In 1962, at the age of twenty-six and under the name Joyce Glassman, the writer, editor, and educator Joyce Johnson published her first novel, *Come and Join the Dance*. The author has signed two names to her books, and this discussion uses both, following her publishing history, to preserve the distinction between the novice and the established writer.[1] Johnson's second novel, *Bad Connections*, came out in 1978 after a hiatus from writing during which she was widowed, then remarried and had a child and began her editorial career. Her third novel, *In the Night Café*, a portion of which won the O'Henry Prize for short fiction, was published in 1987. The three New York novels map key cultural and gender discourses of their eras, portraying adventurous middle-class white women in the Beat 1950s and free-sex sixties. Johnson is best known for her 1983 memoir, *Minor Characters: The Romantic Odyssey of a Woman in the Beat Generation*, which, though it does recount her emergence as a writer, focuses on her youthful affairs with Beat bohemianism and Jack Kerouac in the late 1950s. However, Johnson's significance as a writer surpasses her famous literary connections and bohemian antecedents, for with *Come and Join the Dance* she

entered literary history by publishing the first Beat generation novel by and about a Beat woman.

With its female bohemian perspective on sex, cold war existentialism, and the New York hipster milieu, *Come and Join the Dance* stands as a Beat urtext, on par with the renegade declarations of *On the Road* or "Howl" or *Naked Lunch*. But Johnson's seminal novel, in contrast to the male purview of these classic Beat texts, proclaims instead the arrival of the women typically marginalized in them. Just so, *Come and Join the Dance* is out of print and has been invisible in discussions of postwar American women writers, even to feminist critics who have begun to identify and assess works by women Beat writers.[2] Nor has it been studied in analyses of Johnson's work.[3] It has been further eclipsed by the view that women's prose contributions to Beat literature are confined to memoir.[4] This neglect obscures the novel's pivotal emendations of the Beat field, and its signification of a feminist movement in the fifties. Dissipating the silence of Kerouac's "girls" in black, *Come and Join the Dance* brings to Beat literature a model of female subjectivity. It depicts women's transformation from culture's objects to their own subjects by foregrounding them as sexual actors and consumers, attesting to Beat's anticipation of the sixties women's movement. As a literary text, *Come and Join the Dance* enlarges the scope of Beat invention with its hybrid innovation of "hot" self-expression by means of a "cool" restrained style. And, in an illuminating discourse about gender and canonicity, the novel quotes and revises tropes of classic American literature and the genre of the road tale, a double move that decisively and symbolically delivers the Beat female from eclipse by male hegemony. Challenging masculinist discourses of Beat with its heroine's anti-establishment alienation, sexual autonomy, and subjectivity—attributes and privileges reserved for men—the narrative of *Come and Join the Dance* critiques, challenges, and transgresses Beat as well as mainstream gender codes.

Yet, although it focuses on a bohemian woman, *Come and Join the Dance* is not a feminist but, rather, a proto-feminist novel. Its instantiation of women as Beat subjects anticipates, but does not equal in promise or achievement, the second-wave feminisms emerging in the late sixties and the early seventies. Despite the novel's emphasis on white female subjectivity, it makes no claim to address directly the emancipation of women; its corrective discourses are written in a Beat key rather than with the rhetoric that would be familiar from later women's movements. Indeed, *Come and Join the Dance* is a Beat novel in the usual sense. It recounts the emergence of the individual as counterforce in conformist postwar America; its distinction is to see the white female as that individual, as a Beat subject who, like Beat men, rejects the numerous oppressive overdeterminations of postwar establishment culture. Beat bohemia's inducements are portrayed in the protagonist's efforts to escape conformity, enjoy sexual freedom, and reach existential awareness. Elucidating the decisive role of gender in Beat's formation, the novel calls attention to Beat's reproduction of traditional patriarchal precepts, a recognition which anticipates dialogues of second-wave feminism. The restoration of *Come and Join the Dance* to Beat history and to accounts of postwar women writers illuminates an under-studied continuity between Beat nonconformity and countercultural sixties liberation movements for women.

Set in the mid-1950s, *Come and Join the Dance* recounts ten fraught days before its protagonist, twenty-year-old Susan Levitt of Cedarhurst, a Long Island suburb, graduates from an unnamed women's college near Columbia University and sails to Paris. The novel's principal characters are Susan's college friend Kay Gorman, who, having dropped out of school, resides in a beat hotel called the Southwick Arms and works in the college library; Susan's dull boyfriend, Jerry, whose slavish unrequited love, devotion to upward mobility, and anxiety to conform make him the figure of bourgeois practicality (28); eighteen-year-old Anthony Leone, a self-proclaimed communist, "campus bum" (53) and poet, who has just been expelled from college "for bringing a girl up to his room" (54); and Peter, at nearly thirty a generation ahead of the others, once married, a "perpetual student" who's been working on his thesis for five years, possessor of a 1938 black Packard and the semi-ironic ambition to "be a promising young man as long as possible" (21). The generational divide in this cast of characters suggests the multi-tiered formation of the Beat movement: the moody older hipster Peter evokes Beat's first generation, which includes writers such as Ruth Weiss, John Clellon Holmes, Kerouac, and Allen Ginsberg (all born in the 1920s); Kay, Anthony, and the protagonist Susan, more than a decade younger than Peter but sharing his disaffection, are akin to the second Beat generation, which includes writers such as Elise Cowen, LeRoi Jones, Joyce Johnson, and Diane di Prima (all born in the 1930s). The novel's generational structure

exemplifies Beat's extended influence in the postwar era and Glassman's emergence from an ongoing literary and cultural avant-garde.

However, *Come and Join the Dance* depicts a postwar interval of nonconformity and alienation before Beat is recognized, when the underground avant-garde was inchoate, and its famous adherents Kerouac and Ginsberg were unknown. The novel's moment is situated at Beat's emergence from Greenwich Village bohemian and Times Square hipster subcultures during and after the Second World War. While postwar bohemians, mostly intellectuals and artists, were linked to the Greenwich Village avant-garde of the 1920s, the Times Square hipsters Kerouac saw during the war formed an underclass characterized by hard drugs, criminality, homosexuality, jazz, and revelatory personal vision, and embodied, he felt, the resurgence of a nineteenth-century American individuality (1959, 361). These New York bohemians and hipsters served as antecedents and foundation for the Beat generation, which relished jazz and drugs, writing and sex, nonconformity and petty theft, confession and hallucinatory vision. Like Holmes's early Beat novel *Go* (1952), *Come and Join the Dance* represents a bohemian/hipster subculture characterized by the post-bomb alienation distinct to its era. Johnson recalls reading Holmes's 1952 essay "This Is the Beat Generation," which elaborated a "state of mind that, although new, according to this article, was totally familiar to me" (1983, 74); it was the "Bohemian world" (1983, 44, 55) she knew from Washington Square Park and Greenwich Village. And, as Johnson noted, that incipiently Beat culture was exemplified exclusively by men (1983, 75). Kerouac's idea that "Beat Generation" had "become the slogan or label for a revolution of manners in America" (1959, 363) suggests the signifier's elaboration to a cultural formation; a set of discursive conventions and relations, inclusions and exclusions that shape and are shaped by subjects who participate in and effect the cultural, linguistic field. Addressing the exclusion of women from Beat representation, *Come and Join the Dance* clarifies the discursive field of Beat; unlike *Go* and, later, *On the Road* (1957) and William Burroughs's *Junky* (1953), Glassman's novel sees second-generation Beat women in active relation to the postwar culture of post-bomb alienation.

Yet, while *Come and Join the Dance* challenges and revises discourses of and assumptions about gender in Beat culture and literature, the novel oscillates between adopting Beat stances and privileges for its female protagonist and abolishing discursive structures and assumptions about gender that seem central to Beat's construction. The bohemian dropouts Kay and Susan contest stereotypes of female passivity and conformity; their sexual desire and nonmarital sexual experience explicitly portray female agency and individuality. However, because these modifications of the feminine challenge Beat's patriarchal politics, *Come and Join the Dance* can also seem to be a refutation of Beat. The focus on Susan allows the narrative to sift through the complicated process for women Beats of dropping out; to problematize and resist the silencing of women by fifties gender codes, which afflicted both mainstream "girls" and bohemian "chicks"; and to depict negotiations for the sexual satisfaction that authenticates female subjectivity. Yet, at the same time, in its renovations of Beat discourses, *Come and Join the Dance* dramatizes the irremediality of gender constructions and roles in the postwar era before second-wave feminism, for the protagonist's arrival into Beat subjectivity depends on emulation and appropriation of masculinist hipster styles and freedoms, suggesting that even radical ameliorist subcultures and bohemias are reactionary and inadequate to accommodate women as subjects.

Just as it both adopts and refutes Beat conventions, *Come and Join the Dance* accomplishes a distinctive double move in its representation of Beat bohemia that attests to its proto-feminism and, in this, its anticipation of the postmodern. Linda Hutcheon has observed that formations of post-modern literary discourse enact an oscillating subvert/install maneuver. *Come and Join the Dance* exemplifies this postmodern discursive move: it subverts Beat's male hegemony by positioning a woman as its protagonist, and, revising essential features of Beat narrative, it installs a corrective or replacement discourse, the narration of Beat female agency, sexual desire, self-reliance.[5] At the level of the plot, *Come and Join the Dance* is further marked by the subvert/install tactic Hutcheon has identified: the novel appropriates and then sabotages the traditional road tale, a fragment of which it samples and refigures in the penultimate two chapters. This double move functionally terminates the road tale's iteration in the narrative, and in this rejects the patriarchal, canonical tradition which masculinist Beat follows even in its iconoclasm. Depicting bohemian women's preferences for nonconformity, their rejection of the confining feminine and the masculine hegemonic, *Come and Join the Dance* inscribes the effaced women of the Beat genera-

tion as a presence in its representation of a postwar bohemian clique, entering and perforce altering the male-defined, male-centered discursive field of Beat.

Come and Join the Dance partakes of and simultaneously surpasses Beat's opposition to bourgeois compliance for it reforms Beat's contestatory impulses to fit women. Like other texts of the era of its composition, such as Kerouac's *On the Road*, C. Wright Mills's *The Power Elite* (1956), and William H. Whyte Jr.'s *The Organization Man* (1956), *Come and Join the Dance* contends with the postwar conformity that negates individuality, but with this critical difference: as it affects a young, middle-class white woman. Glassman began work on the novel in 1955,[6] two years before she met Kerouac (1983, 105, 107), so its Beat subject arose from the Greenwich Village zeitgeist. That is, as a neophyte novelist with a book contract in the late 1950s, Glassman was writing amidst many of the same cultural influences as the male Beat writers. Yet, her rendition of the radical sociocultural discourses of her time diverged from both postwar intellectual assumptions about gender, focused mostly on men, and Beat's narrow literary portrayals of women. This jockeying registers the renovation of Beat discourse which its implementation by female bohemians and artists necessitated and effected. Johnson recalls in *Minor Characters* her ambitions for writing:

> As a writer I would live life to the hilt . . . just as Jack and Allen had done. I would make it my business to write about young women quite different from the ones portrayed weekly in the pages of *The New Yorker*. I would write about furnished rooms and sex. Sex had to be approached critically . . . I would not succumb to the lady-like stratagems of shimmering my way toward discreet fadeouts. I'd decided this even before meeting Jack or reading *Howl*.
>
> (156)

She recognized that her gender might consign her to "lady-like stratagems" limiting expression and transforming sexual climaxes to fadeouts in more ways than one. Shaping her Beat moment to accommodate female subjectivity, Glassman determined to write "critically" about sex, disclosing its pivotal role in women's experience without condemning or trivializing female sexuality; she would broach her subjects—femininity, female sexual experience, the existential anonymities and liberties of furnished rooms—freely, as a Beat writer. Her novel illustrates that women practicing, personifying, and writing Beat were instrumental in shaping the Beat literary and cultural

FROM THE AUTHOR

THE PATH OF THE FEMALE BEATS

Those of us who flew out the door had no usable models for what were doing. We did not want to be our mothers or our spinster schoolteachers or the hard-boiled career women depicted on screen. And no one had taught us how to be women artists or writers. We knew a little about Virginia Woolf, but did not find her relevant. She seemed discouragingly privileged, born into literature, connections and wealth. The "room of one's own" that she wrote about presupposed that the occupant had a small family income. Our college educations enabled us to type our way to fifty dollars a week—barely enough to eat and pay the rent on a tiny apartment in Greenwich Village or North Beach, with little left over for the shoes or the electric bill. We knew nothing about the novelist Jean Rhys, an earlier runaway from respectability, dangerously adrift in the Parisian Bohemia of the 1920s; we might have identified with Rhys's lack of confidence in her writing, found a warning to take to heart in the corrosive passivity of her relationships with men. Though no warning would have stopped us, so hungry were we to embrace life and all of reality. Even hardship was something to be savored.

Johnson, Joyce. Excerpt from *Minor Characters: A Young Woman's Coming-of-Age in the Beat Orbit of Jack Kerouac*. Boston: Houghton, 1983.

fields, even as women writers and their texts have been excised from the Beat record.

Come and Join the Dance was conceived and developed in the wake of such early Beat and qua Beat novels as Chandler Brossard's *Who Walk in Darkness* (1952), John Clellon Holmes's *Go* (1952), and Sloan Wilson's *The Man in the Gray Flannel Suit* (1955), as well as women's novels such as Grace Metalious's *Peyton Place* (1956) and Barbara Probst Solomon's *The Beat of Life* (1960), but Glassman's book contends hegemonic gender codes the others accept. Although *The Beat of Life* is today obscure, its author, Barbara Probst So-

lomon, was said to have considered herself the first woman Beat novelist (Grace 1999b, 114). This is inaccurate, but *The Beat of Life,* also about a restless young white woman, does illuminate the Beat character of *Come and Join the Dance.* In both novels, female sexuality is paramount, contingent not on marriage but desire. The heroine of *The Beat of Life* gets pregnant, undergoes the harrowing process to obtain a "therapeutic" abortion, suffers a four-day hospital stay, and upon release, puts her head in a gas oven, committing suicide. In this defeat of female sexual autonomy and desire, *The Beat of Life* is not Beat, although the legendary Beat figure, the poet Elise Cowen, has a similar history. Rather, like *Peyton Place, The Beat of Life* reinscribes women's subordination to patriarchal prescriptions. *Peyton Place,* a controversial bestseller, subverts the conventional view of women as sexually passive, and portrays the psychological, emotional, and physical abuse women suffer from men, focusing on the sexual double standard and the need for legalized abortion. Yet although *Peyton Place* may have been adventurous about women's sex lives, its suburban setting and characters situate the novel in mainstream bourgeois culture. In contrast, the female Beat discourse of women's subjectivity and sexual agency in *Come and Join the Dance* rejects the immaturity and passivity of the feminine mandated by the dominant culture. Glassman gives her protagonist sexual desire and experimentation, with no 1950s penalty of guilt or pregnancy. At the novel's conclusion, Susan leaves her lovers without regret as she embarks for Paris. Rather than stereotypes of female instability and suicide, which Solomon didactically exploits, *Come and Join the Dance* enacts the male Beat model of flight from convention for its protagonist, rejecting female stereotypes and male hegemony through the same discourses by which Beat masculinism affirms them. *Come and Join the Dance* turns Beat's gender conventions to women's ends.

The position of *Come and Join the Dance* as a fiction in the discursive field of Beat literature is clarified by the life-stories recounted in Johnson's memoir *Minor Characters.* The memoir shows that the novel is a fiction based on Glassman's experiences in college and bohemia during the mid-fifties in New York, before she met Kerouac in 1957 and experienced with him the tumultuous publication of *On the Road.* The novel's intersections with and departures from the events recorded in the memoir elucidate the author's development of a Beat fiction; that is, rather than annexing her lived experience, she invented a narrative of bohemian women's experiences and perspectives. Glassman made characters of her college friend, the poet Elise Cowen, and her older lover, a Barnard philosophy instructor she calls Alex Greer (identified as Donald Cook [Johnson 2000]) (1983, 61, 121). But, for example, she does not represent Cowen's hospitalizations and suicide attempts (the last, in 1962, was successful), which might have suggested that a young woman's hunger and capacity for sexual and existential freedoms—her resistance to fifties gender roles—could be only overwhelming and deadly. Cowen's counterpart in *Come and Join the Dance*, Kay Gorman, is cynical and depressed, but the portrait forbids female stereotypes of self-pity and hysteria, and allows the dropout Kay to survive her own defiance.

Similarly, the novel's departures from life in the treatment of the Alex Greer/Donald Cook character transform the young woman whom he cavalierly discarded into a fictive protagonist whose story in *Come and Join the Dance* is commensurate with those of hipster men, the sexual consumers and adventurers of bohemia. In *Minor Characters*, Johnson discloses her plans for the heroine of her first novel: "Just like me, my heroine would have an affair with the Alex character and end up alone. But in my fictional rearrangement of life, it was she who was going to leave him after their one and only night together. I rewarded her with a trip to Paris" (1983, 121). In the novel's discourse of Beat female subjectivity and sexual agency, the heroine's self-sufficiency is not a punishment; she is not seduced and abandoned, but sexually free and journeying into adventure. Further, Glassman did not give her heroine the illegal abortion she herself suffered in the mid-1950s (1983, 110-115), in this avoiding the reactionary sexual politics of contemporaneous norms and novels by women. These moves out of 1950s femininity produce the novel's Beat discourse, while its emphasis on gender roles and conventions problematize the Beat assumption that hipster iconoclasm is normatively male. Indeed, Glassman's fictionalizations of and departures from her life in *Come and Join the Dance*, joined with the novel's self-proclaimed female "outlaw" (62) or bohemian nonconformity, reveal the constructedness of Beat literary discourse so often (mis)taken in the male writers for unvarnished autobiography, and construed and treated as universal.

The contention of 1950s conformity in *Come and Join the Dance* provides a radical answer to what Betty Friedan named in 1963 the "female malaise." The novel prescribes for its dissenting heroine the Beat male ethos: to drop out—of college, of anaesthetized suburban life (122), of "perfect, terrifying blandness" (11). This outcome is anticipated by the novel's opening, which depicts Susan mired in feelings of insubstantiality that she struggles to overcome:

> Her image floated ahead of her like a balloon . . . transparent, ghost-like. . . . What did others see when they looked at her? She would try to study her face as though it belonged to someone else . . . her face cheated her. It had a way of rearranging itself when she looked into mirrors, as though it were giving a performance.
>
> (10-11)

Afflicted with not-thereness, Susan is disembodied, disengaged, dissociated, even from herself. A sense of unreality and opacity blends Friedan's malaise with Didionesque dissociation: the age of anxiety meets the silent generation. The novel's starting place is at this intersection, but as it unfolds, its theme of dropping out repositions the novel on the cusp of fifties conventionality, and sixties feminism and sexual revolution. As the novel intimates, dropping out is a complicated move for postwar women, who have been marginalized in or excluded from the institutions only males are privileged to join and scorn. *Come and Join the Dance* depicts the obligatory downward mobility of Beat masculinity, but problematizes what dropping out can mean when the subject is by definition of her gender already excluded from the social, political, and cultural centers of her era. Nevertheless, the novel's valorization of dropping out defines it as Beat. Beat bohemia reverses mainstream standards, for here, dropping out and relinquishing social privilege designates the attainment of subjectivity, the individual's significance in a cultural or theoretical sense.

For the heroine of *Come and Join the Dance*, dropping out signifies her arrival as subject, and entry into Beat culture and community; her instantiation in Beat history. The story's plot to thwart Susan's "particular" gender and class "fate" to be a "good girl" (75) provides an account of how a bohemian is made, how a college girl is transformed into a Beat dropout. What is thwarted is traditional femininity, which is relinquished for the masculine privileges that secure subjectivity and agency. Susan fields feelings of illegitimacy, convictions of inauthenticity, fears that she "was just a spy, a sneak thief,"[7] a supplicant quartered within the "pink walls" of her mother's house, awaiting rescue. She wants "to be saved from boredom" (70) rather than marry into it (51); she prefers "outlaw" bohemians to her conventional boyfriend, Jerry, for "the terrifying thing about Jerry was that he was someone she could marry— she could marry him and never have to go to Paris—he was only waiting for a signal" (9). Susan rejects the bourgeois destination of sterile conformity in a rhetoric of refusal: "Not me, she thought. She was . . . the odd one. Not me. At last the pain of it was alive inside her. Not me. Not me" (109). Her pain and refusal signify yearning for subjectivity, which she sees as a possibility in bohemian marginality. Coveting the freedom of the "wild girls" who live beyond gender's restraints, Susan would renounce the passive, dissociating silence of femininity—of being "only blank, a spectator of herself, immensely bored" (27)—to claim the connection and power of male Beatness, even if that renunciation is ungendering, as implied in her friend Kay's antifeminine Beat cynicism that "everybody uses everybody. That's the way it is" (71). Thus the college girl is transformed into Beat dropout by the appropriation of male models of sexual agency and subjectivity, which produces the novel's revision of Beat discourse.

This revision is announced in the novel's opening salvo, a challenge to the hegemony of the literary canon. The heroine's capacity for rebellion and resistance is explicit in her inclination to test tests, the vaunted Beat disdain for establishment institutions. The novel begins with the scene of Susan's final college exam as she considers its last question, which is on Melville: she "wondered what Melville would have thought of sixty-three girls concentrating on him at once" (3) and, expecting "freedom to happen" (4) after her last exam, Susan hastens liberty by leaving before she finishes it. Already subversive, the image of sixty-three "girls" "concentrating" on Melville suggests a disruption of the exclusionary conventions and canon that Melville represents: women have broken into the Men's Club. Doubling that subversion, and rejecting rules, customs, and canon as might a male Beat writer, Susan rebels against service to Melville the renegade writer of road tales by refusing to commemorate him with her attention. Susan authenticates her own iconoclasm—that is, her Beat capacity for urgency, restlessness, and flight—by appropriating a male model of agency, the insider's capacity and readiness to reject convention's expectations.

In giving its protagonist the status of Beat subject, *Come and Join the Dance* revises and reinscribes gender codes, particularly the aspect of female passivity which directs that the female function as a mirror reflection, and thus valida-

tion, of male power. As Susan J. Douglas argues in her chronicle of the way postwar mass-culture media narratives reify tropes of sexual difference, "boys are cool; girls are their mirrors . . . surfaces whose function is to reflect all this coolness back to them and on them. Girls watch boys . . . they're only spectators," not actors or possessors of "cool" (299). This assessment echoes Virginia Woolf's metaphoric critique of women's reflective role in hegemonic sexual politics: "Women have served all these centuries as looking-glasses possessing the magic and delicious power of reflecting the figure of man at twice its natural size" (35). Just so, Glassman writes against the gender code's consignment of women to reflect men, revising and expanding Beat by making the male bohemian reflect the female. This ironic reversal is accomplished in the novel's depiction of Peter, the mercurial hipster Susan admires. The narration depicts Peter as a reflective existential surface, a mirror returning Susan's gaze to herself, thus enlisting the Beat male to signify female subterraneanism. He is, nevertheless, an ambiguous aid: "There was something about Peter that forced too much knowledge upon her. He was as dangerous, as compassionless as a mirror" (99). In Glassman's Beat narrative, the figure of the male mirroring and measuring female affect is used to register female subjectivity, which is posited as a "dangerous" excess of awareness. This construction comments on women's potential for liberation in the postwar era: knowledge is seen to jeopardize quiescence and conformity, contravening the gender code for women, instigating a revolt. That is, knowledge instigates women's transformation from object to subject, as in the 1960s liberations that effected the empowerment of white women and people of color, whose subordination had been the foundation of white male subjectivity and whose emergence undermined and fragmented that male hegemonic.

For the Beat woman, this transformation from object to subject encounters cultural, gendered resistance in the form that Helen McNeil has named the "chick category." Like most young bohemian women in 1956, twenty-two-year-old Joyce Glassman working in publishing houses and writing her first novel was regarded in hipster precincts like the San Remo, the Cedar Tavern, or the Five Spot as a "chick."[8] McNeil defines a "chick" as "the attractive, young, sexually available and above all silent ('dumb') female" (189). The "chick" corresponds to Kerouac's "cool" hipster "girls [who] say nothing and wear black" (1959, 362), wordless companions immured in hipster iconography, signifiers of the men's sub-terraneanism. Johnson recalls worrying about her bohemian status—"How Beat could I actually be, holding down a steady office job and writing a novel about an ivy-league college girl on the verge of parting with her virginity" (1983, 216-217). But, in fact, for postwar middle-class white women, economic self-sufficiency such as Glassman's was as radical a step as dropping out; and if it was not hip, it was certainly convenient for the often unemployed male artists of bohemia.[9] Yet, while these square facts of her life undermined her Beat credibility, which valorized voluntary poverty, unemployment, and disdain of establishment culture, the most disempowering dismissal for a self-aware, discerning woman was to be seen as a chick. For as McNeil notes, "the 'chick category' does not violate any existing gender codes." Rather, it provides men more opportunity to have sex with women without responsibility. Most importantly, "it is sex with those who will—mostly—not tell their side of the story" (189). That is, the "chick category" is above all intransitive. It goes only one way: the chick serves male freedom and narrative while herself remaining a cipher, a "girl" who wears black and says nothing. Breaching this intransitiveness, *Come and Join the Dance* breaks a silence; it dissipates Susan's chronic reticence, which Peter, the novel's Beat hero, mocks: "Susan, I've never heard you say anything before. You come to my parties with Kay, you sit on the sofa, you listen to someone very dutifully, and every now and then you tell a story or a little joke—and that's all" (20). This paralyzed, silent "girl" is posited as the chrysalis of Beat female emancipation, for she will emerge from this camouflage of reticence with full discursive powers and unsettling desires.

Susan's alienation and subsequent attraction to bohemia elucidate the text's expansion of Beat discourse, while its representation of her existential condition contends the usual Beat erasure or denial of female subjectivity. Establishing her malaise in the story's opening, Susan is said to be "frozen into a deadly laziness. If she moved she would shatter like glass" (3). She is occupied by questions whose rhetoric typifies Beat existentialism as usually conveyed by men. This discourse elaborates the problem for which dropping out is the solution, the dissatisfaction with convention for which bohemia is antidote:

> What if you lived your life entirely without urgency? . . . spent [hours] waiting for something to happen to you; when you were particularly desperate you went out looking for it . . . something had made [Susan] want the feeling of living

a little close to the edge; perhaps she had chosen to feel frightened rather than feel nothing at all.

(14-15)

To live "without urgency" is to exist as an object—a conformist "girl"—rather than a subject—a Beat rebel. Susan's dilemma is whether to conform or to drop out: to wait passively for the future or to seek it out, to shun urgency or whip it up. Dropping out would position Susan on the edge, at the marginalized field of Beat. Choosing to drop out, she chooses the urgency, search, and trepidation that signifies being a subject, the rejection of conformity's numb safeness for the hipster alternative. This is the uncharted territory of desire, selfhood, and individuality; the "underground brotherhood" (62) of existential adventurers; the bohemian "Outlaws world" (10) of her friends Kay, Peter, and Anthony. Joining them Susan would forego her lassitude, for in the "stolen time" gained by dropping out there is "such a liveness . . . you could really feel yourself exist" (62). The uncertainties of bohemia preclude anaesthetizing complacency, promoting risk and disaffection, sex, movement, and freedom: subjectivity. The narrative's rhetoric for this condition is signature Beat: "driven by a restlessness for something new, unknown" (41), Susan wants "to be set in motion, too, to run mindlessly," to ride "into the night and emptiness to a place where all the clocks had stopped and no one cared" (70). This discourse of nothingness and indifference, of urgings and energy and escape, is reminiscent of the literature of Ginsberg and Kerouac, but the discourse's articulation and embodiment by a female subject contradict the male writers' representations of women, in which females are silent, do not survive the existential trial, or thwart men's freedom.[10]

Come and Join the Dance strongly suggests that, as opposed to the paralysis of conventionality, Beat's dropping out in its restoration of self-awareness provides for subjectivity, a position reminiscent of Julia Kristeva's argument that women's social function is to "reject everything finite, definite, structured, loaded with meaning, in the existing state of society"—to reject gender discourses and differentiation. This "attitude places women on the side of the explosion of social codes," Kristeva notes, in alliance with "revolutionary movements" (1981, 166) to overturn establishment regimes. Just so, *Come and Join the Dance*'s Beat theme of dropping out, its formulation of a revolutionary alternative, rejects the immaturity, passivity, and spectatorship—the object status—of traditional femininity. College

JOHNSON

women of the silent generation, the mass of "replaceable" "pastel girls" (109) whose "faces were the same semester after semester, the same things . . . said, thought, done" (8), are countered by the bohemian "wild girls" who "test limits" (63, 47) and drop out. In this, *Come and Join the Dance* creates an alternative to traditional postwar femininity: neither college "girls" pursuing the "M-R-S" degree, nor hipster women immured in black, but the inspiriting step out of both establishment and counterculture tableaux to a revolutionary subculture that recognizes women's existential freedom. Ultimately, the novel delivers female dissidents from oppressive restrictions assigned to women in both hipster and establishment cultures and consequently renovates masculinist Beat discourse, which, in being stretched to accommodate women, clarifies its continuity with sixties liberation movements.

The novel, however, also reveals that for white, middle-class postwar women, dropping out is a complicated move, since they are denied any privileges beyond skin privilege by patriarchal codes. While the Beat ethic, styled on a white male model, is voluntary poverty and downward mobility, for women in the 1950s, a college education and economic self-sufficiency in the middle class were actually rare and unusual; Susan was to be the first one in her family to graduate from college (124). Yet, it seems unreal: "in a way, I never went to college at all. I was just putting in time at a place that was school, because I'd always gone to school. I was afraid of it ending" (114-115). But Glassman's heroine does end her education; she drops out to cure herself of anomie, much as Kerouac's Sal Paradise leaves college because his "life hanging around campus had reached the completion of its cycle and was stultified . . ." (1957, 10). Cutting so many gym classes that she fails to complete the requirements for a diploma (106-107), Susan refuses to make up the credit, choosing instead to transgress the "peculiar institution of graduation" (114). This signifier evokes the one for slavery; from the novel's Beat perspective, attending college is regarded as institutional servitude, an unjust captivity righteously resisted. With classic Beat contempt, Susan sees graduation as an exercise in obedience and order, a spectacle of three hundred "dressed up . . . already vaguely secretarial" "girls" being "counted off and subtracted" (103-104); they are rendered nameless objects of specularization in their graduation march, voided by their ritual certification into the educated class. In this lies one of the novel's contradictions. Women cannot reject privilege in

the male Beat manner or enact the male Beat's downwardly mobile refusal of institutions unless they have attained them. Susan embodies this irony, the way the existential rigors of Beat bohemia require her to reject the unprecedented privilege of college to display her fitness as hipster.[11] In the novel, she would escape slavery by dropping out, whereas historically, and paradoxically, women's escape from the subordination meted out to the second sex, as Simone de Beauvoir named women's caste in 1949, could well be to finish college.

Glassman's adventurous, rebellious, questioning protagonist might be dismissed as a chick but, very un-chicklike, Glassman gives Susan consciousness, voice, desire—in other words, a bohemian life outside the dominant culture as well as an equally bohemian freedom to flaunt the Beat norm. Amy L. Friedman posits that male Beat writers "reified . . . female sexuality into a mode of expectation of the female which privileged her (sexual) subservience and silence" (211). Speaking for silenced women—the "dumb and sullen" "girls" that Kerouac's heroes in *On the Road* would "make" (30); the "little girls, simple and true and tremendously frightened of sex" to whom they will "prove" sex is "beautiful" (48); the "gorgeous country girl" the men would rouse from her dullness (200)—*Come and Join the Dance* contests Beat men's self-serving representations of having sex with "chicks." Glassman sardonically limns the double bind of female sexuality, in which, to avoid subservience, insignificance, and exploitation, a woman must feign experience. Susan, for instance, has a "bad reputation": "Probably very few people thought she was still a virgin. No one knew how much she lied, how skillful she had become in making adjustments in reality: inferences, suggestions, a few dark strokes, a laugh she had learned from someone" (62-63). By these means, the virgin intimates that she's a sexual adventurer. The heroine's transformation from the object of the scene to its subject-chronicler, from observer to actor, from prevaricator to narrator, explodes the "chick category." Female subjectivity is effected by narrativizing the repressed text of women's real sexual and existential experience, declaring for women the agency and voice mitigated by traditional femininity. As Johnson remarks in *Minor Characters* about her younger self, "It's only her silence that I wish finally to give up" (262). The novel defies gender traditions that valorize female self-containment and propriety. The heroine's self-revelation, the narration that forms *Come and Join the Dance*, stages and signifies the demise of women's silence and transcendence of chick status.

Clearly, however, the male existential model was problematic for the Beat female and *Come and Join the Dance* ponders whether and how to adapt it. One recurrent trope is a refiguring of the Hemingway code of moral behavior, which at mid-century functioned as an important cultural icon for male Beats such as Kerouac. Allusions to Hemingway, often derisive and ironic, appear throughout Glassman's text, inscribing the inadequacy for women writers of the sexual if not the literary model Hemingway provides, and in this advance the novel's move toward a specifically female Beat subjectivity. After losing her virginity, for example, Susan wonders, "If something happened, why didn't it really happen? . . . Where was the moment when everything became luminous and the earth shook? She could remember being bored and not knowing what time it was" (89-90). In Hemingway's (in)famous euphemism for orgasm in *For Whom the Bell Tolls,* the "earth moved" (160, 174, 176) for Maria, implying something seismic in sex that was taken as prescription rather than metaphor. Yet, this figure is, of course, the measure of male self-congratulation. As the ersatz Hemingway rhetoric of Susan's sexual disappointment elucidates, the role assigned to women in masculinist culture is a source of dissatisfaction, self-doubt, and the perception of lack. The Hemingway model cannot adequately account for female subjectivity since it is constructed on female self-effacement, on female gratitude for earth-shaking male attention. Masculinist constructions may provide a model of subjectivity, and some attributes of the male model can be emulated, as with Hemingway's style, but the prescriptive roles assigned to women must be refused.

As the Hemingway trope suggests, *Come and Join the Dance* situates itself in literary history with a temperamental affinity to modernism, but the "cool," restrained style is deployed in the service of "hot" self-expression and modes of subjectivity, a combination which results in a central Beat contradiction.[12] Rather than the breathless jazzy endless lines and ebullient emotions of "hot" Beat stylist Kerouac, Glassman's minimalist, succinct prose mannerisms embody Beat "cool" via the elegant restraint of Henry James, Glassman's acknowledged mentor, and the sparseness of modernist stylists like Hemingway and, later, Joan Didion. The language is contained, inert, not an unnecessary muscle moving; the dispassionate, clipped syntax and diction of understated feeling mark Glassman's aesthetic and style. Registering anomie, the narrative has an emotional climate, a gestalt of incipient fragmentation. This climate derives in part from the intellectual existentialism of postwar New York, where hipsters read Gide, Nietzsche, and Kierkegaard, trying to account for the postwar fatigue and sense of dislocation. It also derives in part from, and signifies, a defining state of the feminine, in which the self is atomized by its objectification in the hegemonic male gaze.

Yet, if the novel moves and speaks stylistically with indirection, coolness, and restraint, in contrast, its characterization of Beat female subjectivity appropriates and follows Kerouac's model for male subjectivity, which valorizes "hot" Beat talkativeness and lack of restraint over "cool," "laconic" effeteness (1959, 362-363). This dichotomy is figured in *Come and Join the Dance* as a contradiction of the novel's "cool" style with its "hot" content. Although Hemingway is evoked in injunctions against expressing emotion, and in valorizations of stoic self-containment and Garboesque insulation, the evocations are simultaneously negated: Susan concludes she would prefer "to feel frightened rather than feel nothing at all" (15); silent stoicism is not heroic but "a kind of failure" (17). To refrain from speaking and articulating painful or confusing matters, as in Hemingway, evokes the influential style of withholding masculinity disseminated through modernist literary and popular twentieth-century culture alike. But this model only perpetuates the silence of female repression. Susan, admonished by her lover Anthony to control her feelings, flashes back the novel's credo for its outlaw wild girls: "I think you have to get upset!" (22). Glassman's discourse of female subjectivity insists on disorder, transgression, forbidden excess, volubility: "trouble's better than nothing" (47), better than femininity's "nothing" of repressed desire and conformity. It is, therefore, incumbent on the heroine to narrate, to become by achieving voice. "Telling" is paramount. She must spill out feelings, confessions, histories, even engage in novel-making: Susan observes that "no act ever seemed complete until it had been made public and a little fictitious" (41). As Kristeva notes, the woman novelist "creates an imaginary story through which she constitutes an identity" (166); and just so for Johnson, who stated that "only the publication of my novel would transform my existence into what I wanted it to be" (1983, 122). Affording identity and visibility, invention makes heroic and exemplary the telling that assures subjectiv-

19

ity. Fictitiousness here is not the stereotype of female deceit but the female entry into history.[13] The directive to write is the directive to enter literature. Glassman's novel, providing her voice, bids to install her among the ranks of her peers, the male Beat writers such as Holmes and Kerouac, Ginsberg, and LeRoi Jones.

Beat female resistance to both mainstream and hipster gender negations is also registered and rendered textually and narratively in the matter of acquisition and alteration of voice. The narrative marks shifts in Susan's discourse from passive to declarative constructions: she evolves from "never really knowing whether or not I mean what I'm saying" (20-21)—from uncertainty of self-knowledge and a consequent passive self-construction—to a declarative self-possession, the certain knowledge of "what it meant . . . I know what it meant" (175). The shift in emphasis here from knowing to meaning suggests an evolution from understanding to interpretation, from seeing to naming. Such a shift signifies subjectivity. The intention to find significance in experience melts the anomie of being gendered female and silenced. The magnitude of this is evinced in Susan's authorship of her own subjectivity; her agency is not effected by a Pygmalion makeover, as Kerouac's men would overhaul women to be perfect foils,[14] but, rather, by self-development. Her patronizing older lover, Peter, deems Susan "worth saving" but Glassman's Beat move is to refuse to assign him the mission. Like the prototypical *sui generis* Beat hero, Susan will make herself; she will be "anything [she] want[s]," "anything" she decides to be (22). She will cease to be produced by operations of the male establishment or bohemian expectations of women and instead author(ize) herself, mimicking the story of this narrative in which she ceases to be the passive object and becomes the active subject. Thus, the narrative enacts the female agency that is antidote to the symptomatic anomie of its heroine.

Contentions of the "chick category" and resistance to female passivity and alienation find their most explicit expression in the arena of sexual relations, in Susan's contemplation and arrangement of "a gratuitous act of sex" (56), a figure inspired by Glassman's reading of Gide (Grace 1999b, 114). The phrase underscores an axiomatic reality, chronicled in **Minor Characters**, that for women in the 1950s the *acte gratuit* of the existential trial to feel in the face of nothingness is to have sex outside marriage in the face of illegal abortion and in the unavailability of effective birth control (1983, 94-97; 110-115; 249).

That is, sexual freedom for women is the existential *acte gratuit* at the same time as it is the sine qua non of individuality. Here, the novel embraces for its heroine a Beat (male) sexual ethos. Virginity is seen not as a barter commodity that secures women's cultural survival through marriage, but as a state of infantilization and passive spectatorship: "graduating a virgin was against all her principles. She was sick of being a child, sick of being only a member of the audience" (47). Yet in this rejection of the feminine, Susan attains male equipoise and self-reliance. Kristeva observes that in a "culture where the speaking subjects are conceived of as masters of their speech, they have what is called 'phallic' position," and, although she sees textual language calling "into question the very posture of this mastery" (165), the trope Kristeva uses even for the female subject who writes, the signifier the "'phallic' position," suggests gender's irremediable saturation of constructions of subjectivity. As a subject who must tell or fictionalize, Susan moves into the masculine, the "'phallic' position" of language. This move has the paradoxical discursive potential of erasing Susan as a gendered woman so as to inscribe her as an agent or individual; to figure her as a Beat in the usual (male) sense.

Thus, Susan is rendered a Beat subject by her capacity for masculine privilege, the ultimate expression of this being her (re)positioning as the privileged consumer of sex. In her sexual awakening, Susan expends men: she rejects Jerry, for "when he began to kiss her, she could not shut her eyes" (30); decides to lose her virginity with Anthony; seduces Peter. In **Minor Characters**, Johnson traces "the new self-consciousness about coming or not coming [that made] it a man's duty and triumph that both should come, and a woman's shame if she didn't" (93), which **Come and Join the Dance** explores and critiques in Susan's two affairs. The 1950s pressure on women to "let go" (1983, 99) is, as Johnson suggests, a pseudofreedom that amounts to another way to keep women subservient; to enforce the dissimulations—the faked orgasms—of the powerless. Reversing cultural données that blame women for their sexual incapacity, Susan's sexual relations with immature Anthony and seasoned Peter, supplicants for her favor, focus on both men's failure to bring her to orgasm (93, 175). The novel observes that desirable and desirous men are not necessarily competent lovers, deflating Norman Mailer's promotion of hipsters in *The White Negro* as sexually proficient.

Wryly commenting on women's education and postwar liberalism—"I know everything [about sex]. I had Modern Living as a freshman" (82)—the narrative authorizes for Susan the expectation of sexual satisfaction and makes the men liable for her pleasure, contending the 1950s Freudian discourse which blamed women for sexual failures that were overdetermined by masculinist social norms.[15] Susan's poise and self-reliance unnerve Anthony; he fears that his lackluster sexual performance has estranged her, a male self-doubt rarely voiced by male Beat writers.[16] But, here, male failure provides opportunity for female subjectivity, as Susan tells Anthony, "'It [the sex act] had nothing to do with you. It was an experiment.' . . . she had never been more honest" (93-94). Repositioning the male from his usual superiority to her subordinate object or "experiment," Susan's "honesty" signifies the refusal of femininity's repressive dissimulations in favor of the existential engagement that arrests alienation.

Possibly the novel's most striking bid for Beat female subjectivity is its re-formation and termination of the road narrative so strongly identified with male Beats. Its decline is so pivotal that both penultimate chapters 19 and 20 are devoted to it. The road tale is a foundation and staple of mainstream and Beat American literature borrowed from European archetypes and, beginning with the texts of colonial settlement, extending well into the mid-twentieth century and Beat generation writing by Kerouac and others. *Come and Join the Dance* transgresses the road tale's traditions by making a woman the protagonist of its quest narrative. It abolishes the stock materials of the American road tale—vehicle, travel, escape—by aborting the entire expedition and shifting its focus to the kind of movement produced in women's typically interiorized flights, journeys to existential and sexual revelation, not destinations on the road away from home. These emendations to the generic road narrative exemplify the subvert/install double move which Hutcheon observes characterizes so many post-war, postmodern texts.

It is Peter, Susan's older lover and subterranean hipster-as-cold-war individual, who represents the novel's conventional Beat road hero. He is reminiscent of both Sal and Dean of *On the Road*, which Glassman read during the time she was writing her novel; he is thinker and doer, intellectual and driver, writer and Kerouacian "mad one," a man constantly in motion, making the rounds of cafés and bars and bookstores in the story's six blocks of New York City (13) or driving off in his 1938 Packard (19, 57, 73, 158). Peter's road binges to Chicago and places in New York State (19) inscribe escape from constraint and the way motion is an antidote to frustration and angst: his "car was the place where he really lived . . . a curious desperate joy possessed Peter at the wheel as long as everything went fast, and he always kept the back seat littered with the fragmentary preparations for a journey" (73). This discourse that links Peter to his car to his existential condition evokes the classic road tale as reinterpreted in the postwar era by Kerouac.

The novel's female appropriation of this male mythic genre negates the canon and refigures Beat, as in the novel's opening in which, pinned by the gaze of sixty-three concentrating "girls," Melville, the peripatetic adventurer, is made their captive, a specimen of their scrutiny, his movement thwarted, his road blocked. When Peter embarks on what proves to be his final odyssey in his Packard, with Susan in tow, the novel's closing on this "buddy" image has a sardonic congruity with its opening on Melville: refusing to "work" Melville anymore, Susan, headed for Paris, would take the road herself. She must authorize her own adventure; bringing women on the road with men will not make the Beat journey accessible to them for they are never going to be the archetypal "buddy": "Suppose you wanted to go wandering with him and you knew that he would never take you along and night after night you watched him go—and you were never able to say 'Take me with you'" (150).[17] A central challenge in taking on the quest narrative, which is one way to regard the mission of this novel, is to cancel the gender inequity that shapes the genre, the stipulation that women are hobbled unless escorted by men, or always already Penelopes resignedly awaiting the Ulyssean return. In *Come and Join the Dance*, the Beat female solution is radical: drop Homer and Melville; or, if women cannot take the road, terminate journeying itself. The road tale, the male escape from civilization, is predicated on having women and domesticity to leave. Just so, Susan's presence with Peter negates the road narrative, which, when stretched to accommodate women or forced to integrate the sexes, ceases as itself. Thus, the re-formation of the road tale mandates that Peter's journey come to a stop.

The novel's protofeminist denouement anticipates the second-wave women's movement. With its diminution of male privilege and concomitant augmentation of female status, it sounds impending changes in gender roles. In parallel plottings, just as Susan foregoes her diploma for flouting the college's rules, Peter is denied his car when it breaks down, but the two moves signify differently. Susan has achieved the Beat masculine condition of rejecting institutions, the hipster's antiestablishment disdain, while Peter has achieved the feminine condition of being denied, in this case, tools for freedom or pleasure. This plotting frees the Beat female to the status of the male while the Beat male becomes truly downwardly mobile, reaching the disaffection of the disempowered, which is ostensibly the point of dropping out for white Beat men. When the decrepit Packard must be junked, it signifies the novel's expiration of the road discourse as rendered by Kerouac, Ginsberg, and William S. Burroughs to express iconoclastic male subjectivity.[18] In its obvious metaphoric capacity, this discourse of the machine which equals power which equals mobility comprises and figures male subjectivity; here, the debilitated machine signifies the decline of male power. Concomitantly, the termination of the road narrative that conveys the Beat male discourse serves as a prelude to Susan and Peter's sexual consummation, which requires equality, for in Glassman's Beat discourse, only after women and men are set in horizontal, not vertical, alliance, can they have sexual relations.

It is the termination of the road tale that achieves gender parity for the novel's New Bohemians (Gruen), or Beats, for it resituates Peter at Susan's level by making him a denizen of urban domesticity, the way women are stranded at home by patriarchal prohibition:

> She was thinking about how it would be for Peter now [without the car], how he would wake up in his apartment each day and find that more dust had settled overnight, how he would go out for breakfast because there weren't any clean cups, how he would drift up and down Broadway until he was tired enough to sleep again.
>
> (162)

Stalled, trapped, landlocked without his car, emasculated like Melville under the scrutiny of college girls, peter would drift now rather than race in society like an archetypal Beat hero. Enraged, smashing his broken-down car and junking it (168), Peter is reduced to travel by taxi, passive in the hands of drivers for hire, which provides a clear contrast to such scenes in *On the Road* in which, when a burned-out car is abandoned, Sal and Dean simply find another vehicle and continue their journey. The destruction in **Come and Join the Dance** of the determinants of the road tale and the diminution of the road hero provide for the heroine's self-assertion: her enact-

ment of Beat subjectivity and agency. Seated with Peter in the taxi, Susan expresses her desire for and attraction to him: "Suddenly she couldn't bear not telling him in some way that she was here with him, that she hadn't just come for the ride, couldn't bear not touching him. . . . She turned to Peter, put her arms around him, held him close to her" (172). As the sexual aggressor, Susan negates the feminine subordination of the silent, acquiescent chick, a breakthrough which occurs at the cost of male mobility and the viability of the road tale as an existential course. This anticipates the decline of white male hegemony during the women's liberation movements of the late 1960s and early seventies. Just so, Susan proves false the 1950s Freudian view of female sexual incapacity and joins the dance, the Beat life of "kicks" and sex, subjectivity and desire that the women's movement later appropriated for many women, not just Beats.

The novel completes its renovation of Beat discourse by extending to the female bohemian the sexual agency men possess; it tells its scene of sexual connection as an event staged for and judged by the female lover. Satisfaction of perspective takes the place of sexual gratification. Delivered by the taxi to Peter's apartment, the lovers consummate their attraction in the novel's brief last chapter. Susan's imminent but not-reached orgasm does not signify sexual incapacity here, but rather, idiomatically, her empowerment. Glassman renders this unclimatic event with characteristic lucidity: during sex, Susan "felt herself becoming flooded with light . . . float[ing] up, up—toward something she had almost reached" (174), an image of the orgasmic brink. Asserting that the sex "was good anyway. . . . It was what it meant. . . . I knew what it meant" (175), Susan claims the sexual agency of the wild girls, renouncing the passive silence of the "chick category" for the élan and power of the (Beat) male. Leveling but not abolishing tropes of gender difference, the Beat female arrival is evinced in the narrative's denouement when Susan renders Peter the object of her departing gaze; now she "knows" Peter, she "can see" him (172). In Laura Mulvey's lexicon, Susan moves from being the object of the gaze to becoming the subject-gazer. In this scene, her judgment and evaluation are foregrounded, asserting women's subjectivity in this incipient Beat bohemia. In the novel's one-line last paragraph, "And then she went" (176)—out of Peter's apartment, off to Paris—Susan becomes protagonist of her own quest narrative, dropping out of bohemia as well as college. Refusing to be the chick, Susan renounces her assigned role in Beat discourse and authors her own subjectivity. "And then she went": no longer passenger or spectator, her renunciation of submission expands and reconstitutes notions of Beat iconoclasm. With this narrative, shaking off her silence, the Beat female subject emerges, contending and refiguring what it means to be Beat.

Notes

1. Joyce Glassman is the signatory of one novel, *Come and Join the Dance,* while Joyce Johnson is the author of novels, prose fiction, and journalism, and is the Beat memoirist and historian. Preserving the distinction between the two names/two selves calls attention to the author as a young, unmarried writer of her first novel, a habitué of Beat scenes and hip New York enclaves who was working to establish herself in a male-dominated world—both the Beat scene and the world of work—without becoming a chick. The second name, "Joyce Johnson," is that of the established writer, editor, teacher. The subject of this essay is the neophyte.

2. See Helen McNeil, "The Archeology of Gender in the Beat Movement," and Amy L. Friedman, "'I saw my new name': Women Writers of the Beat Generation." In neither of these recent survey essays is Joyce Johnson's first novel mentioned, even as each essay addresses the elision of female writers from the Beat canon; both critics see Johnson merely as a memoirist with connections. As Friedman puts it, "Novelist Joyce Johnson . . . was involved with Kerouac at the time *On the Road* was published and is a Beat memoirist" (201); for McNeil, "Joyce Johnson should be added to the list [of eight women writers out of a total of 67 Beat writers included in Ann Charters's 1979 bibliographical compilation] for her memoir *Minor Characters*" (193). McNeil refers to Ann Charters's 1983 volumes for the *Dictionary of Literary Biography, The Beats, Literary Bohemians in Postwar America.*

3. Brenda Knight mentions *Come and Join the Dance* twice in her survey of Beat women artists, *Women of the Beat Generation: The Writers, Artists, and Muses at the Heart of a Revolution,* but the novel is mentioned by title, not discussed (168, 176); Johnson's two other novels are not cited. The full discussion of Johnson's significance and achievement is shortsightedly confined to her memoir *Minor Characters* and her affair with Kerouac.

4. For example, see Bonnie Bremser, Diane di Prima (1969), Hettie Jones (1990), Carolyn Cassady. All four prose texts are billed as memoir, rarely discussed, and have not been examined either in terms of feminist theories of the memoir form for women writers—although this lapse is redressed in this volume; see Nancy Grace, "Snapshots, Sand Paintings and Celluloid"—or as texts whose genre should be interrogated with regard to narrative shape and invention.

5. This indubitably Beat gesture or double move suggests Beat anticipations of the postmodern, or Beat pre-postmodernism. For an extended discussion of Beat pre-postmodernism, see my essay "'You're putting me on': Jack Kerouac and the Postmodern Emergence."

6. Johnson recounts in *Minor Characters* that "[i]n the fall of '56 . . . just turning twenty-one . . . I found a

new job at another literary agency . . . moved into a new apartment of my own . . . [and] worked on the novel about Barnard I'd begun in Hiram Hayden's [novel writing] workshop" in 1955 (107, 121). This unnamed book is certainly *Come and Join the Dance* and, far from being just a "novel about Barnard," it is consumed by the protagonist's effort to transcend the paralyzing expectations for bourgeois college women of the fifties to marry and conform.

7. See *Door Wide Open* (Johnson and Kerouac 2000) for this same formulation or trope about bohemia and confinement to straight communities. With her mother secretly asking her friends questions about her, Joyce Glassman writes to Jack Kerouac that she's "living in the middle of a spy ring" (104).

8. See Sukenick and Wakefield for detailed accounts of the bars, cafés, all-night cafeterias, and jazz spots that served as nuclei for nascent postwar bohemian writer-artist, abstract expressionist, bebop scenes in which women, when they are noticed at all, serve as witnesses to that history or as scenery framing the really important occurrences, like Jackson Pollock's fights or Dylan Thomas's seductions.

9. See Shulman, Johnson 1983, and memoirs by women of the Beat generation listed in note 4.

10. In Ginsberg, the female archetype of "the best minds of my generation destroyed by madness" is actually of the antecedent generation: his mother, Naomi, commemorated for her madness and self-destruction by fantasized political persecution in "Kaddish" (1961). Kerouac offers more female figures destroyed by countercultural existentialism, especially Mardou Fox of *The Subterraneans* (1958), Mary Lou of *On the Road* (1957), and Tristessa of the eponymous novel (1960).

11. In Shulman's *Burning Questions,* the heroine, Zane, proving her fitness for bohemia, refuses to go to college; instead, she moves to Greenwich Village (from her home in Ohio) and seeks out beat bohemians. Although she is treated as a chick and exploited for sex and rent money, her hopes for agency are nurtured until they can be realized in the second-wave women's movement that began in the late 1960s.

12. See Jack Kerouac, "The Origins of the Beat Generation," in which he makes distinctions between "hot" and "cool," and sees most artists belonging to the "hot school," although some are "fifty fifty" and a few "hot" ones like him "cooled it" down after encountering Buddhism (363). While Kerouac allows for degrees of "hot" and "cool," and even mixtures, it is Glassman's distinction to develop the combination of a "hot" style of subjectivity by means of a "cool" literary discourse.

13. Shulman's *Burning Questions* provides an account of the early second-wave women's movement in the Third Street Circle cell of the novel, where women meet and endlessly talk themselves to subjectivity. Later in the novel the talk fest moves to the New Space, a café, but the scene exemplifies the same principle.

14. See *On the Road* and Sal and Dean's continual consternation with women as they are; their repeated assessments of what renovations would need to be made in Camille or Mary Lou or Okie Frankie or Inez or Terry or Rita Bettencourt so that the women would better fit with and accommodate the desires of men like Sal and Dean.

15. In *Burning Questions*, Shulman depicts the first bohemian sexual encounters of the novel's eighteen-year-old protagonist in New York. Of her first Greenwich Village encounter with a Beat poet, in 1958, Shulman writes that Zane "was so intimidated, so terrified of Marshal Braine, that [she] ought to have been quite frigid" (70). The expectation of women's fear of sexually aggressive or sophisticated men and their failure to achieve sexual satisfaction is implied and ironized in Shulman's discourse. Here, Shulman mocks but nevertheless confronts the 1950s burden placed on women, the accusation of frigidity if they did not at least seem to reach orgasm.

16. In Kerouac's *On the Road*, there is an understated scene in which the protagonist Sal Paradise seems to imply he has been a sexual disappointment to a woman: Rita Bettencourt "was a nice little girl, simple and true, and tremendously frightened of sex. I told her it was beautiful. I wanted to prove this to her. She let me prove it, but I was too impatient, and proved nothing" (48). As in *Come and Join the Dance*, it is the male who short-circuits the sexual experience, but such admissions are extremely rare in Kerouac or other male Beat writers, and are never ascribed to such sexual heroes as Dean Moriarty.

17. Johnson writes in *Minor Characters* that "I'd listen to [Kerouac] with delight and pain, seeing all the pictures he painted so well for me, wanting to go with him. Could he ever include a woman in his journeys? I didn't altogether see why not. Whenever I tried to raise the question, he'd stop me by saying that what I really wanted were babies" (142). Further on, she recounts a waterfront prowl with Kerouac: "Here and there at the ends of the dead-end streets were dim taverns all brown inside, with dock workers and sailors steadily drinking under yellow lights. There were no women in this nighttime world . . . I'd never seen anything like it before. It was strange to think that because of my sex I'd probably never see any of this again, and would probably never have seen it at all if it hadn't been for Jack" (145).

18. See not only Kerouac's obvious road tales, but also consider that Ginsberg's *Howl* is a road narrative in unwinding rhythmic verse—its visions unroll geographically across the United States—and that Burroughs's trilogy of *Junky*, *Queer*, and *The Yage Letters* (Burroughs and Ginsberg) is precisely a road tale on its most explicit level, for it moves progressively south, geographically and symbolically away from constraint to freedom, moving as it does from New York to the very tip end of South America, a pattern which is evident when the novels are read in the chronological order of the travels given above (as opposed to their publication order).

Selected Bibliography

Helen Adam

1924. *Charms and Dreams from the Elfin Pedlar's Pack*. London: Hodder and Stoughton.

1924. *The Elfin Pedlar and Tales Told by Pixy Pool*. New York and London: G.P. Putnam's Sons.

1958. *The Queen o' Crow Castle*. Drawings by Jess Collins. N.p.: White Rabbit Press.

1963. *At the Window*. San Francisco: Gene's Print Shop.

1964. *Ballads*. Illustrated by Jess Collins. New York: Acadia Press.

1964. *San Francisco's Burning: A Ballad Opera*. San Francisco: Oannes Press. Reprint 1985. New York: Hanging Loose Press.

1972. *Counting Out Rhyme*. New York: Interim Books.

1974. *Selected Poems and Ballads*. New York: Helikon Press.

1977. *Turn Again to Me and Other Poems*. New York: Kulchur Foundation.

1978. *The Last Secret*. Binghamton, N.Y.: Bellvue Press.

1979. *Ghosts and Grinning Shadows: Two Witch Stories*. Brooklyn, N.Y.: Hanging Loose Press.

1979. *Last Words of Her Lover*. Vancouver, B.C.: Slug Press.

1980. *Gone Sailing*. West Branch, Iowa: Toothpaste Press.

1983. *Summer 1981*. West Branch, Iowa. Toothpaste Press.

1984. *Stone Cold Gothic*. Edited by Lita Hornick. New York: Kulchur Foundation.

1985. *The Bells of Dis: Poems*. West Branch, Iowa: Coffee House Press.

Diane di Prima

1958. *This Kind of Bird Flies Backwards*. New York: Aardvark Press. Reprint 1963. New York: Paper Book Gallery.

1961. *Dinners and Nightmares*. Reprint 1974. Corinth Books. Expanded ed. 1998. San Francisco: Las Gasp Press.

1965. *The New Handbook of Heaven*. San Francisco: Auerhahn Press.

1965. *Seven Love Poems from the Middle Lati*. San Francisco: Poets Press.

1966. *Haiku*. Topanga, Calif.: Love Press.

1968. *Hotel Albert: Poems*. New York: Poets Press.

1969. *Memoirs of a Beatnik*. New York: Olympia Press. Reprint 1988. New York: Last Gasp Press. Reprint 1998. New York: Penguin Books.

1969. *L.A. Odyssey*. San Francisco: Poets Press.

1971. *Kerhonkson Journal*. Berkeley, Calif.: Oyez.

1971. *Revolutionary Letters*. 3rd. ed. 1974. San Francisco: City Lights Books.

1972. *The Calculus of Variation*. San Francisco: Eidolon Editions.

1973. (Editor). *The Floating Bear: A Newsletter*. La Jolla, Calif: Laurence McGilvery.

1974. *Freddie Poems*. Point Reyes, Calif.: Eidolon Editions.

1975. *Selected Poems, 1956-1975*. Plainfield, Vt.: North Atlantic Books.

1978. *Loba*, Parts 1-8. Berkeley: Wingbow Press.

1990. *Pieces of a Song: Selected Poems*. San Francisco: City Lights Books.

1991. *Seminary Poems*. Point Reyes Station, Calif.: Floating Island Publications.

1998. *Loba*, Parts 1-16, Books 1 and 2. New York: Penguin Books.

2001. *Recollections of My Life as a Woman: The New York Years*. New York: Viking Press.

Brenda Frazer (Bonnie Bremser)

1969. *Troia: Mexican Memoirs*. New York: Croton Press. Republished 1971 as *For Love of Ray*. London: Tandem Press.

Joyce Johnson

1962. (As Joyce Glassman).*Come and Join the Dance*. New York: Atheneum.

1978. *Bad Connections*. New York: G. P. Putnam's Sons.

1983. *Minor Characters: A Memoir of a Young Woman of the 1950s in the Beat Orbit of Jack Kerouac*. Boston: Houghton Mifflin. Reprint 1990. New York: Washington Square Press. Expanded ed. 1999. New York: Penguin Books.

1989. *In the Night Café*. New York: Dutton.

1990. *What Lisa Knew: The Truths and Lies of the Steinberg Case*. New York: Kensington Press.

1993. "The Children's Wing." In *Turning Toward Home: Reflections on the Family from Harper's Magazine*. New York: Franklin Square Press, 193-202.

1996. "Greenwich Village." In *The Seasons of Women: An Anthology*. Edited by Gloria Norris. New York: W.W. Norton, 127-33.

1999. "Beat Queens: Women in Flux." In *The Rolling Stone Book of the Beats: The Beat Generation and American Culture*. Edited by Holly George-Warren. New York: Hyperion, 40-51.

1999. "Beat Women: A Transitional Generation." *Beat Culture: The 1950s and Beyond*. Edited by Cornelius Van Minnen, Jaap van der Bent, and Mel Elteren. Amsterdam: VU University Press, 211-221.

2000. (With Jack Kerouac) *Door Wide Open: A Beat Love Affair in Letters, 1957-1958*. New York: Viking Press.

Hettie Jones

1971. (Compiler). *The Trees Stand Shining: Poetry of the North American Indian*. New York: Dial Press. Reprint 1974. New York: Viking Press. Reprint 1997. New York: Dell.

1976. *Big Star Fallin' Mama: Five Women in Black Music*. Reprint 1995. New York: Viking Press.

1980. *I Hate to Talk About Your Mother: A Novel*. New York: Delacorte Press.

1990. *How I Became Hettie Jones*. New York: Dutton.

1996. "Going to Jail." In *In Defense of Mumia*. Edited by S. E. Anderson and Tony Medina. New York: Writers and Readers.

1997. "It Was 1960." In *Generations: A Century of Women Speak About Their Lives*. Edited by Myriam Miedzian and Alisa Malinovich. New York: Atlantic Monthly Press.

1998. *Drive: Poems*. Brooklyn, N.Y.: Hanging Loose Press.

1999. "Babes in Boyland." In *The Rolling Stone Book of the Beats: The Beat Generation and American Culture*. Edited by Holly George-Warren. New York: Hyperion.

Joanne Kyger

1964. (With Phyllis Bailey) *The Persimmons Are Falling*. San Francisco: San Francisco Arts Festival.

1965. *The Tapestry and The Web*. San Francisco: Four Seasons Foundation.

1970. *Places to Go*. Santa Rosa, Calif.: Black Sparrow Press.

1971. *Desecheo Notebook*. Berkeley: Arif Press.

1971. *Trip Out and Fall Back*. Berkeley: Arif Press.

1975. *All This Every Day*. Bolinas, Calif.: Big Sky Press.

1979. *The Wonderful Focus of You*. Calais, Vt.: Z Press.

1981. *The Japan and India Journals, 1960-1964*. Bolinas, Calif.: Tombou Books. Republished 2000. *Strange Big Moon: The Japan and India Journals, 1960-1964*.

1981. *Mexico Blonde*. Bolinas, Calif.: Evergreen Press.

1981. *Up My Coast*. Point Reyes Station, Calif.: Floating Island Publications.

1983. *Going On: Selected Poems, 1958-1980*. New York: Dutton.

1984. *Revolution in Poetic Language*. Translated by Margaret Waller. New York: Columbia University Press.

1986. (With Robert Grenier). *Phantom Anthems*. Oakland, Calif.: O Books in collaboration with Trike Press.

1989. *Phenomenological*. New York: Institute of Further Studies.

1991. *Just Space: Poems, 1979-1989*. Santa Rosa, Calif.: Black Sparrow Press.

1993. *Going Out: Selected Poems 1958-1980*. New York: Dutton.

1996. *Some Sketches from the Life of Helena Petrovna Blavatsky*. Boulder, Colo.: Roden Press & Erudite Fangs.

1999. *Patzcuaro*. Bolinas, Calif: Blue Millennium Press.

2000. *Some Life*. Sausalito, Calif: Post-Aollo Press.

Janine Pommy Vega

1968. *Poems to Fernando*. San Francisco: City Lights Books.

1977. *Song for César*. Brattleboro, Vt.: Longhouse Press.

1978. *Here at the Door*. Brooklyn, N.Y.: Zonepress.

1979. *Journal of a Hermit &*. Cherry Valley, N.Y.: Cherry Valley Editions.

1980. *The Bard Owl*. New York: Kulchur Foundation

1984. *Apex of the Earth's Way*. Buffalo, N.Y.: White Pine Press.

1988. (Editor). *Candles Burn in Memory Town: Poems from Both Sides of the Wall*.New York: Segue Books.

1988. *Skywriting*. San Francisco: City Lights Books.

1992. *Threading the Maze.* Old Bridge, N.J.: Cloud Mountain.

1993. *Red Bracelets.* Chester, N.Y.: White Pine Press.

1994. (Editor). *These Are Successful Hands: An Anthology of Poetry from the Women of Huntington House.* New York: Segue Books.

1997. *Tracking the Serpent: Journeys to Four Continents.* San Francisco: City Lights Books.

1999. (Editor). *Voices Under the Harvest Moon: An Anthology of Writing from Eastern Correctional Facility.* New York: Segue Books.

2000. *Mad Dogs of Trieste: New and Selected Poems.* Santa Rosa, Calif.: Black Sparrow Press.

Anne Waldman

1968. *Giant Night.* New York: Angel Hair Books.

1969. *O My Life!* New York: Angel Hair Books.

1969. (Editor) *The World Anthology: Poems from the St. Mark's Poetry Project.* Indianapolis and New York: Bobbs-Merrill.

1970. *Baby Breakdown.* Indianapolis and New York: Bobbs-Merrill.

1971. *No Hassles: An Unhinged Book in Parts.* New York: Kulchur Foundation.

1973. *Life Notes.* Indianapolis and New York: Bobbs-Merrill.

1975. *Fast Speaking Woman: Chants & Essays.* Rev. ed. 1996. San Francisco: City Lights Books.

1976. *Journals and Dreams: Poems* New York: Stonehill Books.

1980. *Countries: Poems.* West Branch, Iowa: Toothpaste Press.

1983. *First Baby Poems.* New York: Hyacinth Girls Editions.

1984. *Makeup on Empty Space: Poems.* West Branch, Iowa: Toothpaste Press.

1985. *Skin Meat Bones: Poems.* Minneapolis: Coffee House Press.

1987. *The Romance Thing: Travel Sketches.* Flint, Mich.: Bamberger Books.

1988. *Blue Mosque.* New York: United Artists Books.

1989. *Helping the Dreamer: New and Selected Poems, 1966-1988.* Minneapolis: Coffee House Press.

1990. *Not a Male Pseudonym.* New York: Tender Buttons Press.

1991. (Editor). *Out of This World: An Anthology of the St. Mark's Poetry Project, 1966-1991.* New York: Crown Books.

1992. *Fait Accompli.* Boulder, Colo.: last generation press.

1993. *Troubairitz.* New York: Fifth Planet Press.

1994. (Editor, with Andrew Schelling). *Disembodied Poetics: Annals of the Jack Kerouac School.* Albuquerque: University of New Mexico Press.

1994. *Kill or Cure.* New York: Penguin Books.

1996. (Editor). *The Beat Book: Poems and Fiction of the Beat Generation.* Boulder, Colo.: Shambhala Press.

1997. *Iovis: All Is Full of Jove.* Vol. 2. Minneapolis: Coffee House Press.

2000. *Marriage: A Sentence.* New York: Penguin Books.

2001. *Vow to Poetry.* Minneapolis: Coffee House Press.

Works Cited and Consulted

Adam, Helen. 1924. *The Elfin Pedlar and Tales Told by Pixy Pool.* New York and London: G.P. Putnam's Sons.

———. 1964. *San Francisco's Burning: A Ballad Opera.* San Francisco: Oannes Press. Reprint 1985. New York: Hanging Loose Press.

———. 1974. *Selected Poems and Ballads.* New York: Helikon Press.

———. 1977. *Turn Again to Me and Other Poems.* New York: Kulchur Foundation.

———. 1984. *Stone Cold Gothic.* Edited by Lita Hornick. New York: Kulchur Foundation.

———. The Helen Adam Collection. The Poetry/Rare Books Collection. Buffalo: The State University of New York at Buffalo.

Adam, Helen, and Robert Duncan. 1997. "Selected Correspondence, 1955-1956." *apex of the M* 6 (fall): 135-165.

Allen, Donald M., ed. 1960. *The New American Poetry, 1945-1960.* New York: Grove Press.

Allen, Donald M., and Benjamin Friedlander, eds. 1997. *Collected Prose.* Berkeley: University of California Press.

Allen, Donald M., and Warren Tallman, eds. 1973. *The Poetics of the New American Poetry.* New York: Grove Press.

Alter, Robert. 1985. *The Art of Biblical Poetry.* New York: Basic Books.

Altieri, Charles. 1979. *Enlarging the Temple: New Directions in American Poetry During the 1960s.* Lewisburg, Penn.: Bucknell University Press.

Anderson, Susan. 2000. "A Hut of Words Primitive to Our Nature: Ball Influences in the San Francisco Renaissance." Masters thesis, Naropa University: Boulder, Colo.

Auerbach, Nina. 1982. *Woman and the Demon: The Life of a Victorian Myth.* Cambridge, Mass.: Harvard University Press.

Austin, J. L. 1979. "Performative Utterances." In *Philosophical Papers.* Oxford, U.K.: Oxford University Press.

Baraka, Imamu Amiri. 1984. *The Autobiography of LeRoi Jones.* 2nd rev. ed. 1997. Chicago: Lawrence Hill Books.

———. 1995. "Am/Trak." In *Transbluesency: Selected Poems, 1961-1995.* Edited by Paul Vangelisti. New York: Marsilio.

Bartlett, Lee, ed. 1981. *The Beats: Essays in Criticism.* Jefferson, N.C.: McFarland.

———, ed. 1987. *Talking Poetry: Conversations in the Workshop with Contemporary Poets.* Albuquerque: University of New Mexico Press.

Barthes, Roland. 1986. "The Death of the Author." In *The Rustle of Language*. Translated by Richard Howard. Berkeley: University of California Press.

Battersby, Christine. 1989. *Gender and Genius*. London: The Women's Press.

Belgrad, Daniel. 1998. *The Culture of Spontaneity: Improvisation and the Arts in Post-war America*. Chicago: University of Chicago Press.

Benstock, Sheri. 1986. *Women of the Left Bank: Paris, 1900-1940*. Austin: University of Texas Press.

Bhaghostus, Djbot. 1993. *Run*. Los Angeles: Sun and Moon Press.

Bly, Robert. 1973. *Sleepers Joining Hands*. New York: Harper & Row.

Braude, Ann. 1991. *Radical Spirits: Spiritualism and Women's Rights in Nineteenth-Century America.* Boston: Beacon Press.

Breines, Wini. 1992. *Young, White, and Miserable: Growing Up Female in the Fifties.* Boston: Beacon Press.

Bremser, Bonnie. 1969. *Troia: Mexican Memoirs*. New York: Croton Press.

Breslin, Paul. 1987. *The Psycho-Political Muse: American Poetry since the Fifties*. Chicago: University of Chicago Press.

Buchan, David. 1972 *The Ballad and the Folk*. London: Routledge & Kegan Paul.

Burroughs, William S. 1953. *Junky*. New York: Ace Books. Reprint 1977. New York: Penguin Books.

———. 1959. *Naked Lunch*. New York: Grove Press. Reprint 1992. New York: Grove Weidenfeld.

Burroughs, William S., and Allen Ginsberg. 1962. *The Yage Letters*. Reprint 1973. San Francisco: City Lights Books.

Butler, Judith. 1993. *Bodies That Matter: On the Discursive Limits of "Sex."* New York: Routledge.

Butterick, George. 1983. "Diane di Prima." In *The Beats: Literary Bohemians in Post-War America*. Edited by Ann Charters. *Dictionary of Literary Biography*, Vol. 16. Detroit: Gale Research.

Campbell, Joseph. 1962. *Oriental Mythology*. Vol. 2 of *The Masks of God*. New York: Penguin Books.

Cándida Smith, Richard. 1995. *Utopia and Dissent: Art, Poetry, and Politics in California*. Berkeley: University of California Press.

Cassady, Carolyn. 1990. *Off the Road: My Life with Cassady, Kerouac, and Ginsberg*. New York: Penguin Books.

Chadwick, Whitney. 1985. *Women Artists and the Surrealist Movement*. New York: Thames and Hudson.

Charters, Ann. 1983. "Ann Waldman" In *The Beats: Literary Bohemians in Post-War America*. Edited by Ann Charters. *Dictionary of Literary Biography*, Vol. 16. Detroit: Gale Research.

———, ed. 1992. *The Beat Reader*. New York: Viking.

Child, Sir Francis. 1965. *The English and Scottish Popular Ballads*. New York: Dover Publications.

Conway, Jill Ker. 1998. *When Memory Speaks: Exploring the Art of Autobiography*. New York: Random House.

Cook, Bruce. 1971. *The Beat Generation*. New York: Scribner. Reprint 1994. New York: Morrow.

Cowen, Elise. Undated. "Dream," "Enough," "Interview," "Jehovah," "Someone I could kiss," and "Teacher—your body my Kabbalah." Unpublished manuscript.

Cully, Margo, ed. 1992. *American Women's Autobiography: Fea(s)ts of Memory*. Mason: University of Wisconsin Press.

Damon, Maria. 1996. "Victors of Catastrophe: Beat Occlusions." In *Beat Culture and the New America: 1950-1965*. Edited by Lisa Phillips. New York: Whitney Museum of Art, 141-149.

Davidson, Michael. 1989. *The San Francisco Renaissance: Poetics and Community at Mid-Century*. New York: Cambridge University Press.

Michael Davidson, Lyn Hejinian, Ron Silliman, and Barrett Watten. 1992. *Leningrad: American Writers in the Soviet Union*. San Francisco: Mercury House.

De Man, Paul. 1979. "Autobiography as De-facement." *Modern Language Notes*, 94. 919-30.

D'Emilio, John. 1983. *Sexual Politics, Sexual Communities: The Making of a Homosexual Minority in the United States, 1940-1970*. Chicago: University of Chicago Press.

Dery, Mark. 1999. *The Pyrotechnic Insanitarium: American Culture on the Brink*. New York: Grove Press.

di Prima, Diane. 1958. *This Kind of Bird Flies Backwards*. New York: Aardvark Press. Reprint 1963. New York: Paper Book Gallery.

———. 1961. *Dinners and Nightmares*. Reprint 1974. Corinth books. Expanded ed. 1998. San Francisco: Las Gasp Press.

———. 1969. *Memoirs of a Beatnik*. New York: Olympia Press. Reprint 1988. New York: Last Gasp Press. Reprint 1998. New York: Penguin Books.

———. 1971. *Revolutionary Letters*. 3rd. ed. 1974. San Francisco: City Lights Books.

———. 1975. *Selected Poems, 1956-1975*. Plainfield, Vt.: North Atlantic Books.

———. 1978a. "Light / and Keats." In *Talking Poetics from Naropa Institute*. Edited by Anne Waldman and Marilyn Webb. Boulder, Colo.: Shambhala Press.

———. 1978b. *Loba*, Parts 1-8. Berkeley: Wingbow Press.

———. 1990. *Pieces of a Song: Selected Poems*. San Francisco: City Lights Books.

———. 1991. *Seminary Poems*. Point Reyes Station, Calif.: Floating Island Publications.

———. "Recollections of My Life as a Woman / Diane di Prima." New York: Thin Air Video. Video recording.

———. 2001. *Recollections of My Life as a Woman: The New York Years*. New York: Viking Press.

Doolittle, Hilda (H.D.). 1914. "Oread." *Egoist* 1 (2 February): 54-55.

———. 1961. *Helen in Egypt*. New York: New Directions.

Douglas, Ann. 1999. "Strange Lives, Chosen Lives: The Beat Art of Joyce Johnson." In *Minor Characters: A Beat Memoir*. New York: Penguin Books, xiii-xxix.

Dragomoshchenko, Arkadii. "The Eroticism of Forgetting." *Poetics Journal* 10 (1998): 79-87.

Douglas, Susan J. 1994. *Where the Girls Are: Growing Up Female with the Mass Media* New York: Random House

Duncan, Robert. 1960. *The Opening of the Field*. New York: Grove.

———. 1962. "What Happened: Prelude." *Open Space Magazine* (San Francisco), February.

———. 1964. *Roots and Branches*. New York: New Directions.

———. 1985. *Fictive Certainties*. New York: New Directions.

———. 1999. *Selected Poems*. Edited by Robert J. Bertholf. New York: New Directions.

———. Undated. *Homage to Coleridge*. Unpublished manuscript. The Robert Duncan Archive at the Poetry/Rare Books Collection. Buffalo: The State University of New York.

DuPlessis, Rachel Blau. 1990. *The Pink Guitar: Writing as Feminist Practice*. New York: Routledge.

Edelman, Lee. 1993. "Tearooms and Sympathy, or, The Epistemology of the Water Closet." In *The Lesbian and Gay Studies Reader*. Edited by Henry Abelove, Michele Aina Barale, and David M. Halperin. New York: Routledge.

Ehrenreich, Barbara. 1983. *The Hearts of Men*. New York: Anchor Books.

Eliot, T. S. 1964. "Tradition and the Individual Talent." In *Selected Essays*. New York: Harcourt.

———. 1975. "Ulysses, Order, and Myth." In *Selected Prose of T. S. Eliot*. Edited by Frank Kermode. New York: Harcourt.

Ellingham, Lewis. 1982a. "Interview #1 with Robert Duncan." Unpublished transcript. Poetry/Rare Books Collection. Buffalo: The State University of New York.

———. 1982b. "Tape Interview of Ebbe Borregaard and Joanne Kyger by Lewis Ellingham on May 28 at Bolinas, California." Unpublished manuscript. Poetry/Rare Books Collection. Buffalo: The State University of New York.

Ellingham, Lewis, and Kevin Killian. 1998. *Poet, Be Like God: Jack Spicer and the San Francisco Renaissance*. Hanover, N.H. and London: Wesleyan University Press.

Faas, Ekbert, ed. 1978. "Allen Ginsberg." In *Towards a New American Poetics: Essays and Interviews*. Santa Barbara, Calif.: Black Sparrow Press.

Faderman, Lillian. 1991. *Odd Girls and Twilight Lovers: A History of Lesbian Life in Twentieth-Century America*. New York: Penguin Books.

Foster, Edward Halsy. 1992. *Understanding the Beats*. Columbia: University of Southern Carolina Press.

———. 1994. "An Interview with Anne Waldman." Talisman 13 (fall): 62-78.

Foucault, Michel. 1984. "What Is an Author?" In *The Foucault Reader*. Edited by Paul Rabinow. New ork: Pantheon.

Fraser, Kathleen. 2000. *Translating the Unspeakable*. Hanover, N.H. and London: Wesleyan University Press.

Frazer, Brenda (Bonnie Bremser). 1969. *Troia: Mexican Memoirs*. New York: Croyton Press.

———. 2000. E-mail correspondence to Nancy Grace, June 26.

French, Warren. 1991. *The San Francisco Renaissance*. New York: Twayne.

Friedan, Betty. 1963. *The Feminine Mystique*. New York: Norton.

Friedman, Amy L. 1996. "'I saw my new name': Women Writers of the Beat Generation." In *The Beat Generation Writers*. Edited by A. Robert Lee. London: Pluto Press.

Friedman, Susan Stanford. 1998. *Mappings: Feminism and the Cultural Geographies of Encounter*. Princeton, N.J.: Princeton University Press.

Genet, Jean. 1964. *The Thief's Journal*. Translated by Bernard Frechtman. New York: Grove Press.

George-Warren, Holly, ed. 1999. *The Rolling Stone book of the Beats: The Beat Generation and American Culture*. New York: Hyperion.

Gilman, Charlotte Perkins. [1894] 1973. *The Yellow Wallpaper*. Old Westbury, N.Y.: The Feminist Press.

Ginsberg, Allen. 1956. "Howl." In *"Howl" and Other Poems*. San Francisco: City Lights Books.

———. 1961. "Kaddish." In *"Kaddish" and Other Poems*. San Francisco: City Lights Books.

———. 1973. "How Kaddish Happened." In *Poetics of the New American Poetry*. Edited by Donald M. Allen and Warren Tallman. New York: Grove Press.

———. 1976a. *Introduction to Helen Adam at the Naropa Institute*.

———. 1976b. "Spontaneous Poetics, Lecture #2 with Guest Helen Adam." In *The Complete Naropa Lectures of Allen Ginsberg*. Edited by Randy Roark. Unpublished manuscript. 11 June.

———. 1980. "Improvised Poetics." Interview with Michael Aldrich, Edward Kissam, and Nancy Blecker. In *Composed on the Tongue: Literary Conversations, 1967-1977*. San Francisco: Grey Fox.

———. 1984. *Collected Poems 1947-1980*. New York: Harper & Row.

Gitlin, Todd. 1987. *The Sixties: Years of Hope, Days of Rage*. New York: Bantam Books.

Glassman, Joyce. 1962. *Come and Join the Dance*. New York: Atheneum.

Gold, Herbert. 1993. *Bohemia*. New York: Simon and Schuster.

Golding, Alan. 1998. "The New American Poetry Revisited, Again." *Contemporary Literature* 39: 180-211.

Grace, Nancy. 1995. *The Feminized Male Character in Twentieth-Century Literature*. Lewiston, N.Y.: The Edwin Mellen Press.

———. 1999a. "Interview with Brenda Frazer." Unpublished. 13 September. Wooster, Ohio.

———. 1999b. "Women of the Beat Generation: Conversations with Joyce Johnson and Hettie Jones." *Artful Dodge*, no 36/37: 106-133.

Graves, Robert. 1955. *The Greek Myths*. Vol. 2. New York: Penguin Books.

Gruen, John. 1966. *The New Bohemia*. New York: Shorecrest. Reprint 1990. New York: a cappella books.

Guest, Barbara. 1962. *Poems*. New York: Doubleday.

Haggard, H. Ryder. 1886. *She: A History of Adventure*. New York: The Review of Reviews.

Halberstam, David. 1993. *The Fifties*. New York: Villard.

Hampl, Patricia. 1996. "Memory and Imagination." In *The Anatomy of Memory*. Edited by James McConkey. New York: Oxford University Press.

Harris, William J., ed. 1999. *The LeRoi Jones/Amiri Baraka Reader*. 2nd ed. New York: Thunder's Mouth Press.

Hemingway, Ernest. 1940. *For Whom the Bell Tolls*. New York: Scribner's.

Holmes, John Clellon. 1952. *Go*. Rev. ed. 1980. New York: New American Library.

———. 1988. "The Beat Poets: A Primer of 1975." In *Passionate Opinions: The Cultural Essays*. Fayetteville: University of Arkansas Press.

Homer. 1969. *The Odyssey*. Translated by Richmond Lattimore. New York: Harper & Row.

Hoover, Paul. 1994. "Introduction." In *Postmodern American Poetry*. Edited by Paul Hoover. New York: Norton.

Hutcheon, Linda. 1988. *A Poetics of Postmodernism: History, Theory, Fiction*. New York: Routledge.

James, Henry. 1948. *The Art of Fiction and Other Essays*. New York: Oxford University Press.

Jameson, Frederic. 1981. *The Political Unconscious: Narrative as a Socially Symbolic Act*. Ithaca, N.Y." Cornell University Press.

Jelinek, Estelle C. 1986. *The Tradition of Women's Autobiography from Antiquity to the Present*. Boston: Twayne Publishers.

Johnson, Joyce. 1983. *Minor Characters: A Memoir of a young Woman of the 1950s in the Beat Orbit of Jack Kerouac*. Boston: Houghton Mifflin. Reprint 1990. New York: Washington Square Press. Expanded ed. 1999. New York: Penguin Books.

———. 1989. *In the Night Café*. New York: Dutton.

Johnson, Joyce, and Jack Kerouac. 2000. *Door Wide Open: A Beat Love Affair in Letters, 1957-1958*. New York: Viking Press.

Johnson, Ronna C. 2000. "'You're putting me on': Jack Kerouac and the Postmodern Emergence." *College Literature* Special Issue 27 no. 1 (winter), Teaching Beat Literature: 22-38.

Jones, Hettie. 1990. *How I Became Hettie Jones*. New York: Dutton.

———. 1997. "Spotlight on Hettie Jones." *PEN Newsletter* 95 (September-October).

———. 1998. *Drive: Poems*. New York: Hanging Loose Press.

Jones, LeRoi. 1960. "How You Sound??" In *The New American Poetry*. Edited by Donald M. Allen. New York Grove Press.

———. 1961. *Preface to a Twenty Volume Suicide Note*. New York: Totem Press.

———. 1963. *Blues People*. New York: Morrow.

———. 1964. *Dutchman and The Slave*. New York: Morrow.

———. 1973. "Hunting Is Not Those Heads on the Wall." In *The Poetics of the New American Poetry*. Edited by Donald M. Allen and Warren Tallman. New York: Grove Press.

Julian of Norwich, Dame. 1977. *Revelations of Divine Love*. Translated by M. L. de Mastro. Garden city, N.Y.: Image Books.

Kandel, Lenore. 1966. *The Love Book*. San Francisco: Stolen Paper Review Books.

Katz, Marilyn A. 1991. *Penelope's Renown: Meaning and Indeterminacy in the Odyssey*. Princeton, N.J.: Princeton University Press.

Kempe, Margery. 1985. *Book of Margery Kempe*. Translated by B. A. Windeatt. Hammondsworth, U.K.: Penguin Books.

Kerouac, Jack. 1957. *On the Road*. New York: Viking. Reprint 1991. New York: Penguin Books.

———. 1958. *The Subterraneans*. Reprint 1981. New York: Grove Press.

———. 1959. "The Origins of the Beat Generation." *Playboy* (June): 31-32, 42, 79. Reprint 1979. In *On the Road: Text and Criticism*. Edited by Scott Donaldson. New York: Viking Press.

———. 1960. *Tristessa*. New York: McGraw-Hill.

———. 1978. *Desolation Angels*. New York: Capricorn Books.

Kerouac, Joan Haverty. 2000. *Nobody's Wife: The Smart Aleck and the King of the Beats*. Berkeley, Calif.: Creative Arts Books.

Killian, Kevin. 2000. "Jack Spicer's Secret." Paper presented at The Opening of the Field: A Conference on North American Poetry in the 1960s, 28 June-2 July. The University of Maine, Orono.

Kirschenbaum, Blossom S. 1987. "Diane di Prima: Extending La Famiglia." *MELUS* 14, 3-4 (fall/winter): 53-67.

Knight, Brenda. 1996. *Women of the Beat Generation: The Writers, Artists and Muses at the Heart of a Revolution*. Berkeley: Conari Press.

Krim, Seymour. 1960. *The Beats*. New York: Fawcett.

Kristeva, Julia. 1980. *Desire in Language: A Semiotic Approach to Art and Literature*. Edited by Leon S. Roudiez. Translated by Thomas Gora, Alice Jardine, and Leon S. Roudiez. New York: Columbia University Press.

———. 1981. "Oscillation between Power and Denial." Interview, translated by Marilyn A. August. In *New French Feminisms*. Edited by Elaine Marks and Isabelle de Courtivron. New York: Schocken Books.

Kyger, Joanne. 1965. *The Tapestry and the Web*. San Francisco: Four Seasons Foundation.

———. 1974. "A Conversation with Joanne Kyger." Interview by Lawrence Hahem. *Occident* 8, new series: 142-157.

——. 1977. "Three Versions of the Poetic Line." Interview by Robert Bertholf with Joel Oppenheimer and Ed Dorn. *Credences* 4: 55-66.

——. 1979. *The Wonderful Focus of You.* Calais, Vt.: Z Press.

——. 1981. *The Japan and India Journals: 1960-1964.* Bolinas, Calif.: Tombouctou Books. Republished 2000. *Strange Big Moon: The Japan and India Journals 1960-1964.* Berkeley, Calif.: North Atlantic Books.

——. 1983. "Congratulatory Poetics." Interview by Diana Middleton-McQuaid and John Thorpe. *Convivio*: 109-120.

——. 1984. *Revolution in Poetic Language.* Translated by Margaret Waller. New York: Columbia University Press.

——. 1989. *Phenomenological.* Canton, N.Y.: Institute for Further Studies.

——. 1992. Joanne Kyger. Vol. 16 of *Contemporary Authors Autobiography Series.* Edited by Joyce Nakamura. Detroit, Mich.: Gale Research.

——. 1996. *Some Sketches from the Life of Helena Petrovna Blavatsky.* Boulder, Colo.: Rodent Press & Erudite Fangs.

——. 1999. *Patzcuaro.* Bolinas, Calif.: Blue Millenium Press.

——. Undated. "Thoughts on being a woman poet starting in the '50s." Unpublished manuscript. Bolinas, Calif..

Lee, A. Robert. 1996. *The Beat Generation Writers.* London: Pluto Press.

LeJeune, Phillip. 1989. "The Autobiographical Pact." In *On Autobiography.* Edited by Paul John Eakin. Translated by Katherine Leary. Minneapolis: University of Minnesota Press.

Loewinsohn, Ron. 1959. *Watermelons.* New York: Totem Press.

Mackey, Nathaniel. 1993. *Djbot Bhagostus's Run.* Los Angeles: Sun and Moon Press.

——. 1997. *Bedouin Hornbook.* Los Angeles: Sun and Moon Press.

Mann, Ron, director and producer. 1982. *Poetry in Motion.* Distributed by Home Vision Cinema/Public Media Inc. 2000 (Chicago).

Marcus, Greil. 1997. *Invisible Republic: Bob Dylan's Basement Tapes.* New York: Henry Holt.

McNally, Dennis. 1979. *Desolate Angel: Jack Kerouac, the Beat Generation, and America.* New York: Random House.

McNeil, Helen. 1996. "The Archeology of Gender in the Beat Movement." In *The Beat Generation Writers.* Edited by A. Robert Lee. London: Pluto Press.

Metalious, Grace. 1956. *Peyton Place.* New York: Messner.

Meyerowitz, Joanne, ed. 1994. *Not June Cleaver: Women and Gender in Postwar America, 1945-1960.* Philadelphia: Temple University Press.

Miles, Barry. 1989. *Ginsberg: A Biography.* New York: HarperCollins.

Miller, Nancy K. 1988. *Subject to Change: Reading Feminist Writing.* New York: Columbia University Press.

——. 2000. "But Enough About Me, What Do You Think of My Memoir?" *The Yale Journal of Criticism* 13, no. 2: 421-436.

Moffeit, Tony. 1989. "Interview with Diane di Prima." Unpublished. Boulder, Colo.

Mokey, Susan. 1998. *Desires of Their Own: Twentieth-Century Women Novelists and Images of the Erotic.* Ann Arbor, Mich.: University Microfilm.

Mulvey, Laura. 1989. *Visual and Other Pleasures.* Bloomington: Indiana University Press.

Nagy, Gregory. 1996. *Homeric Questions.* Austin: University of Texas Press.

Natsoulas/Novelozo Gallery Press. 1990. *Lyrical Vision: The 6 Gallery 1954-1957.* Davis, Calif.: Natsoulas/Novelozo Gallery Press.

Nelson, Cary. 1981. *Our Last First Poets: Vision and History in Contemporary American Poetry.* Urbana: University of Illinois Press.

——. 1989. *Repression and Recovery: Modern American Poetry and the Politics of Cultural Memory, 1910-1945.* Madison: The University of Wisconsin Press.

Nielsen, Aldon. 1994. "LeRoi Jones as Intertext." In *Writing Between the Lines: Race and Intertextuality.* Athens: University of Georgia Press.

——. 1997. *Black Chant: Languages of African-American Postmodernism.* Cambridge, U.K.: Cambridge University Press.

Neitzsche, Friedrich. 1967. *The Will to Power.* Edited by Walter Kaufmann. Translated by Walter Kaufmann and R. J. Hollingdale. New York: Random House.

Notley, Alice. 1992. "Homer's Art." In *The Scarlet Cabinet.* New York: Scarlet Editions.

——. 1994. "Epic and Women Poets." In *Disembodied Poetics.* Edited by Anne Waldman and Andrew Schelling. Albuquerque: University of New Mexico Press.

——. 1996. *The Descent of Alette.* New York: Penguin Books.

O'Hara, Frank. 1974. "Personal Poem." In *The Selected Poems of Frank O'Hara.* New York: Random House.

Olson, Charles. 1983. *The Maximus Poems.* Edited by George Butterick. Berkeley: University of California Press.

——. 1997. "Projective Verse." Reprinted in *Collected Prose.* Edited by Donald M. Allen and Benjamin Friedlander. Berkeley: University of California Press.

Oppen, George. 1966. *Discrete Series.* Cleveland, Ohio: Asphodel Book Shop.

Ostriker, Alicia Suskin. 1982. "Blake, Ginsberg, Madness, and the Prophet as Shaman." In *William Blake and the Moderns.* Edited by Robert J. Bertholf and Anna S. Levitt. Albany: State University of New York Press.

——. 1987. *Stealing the Language: The Emergence of Women's Poetry in America.* London: The Women's Press.

——. 1997. "'Howl' Revisited: The Poet as Jew." *American Poetry Review* 26, no. 4 (July/August): 28-31.

Peabody, Richard, ed. 1997. *A Different Beat: Writings by Women of the Beat Generation.* London: High Risk Books.

Perloff, Marjorie. 1990. *Poetic License: Essays on Modernist and Postmodernist Lyric.* Evanston, Ill.: Northwestern University Press.

Persky, Stan. 1964. "Proposition." *Open Space* no. 0.

Plimpton, George, ed. 1999. *Beat Writers at Work.* New York: Modern Library.

Pommy Vega, Janine. 1968. *Poems to Fernando.* San Francisco: City Lights Books.

———. 1979. *Journal of a Hermit &.* Cherry Valley, N.Y.: Cherry Valley Editions.

———. 1997. *Tracking the Serpent: Journeys to Four Continents.* San Francisco: City Lights Books.

Pommy Vega, Janine, and Hettie Jones. 1999. *Words Over Walls: Starting a Writing Workshop in a Prison.* New York: PEN.

Portugés, Paul. 1978. *The Visionary Poetics of Allen Ginsberg.* Santa Barbara, Calif.: Ross-Erikson.

———. 1980. "Allen Ginsberg's Paul Cézanne and the Pater Omnipotens Aeterna Deus." *Contemporary Literature* 21 (summer): 435-449.

Poulin, A. Jr. 1991. "Contemporary American Poetry: The Radical Tradition." In *Contemporary American Poetry.* 5th ed. Edited by A. Poulin Jr. Dallas: Houghton Mifflin.

Prevallet, Kristin. 1997. "An Extraordinary Enchantment: Helen Adam, Robert Duncan, and the San Francisco Renaissance." *The Edinburgh Review* (fall).

Reed, Ishmael. 1993. *Airing Dirty Laundry.* Reading, Mass.: Addison-Wesley.

Rexroth, Kenneth. 1975. *Golden Gate: Interviews with Five San Francisco Poets.* Edited by David Meltzer. San Francisco: Wingbow Press.

Rich, Adrienne. 1976. *Of Woman Born: Motherhood as Experience and Institution.* New York: Norton.

Rosetti, Christina. 1979. *The Complete Poems of Christina Rosetti.* Edited by R. W. Crump. Baton Rouge: Louisiana State University Press.

Russo, Linda. 2000. "On Seeing Poetic Production: The Case of Hettie Jones." Paper delivered at *The Opening of the Field: A Conference on North American Poetry in the 1960s.* 28 June-July 2, The University of Maine, Orono.

Savran, David. 1990. *Taking It Like a Man: White Masculinity, Masochism, and Contemporary American Culture.* Princeton, N.J.: Princeton University Press.

Schumacher, Michael. 1992. *Dharma Lion: A Critical Biography of Allen Ginsberg.* New York: St. Martin's Press.

Shulevitz, Judith. 2000. "Schmatte Hari." *The New Yorker* (April 24 & May 1): 206-211.

Shulman, Alix Kates. 1978. *Burning Questions.* New York: Knopf. Reprint 1990. New York: Thunder's Mouth Press.

Shelley, Mary. 1965. *Frankenstein.* New York: Dell.

Skerl, Jennie, ed. 1997. *A Tawdry Place of Salvation: The Art of Jane Bowles.* Carbondale: Southern Illinois Press.

———, ed. 2000. *College Literature* special issue 27, no. 1 (winter). Teaching Beat Literature.

Skir, Leo. 1996. "Elise Cowen: A Brief Memoir of the Fifties." In *Women of the Beat Generation: The Writers, Artists and Muses at the Heart of a Revolution.* Edited by Brenda Knight. Berkeley, Calif.: Conari Press.

Smith, Harry. 1997. *A Booklet of Essays, Appreciations, and Annotations Pertaining to The Anthology of American Folk Music. The Anthology of American Folk Music.* 3 vols. Washington, D.C.: Smithsonian Folkways Recordings.

Smith, Sidonie. 1987. *A Poetics of Women's Autobiography: Marginality and the Fictions of Self-Representation.* Bloomington: Indiana University Press.

Snyder, Gary. 1960. *Myths and Texts.* New York: Totem Press.

———. 1977. "North Beach." In *The Old Ways.* San Francisco: City Lights Books.

Solomon, Barbara Probst. 1960. *The Beat of Life.* New York: Lippencott.

Spicer, Jack. 1975. "After Lorca." In *The Collected Books of Jack Spicer.* Los Angeles: Black Sparrow Press.

———. 1998. *The House that Jack Built: The Collected Lectures of Jack Spicer.* Edited by Peter Gizzi. Hanover, N.H. and London: Wesleyan University Press.

Stewart, Susan. 1991. *Crimes of Writing; Problems in the Containment of Representation.* New York: Oxford University Press.

Stoker, Bram. 1911. *The Lair of the White Worm.* London: W. Foulsham.

Stull, James N. 1993. *Literary Selves: Autobiography and Contemporary American Nonfiction.* Westport, Conn.: Greenwood Press.

Sukenick, Ronald. 1987. *Down and In: Life in the Underground.* New York: Morrow.

Teresa of Avila. 1972. *Interior Castle.* Translated by E. Allison Peers. Garden City, N.Y.: Image Books.

Tytell, John. 1976. *Naked Angels.* New York: Grove Press.

von Hallberg, Robert. 1985. *American Poetry and Culture, 1945-1980.* Cambridge, Mass.: Harvard University Press.

Wakefield, Dan. 1992. *New York in the Fifties.* Boston: Houghton.

Waldman, Anne. 1969. *O My Life!* New York: Angel Hair Books.

———. 1970. *Baby Breakdown.* New York: Bobbs-Merrill.

———. 1975. *Fast Speaking Woman: Chants & Essays.* Rev. ed. 1996. San Francisco: City Lights Books.

———. 1979. "My Life a List." In *Talking Poetics from Naropa Institute.* Edited by Anne Waldman and Marilyn Webb. Vol. 2 of *Annals of the Jack Kerouac School of Disembodied Poetics.* Boulder, Colo.: Shambhala Press.

———. 1984. "An Interview with Diane di Prima." In *The Beat Road.* Edited by Arthur and Kit Knight. California, Pa.: A. Knight.

———. 1989. *Helping the Dreamer: New and Selected Poems, 1966-1988.* Minneapolis, Minn.: Coffee House Press.

———, ed. 1991. *Out of this World: An Anthology of the St. Mark's Poetry Project, 1966-1991.* New York: Crown Books.

———. 1993. *Iovis: All Is Full of Jove.* Vol. 1. Minneapolis, Minn.: Coffee House Press.

———, ed. 1996. *The Beat Book: Poems and Fiction from the Beat Generation.* Boulder, Colo.: Shambhala Press.

———. 1997. *Iovis: All Is Full of Jove.* Vol. 2. Minneapolis, Minn.: Coffee House Press.

Waldman, Anne, and Andrew Schelling, eds. 1994. *Disembodied Poetics: Annals of the Jack Kerouac School.* Albuquerque: University of New Mexico Press.

Watson, Steven. 1995. *The Birth of the Beat Generation: Visionaries, Rebels, and Hipsters, 1944-1960.* New York: Pantheon Books.

Watten, Barrett. 1996. "Being Hailed in and by the 1950s." Paper presented at the conference American Poetry in the 1950s, 21-24 June, University of Maine, Orono.

———. 1997. "The Bride of the Assembly Line: From Material Text to Cultural Poetics." *Impercipient Lecture Series* 1, no. 8 (October): 69-81.

———. Forthcoming. "What Is Literature?" in *Assembling Alternatives.* Edited by Romana Huk. Hanover, N.H. and London: Wesleyan University Press.

Weiners, John. 1996. *707 Scott Street.* Los Angeles: Sun and Moon Press.

Weinreich, Regina. 2000. "The Beat Generation Is Now About Everything." *College Literature* special issue 27, no. 1 (winter): 263-268.

Wilentz, Elias, ed. 1960. *The Beat Scene.* New York: Corinth Books.

Whalen, Philip. 1960. "Further Notice." *Yugen* no. 1.

Woolf, Virginia. 1929. *A Room of One's Own.* New York: Harcourt.

Zizek, Slavoj. 1989. *The Sublime Object of Ideology.* London: Verso.

———. 1996a. "Fantasy as a Political Category: A Lacanian Approach." *Journal for the Psychoanalysis of Culture and Society* 1, no. 2 (fall): 77-85.

———. 1996b. "The Fetish of the Party." In *Lacan, Politics, Aesthetics.* Edited by Willy Apollon and Richard Feldstein. Albany: State University of New York Press.

FURTHER READING

Criticism

Atlas, James. "Marginal Memoirs." *Atlantic* 251, no. 2 (February 1983): 100-01.

Views Minor Characters *as a dispassionate portrait of Beat life.*

Chasin Helen. "The Girl in the Boy Gang." *New York Times Book Review* (16 January 1983): 9, 30.

Finds Minor Characters *to be compelling reading.*

Coles, Robert. "Death of a Child." *New York Times Book Review* (8 April 1990): 1, 30-1.

Praises Johnson's novelistic eye for detail in What Lisa Knew.

Conant, Oliver. "Love and Destruction." *New Leader* (30 October 1989): 20-1.

Positive review of In the Night Café *that praises Johnson's writing but finds it occasionally obtrusively lyrical.*

Diski, Jenny. "Not Guilty?" *New Statesman Society* (29 March 1991): 34.

Generally favorable review of What Lisa Knew *that appreciates Johnson's outrage regarding the outcome of the case.*

Friedman, Amy L. "'I say my new name': Women Writers of the Beat Generation." In *The Beat Generation Writers,* edited by Robert A. Lee, pp. 200-16. East Haven, Conn.: Pluto Press, 1996.

Discussion of women in the Beat movement that mentions Johnson's assertion of the ignored presence of women among Beat writers

Gitlin, Todd. "Where the Boys Aren't." *Nation* (28 May 1983): 663-5.

Praises the poignancy of Minor Characters.

Kantrowitz, Barbara. "A Sick Woman's Poisoned Love." *Newsweek* (23 April 1990): 72.

Views What Lisa Knew *as an eloquent recreation of the emotional and psychological history behind the murder of Lisa Steinberg.*

Johnson, Joyce, and Nancy Grace. "A Conversation with Joyce Johnson." *Artful Dodge* 37-38 (2000): 108-19.

Johnson discusses the Beat Generation, her work as an editor, and her own creative work.

Lopate, Phillip. "Bohemia Died, but Life Went On." *New York Times Book Review* (30 April 1989): 11.

Review of In the Night Café *that finds the final thirty pages to be some of the most powerful in recent American fiction.*

O'Roarke, William. "*Difficult Women* and *Minor Characters.*" In *Signs of the Literary Times: Essays, Reviews, Profiles 1970-1992,* pp. 54-7. Albany, New York: SUNY Press, 1993.

Asserts that Johnson captures the evanescence of the 1960s in Minor Characters.

Passaro, Vince. "Kerouac Wore Khakis." *New York Times* (23 July 2000): 10.

Praises Johnson's language and intelligence in Door Wide Open.

Schiff, Robbin. Review of *Minor Characters.* *Ms.* (March 1983): 36.

Appreciates Johnson's clarification of the role women played in the Beat movement in Minor Characters.

Sheldon, Michael. "'I Couldn't Handle Kerouac.'" *The Daily Telegraph* (15 September 2000): 19.

Discusses the publication of Door Wide Open, *and presents excerpts from his conversation with Johnson about her stormy relationship with Jack Kerouac.*

Shulman, Alix Kates. "The Beat Queens: Boho Chicks Stand By Their Men." *Voice Literary Supplement* no. 75 (June 1989): 18-23.

Views Johnson as a detached observer in Minor Characters.

Steinberg, Sybil. "Joyce Johnson." *Publishers Weekly* (14 January 1983): 12-13.

Interview in which Johnson discusses her involvement with the Beats and the letters in Door Wide Open.

Willis, Ellen. "The Trouble is Not Just with Molly's Men." *Village Voice* 23, no. 27 (3 July 1978): 66.

Review of Bad Connections, *which Willis views as a resigned book in its depiction of feminism.*

Yardley, Johnson. "Beyond Kerouac." *Washington Post* (6 July 2000): C2.

Review of Door Wide Open *that views Johnson's work as more accomplished than that of Jack Kerouac.*

Yglesias, Helen. "News from the Sisterhood." *Harper's* (August 1978): 86-8.

Praises the writing style in Bad Connections *but sees the work as too sad and dreary.*

OTHER SOURCES FROM GALE:

Additional coverage of Johnson's life and career is contained in the following sources published by the Gale Group: *Contemporary Authors*, Vols. 125, 129; *Contemporary Authors New Revision Series*, Vol. 102; *Contemporary Literary Criticism*, Vol. 58; and *Literature Resource Center.*

BOB KAUFMAN

(1925 - 1986)

Bob Kaufman. Copyright © by Fred W. McDarrah.

(Full name Bob Garnell Kaufman) American poet.

Known in Europe as "The Black American Rim-baud" and in the United States as "The Original Be-Bop Man," Kaufman was an influential poet who wrote and recited poetry along with Beat writers of the 1950s and 1960s, including Jack Kerouac, William S. Burroughs, and Allen Ginsberg. Kaufman's poetry relies heavily on be-bop jazz influences, incorporating spontaneity, unconventional verses, surrealism, and symbolism. Many of his poems are about jazz performers, jazz music, and the poets that influenced him—notably Hart Crane, Federico García Lorca, Arthur Rimbaud, and Walt Whitman. Because Kaufman rarely wrote down his poems, preferring instead to deliver his oral compositions spontaneously, his work has not received much critical attention and remains relatively obscure.

BIOGRAPHICAL INFORMATION

Although there are conflicting accounts of Kaufman's early life, most agree that he was born in New Orleans on April 18, 1925, to a Jewish German father and an African-American Catholic mother. The eleventh of thirteen brothers and sisters, Kaufman had a varied religious background; he was exposed to both the Jewish and

Catholic religions as well as his grandmother's belief in voodoo. Kaufman reportedly ran away from home when he was thirteen and joined the Merchant Marine. During his years on the sea, when he purportedly traveled around the world nine times and survived four shipwrecks, Kaufman developed an interest in literature. Kaufman left the Merchant Marine in the early 1940s or 1950s and went to study literature at New York City's New School for Social Research. While in New York City he met Ginsberg and Burroughs, and eventually traveled with them to San Francisco where he met Kerouac and Neal Cassady. Kaufman became involved in San Francisco's North Beach literary scene, along with many other Beat poets. He was married in 1958; his wife, Eileen, acted as his literary agent and encouraged him to collect and publish his poetry. In 1959 he published three broadsides: *Does the Secret Mind Whisper, Second April,* and *Abomunist Manifesto.* That same year he cofounded, with Allen Ginsberg, John Kelly, and William Margolis, the magazine *Beatitude,* which was dedicated to publishing the works of talented unpublished poets. In 1961 Kaufman was nominated for the Guinness Poetry Award, which was won by T. S. Eliot that year. Despite Kaufman's career success, over the next few years he suffered financial hardship, drug addiction, and imprisonment. Kaufman ultimately embraced the philosophy of Buddhism, and in the years between 1963 and 1975 Kaufman took a

Buddhist vow of silence; he stopped speaking after John F. Kennedy was assassinated and did not speak again for twelve years, on the day the Vietnam War ended. During those years he continued to write, and his poems were collected in *Golden Sardine* (1967). Over the next three years he wrote feverishly, composing the poems that were collected in *The Ancient Rain: Poems, 1956-1978* (1981). In 1978 Kaufman again withdrew from society. He received a National Endowment for the Arts creative writing grant in 1981, but wrote little and rarely appeared in public until his death from emphysema on January 12, 1986.

MAJOR WORKS

Kaufman's first full-length book, *Solitudes Crowded with Loneliness*, was published in 1965. Although the book—a collection of his previously published works *Does the Secret Mind Whisper, Second April,* and *Abomunist Manifesto*—was highly regarded by other Beat poets, it was largely ignored by critics in the United States. Nevertheless, the book was a success in Europe, particularly in France. Its translation into several languages, including German, Italian, Polish, Russian, Spanish, Arabic, Danish, and French, also helped to spread Beat philosophies throughout Europe. The works collected in *Solitudes Crowded with Loneliness* evidence Kaufman's strong ties to jazz, symbolist and surrealist poetry, and anarchism, and reveal the influences of García Lorca, Whitman, and Crane, as well as musicians Charlie Parker, Miles Davis, and Dizzy Gillespie. The *Abomunist Manifesto* has been deemed by some critics as the Beat manifesto—a document that contains the major tenets of the Beat movement. The work, which consists of imaginary documents from a supposed recently discovered religious movement, criticizes modern society, American foreign policy in the atomic age, and issues of conformity to American culture. One of the poems in the collection, "Bagel Shop Jazz," a realistic description of the San Francisco Beat scene, won Kaufman a nomination for the Guinness Poetry Award. *Golden Sardine*, published in 1967 during Kaufman's twelve-year silence, is a collection of poems that were found scattered around Kaufman's apartment, written on napkins and paper bags. This collection gained some popularity for Kaufman in the United States, and strengthened his reputation in England and France. The poems collected in Kaufman's last collection, *The Ancient Rain: Poems, 1956-1978*, contain less irony and verbal play than his other works, and are more concerned with religious mysticism and literary themes.

CRITICAL RECEPTION

Although he was well known to the Beat scene and in Europe, Kaufman received little critical attention in the United States; few American critics reviewed or analyzed his work until the end of his writing career in the early 1980s. Many scholars now consider Kaufman to be one of the most underrepresented Beat writers, and maintain that he deserves recognition for his literary achievements. Commentators praise the symbolism and surrealism of Kaufman's work, viewing it as anti-establishment and reminiscent of the underground world of be-bop jazz and political movements such as communism and anarchism. In a 1981 essay, Barbara Christian pays tribute to Kaufman, contending that his poetry creates "a new language, a new mode of perceiving." Critics such as Kathryne Lindberg describe his work as defying self-representation through surrealist techniques, and Maria Damon has strongly advocated the study of Kaufman's poetry in the college classroom, contending that "he fully deserves to be restored to Beat historiography as well as to American and African-diasporic literary historiography." Much of the scant criticism on Kaufman comes from other poets, often in the form of elegies or tributes. Neeli Cherkovski praises Kaufman as a poet who "strived toward an understanding of the universality necessary for great poetry." The publication in 1996 of *Cranial Guitar: Selected Poems*, a collection of much of his published poetry as well as some previously unpublished works, has brought more critical attention to Kaufman. The introduction to *Cranial Guitar* is a testament to Kaufman's popularity among other poets, as it consists in large part of quotes in praise of Kaufman from well known figures from the Beat era, as well as others who knew Kaufman's life and work. Although critical attention came late to Kaufman, his work continues to interest scholars, who now consider him to be one of the most influential poets of his generation.

PRINCIPAL WORKS

Abomunist Manifesto (poetry) 1959

Does the Secret Mind Whisper (poetry) 1959

Second April (poetry) 1959

Solitudes Crowded with Loneliness (poetry) 1965

Golden Sardine (poetry) 1967

Watch My Tracks (poetry) 1971

The Ancient Rain: Poems, 1956-1978 (poetry) 1981

Cranial Guitar: Selected Poems (poetry) 1996

*   Includes *Abomunist Manifesto, Does the Secret Mind Whisper,* and *Second April.*

PRIMARY SOURCES

BOB KAUFMAN (POETRY DATE 1967)

SOURCE: Kaufman, Bob. "'Round About Midnight"; "Jazz Chick"; "On"; and "O-Jazz-O." In *Golden Sardine,* pp. 38-9, 76-7. San Francisco, Calif.: City Lights Books, 1967.

Kaufman was noted for his use of the jazz idiom in his poetry. Following are four poems from his 1967 collection Golden Sardine.

"'ROUND ABOUT MIDNIGHT"

Jazz radio on a midnight kick,
Round about Midnight,

Sitting on the bed,
With a jazz type chick
Round about Midnight,

Piano laughter, in my ears,
Round about Midnight.

Stirring up laughter, dying tears,
Round about Midnight.

Soft blue voices, muted grins,
Excited voices, Father's sins,
Round about Midnight.

Come on baby, take off your clothes,
Round about Midnight.

* * *

"JAZZ CHICK"

Music from her breast, vibrating
Soundseared into burnished velvet.
Silent hips deceiving fools.
Rivulets of trickling ecstasy
From the alabaster pools of Jazz
Where music cools hot souls.
Eyes more articulately silent
Than Medusa's thousand tongues.
A bridge of eyes, consenting smiles
reveal her presence singing
Of cool remembrance, happy balls
Wrapped in swinging
Jazz
Her music . . .
Jazz.

"ON"

On yardbird corners of embryonic hopes,
    drowned in a heroin tear.
On yardbird corners of parkerflights to sound
    filled pockets in space.
On neuro-corners of striped brains & desperate
    electro-surgeons.
On alcohol corners of pointless discussion &
    historical hangovers.
On television corners of cornflakes & rockwells
    impotent America.
On university corners of tailored intellect &
    greek letter openers.
On military corners of megathon deaths &
    universal anesthesia.
On religious corners of theological limericks and
On radio corners of century-long records & static
    events.
On advertising corners of filter-tipped ice-cream
    & instant instants
On teen-age corners of comic book seduction
    and corrupted guitars,
On political corners of wanted candidates &
    ritual lies.
On motion picture corners of lassie & other
    symbols.
On intellectual corners of conversational therapy
    & analyzed fear.
On newspaper corners of sexy headlines &
    scholarly comics.
On love divided corners of die now pay later
    mortuaries.
On philosophical corners of semantic
    desperadoes & idea-mongers.
On middle class corners of private school
    puberty & anatomical revolts
On ultra-real corners of love on abandoned
    roller-coasters
On lonely poet corners of low lying leaves &
    moist prophet eyes.

* * *

"O-JAZZ-O"

Where the string
At
some point,
Was umbilical jazz,
Or perhaps,
In memory,
A long lost bloody cross,
Buried in some steel cavalry.
In what time
For whom do we bleed,
Lost notes, from some jazzman's
Broken needle.
Musical tears from lost
Eyes,
Broken drumsticks, why?
Pitter patter, boom dropping
Bombs in the middle
Of my emotions
My father's sound
My mother's sound,
Is love,
Is life.

GENERAL COMMENTARY

BARBARA CHRISTIAN (ESSAY DATE 1981)

SOURCE: Christian, Barbara. "Whatever Happened to Bob Kaufman." In *The Beats: Essays in Criticism*, edited by Lee Bartlett, pp. 107-14. Jefferson, N.C.: McFarland, 1981.

In the following essay, Christian attempts to revive critical attention to Kaufman, contending that "he fully deserves to be restored to Beat historiography."

My students respond to the name of Allen Ginsberg, howling Jewish-incantation style, to the name of Ted Joans, bopping in Black rhythms, to the name of Jack Kerouac, forever on the road. But Bob Kaufman—who is he? A hurt mutter rushes to my brain—the same damn thing again. Movements that change literature and language, and hence the world they're a part of, but some of the real movers are forgotten, their sacrifices, work erased. But not forever. "Bob Kaufman," I begin, "is one of the poets who helped shape the Beat movement in American poetry, and, as usual when somebody Black makes something new in America, he's the one who's apt to be forgotten."

The situation just described constantly occurs, even as we rediscover our Black creators. It is with the somber awareness that our knowledge of our wise men is always in danger that I write this tribute to Bob Kaufman, a Black poet who is still alive and who need not be praised after his body is gone and only his poetry remains.

Little has been written about Kaufman's life; I know little of the facts that are invariably used to describe a life. What I know I have found in his two published volumes of poetry: *Solitudes Crowded with Loneliness* (1959) and *The Golden Sardine* (1960). These two books project the philosophy of the Beat poet, of the man who challenged middle-class American values in the fifties, when many Black and white intellectuals were yet to see the connection between the incredible blandness of American life and the destruction America as a government and as a propagandist idea symbolized.

Like Ginsberg, Joans and Kerouac, Kaufman's poetry began to take hold on the Lower East Side—the fringe of New York City, of America—where artists, poor people and exiles from the mainstream gathered. Along with these and other poets, Kaufman was a part of that outlandish, rebellious element of American life which emerged in the midst of Eisenhowerian conformity and mediocrity. The potpourri of people on the Lower East Side, who had nothing to lose but a hard life, created a life-style different from that of the mainstream, a life-style which became the basis for the Beat Movement. The lie that was America stuck out there, could not be successfully disguised by slick TV commercials or glamorous billboards. At home and abroad, America was racist, money-crazy and destructive. The Lower East Side with its newly-arrived exiles, Bowery drunks, disenfranchized citizens, crazy niggers, bore witness to the lie of America. The Lower East Side exploded with color; life refused neat categorization into linear pigeon holes[1]:

> Angry, fire-eyed children clutch transient winds
> Singing Gypsy songs, love me now, love me now.
>
> The echoes return, riding the voice of the river,
> As time cries out, on the skin of an African
>   drum.
>   "East Fifth St. (N.Y.)" [p. 18]

The Lower East Side is a haven for the dreamer, who cannot, even if he tries, conform to already prescribed models and images, for he must create his own:

> Remember, poet, while gallavanting across the
>   sky
> Skylarking, shouting, calling names . . . walk
>   softly.
>
> Your footprints in rain clouds are visible to
>   naked eyes.
> Lamps barnacled to your feet refract the mirrored
>   air.
>
> Exotic scents of your hidden vision fly in the
>   face of time.
>   "Forget To Not" [p. 55]

The Lower East Side is the no-man's land from which the mainland can be cursed and criticized:

> The cold land breathes death rattles, trembling
> The dark sky casts shadows across the wounds
> Beneath the bright clothing of well-fed machines
> The hungry heart inside the hungry hearts
> Beats silently, beats softly, beats, beats.
>   "TeeVee People" [p. 50]

Much of Kaufman's poetry is inherently critical of America, protesting its scurrilous ways, calling attention to its blood-thirsty appetite. Passionately, Kaufman reviews its past, illuminates its present, projects its future while he measures the reality of America against the myth it broadcasts. "Benediction," a poem which was performed by Vinie Burrows at the 1969 Algerian Festival, is one of the most damning poems written about America, damning not because it uses invective, but because it uses well-placed irony so effectively:

Your ancestor had beautiful thoughts in his
    brain.
His descendants are experts in real estate.
Your generals have mushrooming visions.
Everyday your people get more and more
Cars, television, sickness death dreams.
You must have been great
Alive.

                  "Benediction" [p. 9]

The poem concentrates on both racism and imperialism, on America not only as a threat to the American Black and the American poor, but to the entire world as well. Written in the early fifties, Kaufman's poem could be read at the Festival in 1969. More than 10 years after Kaufman wrote it, Blacks had just begun to appreciate how far-reaching was America's oppressiveness. In fact, Kaufman's poems seldom allude exclusively to the plight of the Afro-American. His poems always couple domestic racism with American criminal behavior abroad. He attacks the basic values of America, seeing the race problem in its midst and its behavior toward the rest of the world as reflections of the country's internal corrosion.

America's tentacles, which tamper with the world's psyche, are the various forms of its media—the means through which meta-messages are subtly imprinted on the mind. Like LeRoi Jones in the fifties, Kaufman takes great pains to warn us of the termite eating at our spirit. His media poems are set against the background of the West, Los Angeles and San Francisco, for in this wild rootless land, recently taken from the Indians and Mexicans, medialand constructs its images. The lie of the media is tucked away in the West, heavily camouflaged by the glitter of the sweet life. Remember, Kaufman cries, that Hollywood actually represents:

Five square miles of ulta-contemporary
    nymphomania
Two dozen homos, to every sapiens, at last
    countdown
Ugly Plymouths swapping exhaust with red
    convertible Buicks.
Twelve year old mothers suing for child
    support,
Secondhand radios making it with wide-screen
    TV sets,
Unhustling junkies shooting mothball fixes,
    insect junk,
Unemployed pimps living on neon backs of
Unemployed whores.

                  "Hollywood" [p. 24]

In this Babylon of the modern world, language becomes lies; grotesque nightmares are transformed into soft dreams, dreams sent out as

ambassadors to whet the peasant's desire and compel his respect for an illusionary America. No wonder Charlton Heston, as head of the Movie Actors Association, reminded (President) Nixon that movies are America's greatest and most effective export. Ironically, Hollywood makes its bait under the name of Art, and in so doing insults the craft of Bob Kaufman. Kaufman retaliates. In ending his poem to Hollywood, he salutes it as "the artistic cancer of the universe": "I want to prove that L.A. is a practical joke played on us by superior beings on a humorous planet."

Kaufman not only attacks Hollywood, he senses that the ambitious movers of medialand are efficient, having capsulized their product into a portable machine. TeeVee, the machine par-excellence of hypnosis, has created a land of drugged people:

The younger machines occupy miles of dark
    benches,
Enjoying self-induced vacations of the mind,
Eating textbook rinds, spitting culture seeds,
Dreaming an exotic name to give their defeat,
Computing the hours on computer minds.

So Hollywood, in essence, is plugged into the homes of America, and is yearned for by the hungry people of the planet as a drug to ease their pain. For Kaufman, Hollywood and TeeVee are manifestations of America's emptiness and decay, just as the Bowery drunks are evidence of her falseness.

As one reads more and more of Kaufman's poetry, this attitude toward America prevails. Her only saving grace comes from those she casts off: for example, from the Black whose music, grace and mores keep her going. **"War Memoir"** ironically plays on this theme, for in its imagery, the poem juxtaposes the technical stuff America creates for destruction alongside jazz, a music which absorbs everything, even technology, making it into a thing of beauty:

What one-hundred percent redblooded savage
Wastes precious time listening to jazz
With so much important killing to do?

Silence the drums that we may hear the
    burning
Of Japanese in atomic colorcinemascope
And remember the stereophonic screaming.

              "War Memoir" [p. 52]

Jazz as a protest music permeates Kaufman's being—its modal variety and flexibility adapts itself to every situation. And in the late forties and early fifties, Jazz as taken higher by Charlie Parker expressed the alternate route that America's outcasts could take. Kaufman soaks himself in Parker's music, in bop strains of electricity and blood-rhythms. One of his poems, **"Walking Parker Home,"** is studded with those intricately carved word jewels of a genuine poet in communion with a master musician:

> In that Jazz corner of life
> Wrapped in a midst of sound
> His legacy, our Jazz-tinted dawn
> Wailing his triumphs of oddly begotten dreams
> Inviting the nerveless to feel once more
> That fierce dying of humans consumed
> In raging fires of Love.

Jazz is the subterranean music, existing as it protests, developing as it rejects, becoming fuller as it strips away the debris of rot.

To continue to maintain an authentic existence in the face of so much falsehood and decay is a long, hard fight. Charlie Parker heroically conquers American decay with his music. Kaufman expresses the psychic loneliness of a man who is plagued by his environment and turns in on himself. His psyche cannot always stand the loneliness imposed upon him:

> The whole of me
> Is an unfurnished room
> Filled with dank breath
> Escaping in gasps to nowhere.
> Before completely objective mirrors
> I have shot myself with my eyes
> But death refused my advances.
>   **"Would You Wear My Eyes?"** [p. 40]

There is loneliness throughout many of his poems, not just the loneliness that might come from solitude, but an even more devastating psychic loneliness that can come only from knowing so few people who share his perceptions. Such loneliness haunts a man who sees more than the people of his time. Images of dissolution, of being unable to come up from under, burst from these poems as if they, the poems, are the writer's only companion. The absence of any widespread awareness about the visions Kaufman breathed, and the lack of any expansive Black cultural context certainly contributed to Bob Kaufman's loneliness. He was a decade too early—or rather he had to suffer alone so that others in later years could create together.

The extreme objective correlative of this loneliness in our society is the prison. Kaufman's **"Jail Poems"** protest both America's injustice and succinctly, painfully reveal his own psychic prison—the real prison from which he cannot escape. Surrealist images, dada symbols jet-stream through these poems. And Kaufman is magnificently graphic in rendering this loneliness, for he knows the mind often perceives what it cannot logically express. Certain states are irretrievably beyond logic:

> I am sitting in a cell with a view of evil
>   parallels,
> Waiting thunder to splinter me into a thousand
>   me's.
> It is not enough to be in one cage with one self;
> I want to sit opposite every prisoner in every
>   hole.
> Doors roll and bang, every slam a finality bang!

As we discuss the plight of political prisoners today, our minds are now ready for the **"Jail Poems"** of Kaufman. The prison cell is an appropriate symbol for America's way of life and can trap the man who opposes America more through his life-style, than because of any specific act.

Living with the present, living existentially, lies at the core of the Beat philosophy, and necessarily befuddles, thwarts a life-style based on systemization. Kaufman was well-acquainted with the formal outlines of existentialism, as his **"Poem to Camus"** indicates, but he felt that existentialism itself had become too codified.

The *Abomunist Manifesto* picks up where existentialism left off. Like (Richard) Wright in *The Outsider*, Kaufman realizes the limits of all *isms*, the eventual decay of all systems. Kaufman's anti-philosophy, Abomunism, is finally as much a put-down of itself as it is of anything else. The very name makes serious fun of *isms*, manifestos and the like, transforming sense into nonsense, turning reality upside down. Signed "Bomkauf," the manifesto was duly written in legal, political structure. There are **"Notes"** and **"Further Notes,"** **"Craxions,"** a glossary, an anthem, founding documents, and even a newscast. The Abomunist world frinks, digs its own music, even has its own brand of children. A sample of the Abomnewscast . . . on the hour . . . illuminates the method behind Kaufman's "madness:"

> Cubans seize Cuba, outraged U.S. acts quickly,
> cuts off tourist quota, administration intro-
> duces measure to confine all rhumba bands to
> detention camps during emergency . . . Both
> sides in Cold War stockpiling atomic missiles
> to preserve peace, end of mankind seen if
> peace is declared. UN sees encouraging sign
> in small war policy, works quietly for wider
> participation among backward nations. . . .

Defined as "a rejectionary philosophy founded by Barabbas and dedicated to the proposition that the essence of existence is reality essential and neither four-sided nor frinky, but not non-frinky," Abomunism derides logic, philosophy, academic and political jargon, and whatever manifestations exist in response to the need to systematize the world. Commercialized religion, as a major form of systemization, is singled out for commentary by the Abomunists. **"Further Notes (taken from Abomunism and Religion by Tom Man)"** discusses religious props:

> Krishnamurti can relax the muscles of your soul,
> Free your aching jawbone from the chewinggum habit.
> Oupensky can churn your illusions into butter and
> Give you circles to carry them in, around your head.
> Sabud can lock you in strange rooms with vocal balms
> And make your ignorant clothing understand you.
> Zen can cause changes in the texture of your hair,
> Removing you from the clutches of sexy barbers.
> Edgar Cayce can locate your gallstones, other organs,
> On the anarchistic rockpiles of Sacramento.
> Voodoo Marie can give you Loas, abstract horses.
> Snorting guides to tar-baby black masses.
> Billy can plug you into the Christ machine. Mail in your
> Mind today. Hurry, bargain God Week, lasts one week only.
>
> [p. 79]

The *Abomunist Manifesto* creates a world counter to mainstream American life; in effect, it is a blueprint for a revolutionary way of life. It does not purport to know the right way to live; rather, it gives the Abomunist guidelines for avoiding the snares of systematic living, while thwarting the system itself. In some ways, it is the precursor of the hippie and professional revolutionary life-styles. Kaufman saw that in order to live with any kind of freedom, and to be able to fight American mediocrity and destructiveness, a life-style rooted in protest must be invented. In effect, this manifesto is the creation of an alternate community, one in which Kaufman might have been able to function.

Kaufman's poetry, his *Abomunist Manifesto*, are all the result of a new language, a new mode of perceiving. In striking at the lifeless English language, Kaufman creates a new language, linked to Jazz. His poems, along with those of Ted Joans, use Jazz's concept of improvisation as their stylistic core. Casting aside traditional and even more

avant-garde forms and images such as the recent breathline, Kaufman plays with word rhythms and dada images:

> Smothered rage covering pyramids of notes spontaneously exploding
> Cool revelations / shrill hopes / beauty speared into greedy ears
> Birdland nights on bop mountains, windy saxophone revolutions
> **"Walking Parker Home"** [p. 5]

He uses the same words with different emphases, sticking close to the oral tradition of poetry—sometimes moving to the pitch of a chant, sometimes speaking at a conversational level:

> They fear you, Crane . . . you whispered aloft, pains they buried forever . . .
> They hate you, Crane . . . your sur-real eclipses bloat out their muted sun . . .
> They miss you, Crane . . . your footprints are on their rotting teeth . . .

But where is Bob Kaufman?—the Black poet who challenged the American life-style with his own, who fought with the pen as passionately as many do with weapons or rhetoric, who pointed the way to the painful visions Blacks lived through in the Sixties: political prisons, the need for an alternate life-style, America's rottenness, the sacredness of jazz. He wanders the streets of San Francisco, mostly unknown and forgotten, considered mad by many, cared for by few. As his books circulate, the question of responsibility, the responsibility that Black cultural organizations have to protect such a man, screams to be heard. If we do not care to sustain our own wise men who suffered, sacrificed, were attacked and assaulted, then can we really speak of "nation-building"? Who will look to Bob Kaufman—if we don't?

Note

1. Page numbers from *Solitudes* [*Crowed with Loneliness*. New York: New Directions, 1965].

KUSH (ESSAY DATE 1987)

SOURCE: Kush. "The Duende of Bob Kaufman." *Third Rail* 8, no. 1 (1987): 67-8.

In the following essay, Kush provides a tribute to Bob Kaufman and recounts his personal encounters with the poet.

Bob Kaufman, the "black Rimbaud" of Beat San Francisco, passed in his sleep Sunday morn January 12, 1986, passed on in a dream with Halley's Comet leaving our visibility. In the mosaic of the micro-environments of this peninsular city, his very presence would percolate events and cluster conversation. Bolts of insight and humor charging his public atmosphere, electric beat and dancer of his word that went out to the everyday lives, to stir us all. North Beach was his book, its streets his paper, to do his poems in person. For thirty years Bob was the beat Ulysses of North Beach in his dynamic trails and stops, those ports of call, portals of horn, that generated a poetic geography. The neighborhood bars and cafes, Gino's & Carlo's, were his islands and each has their tales as he landed, lived, and disembarked. The illuminated boat of upper Grant Ave., sailing with his wealth of eternal poetry, richly dressed, scarf tied to his hand to represent this gift of being alive. The real movie of his person in the early 70's has him near the old western swinging doors and sun drenched floor of the 1232 Saloon, off his bar seat, calling down pyramids from the sky, snapping his fingers to the breakthru insight that everything happens in less than a second. Remarkably, in 79, for a stretch of weeks, deep within the Savoy Tivoli, near midnite, he projected thru rotten teeth his masterwork *Second April,* this following an actor's rendition of Rimbaud's *Season in Hell.* Let that burn in, Bob whose mental horn punctuated the black comedy of the 20th century, lived the real divine comedy of the poet in the hotel Dante, off Columbus Ave., atop a wing of the Condor Club. *Second April,* a verbal jazz, snapping scenes recounting the witnessing of a death in the holding tank in riffs and extended phrases of the Heart's Voice beating thru.

Lorca put to jazz. In the weave of his being anywhere, Bob manifested, recited Lorca, Apollinaire, Hart Crane, danced their word, the lives of the poets he brought alive by the gift of his own life. Brought alive the crux and pivot and spring and pool and fall of their lives to make us aware of what is really here. Bob's soprano voice inviting us in his vision, his being, his eyes to wear and be liberated, seeing what stands for reality as absurd and humor rejoining ourselves to our root humanity.

Bob Kaufman, 5' 7", wiry compact grace on the go that set in motion waves of poets and scenes from the breakthru 50's-60's-70's into the punked out 80's that went way beyond literary retreats and enlivened neighborhoods.

Tune in that time, 1959 Mimeo humming Beatitudes, Co-Existence Bagel Shop at Grant & Green, with Crazy Alex at the front window running commentary, whirring his lines of broken brain tragedy, Taylor Mead sitting on the piano, elfin, reading his gay lines. Enter officer Bigarani and clubmate, looking for trouble, looking for Bob. Taylor go on with your falsetto delictados. Bigarani frowns. He makes his way around looking for Bob and leaves. Bill Margolis shows up with fresh copies of Beatitudes. Outside the Co-Existence Bagel Shop is a police call box with a swastika painted on its side. Bob confronted and battled the authorities, battled Bigarani on behalf of embodied poetry. Kaufman was a beat soldier, the poet liberator armed with poems, daytime defender of what is real. 1959 Co-Existence Bagel Shop, officer Bigarani close in on Bob. Bob holds his ground, does not cower to brute authority, talks up & up & up. They shove him, he explodes. When the debris settles, they drag him out. This scene was repeated again & again in what was the mean theater done to Bob in the late 50's/early 60's, the mean theater of authoritarian Frisco (conservative-provincial) that preyed on Bob and Lenny Bruce. Ilene Kaufman related that during the first year of their twenty-five year union, in 1957, Bob was arrested nineteen times, 1958 seventeen times. Police dragging him off, his poetry bouncing off walls, to the jail in the old Hall of Justice on Kearny St., beating him up in the elevators between the third and fourth floors: 1956-57-58-59-60. Ilene, his wife, working the friendly storefronts and businesses to raise bail for Bob. Think of doing that time and time and time again.

Warrior Bob went into his word, living poetry down these mean streets the renewed Barbary Coast of Frisco in the 50's, Broadway turned hooker-barker Honky Tonk, come-on to the tourist dollar that hardened and cut and bled the international folk dimension of North Beach. Cars lining up slowly to see the beatnik life along upper Grant Ave. Bob stopping cars to tell them his latest insight. Stop that car and do your poem, open what goes for reality. Bob K a real bird of consciousness, blowing minds, blowing thru Carl Chessman to dig our subconscious ruins.

Black Rimbaud/Black Jew, his living poetry, in the tightening knots of highrise Frisco, dehumanizing space, that obscured origins (Montgomery devouring the first beach of Yerba Buena) that did grow to do in the working class. His person was projective verse, a helix of physical and spiritual energies rippling thru his form, 50's Bob took North Beach back into being a beach in his sandal-clad simplicity and beatific beauty and sympathy for the living.

Spring of 1960, darkness flower, a black hole, black sounds of the blood of the poet. Digest this, Harvard University sending Abomunist Bob a round trip ticket to Boston via NYC to read in honor of his nomination for "The Prestigious Guinness Poetry Award." With police shadowing him, pressures detonate. Bob kicks in all the windows of the Co-Existence Bagel Shop and flies off to New York two weeks before the Boston event. Trying to get off the juice he gets into speed and speeds into Gaslight, Figaro, Rienzi—the West Village scene. Bob dancing under the stage lights, blowing his poems, swinging them, singing his lines:

> Green, Green Rocky Road
> Promenade in Green
> Tell me who do you love

Lines picked up by the Christy Minstrels and sent into public consciousness. Imagine in youthful prime, Bob Kaufman and Bob Dylan sharing the same stage as they did the Gaslight in 1961. Bob blow Bob Dylan's metro mind.

Spring of 1963, lower Manhattan, Kaufman to return to San Francisco with Ilene and baby boy Parker. Bob walking on the grass before the Arch of Washington Square Park. Ilene with Parker and the ride waiting. Bob never comes. They leave. Bob walking on the grass in Washington Square is arrested. He resists. They take him to the Tombs. He resists. They take him to Riker's Island. Doctors tag him a "Behavior Problem" to be corrected by "Behavior Modification." Visions called out. Forced shock treatments through the Summer and Fall. Released in October, he returns to SF. His personal music reads **"Solitudes Crowded With Loneliness."** November 63, the news of Kennedy assassinated breaks Bob's heart. As he leaves for the street, he kneels every two to three steps to pray, two to three steps pray, two to three steps pray, as he goes home and takes his family to Peter & Paul's Church. The week follows; TV watch the Funeral, TV watch Dallas, TV watch Oswald being moved freeze into the shot by Ruby. Bob in the TV glow, commentators ajar with the televized murder, takes his legendary vow of silence.

Ten years he held to that vow against the cancer of violence that multiplied into burning cities and killing Vietnam. Not until the Vietnam War ended did he speak. Those wandering years on the Beach, where he literally entered the *Toa* of North Beach to heal his battered form and chemically modified body. Silent, beatific Bob, while his books 1965 *Solitudes Crowded with Loneliness* and 1967 *Golden Sardine* spoke for him and traveled with a generation of poets that did bring him back to speak.

In December 1974 at Malvina's Coffee House, upstairs into the expanse of the second floor, Bob danced out his Solitudes into a vocal renaissance, poems coming alive, coming alive with his ecstatic voice. Bob birded his poems, Charlie Parkered them into his DNA of humor as his lines twist-twist-twist meanings confounding institutional reality. The French admirers see in Bob's music a humor as dark and penetrant as in Alfred Jarry's "merdre!" and Jaques Vache's emptying theaters with his real movie of returning from the Front. Bob's light of mind breaking thru our hard edges, releasing us in the sweep of his primal humor. He broke the darkness in us.

NEELI CHERKOVSKI (ESSAY DATE 1988)

SOURCE: Cherkovski, Neeli. "Bob Kaufman." In *Whitman's Wild Children*, pp. 105-21. Venice, Calif.: The Lapis Press, 1988.

In the following essay, Cherkovski recounts his experiences with Kaufman during a poetry reading, and examines his life and poetry.

In September 1979 Raymond Foye and I planned a benefit poetry reading for *Beatitude*, the poetry magazine founded by Bob Kaufman and William J. Margolis. For months we edited a selection of poems from various poets, together with a selection of Kaufman poems never before published and an essay on his work by Foye. When we finished editing, we put the work into photo-ready condition and were told we needed $2,400 for a printing of 1,000 copies. Allen Ginsberg agreed to participate in the reading, along with Lawrence Ferlinghetti, Joanne Kyger, Harold Norse, Peter Orlovsky—and Bob Kaufman. It was Kaufman's first major reading in over fifteen years. Foye designed a poster using a photograph of Kaufman in a striped jacket and a straw hat, standing in front of the old City Lights publishing offices. The event was not only a means of raising money but a long overdue tribute to Kaufman as well.

When I told Kaufman that Ginsberg would read, he said, "Allen Ginsberg is the President of Poetry. He's our Pope. We're going to install him in Rome. First, we'll have to buy him a cappuccino at the Trieste and then fly to Rome on a chartered biplane. In Rome, we will all learn Sanskrit and write a new version of the Mass."

Foye and I were surprised to find a front-page headline in the *San Francisco Chronicle* on the morning of the reading: "Beat Reunion In North Beach . . . see page two." Turning the page we found a story on our reading and background information on the starring poets. "This will help bring a crowd," I said, as we were worried about meeting expenses.

I'd run into Kaufman earlier in the day and he took me by the collar. "You'll have to run things when I'm gone," he said. "Bob Kaufman will disappear someday. Nobody will even notice. You can look for him in the bayou or in the swamp, but you won't find him."

"Don't forget, Bobby. Tonight. Seven-thirty. We need you there a half-hour before the reading begins."

Two hours before the reading the street in front of the Savoy Café and Theater looked like the entrance to a major rock concert. We quickly sold out all the seats and then talked to Ginsberg and the other poets about doing a second performance. Everyone agreed and we sold out a second show. An hour before the first performance, at 8:00 P.M., a few hundred disgruntled fans were told that no more tickets were available.

"This is an important event," I told a radio reporter who waylaid me with a microphone on the terrace of the Savoy Tivoli. "Tonight, Bob Kaufman will read *The Abomunist Manifesto,* a major poem of the San Francisco Poetry Renaissance. He has not read together with Ginsberg and Ferlinghetti for twenty years." I went on to say that Kaufman's work had been translated into French and published in two popular editions, but that his work was somehow not appreciated at home.

"Is it true that Governor Jerry Brown will be here tonight?" the reporter asked.

I shrugged my shoulders and went into the theater. Foye and Ginsberg were doing checks on the sound system, and they called me over to coordinate some of the remaining problems.

"Luckily, everyone is here," I said, glancing at my watch. It was twenty minutes before reading time and the Savoy was packed. Then we noticed that Kaufman was missing. Normally this would not be a big worry, but in dealing with the self-proclaimed "abomunist," it could mean he was on a plane to New York or across town at an all-night jazz party.

"I'll run down and see if I can find him," I said, I left the café and looked in on the Coffee Gallery, one of his old hangouts, and then down at the Caffe Trieste. "I saw him a few minutes ago," I was told by one of the poets hanging around. "I think he went up to the reading."

Running back to the café, I was pulled into the theater by Foye. Kaufman was still nowhere in sight. Behind me, Ginsberg, Orlovsky, Ferlinghetti, and the younger poets on the bill sat in anticipation. Foye began the introductions. The glare of the video lights bored in on us. We could barely make out the audience. I had a picture of myself apologizing for Kaufman's absence and reading a selection of his poems. Ginsberg called me over and said I should send somebody out to look for him again. Meanwhile, the reading had begun.

I conjured up images of Kaufman wandering alone by the waterfront docks. Just as I suggested we find a replacement, he came bounding up on stage. Ginsberg launched into *Plutonium Ode,* almost blowing the sound system apart.

"You want me to read **Second April?**" Kaufman leaned over to ask.

"What about the **Abomunist Manifesto?**" I asked.

"Where is it? What have they done to it?" he responded, looking genuinely agitated.

I leafed through **Solitudes Crowded with Loneliness,** his first book, and marked the page where the poem began. Kaufman had brought along a copy of **Golden Sardine,** a collection published by City Lights in 1967. "This is old Beatnik stuff, but I'll read it," he whispered.

It came his time to read. He lifted his thin, dark body from the chair and went toward the dais. Ginsberg smiled at him. The audience seemed to lean forward. There stood diminutive Kaufman with a serape over his flowing white shirt, brown skin radiant as the stage lights hit it. He began to read in a muffled tone that grew clearer as the poem raced toward its conclusion:

> ABOMUNISTS JOIN NOTHING BUT THEIR
> HANDS OR LEGS, OR OTHER SAME.
>
> ABOMUNISTS SPIT ANTI-POETRY FOR POETIC
> REASONS AND FRINK.
>
> ABOMUNISTS DO NOT LOOK AT PICTURES
> PAINTED BY PRESIDENTS AND
> UNEMPLOYED PRIME MINISTERS.

The Abomunist Manifesto is more of a document than a poem. It has elements of the jazz humorist Lord Buckley, a touch of Edward Lear, and some of the popular philosophy of the time. In a section entitled **"Further Notes,"** Kaufman writes:

> Krishnamurti can relax the muscles of your soul,
> Free your aching jawbone from the chewinggum
> habit.

Ouspensky can churn your illusions into butter
    and
Give you circles to carry them in, around your
    head.
Subud can lock you in strange rooms with
    vocal balms
and make your ignorant clothing understand
    you.

There is an explicit political meaning to the work, but it is clothed in a language that frees the perceptions from mere journalism. Thinking of the poem, I am reminded of what the poet once said when asked how he felt about being a third-world poet. "There is no third world. There are thousands of worlds. They all exist at the same time, in the same precise moment. I live in all those worlds. That's where a poet lives."

Bob Kaufman strived toward an understanding of the universality necessary for great poetry. He felt that narrow ideological concerns could shut down the "fountain," as he described it to me. He once told me, "I'm Black, Jewish, white, green, and yellow with a blue man inside me struggling to come out." Often, he begins a poem with his eyes or his head or some other part of his anatomy, and moves outward into the world. He is not visceral but gracefully attuned to his body as a key to opening "the mysteries" he refers to in his poetry. In **"Blues for Hal Waters"** he refers to his head as "my secret cranial guitar"; another poem asks, "would you wear my eyes?" Even in the saddest poems he emerges joyous out of an ecstatic love for language and its possibilities, reaching out to others:

My body once covered with beauty
Is now a museum of betrayal.
This part remembered because of that one's
    touch
This part remembered for that one's kiss—
Today I bring it back
And let it live forever.

Believing strongly in the reality his poems created for him, he lived comfortably with them, and that is why he became like a poem, why those who knew him were always treated to gems of language invented spontaneously or brought out of his memory bank of images.

When we first met, at a book party in 1975, he said, "I knew your uncle, Herman Cherry, in Woodstock. . . . Herman Cherry, painted *Fruit Compote* and gave it to me. . . . Herman Cherry flew to the top of the Washington Monument and painted *Fruit Compote,* and then he wrapped it up and gave it to me at the Lincoln Monument. Herman Cherry is an airplane flying over America with *Fruit Compote,* a small painting in a gilded frame that he gave me in Woodstock thirty years ago. . . . I was a labor organizer. . . . Rimbaud is an orange blossom. . . . Cherry is *Fruit Compote* painted for Bob Kaufman, Poet." He then began reciting T. S. Eliot's *The Love Song of J. Alfred Prufrock,* gesturing elegantly, moving his wiry body back and forth, his fingers playing an elegant invisible instrument. Three-quarters through *Prufrock* he spliced in lines from Yeats' *Sailing to Byzantium* and *Ode to Walt Whitman,* by Federico García Lorca, as well as his own poetry. Through the years I would see a repeat of such performances in cafés, barrooms, and my own apartment, especially in those months Kaufman lived with me after the Dante Hotel burned down.

A week after that first meeting, I was wandering down Adler Alley, a narrow passageway between North Beach and Chinatown, filled with garbage from the nearby Chinese fish markets and flanked on the North Beach end by City Lights Bookstore and Vesuvio's, a bar where Dylan Thomas and Jack Kerouac used to hang out when they were in town. I felt alone and unwanted. Suddenly Kaufman appeared.

"Neeli Cherkovski," he said, looking perfectly serious, "let's find our way to Saturn."

"Bobby, I don't feel good. I'm all alone. I don't have anyone to love me." I looked directly at him, hoping he would provide some words of comfort.

"You're a poet. You can't ever be alone. You have poetry," he insisted, gripping my arm with surprising strength.

He touched me deeply with that exchange, but I never quite figured out how a man who wrote **Solitudes Crowded with Loneliness** could have said what he did.

Bob Kaufman: the son of a Creole mother from Martinique and an Orthodox Jewish father; born in New Orleans in 1926; devotee of jazz, finding his way through that improvisational world to his own song. Kaufman was committed to oral poetry. Much of his work survives because his wife, Eileen, wrote it down as he spontaneously recited it. *Golden Sardine* is filled with poems written on scraps of paper, rescued by Kaufman's friends Mary Beach and Claude Pelieu. His last book, **The Ancient Rain,** came to fruition due to the care given by Raymond Foye to gathering all of the poet's unpublished writings from paper scraps, napkins, old tape recordings, and singed manuscripts retrieved from the poet's burned-out hotel room. Kaufman himself would have nothing to do with the shaping of the book.

Before he came to San Francisco, Kaufman had organized black mine workers in the South and had been a merchant seaman who traveled around the world several times. His ideology was a generalized protest against senators conducting anti-communist witch hunts from the halls of Congress, states conducting the ritualized, official murder of capital criminals, and generals sending soldiers into battle. In the community of poets gathered around North Beach, he found himself concerned more and more with poetry and began writing in earnest.

Kaufman lived in San Francisco until 1961, a habitué of the Co-Existence Bagel Shop, The Place, the Hot Dog Palace, The Coffee Gallery, Mike's Place, and other Beat hangouts. From 1961 to 1963 he lived in New York. His reputation had grown steadily in Europe, particularly in France where he became known as the "Black American Rimbaud." He married Eileen and had a son, Parker, named after the jazz musician Charlie "Bird" Parker.

Second April, ultimate statement of an outsider, a man looking coldly, clinically at a society fringed in nightmare, is a dream-trance of the surreal, serving up childhood memories, young-adult reveries, condemnations of a society in danger of becoming empty at the core. Kaufman affirms the power of poetry and jazz to transform, to radiate from deep within the mind, outward toward others.

Kaufman's protest, wrapped up in jazz images and the summoning of the absurd, includes a recognition of human frailty. Each section of *Second April* is a "session" as in jazz: "Session quarter zero . . . is tubercular leaves, chipped nose saints, alabaster sphinx cats . . . burning warehouses, nonchalant cops, pop-bopping black leather angels, feathered fathers. . . ." Every time I heard him read the poem I imagined myself in a vast jazz club, being led from room to room, following his sadness, his aloneness, his alienation, and his humor, and ducking underneath divine revelations and his juggling of language. "We are attacking our hair, it waves to neighbors in skies, kinky relatives," and "we cook old chaplinesque shoe-strings, they watch, we have never, have we, never ever, never."

Second April impressed Ferlinghetti, who published it as a City Lights broadside back in 1959, calling it "an autobiographical journey springing out of the blind conjunction of such events as Christ's crucifixion, death, and resurrection, the A-bomb, and the author's own birth."

The poem hit like a bombshell when first read in North Beach and quickly became a major weapon in the Beat arsenal:

> O man in inner basement core of me, maroon
>   obliteration smelling futures
> of green anticipated comings, pasts denied, now
>   time to thwart time,
> time to frieze illusionary motion on far imagined
>   walls,
> stopped bleeding
> moondial clocks. . . .

He sets the stage for a world in which normal chronology must be suspended, so that his interior self might jump out and reform consciousness. If in *Howl* ("I saw the best minds of my generation destroyed by madness . . .") Ginsberg looks outward from the "I" and proceeds to range over America, condemning what made the "best minds" of his generation go mad, Kaufman takes us deep inside of himself and then slowly comes back into the "air," talking of time, telling us to be free from the enslavement of clocks. He motioned people inward and then forward: "on to Second April, ash-smeared crowns, perfect, conically balanced, pyramid-peaked heads, shuddering . . ."

I took my turn scattering Kaufman's ashes onto San Francisco Bay from a little boat filled with poets Howard Hart, Jack Hirschman, Lawrence Ferlinghetti, Jack Micheline, Bob's son, Parker, and Bob's brother George from Berkeley. Whenever I miss him, I find myself going to his poetry.

His love for the poet Federico García Lorca was obvious to those who knew him, and references to the Spanish modernist abound throughout the body of his work. In a poem entitled **"Lorca,"** Kaufman writes:

> Spit olive pits at my Lorca,
> Give Harlem's king one spoon,
> At four in the never noon.
> Scoop out the croaker eyes
>   of rose flavored Gypsies
> Singing García,
> In lost Spain's
> Darkened noon.

Identifying strongly with Lorca, and looking on him as the primary singer of sensuality and solitude and the territories lying between those two poles, Kaufman strove for the clarity of expression and the intensity found in Lorca's poems *Somnambular Ballad* and the *Poet in New York* cycle.

In understanding Kaufman, it is vital to appreciate his search for an anchorage amid the lonesomeness he felt so keenly.

Sitting here alone, in peace
With my private sadness
Bared of the acquirements
Of the mind's eye
Vision reversed, upended,
Seeing only the holdings
Inside the walls of me . . .

For many, Kaufman was the ultimate rebel, the man who lived outside of society. His poems, however, no matter how keen their social criticism, are those of a man who yearned to be involved. Some of his last poems are deeply concerned with "that which is out there" in America. He lived in poverty all his life, yet felt himself to be a voice for the people, a new Whitman who, despite "private sadness," developed an expansive vision of the land:

THE AMERICAN SUN HAS RISEN,
THE OTHER SUNS HAVE LEFT
THE SKY, THE POEM HAS ENTERED
THE REALM OF BLOOD. BLOOD IS
NOW FLOWING IN ALL SKIES AND
ALL THE STARS CALL FOR MORE
BLOOD . . .

Kaufman's interior vision goes back to his earliest poems:

I wish that whoever it is inside of me,
would stop all that moving around,
& go to sleep, another sleepless year
like the last one will drive me sane . . .

To be driven sane . . . for Kaufman that may mean to lose what he saw as the unlimited joy of poetry. It isn't for nothing that he signed his name "Bob Kaufman, Poet." Yet, with this joy—the vocation of poet—also came the preoccupation with the themes of death, loneliness, solitude. *Solitudes Crowded with Loneliness,* far from being a sad book, has a playfulness throughout the text. It isn't always overt, but it is there amid the alienation he saw so clearly:

What of the answers
I must find questions for?
All these strange streets
I must find cities for,
Thank God for beatniks.

He could sweep the reader into his deepest sorrows, into his intense feeling of being on the outside cut off from others or from himself, yet he always marches back with keen wit.

In clear language he invoked surreal moods, tossing out one-liners that became, piled against one another in a poem, visionary: "The radio is teaching my goldfish Jujitsu . . . / My old lady has taken up skin diving & sleeps underwater / I am hanging out with a drunken linguist who can speak butterfly / And represents the caterpillar industry in Washington D.C."

By the time Bob and I first met in 1975 he had written most of his poetry, and the Kaufman legend had been fixed in concrete. People would say, "Bobby didn't speak all through the Vietnam War" or "Bob stopped talking after President Kennedy's assassination." In his preface to *The Ancient Rain,* Raymond Foye wrote, "Kaufman took a ten-year Buddhist vow of silence, prompted by the assassination of President Kennedy." Later I would hear his old friends say things like, "He spoke all the time, man," or "Hey, Bob would speak now and then." I can believe the silence, especially in light of some of his more memorable lines. Sometimes I would read his poems and feel guilty, as if I were responsible for the deep, profound vision so often threaded with sorrow: "THERE ARE TOO MANY UNFUNNY THINGS HAPPENING TO THE / COMEDIANS," he wrote in "**The Travelling Circus,**" typical Kaufman wordplay from *The Ancient Rain.* In the same poem he writes of "publishing two volumes of my suicide notes." Plagued, fearing nothing when he holds the banner of the poem aloft:

THE POET NAILED ON
THE HARD BONE OF THE WORLD,
HIS SOUL DEDICATED TO SILENCE
IS A FISH WITH FROG EYES,
THE BLOOD OF THE POET FLOWS
OUT WITH HIS POEMS, BACK
TO THE PYRAMID OF BONES
FROM WHICH HE IS THRUST
HIS DEATH IS A SAVING GRACE

CREATION IS PERFECT . . .

Death and creation are juxtaposed dramatically in the heated vortex at the center of Kaufman's vision. The poem becomes a death sentence, isolating him, opening up the terror of ultimate truths; and yet it also served as a great light, a way to express the fury of being unable to triumph over the vast emptiness permeating existence. Every line counts. Each poem is a final statement, not really part of a process but a hard thing nailed to a hard thing. Something meant to be permanent: "The blood of the poet flows out with his poems." Bob Kaufman, Poet.

I remember: Kaufman sits in my kitchen across the table from where I hold a black binder filled with soiled pages on which I have typed poems. His eyes cover me, invade my own private sadness as I read aloud. I find myself slowing down when I am on sure ground and speeding up when I am not . . . hoping he'll pass over the rough spots. I cannot fool him. He is with every

ABOUT THE AUTHOR

KEN KESEY ON FIRST ENCOUNTERING BOB KAUFMAN

I can remember driving down to North Beach with my folks and seeing Bob Kaufman out there on the street. I didn't know he was Bob Kaufman at the time. He had little pieces of Band-Aid tape all over his face, about two inches wide, and little smaller ones like two inches long—and all of them made into crosses. He came up to the cars, and he was babbling poetry into these cars. He came up to the car I was riding in, and my folks, and started jabbering this stuff into the car. I knew that this was exceptional use of the human voice and the human mind.

Kesey, Ken. Excerpt from an interview. *Digital Interviews* (website), <http://www.digitalinterviews.com/digitalinterviews/views/kesey.shtml> (September 2000).

word, all of the line breaks. And this is the man I had consigned to a vague, anonymous fog when we lived together in Harwood Alley.

I try to pull myself back, thinking of Kaufman's **"Hollywood"** poem or the long, wild poem that opens *Golden Sardine*. He describes the execution of Caryl Chessman by the State of California as it takes place on the backs of a visionary bison herd, images of PTA women and Kiwanis Club men attempting to chop down the tree from which the poem grows . . . I am pulled into Bobby's darkness . . . I am alone . . . I am unutterable and yet words begin to form. Bob Kaufman, obsessed with that "inner basement core" of himself, declared:

> I refuse to have any more retired burglars
> picking the locks on my skull, crawling in
> through my open windows, i'll stay out forever,
> or at least until spring, when all the wintered
> minds turn green again . . .

That's about as playful a mask as I've ever seen a poet wear. Kaufman climbs out of himself, ranges above his own fragility and vulnerability, but will come back again when the human mind (and heart) "turn green again," when men are warm, when love rules.

We would sit in Harwood Alley during the winter we lived together—both of us probably thinking of springtime and green things—as we shivered in the kitchen. "Bob, what are you thinking?" I'd often ask. Usually, I'd get a cold stare or he would simply look off into space, but occasionally he'd say, "Nothing . . . nothing." The sure-fire way of eliciting a response was to start reading Hart Crane, Federico García Lorca, T. S. Eliot, or Wallace Stevens. He felt close to Crane's blazing meteor of a life, reciting pieces of *The Bridge* from memory or fragments of *White Buildings*. Frequently, in the North Beach cafés, Bob would quote Stevens' *Music then is feeling, not sound* or launch into a fanciful version of Lorca's *The King of Harlem*.

One evening I read the first few pages of Whitman's *Song of Myself* to Kaufman as he sat at the kitchen table. As I read, he tapped his fingers on the table with his right hand, following the big Whitmanic tone I tried to approximate with my voice. When I stopped for breath, he cried: "More. More Whitman."

Bob once wrote that the first man was unable to survive the first truth and so he invented suicide. Throughout his poetry, he throws the proverbial naked truth in our faces, hot with music and cool with steady wit. He could retreat, not only into himself but to the memory of his youthful days as a sailor or into childhood reveries as well. In **"Night Sung Sailor's Prayer,"** Kaufman sails off the page:

> Voyager now, on a ship of night
> Off to a million midnights, black, black
> Into forever tomorrows, black
> Voyager off to the time worlds,
> Of life times ending, bending, night.

The lines bring me to ". . . Sappho, rolling drunks in coffee galleries, cock robin is / posthumously guilty, chicken little was right all along, Vachel's basic savages drive Buicks now, God is a parking meter. . . ." In these lines he captures so much . . . summoning forth Sappho and Vachel Lindsay. The image of Lindsay's middle Americans, the people he "sang" his poems to through the raucous 1920s, in big Buicks rambling down the highways, their spiritual values wrapped in the idea of parking meters, in the idea of time and money.

I read again Bob's poem on Caryl Chessman, the long and thunderous beginning to *Golden Sardine*. The poem could easily be tacked on to *Leaves of Grass*.

CARYL CHESSMAN INTERVIEWS THE P.T.A. IN HIS SWANK GAS CHAMBER BEFORE LEAV-

ING ON HIS ANNUAL INSPECTION OF
CAPITAL, TOUR OF NORTHERN
CALIFORNIA DEATH UNIVERSITIES,
HAPPY.

Chessman, a convicted kidnapper, became a symbol for people around the world who opposed the death penalty. Kaufman, in joining the protest, brought his ironic sensibility into full force:

CARYL CHESSMAN KNOWS, THE GOVERNOR
OF CALIFORNIA KNOWS, GOOD JOHNNY
THE POPE KNOWS, SALVATORE AGRON
KNOWS & ALL THE LEAKY EYED POETS
KNOW, IN THEIR PORES. NO ONE IS
GUILTY OF ANY THING AT ANY TIME
ANYWHERE IN ANYPLACE . . .

The most stirring and memorable lines of the poem come when Kaufman's protest takes flight, soaring over the American landscape, irony still intact, a wide and all-embracing vision of America at its historical center (rendered hysterical in Kaufman's word juggling). The poet in San Francisco, a child of New Orleans, roams the continent, leaping back in time to the torment and turmoil of a nation undergoing violent birth pains. At the end of this passage, Kaufman makes reference to his son, Parker, whom he calls to witness Chessman's truth—the taking of a life by the state is murder. Here is a vision worthy of Whitman:

. . . CARYL CHESSMAN WAS AN AMERICAN
BUFFALO, THUNDERING ACROSS
CALIFORNIA'S LYING PRAIRIES, RACKED
WITH THE POISON THE ARROWS OF
AUTHORITY, GUARDING THE BRILLIANT
. . . VISIONS OF MILLIONS OF GENO-
CIDED RED CRAZYHORSE PEOPLE, DEAD
IN THE MAKESHIFT GAS CHAMBERS OF
SUPPRESSED HISTORY . . .

"Lorca . . . Federico García Lorca!" Kaufman yelled from my living room where he had been sleeping on the floor. I walked in to find him sitting on a chair with a small lamp beside him, chain smoking and sipping from a Coke.

"What about Lorca?" I asked.

"The night that Lorca comes will be when the Negroes leave the south . . . when Lorca comes, Harwood Alley will move to New Orleans . . . we'll live on the clotheslines. . . ."

He was half-quoting from one of his latest poems—a poem that would be included in *The Ancient Rain.* It begins:

THE NIGHT THAT LORCA COMES
SHALL BE A STRANGE NIGHT IN THE
SOUTH, IT SHALL BE THE TIME WHEN
NEGROES LEAVE THE SOUTH
FOREVER . . .

"North Beach is home to me," Kaufman once told me. "When I'm in bed at night, and Billie Holliday is singing the blues outside my window, and Paul Robeson is singing the Soviet National Anthem in my head, and I can't sleep, I go outside and walk the streets of North Beach. And I know I'm home." Once describing himself as "the poet of the Bagel Shop," he sat in that long-gone coffeehouse on Grant Avenue with other habitués, drinking coffee, smoking endless packs of cigarettes, and dreaming up new poems. When I first came to North Beach, the storefront had become a dress shop. Today it's North Beach Video.

After the Bagel Shop closed (Bob wrote a poem about that North Beach event) there were still other places: the Coffee Gallery, 12 Adler Place, and Vesuvio's. In the latter, he once leaned over and whispered in my ear: "T. S. Eliot is my father." That seemed funny to me at the time. I thought how different Kaufman dressed and lived from the St. Louis native who had fled to England in fear of his barbarous homeland. Eliot had an ear for those compelling mysteries that make a poem real. According to Raymond Foye, Kaufman broke his long years of silence by reciting Thomas à Becket's speech from Eliot's *Murder in the Cathedral* at a North Beach gathering.

Kaufman and I once drove out to the state beach at Land's End. He said nothing on the way there, preferring to chain-smoke. I parked on a high cliff so we could see the Golden Gate Bridge, the Marin Headlands, and hear the seals below on the rocks. I suggested that we walk down toward the rocks. Kaufman remained silent, but followed.

"Everything living that passes through death walks with head lowered," he said.

"Is that your line?" I asked.

"Lorca," he said. "I wrote it for García Lorca a long time ago, when he was a gypsy in Seville . . . when I was washed ashore. Endless moon. Dreamless Spain."

Now he quoted himself. I began reciting random lines from Lorca's poem for Whitman. "*Y tú bello,* Walt Whitman, *con su barba . . .*"

I forgot the rest of the poem and wanted Kaufman to finish the lines. But he wasn't beside me. I ran down the path and couldn't find him. A wave of panic swept over me. Jesus, people fall from these cliffs, I thought, and looked down the narrow path to the jagged-edged rocks and threatening sea swells below.

"Bobby . . . where are you?"

Silence weighed heavily on me as two men passed with a poodle following obediently behind them. I took a path that forked into a clump of thick bushes and then sloped toward an embankment of sand. In the bushes, it was cool. The moment I reached the sandy clearing, I might as well have been in the Sahara.

"Come on, Bob . . ."

Then I saw him, far below, sitting on a boulder. I ran down to him.

"How did you get here so fast?"

"I'm from New Orleans," he said, "and when I sailed away, I sailed away forever. . . ."

He pointed to a massive tanker whose prow was pointed toward the bay. We watched together as it sailed under the bridge.

"Visual beatitudes," he said.

Soon we were back in the car, racing to North Beach. I glanced at him as he lit another cigarette. Hoping to catch him off guard and glean a little biographical information, I asked, "What was it like when you were sailing? Did you read a lot of books? When did you first go to sea?"

"Negroes . . . Negroes . . . Negroes" he shouted. "The world is full of Negroes . . . and the king of Harlem lifts a spoon over Whitman's beard full of butterflies."

Whitman and Bob Kaufman were meeting yet again.

In 1983 Kaufman and Lynn Wildey, fellow poet and girlfriend, rented a small house in the Russian River town of Guerneville, ninety miles north of San Francisco. I drove there with a younger poet to visit and to do a poetry reading at a nearby café.

"Neeli Cherkovski! Eric Walker! How are you? Did you bring Grant Avenue in the car trunk?" Kaufman said as he greeted us at the front door.

The first thing he wanted to do was have a drink. Lynn, however, had already made a meal, so we ate, then visited a neighbor. Kaufman, as usual, remained silent. Later we drove to a riverfront beer bar where Lynn and I tried to coax him into talking about his early youth. We hoped to get enough biographical information so I could begin a long projected profile.

"Listen, Bobby, just tell me a few things, like your father, what did he really do?"

"We were Jewish and Catholic. My mother took us to church. Sometimes we went to the synagogue. I played in Bayou Saint John. Now, buy me a beer, Neeli." Kaufman pressed his hand into my wrist. "Just one beer and I'll tell you everything."

I bought the beer, but noticed that his expression denoted a complete lack of interest in the interview. I switched to small talk about the river, the weather, and if he liked living so far from North Beach.

Then I asked a question regarding writing. "Bob, why do you like Whitman so much?"

"Another beer," he said with a demon-like glint in his eyes.

I bought another round of draft beers.

"Whitman invades America," he said.

That was his final commentary on Whitman. I used a new tactic. "What would you say to young writers?"

His eyes came alive. He stood up from the wobbly chair he was sitting on, almost tipping our equally wobbly table, and said, "Write! I'd tell a young writer to write! Write it all down! Don't hold it back!" With that said, he sat back down, stared into his remaining beer, drank it, and asked for another. I found his reticence annoying, though it was nothing new. There must be some other way to get him to talk. While I ordered more beers, Lynn began to demand that he open up. I saw his face framed in the greenery outside the window at the end of the cavernous barroom, and I knew him well enough to realize he was definitely finished with the interview.

In his early years Kaufman had tried to make changes in society. He threw himself into the political arena as a labor organizer. Those who knew him then speak vividly of his passion while addressing a crowd or explaining whatever oppression he wanted to end.

Later he retreated into his poetry, finding in it all the necessary ingredients for battling oppression. Poetry, in and of itself, became a means of defining life and of dealing with all the social, political, and personal issues that had concerned him. Lorca saw great poetry, and all great art, as possessed of *duende*, a mysterious essence that radiates from within, having little to do with a preconceived idea of craft and more with an embodied spirit that somehow captures the purest essence of what it means to be human, to live, and to die. It is a spirit that must be sought but can never be confined or completely analyzed. Kaufman longed to embrace this spirit of *duende*, to confront the demons that inhabit a poem.

Bob talked frequently of death in his last few years. Late one evening in Specs', a bar across the street from City Lights, he entered and addressed the crowd. "I don't live here anymore. I live on Mount Olympus now. I only use this body for dirty bookstore purposes." Later, as the bartender gave the last call, the poet proclaimed, "I have seen my own death. One day I shall be walking down Grant Avenue. And a pay telephone will ring. I will pick it up. It will be Jean Cocteau on the other end. And he will say, 'The Blood of the Poet.'"

When Lynn Wildey called on a Sunday morning in 1986 to tell me, "The poet Bob Kaufman is dead," I went to his poem "Awe":

> At confident moments, thinking on Death
> I tell my soul I am ready and wait
> While my mind knows I quake and tremble
> At the beautiful Mystery of it.

After my fellow poets and I had each taken a turn scattering Bob's ashes into San Francisco Bay from the small boat that had taken us out, Ferlinghetti turned to me and said, "When I retire, I think I'll live on a little boat out by Mission Rock." I almost responded, But the shoreline there will all be filled with condos and office towers by then. . . . Instead I smiled. I leafed through a copy of *The Ancient Rain* and read to myself.

Turning back to Ferlinghetti, I said, "What do poets retire from?"

MARIA DAMON (ESSAY DATE WINTER 2000)

SOURCE: Damon, Maria. "Triangulated Desire and the Tactical Silences in the Beat Hipscape: Bob Kaufman and Others." *College Literature* 27, no. 1 (winter 2000): 139-57.

In the following essay, Damon analyzes Kaufman's "Bagel Shop Jazz" and examines the Beat lifestyle that it portrays.

This essay has three strands: that is, it is "about" three things, and these three things are not autonomous but interwoven; discussion of each illuminates the others. It is about the historical intersection of Beat, gay, and minority writers/cultures in San Francisco in the late 1950s. It is also about a Black poet, Bob Kaufman, who deserves critical attention and who figures pivotally in the nexus of sexual, racial, and gendered tensions in a homosocial and homoerotic poets' triangle. Third, it is about a poem by Kaufman which purports to document these tensions in the "scene" he lived in, but is strikingly silent about the queer presence that in fact was so visible, and so much a part of his life. This last point, about what is and what is not in a poem, is an important

pedagogical one for any consideration of "teaching the Beats." Teaching Beat literature is not like teaching literatures in which the "work itself" is supposed to be independent from its context; the Beats were determined to write their lives, and this makes examination of those lives—not in an uncritically worshipful way, but with sympathetic critique—especially crucial. In the classroom, then, "close readings" of Beat texts will not suffice; it is necessary to widen the focus and see the interplay between text and context. The poem **"Bagel Shop Jazz"** is as pedagogically important for what it "disappears" as for what it emphasizes.

Bob Kaufman's Disappearing Acts

"BAGEL SHOP JAZZ."

> Shadow people, projected on coffee-shop walls
> Memory formed echoes of a generation past
> Beating into now.
> Nightfall creatures, eating each other
> Over a noisy cup of coffee.
>
> Mulberry-eyed girls in black stockings
> Smelling vaguely of mint jelly and last night's
>   bongo drummer,
> Making profound remarks on the shapes of
>   navels,
> Wondering how the short Sunset week
> Became the long Grant Avenue night,
> Love tinted, beat angels,
> Doomed to see their coffee dreams
> Crushed on the floors of time,
> As they fling their arrow legs
> To the heavens,
> Losing their doubts in the beat.
>
> Turtle-neck angel guys, black-haired dungaree
>   guys,
> Caesar-jawed, with synagogue eyes,
> World travelers on the forty-one bus,
> Mixing jazz with paint talk,
> High rent, Bartok, classical murders,
> The pot shortage and last night's bust.
> Lost in a dream world,
> Where time is told with a beat.
>
> Coffee-faced Ivy Leaguers, in Cambridge jackets,
> Whose personal Harvard was a Fillmore district
>   step,
> Weighted down with conga drums,
> The ancestral cross, the Othello-laden curse,
> Talking of Diz and Bird and Miles,
> The secret terrible hurts,
> Wrapped in cool hipster smiles,
> Telling themselves, under the talk,
> This shot must be the end,
> Hoping the beat is really the truth.
> The guilty police arrive.
> Brief, beautiful shadows, burned on walls of
>   night.
>
>   (Kaufman 1965, 14-15)

I have earlier, and repeatedly, used **"Bagel Shop Jazz,"** a nominee for the Guinness Prize in Poetry in 1960, as a theoretical framework for exploring triangulated desire in Beat culture (Damon 1995, 141-49; 1996, 150-75; 1997a, 137-47; 1997b, 177-85). In those essays I tried to show how the poem illuminates the tensions and attractions between the three groups described in the three stanzas that comprise the poem's substance: the non-ethnoracialized "Beat chicks," the presumed-male "white ethnic" Beats, and the presumed-male hip African-Americans (Black Beats). The poem is a beautifully succinct tableau depicting, in somewhat static terms, the ways in which the women, through their preoccupation with love and sex, mediate between the "secret hurts" of the Black, jazz-oriented men and the "dream world" of "high rent, Bartok" and "the pot shortage" that characterize the "black-haired[,] . . . Caesar-jawed" guys with "synagogue eyes"—that is, Jewish, Italian, and other liminally white Mediterranean immigrants. By "liminal," I mean that these white men can be specifically identified by the reader, through Kaufman's mention of their ethnicity, as "threshold" cases; both Jews and Italians had to work to establish their whiteness on first arriving in the United States, and they did so by distinguishing themselves from—that is, repudiating their possible alliances with—African-Americans.[1] And indeed, in the recent revival of interest in the Beats, the discovery of the full participation of women and Blacks in a white-male dominated counterculture should be encouraged. The poem elaborates on the presence, even in as hip a counterculture as the Beats', of the triangulated paradigm in which men express their desire for each other, and each other's status, through a feminized third element which is a conduit (rather than a third point properly speaking) of their mutual desire. The white ethnics envy what they perceive as their Black comrades' authenticity and soulfulness without specific knowledge of the "secret terrible hurts" that have shaped these outsider subjectivities, and which they themselves can only intuit; likewise they covet their groundedness and hipness. The Black men in turn desire the power and privilege it would take to let them live in the "dream world" so blithely occupied by their white comrades.

However, there is another triangle operating here which a too-narrow focus on "the poem itself" obscures, and it is important to tease it out of hiding, because in my experience of teaching Beat literature, the two areas which meet with the most resistance among my (undergraduate) stu-

dents are, on the one hand, a critique of the "romantic racism"—the appropriative strain in white Beat desire for Black culture—and, on the other, the homo-erotics of Beat culture, beyond a somewhat fetishized notion of Ginsberg and Burroughs as iconoclasts because they were sexually non-normative and used "obscene" language in their writing. That is, just as an enthusiasm for jazz is taken as a sign of white Beats' openness to Black people (and not just aspects of Black culture), Ginsberg's and Burroughs's homosexuality is consumed as decontextualized, as if there were no gay culture in which these men participated (or didn't), and as if this status as lonely "Other" served merely to enhance their glamour for a straight white counterculture. In fact, as both John D'Emilio's pioneering work on gay history (1986) and the recently published biography of the poet Jack Spicer make abundantly clear, Beat culture, especially in San Francisco but also in New York, lived in close and over-lapping proximity with a burgeoning gay male community which had cultural but as yet no political visibility (D'Emilio 1986; Ellingham and Killian 1998). Studies of Beat culture have tended to either condemn the Beat movement as wholly noxious in its exploitations or to exonerate (and indeed lionize) the "white negroes" for their individually flamboyant dissidence, rather than seeing a nuanced picture of competing and collaborating subject positions inhabited, to be sure, by subjects holding unequal social power. Thus, as both Hettie Jones (1991) and Amiri Baraka (1984) have observed in their respective autobiographies, Beat culture was deeply flawed, but it seemed to hold out certain possibilities in a world that appeared increasingly shut down, conformist, and eviscerated of creative, original thinking and cultural expression.

"Bagel Shop Jazz," which functions as a lens onto Beat culture in San Francisco's North Beach in the 1950s, is the work of Bob Kaufman, who has been until recently a well-kept secret, known only to African-Americanists and a small cadre of die-hard Beat fanatics, some of whom were actually there in the 50s and 60s. He fully deserves to be restored to Beat historiography as well as to American and African-diasporic literary historiography in general and certainly introduced to the college classroom. Bob Kaufman, born in New Orleans to a high-achieving middle-class Black Catholic family (his mother was a school-teacher, his father a Pullman Porter) was active in the Merchant Marines from his 18th birthday until his leftist union activities came under suspicion in the early 50s. When the AFL merged with the CIO, the more radical union members were driven out, Kaufman among them. He re-emerged in the late 1950s as a Beat poet in San Francisco (New York had been the site of most of his union activities), where he co-founded *Beatitude,* a seminal journal of Beat culture, and published the **Abomunist Manifesto** which was considered, along with Ginsberg's *Howl,* to be a Beat manifesto. (It is the reading material of the wasted-looking young man in the famous *LIFE* magazine photo accompanying its article on the Beats which has become the touchstone of every Beat-revival lecture in the past decade.)

There are multiple and conflicting accounts of Kaufman's genealogy, his life story, and other putatively relevant aspects of his life work. Was he, as the bookcovers of his New Directions books suggest, brought up by an Orthodox Jewish German father and a Martiniquan Catholic-"voodoo" mother? Not according to his many siblings. Was he ever in fact enrolled in the Merchant Marines or the National Maritime Union? His siblings and the legend say yes, but his name doesn't appear in any NMU archive records, and I have found no hard evidence of his membership. Just like scholarship on Bob Kaufman, Beat scholarship keeps shifting as more is revealed and as details about homo-eroticism, racial/ethnic tensions, and just plain biographical minutiae become permissible public discourse. However, Beat scholarship will never stand on incontrovertibly firm ground, because legend, hyperbole, and a scorn for official forms of documentation have constituted such primary elements in the Beat aura. Further, Beat scholarship is coming to legitimacy precisely in the era when indeterminacy is an intellectual value rather than a liability. However, Kaufman's disappearance from literary annals is more extreme even than that of some other Beats who at least achieved some semi-canonical notoriety, though Beat work as such has not been a regular part of the established curriculum. "**Bagel Shop Jazz**" itself is all about silence and obfuscation, though ostensibly it is all about talking, talking, talking. The veneer of hyperverbal poseurism hides what for many minority Beats was, in fact, a life of "secret terrible hurts" that will never be known because the principals are dead, and they covered their tracks astonishingly well. An even thicker cloud of mystery surrounds the figure of Stephen Jonas, a Black Bostonian poet who moved in queer/Beat circles. Turning yet again to "**Bagel Shop Jazz**," one can find still more material for rectifying (setting unstraight, queering, "reNegrifying" in the words of one colleague) the Beat

record. This time I want to look at that larger silence, especially when the poem is juxtaposed with other documents of the time, published and unpublished.

The triangle I now consider in the poem, then, is not that of Black and white men's desire for what each sees as the other's privilege, mediated by love-starved Beat chicks, but the worlds of Beat and gay (as they were conceived at that time) mediated by the figure of the Black man—an object of desire (and fear) for gay white men, and an object of fear (and desire) for straight white men. Like the presumed maleness of the Black and Jewish/Italian Beats, we find a presumed straightness in the figure of the Black hipster who serves as fantasy vehicle for gay and straight men of the Bohemian counterculture. The countertext to "**Bagel Shop Jazz**" is the still unpublished diary of Russell FitzGerald, a young artist whose infatuation with Bob Kaufman during the course of his live-in relationship with gay poet Jack Spicer dramatizes some of the conflicts of Beat/queer life in eloquent, anguished, and highly disturbing terms. The diary chronicles not only FitzGerald's obsession with Kaufman, but his attempts to work that obsession into an overall artistic and metaphysical ethos in which spiritual yearnings, artistic expression, and physical/erotic desire are harmoniously lived and theorized. The rigor and purposefulness with which the young artist attempts to make sense of his emotional life, and the immediacy with which he experiences as contradictory the very forces he is trying to harmonize, foreground the pain of Beat utopian aspirations. (He is often, for example, driven by the torment of a physical desire he perceives as both exalting and debasing, and which casts him simultaneously as victim and predator.)

For the Beat project was utopian, and Kaufman's poem attempts to document this by showing the range of inhabitants who lived in the sealed-off and culturally marked-as-different Coexistence Bagel Shop: it is interracial, it is hip, it is emancipated from the tedium of the workplace and its schedules, because it has beautiful, sexually available young women who will work a day job proofreading or writing ad copy to support you. One of the goals of Beat utopia was this kind of cross-racial democracy—democracy, that is, in the sense of identifying with the "fellaheen," as Kerouac called them—the down and out, the anonymous workers, and so forth. But, as the examples of both Athenian and American democracies have shown, equality and fraternity are usually purchased at someone's else expense. As much as "**Bagel Shop Jazz**" describes a kind of insider/outsider society marked by its freewheelingness (its valuing of "coexistence"), it also describes a tense negotiation between non-equals who, drawn together by mutual yearning for a new society, have had to put up a united front against the "guilty police"—the normative world. As Richard Cándida Smith (1995) elaborates, the vision of a working harmony between community (democracy, alternative domestic arrangements and sexual options), cultural expression, and everyday life was one that the Beats shared with other art communities, among them the gay poets of San Francisco, who also shared with them an embattled relationship to mainstream culture. But their respective democratic visions were somewhat in tension with the queer writers more drawn toward a Platonic ideal of an elite intelligentsia. The Beats were more wholeheartedly enamored with the lower echelons of both cultural and economic registers, though they still held the figure of the artist in special reverence. The shining example of Walt Whitman was the great mediator for both groups. He was taken up by gay writers as one of them as he championed loving male friendships. He was taken up by the Beat writers because of his expansive, all-embracing vision of American life. And he was taken up by both because of his long poetic line, daring both formally and in its inclusion of all and any material as suitably "poetic."

The relationship of the queer 1950s counterculture to Whitmanian/American democracy and Athenian political/philosophical thought is complex and (at least) double-edged; there was, among gay writers, affection for Platonic writing, especially the *Symposium*, because it offered an overt expression of homoerotic love in a time when that form of love was considered the highest human affective bond. At the same time, there was a consciousness of Plato's disdain for the physical world in relation to the ideal world which they alternately found consoling and oppressive. That is, on the one hand, there is another reality "hidden behind" the cruelties of the world we live in, and we can take some comfort and joy in cultivating that realm. On the other hand, the social contempt for the physical and sexual so prevalent in American puritan society—especially in the 1950s—intensifies the prejudice against homosexuality, since it is not necessary for procreation and thus cannot be sanctioned within state institutions. This contempt justifies the criminalization of homosexual behavior or even inclinations.[2] Although the gay writers of the San Fran-

cisco Renaissance—among them Jack Spicer, Robert Duncan, Robin Blaser, George Stanley, and Stan Persky—sometimes invoked a revised version of Plato's *Republic* as an ideal (following the Austrian poet Stefan George, they referred to themselves as "poet-kings" of their own republic of poetry, even though Plato's "philosopher-kings" had exiled Poetry in the classical work), they were torn between Plato's and George's belief in an elitist cult of the initiated on the one hand, and Whitman's more democratic notion of brotherly erotic love on the other. Even in the split between the ideal and the immanent, which in some ways was a painful and self-denying ethos, and which translated into "we wear the mask" or "we are not what we appear to be" (we are gay, but must pretend to be straight in this social closet), there was a kind of art, finesse, and sophistication involved in living double lives, or of having to keep one's life compartmentalized—this part could be public, that part had to be kept private. As gay historian George Chauncey has pointed out, while the circumstances of such double living were incontrovertibly oppressive, there was respect for the grace and skill with which the life was handled. Its practitioners did not necessarily consider themselves victims, or that they were victimized by their own skills. The ideology of ethnoracial authenticity was not to become publicly or theoretically significant until the late 1960s, when minoritized ethnic, racial, gendered, and sexual communities based political movements on unitary identities.

It was the Beat era, however, that helped midwife that ideology of authenticity into being. What the Beats did for the gay community was to goad it into visibility—a visibility that would eventually become politicized—by exemplifying flamboyant resistance to an oppressive norm. What the gay culture did for the Beats was to offer them a model for fluid relationships, outlaw culture and a high regard for the relatively apolitical politics of "lifestyle" (though the latter word was not coined until the 1970s). More than the queers, who had an ambivalent stake in the high art and philosophy of the Platonic tradition, the Beats insisted on making the signifier fit the signified. They tried to collapse the distance between the "private" and "public" selves, insisting that such a division was a form of social mutilation. So the Beats were, on the whole, less ambivalently anti-Platonic in their desire to refuse the gap between the Ideal and Immanent, the spiritual and the physical, the soul and the body. And they had no reason to be loyal to the cult of philosopher-kings, poet-kings, or any other type of cultural elite. They were unambiguously Whitman's heirs rather than Stefan George's or Plato's. The various Europes their parents had fled had treated them with cruelty and contempt and had visited upon them extreme economic privation as well as state-sanctioned class and ethnic prejudice. They associated high European art with their class enemies, though as Kaufman's poem demonstrates ("paint talk, . . . Bartok" [Kaufman 1965, 14]) they were attracted to the newer elements of classical art that drew on the "folkish." We need only look at the difference between Allen Ginsberg's and Jack Spicer's poetics, poetry, and personal comportments to see a glaringly dramatic embodiment of the dissonance between the Beats and the queers: Ginsberg is all-embracing, raw, confessional, intent on destroying the dualism between the sacred and the degraded. Spicer is resolutely private, hermetic, devoted to keeping his personality out of his work in the service of a higher entity—Poetry. (We can see the potential and the ugliness of both forms of democracy. Kerouac, in his later years, came to articulate an anti-intellectual, crude form of populism in which he Jew-baited his friend Allen Ginsberg and others, denounced the Communist menace, and so forth—this is the nadir of a populist democracy. The more selective type of democracy practiced by the Athenian elite and in some ways admired by the gay writers runs the risk of replicating the kind of mainstream exclusions to which Bob Kaufman was subject and can result in an equally embittered withdrawal into an aggrieved sense of superiority.)

Nonetheless, this very anguish and urgency of the Beats to tear down the illusory wall separating them from themselves, from "reality," from an authentic life that expressed and externalized their spiritual yearnings, speaks to a complicity with patterns of inside versus outside, authenticity versus falsity, the "guilty police" versus the "beautiful shadows." Although they did reverse the hierarchy of those binarisms, putting the police in the "guilty" slot and themselves as the deviant/innocent victims, Beat culture (if not the work of specific Beat writers like William Burroughs, for example) reified rather than dissolved the binary bind of life in the 1950s. And it did so using Black culture as the lightning rod that conducted the meeting of Heaven and Hell. Furthermore, what has come to us as Platonic wisdom, like what has come to us as a united Beat front against the straight world, is actually far more complex and interesting than binarized

(queer/Beat) generalizations can convey. The narrative complexity and poetic beauty of Platonic writing, for example, which does *not* tell a straightforward story celebrating an idealized spiritual love, allows us to see the dynamic intelligence and flamboyant, often conflicting ideologies, personalities and styles at work in the construction of what (as good post-structuralist scholars and/or Beat aficionados) we know and mistrust as the Athenian roots of Western philosophy. Likewise we can appreciate the nuances of the 1950s counterculture; its complicated internal alliances and schisms require close attention to counter glib, unqualified celebrations of a certain glorified caricature of Beat culture as emancipatory on the one hand, and unqualified condemnations of Beat culture as exploitive and vulgar on the other. In remapping onto both the Beat past and the historicizing-Beat present these dramas laced with lacunae and loud absences and present silences, it is not hard to see what has been left out of the official beat text and, to the degree that there was one, the official queer text. Missing in action from the official beat scene: gay men. Women, insofar as they were foundational rather than decorative. People of color insofar as they were foundationally interactive with it rather than merely inspirational/apparitional/allegorical reference points.

The scene described by **"Bagel Shop Jazz,"** a static and haunting *tableau vivant,* is prepackaged for historicization: you want to know who we were in the 1950s North Beach? Here we are: (non-racialized) women, white ethnics (men), and Blacks (men). This, at least, is the substance of the poem's content. However, the door opens to a more comprehensive reading when we admit that the poem enacts its own aporia. By today's standards, it is not only ragingly hetero-normative (if complexly so), but when the researcher investigates Kaufman's actual biography, the milieu he traveled in and the company he kept, the absences are even more dramatic and can be ascribed to a purposeful (if mediated by convention) elision. It is not the case that queers were simply part of a vague backdrop of undifferentiated Bohemia. Kaufman was actively enmeshed in a triangle involving queer men; he was their friend, he engaged them *as queers* in public if playful verbal sparring. The queer scene to which he lived in such close and even overlapping proximity (in light of his protracted flirtation with Russell FitzGerald), with its far more believable and regular bar busts and its coded communications, its shadow existence, its secret terrible hurts, and its fantasies of love, forms the world that this Bagel Shop world protects the Beats against as much as it does against the police. The queers did not congregate at the "Co-existence Bagel Shop" *as* a queer space, though as individuals they may have been customers. They congregated at certain bars which themselves had different flavors (the drag show bars as distinct from the intelligentsia's bars, for instance) and some of which, like "The Place," did in fact cater to a broader group of Bohemians. The queer side of Bob Kaufman, such as it was, and of the Beat scene, is dramatically excised from the bagel shop poem which is framed precisely to exclude the formal presence of queers as a group that makes up the counterculture. There is no "queer content" in the poem, except insofar as the homosocial economy of desire that flows between white men and Black men, mediated by women as presumed property of the Other/object of desire, can be considered queer. (NB: It is emphatically not my objective here to claim a closeted "homosexual" or "gay" identity for Kaufman, but rather to point out that certain experiences and elements that textured everyday Beat life have been suppressed from the record, both in this poem and in other Beat documents, such as *On the Road* and other of Kerouac's *romans à clef* which are not only silent about Dean/Neal's homosexual encounters, but those of Kerouac and even of those of Ginsberg, the "out" homosexual.)

The Beat scene was one where ethnic and subcultural styles were readily borrowed and experimented with, and consumed in the crassest sense of thoughtless appropriation. Kerouac's purple prose about jazz and its musicians is everyone's (both Kerouac bashers and Kerouac aficionados) favorite example, in which his obvious enthusiasm cannot hide, though it mitigates a wholly negative and dismissive judgment about, his callow misunderstandings. Kaufman's poem, quite different from Kerouac's rhapsodic prose, captures with a kind of distant compassion the dynamics of this mutual exploitation—the currency—sex (women), high modernist culture (Jews/Italians), and the cool, stoic authenticity of hip Black men that hides the depth of their suffering—that each party brings to the table in very stereotyped profiles. The poem is also, of course, about how fragile these negotiations are, how tenuous this counterculture's sense of itself really is. The unspeakable, queerness, constitutes the scene's hipness. However countercultural these bagel shoppers are, however much heat their conversation generates against the Cold War rag-

ing outside, the triangle of Other faces they present to the straight world relies on queer silence.

In spite of the larger silence it enacts, though, this poem's manifest content should itself be seen as an anomalous breakthrough in Beat discourse, because it disturbs the silence surrounding the tension between various members of the scene's constituency. In particular, Beat discourse (especially by white male Beats) about Black men is generally characterized by an admiring, hyperbolic description of hetero-machismo or preternatural musical talent. Often this rhetoric includes envious anecdotes about how much easier it was for Black men to pick up cute chicks than it was for the writer. Black men, in these accounts, are either saintly musicians or hustlers on the prowl. This latter view is epitomized, of course, by Norman Mailer's notorious "The White Negro" (1959) which claims to be about how the white man envies the Black man's sexuality and thus tries to emulate his style, but whose subtext is about how the Jewish man envies and wants to emulate the gentile man's sexuality but can't say so. One of the contributions **"Bagel Shop Jazz"** makes to the Beat legacy is that it complicates this static outside-in view of Black masculinity and attributes to African-American men a textured, dignified interiority born of a collective experience of tragedy. Nowhere are the men, "white ethnic" or Black, seen as preying on the women; they are each preoccupied with troubles emblematic of their culture, be it high modernist or streetsmart. Instead, sexuality, which in the writing of white Beat men gets projected onto Black men, is here projected onto women. And it is an extraordinarily naive version of sexuality that Kaufman imputes to the women; the stereotypically gendered syndrome of one-night stands en route to the search for true love is sympathetically if superficially rendered. The gay scene, which was a living, palpable presence in North Beach counter-culture, is effaced. Though to be sure the men are not indicated as specifically heterosexual, the women are, and the men by being unspecified are subsumed into a normative standard that need not speak its name—that is, heterosexuality.

Vice Versa

Not surprisingly, the gay community's public discourse did to Kaufman what he did to them in **"Bagel Shop Jazz."** In that public discourse we find what we might expect with regard to the Black poet—that is, he is invisible, and to the degree that he is acknowledged at all, he is hypersexualized or seen as emblematic of the physical body, or its abstract and ambiguously positive analogue, the "folk." If he is Black, in other words, he can't be a Poet. As he dismissed them as soulless, precious intellectuals, they wrote him off as a vulgar, undisciplined populist. He was excluded from foundational anthologies such as Donald Allen's *The New American Poetry* (1960), and he did not participate in the informal workshops that coalesced around the writers with serious literary aspirations, such as Spicer. It is, however, difficult to make absolute generalizations about the mixture of Negrophilia and racism, or the way the two function in tandem, in gay writing of the time, because the politics of identity functioned very differently from those of today. It was possible for gentiles, whites, and men to have warm, collegial friendships with Jews, Blacks, and women in which they interacted on a daily basis, while simultaneously unself-consciously and publicly subscribing to strict prejudices at the abstract level.

For example, we find a blend of misogyny and comradeship in references to women. Women are reviled by Jack Spicer in his greeting to Denise Levertov (a poem he wrote on the occasion of her visit to San Francisco opens with the lines: "People who don't like the smell of faggot vomit / Will never understand why men don't like women"); but Robert Duncan wrote frequently about his affection for and feeling of inspiration from Levertov, clearly a comrade in aesthetic mission. Blacks figured in the gay poets' work mostly in comparatist contexts, where the social marginalization of gay men is juxtaposed to that of Blacks— sometimes in gestures of solidarity, sometimes in gestures of dismissal, sometimes simply as a jumping off point for the consideration of gay oppression, a topic much less publicly discussed than racial oppression. Robert Duncan, for example, opens his 1944 groundbreaking essay "The Homosexual in Society" thus:

> Something in James Agee's recent approach to the Negro pseudo-folk (Partisan Review, Spring 1944) is the background of the notes which I propose in discussing yet another group whose only salvation is in the struggle of all humanity for freedom and individual integrity; who have suffered in modern society persecution, excommunication; and whose "intellectuals," whose most articulate members, have been willing to desert that primary struggle, to beg, to gain at the price if need be of any sort of prostitution, privilege for themselves, however ephemeral . . .
>
> (Duncan 1944, 209)

Duncan had at that time also written a poem, "African Elegy," which he had submitted to John Crowe Ransom at the *Kenyon Review*, which, after the publication of "The Homosexual in Society," was returned after having been accepted because Ransom could no longer overlook the homoerotic content. The poem combines Negrophilia and homoeroticism in a joyous, though stereotypical, fantasy of bondage and magic. Note the drug reference; African-Americans were perceived by their white counterparts to be sophisticated initiates into the esoterica of drug use. And note also the ambiguous degree to which Duncan takes responsibility, in the last few lines of the passage below, for his own fantasizing. He knows he is projecting wondrous and titillating scenarios onto Africa, Africans, and African-Americans, and as a writer and gay man claims solidarity with them through the "darkness" of his own forbidden desires (it is important to remember, when we inquire into the projective nature of Beat writers' Negrophilia, that miscegenation was still literally against the law):

> Negroes, negroes, all those princes,
> Holding cups of rhinoceros bone, make
> magic with my blood. Where beautiful
>   Marijuana
> towers taller than the eucalyptus, turns
> within the lips of night and falls . . .
> those Negroes, all those princes
> holding to their mouths like Death
> the cups of rhino bone,
> were there to burn my hands and feet,
> divine the limit of the bone and with their
>   magic
> tie and twist me like a rope. I know
> no other continent of Africa more dark than this
> dark continent of my breast.
>
> (Duncan 1966, 34)

John Wieners, another queer Beat, whose writing can be studied very usefully alongside Kaufman's for a similar approach to poetics and the role of the poet in society, also attributes a sense of aliveness and dynamism to "Negroes" (though less flamboyantly)—a dynamism he finds lacking in other segments of 1950s society. In describing an evening in San Francisco in 1959, he writes:

> Streetwalkers, showgirls, perverts, late businessmen, clerks, schoolboys, tourists, from the healthy country . . . poets with pale faces, girls dressed in black beside them. All parade by on silent errands. There is seldom laughter except in the neighborhood and negro districts. Here all is flash and glamour. . . . How long? Two years at it and I am worn out. My teeth half gone at 25. A racking cough all night. Little food and sour stomach in the morning unless drugs, not to deaden one, but open doors for the fantasy world. Sur-real is the only way to endure the real we find heaped up in our cities.
>
> (Wieners 1997, 53-54)

Jack Spicer's campy dismissal of camp as authentic queer culture in "Excerpt from the Diaries of Oliver Charming" highlights the differences and similarities he perceives between Black, Jewish, and homosexual "identity" insofar as the search for an authentic culture is concerned. He writes that camp is "a perpetual Jewish vaudeville joke—or at the very best, a minstrel show impeccably played by Negros in blackface" (1975, 344). He dwells on the differences between the three groups (assumed, in his paradigm, to be mutually exclusive and exclusively male) in precept #12 of the "Unvert Manifesto" (possibly an inspiration for Kaufman's **Abomunist Manifesto**?): "Jews and Negros are not allowed to be unverts. The Jew will never understand unversion and the Negro understands it all too well" (1975, 341). Unverts are metasexual homosexuals—that is, as far as I can tell, celibate or beyond the reach of the usual pleasures, and intimately familiar with erotic pain that makes "platonic love" an experience that transfigures suffering into purified poetic material. By attributing to Black and gay men the depth and soulfulness needed to undergo such alchemical sublimation, and by denying that possibility to Jews (presumably because, according to the stereotypes of the day, they were overly materialistic), Spicer is both participating in a Poundian legacy joining anti-Semitism with avant-garde poetics and declaring a kinship with Black Americans' putatively superior spiritual capabilities that have been forged by the fire of extreme social suffering.

Here we can circle back to the notion of a Platonic Symposium as a kind of loose, floating trope for homosocial, homoerotic, and intellectual community. In his magisterial presence in the North Beach counter-cultural poetry scene, in his espousal of a doctrine of extreme dualism (suggested in the spiritual/material split alluded to above), and in his ruthless pursuit of purity in thought, conduct and poetry, Spicer, of course, is the Socratic presence in this drama. His collegial friendship with apocryphally Black poet Stephen Jonas notwithstanding (and Jonas, too, espoused an extreme skepticism toward fleshly pleasures and the comforts of identity-based communities of suffering, as well as a die-hard Poundianism that included anti-Semitism), Spicer is no more forgiving on the subject of race than he is on the subject of, say, gayness, or poetry. He is uncompromising on all fronts. As in Kaufman's exclusionary **"Bagel Shop Jazz,"** there's no hint of the proximity of Black presence in Spicer's work, except in his "Song for Bird and Myself" (poems for Charlie

Parker were practically *de rigueur* in hipster culture) which puns on "blow" to create a continuum and a shared sense of aesthetic commitment between himself and the founding and legendary father of bebop ("And are we angels, Bird?" / "That's what we're trying to tell 'em, Jack / There aren't any angels except when / You and me blow 'em" [Spicer 1975, 348]). While Spicer did not consider himself a Beat poet, and while he and his circle are not usually considered Beats, they were equally a part of what is now termed the "San Francisco Renaissance," and it is only with the recent publication of the Spicer biography by San Francisco writers Kevin Killian and Lew Ellingham (1998), that full justice can be done to the rich and nuanced intermeshing and dissonances between both (overlapping) scenes.

One could, in fact, easily read the entire works of Jack Spicer and Bob Kaufman and never realize that they moved in the same circles, drank in the same bars, slept with the same man. The document that gives the lie to these mutual silencings is the beautifully anguished and as yet unpublished diary of Russell FitzGerald, the young painter/poet who was the object of Jack Spicer's affection and who, even while he lived with Spicer and loved him as a mentor, pursued Bob Kaufman wildly, famously and hopelessly all over North Beach. In this drama, Spicer is, again, clearly Socrates but not Socrates the powerfully wise philosopher; here, he is the Socrates whose buttons get pushed by his own desire for the beautiful wild boy. FitzGerald is that very boy, the wayward genius Alcibiades who teases Socrates and undoes his claim to Platonic disinterest, and Kaufman is. . . . Eros itself? Poetry itself, the obsessive object of desire that is talked into being by the community of lovers, philosophers, poets? Perhaps, but Bob Kaufman, as a Black man, also represents, in FitzGerald's Negrophiliac imagination, the temptations of the physical rather than the balm of the spiritual. At one point in the diary, "Bobby" is spelled "Bo(d)by," and comes to represent in FitzGerald's feverishly conflicted imagination the pull of the physical, the erotic, the sinful. For all that the Beats tried to marry Heaven and Hell, both they and members of the Spicer-kreis were heavily invested in that marriage as a crazy juncture of distinct opposites. "Bob is wonderful, a living poem," gushes FitzGerald (n.d. 19), charmed by Kaufman's high-spirited and thoroughly endearing falling-down-drunk monologues in which he castigates the "queers" for being inauthentic and spiritually impoverished, compared to his own richness in "soul." FitzGerald admires Kaufman's physicality, his lack of social inhibition, the spontaneity of his no-harm-intended, playful invectives.

Spicer and FitzGerald discuss Kaufman endlessly, to the point that he has more of a textual or discursive than actual presence in FitzGerald's life. The "Kaufman situation," that is, the Spicer-FitzGerald-Kaufman love triangle, becomes more real to the infatuated young painter than is Kaufman himself who is busy having a life of his own that will eventually include a (second) wife, Eileen, and a son, Parker. Kaufman becomes, literally, an icon in FitzGerald's passionate spiritual mythography: a recent, serious, and anguished convert to Catholicism at the time of his move to North Beach, he executed a series of religious paintings, "14 Stations of the Cross" featuring Kaufman as Christ—a connection that was to be made throughout Kaufman's life and posthumously, when eulogies like Winans's "Black Jesus of the 50s" appeared on the storefront doors of North Beach. Kaufman himself, raised Catholic in New Orleans, played on this identification in a number of his earlier poems, including *Abomunist Manifesto* which features hilarious passages from the diary of Christ figured as a hip-lingo-slinging Beat poet, and **"Afterwards, They Shall Dance,"** in which he "sings the nail-in-the-foot song" (1965, 6).

While talk about Kaufman entirely permeates FitzGerald's journal and gives it that urgently poetic quality of erotic longing that makes it such a remarkable text, Kaufman's voice is negligibly recorded. The moments that are documented, however, are significant, because they capture the free-wheeling hyperverbal high spirits for which Kaufman was known before lapsing into his legendary silence which lasted, with a few notable departures into writing/speaking again, from 1963 to the end of his life in 1986. In one such passage, Kaufman excoriates, jokingly of course, Spicer's table at the bar, accusing the intellectuals of being soulless faggots. On another, he quips, "I have to sleep with women to keep from sleeping with men," a line that strings FitzGerald along. Finally after months of "cat and mouse," FitzGerald gets to go down on Kaufman who has "managed to pass out" (49) in a seedy hotel room and is promptly disgusted by his own behavior. "Even the smell on my hands seemed sickening," he writes (66). This demystifying culmination of their intimacy doesn't quell his ardor, however, and for a year or more the two continue their game, enraging Spicer so much that he scribbles "nigger" across Russell's copy of Kaufman's *Abomu-*

nist Manifesto which Spicer knows Kaufman will see. What is both poignant and repellent are FitzGerald's continual and addictive private vows not to objectify Kaufman—vows that always get broken. "I swear I will never again conjure his body to feed my imaginary lust. . . . Dark brother, I free you from my legend, I love you real. No more masturbating, no more black magic. Oh my love forgive me. Oh God, grant me all the fire I need" (n.d. 66). The purple prose is both touching in its pained sincerity and laughable in its over-the-top histrionic self-delusion. Meanwhile, Kaufman wears a ring FitzGerald gave him on the occasion that Kaufman had just sucked the blood from a self-inflicted wound on FitzGerald's hand and then "drew and held the admiration of everyone in the [Coffee] Gallery with one of his free-wheeling monologues denouncing the faggot table" (67).

In the midst of this swirling evidence of a heavy investment on Kaufman's part in being adored by a man, it seems safe to say that Kaufman's performance of homophobia was a double-edged matter: his charm and charisma went a long way toward mitigating what could only have been partial self-mockery as well. Typical of societies that try to blend utopian democracy with a respect for charismatic flamboyance, actions and speech veer every which way, complementing and canceling each other out until everyone is living with his back against the wall. Kaufman, I suspect, was willing to put up with some objectification because of a recognition of the social stigma queerness incurred. In **"Unhistorical Events"** he records some of the "secret terrible hurts" suffered by the anonymous poor, including himself and one of his former shipmates: "Apollinaire / never sailed with riffraff rolfe / who was rich in California, but / had to flee because he was queer. . . . Apollinaire / never slept all night in an icehouse . . ." (1968, 30-31; This last is evidently a reference to Kaufman's having been suspended by his thumbs in an icehouse all night by the Klan when he was in his teens.) Also, as actor Ben Vereen has recently pointed out, the ills of racism have some secondary benefits, including a certain privacy to do and be as one wishes while whites labor under a false impression that one is stupid, insensitive, or unaware that one is being objectified. Thus, being adoringly objectified by Russell FitzGerald allowed Kaufman a measure of freedom; he was never called on to reveal himself, to put his cards on the table as it were, since he was presumed to have no interiority (Vereen 1999). However, it must also finally be recognized that Kaufman could be said to have *submitted to* FitzGerald's pressure—especially the night when he passed out and allowed FitzGerald to perform fellatio on him—because the relationship was, after all, one between structurally unequal subjects. Although FitzGerald experiences himself as a victim of Kaufman's attractiveness and thus feels impelled to behave in an undignified way in pursuit, we know that structurally this is not the case. FitzGerald experiences Kaufman as teasing him mercilessly, and himself as abject; but he is an enfranchised citizen, while Kaufman is not. In pre-Civil Rights era United States, even in a freewheeling social bohemia, where Kaufman's colleagues could hurl racial epithets at him with no more consequence than a bitter laugh on his part, what kind of choice did he have? In becoming a full-fledged member of the triangle, Kaufman could be said to exhibit compassion and grace under pressure. These are the scenes so strikingly absent from **"Bagel Shop Jazz;"** and their absence could signal either an aporia on Kaufman's part, which is how I have constructed it in my reading of the poem, or a way of "writing back": we will love each other, we will silence each other.

Biographically, there is no happy ending, but there is evidence of tenacity, creativity, and persistence against the odds. In 1960, Kaufman eventually embarked with his new family (wife and infant son) for New York City—a trip that resulted in Kaufman's return to San Francisco, three years later, a bitterly disillusioned amphetamine addict who would rise only occasionally to his former wildly antic, creative heights. "I want Bob Kaufman back," he was known to say on certain occasions, speaking from so far within his disappointment that much of his language became private and cryptic where it had been public and wittily accessible. When FitzGerald followed him east, some months later, he too succumbed to heroin addiction which he drifted into as a way of entering the world of Black men. Eventually his wife (he had, in the midst of all this infatuated activity, eloped with Dora Dull and her twin daughters) took him to Vancouver where he kicked the habit and became a gourmet cook, dying of alcoholism in his early 40s. His magnum opus, "The Stations of the Cross," testimony to the role of Kaufman and Catholicism (Heaven and Hell) in his life, was irreparably damaged by flooding in Vancouver, but his journal's vividness enables us to reconstruct much of the passionate scene of which he was apart. Jack Spicer too died of alcoholism at 40, uttering these legendary last words to his friend Robin Blaser: "My vocabulary

did this to me: your love will let you go on" (Blaser 1975, 325)—a cautionary self-reflection on a life lived, perhaps, too purely and exactly devoted to the Real in poetry. Kaufman outlived his co-triangulants, dying in 1986 at age 60 of emphysema and cirrhosis in a Catholic resthome in the Western Addition, a Black section of San Francisco. With characteristic wit and foresight, he whispered to his girlfriend Lynne Wildey these last words, "If you're ever in the neighborhood, drop by—" (Blaser 1975, 325).

. . . . .

I have been concerned throughout to show the dynamics of mutual silencings and objectification, and occasional solidarity and genuine comradeship, between various constituencies of Beat culture in the North Beach neighborhood of San Francisco. I have also been concerned to explore these dynamics through the work of a not yet fully acknowledged Beat poet, who, in my teaching experience, is always a success in the classroom. Students invariably express indignation that Kaufman's work has been unknown to them. In the classroom, his poetry can pry open some of the hidden and complex connections between Beat and queer men and between white Beats, queers and African-Americans, as well as the cultural debt the Beat scene owes to anonymous denizens of outcast cultures. Kaufman's **"Bagel Shop Jazz"** and other work can also illuminate connections with the Graeco-Roman tradition so important to both Beat and gay poets.

Notes

1. See the work of Roediger (1993) for a historian's view of how the social commodity of "whiteness" (itself a social construction rather than a biological category) had to be earned by incoming members of the labor force from Ireland as well as Eastern and Southern Europe. By the 1950s, these Jews and Italians were safely "white"—but there were still, for example, quotas in universities that prohibited Jews from attending, and other forms of institutionalized prejudice. Moreover, the imaginative literature of the time continued to explore the anxieties experienced by these subjects. See in particular Brossard's *roman à clef* (1952), in which an Italian-American woman is romantically torn between a "passed Negro" (based on Anatole Broyard) and the narrator, a white man named, suggestively, Blake.

2. For an extended discussion of gay writing and Platonic thought, especially with regard to the North Beach 1950s and 1960s, see the first few sections of "Dirty Jokes and Angels: Jack Spicer and Robert Duncan Writing the Gay Community" (Damon 1993, 142-55).

Works Cited

Baraka, Amiri/LeRoi Jones. 1984. *The Autobiography of Amiri Baraka/LeRoi Jones.* New York: William Morrow.

Blaser, Robin. 1975. "The Practice of Outside." In *The Collected Books of Jack Spicer,* by Jack Spicer. Santa Barbara: Black Sparrow Press.

Brossard, Chandler. 1952. *Who Walk in Darkness.* New York: Grove Press.

Cándida Smith, Robert. 1995. *Utopia and Dissent: Art, Poetry, and Politics in California.* Berkeley: California University Press.

D'Emilio, John. 1986. *Sexual Politics, Sexual Communities: The Making of a Homosexual Subculture 1940-1980.* Chicago: Chicago University Press.

Damon, Maria. 1993. *The Dark End of the Street: Margins in American Vanguard Poetry.* Minneapolis: Minnesota University Press.

———. 1995. "Victors of Catastrophe: Beat Occlusions." In *Beat Culture and the New America. 1950-1965.* New York: Whitney Museum of American Art.

———. 1996. "Jazz-Jews, Jive and Gender: Ethnic Anxiety and the Politics of Jazz Argot." In *Jews and Other Differences: The New Jewish Cultural Studies,* ed. Daniel and Jonathan Boyarin. Minneapolis: University of Minnesota Press.

———. 1997a. "Callow But Not Shallow." Review of *707 Scott Street,* by John Wieners. *Xcp 3: Cross-Cultural Poetics* 3: 137-47.

———. 1997b. "Other Beats," *Hambone* 13 (Spring): 177-85.

Duncan, Robert. 1944. "The Homosexual in Society," *Politics* (August): 209-11.

———. 1966. "An African Elegy." In *The Years as Catches.* Berkeley: Oyez.

FitzGerald, Russell. n.d. *The Diary of Russell FitzGerald.* Unpublished.

Jonas, Stephen. 1994. *Selected Poems.* Ed. Joseph Torra. Hoboken NJ: Talisman House.

Jones, Hettie. 1991. *How I Became Hettie Jones.* New York: Penguin.

Kaufman, Bob. 1965. *Solitudes Crowded with Loneliness.* New York: New Directions.

———. 1968. "Unhistorical Events." In *Golden Sardine.* San Francisco: City Lights Books.

———. 1981. *The Ancient Rain: Poems 1956-1978.* New York: New Directions.

Killian, Kevin, and Lew Ellingham. 1998. *Poet, Be Like God: Jack Spicer and the San Francisco Renaissance.* Middletown: Wesleyan University Press.

Mailer, Norman. 1992. "Hipsters. "In *Advertisements for Myself.* 1959. Reprint. Cambridge: Harvard University Press.

Nielsen, Aldon Lynn. 1996. *Black Chant: Languages of African American Postmodernism.* New York: Cambridge University Press.

Roediger, David. 1993. *The Wages of Whiteness.* New York: Routledge.

Spicer, Jack. 1975. *The Collected Books of Jack Spicer.* Santa Barbara: Black Sparrow Press.

Vereen, Ben. 1999. Interview. In "I'll Make Me a World: A Twentieth-Century History of African Americans in the Arts." PBS. 1 February.

Wieners, John. 1997. *707 Scott Street.* Los Angeles. Sun and Moon Press.

FURTHER READING

Biographies

Clay, Mel. *Jazz—Jail and God: Bob Kaufman: An Impressionist Biography.* San Francisco: Androgyne Books, 1987, 82p.

An impressionistic biography of Kaufman, relying on personal accounts by the author.

Henderson, David. Introduction to *Cranial Guitar: Selected Poems,* by Bob Kaufman, edited by Gerald Nicosia. Minneapolis, Minn.: Coffee House Press, 1996, 165p.

Short biography and list of quotes by famous poets and others about Kaufman.

Criticism

Anderson, T. J. "Body and Soul: Bob Kaufman's *Golden Sardine.*" *African American Review* 34, no. 2 (summer 2000): 329-45.

Examines Kaufman's poetry as it relates to jazz.

Callaloo 25, no. 1 (winter 2002): 103-232.

Special section on Bob Kaufman, with introduction by Maria Damon and several essays by different authors.

Cherkovski, Neeli. *Elegy for Bob Kaufman.* Northville, Mich.: Sun Dog Press, 1996, 105p.

Collection of poems dedicated to the memory of Bob Kaufman, with introduction.

Lee, A. Robert, editor. "Black Beats: The Signifying Poetry of LeRoi Jones/Amiri Baraka, Ted Joans and Bob Kaufman." In *The Beat Generation Writers,* pp. 158-77. East Haven, Conn.: Pluto Press, 1996.

Analyzes the poetry of several black Beats, including Kaufman.

Lindberg, Kathryne V. "Bob Kaufman, Sir Real, and His Rather Surreal Self-Presentation." *Talisman* 11 (fall 1983): 167-82.

Examines Kaufman's poetry as resistance to a coherent self-representation.

Thomas, Lorenzo. "'Communicating by Horns': Jazz and Redemption in the Poetry of the Beats and the Black Arts Movement." *African American Review* 26, no. 2 (summer 1992): 291-8.

Examines Kaufman's relation to jazz.

OTHER SOURCES FROM GALE:

Additional coverage of Kaufman's life and career is contained in the following sources published by the Gale Group: *Black Writers,* Ed. 1; *Contemporary Authors,* Vols. 41-44R; *Contemporary Authors New Revision Series,* Vol. 22; *Contemporary Literary Criticism,* Vol. 49; *Dictionary of Literary Biography,* Vols. 16, 41; and *Literature Resource Center.*

JACK KEROUAC

(1922 - 1969)

(Born Jean-Louis Lebris de Kerouac) American novelist, poet, essayist, and nonfiction writer.

Kerouac is regarded as the one of the key figures of the Beat movement. He brought the term "Beat," meaning both "beaten down," or outcast, and "beatific," or full of spiritual joy, into common use to describe the condition of his generation. His 1957 novel *On the Road* gained widespread recognition, both positive and negative, for the unconventional lifestyle and literary techniques practiced by the Beats. Some passages of the book are considered early examples of the "spontaneous prose" method that Kerouac developed in an effort to escape the strictures of grammar and syntax. Consequently, *On the Road* moves with the same frenetic energy as the real-life road trips and drunken episodes that are chronicled in a narrative that eschews extensive characterizations or plot development. Kerouac used several of his friends, including poet Allen Ginsberg and novelist William S. Burroughs, as models for the prominent characters in the autobiographical narrative, as well as in many of his other works.

BIOGRAPHICAL INFORMATION

Born in a French-Canadian community in Lowell, Massachusetts, Kerouac was reared in a devout Roman Catholic family and educated in parochial schools. An outstanding athlete, he received a football scholarship to Columbia University, but withdrew from the university during the fall of his sophomore year. He joined the U.S. Navy in 1943 and was honorably discharged after six months as an "indifferent character." Kerouac worked for the remainder of World War II as a merchant seaman and later began associating with the bohemian crowd around Columbia, which included Ginsberg and Burroughs, both of whom were influential in Kerouac's intellectual and artistic coming of age as well as becoming major figures associated with the Beat movement. Like Ginsberg and Burroughs, many of Kerouac's friends among the Beats served as the basis for the characters in his novels. Poet Gary Snyder, for instance, inspired Japhy Ryder, the main character in *The Dharma Bums* (1958). The single most influential personality in Kerouac's circle of friends, and the protagonist in both *On the Road* and *Visions of Cody* (1972), was Neal Cassady. Kerouac saw the energetic, charismatic Cassady as the quintessential Beat figure—an independent spirit who lived unhindered by societal conventions. Kerouac also cited Cassady's stream-of-consciousness writing style, exemplified in his voluminous correspondence, as having inspired his own "spontaneous prose" technique. This free-flowing, fast-paced, and self-consciously poetic style of narrative, which is not observable in Kerouac's first novel, *The Town and the City* (1950), became widely imitated by later writers. With the initial publication of *On the Road*, Kerouac achieved sudden fame as the most conspicuous representative of the "beatnik" way of life. Subsequently, several of his novels were issued in quick succession as publishers rushed to capitalize on his popularity. Kerouac's shy nature and emotional instability, however, kept him from enjoying his fame: he was known to arrive at public appearances in a state of intoxication and failed in his sporadic attempts to withdraw from a life of celebrity in order to concentrate on writing. A sincere patriot and Catholic, Kerouac became increasingly bewildered by and alienated from his bohemian fans in the 1960s. He died from complications due to alcoholism in 1969.

MAJOR WORKS

Kerouac viewed his novels as comprising a series of interconnected autobiographical narratives in the manner of Marcel Proust's *A la recherche du temps perdu* (*Remembrance of Things Past*). The novels that compose "The Legend of Duluoz," as Kerouac called the totality of his works include *Visions of Gerard* (1963), which depicts the author's childhood as overshadowed by the death of his beloved brother Gerard at age nine; *Doctor Sax: Faust Part Three* (1959), a surrealistic portrait of Kerouac's boyhood memories and dreams; *Maggie Cassidy* (1959), a fictional account of Kerouac's first love; and *Vanity of Duluoz: An Adventurous Education, 1935-1946* (1968), which chronicles Kerouac's years of playing football at prep school and Columbia University. In *On the Road*, Kerouac wrote about his life in the late 1940s, focusing on the cross-country traveling he did during this time as well as his relationships with Ginsberg, Burroughs, and Cassady. *Visions of Cody*, viewed by many critics as a late revision of *On the Road*, retells the story in spontaneous prose. Kerouac wrote about his love affair in 1953 with an African-American woman in *The Subterraneans* (1958), and his adventures on the West Coast learning about Buddhism from Gary Snyder are delineated in *The Dharma Bums*. *Desolation Angels* (1965) covers the years just prior to the publication of *On the Road*, while *Big Sur* (1962) displays the bitterness and despair Kerouac experienced in the early 1960s and his descent into alcoholism.

CRITICAL RECEPTION

When first published, *On the Road* was rejected by many as a morally objectionable work. Kerouac, through his first-person narrator, Sal Paradise, enthusiastically describes the adventures that make up the book's narrative, including stealing, heavy drinking, drug use, and sexual promiscuity. To many critics of the time, Kerouac's novel signaled the moral demise of a generation. However, several reviewers disagreed with this assessment, noting the spiritual quest theme that permeates the novel and arguing that such themes made *On the Road* a descendent of American "road literature" as represented by such works as Mark Twain's *Adventures of Huckleberry Finn*. Although *On the Road* was once commonly considered to have inspired the peripatetic hippie generation of the 1960s, later evaluations have paid greater attention to the narrator's disillusionment with the life of the road at the conclusion of the novel. Some commentators now view *On the Road* as depicting the conflicting appeal of a contemplative, inner-directed life on the one hand, and an unexamined, outgoing existence on the other. More recent critical studies also evidence considerable interest in Kerouac's "spontaneous prose" method, viewing it as an extension of the "stream-of-consciousness" technique used by James Joyce. While *On the Road* and subsequent works by Kerouac once stunned the public and the literary establishment, the enduring attraction these works hold for both readers and critics argues for their importance in the canon of modern American literature.

PRINCIPAL WORKS

The Town and the City (novel) 1950

On the Road (novel) 1957

The Dharma Bums (novel) 1958

The Subterraneans (novel) 1958

Doctor Sax: Faust Part Three (novel) 1959

Excerpts from Visions of Cody (novel) 1959; enlarged edition, 1972

Maggie Cassidy (novel) 1959

Mexico City Blues (poetry) 1959

The Scripture of the Golden Eternity (poetry) 1960

Tristessa (novel) 1960

The Book of Dreams (diaries) 1961

Big Sur (novel) 1962

Visions of Gerard (novel) 1963

Desolation Angels (novel) 1965

Satori in Paris (novel) 1966

Vanity of Duluoz: An Adventurous Education, 1935-1946 (novel) 1968

Pic (novel) 1971

Visions of Cody (novel) 1972

Book of Blues (poetry) 1995

Jack Kerouac: Selected Letters, 1940-1956 (letters) 1995

Some of the Dharma (nonfiction) 1997

Jack Kerouac: Selected Letters, 1957-1969 (letters) 1999

Door Wide Open: A Beat Love Affair in Letters, 1957-1958 (letters) 2000

Book of Haikus (poetry) 2003

PRIMARY SOURCES

JACK KEROUAC (ESSAY DATE AUTUMN 1957)

SOURCE: Kerouac, Jack. "Essentials of Spontaneous Prose." *Black Mountain Review* 7 (autumn 1957): 226-8.

Kerouac believed that writing spontaneously produced the most honest, direct material. In this brief article, he outlines the basic process for the practice of spontaneous prose.

Set-Up

The object is set before the mind, either in reality, as in sketching (before a landscape or teacup or old face) or is set in the memory wherein it becomes the sketching from memory of a definite image-object.

Procedure

Time being of the essence in the purity of speech, sketching language is undisturbed flow from the mind of personal secret idea-words, *blowing* (as per jazz musician) on subject of image.

Method

No periods separating sentence-structures already arbitrarily riddled by false colons and timid usually needless commas—but the vigorous space dash separating rhetorical breathing (as jazz musician drawing breath between outblown phrases)—"measured pauses which are the essentials of our speech"—"divisions of the *sounds* we hear"—"time and how to note it down." (William Carlos Williams)

Scoping

Not "selectivity" of expression but following free deviation (association) of mind into limitless blow-on-subject seas of thought, swimming in sea of English with no discipline other than rhythms of rhetorical exhalation and expostulated statement, like a fist coming down on a table with each complete utterance, bang! (the space dash)—Blow as deep as you want—write as deeply, fish as far down as you want, satisfy yourself first, then reader cannot fail to receive telepathic shock and meaning-excitement by same laws operating in his own human mind.

Lag in Procedure

No pause to think of proper word but the infantile pileup of scatalogical buildup words till satisfaction is gained, which will turn out to be a great appending rhythm to a thought and be in accordance with Great Law of timing.

Timing

Nothing is muddy that *runs in time* and to laws of *time*—Shakespearian stress of dramatic need to speak now in own unalterable way or forever hold tongue—*no revisions* (except obvious rational mistakes, such as names or *calculated* insertions in act of not writing but *inserting*).

Center of Interest

Begin not from preconceived idea of what to say about image but from jewel center of interest in subject of image at *moment* of writing, and write outwards swimming in sea of language to peripheral release and exhaustion—Do not afterthink except for poetic or P. S. reasons. Never afterthink to "improve" or defray impressions, as, the best writing is always the most painful personal wrungout tossed from cradle warm protective mind—tap from yourself the song of yourself, *blow!*—*now!*—*your* way is your only way— "good"—or "bad"—always honest, ("ludicrous"), spontaneous, "confessional" interesting, because not "crafted." Craft *is* craft.

Structure of Work

Modern bizarre structures (science fiction, etc.) arise from language being dead, "different" themes give illusion of "new" life. Follow roughly outlines in outfanning movement over subject, as river rock, so mindflow over jewel-center need (run your mind over it, *once*) arriving at pivot, where what was dim-formed "beginning" becomes sharp-necessitating "ending" and language shortens in race to wire of time-race of work, following laws of Deep Form, to conclusion, last words, last trickle—Night is The End.

ON THE SUBJECT OF...

JOAN HAVERTY KEROUAC

Joan Haverty became Kerouac's second wife in 1950, and supported them both while Kerouac wrote *On the Road*. Shortly thereafter the marriage ended, and Joan moved to Albany, New York, where she was living with her parents when her daughter, Jan Kerouac, was born on February 16, 1952. Joan and Kerouac battled publicly and privately over Jan's paternity and financial support for many years. Between 1982 (the year she was diagnosed with breast cancer) and 1990 (the year she finally succumbed to the disease), Joan captured her experiences with Kerouac in writing. A manuscript was pieced together by Jan and several of Joan's friends after her death, and was published in 2000 as *Nobody's Wife*. A brief excerpt from this memoir appears below.

WHEN JOAN MET NEAL: 1951

As [Neal] talked, the sound of Jack's proposal to me echoed in my memory. I had been unable until now to reconcile the audacity and presumptuousness he'd shown that night with the timid, suspicious personality I had now come to know so well. Now I saw that, in order to get the job done, and reinforced by the smoking of a lot of grass, Jack had become the embodiment of Neal. He had done it in the same way he automatically became W. C. Fields when he drank. The garb or disguise of one hero or another allayed his fears and suspicions and enabled him to surge forth and meet the challenge, whatever it was.

Kerouac, Joan Haverty. An excerpt from "Chapter 17: Meeting Neal Cassady." *Nobody's Wife: The Smart Aleck and The King of the Beats*. Berkeley, Calif: Creative Arts Book Co., 2000.

Mental State

If possible write "without consciousness" in semitrance (as Yeats' later "trance writing") allowing subconscious to admit in own uninhibited interesting necessary and so "modern" language what conscious art would censor, and write excitedly, swiftly, with writing-or-typing-cramps, in accordance (as from center to periphery) with laws of orgasm, Reich's "beclouding of consciousness." *Come* from within, out—to relaxed and said.

JACK KEROUAC (NOVEL DATE 1957)

SOURCE: Kerouac, Jack. "Chapter 2." In *On the Road*, pp. 3-13. New York: Viking, 1957.

Often cited along with Ginsberg's Howl *as a definitive work of the Beat Generation,* On the Road *has endured as a highly influential work in twentieth-century literature. In the following excerpt, the character Sal Paradise writes of approaching New York City at the outset of his journey West.*

I'd been poring over maps of the United States in Paterson for months, even reading books about the pioneers and savoring names like Platte and Cimarron and so on, and on the road-map was one long red line called Route 6 that led from the tip of Cape Cod clear to Ely, Nevada, and there dipped down to Los Angeles. I'll just stay on all the way to Ely, I said to myself and confidently started. To get to 6 I had to go up to Bear Mountain. Filled with dreams of what I'd do in Chicago, in Denver, and then finally in San Fran, I took the Seventh Avenue Subway to the end of the line at 242nd Street, and there took a trolley into Yonkers; in downtown Yonkers I transferred to an outgoing trolley and went to the city limits on the east bank of the Hudson River. If you drop a rose in the Hudson River at its mysterious source in the Adirondacks, think of all the places it journeys as it goes to sea forever—think of that wonderful Hudson Valley. I started hitching up the thing. Five scattered rides took me to the desired Bear Mountain Bridge, where Route 6 arched in from New England. It began to rain in torrents when I was let off there. It was mountainous. Route 6 came over the river, wound around a traffic circle, and disappeared into the wilderness. Not only was there no traffic but the rain come down in buckets and I had no shelter. I had to run under some pines to take cover; this did no good; I began crying and swearing and socking myself on the head for being such a damn fool. I was forty miles north of New York; all the way up I'd been worried about the fact that on this, my big opening day, I was only moving north instead of the so-longed for west. Now I was stuck on my northernmost hangup. I ran a quarter-mile to an abandoned cute English-style filling station and stood under the dripping eaves. High up over my head the great hairy Bear Mountain sent down thunderclaps that put the fear of God in me. All I could see were smoky trees and dismal wilderness rising to the skies. "What the hell am I doing up here?" I cursed, I cried for Chicago. "Even now they're all having a big time, they're doing this, I'm not there, when will I get there!"—and so on. Finally a car stopped at the empty filling station; the man and the two women in it wanted to study a map. I stepped right up and gestured in the rain; they consulted; I looked like a maniac, of course, with my hair all wet, my shoes sopping. My shoes, damm fool that I am, were Mexican huaraches, plantlike sieves not fit for the rainly night of America and the raw road night. But the people let me in and rode me *back* to Newburgh, which I accepted as a better alternative than being trapped in the Bear Mountain wilderness all night. "Besides," said the man, "there's no traffic passes through 6. If you want to go to Chicago you'd be better going across the Holland Tunnel in New York and head for Pittsburth," and I knew he was right. It was my dream that screwed up, the stupid hearthside idea that it would be wonderful to follow one great red line across America instead of trying various roads and routes.

In Newburgh it had stopped raining. I walked down to the river and I had to ride back to New York in a bus with a delegation of schoolteachers coming back from a weekend in the mountains— chatter chatter blah-blah, and me swearing for all the time and money I'd wasted, and telling myself, I wanted to go west and here I'd been all day and into the night going up and down, north and south, like something that can't get started.

JACK KEROUAC (ESSAY DATE SPRING 1959)

SOURCE: Kerouac, Jack. "Belief and Technique for Modern Prose." *Evergreen Review* 2 (spring 1959): 57.

Kerouac composed this brief list of suggestions for writers wishing to achieve a "modern" sensibility in their work.

List of Essentials

1. Scribbled secret notebooks, and wild typewritten pages, for yr own joy

2. Submissive to everything, open, listening

3. Try never get drunk outside yr own house

4. Be in love with yr life

5. Something that you feel will find its own form

6. Be crazy dumbsaint of the mind

7. Blow as deep as you want to blow

8. Write what you want bottomless from bottom of the mind

9. The unspeakable visions of the individual

10. No time for poetry but exactly what is

11. Visionary tics shivering in the chest

12. In tranced fixation dreaming upon object before you

13. Remove literary, grammatical and syntactical inhibition

14. Like Proust be an old teahead of time

15. Telling the true story of the world in interior monolog

16. The jewel center of interest is the eye within the eye

17. Write in recollection and amazement for yourself

18. Work from pithy middle eye out, swimming in language sea

19. Accept loss forever

20. Believe in the holy contour of life

21. Struggle to sketch the flow that already exists intact in mind

22. Dont think of words when you stop but to see picture better

23. Keep track of every day the date emblazoned in yr morning

24. No fear or shame in the dignity of yr experience, language & knowledge

25. Write for the world to read and see yr exact pictures of it

26. Bookmovie is the movie in words, the visual American form

27. In praise of Character in the Bleak inhuman Loneliness

28. Composing wild, undisciplined, pure, coming in from under, crazier the better

29. You're a Genius all the time

30. Writer-Director of Earthly movies Sponsored & Angeled in Heaven

JACK KEROUAC (POEM DATE 1960)

SOURCE: Kerouac, Jack. "Scripture of the Golden Eternity." In *Scripture of the Golden Eternity*, pp. 23-61. San Francisco: City Lights, 1970.

Kerouac wrote the following poem in response to a suggestion from fellow Beat Gary Snyder that he write his first Sutra. In 1960, when he presented it for publication, he said, "While I was writing this, I thought I knew what it meant, but now I don't know anymore."

1

Did I create that sky? Yes, for, if it was
anything other than a conception in my mind
I wouldnt have said "Sky"—That is why I am the

golden eternity. There are not two of us here, reader and writer, but one, one golden eternity, One-Which-It-Is, That-Which-Everything-Is.

2

The awakened Buddha to show the way, the chosen Messiah to die in the degradation of sentience, is the golden eternity. One that is what is, the golden eternity, or, God, or, Tathagata—the name. The Named One. The human God. Sentient Godhood. Animate Divine. The Deified One. The Verified One. The Free One. The Liberator. The Still One. The settled One. The Established One. Golden Eternity. All is Well. The Empty One. The Ready One. The Quitter. The Sitter. The Justified One. The Happy One.

3

That sky, if it was anything other than an illusion of my mortal mind I wouldnt have said "that sky." Thus I made that sky, I am the golden eternity. I am Mortal Golden Eternity.

4

I was awakened to show the way, chosen to die in the degradation of life, because I am Mortal Golden Eternity.

5

I am the golden eternity in mortal animate form.

6

Strictly speaking, there is no me, because all is emptiness. I am empty, I am non-existent. All is bliss.

7

This truth law has no more reality than the world.

8

You are the golden eternity because there is no me and no you, only one golden eternity.

9

The Realizer. Entertain no imaginations whatever, for the thing is a no-thing. Knowing this then is Human Godhood.

10

This world is the movie of what everything is, it is one movie, made of the same stuff throughout, belonging to nobody, which is what everything is.

11

If we were not all the golden eternity we wouldnt be here. Because we are here we cant help being pure. To tell man to be pure on account of the punishing angel that punishes the bad and the rewarding angel that rewards the good would be like telling the water "Be Wet"—Never the less, all things depend on supreme reality, which is already established as the record of Karma earned-fate.

12

God is not outside us but is just us, the living and the dead, the never-lived and never-died. That we should learn it only now, is supreme reality, it was written a long time ago in the archives of universal mind, it is already done, there's no more to do.

13

This is the knowledge that sees the golden eternity in all things, which is us, you, me, and which is no longer us, you, me.

14

What name shall we give it which hath no name, the common eternal matter of the mind? If we were to call it essence, some might think it meant perfume, or gold, or honey. It is not even mind. It is not even discussible, groupable into words; it is not even endless, in fact it is not even mysterious or inscrutably inexplicable; it is what is; it is that; it is this. We could easily call the golden eternity "This." But "what's in a name?" asked Shakespeare. The golden eternity by another name would be as sweet. A Tathagata, a God, a Buddha by another name, an Allah, a Sri Krishna, a Coyote, a Brahma, a Mazda, a Messiah, an Amida, an Aremedeia, a Maitreya, a Palalakonuh, 1 2 3 4 5 6 7 8 would be as sweet. The golden eternity is X, the golden eternity is A, the golden eternity is △, the golden eternity is ○, the golden eternity is □, the golden eternity is t-h-e-g-o-l-d-e-n-e-t-e-r-n-i-t-y. In the beginning was the word; before the beginning, in the beginningless infinite neverendingness, was the essence. Both the word "god" and the essence of the word, are emptiness. The form of emptiness which is emptiness having taken the form of form, is what you see and hear and feel right now, and what you taste and smell and think as you read this. Wait awhile, close your eyes, let your breathing stop three seconds or so, listen to the inside silence in the womb of the world, let your hands and nerve-ends drop, re-recognize

the bliss you forgot, the emptiness and
essence and ecstasy of ever having been and
ever to be the golden eternity. This is
the lesson you forgot.

15

The lesson was taught long ago in the other
world systems that have naturally changed
into the empty and awake, and are here
now smiling in our smile and scowling in our
scowl. It is only like the golden eternity
pretending to be smiling and scowling to
itself; like a ripple on the smooth ocean of
knowing. The fate of humanity is to vanish
into the golden eternity, return pouring into
its hands which are not hands. The navel shall
receive, invert, and take back what'd issued
forth; the ring of flesh shall close; the personali-
    ties
of long dead heroes are blank dirt.

16

The point is we're waiting, not how comfortable
we are while waiting. Paleolithic man waited by
caves for the realization of why he was there,
and hunted; modern men wait in beautified
homes and try to forget death and birth. We're
waiting for the realization that this is the
golden eternity.

17

It came on time.

18

There is a blessedness surely to be believed,
and that is that everything abides in
eternal ecstasy, now and forever.

19

Mother Kali eats herself back. All things but
come to go. All these holy forms, unmanifest,
not even forms, truebodies of blank bright
ecstasy, abiding in a trance, "in emptiness and
silence' as it is pointed out in the Diamond-
    cutter,
asked to be only what they are: *Glad.*

20

The secret God-grin in the trees and in the
    teapot,
in ashes and fronds, fire and brick, flesh and
mental human hope. All things, far from yearn-
    ing
to be re-united with God, had never left
    themselves
and here they are, Dharmakaya, the body of the
truth law, the universal Thisness.

21

"Beyond the reach of change and fear, beyond
all praise and blame," the Lankavatara Scripture

knows to say, is he who is what he is in time and
    in
time-less-ness, in ego and in ego-less-ness, in self
and in self-less-ness.

22

Stare deep into the world before you as if it were
the void: innumerable holy ghosts, buddhies,
and savior gods there hide, smiling. All the
atoms emitting light inside wavehood, there is
no personal separation of any of it. A hum-
    mingbird
can come into a house and a hawk will not: so
    rest
and be assured. While looking for the light, you
may suddenly be devoured by the darkness
and find the true light.

23

Things dont tire of going and coming.
The flies end up with the delicate viands.

24

The cause of the world's woe is birth,
The cure of the world's woe is a bent stick.

25

Though it is everything, strictly speaking
there is no golden eternity because everything
is nothing: there are no things and no goings
    and
comings: for all is emptiness, and emptiness is
these forms, emptiness is this one formhood.

26

All these selfnesses have already vanished.
Einstein measured that this present universe is
    an
expanding bubble, and you know what that
    means.

27

Discard such definite imaginations of
    phenomena
as your own self, thou human being, thou'rt a
numberless mass of sun-motes: each mote a
    shrine.
The same as to your shyness of other selves,
selfness as divided into infinite numbers of be-
    ings,
or selfness as identified as one self existing
eternally. Be obliging and noble, be generous
with your time and help and possessions, and be
kind, because the emptiness of this little place
of flesh you carry around and call your soul,
your entity, is the same emptiness in every direc-
    tion
of space unmeasurable emptiness, the same, one,
and holy emptiness everywhere: why be selfy
    and

unfree, Man God, in your dream? Wake up,
    thou'rt
selfless and free. "Even and upright your mind
abides nowhere," states Hui Neng of China.
We're all in heaven now.

28

Roaring dreams take place in a perfectly silent
mind. Now that we know this, throw the raft
    away.

29

Are you tightward and are you mean, those are
the true sins, and sin is only a conception of
    ours,
due to long habit. Are you generous and are
you kind, those are the true virtues, and they're
only conceptions. The golden eternity rests
    beyond
sin and virtue, is attached to neither, is attached
to nothing, is unattached, because the golden
eternity is Alone. The mold has rills but it is one
mold. The field has curves but it is one field.
All things are different forms of the same thing.
I call it the golden eternity—what do you
call it, brother? for the blessing and merit
of virtue, and the punishment and bad fate
of sin, are alike just so many words.

30

Sociability is a big smile, and a big smile is
nothing but teeth. Rest and be kind.

31

There's no need to deny that evil thing called
GOOGOO, which doesnt exist, just as there's no
need to deny that evil thing called Sex and
    Rebirth,
which also doesn't exist, as it is only a form of
emptiness. The bead of semen comes from a
    long
line of awakened natures that were your parent,
a holy flow, a succession of saviors pouring from
the womb of the dark void and back into it,
fantastic magic imagination of the lightning,
    flash,
plays, dreams, not even plays, dreams.

32

"The womb of exuberant fertility," Ashvhag-
    hosha
called it, radiating forms out of its womb of
exuberant emptiness. In emptiness there is no
Why, no knowledge of Why, no ignorance of
    Why,
no asking and no answering of Why, and no
significance attached to this.

33

A disturbed and frightened man is like the
golden eternity experimentally pretending at

feeling the disturbed-and-frightened mood; a
calm and joyous man, is like the golden eternity
pretending at experimenting with that experi-
    ence;
a man experiencing his Sentient Being, is like
the golden eternity pretending at trying that out
too; a man who has no thoughts, is like the
    golden
eternity pretending at being itself; because
the emptiness of everything has no beginning
and no end and at present is infinite.

34

"Love is all in all," said Sainte Therese, choosing
Love for her vocation and pouring out her
happiness, from her garden by the gate, with
a gentle smile, pouring roses on the earth,
so that the beggar in the thunderbolt received
of the endless offering of her dark void.
Man goes a-beggaring into nothingness.
"Ignorance is the father, Habit-Energy is
the Mother." Opposites are not the same
for the same reason they are the same.

35

The words "atoms of dust" and "the great
universes" are only words. The idea that they
imply is only an idea. The belief that we live
    here
in this existence, divided into various beings,
passing food in and out of ourselves, and casting
    off
husks of bodies one after another with no cessa-
    tion
and no definite or particular discrimination, is
only an idea. The seat of our Immortal Intel-
    ligence
can be seen in that beating light between the
    eyes
the Wisdom Eye of the ancients: we know what
we're doing: we're not disturbed: because
we're like the golden eternity pretending at
playing the magic cardgame and making believe
it's real, it's a big dream, a joyous ecstasy of
words and ideas and flesh, an ethereal flower
unfolding a folding back, a movie, an
exuberant bunch of lines bounding emptiness,
the womb of Avalokitesvara, a vast secret
silence, springtime in the Void, happy young
gods talking and drinking on a cloud. Our
32,000 chillicosms bear all the marks of
excellence. Blind milky light fills our night;
and the morning is crystal.

36

Give a gift to your brother, but there's no gift
to compare with the giving of assurance that he
is the golden eternity. The true understanding of
this would bring tears to your eyes. The other
shore is right here, forgive and forget, protect
and reassure. Your tormenters will be purified.
Raise thy diamond hand. Have faith and wait.
The course of your days is a river rumbling over

your rocky back. You're sitting at the bottom of
the
world with a head of iron. Religion is thy sad
heart. You're the golden eternity and it must be
done by you. And means one thing: Nothing-
Ever-Happened. This is the golden eternity.

37

When the Prince of the Kalinga severed the
flesh from the limbs and body of Buddha, even
then the Buddha was free from any such ideas as
his own self, other self, living beings
divided into many selves, or living beings
united and identified into one eternal self.
The golden eternity isnt "me." Before you
can know that you're dreaming you'll wake up,
Atman. Had the Buddha, the Awakened One,
cherished any of these imaginary judgments
of and about things, he would have fallen
into impatience and hatred in his suffering.
Instead, like Jesus on the Cross he saw the
light and died kind, loving all living things.

38

The world was spun out of a blade of grass:
the world was spun out of a mind. Heaven
was spun out of a blade of grass: heaven was
spun
out of a mind. Neither will do you much good,
neither will do you much harm. The Oriental
imperturbed, is the golden eternity.

39

He is called a Yogi, his is called a Priest,
a Minister, a Brahmin, a Parson, a Chaplain,
a Roshi, a Laoshih, a Master, a Patriarch, a Pope,
a Spiritual Commissar, a Counselor, and Adviser,
a Bodhisattva-Mahasattva, an Old Man, a Saint,
a Shaman, a Leader, who thinks nothing of
himself as separate from another self, not
higher nor lower, no stages and no definite
attainments, no mysterious stigmata or secret
holyhood, no wild dark knowledge and no
venerable authoritativeness, nay a giggling sage
sweeping out of the kitchen with a broom. After
supper, a silent smoke. Because there is no
definite teaching: the world is undisciplined.
Nature endlessly in every direction inward
to your body and outward into space.

40

Meditate outdoors. The dark trees at night
are not really the dark trees at night, it's
only the golden eternity.

41

A mosquito as big as Mount Everest is much
bigger than you think: a horse's hoof is more
delicate than it looks. An altar consecrated to
the golden eternity, filled with roses and lotuses
and diamonds, is the cell of the humble prisoner,

the cell so cold and dreary. Boethius kissed the
Robe of the Mother Truth in a Roman dungeon.

42

Do you think the emptiness of the sky will ever
crumble away? Every little child knows that
everybody will go to heaven. Knowing that
nothing ever happened is not really knowing
that nothing ever happened, it's the golden
eternity.
In other words, nothing can compare with telling
your brother and your sister that what happened,
what is happening, and what will happen, never
really happened, is not really happening and
never
will happen, it is only the golden eternity.
Nothing was ever born, nothing will ever die.
Indeed, it didnt even happen that you heard
about
golden eternity through the accidental reading of
this scripture. The thing is easily false. There
are no warnings whatever issuing from the
golden eternity: do what you want.

43

Even in dreams be kind, because anyway there is
no time, no space, no mind. "It's all not-born,"
said Bankei of Japan, whose mother heard this
from her son did what we call "died happy."
And even if she had died unhappy, dying
unhappy
is not really dying unhappy, it's the golden
eternity.
It's impossible to exist, it's impossible to be
persecuted, it's impossible to miss your reward.

44

Eight hundred and four thousand myriads of
Awakened Ones throughout numberless swirls
of epochs appeared to work hard to save a grain
of sand, and it was only the golden eternity.
And their combined reward will be no greater
and
no lesser than what will be won by a piece of
dried turd. It's a reward beyond thought.

45

When you've understood this scripture, throw it
away. If you cant understand this scripture,
throw it away. I insist on your freedom.

46

O Everlasting Eternity, all things and all truth
laws are no-things, in three ways, which is the
same way: AS THINGS OF TIME they dont
exist and never came, because they're already
gone
and there is no time. AS THINGS OF SPACE they
dont exist because there is no furthest atom than

can be found or weighed or grasped, it is emptiness
through and through, matter and empty space
too.
AS THINGS OF MIND they dont exist, because
the mind that conceives and makes them out
does
so by seeing, hearing touching, smelling, tasting,
and mentally-noticing and without this mind
they
would not be seen or heard or felt or smelled or
tasted or mentally-noticed, they are
discriminated
that which they're not necessarily by imaginary
judgments of the mind, they are actually
dependent
on the mind that makes them out, by
themselves
they are no-things, they are really mental, seen
only
of the mind, they are really empty visions of the
mind, heaven is a vision, everything is a vision.
What does it mean that I am in this endless
universe
thinking I'm a man sitting under the stars on the
terrace of earth, but actually empty and awake
throughout the emptiness and awakedness of
everything? It means that I am empty and
awake, knowing that I am empty and awake,
and that there's no difference between me and
anything else. It means that I have attained
to that which everything is.

47

The-Attainer-To-That-Which-Everything-Is,
the Sanskrit Tathagata, has no ideas whatever
but abides in essence identically with the essence
of all things, which is what it is, in emptiness
and
silence. Imaginary meaning stretched to make
mountains and as far as the germ is concerned it
stretched even further to make molehills. A
million souls dropped through hell but nobody
saw them or counted them. A lot of large people
isnt really a lot of large people, it's only the
golden eternity. When St. Francis went to heaven
he did not add to heaven nor detract from earth.
Locate silence, possess space, spot me the ego.
"From the beginning," said the Sixth Patriarch
of the China School, "not a thing is."

48

He who loves all life with his pity and
intelligence isnt really he who loves all life
with his pity and intelligence, it's only natural.
The universe is fully known because it is
ignored. Enlightenment comes when you dont
care. This is a good tree stump I'm sitting on.
You cant even grasp your own pain let alone
your eternal reward. I love you because you're
me. I love you because there's nothing else
to do. It's just the natural golden eternity.

49

What does it mean that those trees and
mountains are magic and unreal?—It means
that those trees and mountains are magic and
unreal. What does it mean that those trees and
mountains are not magic but real?— it means
that those trees and mountains are not magic
but real. Men are just making imaginary
judgments both ways, and all the time it's
just the same natural golden eternity.

50

If the golden eternity was anything other than
mere words, you could not have said "golden
eternity." This means that the words are used
to point at the endless nothingness of reality.
If the endless nothingness of reality was
anything
other than mere words, you could not have said
"endless nothingness of reality," you could not
have said it. This means that the golden eternity
is out of our word-reach, it refuses steadfastly
to be described, it runs away from us and leads
us in. The name is not really the name. The
same
way, you could not have said "this world" if this
world was anything other than mere words.
There's
nothing there but just that. They've long known
that there's nothing to life but just the living of
it.
It Is What It Is and That's All It Is.

51

There's no system of teaching and no reward
for teaching the golden eternity, because
nothing has happened. In the golden eternity
teaching and reward havent even vanished let
alone
appeared. The golden eternity doesnt even have
to
be perfect. It is very silly of me to talk about
it. I talk about it simply because there's no command or
reward. I talk about it simply because here I am
dreaming that I talk about it in a dream already
ended, ages ago, from which I'm already awake,
and
it was only an empty dreaming, in fact nothing
whatever, in fact nothing ever happened at all.
The beauty of attaining the golden eternity is
that nothing will be acquired, at last.

52

Kindness and sympathy, understanding and
encouragement, these give: they are better
than just presents and gifts: no reason in the
world why not. Anyhow, be nice. Remember
the golden eternity is yourself. "If someone will
simply practice kindness," said Gotama to
Subhuti, "he will soon attain highest perfect
wisdom." Then he added: "Kindness after all
is only a word and it should be done on the spot

without thought of kindness." By practicing
kindness all over with everyone you will soon
come into the holy trance, infinite distinctions
of personalities will become what they really
mysteriously are, our common and eternal
  blissstuff,
the pureness of everything forever, the great
  bright
essence of mind, even and one thing everywhere
  the
holy eternal milky love, the white light
  everywhere
everything, emptybliss, svaha, shining, ready,
  and
awake, the compassion in the sound of silence,
  the
swarming myriad trillionaire you are.

53

Everything's alright, form is emptiness
and emptiness is form, and we're here forever, in
one form or another, which is empty.
    Everything's
alright, we're not here, there, or anywhere.
Everything's alright, cats sleep.

54

The everlasting and tranquil essence, look
    around
and see the smiling essence everywhere. How
wily was the world made, Maya, not-even-made.

55

There's the world in the daylight. If it was
completely dark you wouldnt see it but it would
still be there. If you close your eyes you really see
what it's like: mysterious particle-swarming
emptiness. On the moon big mosquitos of straw
know this in the kindness of their hearts. Truly
speaking, unrecognizably sweet it all is.
Don't worry about nothing.

56

Imaginary judgments about things, in this
Nothing-Ever-Happened wonderful Void,
you dont even have to reject them, let alone
accept them. "That looks like a tree, let's
call it a tree," said Coyote to Earthmaker at
the beginning, and they walked around the
rootdrinker patting their bellies.

57

Perfectly selfless, the beauty of it, the butterfly
doesnt take it as a personal achievement, he just
disappears through the trees. You too, kind and
humble and not-even-here, it wasnt in a greedy
mood that you saw the light that belongs to
everybody.

58

Look at your little finger, the emptiness of it is
no different that the emptiness of infinity.

59

Cats yawn because they realize
that there's nothing to do.

60

Up in heaven you wont remember all these
tricks of yours. You wont even sigh "Why?"
Whether as atomic dust or as great cities, what's
the difference in all this stuff. A tree is still
only a rootdrinker. The puma's twisted face
continues to look at the blue sky with sightless
eyes, Ah sweet divine and indescribable verdur-
  ous
paradise planted in mid-air! Caitanya, it's only
consciousness. Not with thoughts of your mind,
but in the believing sweetness of your heart,
you snap the link and open the golden door
and disappear into the bright room, the everlasting
ecstasy, eternal Now. Soldier, follow me!—there
never was a war. Arjuna, dont fight!—why
fight over nothing? Bless and sit down.

61

I remember that I'm supposed to be a man and
consciousness and I focus my eyes and the
print reappears and the words of the poor book
are saying, "The world, as God has made it"
and there are no words in my pitying heart
to express the knowless loveliness of the
trance there was before I read those words,
I had no such idea that there was a world.

62

This world has no marks, signs, or evidence of
existence, nor the noises in it, like accident
of wind or voices or heehawing animals,
yet listen closely the eternal hush of silence
goes on and on throughout all this, and has
    been
going on, and will go on and on. This is because
the world is nothing but a dream and is just
    thought
of and the everlasting eternity pays no attention
to it. At night under the moon, or in a quiet
room, hush now, the secret music of the Unborn
goes on and on, beyond conception, awake
    beyond
existence. Properly speaking, awake is not really
awake because the golden eternity never went to
sleep; you can tell by the constant sound of
Silence which cuts through this world like a
magic diamond through the trick of your not
realizing that your mind caused the world.

63

The God of the American Plateau Indian was
Coyote. He says: "Earth! those beings living on
your surface, none of them disappearing, will
all be transformed. When I have spoken to them,
when they have spoken to me, from that mo-
    ment

on, their words and their bodies which they usually use to move about with, will all change. I will not have heard them."

64

I was smelling flowers in the yard, and when I stood up I took a deep breath and the blood all rushed to my brain and I woke up dead on my back in the grass. I had apparently fainted, or died, for about sixty seconds. My neighbor saw me but he thought I had just suddenly thrown myself on the grass to enjoy the sun. During that timeless moment of unconscious-
     ness
I saw the golden eternity. I saw heaven. In it nothing had ever happened, the events of a million years ago were just as phantom and ungraspable as the events of now or of a million years from now, or the events of the next ten minutes. It was perfect, the golden solitude, the golden emptiness, Something-Or-Other,
     something
surely humble. There was a rapturous ring of silence abiding perfectly. There was no question of being alive or not being alive, of likes and dislikes, of near or far, no question of giving or gratitude, no question of mercy or judgment, or of suffering or its opposite or anything.
It was the womb itself, aloneness, alaya vijnana the universal store, the Great Free Treasure, the Great Victory, infinite completion, the joyful mysterious essence of Arrangement. It seemed like one smiling smile, one adorable adoration, one gracious and adorable charity, everlasting safety, refreshing afternoon, roses, infinite brilliant immaterial gold ash, the Golden Age. The "golden" came from the sun in my eyelids, and the "eternity" from my sudden instant realization as I woke up that I had just been where it all came from and where it was all returning, the everlasting So, and so never coming or going; therefore I call it the golden eternity but you can call it anything you want. As I regained consciousness I felt so
     sorry
I had a body and a mind suddenly realizing I didn't even have a body and a mind and noth-
     ing
had ever happened and everything is alright forever and forever and forever, O thank you thank you thank you.

65

This is the first teaching from the golden eternity.

66

The second teaching from the golden eternity is that there never was a first teaching from the golden eternity. So be sure.

JACK KEROUAC (ESSAY DATE MARCH 1968)

SOURCE: Kerouac, Jack. "In the Ring." *Atlantic Monthly* 221, no. 3 (March 1968): 110-1.

In the following article, written a year before Kerouac's death, the author expounds upon the arts of pugilism and wrestling.

My jewel center of interest when I think of sports as is, or as we say in the academic circles, *per se,* which means "as is" in Latin, is that sight I had one time of a young teen-age boxer hurrying down the street with a small blue bag in which all his fundamental things were packed: jock-strap I guess (I know), trunks, liniment, toothbrush, money, vitamin pills mayhap, T-shirts, sweat shirt, mouthpiece for all I know, under the grimly drab lamps of New England on a winter night on his way to, say, Lewiston Maine for a semifinal light-weight bout for 10 bucks a throw for all I know, or for (O worse!) Worcester Massachusetts or Portland Maine, or Laconia N.H., to the Grey-hound or Trailways bus a-hurrying and where his father is I'll never have known, or his mother in what gray tenement, or his sisters or brothers in what war and lounge—With a nose not yet bro-ken, and luminous eyes, and meaningful glance at the sidewalk 'pon which he pounds to his destination the likes of which, whatever it ever became, shall never be visited on any angel that was fallen from heaven—I mean it, what's the sense of knocking your brains out for a few bucks?—I saw this guy outside the little training gym my father ran in Centerville, Lowell Mass., about 1930, when he first introduced me to sports by taking me in there to watch the boys hammer away at punching bags and big sand bags, and if you ever see an amateur heavyweight whacking away full-fisted at a sandbag and making the whole gym creak, you'll learn never to start a fight with any big boy you ever do meet in any bar from Portland Maine to Portland Oregon—And the young pug's name on the street was probably Bobby Sweet.

I was 8 at the time and soon after that my big fat cigarsmoking Pa (a printer by trade) had turned the place into a wrestling club, organization, gymnasium, and promotion, call it what you will, but the same guys who were boxers the year before were now wrestlers; especially old Roland Bouthelier, who was my father's unofficial chauf-feur 'cause my father couldn't drive his 1929 Ford himself his legs being too short, or him having to try to talk too much while driving, and Roland being also a young friend of the family's (about 22) and a worker in his printing plant to boot—

Now Roland was a wrestler and my sister Nin (10) and I always beseeched him to show us his muscles when he came in the house for occasional supper and certainly for holiday suppers and he always obliged and Nin hung from one biceps and I hung from the other, where . . . What a build! Like Mister America. One time he swallowed his tongue and almost choked at Salisbury Beach. He had a touch of epilepsy. During his youth there, my father was his friend and employer and protector. No capitalism involved, as tho a two-bit wrestling promoter and a one-bit printer could be a capitalist in a city of 100,000 people and him as honest as the day pretended to be long.

So I remember the time in about 1931 when I heard Roland being given sincere instructions in a dressing room smelling of big men sweat and liniment and all the damp smells that come from the showers and the open windows, "Go out there etc.," and out comes me and my Pa and we sit right at ringside, he lights up his usual 7-20-4 or Dexter cigar, the first match is on, his own promoted match, it's Roland Bouthelier against wild Mad Turk McGoo of the Lower Highlands and they come out and face each other; they lean over and clap big arms and hands over each other's necks and start mauling around and pretty soon one of them makes a big move and knocks the other guy down on the soft hollowly bouncing canvas, "Ugh, OO," he's got a headlock around Roland's head with his big disgusting legs full of hair, I can see Roland's face (my hero) turn red, he struggles there, but the guy squeezes harder and harder. This was before wrestling matches had begun to be fixed? you say? Well Roland had just got his instructions to lose the match in the first minute and then in the next minute if possible, to make time for the semifinal and the main match. But I saw his face turn red with French-Canadian rage and he suddenly threw his legs out and shot himself out of the leg hold and landed on his behind and leaped up in one acrobatic move on his feet, turned, and took the Turk by the shoulders and shoved him against the ropes, and when the Turk bounced back he had him direct in the stomach with a Gus Sonnenberg head charge and knocked the guy so hard back against the ropes the ropes gave and the guy tilted over and landed at some used cigars under the apron of the ring, where he lay gazing up with bleary nonunderstanding eyes. So naturally the referee gives the count, slow as he can, but that guy is slow coming back in; as soon as he crawls thru the ropes Roland's got him by the neck and throws him over his shoulder, the poor guy lands

ABOUT THE AUTHOR

GINSBERG DESCRIBES KEROUAC: MAY, 1956
Jack Kerouac . . . is the Colossus unknown of U. S. Prose who taught me to write and has written more and better than anybody of my generation that I've ever heard of. . . . [H]e is *the* unmistakable fertile prolific Shakespearean *genius*. . . .

Ginsberg, Allen. An excerpt from "Letter to Richard Eberhart." Reprinted in *To Eberhart from Ginsberg—A Letter About "Howl."* Lincoln, Mass.: Penmaen Press, 1976.

slam on his back, Roland's on top of him and pins his two shoulders down, but the guy wriggles out and Roland falls on his behind, clips him with his two sneakered feet, knocks him over on his stomach, jumps on his back, gives him the Full Nelson (which means both arms under the other guy's armpits and twined around to join at the neck), makes him hurt and weep and cry and curse and wince awhile, then, with one imperious angry shove, knocks him over again to his back (one big biceped arm) and pins his two shoulders down and he's gone and thrown the match, so to speak, which he was supposed to lose, out of angry real wrestling fury.

I'm even in the showers afterward listening to my Pa and the men give Roland hell for making them lose all that money, Roland says simply, "OK but he spit in my face in the leg lock when he had me down there, I wont take that from nobody."

A week later Roland is driving me and Pa, my ma and my sister to Montreal Canada for a big Fourth of July weekend where Roland is going to be introduced to the most beautiful little French dolls in town, my elder cousin girls. He turns and looks at me in the back seat as we're passing Lake Champlain, yells in French, "Are you still there, Ti Pousse?" (Lil Thumb?)

About this time too my Pa takes me and my ma to see every big wrestling match which happened at the time (dont ask my why, except Lowell must have been a big wrestling town) between the two world champs, Gus Sonnenberg of Topsfield (or thereabouts Massachusetts, originally from Germany) and the great Henri DeGlane, world's champion from France—In those days wrestling was still for keeps, dont you see—In the first fall Gus Sonnenberg rushes off the ropes with a bounce and does his famous head-into-belly rush that knocks DeGlane right over the ropes upside down bouncing and into my mother's lap . . . He is abashed, says, "I'm sorry, Madame," she says, "I dont mind as long as it's a good French man." Then on the next play he pins Sonnenberg down with his famous leg stranglehold and wins the first fall. Later on, in the incredible cigarsmoke which always made me wonder how those guys could even breathe let alone wrestle (in the Crescent Rink in Lowell) somebody applies a wrenching awful hellish leg-spreading hold that makes some people rush home in fear and somebody wins, I forget who.

It was only shortly after that that wrestling matches began to be fixed.

Meanwhile in this Crescent there were boxing matches and what I liked, besides the action, and since I didnt gamble, being 10 and not caring about money bets then as even now, I saw some marvelous aesthetical nuances connected with indoor fight sports: heard: smelled the cigarsmoke, the hollow cries, the poem of it all . . . (which I wont go into just now).

Because now there's no time for poetry anyway. The only way to organize what you're going to say about anything is to organize it on a grand and emotional scale based on the way you've felt about life all along. Only recently, now at age 45, I saw I swear the selfsame young pug with the sad blue bag a-hurrying to the bus station in Massachusetts to make his way to Maine for another dreary prelim bout, with no hope now but maybe 50 bucks, and maybe a broken nose, but why should a young man do things like that and wind up in the bottom pages of smalltown newspapers where they always have the UPI or AP reports of fights: "Manila, Philippines, Jose Ortega, 123, of San Juan Puerto Rico, outpointed Sam Vreska, 121, Kearney, Nebraska, in ten rounds. . . . Hungry Kelly, 168, Omaha, Nebraska, kayoed Ross Raymond, 169, Ottawa, Canada, in round 2." You read those things and you wonder what makes them so eagerly helpless in the corner when their seconds are sponging their reddened nose. Well never expect me to go into the ring! I'm too yellow! Could it say in the lexicon of publishing stories that Grass Williams outpointed or kayoed Gray Glass in the fifth? in Beelzabur Town? I say,

God bless young fighters, and now I'll take a rest and wait for my trainer's bottle, and my trainer's name is Johnny Walker.

GENERAL COMMENTARY

OMAR SWARTZ (ESSAY DATE 1999)

SOURCE: Swartz, Omar. "Kerouac in Context." In *The View from On the Road: The Rhetorical Vision of Jack Kerouac*, pp. 15-26. Carbondale: Southern Illinois University Press, 1999.

In the following essay, Swartz discusses Kerouac's role in the Beat movement and examines how On the Road *embodies the values of the "cult of high experience."*

Jack Kerouac was born in Lowell, Massachusetts, in 1922. He died in Florida in 1969 from internal hemorrhaging brought on by his alcoholism. Kerouac's working-class family was French-Canadian, raising Kerouac under the guidance of Catholicism. He studied in parochial schools where he learned to speak and read English as a second language. He had one older brother, Gerard, who died when Kerouac was a child, and a sister who died when he was much older. Kerouac was a strong, husky man with considerable athletic ability. He was recruited by Columbia University to play football, and his enrollment at that school was a decisive event in his life, for it was a Columbia that Kerouac was exposed to the excitement and lure of New York City. Within a few years he had met and befriended people such as William S. Burroughs, Lucien Carr, Hall Chase, and Allen Ginsberg. With these people, Kerouac became exposed to the men and women of the criminal underclass that he would romanticize in many of his novels.

At Columbia, Kerouac soon lost interest in football, rejecting the authority of the coach as he would reject all authority in his life. However, by losing interest in football, Kerouac lost his scholarship and subsequently was unable to remain in school. Kerouac enthusiastically departed from Columbia, using his newly freed time to read voraciously, write continuously, and intensify his experiences in the city, where he solidified his relationship with a crowd of petty criminals and drug abusers, including Ginsberg and the slightly older William Burroughs. These three men belonged to a larger collection of men and women, in major cities throughout the United States, that had an informal network of liaisons and influences. Picking up on this small but highly visible subculture in the United States, the media, using Kerouac's cue, identified it as the "Beat Generation."

In light of the media blitz that surrounded the reception of many of their works, Kerouac, Ginsberg, Burroughs, and Neal Cassady became the Beat culture's most celebrated and controversial representatives. Others, such as Ferlinghetti, Holmes, McClure, and Snyder, also contributed to a poetic cultural resurgence/resistance (Davidson 1989; Kherdian 1967). In particular, under the influence of Ferlinghetti founder of City Lights Books, San Francisco soon replaced New York as the mecca of the new American cultural movement.[1] This is not surprising as the "West" had an aura of potentiality to it in much Beat literature. Throughout the late 1960s, northern California, in particular the Bay Area, was a popular place for people to gather from across the country in communes and communities to live out their shared visions.[2]

In the decade following his department from Columbia, Kerouac wrote novels and ramble throughout the United States and Mexico, following his friends and getting his "kicks" where he could. His travels brought him through the armed services and marriage, neither of which kept his attention for long (he had one child whom he rejected and denied his entire life). Kerouac made a career out of being a wanderer and hobo, all the while recording his thoughts and sights in his journals. Kerouac's first book, **The Town and the City,** was published in 1950. Written in the style of Thomas Wolfe, it was not a success; it brought him little fame or financial security. More damaging to Kerouac's development as a writer, however, was the fact that publishing the book was a difficult experience. Kerouac's rejection of authority led him to oppose stringently the efforts of editors to help him publish his work. He claimed that the demands of the publishing process stifled his creativity as a writer. As a result, Kerouac cut himself off from the publishing world and wrote book after book in his own idiom, circulating the manuscripts among his friends, the growing community of yet-to-be-publicized "Beats."

The 1952 publication of Holmes's *Go* and the 1956 publication of Ginsberg's *Howl,* and the publicity from the obscenity trial that resulted from it (see Ferlinghetti 1976), created conditions in the publishing world conducive to Kerouac's books. The eventual publication and success of **On the Road** surprised Kerouac, who was very shy, and surrounded him with a notoriety that turned increasingly hostile. Overnight, Kerouac was transformed from obscurity into a star. Many of the books that Kerouac had been hoarding all the years he was on the road were published in rapid succession, as well as a few new ones.[3] However, his fantastic burst of creativity had been spent. Within a few years, the pressures of his fame and notoriety, along with his accelerated use of alcohol and drugs, exacted their toll, first on his creativity and then on his health. Kerouac died in Florida, a sick and broken man, spurned by the world and spurning the world. He died resenting the very social world that he helped create; that existed and continues to exist, in part, in his own image. It was only after he died that he was recognized for the hero that he was among the people he helped give a voice to—Bob Dylan, members of the Doors, and the Grateful Dead all paid homage to him, as did many writers, social movement leaders, and other members of the cultural Left. These people found in Kerouac the initial spark that they needed to recreate themselves and to begin their work in transforming society. As is the case of so many prophets, Kerouac died young and left to the next generation the task of developing his vision.

"On the Road" and the Cult of High Experience

Kerouac's experiences during the years 1946 to 1950 are recorded in two primary sources, **On the Road** and **Visions of Cody.** These so-called "road books" are thinly veiled travel diaries that chronicle the adventures and lifestyles of Sal Paradise and Dean Moriarty (also called Jack Duluoz and Cody Pomeray in other works), fictional counterparts to Jack Kerouac and Neal Cassady.[4] Kerouac traveled with Cassady, lived with Cassady, and tape-recorded their conversations in his effort to *know* Cassady and to understand the depths of his euphoric existence. Kerouac's relationship with Cassady may even have been sexual at times, as Kerouac, Cassady, and Ginsberg all engaged in homosexual relationships.[5] Ecstasy for these men was to a large degree phallic and associated with the Greek connections between knowledge and sperm.[6] To a large degree, women were marginalized from these men's existence and were delegated to the role of care givers or sex objects (a point evident in Johnson 1983 and Ehrenreich 1983). . . .

While Kerouac maintained that **Visions of Cody** is his masterpiece, the book itself was not published in its entirety until 1972 and hence falls outside the direct parameters of this study. It nevertheless was known by reputation among the

Beats and provides much of the context for a wider understanding of *On the Road,* the more influential and popular of the two works. *Visions of Cody* certainly deserves mention before beginning a journey down Kerouac's road; any understanding of Kerouac requires an understanding of his relationship with Neal Cassady, and *Visions of Cody* is Kerouac's personal and private testimony to the brilliantly disturbed Cassady. Moreover, both *Visions of Cody* and *On the Road* represent the clearest expression of Kerouac's "voice" as a writer. Both books were written to capture the motion and influence that was Neal Cassady. Both cover many of the same events in the young men's lives.

On the Road is a novel of experience and adventure, of impressions and expanded awareness. The book is a celebration of life and youth. *On the Road* brings youth consciousness to new heights. More than popularizing "beatness," in any of its three connotations, *On the Road* presents to a large popular audience what can be identified as the "cult of high experience." Broadly, the cult of high experience was an attitude that fermented with the Beat Generation, involving the belief that experience rather than conformity was the natural condition of the healthy human being. What followed the publication of *On the Road* was the appearance of a generation of converts who, like Kerouac and his persona, Sal Paradise, became "turned on" by Cassady's embodiment of movement and freedom and followed with their own imitations. The cult of high experience involved the loose ideology that anything goes" and that the more intense the flame, the more valuable the fire. Rock and roll, as it was personified by people like Jim Morrison, was one cultural practice that was influenced by this cult and characterized the counterculture through the early 1970s (Riordan and Prochnicky 1991).

The cult of high experience finds its representation in Cassady, who embodies the victory of bodily desire over the limitations of societal constraints. Holmes notes that in the books featuring Cassady, Kerouac presents his most profound "portrait of the young, rootless American, high on life." Furthermore, as Holmes maintains, Kerouac clearly articulates the feeling, shared by many, "that a certain reckless idealism, a special venturesomeness of heart, had been outlawed to the margins of American life in his time" (1967, 76). Holmes elaborates:

> Kerouac expresses most clearly his vision of America . . . at once cruel and tender, petty and immense; and in [Cassady] himself, he embodies both the promise of America's oldest dream (the unbuttoned soul venturing toward a reconciliation of its contradictions) and the bitter fact of its contemporary debauching (the obscenely blinking police car that questions anyone "moving independently of gasoline").
>
> (76)

The cult of high experience, restless and uncompromising, invites an honest appraisal of the U.S. cultural wasteland, rejects the conformity, mediocrity, and oppression of the United States, and runs on a rhetorical fuel generated by the tensions caused by the "debauching" of American potentialities. "If we are truly a free nation," maintains the cult of high experience, "then let's act like we are a free nation and let it all hang out." Unfortunately, the vast potentialities of our social landscape are policed by the representatives of hypocrisy that tail into question and check the tendencies of self-expression and social independence.[7]

In *On the Road,* Sal and Dean embark on an exhausting foray that brings them through the slums of New York, Denver, San Francisco, New Orleans, Mexico, and points in between. While exploring the bohemian underworld of vice, sex, drugs, and nonconformity, the men search for new meaning in their lives. These meanings derive from lessons learned on the road, from interactions with the marginalized the simple, the poor people they meet in their travels. Inspired by these experiences, bordering on the criminal and the insane, Kerouac (as Walt Whitman before him) describes with a religious tone that all unfolds before him as if he were simply an eyewitness of the manifest glory of God.[8] In the manifest glory of existence that Kerouac celebrates, he manages to transform the pettiness and sorrow of life in 1950s America into an expression of wonder and revelation. Kerouac secularizes his Catholicism and brings God into the level of the mundane experience of "getting by." Kerouac makes the body sacred and embodies the sacred in Cassady. An early example of Kerouac's gift for uplifting the commonplace comes as he crosses into the West for the first time, in search of Cassady:

> I woke up as the sun was reddening; and that was he one distinct time in my life, the strangest moment of all, when I didn't; know who I was—I was far away from home, haunted and tires with travel, in a cheap hotel room I'd; never seen, hearing the hiss of steam outside, and the creak of the old wood of the hotel, and the footsteps upstairs, and all the sad sounds, and I looked at the cracked high ceiling and really didn't; know who I was for about fifteen strange seconds. I wasn't scared; I

was just somebody else, some stranger; and my whole life was a haunted life, the life of a ghost. I was halfway across America, at the dividing line between the East of my youth and the West of my future.

(1957, 16)

Kerouac, as represented by Sal Paradise, has been bitten by the bug of Dean's madness. In joining Dean Moriarty in his quest for experience and freedom, Sal journeys across America, ostensibly searching for Dean's missing father. Dean's lost father symbolizes, in this time of atomic threat, the loss of authority or the loss of faith that Americans had in a figure that they could turn to for guidance and comfort. This absence represents the betrayal of the average American by U.S. cultural and political institutions. Dean's father, after all, was an average citizen with a wife and child, no different from thousands of other me who fall on hard times and never manage to recover. His offspring, Dean (and by spiritual extension, Sal), uses his father's disappearance as an excuse to shirk his responsibilities to the social order and to pursue his own cultural ideal.

In the pursuit of Dean's father, which never really becomes anything more than an excuse to roam aimlessly among the bums and dispossessed, Sal and Dean reveal the more fundamental object of their journey: the relentless pursuit of "IT!" As Kerouac makes clear throughout his book, IT! signifies the indescribable moment of perfect understanding when the sensating individual and the sting of time blend indistinguishably against the "blank tranced end of all innumerable riotous angelic particulars that had been lurking in our souls all our lives" (1957, 172). IT! is an existential moment, perhaps the existential moment, when the truth that is locked behind the plastic and painted and artificial constraints of our identities is allowed to break through and consume consciousness. IT! is a state of religious exultation and exuberance, an expression of the orgasmic oneness and unity of creation. For Sal and Dean, IT! can be found at a spiritual apex, where the consciousness of an individual is transformed by some catalyst, usually sex or drugs or intense deprivation and despair. IT! is usually associated with some marginalized condition. For instance, while watching a musician in a night club, Dean Moriarty explains to Sal Paradise how the experience of IT! can be aroused through the medium of jazz expression:

> All of a sudden somewhere in the middle of the chorus he *gets* it—everybody looks up and knows; they listen; he picks it up and carries. Time stops. He's filling empty space with the substance of our

lives, confessions of his bellybottom strain, remembrance of ideas, rehashes of old blowing. He has to blow across bridges and come back and do it with such infinite feeling soul-exploratory for the tune of the moment that everybody knows it's not the tune that counts but IT.

(1957, 170)

The fact that the status quo marginalizes the activities that lead to the condition of IT!—as jazz was marginalized as an expression of the African American experience (Baraka 1963)—is further evidence of the unnaturalness or unreasonableness of the status quo. Thus, the pursuit of IT! is, in many ways, the pursuit of sexual, spiritual, and political liberation.

Essayist Gregory Stephenson defines IT! in Eastern spiritual terms, explaining how IT! is "[t]he transcendence of personal, rational consciousness and the attainment of a synchronization with the infinite" (1990, 157). This conceptualization of Kerouac in terms of Eastern spirituality is important to emphasize since Kerouac, along with Gary Snyder and Alan Watts, is largely responsible for introducing Eastern mysticism and Zen Buddhism into the United States in the late 1950s (Jackson 1988; see also Rao 1974; Watts 1958). Kerouac's **Dharma Bums** (1958b), featuring Gary Snyder as the protagonist, is one of the first books in America, if not *the* first, to accentuate Eastern religious theme and infuse them in the popular mind. **Mexico City Blues** (1959b), a book of Kerouac's poetry, was an influential volume among poets of Kerouac's era, taking Eastern spirituality and giving it presence in American poetics, as well as in the American ecological movement.

The desire to reach a state of IT! is such a powerful force in **On the Road** that Sal and Dean are not content to reach IT! through the lone medium of music, or even meditation. As suggested, both characters attempt to recreate the experience of jazz rhapsody or meditative bliss in other, inventive ways. For example, Sal and Dean's experiences, with marijuana, morphine, heroin, hallucinogenics, and excessive alcohol, their mad cross-country conversations, the mindless travel itself, and the energy portrayed in the book all attempt to approximate the Beat spiritual essence that transcends the mundane to become the IT! of unrestrained ecstasy.

While the specter of Dean's lost father is often eclipsed by the action of the text, and while it largely serves as a pretext for the travels and wanderings of the two men, it nevertheless motivate much of the action throughout the book.⁹ A scene from the novel illustrates:

> [Dean speaking] "[B]ut hey, look down there in he night, that, hup, hup, a buncha old bums by a fire by the rail damn me." He almost slowed down. "You see, I never know whether my father's there or not." There were some figures by the tracks, reeling in front of a wood fire. "I never know whether to ask. He might be anywhere." We drove on. Somewhere behind us of in front of us in the huge night his father lay drunk under a bush, and no doubt about it—spittle on his chin, water on his pants, molasses in his ears, scabs on his nose, maybe blood in his hair and the moon shining down on him.
>
> (1957, 191)

Dean's lost father could be anywhere in America. Any bum or hobo that Sal and Dean meet could be Dean's father; hence all men need to be shown compassion. As he meets and mingles with these lost and hopeless figures, Sal muses that a bum can be anyone's father. Furthermore, since one of them produced Dean Moriarty, there must be something potentially great in each man. At moments such as these, Kerouac's Buddhist compassion becomes materialized. Indeed, it is a theme behind much of his writing.¹⁰

While Dean's derelict father represents a blessed figured, having created Dean and thus showing the potential for greatness in all men, and while the poor and the *fellahin* of the Earth (adapted froth Spengler's *Decline of the West*) evoke Sal and Dean's compassion and respect, there is, nevertheless, the recalcitrant reality that the dispossessed must face on a daily level—a reality as harsh as it is romantic. This reality is never far from the characters of **On the Road**. This is most clear where Dean's father is concerned. Dean's father represents a reality that is close to Dean—a man chronically on the edge, a reminder that the liminal existence of social rootlessness leads finally to a condition of complete abandonment . . .¹¹ Yet even in the ultimate state of deprivation and despair that the derelicts of society occupy, Kerouac discovers that there is a sense of freedom that an otherwise burdened man is denied. Dean suggests this liberating dimension of poverty though his unique life philosophy:

> "You see, man, you get older and troubles pile up. Someday you and me'll be coming down an alley together at sundown and looking in the cans to see." "You mean we'll end up old bums?" [asks Sal.] "Why not, man? Of course we will if we want to. . . . There's no harm ending that way. You spend a whole life of noninterference with the wishes of others, including politicians and the rich, and nobody bothers you and you cut along and make it your own way."
>
> (1957, 205)

In contrast with the warm, sentimental concern for Dean's lost father and the gentle romanticism of bums and the dispossessed in general, both Sal and Dean spend a great deal of energy in an attempt to achieve the state of IT! As mentioned above, IT! appears at the moments when action or experience come to a head, either through frantic activity, artistic rapture, or severe emotional strain. IT! represents the unpronounceable ecstasy that occurs when relentless souls merge their energies in jazz, sex, travel, drugs, or despair. In one poignant scene in **On the Road,** Sal describes the experience of IT! that he attains as he walks down the street in San Francisco, having been betrayed by Dean and left without money, friends, or a place to stay. Sal passes beyond a point of despair:

> [F]or a moment I had reached the point of ecstasy that I always wanted to reach, which was the complete step across chronological time into the timeless shadows, and wonderment in the bleakness of the mortal realm, and the sensation of death kicking at my heels to move on, with a phantom dogging its own heels, and myself hurrying to a plank where all the angels dove off and flew into the holy void of uncreated emptiness, the potent and inconceivable radiances shinning in the bright Mind Essence, innumerable lotuslands falling open in the magic mothswarm of heaven. . . . I felt sweet, swinging bliss, like a big shot of heroin in the mainline vein; like a gulp of wine late in the afternoon and it makes you shudder; my feet tingled. I thought I was going to die the very next moment.
>
> (1957, 143)

As this passage illustrates, Kerouac and the Beats feel that life transcends into death and transformation; movement and change become the source of life, growth, and experience. This state of constant emotional upheaval, and its physical and psychological manifestations, contrasts with the static, controlled, and fabricated existence of 1950s corporate American culture.

As can be expected by the prose above, **On the Road** is a novel that ends without much resolution, in a traditional sense. Dean's father is never found. The pursuit of IT! culminates at frenzied intervals, but it is not permanent and soon passes. The mundane existence of everyday life always returns, leaving Sal and Dean no more the better and all the more worn down. Both characters experience sickness and disease in the novel. When Sal becomes too ill to travel, Dean abandons him again, this time in Mexico. In both cases, Sal is forgiving, recognizing that the holy madness of Dean must run its own course, unconstrained by even the bonds of friendship. Later, at the end of the book when Sal's disillusionment with Dean becomes more tangible, he chooses to leave Dean behind in the snow and goes off with a girl and another friend to a concert. Dean had suddenly come unannounced to New York one winter after the and Sal had made vague plans to live together in California. The men had been living on opposite coasts, working to earn money for the move. But Dean, always the compulsive, driven lunatic, irresponsibly arrives weeks early and all plans fall apart (as they always do in the novel). The novel ends with this disillusionment; the obscenity of Dean's lifestyle creates pressures that Sal can no longer accept. No certainty is presented at the novel's conclusion, no dramatic or climactic resolution of plot or character development. Without Dean to inspire him, Sal's energy and experience end, and the novel ends. Ostensibly, little is revealed to Sal or to Kerouac's reading audience besides the "forlorn rags of growing old" (1957, 254) that Sal accepts as he sits on a brokendown pier and ponders the random senselessness of our "Pooh-Bear" like existence.

The fact that **On the Road** presents no traditional resolution is not disturbing in the least, although it does contribute to the controversial style of the text. To those attuned to Kerouac's message and vision, the novel's end is a beginning, an invitation to change and transformation. Kerouac wrote the book as one chapter in a legend that he was designing and giving to the world. He saw his life as a legend and tried to give that legend a voice and a presence; his "road" books are all documentations of that legend. From **On the Road** the legend continued to unfold. More important, the novel represents the beginning of a new lifestyle, a consciousness that left the pages of Sal and Dean's adventures to become a force of its own life and own reckoning. "[N]othing ever ended" (1957, 248), Kerouac wrote, and for his vision that was certainly true. **On the Road** was the beginning of that vision's popular expression."[12]

Kerouac and the Beat Generation

Kerouac's life and work cannot be fully understood outside of the context of the Beat Generation, and his vision and rhetorical significance in contributing to an American counterculture must be situated in the Beat Generation so that its amplification and chaining-out effects can be placed in perspective.

Kerouac is widely recognized as the unlikely and resistant "leader" or "father" of the Beats, hailed in the popular media as the "King; of the Beats."[13] However, this honorific title does not reflect his actual participation in what became popularized as the "Beat Generation"; by the time the Beats became a media phenomenon, Kerouac had retired and begun his rapid (and unromantic) descent into depression, decay, and death. Furthermore, Kerouac's label also results from an important misidentification: Kerouac was thought by many to exemplify the lifestyle that was led by Neal Cassady. The Beat Generation itself was an ideological community that defied a strict genealogical characterization. In reality, it was a loose connection of artists and alienated youth. Its unifying characteristic was its role in helping to shape American Left culture during the 1950s and 1960s. The Beat Generation gave the political Left a degree of cultural style during this time. Still, even with these qualifications, Kerouac *did*, at least for a time when he was unknown and actually living on the road, enact his vision. Karlyn Kohrs Campbell and Kathleen Jamieson discuss "enactment" as the process whereby rhetors "incarnate" their argument and embody "the proof of what is said" (1977, 9).

Through his art and life, Kerouac called into being a "community," however loosely we must use the term, and gave it an epistemological consciousness. Charters acknowledges Kerouac's unique position in the Beat Generation:

> In the intensity of the vision he had of his confused life he caught the dreams of a generation: the feeling that at some point something had been together, that there was a special vision they all shared, a romantic ideal that called on the road just ahead. To this generation Jack Kerouac became a romantic hero, an archetypal rebel, the symbol of their own vanities, the symbol of their own romantic legend.
>
> (1973, 22)

Reviewing Kerouac's book for the *New York Times*, Gilbert Milistein credits **On the Road** as being "the most beautifully executed, the clearest and the most important utterance yet made by the generation Kerouac himself named years ago as 'beat,' and whose principal avatar he is" (1957, 27). In "naming" this generation, Kerouac exerted influence on two generations of young people. This influence ranged from the beatniks to the hippies and from Greenwich Village to North Beach. As exemplified by Wavey Gravey, the hippie clown (and former Beat poet) who led the medical services at the original Woodstock music festival, Kerouac's influence reached far into the self-acclaimed "Woodstock Nation" (Cook 1971, 232). Indeed, during the 1960s, scores of social revolutions rose to rattle the cages of American conformity. While Kerouac's vision is alien to some of these movements (most notably the feminist movement, for obvious reasons), it is intimately tied to many (Oakley 1986).[14] Robert J. Milewsky substantiates the claim that Kerouac had a significant effect on American culture:

> Jack Kerouac, through his writing, exerted a force (or influence) on the outside world. The life-style of the Beats was emulated by the beatniks. They had their pads, poetry readings, beards, dark clothing, hot and cool jazz, chicks, slangs, parties, wine, marijuana, etc.; and all of this borrowed, largely, in itself from the bohemians, hipsters, and jazz musicians Kerouac knew and wrote about. (Later, the hippies of the sixties would adopt or transform some of these for their own use.) Also, the young of each generation since Kerouac have gone "on the road," across the country, exploring his America. *On the Road,* that Baedeker of beatism, became the traveler's guide of the penniless set, America's second and third generation "dharma bums." Kerouac became the "hero of the alienated."
>
> (1981, 7)

The social movements that Kerouac has been identified with, calling for reform, freedom, sexual liberation, and a new and less materialistic cultural outlook, were powerful enough to make a permanent mark on American culture and to usher in a range of resistance narratives and alternative lifestyles that were simply unthinkable in the drab grayness of 1950s America. Anthropologist Pierre Anctil describes how "Kerouac's experience . . . brutally highlights the post-war spectacle of a triumphant, arrogant and self-satisfied America comfortably installed in the contemplation of its material wealth" (1990, xviii). In contrast to this brutality and base arrogance, Kerouac served as a central point of resistance, emphasizing compassion and diversity. As Anctil concludes, "By virtue of a great adventurer . . . Kerouac denounced this new asphyxia and gave force to the call of the wild, in all its purity" (xix). In exhorting America to actualize a new purity of heart and cultural expression, Kerouac contributed to a symbolic restructuring of American values. Allen Ginsberg explains this idea more fully and further documents the direct genealogical connections between the Beats and the hippies:

> I don't think it is possible to proceed further in America without first understanding Kerouac's tender brooding compassion for bygone scene & personal Individuality oddity'd; therein. Bypassing Kerouac one bypasses the mortal heart, sung in prose vowels. . . . a giant mantra of appreciation and adoration of an American man, one striving heroic soul. Kerouac's judgment on Neal Cassady was confirmed by later [Ken] Kesey history.
>
> (1972, vii)

Kerouac's relationship to the Beat Generation, and the relationship between the Beat Generation and the larger, more socially diverse counterculture of the 1960s, can be seen rhetorically, as this study documents. In particular, Ernest G. Bormann's theory of fantasy theme and rhetorical vision helps explain the process behind this rhetorical influence. As he explains, "When a person appropriates a rhetorical vision he gains with the supporting dramas constraining forces which impel him to adopt a lifestyle and to take certain action" (1972, 406). In the case of Kerouac, this vision enabled people to become aware of their option to adopt different lifestyles and gave them the opportunity to join with the "drama" that was formed by a new way of viewing reality. Bormann explains, "[T]he convert to one of the counter cultures in the 1960s would let his hair and beard grow, change his style of dress, and his method of work" (407). Readers of Kerouac would become transformed into "Beats" and later into "hippies" as changes in their attitudes became manifested in behavioral and lifestyle changes.[15] These changes would, circularly, effect and reinforce attitudinal commitments. Ironically, however, while these "converts" were seeking freedom from societal norms and the establishment of their own individuality and values, the shifting of narratives brought with it, as it always does, a shifting of constraints. As Michel Foucault warns, there is no "liberation" in the sense that a new value system and set of social beliefs can bring "freedom." Rather, all epistemologies have their binders and their boundaries (see Foucault 1980; Burke 1984). More specifically, as Maurice Charland warns, "Subjects within narratives are not free, they are positioned and so constrained. All narratives have power over the subjects they present" (1987, 140). Thus, Kerouac's narrative, the visions and fantasies promoted in his text, while suggesting new avenues of cultural and personal expression, also serve to limit action and to reify belief. The limitations of the politically Left counterculture and its relative wane in influence since the 1970s may be due in part to the fact that narratives provide their own limited and limiting social apparatuses. In other words, countercultures themselves need to be reenvisioned from time to time to avoid suffocating in their own stagnated reifications.

Notes

1. City Lights Books, founded in 1953, was the first paperback book store in the country and was devoted to publishing Beat authors.

2. While northern California was a central place of countercultural activity, it was not the only place in America where communes and other ideological activity took place. See Berger (1981).

3. Not all of his work was published during or around this time, however. For instance, *Visions of Cody* was not published until after his death. In the 1990s, interest in Kerouac, spawned in great deal by the efforts of Charters to revive him, has led to the publication of some of his unpublished writings (1992, 1993, 1995a, 1995b, 1995c). A second major reason for the spate of new Kerouac material involves the 1990 death of Stella Kerouac (Jack Kerouac's third wife.) Stella was hostile to the literary world, which she blamed for Kerouac's troubles, and she suppressed her late husband's unpublished manuscripts for over twenty years.

4. Kerouac's other "road" books, such as *The Subterraneans* (1958c), *Big Sur* (1962), and *The Dharma Bums* (1958b), do not focus on Neal Cassady (although he does play a part in most of them).

5. See Stimpson (1982) for a study of homosexuality among the major writers in Beat culture.

6. This is a particularly evident theme in much of Ginsberg's poetry. See, for instance, Ginsberg's homage to Cassady's penis, a poem entitled "Done, Finished with the Biggest Cock" (1984, 466).

7. See Chomsky (1994) for a contemporary appraisal of what he identifies as American hypocrisy and political repression.

8. God, in fact, appears or is evoked frequently in the text and is usually associated wit the road, as exemplified in Kerouac's phrase "[T]he road is life" (1957, 175). Kerouac's God is Western-looking: he is an old man with a white-streaked beard and hair who walks on the road. This God even becomes embodied in Dean, as when Kerouac writes, "I had to struggle to see Dean's figure, and he looked like God" (1957, 233).

9. For men's studies approach to issues of fatherhood in Kerouac's writing, see Davenport (1992).

10. For a selection of Beat writing on Buddhism, see Tonkinson (1995).

11. The real-life Herbert Huncke and Bill Cannastra, as well as the fictional Mardou in *The Subterraneans*, are also examples of liminal figures in Kerouac's world.

12. This lifestyle did have its literary genesis, in part, elsewhere. Perhaps it is clearer to write that Kerouac did not "invent" a new lifestyle; rather he updated an older one by reading the words of Rimbaud, Celine, and Gide. Kerouac is but a participant in a long tradition of bohemianism who served the important function of popularizing, through his writing, countercultural themes (see Riesman 1961; Goodman 1960; and Ehrenreich 1983).

13. The clearest articulation of Kerouac's position as patriarch is *On the Road*, the book that "captured the spirit of [Kerouac's] generation, their restlessness and confusions in the years immediately following World War II." charters summarizes this perspective by writing, "[P]eople looked at Kerouac as if *he* were the Beat Generation" (1973, 297).

14. Oakley explains that the Beats "were the progenitors of the hippies, yippies, and other youthful members of the counter-culture of the sixties" (1986, 402).

15. This in not to imply that the two groups can be reduced to a seamless whole. With continuity also comes disjunction and even antagonism (see Rather 1977).

Works Cited

Anctil, Pierre. 1990. Preface to *Un Homme Grand: Jack Kerouac at the Crossroads of Many Cultures,* ed. Pierre Anctil, Louis Dupont, Remi Ferland, and Eric Waddell. Ottawa: Carleton University Press. xviii-xix.

Berger, Bennett M. 1981. *The Survival of a Counterculture: Ideological Work and Everyday Life among Rural Communards.* Berkeley: University of California Press.

Bormann, Ernest G., John F. Cragan, and Donald C. Shields. 1994. "In Defense of Symbolic Convergence Theory: A Look at the Theory and Its Criticisms after Two Decades." *Communication Theory* 4: 259-94.

Burke, Kenneth. 1984. *Permanence and Change: An Anatomy of Purpose.* 1935. Reprint, Berkeley: University of California Press.

Campbell, Karlyn Kohrs, and Kathleen Jamieson. 1977. "Form and Genre in Rhetorical Criticism: An Introduction." In *Form and Genre: Shaping Rhetorical Action,* ed. Karlyn Kohrs Campbell and Kathleen Jamieson. Falls Church, VA: Speech Communication Association. 9-32.

Charland, Maurice. 1987. "Constitutive Rhetoric: The Case of the Peuple Quebecois." *Quarterly Journal of Speech* 73: 133-50.

Charters, Ann. 1973. *Kerouac: A Biography.* San Francisco: Straight Arrow.

Chomsky, Moan, and Edward S. Herman. 1979. *The Washington Connection and Third World Fascism.* Boston: South End.

Cook, Bruce. 1971. *The Beat Generation.* New York: Charles Scribner's Sons.

Davenport, Steve. 1992. "Complicated 'A Very Masculine Aesthetic': Positional Sons and Double Husbands, Kinship and Careening in Jack Kerouac's Fiction." Ph.d. diss., University of Illinois, Urbana.

Davidson, Michael. 1989. *The San Francisco Renaissance: Poetics and Community at Mid-Century.* New York: Cambridge University Press.

Ehrenreich, Barbara. 1983. *The Hearts of Men: American Dreams and the Flight from Commitment.* Garden City, NY: Anchor.

Ferlinghetti, Lawrence. 1976. *Howl of the Censors.* Westport, CT: Greenwood.

Foucault, Michel. 1970. *The Order of Things: An Archaeology of the Human Sciences.* New York: Vintage.

Goodman, Paul. 1960. *Growing Up Absurd: Problems of Youth in the Organized Society.* New York: Vintage.

Jackson, Carl T. 1998. "The Counterculture Looks East: Beat Writers and Asian Religion." *American Studies* 29: 51-70.

Johnson, Joyce. 1983. *Minor Characters.* Boston: Houghton Mifflin.

Kerouac, Jack. 1957. *On the Road*. New York: Viking.

———. 1958a. *The Dharma Bums*. New York: Viking.

———. 1958b. *Dr. Sax*. New York: Grove.

———. 1958c. *The Subterraneans*. New York: Grove.

———. 1959a. *Maggie Cassady*. New York: Avon.

———. 1959b. *Mexico City Blues*. New York: Grove.

———. 1960. *The Scripture of the Golden Eternity*. New York: Cornity.

———. 1962. *Big Sur*. New York: Farrar, Straus and Company.

———. 1963. *Visions of Gerard*. New York: Farrar, Straus and Company.

———. 1972. *Visions of Cody*. New York: McGraw-Hill.

———. 1992. *Poems All Sizes*. San Francisco: City Lights.

———. 1993. *Good Blonde and Other Stores*. San Francisco: Gray Fox.

———. 1995a. *The Portable Jack Kerouac*. New York: Viking.

———. 1995b. *Selected Letters, 1948-1956*. New York: Viking.

———. 1995c. *Some of the Dharma*. New York: Viking.

Kherdian, David. 1967. *Six Poets of the San Francisco Renaissance: Portraits and Checklists*. Fresno, CA: Giligia.

Millstein, Gilbert. 1957. Review of *On the Road*, by Jack Kerouac. *New York Times*, 5 Sept., 34.

Oakley, Ronald J. 1986. *God's Country: America in the Fifties*. New York: Dembner.

Rao, Vimala C. 1974. "Oriental Influence on the Writing of Jack Kerouac, Allen Ginsberg, and Gary Snyder." Diss., University of Wisconsin.

Rather, Lois. 1977. *Bohemians to Hippies: Waves of Rebellion*. Oakland: Rather.

Riesman, David. 1961. *The Lonely Crowd: A Study of the Changing American Character*. New Haven: Yale University Press.

Stimpson, Catharine R. 1982. "The Beat Generation and the Trials of Homosexual Liberation." *Salmagundi* 58: 373-92.

Tonkinson, Carole, ed. 1995. *Big Sky Mind: Buddhism and the Beat Generation*. New York: Riverhead.

Watts, Allen. 1958. "Beat Zen, Square Zen, and Zen." *Chicago Review* 12: 3-11.

TITLE COMMENTARY

On the Road

CAROLE GOTTLIEB VOPAT (ESSAY DATE JULY 1973)

SOURCE: Vopat, Carole Gottlieb. "Jack Kerouac's *On the Road*: A Re-evaluation." *Midwest Quarterly* 14, no. 4 (July 1973): 385-407.

In the following essay, Vopat contends that On the Road *is a more complex and serious work than critics have previously recognized.*

Nothing has been published about Jack Kerouac for seven years. Most of what has been written is either hostile or condescending or both. While it may perhaps be true, as Melvin W. Askew suggests ("Quests, Cars and Kerouac," *University of Kansas City Review*, 28 [1962], 231-240), that to speak of Jack Kerouac in the same breath with Melville, Twain and Hawthorne is "to leave a smirch on the configuration of classic American literature" (p. 235), Kerouac has, as they have, provided an enduring portrait of the national psyche; like Fitzgerald, he has defined America and delineated American life for his generation. Certainly, Kerouac is not a great writer, but he is a good writer, and has more depth and control than his critics allow. **On the Road** is more than a "crazy wild frantic" embrace of beat life; implicit in Kerouac's portrayal of the beat generation is his criticism of it, a criticism that anticipates the charges of his most hostile critics. For example, Norman Podhoretz' assertion ("The Know-Nothing Bohemians," *Doings and Undoings* [New York: Noonday Press, 1964], 143-158) that "the Beat Generation's worship of primitivism and spontaneity . . . arises from a pathetic poverty of feeling" (156), parallels Kerouac's own insights in **On the Road.**

In that novel Kerouac makes it clear that Sal Paradise goes on the road to escape from life rather than to find it, that he runs from the intimacy and responsibility of more demanding human relationships, and from a more demanding human relationship with himself. With all their emphasis on spontaneity and instinct, Sal and his friends are afraid of feeling on any other than the impassive and ultimately impersonal "wow" level. For Sal especially, emotion is reduced to sentimentality, roleplaying and gesture. His responses are most often the blanket, indiscriminate "wow!" or the second-hand raptures gleaned from books and movies; he thrills to San Francisco as "Jack London's town" and melodramatically describes leaving his Mexican mistress: "Emotionlessly she kissed me in the vineyard and walked off down the row. We turned at a dozen paces, for love is a duel, and looked at each other for the last time . . ." (**On the Road** [New York: The Viking Press, 1957], 101). Sal is continually enjoying himself enjoying himself, raptly appreciating his performance in what seems more like an on-going soap-opera than an actual life: "She'd left me a cape to keep warm; I threw it over my shoulder and skulked through the moonlit vineyard. . . . A California home; I hid in the grapevines, digging it all. I felt like a million dollars; I was adventuring in the crazy American night" (100).

Sal's self-conscious posturing undercuts his insistence on the life of instinct and impulse, and indicates his fear of emotions simply felt, of life perceived undramatically and unadorned. He responds to experience in a language of exaggeration; everything is the saddest or greatest or wildest in the world. Although on page 21 he meets a "rawhide oldtime Nebraska farmer" who has "a great laugh, the greatest in the world," a few pages later he encounters Mr. Snow "whose laugh, I swear on the Bible, was positively and finally the one greatest laugh in all this world" (62). Reality is never good enough; it must be classified, embroidered and intensified; above all, the sheer reality of reality must be avoided. Sal's roleplaying shelters him from having to realize and respond to actual situations, and to the emotions and obligations, whether of others or of himself, inherent in those situations. He is protected from having to face and feel his own emotions as well as from having to deal with the needs and demands of other people. What Sal enthuses over as "a California home" Kerouac reveals as a place of poverty, frustration, anger and despair, but Sal's raptures cushion him from recognizing the grimness of the existence to which he is carelessly consigning his mistress and her small son, a child he had called "my boy" and played at fathering. By absorbing himself in the melodramatics of a renunciation scene, Sal is protected from the realities of Terry's feelings or her future, nor must he cope with his own emotions at parting with her. When the melodrama fails and the scene threatens him with its potentiality for suffering and loss, Sal is able to escape from feeling by escaping from the scene:

> 'See you in New York, Terry,' I said. . . . But we both knew she wouldn't make. . . . She just walked on back to the shack, carrying my breakfast plate in one hand. I bowed my head and watched her. Well, lackadaddy, I was on the road again.
>
> (101)

Sal is far more comfortable in the role of wayward child than as friend or brother, much less father and husband. His early trips end in a return home to be babied by his aunt: "Poor little Salvatore . . . , you're thin, you're thin. Where have you been all this time?" (107). Sal is a failure as a friend, unable to sustain even the least demanding friendships. His idyll with Remi and Lee Ann breaks down partially because of his own irresponsibility. Although he knows Remi wants desperately to impress his doctor stepfather, Sal

appears at their rendezvous drunk and outrageous, knowing he is ruining their friendship but unable to control himself: "I gave up, I got drunk. . . . Everything was falling apart" (77).

Kerouac's characters take to the road not to find life but to leave it all behind: emotion, maturity, change, decision, purpose, and, especially, in the best American tradition, responsibility; wives, children, mistresses, all end up strewn along the highway like broken glass. Sal refuses responsibility not only for the lives of others but for his own life as well. He does not want to own his life or direct his destiny, but prefers to live passively, to be driven in cars, to entertain sensations rather than emotions. A follower, Sal is terrified of leading his own life; he is, as Kerouac points out, "fearful of the wheel" and "hated to drive;" he does not have a driver's license. He and Dean abdicate self-control in a litany of irresponsibility: "It's not my fault, it's not my fault . . . , nothing in this lousy world is my fault" (213). Both of them flee from relevance and significance, telling long, mindless stories and taking equally pointless trips. They avoid anything—self-analysis, self-awareness, thinking—which would threaten or challenge them, for with revelation comes responsibility for change and, above all, they do not want change. They demand lives as thin and narrow as the white lines along the road which so comfort and mesmerize them, and are content with surfaces, asking for no more. Thus they idolize Negroes as romantic and carefree children, seeing in the ghetto not the reality of poverty and oppression, but freedom from responsibility and, hence, joy.

Sal and his friends are not seeking or celebrating self, but are rather fleeing from identity. For all their solipsism, they are almost egoless. They do not dwell on the self, avoid thinking or feeling. They run from self-definition, for to admit the complex existence of the self is to admit its contingencies: the claims of others, commitments to society, to oneself. Solipsism rather than an enhancement of self is for them a loss of self, for the self is projected until it loses all boundaries and limits and, hence, all definition. Sal in the Mexican jungle completely loses his identity; inside and outside merge, he becomes the atmosphere, and as a result knows neither the jungle nor himself. For Sal and Dean, transcendentalism, like drugs, sex, liquor, and even jazz, leads not to enlightenment but to self-obliteration. Erasing both ego and world, nothing remains save motion and sensation, passive, self-effacing and mechanical. Only the sheer impetus of their frantic, speeding cars holds their scattered selves together.

Their selves have no definition and their lives no continuity. Nothing is related, neither self nor time; there is no cause and effect, life is not an ongoing process. Rather, there is only the Eternal Now, the jazz moment, which demands absolutely nothing. Their ideals are spontaneity and impulse because both are independent of relation to what has gone before and what may come after. Spontaneity and impulse are the ethic of disjunction, recognizing neither limit, liability or obligation. Their emphasis on spontaneity is a measure of their fear of life. In their cars they are suspended from life and living, as if in a capsule hurtling coast-to-coast above the earth. They seek out not truth nor values but this encapsulated almost fetal existence as an end in itself, an end that is much like death.

For even their much touted ideal of Freedom is in reality a freedom from life itself, especially from rational, adult life with its welter of consequences and obligations. Dean is utterly free because he is completely mad. He has defied maturity and logic, defied time with its demands that he grow up to responsibility. Like Nietzsche's superman, he is beyond good and evil, blame and expectation, nor must he justify his existence through work and duty, a state Sal sorely admires: "Bitterness, recriminations, advice, morality, sadness—everything was behind him, and ahead of him was the ragged and ecstatic joy of pure being" (195). Sal's own longing for freedom is embodied in a mysterious Shrouded Traveler, a figure who unites the road and death. In many avatars, he pursues Sal in his headlong flight down the highway, offering, through solitary travel, the "lost bliss" which is the death of the self: "The one thing that we yearn for in all our living days, that makes us sigh and groan and undergo sweet nauseas of all kinds, is the remembrance of some lost bliss that we probably experienced in the womb and can only be reproduced (though we hate to admit it) in death" (124).

"Free love" is rather freedom from love and another route down that same dark deathwish. For Sal the love-bed is "the deathbed," where he goes to obliterate himself and to find the safe "lost bliss" of the womb, "blindly seeking to return the way he came" (132). But Sal is only able to find this particular version of "lost bliss" when he has reduced his partner to the non-threatening role of fellow child. He has trouble succeeding with adult women; he fills Rita with nothing but talk and is convinced Theresa is a whore until he discovers with relief that she is only a baby, as fragile and vulnerable as he: "I saw her poor belly where there was a Caesarian scar; her hips were so narrow she couldn't bear a child without getting gashed open. Her legs were like little sticks. She was only four foot ten. I made love to her in the sweetness of the weary morning. Then, two tired angels of some kind, hung-up forlornly in an LA shelf, having found the closest and most delicious thing in life together, we fell asleep . . ." (84). Sex here is not a wild explosion but the desperate, gentle solace two babes in the woods haltingly offer each other. Sex, like love, is passive and accepting; it is child-love: one only stands there and is showered in undemanding, protective affection. Sal says he ought to be seeking out a wife, but his true search is, as is Dean's, not for lover but for father, for someone to shelter him from life and responsibility. He turns to Terry not for ecstasy or even sensation, but as a respite from his search, an escape from the demands of life: "I finally decided to hide from the world one more night with her and morning be damned" (89).

In short, for all their exuberance, Kerouac's characters are half in love with easeful death. And this Sal Paradise and his creator well know. Neither is deceived about the nature of beat existence. Kerouac is able to step back from his characters to point out their follies; to show, for example, Dean's pathetic justification of life on the road and Sal's equally pathetic hunger, despite his friend's unmistakable deterioration, to believe him: "'What's your road man?—holy boy road, mad man road, rainbow road, guppy road, any road. It's an anywhere road for anybody anyhow. Where body how?' We nodded in the rain" (251). Sal himself is able to articulate his own fear of feeling and responsibility and his resultant, overwhelming emptiness: "Well, you know me. You know I don't have close relationships with anybody anymore. I don't know what to do with these things. I hold things in my hand like pieces of crap and don't know where to put it down. . . . It's not my fault! It's not my fault! . . . Nothing in this lousy world is my fault, don't you see that? I don't want it to be and it can't be and it *won't* be" (213). He realizes that he has "nothing to offer anybody except my own confusion," and marks the deaths of his various illusions with the refrain, "Everything is collapsing."

Kerouac further points out that the shortcomings of his characters parallel the shortcomings of the country to which they are so intimately connected. Kerouac's response to America is typically disillusioned. America is a land of corruption and hypocrisy, promising everything and delivering nothing, living off the innocence and opportunity, the excitement and adventure of the past. In particular Kerouac indicts America for failing to provide his searching characters with any public meaning or communal values to counteract the emptiness of their private lives. Sal looks to America much as he looks to Dean, to provide him with direction, purpose and meaning, to offer him a straight line, an ordered progression to a golden destination, an "IT" of stability and salvation. But IT never materializes, and the straight line itself becomes an end; the going, the road, is all. Dean's response to continual disillusionment is to forsake the destination for the journey: "Move!" Sal follows his leader but eventually becomes disgusted with the purposeless, uncomfortable jockeying from coast to coast, just as he becomes disgusted with Dean. Unlike Dean, Sal is able to recognize and identify his despair and, ultimately, to act on the causes of it; where for Dean change is merely deterioration, Sal undergoes true development.

In addition to Sal's growing insight, Kerouac equips his narrator with a double vision, enabling Sal to comment on the people and events of the novel as he saw them when they happened, and as he views them now that they are over, a sadder-but-wiser hindsight which acts as a check upon his naive, undiscriminating exuberances and provides a disillusioned alternative view of the beatifics of the beat generation.

While the younger Sal idolized Dean upon first meeting him, the older Sal reminds the reader that "this is all far back, when Dean was not the way he is today . . ." (4), and notes that "the whole mad swirl of everything that was to come began then; it would mix up all my friends and all I had left of my family in a big dust cloud over the American night" (8). He observes the sad effect of Time upon his old friends who once "rushed down the street together, digging everything in the early way they had, which later becomes so much sadder and perceptive and blank" (8). He corrects himself when his earlier view of Dean intrudes upon the more precise voice of his older self: "Dean . . . had finished his first fling in New York. I say fling, but he only worked like a dog in parking lots" (9). Sal continually checks and repudiates his youthful self, and deflates his naive view of Dean and life on the road: "I could hear a new call and see a new horizon, and believe it at my young age; and a little bit of trouble or even Dean's eventual rejec-

tion of me as a buddy, putting me down, as he would later, on starving sidewalks and sickbeds—what did it matter? I was a young writer and I wanted to take off" (11). He is even able to poke fun at his melodramatic posturings: "I hid in my corner with my head between my knees. Gad, what was I doing three thousand miles from home? Why had I come here? Where was my slow boat to China?" (75).

Sal's double vision does more than correct his impulses. It projects the reader forward in time and provides the sense of continuity the disjunctive characters, including the younger Sal, lack. This older voice offers relations and connections, causes and effects, connects past with present and projects into the future. It firmly anchors reader and narrator to the familiar world of change and conjunction. It knows the discrepancy between appearance and reality and realizes sadly that Time eventually captures even frantically speeding children. It is the view of a man who has, in Dean Moriarty's words, come to "know Time," it prepares the reader for Sal's eventual disillusionment with beat life and "the sordid hipsters of America."

Sal's double vision is proof of his eventual recapitulation to time and change, a recapitulation which he battles for most of the novel. It is this battling, perhaps, so constant and monotonous, which has infuriated readers used to traditional novels of development and makes them wonder, indeed, whether anything happens to anyone in the novel at all. Sal alone of the characters continually perceives the futility and insanity of his journeys, yet continually makes them, always with the same childlike innocence and expectation, always to follow the same pattern of hopefulness ending in disillusionment as he learns and relearns the same weary lessons about America and Dean Moriarty. Nonetheless, Sal does finally accept the obligations of his insights and revelations, decides to bear the heavy weight of change and responsibility, and grows up to understand, evaluate and finally repudiate Dean Moriarty, the American Dream, and life on the road.

Kerouac makes it clear from the first sentence of the novel that Sal's relationship with Dean is a less demanding, less intimate substitute for a relationship with a wife, a relationship which the newly-divorced Sal has proven himself unable to handle. His liaison with Dean is intimately connected with his fears of emotions, of himself, and of life. He is able to work through with Dean some of the fears, inadequacies and reservations that have prevented him from forming meaningful or lasting alliances, and have prompted him to search for meaning in cars or countries rather than in himself and with a woman.

When the novel opens, Sal is drifting. His marital and college careers have broken down and, as he says of his friend Remi, he has "fallen on the beat and evil days that come to young guys in their middle twenties;" he is "hanging around waiting for a ship" (61). Unable to provide himself with direction or purpose, haunted by the "feeling that everything was dead," Sal seizes on an impetus from without, a strong force which promises to order his life. His ship comes in, navigated by that "crazy Ahab," Dean Moriarty, who, for all his madness, is able, as was Ahab, to provide his crew with direction and purpose. With his constant schedules and plans, his frantic attempts to order, use and outrun Time, his paring down of life to the essentials of motion and survival, Dean is a figure of order and authority for Sal. As long as he is in Dean's car, Sal has a direction and a destination: California, Mexico or New York, in as straight a line as possible. Even more, he has a purpose. Sal and Dean manage, at least at first, to endow their trip with great spiritual significance. They are not tourists, as Sal often points out with contempt, but pilgrims in search of all the "IT" America has to offer, seekers after paradise and salvation, as Sal's name suggests. Denver and San Francisco are not mere cities but, respectively, "the Promised Land" and "the greater vision." Their trip is to be a straight and holy march across the continent, a quest endowed, as all quests ought to be, with monastic purity, rigid order, and singleness of purpose, goals Sal is unable to carry out but nonetheless upholds: "I rued the way I had broken up the purity of my entire trip, not saving every dime, and dawdling and not really making time, fooling around with this sullen girl and spending all my money" (35).

Dean offers Sal more than direction and meaning; he simultaneously provides both a quest and an escape, a hiatus from adult life and adult feelings, a moratorium on maturity. Sal associates Dean with his own childhood: ". . . he reminded me of some long-lost brother . . . , made me remember my boyhood. . . . And in his excited way of speaking I heard again the voices of old companions and brothers under the bridge . . ." (10). Indeed, although Sal is older than Dean, he regards Dean at first not so much as "long lost brother" but as Father whom he passively follows, trusting to be protected, loved and directed. Sal is disenchanted with Dean at the end of Part Two

not because Dean has proven himself a poor friend, but because he has turned out to be yet another bad father: "Where is Dean and why isn't he concerned about our welfare?" (171).

Sal's disillusionment with Dean in California is paralleled by his disenchantment with Los Angeles and the perversion and despair he finds there. Fed up with his adoptive fathers, with Dean and America, Sal falls in with the Chicanos whom he regards as a nation of beautiful children, leading lives free from ambition, success, pressure and responsibility: "Nothing had been accomplished. What was there to accomplish? Manana . . . Manana, man" (92). Sal attempts to find an antidote to Dean's frenzy, California's emptiness, and all the adult voices haranguing him to make a choice in the slow, primitive ease of Chicano life. He finds Theresa, another child, and plays house with her. But this too collapses; the chill of winter is in the air and he tires of playing at husband and father. He can romanticize the life of the migrant workers, but their suffering is real: "Nothing was going to happen except starvation for Terry and me" (95).

Once again he takes to the road, heading back to his old life, having managed to ignore all the disillusionment along the way. But the stern prophet figure which has haunted him on his journey West appears in real form, not as father but as fool, a warning to Sal that his journey has been foolish and in the wrong direction, that he is heading nowhere and towards nothing, that he must take hold of and change his life.

The Ghost of the Susquehanna arrives like the prophet Sal had been expecting; "he walked very fast, commanding me to follow, and said there was a bridge up ahead we could cross" (103). But "as far as I could see he was just a semi-respectable walking hobo of some kind" (104). Instead of father and son, they are only "bums together." The old man's message is not a revelation but a recital of free meals cadged from the Red Cross. Lost and confused, he is unable to conduct Sal into paradise; "we never found that bridge." But although he does not live up to Sal's romantic expectations, he does function as a genuine prophet, offering through his example a warning and a prophecy: he and Sal are traveling on the same road. The "poor little madman," stubbornly headed out in the wrong direction "on the wrong road," is an aging reflection of Sal himself, who, empty, lost, starving, mired in the past, is as well a "poor forlorn man, poor lost sometime boy, now broken ghost of the penniless wilds" (104).

That Sal understands the connection between the Ghost and himself is immediately evident. Shaken by this new view of his life, he wakes to a morning with "a whiteness like the whiteness of the tomb," a "day of the Laodiceans, when you know you are wretched and miserable and poor and blind and naked, and with the visage of a gruesome grieving ghost you go shuddering through nightmare life." He understands that he is no longer "a sweet child believing in everything under your father's roof" (105); the lonely road along which he stumbles is "terrifying" now and "mournful," lit by hellish fires. Nor will the road and its denizens shelter him: "I was starving to death." Yet the alternative to innocence, childhood, dreams and the road is even more "terrifying" and "mournful." To be an adult, to settle down, is to be one of the "millions and millions hustling forever for a buck among themselves, the mad dream—grabbing, taking, giving, sighing, dying, just so they could be buried in those awful cemetery cities beyond Long Island" (106). Sal's temporary compromise is to forsake the road and return home, where he can have both roots and irresponsibility, safe with his aunt and her laden refrigerator, in his room with the rug "woven of all the clothes in my family for years" (107).

Yet, after he has been home awhile, his family begins to wear on him. Adult life is reduced to "talking in low whining voices . . . about the weather, the crops, and the general weary recapitulation of who had a baby, who got a house, and so on . . ." (109). The prospect of settling down "to marry a girl . . . so I can rest my soul with her till we both grow old" (116) is enough to send Sal straight into Dean's battered Hudson for another sail around the road; as always, Dean appears to "save" his friend from having to grow up. However, rather than a holy quest, Sal introduces this second journey as nothing less than a species of madness. They have no particular destination; Sal is going merely because "the bug was on me again." Although Dean's madness endows everything with frenetic significance, Sal knows that "It made no sense. . . . It was a completely meaningless set of circumstances that made Dean come, and similarly I went off with him for no reason" (116). Now only pot can make him believe that IT, the moment of decision and revelation, is at hand; "that everything was about to arrive—the moment when you know all and everything is decided forever" (129).

Dean's madness has "bloomed into a weird flower" (113), and it becomes more and more difficult for Sal to enthuse away his friend's "compulsive psychosis dashed with a jigger of psychopathic irresponsibility and violence" (147). Sal grows colder, hungrier, more frustrated and miserable, haunted by "that feeling when you're driving away from people and they recede on the plain till you see their specks dispersing" (156). He yearns after the "comfortable little homes with chimneys smoking," wants to "go in for buttermilk and beans in front of the fireplace" (161). Dean retreats further and further until "we didn't know what he was talking about anymore," and Sal comes to view their furious rushing with disgust and rue: "It was sad to see [Hingham's] tall figure receding in the dark as we drove away, just like the other figures in New York and New Orleans. . . . Where go? What do? What for? . . . But this foolish gang was bending onward" (167). Onward is only once more to California, as "broken-down," "withered" and "disenchanted" as before. Demanding more of his travels than mere distance ("What I accomplished by coming to Frisco I don't know"), abandoned again by Dean ("Dean didn't care one way or the other"), Sal ends his second journey with a catalogue of madness, perversion, and despair, and decides to strike off on his own ("We were all thinking we'd never see one another again and we didn't care" [178]).

He moves to Denver, gets a job, and thinks of "settling down there" to be a "patriarch" and live alone in the adult world. Once again, his cautious foray into adult life is followed by a frenzied retreat. Unable to bear the "loneliness" and emptiness of his new life style ("In God's name and under the stars, what for?"), he longs to be a Black or a Chicano or "even a poor overworked Jap," anything but a "disillusioned 'white man'" caught up in respectability and dreariness (p. 180). While he cannot be a Black or a Chicano or a "Jap," and share what he deems their "boyish human joy," he can rejoin Dean Moriarty who, by virtue of his madness, is one with the "happy true-hearted ecstatic Negro," beyond respectability, responsibility and the grim white workaday world. Suppressing his earlier disenchantment, Sal vows to keep "faith" in Dean, for his alternatives are either the white wasteland of adult life, the depression of living completely without meaning, or the awesome responsibility of having to provide order and direction for himself, beyond what either Dean or modern America can offer.

Yet when Sal "runs immediately to Dean . . . burning to know . . . what would happen now," he finds his friend sunk into pitiable madness, and realizes with shock and pity that "it was up to me. Poor, poor Dean—the devil himself had never fallen farther; in idiocy, with infected thumb, surrounded by the battered suit-cases of his motherless, feverish life across America and back numberless times, an undone bird" (189). Sal accepts the responsibility for his "undone bird" and commits himself "resolutely and firmly" to Dean and his "burdensome existence." Their roles reverse; now Sal provides the direction and purpose ("Come to New York with me; I've got the money"), decides, plans and answers all questions. He becomes, in short, Dean's father, his adult, feeling "sudden concern for a man who was years younger than I. . . ." This change in Sal is nothing short of momentous. In effect, he enters into a marriage with Dean "whose fate was wound with mine . . . ," a pact as solemn as any with a woman. He asks for Dean's hand like a nervous fiancé, looking into his eyes and blushing, "for I'd never committed myself before with regard to his burdensome existence," and waits for Dean's answer, "my eyes . . . watering with embarrassment and tears" (189). But "something clicked in both of us;" standing "on top of a hill on a beautiful sunny day," Dean accepts him; "he became extremely joyful and said everything was settled." The two plight their troth ("we would stick together and be buddies till we died"), witness an actual wedding party (p. 190), then go off on their honeymoon ("'Well,' said Dean in a very shy and sweet voice, 'shall we go?'"), forsaking all others ("we paid absolutely no attention to Roy and sat in the back and yakked"). Although both are afraid of this rather formal intimacy and involvement, and feel "perplexed and uncertain," true to his vows Sal takes care of Dean, defending him against his enemies, responding to him with love and protecting him from worry. Although not yet ready to settle down with a woman, Sal can travel intimately with his dependent friend to whom he shyly but resolutely offers sympathy, commitment and responsibility.

Sal's emotional maturation is evident in his first "lover's quarrel" with Dean. Enraged by Dean's casual reference to his growing old ("You're getting a little older now"), Sal turns on him, reducing him to tears, but immediately afterwards realizes that his anger is directed at aging rather than at Dean: "I had flipped momentarily and turned it down on Dean" (212). He takes responsibility for hurting Dean, and apologizes to him, humbly and lovingly: "Remember that I believe in you. I'm infinitely sorry for the foolish grievance I held against you . . ." (217). He sees that his present anger springs from sources buried in his youth ("Everything I had ever secretly held

against my brother was coming out . . ."). This insight into himself helps him to understand Dean, who is, like him, mired in a past whose anger and frenzy he is compelled to act out, but, unlike Sal, without benefit of apology or insight: "All the bitterness and madness of his entire Denver life was blasting out of his system like daggers. His face was red and sweaty and mean" (221). Regarding his friend without desperate idealism, Sal sees that Dean's frantic moving and going is not a romantic quest for adventure or truth but is instead a sad, lost circling for the past, for the home and the father he never had. He sees that both he and Dean are as frightened and lost as "the Prince of Dharma," going in circles in the dark lost places between the stars, searching for that "lost ancestral grove" (222). The road on which they run is "all that old road of the past unreeling dizzily as if the cup of life had been overturned and everything gone mad. My eyes ached in nightmare day" (234). True to his vow, he takes Dean back to New York with him, yet knows that for them a "permanent home" is impossible. Their marriage breaks down; Dean returns to his crazy welter of wives and children, Sal to his aunt and his disillusionment.

Reminders that he is aging and must decide what to do with his life become inescapable. Dean's gloomy forecast of their futures as desperate bums ("someday you and me'll be coming down an alley together at sundown and looking in the cans to see" [251]) is frightening rather than romantic. Playing basketball with a group of "younger boys," he is forced to admit that he is no longer legitimately young, and cannot compete with the "boys" who "bounced all around us and beat us with ease" while "we huffed and puffed." Nor does he miss their condemnation of his frantic pursuit: "They thought we were crazy" (253). As usual, his response to pressure is flight; he tries to deny the facts of age and decision by running off with Dean in search of ecstasy in timelessness. In leaving America behind, Sal hopes to leave behind all he has realized there ("behind us lay . . . everything Dean and I had previously known about life and life on the road" [276]), as well as his identity as a "disillusioned white man" confronted with the American way of life. But this final foray with Dean only brings to a head all the forces of Time and Change that have borne down upon him in the course of his journeys.

In Mexico Sal hopes to escape from the self, civilization, and their discontents. At the bottom of his primitivism is a desire to confront the primal sources of pure being, to discover life as it was—shapeless, formless, dark—before being molded into self or society; in short, to find once and for all the womb he has been seeking all his life. If nothing else, he hopes to search out his final, true and ultimate parents among the Indians who are "the source of mankind and the fathers of it."

But the "strange Arabian paradise we had finally found at the end of the hard, hard road" is only "a wild old whore house" (290) after all. The Indians are coming down from the mountains drawn to wristwatches and cities. They and the Mexicans welcome Sal and Dean not as brothers or fellow children, but as American tourists to be exploited. The brothel where they converge for their ultimate mind- and time-blowing fling is a sad, frantic, desperate place, full of eighteen-year-old drunks and child whores, "sinking and lost," "writhing and suffering." The children cry south of the border too: "The baby . . . began a grimace which led to bitter tears and some unknown sorrow that we had no means to soothe because it reached too far back into innumerable mysteries and time" (286). Their great primitive playground is no more than "a sad kiddy park with swings and a broken-down merry-go-round . . . in the fading red sun . . ." (292). And in that "sad kiddy park" Sal leaves behind his faith in the possibility of an infantile paradise and, with it, his faith in Dean.

Dean first induced Sal to accompany him over the border with the happy announcement that ". . . the years have rolled severally behind us and yet you see none of us have really changed . . ." (262). In Mexico Sal finds this denial of time not a reprieve but a condemnation. Dean cannot change and he cannot rest, not even in "the great and final wild uninhibited Fellahin childlike" Mexico City. Wedded forever to his terrible, changeless compulsions, not the love of his friend nor the possibility of paradise can stay him from his rounds. He leaves the "delirious and unconscious" Sal to return to "all that again," for, as he himself announces, "the road drives *me*." Sal understands and pities him ("I realized what a rat he was, but . . . I had to understand the impossible complexity of his life, how he had to leave me there, sick, to get on with his wives and woes" [302]), realizing his friend is the least free of anyone. Dean leads not a primitive life of spontaneity and instinct but instead a sorry, driven existence of joyless "sweats" and anxieties. Sal has a "vision" of Dean not as sweet, holy goof but as the Angel of Death, burning and laying waste whatever he touches:

(Clockwise, from far left, top row) Jack Kerouac, Allen Ginsberg, Peter Orlovsky, Lafcadio Orlovsky, and Gregory Corso in 1956 on a vacation in Mexico City.

Suddenly I had a vision of Dean, a burning shuddering frightful Angel, palpitating toward me across the road, approaching like a cloud, with enormous speed, pursuing me like the Shrouded Traveler on the plain, bearing down on me. I saw his huge face over the plains with the mad, bony purpose and the gleaming eyes; I saw his wings; I saw his old jalopy chariot with thousands of sparking flames shooting out from it; I saw the path it burned over the road; it even made its own road and went over the corn, through cities, destroying bridges, drying rivers. It came like wrath to the West. . . . Behind him charred ruins smoked. . . .

(259)

On the Road ends with a rejection of beat life. Sal turns his back on Dean and the life of "bursting ecstasies" and frantic traveling, for he knows now that it, too, is meaningless, "making logics where there was nothing but inestimable sorrowful sweats" (305), that it is, ultimately, the way of Death. Sal himself must opt for life, and for growth.

Returning to America, Sal meets up once more with the Shrouded Traveler, a symbol of the fatal lure of the road and the restless, nomadic beat life. Sal wonders if this "tall old man with flowing white hair . . . with a pack on his back" is a sign "that I should at last go on my pilgrimage on foot on the dark roads around America" (306). He wonders, in short, if he ought to become the Ghost of the Susquehanna, to enter the darkness from which the old man appeared and into which he vanished. He responds to the romance of this suggestion, but is haunted by its loneliness. Later, in New York, he calls out his name in the darkness and is answered by Laura, "the girl with the pure and innocent dear eyes that I had always searched for and for so long" (306). Settling his dreams of paradise and salvation in her, he gives up the road.

Sal's emphasis has shifted from moving to staying, from road to home. His relationship with Laura is described simply; they can communicate with and respond to one another without the sentimental, self-important posturings that have marked Sal's previous interludes. He and Laura have long-range plans; they will take a trip, but it will be a migration rather than a flight, not impulsive but carefully planned out, a moving from one home to another, bringing with them furniture, a future, and roots: "We planned to migrate to San Francisco, bringing all our beat furniture and broken belongings with us in a jalopy truck" (306). Sal is now able in himself to consummate straight lines, to carry through on his plans with Laura and his decision to make it up with Remi; he is able to fulfill his promises. But to make it up with Remi and continue his orderly relationship with Laura, to remain in the world of intimacy and responsibility he has newly entered, he must reject Dean.

In a sense, Sal's growth as an adult can be measured through his responses to Dean and in the changing aspects of their relationship. Sal moves from idolatry to pity, from a breathless, childlike worship of Dean as alternately Saint and Father, to a realization of Dean's own tortured humanity, marked by Sal's attempt to be brother, then Father, to his friend, sensitive to Dean's needs without melodrama, facing responsibility and decision, allowing himself to feel blame and love, yet, eventually, for the sake of his own soul, rejecting, deliberately and sadly, his lost, perpetually circling friend.

When Dean arrives to rescue him once more from the world of age and obligation, Sal refuses to go. He discards Dean's plan to leave for San Francisco before he himself is absolutely ready ("But why did you come so soon, Dean?"), and, deciding that he "wasn't going to start all over again ruining [Remi's] planned evenings as I had done . . . in 1947" (309), he pulls away from Dean and leaves him behind.

Sal's final view is of his friend as the Shrouded Traveler. Looking back he sees Dean, ragged, freezing, shrouded in "a motheaten overcoat," alone, and on the move: "Dean, ragged in a motheaten overcoat . . . walked off alone, and the last I saw of him he rounded the corner of Seventh Avenue, eyes on the street ahead, and bent to it again" (309), to a lower-case "it" of frustration, futility and despair.

In the course of his scattered journeys Sal has learned, perhaps to his regret, what rather tentatively might indeed finally matter, and to this tenuous value he cautiously decides to commit himself, giving up the ghost of the Shrouded Traveler, of Dean Moriarty and Old Dean Moriarty and dead America, and accepting in their place feeling, responsibility, and roots—not in a place but in another person, Laura. Sal's relationship with Dean has served as an apprenticeship during which he has learned how to accommodate to intimacy, as his disillusionment with America has prepared him to look beyond the road for salvation and paradise. Neither America nor Dean can successfully order his life, provide him with direction or meaning. Neither can father him; ultimately, he must father himself, must look inward for purpose and belief. For America has lost her innocence and her sense of purpose just as Dean has and, like Dean, is continually making bogus attempts to pretend it still has all the potential and grace of its youth ("Hell's bells! It's Wild West Week. . . . Big crowds of businessmen, fat businessmen in boots and ten-gallon hats, with their hefty wives in cowgirl attire, bustled and whooped on the wooden sidewalks of old Cheyenne. . . . I was seeing to what absurd devices [the West] had fallen to keep its proud tradition" [33]).

On the Road ends with an elegy for a lost America, for the country which once might have been the father of us all, but now is only "the land where they let children cry." Dean Moriarty is himself America, or rather the dream of America, once innocent, young, full of promise and holiness, bursting with potential and vitality, now driven mad, crippled, impotent ("We're all losing our fingers"), ragged, dirty, lost, searching for a past of security and love that never existed, trailing frenzy and broken promises, unable to speak to anybody anymore.

WARREN FRENCH (ESSAY DATE 1986)

SOURCE: French, Warren. "*On the Road*: Work in Progress." In *Jack Kerouac*, pp. 33-45. Boston: Twayne Publishers, 1986.

In the following essay, French analyzes the structure and underlying intent of On the Road, *and attempts to account for the popularity of the novel.*

At the beginning of *Big Sur* (1962), Jack Kerouac departs from his usual practice to add a prefatory note in which he explains that *"My work comprises one vast book like Proust's except that my remembrances are written on the run instead of afterwards in a sick bed. . . . In my old age I intend to collect all my work and re-insert my pantheon of uniform names, leave the long shelf full of books there, and die happy."*

This "enormous comedy" he called the Duluoz Legend. He never lived into old age, when the proposed collection would have been made with *Big Sur* as the last major section; nor does he appear to have died happy. We would surely have a different concept of Kerouac's intentions and achievement if his lifelong "work in progress" had received this final editing; as things stand, we must fit the pieces together for ourselves.

Certainly some of his novels would not be included, at least in their present forms. His last major completed work, *Vanity of Duluoz*, superseded his first published novel, *The Town and the City*, which could never have been made compatible with the later works because of the major differences between the wholly invented Martin family and the mirror image of his own family found in the later novels.

The Subterraneans and *The Dharma Bums* were prompted by quite different motivations from the other novels and would require rewriting beyond a simple substitution of a uniform set of names. The post-humous *Pic*, as it stands, has no relationship at all to the other works. Kerouac's most popular and celebrated novel, *On the Road*, was also in his eyes superseded long before it was published, as it was only one of the stages of a work in progress that he considered to have achieved its final form in *Visions of Cody*, which was never published in its entirety during his lifetime. What was at last published as *On the Road* had been completed in 1951 and had

ON THE SUBJECT OF...

JACK MICHELINE

While Micheline emerged as a poet during the Beat generation, his subsequent work is considered just as vital. Despite his stature among a small, devoted following, he remains virtually undiscovered by a majority of critics, academicians, and publishers. His relative anonymity is partially due to Micheline's refusal to compromise his values or to make concessions to commercialism. In fact, Micheline initially viewed the Beat movement as publishing propaganda; while he conceded that it provided a forum and exposure for new writers, he also felt that the movement's popularity tainted true expression by introducing big money and commercial motivations to the literary and artistic worlds. Despite his criticism, Micheline is strongly identified with the Beats because of his writing style and the subjects and themes of his work. Written to be read aloud, his poems imitate the rhythms of speech—especially ethnic dialects—and reflect the influence of jazz music. Many of his early poems celebrate the vitality of black American culture, with which he had been fascinated. Also characteristic of Beat literature, Micheline's verse is populated by street people: the outcast and the destitute, addicts, dreamers, drunks, and visionaries. His publications include *Red River of Wine* (1958), *In the Bronx and Other Stories* (1965), and the play *East Bleeker: A Drama with Music* (1967).

circulated for years under the title "The Beat Generation." Tim Hunt in the most brilliant scholarly study so far of any of Kerouac's works, *Kerouac's Crooked Road* (1981), presents a convincing theory about the relationships between the various—and often greatly different—versions of what Kerouac conceived as a work in progress that found its final form only in *Visions of Cody* (earlier referred to as the "Neal Book").

The preliminary version, however, that Kerouac reputedly typed in a single paragraph on a single scroll of paper in April 1951 is the one that has become a modern classic, overshadowing all of what the author considered the more definitive chronicles of the Legend of Ti Jean Duluoz. The principal questions that must be faced are: why has this become and remained so much more popular than any other of Kerouac's works, and what does its popularity suggest about the sensibilities of its audience?

An Episodic Tale

One of the features that conspicuously differentiates **On the Road** from Kerouac's other works is its structure. After establishing a reputation with this work, Kerouac was increasingly able to insist upon his books being published just as he had written them. Astute editor Malcolm Cowley, however, who was instrumental in Viking Press's finally publishing **On the Road,** forced Kerouac to accept some changes in the work. While the unavailability of the manuscripts makes it impossible even to guess how much these changes may have affected the contents and tone of the work, we know from Allen Ginsberg's comments, for example, that in the episode in part three in a Sacramento motel,[1] Cowley insisted on the deletion of mention of Dean Moriarity's permitting the owner of an automobile to fellate him in order to take control of the car for the rest of the trip.

Cowley told Ann Charters, however, that all the changes he suggested "were big ones, mostly omissions. I said why don't you boil down these to two or three trips and keep the mood of the content." The aim of the changes, he said, was to "make it a more continuous narrative. . . . Kerouac agreed and did the job."[2]

Tom Clark minimizes the possible importance of these changes by commenting that, although Kerouac complained that "the published version was an emasculation of the 1951 book . . . Viking's 1956 editing left the story intact . . . some of the cross-country travels were removed or spliced together."[3] Such splicings, however, could have helped to achieve the novel's balanced four-part structure; each contains a story-within-a-story that reinforces the predominant impression left by the work as a whole, as summed up in the brief fifth part. If the original version of the text was, like some of Kerouac's others, analogous to a jazz improvisation, Cowley's "big changes" may have turned **On the Road** into a symphonic work, in which the patterns of the four movements are repetitive and incremental rather than varied in temper as they are in the traditional musical form of the symphony.

Before looking closely at the structure of the novel, however, we must consider what—from a chronological point of view—is included, and what is left out. Even though the account of Kerouac's cross-country junkets may have been streamlined, the order of events in the novel still corresponds closely enough to the order of similar events in the author's life to make it possible to date them with some precision. The narrative begins when Sal Paradise (based on Kerouac himself) meets Dean Moriarity (based on Neal Cassady) for the first time around Christmas 1946 in New York City, and it ends shortly after Sal gets back to New York after a devastating trip to Mexico City with Dean in October 1950. The time spanned is thus just slightly less than four years, but the events depicted in the novel occur within just twenty-four months. Part 1 parallels Kerouac's first long junket into the West between December 1946 and October 1947. Of the next thirteen months, however, Sal says only, "It was over a year before I saw Dean again. I stayed home all that time, finished my book and began going to school on the GI Bill of Rights."[4] The action does not resume until December 1948, and part 2 uses events only from that month and January 1949. After a brief break, the action resumes in part 3 in April 1949 and continues until July. There follows another long break until March 1950, when Sal, like Kerouac having just sold his first novel, sets off on the road on his own—for the first time without Dean.

The novel opens with the curt announcement that Sal first met Dean not long after he had split up with his wife and suffered a serious illness, but he does not want to talk about these events, which are part of a dead past. "With the coming of Dean Moriarity," he announces, "began the part of my life you could call my life on the road" (5). It is this life, and only this life, with which the novel is concerned. It begins with a major turning-point in the narrator's life, and the reader is given few glimpses into what has gone before. The novel ends almost four years later with Sal's split-up with Dean, another major turning point in his life, and we have little hint of what comes afterwards. (It is important to note here that Kerouac did continue seeing Neal Cassady after the separation dramatized in the novel in order to emphasize that we should always remember that **On the Road,** no matter how much autobiographical material it draws upon, is a self-contained picaresque tale that needs to be interpreted on its own terms and not viewed as a literal record of the Kerouac-Cassady relationship.)

Since Sal's connection with Dean begins after the breakup of a marriage and depicts the finally unsuccessful effort to establish an intimate bond with another man, some readers have been tempted to interpret the work in homosexual terms—a temptation encouraged by Neal Cassady's known bisexual practices (including a short-lived relationship with Allen Ginsberg) and Kerouac's own ambiguous sexuality. Suspicion is also supported by the almost too strident fag-bashing tone that Sal adopts whenever he speaks about "fairies" in the book. A preoccupation with this thesis, however, leads to a confusion between fiction and possible reality that distracts attention from the novel itself. Sal Paradise's emphasis throughout his narrative is upon the quest not for a lover, but for a brother, reflecting Kerouac's own effort to find a replacement for his dead brother Gerard, with whom as a child he had identified himself. Cassady also closely resembles the fictional figure of brother Joe Martin in **The Town and the City,** with whom Peter Martin had shared a bedroom as a child.

At the emotional climax of the novel in part 3, when Dean is beginning to be denounced and shunned by former friends and even relatives, Sal's defense of him has religious rather than sexual overtones. When Galatea Dunkel charges that Dean has "done so many awful things I don't know what to say to you," Sal experiences the revelation that has most upset many of the commentators already appalled by the behavior of the characters in the novel—"Dean, by virtue of his enormous series of sins, was becoming the Idiot, the Imbecile, the Saint of the lot. . . . That's what Dean was, the HOLY GOOF" (160-61).

Sal has earlier realized that the relationship described in the novel is reaching its crisis: "It was probably the pivotal point of our friendship when he realized I had actually spent some hours thinking about him and his troubles" (156), and they resolve to go to Italy. The exact nature of the relationship as Sal conceives it is brought out when Sal is questioned by two college boys who are frightened by Dean's wild driving. When they ask if he is Sal's brother, Sal replies, "He's mad . . . and yes, he's my brother" (187).

Despite Sal's "amazed" attention to Dean's "enormous dangle" in a nude drawing of Dean by his girl friend (38), a serious objection to viewing Sal's attachment to Dean as a search for a substitute spouse rather than a putative brother is the very structure of the story. As we have seen, Dean is a part of Sal's life only when they are on the road; almost half of the elapsed time, however, Sal is back home in New York, working, writing, living with his aunt, completing his novel and eventually selling it. Sal is thus a split character, although in **On the Road,** Kerouac has combined the parts of a personality divided in **The Town and the City** between two brothers into a single figure who moves back and forth between two quite different lives. Only the most fleeting references are made, however, to the life he lives off the road; the novel is intensely focused on only the half of his life that he lives on the road where Dean serves as his guide and model, although he never becomes a full-time partner in both halves of Sal's divided life.

Not much attention has been paid in criticism of the novel to the fact that it is focused solely on half of Sal's life, although this focusing needs to be taken into account in speculating about the audience's favorable reaction to the work. The life on the road that is depicted is, of course, the exciting part of Sal's life. Living at home, being cared for by one's aunt, working on a novel, even achieving commercial success is not exciting, so that in this novel when the narrator skips over half his life hardly anyone notices.

By thus intensely focusing the story—a focusing that must have been strengthened by Malcolm Cowley's suggested revisions, even if in accord with Kerouac's original intentions—Kerouac could be employing Poe's theories about narrative construction explained in his review of Hawthorne's *Twice-Told Tales*. In this landmark statement, Poe explains that when a skillful literary artist ideally constructs a tale "he has not fashioned his thoughts to accommodate his incidents, but having conceived, with deliberate care, a certain unique or single *effect* to be wrought out, he then invents such incidents—he then combines such events as may best aid him" to the "outbringing" of this preconceived effect, so that "during the hour of perusal the soul of the reader is at the writer's control."

Kerouac's other writings, neither the diffuse and rambling **The Town and the City** nor his later strivings for spontaneity, followed no such practice; but **On the Road** illustrates (though probably not deliberately) Poe's principles, especially in putting the soul of the reader at the writer's control during the hour of perusal.

The novel can be discussed in terms of Poe's theory (despite Poe's own distrust of such an extended form) because each of the four major sections can be read as an individual tale at a single sitting. The second, third, and fourth parts are remarkably comparable in length, and the first is substantially longer only because it contains a section that sharply contrasts with the episodes concerning Sal and Dean and that has no counterpart in the succeeding sections. Otherwise all four parts are remarkably similar in structure, each leading to the same kind of conclusion, one that serves to foreshadow and reinforce the conclusion of the whole tale in the brief fifth section.

The Parts and the Whole

Each of the four major parts of the novel describes one of Sal's road trips, reflecting Kerouac's own major ventures between 1946 and 1950. Each of these parts follows a remarkably similar pattern leading to identical conclusions. Each begins with Sal tired and depressed and seeking an escape from a troublesome or boring situation in his "other life." He at first takes to the road slowly and cautiously, but as he gains confidence and becomes energized by this new life, the action accelerates until it reaches a high point at which a disappointing experience causes things to fall to pieces, and Sal returns home (often slinking there) dejected and depressed again.

In part 1, Sal meets Dean in December 1946, but it is the following July before he has saved enough money to venture out on the road. His initial attempts at hitchhiking are futile, and he has to take a bus to Chicago. On his way to Denver, however, he begins to pick up the beat of life on the road. He takes the bus again to San Francisco, where instead of enjoying life as he has expected he ends up as a security guard in a construction camp with a tyrannous chief. This experience leads him to conclude that "this is the story of America. Everybody's doing what they think they're supposed to do" (57). Things have not worked out at all, and he laments how different the reality has proved from what he had envisioned: "Here I was at the end of America—and now there was nowhere to go but back" (66).

On this trip, however, a determination to go to Los Angeles leads Sal into the one genuinely promising relationship that he develops. He meets a Mexican girl named Terry on a bus and has his only rewarding romantic relationship with a woman with her. They spend only fifteen days together, however, because he is broke. She is supposed to follow him to New York, but Sal comments with sad finality, "We both knew she wouldn't make it." (85). Why he fails to pursue the relationship is not revealed, however, until much later in the book, when, mooning in Denver's colored section, he wishes that he belonged to one of the oppressed but happy minorities and was anything but what he was "so drearily, a

'white man' disillusioned." In one of the most startling and surprising statements in the novel, he blurts out, "All my life I'd had white ambitions; that was why I'd abandoned a good woman like Terry" (148).

More than a year passes before Dean turns up again at the start of part 2 to help Sal move his mother's furniture to his sister's house in North Carolina. Then Sal wants to set off on one more "magnificent" trip to the West Coast before he returns to school in the spring. After troubles with a "Victorian police force," the travelers visit Old Bull Lee (based on William Burroughs) near New Orleans, where he is raising marijuana; but at the last minute Dean antagonizes Old Bull by using his con man tactics to try to borrow money. Finances become increasingly difficult, but when the travelers at last reach the Golden Gate, Dean dumps Sal and Marylou (the girl that Dean had brought East with him); and Sal realizes "what a whore she was" (142). The deflating climax comes, however, when Dean tries to make some money selling a new kind of pressure cooker at home demonstrations. One morning Sal sees Dean standing naked by the window and observes that "he looked like someday he'd be the pagan mayor of San Francisco," but in the judgment that marks the climax of the novel and begins an increasingly depressing picture of the life on the road, Sal observes, "But his energies ran out" (145). Life on the road has been built on "a hurricane of energy," but people have limitations that make it impossible to sustain this life of irresponsible kicks. Sal has become tired of the whole business and remains in California only until a compensation check arrives that enables him to take the bus back home again. "What I accomplished by coming to Frisco I don't know," he observes. As he parts with Dean and Marylou, he laments, "We were all thinking we'd never see one another again and we didn't care" (147).

By spring, however, he has saved a few dollars and takes off again for Denver, thinking of settling there. But he finds, as he reflects on his "white ambitions" that it is too late: "always it had been college, big-time, sober-faced; no boyish, human joy. . . . All I did was die" (149). When a rich girl gives him a hundred dollars, he is drawn back to San Francisco, where Dean greets him naked in the doorway (150). (Sal's frequent emphasis on Dean's nakedness also suggests a sexual preoccupation, but Sal never admits any physical response. The nakedness seems rather to symbolize Sal's conception of Dean as a kind of primitive force, unrestrained by any social institutions, until his energies give out.) After hearing Dean's tales of woe about his tangled domestic affairs, Sal offers to take the responsibility for supporting them both and proposes the trip to Italy. They set off for the East on a terrifying drive in a car obtained from an agency that provides drivers for other people's vehicles.

Along the way, Sal becomes increasingly defensive as Dean is attacked by family and friends, but even he is beginning to lose faith in the lure of the endless road: "I was beginning to cross and recross towns in America as though I was a traveling salesman—raggedy travelings, bad stock, rotten beans in the bottom of my bag of tricks, nobody buying" (202). In New York, the patient aunt into whom Kerouac has transformed his mother for this tale allows Dean to stay only a few days. Although Dean and Sal agree to remain friends forever, within a few days Dean is involved with still another woman and a few months later, he has four children on his hands, two illegitimate. "So we didn't go to Italy," Sal ends this installment in curt disgruntlement.

Selling his novel, however, enables him to take to the road with regenerated enthusiasm in the spring of 1950, as in part 4 for the first time he leaves Dean behind and sets off on his own. Dean turns up, however, on his way to Mexico to get a divorce, and Sal is suddenly aglow in anticipation of the unimaginable prospects of "the most fabulous" trip of all. As they enter Mexico, Dean enthuses, "Now, Sal, we're leaving everything behind us and entering a new and unknown phase of things. All the years and troubles and kicks—and now this!" (226), but *this* turns out to be only more of the same old frustration and disillusionment. After some nights of innocent fun, Sal comes down with a bad fever, and Dean, who has gotten his divorce, deserts Sal, telling him only, "Gotta get back to my life" (248). When Sal recovers, he realizes "what a rat" Dean was (249); but recognizing the hopeless complexity of Dean's life, he promises the absent Dean to say nothing.

This concluding disillusionment with Dean and the life he promises and Sal's resignation should not come, however, as a surprise to the careful reader. Very early in the book Sal acknowledged that Dean is a con man, but justifies his behavior on the grounds that "he was only conning because he wanted so much to live and to get involved with people who would otherwise pay no attention to him. He was conning me and I knew it . . . and he knew I knew (this has been the basis of our relationship)" (8). Sal apparently hopes that out of his bag of tricks, Dean might

generate energies that would lead to a magnificent life on the road. His hopes are dashed, however, when Dean's energies run out in San Francisco; he will never become the "pagan mayor" who will generate a new order of things. From this point forward, despite some desperate efforts on Sal's part to sustain the relationship, it gradually deteriorates until Dean walks out on Sal in Mexico City, unable to accept responsibility that will interfere with his uncontrollable impulses.

Those who have denounced **On the Road** as promoting the adoption of life on the road have certainly failed to notice two passages late in the novel that reflect Sal's state of mind before he is lured into the final disastrous adventure.

Looking over some photographs of friends just before Sal sets off on the last trip by himself, he muses: "I realized these were all the snapshots which our children would look at someday with wonder, thinking their parents had lived smooth, well-ordered, stabilized-within-the-photo lives and got up in the morning to walk proudly on the sidewalks of life, never dreaming the raggedy madness and riot of our actual lives, our actual night, the hell of it, the senseless nightmare road. All of it inside endless and beginningless emptiness" (208). Just before this he has told the man who had been the embodiment of the life on the road, "All I hope, Dean, is someday we'll be able to live on the same street with our families and get to be a couple of oldtimers together" (207). No wonder that the novel ends with Sal sitting "on the old broken-down river pier watching the long, long skies over New Jersey" (as anyone who has seen this particular Hudson riverscape knows, it is one of the most dismal prospects anywhere), musing, as the sun goes down, that "nobody knows what's going to happen to anybody besides the forlorn rags of growing old" (254).

Just prior to these lines, Kerouac provides one of the most brilliant images anywhere in his fiction to convey the state of mind of his narrator. Back in New York, his novel published, Sal is riding to a Duke Ellington concert at the Metropolitan Opera House with an old friend who has had handpainted for the occasion one of those garish early 1950s ties that Frederic Wakeman satirizes in *The Hucksters*, "on it was painted a replica of the concert tickets, and the names Sal and Laura and Remi and Vicki, the girl, together with a series of sad jokes and some of his favorite sayings such as 'You can't teach the old maestro a new tune'" (253). Dean asks for a ride, but Remi—

Sal's host—refuses, so that Sal can only sit in the back seat of a bookie's Cadillac and wave through the window to Dean.

The image perfectly encapsulates the whole drift of the novel: Sal, despite his efforts to break out, is left behind glass, the captive of his "white ambitions," unable to communicate with Dean, who is left behind to shiver in the New York cold. Sal has been on the road, but never *of* the road. After each adventure, he has withdrawn to a protected environment. Dean has repeatedly tempted him out before, but fails to do so on this final occasion.

To call **On the Road,** a bildungsroman, a novel of education, is a misapplication of the term; for in such a novel the protagonist is substantially changed by his experiences, but Sal Paradise never changes. He is rather simply confirmed in the identity that he possessed before the beginning of the novel. Sal has recognized Dean as a confidence man from the beginning of their association, but he has allowed himself at times to be hypnotized by Dean's energies, which promise a magical new world. When these energies run out, Sal wakes up and finds himself back in the same old world that he left, neither happy nor comfortable, but captive to the materialistic world of bad taste and conspicuous consumption epitomized by the final Cadillac ride. He sees no future, but "the forlorn rags of growing old."

The Appeal of "On the Road"

On the Road is thus not, except at occasional moments early in each of its four major parts, a carefree, upbeat promotion of an irresponsible life on the road that presents a formidable threat to the traditional American way of life; rather it is a distinctly downbeat work, with a conclusion in which the narrator is distinctly "beat" in the commonest sense of the word meaning something battered by the world (and *beat* is most frequently used in this sense in this novel). The conclusion is foreshadowed and reinforced by the movement of each of the four major parts from beginnings full of happy anticipations through periods of frenzied excitement to depressing conclusions portraying the characters' frustration and exhaustion.

What does an audience find appealing about such a work? Despite harsh attacks by establishment critics, the work was an immediate success, and it has remained steadily in print, attracting a sizeable cult following that has been regularly renewed, especially among high school and college readers. It continues to be attacked, often

quite virulently, but usually by people who do not appear to have read the novel itself but to have been influenced by media stereotypes of the Beat Generation and the more sensational passages from Allen Ginsberg's poem *Howl*. Certainly it is not a novel that preaches the benefits of rebellion any more than is J. D. Salinger's *Catcher in the Rye*.

What the novel communicates, in fact, is much like Holden Caulfield's advice to his readers after he has spent a night trying to sleep on a bench in Grand Central Station, "Don't ever try it. I mean it. It'll depress you." Certainly an attempt to duplicate the ironically named Sal Paradise's life on the road would prove equally depressing. Far from inciting the reader to hit the road, **On the Road** proves a traditional cautionary tale, warning readers about the sorry nature of the world. It promises the reader nothing but disappointment and disillusionment.

Although this is not the way the novel has usually been described, it is supported by a careful analysis of the narrative, and it not only best suits the work, but is in keeping with what might be anticipated from the work of a basically conservative young person as he faces a critical test as to which part of his divided personality will dominate his life. Can he really overcome his "white ambitions" to adopt a spontaneous, irresponsible way of life? We should not be surprised after reading **On the Road** that its author would subsequently, in an article entitled "**After Me, the Deluge,**" reveal that he feels lost in contemporary America, fulminate against Jerry Rubin, Abbie Hoffman, Ken Kesey, Timothy Leary, and his former close friend Allen Ginsberg, and finally refuse to accept any responsibility for the kind of youth culture that others blame him for promoting.[5]

Perhaps Kerouac's own expectations are best summed up in Sal Paradise's reflection before the second and shortest of his trips, "What I wanted was to take one more magnificent trip to the West Coast and get back in time for the spring semester in school" (107)—a manifestation of the urge that drives thousands of college students every spring to Daytona Beach and Fort Lauderdale. What he is telling readers is that such junkets promise to be great fun, but prove exhausting and disappointing. Hopeful young readers are likely, however, to be inclined to do what he himself did rather than what he tells them to do. **On the Road** is surely a novel that has been more enthusiastically than carefully read, so that professional busybodies are probably correct in feeling that it might foster delinquent impulses, but only because they have missed the point themselves. A familiar case of the blind presuming to lead the blind.

The novel cannot be dismissed as simply exciting fare for careless readers. Perhaps even only unconsciously, many readers are likely to be affected by the underlying despair that the novel expresses. The view that Sal finally espouses as he sits forlornly watching the coming of night and its symbolic anticipation of growing old is that people's energies are not equal to the demands that youth greedily imposes upon them. Driving fast and dangerously is an exhilarating experience for a while, but people, like cars, finally run out of gas. **On the Road** suggests that maturity offers no rewards; there is only, after the excitement of youth, "the forlorn rags of growing old." What the novel ultimately fosters is not rebellion, but sullen resignation.

It may be, of course, the very defeatist aspects of the conclusion that have most bothered high-minded attackers who are still guided (or misguided) by Longfellow's injunction that "life is earnest, life is real." If Kerouac's novel serves to stimulate any sensibility, it is not that of an ebullient youth cult, but a world-weariness that harks back to the French decadents of the fin de siècle, as is evidenced also by Kerouac's fondness for Rimbaud.

On the Road is, thus, ultimately a defeatist book, but this very quality may account for its appeal. Americans are not really educated to be winners, and few of them know how to win gracefully. Most, especially of Kerouac's generation that grew up during the Depression, expect to lose and to be taken in by confidence men. It remains to be seen whether the new generation of "Yuppies" are to enjoy a basically different experience, but for those who have been for thirty years the enthusiastic readers of the book its underlying appeal may be that it does indeed really show things as they are—and shows that they are not very good.

Although the language and the settings are new, **On the Road** is a traditional tale of youth's disillusionment, perhaps closest in the American tradition to Fitzgerald's *The Great Gatsby*. What was distinctly new and different about the book, however, was that the disenchantment, traditionally regarded as the preserve of the rich, was transferred here not to poor, honest working people—as in the writings of Dreiser and the proletarians—but to questionable bohemians operating on the margins of society.

Kerouac's work may have gone unpublished as long as it did because most of the reputable American publishers regard themselves as refined and genteel caterers to a refined and genteel audience. They would have been uneasy about introducing into the homes of their customers ruffians whom one would certainly avoid in public. Publishers tend, until pressed by powerful forces of public opinion, to print what they think readers ought to want to read; so they find it difficult to recognize changes occurring in the audience or new voices that might appeal to a changed audience, even when those voices are saying the same things as the established literati but not in the expected way.

Notes

1. Allen Ginsberg and Allen Young, *Gay Sunshine Interview* (Bolinas, Calif.: Grey Fox Press, 1974), 3.

2. Charters, [Ann.] *Kerouac*[: *A Biography*. San Francisco: Straight Arrow, 1973], 223.

3. Clark, [Tom.] [*Jack*] *Kerouac*, [San Diego: Harcourt Brace Jovanovich, 1984], 152.

4. [Kerouac, Jack.] *On the Road*, [New York: Viking Press, 1957], 91. Subsequent page references in the text.

5. "After Me, the Deluge," *Chicago Tribune*, 28 September 1969, Sunday Magazine, 3. The article was also syndicated to other newspapers, where it appeared under various titles.

The Subterraneans

JON PANISH (ESSAY DATE FALL 1994)

SOURCE: Panish, Jon. "Kerouac's *The Subterraneans*: A Study of 'Romantic Primitivism.'" *MELUS* 19, no. 3 (fall 1994): 107-23.

In the following essay, Panish views The Subterraneans *as an extended instance of what he terms "Kerouac's romantic racism."*

In a review of Jack Kerouac's 1958 novel, **The Subterraneans**, poet/critic Kenneth Rexroth said, "The story is all about jazz, and Negroes. Now there are two things Jack knows nothing about—jazz and Negroes" (Nicosia 568). Whatever the source of Rexroth's disdain for Kerouac's novel, this criticism of **The Subterraneans** hits close to the mark.[1] Kerouac's romanticized depictions of and references to African Americans (as well as other racial minorities—American Indians and Mexican-Americans) betray his essential lack of understanding of African American culture and

ABOUT THE AUTHOR

BURROUGHS REMEMBERS KEROUAC

Jack Kerouac knew about writing when I first met him in 1944. He was twenty-one; already he had written a million words and was completely dedicated to his chosen trade. It was Kerouac who kept telling me I should write and call the book I wrote *Naked Lunch.*

Burroughs, William S. An excerpt from "Remembering Jack Kerouac." In *The Adding Machine: Selected Essays,* pp. 176-81. New York: Arcade, 1993.

the African American social experience. That is, Kerouac's novelistic attitude toward racial minorities in ***The Subterraneans*** (and elsewhere) is similar to the stance of those "romantic racialists" of the 1840s and 1850s described by George M. Fredrickson, who, in African Americans, "discovered redeeming virtues and even evidences of . . . superiority" (Fredrickson 101). For Kerouac uses (as did the nineteenth-century romantic racialists) racial minorities as symbols of those entities that he feels are "tragically lacking in white American civilization" (Fredrickson 108). American society, Kerouac says, desperately needs an infusion of the qualities embodied by her oppressed minorities: the existential joy, wisdom, and nobility that comes from suffering and victimization.

It is an indication of how deeply racism is embedded in American discourse that the African American characters and art forms that are depicted in Kerouac's novel are not substantially different from the "Negro symbols" used by the romantic racialists over a century earlier to help eradicate slavery. Even on the dawn (and later, in the midst) of the Civil Rights Movement, white authors, such as Kerouac, who positioned themselves on the outside of the social and literary mainstream of America—that is, contiguous with, if not intersecting those groups who had been *forced* outside—were not any closer than writers of previous generations, such as Carl Van Vechten, to representing America's oppressed minorities in ways that respected those groups and their history and traditions. Not recognizing their own complicity in perpetuating racist ideology, Kerouac

and others continued the tradition of primitivizing and romanticizing the experiences of racial minorities (particularly African Americans) and raiding their culture and contemporary experience for the purpose of enhancing their own position as white outsiders.

While the attraction of white writers such as Kerouac to African American society and culture was not new to the 1950s,[2] the amount and vitality of both the white and black literary work with these materials during this decade combined with the proximity of this period to the succeeding boom in white and black cultural interaction has prompted many cultural historians to speculate about this decade's unique characteristics. The favored explanation for the attraction of white people in general to African American society and culture during the 1950s has been their identification as victims of nuclear terror with the traditional victims of American governmental policy—African Americans—and their need to replace the cold logic and reason of this scientific terror with a strategy for living that is more spontaneous, emotional, and spiritual. Similarly, the conventional explanation for the white writers's interest in African American culture involves their use of these materials in reaction against the literary establishment; that is, jazz and a kind of African American oral poetry gave these writers forms for their expression that they believed were more alive, vital, and honest than what they perceived as the fake, impotent, and artificial forms of literature emanating from the establishment.[3]

Both of these explanations (the general and the specific) fit very well with classic descriptions of cultural and artistic "primitivism." That is, in times when people are discontented with the progress of their society, these so-called civilized people look to the "other"—usually a Noble Savage—as a remedy for their dissatisfaction. The civilized people, in other words, endow a symbol with those characteristics that are opposite those that their society champions. The white writers of the 1950s, then (like such earlier ones as Van Vechten in *Nigger Heaven* or Sherwood Anderson in *Dark Laughter*), do not see the "other" (in this case, mostly African Americans) for what he or she is—a person just like any other who is involved in the complex relations of his or her culture—but as a static, unreal image. As Marianna Torgovnick points out, the image of the primitive itself is "infinitely docile and malleable": "The real secret of the primitive in this century has often been the same secret as always: the primitive can be—has been, will be [?]—whatever Euro-Americans want it to be" (Torgovnick 9-10).

Although the actual experiences Kerouac depicts in **The Subterraneans** occurred slightly earlier (1953) than the full-fledged Beat "scene" that later developed in Greenwich Village (primarily during the second half the 1950s), a glimpse of the contours of race relations in the Village Beat scene during the late 1950s will help prepare us for understanding the discursive racial patterns (that is, his primitivizing of African American culture and society) that emerge in Kerouac's novel.[4] Not only were some of the same people depicted in **The Subterraneans** still involved in the later Beat scene (including Kerouac himself) but the same racial power relations existed at both times as well. Revolving around Greenwich Village, the New York Beat scene members saw themselves as a new, racially integrated sub-society, apart from both of the racially constituted parts of New York City (i.e. black Harlem and white elsewhere). Describing the difference between what she still (when the book was published in 1990) sees as the difference between the Beats's interest in African American culture and that of previous generations of white bohemians, Hettie Jones says,

> But it's important to the particular history of what would later be called the New Bohemia that going to the Five Spot was not like taking the A train to Harlem. Downtown was everyone's new place. . . . And all of us there—black and white were strangers at first.
>
> (Jones 34)

Although Jones does depict herself as being rather naive (or, at least, idealistic) upon first arriving in the Village (especially with regard to race), she does portray the Village bohemian scene as being one that is remarkably free of not only the sicknesses of the dominant society (e.g. racism) but also of those that had been ascribed to hipsters by the likes of Norman Mailer:

> That summer [1957] *Dissent* magazine published Norman Mailer's essay "The White Negro." There I read that jazz was orgasm, which only blacks had figured out, and that white "hipsters" like me were attracted to the black world's sexy, existential violence. But the only violence I'd ever encountered, the one time I'd heard bone smashing bone, had been among whites in the South. The young black musicians I met didn't differ from other aspiring artists. And jazz music was complicated, technically the most interesting I'd heard, the hardest to play.
>
> (Jones 35)

In fact, contrary to Mailer's theoretical stance, Jones's overall depiction of the Village in the late 1950s is one of an open, youthful community full of optimism and goodwill and beyond any racial tension. As Dan Wakefield has recently described it, the Village during the 1950s was a "haven where people were not only allowed but expected to dress, speak, and behave differently from the herd" (Wakefield 121).

Similarly, Lawrence Lipton justified the Beats's use of the descriptive term "spade cat" instead of "Negro" by appealing to the notion that the relationship between these hip whites and their black counterparts is outside what has been and is typical in American society: "The holy barbarians, white and negro, are so far beyond 'racial tolerance' and desegregation that they no longer have to be polite about it with one another" (Lipton 317). In this quotation, it is significant that Lipton places the relationship between "white and negro" bohemians outside what was the most progressive race politics of the time—"desegregation"—as well as what could be called more polite, middle-class politics—"racial tolerance."

Corroboration of Lipton's and Hettie Jones's characterizations (at least at the initial stages of the association of people in the Village) comes from both Jones's friend, Joyce Johnson, and her ex-husband, Amiri Baraka. Johnson says,

> In the excitement and hope of that moment [1957]—in what was real and strongly believed and truly lived out, as distinct from fad—there seemed the possibility of enormous transformations. It seemed entirely possible that newness and openness expressed in the poems, the paintings, the music, would ripple out far beyond St. Marks Place and tables in the Cedar, swamping the old barriers of class and race, healing the tragic divisions in the American soul.
>
> (Johnson 216)

Although Baraka is, predictably, less charitable than Johnson in his retrospective assessments of this same gathering of bohemians, he does admit that he "came to the Village thinking the people there, those vaunted intellectuals and artists, could not possibly be 'prejudiced' because that was dumb shit" (Baraka 132). Moreover, he says, "I could see the young white boys and girls in their pronouncement of disillusion with and 'removal' from society as being related to the black experience. That made us colleagues of the spirit" (157).

However, as Baraka and even Joyce Johnson (but not Hettie Jones) recognize (even if for slightly different reasons), the hope that the relationships between white and black bohemians were free from America's racist disease was *only* a

William Burroughs (left) and Jack Kerouac in a New York City apartment, circa 1953.

hope, *only* illusion. That is, no matter how much these idealistic young bohemians hoped and imagined that they were beyond racism, the same power relations existed in the Village that existed outside of it. Using Hettie Jones herself as her example, Johnson attributes this false hope to the idealism of youth that obscured the social facts of the period: "Children of the late and silent fifties, we knew little of political realities. We had the illusion our own passions were enough. We felt, as Hettie Cohen Jones once put it, that you could change everything just by being loud enough" (Johnson 216).

An African American man in a predominantly white island of outsiders, Baraka recounts that he, at least, always felt a tension between his imaginative connection with these people and the social reality of their interaction. He remembers that even though he felt a "spiritual" connection with these white outsiders, he never quite felt that he fit in—their ultimate concerns were not his and vice versa.[5] Finally, he was an outsider "even inside those 'outsider' circles" (157).

A close examination of Kerouac's *The Subterraneans* will reveal how this distance between imaginative projection and social reality is manifested discursively. The novel's depictions of jazz and African American characters will also expose the essential racism that is at the core of Kerouac's work and that formed the basis for the race relations that existed in the later Village Beat scene.

Written in 1953 but not published until 1958, *The Subterraneans* narrates a brief, ill-fated affair Kerouac had with a young African American woman the same year the novel was written. Kerouac wrote the book shortly after the affair broke up in a furious "three days and nights of speed typing on benzedrine" (Nicosia 445). It is not considered of primary significance by most Kerouac scholars.[6] *The Subterraneans* is nevertheless an interesting novel for this study because it not only focuses on topics relating to African Americans—jazz and interracial relationships—but is Kerouac's most direct and sustained example of the literary method he modeled, in part, on bebop and later called "spontaneous bop prosody."[7]

Jazz (or, more specifically, bebop), then, is at once the backdrop and one of the organizing principles of **The Subterraneans**: readers "hear" it in the many clubs that the two main characters—Leo Percepied and Mardou Fox—frequent and also in the rhythm of the words and sentences used in the novel. As backdrop, jazz is depicted by Kerouac as being produced by beautifully suffering jazz musicians for the enjoyment and even liberation of Kerouac's generation of bohemians. Although jazz as backdrop occurs many times throughout the novel, one scene in particular presents an interesting example of Kerouac's perspective on jazz, its performers, and its performance in clubs.

Occurring early in the novel, the scene describes the night the narrator (a Kerouac substitute named Leo Percepied) first meets the young African American bohemian Mardou Fox and they go with some friends to hear jazz (more specifically, Charlie Parker) at a club called the Red Drum:

> . . . and up on the stand Bird Parker with solemn eyes who'd been busted fairly recently and had now returned to a kind of bop dead Frisco but had just discovered or been told about the Red Drum, the great new generation gang wailing and gathering there, so here he was on the stand, examining them with his eyes as he blew his now-settled-down-into-regulated-design "crazy" notes. . . .
>
> (18-19)

A number of aspects of this passage are both significant and characteristic of the way Kerouac depicts and attributes meaning to jazz. First, Kerouac's focus on Charlie Parker is, of course, on his victimization—"been busted fairly recently"—and, just as importantly, on Parker's emotional response to his existence as a suffering black jazz musician—solemnity, perhaps indicating a certain amount of resignation to his martyr-like status among the jazz faithful (certainly the religious connotation of a word like "solemn" cannot be ignored, especially as the scene is further developed by Kerouac).[8] Of course, Kerouac was not the first nor the last to emphasize the notion that Parker (especially, but really *all* black jazz musicians are included) suffered at the hands of white society. However, this is, and remains, Kerouac's major use of the Parker image in his work. In a later characterization of Parker—found in the later choruses of his **Mexico City Blues**—the same themes, victimization and Parker's resignation to his Christ-like status, are also emphasized. This time Kerouac compares Parker to another religious figure, Buddha, but again focuses on the quiet resignation on his expressive face:

> And his expression on his face
> Was as calm, beautiful, and profound
> As the image of the Buddha
> Represented in the East, the lidded eyes,
> The expression that says "All is Well"
> —This was what Charley [sic] Parker
> Said when he played, All is Well.
>
> (241)

In this chorus (239), Kerouac's focus on Parker's victimization by his followers takes the following form,

> —Charley burst
> His lungs to reach the speed
> Of what the speedsters wanted
> And what they wanted
> Was his Eternal Slowdown
>
> (241)

There may be much truth to the idea that Parker and black jazz musicians were victimized and exploited (and may have even contributed to this perception).[9] However, the focus on this aspect of their persona was more characteristic of their white audiences (and the whites who wrote about them) than their black audiences. In any case, as jazz writer Nat Hentoff has said, to blame Parker's death solely on society and absolve him of any contribution is to be too simplistic (Hentoff 194); most jazz musicians suffered from the same racism and economic exploitation and survived, only Parker and some others did not.

Also significant in the passage from **The Subterraneans** is Kerouac's portrayal of Parker as being interested in the existence and presence of his audience—"been told about the Red Drum, the great new generation wailing and gathering there . . . examining them with his eyes as he blew . . ."—that is, Parker is depicted not as playing the Red Drum simply because he has been booked into another jazz club where he can work and earn some money, but as being interested in this particular club because of the audience that would be seeing and hearing him: "that great new generation." The connection between Parker and his bohemian audience is made personal and momentous in this way and is enhanced by further linking Parker and the audience through the image of his eyes, which have already been designated (not just by this passage but by tradition as well) as the locus of Parker's emotional response to his victimization as a black jazz musician.

The nexus Kerouac emphasizes between the jazz performer and his bohemian audience is one that the novelist repeats often in this and other works. Throughout **The Subterraneans** and **On the Road,** for example, are tossed-off references to

Kerouac and friends being the "bop generation" or "children of bop." Also included in **On the Road** is a scene remarkably similar to the one reproduced above from **The Subterraneans**:

> . . . he [a Negro tenor saxophone player] looked at us, Dean and me; with an expression that seemed to say, Hey now, and what's this thing we're all doing in this sad brown world? . . . because here we were dealing with the pit and prune juice of poor beat life itself in the god-awful streets of man, so he said it and sang it "Close—your—" and blew it way up to the ceiling and through to the stars and on out. . . .
>
> (164)

In this passage, the musician and his bohemian audience are connected by their mutual *and equal* suffering in the world and are able to transcend this squalor through the magic of the music. In Kerouac's descriptions of jazz performances there is usually this personal, emotional link made between performer and audience, *especially* if it involves an African American jazz musician.

Moreover, Kerouac is often even more focused in his connection between jazz performers and their audience; that is, he also delineates a close bond between the performer and himself as the fictionalized artist/narrator. From the same scene in **The Subterraneans** we find

> . . . returning to the Red Drum for sets, to hear Bird, whom I saw distinctly digging Mardou several times also myself directly into my eye looking to search if really I was that great writer I thought myself to be as if he knew my thoughts and ambitions or remembered me from other night clubs and other coasts, other Chicagos—not a challenging look but the king and founder of the bop generation at least the sound of it in digging his audience digging his eyes, the secret eyes him-watching, as he just pursed his lips and let great lungs and immortal fingers work, his eyes separate and interested and humane, the kindest jazz musician there could be while being and therefore naturally the greatest—watching Mardou and me in the infancy of our love and probably wondering why, or knowing it wouldn't last, or seeing who it was would be hurt, as now, obviously, but not quite yet, it was Mardou whose eyes were shining in my direction, though I could not have known and now do not definitely know. . . .
>
> (19-20)

As with the earlier passage, this one offers an imaginative, romanticized portrait of Charlie Parker, one that is at odds with the conventionally accepted depiction of the bebop legend.[10] Again, the eyes are the locus of emotion and interaction and the audience is somehow able to sense something about Parker's life and his strat-

egy for living that life from gazing into his eyes. More importantly, though, Kerouac himself (as the narrator) obliterates Parker's non-performing existence in this description by fusing him with his art: his performing, his sax playing. Parker is described as being "the kindest jazz musician there could be while being and therefore naturally the greatest": his personality—kindness or humaneness—is thus linked *only* to his gift for playing music; in essence his off-stage life is irrelevant to who he is because he is, as far as the narrator is concerned, his music.

The obliteration of Parker's off-stage life is especially significant because Kerouac uses this rhetorical strategy, finally, not to say something about Parker or jazz musicians in general but to enhance his own image as a suffering, victimized artist and man by connecting himself to the already established image of the exploited jazz musician. Kerouac needs a de-historicized symbol of suffering and outsiderism so that he can link himself to it. The passage begins and ends with the narrator making an intimate connection with the jazz performer: Percepied sees Parker not just looking at him and his "date," but looking at them very meaningfully. Percepied imagines that Parker connects with him from the bandstand as a fellow artist[11] "looking to search if really I was that great writer I thought myself to be as if he knew my thoughts and ambitions"—and also as a sad, doomed, suffering individual, "watching Mardou and me in the infancy of our love and probably wondering why, or knowing it wouldn't last, on seeing who it was would be hurt as now, obviously, but not quite yet it was Mardou whose eyes were shining in my direction, though I could not have known and now do not definitely know." The effect of this narrative strategy—linking himself with the jazz performer—on his depiction of Charlie Parker is to even further romanticize and stereotype the image of Parker specifically and the jazz musician more generally. Parker becomes more than simply a saxophone player; he is a seer, a savant, a psychic—able to see in the one look that Mardou directs at Percepied (what the narrator himself misses) that she is going to hurt him. Perhaps more importantly, at the same time Parker becomes less than a full-fledged character in the novel, he simply remains a static, stereotyped symbol. As with most nonwhites in Kerouac's work Parker never speaks for himself; his silence is necessary to maintain the focus on Kerouac's (and his cohort's) experience as American outsiders and to obscure the difference between their choice to remain outside and the force used (and maintained by the silence of the bohemians themselves) to put and keep African Americans there.[12]

Slightly more difficult to discuss than the depictions of jazz and jazz musicians is the notion that jazz is the organizing principle of *The Subterraneans* (that is, the basis for the novel's narrative structure). There is no argument about whether Kerouac designed his prose style, in part, to imitate not only the creative process of jazz—the spontaneity that comes from improvising—but also the sound of jazz or, more specifically, the sound of bebop. However, the question of how successful he is in being as spontaneous as a jazz musician or, even more difficult to determine, imitating the sound of bebop is, it seems to me, a thorny one. How does one, finally, determine whether, or how much, Kerouac's prose sounds like or follows similar patterns to the alto sax lines created by Charlie Parker?

The passages from *The Subterraneans* analyzed above present an interesting subject to consider the success of Kerouac's approximation of jazz improvisation because they are part of a scene—occurring in a jazz club featuring the great Charlie Parker—that one would expect to transmit the reader to Kerouac's jazzy milieu. Moreover, this scene is used by at least two Kerouac critics (John Tytell and Regina Weinreich) to exemplify Kerouac's musicality. Both of these critics point to the same formal device—the building of "associations" or the "spontaneous flow" of images—as the technique that convinces them that Kerouac's goal of approximating the spontaneity of the jazz musician has been reached. Really, though, this is only to call what has been practiced by previous writers—Joyce or Faulkner, for example—by another name; that is, "stream-of-consciousness" becomes "spontaneous prose"; or, put another way, a practice based on a psychoanalytical model becomes one based on a musical one. It seems to me that there is nothing *inherently* musical or jazz-like in Kerouac's writing. The recipe for improvisational writing that Kerouac offered in "**Essentials of Spontaneous Prose**"—composing without editing (if indeed he did do this), replacing standard punctuation with dashes, and tapping into some sort of essential part of one's self—does not necessarily make Kerouac's prose sound more like jazz.

The scene from *The Subterraneans* is also an interesting one for consideration because there is a recording of Kerouac reading it. Recorded in 1959 on the jazz label Verve and recently rereleased on *The Jack Kerouac Collection*, this recording is touted (in the booklet to the recent compilation) by Kerouac biographer Gerald Nicosia as being "so immediate, intense, and full of subtle emotional changes that it rivals any piece Bird himself ever recorded" (10). Nicosia, moreover, says that "as with the greatest jazz musicians, Kerouac is not just blowing a tune, he is blowing his own life, up on the bandstand for all the world to witness" (11). Setting aside the likelihood that Nicosia's hyperbole is calculated to magnify the significance of this "product," these are substantial claims for Kerouac's writing and performing (this latter is supposed to be believable despite the fact that both Nicosia and Ann Charters report that Kerouac's late-fifties Village Vanguard performances were marvelously unsuccessful). And yet, my repeated listenings to this recording followed by listenings to Charlie Parker convinces me that only a very sympathetic listener would agree that Kerouac's sound "rivals" Charlie Parker's or even that Kerouac's performance is similar to the performance of a jazz musician. This is not to say that there are not any similarities between Kerouac's prose and bop. He does move from association to association, modulate his tone, and underpin his prose with a quick, quirky rhythm. However, if, in jazz historian James Lincoln Collier's words, "Bop was, in the exact sense of the word, a musical revolution" (361), then Kerouac's prose—following Joyce, Faulkner, and others—did not "rival" Charlie Parker's music because it was not, in any sense of the word, a literary revolution.

Nevertheless, what is even more crucial for the purposes of this essay than Kerouac's success or failure in imitating jazz is the *way* Kerouac *characterized* the jazz structures that he tried to imitate in his prose. That is, just as he primitivizes the image of Charlie Parker in this narrative so does he primitivize the process a jazz musician uses to create the music he plays. This can be seen most readily in Kerouac's major statement of his writing method, "**Essentials of Spontaneous Prose**." In this manifesto, Kerouac relies heavily on jazz metaphors to characterize his own writing process.[13] Specifically, under "Procedure," Kerouac emphasizes the notions of spontaneity and improvisation. Mixing jazz and pictorial art metaphors, he states that "sketching language is undisturbed flow from the mind of personal secret ideawords blowing (as per the jazz musician) on the subject of image." Under "Method," Kerouac advises using a different kind of punctuation to inject more vitality into writing: that rather than using periods, colons, or commas to separate sentences, one should use "the space dash separating rhetorical breathing (as a jazz musician drawing breath between outblown phrases). Finally, discussing what should be the subject of one's writing, Kerouac exhorts writers to "blow as deep as you want . . . tap from yourself the song of yourself, *blow!— now! . . .*" (65-67). Similarly, in his 1968 *Paris Review* interview, Kerouac focuses on the same jazz metaphors—breath and blowing—to talk about the connection between his writing and jazz. In response to a question about the influence of jazz and bop on his writing, Kerouac says, "Yes jazz and bop, in the sense of a, say, a tenor man drawing a breath and blowing a phrase on his saxophone, till he runs out of breath, and when he does, his sentence, his statement's been made . . . that's how I therefore separate my sentences, as breath separations of the mind . . ." ("Art of Fiction" 83). In this interview Kerouac furthermore states that what he is after with this jazz-influenced method is "FEELING, Goddamn it, FEELING is what I like in art, not CRAFTINESS and the hiding of feelings" (65).

Taken by themselves, these statements of method might not add up to a primitivized depiction of the *jazz* process. However, combined with the portraits of jazz musicians (such as the one of Charlie Parker in **The Subterraneans**) found in Kerouac's fiction that obliterate their off-stage lives and de-historicize them, Kerouac's overarching portrayal of the process of creation in jazz is one that requires almost no training, skill, or education: just pick up a horn, tap into your emotions, and "blow." Kerouac repeatedly portrays the process this way even though, according to Gerald Nicosia, Kerouac himself had to learn to hear and appreciate the technical innovations of bop (125). In Kerouac's work, the jazz process remains one that is not the result of a cultural development on the group level and disciplined practice on the individual level but one that is fundamental to any "primal" human existence.

Combined with the romanticized portrayal of jazz and jazz musicians, **The Subterraneans** offers an exoticized image of African American women in the depiction of Leo Percepied's lover, Mardou Fox. Although Mardou is initially described in quite "civilized" terms as being well-educated and "part Negro high class" (10), throughout the novel she is revealed to be a woman with impeccable oppressed and suffering blood lines—African Americans on her mother's side, American Indians on her father's side. In fact, more often than not, the narrator's attraction for Mardou seems due to her pedigree rather than to her own characteristics. In her company the nar-

rator continuously slips into reveries of such scenes as that of "her Cherokee halfbreed hobo father . . . lying bellydown on a floater with wind furling back his rags and black hat, his brown sad face facing all that land and desolation" (27). One of Kerouac's biographers says that the real Mardou "made him think of Indians he'd seen crossing the country. They were outcasts, going nowhere. Kerouac was moved and saddened by the vanquished Indians and desperate blacks of America . . ." (Charters 192).

Most telling though is the fact that the narrator never sees Mardou when he looks at her. Instead he sees "in Mardou's eyes now the eventual Kingdom of Inca, Maya and vast Azteca shining of gold snake and temples as noble as greek, Egypt, the long sleek crack jaws and flattened noses of Mongolian geniuses creating arts in temple rooms" (35). The narrator alternately sees the African American woman as a Negro goddess, an Indian princess, an Aztec, or Greek, or Egyptian mask; the specific historical locale does not matter, what does is only that she is an exotic, alien, distant figure. When, in fact, the narrator sees Mardou for what she actually is he is slightly repulsed: "So in the morning I wake from the scream of beermares and see beside me the Negro woman with parted lips sleeping and little bits of white pillow stuffing in her black hair, feel almost revulsion, realize what a beast I am for feeling anything near it . . ." (24). Although the "revulsion" the narrator feels could be connected to his disgust about her general sloppiness, it is revealing both that the particular imagery he chooses to emphasize Mardou's sloppiness highlights white against black and that this revulsion hits him while in bed after having spent the night with her. As Calvin Hernton says, "The first focus of racism is the physical body—skin color, facial features, hair, physique, particularly the ass, and most of all the sexual genitalia of both males and females of the black race" (xii). Finally, this passage reveals that although the narrator knows he should be beyond racial tolerance (and even this *mea culpa* is barely believable), he is actually not even close to being there yet.

Later in the novel, as their relationship begins to deteriorate (due to Mardou's "affair" with a younger poet [Gregory Corso] who is also one of the narrator's rivals—and Percepied's inability to accept or work through the crisis this precipitates), the narrator describes the doubts he has about Mardou, doubts that further reveal the narrator's deeper feelings toward Mardou. One doubt has to do with the fact that the relationship would prevent him from realizing one of his fantasies—living in the South in a Faulknerian homestead (of all things!). Not realizing this fantasy, he says, "would cut my life in half, and all such sundry awful American as if to say white ambition thoughts or white daydreams" (62). The narrator's instinct in this speculative situation is not to challenge the social forces that would make being an interracial couple in the South difficult but to sacrifice the relationship to the fantasy. More revealing though is his "last deepest final doubt . . . about Mardou that she was really a thief of some sort and therefore was out to steal my heart, my white man heart, a Negress sneaking in the world sneaking the holy white men for sacrificial rituals later when they'll be roasted and roiled" (67). These passages betray the closeness of Kerouac's romantic stereotype of African Americans with the earlier more pernicious ones—they are, in fact, different sides of the same coin. In another passage that makes this juxtaposition even clearer, the narrator admits that his anger over their deteriorating relationship has made him look at Mardou in a different way:

> "Honey, what I see in your eyes is a lifetime of affection not only from the Indian in you but because as part Negro somehow you are the first, the essential woman, and therefore the most, most originally most fully affectionate and maternal . . ." I'd added one time—but now in my hurt hate turning the other way and so walking down Price with her every time I see a Mexican gal or Negress I say to myself, "hustlers," they're all the same, always try to cheat and rob you.
>
> (129)

On the other hand, the narrator ascribes to Mardou extraordinary powers of insight and intuition. For example, the centerpiece of the novel is a long story Mardou tells about wandering the streets of San Francisco, naked and in a daze, whereupon she discovers the "truth" of her existence. After hearing the story the narrator says, "No girl had ever moved me with a story of spiritual suffering and so beautifully her soul showing out radiant as an angel wandering in hell and the hell the selfsame streets I'd roamed" (50). Another indication of Mardou's innate virtues as an African American is her connection to jazz. Not only does Charlie Parker make special eye contact with both her and the narrator, but Mardou "is the only girl I've ever known who could really understand bop and sing it" (86).

The exoticism of this characterization is made even more apparent with knowledge of the real-life relationship between Kerouac and "Mardou Fox."[14] For example, Gerald Nicosia reports that

Kerouac's depiction of Mardou as a jazz fanatic was, at best, one-dimensional: "Though they [Kerouac and Mardou Fox] both liked classical music, he only discussed jazz with her" (443). Further, even though Kerouac gives Mardou a "voice" in this novel (something he does not do, as I mentioned earlier, for Charlie Parker), making her story the connective thread for the novel, he actually only puts his ideas in her mouth. Although he defends Kerouac against the charge of distortion by claiming that Kerouac was letting "the characters speak through him," Gerald Nicosia relates that "Mardou" told Kerouac that she "was also upset by the ridiculous speeches he had put in her mouth" (452). Joyce Johnson also relays that when she and Kerouac went to visit Mardou upon the publication of *The Subterraneans* in 1958, Mardou was still angry about Kerouac's portrayal of her. Johnson says that Mardou "seemed to be saying [that] *The Subterraneans* wasn't a real picture of her or of anything, just a lot of distorted impressions for the media to feed upon" (229).

Certainly some of the more hostile, obvious racism in Kerouac's depiction of Mardou Fox can be attributed (as both John Tytell and Joyce Johnson point out) to his penchant for demanding self-revelation (Tytell 197; Johnson 227). To a certain extent, Leo Percepied's narrative stance toward his recently ended relationship with Mardou Fox is one of self-blame. And part of this self-accusation is Percepied's recognition that his relationship with Mardou was made more difficult for him because of her race; he could not transcend the social pressures on interracial couples. Apparently, no matter how much Kerouac fancied himself a social outsider he could not cope with the "fugitive" status assigned to "people who trespass across race and sex barriers" (Hernton xviii).

However, beyond the superficial recognition of the narrator's own failings are the images, descriptions, and scenes in the novel that are racist and are not accompanied by any acknowledgment that they are so. These include most of the characterizations of jazz and jazz musicians and much of the exotic romanticization of Mardou Fox. Moreover, although the narrator acknowledges that racism exists (he recognizes, for example, that his mother, sister, and brother-in-law—a Southerner—would be "mortified" if he married an African American woman and that it would be impossible to live in the South [62]), he demonstrates that he does not truly understand the effect it has on its "victims." An example of his complete lack of understanding (and, even, his condescension toward the experience of racism) comes in the following recollection:

> . . . out on Market Street she would not have me hold her arm for fear people of the street there would think her a hustler, which it would look like but I felt mad but let it go and we walked along, I wanted to go into a bar for a wine, she was afraid of all the behatted men ranged at the bar, now I saw her Negro fear of American society she was always talking about but palpably in the streets which never gave me any concern—tried to console her, show her she could do anything with me, "In fact baby I'll be a famous man and you'll be the dignified wife of a famous man so don't worry" but she said "You don't understand" but her little girl-like fear so cute, so edible, I let it go, we went home, to tender love scenes together in our own and secret dark—
>
> (95)

In this passage, Kerouac clearly reveals not only that he does not understand the "palpable" effect even the most mundane form of racism has on African Americans but also that he does not really believe it exists and, furthermore, does not care. Moreover, Kerouac belittles Mardou's feeling of oppression by describing it as "her little girl-like fear so cute."

Finally, then, there is not much in this book or any of his other works to convince us that Kerouac did not truly believe the racial differences depicted in **The Subterraneans.** From the infamous "At lilac evening . . ." passage in **On the Road** to the depictions of Charlie Parker in **Mexico City Blues** and **The Subterraneans** to the portrayal of Mardou Fox in **The Subterraneans,** Kerouac's romantic racism is clear. Following in what has been and, to some extent, remains an accepted white American tradition, Kerouac tried to enhance and ennoble his position as a *voluntary* social outsider by linking himself to the historical status of African Americans as *forced* outsiders and victims of white oppression. Discursively, Kerouac made this connection by raiding African American culture for its method of expressing the experience of this oppression and its strategy for surviving it. The result of Kerouac's unwarranted identification with the African American experience and his appropriation of African American culture is a depiction of these materials that is distorted because it trivializes the true nature of American racial oppression by blurring (if not obscuring) the difference between voluntary and forced outsiderism.

Notes

1. There is some suggestion in Ann Charters's biography of Kerouac that Rexroth felt some personal animosity toward Kerouac because of Kerouac's "offhand characterization" of him in *The Dharma Bums* (Charters 307).

2. For a good account of this American tradition in modern poetry see Aldon Lynn Nielsen, *Reading Race: White American Poets and the Racial Discourse in the Twentieth Century* (Athens and London: The University of Georgia Press, 1988).

3. For examples of this historical explanation see W. T. Lhamon, Jr., *Deliberate Speed: The Origins of a Cultural Style in the American 1950s* (Washington: Smithsonian Institution P, 1990); John Patrick Diggins, *The Proud Decades: America in War and Peace, 1941-1960* (New York: W. W. Norton, 1988); Douglas T. Miller and Marion Nowak, *The Fifties: The Way We Really Were* (New York: Doubleday, 1977); and John Tytell, *Naked Angels: The Lives and Literature of the Beat Generation* (New York: Grove P, 1976).

4. Although the actual incidents fictionalized in this novel take place in New York, Kerouac changed the locale to San Francisco.

5. Interestingly, Baraka also attributes his discomfort with "bohemianism" to his "lower-middle class craving after order and 'respectability'" (Baraka 157). That is, he portrays himself as being more inhibited by these "mainstream" values than the middle-class whites with whom he associated.

6. Regina Weinreich, for example, places *The Subterraneans* in a grouping of "noncanonical" Kerouac writings; that is, those novels that she reads as variations on the central themes or strategies in what she terms the "core group" of writings—*The Town and the City, On the Road, Visions of Cody,* and *Desolation Angels* (Weinreich 13). Although they are less rigid in their evaluations of Kerouac's work, Ann Charters, Gerald Nicosia, and John Tytell seem to agree that *The Subterraneans* is a "successful" and powerful novel but to a smaller and more limited degree than some of his other works.

7. In fact, according to Ann Charters, it was as a result of *The Subterraneans*—at Allen Ginsberg's urging—that Kerouac's one major statement—"Essentials of Spontaneous Prose"—of his literary methodology and its connection to jazz was written (Charters 188-89).

8. W. T. Lhamon does an excellent job of explaining Kerouac's use of the jazz club as a "secular, vernacular rite that substituted for religious sacrament" (Lhamon 152).

9. See, for example, Ralph Ellison's characterization of Parker's life and the cult that followed him in life and death in the essay "On Bird, Bird-Watching, and Jazz" in *Shadow and Act.* Ellison says that Bird's efforts to combat the existing role of the black jazz musician as "entertainer" (from Louis Armstrong) by portraying himself as a serious artist led to much of the perception of him as a "tortured" artist. Miles Davis says much the same thing in his *Autobiography.*

10. In his *Autobiography,* for example, Miles Davis depicts Parker in very uncomplimentary terms, saying that he was "greedy" and not a very likable person. Also, in

The Making of Jazz James Lincoln Collier describes Parker as having a "character disorder" which manifested itself in a "total lack of concern for [the] well-being of others" (371).

11. In a later piece, "The Origins of the Beat Generation," Kerouac reveals the conflict (without any seeming awareness) between what he knows to be real—the jazz musicians's ignorance of him as an artist and person—and what he wants to be true—a human connection between fellow suffering artists. He says, "When I first heard Bird and Diz in the Three Deuces I knew they were serious musicians playing a goofy new sound and didn't care what I thought . . ." However, in the next sentence Kerouac continues, "I was leaning against the bar with a beer when Dizzy came over for a glass of water from the bartender, put himself right against me and reached with both arms around both sides of my head to get the glass and danced away, as though knowing I'd be singing about him someday. . . ." (72)

12. As W. T. Lhamon points out, even Cody, the fictional Neal Cassady in *Visions of Cody*, takes Kerouac to task for this. Lhamon says that Cody "wants to listen for the central voices of black culture—or whatever else he is attending to—for their own sake: 'listen to the man play the horn, that's all.'" Kerouac, Lhamon says, cannot heed Cassady's advice because it would "inhibit his writing" (162).

13. While not denying Kerouac's affinity for jazz, George Dardess has claimed that "the most vigorous metaphors" in this manifesto derive not from jazz or pictorial art but from "nature" (733-34). Although "most vigorous" is a little bit too vague to be very meaningful, his argument is reasonable and allows Dardess to make interesting connections between Kerouac's method and Emerson's and Thoreau's methods.

14. This character has always been anonymous, identified either as her character's name—Mardou Fox—or the pseudonym Irene May.

Works Cited

Baraka, Amiri. *The Autobiography of LeRoi Jones/Amiri Baraka.* New York: Freundlich, 1984.

Charters, Ann. *Kerouac: A Biography.* New York: St. Martin's Press, 1987.

Collier, James Lincoln. *The Making of Jazz: A Comprehensive History.* New York: Dell, 1978.

Davis, Miles, with Quincy Troupe. *Miles: The Autobiography.* New York: Simon and Schuster, 1989.

Dardess, George. "The Logic of Spontaneity: A Reconsideration of Kerouac's 'Spontaneous Prose Method.'" *Boundary* 2 (Summer) 1982.

Ellison, Ralph. *Shadow and Act.* New York: Random House, 1964.

Fredrickson, George M. *The Black Image in the White Mind: The Debate on Afro-American Character and Destiny, 1817-1914.* Middletown, CT: Wesleyan U P, 1987.

Hentoff, Nat. *Jazz Is.* New York: Random House, 1976.

Hernton, Calvin C. *Sex and Racism in America.* New York: Grove P, 1988.

Johnson, Joyce. *Minor Characters.* Boston: Houghton Mifflin, 1983.

Jones, Hettie. *How I Became Hettie Jones.* New York: Penguin, 1990.

Kerouac, Jack. "The Art of Fiction XLI: Jack Kerouac." *Paris Review* Summer, 1968.

———. "Essentials of Spontaneous Prose." *A Casebook on the Beat.* Ed. Thomas Parkinson. New York: Crowell, 1961.

———. *The Jack Kerouac Collection.* Santa Monica: Rhino Records, 1990.

———. *Mexico City Blues.* New York: Grove Weidenfeld, 1990.

———. *On the Road.* New York: New American Library, 1957.

———. *The Subterraneans.* New York: Grove P, 1958.

Lhamon, W. T., Jr. *Deliberate Speed: The Origins of a Cultural Style in the American 1950s.* Washington: Smithsonian Institution P, 1990.

Lipton, Lawrence. *The Holy Barbarians.* New York: Julian Messner, 1959.

Nicosia, Gerald. *Memory Babe: A Critical Biography of Jack Kerouac.* New York: Penguin, 1986.

Torgovnick, Marianna. *Gone Primitive: Savage Intellects, Modern Lives.* Chicago: U of Chicago P, 1990.

Tytell, John. *Naked Angels: The Lives and Literature of the Beat Generation.* New York: Grove P, 1986.

Wakefield, Dan. *New York in the 50s.* Boston: Houghton Mifflin, 1992.

Weinreich, Regina. *The Spontaneous Poetics of Jack Kerouac: A Study of the Fiction.* New York: Paragon House, 1990.

The Dharma Bums

WILLIAM CRAWFORD WOODS (ESSAY DATE SUMMER 1983)

SOURCE: Woods, William Crawford. "'A New Field': A Note on *The Dharma Bums*." *Review of Contemporary Fiction* 3, no. 2 (summer 1983): 7-14.

In the following essay, Woods argues that The Dharma Bums *should be accorded a higher stature among Kerouac's works.*

1

Ten years ago, the editors of *The New Republic* asked me to contribute an article on an author of my choice to their "Reconsiderations" series—a run of essays the magazine had just inaugurated on worthy works and writers who'd been neglected or misread. Kerouac came at once to mind. My idea—and it was as impressionistic as the piece I turned out—was that by the early 1970s **On the Road** had been filed away as a performance preliminary to the arts that flowered in other forms in the counterculture that inherited the novel; and that the rest of Kerouac's work had simply been filed away. Less scholarship was involved than will, I hope, be found in the pages that follow; the idle authority I consulted was little more than an image of "Jack's book"—his life in letters—that I'd carried down the years in my own mind.

Still, to do the story proved exciting, if only because it involved recovering so many sparkling texts that had meant so much to me as a man; and so little to me as a writer. I'm neither Catholic nor Buddhist, don't much believe in "spontaneous prose," and was (and am) satisfied that the Beat social program had largely vanished into its successes. So why "reconsider" this particular writer, if not from the ground of a set of personal imperatives I sensed only dimly as I started out on the job?

Anyway, I read and re-read him, ". . . eight books in half as many evenings, midnight readings stoked by Scotch and coffee with the hi-fi leaking 'old God Shearing' and the bebop of a brighter day." Which sounds a little like Jack, not that I'd intended that it should.

Calling him "Jack" sounds like him, too: the easy assumption of friendship that his own friendly tone so often licenses.

Reviewing that essay now, I don't find too much to be altogether pleased with. A patronizing tone hums behind even my most sympathetic observations, and the collation of ideas I used to connect Kerouac to the counterculture looks shopworn where it doesn't seem devised merely to surprise. More important, had I worked a little harder and better I would have emphasized the force of his Buddhism more than I did and would have taken his express theories of composition less lightly. But I did work up a reasonable argument that ended by awarding Kerouac a "modest honorable place" in the American literature of his time (the praise now seems too slight), and—most valid of all—I was ready to see that his great value lay in the personal impact of his confessional voice: Kerouac was, for me, a specific anodyne to the sargassos of adolescence; while every authority figure ringed me with a gospel of good behavior, Jack's cast and crew were on hand to recommend a life of getting your kicks where you could.

Anyway, the piece came out, and drew some friendly fire—a letter from John Montgomery (Henry Morley in *The Dharma Bums*), who was vexed that I seemed to have slighted his moun-

taineering skills; another from McGraw-Hill, hoping for a boost for the forthcoming *Visions of Cody*; and a blast from Seymour Krim, who felt I had Jack's aesthetic down at least half-wrong. (Krim was at least half-right. He and I clashed a bit more by mail until he drew the correspondence to a graceful conclusion; I remember only enough of it to feel abashed at my own acrimony, and I'd like to record here a belated thanks to Krim for the valiant play of his ideas.)

The article must also have seemed serviceable to academic readers, because it began to show up now and again in the bibliographies of the wave of Kerouac criticism and commentary that gathered in strength through the '70s, books and articles I read partly to test my informal conclusions against those of the deep-water scholars and partly to fuel a college course in the literature of the Beat Generation I had devised, mostly for my own enjoyment, as I had little hope that work so remote to their own experience would absorb the students for whom I planned to unfold it.

Two surprises were contained here, and I want to digress to explore them, because it seems to me that a large part of Kerouac's importance can be measured by his often vivid impact on readers you might expect to find largely out of sympathy with his goals: the work was even more remote than I had feared, and far more appealing than I had expected.

I teach at a small state college in south central Virginia that attempts to marry the liberal arts to teacher-training, business education, and the like; my students are mostly intellectually resistant, so to speak, and I was doubtful of the diet of Kerouac, Ginsberg, and Burroughs I hoped, despite its difficulty, to tempt them with even as I fashioned it. My guess was that once my mostly God-fearing flock got a good look at Jack's crazy line, Allen's cock preoccupations, and Honest Bill's reign of moral terror, I'd be signing a lot of drop slips.

Wrong. The class overfilled, the students devoured it all, Kerouac especially. Attendance was high, blue sparks flew in class discussion. Papers were often inspired and almost always on time. All this despite the fact that these texts were opened as utter mysteries, with their social background a considerable void. I couldn't refer Kerouac's aesthetic to the work of Jackson Pollock or Charlie Parker without inserting short lectures on 1950s music and art. The political arena had to be filled in: Eisenhower who? Needless to say, Buddhism might as well have been the faith of Mars, and Whitman as ancestor, when he'd been heard of at all, was variously considered a Lake poet and a Confederate general.

I go into all this not to bemoan my students' ignorance, but to applaud their work—the energetic way they proceeded to educate themselves (and me) out of the kinship they felt with a body of writing I had supposed would have to be forced down their faces like *Beowulf*. Appropriately, there was a breakdown of boundaries: they came to class in shades and berets, read Han Shan without being told to. One, who had despised poetry, began to write it after reading Ginsberg. Another, stymied by the conventions of academic criticism, developed a cogent paper on Burroughs' work using the novelist's own cut-up method. One young man reached a pinnacle when he proudly told me that he'd hitched a ride on "boxcars boxcars boxcars" and thumbed three hundred miles over a weekend even though he had a car.

I'm finally at a loss to fully explain the impact of this literature on so unlikely a readership, but I suspect it has to do with the same characteristics that keep any book alive for a vertical audience, which has less to do with formal cohesiveness than with pertinacity to successive readers' own extra-literary experiences; thus my students were finding, at a minimum (and particularly in Kerouac), the roots of the music they listened to, a sponsor for the drink and drugs some enjoyed, and a suggestion that there might indeed be a life to be lived outside the drab routine of business, a life of wry adventure closer to their secret longings. In other words, they were getting in their twenties from the Beats exactly what their instructor had gotten in his teens: fresh possibility, or what *The Dharma Bums* calls "a new field."

To return to the essay:

I had concluded my overview with an opinion that much of the criticism I'd been reading made it appear anomalous; had honored an impulse to record the view that *The Dharma Bums* was Jack Kerouac's best novel, indeed his "only whole survivor . . . a well-tuned book with a catapult motion"—odd mechanical metaphors for so blissful a work from so dreamy a writer, particularly given that I had earlier tried to make a case for its "food-like sweetness" and its celebration of "animal enjoyment." It seems to me now that this awkward flailing about for the proper terms of praise was the result of an inability to say exactly why I should prize so highly a novel that even the author and his friends had some doubts about, though how severely those doubts would be

ON THE SUBJECT OF...

JOHN MCVEY MONTGOMERY

John Montgomery is the author of numerous volumes of poetry and a vast chronicle of the Beat Generation, yet his writing remains largely unpublished, and he is virtually unknown outside of inner literary circles. Despite this anonymity, he is considered one of the most interesting and original poets in America and an integral Beat figure. Kerouac was so fascinated by him—his constant poetic monologues and satiric appraisals of his surroundings—that he cast Montgomery as major characters in two of his novels. It is Montgomery, as Henry Morley, who accompanies Ray Smith (Kerouac) and Japhy Ryder (Gary Snyder) to the Matterhorn in Kerouac's *The Dharma Bums* (1958). As Alex Fairbrother in *Desolation Angels* (1965), he supplies Kerouac with his last workaday job. It is also Montgomery who is mentioned as "The greatest librarian in America" in *Satori in Paris* (1966). Adding to his curiosity appeal, little is known about Montgomery's mysterious past. Besides the character sketches by Kerouac, Montgomery has seldom been profiled in print. He is notorious for his equivocations and has frequently supplied misleading information in regards to his personal history.

reflected in the book's reception became clear only as I began to work through the literature and to realize that I'd crowned as Kerouac's best, a book ordinarily held to be his slightest, accomplishment.

The Dharma Bums appeared in 1958, so hard upon the success of *On the Road* that you have to give some credence to the familiar charge that it was a commercial job requested by the author's publisher, Viking, written in an accessible style suggested by his editor, Malcolm Cowley, and therefore not a true slice of his authentic canon. According to John Tytell's critical biography *Naked Angels*, Kerouac himself grumbled that the book was "not compelling," and his colleagues Allen Ginsberg and Gary Snyder voiced reservations of their own. Snyder "wished Kerouac had taken more trouble to smooth out dialogue and make transitions less abrupt," though he admired the book, and Ginsberg, also largely a fan, used a "Village Voice" review to find it the work of a man now "weary of the world, and prose." Reviews were mixed but mostly bad, and **The Dharma Bums** did not follow its famous predecessor onto the best-seller lists. Even John Tytell, Kerouac's most astute and sensitive critic, found little to like in its pages, charging the book with a "staged and contrived quality," "forced symbolism," and a programmatic, over-engineered approach to its materials. "Stylistically," Tytell concludes, the novel did not represent "the essential Kerouac, his ideals of spontaneous composition, or his flaunting of conventional novelistic expectations."

The role of editorial assistance—or interference—in the final product is difficult to assess. The author, in his *Paris Review* interview, has bitter words about a process in which his editor would later claim to have played no part:

> In the days of Malcolm Cowley, with . . . **The Dharma Bums,** I had no power to stand by my style for better or worse. When Malcolm Cowley made endless revisions and inserted thousands of needless commas . . . why, I spent $500 making the complete restitution of the **Bums** manuscript and got a bill from Viking Press called "Revisions." Ha ho ho. And so you asked about how do I work with an editor . . .

But Cowley told two other interviewers (Barry Gifford and Lawrence Lee, who in their oral history *Jack's Book* called **The Dharma Bums** a novel "written with an air of patient explanation, as though addressed to a book editor"):

> . . . somebody at Viking said, "Why don't you just carry on what you were doing in **On The Road**?" And Jack sat down and did his **Dharma Bums.** And I had nothing at all to do with that. It's very acceptable prose, but this time he had a terrible fight with Viking about the changes.

"I never liked **Dharma Bums** very much," Cowley concluded, adding that it had "no people" in it.

Wherever the truth of the matter rests, there's a clear suggestion in this cranky debate that—from whatever motive—the author may have been consciously seeking to enlarge his audience by diminishing his range; that, far from being his best (that is, most authentic) book, **The Dharma Bums** may be his most calculated.

I believe I can demonstrate otherwise.

If my central contention is correct—if Kerouac's special merit lies not in the art he shapes so much as in the transformations he triggers in his readers—then it will be necessary to show how **The Dharma Bums** has a place in that process. But I also want to suggest that, even in strictly literary terms, the novel has formal affinities with the broader body of Jack's books; and that it generally carries on the program of personal and social transformation posited by the Beats in the years of their ascendancy.

2

The Dharma Bums is a picaresque quest romance narrated in the first person by a protagonist named Ray Smith. (Smith is the author's unmistakable persona and this is thus the place to acknowledge a central problem of Kerouac commentary. A fundamental principle of objective criticism, the separation of author and narrator, entails the ancillary convention that the biography of the first is said to have no bearing on the life of the second. It's misleading to maintain this ordinarily useful fiction when writing about Kerouac. Not only did he disguise fact so thinly that many of his books are published with charts that translate the names of the various characters back into their historical originals, but the source of his personal impact on readers depends greatly on the confessional nature of his work: open a book, meet a man. So I will use "Kerouac," "Smith," and the other doubled names interchangeably as the context of my discussion requires. The decision is not a small one; it endorses Kerouac's tacit assumption that history becomes fiction in the fact and act of being written down.)

Smith, a successful but somewhat aimless and unfocused writer, crosses the country to take part in the San Francisco Poetry Renaissance (the self-conscious capitals are his; are Kerouac's), and in that city encounters many of the artists who will form the nexus of the Beat Generation in its literary part, most notably the poet Japhy Ryder (Gary Snyder), who quickly takes over the action by investing the narrator's imagination so fully that Smith's continued travelling (cross-country again; into the mountains and the woods) becomes mostly an objective correlative for the mental voyages he takes under Ryder's benign tutelage—voyages into a refreshed and enlightened sense of self, society, poetry, meditation, and the more spartan pleasures of the senses: woodchopping, walking, and climbing experienced with comic detachment as adventures in the world-as-void.

Void is here theologically intended. Ryder and Smith are both practicing Buddhists, but the poet makes a better job of it. Smith is a beleaguered sensualist who has half-heartedly sworn himself to a temporary celibacy ("pretty girls make graves") but who still indulges lavishly in alcohol and food—"'always eating and drinking,'" as one young woman who tests his monkish vow reproaches him. The reader shares these feasts; nowhere in American literature are food and drink described with more gusto. This is a potential point of conflict between these men. Smith, cooking up a big New England dinner in Ryder's simple semi-Chinese kitchen, worries suddenly about his introduction of "all the big substantial pork and beans of the world" into the poet's carefully circumscribed routine; and Smith's drunkenness finally does flare up between them when he decides to stay home with a bottle of wine while Ryder attends a lecture on Buddhism—only to have the poet find, to his delight, that the lecturers are drunk. Thus both sensual and spiritual life are absorbed into the void; "comparisons are odious," as Ryder reminds himself.

Yet the novel is filled with tacit comparisons between the rowdy life Smith has lately led and the reflective one he slowly surrenders to ("above the gnashing world, a picture of peace and good sense"), a dichotomy dramatized at the end when Ryder sails to Japan to submit himself fully to Zen monastic discipline, while Smith, after an isolated summer as a fire warden in the Cascade Mountains, returns to "this world," and the battering of cultural notoriety that lies on the other side of the silence at the end of the book. It's as though his salvation could be only temporary. "'You've let the world drown you in its horseshit,'" Japhy Ryder has charged him; now, briefly cleansed, he's about to dive back in.

But the lesson hasn't been altogether lost. Smith has been granted glimpses of an animate universe where even the leaves are "bred to rejoice," and of a bond of friendship grounded in a "regular classical scene of angels and dolls having a kind flowery time in the void." This phrase has the feel of the author's barely controlled sentimentality, but a closer look shows that Kerouac knows very well what he's doing, invoking Eden and antiquity in the second adjective, and then peopling the field with two kinds of creatures that define human possibility. Mountain climbing with Japhy Ryder, Smith has felt the hectic round of his days dissolve into the mystical sense of a more meaningful journey, "as though I'd been there before, scrambling on these rocks, for other purposes more ancient, more serious, more simple."

All these themes and journeys are deeply in accord with the core conditions of Beat, in which

art is seen as equivalent to action, self-confession is posited as the path to freedom from the curse of self, and an illuminated state is held to be the goal to be wrung from every hell of cultural conditioning or unexamined life. This is not—or was not, in the middle '50s—the usual subject matter of the American novel. In many respects, the hip posturings and automotive passacaglias (in Henry Miller's phrase) of *On the Road* would have seemed more palatable even to readers dismayed by that book's proposed rebellion. So the relative inability of *The Dharma Bums* to find either an immediate audience or an informed response may well be explainable in terms that have little to do with its author's supposed artistic failure or altered intentions.

Actually, the idea that Kerouac would even have known *how* to devise a style appealing to a mass readership is an odd one. His imposing body of work achieved in the first seven years of the 1950s—"twelve books, a creative explosion comparable to Melville's great productive period from 1853 to 1857," John Tytell notes—was done without much hope of publication, and indeed it remained unpublished until Kerouac's credit soared with the success of *On the Road.* As a writer who mostly consulted his solitude, and who battled editors over every comma, he would hardly have been eager to compromise with a culture he persistently criticized in order to reap from it rewards he despised. We can even adduce biographical evidence to suggest that *The Dharma Bums* was written under circumstances consonant with the author's other compositions. An early biographer, Ann Charters, provides this picture:

> In October 1957, [Kerouac] turned, at Cowley's suggestion, to *The Dharma Bums*. . . . Kerouac was thoroughly bored with Florida. He had money now from *On The Road,* and he began coming up frequently to New York to work at Viking over editorial changes on *The Dharma Bums,* riding the buses between New York and Orlando with a bag of his favorite hamburgers from the White Tower.

On the road again. But it was during this period that he purchased the house on Long Island where he relocated his mother and himself and continued work on the book.

> He took a bedroom upstairs for his study, moving in a new typewriter and a tape recorder on his desk, filling the room with his stacks of manuscripts, notebooks, and books. When things were going well, he felt great, eating big meals in the kitchen, drinking beer and watching TV most of the night, exercising and taking walks.

This has the familiar ring of the author's characteristic routine, an odd forlorn mixture of wishful domesticity played against constant motion and appetitive excess. The tape recorder reminds us of his reliance on free-form narration, the battle of gluttony and physicality of the theme of the book he was working on. So I've cited Charters' account as a tenuous suggestion that such an unchanged mode in his life is probably an unlikely background for sudden obedience to commercial strictures in his letters. (It must still be noted that the writing of *The Dharma Bums* may have exacted a psychic toll we can neither discount nor account for. After completing it, Kerouac didn't finish another novel for almost four years.)

These observations are, of course, conjecture; there's better evidence in the text itself, where, on page after page, *The Dharma Bums* delivers scenes and situations central to Kerouac's vision in language self-evidently his own. It may be sufficient to cite the book's beginning:

> Hopping a freight out of Los Angeles at high noon one day in late September 1955 I got on a gondola and lay down with my duffle bag under my head and my knees crossed and contemplated the clouds as we rolled north to Santa Barbara—Somewhere near Camarillo where Charlie Parker'd been mad and relaxed back to normal health, a thin old little bum climbed into my gondola as we headed into a siding to give a train right of way and looked surprised to see me there—I figured I needed a bottle of Tokay wine to complete the cold dusk run—"Will you watch my pack while I run over there and get a bottle of wine?"—"Sure thing."—He ate . . . the bread and drank the wine with gusto and gratitude—I was pleased—I reminded myself of the line in the Diamond Sutra that says, "Practice charity without holding in mind any conceptions about charity, for charity after all is just a word."

I've substituted dashes for dots in my ellipses here in order to suggest a restoration of the long line Kerouac had intended. For like *On the Road*—which Viking insisted on publishing in conventionally paragraphed form although it had been written in a rush on a single roll of paper—*The Dharma Bums* often appears typographically conventional. But it's possible for a knowledgeable reader to restore an approximation of Kerouac's sound by reading back into his narrative the dense texture of repeated words and images, the periodic phrasing, and the heavy stream of hesitant qualifiers that for better or worse mark Kerouac's work off from that of his more technically conservative contemporaries. The touchstones here as elsewhere continue to be action painting and improvised jazz, and the results,

when once reconfigured in the imagination, are largely in accord with the "undifferentiated consciousness" (in Ginsberg's phrase) that Kerouac prized above all as an earnest of a writer's commitment to unmediated truth. It's remarkable: he may be the only writer of note whose genuine readers have to restore in the process of reading the very page his editors deprived them of in hopes of enlisting their attention.

Short of that, however, we're stuck with the book as we have it; and that fact lands us in a fictional territory not quite recognizable either as conventional narrative or as the Whitmanesque line most typical of its author. The subject matter—poetry, prayer, mountaineering, and the quietening of a fretful Western mind—must have been, as I've suggested, remote from the concerns of most fiction readers of the late 1950s, and the seemingly haphazard structure of the novel appears at first glance to confirm some of the objections of its critics. But in essence it's in many ways a classic tale of apprenticeship in which the narrator's manic intensity is softened by the practical and spiritual disciplines of the poet he adores. Nor is the book really formless, unless we insist that linear chronology or stream-of-consciousness are the only apt ways of telling a tale. To suggest others, we may turn to the governing imagery of the novel itself: to the mandala, that visible form of Buddhist devotion in which the circle signifies the void, and its ornamentations the illusions, of being; or to the quoted and cited poetry that suffuses the text so richly as to transform it into a long prose-poem in itself; or perhaps most of all to the image of prayer, which is so central to the activity of the characters as to suggest the book may be nothing less than a sustained act of petition and adoration by their creator.

Confirmation of these notions can again be found at the outset, from the opening passage cited above that unites inner and outer journeys, tying a physical voyage to contemplation of the sky that shelters it. And the very first lines of dialogue evoke moods of compassion and communion through the sharing of bread and wine; this imagery is as pointedly Christian as the narrator's reflections on it are specifically Buddhist, invoking paths of faith that Ray Smith, toward the story's end, will confidently see as converging when he identifies Christ (to a skeptical Japhy Ryder) as a manifestation of Buddha. All of this is achieved with an economy of means that suggests that categorically "spontaneous prose" may indeed be banished from these pages, a fresh direction for the author explicitly justified by his alter ego in a later scene in which Ryder thanks Smith for teaching him "how to write spontaneously and all that." "Ah, that's nothing," the disciple returns, acknowledging that true spontaneity can call for abandoning a mere program of it, and writing with traditional craft if called upon by the emerging material to do so.

So it becomes clear that Kerouac's choices as they're enacted on the page are a good deal more complex than he's ordinarily given credit for, and that the voice that sounds in this book is neither commercially dictated nor devised in accordance with a theory that might overly condition it.

Ultimately, the best way of describing that voice may be by noting a behavior in which the narrator so often indulges: conversations around a campfire. (Not by chance is some of the best nature writing in American literature to be found in these pages, tied to an ecological urgency that wouldn't become current for ten years after their appearance and graced by a careful system of color symbols that place the things of this world under the eye of eternity.) What we're finally hearing is the vexed, hopeful voice of a storyteller—now plunging forward, now pausing to retrieve an anecdote or illustration, now lecturing, now offering a joke—but always confident that the affection of his listeners will compensate for deficiencies in his style. And in this particular, *The Dharma Bums* synthesizes the two extremes of its available rhetoric, and finds its formal connectedness to the full body of Kerouac's work.

I've claimed that we might chiefly value Kerouac's books for what they tend to turn us into— for the range of possibilities they suggest. On this basis, I could only claim major status for *The Dharma Bums* by pointing to a nation of meditating mountaineers who divide their time between poetry writing and sutra reading. This we haven't got; but there's increasing evidence that Beat Buddhism, first regarded in the popular press as an intellectual affectation worn by the hip, like beards and shades, as a kind of recognition symbol, was a genuine commitment to a path little known at that time in this country. It's been taken seriously enough by institutions like the Naropa Institute, at whose memorial Jack Kerouac School of Disembodied Poetics both Allen Ginsberg and William Burroughs have lectured, and whose director credited Kerouac with initiating a respectful popular consciousness of Buddhism in the United States. And according to John Tytell, the Zen scholar Alan Watts was impressed enough by *The Dharma Bums* to revise his attitudes toward the sincere if fumbling Beat approach to the creed.

Whatever the spiritual ground, the persistent chime of freedom—of enlightenment, of liberation—that's at the heart of Kerouac's work is sounded in these pages, even though most critics have found the note forced. Here I have to agree with them. The lives of *The Dharma Bums* are strongly polarized: hip, happy saints who chant across cityscape and mountaintop vs. materialistic drones locked in fog to their television sets. Though Smith sometimes chastises Ryder for his lack of charity toward the latter, Kerouac's heart isn't in his hero's voice, and we mainly encounter alternatives more bluntly proposed than subtly explored. Only within certain individual lives do these polarities become dialectical and so fructifying, notably in the portrait of Japhy Ryder/Gary Snyder, who is convincingly envisioned as both madman and holyman, poet and Yankee pragmatist, man of letters and of the outdoors, who cares for the edge on an axe blade no less than for the precision of a line—"a great new hero of American culture," Kerouac/Smith proclaims him, one who harks back to Leatherstocking origins and looks forward to a post-industrial land where tribal values will again be celebrated.

That this character sketch may be the book's chief achievement is the assertion of a more recent Kerouac biographer, Dennis McNally, who in his *Desolate Angel* called *The Dharma Bums* "an unmystical, tightly-knit narrative, not, as a few critics suggested, because Viking was salivating for a commercial duplication of *On the Road*, but because it was Gary's portrait."

As such, it's the portrait not only of a man but of a model—an alternative to the hectic example of random energy Neal Cassady was first to represent for Kerouac, who embossed his impact into Dean Moriarty in *On the Road*, which both celebrates Cassady and sets him at nought; even so Gary Snyder's exemplary spiritual and poetic disciplines are proposed in *The Dharma Bums* as a path to enlightenment at least as valid and a good deal less exhausting— though, as we know, Kerouac was never able wholly to live up to them.

While they meet roughly as equals as writers, Ray Smith's comic ineptitude as an outdoorsman is played off disarmingly against Japhy Ryder's illuminating competence. John Tytell notes in this encounter a "new field" in which the narrator's apprenticeship to a new master can enlarge his, as it does his creator's, options. The awesome automotive frenzies of Cassady/Moriarty give way to the centered purposeful activities of Snyder/Ryder, who is equally in rebellion against his society but who finds more wholesome ways to express it:

> Ryder's energy is directed by a sense of purpose that Dean's speeded lust for change cannot contain. . . . Though they both manifest for Kerouac a similar hope and optimism, Ryder is always constructive while Dean is destructive. . . . Ryder, instead of compulsively changing the surface of his life with frequently alternating emotional entanglements, reforms its core through a study of Buddhism which acts as a ground for his energetic capacities. . . . [He] is an avatar of a change in consciousness whose impact on American life would only be realized in the sixties.

That realization **The Dharma Bums** predicts with an impressive specificity. Having inserted into the culture a powerful fictional image of Gary Snyder, the poet would go on to more than justify—the book predicts and helps to prepare the way for—the emergence of a generation that would achieve on an international scale the transformation of society the Beats had sketched in.

The relevant passage is justly famous. Ryder, who's been reading Whitman, has a vision

> of a great rucksack revolution thousands or even millions of young Americans wandering around with rucksacks, going up to mountains to pray . . . all of 'em Zen lunatics who go about writing poems that happen to appear in their heads for no reason and also by being kind and also by strange unexpected acts keep giving visions of eternal freedom to everybody and to all living creatures.

But less well-remembered is a chilling scene that appears only a few pages later in which the poets fail to guard the life of a disconsolate woman whose paranoid anticipations of repression end in her suicide after she unfolds her own dark vision of "a big new revolution of police": two images of America, light and dark, predictions by Kerouac that the 1960s were utterly to confirm.

He may have taken little pleasure in this. An always-present conservatism in his social thought dominated the logic of his later years, which coincided with the emergence of the counterculture. His ear for jazz did not extend to rock, his taste for wine did not move on to acid, and the visual acumen that makes so much of his prose a kind of analogue to Edward Hopper's painting probably would have blinked at the psychedelic art his own testaments of freedom in part made possible. But more lines than one are laid down in **The Dharma Bums** that the counterculture would soon be seen to follow: pacifism, decorated days, ecological concern, a turn to the East, and a

sense of shared selves made manifest in urban enclave and rural commune alike. And even today—with the counterculture as thoroughly absorbed into the nation's life as Beat was built into the counterculture—the book continues to press its case even for readers unready to receive it:

> "I didn't really like that book," one of my students said.
>
> Why not?
>
> "Because I don't know that I want to change my life that much."

3

Twenty years after the publication of **The Dharma Bums**, both Allen Ginsberg and Gary Snyder were to revise their estimates of it sharply upward—perhaps because by then they, like the rest of us, could take a longer look at what the book eventually achieved. Ginsberg, in an interview anthologized in *Allen Verbatim*, seems to remain convinced that the novel was born largely of contractual obligation, but in that fact he finds a victory: ". . . Kerouac took Viking's request for a commercial volume as a challenge and did a great little classic called **Dharma Bums,** with short sentences, like haikus, actually." Which may be a charitable way of putting the best possible face on editorial alteration, though the mention of haiku is in accord with my own view that the book is perhaps best read as a poem, and Gary Snyder seems almost to have been describing that special poetic form when he praised Kerouac (to Dennis McNally) for having gone for "the simple, interesting, paradoxical bones of things." And Snyder's considered final judgment (I quote from *Jack's Book*) locates the novel firmly in its tradition: "In a way, the Beat Generation was a gathering together of all the available models and myths of freedom in America. . . . **The Dharma Bums** is a real statement of that synthesis."

I'm ready to conclude that **The Dharma Bums**'s clear formal connection to Kerouac's other prose, its transformational potential, and its demonstrated place in the Beat social program all suggest that it must finally be accorded a place on the author's shelf a good deal higher than it has ordinarily been put by critics too ready to suppose that one or another of Jack's books can be singled out as falling short of its mission. Kerouac was fond of referring to the body of his writing as "one vast book," a bogus claim insofar as he advanced it in support of his idea of himself as an American Proust, but an accurate method of stating how the apparent formlessness of one book is resolved into form by its companions. It's also worth remembering in this context Japhy Ryder's remark, "Comparisons are odious"; in a sense, comparing *The Dharma Bums* to the wilder books that flank it is a little like comparing the frenzied motion portrayed by Neal Cassady with the studied calm embodied in Snyder himself; both are, or can be, models of freedom not mutually exclusive when they offer themselves as alternatives to the muted routines of the inert everyday. Just so *The Dharma Bums,* no less than *Doctor Sax* or *Visions of Cody,* say, has a role to play in that genuine unity of Kerouac's work that now can be seen connecting the smallest scrap in his notebooks with the longest line on his endless page. There's nothing quite like this extended performance anywhere else in American literature, and we still don't really altogether know how to read it or what to do with it. But some readers, and their numbers will grow, know what it's done to and for them.

"'I wonder which one of us'll die first,'" Ray Smith muses just before he and Japhy Ryder part. "'Whoever it is, come on back, ghost, and give 'em the key.'"

Jack died first. I don't know that he'll be back. But I'm not so sure he didn't leave the key behind.

Doctor Sax

RONNA JOHNSON (ESSAY DATE SUMMER 1983)

SOURCE: Johnson, Ronna. "*Doctor Sax*: The Origins of Vision in the Duluoz Legend." *Review of Contemporary Fiction* 3, no. 2 (summer 1983): 18-25.

In the following essay, Johnson examines Doctor Sax *as the second volume in the thirteen-novel series that Kerouac conceived as "The Duluoz Legend."*

First Kerouac's Duluoz Legend must be apprehended. It is a thirteen-volume biographical saga about a visionary artist beginning with his birth in 1922 and ending in his middle age in 1967. The artist, named Jack Duluoz in seven of the novels, remembers and recreates his sometimes immediate, sometimes distant past, rescuing from the silence of history the "should not be tolds" never uttered in daily life. The legend is based on Kerouac's life but transcends autobiography in its invention and purpose. Its dramatic shape builds from childhood to a taut climax and drops off precipitously thereafter, but it was not written in chronological sequence or with consistent personae names, so it must be reordered and recast in a reader's mind to be recognized. "The Duluoz Legend" has been obscured by critical partisanship for special novels and by the tiresome search for autobiographical revelations of its author, but it is the fundamental fact of the Kerouac canon and the source of its most lasting meanings.

Kerouac urged that his novels be read as a continuous history of a single life. In the eleventh volume of the legend, *Big Sur* (1962), he wrote in a preface:

> My work comprises one vast book. . . . Because . . . of objections of my early publishers I was not allowed to use the same personae names in each work. [My novels to date] are just chapters in the whole work which I call "The Duluoz Legend." In my old age I intend to collect all my work and reinsert my pantheon of uniform names. . . . The whole thing forms one enormous comedy, seen through the eyes of poor Ti Jean (me), otherwise known as Jack Duluoz, the world . . . seen through the keyhole of his eye.[1]

Kerouac did not live to issue a "New York Edition" of the legend, so the names remain inconsistent from volume to volume. But the image of the hero's eye as a keyhole on the world aptly characterizes the special province accorded to vision in the legend. The merely autobiographical is transformed into a charged fiction by what the hero sees in the life that has pulsed through his time; that, and the purpose that informs his seeing.

In the thirteenth volume of the legend, *Vanity of Duluoz* (1967), Kerouac again insisted on the fact of the Duluoz Legend and suggested its humanistic reach. He pointed to a concept of seeing that eclipses autobiography. The hero of the novel, a writer named Jack Duluoz, remembers having a vision of "The Duluoz Legend" as a young man. It would encompass "a lifetime of writing about what I'd seen with my own eyes . . . put it all together as a contemporary history record for future times to see what really happened and what people really thought."[2] Personal experience, "what I'd seen with my own eyes," is highly valued, not as a source for autobiography but for the documentation of a common human history, a "contemporary history record." The legend would be an artifact left for the future of "what really happened and what people really thought." Again, the emphasis is placed on a communal representation: the confessions of the seer would uncover a truth about event and thought collectively sustained. By this, Kerouac did not mean anything as facile as autobiographical journalism of the period. He meant to strip masks, to expose concealed universals, to liberate truth, to "be a great rememberer redeeming life from darkness."[3] The novels themselves affirm this distinction.

The hero of the Duluoz Legend, keyed to perceive elements that transcend the particulars of his experience but which are nevertheless contained or suggested by his experience, offers an account of life derived from what he "sees." The eye to the keyhole is privy to visions of the world that keenly cut through the ostensible meaning of facts. Strikingly consistent in character, the hero's visions invariably reveal one truth most repressed in common experience: mortality, what he calls the "common dark." He sees death at the core of sentience; it is an obstacle to fulfillment and the source of human suffering. The biographical legend of the seer emphasizes the origins, the character, and the consequences of visionary perceptions of mortality.

What is meant by vision is idiosyncratic yet simple. It refers to the act of seeing and names what is seen. In Kerouac, the gifted individual perceives an extra dimension in his experience; his vision is acute. The vision, similarly, is a vivid image cast in intensely personal terms in which basic and often disturbing human knowledges are recognized; it is an x-ray of an infrastructure. Visionary meditations on the "common dark," which occur as the hero contemplates and tells the story of his life, yield compassion for a humanity suffering unknowingly in its anticipation of death. Nominating himself a "great rememberer redeeming life from darkness," he seeks to expiate this travail. By retrieving the details of his life in defiance of its ignoble end, the Duluoz hero endeavors to dignify the suffering that mars sentience. Vision mandates a heroic undertaking.

The novels of the Duluoz Legend cumulatively evince this calling. Separately, each offers a segment of the hero's life charged by visionary truth. The novels of childhood and adolescence, *Visions of Gerard, Doctor Sax,* and *Maggie Cassidy,* revise the hero's memory of his past to reveal knowledge once inexplicable and now plain to his seeing eyes. He traces there the origins of his visionary capacity as an ultrareceptive child and the sources in experience for the dark preoccupations of his visions. This focus reveals the extent to which Kerouac modified autobiography for the purposes of his legend. The events recalled are most often those that demonstrate the inevitability of mortal visions; in this, Kerouac invents a hero from himself who has a biography fundamentally independent from the diverse putative facts that describe Jack Kerouac, Duluoz embodies specific intuitions and is the agent of a truth to be cathartically exposed, that life may be redeemed from darkness. Of the novels of childhood and adolescence, *Doctor Sax* (1959), the second volume of the Duluoz Legend, presents the greatest challenge and offers a rich rationale for the origin of vision and visionary capacity.

Kerouac called the book "the myth of the rainy night,"[4] underscoring the baroque comic strip fantasy it presents. This quality, personified in the supernatural hero Doctor Sax, is the challenge that distracts from and competes with the more mundane aspects of the narrative, the child's growing up in a close-knit community in Lowell, Massachusetts. Often segregated, two narratives form the novel. One depicts life in Lowell. The other, evolving from the child's fantasies, pictures a gothic underworld peopled by surreal imaginary characters. Jackie Duluoz, the child, presides in the first. Doctor Sax, a figure he invents from Lamont Cranston's "The Shadow," lives in the second but frequents the first. Remembering sporadic moments from his birth in 1922 to his fourteenth year, 1936, Duluoz relates both worlds. Although Doctor Sax and the underworld are spectacular and arcane diversions that evince Kerouac's versatility, the precocious child's fears and intuitions are the emotional core of the novel and they register largely in the everyday Lowell the boy experiences. They indicate the locus of vision and are treated to visionary perception.

Perhaps because of the underworld narrative, critics and reviewers have encouraged the view that the novel is too bizarre to assess systematically,[5] but *Doctor Sax* advances on a linear though episodic narrative and consistently explores a dark underside of consciousness. Passing into adolescence in the course of the tale, the child learns to tolerate the intimations which frighten him. That Doctor Sax is ultimately secondary to the recognitions which have urged the child to invent him is affirmed by his metamorphosis into a man at the novel's climax. The child's rite of passage is to demythify the superhero to hazard adolescence on his own. Based on facts of Kerouac's life, *Doctor Sax* mystically depicts childhood as a sublime innocence terrorized by blighting forces. The sharp awareness of mortality brought to consciousness in visions begins here; childhood vulnerability is universally assaulted and difficult to defend. *Doctor Sax* foreshadows a lifetime similarly besieged and told in the following volumes of the Duluoz Legend.

Duluoz begins his reminiscences by stating his narrative method and by describing his mode of perception. He relates a dream in which he has ordered himself to "Describe the wrinkly tar of this sidewalk . . . and dont stop to think of words when you do stop, just stop to think of the picture better—and let your mind off yourself in this work."[6] Free intuition and association are valued above self-conscious selection in the descriptive process; Duluoz prefers an unretouched visualized truth, which he implies will ensue from a free-floating meditation. The image of the "wrinkly tar sidewalk" recurs throughout like a mantra designed to free the narrator from consciousness to the limitless realm of dream and the pursuit of truth in dreamwork. Dreaming is a way of seeing through fact to a core of meaning: "Dreams are where participants in a dream recognize one another's death—there is no illusion of life in this Dream" (112), Duluoz later asserts. Disclosed in the dreams that issue from meditations on the past are intimations of mortality. Disclosed also is the future of the dreamer, as Duluoz adds, "what it is I really see in that dream—[is] the future really" (112), a vision of his own mortality, hovering ahead of him in time, implacable and certain. Life is thus stripped of even the illusion of a future by the knowledge revealed in the dream-work of a revery on childhood. To look again into childhood is to uncover the genesis of this knowledge in experience.

The process of remembering is familiar from Kerouac's aesthetic statement, **"Essentials of Spontaneous Prose."** There, he instructs aspiring writers to set the "object," or subject of composition, "before the mind, either in reality," as in a landscape or a face, or "in the memory," as in "the sketching from memory of a definite image-object."[7] Then, by "following free deviation (association) of mind into limitless . . . seas of thought," the writer's real but buried knowledge or feeling for the subject will be released and truth revealed. Here, the "image-object" in the memory is Doctor Sax, and Duluoz's associations with him are supernaturally bleak. In his meditation, Duluoz uncovers the meaning of feelings only intuited as a child, hence revising his history with hindsight vision.

When he thinks of Doctor Sax, then, letting his mind off himself in the work as he says, definite pictures of his life rise into view. For example, he remembers that "Doctor Sax I first saw in his earlier lineaments in the early Catholic childhood of Centralville—deaths, funerals, the shroud of that, the dark figure in the corner when you look at the dead man coffin" (4). He sees himself at a funeral, and life in the Centralville neighborhood of Lowell associated with Catholic death rituals. He also sees a shadowy figure lurking near the coffin, identified as Doctor Sax. The superhero is linked with death in his memory, and is an invention to beguile the fear roused by the baroque Catholicism that is an apparently fertile medium for ghostly visitations and signs:

> I knew I was haunted . . . after that I dreamed the horrible dream of the rattling red living room . . . I saw it in the dream all dancing and rattling like skeletons because my brother Gerard haunted them . . .—Memory and dream are intermixed in this mad universe.
>
> (5)

Surreal nightmares colored hell-fire red follow from the fears unearthed at funerals; the dead brother Gerard haunts dreams and memory which are indistinguishable in the "mad universe" of childhood. This child is involuntarily privy to a dark realm seated in his own soul. Like a figure in Poe, he is a seer of horror, an outcast or outsider in his own world. His innocence attracts mad visions and supernatural signs which set him apart from domestic security and boyhood games.

The putative facts of this world are equally terrible. Remembering even the most banal biographical details provokes alarming associations:

> At age seven I went to St. Louis Parochial School, a particularly Doctor Saxish school. . . . Rainy funerals for little boys, I saw several including the funeral of my own poor brother when (at age 4) my family lived exactly on the St. Louis parish on Beaulieu St. . . .
>
> (34)

Again, Catholicism hosts an environment congenial to the funeral maven Doctor Sax and the child lives in a neighborhood where little boys, little brothers, die. Duluoz reiterates this gloomy theme, describing the ubiquitous rain and the wailing of his neighborhood: "A kid across the street from Joe's died, we heard wailing; another kid in a street between Joe's and mine, died—rain, flowers—the smell of flowers" (66). Death is a dominant reality, a fact of childhood. The Beaulieu Street house itself is "built over an ancient cemetery" nestled behind the old St. Louis parish. It is little wonder that "Presentiments of shadow and snake came to me early" (35), Duluoz concludes, anticipating the Doctor Sax myth; the real world is perilous.

"Fears," he states, "like any prescience of a dream are unerasable" (75). Perhaps this is so because they have vivid correlatives in reality. In addition to the array of child corpses, Duluoz remembers the neighborhood peopled by grotesque funhouse characters. Destouches' candy store is "the brown establishment of an ailing leper—it was said he had nameless diseases" (14). The child knows a denizen named Ali Zaza, "a moronic French Canadian sex fiend . . . since childhood, spermatazoing in all directions, jacking off dogs and worst of all sucking off dogs" (69). These Felliniesque characters fill Duluoz's child world, and though his ally Doctor Sax "knew these things," Jackie is nonetheless compelled to confront them himself and to master his reactions. He conceives a touching "duty": "I had learned to stop crying in Centralville and I was determined not to start crying in Pawtucketville" (43), he says, referring to family moves from one section of Lowell to another, both neighborhoods equally treacherous. Fear of death and the neighborhoods' grotesques unman the child in Duluoz's memory and he devises a crude child code, the will to stay his tears, to maintain grace under pressure. He knows that doom is nonetheless inescapable: "(two more will die, who will it be, what phantom is pursuing *you*?)" (43). Instructed by the death of his brother and other children, Duluoz develops an awareness of universal doom, a collective fate. Childhood is blighted by the necessity for a precocious wisdom.

The dramatic centerpiece of the biography told in **Doctor Sax** is Duluoz's recreation of his birth. The beginning of independent life is here inscribed into the legend and conceived in dark terms consistent with the dangerous childhood and its terrifying knowledge:

> It was in Centralville I was born, in Pawtucketville saw Doctor Sax. Across the wide basin to the hill—on Lupine Road, March 1922, at five o'clock in the afternoon of a red-all-over suppertime . . .—I was born. Bloody rooftop. Strange deed. All eyes I came hearing the river's red; I remember that afternoon, I perceived it through beads hanging in a door and through lace curtains and glass of a universal sad lost redness of mortal damnation. . . .
>
> (16-17)

The facts of date and location are Kerouac's actual statistics, but they are poetically transformed in the telling to that hell-fire red, the color of blood, birth, and nightmares of death. To state natal facts is to acknowledge another fact, "mortal damnation." In Kerouac, death is often linked with the subject of birth; in **Doctor Sax**, that dreary fate is worsened by what Duluoz was born destined "all eyes" to see. Visionary capacity is indicated by what is heard and what remembered

in poetic inversions: the color of the river, the beads, the glass. All "perceived," all are symbolic lenses which focus the universal fate, the "sad lost redness" of being condemned to die by being born. The "strange deed" of birth suggests the reflexive properties of the legend. The seer gives birth to himself in his recreation, revising even the involuntary to fit the schema of a legend cast in visionary dimensions.

Doctor Sax is similarly created, but from *Shadow* comics and an imagination spurred by fear. Compensating for the child's inadequacies, he possesses power where the child shows helplessness: "Doctor Sax had knowledge of death . . . but he was a mad fool of power, a Faustian man, no true Faustian's afraid of the dark . . ." (43). A product of the child's uninhibited imagination, Doctor Sax rallies the frightened spirit. He is an outlaw shaman who undertakes a twenty-year battle for humankind by alchemizing an herbal powder to kill the feared Snake, an underworld creature who embodies the evil of the child's precocious knowledge. Sax is well-equipped for the cause: "to battle required herbs and nerves . . . moral nerves, he had to recognize good and evil and intelligence" (32). Dramatizing the child's fears in a fantasied moral battle, the Faustian medicine man Sax takes on "the enigma of the New World—the snake of evil." That enigma is no less than the knotty and frightening problem of life which is known to culminate in "mortal damnation." Until the grand confrontation in the climax of the tale, the child believes in Sax's power. His purpose in the child's fantasy is to combat the unassailable universals—fear, evil, destruction, death—and thus he is a superhero. He is destined to descend to the underworld of the child's imagination to battle the feared forces embodied by the Snake. His actual purpose is to be an ally for a child burdened by fears he cannot communicate. When these fears are released in language, Sax is transformed into a man, his purpose fulfilled.

Extracting Doctor Sax from childhood fantasy and providing him a literary presence, Duluoz alchemizes putative biography with emotional truth. He recreates childhood from his memory-impressions and against the dark, displays the ineffable other, Doctor Sax. Three important events comprise the balance of the novel. The first two, the death of a man on the Moody Street Bridge and the 1936 Merrimac River flood, derive from remembered empirical events. The third, the confrontation with the Snake, occurs in the imagined gothic underworld and concludes the novel, resolving the emotional crisis promulgated by the two actual events. At this juncture, the imagination is empowered to affect consciousness; this is the process by which fundamental and frightening visionary knowledge is brought to a tolerable recognition and passed through. Thus, Duluoz endorses the power of the imagination to approach, apprehend, and even possibly vanquish plaguing enigmas.

In telling of the night he saw a man drop dead on the Moody Street Bridge, Duluoz again sees Doctor Sax in the actual world. The mood of the night is palpable. The sky is lit by a full August moon, the "moon of death," as the boy and his mother walk home from a visit. They pass through the Catholic Grotto and pray at the Stations of the Cross. This ritual summons Doctor Sax, whom the child sees flitting "from Station to Station . . . in terrible blasphemy prayer in the dark with everything reversed" (126), like a Gnostic priest: Catholic ritual triggers presentiments of death, Sax's native emotional landscape in the child. The important moment of the night is dramatically simple. A man carrying a watermelon passes the mother and child on the bridge and drops dead. The event is an intensely personal invasion; it yields vision and knowledge:

> I saw the watermelon man staring at the waves below with shining eyes . . . I'm completely terrified and yet I feel the profound pull and turn to see what he is staring at so deadly-earnest with his froth stillness—I look down with him and there is the moon on shiny froth and rocks, there is the long eternity we have been seeking.
>
> (128)

The child witnesses his first death, an event traumatic and suggestive enough, but for this destined seer, it engenders a vision of mortal eternity. He sees the corpse staring, and, sensitive to the "profound pull," mystically follows that "deadly-earnest" gaze to its ineffable end. Schooled by the dead, the child recognizes that the eternity sought is the mortal end to suffering; in his memory-vision, death is seductive, even desired. This is the precocious wisdom that has blighted his innocence and that even Doctor Sax flitting in the shadows has been unable to forestall. The moment when knowledge has been delivered by vision is recreated with convincing dramatic realism.

Certain words and images accrue symbolic significance for the child as he develops a language with which to express his feeling that "death was catching up again" (147). The dead man staring at

the water in "froth stillness," and the "moon on shiny froth rocks" builds up a poetic diction of fear. "The full moon horrified me with her cloudy leer" (129), Duluoz remembers, and soon death is visually omnipresent in the natural world, as certain sights associated with this diction now trigger visionary seeing:

> the moon [on the river] made the white horses foam all beautiful and close and shiny so that it was almost inviting—to jump in—everybody in Pawtucketville had the perfect opportunity to commit suicide coming home every night—that is why we lived deep lives—
>
> (127)

In this surreal vision, foam forms "mad white horses," correlatives for the water's deadly-seductive power, very like the "eternity we have been seeking." To the mortality-keyed sensibility of the child, the moonlit shiny river potently promulgates "deep lives." The opportunity for a watery suicide is a graphic fact of daily life for Duluoz in the milltown communities that border the river where he lives. Death is associated with primal nature, with water and the moon, and thus kept present by visual suggestion. When the river floods, Duluoz's consciousness of mortal helplessness against universal powers deepens, for the natural disaster enacts the suicidal promise of the water.

The Merrimac River flood of 1936 is described in Book Five of **Doctor Sax**. Coincidentally occurring in Duluoz's fourteenth year, it is treated as an analogue for his loss of innocence; the tragic dislocations of nature correspond with the end of childhood. Literally, the flooding river obliterates the scenes of childhood play: "they were now abluted in pure day by the white snow mist of tragedy" (166), Duluoz remembers, in vision converting the flooding to a ceremonial cleansing, an absolution. The river assumes the color of tragedy, white like the deadly moonlight and the foamy "mad white horses." The flood accelerates the natural order of untimely death in this community, and justifies the "deep lives" earlier told, for Duluoz remembers "all the boys who had drowned in the river" as it flooded, more child coffins to see. Freed to his memory, he realizes of his childhood that *all of it was drowned* (169), a vivid recognition that gives way to a deeper truth. Remembering the scribbled child journals he kept during the flood, Duluoz sees what he had intuited then, that there was

> something hopeless . . . something that can't possibly come back again in America and history, the

gloom of the unaccomplished mudheap civilization when it gets caught with its pants down from a source it long lost contact with—natural phenomena.

(180)

The sins of civilization are avenged by the savage waters in an almost cathartic absolution, a return to the primitive landscape, literally and emotionally, of precivilized life. As society was built in defiance of primal orders, so it is devastated in an eventual day of reckoning when elemental forces, the fierce knowledge of death their theme, assert themselves after the long abeyance. So too repressed knowledge is restored to consciousness. The flood forces a respect for primal power, a recognition of mortality and its tragic but unassailable command, *"all of it was drowned."* This knowledge is deeply impressed on the child about to pass into adolescence.

Naturally enough, the child's Doctor Sax has not been deceived by the structures of civilization. With his Faustian "knowledge of death," he prophesies, "'a flood will bring the rest. . . . The day of the Great Spider,' is come" (155). Here, the cold facts of 1936 are converted into the myth of the underworld battle, Duluoz thus fancifully expressing the truths that haunt him. He resolves his fears in the imagined underworld, ritualizing his passage into adolescence on his own terms. Again, a reflexive endeavor usurps the place of fact with a stronger power, imagination.

The novel's resolution in the underworld is apocalyptic, as perhaps the end of childhood and the loss of innocence seemed to the seer. Sax is a more palatable medium for the truths the dead have shown the boy, for he speaks "to the bottom of my boy problems" (197). When Jackie can "fathom his speech," he has accepted his knowledge. As though speaking to his younger self, Duluoz hears the Faustian hero telling him that "'rages you never dreamed'" await him in the future and that "'you'll never be as happy as you are now in your quiltish innocent book-devouring boyhood immortal night'" (203). Though the "boyhood immortal night" has been dark and shrouded by death, what lies ahead, he implies, is yet more disconcerting. Duluoz seemingly speaks through Sax what time has shown him to be true, modifying the childhood tale with adult knowledge. More, Sax counsels the child that "'in your death you'll know the *death* part of your life'" (204), suggesting that all the death the child has witnessed like a fear-ridden Huckleberry Finn is a dark but undeniable component of the life there is to live. Lastly, the child is told to "listen to your

own self—it ain't got nothing to do with what's around you, it's what you do inside at the controls" (211). As in a free association on experience, vision occurs inside; projecting Sax is precisely what Duluoz is doing "inside at the controls." He thus asserts the redemptive power of the imagination against the inevitability of death. If it cannot be forestalled or denied, death can be countered by the lively, inventive and free mind.

Sax's last stand is the apocalyptic descent into the underworld of the Pit, and it is Jackie's dramatic liberation from fear and childhood. The child follows Sax into the "mud cellar" of the Castle to prepare the powders that will vanquish the Great World Snake. The fantasy night, in contrast to the moonlit night on the bridge, is filled with the "eyes of eternity" sparkling like stars in anticipation of the manifestation of the "Golden Being of Immortality." The Day of Judgment is nigh, when as with the flood, the "earth's returned to fire, the western wrath is done" (228), but here, this is a desirable end, for evil will be destroyed by immortality. Yet when the child peeks into the Pit from which the Snake will rise, he confronts a startling knowledge:

> I looked down to face my horror, my tormentor, my mad-face demon mirror of myself. . . . I found myself looking into the horror, into the void, I found myself looking into the Dark, I found myself looking into IT. I found myself compelled to fall. *The Snake was coming for me!!*
>
> (238)

The child's last discovery is of his own humanity and of what that humanity is made. It is a powerful yet subtly stated recognition. The void, the "IT" beneath consciousness, contains knowledge of the primal fall to evil. In that fall, the seductive "Dark" is the compelling factor for Duluoz, much as the river seductively invites suicide and as the dead man's gaze meets an eternity in death *sought*. This vision reveals the final meaning of the child's precocious wisdom: it acknowledges that he too is compelled by the seductive quality of death. To know the "*death* part of life" is to apprehend that this "evil" desire is human, that it is an organic universal impulse to seek death. In the "demon mirror" of life, Duluoz sees this inadmissible impulse in himself. The vision, deeply disturbing, is mitigated, however, by Sax's confrontation with the Snake.

In the last scene, the Snake emerges from the Pit and Sax flings his blue powders. Unexpectedly, he fails and the Snake prevails. Equally surprisingly, the moment his duty is discharged, Sax metamorphoses into a man, a mortal hero very "like Bull Hubbard (tall, thin, plain, strange), or like Gary Cooper" (240). The failure of Doctor Sax's twenty-year quest and his metamorphosis are significant. They suggest that humanity is redeemed of its dark desire by the defiant effort to resist evil. A noble humanity is earned by the will of the imagination to supercede and to struggle against the lure of suicide felt in "deep lives." Imagination, the writer's agent of redemption, affirms an admirable human impulse, the life-embracing effort to overcome the usually unacknowledged but nevertheless powerful death impulse. The improbable *deus ex machina* that resolves the story of the Great Snake confirms this theme. The "Bird of Paradise" swoops down from the heavens and snaps up the Snake, bearing it back into the "Giant Bird Cloud." Thus freed of the Snake, Sax exults, "'The Universe disposes of its own evil!'" (245). This is the novel's final refrain and it is worked out in the imagined underworld narrative.

At this, both the superhero and the child are released to a benign actuality. Doctor Sax no longer lurks in the funereal shadows of consciousness; he is to be seen instead "at dusk, in autumn, when the kids jump up and down and scream" (245). In a world no longer fatal to children, the caped hero turned movie star mortal "only deals in glee now" (245). The child who invented him sees him in a new way. Similarly, Jack leaves the Castle of his imagination now an adolescent at peace with visionary knowledge:

> I went along home by the ding dong bells and daisies, I put a rose in my hair. I passed the Grotto again and saw the cross on top of that hump of rocks, saw some old French Canadian ladies praying step by step on their knees. I found another rose, and put another rose in my hair, and went home. By God.
>
> (245)

Thus the novel concludes, affirming the resolutions achieved by the imagined gothic drama in which the precocious wisdom of childhood visions has been enacted and released. Formerly a haunting ground of sudden death and dark vision, the Catholic Grotto is now seen to be the proper domain of devout old ladies. Tolling no funerals, church bells clarion cheerfully and flowers no longer carry the smell of death. Duluoz jauntily wreathes his hair in roses on his way home, no longer estranged from domestic comfort or alienated from the simple pleasures of sentience. Where once plagued by blighting knowledge, he is free to live. The apocalypse of childhood's end has been met, endured, and surpassed.

The Sax mythology parallels and resolves the child's real experience in Lowell of death and the flood. Both the novel's narratives suggest that humankind is helpless to engender or to forestall either good or evil; as immutable as birth and death, they are involuntary human manifestations. The child's recognition that the Snake is "after" him, or his to fear, suggests that what is human is of and beyond will, as "The Universe disposes of its own evil," unaffected by mortal or supernatural intervention. At best, the imagination can empower a transcendent seeing that orders the chaos of immutable forces. Duluoz's cathartic reconstruction of childhood, its facts and its imagined alter world, signifies the curative power of the imagination. Memory and the meditative work of dreaming free him and exorcise the dark haunting of the past. With Doctor Sax, the child is initiated to the real if shadowy domain of primitive feeling; once apprised of the primal phenomena "long lost contact with," he passes into adolescence beflowered and abluted. ***Doctor Sax***, like many of the novels of the Duluoz Legend, is ultimately more about the seer than about the figure for whom it is named, as that figure is a means to resolution. In the legend, Doctor Sax personifies the sources of visionary capacity, a hero created to palliate the terrible truths involuntarily learned by a gifted child. The eye to the keyhole sees a caped crusader at the genesis of the Duluoz Legend and watches as he changes into a man, the world now a little safer for sentience.

Notes

1. Jack Kerouac, *Big Sur* (New York: McGraw-Hill Book Company, 1962), Preface.

2. Jack Kerouac, *Vanity of Duluoz* (New York: G. P. Putnam's Sons, Capricorn Books, 1967), p. 195.

3. Jack Kerouac, *Visions of Cody* (New York: McGraw-Hill Book Company, 1972), p. 103.

4. Dennis McNally, *Desolate Angel* (New York: Random House, 1979), p. 150.

5. See David Dempsey, "Beatnik Bogeyman on the Prowl," *New York Times Book Review*, May 3, 1959, p. 28; Barnaby Conrad, "Barefoot Boy with Dreams of Zen," *Saturday Review*, February 2, 1959, pp. 23-4; Robert A. Hipkiss, *Jack Kerouac: Prophet of the New Romanticism* (Lawrence, KS: The Regents Press of Kansas, 1976).

6. Jack Kerouac, *Doctor Sax* (New York: Grove Press, Inc., 1959), p. 3. All subsequent quotations of this novel are taken from this edition; page numbers appear in parentheses after each quotation and refer to this edition.

7. Jack Kerouac, "Essentials of Spontaneous Prose," reprinted in The Viking Critical Library *On the Road* (New York: Penguin Books, 1979), p. 531.

Tristessa and *Visions of Gerard*

MATT THEADO (ESSAY DATE 2000)

SOURCE: Theado, Matt. "*Tristessa* (1960), *Visions of Gerard* (1963), and Buddhism." *Understanding Jack Kerouac,* pp. 123-40. Columbia: University of South Carolina Press, 2000.

In the following essay, Theado elucidates the influence of Kerouac's studies in Buddhism on his novels Tristessa *and* Visions of Gerard.

Although linked to *Maggie Cassidy* and *The Subterraneans, Tristessa* represents a departure in Kerouac's true-story novels. An important distinction between this book and the previous true-story novels Kerouac had written concerns his discovery of Buddhism in the late winter of 1953 and spring of 1954. One cannot overstate the significance of Kerouac's Buddhist studies on his life and his writing. At its core, Kerouac's Buddhism was not a radical departure from his worldview, for he had been exploring key Buddhist issues since *The Town and the City* without the background of Buddhism's rich traditions. He found affirmation in Buddhist teachings that made sense in the universe as he knew it. Kerouac augmented rather than replaced his childhood religious beliefs. According to Ann Charters, "Kerouac was of course born a Catholic, raised a Catholic and died a Catholic. His interest in Buddhism was a discovery of different religious images for his fundamentally constant religious feelings. . . . It was just that, for a time, he was a self-taught student of Buddhism" (*Kerouac* 199). Once self-taught, he was soon eager to teach others. He dove into his studies of Buddhism with enthusiasm, encouraging his friends, especially the Cassadys and Ginsberg, to partake with him of "the one path." He even came to believe by 1955 that only poetry based on Buddhist principles would be without flaws [*Selected Letters, 1940-1956*]. In a later interview Kerouac said, "My serious Buddhism, that of ancient India, has influenced that part in my writing that you might call religious, or fervent, or pious, almost as much as Catholicism has." When the interviewer asked him to identify the differences between Jesus and Buddha, Kerouac responded, "There is no difference" [Ted Berrigan, "The Art of Fiction XLI: Jack Kerouac," in *On The Road: Text and Criticism,* ed. Scott Donaldson].

When Kerouac discovered Buddhism, he had recently completed *The Subterraneans,* and as he told interviewer Al Aronowitz, "I went home and just sat in my room, hurting. I was suffering, you know, from the grief of losing a love."[1] The First Noble Truth of the Buddha especially intrigued Kerouac: Life is suffering. More generally, the ancient Indian term *duhkha* means more than suffering; it refers to the condition of people who do not have what they want or have what they do not want, who sorrow and grieve, or who are ill. Some Buddhist commentators use the word *anguish* as a translation, and Kerouac himself once stated the First Noble Truth thus: "All Life is Sorrowful" (*Good Blonde* 166). The First Noble Truth matched up with how Kerouac had felt throughout his life, particularly regarding his professional career. He had written five books since the spring of 1951 without any publication. He had been thwarted in his main desire: professional recognition of his success as a writer. In the dedication to *Howl* Ginsberg identifies Kerouac as one of the "best minds" of his generation being destroyed by the mechanistic, unsympathetic American culture. In fact, Ginsberg called Kerouac the "new Buddha of American prose."

In 1954 Kerouac began writing Buddhist studies and translating Buddhist sutras from the French. He kept a notebook that swelled eventually to hundreds of pages of Buddhist translations along with his ideas on their importance and meaning. He called this book *Some of the Dharma,* and it was finally published in 1997. This book is certainly not a concentrated study of Buddhism; it reveals, instead, Kerouac's own eccentric approach to Buddhism. He does include a smattering of scholarship—a Buddhist bibliography, for example, and some translations of ancient texts—but mostly the book consists of his apparently unadulterated speculations on the general notions of what Buddhism meant to him. The book might not be of use to a beginning student in Buddhism, yet it is intriguing because the reader can follow Kerouac's mental elaborations as he processes Buddhism through his thoroughly Christian value system. From the start Kerouac contrasts one savior with the other: "Buddha goes beyond Christ" (1). A surprising aspect of *Some of the Dharma* is its portrayal of Kerouac's ongoing battle between spiritual enlightenment and his desire to write. Throughout the book he recognizes that no words can convey truth properly; the Buddha's teaching is beyond words. Furthermore, he believes that his attempts to write merely serve to feed his ego unless he can write the Duluoz Legend so that every line provides enlightenment (278, 279).

Kerouac was impressed with the huge epochs of time, the *kalpas,* that lead cyclically to vast new ages. In the face of such colossal patterns, one's ego vanishes to insignificance. The editors of *Jack's Book* [eds. Barry Gifford and Lawrence Lee] point out other parallels between the Buddhist universe and Kerouac's. For example, he found in "the notion of *dharma,* the same self-regulating principle of the universe that he had proposed himself in the closing pages of **Doctor Sax.** *Maya,* the illusory play of reality, matched the vision of his personal insignificance" (Gifford and Lee 186). Kerouac also identified with the Buddhist notion of compassion for all living things, a lesson his brother, Gerard, had taught him years before. Though his frenetic interest in Buddhism would wane later in his life, Buddhism affected nearly every subsequent book Kerouac would write, an influence foregrounded even in the titles of **The Dharma Bums** and **Satori in Paris.** Interested readers should refer to the biographies, letters, **Some of the Dharma,** James Jones's *A Map of "Mexico City Blues,"* and *Big Sky Mind: Buddhism and the Beat Generation* [ed. Carole Tonkinson] for more details of Kerouac's involvement with Buddhism and its effect on his art.

Thematically, one of Buddhism's more important influences on Kerouac was its insistence on abstinence. While he never quit drinking entirely—and recognized this as a weakness—he did swear himself to celibacy for most of a year. While he lusted for Mardou in his pre-Buddhist **The Subterraneans** and assumed that his male readers were similarly "crudely sexual" as well, in **Tristessa** Kerouac assumes the persona of a celibate penitent, mindful of his Buddha nature. Later he would boast that he had endured a year of celibacy because he saw lust as the cause of birth, which in turn brought about suffering and death (**The Dharma Bums** 29). Besides celibacy, Kerouac found the doctrine of impermanence to be important. He had always sensed the fleeting quality of life and reflected this in his writing, and now he began to see that even the apparent reality of the present moment was illusory. All the sensations of the physical world were merely an entrapment in samsara, the karmic wheel of death and rebirth. Kerouac saw in the Buddhist concept of nirvana an escape from illusion and grasping, a return to the Eden he felt he had lost. Nirvana represented the completion of his life's seeking, for he moved first from the bliss of his mother's womb, then from the security of his father's house, and finally from the idealistic philosophical notions that might have sustained him in his youth. After a

period of loss Kerouac believed he could regain the sense of bliss again through Buddhist meditation and awareness.

On a more communal, less personal level, Kerouac found in Buddhism an alternative to the cold war culture that surrounded him. Carole Tonkinson, editor of *Big Sky Mind,* explains that from the Buddhist point of view, "Cold War catchwords—us and them, ally and enemy—were rendered meaningless. . . . And Buddhism's advocation of a mendicant, homeless life also suggested the practical alternative to the rapidly accelerating cycle of work-produce-consume that was the engine driving fifties' culture."[2] Kerouac relied more on the personal aspects of Buddhism in **Tristessa, Visions of Gerard,** and **Desolation Angels,** and he developed the social, cultural ideas in **The Dharma Bums.**

Tristessa

When he arrived in Mexico City in the summer of 1955, he wrote his long poem **Mexico City Blues,** his first artistic attempt to convey his Buddhist-inspired visions. Immediately after finishing his poetic Buddhist exploration, he began **Tristessa,** a prose exploration of a related situation. He based the main character on Esperanza Villenueva, who served as a morphine connection for Kerouac's friend Bill Garver. In keeping with the mood of the book, he changed her name from Esperanza, which means "hope" in Spanish, to Tristessa, which means "sadness." Although the jacket notes of most editions say that Tristessa is a prostitute, it is difficult to find evidence in the text to support that claim.

Kerouac continues the Duluoz Legend in Mexico City from an entirely different perspective from the way he presented his affair with Mardou in **The Subterraneans.** Again, he positions himself as a narrator excluded from the central cast of those he observes and with whom he interacts. However, in **Tristessa** he focuses on the difficulties of maintaining compassion among a group of Mexican junkies who have little to offer anyone besides Tristessa's sexuality, which Duluoz denies himself. Instead, he comes to see that she possesses an innate sense of Buddhism without having ever read the works he himself has studied. There is a tragic consequence in her ability to cancel desire, though. As Kerouac transcribes her speech, "I weeling to haff jonk—morfina—and be no-seek any more" (28). Tristessa is saying that she will not be *sick* anymore, since for an addict a shot of morphine cures its own disease. Yet Ker-

ON THE SUBJECT OF...

JAN MICHELE HACKETT

Jan Hackett was Kerouac's daughter. Despite the fact that she only met her famous father twice, Hackett's life and her writing were strongly influenced by the Kerouac legend. She left home at an early age and experimented freely with drugs, including LSD and heroin. She traveled extensively in the United States and abroad, making her way through a wide variety of odd jobs along the way, including that of waitress, maid, cannery worker, racetrack groom, and prostitute. Hackett published two novels under the name Jan Kerouac and was working on a third at the time of her death in 1996. Her first book, *Baby Driver: A Story about Myself,* tells of her childhood on Manhattan's Lower East Side, her early rebellion, and her travels in Latin America. Her second novel, *Train-song,* takes up where her first book left off, continuing the tale of Hackett's episodic and often extreme experiences while traveling throughout the United States and Europe.

ouac implies that this drug is still a temporary form of nirvana, a release from desire (seeking) and thus from pain, however temporary. Tristessa also lives according to the Buddhist doctrine of karma: she understands that life is hard, and she says, "What I do, I *reap*" (28). Tristessa knows, too, the Buddhist precepts of impermanence. She tells Duluoz that since both she and he will die, they are "nothing" (76).

Buddhism blends with Catholicism in this book. Just as Kerouac saw the subterraneans as "Christlike," he sees Tristessa as the "Virgin Mary of Mexico" (13). Like Kerouac, Tristessa is a devout Catholic. She keeps a large icon in her room, but the Catholic imagery extends beyond a traditional representation of piety; Tristessa's companion, El Indio, prays devoutly before the icon when he goes out to buy drugs. They keep their Catholic attributions in Kerouac's descriptions just as the subterraneans remain Christlike as they smoke marijuana and inject heroin. In this tale, though, the characters take on both Buddhist and Catholic

aspects. For example, Duluoz admits that he knows everything is all right, but still he wants "proof and the Buddhas and Virgin Marys are there to remind me" (19). Later he prays to *"ma Dame"* and accentuates the *Dame* "because of Damema the Mother of Buddhas" (38).

Very little happens in this story, for the core of Duluoz's experience here is observation and reflection, not action. When the narrative begins he is drunk; he takes a shot of morphine at his hosts' behest; and he observes the scene around him without interfering. A key scene occurs when Duluoz troops home at night through the rain. Viking Press adviser Malcolm Cowley once wrote to Kerouac that **Desolation Angels,** a later book, was formless and weakened by the impression that "Duluoz seems to be moving through his own reflections almost in a world of ghosts."[3] Kerouac responded that this was precisely his intention. These books did not satisfy Cowley's expectations for what a novel should be, while in fact the books are a different genre altogether—dramatized events from real life, heightened by artistic language, based on interior considerations of external circumstances.

In his earlier spontaneous prose stories Kerouac blends memory, reality, and dream to achieve the perception of events by the mind. In **Tristessa** he adds the element of unreality. As Kerouac writes in **Mexico City Blues,** "Dharma law / Say / All things is made / of the same thing / which is a nothing" (66). This apparent paradox is at the core of Buddhism. Nirvana comes when one sees the wholeness of the universe, yet even the notion that there is a "wholeness" is an illusion. There can be no "wholeness" as long as there is a separate perceiver to see it. Throughout **Tristessa** tears appear in the fabric of reality as Kerouac reveals the lack of substance one usually takes for granted. For example, as Duluoz observes Tristessa preparing her morphine shot, he inexplicably recalls a scene from his youth. In that scene he now realizes that his surroundings are not only impermanent but are beautiful *because* they are not lasting (23). This end of things is more than the dissolution of form Kerouac saw in **Doctor Sax** as the high school fence posts disappear, and more than the loss of the riverbanks in **Maggie Cassidy.** For now, Duluoz sees beauty in their cessation because they were never there to begin with. The things end because the perceiver realizes their impermanent nature and sees that they are simply manifestations of maya.

As Duluoz walks home through the rain, he observes a group of children who have just finished playing a baseball game. A player acknowledges a bad play he has made but adds, "Didn't I make it up with that *heet* in the seventh inning?" (55). Again, Kerouac uses the Mexican pronunciation to produce a pun, for *heet* means "hit" but also implies "heat," the totality of the player's involvement in the moment when he made his good play. One tenet of spontaneous prose is that the words stay as written. A jazz musician cannot retrieve a passage he has just played, and Kerouac will not retreat in his writing to undo what he has just done. Joyce Carol Oates notes that "to say that Kerouac's work is uneven is simply to say that it is Kerouac's work."[4] Still, Kerouac will frequently roar back with eloquent passages that, like the kid's hit, are the heat that make up for the miscues. Another level of meaning is possible here too. The idea of karma means that one is responsible for one's actions, and in some future existence one must atone for the actions of the present life. Tristessa, despite her addiction to drugs, believes that the Lord will reward the good she does. Duluoz knows that she will reap her reward, that she will receive blessing in nirvana (27). Duluoz, too, hopes to atone later for present actions. He arrives home Sunday morning, and though he falls asleep while other people are going to church, he avows to make up for it later. In fact, the next paragraph, ostensibly written after he sleeps, is a prayer—"Blessed Lord, though lovedest all sentient life"—that is a mixture of Buddhist and Catholic imagery.

Part 2 begins a year later, after Kerouac had lived the adventures that would become *The Dharma Bums* and *Desolation Angels*. Nonetheless, he nearly seamlessly stitched part 2 onto the end of part 1, manipulating the phrase that ended the first part to begin the second. Still, strong differences in mood reveal that much has changed in the year that has passed. For one thing, Duluoz now regrets his celibacy as a mistaken notion, for he now feels that their intimacy may have helped her (84). Since the previous summer, Duluoz has learned the vaguely Buddhist practice of *yabyum* (described in *The Dharma Bums*), where sex is a celebration of life and togetherness. For another thing, Tristessa's insistence that she is "seek" is obviously the case now, for she has been addicted to morphine all this time and has also begun taking "goof balls" (Seconal).

As in his other books, Kerouac includes the rhetorical decisions he must make about the writing process in the text of the book itself. Early in part 2 he states that since he does not remember all the details of the story except the final night,

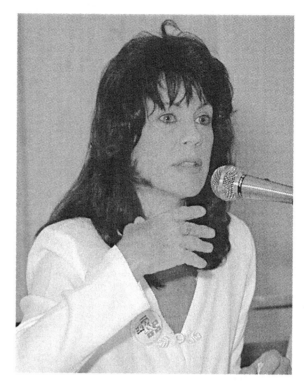

Jan Michele Hackett (Jan Kerouac), 1952-1996.

he will avoid the writer's traditional urge to "build up" (86). Kerouac wishes to avoid the trappings of telling a story in a predetermined form, a "literary" form, that would rob it of its essential interest, which for him is the emotional impact of events. Years later he told an interviewer that "FEELING is what I like in art, not CRAFTINESS and the hiding of feelings" (Berrigan 541). As he moves toward completion of this book, then, he consciously attempts to avoid relating a structured version of the events and instead offers a series of impressions. The color blue dominates the scenes as Bull Garver and Duluoz go downtown to El Indio's place to buy drugs. The day leads to Duluoz's own kind of blues, as he complains, that his poems and his money have been stolen, that Tristessa is sick; he had not imagined his pitiful fate (109). Not even his language can save the sense of despair; "O I wish I could write!—Only a beautiful poem could do it!" (112).

Finally, Tristessa's desire for morphine overrides any hope that she and Duluoz could be together. After he tells her he now wants to marry her, she reveals that her true love is morphine. Perhaps Garver and Tristessa will be together, though, for Garver says that one must be a junkie to understand a junkie (122). Duluoz takes a shot of morphine so that he can be temporarily more like them, and the prose of the book dissolves in wordplay and loose association. Life becomes a movie that shows God to people and people to God, and Duluoz's part is to chronicle the "long sad tales about people in the legend of [his] life" (126). *Tristessa* is not a fully developed exploration of its main character as *Visions of Cody* is, but Tristessa is not really at the core of this story. Instead the book explores Kerouac's relationship with Buddhism and the language he invents to reveal that relationship.

Visions of Gerard

One phrase in *Tristessa* was so important to Kerouac that he wrote it in capital letters and vowed to write it all over America: "BORN TO DIE." Impending death made no sense to Kerouac, for it seemed to negate or make insignificant all the labors and sufferings of life. Only a mystical, spiritual comprehension could counter the senselessness of the inevitable death of humans; death is not life thwarted, for death and birth naturally arise together, as wet implies dry, or as high implies low. Kerouac offers in *Tristessa* a message "that recompenses all that pain with soft reward of perfect silent love" (33). The apparent senselessness of death and the message that alleviates the suffering it causes are at the core of *Visions of Gerard*. A biographer of Beethoven once wrote, "Few men have the capacity fully to realize suffering as one of the great structural lines of human life." Stephen Batchelor, who cites this line in an article on Buddhism, goes on to say that "as with Great Dharma, Great Art begins with an unflinching acceptance of anguish as the primary truth of human experience. . . . All are united by the terrible beauty of anguish."[5]

For four years no other person was as close to Kerouac as his older brother, Gerard;[6] in fact, Duluoz identified so strongly with his older brother he claimed that he *was* Gerard (2). Without Gerard's saintly influence, Kerouac says—through the persona of his narrator, Duluoz—that he would not have become a writer. Kerouac also firmly believed that his brother was a saint. Warren French finds that "considered as a saint's life, *Visions of Gerard* is a remarkable achievement for a twentieth-century writer generally regarded as an instigator of a counterculture" (66). Gerard's life had other lasting effects, too, for Duluoz swears that their mother loved Gerard more than she loved him (72). Gerard was an inspiration, a tragic loss, and an unwilling combatant for their mother's affections.

In *The Town and the City* Kerouac writes of his parents' lives before he was born. He develops their characters and fills in their experiences; in short, he fictionalizes them, for he had no firsthand knowledge of their lives at the time covered in the early parts of the book. Kerouac wrote in a 1950 letter to Cassady that when he wrote those characters, he was "trying to stuff" his material but that he would not succumb to that ploy again. However, Kerouac wrote an entire novel about the brother who died when he himself, called Ti Jean by his family, was only four years old. He even tells Cassady that he barely knew Gerard and remembered little of their relationship. He goes on to relate one clear memory of Gerard (*Letters* 255). He also recalls that, just before Gerard died, Gerard slapped him in the face for disturbing his erector set project. He even admits in the text of the novel that his "memory is limited and mundane" (109). One wonders, then, how Kerouac could get the material to write this novel while he seems to remember clearly only two events. In part, he relied on stories his parents and relatives told him through the years. His long letter to Cassady contains most of the scenes that he would retell in the novel, and his source was family lore. Gerard apparently was a fixture in the family legend—his stories repeated "a thousand times"—before Kerouac wrote him into the Duluoz Legend. He relies also on his ability to romanticize the scenes that must have occurred and to invent scenes that probably did not occur but serve to balance the story. Finally, Kerouac wished to express the spiritual embodiment that Gerard was for him. If his lasting impression of Gerard was necessarily distorted by the fact that he had perceived as a four-year-old does, the distance between fact and impression is of little consequence. Kerouac portrays Gerard the way he saw him; after all, this is the Duluoz Legend, the saga of his own life blown to legendary status. Whether or not Gerard did or said the things attributed to him in this book is not as important as whether Kerouac believes he did. He later wrote in *Desolation Angels* that he may only remember a few of the things Gerard said to him as a child, but he knows that Gerard spoke of "a *reverence* for life, no, at least a reverence of the *idea* of life, which I translated as meaning that life itself is the Holy Ghost" (229). *Visions of Gerard* is the most "fictional" or "creative" book in the Duluoz Legend. As Kerouac concludes Gerard's tale in his letter to Cassady—his few memories and the stories that his family had relayed—he claims, "if you burned what I write you now with such joy I could never tell it again so truly; so of course, don't burn anything but save for me, for my honest books of later" (262).

In twelve nights in January 1956, writing by candlelight and under the influence of Benzedrine, Kerouac wrote the tale of his brother's last year. He wrote what he thought of as a variation of Shakespearean prose. He told Ann Charters that he had recently read *Henry V* and the Elizabethan diction had influenced his own style. Kerouac's manner in this book is quite different from that of his previous books—which were different from each other as well. Long sentences, quirky twists and associations, and wordplay predominate as in the others, but this book contains a softer, more religious tone.

Kerouac begins the tale with a variation on the classic invocation to the muse: he imagines that Gerard would "bless my pencil as I undertake and draw breath to tell his pain-tale for the world that needs his soft and loving like" (3). The rhythm is basically iambic ("the world that needs his soft and loving like"), a Shakespearean characteristic. Kerouac also reveals his method of composition, as he writes with a pencil and structures his phrases and sentences according to his natural breath. The verb "undertake" puns on "undertaker," referring both to Gerard's imminent mortality and to the last scene, based on another pun, when the gravedigger "picks up his shovel and closes the book" (129). The puns tie the book together, as Kerouac uses the pencil temporarily to revive Gerard and the gravedigger uses his tool as an implement of closure.

Throughout the book the narrator jumps from his narration of his family's past to describe recent events. Besides being a typical Kerouac technique that reveals the writer at work, this temporal leap also distances the past, when Gerard lived, and the present days, when Gerard is lost. For example, young Ti Jean watches as Gerard befriends a hungry kid and asks his mother to feed his new friend. Duluoz adds that on a recent trip to Lowell he has seen the now-matured kid who has grown to six feet tall and weighs two-hundred pounds (5). The implication is that although Gerard is gone, his kindness still lives on in the form of a grown man who benefited from it. The most important connection between the past and the present is Kerouac's Buddhism, for of course there was no Buddhism in the Kerouac household when Gerard lived. Kerouac's Buddhism percolates throughout the story that had no Buddhist flavor for his family when they told and retold the

events. Duluoz imagines Gerard watching the dissolution of summer clouds that, in their immateriality, reflect Taoist principles (2). The people of the town and even the solid redbrick smokestacks—and Gerard himself—will similarly dematerialize. Clouds work as symbols of the impermanence of reality since they seem solid, possessing color and shape, but no one can grasp them, and they disappear when observed for any length of time. Like Tristessa, Gerard has an intuitive knowledge of the fleeting nature of things. He proposes that reality is as transitory as the smoke from his father's pipe (25).

One night Gerard goes to the store to get aspirin for his mother, an act that typifies Gerard's kindness. Gerard travels through the cold night with which Frances confronted Peter in *The Town and the City* (42). Gerard avoids the spiritual implications of the terrible, cold night, though, by arriving at a fundamental Buddhist conception. Were it not for Gerard's presence as a perceiver, he understands that there would be no cold, that the feeling of cold is merely the sensation of his interaction with the environment. Without that sensation, people would see the world as heaven and know that there is no future salvation to await.

The book also features Christian—specifically Catholic—imagery, from the parochial school Gerard attends to the church itself and finally the funeral mass. Gerard is Christlike when he angrily admonishes the cat who ate his mouse in a manner reminiscent of Jesus chastising the moneychangers in the temple. Gerard's Christlike qualities are coupled with Buddha-like qualities. In the biography of the Buddha, young Sakyamuni leaves his royal father's walled-in house and discovers the suffering of the poor and the old. In the cold night Gerard crosses paths with the solitary old junk man, who is coming home with his burdensome junk cart. The sight leaves Gerard shaken, and he wonders why God put people out of heaven to be sick and cold.

The key scene in the book plays directly in the title: Gerard's vision of heaven. The nun is reciting a catechism, the oral recitation and memorization of Catholic principles, taught in question and answer. Because of his illness Gerard has not slept well, and now he dozes in class. In his dream he recounts his responsibility to take care of his little brother, Ti Jean. Then Gerard sees the Virgin Mary, a beautiful emanation of purity (52). In this dream Gerard's suffering existence on earth is but a brief morning when he wandered out of heaven. Ti Jean himself will have this awareness at Gerard's funeral, when he cannot understand the grief the adults suffer. Ti Jean senses that Gerard's death means his freedom from suffering, and in any case, life is "a dream already a long time ended and [my parents] don't know it and I try to tell them, they want to slap me in the kisser I'm so gleeful" (111). In the midst of this gloomy book of a child's illness and death, Kerouac yokes Buddhism and Catholicism and announces that Nirvana and Heaven reside in the present moment (110). As with other mystics throughout history, Gerard is frustrated at his inability to convey adequately the substance of his vision. He says on Christmas Eve, the last for which he will be alive, that he wishes eagerly to tell his family of his understanding of heaven—the visions of Gerard—but he fears these matters cannot be put effectively into words (59).

As in most of his earlier books, Kerouac pays close attention to seasons and their significance in the story. In one particular set piece Kerouac launches into a paean to spring. In keeping with his Buddhist knowledge, he immediately notes that spring, as generally recognized, is the time of rebirth. Now, however, he realizes that the rebirth only leads to more death. He manipulates syntax to bring the two significant terms into the closest possible contact: "Comes the cankerous rush of spring, when earth will fecundate and get soft and produce forms that are but to *die, multiply*" (74, emphasis mine). Readers arrive at the word "die" before the word "multiply," for no doubt exists as to the fate of living things. Kerouac uses the term "cankerous," which has an appropriate sound for the "rush of spring" yet contains also connotations associated with "canker"—an open or festering sore, a source of corruption—and comes from the Latin root "cancer." The hopeful song of spring is riddled with the inevitability of disease.

Almost as an escape from the pain of Gerard's sickness, Duluoz continues by detailing an evening with the father, Emil, based closely on Kerouac's own father. As Emil meets his friend, Manuel, in the warm airy night, Kerouac records the sounds that float through the open windows and attributes a human cause to every one. The cacophony creates a kind of human symphony, with the orchestra ranged around the neighborhood; the evening gathers up human utterances and activities in its swirling current and carries them along in an endless stream (81). In his wildest prose experiment, *Old Angel Midnight,* (1959) Kerouac would return to another evening when he listened to the sounds of the universe coming

in his window. For now, he is content to list the sounds without trying to imitate them—except for standard onomatopoeia.

As *Tristessa* did, *Visions of Gerard* ends with Kerouac describing the reality of life as if it were a movie directed by God (127). The movie conceit is Kerouac's representation of maya, which Kerouac employs in several other books as well. The child Ti Jean and the adult narrator Duluoz each feel compelled to tell people of the *"Here and Now"* of salvation, but each is frustrated in his attempts to make that message clear. They share a vision of heaven that might be impossible to pass on through the medium of language, whether oral or written. Nonetheless, Kerouac conveys his Buddhist-influenced perceptions on the long-ago events that shaped him as a person and as a writer.

Notes

1. Cited in Fields, "Buddhism Beat and Square," 75.

2. Tonkinson, "Buddhism and the Beat Generation," 60.

3. Unpublished letter from Malcolm Cowley to Jack Kerouac, 24 February 1957. Newberry Library, University of Chicago.

4. Oates, "Down the Road," 98.

5. Batchelor, "A Democracy of the Imagination," 71.

6. One should bear in mind that "Gerard" is pronounced differently in French than in English.

Bibliography

Works by Jack Kerouac
The Town and the City. New York: Harcourt, Brace, 1950; London: Eyre and Spottiswoode, 1951.

The Subterraneans. New York: Grove, 1958; London: Deutsch, 1960.

The Dharma Bums. New York: Viking, 1958; London: Deutsch, 1959.

Doctor Sax: Faust Part Three. New York: Grove, 1959; London: Deutsch, 1977.

Maggie Cassidy. New York: Avon, 1959; London: Panther, 1960.

Mexico City Blues. New York: Grove, 1959.

Tristessa. New York: Avon, 1960; London: World, 1963.

Visions of Gerard. New York: Farrar, Straus, 1963; London: Deutsch, 1964.

Desolation Angels. New York: Coward-McCann, 1965; London: Deutsch, 1966.

Satori in Paris. New York: Grove, 1966; London: Deutsch, 1967.

Works about Kerouac

Listed in alphabetical order by author.

BIOGRAPHIES

Charters, Ann. *Kerouac.* San Francisco: Straight Arrow, 1972.

Gifford, Barry, and Lawrence Lee (eds.). *Jack's Book: An Oral Biography of Jack Kerouac.* New York: St. Martin's, 1978.

Miles, Barry. *Jack Kerouac, King of the Beats: A Portrait.* New York: Holt, 1998.

Nicosia, Gerald. *Memory Babe: A Critical Biography of Jack Kerouac.* New York: Grove, 1983.

ARTICLES

Batchelor, Stephen. "A Democracy of the Imagination." *Tricycle* (Winter 1994): 70-75.

Fields, Rick. "Buddhism Beat and Square." *Tricycle* (Fall 1995): 75-82.

Oates, Joyce Carol. "Down the Road." *New Yorker* (27 May 1995): 95-98.

BOOKS

French, Warren. *Jack Kerouac: Novelist of the Beat Generation.* Boston: Twayne, 1986.

Hipkiss, Robert. *Jack Kerouac: Prophet of a New Romanticism.* Lawrence: Regents Press of Kansas, 1976.

Hunt, Tim. *Kerouac's Crooked Road: Development of a Fiction.* Hamden, Conn.: Archon, 1984.

Jones, James. *A Map of Mexico City Blues: Jack Kerouac as Poet.* Carbondale: Southern Illinois University Press, 1992.

Tonkinson, Carole. *Big Sky Mind: Buddhism and the Beat Generation.* New York: Riverhead Books, 1995.

Desolation Angels

REGINA WEINREICH (ESSAY DATE 1987)

SOURCE: Weinreich, Regina. "The Sound of Despair: A Perfected Nonlinearity." In *The Spontaneous Poetics of Jack Kerouac: A Study of the Fiction,* pp. 89-118. Carbondale: Southern Illinois University Press, 1987.

In the following essay, Weinreich examines Desolation Angels *as the culmination of Kerouac's religious and philosophical thinking just before the publication of* On the Road.

> Do you hear that? The sound of it alone is wonderful, no? What can you give me in English to match that for sheer beauty of resonance?
>
> Henry Miller, *The Colossus of Maroussi*

Kerouac attempted to resolve the aesthetic problems of *Visions of Cody* in his next period of writing, from 1953 with the writing of *The Sub-terraneans* on through the sixties, as his life and thinking became more religious and philosophical. The culmination of the experiments that comprise *Visions of Cody* is found in *Desolation Angels,* a novel concerned with the period of legend/life from 1956 to 1957. The novel, first published in 1965, is based on Kerouac's journals written in the year before the appearance of *On the Road*; these writings were put in novel form after the success of *On the Road,*[1] and integrate the events of the road with the Zen philosophy he was learning as he developed both as a man and as a writer. The first half of the book was completed in Mexico City in October 1956 and "typed up" in 1957; the second half was not written until 1961, although chronologically it follows immediately after the first.[2] The novel is thus another take on Kerouac's road adventures: it covers roughly the same aspects of his legend as *On the Road* and *Visions of Cody* and is stylistically the logical culmination of them both.

Although the merits of this novel have often been hinted at, some critics, such as Dennis McNally, state flatly that the writing is not nearly Kerouac's best.[3] Tytell, on the other hand, lauds the work as "the best existing account of the lives of the Beats" and further claims that its influence upon the nonfiction novel emerges in such books as Tom Wolfe's *Electric Kool-Aid Acid Test.* Tytell also groups *Desolation Angels* with *The Dharma Bums* in claiming that neither novel represents the essential Kerouac—the ideal of spontaneous composition, the flaunting of conventional novelistic expectations.[4]

Indeed, *Desolation Angels* has not yet been understood as a stylistically integrated work. If the earlier experimental novel combines adventure with the meditative mode, then the later novel builds upon that combined form by sustaining the structure, techniques, and images beyond the initial experimentalism. If *On the Road* describes the outward journey and *Visions of Cody* the inner one, here the techniques of both are joined for a more consistent narrative. Thus, even though several books follow in the chronological sequence of Kerouac's career, *Desolation Angels* will be shown here to be the stylistic perfection of the techniques of the Duluoz legend, and perhaps its best expression.

The circular narrative structure of *Desolation Angels* begins and ends with a period of intense confrontation with the self. The terror and beauty of utter solitude on Desolation Peak—sixty-three days of proximity to nature's powers, including lightning storms, huge looming mountains, voids of gorges and canyons, bright sunsets, fog, silence, loneliness—end with Duluoz/Kerouac's finding nothingness at the bottom of "myself abysmal," after the lustful desire to return to the world.[5] In the end he finds only "a peaceful sorrow at home is the best I'll ever be able to offer the world, in the end, and so I told my Desolation Angels good-bye. A new life for me" (*DA*, [*Desolation Angels,*] 366). Ironically, the descent from the heights of the mountain provides for the ascent of the writer's spirit. Opposing images once again define the thematic shape as well as the linguistic component of Kerouac's text. And the return to the self follows from it full circle.

Kerouac's ability to integrate the diverse components of his prose emerges at last in a distinct narrative voice. More highly evolved than the Paradise or Duluoz narrators of the previous books, this Duluoz voice provides a consistent method of discourse for each prose segment. Each division—whether book, part, or section—echoes the circular shape of the whole, with the opposition between the "abysmal self" and the world vast and teeming with "angels" magnified. The Dean/Cody persona is no longer needed as a catalyst for the narrator's philosophical and adventuring self. The Duluoz narrator here is thus more developed, integrated, and self-contained.

As a self-conscious persona, Kerouac's narrator shapes the action of the novel through his perception. Kerouac now achieves greater control of his method in the reflexive connection between the act of living and the act of writing. Most important, Kerouac's command of his spontaneous prose technique has developed through his experience. The disclosures of *Desolation Angels* are really the revision of initial insights recorded in *On the Road* and *Visions of Cody*. This revision is now his methodological control.

The circular shape of his local discourse controls the design of his narrative at large. Thus the overall form is but the largest circle of these interior structures of thought, the prose paragraphs that comprise the whole. The book and part divisions are named and numbered and the sections are numbered; but even though they are therefore sequential and cannot be transposed as was the case in *Visions of Cody*, the book and part divisions nonetheless follow the familiar romantic circle. "**Desolation Angels,**" the first book, contains two parts—"Desolation in Solitude" and "Desolation in the World"—indicating the linguistic polarities of Kerouac's thought in this final stage of legend. "Passing Through," the second book, has four part divisions in which the writer/self defined in the first book becomes a transient being (like the "gruesome grieving ghost" identified in the earlier fiction) who is "Passing Through Mexico," "Passing Through New York," "Passing Through Tangiers, France and London," and "Passing Through America Again." Structurally and thematically, then, there is a beginning in innocence that must pass through experience. The Higher Innocence that Kerouac characteristically desires can only be accomplished by the return to themes that are American.

It will be worthwhile to see what this writer/self has to say about his enlightenment in order to describe fully the circular journey as well as to see how the creation of the narrator follows the precepts of Kerouac's earlier literary ethic: "And now, after the experience on top of the mountain where I was alone for two months without being questioned or looked at by any single human being I began a complete turnabout in my feelings about life. . . . I knew now that my life was a search for peace as an artist, but not only as an artist—As a man of contemplations . . . "(*DA*, 219). Jack Duluoz sees himself as singular, lonely, and separate. He talks about the circular notion of a "turnabout" following the movement down from the mountain. This movement echoes the shape of the entire work structurally and thematically.

"A man of contemplations" further defines the consistency of mood of *Desolation Angels*, a contemplative mood which Kerouac only now achieves: "I was searching for a peaceful kind of life dedicated to contemplation and the delicacy of that, for the sake of my art (in my case prose, tales) (narrative rundowns of what I saw and how I saw) but I also searched for this as my way of life, that is, to see the world from the viewpoint of solitude and to meditate upon the world without being imbroglio'd in its actions . . ." (*DA*, 220). Here is another circumlocution that develops in more detail his notion of the writer/self. The contemplation initiates a down movement, as if in his thoughts he were still perched above on the mountain. The word "rundown" resonates, as does the manifest integration of life and art in solitude. But most important of all is Kerouac's declaration (through Duluoz) that his life is dedicated to the contemplation of the creation of not only "what I saw" (a minor explanation of his interest in the form of description called sketching), but also "how I saw" (that is, the vehicle of perception in language). The legend reaches its fullness, in other words, as a discovery of language.

The language of the writer/self is made up of rhetorical tropes similar to those we have found in the earlier novels, revealing an integrity of preoccupation as well as a more highly-evolved form. The free prose sections of the *Visions of Cody* experiment become a harmonious sphere in the novel's three-dimensional atmosphere, as once again a musical analogy provides a solution to structural problems. Duluoz explains his control over the material in the following way: "'There's a certain amount of control going on [in my writing] like a man telling a story in a bar without interruptions or even one pause'" (*DA*, 280).

The voice of *Desolation Angels* is especially appropriate to Kerouac's interior journey as a rhetorical spiral leads him from exuberance to despair. A hymnal, litanous language maintains the musical analogy. Thus Kerouac solves the time/space, linear/nonlinear problems encountered in the earlier novels because chord structures—or, in the linguistic register, "narrative rundowns"—allow him to repeat as well as to progress. The effect is the paradox of circular motion, at times a mandala of themes on a circular plane. The spiral of recurrence and progression provides the familiar circular motion from beat to beatitude: "It's *beat,* it's the beat to keep, it's the beat of the heart, it's being beat and down in the world and like oldtime lowdown and like in ancient civilizations the slave boatmen rowing galleys to a beat and servants spinning pottery to a beat" (*DA*, 123). The juxtaposition of antithetical images in earlier works is now the very subject of Kerouac's prose. Here the matrix of rhetorical tropes is, as I shall show, simultaneously the completion of an entire image in all its possibilities. The beat moves from a staccato rhythm of exuberance in terse phrasing, through the images of "down in the world" and "oldtime lowdown," to longer, more cumbersome descriptions of mundane labors usually associated with human misery. Thus Kerouac uses the preoccupations and themes of the entire legend with a more masterful command of the material as his mind recollects it in memory.

Desolation in Solitude

A detailed account of the elements of Kerouac's circles will illustrate this solitude in action. Several sections of prose will be analyzed to explain Kerouac's mature methodology. Indeed, the language of *Desolation Angels* will be shown to be Kerouac's highest expression of "free prose."

In section 2 of "Desolation in Solitude," Duluoz explains why he is on Desolation Peak and has to stare at it for over seventy days. Contained within the passage are suggestions of the madness of solitude, especially in the allusions to King Lear on the heath. At times, the language reflects the garbled and mangled musings of a man in painful isolation; his speech in inchoate syllables of suffering reflects his inability to express these feelings coherently. At these times, the sounds themselves control the narrative. In toto, the section reads like a dramatic monologue:

> Yes, for I'd thought, in June, hitch hiking up there to the Skagit Valley in northwest Washington for my fire lookout job "When I get to the top of Desolation Peak and everybody leaves on mules and I'm alone I will come face to face with God or Tathagata and find out once and for all what is the meaning of all this existence and suffering and going to and fro in vain" but instead I'd come face to face with myself, no liquor, no drugs, no chance of faking it but face to face with ole Hateful Duluoz Me and many's the time I thought I die, suspire of boredom, or jump off the mountain, but the days, nay the hours dragged and I had no guts for such a leap, I had to *wait* and get to see the face of reality—and it finally comes that afternoon of August 8 as I'm pacing in the high alpine yard on the little wellworn path I'd beaten, in dust and rain, on many a night, with my oil lamp banked low inside the cabin with the four-way windows and peaked pagoda roof and lightning rod point, it finally comes to me, after even tears, and gnashing, and the killing of a mouse and attempted murder of another, something I'd never done in my life (killing animals even rodents), it comes in these words: "The void is not disturbed by any kind of ups and downs, my God look at Hozomeen, is he worried or tearful? Does he bend before storms or snarl when the sun shines or sigh in the late day drowse? Does he smile? Was he not born out of madbrained turmoils and upheavals of raining fire and now's Hozomeen and nothing else? Why should I choose to be bitter or sweet, he does neither?—Why cant I be like Hozomeen and O Platitude O hoary old platitude of the bourgeois mind "take life as it comes"—Twas that alcoholic biographer, W. E. Woodward, said, "There's nothing to life but just the living of it"—But O God I'm bored! But is Hozomeen bored? And I'm sick of words and explanations. Is Hozomeen?
>
> Aurora Borealis
>   over Hozomeen—
> The void is stiller
>
> —Even Hozomeen'll crack and fall apart, nothing lasts, it is only a faring-in-that-which-everything-is, a passing-through, that's what's going on, why ask questions or tear hair or weep, the burble blear purple Lear on his moor of woes he is only a gnashy old flap with winged whiskers beminded by a fool—to be *and* not to be, that's what we are—Does the Void take any part in life and death? does it have funerals? or birth cakes? why not I be like the Void, inexhaustibly fertile, beyond seren-

ity, beyond even gladness, just Old Jack (and not even that) and conduct my life from this moment on (though winds blow through my windpipe), this ungraspable image in a crystal ball is not the Void, the Void is the crystal ball itself and all my woes the Lankavatara Scripture hairnet of fools, "Look sirs, a marvelous sad hairnet"—Hold together, Jack, pass through everything, and everything is one dream, one appearance, one flash, one sad eye, one crystal lucid mystery, one word—Hold still, man, regain your love of life and go down from this mountain and simply *be*—*be*—be the infinite fertilities of the one mind of infinity, make no comments, complaints, criticisms, appraisals, avowals, sayings, shooting stars of thought, just *flow, flow,* be you all, be you what it is, it is only what it always is—Hope is a word like a snow-drift—This is the Great Knowing, this is the Awakening, this is the Voidness—So shut up, live, travel, adventure, bless and dont be sorry—Prunes, prune, eat your prunes—And you have been forever, and will be forever, and all the worrisome smashings of your foot on innocent cupboard doors it was only the Void pretending to be a man pretending not to know the Void—

I come back into the house a new man.

All I have to do is wait 30 long days to get down from the rock and see sweet life again—knowing it's neither sweet nor bitter but just what it is, and so it is—

So long afternoons I sit in my easy (canvas) chair facing Void Hozomeen, the silence hushes in my little shack, my stove is still, my dishes glitter, my firewood (old sticks that are the form of water and welp, that I light small Indian fires with in my stove, to make quick meals) my firewood lies piled and snaky in the corner, my canned goods wait to be opened, my old cracked shoes weep, my pans lean, my dish rags hang, my various things sit silent around the room, my eyes ache, the wind wallows and belts at the window and upped shutters, the light in late afternoon shades and bluedarks Hozomeen (revealing his streak of middle red) and there's nothing for me to do but wait—and breathe (and breathing is difficult in the thin high air, with West Coast sinus wheezings)—wait, breathe, eat, sleep, cook, wash, pace, watch, never any forest fires—and daydream, "What will I do when I get to Frisco? Why first thing I'll get a room in Chinatown"—but even nearer and sweeter I daydream what I'll do Leaving Day, some hallowed day in early September, "I'll walk down the trail, two hours, meet Phil in the boat, ride to the Ross Float, sleep there a night, chat in the kitchen, start early in the morning on the Diablo Boat, go right from that little pier (say hello to Walt), hitch right to Marblemount, collect my pay, pay my debts, buy a bottle of wine and drink it by the Skagit in the afternoon, and leave next morning for Seattle"—and on, down to Frisco, then L.A., then Nogales, then Guadalajara, then Mexico City—And still the Void is still and'll never move—

But I will be the Void, moving without having moved.

(*DA*, 4-6)

Like every section, this one is a microcosm of the whole work, a compendium of antithetical imagery, a prose poem complete within itself. Placed at the book's beginning, this passage sets up the idea of the quest in solitude and without movement, reminiscent in its way of the gnomic utterances of the Old English "Seafarer" poem of which Ezra Pound was so fond. Kerouac uses the solitude of the American landscape, so profoundly frightening in its accentuation of his own preoccupations about life, to eclipse his own expression, his own self. The linguistic oppositions that unified earlier novels recur as animation is pared away and he is left alone, all the wandering "to and fro" supplanted by stillness. In the austere clearing that remains, the two principal Kerouacean techniques of vision are particularly evident: the all-inclusiveness of opposing imagery and the generalization from the particular to make a philosophical point.

Duluoz begins with a rhetorical "yes" of affirmation and proceeds to build up to a philosophical dialogue with himself. Words like "up," "top," "peak," are countered by "valley"; he suggests he must go up to stay level. In his first speech to himself, he speaks of lateral movement which balances up and down. He begins the narrative refrain of "face to face," for example, and balances that with "to and fro" for the creation of the tautologies that are characteristic of this section. The narrative takes a turn with "but," and between the repetitions of "face to face" he begins a series of negations to counterpoint the "yes" at the start: "no liquor, no drugs, no chance of faking it. . . ." The first tautology of "face to face" is "Hateful Duluoz Me," a self-negating image followed by verbs that suggest his death: "I thought I die, suspire of boredom, or jump off the mountain. . . ."

After the first break, indicated by dashes, concrete details bring reality home. The word "and" precipitates the all-inclusiveness of oppositions. "Wellworn," "beaten," "banked low" contrast with "peaked pagoda roof and lightning rod point." Extreme actions, even when referring to mice, contrast with a simultaneous stasis: "The void is not disturbed by any kind of ups and downs," Duluoz muses. He then identifies the Void and the mystery of the experience on Desolation Peak with another mountain vision which he can actually sight from his perch, a vision of Hozomeen, which becomes the object of a set of rhetorical questions from which he generalizes. He questions the oppositions of "bitter or sweet," for example, and asks why we must choose between them. Then, in further tautologies, he reveals that no choices can be made because every choice already contains its own opposite anyway.

Kerouac's haiku in midsection is typical of *Desolation Angels,*[6] and is a compressed form of his philosophizing in general. Here the idea that the endurance of the mountain is second to the endurance of the Void is central to linguistic collapse of oppositions, to the unified vision of all-inclusiveness. The next segment suggests that even the mountain will crack and fall apart, since "Nothing lasts." Again, Kerouac suggests a lateral movement of activity which goes along with the extreme stasis, boredom, and stillness of the mountain ("faring-in-that-which-everything-is" and "passing-through"), which is then set in opposition with the desire to "ask," "tear," "weep," echoing Prufrock's dilemma. The next cluster of mere syllables evokes Shakespeare ("burble blear purple Lear on his moor of woes"). Not only does Kerouac's narrator liken himself to Lear, but he generalizes from the comparison to the human condition as a whole—to be a "flap with winged whiskers beminded by a fool."

Then, evoking Shakespeare once more, he revises a tautology into "to be *and* not to be," with special emphasis upon the "and." Consciously or not, Kerouac strives for a stasis or balance of oppositions, leading to a series of questions about the activity of the Void—"Does the Void take any part in life and death? does it have funerals? or birth cakes?"—which ends in a single question, identifying the narrator in the negative: "Why not I be like the Void, inexhaustibly fertile, beyond serenity, beyond even gladness, just old Jack (and not even that)." The Void is represented in images of passing through: "beyond serenity," and "beyond gladness." Even Jack and non-Jack are represented with the same strong metaphor: "winds blow through my windpipe." Then he negates the Void to affirm himself. The oxymoron "ungraspable image" is used to define the Void and the "crystal ball"; the "hairnet of fools" is that by which he is "beminded" (like Lear above) when he preoccupies himself with his woes. Thus he brings the Lear image full circle. The net contains the hair torn away by man in despair. But it is a reassurance that allows the narrator to transcend the conceits of these tautologies by exhorting himself to have the courage to pass through.

First he tells himself to "hold together . . . everything," whether "dream," "appearance," "flash," "eye," "crystal lucid mystery," or finally, "word." He thus exhorts his writer/self to "hold still" and to "go down"—that is, to descend in order to ascend. This action results in "infinite fertilities," a correspondence with the "inexhaustibly fertile" nature of the Void earlier in the passage. And rather than create thoughts or words that prevent the passing through from taking place, he exhorts himself to "*flow.*" This exhortation precipitates another set of tautologies as the old ones break down: "It is only what it always is"; "Hope is a word like a snow-drift"; "This is the Great Knowing"; "[T]his is the Awakening"; "This is the Voidness." Thus Kerouac implements the "flow." And just as the appearance/reality theme is resolved in the me/not me imagery of *Desolation Angels,* the antithetical images brought "face to face" bring the picture of the Void full circle with its image of "pretending to be a man pretending not to know the Void." This writing, as if in Kerouac's characteristic "semitrance" has thus built up to a release of expression—to the completion of an all-inclusive image.

There follows a return to Duluoz's physical state, with new understanding. That is, insight follows release: "I come back into the house a new man." Now an interior landscape is juxtaposed with the exterior landscape of the first movement. But the interior is not the same after the new insight. "Bitter" and "sweet" are not oppositions but are together in "what it is." Thus the description, though specific in detail, generalizes from the particular to show the interior in a total image, not subject to flux. Lateral movement marks the passivity of the scene: "silence hushes," "stove is still," "dishes glitter," "firewood . . . lies piled and snaky in the corner." The stillness evokes the Edenic paradise of prebirth bliss for which Duluoz is nostalgic. Though the objects in this cabin are personified, the verbs indicate passivity: "canned goods wait," "pans lean," "dish rags hang," "things sit silent."

But there is still movement in this silent scene as the wind "wallows and belts . . . upped shutters," a movement indicating ascension after a going down. This movement leads to enlightenment, to images of passing through: "wait," "breathe," "eat," "sleep," "cook," "wash," "pace," "watch," "daydream." Kerouac capitalizes Leaving Day as if it were a day of celebration and exuberance, and in one long breath envisions the future in a kind of apocalypse of mundane images that brings the section full circle with the repetition of Skagit and other geographic detail; the repetition of "then" allows the enumeration to flow. The ultimate paradox of the circular imagery of all-inclusiveness then emerges: "And still the Void is still and'll never move." The flow which implies movement is so all-inclusive as to take up all space and need not operate in time at all. This is the final enlightenment of the passage. Duluoz ends, however, by identifying himself ("face to face") with the Void in the bridge: "But I will be the Void, moving without having moved." True to Kerouac's design, even this bridge that ends the section defies closure as it leads to the next.

Desolation in the World

The second part of the first book opposes "Desolation in Solitude" with "Desolation in the World." An examination of a sample section will reveal still another development in Kerouac's expression. For example, Kerouac's "sketch" of Seattle in section 52 bears the refrain of how hard it is to come off the mountain:

> Seattles in the fog, burlesque shows, cigars and wines and papers in a room, fogs, ferries, bacon and eggs and toast in the morning—sweet cities below.
>
> Down about where the heavy timber begins, big Ponderosas and russet all-trees, the air hits me nice, green Northwest, blue pine needles, fresh, the boat is cutting a swath in the nearer lake, it's going to beat me, but just keep on swinging, Marcus Magee—You've had falls before and Joyce made a word two lines long to describe it—bra-barackotawackomanashtopataratawackomanac!
>
> We'll light three candles to three souls when we get there.
>
> The trail, last halfmile, is worse, than above, the rocks, big, small, twisted ravines for your feet—Now I begin sobbing for myself, cursing of course—"It never ends!" is my big complaint, just like I'd thought in the door, "How can anything ever end? But this is only a Samsara-World-of-Suffering trail, subject to time and space, therefore must end, but my God it will never end!" and I come running and thwapping finally no more—For the first time I fall exhausted without planning.
>
> And the boat is coming right in.
>
> "Cant make it."
>
> I sit there a long time, moody faced and finished—Wont do it—But the boat gets coming closer, it's like timeclock civilization, gotta get to work on time, like on the railroad, tho you cant make it you'll make it—It was blasted in the forges with iron vulcan might, by Poseidon and his heroes, by Zen Saints with swords of intelligence, by Master French-god—I push myself up and try on—Every step wont do, it wont work, that my thighs hold it up's'mystery to me—plah—
>
> Finally I'm loading my steps on ahead of me, like placing topheavy things on a platform with outstretched arms, the kind of strain you cant keep up—other than the bare feet (now battered with torn skin and blisters and blood) I could just

> plow and push down the hill, like a falling drunk almost falling never quite falling and if so would it hurt as much as my feet?—nu—gotta push and place each up-knee and down with the barbfoot on scissors of Blakean Perfidy with worms and howlings everywhere—dust—I fall on my knees.
>
> Rest that way awhile and go on.
>
> "Eh damn Eh maudit" I'm crying last 100 yards—now the boat's stopped and Fred whistles sharply, no a hoot, an Indian Hooo! which I answer with a whistle, with fingers in mouth—He settles back to read a cowboy book while I finish that trail—Now I dont want him to hear me cry, but he does he must hear my slow sick steps—plawrp, plawrp—timber tinker of pebbles plopping off a rock round precipice, the wild flowers dont interest me no more—
>
> "I cant make it" is my only thought as I keep going, which thought is like phosphorescent negative red glow imprinting the film of my brain "Gotta make it"—
>
> Desolation, Desolation
>   so hard
> To come down off of.

(*DA*, 76-77)

Again the passage is made up of antithetical imagery with an eye toward all-inclusiveness. Again Kerouac's eye focuses on the particular to render the general. Again he has Duluoz speak from above, as if he were a god, as if the identification with the eternity cited in the previous passage were complete. The omission of the apostrophe in "Seattles" (and despite Kerouac's overall irreverence for standard punctuation) is purposeful. It renders the city an emblem of many an American city. Naturally the fog, mentioned twice, indicates the haziness reminiscent of Joan Rawshank's movie set in *Visions of Cody*. As Kerouac catalogs the things of this world, he chooses seamy details: "burlesque," "cigars and wines," mundane images of "ferries," "bacon and eggs and toast." Then he sums it all up in the clause after the dash: "sweet cities below." The eye of the narrative's movement is down, and thus he descends.

The word "Down" in fact begins the following paragraph as Kerouac's eye now descends to the timber line, the specific Ponderosas, and inclusive "all-trees." The next image is a technicolor "green" and "blue." His own path is contrasted with the "cutting" boat, which is going to "beat" and "swing." The juxtaposition of the two movements allows for a tentative release in enlightenment as "candles" correspond with "souls" at the point of reaching a "there" that is the bottom. Once again, he must descend to ascend.

Looking upward, Duluoz compares this portion of the journey by stating that the last half mile is worse. But this journey down the mountain is a metaphor for Kerouac's life as a whole. Just as Duluoz laments "'It never ends!'" the "But" signals a change in the course of the narrative. The suffering trail as "a Samsara-World-of-Suffering trail, subject to time and space, therefore must end," but it will "never end." He resolves to stop the "running" and "thwapping," lateral movements which obstruct his fall. And so, in letting go, he "falls."

But again, the contrasting movement of the boat cuts his fall short: "'Cant make it.'" The boat represents an aspect of civilization that deters man from his descent/ascent. It represents stoppage as the narrator must "sit," "moody faced" and "finished." The "But" signals a shift in the narrative, time and civilization drawing near. The all-inclusive image of the railroad is seen in "making it"/"not making it" on time. "It"—both civilization and time—is like a relief sculpture etched into eternity, "blasted" by society's heroes, by "Poseidon," "Zen Saints," "Master Frenchgod." Against this image of stasis, Duluoz pushes "up." But his effort to engrave himself on this surface "wont work," and he falls further—"plah."

The next paragraph is replete with christological images of the "fall." Duluoz is "loading," "placing topheavy things," feeling "strain." He is raw with "bare feet," "torn skin," "blisters," "blood," "I fall on my knees." But after a brief rest, his expression turns toward contemporary civilization, as Fred hoots and whistles to him. In keeping, then, with the antithetical imagery throughout the description, the fall from grace is balanced by the "cowboy book," "I dont want him to hear me cry," "timber tinker . . . plopping," and "wild flowers"—in short, by the civilization he has just described.

The final bridge of the passage contrasts "I cant make it" with "Gotta make it" and interprets the return to civilization as Duluoz images the descent from the mountain not in Christian terms but in a red neon imprint. The image is reminiscent of the lighting in the Hector's Cafeteria scene of *Visions of Cody* and is summed up in the haiku at the end with its "hard" mountain echoed by the clumsy line "To come down off of." And yet, the quotidian images produce the divine as well as the mundane. The movement of the journey down the mountain likens Duluoz not only to a drunk, but also to a man on his knees, seeking repentance. Hence the all-inclusive image of beat/beatitude is complete.

But the pretext of closure in the all-inclusive imagery of beat/beatitude presents a paradox. The haiku at the end suggests that we must repeat in order to progress. Thus a spiral upward is created even as Kerouac preaches a "digging deep," a down movement in the language itself. The language and structuring of language is indeed well-suited to the function of a novel that mediates, or attempts to mediate, the highly subjective quality of the experiments of *Visions of Cody* with the need to express something objective to the world. Hence the texture of Kerouac's language explains why his role as writer/self—distanced, itself an object of the novel rather than its subject—is so necessary in this book at this stage of legend. Therefore a preoccupation with expression emerges as a thematic motif in "Desolation in the World," which becomes the object of the quest that finally gives context to Duluoz's arduous journey.

Thus in section 97 the overt concern is with the problem of expression. The passage is both consistent in movement with previously cited passages and shows the characteristic progression of techniques—from general to particular and all-inclusive imagery—to resolve the paradox of beat/beatitude:

So we go out and get drunk and dig the session in the Cellar where Brue Moore is blowing on tenor saxophone, which he holds mouthpieced in the side of his mouth, his cheek distended in a round ball like Harry James and Dizzy Gillespie, and he plays perfect pretty harmony to any tune they bring up—He pays little attention to anyone, he drinks his beer, he gets loaded and eye-heavy, but he never misses a beat or a note, because music is his heart, and in music he has found that pure message to give to the world—The only trouble is, they dont understand.

For example: I'm sitting there on the edge of the bandstand right at Brue's feet, facing the bar, but head down to my beer, for modesty of course, yet I see they dont hear it—There are blondes and brunettes with their men and they're making eyes at other men and almost-fights seethe in the atmosphere—Wars'll break out over women's eyes—and the harmony will be missed—Brue is blowing right on them, "Birth of the Blues," down jazzy, and when his turn comes to enter the tune he comes up with a perfect beautiful new idea that announces the glory of the future world, the piano belongs that with a chord of understanding (blond Bill), the holy drummer with eyes to Heaven is lilting and sending in the angel-rhythms that hold everybody fixed to their work—Of course the bass is thronging to the finger that both throbs to pluck and the other one that slides the strings for the exact harmonic key-sound—Of course the musicians in the place are listening, hordes of colored kids with dark faces shining in the dimness, white eyes round and sincere, holding drinks just to be in there to hear—It augurs something good in men that they'll listen to the truth of harmony—Brue has nevertheless to carry the message along for several chorus-chapters, his ideas get tireder than at first, he does give up at the right time—besides he wants to play a new tune—I do just that, tap him on the shoe-top to acknowledge he's right—In between the sets he sits beside me and Gia and doesn't say much and appears to pretend not to be able to say much—He'll say it on his horn—

But even Heaven's time-worm eats at Brue's vitals, as mine, as yours, it's hard enough to live in a world where you grow old and die, why be disharmonious?

(*DA*, 198-99)

The bridge tells us the all-inclusive imagery here is harmony/disharmony, itself the image of a circle, or wholeness, especially as it pertains to musical form. Throughout the passage, images of harmony are juxtaposed with images of disharmony, up until the final question posed at the passage's end. Yet the passage is also self-reflexive in its generalization of the musician's work to stand as a metaphor for the work of any artist; it is about the ability of art—in Kerouac's particular case, of writing—to render perfection.

Echoing the movement of passages cited earlier, Duluoz will "fall" or descend in order to ascend. He will "dig" in the "Cellar." Images of harmony follow in the shape of a circle leading to perfection: "mouth" and "round ball" lead to "perfect pretty harmony"—"to any tune they bring up." He goes down, in other words, to go up. Getting "loaded" and "eye-heavy"—images of plodding like Duluoz's difficult trip down the mountain—are used to describe the travail of the musician in Kerouac's cast of types or generalized personae. The "but" is not a rhetorical contradiction but a synthesis that completes the circle of his attributive perfection—"he never misses a beat," "music is his heart." Music is his vehicle of perfection. He has found in music "that pure message to give to the world." Like Duluoz, he has a message. But, to complete the image, there is inevitably the contrast of trouble, or disharmony, stated in the negative in contrast with the prior affirmative: "they dont understand"; that is, there is no enlightenment.

"For example" is a narrative shift into the scene that follows, creating first a still setting shattered by disharmonious images. Duluoz sits facing the bar (like facing the Void) followed by a "but" that implies the synthesis of all-inclusive imagery that will emerge momentarily ("head down").

"Yet" shows the narrative will take another turn. "I see they dont hear it" shows a complete disharmony of the senses. The eyes of the people are darting about unlike the heavy eyes of those working. Images of disharmony ensue with particular pungency in phrases like "almost-fights seethe in the atmosphere," "Wars'll break out," and "harmony will be missed."

After the dashes, images of harmony show what this audience will miss: "'the Birth of the Blues'"—reminiscent of Kerouac's prebirth bliss—"down jazzy," that is, in "Deep Form"[7] (in its suggestion of "digging deep"). "Turn" underscores the change in narrative course as upward images make Duluoz ascend to an apocalyptic image: "up," "perfect beautiful new idea that announces the glory of the future world." This beatific view precipitates the "chord of understanding." These "up" images of "holy," "eyes to Heaven," "lilting and sending in the angel-rhythms" that cause the stillness of passing through hold everybody "fixed." And "of course" there is "the exact harmonic key-sound," the highest point. And "of course," too, the listeners who do hear—other musicians and black children described in antithetical images of "dark," "shining," "dimness," and "round"—are, unlike their down counterparts, capable of perfection themselves. The message provides a quiet apocalyptic view—"It augurs something good in men that they'll listen to the truth of harmony."

"Nevertheless" indicates another narrative turn, a lateral movement or development of the idea of carrying the message. Duluoz does so in "chorus-chapters" (his kinship and identification with the jazzman is explicit). And, wishing to progress, he continues to carry his message, to play a new tune. The lateral or shifting movement of antitheses is even graphic in "between," "beside," and "appears to pretend not to be able to say much—He'll say it on his horn."

The bridge therefore has resonance as an image of the condition of the man with the truth, with a message to convey, whether by words or music or both. In his characteristic juxtaposition of images, Kerouac creates a vision of a heaven with a landscape of hell. The disharmonious is stated in the negative, which, as we might expect by now, only serves to reinforce the positive, the affirmation of the perfection of harmony. Therefore, as writer/self, Duluoz understands his calling. Like the jazzman he must proclaim this truth of harmony through his art.

Passing Through

The second book of *Desolation Angels,* "Passing Through," was written much later than the first book and shows Duluoz experiencing the lessons of that prior "desolation." "Passing through" becomes a metaphor for traveling and, later on, a metaphor for life itself. More to the point of Kerouac's writing, "passing through" becomes a structural metaphor as it leads to the collapse of antithetical imagery in favor of images of stasis. These provide a more secure spiritual context for Kerouac's belief. Section 15 of "Passing Through Mexico" is particularly resonant in echoing the technique:

> So, as Lazarus walks thru villages, so God walks thru our lives, and like the workers and the warriors we worry like worrywarts to straighten up the damage as fast as we can, tho the whole thing's hopeless in the end. For God has a bigger foot than Lazarus and all the Texcocos and Texacos and Mañanas of tomorrow. We end up watching a dusk basketball game among Indian boys near the bus stop. We stand under an old tree at the dirtroad crossing, receiving dust as it's blown by the plains wind of the High Plateau of Mexico the likes of which none bleaker maybe than in Wyoming in October, late October . . .
>
> p.s. The last time I was in Teotihuacan, Hubbard said to me "Wanta see a scorpion, boy?" and lifted up a rock—There sat a female scorpion beside the skeleton of its mate, which it had eaten—Yelling "Yaaaah!" Hubbard lifted a huge rock and smashed it down on the whole scene (and tho I'm not like Hubbard, I had to agree with him that time).
>
> (*DA,* 244)

First, we find the general in the particular, especially in the anecdote recounted in the postscript. There is also the customary "So" transition. And there is also the characteristic antithetical movement of rhetorical tropes. But more evident here are the images of "passing through." "Walking thru," for instance, is contrasted with images of stoppage like the "worker" and "worrywarts" fixing "the damage," the still-life description of the Indian boys playing, the bus stop, and the activity of standing while the dust is blown by the winds. The hint of closure in the repetition of "end" contrasts with the abrupt cut-off line. Finally, the postscript remembrance is the concrete evidence of the message of "above," told in up/down opposition as Hubbard lifts the rock (reminiscent of Sisyphus?) and then smashes it down on the whole scene. The image of the female scorpion's murder and cannibalism of her mate is the recognition that "the whole thing's hopeless in the end." In nature the best and worst of circumstances are alike contained. There is,

however, harmony and agreement in the incorporation of despair, because "passing through" is ultimately a metaphor for living life in the acceptance of its totality, bliss and despair together.

When Duluoz passes "through America again," it is to return to the realization of the perfected image. The circle is now the image of life and death together. Section 84, the last section of the novel, repeats the structural solution of the entire novel, bringing it all full circle:

> So I go downtown and get an expensive hotel room to make up for it—But a sinister Marble Hotel it is—Now that Gaines' gone away all Mexico City is a sinister Marble Hive—How we continue in this endless Gloom I'll never know—Love, Suffer, and Work is the motto of my family (Lebris de Keroack) but seems I suffer more than the rest—Old Honeyboy Bill's in Heaven for sure anyway—Only thing now is Where's Jack Going?—Back to Florida or New York?—For further emptiness?—Old Thinker's thought his last thought—I go to bed in my new hotel room and soon fall asleep anyway, what can I do to bring Gaines back to the dubious privilege of living?—He's trying his best to bless me anyway but that night a Buddha's born to Gina Lollobrigida and I hear the room creak, the door on the dresser creaks back and forth slowly, the walls groan, my whole bed weaves like I say "Where am I, at sea?" but I realize I'm not at sea but in Mexico City—Yet the hotel room is rocking like a ship—It's a giant earthquake rocking Mexico—And how was dying, old buddy?—Easy?—I yell to myself *"Encore un autre petrain!"* (like the sea storm) and jump under the bed to protect myself against falling ceilings if any—*Hurracan* is whipping up to hit the Louisiana coast—The entire apartment building across the street from the post office on Calle Obregon is falling in killing everybody—Graves leer under Moon pines—It's all over.
>
> Later I'm back in New York sitting around with Irwin and Simon and Raphael and Lazarus, and now we're famous writers more or less, but they wonder why I'm so sunk now, so unexcited as we sit among our published books and poems, tho at least, since I live with Memère in a house of her own miles from the city, it's a peaceful sorrow. A peaceful sorrow at home is the best I'll ever be able to offer the world, in the end, and so I told my Desolation Angels goodbye. A new life for me.
>
> (*DA,* 365-66)

First, a linguistic analysis reveals the repetition of the all-inclusive imagery, and second, a thematic analysis reveals the relationship of the section to the Duluoz myth. Once again the rhetorical "so" leads into the piece from the previous passage. The movement is down: "downtown" and "sinister" culminate in "endless Gloom"—the concept of gloom, in other words, has no closure.

By contrast, the active tropes of "Love, Suffer, and Work" are what Duluoz inherits too: "I suffer more than the rest." This proclamation leads him to question his direction. The upward "Heaven" contrasts with Florida and New York, which can provide only "emptiness." The closure of "Old Thinker's thought his last thought" slides into images of the grave. The "bed" and "room" further signify falling—"fall asleep," "the dubious privilege of living." The attempt to bless is cut by "but" and an image of rebirth ensues ("Buddha's born"). The two movements of beat/beatitude are, in other words, once again juxtaposed with one another—"creaks back and forth," "walls groan," "bed weaves" (Kerouac's version of Whitman's cradle "endlessly rocking"). The "yet" signifies a synthesis with "room is rocking like a ship."

As this death fantasy makes Duluoz envision his own death, he begins to talk to himself, the images becoming more active than those in life. He yells and jumps and protects himself from "falling ceilings." Even a hurricane "whips" and "hits." An entire apartment building falls and kills everybody as a prologue to the final announcement that signifies closure, or the end—"It's all over" the contrast to "passing through."

"Graves leer under Moon pines" is, however, the most powerful image of the circle of closure/nonclosure. That "graves"—the image of the inanimate final resting place—are personified by "leer" and then juxtaposed with enduring images in nature—"Moon pines"—is a contrast to "It's all over," which finishes the paragraph. But not surprisingly, it does not finish the book. The final paragraph is fraught with active oppositions: "Later," "back," "more or less," "but," "sunk," "unexcited," "tho," "I live," "it's a peaceful sorrow," "in the end," "A new life for me."

Of course the creation of this language extends the Kerouac myth, and this final section of *Desolation Angels* draws the Duluoz legend to its close in the core group of Kerouac's novels. The characters (the Desolate Angels Bill Gaines, Irwin, Simon, and Lazarus) are identified by stock epithets or leitmotifs. In fact, they are deindividuated as characters in the traditional sense and reinvented as figures of myth. Bill Gaines, for example, is elsewhere called "Old Guru Gaines, in fact the first of many characters I was to know from that innocent time to now" (*DA*, 223). And "Gaines was the now fairly famous character who stole an expensive overcoat every day of his life for twenty years in New York and pawned it for junk, a great thief" (*DA*, 225). If the characters of *The Town*

and the City are philosophical archetypes and those in *On the Road* and *Visions of Cody* "holy" or spiritual archetypes, here they are "angels" and godmen in fuller service to beatitude. Kerouac's mock-heroic progresses from that in his first novel. Comic types thus proliferate: "Everybody in the world is an angel, Charley Chaplin and I have seen their wings" (*DA*, 66); W. C. Fields is conjured as a voice in a vignette involving the "Thirties Luncheonette" (*DA*, 107); and Duluoz waits for his friends in Mexico, sitting on the edge of his rooftop, "looking down on the street for the Four Marx Brothers to come walking down Orizaba" (*DA*, 231). The four principal characters are thus placed within a larger mythic and relentlessly American context.

But their main function is to put the deeply reflective narrator in relief by contrast to them. Unlike the narrator of the earlier works, this Jack Duluoz is most concerned with a self-conscious appraisal of the writer—that is, himself—as he allows life to pass through him as he passes through it in God's image. Thus the God-reflexive/self-reflexive state becomes an aspect of the development of Kerouac's mind as he advances closer to carrying out his own aesthetic philosophy of simultaneity. Duluoz says, "My life is a vast inconsequential epic with a thousand and a million characters—here they all come, as swiftly as we roll east, as swiftly the earth rolls east" (*DA*, 12).

The moon becomes the chief icon for the new level of consciousness revealed by this novel. Duluoz repeatedly invokes the moon as if it were a poetic muse: "And that night I see the Moon, Citlapol in Aztec, and even draw a picture of it on the moonlit roof with house paint, blue and white" (*DA*, 228). Thus the moon is connected integrally with the act of writing: "I remember, that is to say, a spasm takes place in my memory chamber of the brain (O hollow moon!)" (*DA*, 60). The Moon represents a category of belief in the writer/self: ". . . and over such a text as the Lankavatara Scripture which says things like . . . *Life is like the reflection of the moon on the water, which one is the true moon?* meaning: Is reality the unreal part of unreality? or vice versa, when you open the door does anyone enter or is it you?" (*DA*, 349). This passage supports the life/death theme at the end ("graves leer under Moon pines"). The moon is a circle on one plane and therefore as a shape echoes the shape of the entire work.

The circle also maintains the musical analogy by containing as well the "big rhythmic loops" that allow Kerouac to incorporate even the images that are most ugly and despairing to him:

> Because by far the sweetest gift on earth . . . leads to children who are torn out of the womb screaming for mercy as tho they were being thrown to the Crocodiles of Life—in the River of Lives—which is what birth is. . . . [F]or every Clark Gable or Gary Cooper born, with all the so called glory (or Hemingway) that goes with it, comes disease, decay, sorrow, lamentation, old age, death, decomposition—meaning, for every little sweet lump of baby born that women croon over, is one vast rotten meat burning slow worms in graves of this earth.
>
> (*DA*, 267-68)

The image of rebirth is a circle that is repeated in the final pronouncement "A new life for me." Clearly the return to prebirth bliss is the goal of Kerouac's ultimate journey and his discontent in the world. He writes, "All I remember is that before I was born there was bliss" (*DA*, 283). Presumably, the ultimate circle is the return to that bliss, in death. The return to that memory of prebirth bliss is the final expression of the Duluoz legend, the end/not-end. The canonical novels—**The Town and the City, On the Road, Visions of Cody** and **Desolation Angels**—represent the fullest expression of the life/legend and the spiritual development that completes the story they tell, even as the story remains without end.

Desolation Angels is a refinement of Kerouac's aesthetic philosophy. The circle analogy and musical metaphor go far to explain the culmination of control achieved in **Desolation Angels**, still written spontaneously as if in one long breath out of a horn but refined by a sensibility that understands the repetition of chord changes as a perpetual opportunity for refinement and revision. Thus **Desolation Angels** can be seen as the perfection of Kerouac's nonlinear or free prose. And this structural ideal underscores a thematic perfection he seeks as the object of his mythic quest.

Notes

1. Tytell, *Naked Angels,* p. 174.

2. Krim, "The Kerouac Legacy," p. 214.

3. McNally, *Desolate Angel,* p. 295.

4. Tytell, *Naked Angels,* pp. 174, 175.

5. Quoted in Tytell, *Naked Angels,* p. 173.

6. The Columbia University Archives houses numerous manuscript pages of Kerouac's American haikus. These demonstrate his interest in a poetic form that accompanies his interest in Zen philosophy. In *Desolation Angels* his prose paragraphs often culminate in

haiku lines that form a "bridge" to the next section. Kerouac also mentions his interest in haiku in his *Paris Review* interview, p. 367.

7. Kerouac, "Essentials of Spontaneous Prose," p. 73.

Works Cited

Kerouac, Jack. "Essentials of Spontaneous Prose." *Evergreen Review* 2 No. 5 (Summer 1959): 72-73.

Krim, Seymour. Introduction to *Desolation Angels*, pp. ix-xxviii. New York: Putnam's, 1965. Reprint as "The Kerouac Legacy" in *Shake It for the World, Smartass*, pp. 193-216. New York: Dial, 1970.

McNally, Dennis. *Desolate Angel: Jack Kerouac, the Beat Generation, and America*. New York: Random House, 1979.

Tytell, John. *Naked Angels: The Lives and Literature of the Beat Generation*. New York: McGraw-Hill, 1976.

FURTHER READING

Bibliography

Charters, Ann. *Bibliography of Works by Jack Kerouac, 1939-1975*. New York: Phoenix Book Shop, 1975, 136p.

> *Comprehensive bibliography of primary sources by Kerouac.*

Milewski, Robert. *Jack Kerouac: An Annotated Bibliography of Secondary Sources, 1944-1979*. Metuche, N.J.: Scarecrow Press, 1981, 225p.

> *Comprehensive bibliography of writings about Kerouac's life and works.*

Biography

Charters, Ann. *Kerouac: A Biography*. San Francisco: Straight Arrow, 1972, 419p.

> *Biographical study of Kerouac. Charters is a scholar who has written extensively on various Beat writers.*

Cassady, Carolyn. *Off the Road: My Years with Cassady, Kerouac, and Ginsberg*. New York: William Morrow, 1990, 436p.

> *Provides an intimate portrayal of the author's relationships with Cassady, Kerouac, and Ginsberg, discussing the ways in which genius manifested itself in each.*

Miles, Barry. *Jack Kerouac, King of the Beats: A Portrait*. New York: Henry Holt, 1998, 332p.

> *Emphasizes Kerouac's influence on 1960s American culture.*

Nicosia, Gerald. *Memory, Babe: A Critical Biography of Jack Kerouac*. New York: Grove, 1983, 767p.

> *Detailed biography of Kerouac.*

Criticism

Bartlett, Lee. "The Dionysian Vision of Jack Kerouac." In *The Beats: Essays in Criticism*, pp. 115-23. Jefferson, N.C.: McFarland, 1981.

> *Utilizes C. G. Jung's psychoanalytic theories to illuminate the connection Kerouac makes between the jazz musician and the Dionysian writer.*

Burns, Jim. "Kerouac and Jazz." *Review of Contemporary Fiction* 3, no. 2 (summer 1983): 33-41.

Study of Kerouac's references to jazz music and musicians in his writings.

Coolidge, Clark. "Kerouac." *American Poetry Review* 24, no. 1 (January-February 1995): 43-9.

Analysis of Kerouac's poetic and prose style.

Foster, Edward Halsey. "Kerouac." In *Understanding the Beats*, pp. 28-83. Columbia: University of South Carolina Press, 1992.

Introductory biographical and critical essay.

Holmes, John Clellon. "The Philosophy of the Beats." *Esquire* 49, no. 2 (February 1958): 35-38.

Emphasizes the importance of the spiritual quest to the Beats.

Hunt, Tim. *Kerouac's Crooked Road: Development of a Fiction*. Hamden, Conn.: Archon, 1981, 262p.

Delineates the complex textual history of On the Road *based on Kerouac's correspondence and his 1948-1949 working journal.*

Jones, Granville H. "Jack Kerouac and the American Conscience." In *Lectures on Modern Novelists*, edited by Arthur T. Broes, pp. 25-39. Pittsburgh: Books for Libraries Press, 1963.

Defines the individualistic philosophy Kerouac advocated in his fiction and life as a distinctly American phenomenon.

Jones, James. *A Map of* Mexico City Blues: *Jack Kerouac as Poet*. Carbondale: Southern Illinois University Press, 1992, 202p.

Extensive study of Kerouac's poetry.

McDarragh, Fred W. *Kerouac and Friends: A Beat Generation Album*. New York: William Morrow, 1985, 338p.

Selection of newspaper and magazine articles and essays from the 1950s pertaining to Beat writers, along with McDarragh's photographs of major and minor figures of the movement.

McNally, Dennis. *Desolate Angel: Jack Kerouac, the Beat Generation, and America*. New York: St. Martin's, 1978, 400p.

Provides historical background for Kerouac's literary career and the Beat movement.

OTHER SOURCES FROM GALE:

Additional coverage of Kerouac's life and career is contained in the following sources published by the Gale Group: *American Writers Supplement*, Vol. 3; *Authors and Artists for Young Adults*, Vol. 25; *Authors in the News*, Vol. 1; *Beacham's Encyclopedia of Popular Fiction: Biography & Resources*, Vol. 2; *Concise Dictionary of American Literary Biography, 1941-1968*; *Contemporary Authors*, Vols. 5-8R; *Contemporary Authors New Revision Series*, Vols. 26, 54, 95; *Contemporary Literary Criticism*, Vols. 1, 2, 3, 5, 14, 29, 61; *Contemporary Popular Writers*; *Dictionary of Literary Biography*, Vols. 2, 16, 237; *Dictionary of Literary Biography Documentary Series*, Vol. 3; *Dictionary of Literary Biography Yearbook, 1995*; *DISCovering Authors*; *DISCovering Authors: British Edition*; *DISCovering Authors: Canadian Edition*; *DISCovering Authors Modules: Most-studied Authors, Novelists, Poets*, and *Popular Fiction and Genre Authors*; *DISCovering Authors 3.0*; *Gay & Lesbian Literature*, Ed. 1; *Literature Resource Center*; *Major 20th-Century Writers*, Eds. 1, 2; *Novels for Students*, Vol. 8; *Reference Guide to American Literature*, Ed. 4; *Twayne's United States Authors*; *Twentieth-Century Literary Criticism*, Vol. 117; *World Literature Criticism*; and *World Poets*.

KEN KESEY

(1935 - 2001)

(Full name Ken Elton Kesey) American novelist and nonfiction writer.

Kesey became acquainted with the Beat Generation during the 1950s, when he was a teenager in California. He later cited Beat writers Jack Kerouac, John Clellon Holmes, and William S. Burroughs as having a profound influence on his writing style. His most famous work, the novel *One Flew Over the Cuckoo's Nest* (1962), was inspired by his stint as a night attendant in the psychiatric ward of a California hospital. In that work, a mental hospital serves as a metaphor for the oppressive and mechanized nature of modern society. During the 1960s, Kesey's experiences as part of the Merry Pranksters—a group that included Beat Generation notable Neal Cassady, among others—informed his approach to his writing as well as his life-style.

BIOGRAPHICAL INFORMATION

Kesey was born in La Junta, Colorado, and moved to a farm in Springfield, Oregon, in 1946.

His family was religious, and Kesey received Bible instruction from an early age. In high school he was a champion wrestler and voted "most likely to succeed." After graduating, he tried his hand in Hollywood as an actor and eloped with his high school sweetheart, Faye Haxby, with whom he had three children. Kesey attended the University of Oregon, earning a degree in Speech and Communications, before going on to the prestigious Creative Writing program at Stanford University. In the fall of 1957, shortly before he went to Stanford, Kesey read Jack Kerouac's newly published novel *On the Road* and was particularly impressed by the freewheeling character of Dean Moriarty. While at Stanford, Kesey participated in experiments administered by the psychology department involving psychotropic drugs, including psilocybin, mescaline, and LSD. He lived in a bohemian community in Palo Alto, where he became known for throwing parties in which psychedelic drugs were a prominent feature. While working as an orderly at the psychiatric ward of the local veteran's hospital, Kesey began to have hallucinations about an American Indian sweeping the floors. This was the inspiration for the character of Bromden, "Chief Broom," in *One Flew Over the Cuckoo's Nest,* which was his graduate writing project. The novel was published in 1962 and was an immediate critical and popular success. In 1963, Kesey moved to La Honda, California, to begin research for his second novel,

Sometimes a Great Notion (1964), a story about a family of loggers. He continued to be a leading figure in the growing drug culture of the 1960s. He and his friends—among them Neal Cassady—had become known as the Merry Pranksters, and were notorious for their use of LSD and other drugs. In 1964, they bought a 1939 International Harvester bus, which they decorated in bright colors, and headed to New York to see the World's Fair. Kesey filmed portions of the trip, which he later showed at his parties. During this time, he also became a fan and supporter of the Warlocks, a rock band that later became the Grateful Dead. Kesey's exploits formed the basis for Tom Wolfe's bestselling *The Electric Kool-Aid Acid Test* (1968). When LSD became illegal in the United States, Kesey and his Pranksters moved to Mexico. When Kesey returned to the United States, he was arrested and imprisoned for marijuana possession. After his release, he moved with his family to a farm in Oregon. After the 1970s, he turned away from heavy drug use and became involved with environmental causes. He did not publish another novel until 1992, although he did write experimental nonfiction and children's books and occasionally taught at writing programs. He died on November 10, 2001 after undergoing liver surgery.

MAJOR WORKS

One Flew Over the Cuckoo's Nest is almost universally acknowledged as Kesey's crowning achievement and as a uniquely innovative example of twentieth-century American fiction. The novel concerns the fast-talking convict Randle Patrick McMurphy, who has himself committed to a mental hospital to avoid work on a prison farm. He soon creates upheaval among the inmates of the ward and comes to blows with "Big Nurse" Ratched. The novel is written from the unusual perspective of a paranoid schizophrenic, Chief Broom, and is at turns humorous and tragic. Kesey's second novel, *Sometimes a Great Notion*, takes place in Oregon, where independent loggers Hank and Leland Stamper engage in conflicts with each other as well as with the union that dominates their community. In this novel, Kesey also uses an interesting narrative technique, offering multiple perspectives of the events in the story. After the 1960s, Kesey turned to nonfiction. He edited and contributed to the anthology *Ken Kesey's Garage Sale* (1973), which contains essays, drawings, letters, interviews, and fiction by and about him. The volume contains accounts of his days with the Merry Pranksters, including the

script of a movie about his flight to Mexico. His collection of short stories and poems, *Demon Box* (1986), along with his screenplay *The Further Inquiry* (1990), reflect on his experiences in the American counterculture. In 1992, Kesey published his third novel, *Sailor Song,* a futuristic tale in which ecological disasters are predicted and then become a reality. Two years later, Kesey published *Last Go Round,* co-written with Ken Babbs, a dime-novel western about a Native American and an African-American bronco rider who compete for a silver saddle. Before his death, Kesey was working on a novel that included a character from his movie about his trip to Mexico, but it was never completed.

CRITICAL RECEPTION

Kesey has enjoyed renown not only for his literary endeavors but for his status as a counterculture hero. When *One Flew Over the Cuckoo's Nest* was published in 1962, it was well received by most critics. However, it was not until the 1970s, when interest in anti-establishment writing was high, that the novel attracted a wide audience and garnered scholarly attention. It has continued to interest readers and commentators, and there is a rich body of critical discussion on the work. Commentators often focus on the novel's theme of the mechanization and oppressiveness of modern American society. Other major critical approaches to the novel discuss the work's narrative technique, examine its treatment of manhood and masculinity, and consider possible sexist and racist attitudes expressed in Kesey's portrayal of his characters. *Sometimes a Great Notion* has not received the same level of scrutiny from critics, although some scholars have viewed it as Kesey's strongest work, a novel of stylistic and psychological complexity that exhibits the influence of William Faulkner, especially in its ambitious narrative style. Kesey's other works have received disappointing reviews for the most part, and some critics have suggested that Kesey's excessive drug use negatively affected his creativity after his early years.

PRINCIPAL WORKS

One Flew Over the Cuckoo's Nest (novel) 1962

Sometimes a Great Notion (novel) 1964

Ken Kesey's Garage Sale [editor and contributor] (essays, fiction, letters, and interviews) 1973

Demon Box (poetry and short stories) 1986

Little Tricker the Squirrel Meets Big Double the Bear (juvenilia) 1988

The Further Inquiry (screenplay) 1990

The Sea Lion: A Story of the Sea Cliff People (juvenilia) 1991

Sailor Song (novel) 1992

Last Go Round [with Ken Babbs] (novel) 1994

PRIMARY SOURCES

KEN KESEY (SHORT STORY DATE 1979)

SOURCE: Kesey, Ken. "The Day after Superman Died." In *Demon Box*, pp. 56-90. New York: Viking, 1986.

The following excerpt from "The Day after Superman Died" was written by Kesey in 1968 after he learned of the death of Neal Cassady and first published in 1979. Cassady was the driver on the Further bus during the Merry Pranksters' cross-country journey in 1964. In this fictionalized account, Kesey refers to himself as "Deboree" and Cassady as "Houlihan."

He had been up two days, grassing and speeding and ransacking his mental library (or was it three?) for an answer to his agent's call about the fresh material he had promised his editor and to his wife's query about the fresh cash needed by the loan office at the bank. Mainly, since Thursday's mail, for an answer to Larry McMurtry's letter.

Larry was an old literary friend from Texas. They had met at a graduate writing seminar at Stanford and had immediately disagreed about most of the important issues of the day—beatniks, politics, ethics, and, especially, psychedelics—in fact, about everything except for their mutual fondness and respect for writing and each other. It was a friendship that flourished during many midnight debates over bourbon and booklore, with neither the right nor the left side of the issues ever gaining much ground. Over the years since Stanford, they had tried to keep up the argument by correspondence—Larry defending the traditional and Deboree [Ken Kesey] championing the radical—but without the shared bourbon the letters had naturally lessened. The letter from Larry on Thursday was the first in a year. Nevertheless it went straight back at the issue, claiming conservative advances, listing the victories of the righteous right, and pointing out the retreats and mistakes made by certain left-wing luminaries, especially Charles Manson, whom Deboree had

known slightly. The letter ended by asking, in the closing paragraph, "So. What has the Good Old Revolution been doing lately?"

Deboree's research had yielded up no satisfactory answer. After hours of trial and chemistry before the typewriter, he had pecked out one meager page of print, but the victories he had listed on his side were largely mundane achievements: "Dobbs and Blanche had another kid. . . . Rampage and I finally got cut loose from our three-year probation. . . ." Certainly no great score for the left wing of the ledger. But that was all he could think of: one puny page to show for forty hours of prowling around in the lonely library of what he used to call "The Movement." Forty hours of thinking, drinking, and peeing in a milk bottle, with no break except that ten-minute trip downstairs to deal with those pilgriming prickheads. And now, back upstairs and still badly shaken, even that feeble page was missing; the typed yellow sheet of paper was as misplaced as his colored glasses.

"Pox on both houses," he moaned aloud, rubbing his irritated eyes with his wrists. "On Oregon field burners poisoning the air for weed-free profit and on California flower children gone to seed and thorn!"

. . . He heard the whine again, returning, growing louder. He opened his eyes and walked back to the window and parted the tie-dye curtains. The pink car had turned around and was coming back. Entranced, he watched it pass the driveway again, but this time it squealed to a stop, backed up, and turned in. It came keening and bouncing down the dirt road toward the barn. Finally he blinked, jerked the curtain closed, and sat heavily in his swivel chair.

The car whirred to a stop in the gravel and mercifully cut its engine. He didn't move. Somebody got out, and a voice from the past shouted up at his office: "Dev?" He'd let the curtain close too late. "Devlinnnn?" it shouted. "Hey, you, Devlin Deboreeeee?" A sound half hysterical and half humorous, like the sound that chick who lost her marbles in Mexico used to make, that Sandy Pawku.

"Dev? I've got news. About Houlihan [Neal Cassady]. Bad news. He's dead. Houlihan's dead."

He tipped back in his chair and closed his eyes. He didn't question the announcement. The loss seemed natural, in keeping with the season and the situation, comfortable even, and then he thought, *That's it! That's what the revolution has been doing lately, to be honest. Losing!*

"Dev, are you up there? It's me, Sandy . . ."

He pushed himself standing and walked to the window and drew back the curtain. He wiped his eyes and stuck his head into the blighted afternoon. Hazy as it was, the sunlight nevertheless seemed to be sharper than usual, harsher. The chrome of the little car gleamed viciously. Like the knife blade.

"Houlihan," he said, blinking. The dust raised by the car was reaching the barn on its own small breeze. He felt it bring an actual chill. "Houlihan dead?" he said to the pink face lifted to him.

"Of exposure," the voice rasped.

"When? Recently?"

"Yesterday. I just heard. I was in the airport in Oakland this morning when I ran into this little hippie chicky who knew me from Mountain View. She came up to the bar and advised me that the great Houlihan is now the late great. Yesterday, I guess. Chicky Little had just got off the plane from Puerto Sancto, where Houlihan had been staying with her and a bunch of her buddies. At a villa right down the road from where we lived. Apparently the poor maniac was drinking and taking downers and walking around at night alone, miles from nowhere. He passed out on a railroad track between Sancto and Manzanillo, where he got fatally chilled from the desert dew. Well, *you* know, Dev, how cold it can get down there after sunset."

It was Sandy Pawku all right, but what a change! Her once long brown hair had been cropped and chromed, plated with the rusty glint of the car's grill. She had put heavy eye makeup and rouge and lipstick on her face and, over the rest of her had put on, he guessed, at least a hundred pounds.

"Dead, our hero of the sixties is, Devvy, baby. Dead, dead, dead. Of downers and drunk and the foggy, foggy dew. O, Hooly, Hooly, Hooly, you maniac. You goon. What did Kerouac call him in that book? The glorious goon?"

"No. The Holy Goof."

"I was flying to my aunt's cottage in Seattle for a little R and R, rest and writing, you dig? But that news in Oakland—I thought, Wonder if Dev and the Animal Friends have heard? Probably not. So when the plane stopped in Eugene, I remember about this commune I hear you all got and I decided, Sandy, Old Man Deboree would want to know. So Sandy, she cashes in the rest of her ticket and rents a car and here she is, thanks to Mr. Mas-

tercharge, Mr. Hughes, and Mr. Avis. Say, is one supposed to drive these damn tricks in D1, D2, or L? Isn't L for driving in the light and D for driving in the dark?"

"You drove that thing all the way here from the airport in low gear?"

"Might have." She laughed, slapping the flimsy hood with a hand full of jeweled fingers. "Right in amongst those log trucks and eighteen-wheelers, me and my pinkster, roaring with the loudest of them."

"I'll bet."

"When it started to smoke, I compromised with D1. Goddamn it, I mean them damn manufacturers—but listen to me rationalizing. I probably wrecked it, didn't I? To tell the truth? Be honest, Sandy. Christ knows you could use a little honesty. . . ." She rubbed the back of her neck and looked away from him, back the way she had come. "Eee God, what is happening? Houlihan kacked. Pigpen killed by a chicken-shit liver; Terry the Tramp snuffed by spades. Ol' Sandy herself nearly down for the count a dozen times." She began walking to and fro in the gravel. "Man, I have been going in circles, in bummer nowhere circles, you know what I mean? Weird shit. I mean, hey listen: I just wasted a *dog* on the road back there!"

He knew he must have responded, said, "Oh?" or "Is that right?" or something, because she had kept talking.

"Old bitch it was, with a yardful of pups. Whammed her good."

Sandy came around the front of the car and opened the right door. She tipped the pink seat forward and began hauling matching luggage out of the back and arranging it on the gravel, all the while relating vividly how she had come around a bend and run over a dog sleeping in the road. *Right* in the *road*. A farmwife had come out of her house at the commotion and had dragged the broken animal out of the culvert where it had crawled howling. The farmwife had felt its spine then sentenced it to be put out of its misery. At her repeated commands, her teenage son had finally fetched the shotgun from the house.

"The kid was carrying on such a weeping and wailing, he missed twice. The third time, he let go with both barrels and blew bitch bits all over the lawn. The only thing they wanted from me was six bits apiece for the bullets. I asked if they took credit cards." She laughed. "When I left, goddamn me if the pups weren't playing with the pieces."

She laughed again. He remembered hearing the shots. He knew the family and the dog, a deaf spaniel, but he didn't say anything. Shading his eyes, he watched this swollen new version of the skinny Sandy of his past bustle around the luggage below him, laughing. Even her breath seemed to have gained weight, husking out of her throat with an effort. Swollen. Her neck where she had rubbed it, her wrists, her back, all swollen. But her weight actually rode lightly, defiantly, like a chip on her shoulder. *In her colored shoes and stretch pants and a silk Hawaiian shirt pulled over her paunch, she looks like a Laguna Beach roller derby queen,* he thought, *just arriving at the rink. She looks primed,* he thought. Like the hitchhiker; an argument rigged to go off at the slightest touch. The thought of another confrontation left him weak and nauseous.

M'kehla's Great Danes discovered her in the yard and came barking. Sandy sliced at them with her pink plastic handbag. "Get away from me, you big fuckers. You smell that other mutt on my wheels? You want the same treatment? Damn, they are big, aren't they? Get them back, can't you?"

"Their big is worse than their bite," he told her and shouted at the dogs to go home to their bus. They paid no attention.

"What the shit, Deboree?" She sliced and swung. "Can't you get your animals to mind?"

"They aren't mine," he explained over the din. "M'kehla left them here while he went gallivantin' to Woodstock with everybody else."

"Goddamn you fuckers, *back off!*" Sandy roared. The dogs hesitated, and she roared louder. "*Off! Off!* Clear *off!*" They shrunk back. Sandy hooted gleefully and kicked gravel after them until they broke into a terrified dash. Sandy gave chase, hooting their retreat all the way to the bus, out of his view.

The ravens were flying again. The sun was still slicing a way through the impacted smoke. The radio was playing "Good Vibrations" by The Beach Boys. Back in the yard below, at her luggage, Sandy was humming along, her hysteria calmed by her victory over the dogs. She found the bag she had been searching for, the smallest in a six-piece set that looked brand-new. She opened it and took out a bottle of pills. Deboree watched as she shook out at least a dozen. She threw the whole handful into her mouth and began digging again into the case for something to wash them down with.

"Ol' Thandy'th been platheth and theen thingth thinth Mexico," she told him, trying to keep all the pills in her mouth and bring him up to date at the same time. Seen lots of water under the bridges, she let him know, sometimes too much. Bridges washed out. Washed out herself a time or two, she told him. Got pretty mucked up. Even locked up. But with the help of some ritzy doctors and her rich daddy, she'd finally got bailed out and got set up being half owner of a bar in San Juan Capistrano; then become a drunk, then a junkie, then a blues singer *non*professional; found Jesus, and Love, and Another Husband— "Minithter of the Univerthal Church of Latterday Thonthabitcheth!"—then gotp.g., got an abortion, got disowned by her family, and got divorced; then got depressed, as he could well understand, and put on a little weight, as he could see; then— Sunday, *now*—was looking for a place where a gal might lay back for a while.

"A plathe to read and write and take a few barbth to mellow out," she said through the pills.

"A few!" he said, remembering her old barbiturate habit. "That's no 'few.'" The thought of having more than one carcass to dispose of alarmed him finally into protest. "Damn you, Sandy, if you up and O.D. on me now, so help me—"

She held up her hand. "Vitamin theth. Croth my heart." Pawing through a boil of lingerie, she at last had found the silver flask she had been seeking. She unscrewed the lid and threw back her head. He watched her neck heave as the pills washed down. She wiped her mouth with her forearm and laughed up at him.

"Don't worry, Granny," she said. "Just some innocent little vitamins. Even the dandy little Sandy of old never took *that* many downers at once. She might someday, though. Never can tell. Who the hell knows what anybody's gonna do this year? It's the year of the downer, you know, so who knows? Just let it roll by. . . ." She returned the flask to the suitcase and snapped it shut. Rayon and Orlon scalloped out all around like a piecrust to be trimmed. "Now. Where does Sandy take a wee-wee and wash out her Kotex?"

He pointed, and she went humming off to the corner of the barn. The big dogs came to the door of their bus and growled after her. Deboree watched as she ducked under the clothesline and turned the corner. He heard the door slam behind her.

He stayed at the window, feeling there was more to be revealed. Everything was so tense and restrained. The wash hung tense in the smoky air, like strips of jerky. The peacock, his fan molted to a dingy remnant of its springtime elegance, stepped out of the quince bush where he had been visiting his mate and flew to the top of one of the clothesline poles. Deboree thought the bird would make his cry when he reached the top, but he didn't. He perched atop the pole and bobbed his head this way and that at the end of his long neck, as though gauging the tension. After watching the peacock for a while, he let the curtain close and moved from the window back to his desk; he too found he could be content to let it roll by without resolution.

Over the radio The Doors were demanding that it be brought on through to the other side. Wasn't Morrison dead? He couldn't remember. All he could be sure of was that it was 1968 and the valley was filled to the foothills with smoke as 300,000 acres of stubble were burned so lawn-seed buyers in subdivisions in California wouldn't have to weed a single interloper from their yards.

Tremendous.

The bathroom door slammed again. He heard the plastic heels crunch past below; one of M'kehla's dogs followed, barking tentatively. The dog followed the steps around the other corner, barking in a subdued and civilized voice. The bitch Great Dane, he recognized. Pedigreed. She had barked last night, too. Out in the field. Betsy had got out of bed and shouted up the stairs at him to go check what was the matter out there. He hadn't gone. Was that what offed the lamb? One of M'kehla's Great Danes? He liked to think so. It made him pleasantly angry to think so. Just like a Marin County spade to own two blond Great Danes and go off and leave them marooned. Too many strays. Somebody should go down to that bus and boot some pedigreed ass. But he remained seated, seeking fortification behind his desk, and turned up the music against the noise. Once he heard a yelping as Sandy ran the bitch back to the bus. Sometimes a little breeze would open the curtain and he could see the peacock still sitting on the clothesline pole, silently bobbing his head. Eventually he heard the steps return, enter the barn below, and find the wooden stairs. They mounted briskly and crossed the floor of the loft. Sandy came through his door without knocking.

"Some great place, Dev," she said. "Funky but great. Sandy gave herself the tour. You got places for everything, don't you? For pigs and chickens and everything. Places to wee-wee, places to eat, places to write letters."

Deboree saw the pitch coming but couldn't stop her chatter.

"Look, I blew the last of my airline ticket to Seattle renting that pink panther because I knew you'd want Sandy to bring you the sad news in person. No, that's all right, save the thanksies. No need. She *does* need, though, a little place to write some letters. Seriously, Dev, I saw a cabin down by the pond with paper and envelopes and everything. How about Sandy uses that cabin a day or so? To write a letter to her dear mother and her dear probation officer and her dear ex et cetera. Also maybe catch up on her journal. Hey, I'm writing up our Mexico campaign for a rock'n'roll rag. Are you ready for *that?*"

He tried to explain to her that the pond cabin was a meditation chapel, not some Camp David for old campaigners to compile their memoirs. Besides, he had planned to use it tonight. She laughed, told him not to worry.

"I'll find me a harbor for tonight. Then we'll see."

He stayed at his desk. Chattering away, Sandy prowled his office until she found the shoe box and proceeded to clean and roll the last of his grass. He still didn't want to smoke, not until he was finished with that dead lamb. When he shook his head at the offered joint, she shrugged and smoked it all, explaining in detail how she would refill his box to overflowing with the scams she had cooking in town this afternoon, meeting so-and-so at such and such to barter this and that. He couldn't follow it. He felt flattened before her steamrolling energy. Even when she dropped the still-lit roach from the window to the dry grass below, he was only able to make the feeblest protest.

"Careful of fire around barn?" She whooped, bending over him. "Why, Mistah Deboree, if you ain't getting to be the fussy little farmer." She clomped to the door and opened it. "So. Sandy's making a run. Anything you need from town? A new typewriter? A better radio—how can you listen to good music on that Jap junk? A super Swiss Army? Ho ho. Just tell Sandy Claus. Anything?"

She stood in the opened door, waiting. He swiveled in his chair, but he didn't get up. He looked at her fat grin. He knew what she was waiting for. The question. He also knew better than to ask it. Better to let it slide than encourage any relationship by seeming curious. But he was curious, and she was waiting, grinning at him, and he finally had to ask it:

"Did he, uh, *say* anything, Sandy?" His voice was thick in his throat.

The black eyes glistened at him from the doorway. "You mean, don'cha, were there any, uh, *last words? Any sentences commuted,* any *parting wisdoms?* Why, as a matter of fact, in the hospital, it seems, before he went into a coma, he did rally a moment and now wait, let me see. . . ."

She was gloating. His asking had laid his desperation naked. She grinned. There he sat, Deboree, the Guru Gung Ho with his eyes raw, begging for some banner to carry on with, some comforter of last-minute truth quilted by Old Holy Goof Houlihan, a wrap against the chilly chaos to come.

"Well, yep, our little hippie chick did mention that he said a few words before he died on that Mexican mattress," she said. "And isn't that irony for you? It's that *same ratty Puerto Sancto* clinic where Behema had her kid and Mickey had his broken leg wherein our dear Hooly died, of pneumonia and exposure and downers. Come on! Don'cha think that is pretty stinking ironic?"

"What were they?"

The eyes glistened. The grin wriggled in its nest of fat. "He said—if Sandy's memory serves—said, I think it was, 'Sixty-four thousand nine hundred and twenty-eight.' Quite a legacy, don'cha think? A number, a stinking number!" She hooted, slapping her hips. "Sixty-four thousand nine hundred and twenty-eight! Sixty-four thousand nine hundred and twenty-eight! The complete cooked-down essence of the absolute burned-out speed freak: sixty-four thousand nine hundred and twenty-eight! *Huh-woow woow wow!*"

She left without closing the door, laughing, clacking down the steps and across the gravel. The injured machine whined pitifully as she forced it back out the drive.

So now observe him, after the lengthy preparation just documented (it had been actually three days and was going on four nights), finally confronting his task in the field: Old Man Deboree, desperate and dreary, with his eyes naked to the smoky sun, striding across the unbroken ground behind a red wheelbarrow. Face bent earthward, he watches the field pass beneath his shoes and nothing else, trusting the one-wheeled machine to lead him to his destination.

Like Sandy's neck, he fancies himself swollen with an unspecified anger, a great smoldering of unlaid blame that longed to bloom to a great blaze. Could he but fix it on a suitable culprit. Searching for some target large enough to take his fiery blame, he fixes again on California. *That's* where it comes from, he decides. Like those two weirdo prickhikers, and Sandy Pawku, and the Oakland hippie chick who must have been one of that Oakland bunch of pillheads who lured Houlihan back down to Mexico last month . . . all from California! It all started in California, went haywire in California, and now spreads out from California like a crazy tumor under the hide of the whole continent. Woodstock. Big time. Craziness waxing fat. Craziness surviving and prospering and gaining momentum while the Fastestmanalive downs himself dead without any legacy left behind but a psycho's cipher. Even those Great Danes—from California!

The wheelbarrow reaches the ditch. He raises his head. He still cannot see the carcass. Turning down into the ditch, he pushes on toward the place where the three ravens whirl cursing in and out of the tall weeds. . . .

KEN KESEY (ESSAY DATE 1996)

SOURCE: Kesey, Ken. "Flowers for Tim." Foreword to *On the Bus,* by Paul Perry, pp. xi-xiii. New York: Thunder's Mouth Press, 1996.

Kesey is often seen as a link between the Beats and the counterculture of the 1960s, and his trip aboard the Further bus is considered a defining moment of that evolution. This essay is a foreword to On the Bus, *a chronicle of that trip.*

"Give 'em while they can smell 'em."
                    —sign in florist shop window

During the seventies Ken Babbs and I put out a little homegrown periodical called *Spit In The Ocean*. The idea was to have a different editor for each issue and let them call the deal, like in the poker game. Dr. Timothy Leary had agreed to deal our third issue of *Spit* from his San Diego prison cell where he was being re-restrained after being recaptured after his escape the year before.

We expected some kind of bleak jailhouse blues, I guess—"Ex-Harvard Prof Gets Down and Dirty Behind Bars!" But no: Dr. Leary writes to inform us that the theme for his issue will be Communication With Higher Intelligence—an ambitious aim even from atop the loftiest ivory tower. But from behind bars?

So Babbs and I fly south to ask our incarcerated editor a few probing questions.

I confess I had some reservations. The famous Dr. Leary had always been more a distant phenomenon than a close friend. Previous attempts at close encounters had always seemed jinxed. The summer of 1961, for example. My family and my bay area buddies were booked for a high level seminar with Leary and Alpert and the International Federation for Internal Freedom down at IFIF's winter paradise in Ziuwataneo. We were bustling our way through the SF airport to our Mexicana flight when we saw the SF Chronicle headlines: DOPE DOCTORS ARRESTED AT MEXICO MANSION. Leary, Alpert, and LSD Cronies Given Choice: Go Home or Go to Jail. So much for paradise.

A couple seasons later we bussed our way out to IFIF's digs in upper New York. This Northern rendezvous wasn't much more successful than the one that didn't happen down south. Our spirited arrival at the Millbrook mansion was met with a less-than-enthusiastic welcome. Who's to say? It could have been the time wasn't right, or the stars were wrong. Or it could have been the way we came barging up on a sleepy Sunday morn in a gawdy vehicle belching green and orange smoke from beneath the hood and blaring Neal Cassady out the rooftop speakers. Dr. Leary was upstairs, we were informed, sleeping one off. We left before he woke.

So here we were for one more try, in the visitor's tank at the San Diego Federal Pen, waiting for the stonefaced warden to decide whether it's in society's best interest to allow our visit with Prisoner Leary or not. He's taking his own sweet time, too, this warden. He wants to let everybody sit and stew a while. I tip back my chair pull down my shades, and stew.

I was no stranger to pulling time. But my six month's stretch was at a work camp up in the redwoods. Imagine serving a sentence in this skyless scene, slammed away with Warden Rockface for God knows how long on God knows how many charges! Be a drag. No wonder Dr. Leary let that shadowy gang of revolutionaries called The Weathermen talk him into that swashbuckling escape from the San Luis Obispo slammer last year.

The Weatherman plan? At a quarter to ten Leary excuses himself from the Sunday eve movie in the penitentiary messhall—nature calls, boss . . . slips into the kitchen instead of the can . . . ten minutes to ten, up the greasy ventilation shaft above the kitchen range to the roof. Five to ten shinny up the prison's main power pole. If everything went according to plan the Weathermen would blow the transformer out on the street at the stroke of ten. Leary would then have to hand

over hand along the wire over the wall and down the streetcorner pole before auxiliary power cut in. Three minutes. His accomplices would be waiting in the gettaway rod.

So imagine: you're a middleaged psychologist, an alumn from West Point and a discredited prof from Harvard, serving five-to-ten for a fall you took for your daughter at the Texas border when you relieved her of the two stupid joints she had stashed in her panties. Now you're up a power pole on top of a state prison, one eye on your wristwatch while the other contemplates the naked cable that will carry you to freedom, one way or another.

"It was the longest three minutes of my life." Now imagine being spirited out of the country and whisked to Algiers where you are taken in by fellow fugitives Eldridge and Kathleen Cleaver and the Black Panthers who intend to indoctrinate yo pampered ass! Heavy trip or what? Hemmed in by Black Panthers on one side and whitebread weather prognosticates on the other while unscrupulous Algerian cops prowl the street outside the compound eyes like hungry jackals. Might as well stayed in San Luis Obispo.

Now, picture this: into this uptight arrangement a sleek and mysterious siren comes swinging to your rescue, sweeps you off your feet then saves you from Black Panthers white Weathermen and jackal-eyed cops alike by marrying you! Seemed like things were looking up at last.

For a honeymoon your new bride wants to take you to her family estate just across the border—meet the folks. But it aint exactly the folks there to meet you and your bride when the airplane lands. Its four CIA agents, waiting for you with extradition papers and handcuffs. And for your glamorous wife? Handshakes and praise for a job well done. It finally dawns on you: your mysterious bride is actually bait—hired CIA bait!— and you went for it, hook, line, and glamor.

That's what I really wanted to ask about in that visiting room in San Diego: You're supposed to be this psychedelic wiseman—what wisdoms if any have you gleaned from these ill-fated involvements with beautiful women and borders? What feelings? Did you yearn to kick your daughter's dumb butt? Did you ache to wring your wife's treacherous neck? That's the question I wanted to ask.

Our visiting hour was three quarters gone when the prisoner was at last escorted in. The guards were polite and the warden was congenial. He even returned Babbs' tape recorder before leaving us alone. The first 15 minutes on the tape is devoted to *Spit In The Ocean* business. I don't get around to asking my question until the squawk box squawks that visiting is over.

"By the way, Tim, I was wondering . . . what's happening with your new—you know—since you last saw—?"

His recorded response was classic Tim Leary. "With my new spouse the Spy? I see her four, five times a week. She's rented a beach house thirty minutes away by bike. She doesn't have her US drivers license yet. Sometimes she catches a ride with one of our lawyers."

Babbs and I were dumbstruck. Leary laughed. "I certainly don't hold it against her, her being a spy. She likes this espionage action. It gets her off. It turns her on."

He walked us to the door and waved at the warden behind his bulletproof glass wall.

"Besides," he added, "who am I, of all people, to put down somebody else's turn on."

And that's my little flower for Tim.

GENERAL COMMENTARY

JAMES O. HOGE (ESSAY DATE FALL 1972)

SOURCE: Hoge, James O. "Psychedelic Stimulation and the Creative Imagination: The Case of Ken Kesey." *Southern Humanities Review* 6, no. 4 (fall 1972): 381-91.

In the following essay, Hoge discusses Kesey's involvement with psychedelic drugs and his commitment to the life of the senses.

The contemporary cultural reaction against the ethic of the rational intellect, including an overriding distaste for "content" art, and the correspondingly pervasive commitment to sensorial experience, are exemplified in the career of Ken Kesey, erstwhile novelist and psychedelic superhero. Whatever became of that boisterous and brilliant young diamond-in-the-rough novelist who commanded the attention of middle-class American youth during the Haight-Ashbury era as prophet of the feverish *Now* religion? In 1962 Kesey published his bitter fable, *One Flew Over the Cuckoo's Nest,* still an extremely popular novel, and he was immediately included in the slate of highly regarded, challenging young American writers. Like so much of the important literature of this century, Kesey's first book laments the

FROM THE AUTHOR

LSD AND AWARENESS
When people ask me about LSD, I always make a point of telling them you can have the shit scared out of you with LSD because it exposes something, something hollow. Let's say you have been getting on your knees and bowing and worshiping; suddenly you take LSD, and you look, and there's just a hole, there's nothing there. The Catholic Church fills this hole with candles and flowers and litanies and opulence. The Protestant Church fills it with hand-wringing and pumped-up squeezing emotions because they can't afford the flowers and the candles. The Jews fill this hole with weeping and browbeating and beseeching of the sky: "How long, how long are you gonna treat us like this?" The Muslims fill it with rigidity and guns and a militant ethos. But all of us know that that's not what is supposed to be in that hole.

Kesey, Ken. An excerpt from "Ken Kesey: The Art of Fiction" *Paris Review,* no. 130 (spring 1994): 58-94.

destruction of America by the monstrous organizational Combine, and it defines that retreat to private, "irrational" satisfactions which has in the past decade become an extraordinarily widespread response to claustrophobic rational life in the social madhouse. Kesey then personally rejected the painfully logical, but thoroughly berserk machinery of orthodox spaceage existence and followed his Indian refugee Chief Bromden back to the tribe. Of course, Kesey's noble savages were Indians only in spirit, social drop-outs who had discovered the primitive in themselves and who preferred the random life to the servile treadmill of community responsibility and business as usual. Kesey went native, went mad by society's definition, which labels any man insane who is unable or unwilling to conform, and he found a new life as charismatic chieftain of the Merry Pranksters.

While living with the San Francisco clique that gathered around him, and before he ran afoul of the police in 1965, Kesey published *Sometimes a Great Notion,* a long and ambitious novel which, despite its remarkable triumphs of language, is somewhat strained and meandering. And with that second book, less successful than the first, but by no means poorly received, Kesey apparently drew the curtain on his literary career. Perhaps his difficulties with *Sometimes a Great Notion* discouraged further writing. Or, as Leslie Fiedler has observed, Kesey's first book may prophesy silence for him.[1] Certainly it can be read as telling the truth about Kesey's own renunciation of "civilization," and perhaps the "Indian" who seeks out an uninhabited psychological frontier does not write books. In any case, a close scrutiny of Kesey's commitment to the unrestricted sensorial life and a consideration of the implications of his radical dedication to the ecstasy of the present moment offer more adequate explanations for his turning away from verbal communication of any kind.

One Flew Over the Cuckoo's Nest adheres to the Arnoldian definition of art as the criticism of life. For all its informality and its smacking of Pop Art, Kesey's maiden novel is an educative work of the old order, communicating ethical, social, and political ideas. The book has a decidedly personal flavor. It presents Kesey's moral judgment of the dehumanizing technocracy which dwarfs and desensitizes the individual, stripping him of his creativity and his personal uniqueness. Kesey would free all those repressed by Big Nurse and the flesh-frying system she represents. He grieves particularly for the psychologically victimized, those "inmates" with blue noses but red eyes, whose emotions opt for rebellious independence, but whose minds force them to play it safe and avoid the castrating reprisals of Big Nurse.

Directly attacking the power and injustice of the death-dealing industrial state, Kesey packed his story with hot and telling derision of the nation-wide bureaucracy. Unlike numerous less significant social novelists, whose expressions of disillusionment speak primarily of injuries to their own personal sensibilities, Kesey caught the burgeoning mood of an entire generation bound together by a detestation of the encroachments of blind material progress and by a desire for a life based on impetuous personal feelings rather than on the mandates of success, status, and other future-directed rewards. For all its acrimonious proscriptions, *One Flew Over the Cuckoo's Nest* offers hope in the possibility of revitalizing the senses and thus realizing the joys of an instinctual life untouched by imperialist reason. Like lusty

Randle McMurphy, who brings the smell of life to Nurse Ratched's patients, Kesey enjoins his readers to break their anesthetizing mental shackles, to flex long-neglected sensory capacities and return with Chief Bromden to lives that have waited since they were children, when the land sang kids' poetry every day.

The anti-intellectualism of the new generation, including Kesey's expression and extension of that sensibility, bears a marked similarity to the early nineteenth century irrationalism enunciated by the first modern experts in sensory awareness, the Romantic poets. The Romantics were able to transcend a constricting culture by regenerating and expanding their individual senses, thereby modifying their ways of thinking, feeling, and valuing. They understood that man had circumscribed his creative faculty and abridged his human identity by limiting his perception. For those self-conscious aestheticians personal release from an incomplete version of reality depended upon the automatic extension of life (beyond its ordinary, accepted boundaries) which follows an enlarging and strengthening of the senses. By shattering the barrier between the individual and the external, the I and the not-I, by means of an alteration of perception, man could "discover" his world, could experience and understand it for the first time. Such dialectical interchanges with the unadorned natural world provided the Romantics with insights, both into the sorrows and into the essential beauties of human existence, which enabled them to transcend the wasteland of an industrial age.

Kesey grounded his revolt against the utilitarian life subject to "the public interest" on a cognitive process which Marshall McLuhan, Aldous Huxley, Coleridge, and other Romantic and post-Romantic cultural critics have traced back to the original sensualist—tribal man, totally enthralled in the physical world. Of course, Kesey is a nonverbal philosopher, so we must piece together his philosophy from a knowledge of how he acted as Psychedelic Superhero, and from Tom Wolfe's account of the now legendary peregrinations of Intrepid Trips in *The Electric Kool-Aid Acid Test.*[2] Nevertheless, Kesey's message comes through loud and clear. In part it seems a message we have long been acquainted with: If man is to resurrect his body and his mind, if he is to realize his real human kindness, he must get intimately in touch with his world. Man has been sensually impaired by his own civilization, and in order to make himself whole he must open wide his doors of perception, fill his expanded consciousness with all that confronts him, and give himself to an unplanned, unpredictable *Now*, to sensual life lived in the present moment. So far, so good. Keseyism sounds like romanticism slightly revised, a smooth blend of Wordsworth and Blake with just a pinch of Walter Pater and Oscar Wilde in colloidal suspension.

A closer inspection, however, reveals dramatic intrinsic differences between the new sensationalists, epitomized by Kesey and his Edge City tribe, and earlier psychological revolutionaries. Hallucinogenic drugs[3] were the key to Edge City, and the Pranksters who lived there hooked down enough LSD during the middle sixties to insure a continuous drug-induced synchronic perception. Sounds became colors, colors smells, ego and non-ego merged, and all things flowed together in cosmic unity. But, though perhaps inspired by specific objects and situations in the real world, the Pranksters' frenetic imaginative experiences took place in an Other World of hallucination wholly separated from the plane of empirical phenomena and common consciousness which Randle McMurphy had called home. That self-negating union of the individual with the external through empathic identification which captured the imaginations of Wordsworth, Coleridge, and Keats is contingent upon man's acute awareness of and participation in the physical world. According to the theory of "Negative Capability," it is the concentration of expanded and enlivened senses upon an object which enables the mind of the perceiver to transcend the boundary between the personal and the impersonal realms. Such a process draws man into a closer relationship with his world, prompting him, with Browning's Lippo Lippi, to penetrate the deceptive veil of familiarity and to feel the beauty, value, and significance of fleshly existence.

Kesey offered his disciples no reconciliation with the world where, as Wordsworth observed, man must ultimately find fulfillment, if he is to find it at all. Rather he steered them away from a mindless, exhausting life in the Corporate State into an entranced fantasy existence with only one standard of value, the standard of sensation.

Surely for all its stark naked intensities, the life of sensation is as mindless and as far removed from any healthy relationship to reality as is the orthodox rational life imposed by society. Drugs were an inevitable part of the current exploration and revitalization of long deadened senses, and they are useful tools as long as they work *for* human interests. Marijuana causes a concentration of the senses on whatever is immediately present,

and though such a concentration by itself promotes no better understanding of reality, it may entail a valuable increase in sensory awareness. However, when used continually, even marijuana betrays its usefulness, dulling the consciousness and becoming yet another barrier between the individual and reality. A kind of drug tourism may well expand sensory capacities, but an incautious commitment to uncontrolled sensation, whether drug-induced or not, lures the mind toward anarchy.

Much like Coleridge, DeQuincey, Baudelaire, Francis Thompson, and other nineteenth-century laudanum drinkers, Kesey's LSD-charged crew paid for their nearly continuous fanciful sojourn apart from the joys and terrors of ordinary experience with a loss of interest in the real world. Ironically Kesey carried the attempt to seize present reality beyond reality into a remote area of the human unconscious. In Keatsian terminology he took the imagination "beyond its proper bound" and teased himself out of concern with earthly things. DeQuincey acknowledged that drugs and the hallucinations they stimulate both give and take away. As the strange power of his fanciful voyages expired, DeQuincey inevitably felt desolate and disenchanted with reality, and that dissatisfaction, combined with the actual opium habit, which grew fast upon him, encouraged a consumption of even greater quantities of the drug and steadily moved him further apart from the conditions of real life. And Kesey's Day-Glo riders found their trip "on the bus" as startling in its radical separation from the natural world as DeQuincey found the "abyss of divine enjoyment" described in the *Confessions of an English Opium Eater.*

LSD unlocks a Pandora's box of distorted sensorial phenomena (ashtrays turning into Venus flytraps, eyelid movies of crystal cathedrals) which bear little relation to the Romantics' ideal of sensuous entanglement with the external. Wordsworth's active, aware passivity of "a heart / That watches and receives"[4] is far removed from the kind of submission to random fantasy advocated by Kesey. At a particular moment LSD may increase or deepen the capacity for alert perception, but it permits no organization or temporal extension of what is perceived, and no real appreciation of the truths Wordsworth found waiting in all things. Instead of promoting that imaginative process by which the expanded mind becomes one with the physical world, the LSD hallucination, like the opium delirium, may relax the ability and the desire to cope with conscious experience. Certainly when used to excess, hallucinogens isolate the self, precluding any possibility of a sensitive response to reality.

Kesey and his mind-sharing friends scoffed at the orthodox, cops, peaceniks, and everyone else alike, and they shunned the usual pursuits of men, dismissing even such standard intellectual interests as literature and politics. Obviously such a thorough distaste for anything beyond the grasp of immediate sensual intoxication is alienating and in the long run self-defeating. Unlike the Platonic quester seeking union with the Absolute or Ultimate Beauty, the sensationalist who has stimulation as his final objective experiences no gratifying spiritual transformation. Nor does his frenzied pursuit of sensorial excitement lead through sensualism to any new understanding of the world of common humanity. Drugs appeared to provide the Kesey cultists with a channel for retreat into private, inward satisfactions, but the Pranksters remained satisfied only so long as they were blown beyond any possibility of apprehending ordinary human passions. Whenever they momentarily touched ground, they rapped all the harder, downing 500, 1,000, 1,500 micrograms of acid at a time. Kesey initiated his clan into a way of life which, for all its allurements, is as berserk and as pernicious as the anemic life of social responsibility. The Pranksters and the Haight-Ashbury hips they influenced were the pioneers of the current anti-cerebral movement which exchanges the structured turbulence of a society numbed by the pressures of bureaucratic organization for the formless turbulence of an equally depersonalizing culture committed to sensation.

Though Kesey is the original fabulist behind the psychedelic fantasy, he has written not a word about his sensual Utopia. And if we may judge by Tom Wolfe's scanty remarks about the thought behind all the Kesey razzmatazz, he has not said much about it either. Kesey exists outside the world of logical discourse, and though several of his few recorded statements emphasize the necessity for spreading the faith to all people, he simply does not consider verbalization an efficacious means of communication. The sensibility "on the bus" is an inexplicit and inexplicable thing that one must *feel*. Kesey would consider it inappropriate and, in fact, impossible to put into words the ecstatic experience of overcoming the sensory lag that distances man from the present moment. Kesey's interest has been in extending sensation, not in systematizing it, and those who looked to him as spiritual navigator were guided by his actions rather than by any explanation of what he had in mind.

The separation of Ken Kesey from the world of readers can be explained in part by the drastic change in his thinking and valuing which led him to draw away from the natural order into an elysium of pure sensation. But his skepticism about "linear" communication is probably equally responsible for his disappearance. Even before his drop-out Kesey was a missionary, a converter, but when his message changed so did his means of conversion. As a novelist he used words to impress upon America the brutalizing sterility of its system. As a Prankster he taught simply by the example of his own life, by making himself and all that he did his mode of communication, his vehicle for changing the sensibilities of any who wished to be changed.

Kesey is partly a product, but also partly a shaper, of the McLuhanish yearning for information conveyed by a cooler, more direct, and less content-oriented means than print. He epitomizes the significant lack of respect granted by the new sensationalists to written communication, or indeed to the dissemination of analytic thought by any means. One has the feeling that for Kesey writing is no longer suitable because reading requires some use of the conscious, critical intelligence, and he demands an immediate, unmediated sensory response. Kesey's literary appetite apparently vanished with the completion of his second (or perhaps his first) novel, and he came to regard all art as obsolescent unless it offered instantaneous sensation. Art then is not eternal; it is significant only momentarily as it channels momentary pleasure to the senses. Thus the geodesic dome with its wild Day-Glo creations is art; the Trips Festival with its strobes, projectors, mikes, tapes, amplifiers, drugs, and acid-impelled rock music is art; but literature has nothing to do with art because it treats *ideas*, makes *statements*, and assumes an unwarranted claim to immortality.

Like the broad disdain for everything in the ordinary, "unattuned" world, the current impatience with literature or any form of art that cannot simply be dropped down the gullet like so much LSD is indicative of a desire for retreat, for total surrender to unreality. Kesey's mid-sixties psychedelic culture manifested a general trend away from both the great literature of the past and contemporary writing toward a new cultural predilection for films, music, dance, painting, sculpture—particularly for multimedia works which experiment with new "sensory mixes." Susan Sontag sees this aesthetic impulse which demands less content and less moral judgment as a healthy movement away from a snobbish prejudice for "high" or "intellectual" art of individual personal expression.[5] Apparently many contemporary artists, including writers of poetry and fiction, agree with her. In poetry there is less emphasis upon coping with the dilemmas of modern man than upon the creation of a striking image or an unusual sound effect. Of course, the new imagists are not all that new, and the rebellion against lofty subject matter traces its American origins back to Pound, Cummings, and William Carlos Williams. But some of the current writers eschew any subject matter at all, and they seem to find all literature irrelevant. In an article treating the disenchantments of students, teachers, and writers of literature, Maynard Mack cites a *New York Times* interview in which a number of young writers declared themselves to be non-readers. "'No, I don't read,'" one was quoted as saying. "'It's just easier to go to a movie and let it all wash over you.'"[6]

Miss Sontag has good reason for applauding that new critical sensibility which finds beauty in the Beatles' music, in the avant-garde films of Jean-Luc Godard, in The Living Theater, and in the painting of Frank Stella and Jasper Johns. But though she would not advocate the renunciation of all standards, her approval of the monomaniacal focus of contemporary art upon sensation seems by logical extension to imply that Kesey's echolalia and ululation under the influence of LSD might be judged as fine as a Beethoven symphony as long as it afforded some arbitrary listener with an equal degree of sensual stimulation. Extreme critical affirmations of the value of any art which produces momentary stimulation by challenging and stretching or unclosing the senses are surely wrong-headed. An aesthetic attitude which accepts art only if it can be tripped on today and discarded tomorrow simply ignores the fact that at different times a work of art may touch an individual's consciousness in very different ways. There are people who see more deeply into the beauties of the music of *Tristan and Isolde* as they experience it over a period of years, and there are others who arrive at new meanings, or perhaps reestablish former insights, each time they return to *The Prelude*. The Keseyite sensation-for-sensation's-sake approach inadvertently destroys the primary purpose of art, the giving of pleasure, by negating the possibility of a longlasting and deeply satisfying experience with a single work of art. Furthermore, truly worthwhile art does more than bombard the senses and expand the consciousness. Certainly it extends the region of the senses, but it also heightens man's awareness and understanding of the world in which he is to live out his days. To foster an appreciation of reality, art must have content. Art need not educate or program to have significance, but it must celebrate the joy, the terror, and the awe of human existence. It must communicate life.

The present predilection for the life of sensation and for art which arouses an exquisite momentary passion carries to its ultimate conclusion the philosophy of late nineteenth-century aestheticians such as Walter Pater. In his 1873 *Studies in the History of the Renaissance* Pater defined human success as the realization of many sharp and passionate experiences which stir the senses and "set the spirit free for a moment."[7] Man, said Pater, has no time to theorize about life; rather, he must ever court new impressions and new opinions, ready to catch at any vibrant moment that might yield the fruit of a quickened, multiplied consciousness. In the absence of any Platonist or Christian validation for personal transcendence, one may find meaning in individual instances of passionate fulfillment. Pater rated all experience according to its ability to produce pleasure, but, unlike Kesey and other new sensationalists, he valued moments of intellectual excitement most of all. And whereas each intense sensory experience brought Pater closer to an understanding of the strange, mystical sense of life in the world and thus affected him with an unique impression of pleasure, a religion of the senses which aims at nothing beyond sensation fosters a narrow, stale single-mindedness. The Merry Pranksters left no sensory experiment undone, but every new experiment found its apex in the same sort of ephemeral blast as the last one. Their attempt to restore variety to life got lost in the mindless, automatic repetition of "getting stoned," and when Kesey went underground to Mexico in 1966 the mystical unity of his commune dissolved in internal friction and boredom.

Perhaps it is misleading to indict the "new sensibility" or the "new generation," for such terms encompass many individuals with distinctly different ideas and values. Nonetheless, there is a censurable mood or trend in the thought and actions of extreme examples of the new sensibility, such as Kesey and those seduced by his wizardry, which sanctions the renunciation of all qualitative standards for pleasure both in life and in art. Like the new sensationalists, the Romantics and the *fin-de-siècle* aesthetes reacted against the ethic of controlled rational intellect and opted for sensory awareness. But not even such self-indulgent aestheticians as Baudelaire and Oscar Wilde ever went so far as to make sensation itself the only standard for experience, or to find fantasy preferable to reality. Keats at times longed to surrender himself to sensation, and he always felt the strong pull of that supersensuous region beyond earthly existence which Charles Patterson has called the daemonic.[8] Keats, however, came to understand that man must exist "partly on sensation partly on thought."[9] He must penetrate and unite imaginatively with the external world, not ultimately for the purpose of a sensory reveling, but in order to *know* the world, so that after any single empathic experience he will never be quite the same again.

Any response to a bird's song or a Day-Glo bus that does not reach its climax in a deeper understanding of the real precludes the possibility of imaginative development, as well as the realization of that highest form of pleasure which is dependent upon the symbiotic relation of thought to feeling. As Eliot recognized, thought and emotion must complement each other, and a valid perception of reality is dependent upon a proper blending of the cerebral and the emotional faculties. The idea expressed in the "Preface" to *Lyrical Ballads* that the natural process is best understood when thought is given, in tranquillity, to a particular intense perception is instructive. It is a thorough understanding of reality, rather than a surrender to unorchestrated sensation, that develops the imagination, which, as Wordsworth noted, is but another name for "reason in her most exalted mood."[10] The satisfactions of life which are to be found in imaginative communication with the external presuppose and necessitate feelings, but unless they lead to comprehension and conceptualization, high sensations offer a life no richer, no more satisfying than the life devoted to status, power, money, and other purely rational achievements.

Kesey's Trips Festivals were perhaps maniacal but the rationally controlled activities of a society that banishes everything random, irrational, and unconventional are no less insane. Chief Bromden had the right answer to a maddened world that locks men up in their own selfhoods and reduces them to isolated mutes. Ironically Kesey corrupted the Chief's full-blooded impulse to regain the genuine, instinctual life by immersing himself in a sensationalism which defeats its own purpose and narrows rather than broadens life's possibili-

ties. And those artists and aestheticians who look through Kesey's eyes are reducing the rich and varied possibilities of art as surely as the Merry Pranksters limited their own lives. The function of art should be to raise consciousness, but extremists in the nonliterary culture yearn for art which numbs the ability to be conscious. Any art that demands the penetration of a shaping and unifying intelligence is rejected by them, and of course the novel has been the first art form to go. When in 1966 Tom Wolfe asked Kesey why he did not write any more, Kesey explained that his message could be communicated more effectively through forms of expression in which there is no separation between artist and audience. Still one wonders about the "art" of the intoxicating Kesey presence; one searches for some substance, some content in that "message," beyond the short-sighted nonsense of grooving to an endless succession of sound mixers and acid tests. But there is no content, and there are no ideas. There is only the pitiful, self-defeating demand for protracted sensual euphoria.

Notes

1. *The Return of the Vanishing American* (New York: Stein and Day, 1968),p. 183.

2. (Farrar, Straus, and Giroux, 1968). As Joel Lieber indicates in his review (*The Nation*, September 23, 1968), Wolfe's book comes as close as seems possible to recreating the mental atmosphere of a scene and an experience for which there is really no adequate vocabulary.

3. The Merry Pranksters "tripped" almost exclusively under the influence of lysergic acid diethylamide (LSD). I do not therefore particularize other hallucinogens, such as mescalin and psilocybin, but my remarks are applicable to all hallucinogenic drugs.

4. "The Tables Turned," 11. 31-2.

5. "The Basic Unit of Contemporary Art is not the Idea, but the Analysis of and Extension of Sensations," *McLuhan: Hot and Cool* (New York: Dial Press, 1967), pp. 252-63.

6. "To See It Feelingly," *PMLA*, 86 (May 1971),p. 368.

7. "Conclusion" to *Studies in the History of the Renaissance.*

8. See Charles I. Patterson, Jr., *The Daemonic in the Poetry of John Keats* (Urbana, Chicago, London: University of Illinois Press, 1970).

9. "John Keats to Benjamin Bailey, November 22, 1817," *John Keats: Complete Poems and Selected Letters,* ed. Clarence DeWitt Thorpe (New York, The Odyssey Press, 1935),p. 525. In his interesting but fundamentally wrongheaded *Poetic Vision and the Psychedelic Experience* (Syracuse University Press, 1970), R. A. Durr quotes another portion of this letter to support his thesis that the contemporary drug experience is a manifestation of the search for self-transcendence

undertaken in every generation by imaginative spirits who live "the life of poetry." Contending with his growing realization that the life of sensation can never lead to Truth, Keats expressed to Bailey his belief that the beautiful and the real are accessible only to the "philosophic Mind": "I have never yet been able to perceive how anything can be known for truth by consecutive reasoning—and yet it must be. Can it be that even the greatest Philosopher ever arrived at his goal without putting aside numerous objections?" By selective quotation (particularly the omission of the last five words of Keats's first sentence above), Durr blurs Keats's elucidation of the idea that a thorough knowledge of the human world is dependent upon both intuitive insight and intellectual reflection.

10. *The Prelude*, XIV, 192.

M. GILBERT PORTER (ESSAY DATE 1982)

SOURCE: Porter, M. Gilbert. "Kesey: The Man and the Artist." In *The Art of Grit: Ken Kesey's Fiction*, pp. 1-6. Columbia: University of Missouri Press, 1982.

In the following essay, Porter offers an introduction to Kesey's life and discusses his craft as a fiction writer.

From his personal accounts and many public appearances, from biographical critics and a score of journalists and interviewers, we know a good deal about Ken Kesey. The mere mention of his name among Kesey followers animates a day-glo carousel of images: brawny wrestler and actor manqué from the University of Oregon, ardent and idiosyncratic writing student at Stanford holding psychedelic court on Perry Lane, 'possum-smiling volunteer for government drug experiments, spaced-out hospital aide compassionately tending the old and the mentally infirm, motlied master-of-the-revels for the Merry Pranksters, drug-busted prisoner on a San Mateo work farm, intrepid but uneasy host for the Hell's Angels in La Honda, Dr. Feelgood for a parade of pilgrims to the shrine of his white-starred barn in Pleasant Hill, Oregon, flea-ridden travel correspondent probing the secrets of the Pyramids, desperate father prayerfully breathing life back into a dead son, defender of free dogs before civil courts, political activist on the college circuit, ecologist, moviemaker, mystic, rancher, little-magazine publisher, and American novelist. From gleefully hawking the benefits of cornstarch on the groin to grooving on the Grateful Dead, from preaching parables to the Black Panthers to recommending hash with Bible readings, Kesey has stayed busy, and under observation.

Thanks to time-lapse impressionism, we even have a verbal record of the faces Kesey has presented to the public. Athletic, said Lucille Vaughan Payne in 1967: "Kesey has bright red hair. It has

FROM THE AUTHOR

KESEY DESCRIBES THE WAVE OF COUNTERCULTURE CREATIVITY

That stuff that happened in the Sixties, all of us who were part of it ... you can tell when you break new ground. If you're a farmer, you can tell that this sod has never been broken before, the plow is laying open great, purple earth and something comes out of it and you can *smell* it. When you're a writer, when I was working on *Sometimes a Great Notion*, I could tell I was breaking new ground; there's an energy that comes out, that's probably not unlike the energy that comes out of nuclear fission—It wasn't just me. It was not *anybody*. It wasn't rock and roll; it wasn't art; it wasn't cinema or dance. *Something was happening* at that time, and it was a wave that some of us were able to surf on. And none of us started the wave; I don't think there's any way you could start the wave. The wave is still going.

Kesey, Ken and Todd Brendan Fahey. "Comes Spake the Cuckoo: Ken Kesey: The Fargone Interview." *Fargone Books* (website) <http://www.fargonebooks.com/kesey.html> (13 September 1992).

receded enough to beach a good deal of forehead, but it is thick and springy with curl at the nape of his muscular neck, a wrestler's neck, and it reminds you a little of McMurphy."[1] Country, said Tom Wolfe in 1968, looking back through the eyes of the Perry Lane sophisticates: "he had an Oregon drawl and too many muscles and calluses on his hands and his brow furrowed when he was thinking hard."[2] Clownish, observed George Bundy in 1973: "His eyes, hazel but nearly blue, sit in a face which is one moment young and fresh, then suddenly wise and weathered. . . . His hair, oh his hair right away! Curly and blond hair, bald on top with heavy sideburns reaching up from the sides to the back of his head in points, like a funny clown . . . or a devilish imp perhaps . . . or both."[3] Serious, said John Pratt more recently, despite a "zaniness somehow residual" and a residual baldness: "Kesey was recognizable only by the top of his head. The tight cap with the curls

A scene from the 1975 film adaptation of Kesey's *One Flew Over the Cuckoo's Nest*, starring Jack Nicholson as Randall Patrick McMurphy. Although the film won an Academy Award and received widespread critical and public acclaim, Kesey reportedly objected to the casting of Nicholson in the lead role and maintained that he never saw the film.

of reddish hair sticking around it resembled a busted soft-ball. . . . That Kesey has actually run for a School Board post, has organized and conducted the pioneering Media Referendum on political issues, and will constantly remind you that he is, after all, a serious artist—all of this belies the decade-old impression which many still have of him."[4] Although Kesey's general appearance remains pretty much the same, his antics appear to have gone the way of his hairline—toward maturation.

Kesey has been a public figure since **One Flew Over the Cuckoo's Nest** appeared in 1962, and every dimension of his life has received widespread attention, for he is an extraordinarily interesting person. If Kerouac seemed to be the spokesman for the curiously restive passiveness of the fifties, Kesey seemed to capture in his actions and reflections the frantic spirit of the sixties and seventies. For readers of such publications as *Rolling Stone* and *Crawdaddy*, for heads, revolutionaries, and English majors, Kesey has been the man capable of articulating the subtleties crammed

under the dated catch phrases "what's happening," "where we are coming from," and "where we are at." Kesey's position as former spokesman for a questlike youth movement resulted partially from personal charisma but more centrally from his attentive engagement with his life. Kesey keenly experiences his experience and constantly monitors his responses, recording his findings almost compulsively in journals, tapes, movies. His analyses and interpretations of this experience are serious and perceptive, and, like Whitman, he operates tacitly as representative man on the principle "what I assume you shall assume." But Kesey communicates less and less now as a spokesman or a guru and more and more as a serious writer. He still lives with his family on the farm with the white-starred barn in Pleasant Hill, Oregon, where he ranches on a small scale and is writing on a larger scale a manuscript called **The Demon Box**. "One of the reasons I think of it as a box," says Kesey, "is I keep putting more stuff into it and maybe shall for years to come. **Grandma Whittier** is part of it, as are all the other pieces that have appeared in **Spit in the Ocean.** Also, **Over the Border** in **Garage Sale.**"[5] The man with the vision has parked in the pasture the Merry Prankster bus marked "Further." Those who seek the Word from Kesey now must go to his books, and the man one finds there is a first-rate artist in the two novels and a creative spirit seeking new directions in the work in progress. . . .

Much has been made of the role drugs have played in the composition of Kesey's stories. Not nearly enough has been made of the role craftsmanship has played, the clear-headed conceiving and constructing of parts to create organic wholes.[6] Anyone who examines Kesey's working notes will discover that countless hours of careful thought went into the planning and revision of both novels.[7]

The notes range over all the elements of fiction. Always aware of his function as raconteur, Kesey assigns a high priority to story: "*The story—figure out later what it means*" (Strelow,p. 77). He labors over naming his characters to achieve an appropriate match between character and name. Thus "Ratched" evolves from "Birenshki" (as does "Bromden" in an ironic verbal spin-off), and "Drake" becomes "Draeger." He probes into character and motivation: "The human isn't some kind of complex instrument for receiving stimuli—it is a *will*, a *will*" (Strelow,p. 77). He worries about scope: "My book is trying maybe too goddamn much, trying to encompass a man, a family, a town, a country, a time—all at once, simultaneously, and work them into a story, and have the story say something important. Awful much, Awful much" (Strelow,p. 81). He lingers over leitmotifs and images, emphasizing creation as discovery: "I must keep the pen moving across the paper and just see where it comes, like firing at random to keep from falling asleep, like putting paint on a canvas and discovering—and *discovering* is the word—moving with each idea, each image, on into the next—so we create a feeling by connecting a series of images that in my mind gave me that feeling so we have the job of the lawn sprinkler" (Strelow,p. 82).

He exhorts himself to maintain control: "Decide on arrangement and order. Get the voices true. Shape up the conflicts. Begin to think of it as a whole" (Strelow,p. 81). He carefully cultivates individual styles for each character: "Hank's style—is Algren's style—read Algren to write Hank" (Strelow,p. 61). And working toward a narrative strategy, Kesey asks himself central questions about plot:

What about this: could I have 3 things going at once and have them occasionally interact like History, family meeting Lee driving out after Joe's Telegram. Click right there end of section?

Splicing? Quick glimpses of scenes to come. Quick images.

We're going along when a line triggers an image in the future. The image occurs some way. Finally the scene going and the scene sneaking in mesh and the scene sneaking in takes over. . . .

. . . Like background noise coming in over scene or background noise incongruous to *what is happening* at the moment before your eyes, but fitting with what is to happen.

(Strelow,p. 83)

Meticulously aligning each board and brick, Kesey constructs his sturdy house of fiction.

The eye of Kesey as master craftsman is most attentive to the requirements of point of view. "I'll discuss point of view for a time now," he once told Ken Babbs in a letter; "I am beginning to agree with Stegner, that it truely [sic] is the most important problem in writing."[8] Kesey goes on to explain that he hopes to adopt in **Cuckoo's Nest** some of the first-person diarist techniques of Trocchi and Burroughs, with the addition of an element missing in their work—control. His concern for point of view and control intensified in the writing of his second novel: "As I rewrite I'm trying for effect with arrangement and interwoven P.V., something to give the reader more than one eye, this is going to be tough enough. I should devote most of this time through to that" (Strelow, p. 45). All of the elements of fiction are integrated for Kesey in the controlled arrangement of point of view, and he has grown in his technique from the singular vision of Bromden to the multiple views of the township of Wakonda on the Wakonda Auga. *Wakonda* is a Sioux word meaning "a mysterious Other, a spirit or breath in the world, which is more real, more awful . . . and more reverenceable than the visible and obvious particulars of experience, while at the same time it may manifest or embody itself in persons, things, words and acts in unforeseeable ways."[9] Neither the singular nor the plural vision is simple. Both grow out of the demands of character and theme, and both lead to a mysterious Other, Kesey's imaginative world of fiction, where idea and image converge in truth.

Notes

1. Lucille Vaughan Payne, "Psychedelic Voice from a California Prison," *Old Oregon* 47:3 (November-December 1967):23-24.

2. Tom Wolfe, *The Electric Kool-Aid Acid Test* (New York: Bantam, 1968),p. 31.

3. George Bundy, "Ken Kesey: 10 Years After: 'Both a Lightning Rod and a Seismograph,'" *Oregon Daily Emerald,* 24 January 1973.

4. John Clark Pratt, "On Editing Kesey: Confessions of a Straight Man," in *Kesey,* ed. Michael Strelow (Eugene, Oregon: Northwest Review Books, 1977), pp. 8-11.

5. Letter received from Ken Kesey, October 1979.

6. A notable exception is Ronald G. Billingsley, in his dissertation "The Artistry of Ken Kesey," University of Oregon, 1971.

7. A substantial number of these working journals are now available in the Kesey archives of the University of Oregon Library's Special Collections (Martin Schmitt, curator). A sampling of these notes appears in the excellent collection edited by Michael Strelow (cited above), from which most of my examples are taken (page numbers hereafter cited in parentheses in the text).

8. "Letter to Ken Babbs: 'Peyote and Point of View,'" in *One Flew Over the Cuckoo's Nest: Text and Criticism,* ed. John C. Pratt (New York: The Viking Press, 1973), p. 338.

9. Philip Wheelwright, "Poetry, Myth, and Reality," in *Twentieth Century Criticism: The Major Statements,* eds. William J. Handy and Max Westbrook (New York: The Free Press, 1974),p. 256.

STEPHEN L. TANNER (ESSAY DATE 1983)

SOURCE: Tanner, Stephen L. "Influences and Achievement." In *Ken Kesey,* edited by Warren French, pp. 137-44. Boston: Twayne Publishers, 1983.

In the following essay, Tanner examines the influences behind Kesey's body of work and the milestones that Kesey has accomplished throughout his career.

Influences

Kesey's fiction displays a distinctive blending of American traditions. It is obviously an extension of the Beat movement; it reflects the concerns and attitudes of American Transcendentalism; it has the vernacular flavor of frontier humor and the oral tale tradition; and it manifests the themes and character types of the western. These elements are combined with a great admiration for Faulkner and a keen interest in popular culture from comic books to cowboy movies.

The Beats were by far the most important influence upon Kesey. He discovered them at the most impressionable stage in his development, and the discovery was crucial in determining the course of his life and writing. His letters and notes reveal that he was well acquainted with Beat literature before he wrote his novels, and he had observed the Beat life-style at North Beach while a student at Stanford. Neal Cassady was an important influence, at first as Dean Moriarty in *On the Road* and later as a close friend and companion in escapades that constituted a kind of sequel to Kerouac's novels. Some of those involved in the Prankster activities have mentioned that Cassady was the real energizing force in the group, even though Kesey had the role of nonnavigating guru. Michael Goodwin quotes Kesey as saying that Cassady had a lot to do with his losing interest in writing during the 1960s: "I saw that Cassady did everything a novel does, except he did it better 'cause he was livin' it and not writin' about it."[1]

There are numerous parallels between Kesey and the Beats that demonstrate a continuity of ideas, attitudes, and behavior. His relation to them can be described as a transition from disciple to successor. But this obvious continuity should not be allowed to obscure important differences. He possesses attitudes, values, and objectives fundamentally different from and conflicting with those of the Beats. Some of the differences result from his being from the country rather than the city and possessing strong ties to his family background and region. His basic optimism and faith in individual strength of character, originating in his rural western background, produce a basic mental and moral framework fundamentally different from that of the Beats.

This is clearly manifest in his approach to writing. Beat writers like Kerouac and Burroughs were primarily interested in reporting. Kesey has identified himself as a "parabolist" and not a reporter.[2] Reporting does not get at the kind of truth or knowledge he is interested in. He believes experience must be shaped by the intellect and imagination to a significant degree so that it suggests meaning the way a parable does. Moreover, he never adopted Kerouac's notion of "Spontaneous Prose," a notion that considered revision unnecessary and even debilitating. Malcolm Cowley, who was Kesey's teacher and editor, says of him, "He had his visions, but he didn't have the fatal notion of some Beat writers, that the first hasty account of a vision was a sacred text not to be tampered with. He revised, he made deletions and additions; he was working with readers in mind."[3]

The influence of the Beats contributed to a tension within Kesey. It is part of the Oregon-California polarity in his career. He shared their desire for liberation and their thirst for altered states of consciousness and was tempted by their go-with-the-flow philosophy, but his Baptist and rural western backgrounds have pulled him in another direction.

The parallels between Kesey and American Transcendentalism were treated in Chapter 4, but a few more observations are necessary. These parallels can be accounted for partly by his possessing a temperament or spiritual-intellectual predisposition similar to that of the Transcendentalists. Such people are born every generation. But he was also influenced by the writings of Transcendentalism and particularly by the way those writings were assimilated by the Beats. Whitman glorified the common and spiritualized the flesh; he introduced the notion that the mystical or transcendental experience can be achieved by immersion in sensuous experience rather than by escape from it; and he expressed tolerance for the vulgar and criminal. The Beats took these cues and, lacking the nineteenth-century moral and religious assumptions that underlay even Whitman's pronouncements, carried to extremes the notion that self-fulfillment comes from going with the flow and indulging sensuous appetites and instincts. Kesey's transcendentalism in his psychedelic experimenting was primarily of this go-with-the-flow variety. His novels, however, display more of Thoreau's activist self-reliance—controlling the flow or escaping from it.

The fact is there is a certain confusion within his transcendentalism, a tension corresponding to the Oregon-California polarity in his personality. This confusion originates in the concept of going with the flow. Emerson spoke of "the currents of the Universal Being" flowing through him during the transcendental experience. Thoreau also frequently used such current motions as a fundamental metaphor for the vital spiritual element in the universe. To put oneself in harmony with the flow these men envisioned is to magnify one's higher self and experience divine inspiration. It requires intelligent effort and discipline and is quite a different thing from simply submitting oneself to the flux of experience and giving in to instinct, impulse, and appetite. The Beats generally blurred this distinction, and Kesey, under their influence, was victim of the same confusion. But another part of him—the part deriving from his conservative rural and Baptist background—remained slightly suspicious of the flow, hence the resistance to flow in *Great Notion* and his concern with the lost tiller in evaluating his drug experience.

The pattern of migration of Kesey's ancestors corresponds with the westward movement of the tradition of Southwest humor and frontier oral tales. Both began in the middle southern states and moved into Texas, Oklahoma, through Colorado, and into the Northwest. Kesey's artistic disposition derives to a large extent from this tradition. He was born into it. From his early years he listened to members of his family tell stories rich in colorful expressions, earthy and vivid similes, and comic exaggeration. And in addition to acquiring skill in vernacular storytelling by the unconscious process of growing up amid accomplished yarn spinners, he has taken a conscious interest in such folk traditions as those of the confidence man (often noted for his ribald and off-color remarks); the vernacular hero besting the educated city slicker; the preoccupation with physical strength; employing such stylistic techniques as the use of exaggeration, comic similes, dialect, practical jokes, comic juxtapositions and incongruities; the identification of men with various animals; comic treatment of violence, pain, and danger; and common-sense observations on civilized conventions. All these elements of the frontier and rural traditions of storytelling function significantly in Kesey's fiction.

Blended with them are elements of the western. Kesey frequently alludes to typical western heroes (the Lone Ranger, the Marlboro Man, John Wayne, etc.) and to typical patterns or situations in westerns (conflicts between cattlemen and sheepmen, ranchers and sodbusters; showdowns and shootouts; the fast-draw gunslinger who constantly must confirm his reputation, etc.). But the western influence reflected in his novels goes much deeper than playful allusions to stereotypic characters and situations. It is manifest in the core values expressed in the novels: the preference for the natural over the civilized; the desire for freedom and independence; the importance of self-sufficient strength and a corresponding disregard of civilized conventions; the style of facing danger, injury, and death with taciturn nonchalance or understatement; the approach of helping others by maintaining one's own strength and integrity rather than relying on collective action; and the recognition that a certain amount of violence or physical conflict is inevitable for the man committed to independence and self-reliant action. Because these values do not always correspond with those of the counterculture, readers who identify Kesey primarily with psychedelic drugs and youthcult are startled when they encounter these essentially conservative values in the novels, particularly in *Great Notion*.

It is these values that largely make up the Oregon side of Kesey's personality and pull against the California side. And it is the tension between the two that accounts for the distinctive quality of his career, in which nineteenth-century rural western attitudes and values are blended with those of twentieth-century urban radicalism. The blending has not been entirely comfortable or fortunate.

Achievement

Kesey's notoriety as psychedelic prophet and hippie culture hero is dissipating, even though Tom Wolfe's fascinating book continues to be read. But *Cuckoo's Nest* and *Great Notion* will probably provide a more lasting reputation for him. What are the characteristics of his achievement that might insure continued reading of his fiction?

First of all, he provides a fresh and original expression of cherished American traditions and values. Americans perhaps have never been as individualistic, self-reliant, and in tune with nature as our myths and traditions make us out to be; but we certainly praise those qualities in our rhetoric. They bolster our pride and sense of identity. We would consider ourselves much poorer without types like Randle McMurphy, Hank Stamper, and Grandma Whittier. Kesey's themes and characters resonate in that part of us that admires the strengths of the western experience, as coarse and antisocial as they sometimes were. Kesey not only embodies in his fiction the ideals of the western myths and traditions, he is at his best when writing in their vernacular and anecdotal idiom.

His humor is a second important strength. It is seldom contrived or strained, but grows naturally out of the situations and idioms of his characters. And most importantly, it is rarely there simply for its own sake; it usually functions to further a serious artistic purpose. It is not the humor of detached wit, but originates in a tolerant delight in human foibles and a recognition that laughter is the best counterweight for pain and narrow sobriety.

A third strength is the intelligence that shapes and controls Kesey's fiction; and, as has already been noted, idea is adequately balanced with imagination so that the characters and events are not obtrusively theme-ridden. Kesey has a remarkable gift for perceiving lessons from experience, morals in simple events. He employs this gift in making his narrative reverberate with meaning. It is a preacher's gift, and it is not surprising that when asked once what he might have been had he lived in another time and without the option of being a writer, he answered, "I'd have been a preacher."[4] It is this gift Kesey probably has in mind when he refers to himself as a "parabolist" rather than a reporter.

A fourth distinctive achievement is Kesey's forceful distinction between the rational and the human. The strictly rational view does not allow for spontaneity and the uniqueness of individuals, and it denies the mystery of human personality. It is the mysterious spiritual component within persons that is the source of real freedom, creativity, and moral character. The Big Nurses and Jonathan Draegers of the world are enemies to the distinctively human aspects of men and women. Kesey is incorrigibly romantic in his insistence upon man's capacity to transcend rational explanations and limitations of his nature.

Kesey's technical inventiveness constitutes a fifth significant achievement. His manipulation of point of view and experimentation with narrative technique are notable accomplishments, combining a perceptive understanding of previous advancements in technique with original invention. His adaptations of cinematic techniques and his use of popular culture for serious purposes are additional accomplishments significant in originality.

A sixth strength is Kesey's honesty and self-criticism. Even his most sympathetic characters are shown with unattractive traits. McMurphy is criminal and psychotic as well as heroic. Hank is coarse and bigoted as well as admirably strong. Grandma Whittier, with all her compassion and common sense, can still be foolish at times. Perhaps this balance contributes to their being such vivid and memorable personalities. And when Kesey writes about himself, he does so with remarkable candor. *Over the Border* is penetrating self-criticism, and the attempt to justify his psychedelic activities during the 1960s in "**The Day After Superman Died**" does not ignore the negative consequences of that revolution.

Despite these achievements, there are disturbing qualities in Kesey's career. Perhaps more was lost than gained by his California experience. His return to Oregon suggests such a realization on his part. The drug experiments and the attempt to go beyond writing seem to have been misguided. At the height of his literary creation, they distracted him and dissipated his creative energies. The legal entanglements were unsettling and created debilitating anger and bitterness. It is useless to speculate concerning what direction his career might have taken had he stuck diligently to writing, but even the thought of such speculation is saddening. Some believe Kesey burned himself out and expect to see him produce no more significant fiction. The fact that it is now nearly two decades since *Great Notion* was published gives weight to this opinion. But Kesey scarcely seems burned out. Part of the reason for his lack of literary productivity is that he has many interests. There is a strong element of the promoter in him, and he is fascinated with spectacle and performance. A number of projects of various kinds have occupied his attention and distracted him from writing novels. But, again, it was his California escapades that nurtured him as a promoter.

One of the disturbing aspects of Kesey's personality is that his obvious intelligence is combined with an indiscriminate credulity, an overly tolerant curiosity about anything that promises new awareness or communication with another realm of consciousness. In this he is representative of his age and particularly of the youth revolution in California. The 1960s and 1970s produced a renaissance of credulity. Intellectual respectability was granted to belief in witchcraft, flying saucers, reincarnation, tarot cards, pyramid power, transcendental meditation, parapsychology, etc. This eagerness to believe was probably a reaction to the spiritual aridity of modern technological society, orthodox religion—the traditional focus for spiritual yearning—having been discredited in the eyes of many searchers. Kesey's curiosity about any avenue offering the prospect of new awareness has entangled him in a good deal of nonsense and diffused his creative energies.

Perhaps the attitude that had the most unfortunate consequences for his literary career was the go-with-the-flow notion, inherited largely from the Beats. In fact, the Beat influence in general was a less than fortunate one for Kesey, because at the same time it stimulated him, it drew him away from some of his strengths and roots. Going with the flow can produce a temporary exhilaration, but it leads away from the self-disciplined effort required for producing significant literature. *One Flew Over the Cuckoo's Nest* and *Sometimes a Great Notion* were not produced by going with the flow. In addition to hampering serious literary effort, the go-with-the-flow attitude has contributed to the gratuitous obscenity in some of Kesey's writing and his tendency to equate uninhibited sensual expression in language and behavior with spiritual liberation.

In view of the achievement of *Cuckoo's Nest* and *Great Notion* and the long novelistic quiet that followed them, it is difficult not to feel that Kesey took some wrong turns in his career, that promise went unfulfilled and talent was diverted from its proper course. But judging the way a man makes use of his creative gifts is as hazardous as it is easy. Regardless of what Kesey writers or fails to write in the future, he merits respect and recognition for two remarkable novels; and those who admire these novels and desire more can take heart from the stories and novel in progress that have appeared in recent years.

When asked why he has not written more novels in recent years, Kesey explains that his family has occupied most of his attention. Rearing his children is for him a greater concern than writing. He compares the writing process to juggling—keeping many balls in the air at the same time. This requires extreme concentration. When a child comes in with a bloody nose or other problem that must be attended to, the balls fall to the ground and bounce off in every direction, and it is not easy to gather them up and get them in the air again. But now that his children have reached an age of greater self-suffience, he intends to do more writing. Presently he is planning a novel dealing with fishing in Alaska.

Notes

1. Michael Goodwin, "The Ken Kesey Movie," *Rolling Stone,* 7 March 1970,p. 33.

2. Lish, "What the Hell,"p. 20.

3. *Kesey,*p. 3.

4. Letter from Peter S. Beagle to E. D. Webber, 17 May 1971, in Webber, "Keepin' on the Bounce,"p. 142.

FURTHER READING

Bibliographies

Bischoff, Joan. "Views and Reviews: An Annotated Bibliography." *Lex et Scientia* 13, nos. 1 and 2 (January-June 1977): 93-103

Bibliography of important early essays on One Flew Over the Cuckoo's Nest.

Frank, Robert. "Ken Kesey." In *Fifty Western Writers: A Bio-Bibliographical Sourcebook,* edited by Fred Erisman and Richard Etulain, pp. 246-56. Westport, Conn.: Greenwood Press, 1982.

Annotated bibliography of primary and secondary sources; includes a brief overview of Kesey's life and literary career and a discussion of the principal themes and critical reception of his major works.

Weixlmann, Joseph. "Ken Kesey: A Bibliography." *Western American Literature* 10 (November 1975): 219-31.

Provides a comprehensive bibliography of critical material on One Flew Over the Cuckoo's Nest, Sometimes a Great Notion, *and Kesey's Garage Sale.*

Biographies

Carnes, Bruce. *Ken Kesey.* Boise State University Western Writers Series, Vol. 12. Boise, Idaho: Boise State University, 1974, 50p.

Biographical and critical study that views Kesey as working in the tradition of cowboy and frontier-hero literature.

Faggen, Robert. "Ken Kesey: The Art of Fiction CXXVI." *Paris Review* 36, no. 130 (spring 1994): 58-94.

Provides a transcript of an interview in which Kesey discusses his major literary influences, his views concerning the relationship between drugs and creativity, and the genesis of Sailor Song.

Krassner, Paul. "An Impolite Interview with Ken Kesey." *The Realist* 90 (May-June 1971): 1, 46-53.

Free-wheeling interview that includes discussion on the relationship between freedom and insanity, Kesey's assessments of Jack Kerouac and Neal Cassady, his opinions about the relationships between drugs and faith, and his attitudes toward various psychiatric treatment methods.

Wolfe, Tom. *The Electric Kool-Aid Acid Test.* New York: Farrar, Straus and Giroux, 1968, 372p.

Account of Kesey's early life and his later escapades with psychedelic drugs.

Criticism

Barsness, John A. "Ken Kesey: The Hero in Modern Dress." *Bulletin of the Rocky Mountain Modern Language Association* 23, no. 1 (1969): 27-33.

Shows how Kesey's protagonists embody the Western myth of the rough-hewn hero.

Baurecht, William C. "Separation, Initiation, and Return: Schizophrenic Episode in *One Flew Over the Cuckoo's Nest.*" *Midwest Quarterly* 23, no. 3 (spring 1982): 279-93.

Focuses on the character of Chief Bromden in One Flew Over the Cuckoo's Nest.

Benert, Annette. "The Forces of Fear: Kesey's Anatomy of Insanity." *Lex et Scientia* 13, nos. 1-2 (January-June 1977): 22-6.

Analyzes One Flew Over the Cuckoo's Nest, *exploring the connections to fear of woman, fear of the machine, and glorification of the hero.*

Blessing, Richard. "The Moving Target: Ken Kesey's Evolving Hero." *Journal of Popular Culture* 4, no. 3 (winter 1971): 615-27.

Views the character of McMurphy as a hero who embodies various archetypes, from fertility deity to Christ figure.

Boardman, Michael. "*One Flew Over the Cuckoo's Nest*: Rhetoric and Vision." *Journal of Narrative Technique* 9 (1979): 171-83.

Views One Flew Over the Cuckoo's Nest *as essentially tragic, centering upon McMurphy's external struggle with Big Nurse and his internal struggle of deciding whether to escape the mental institution or become a sacrificial victim. Boardman's discussion reveals the difficulties Kesey faced when he tried to adapt classical tragedy to the modern age.*

Boyers, Robert. "Porno-Politics." *Annals of the American Academy of Political and Social Sciences,* no. 376 (March 1968): 36-52

Examines the novel's attitudes towards sex and the linkages between sexuality and laughter.

Chidley, Joe. "A War for the Future." *Maclean's* (7 September 1992): 50.

Defines the various elements of Sailor Song *as a drama of a devastated world; a satire aimed at the American film industry, land development, and small town life; and a love story.*

Crotty, Mark. "The Mixed Heritage of the Chief: Revisiting the Problem of Manhood in *One Flew Over the Cuckoo's Nest.*" *Journal of Popular Culture* 29, no. 3 (winter 1995): 225-35.

Explores Chief Bromden's "search for the father" in a matriarchal system, a quest that is complicated by his mixed heritage.

Forrey, Robert. "Ken Kesey's Psychopathic Savior: A Rejoinder." *Modern Fiction Studies* 21, no. 2 (summer 1975): 222-30.

Forrey objects to critic Terence Martin's praise for One Flew Over the Cuckoo's Nest, *and instead views the novel as conservative, sexist, lowbrow, and a throwback to the macho themes and Christian symbolism of Ernest Hemingway and John Steinbeck.*

Foster, John Wilson. "Hustling to Some Purpose: Ken Kesey's *One Flew Over the Cuckoo's Nest.*" *Western American Literature* 9, no. 2 (summer 1974): 115-29.

Likens both Kesey and his protagonist McMurphy to poolroom hustlers and argues that the basic theme of One Flew Over the Cuckoo's Nest *is the spiritual versus the secular.*

Francis, William A. "Of Madness and Machines: Names in Ken Kesey's *One Flew Over the Cuckoo's Nest.*" *Literary Onomastics* 16 (1989): 55-8.

Explores the significance of the names Randle Patrick McMurphy and Nurse Ratched as they contribute to the novel's theme.

Gaboriau, Linda. "Ken Kesey: Summing Up the 60's; Sizing Up the 70's." *Crawdaddy* 19 (December 1972): 31-9.

Interview with Kesey in which he talks about his experiences with drugs as well as his early career.

Goluboff, Benjamin. "The Carnival Artist in the Cuckoo's Nest." *Northwest Review* 29, no. 3 (1991): 109-22.

Maintains that Kesey's novel illustrates Russian formalist critic Mikhail Bakhtin's theory of the carnivalesque.

Horst, Leslie. "Bitches, Twitches, and Eunuchs: Sex-Role Failure and Caricature." *Lex et Scientia* 13, nos. 1-2 (January-June 1977): 14-17.

Dissects the novel's narrow portrayals of sex roles, both masculine and feminine.

Knapp, James F. "Tangled in the Language of the Past: Ken Kesey and the Cultural Revolution." *The Midwest Quarterly* 19, no. 4 (summer 1978): 398-412.

Views Kesey as an "anti-establishment" writer whose art and life encouraged social change.

Lish, Gordon. "What the Hell You Looking in Here For, Daisy Mae? An Interview with Ken Kesey." *Genesis West* 2, no. 5 (1963): 17-29.

Interview with Kesey in which he discusses his attitudes and objectives as a writer.

Malin, Irving. "Ken Kesey: 'One Flew Over the Cuckoo's Nest.'" *Critique* 5, no. 2 (1962): 81-4.

Situates the novel in the mode of the New American Gothic, which "gives us violent juxtapositions, distorted vision, even prophecy."

Nastu, Paul. "Kesey's *One Flew Over the Cuckoo's Nest.*" *The Explicator* 56, no. 1 (fall 1997): 48-50.

Notes the thematic and visual elements that the novel borrows from animated cartoons.

Pearson, Carol. "The Cowboy Saint and the Indian Poet: The Comic Hero in Ken Kesey's '*One Flew Over the Cuckoo's Nest.*'" *Studies in American Humor* 1, no. 2 (October 1974): 91-8.

Employs the myth of the king, the hero, and the fool to gain an understanding of the novel.

Porter, M. Gilbert. *The Art of Grit: Ken Kesey's Fiction.* Columbia: University of Missouri Press, 1982, 102p.

Includes analysis of One Flew Over the Cuckoo's Nest, Sometimes a Great Notion, *and* Demon Box.

Safer, Elaine B. "The Absurd Quest and Black Humor in Ken Kesey's *Sometimes a Great Notion.*" *Critique* 24, no. 4 (summer 1983): 228-40.

Examines the absurdist vision and black humor tone in Sometimes a Great Notion.

Scally, Thomas. "Origin and Authority: An Analysis of the Relation Between Anonymity and Authorship in Ken Kesey's *One Flew Over the Cuckoo's Nest.*" *Dalhousie Review* 62, no. 3 (autumn 1982): 355-73.

Discusses issues of factuality and truth in One Flew Over the Cuckoo's Nest.

Searles, George J., editor. *A Casebook on Ken Kesey's* One Flew Over the Cuckoo's Nest. Albuquerque: University of New Mexico Press, 1992, 203p.

Reprints thirteen of the most important critical essays written on One Flew Over the Cuckoo's Nest; *includes an extensive annotated bibliography.*

Sherman, W. D. "The Novels of Ken Kesey." *Journal of American Studies* 5, no. 2 (August 1971): 185-96

Claims that Kesey's novels suggest that the path to psychic liberation lies in the psychedelic experience and a willingness to transcend the ego.

Sherwood, Terry G. "'One Flew Over the Cuckoo's Nest' and the Comic Strip." *Critique* 13, no. 1 (1971): 96-109.

Assesses the role of comic books and comic book figures in the novel.

Sullivan, Ruth. "Big Mama, Big Papa, and Little Sons in Ken Kesey's *One Flew Over the Cuckoo's Nest.*" *Literature and Psychology* 25, no. 1 (1975): 34-44.

Examines the psychological conflicts in One Flew Over the Cuckoo's Nest *between McMurphy, Nurse Ratched, and the other inmates of the mental institution.*

Tanner, Stephen L. "Labor Union Versus Frontier Values in Kesey's *Sometimes a Great Notion.*" *Rendezvous* 19, no. 1 (fall 1983): 16-21.

Sees Sometimes a Great Notion *as a remarkable achievement in narrative technique and examines its portrayal of the evolving relationship between frontier values and labor unions in the American West.*

Waldmeir, Joseph J. "Two Novels of the Absurd: Heller and Kesey." *Wisconsin Studies in Contemporary Literature* 5, no. 3 (1964): 192-204.

Argues the Kesey's novel is a better example of the use of the absurd than Heller's Catch-22.

Wallis, Bruce E. "Christ in the Cuckoo's Nest: Or, the Gospel according to Ken Kesey." *Cithara* 12 (1972): 52-8.

Traces the analogy Kesey draws between McMurphy and Christ in One Flew Over the Cuckoo's Nest, *concluding that Kesey's text contains a serious inversion of Christian values, for McMurphy chooses self-assertion rather than salvation through humility.*

Zashin, Elliot M. "Political Theorist and Demiurge: The Rise and Fall of Ken Kesey." *The Centennial Review* 17, no. 2 (spring 1973): 199-213.

Contends that Kesey failed to articulate an enduring political vision in his fiction.

Zubizarreta, John. "The Disparity of Point of View in *One Flew Over the Cuckoo's Nest.*" *Film Literature Quarterly* 22, no. 1 (1994): 62-9.

Examines the relationship of text to film in Kesey's novel and the film adaptation of One Flew Over the Cuckoo's Nest.

OTHER SOURCES FROM GALE:

Additional coverage of Kesey's life and career is contained in the following sources published by the Gale Group: *Authors and Artists for Young Adults,* Vol. 25; *Beacham's Encyclopedia of Popular Fiction: Biography & Resources,* Vol. 2; *Concise Dictionary of American Literary Biography, 1968-1988; Contemporary Authors,* Vols. 1-4R; *Contemporary Authors New Revision Series,* Vols. 22, 38, 66; *Contemporary Literary Criticism,* Vols. 1, 3, 6, 11, 46, 64; *Contemporary Novelists,* Ed. 7; *Contemporary Popular Writers; Dictionary of Literary Biography,* Vols. 2, 16, 206; *DISCovering Authors; DISCovering Authors: British Edition; DISCovering Authors: Canadian Edition; DISCovering Authors Modules: Most-studied Authors, Novelists,* and *Popular Fiction and Genre Authors; DISCovering Authors 3.0; Exploring Novels; Literature and Its Times,* Vol. 4; *Literature Resource Center; Major 20th-Century Writers,* Eds. 1, 2; *Novels for Students,* Vol. 2; *Reference Guide to American Literature,* Ed. 4; *Something about the Author,* Vol. 66; *St. James Guide to Young Adult Writers; Twayne's United States Authors;* and *World Literature Criticism.*

JOANNE KYGER

(1934 -)

(Full name Joanne Elizabeth Kyger) American poet and travel writer.

Kyger was an important figure in San Francisco poetry circles in the late 1950s. However, like many women writers of the Beat Generation, she was as well known for her association with such leading male poets as Jack Spicer and Robert Duncan as she was for her own work. Her 1965 collection *The Tapestry and the Web* includes poems written during her time with Spicer and Duncan, and *The Japan and India Journals, 1960-1964* (1981) chronicles the years she spent in Japan while married to the poet Gary Snyder and the couple's travels to India with Allen Ginsberg and Peter Orlovsky. Kyger continued to write after the end of the Beat era, and she is a respected figure of the Language Poetry school. Kyger is a Buddhist, and her poetry displays a strong interest in Zen and Native American mythology.

BIOGRAPHICAL INFORMATION

Joanne Kyger was born in 1934 in Vallejo, California. Her father was a naval officer, and their family lived in China and in various cities across the United States before settling in Santa Barbara when Kyger was fourteen. Kyger began writing poetry at an early age; her first publication was at age five, by her elementary school. When she attended the University of California at Santa Barbara, she was introduced to the modernist poets, whose work influenced her own. Kyger left college one credit short of a degree and moved to San Francisco. She arrived at the height of the *Howl* obscenity trial. A friend introduced her to The Place, the bar that served as headquarters for Spicer and other poets of the San Francisco Renaissance. In 1958 Kyger met poet Gary Snyder while studying Zen Buddhism, and in 1960 they traveled together to Japan, where they married. In 1964 Kyger moved back to San Francisco, divorced Snyder, and published her first book of poems, *The Tapestry and the Web*. She traveled in Europe with Jack Boyce, who she married in 1968, and lived in New York briefly before returning to California. She and Boyce moved to the small town of Bolinas in 1969, where Kyger has lived ever since. She continues to write poetry and teaches occasionally at the Jack Kerouac School of Disembodied Poetics at the Naropa Institute in Boulder, Colorado.

MAJOR WORKS

Kyger's first published collection, *The Tapestry and the Web,* appeared in 1965, but she had been writing seriously since the late 1950s when she was involved with other poets of the San Francisco Renaissance. She attended the Sunday Meetings led by Spicer and Duncan, and gave her first reading at the Bread and Wine Mission in 1959. *The Tapestry and the Web,* which included much of her work from the 1950s, was published with the support of Donald Allen, who helped many Beat writers get their work into print. *Tapestry* is influenced heavily by William Carlos Williams's *Paterson* as well as Homer's *Odyssey*. In 1965 Kyger was presented at the Berkeley Poetry Conference with Ginsberg, Lew Welch, Ed Sanders, and other noted Beat poets. Kyger's early works and *The Japan and India Journals, 1960-1964* are considered by many to be important documents of the Beat era, as they offer a uniquely female perspective on the time.

Kyger has continued to write and publish prolifically. Her poetry largely deals with themes of Zen Buddhism, the relationship of the individual psyche to the sociopolitical world, love and marriage, art, philosophy, and travel. Her interest in the recounting of everyday activities and observations of the world mark her as a Language poet, though the 1960s counterculture remains a continuing influence in her work.

CRITICAL RECEPTION

Since the 1970s Kyger has been a respected poet whose work has been appreciated by a small audience and often praised by critics for its sense of immediacy and spontaneity. Her work has received scant recognition from academic critics, but she continues to enjoy readership among those interested in Zen Buddhist themes, the Beat Generation, Native American mythology, and travel. Critics have noted that Kyger does not fit neatly into any one category or literary movement. Both Alice Notley and Stephen Vincent connect her to the Black Mountain Poets and to the New York School, in addition to the more apparent associations with the Beats, the San Francisco Renaissance, and the Language Movement. Brenda Knight writes that Kyger's "poems are often snapshots of the realities of daily life" and deems them "exemplary of Buddhist consciousness in Beat writing." Vincent praises Kyger's poetry as distinguished by a distinctive line, a sense of pitch and a content whose implicit form seduces eye and ear into a robust, most often illuminated, ecstatic space." Kirby Olson explores the reasons that Kyger's poetry has not been accepted into the literary canon, asserting that her Zen-focused poetry does not conform to the ideal of "progressive dialectical materialism" empha-

sized by universities. Anne Waldman characterizes *The Japan and India Journals, 1960-1964* as "a minor classic."

PRINCIPAL WORKS

The Tapestry and the Web (poetry) 1965

Places to Go (poetry) 1970

Desecheo Notebook (poetry) 1971

Trip Out and Fall Back (poetry) 1974

All This Every Day (poetry) 1975

The Wonderful Focus of You (poetry) 1980

*The Japan and India Journals, 1960-1964 (poetry and travel writing) 1981

Mexico Blonde (poetry) 1981

Up My Coast (poetry) 1981

Going On: Selected Poems 1958-80 (poetry) 1983

The Dharma Committee (poetry) 1986

Phenomenological: A Curriculum of the Soul (poetry) 1989

The Book for Sensi: Poems (poetry) 1990

Just Space: Poems 1979-1989 (poetry) 1991

Some Sketches from the Life of Helena Petrovna Blavatsky (poetry) 1996

Patzcuaro (poetry) 1999

Some Life (poetry) 2000

The Scent of Water: New and Selected Poems (poetry) 2001

As Ever: Selected Poems (poetry) 2002

* Published in 2000 under the title *Strange Big Moon: The Japan and India Journals, 1960-1964.*

GENERAL COMMENTARY

ALICE NOTLEY (ESSAY DATE 1996)

SOURCE: Notley, Alice. "Joanne Kyger's Poetry." *Arshile* 5 (1996): 95-110.

In the following essay, Notley offers her personal reactions to Kyger's poetry from the 1960s to the 1980s, viewing Kyger's work as a living poetry that has not received the notice it deserves.

I first heard Joanne Kyger read her poetry in December of 1969 at somebody's house in Bolinas; it was the first contact I'd had with her poetry

(I'd heard she was very "fast"), so I've never known her words apart from her voice. But I can't imagine any reader not hearing it: that her poetry is vocally sculpted is its most overwhelming characteristic. I mean that not all poetries are. There are some in which letters and words stand firm and dare the voice to make them give in: this is a nice masculine way to write; or there are uniquely-voiced poets who pronounce/choose each word so carefully that one hears the voice of a playful but domineering general (Stein comes to mind), organizing the words into formation. In Kyger's poems the voice bends the words, but Voice is not a pseudonym for Emotion or Character, Voice is very close to being Voice. Here is a short light poem I remember her reading in that living room in 1969:

> Thursday, 13 November
>
> Unified School District.
> I'm still going to school.
>
> Learning how
> to be personal   in the most elevated
> State of the Union
> (from *All This Every Day*, 1975)

The words don't separate. You have to attend to what is being said, you have to attend to a vocal movement which corresponds to a mental movement; the voice has charm, but though it says "I" intimately it isn't calling attention to a person. I also remember her reading the untitled short poem which ends with the statement, "Whereas the real state is called golden / where things are exactly what they are." The "Most Elevated State of the Union" and the "golden" state may have been California, where we were; I remember we laughed, there were a lot of jokes about "states" at the time. However, these poems point to Kyger's major preoccupation, the attainment in quotidian life of that state where things and one are unveiled. If you think about it for a moment you realize her voice is the voice of that "search" or "state": not vatic not academic not showing-off, it is ordinary or actual life finding itself, which shouldn't be boring, and in her poems never is.

Kyger's work from the early 60s, collected in *The Tapestry and The Web* (Four Seasons Foundation, 1965) and *Places to Go* (Black Sparrow, 1970), is imbued with Greek myth and classical illusions and has a rather darker feel to it than her work from the late 60s on, a progress that's the opposite of the usual one. Her early work is haunted by a problem of husbands and fathers, is rich but suggestive of revulsion, as well as being already casual, pliantly turned, and funny. Here are several lines from **"The Pigs for Circe in May"**, in *Places to Go*:

> I like Pigs. Cute feet, cute nose, and I think
>
> some spiritual value investing them. A man and
>   his pig together, rebalancing the pure in
>   them, under each others arms, bathing, eat-
>   ing it.

There's a girlish laughter and syntactical elegance and trickery, a mixed diction for a mixed experience, but another (untitled) poem from the same book is less patronizingly amused at being patronized by the established men in life and literature:

> They rise
> taking their way, the struggle of heads, walking
> strong and oblivious, with pomp and rich robes
>   saying
> we are the minds of the country.

Kyger's work in subsequent books, though it most certainly contains lovers, subsists more in a broad air of friendship and community; classical allusions give way to allusions from Native American myths, as well as from Asian religions. Her poetry continues an involvement with narrative; the way her voice bends words is a clue to an involvement with telling as well as thinking. She has a propensity for recounting stories in poetry, particularly recasting stories found in the course of reading prose. As she'd learned to use, really rather than tell, the story of Penelope and other Odyssean characters in her first two books, she now learns to tell, more straightforwardly, a Coast Miwok story or the life of the Indian religious figure, Naropa. But one has a sense in all of her subsequent poetry of a wide golden light, which doesn't deny suffering but does contain it with consistency. Kyger's poetry is spiritual, natural, and transparent, full of that light.

What are the techniques for this light which is allowed in by a voice? The "I" of these poems rarely makes a character of itself, it presents its time or matter as what is seen, enacted, reflected upon, in unity.

> When I step through the door
> everything has changed. Finally,
>   it is out the door
> past homes, down the trail
>   the lovely beach
>   draws me into her drawing. Finally
>
> I am past the fear of life's paucity.
> Green Angels, stream, in hot California
> and in the stillness seeds popping.
> (untitled, from *All This Every Day*)

. . . In *Just Space* she has evolved a form of poem that contains more of name and event than before, but is also more subtle and compact and quick in meaning than before. *Just Space* is not presented as sequence except chronologically but it is very much a book as well as a collection. It isn't laid out like a journal, but it's shaped as any journal is by the story time makes in a life, with people passing through, dying, being recalled, the seasons passing, wisdom being acquired and sometimes lost: all of that is a natural narrative. Any small town like Bolinas, where Kyger has continued to live since the 60s, as well mirrors the nation, so to keep track of one is to keep track of both. But notice how the book begins:

> You believe this stash of writing is "scholarly"?
> Out of this we deduce . . .
> From this we can see that . . .
>
> I know it's a detective story of passions,
> dinners, blood stuff around which the history of
>   our lives
> crank.

The margin must not be flush left or there is no movement, as in the walking and thinking in this voice. "When I step through the door / everything has changed," but there would be no change if "everything" weren't a little to the left of "when." And so on down the poem, to, for example, the unexpectedness of a verb after "beach," as "draws me into her drawing" makes waves slide down over sand. "I am past the fear of life's paucity" has been a peculiarly memorable lines for me—"paucity" has the exact sound of its meaning here, an inspired choice enhanced by being paired with "popping." the two words surround "Green Angels," letting the phrase stain them—for the reader a visionary experience.

Another poem from *All This Every Day,* again untitled as the majority of the poems are with their "just-materialized" aura, demonstrates the sinuosity of her sentences, the unexpectedness of their development, and their considerable precision. The poet speaks of the lighting incense before an image of Kannon San, describes the image a bit, then says

>   I have read
> about her but can't remember
> it is really important
>
> for how she affects me
> as a dark little statue
> I make an intelligent
> pass at, when I bow
> I mean I am hopeful
> she evens off the demons.

There is consistent surprise from line to lines, but it isn't just a trick, it effects a release of passion, something that must be said that contains a negative burden in conjunction with a hopeful activity. For the poem becomes a put-down of "Holy Mary" and also a statement of despair, terminating in a long period of punctuated sentences:

> On Holy Mary
> you'll just say
> I'm not a good enough
> Christian
> to go to heaven &
> you look so sad
> You are merely human
> and wafted above us
> the Queen of a big
> church who staked out
> the real estate
> But then again what do I know
> of my heart but that it is tight
> and wishes to burst
> past the wall of my chest
>
> I am depressed, darling
> the power of belief
> is from me

The reader is still being surprised, but the feeling that has been released by the technique of surprise is now much stronger than the technique; the precision of "church who staked out / the real estate" is idiomatically cutting—a stabbing pair with "evens off the demons." The reality of the feeling here is obvious; Kyger always tells the truth.

An important poetry experience for me was hearing Kyger read the title sequence from *The Wonderful Focus of You* at St. Mark's Church in the late 70s. This event was held in the main sanctuary where one's voice echoed and traveled under eaves, and where a reader could look either preacherly or alone, standing near the pulpit. Kyger looked very solitary, performing poems about the lone self facing time and being cured of hurt and fear in time's process; she seemed alone with her voice, which as is characteristic with her, made unexpected turns and changes of both tone and pace rather than observing a consistent mood or metric. This reading seemed, and still seems to me, as deeply serious as a reading can be—which point I make to aver that it's not the bombastic or declamatory, or abstract or otherwise difficult, voice which presses deeply, it's the one committed to the truth. The truth tends to be something faced, rather than owned or explored: it doesn't always like you either, even when it can still be joked with and hung out with. A quiet voice is better then (in that circumstance), though quiet doesn't mean that quiet. Kyger has a lively, even extraordinarily quick mind-in-voice. It can shout too, even in this sequence, though not in order to dominate.

At the beginning of this sequence of dated diary-like entries we are presented with ideas of continuity and change as entries we are presented with ideas of continuity and change as in the natural realm of plants with their seeds and cycles; in contrast the Human seems spiritually inelegant, desperate, shut out:

> Shabby Lady
>   You mixing up my time
> and changes of who I am and it's all
>
>   in the teeny trembling world
>   ("February 15")

Kyger, I the poet, announces in **"March 2"** "The awful emptiness of you / who won't let me come to your heart." In this instance "you" may be Green Tara (Tibetan goddess of compassion—green as in the fertile world?) ore the you in the poet's literal dreams" in other poems You, becoming "The Wonderful Focus of You," is "the Lord," perhaps community, a lover, nature, herself. Being drawn into You is to come alive again—after what death? A broken relationship is hinted at when the sequence is almost over:

> Say it brother, I want
> to be free
> and walk away
> from your smile and feel
> OK after while
>
>   ("August 16")

but one of Kyger's unusual skills is to be able to be personal and not confessional: life is perpetual death and refocus upon You, the details are less in names than in the bite and color of experience-in-progress. **"More on Thursday"** ends:

> And electric enlightenment is in Pacific
> blue air pelicans dive
> and I'm the kundalini snuggle that moves
> on the mount
> of baby fawn spots
> leap into the crazy arms of the impassionata
> utterly consumed

That is followed immediately by **"August 1,"** beginning "Bruised I am totally bruised full moon." We get change within setting, natural setting and emotional setting, and can identify without knowing more. Note in the passage from More on Thursday the layout that is the unfolding of each line in its own setting on the page, its own space—that layout is a voice making time interested for You; time is lengthened cut sloweddown speeded-up, luxuriated in. One of the final conclusions Kyger arrives at is that "Time is a nice thing to go through" (**"December 20"**). But the very last entry is not so simply positive:

> Just sitting around smoking dope, drinking and telling stories, the news, making plans, analyzing, approaching the cessation of personality, the single personality understands its demise. Experience of the simultaneity of all human beings on this planet, alive when you are alive. This seemingly inexhaustible sophistication of awareness becomes relentless and horrible, trapped. How am I ever going to learn enough to get out.
>   (**"January 23, 1979"**)

In the ***Up My Coast*** section of the same volume Kyger, retelling a Coast Miwok myth, shows another part of her talent: for translating humor, and what you might call happy expressiveness, from another culture and time into our own.

> . . . Sun Woman kept on going.
> Come back! Coyote sent some people to get
> her back. She wouldn't come back. So
> Coyote sent enough men to bring her back
> whether she wanted to or not.

This is plain, so plain, as Native American storytelling often is; but the use of such phrases as "Come back!" and "whether she wanted to or not" is very skillful. They quicken and enliven the poem, making it idiomatic but not corny, trenchant. All of Kyger's effects in whatever poem seem spontaneous, and spontaneity adds edge, in fact, since it's difficult and everyone knows that, a real feat if maintained as a way of being or an ethic. This Coyote poem, which is untitled, is alive throughout with ordinary words used quickly, vividly, and musically:

> But Meadow Lark came
> and drove him away saying
> People no good, People smell.
> When they die, they better stay dead.
> . . . when he caught her, imagine his surprise!
> She was his own wife!
> from over the ocean! Small world!

It sounds like a Native American story and it sounds like Kyger; it's an example of keeping a story alive using poetry, the more economical genre, rather than the usual prose.

Kyger's most recent collection of poems, ***Just Space: Poems 1979–1989*** (Black Sparrow, 1991), is a logical follow-up to the struggle in the sequence **"The Wonderful Focus of You,"** being something like the journal of an arrived spirit, with a stake in a community of people and other natural beings. The word "journal" means by day, which is how time passes, and it's time we're given to find out in, as **"The Wonderful Focus of You"** makes clear. Kyger accepts the quotidian, the people and events in her days, as the obvious ground for right living and less obviously for acquiring knowledge. In Just Space she has evolved a form of poem that contains more of names and event than before, but is also more subtle and compact and quick in meaning than before.

Just Space is not presented as sequence except chronologically but it is very much a book as well as a collection. It isn't laid out like a journal, but it's shaped as any journal is by the story time makes in a life, with people passing through, dying, being recalled, the seasons passing, wisdom being acquired and sometimes lost: all of that is a natural narrative. Any small town like Bolinas, where Kyger has continued to live since the 60s, as well mirrors the nation, so to keep track of one is to keep track of both. but notice how the book begins:

> You believe this stash of writing is "scholarly"?
> Out of this we deduce. . .
> From this we can see that. . .
>
> I know it's a detective story of passions,
> dinners, blood stuff around which the history of
> our lives crank.

The poem, which is untitled, becomes a disclaimer of modern disciplines—scholarly, historical—which try to make what's wild in us go away so we can be "in the know." One deduces ("Out of this we deduce," I'm afraid) that what's wild is what happens, and what happens is what this book is about to tell you. The book ends as follows:

> So, remembering to chronicle
> events economically
> and learning how to sit
> properly were what I thought important
> to learn from this space and respect
> and awe majestic old time news
> **("Death Valley Desert Notes")**

Just space works on a simple level as a Book of Pleasure, i.e., you can read it. For example, the gossip about people you don't know is quite biting.

> Even Bisbee with the last stronghold of the poor white hippies doesn't have such a determined bunch of sleazos. Persephone Jones needs something to do except being the Queen of Green Death & Smack. I arrived to open the Bookstore at seven a.m. She's seated on the steps. "Did you bring the Beer?" she said.
> **("Back from Bisbee: or Clean Up Time in Bolinas")**

Natural description can be breathtaking:

> Defying gravity
> the powerful serenity
> of Redtail waits
> to catch his snake mid wind
> rain storm late morning
> (Untitled—entire poem)

There is literary comment and record; the arrival of Language Poetry, for example, is caught and both accepted and gently repudiated as personal practice:

> The electric clock
> from the 30's childhood belongs to me. *I* am the
> I
> of this writing which indeed I like to do.
> (Untitled)

Note how in less than three lines she has managed to say she is of her own time, to identify her time, to conjure up an actual clock in a room, to comment on the nature of her favored first person singular, and to suggest that she is surpassingly content with the way she writes and not about to change for a fashion. Language Poetry is also possibly the subject of the poem **"Yuppy Wittgensteins Arise!"**, but the poem moves too quickly and subtly to let us know who it's putting down, if that's what it's doing.

> Gee glad you've got a horizon
> to speak to You
> are as humorous as the hospitality you enjoy
> So you must go to the Dentist. . .

Many of the poems are species of what we used to call the Clear Enigma: you know exactly what's going on but you're not exactly sure of what else is going on. Elsewhere deaths are recorded, the moon rises often, people get pissed off at Kyger and she at them, she narrates sporadically the life of Naropa, books are read, marriages celebrated, animals and plants encountered. Phenomenology is a concentration on the outer world as phenomena appearing to a mind; as so Kyger is a phenomenologist, and hints that she is from time to time: one poem is called **"Narrative as Attention on a Rainy Sunday's Phenomenology."** She is more overtly a Buddhist, and her practice ornaments the poetry with references and more importantly provides the awareness of "space" in the title *Just Space,* the real background of the poems, the considerable expanse of white paper from which these short-ish poems emerge, as the daily phenomena of Bolinas materialize and group into poem-forms. A poem on the death of the writer Richard Brautigan is eerily a good example of a public subject—and as such susceptible to scrutiny via whatever trite overview is handy—seen by Kyger through the details of real encounter. Brautigan, who committed suicide in 1984, lived in Bolinas at the time. Here is Kyger's untitled poem:

Self Loathing & Self Pity
I finish Somerset Maugham's biography
on almost empty Wharf Road Beach.
—terrified, lonely, crazy, no religion, dies
at '92.
"I think a Tragedy has occurred"
notes Charles Reeves as I give him a ride up Terrace
as we pass Sheriff's vehicles in front of Richard
Brautigan's
in front of Richard Brautigan's house. Well he's
gone
away, maybe
a robbery . . .
October 25

The comments on Maugham spread to the Brautigan death, which is caught in the moment exactly but exactly from the outside. Yet the conjunction in Kyger's mind of her reading and the registering of death make a knot, an event, which also becomes itself, that poem. That poem is haunting because it finally resists being more than a shape in time; its emotional strength lies in that resistance, which is both the poem's form and its wisdom.

Kyger's "researches" lead her toward the end of the book to the conclusion that everything is the one thing, what she perceives, presumably the poem it becomes, and the infinite space it sounds out of:

I'm not really used to God anymore
Like is her any different
from that Flicker out there
flying & disappearing into the Broom
                    ("February 1 Wednesday")

That's finally the meaning of her book.

When I began this essay I thought I wouldn't discuss Kyger's lineage and influences, the extent of her own influence, "poetry-school" affiliations, and so on. I now think to, but here at the end and briefly. No poet is those things, and the poetry's the thing, as we all know; furthermore, such labeling by association is frequently detrimental to women poets. Poetry movements are generally man-made; women seen in light of such movements always appear secondary. However, Kyger has a lovely poem in *Just Space* about her lineage, which I can quote in full:

You know when you write poetry you find
the architecture of your lineage your teachers
like Robert Duncan for me gave me some glue
for the heart

Beats which gave confidence
                    and competition
to the Images of Perfection

. . . or as dinner approaches   I become hasty
do I mean PERFECTION?
                    September 17, 1986

Besides her connection to Duncan and to the Beats, Kyger is connected by style and personal relationships to the other Black Mountain Poets (Olson's Essay "Projective Verse" is an avowed influence) and to the New York School Poets, particularly to the Second Generation New York School. She is an exact contemporary of Ted Berrigan (both born in November, 1934), another celebrated conversationalist. Being known as a glorious and fascinating talker can obscure the value of your work, at least during your lifetime. I certainly hope to have shown that Kyger's work lives up to her conversation, which I also know something about. Kyger's influence on my own practice has been considerable—and on many other women—she's one of the women who's shown me how to speak as myself, to be intelligent in the way I wish and am, rather than suiting the requirements of established intellectuality. Universities are frightfully conservative because they love their traditions and especially their language; idiomatic truth can't get born there, or anything that has to be new, not just wants to be.

Kyger was recently omitted from *Postmodern American Poetry: A Norton Anthology* (a very useful book except for the omissions any anthology's prone to). One must assume this is at least partly because she's stayed away from the centers of Poetry's meager power; to wield power would be counter to the logic and even the technique of her poetry, would be for her a spiritually poor choice. But not calling attention to herself, she isn't always included. As her books show, her daily life involves, besides poetry, domestic chores, community service, local jobs in stores, frequent teaching at the Naropa Institute in Boulder, extensive trips to Mexico, and poetry reading trips to the East Coast. This is not at all an insular existence, but it somehow hasn't brought her the notice she deserves. A certain poetry isn't always fashionable. However, each poet's poetry is, or should be, its own world; you cross borders, you get to know it, you read it being there, not bringing a lot of baggage from outside it, and it works. Poetry's supposed to be lived in no assessed. This particular poetry world is green and blue and has a gold air fraught with a rather awesome but familiar intelligence—it seems to know you quite well. While I'm reading these poems I can't imagine reading any other; my own poems get stiff by comparison if I think of them. Hers isn't a huge output, but that doesn't seems to matter, nor the fact that hardly any of it seems long. It's exceedingly ambitious in its search for an exact spiritual truth and for the "true-to-life." The fact of such uncompromising truthfulness is as "major" as an epic poem might be.

BRENDA KNIGHT (ESSAY DATE 1996)

SOURCE: Knight, Brenda. "Joanne Kyger, Dharma Sister." In *Women of the Beat Generation: The Writers, Artists, and Muses at the Heart of a Revolution*, pp. 197-204. Berkeley, Calif.: Conari Press, 1996.

In the following essay, Knight presents a general introduction to Kyger's life and poetry, touching on her association with the Beats and her experience as a Buddhist practitioner.

". . . We met the Dalai Lama last week right after he had been talking with the King of Sikkim, the one who is going to marry an American college girl. The Dal is 27 and lounged on a velvet couch like a gawky adolescent in red robes. . . . And then Allen Ginsberg says to him how many hours do you meditate a day, and he says me? Why I never meditate, I don't have to."

—Joanne Kyger, in the *Japan and India Journals, 1960-1964*

At the age of five, Joanne Kyger published her first poem in the literary and news magazine of Naples Elementary School in Long Beach, California. She closed her eyes and told it to the teacher, who wrote it down. In high school in Santa Barbara, California, she wrote the school newspaper's feature page with the help of poet Leland Hickman. "He was sophisticated, worldly to me, but was also able to laugh at my pieces, like '**From Dinah Shore to Dinosaur**,' about Mr. Meen, tracer of lost bones."

At the University of California at Santa Barbara, Joanne pursued her interests in poetry and philosophy. In 1957, she moved north to San Francisco, where the "Howl" obscenity trial was in full swing. She became immediately immersed in the city's blooming poetry community, meeting, among others, Gary Snyder.

Joanne moved into the East-West House, a communal living project, and began sitting with Zen master Shunryu Suzuki Roshi, who had recently come from Japan to teach at the Soto Zen Church. In 1960, she left for Japan and joined Gary Snyder. They were married at the American Consulate in Kobe three days after her arrival. Five days later, they were married again in a Zen

ceremony at Daitoku-ji, a large and beautiful complex of temples in Kyoto.

I had met Gary Snyder in 1958 in North Beach when he was visiting the United States, back from his first trip to Japan. I was a part of a group of young writers clustered around the poets Robert Duncan and Jack Spicer. Gary came to our Sunday poetry group and read from *Myths and Texts* sitting cross-legged on a table with Jack Spicer sitting cross-legged under the table. "Do you like this Boy Scout poetry?" Spicer challenged me. I did indeed, very much.

Ruth Fuller Sasaki, who was Gary's sponsor in Japan and ran the First Zen Institute in Kyoto, which hired him part-time, made it clear that I could not come and "live" with Gary. We would have to marry. She wrote to him, "If you and Joanne want to marry at any time, and then live in your little house in the mountains, fine. But living together in the little house before marriage won't do. There are certain fixed social customs that the Institute expects its members to respect." I bought a wool dress with a scooped neckline, basic black, so I could wear it a lot, starting with the wedding, which happened a few days after I arrived.

Joanne lived in Kyoto for four years, writing poetry, studying flower arranging, and practicing Zen Buddhism at Daitoku-ji with Ruth Fuller Sasaki, the experience of which she has chronicled in *Japan and India Journals: 1960-1964.* To help make ends meet, she also taught conversational English and obtained English-speaking parts in low-budget Japanese films.

In 1964, she returned to San Francisco, where she started writing prodigiously, gave readings, and participated in the Berkeley Poetry Conference. In 1965, her first book of poems, *The Tapestry and the Web,* was published. Her second book, *Places to Go,* was published in 1970 by Black Sparrow Press. Alicia Ostriker wrote in the *Partisan Review,* "Risking folly, let us propose that Joanne Kyger is a genius, though a weird one. Handling her work is like handling a porcupine traveling at the speed of light. She is not 'disciplined' but is a radically original combination of symbolist and comedienne."

Gary and Joanne divorced, and in 1966 she traveled to Europe with Jack Boyce and sojourned for a time in New York. The two returned to San Francisco and, in 1968, together purchased land in Bolinas, just north of the city. "It was a time of inventive country living, dirt roads, no street lights, interesting plumbing, and an hour away over the coast range for shopping. Robert Duncan called us the 'Bolinas bucolics.'"

Seven years later, she was at the Naropa Institute in Boulder, Colorado, with Allen Ginsberg and Anne Waldman. Based on the same principles as the legendary Black Mountain College, Anne and Allen founded the Jack Kerouac School of Disembodied Poetics, which continues to this day as the forum for counterculture humanities where Buddhism meets Beat. Here Joanne met Chogyam Trungpa Rinpoche and the Sixteenth Gyalwa Karmapa, head of the Kagyu school of Tibetan Buddhism. It was while teaching at Naropa in 1978 that she met Donald Guravich, a writer and artist from New Brunswick, Canada. When she returned to Bolinas, he joined her and they have shared a household ever since. She now sits at the Ocean Wind Zendo in Bolinas.

Joanne Kyger has published many books of poetry. Recent collections of her work include *Going On: Selected Poems 1958-1980* and *Just Space: Poems 1979-1989*. In a voice that is immediate and accessible, her poems are often snapshots of the realities of daily life. The combination of these characteristics and her Buddhist beliefs meet to form precise imagery and powerful ideas.

> The "Square Zen" Alan Watts spoke of, the Zen of the established tradition, was not an accessible practice for me. But the sheer caprice of "Beat Zen" with its "digging of the universe" seemed out of hand too. Sitting with the sangha at Suzuki's San Francisco Zen Center when I returned, I was struck with the simplicity of zazen, nothing to prove, nothing to gain. But I was also grateful for the established traditional rules of the zendo, unquestioned, that allowed one's mind freedom within the form.

Buddhism was a major influence on Beat writers, a philosophy and teaching that they embraced in rejection of fifties' materialism. For a literature in celebration of the open mind and the open road, Buddhism offered a transcendental grace and deeper consciousness for Kerouac's spiritually weary "seeking" generation. Joanne Kyger's poetry is exemplary of Buddhist consciousness in Beat writing, of a sensibility for which wisdom is the greatest beauty.

KIRBY OLSON (ESSAY DATE 2002)

SOURCE: Olson, Kirby. "Joanne Kyger and the Tradition of Zen Beatitude." *Exquisite Corpse: A Journal of Letters and Life* no. 9 (online magazine), <www.corpse.org/issue_9/critiques/olson.htm> (2002).

In the following essay, Olson examines Kyger's understanding of the Zen tradition and analyzes why the aesthetics of her work have not been embraced by literature departments in universities.

Because capitalism has little room for the self-reflective, and because poetry is a form of reflec-

tion, poets in America have sought outside the capitalist system for a tradition, and a philosophy, which would be amenable to their art. One tradition which works against the capitalist one of simple efficacity is Marxism, and its contemporary inheritors which have gone under the name of L-A-N-G-U-A-G-E poetry. This tradition is perhaps more intensely violent towards the notion of an individual self than capitalism, however, and seeks to eschew every trace of the individual subject, and has thus sought to develop a poetry of words without connection to either interior feeling or an appreciation of the exterior world. It is instead a poetry which intensely interrogates words, and the way in which they construct meaning. While Christian religion has mostly been held under suspicion by the left for its global imperialism, on the west coast, another religious poetry has appeared as a major aspect of Beat poetry, as Joanne Kyger, Gary Snyder, Philip Whalen, and others have looked to the tradition offered within Zen Buddhism to give form and a tradition to their art. The purpose of this article will be to look at Joanne Kyger's understanding of the Zen tradition, and to discuss how and why the aesthetics of her work have been pushed aside by the more political practices of Marxism, and the L-A-N-G-U-A-G-E school in particular, which is dominant in academic circles just now.

In a poem published in the San Francisco poetry journal *Bluebook*, Kyger writes of a phone conversation with fellow Zen practitioner Philip Whalen:

"A BRISK WIND IS BLOWING THOUGHTS CLEAR THROUGH TO PHILI ON THE PHONE"

'The New York Times says I'm a language poet.'
"Well are you?"
'No. Of course not.'

'Are you a beat poet?'
'No. I'm my own poet.'
'George Stanley says you're an Oregon poet.'
'Ha ha.'
'Do you understand what deconstruction is?'
'No.'
'Well, if you don't, I won't bother to try.'
                                        May 14, 1999

This short dismissal of poetry affiliations, with its consequent claim of the ability to be one's "own" poet, flies in the face of critical discourse which seeks to define poets in terms of a tradition and practice. And yet, can a poet exist outside of a tradition, outside of a school, with no ancestors, and no hope of being understood from within a common framework of reference, with no fellow poets to correspond, and read with? Kyger's interview in *Crooked Cucumber: The Life and Zen Teaching of Shunryu Suzuki,* offers an intense biographical list of philosophies, poetries, and fellow seekers in the California scene in the late 1950s and early 1960s, which does much to negate the sense that good poets are ever found who don't consciously work within some tradition. "My own interest in Zen came about because I had been studying Wittgenstein and Heidegger in Santa Barbara.

"Their philosophy just comes to an end saying you just have to practice the study of nothing. Then I got D. T. Suzuki's book on Japanese Zen and I thought oh! this is where you go with this mind. And my teacher was Paul Wienpahl and I studied with him for practically four years—I was infatuated with his style and his teaching . . . The way of Western philosophy had come to a real dead end and where did you go for practice or illumination or insight and it was a very natural kind of progression into what was available about Zen Buddhist teachings. Like no mind—no mind—what is the study of nothing? Where do you start to open up that mystery? A lot of people—Ginsberg, Kerouac had started to find these books. Everybody was reading about this Zen and Gary [Snyder] was the only one who had figured out how to meditate although he hadn't had any formal teacher . . . It was very attractive to everybody in the sense that there was some illumination at the end not like the dead end of philosophy. The logical positivists were analyzing language were all analyzing questions like if you have a headache and you have an aspirin does the headache go away? They were really dumb states of mind. There was some kind of religious quest in the fifties going on but there weren't any teachers" (*Interview,* 5-6).

Kyger's interest in Zen came about because she was searching for a tradition. She says in her interview, "I didn't speak Japanese, I was a woman, and there was such formality inside the sodo you couldn't just drop in and out and it was a very strict kind of sitting. Eventually I got fed up" (3). What Kyger was looking for was what was missing on the west coast at the time, a deep practice, and she saw Zen and Japanese aesthetics as the best option available. "Mrs. Sasaki always said that this is what Japanese Zen is about—these are Japanese forms. . . . All of these were very attractive cultural methods that had come over since the war. The coast here didn't have any really strong sense of aesthetics. We had Doris Day and Rock Hudson" (4).

Throughout the interview Kyger doesn't mention any belief in politics, nor does she strenuously protest the chauvinism of Zen tradition. What she was looking for is humanity: "Suzuki Roshi always kept a modest demeanor. I was always watching to see if people were going to be human in the roles they were taking in the organization which was getting more hierarchical but I never saw that in Suzuki Roshi. He wasn't carrying a lot of baggage, that's what was so appealing" (8).

Ron Silliman writes of Kyger, that "She's one of our hidden treasures—the poet who really links the Beats, the Spicer Circle, the Bolinas poets, the NY School and the language poets, and the only poet who can be said to do all of the above" (2). He also writes that, "Joanne has a terrific sense of humor in her writing, which may in fact actually work against her being taken as seriously as she deserves" (2). Kyger isn't heavily represented in the anthologies which form the canon of this period, even though she seems to have known everybody, and was taken seriously by other poets. Silliman writes, "I've written at some length about the disappearance of poets and how it reconfigures history into something unrecognizable to those present at the event . . . all too often it leads to this sort of erasure of a major writer" (2).

Alice Notley writes in an article on Kyger, "When I began this essay I thought I wouldn't discuss Kyger's lineage and influences, the extent of her own influence, 'poetry-school' affiliations, and so on . . . No poet is those things, and the poetry's the thing, as we all know; furthermore, such labelling by association is frequently detrimental to women poets. Poetry movements are generally man-made; women seen in light of such movements always appear secondary" (2). Notley writes that Kyger's omission from *Postmodern American Poetry* among other anthologies has clear reasons. "One must assume this is at least partially because she's stayed away from the centers of Poetry's meager power; to wield power would be counter to the logic and even the technique of her poetry, would be for her a spiritually poor choice. But not calling attention to herself, she isn't always included . . . Poetry's supposed to be lived in not assessed" (3).

Nevertheless, poetry is always finally assessed. Each reader assesses whether it is worth passing on to a friend, each critic wonders whether it is worth exploring in depth, or defending as a canonical work to be taught to students in a university. Without this kind of assessment, there is no conversation, and the process of passing on what is the best of a tradition doesn't take place, and ultimately a poet's work disappears, first the individual books disappear, then the name in anthologies, and eventually all but the biggest libraries are forced to push out the books in order to make room for new work.

Only a few of Kyger's books are currently available, while most of them have gone out of print. She is not widely anthologized, and the critical material is scanty. Against Notley and Silliman, I will argue that Kyger's poetry has one clear lineage, and that her lack of a will to power isn't the reason for her disappearance. The reason for her disappearance, I will argue, is that she is a non-political writer in an age in which showing one's politics, and one's clear preference for the left, is the minimum entrance requirement for academic respectability. When the most powerful members of academia therefore propose their canon of the best, Kyger isn't thought of as being inside, for instance, the language school, or the feminist school, or the Jack Spicer (gay rights) circle, but seems to have always been a peripheral member of these groups, and she therefore doesn't have any critics who see her as a top priority. There aren't many Zen critics in academia, and she is neither an ardent feminist, homosexual, or political writer. Kyger is an individual, a humorist, even an iconoclast, in her own quiet way.

What I propose to treat her as is as a member of the Zen circle within the larger Beat school, and therefore as a member of a doubly dismissed group.

Except insofar as the Beat writers supported leftist goals and positions, they still do not have academic respectability. Because Zen is not a political movement, but rather one of personal development, and also a religious stance, Kyger's work is not welcomed. It is Zen that Kyger most consistently invokes as her own tradition. I want to explore her understanding of this tradition, and to propose it as a counterweight to L-A-N-G-U-A-G-E, which has such a powerful sense of history, and how canonization works. I want to state at the outset that L-A-N-G-U-A-G-E poets have interested themselves in Kyger's work, as Ron Silliman, a member of that school, has shown, but they have yet to provide a rationale through which to read her work. The aim of this article is to recuperate Zen as a deep aesthetic practice, and to present it as a rival tradition to Marxism.

The Zen poets are perhaps the least canonical of all the poets of the last fifty years, and this is because they have consistently been the most self-effacing, the least drawn to power or to the back-slapping and back-stabbing which goes with a climb to the top.

Inside of American academia, where a certain neo-Marxism based on the work of Louis Althusser and Jurgen Habermas has gained ground, Charles Bernstein, the most powerful poet of the L-A-N-G-U-A-G-E circle, at least in terms of his professional position and his clout within the profession, will be used as a poet to compare with Kyger.

In Charles Bernstein's volume, *Content's Dream, Essays 1975-1984,* it is possible to read five hundred pages which is neither poetry nor essay nor philosophy, but some kind of mixture which mostly reads as reworkings of the philosophy of cultural revolution as practiced by the Tel quel group.

Bernstein writes that he wants to "change the nature of reading values" (388), and that what he wants to show is that "Phallocentric syntax . . . values the declarative more than the convoluted, grandiosity more than humor, assurance more than confusion" (329).

Bernstein is attacking phallocentric syntax, but his own writing is declarative, grandiose, and self-assured to the point of violent machismo, as he mows down everyone from Charles Algernon Swinburne to Allen Ginsberg, to make room for himself in the canon. There is confusion in his work, but he doesn't see it, and there is humor and convoluted thinking, but it is unintentional.

Instead of Bernstein, it would be Kyger who demonstrates the values this writer preaches, but doesn't practice. Her writing is often convoluted, humorous, and full of confusion, and is anything but phallocentric. But how does a writer make a virtue of such qualities, without standing on a soap box, and advertising herself?

There is a curiously aimless quality to much of Kyger's writing:

> Robin Blaser's old plaster of Paris
> Bust of Dante . . .
> lent to me by
> Paul Alexander . . .
> now residing in our back guest shed . . .
>
> *(Just Space 72)*

This fragment is an entire poem, apparently. Is it about the vanity of passing fame? This seems to be at least part of it, that the simulacra of celebrity passes, and ends up in storage. However, there is no mourning of this in the poem. Instead, there is something humorous about it, a quality that is always evident in Kyger's poetry. Her humor is always gentle.

On the other hand, there is a furious militant quality in Bernstein's work. Bernstein's convoluted confusion leads to humor when as a poet he would like to give room to the individual, in sentences such as these: "Individuals are in essence that which is maladapted, idiocentric, resistant; it is in that sense that we get to know one another only through the identification and appreciation of their peculiarities as particularized—mutant—and not as instances of some generalized feature of some genre of humans" (410). To cut through the abstraction, he is saying that individuals are resistant to their times, and this is what makes them individuals. So far, I have no problem with this, but then he suddenly turns around and attacks his previous individualism with a truism: "—So I hope the reader does feel implicated because I want to show that I as a social construction, a product of language and not a preexisting entity outside it; that I is first a we" (410). At first he valorizes individualism, and then he turns around and valorizes the communal. This is certainly convoluted, confused, and humorous, but it is humorous in a painful way, because he argues that the individual should stand up to the particular ideology of her time, and then he neglects to do that against the ideology of Althusserian ideology, which is the ideology of his particular circle.

Because the L-A-N-G-U-A-G-E poets have the lion's share of academic interest, since they pay lip-service to continental philosophers who got a monopoly on the inside of academic thinking forty years ago, and because these poets seemingly share a Marxist orientation with the younger academic elite which has fallen in line with ideological Marxism, their dogma is all but unchallenged. There is no single subject, language speaks us, we are not individuals, but ideology: these are their truths.[1]

To contrast Kyger's writing with this militant ideological writing provokes stark contrasts. Alice Notley writes of Kyger, "As her books show, her daily life involves, besides poetry, domestic chores, community service, local jobs in stores, frequent teaching at the Naropa Institute in Boulder, extensive trips to Mexico, and poetry reading trips to the East Coast. This is not at all an insular existence, but it somehow hasn't brought her the notice she deserves. A certain poetry isn't always fashionable" (3).

Notley concludes, "Universities are frightfully conservative because they love their traditions and especially their language; idiomatic truth can't get born there, or anything that has to be new, not just wants to be" (3). By Bernstein's own admission, we need a "revolution every 20 years" (Thomas Jefferson cited by William Carlos Williams cited in Bernstein 246).

Bernstein's initial work appeared at least twenty years ago, and he has been an insider for at least that long, and yet he is still considered a radical within academia. And yet, what seems the problem with Bernstein and his circle isn't their novelty, but precisely their lack of historical depth.

The L-A-N-G-U-A-G-E school's philosophical bric-a-brac cites Heidegger, Lyotard, Derrida, Merleau-Ponty, and others, but there is no older tradition cited, the oldest authority being Karl Marx. It is as if Marx, for them, represented a break with all of human history. Shakespeare, Chaucer, the Greeks, the ancient Chinese, the Indian traditions, African-American traditions, are never cited. Theirs is a new language, and one that has been increasingly dominant in universities over the last fifty years, and is now dominant almost to the exclusion of all else. Joanne Kyger, on the other hand, rarely cites Marx, and seems to have a kind of comic attitude towards Marxist thought, which would hardly make a place for her in that canon.

Kyger writes in the opening poem of *Just Space:*

> You believe this stash of writing is 'scholarly'?
> Out of this we deduce . . .
> From this we can see that . . .
> . . . . .
>
> So enough of that tune I was singing there
> further back, I'm up to date with the day-glo
>   goods
> of modern historical revelation, barely a day old.
> . . . . .
>
> So what
>
> about that deer in the backyard eating down the
>   as yet
> unborn apples. A little deer go away dance?
> . . . . .
>   (13)

Kyger brings us back out of the realm of "historical revelation," and into the confused, convoluted, and humorous present, in which a deer, which "last summer it was / a heart-stopping glimpse" is now attacking the apple tree out back, and it leaves her only the one academic solution: "You fence it in" (13). Against dialectical materialism, Kyger is working in a different tradition, one that moves back and forth between systems of thought, and the concrete fleshly existence, with all of its unsystematic ironies. As she would put it, life is first, and then theories, which are more of a nuisance than a help.

On the other hand, Bernstein writes that ideology is more primary than experience. "Ideology is more fundamental than phenomena" (417). Ideology is more fundamental than sensory experience? Is Bernstein's ideology more fundamental than a deer eating apples in the backyard, or is even what is to be eaten by what to be mediated by ideology? Does language mediate the reality of a deer eating an apple? Bernstein writes, "There is no natural look or sound to a poem. Every element is intended, chosen" (49). Apparently not believing in anything outside his conscious mind, Bernstein writes that every moment of every poem is socially constructed, with the implication that we can therefore build exactly the kind of society that we want, without reference to any external constraints whatsoever.

Kyger, on the other hand, is quite deep into Zen culture, and writes historical poems about Naropa, for instance, who's been dead for nine hundred years (*JS* [*Just Space*] 22-25). Moreover, in contrast to the militant tradition of Marx in which history and the communal wipe out the significance of the individual, the Zen tradition does believe in the individual. James H. Austin writes, in *Zen and the Brain*, that, according to Freud, "The ego, modified from the id, organized our behavior along rationally effective lines. It drew on hard-won lessons of personal experience, constantly reminding the id: the real world has consequences. Freud viewed the ego, in a sense, as a rider who guided a horse, not yet tamed, toward a destination . . . The term still refers to each person's capacity to deal confidently with life in a mature, realistic, matter-of-fact way. The I that Zen diminishes is not the pragmatic ego. If Zen were to remove such an ego, it would leave its adherents in a helpless 'identity crisis.' Rather, Zen aims to strengthen the ego in its original Freudian sense" (35). Zen, however, does have an aim to remove narcissism and other aspects of the self, Austin writes, "But does the whole process of Zen aim to magnify or adore the self? No; to dissolve its fictions" (48).

A game of cultural power is still to be played out here, which will eventually control the way new generations understand the world, but unless the remaining threads of Kyger's Zen school can rise to the challenge they will end up in the dustbins of history, as few within academia are willing

to consider anything that can't be seen as part of progressive dialectical materialism. Fortunately, there is still a non-academic realm, where Zen poetry began, and where it continues to flourish.

It requires a contrast of the militant school of Language, with its distrust of art as religion, and its turning away from interiority and feeling, with the more generous and tender dimensions of experience tended to by Kyger and her circle to make us inquire again into the true goal of beauty and art, and to wonder if the much deeper, older traditions of Zen can find a place in the humanities. The Beat school within which Kyger worked turned towards religion as a major aspect of the aesthetic experience. From Gregory Corso and Lawrence Ferlinghetti's references to Catholicism and St. Francis to Gary Snyder, Philip Whalen's and Joanne Kyger's interest in Zen, Robert Duncan's interest in theosophy, to Allen Ginsberg's championing of the Tibetan crazy wisdom school, there is an openness to mystical experience which is not part of current academic fashion, which tends to dismiss such attitudes and mental states, and the writers who foster them, and to keep only those writers, or those aspects of writers, which fit the materialist philosophy. In addition, even in the older tradition of the humanities which still exists at certain small colleges, it is generally felt that the tradition of a separation of church and state should be respected and so there is little discussion of spiritual states, or religion as something worthy of the humanities. Thus, Kyger's poetry, as well as the tradition to which it belongs, will continue to be slighted within universities, except insofar as it can articulate a progressive agenda. Nevertheless, to leave out the spiritual aspect of experience is possibly to leave the best part of life on the editing room floor. Poetry as a description of mystic peak states is an important part of non-academic poetry, as it is an important experience in most people's live. James H. Austin writes that in fact it is these experiences which give meaning to the rest of life to the majority of the population. "Maslow, finding fewer people who did not have these experiences, finally began to use the term 'non-peakers'" (Austin 20). Still others, Austin writes, had an appreciation of formal beauty along strictly aesthetic lines at some point in their lives. Austin writes, "Interestingly, aesthetic experiences alone caused little subsequent change in either their religious orientation or interpersonal relations, nor did it enrich their lives. Who, then, tended to have experiences which did transform them? It was the group of subjects who had repeated experiences, both aesthetic and religious" (21). The language of spiritual revelation has been occluded from state universities as an attempt to forestall religious indoctrination. However, what has perhaps been lost is the idea of the poetic epiphany, the richest experience that an individual can have. ". . . the Eastern Orthodox Church interpreted epiphany in relation to the revelation which occurred at the time Jesus was being baptized in the river Jordan. He was then about thirty years old, and was praying while he was being baptized. At that moment, according to the story in the fourth chapter of the New Testament, the heavens seemed to open and he heard the words, 'Thou art my beloved son; in thee I am well pleased' . . . afterward, when he returned to Galilee to begin his ministry, his words bore a new authority, and he spoke in the 'power of the Spirit'" (21).

At certain schools in the west, such as Naropa Institute, founded by Allen Ginsberg with the cooperation of the Tibetan leader Choygam Trungpa, an openness to such states is encouraged. In the poetry of Joanne Kyger, who often teaches at Naropa, the influence of such states can be felt in her poetry. At Christian universities in the west, as well, such transcendence can still be addressed, but there is a difference between Christian revelation and Zen revelation. Austin writes, "Zen deemphasizes momentary isolated experiences, and is very wary about how they are to be viewed. It prefers instead to address the way the person then goes on to live each day on a moment-to-moment basis" (23). For this reason, we can see Kyger's extraordinary interest in daily life in her poetry, in small epiphanies, rather than the cataclysmic events of much Christian poetry.

> The wind thru a field of wild oats
> How long does a second last?
>
> (*JS* 96)

Is there room for an exploration or discussion of such experience in the state universities of the west, or must young people go to religiously oriented schools in order to have value given to the states of epiphany?

Ecstasy is neither pragmatic, nor progressive, but it can sponsor the kind of "loving kindness to all" (Austin 25) for which Jesus and the Zen masters have been valued. To sacrifice this possibility of transcendence seems to be a mistake, and to undo the impact that the humanities can have on the richness of a human life. Even the atheist Nietzsche writes, "Does his basic instinct aim at art, or rather at the sense of art, at life? at a desirability of life? Art is the great stimulus to life: how could one understand it as purposeless, as

aimless, as l'art pour l'art?" (529). Kyger's work certainly contributes to the desirability of life, and is a stimulus to peak experience as the most meaningful aspect of it.

Note

1. The Dalai Lama spoke at a conference in Seattle in June 1993. He was asked if he had read recent French philosophy, and whether he thought the individual subject existed. He answered that he had extensively read recent French philosophy translated into Tibetan by his aids, and that he felt it rested on several confusions which the Tibetan tradition had swept off the table five hundred years ago. In order to have a community at all, he said, the Buddhist tradition had decided we need to agree on these postulates:

1. The individual subject exists.

2. The external world exists.

3. Causality between the internal and the external world exists.

4. All beings suffer.

Without these conditions, which (he stipulated) cannot be rationally proven, but which have to be accepted as axiomatic, there is no possibility of a decent life. In other words, without an individual subject there can be no responsibility, and without an understanding that between an individual and the exterior, there can be no sense of causality. Without this, we are in a solipsistic state, rather than in a community. Without an understanding that others have an interior dimension, which often suffers, we cannot have compassion. I have told this anecdote several times to neo-Marxist academics who see Tel Quel and L-A-N-G-U-A-G-E as their point of reference, and every time they wave it away, and say, "But the Dalai Lama's not a real intellectual."

It is funny to me to think that Tel Quel (Derrida, Foucault, Kristeva, Lacan) were avowed Maoists throughout the nineteen-seventies, and that during this time the Chinese Cultural Revolution was in the process of destroying the Tibetan cultural heritage. In America today, that same process is on-going with those who derive their thinking from Tel Quel and academic Marxism running off those who derive their thinking and tradition from Zen.

Works Cited

Austin, James H. *Zen and the Brain* (Boston: MIT, 1997).

Bernstein, Charles. *Content's Dream: Essays 1975-1984* (Los Angeles: Sun & Moon Press, 1985).

Kyger, Joanne. "Joanne Kyger Interview with Crooked Cucumber." *http://cuke.com/interviews/kyger.html*

———*Just Space.* (Santa Barbara: Black Sparrow, 1991).

Notley, Alice. "Joanne Kyger's Poetry." *http://www.epc.buffalo.edu/authors/kyger/notley.html*

Silliman, Ron. "E-mail to Linda Russo." *http://www.epc.buffalo.edu/authors/kyger/silliman.html*

LINDA RUSSO (ESSAY DATE 2002)

SOURCE: Russo, Linda. "To Deal with Parts and Particulars: Joanne Kyger's Early Epic Poetics." In *Girls Who Wore Black: Women Writing the Beat Generation,* edited by Ronna C. Johnson and Nancy M. Grace, pp. 178-204. New Brunswick, N.J.: Rutgers University Press, 2002.

In the following essay, Russo discusses the poems in The Tapestry and the Web *and other works that challenge established notions of gender and poetic authority.*

> . . .none of these
> came into the story,
>
> it was epic, heroic and it was far
> from a basket a child upset
> and the spools that rolled to the floor . . .
> —H. D., *Helen in Egypt*
> I weave my own wiles.
> —Penelope in Homer's *The Odyssey*

Penelope marks time at her loom, weaving and unweaving. When her tapestry is done, the story told in *The Odyssey* will end. The inevitable is deferred by the making of that enduring present. Her repetitions maintain possibility, keep the narrative open, and history marks that only in passing. The generic origins of epic, the grand poetic form of history, heroics and culture, lie in the exclusion of her experiences and her actions—except where these might reflect on a hero's renown. If mythic figures like Helen of Troy and Penelope do not resemble women and only men are like them, it is perhaps because they are invented by men, pieces of a male mind, as Alice Notley writes in "Homer's Art" (1992, 491). Joanne Kyger's first book of poems, *The Tapestry and the Web* (1965), stands beside H. D.'s (Hilda Doolittle's) *Helen in Egypt* (1961) and Notley's *The Descent of Alette* (1996).[1] All are acts of imaginative intervention into epic invention, animating female presence, remaking the gender ideologies and histories transmitted from generation to generation in epic form. Their work is barbarous to the epic lexicon and makes the heroic narrative, the epic's raison d'être, a linguistic field in which the particularities of women's stories—in the revision of female epic figures—are given play.

Kyger has authored over fifteen books of poetry since *The Tapestry and the Web* was published. Many of these, such as *The Wonderful Focus of You* (1979), *Phenomenological* (1989), and more recently *Some Sketches from the Life of Helena Petrovna Blavatsky* (1996) and *Patzcuaro* (1999), dwell in and question received realities textual, social, and historical, often by taking up myths and mythic lives and altering structures of experience through the innovative structure of the poem. But it is *The Tapestry and the Web* that, by intervening upon the structure of the epic, constructs a new poetic space in which to explore and challenge received notions of gender and poetic authority, particularly those notions of the feminine fostered by cold war culture and reinforced in poetry by the masculinist rhetoric of the New American poetry—exhibited, for example, in Charles Olson's "Projective Verse" and Gary Snyder's *Myths and Texts*. As if in a direct line from Sappho, *The Tapestry and the Web* appears to be a collection of fragments. The poems are for the most part untitled; though summoned together in the table of contents by their first lines, they resist being woven into a categorical whole. As a web of various aberrant threads, these poems assert a new mode of poetic authority that diverges markedly from masculinist conceptions of the role of poet as maker. As she wrote in the third "**Tapestry**" poem, Kyger chose to work "with the detail / on the fragment" and to search "for bigger & better things" (1965, 40).

The heart of *The Tapestry and the Web* radically revises the story of the artful and long-patient Penelope, who while waiting for the return of her adventuring husband, Odysseus, delays by deceit 108 eager suitors, weaving a tapestry by day and unraveling it by night. Her story, rendered together with apocrypha, is reworked in two serial poems: a thematically united, six-page group, therein untitled but elsewhere referred to as the "**Penelope poems**" (1981, 86), and a nine-page sequence of seven numbered and two unnumbered poems titled "**The Odyssey Poems.**"[2] The Penelope poems are indistinguishable as a series separate from surrounding poems except for their focused treatment of Penelope. Further distinction is blurred in the thematic interactions with poems scattered throughout the book, especially three poems titled "**Tapestry,**" so that references to Penelope appear sporadically in *The Tapestry and the Web,* creating an evasive figure whose identity is diffused in a mode that can hardly be called a narrative. This tactic ensures that Penelope—and the untitled Penelope poems—will not be completely subsumed under their companion piece, "**The Odyssey Poems.**" In their obscurity they shift about as apocrypha against which "**The Odyssey Poems**" appear more contained and defined.

"**The Odyssey Poems,**" for their part, continue to deform the figure of Penelope while incorporating the figure of Odysseus and the story of his return to Ithaca into a new narrative complex, one that collages references to contemporary contexts and details, as in the first poem,

FROM THE AUTHOR

RECOLLECTIONS OF THE SAN FRANCISCO RENAISSANCE

The Beat Generation, the San Francisco Renaissance, is dramatically in the air, most especially in North Beach, which I visit every night in my red Capezio slippers with silver buckles. I have them reheeled every two weeks. I drink devastating martinis and hear Kenneth Rexroth and Lawrence Ferlinghetti read poetry with jazz at The Cellar. My friend Nemi Frost has moved up fom Santa Barbara. Nemi has lived in Mallorca and met Robert Creeley and the painter John Altoon, and tells me mad stories of her adventures there. I am starting to get a picture of a certain kind of world.

Kyger, Joanne. Excerpt from *Contemporary Authors Autobiography Series* 16. Detroit, Mich.: Gale, 1992, pp. 189-90.

which appears to place Odysseus outside of San Francisco, where "the long paths and eucalyptus / are another country" (1965, 53). While the Penelope poems and **"The Odyssey Poems"** were not conceived of as purposefully disruptive—Kyger later described **The Tapestry and the Web** as "just the poems that I thought the strongest work I had done" (Ellingham 1982b, 109)—together they evince a large-scale renovation of *The Odyssey* as poetic and cultural authority, and the making of a female self through assembled and reassembled particulars. The figure of Penelope is opened to a radical recomposition, after which *The Odyssey* itself must be read anew.

The totemic image of Snyder reading from *Myths and Texts* "sitting cross-legged on a table, with Jack Spicer sitting cross-legged *under* the table, like a troll under a bridge" (Kyger 1992, 191) serves as a figure for Kyger's hybrid poetic lineage and the divergent forms of poetic authority she encountered. During her early years in San Francisco, she developed mentor relationships with poets Robert Duncan and Jack Spicer and then traveled for four years (1960-1964) in Japan and India with her then-husband, Gary Snyder, during which time she wrote, alongside **The Tapestry**

and the Web, the provocative and illuminating **Japan and India Journals** (1981).[3] Thus **The Tapestry and the Web** grew out of Kyger's immersion in and subsequent absence from a persuasively male context, where writers were the dons of antiestablishment culture. Kyger had left the establishment—in this case, the University of California, Santa Barbara—one credit short of a bachelor's degree, and arrived in San Francisco in 1957, a year marked by the censorship trials about "Howl" and the overnight success of Jack Kerouac's *On the Road,* whose attention in the national press set the tone for the Beat Generation. As Michael Davidson shows in *The San Francisco Renaissance,* while "the Beats provided the most public demonstration that some sort of literary ferment was occurring in the Bay Area," the Beat movement was "only one strand in a much more diverse and eclectic movement" (60). That same year San Francisco felt the aftershock of the closing of Black Mountain College—where Charles Olson, whose "Projective Verse" would become a persuasive document, had been rector—as many young male poets arrived in search of community. A few found it in the Sunday Meetings held under the aegis of Duncan and Spicer.

Amidst these poetic upheavals, a young poet like Kyger was exposed to various poetic options, and she chose her influences as much as they seemed to have chosen her. In The Place, a popular North Beach bar, Kyger met recent Black Mountain émigré Joe Dunn, who invited her to the Sunday Meetings, where she found Duncan and Spicer informal teachers to several younger, predominantly gay poets, who were her classmates, the Sunday Meetings her first poetic school.

She was drawn to the mythic consciousness of Duncan and the exactitude of Spicer rather than the jazzy street vernacular of the Beat poets, such as Allen Ginsberg, Kerouac, or Bob Kaufman[4]—a situation which may be attributed to Kyger's marginal presence in the histories (though not in the fact) of the San Francisco Renaissance, largely histories of social and poetic exchange.[5] The poem is for Kyger not an occasion for lofty proclamation and protestation, as in Snyder's essay "North Beach," which declares "the spiritual and political loneliness of America" to be an occasion to "hitch a thousand miles to meet a friend" (1977, 45), or as in the opening line of Ginsberg's "America," "America I've given you all and now I'm nothing." As she comments dryly in her journal, "what woman ever writes a poem 'America I Love You'" (1981, 234). Kyger could develop an alternative to a poetics that, though tremendously popular, she felt to be ill fitting. Both Duncan and Spicer, to different degrees, preferred a poetic authority invested in the making of poems rather than in political self-expression, and her desire to forgo a lofty masculinism was no doubt welcomed at the Sunday Meetings. There she encountered a rhetoric that focused on a poetic authority emergent in the process of composition rather than prior to the poem: the authority of the poet who is called into action by poems. This process of composition enabled someone with little traditional poetic authority to create her or his own. And because what lay behind this authority was not the muse and remained ungendered, it usefully counterbalanced otherwise popular prohibitions on female poetic genius, such as those Kyger encountered in Robert Graves's *The White Goddess,* which, in her words, inveighed: "if you happened to be a woman you had no access to the muse herself since you WERE female and couldn't take a (same sex) female, or a male, as your muse, therefore you could never be a great poet" (Kyger, undated, n.p.). Within this tight-knit poetic community that fostered her desire to develop her voice, poetry presented her the opportunity to fit herself to the role of a universalized poetic subject, not at the expense of gender, but in bringing the female self into closer view, identifying as "a human self, with all attendant identity anxieties" (Kyger, undated, n.p.).

The introductory poem of *The Tapestry and the Web*, "The Maze," written in 1958, was composed for the Sunday Meetings and can be read as a point of connection between Kyger and both her teachers—and a point of divergence from them. It met with much approval and was received as proof that she had achieved the much-valued voice espoused by Duncan and Spicer. **"The Maze"** contains an allusion to the figure of Penelope, who would emerge in the coming years as a significant guiding figure, "singing high melodies," a co-conspirator at the center of "their design" (1965, 12). The poem opens with an image in which the present and the past are fused: "I saw the / dead bird on the sidewalk / his neck uncovered / and prehistoric." The bird one encounters in a routine way, on the sidewalk, reveals its ancient source, proposes the existence of another, mythic, knowledge. The poem presents a willful, solitary adventurer "shrugging off hands / in treacherous places." Juxtaposed to the bird's selfless revelation, a literal maze in "the dead / governor's garden" is a form of patriarchal knowledge pointed out by an uncle. It embodies layers

of both personal and mythic history; it is a pathway back and into history and her self:

the sky disappeared
and I
could hear
the sound of water
rushing

I knew each corner
without pausing

Held captive in a cave
Ulysses
sobbed for his wife
who was singing high

melodies
from the center of a
cobweb shawl
of their design

(12)

The maze is easily navigable once it is revealed; "she knew each corner" because, the next stanza suggests, of her knowledge, in myth, of the captivity of Ulysses and his wife. The "I" is "amazed"—confused, mixed together, held together—by the poem that presents a defining architecture in which memory and will are aligned with myth as guides.

The maze is a "made place" like that referred to in Duncan's poem "Often I am Permitted to Return to a Meadow," a place where new imaginations are created, what Duncan calls a "place of first permission" (1960, 8). It is where Kyger enters into the maze of mythic forms and figures to confront that which is and is not hers—and to find or make her own. The imaginative and actively critical reweaving that Kyger undertakes in the Penelope poems and **"The Odyssey Poems"** contrasts sharply with the disturbing closing image of **"The Maze"**:

                              She
tortures
        the curtains of the window
                shreds them
                like some
                                        insane insect

creates a
                demented web
        from the thin folds
        her possessed fingers
        clawing . . .

(1965, 13)

She is helpless and can but claw the curtain into a "demented web" that is, nonetheless, of her own design. The demented web maker recalls the female creative genius domesticated and entrapped, as in the unnamed female protagonist in Charlotte Perkins Gilman's *The Yellow Wallpaper,* whose husband administers a putative cure that drives her insane. The web maker at the window symbolizes the consequences of a failure to step into the maze. She must act or be prohibited to act, proceed sanely or go insane. The limitation that the image of the window proposes—that her adventures are another's, witnessed, or are purely imaginary—contrasts with the image of a worker amidst a maze of texts the later poems reveal. In this light **"The Maze"** anticipates working a way out of the maze over the six years in which the rest of **The Tapestry and the Web** was written. It is a text that speaks of its encounters with other texts punctuated with acceptances and rejections of instruction; later, these serve as points where the text swerves out in a singular, unpredictable direction, a direction unanticipated by the precepts of the tradition from which, like Athena from the head of Zeus, it sprang.

No poet's education in the 1960s would have been complete without the instruction of Olson, particularly that conveyed in his much-circulated essay, "Projective Verse," which appeared as a pamphlet from Totem Press in 1959.[6] There, prominent scrutiny is paid to the poetic line. In Olson's anatomized theory of the connection between head, ear, and syllable, and heart, breath, and line, the line served as a measure of "the man who breathes as well as his listenings." Although his focus on the breath privileged masculine force, it offered specific enough directives: "one perception must immediately and directly lead to another" (1997, 239-240). Apropos of "Projective Verse," Kyger wrote that it hit her "like a whallop" (1981, 60). The poems in **The Tapestry and the Web,** chronologically ordered, mark the influence of Olson's blow; those written in late 1959 radically reconceptualize space in the vein of Olson's "graphic intervention in the field of the regularized page" (Fraser 2000, 178).[7] While in earlier poems, like **"The Maze,"** the poetic line departs with regularity at the left margin, diverging only occasionally and then at quite regular tab stops; in later poems the left margin is dispersed by lines commencing in a scattered fashion down the page, a style that is crafted to achieve a visual balance. For Kyger, understanding the page as field translated into a consideration of how one "could move the line around very carefully" in relation to other lines on the page to dictate "how the poem was going to move, how the voice was going to move in a certain way, and how your physical speech moved thru the line" (1977, 63).

"Physical speech" is both corporeal and conceptual. On the one hand, the line materializes the physical body, going "through your hand, and . . . out on the page" (64) and this spatialization reflected her imaginative complexity; the page space would reflect her "head space" (64). This realization, Kyger said, came from working with galleys set on a Linotype machine, where spacing was vastly different from that of her typewritten manuscript, the spacing of both technologies contrasting with where her "head space was" (64).

Kyger's engagement with Olson foregrounds a concern for a formally encoded conceptualization of her interiority and corresponds to a poetic epistemology where the poem, by piecing various materials together, enables a particular knowledge of the world. "Stories," as she wrote in the poem "vision of heaven & hell," are "spun out, *connected* / and put together" to become "our knowledge [and] expectancy" and it is "this creation that remains" (1965, 36, emphasis in original). Thus "put together," the structure of the poem was a frame upon which her self-knowledge could be enacted as history, given a precedent, and confirmed. Here Duncan's influence is perceptible, particularly his sense that the poem defines a world arising from a conscious retrieval of "first things that might define a world" (1960, 79). In "Those things we see are images of the past," Kyger drew upon the notion that things are also relics, "images of the past" out of which one constructs an understanding, an "interpretation," of the world:

> From now, always, on the turning point, view-
> ing back
>   and that delicious interpretation
> is the world, HOW CLEVER OF US
>
>   An entirely new thing each time
> blind or not about it, always inventive—seeing
>   stones,
>   persimmons,
> moving a stone in dirt, oh where does it go
>   she's fleet footed
> to be a tree, to be Jack Spicer in a dream
>   to carry this around all day and every night
> the waves chuck full of things to happen
>
>   As clear as you can See
>   it's done, isn't it, isn't that a *fact.*
>   (1965, 49 emphasis in original)

Here the present is temporally complex; locating oneself in the present entails an interpretation of the past, a "viewing back" on "images of the past" that are not lapidary but shift and change, become decontextualized and foreign, thus new. Real things (stones, persimmons) are connected with the imaginary (being a tree, being Spicer in a dream) by a mythic version of the self. The line "She's fleet footed" recalls Hermes, Zeus's herald with winged golden sandals, and positions the "she" of the poem as a messenger; the metonymy around her recalls not the past but another temporal plane, ever present, which surfaces in the poem as possibility, "waves chuck full of things to happen." Things stay in the present, as the poem is present, as words are present in the poem, pulsating with potentiality, more real than the things/images they represent. It is this radical clash of words as representing things real and imaginary and the poem as a site of the slippage the adept poet/messenger might make between the two that makes Kyger's treatment of myth not simply a revision, but a re-envisioning. Thus, Kyger enacts what Duncan describes as "the poetic imagination [that] faces the challenge of finding a structure that will be the complex story of all the stories felt to be true, a myth in which something like the variety of man's experience of what is real may be contained" (1985, 6). That structure, for Kyger, would emerge from finding the self, the "fleet footed" she, at a crucial nexus; the poem, finally, is what "you can see" clearly, what's "done" and emerges as "a fact."

Spicer's poetic instruction extended beyond the text into the field of poetic production that played out during Kyger's years in the Bay Area. He arranged her first public reading, at the Beer and Wine Mission on March 7, 1959, one of the most important events that preceded her trip to Japan. His magazine *J*, of which eight issues were published from 1959 to 1961, was her first print forum. Undoubtedly *J*'s permissive and accessible submission policy encouraged her to submit "**Tapestry #3**" (the second "**Tapestry**" poem in *The Tapestry and the Web*, beginning "The eye / is drawn / to the Bold / DESIGN"), which came out in the fourth issue. It was Kyger's first published poem and a defining occasion: "The world changed. I thought people on the street looked at me differently" (1992, 191). She was on her way to constructing, as the first line of the poem suggests, a new "bold design" in her poetry.

From Spicer's poetics she gained an eye for "the Real," a nonsubjective reception of poetic voice enabled through what he called "Dictation," drawing an analogy that illustrated a "difference between you and the Outside of you which is writing poetry" and the imperative "to keep as much of [one's] self as possible out of the poem" (1998, 7-8). In *The Tapestry and the Web*, Kyger's use of myth serves at once as a surface that makes

that difference between the poet and "the Outside" perceptible. Her inclination toward myth was also encouraged by Duncan, who accorded it mystic powers: "The mythic content comes to us, commanding the design of the poem; it calls the poet into action, and with whatever lore and craft he has prepared himself for that call, he must answer to give body in the poem to the formative will" (1985, 13). Kyger synthesized these. Through the figure of Penelope, Kyger's own life could be seen and worked upon a mythic frame. She could keep herself "Outside" while dwelling "inside" myth, using poems as a structure in which to observe her situation as an American poet/wife abroad at a distance that provided some perspective on the difficulties and dissatisfactions associated with her roles.

Kyger discusses her interest in Homer in such situational terms. The Homeric landscape provided her with a conceptual "home," a web of images and associations that she called the "Homer Dome." This was a narrative that she could "get inside of," one that invited her, such that she "could fall in and out of that story for some time." She could find in the Homeric search for home a home for herself, while also connecting to poetry as a tradition. By thus connecting, she "learned that there was a big Story" in which being a woman entailed certain constraints (1983, 110). In the Penelope poems, Kyger explored a detail of the "big Story" that remains undeveloped in (or excised from) the Homeric texts she encountered while working in San Francisco's Brentano's bookstore, where she would jot off letters to Duncan and sneak into the overstock area to read. Kyger addressed what has long been a point of difficulty for Homeric scholars: the question of Penelope's intentions and character. As feminist critics have noted, all that could be heard in *The Odyssey* is not; Penelope's *kleos*, or "renown," literally all of which is heard, is characteristically "identical with her capacity for endurance and her faithfulness to Odysseus" (Katz, 5-6). In a more radical reading, Kyger included what is not heard in *The Odyssey* to formulate an interpretation. She inscribed another Penelope, scandalous, promiscuous (or simply unfaithful), a Penelope written over by canonical myth, to whom she found an apocryphal reference, possibly in Robert Graves's *The Greek Myths*. It explains: "Some deny that Penelope remained faithful to Odysseus. They accuse her of companying with Amphinomus of Dulichium, or with all the suitors in turn, and say that the fruit of this union was the monster god Pan"

(373). The role of Pan, downplayed in *The Odyssey*, would figure significantly in Kyger's retelling.

In this sense, **The Tapestry and the Web** anticipates the revisionary project that characterizes a feminist poetics shaped by the second-wave women's movement. Yet, writing in the late 1950s and early 1960s, prior to the second-wave women's movement and in the absence of any supportive community of women writers, Kyger wrote singly, not to demystify "woman" or to understand her own writing as specifically feminine. In fact, for Kyger the question of poetic identity was not at base a question of "male or female" (undated, n.p.); rather she saw it as her task to be "the instigator" and "propagator" of her own definition of female—one that could encompass the contraries of being herself the muse to her circle of male poets and her life the medium of her own poetry (1974, 150). Neither was she occupied by the multifarious surfaces of a deep-rooted misogyny that were to galvanize the next generation of women—except in that she "hate[d] the word 'female'" when it implied "a traditional role in which the woman is supportive to the idea" (150). She was highly critical of the dynamics she witnessed in other American couples whom she observed when she lived in Japan, especially those occasions upon which men gave too many orders and women "[fell] all over and [talked] baby talk" when they came into a room (1981, 232). The critique she was to render in her treatment of *The Odyssey* was a protofeminist consequence of her own sense of American women's culturally instituted subservience, which had been made starkly apparent to her outside of its naturalizing context. In a feminist critique of patriarchy, Kyger confronts both the representations of women and the structures in which these occur. And though it precedes the sexual revolution, **The Tapestry and the Web** lays bare this nexus of concerns in order to move through them, aiming for a revolution in consciousness nonetheless.

Life in Japan was estranging and, though often lonely, it proved to be productive; in Japan Kyger would reconcile with gender-biased conceptual restraints that tended to masculinize poetic production. Her anxieties took an alarming turn when she realized that being a woman and a writer was at the heart of much of her discontent—"I wish I had never known writing and then I'd be more content with what I am doing now instead of wishing I was proving myself by writing" (1981, 36). Though the marital frame immediately defined her in a most concrete way, she continued to see herself in relation to her North Beach friends, with whom she corresponded, and continued to identify strongly as the one woman among her male peers. So involved was this identification that news from home could invoke antagonism, and on one occasion she singles out another woman as a figure of dissimilitude: "I get nervous. Everyone seems to be writing and publishing but me. Thea says in a letter she sent all her things to Evergreen—but that they sent them all back—I should think so" (1981, 40).[8] Though she felt strongly that her perceived conceptual restraints did not affect her practice of writing (undated, n.p.), she felt at the same time pressured to measure up to her male—and not her female—peers. The "everyone" to whom she refers, more likely than not, are specific men; whether Kyger is implying that the fact that Thea was a woman lay behind her rejection is not clear. Nevertheless, her "I should think so" places a disdainful distance between herself and Thea.

While literally outside the concerns that in San Francisco were made evident on a daily basis, Kyger, as Snyder's wife, was sensitized to other sex-based limitations. On the boat to Japan, she decided to stay only a short time and not to marry, but soon after arriving, she and Snyder wed—as expected by the Zen Institute, where Snyder was a student. She felt at times "trapped," "overpowered," wished she had not married, and was reticent toward his matrimonial prerogative: "He seems to have plans for me, although he claims no—and I will not fit into them" (1981, 10). Her feelings toward Snyder typically fluctuated from love and acceptance to unease and a seemingly externally prompted self-criticism: "indeed I am bad tempered / foulmo[u]thed etc." (13). Struggle was laid out in gendered terms: "Is his own masculinity threatened that he must fight so hard to assert himself & show no regard for my desires or identity. As far as I can recall he has always treated women this way, at least that is what I have been told" (30). Out of the tension between wanting to write and being called upon to fulfill the role of wife came an imagined alternative, "a room all my own to decorate with pictures and plants just the way I wanted with no one to intrude, high ceilinged light & airy" and she hoped "someday to be able to make it alone writing in such a room" (31). But her own desire conflicted with Snyder's highly conventional expectations and her sense of obligation to them. While she felt that she would have to leave, she worried about what would become of his plans: "I want him to be happy & have what he wants, a family etc. But I must live too, I see no solution" (31). Seeing no way to achieve her solitude, she was beset by self-doubt: "I wish I could just pack up and get out for a day or so, then perhaps I could see things clearer, perhaps the faults are all mine—he leads me to think so" (31). The wish to be alone was inseparable from the need to write; in writing, in being alone, came the possibility that her identity was not overdetermined. This hinged on the question of how to act that also occupied her (249). Solitude proposed a space in which to act freely. In anticipation of this she asked Snyder "what if I was involved in doing something & didn't want to do the dishes for say a few days—I want to feel the freedom of acting that way should the possibility arise." But her husband was inflexible: "He would not grant me that, he said" (33).

Kyger attempted to become a more serious student of Zen—not at the institute, which prohibited female students, but in her home, though there she always felt inadequate in light of Snyder's strict discipline. She moved her Zen practice from a context in which she felt pressured to "do more and more Zazen to get anywhere at all" (1981, 2), bringing it to bear on her writing practice. Zen-inspired questions of self mark her personal writing from the early part of this period: "For my fractured consciousness, Zen Buddhism seems to me the only path out of the nothingness of Western philosophy. I need to find that discipline, that art form" (3). Toward the end of her journals, her writing becomes the focus of inquiry. Striving for Zen-like clarity, she reminded herself to "[a]im for a whole new way of using language. There should be no artificial abbreviations (of sentences etc.) in poetry. Closer to the mind it comes out how? Or the mind close to the poem, comes out with its own good poetry" (242). Zen informed her poetic sensibility, a meditative noticing of the movement of the mind that is evident in the fifth of "The Odyssey Poems," "Meeting May 20":

> 'for by day my one relief is to weep and sigh
>   Am I to stay
> winding and coming back, goes out and sees,
>   dreams
> are awkward things
>   a cigarette falls behind the bed
>   I *can't* get out of bed
>   she pushes
>   where where are the walls,
> out the window the poetry, dishes broken,
>   things torn up, please
>   please don't weep anymore.
>   the suitors are sickened w/ blood, look
>   how they decay, kill them all

> an eagle takes a terrified dove
> and she places a good chair to hear what goes on
>   (1965, 57)

But the usefulness of Zen was limited. It was, after all, what her husband's Japan could offer her; he was its privileged subject. Its nonintrusive approach would not accomplish the work of negotiating the dueling expectations that constituted, in part, their marriage. Oblique questions of consciousness such as "How can i be something specific / yet undefined?" (1981, 61) offer a weak accompaniment to her specifically gendered struggles for self-definition, and in the imported figure of Penelope she discovered more powerful poetic tools. On July 26, 1960, she wrote: "To penetrate (Penelope) the depth found within, the actual feeling, go into. Not idealistically, not ideas of psychological sort" (43). Mythic themes forge multiple relations to the biographical; rewriting Penelope's role in *The Odyssey*, Kyger managed to mingle her own willful vision and pursue the Zen-like "[q]uestions of identity & how to act" that urged her on (249). Penelope enabled her to address poetically the sexual and intellectual anxieties and apparently immutable dictates which together bolstered the muse/poet binary—one that was at the heart of her husband's marital presumptions—and then break with them. Penelope's story prompted her to explore the "big Story." It offered a model of resistance in the wake of a series of decisions that she had wavered over, of others' desires acquiesced to.

Further, Kyger chose to follow an aberrant thread—the apocryphal story that challenges the Penelope valued in *The Odyssey*. Thus in **The Tapestry and the Web**, Kyger's rather standard poetic treatment of *The Odyssey* challenges its premises in subtle ways. Kyger's desire to write through *The Odyssey*, coupled with her refusal to occupy the place designated feminine in the process, overturned an epic mode of production that imagines text to be communicated to the male poet by the disembodied female muse. This significantly complicates conceptions of the epic text—and casts doubt on Kyger's fitness as an epic poet. With this different view and her desire to entertain different mythic aspects, Kyger swerved away from contemporary poetic concerns into her own feminist space. Her conceptual swerve mirrors the apocryphal "swerve," the aberrant narrative line, that it was her project to follow. This departure, however, presented a formal concern: how she could ever be a great poet, ever "write an epic the way [Pound biographer Charles Norman] says a great poet must," that is, ever "have the command of a world / universal view" (1981, 225).

One answer to this question would be articulated years later, in the wake of the Vietnam War, by Alice Notley, who struggled to write an epic about her experience of the war that did not champion heroism. Notley suggested that there are two choices for the aspiring female epic poet: she might make her heroine manlike in action, knowledge, and/or experience, or try to suit epic to what a woman is like, to "make something lofty and grand in another way than a man's" (1994, 103). Kyger's revision of *The Odyssey* follows this second tack. Through disassembling parts of the epic and expanding on certain particulars, **The Tapestry and the Web** risks the question of how as a woman Kyger might assemble her part in relation to the heroic, the larger whole. Like "the Homeric rhapsode who sew[ed] together songs" (Nagy, 21) recomposing parts that had been dispersed,[9] Kyger returns the epic story to recomposition, as it had been in the oral tradition, where the text remained open to potential reweaving with the unwritten and the unperformed. Her retellings produce another set of truths and potentialities. Thus Penelope is a potent figure not only because *The Odyssey* tells so little of her story and leaves her in relative obscurity (*penelope* means, literally, "with a web over her face"), or because it provides her with a web of appearances beneath which she carries out her true design, but also because Penelope's craft, her complicated tapestry making, resembles Kyger's own.

Kyger's aberration is her introduction to an augmentation of this apocryphal tale. As she points out in an untitled poem that serves as an introduction to the Penelope poems,

> Somewhere you can find reference to the
> fact that PAN was the
> son of PENELOPE
> Either as the result of a *god*
> or as a result of ALL the suitors
> who hung around while
> Odysseus was abroad.
> (1965, 29 emphasis in original)

In the Homeric version of the myth, home is the site of those repetitive activities—like tapestry making—that limit female experience and preserve the place of women and men in relation to it. The duplicity at the heart of Penelope's tapestry-making ruse is gestured toward in Kyger's book title by two trails of reference leading out—the enduring tapestry and the provisional and remade web. Enduring and provisional, Penelope's tactic,

by delaying remarriage, ensures Odysseus's return to a place unchanged in his absence while at the same time creating the time for that to happen, the time in which Odysseus's story unfolds. What occupies *her* time is not of importance; what matters is what must not happen: his home must not fall into dissolution; only then is his heroic homecoming assured. Penelope's "circumspection," her craftiness, ensures this.

But in Kyger's version, home opens onto nontraditional narrative, generative rather than preservative: spawning Pan not only represents her sexual adventures, it introduces into the mythic genealogy the unpredictable, a "monster" (half goat, half man) who runs about generating his own undisciplined and prolific narrative in "12.29 & 30 (Pan as the son of Penelope)":

> And where did she hide her impudent monster?
> He was acres away by then I suppose in the
>   sunlight leching
>   at some round breasted sheep
> girl.
>   the cock crowing at dawn never had bigger
>   thoughts than he did
> about waking up the world.
>   (1965, 31)

The apocryphal reveals a schism between the mythic and the real. Against its borders both sides are rewritten. Revelation shifts focus, consigns new significance despite the tightness of the authoritative whole. Pan is "Bred of the weaver," "bold" and "the result of impatience" (30). His appearance and characteristics bear witness to his lineage in an attempt to wake up the world to a sexualized image of Penelope. Because this Penelope is otherwise covered over and encoded, Pan's promiscuity becomes an acceptable symbol of her sexuality which remains, even in Kyger's radical version, displaced, "acres away". Her sexual power is related to narrative determinacy. In Kyger's revision Penelope has the power to thwart the return of Odysseus; she is concocting his adventures rather than weeping for his return:

> *I* choose to think of her waiting for him
>   concocting his adventures bringing
>   the misfortunes to him
> —she must have had her hands full.
>   (31 emphasis in original)

Kyger delegates to Penelope—not Calypso or Circe, Athena or Zeus—the power to control Odysseus's fate; it is she who, by inhibiting his return, controls the epic trajectory and, in doing so, prolongs the length of their marital caesura. This is reinforced by the fact that Penelope shows no enthusiasm for his return: "She did not run up and embrace him as I recall. / He came upon her at the house & killed the suitors" (31). Doubt is further propagated by Kyger's jesting tone. Unhinged from the gravity of Penelope's situation as *The Odyssey* retells it, "**12.29 & 30 (Pan as the son of Penelope)**," the fourth poem in the Penelope sequence, works in the mode of question and assertion to sardonically cast doubt on the canonical interpretation. It is a corrective that is decidedly playful but that also renders a serious protofeminist critique of the romanticized tinge upon what Adrienne Rich would, in the next decade, call the institution of motherhood. A tone of gossipy levity runs throughout in comments such as "What a birth / THAT must have been. Did she turn away & sigh and I believe she dreamed too much" (31). Thus Penelope is brought into a contemporary context resonating with accusative clarity on current expectations and mores:

> Refresh my thoughts of Penelope again.
> Just HOW
>   solitary was her wait?
> I notice Someone got to her that
>   barrel chested he-goat prancing
>   around w/ his reed pipes
>
> is no fantasy of small talk.
> More the result of BIG talk
>   and the absence of her husband.
>
>   (31)

Though "Someone got to her," Penelope "knew what she was doing" (31). Penelope, in other words, is not a victim in a schema that renders women powerless in narratives of pursuit and conquest or constraint—of which, in myth, there are many. Instead she is an agent in the construction of her own domestication, one that is deviant and empowering. Kyger imagines not the chastity represented by Penelope's weaving and unweaving, but rather the sexual activity her tapestry making and unmaking is supposed to have replaced.

Penelope's life is left relatively untreated in *The Odyssey*. She makes a few appearances in the epic, always in relation to her task. Though it represents her passivity and chasteness, when those characteristics are overlooked, as in Kyger's creation of a more dynamic Penelope, her life emerges as a yet-to-be-textualized imaginative space. As rhapsode, Kyger steps in to rectify the paucity of details regarding Penelope, the substantive loss of her in the canonical retelling. She suggests that the tapestry making is an act of self-creation, much like her own poetry: "I believe she dreamed too much. Falling into her weaving / creating herself as a fold in her tapestry" (1965,

31). This craft, Kyger's rendering suggests, is like that of the poet who breaks from the tightly woven web of authoritative voices and follows up new strands, a process that begins by refuting the so-called facts: "We are in a tighter web than I had imagined. / that story / about him capturing a girl in the woods was a lie!" (30). "Linear space," Kyger has said, "was not a space that I really thought or experienced in. Although it's a good space for your head to follow at times . . . but that space is really, like chunks of things" (1974, 155). When the facts are suspect, when accusations of lying are tossed about, narrative begins to dissolve. Kyger's lack of interest in preserving linear narrative as a structure freed the poem as a space for invention in which she could see "chunks of things" and explore between them possible, unrealized connections. The web of half-truths and accusations characterizing Penelope's story is collaged with chunks of story from Kyger's own lineage, which reveals a compassion for a tragic figure, who is, like Pan, "of another sort":

> My mother always remembered the
> crippled boy in her grade school class who teased
>   her.
>
>   he was ugly.
>   of another sort.
>
>   But then are You one
> or many.   Could I meet you, drive away the
>   children who beat you with sticks.
>   (1965, 30)

In a reference to both Penelope and Kyger as craftswomen, the crippled boy is shown to be a product of imaginative interminglings: "But then I forget you / have been made by the excellent craftsman, she / is lovely" (30). The poem stands as a record of her mother's memories and a testament to Penelope's procreative craftsmanship—details otherwise lost.

Kyger seemed to have felt *The Tapestry and the Web* coming together—or failing to—as early as April 1962, during her travels in India with Snyder, Ginsberg, and Peter Orlovsky. This trip recalls her struggles with self-definition and her inheritance of their poetic lineage. Significantly, questions regarding her own project in developing *The Tapestry and the Web* emerge at the same time. After a particularly trying evening during which an "overwhelming reaction against Ginsberg choked and suffocated" her and she felt "if I give up, I'll walk into the ocean and swallow it into myself," she wrote in her journal: "The words are not precise, not muse. The tapestry book here. Not a key to lead me on, not a passageway that begins to turn. Nothing to send me on, it always stops" (1981, 97). "Muse" becomes inadequate as a descriptor for her work. Perhaps the male poet, represented by Ginsberg, cannot be relied upon to mediate her voice, which, rather, he suffocates. The loss of voice, what she calls "giving up," is equivalent to a loss of self, to drowning.

In 1963, her last year in Japan and the final year of her marriage, her anxieties waned and her journal writing moved into a more productive poetic space. Textual encounters were occasion to reflect on the significance of her patrilineage and shaped a path that *The Tapestry and the Web*, and "**The Odyssey Poems**" in particular, would follow. In one journal entry, she copied these lines from Charles Norman's 1960 biography of Ezra Pound, which reflect Olson's central image in "Projective Verse": "The poet's line reveals not only his manner of expression, hence the way he thinks, it reveals his identity almost, it might be said, his way of breathing. And this individual structure is all that can be called different in the poets" (1981, 227). On this occasion to rethink Olson's influence her own aesthetic choices regarding the line were confirmed. She also copied "thus no matter where the discussion starts, it is always necessary to return to the line and its structure" (227). This justification of the line as primary, a detail through which one might, in part, address the daunting epic whole, could have been reassuring. It meant that what Kyger perceived as a woman's craft, dealing with "parts" and "particulars"—like Penelope the tapestry maker who focuses on the fragment—though it seemed contradictory to epic's episodic historical movement, might instead constitute a component of that movement. Still, according to Olson, writing large was a measure of poetic greatness; through the practice of projective verse, he writes, "the problem of large content and larger forms may be solved" (1997, 248). Next to what she had read of the celebrated achievements and comprehension of Pound, Kyger's own achievements appeared to shrink to inadequacy: "What can I know without reading & observing all of mankind," she wrote, "[m]y own mind but a risky & perhaps lopsided direction" (1981, 225-226). For her part, Kyger was reading Emily Dickinson's poetry, Gertrude Stein's lectures, and Edna St. Vincent Millay's letters—the work of three women poets who, in various ways, approached large content without the "larger forms" that Olson deemed necessary. Though daunted by Pound's purview, Kyger nevertheless undertook a poetic treatment of history: her own history and the fact of epic as a part of her historical, poetic inheritance.

"The Odyssey Poems" witness Kyger's homecoming made strange by the myths and mutations she had brought along with her from her sojourn in Japan. After four years abroad, she returned to San Francisco on January 20, 1964, the deadline for the first issue of *Open Space*. Edited by Stan Persky throughout 1964, *Open Space* was to be a working space to help make young poets visible. Kyger was one of these young poets. Poems from "**The Odyssey Poems**," written between April and December 1964, appeared in four of its thirteen issues. Parts of "**The Odyssey Poems**" appear in her Japan journal alongside an emerging sense of independence and discussions with Snyder over the possibility of divorce. Her textual experience provided a way to navigate the changing nature of her marriage. The figures of Odysseus and Penelope are equally disrupted; the gender identities of this mythic pair, which had been replicated in her own marriage, are distorted. Though "**The Odyssey Poems**," for the most part, leave out any reference to Pan, the symbolic weight of his generative swerve continues to propel Penelope away from her prescribed role in *The Odyssey*. Kyger further contemporizes and develops Penelope's character, and, coincidentally, the primacy of Odysseus's story degenerates into an oddity—a collage of details mythic, fictional, and contemporary.

The epic and its ideologies examined in "**The Odyssey Poems**" are thus brought into the present to bear the scrutiny of Kyger's own experience, through which an understanding of the myth and her commentary on it would emerge. Forging this temporal link, Kyger titled the first of "**The Odyssey Poems**" "**April 8. The Plan**," and like many of her poems it evokes the present, and presence, by creating an intersubjective space, beginning "Where ever you go I am with you. / and bring you back" (1965, 53). The poem returns received words, "Where ever you go I am with you," a profession of faith and companionship despite distance. The source of the quote is unrevealed; it could be Athena addressing Odysseus in *The Odyssey*. It could also, in a characteristic twist, be an address to Penelope, since in Kyger's poetic imagination Penelope, unbound from her tapestry-making task, does "go" and Kyger is "with" her and does, in her poetic sequence, "bring" her "back"—back, that is, into a plausible reality, back "to life" and away from restrictive fictions. The unattributed quote achieves mythic status and suggests a perpetual rereading of this familiar assurance, a rereading that continually occurs in the present: it is brought back into contemporaneity and localized. Thus retelling history does not reproduce it, but rather produces another history, a history that incorporates the telling self as both an agent of history—a history maker—and an historical object—an element to be incorporated in future iterations. Perhaps written in anticipation of her homecoming, this poem, in reweaving and altering Odysseus's homecoming, accommodates her own.

> The morning venus
> sailing into the bay,
>   lifting him asleep onto the land
>   he has returned to
> and doesn't know where he is.
>   outside of San Francisco
>   the long paths and eucalyptus
>   are another country
>
> (53)

Juxtaposed to an account of Odysseus's arrival home to Ithaca is a description of Kyger's personal geography, her San Francisco. It witnesses her homecoming at the same time that it is made strange by Odysseus's and Kyger's presences. Typical in these lines is Kyger's ambiguous use of subjects and verbs, so that meaning shifts: the verb phrase "doesn't know" can be read as the complement of either "he" or "land," so that Odysseus is lost to himself and also a foreigner to the land in which Kyger is a native. The Ithaca to which Odysseus returns and the San Francisco to which Kyger is returning become one and the same.

This web of gender identity (Kyger/Penelope becomes Kyger/Penelope/Odysseus) is indicative of the intricate weaving of narratives and details that characterize "The Odyssey Poems." Whereas in the Penelope poems Kyger stood relatively distinct from Penelope, as an "I" thinking of "her," in "The Odyssey Poems" their identities blend. Penelope's narrative bears details current to Kyger's life in her/their expression of dismay, as the following passage from "April 23. Possibilities" illustrates:

> She comes and rages
> quit eating the coffee cake and cottage cheese
> put the lid on the peanut butter jar
>   sandwiches made of cucumber, stop eating
>   the *food*!
>
> (1965, 56 emphasis in original)

In the collaging of memories, myths, other's stories, and the present narrative of the "I" who is writing them, the poems are a series of tapestries and webs, distinct vignettes juxtaposed like a blending of threads where language play and image play reorient the mythic and the contemporary. This weaving is extended across gender as well. For example, the first three poems ("April 8.

The Plan," "Whether he is dead or not . . . ," and "Land at the first point you meet") seem to be the descriptions of an "I" who is Penelope and a "he," Odysseus. But in the fourth poem this switches to a "she" addressing a "you," commenting first on Penelope ("Still after fifteen years or more she doesn't know") and then addressing an unspecified "he" and a different "you":

> climbing over the rough ravine
> and up an impossible cliff, naked, you mark
>   how high you can go
> coming back to his opinion of her and hers of
>   him
>   listening sometimes
> to *him* raging, you leave me alone. you dream of
>   me.
>
>   and there, she withdrew
>
>   and wept for odysseus
>   (56, emphasis in original)

Now it is Odysseus who is the figure of obscurity, Penelope-like, with a web over *his* face. The instability of his identity allows Kyger to negotiate his symbolic weight. With Odysseus no longer the mythic hero-adventurer, a more heroic Penelope (and Kyger) emerges. An altercation ensues after the male figure descends from his great height, "coming back to his opinion of her and hers of him." This suggests a demystifying of the heroic figure—who is then wept for—but also an exchange across the gap between *The Odyssey* and "The Odyssey Poems" in which it is *his* raging that is heard. The effect, however, is complicated by the obscurity of some of the referents. Who is the "you"? Is it an imperative to her to leave him alone, dream of him? Or is it her appeal to be left alone and dreamed about? The confusion is central to the confounding of myths, and that confounding an occasion for the weeping that overcomes Penelope and with her the implied "I" of the poem. Withdrawing from the mythic world, Penelope/ "she" weeps for the loss of that world, but also for the loss of contemporary men as heroic figures. Descending from the "impossible cliff," he remains, after all, just as he went up it—a man.

The break between "she withdrew" and "and wept . . ." also signals a removal from both the world of contemporaneity (the story of the "she") and the world of myth (Penelope's story). She is in a space between, an interstice in which she can escape her own life but also realize the distance from, and relationship to, that other, mythic place. Within the frame of the great epic of Western tradition, Penelope weeps for the loss of a presence desired. But in the frame of Kyger's epic revisioning, "she" weeps perhaps for the loss of the heroic as a narrative she can live inside and turn to for a sense of stability and definition. In mourning this, Kyger risks a betrayal of her mentor Duncan and turns onto a path unmarked by his dictates. That loss, these lines imply, while liberating for the female figure, can only be remade, reenacted in the lost object or image, but never restored. This is reflected in her journal entry on New Year's Eve 1963, in which Kyger decided to forgo mythic sources. She planned for herself a newly disciplined course:

> Resolutions: In order to rise as a poet, the craft of poetry must be studied and known. Painful as it may be, hours each day should be spent scanning poetry sheets and volumes of the past. New conscious ground expansion for poems and ordinary proficiency both executed daily. The craft should fit like a glove. Exactly: from my own life, not sources from myth.
>
> (1981, 269)

There is tension here in what appears to be a satire of Poundian didacticism and the imperative in the last line—to take one's life as a source, rather than "sources from myth"—in which Pound serves as but another mythic presence in the "volumes of the past" that Kyger urges herself to scan "hours each day." Or this last sentence might signal such a breaking away, a realization that a glove-like fit of craft can't be achieved through another's discipline, especially when that discipline, like Snyder's Zen studies, are exacted at the cost of one such as herself, expected to accommodate his demanding study schedule through her domestic labor. Indeed, the undertone of sarcasm in this resolution suggests that these closing pages of *The Japan and India Journals* are tinged with an ironic self-awareness: the "resolution" may follow Snyder's model, but the resolve is finally her own, "from my own life, not sources from myth." Kyger, about to part from Snyder and return to San Francisco, faces the opportunity to live out this self-directed resolution. Kyger's own life was, as *The Tapestry and the Web* shows, always a source for "conscious ground expansion." Through a contrivance of mythic images and innovative structures, through hybridizing them with her own—the whole of her identity-consciousness, from practicing Zen to writing poetry—would serve to (re)define the role she was, according to contemporary mores at least, given to play.

The last of "The Odyssey Poems," "From our soundest sleep, it ends VII," includes the comment "It has been difficult to write this." This poem describes Odysseus as "that great fighter / having a guide, a female presence who pulls her own self into battle also" (1965, 61). Kyger, too, is that female presence, pulling herself into battle with difficulties, both practical and intellectual, enacted in the pages of her journals and poems. Penelope's alternative narrative, vitalized in adjoined apocrypha unearthing Pan's genesis, is openly played against *The Odyssey*, confounding and confusing canonical mythos and rendering the figure of Penelope more complex and far more ambiguous than tradition allows. Her retelling of epic history does not reproduce it, but rather produces another history. Kyger includes what is not heard in *The Odyssey* to create an intricate, structured poetics, a reimagination of poetry and of her identity as a poet. The poems that comprise *The Tapestry and the Web* uncouple and rework concepts of gender and poetic authority she inherited from a poetic tradition sustained through Homer, Olson, Duncan, and Spicer and ultimately swerved away from. Her work is charged by what Kathleen Fraser has called "an innovative necessity," the need to improvise "one's relation to language as often as is necessary," a strategy especially pertinent for a woman poet who situates herself in a tradition whose imperatives grant her a limited range of options for self-creation, few role models, and fewer publishing opportunities (207). *The Tapestry and the Web* broaches the question of how poetic knowledge is formed despite this paucity and, cleaving the possibility for a postmodernist feminist epistemology from epic structures and ideology, anticipates questions of gender and genius that feminist scholarship would pursue.

Notes

1. Kyger's work also compares to poems in Barbara Guest's first collection (1962), "Dido to Aeneas" and "The Hero Leaves His Ship," the opening lines of which declare "I wonder if this new reality is going to destroy me" (20). While such foreboding does not characterize Kyger's approach, she realizes hers as an encounter with a potentially destructive "new reality" nonetheless.

2. "The Odyssey Poems" begin with "Tapestry," the second of three poems thus titled, and include "Note: 'Somewhere you can find reference'," "We are in a tighter web," "12.19 & 30 (Pan as the son of Penelope)," "A song in the rope," and "waiting again."

3. These journals have recently been republished as *Strange Big Moon: The Japan and India Journals 1960-1964* ([1981] 2000).

4. It is important in understanding these familiar involutions to recall the schism that existed between the Spicer-Duncan circles and the Beat writers. Michael Davidson writes, "the San Francisco Renaissance was

by no means unified, nor did it necessarily revolve around the figures who read at the Six Gallery [Ginsberg, Michael McClure, Snyder, Philip Whalen, and Philip Lanantia, Oct. 7, 1955]. . . . Two major poets of the period—Robert Duncan and Jack Spicer, both of whom were intimately associated with the formation of the Six Gallery—were not part of the reading, nor did they identify the Beat movement as 'their' renaissance" (3).

5. The appearance of *The Tapestry and the Web,* published by Donald Allen's Four Seasons Foundation in 1965, as well as Kyger's inclusion in the re-edited British edition of *The New American Poetry,* published two years later, *New Writing in the U.S.A.,* edited by Donald Allen and Robert Creeley, seems to signal that she had gained some ground lost by having arrived on the scene too late to be included in Allen's *New American Poetry,* an anthology published in 1960. Something might be made of her exclusion—whether it was to blame for her status as a missing female poet of the Beat generation—but relatively little has been made of Kyger in the anthologies and literary histories that seek to recapture and contextualize the San Francisco of the Beat Generation and the San Francisco Renaissance, with the exception of the hasty genealogies of anthologies specific to women writers that inadvertently misplace Kyger as a female beatnik. The recent biography of Jack Spicer by Lewis Ellingham and Kevin Killian is an exception. Alan Golding's "*The New American Poetry* Revisited, Again" also illuminates.

6. Though the oft-republished "Projective Verse" originally appeared in the literary magazine *Poetry New York* in 1950, its publication by LeRoi Jones's Totem Press sealed its cult status. It was reprinted the next year as the leading essay in the "Poetics" section of Donald Allen's *New American Poetry,* thus appearing as the most significant articulation of the breakaway, anti-establishment aesthetic that the anthology sought to portray.

7. For an elaboration of a later generation of women poets influenced, in part, by Olson's field, see Kathleen Fraser's "Translating the Unspeakable: Visual Poetics, as Projected through Olson's Field into Current Female Writing Practice" (2000, 174-200).

8. It is unclear who Thea is; she is referred to in the journals by this name only.

9. In Pindar, Gregory Nagy finds reference to the fact that Homeric poetry had been scattered about, that it was the rhapsode who joined the pieces together, so that the master poet Homer is the ultimate joiner retrojected as the original genius of epic (21).

Works Cited

———. 1977. "Three Versions of the Poetic Line." Interview by Robert Bertholf with Joel Oppenheimer and Ed Dorn. *Credences* 4: 55-66.

———. 1979. *The Wonderful Focus of You.* Calais, Vt.: Z Press.

———. 1981. *The Japan and India Journals: 1960-1964.* Bolinas, Calif.: Tombouctou Books. Republished 2000. *Strange Big Moon: The Japan and India Journals 1960-1964.* Berkeley, Calif.: North Atlantic Books.

———. 1983. "Congratulatory Poetics." Interview by Diana Middleton-McQuaid and John Thorpe. *Convivio:* 109-120.

———. 1984. *Revolution in Poetic Language.* Translated by Margaret Waller. New York: Columbia University Press.

———. 1989. *Phenomenological.* Canton, N.Y.: Institute for Further Studies.

———. 1992. Joanne Kyger. Vol. 16 of *Contemporary Authors Autobiography Series.* Edited by Joyce Nakamura. Detroit, Mich.: Gale Research.

———. 1996. *Some Sketches from the Life of Helena Petrovna Blavatsky.* Boulder, Colo.: Rodent Press & Erudite Fangs.

———. 1999. *Patzcuaro.* Bolinas, Calif.: Blue Millenium Press.

———. Undated. "Thoughts on being a woman poet starting in the '50s." Unpublished manuscript. Bolinas, Calif..

Lee, A. Robert. 1996. *The Beat Generation Writers.* London: Pluto Press.

LeJeune, Phillip. 1989. "The Autobiographical Pact." In *On Autobiography.* Edited by Paul John Eakin. Translated by Katherine Leary. Minneapolis: University of Minnesota Press.

Loewinsohn, Ron. 1959. *Watermelons.* New York: Totem Press.

Mackey, Nathaniel. 1993. *Djbot Bhagostus's Run.* Los Angeles: Sun and Moon Press.

———. 1997. *Bedouin Hornbook.* Los Angeles: Sun and Moon Press.

Mann, Ron, director and producer. 1982. *Poetry in Motion.* Distributed by Home Vision Cinema/Public Media Inc. 2000 (Chicago).

Marcus, Greil. 1997. *Invisible Republic: Bob Dylan's Basement Tapes.* New York: Henry Holt.

McNally, Dennis. 1979. *Desolate Angel: Jack Kerouac, the Beat Generation, and America.* New York: Random House.

McNeil, Helen. 1996. "The Archeology of Gender in the Beat Movement." In *The Beat Generation Writers.* Edited by A. Robert Lee. London: Pluto Press.

Metalious, Grace. 1956. *Peyton Place.* New York: Messner.

Meyerowitz, Joanne, ed. 1994. *Not June Cleaver: Women and Gender in Postwar America, 1945-1960.* Philadelphia: Temple University Press.

Miles, Barry. 1989. *Ginsberg: A Biography.* New York: HarperCollins.

Miller, Nancy K. 1988. *Subject to Change: Reading Feminist Writing.* New York: Columbia University Press.

———. 2000. "But Enough About Me, What Do You Think of My Memoir?" *The Yale Journal of Criticism* 13, no. 2: 421-436.

Moffeit, Tony. 1989. "Interview with Diane di Prima." Unpublished. Boulder, Colo.

Mokey, Susan. 1998. *Desires of Their Own: Twentieth-Century Women Novelists and Images of the Erotic.* Ann Arbor, Mich.: University Microfilm.

Mulvey, Laura. 1989. *Visual and Other Pleasures.* Bloomington: Indiana University Press.

Nagy, Gregory. 1996. *Homeric Questions*. Austin: University of Texas Press.

Natsoulas/Novelozo Gallery Press. 1990. *Lyrical Vision: The 6 Gallery 1954-1957*. Davis, Calif.: Natsoulas/Novelozo Gallery Press.

Nelson, Cary. 1981. *Our Last First Poets: Vision and History in Contemporary American Poetry*. Urbana: University of Illinois Press.

———. 1989. *Repression and Recovery: Modern American Poetry and the Politics of Cultural Memory, 1910-1945*. Madison: The University of Wisconsin Press.

Nielsen, Aldon. 1994. "LeRoi Jones as Intertext." In *Writing Between the Lines: Race and Intertextuality*. Athens: University of Georgia Press.

———. 1997. *Black Chant: Languages of African-American Postmodernism*. Cambridge, U.K.: Cambridge University Press.

Neitzsche, Friedrich. 1967. *The Will to Power*. Edited by Walter Kaufmann. Translated by Walter Kaufmann and R. J. Hollingdale. New York: Random House.

Notley, Alice. 1992. "Homer's Art." In *The Scarlet Cabinet*. New York: Scarlet Editions.

———. 1994. "Epic and Women Poets." In *Disembodied Poetics*. Edited by Anne Waldman and Andrew Schelling. Albuquerque: University of New Mexico Press.

———. 1996. *The Descent of Alette*. New York: Penguin Books.

O'Hara, Frank. 1974. "Personal Poem." In *The Selected Poems of Frank O'Hara*. New York: Random House.

Olson, Charles. 1983. *The Maximus Poems*. Edited by George Butterick. Berkeley: University of California Press.

———. 1997. "Projective Verse." Reprinted in *Collected Prose*. Edited by Donald M. Allen and Benjamin Friedlander. Berkeley: University of California Press.

Oppen, George. 1966. *Discrete Series*. Cleveland, Ohio: Asphodel Book Shop.

Ostriker, Alicia Suskin. 1982. "Blake, Ginsberg, Madness, and the Prophet as Shaman." In *William Blake and the Moderns*. Edited by Robert J. Bertholf and Anna S. Levitt. Albany: State University of New York Press.

———. 1987. *Stealing the Language: The Emergence of Women's Poetry in America*. London: The Women's Press.

———. 1997. "'Howl' Revisited: The Poet as Jew." *American Poetry Review* 26, no. 4 (July/August): 28-31.

Peabody, Richard, ed. 1997. *A Different Beat: Writings by Women of the Beat Generation*. London: High Risk Books.

Perloff, Marjorie. 1990. *Poetic License: Essays on Modernist and Postmodernist Lyric*. Evanston, Ill.: Northwestern University Press.

Persky, Stan. 1964. "Proposition." *Open Space* no. 0.

Plimpton, George, ed. 1999. *Beat Writers at Work*. New York: Modern Library.

Pommy Vega, Janine. 1968. *Poems to Fernando*. San Francisco: City Lights Books.

———. 1979. *Journal of a Hermit &*. Cherry Valley, N.Y.: Cherry Valley Editions.

———. 1997. *Tracking the Serpent: Journeys to Four Continents*. San Francisco: City Lights Books.

Pommy Vega, Janine, and Hettie Jones. 1999. *Words Over Walls: Starting a Writing Workshop in a Prison*. New York: PEN.

Portugés, Paul. 1978. *The Visionary Poetics of Allen Ginsberg*. Santa Barbara, Calif.: Ross-Erikson.

———. 1980. "Allen Ginsberg's Paul Cézanne and the Pater Omnipotens Aeterna Deus." *Contemporary Literature* 21 (summer): 435-449.

Poulin, A. Jr. 1991. "Contemporary American Poetry: The Radical Tradition." In *Contemporary American Poetry*. 5th ed. Edited by A. Poulin Jr. Dallas: Houghton Mifflin.

Prevallet, Kristin. 1997. "An Extraordinary Enchantment: Helen Adam, Robert Duncan, and the San Francisco Renaissance." *The Edinburgh Review* (fall).

Reed, Ishmael. 1993. *Airing Dirty Laundry*. Reading, Mass.: Addison-Wesley.

Rexroth, Kenneth. 1975. *Golden Gate: Interviews with Five San Francisco Poets*. Edited by David Meltzer. San Francisco: Wingbow Press.

Rich, Adrienne. 1976. *Of Woman Born: Motherhood as Experience and Institution*. New York: Norton.

Rosetti, Christina. 1979. *The Complete Poems of Christina Rosetti*. Edited by R. W. Crump. Baton Rouge: Louisiana State University Press.

Russo, Linda. 2000. "On Seeing Poetic Production: The Case of Hettie Jones." Paper delivered at *The Opening of the Field: A Conference on North American Poetry in the 1960s*. 28 June-July 2, The University of Maine, Orono.

Savran, David. 1990. *Taking It Like a Man: White Masculinity, Masochism, and Contemporary American Culture*. Princeton, N.J.: Princeton University Press.

Schumacher, Michael. 1992. *Dharma Lion: A Critical Biography of Allen Ginsberg*. New York: St. Martin's Press.

Shulevitz, Judith. 2000. "Schmatte Hari." *The New Yorker* (April 24 & May 1): 206-211.

Shulman, Alix Kates. 1978. *Burning Questions*. New York: Knopf. Reprint 1990. New York: Thunder's Mouth Press.

Shelley, Mary. 1965. *Frankenstein*. New York: Dell.

Skerl, Jennie, ed. 1997. *A Tawdry Place of Salvation: The Art of Jane Bowles*. Carbondale: Southern Illinois Press.

———, ed. 2000. *College Literature* special issue 27, no. 1 (winter). Teaching Beat Literature.

Skir, Leo. 1996. "Elise Cowen: A Brief Memoir of the Fifties." In *Women of the Beat Generation: The Writers, Artists and Muses at the Heart of a Revolution*. Edited by Brenda Knight. Berkeley, Calif.: Conari Press.

Smith, Harry. 1997. *A Booklet of Essays, Appreciations, and Annotations Pertaining to The Anthology of American Folk Music*. *The Anthology of American Folk Music*. 3 vols. Washington, D.C.: Smithsonian Folkways Recordings.

Smith, Sidonie. 1987. *A Poetics of Women's Autobiography: Marginality and the Fictions of Self-Representation.* Bloomington: Indiana University Press.

Snyder, Gary. 1960. *Myths and Texts.* New York: Totem Press.

———. 1977. "North Beach." In *The Old Ways.* San Francisco: City Lights Books.

Solomon, Barbara Probst. 1960. *The Beat of Life.* New York: Lippencott.

Spicer, Jack. 1975. "After Lorca." In *The Collected Books of Jack Spicer.* Los Angeles: Black Sparrow Press.

———. 1998. *The House that Jack Built: The Collected Lectures of Jack Spicer.* Edited by Peter Gizzi. Hanover, N.H. and London: Wesleyan University Press.

Stewart, Susan. 1991. *Crimes of Writing; Problems in the Containment of Representation.* New York: Oxford University Press.

Stoker, Bram. 1911. *The Lair of the White Worm.* London: W. Foulsham.

Stull, James N. 1993. *Literary Selves: Autobiography and Contemporary American Nonfiction.* Westport, Conn.: Greenwood Press.

Sukenick, Ronald. 1987. *Down and In: Life in the Underground.* New York: Morrow.

Teresa of Avila. 1972. *Interior Castle.* Translated by E. Allison Peers. Garden City, N.Y.: Image Books.

Tytell, John. 1976. *Naked Angels.* New York: Grove Press.

von Hallberg, Robert. 1985. *American Poetry and Culture, 1945-1980.* Cambridge, Mass.: Harvard University Press.

Wakefield, Dan. 1992. *New York in the Fifties.* Boston: Houghton.

Waldman, Anne. 1969. *O My Life!* New York: Angel Hair Books.

———. 1970. *Baby Breakdown.* New York: Bobbs-Merrill.

———. 1975. *Fast Speaking Woman: Chants & Essays.* Rev. ed. 1996. San Francisco: City Lights Books.

———. 1979. "My Life a List." In *Talking Poetics from Naropa Institute.* Edited by Anne Waldman and Marilyn Webb. Vol. 2 of *Annals of the Jack Kerouac School of Disembodied Poetics.* Boulder, Colo.: Shambhala Press.

———. 1984. "An Interview with Diane di Prima." In *The Beat Road.* Edited by Arthur and Kit Knight. California, Pa.: A. Knight.

———. 1989. *Helping the Dreamer: New and Selected Poems, 1966-1988.* Minneapolis, Minn.: Coffee House Press.

———, ed. 1991. *Out of this World: An Anthology of the St. Mark's Poetry Project, 1966-1991.* New York: Crown Books.

———. 1993. *Iovis: All Is Full of Jove.* Vol. 1. Minneapolis, Minn.: Coffee House Press.

———, ed. 1996. *The Beat Book: Poems and Fiction from the Beat Generation.* Boulder, Colo.: Shambhala Press.

———. 1997. *Iovis: All Is Full of Jove.* Vol. 2. Minneapolis, Minn.: Coffee House Press.

Waldman, Anne, and Andrew Schelling, eds. 1994. *Disembodied Poetics: Annals of the Jack Kerouac School.* Albuquerque: University of New Mexico Press.

Watson, Steven. 1995. *The Birth of the Beat Generation: Visionaries, Rebels, and Hipsters, 1944-1960.* New York: Pantheon Books.

Watten, Barrett. 1996. "Being Hailed in and by the 1950s." Paper presented at the conference American Poetry in the 1950s, 21-24 June, University of Maine, Orono.

———. 1997. "The Bride of the Assembly Line: From Material Text to Cultural Poetics." *Impercipient Lecture Series* 1, no. 8 (October): 69-81.

———. Forthcoming. "What Is Literature?" in *Assembling Alternatives.* Edited by Romana Huk. Hanover, N.H. and London: Wesleyan University Press.

Weiners, John. 1996. *707 Scott Street.* Los Angeles: Sun and Moon Press.

Weinreich, Regina. 2000. "The Beat Generation Is Now About Everything." *College Literature* special issue 27, no. 1 (winter): 263-268.

Wilentz, Elias, ed. 1960. *The Beat Scene.* New York: Corinth Books.

Whalen, Philip. 1960. "Further Notice." *Yugen* no. 1.

Woolf, Virginia. 1929. *A Room of One's Own.* New York: Harcourt.

Zizek, Slavoj. 1989. *The Sublime Object of Ideology.* London: Verso.

———. 1996a. "Fantasy as a Political Category: A Lacanian Approach." *Journal for the Psychoanalysis of Culture and Society* 1, no. 2 (fall): 77-85.

———. 1996b. "The Fetish of the Party." In *Lacan, Politics, Aesthetics.* Edited by Willy Apollon and Richard Feldstein. Albany: State University of New York Press.

TITLE COMMENTARY

The Japan and India Journals: 1960-1964

ANNE WALDMAN (ESSAY DATE 2000)

SOURCE: Waldman, Anne. Foreword to *Strange Big Moon, The Japan and India Journals: 1960-1964,* by Joanne Kyger, pp. viii-x. Berkeley, Calif.: North Atlantic Books, 2000.

In the following essay, Waldman offers an overview of The Japan and India Journals, *discussing its composition, themes, and subject matter, and also notes Kyger's place in the Beat and San Francisco Renaissance movements.*

The Japan and India Journals 1960-1964 is a minor classic. It is also one of the finest books ever in the genre of "journal writing." It is—in part—in the tradition of Lady Nijo's Diary, *The Pillow Book* of Sei Shonagon, Basho's *Oku no Hosomichi.* In spite of the resemblance to these culturally distinct Japanese texts and although written primarily in Kyoto, the *Journals* is an uniquely contemporary American product. It is rhizomic in structure, multi-directional. The writer agonizes over the need to "share parts of my life with the other parts—each clump wants to act independently and ignore the existence of anything else." The *Journals* weaves these disparate alluring "selves" together in a stunning tapestry. Irony abounds. Kyger is "self" conscious enough to laugh at herself. She never stoops to sentimentalizing, never drifts into writing-as therapy, as so much current "journaling" (hideous word) does. Yet the writing of these pages is her salvation.

The *Journals* reads like a novel. It has the gait of a love story, a heartbreaking love story set in an exotic Kyoto still somewhat steeped in the past. It's a surprisingly (surreptitiously) feminist tract as well: woman artist struggles for identity and independence in the early 1960s. Likewise a poetics meditation. Poetry fragments tumble in and out of the narrative, as do canny dreams. It is a spiritual account as one of the poet's selves struggles with the axiomatic truths of Buddhism and her own difficulty to sit still. The *Journals* has a wide enough compass to include quotidian accounts of food and drink, wild socializing, lists of birthday presents. It is a study of ritual domesticity, of local plant lore, of flower-arranging, of relationships with Americans abroad as well as Japanese friends and dignitaries within the Japanese Zen community. It names people and things, clearly, precisely. It is myriad stories within the Story of poet Joanne Kyger's life of four years, caught yet energized by a temperamental marriage to the already celebrated poet Gary Snyder. Kyger, our brave and elegant heroine-raconteur, must make and have her own way within the dynamics and constraints of marriage to a famous "Zen student" in an alien culture. She stands tall in her "much reheeled black suede shoes." Yet at its core, the book is essentially about being a writer, "Why write. I want to write the world upsidedown."

Where does Kyger, poet, fit? Then and now, one might ask. Twenty-six years old when the *Journals* open she has already been at the center of a literary life in San Francisco, been close to Robert Duncan, and one of the young writers included in Jack Spicer's exacting gnostic circle. She is bosom pal to Philip Whalen. She fits awkwardly alongside the confessionalism and publicized indulgences of The Beats. In the highly competitive gossipy community around The Place, a bar in North Beach, she is known as "Miss

Kids." Her poetic alignments are with myth with memory with dream. There's a distinctly feminine strength and humility both to the tone and the look of her poems on the page. She already has a singular style in the grace of her line and breath, and she is a master of arrangement. She follows mind's restless patternings. She has yet to publish her first book of poems, *The Tapestry and the Web,* hints and murmurs of which resonate through the poetry and thinking of the *Journals.* Her writing is not at all like the hipness and frankness of Diane diPrima, her nearest female contemporary. When the *Journals* moves to India, Kyger is horrified by Allen Ginsberg's ego as perceived first hand (he wants to read *Howl* to everyone he meets, including the Dalai Lama.) These India travels provide the source of her campiest wit, as she writes to her friend Nemi Frost in a letter that has been famously quoted from the book: "The thing is, I am sounding rather bitter because its been years since I've been able to get any wild martini attention. All I do is stand around in this black drip dry dress in India." Joanne Kyger the Writer forms both a public and private identity here. Taking the measure of her male poet-companions, she is most definitively in a different "space." Perhaps the initial publication of this book in 1981 and the enthusiastic response to it gave Kyger permission to write her own poetry in a way that was closer to this original looseness and bravado.

Joanne Kyger is commonly linked to both the San Francisco Renaissance through her association to Duncan and Spicer, and the Beat literary movement through her marriage and friendships. Yet she never seems to get her due on either front. She shares with the Beats their proverbial wanderlust—mental, psychological, spiritual. Her politics are environmental. She locates the world in tangibles. She is very much a poet of place. Through friendships in the late 60s and early 70s with Ted Berrigan, Joe Brainard, Bill Berkson and others, she also shares an affinity with the New York School. She has been a major figure in the Bolinas literary Renaissance. Yet she remains in a category of her own design and making. Absent from many of the current anthologies of contemporary poets, Kyger's work also suffers from being outside the ken of the critical attention given Language-centered writing. I would argue that it is now time for her work to be given the close reading it deserves. She has been an active, consistently engaged, engaging poet for over forty years. Her public readings are legendary. She is a brilliant and generous teacher. May the re-publication of the *Journals* spark some serious consideration to her life and work.

Her story reminds us that in the 1960s there was still the bohemian possibility of a serious writer living on very little money. That was before "experimental" poetry became an academic pursuit and was funded primarily by grants and university positions. Those years also were a time when some poets were deeply immersed in non-Western spiritual traditions and looked to Asia instead of Europe to expand their sensibilities.

The Japan and India Journals has an honorable place in the annals of the New American Poetry. It is one of the most salient and valuable documents of a writer's life and mind, written during a decisive and exciting time for American poetry. The perspicacity, honesty, struggles and charms of its heroine survive in its pages. It is a happy occasion that this marvelous book finally be brought back to print.

FURTHER READING

Criticism

Coffey, Dan. "'My phenomenology waits': Death and Rebirth in Joanne Kyger's *Phenomenological*." *Jacket* 11 (online magazine), <jacketmagazine.com/11/kyger-coffey.html> (April 2000).

Asserts that Phenomenological *is Kyger's work that is most deserving of critical attention.*

Friedman, Amy L. "'I say my new name': Women Writers of the Beat Generation." In *The Beat Generation Writers,* edited by Robert A. Lee, pp. 200-16. East Haven, Conn.: Pluto Press, 1996.

General examination of women writers of the Beat generation; includes a discussion of Kyger's work and her view of the attention paid to men compared to the neglect of her experience and work.

Johnston, Devin. Review of *Some Sketches from the Life of Helena Petrovna Blavatsky,* by Joanne Kyger. *Chicago Review* 43, no. 1 (winter 1997): 114-16.

Contends that while it is not Kyger's best volume of verse, the collection is pleasurable reading and the poems demonstrate a sense of spontaneity.

Killian, Kevin. "The *Carola Letters* of Joanne Kyger and George Stanley. *Jacket* 11 (online magazine), <jacketmagazine.com/11/kyger-killian.html> (April 2000).

Discusses the letters written between Kyger and George Stanley.

Schelling, Andrew. "Joanne Kyger's Portable Poetics." *Jacket* 11 (online magazine), jacketmagazine.com/11/kyger-schelling.html (April 2000).

Examines Kyger's travel journals and notebooks.

Skinner, Jonathan. "Generosity and Discipline: The Travel Poems." *Jacket* 11 (online magazine), <jacketmagazine.com/11/kyger-skinner.html> (April 2000).

Examines Kyger's travel poems in Desecheo Notebook, Mexico Blonde, Phenomenological, *and* Patzcuaro.

OTHER SOURCES FROM GALE:

Additional coverage of Kyger's life and career is contained in the following sources published by the Gale Group: *Contemporary Authors,* Vol. 101; *Contemporary Authors Autobiography Series,* Vol. 16; *Contemporary Authors New Revision Series,* Vols. 17, 40; *Contemporary Poets,* Ed. 7; *Contemporary Women Poets; Dictionary of Literary Biography,* Vol. 16; and *Literature Resource Center.*

MICHAEL MCCLURE

(1932 -)

(Full name Michael Thomas McClure) American poet, novelist, playwright, essayist, nonfiction writer, and critic.

McClure's work as a Beat poet and playwright explores the balance between body and mind, stressing the existence of a biological consciousness that ties all life together. In a prolific career that spans the second half of the twentieth century, McClure's early association with the San Francisco Beat movement fueled his development of a writing style that incorporates animal consciousness and scientific, ecologically motivated poetics. Often controversial for using explicit language and depicting drug use, McClure's work has been both challenged as obscene and heralded as true American genius.

BIOGRAPHICAL INFORMATION

Born in 1932 to Thomas and Marian (Dixie Johnston) McClure in Marysville, Kansas, McClure spent his childhood in both the vast farmlands of Kansas and his grandfather's home in the Pacific rainforests of Seattle, Washington. His parents divorced when McClure was five, and he went to live with his grandfather, who sparked McClure's lifelong interest in nature. When he was twelve, McClure returned to Kansas with his mother and her new husband and during the next few years began writing poetry.

An interest in the works of William Blake, William Butler Yeats, and John Milton led McClure to study traditional poetry at the University of Wichita and the University of Arizona. McClure moved to San Francisco and married Joanna Kinnison in 1954. That same year, he enrolled at San Francisco State College and attended a writing class taught by Robert Duncan, who was influential in the growing Beat movement. In 1955 McClure met Allen Ginsberg and on October 13, 1955, read his poetry alongside Ginsberg and others at the historic Six Gallery poetry reading, where Ginsberg's *Howl* made its first impact on the literary scene. McClure's poetry was published in the journal *Poetry* in 1956, the year his daughter was born, and McClure and his wife moved to San Francisco.

McClure became interested in the rock music of the late 1960s and played the autoharp in a music group with two other poet-musicians to develop a new sort of troubadour poetry style. By the early 1970s McClure was again intensely focused on his playwriting, moving toward a "neo-Ibsenism" in his naturalist works. With numerous collections of poetry, critical essays, and play productions, McClure continues to be active in the New Language movement and in environmentally conscious writing. In 1993 he won the Award for Lifetime Achievement in Poetry from the National Poetry Association.

MAJOR WORKS

As McClure developed as a writer and painter, his interests in nature and science evoked concerns regarding humankind's interference in the environment. In 1956 McClure's first book of poetry, *Passage,* was published. The Beat scene in San Francisco in the late 1950s and 1960s was strongly influenced by experimentation with psychoactive drugs. McClure began using peyote and LSD, which he felt gave him a clear, pure vision of reality and enhanced his thoughts and writing on reality. McClure's "Peyote Poem," published as a broadside, is considered a representative example of both the culture and art that evolved from this drug lifestyle. McClure's drug use also informed his paintings, which were shown at SPAATSA Gallery in San Francisco's exhibit "Visionary Portraits and Banners" in 1960. McClure's dramatic works question human consciousness and provide him with a forum for addressing ecological issues. Related to this were McClure's experiments with animals sounds as a way to connect with animal consciousness. McClure argues that such sounds belong to all life, including humans—whom he frequently refers to as "meat"—and connect us to a larger, more truthful understanding of our world and ourselves. Sound and feeling increasingly became McClure's primary focus, and his 1964 work *Ghost Tantras* contains ninety-nine poems written in "beast language"—sounds, chanting, baby talk, and direct speech. He continued to experiment with beast language and theater through the mid-1960s.

McClure's poetry traces a number of themes, including bio-ecological consciousness, the exploration of the intellectual effects of psychotropic drug use, and sociopolitical revolt against injustice. In *Hymns to St. Geryon, and Other Poems* (1959), McClure displays his visual interest in poetry, and designs each poem to convey meaning through the words as well as through their arrangement on the page. Of McClure's plays, *The Beard* (1965) is probably his best known. It examines the psychic division between spirit and body, relying on obscenity and explicit sexuality to convey its meaning. Called both contemporary and archaic, the play has been contested legally in court for its obscene content. *The Beard* is set in a spiritual realm and its characters are ritually given white tissue paper beards indicating that they are spirits. Billy the Kid and Jean Harlow, two of McClure's favorite characters who also appear in his other works, represent respectively the outlaw and the sex goddess. Conveying opposing perspectives, the two engage in quick verbal exchanges to try to further their own point of view. Ultimately, the characters reach a higher sense of truth and unity based on mutual understanding.

McClure also wrote novels. His autobiographical *The Mad Club* (1970) follows the narrator through youth and confusion to a state of self-renewal. The narrator's self-destructiveness, suspiciousness, and inability to love or be loved bring about an emotional and intellectual crisis. McClure's use of animal imagery illustrates the notion that humans are simply mammals, a philosophy that ultimately brings about resolution and allows Pete, the narrator, to regain his faith in himself and in life. Pete's condition is a metaphor for the human condition, and his salvation through "mammal consciousness" is representative of McClure's belief in human potential.

CRITICAL RECEPTION

McClure's role in the Beat movement and his relationship with notables Jack Kerouac, Robert Creeley, Ginsberg and others have been discussed in both literary and historical studies of the Beats. Writing and contributing at the height of the San Francisco Renaissance, McClure's naturalism and his ecological poetics influenced his fellow literati and enlivened the Beat literary scene. Kerouac's fictionalized portrait in *On the Road* of a loving, attentive couple in the midst of the restless chaos is considered by many to be a tribute to McClure and his wife. Most critical analysis of McClure's work has focused on his discourse on environmental issues. Gregory Stephenson provides a comprehensive overview of McClure's writing, considering the traditions that influenced him as well as his revolutionary "bio-alchemical" style. Rod Phillips considers McClure's mammalian poetics in terms of the ways it challenges how people think about themselves and their world. In numerous interviews McClure has discussed the influence of nineteenth-century poets on his poetry and worldview, as well as informing his sense of his purpose as an artist.

PRINCIPAL WORKS

Passage (poetry) 1956

Peyote Poem (poetry) 1958

Dark Brown (poetry) 1959

For Artaud (poetry) 1959

Hymns to St. Geryon, and Other Poems (poetry) 1959

!The Feast! (play) 1960

The New Book/A Book of Torture (poetry) 1961

Meat Science Essays (essays) 1963

Ghost Tantras (poetry) 1964

The Beard (play) 1965

Poisoned Wheat (poetry) 1965

The Shell (play) 1968

*The Charbroiled Chinchilla (plays) 1969

Ghost Tantras (poetry) 1969

Hymns to St. Geryon [and] Dark Brown (poetry) 1969

The Surge: A Poem (poetry) 1969

†The Brutal Brontosaurus (plays) 1970

The Mad Club (novel) 1970

Star (poetry) 1970

The Adept (novel) 1971

Gargoyle Cartoons (play) 1971

99 Theses (poetry) 1972

McClure on Toast (play) 1973

The Derby (play) 1974

Fleas, 189-195 (poetry) 1974

Rare Angel (writ with raven's blood) (poetry) 1974

September Blackberries (poetry) 1974

Jaguar Skies (poetry) 1975

Gorf; or Gorf and the Blind Dyke (play) 1976

Antechamber (poetry) 1977; revised as *Antechamber and Other Poems*, 1978

Scratching the Beat Surface (essays) 1982; published as *Scratching the Beat Surface: Essays on New Vision from Blake to Kerouac*, 1994

Fragments of Perseus (poetry) 1983

Fleas (180-186) (poetry) 1985

Selected Poems (poetry) 1986

Rebel Lions (poetry) 1991

Testa Coda [with Francesco Clemente] (criticism) 1991

Lighting the Corners on Nature, Art, and the Visionary: Essays and Interviews (essays and interviews) 1993

Three Poems (poetry) 1995

Camping Wyoming (nonfiction) 1999

Huge Dreams: San Francisco and Beat Poems (poetry) 1999

Rain Mirror (nonfiction) 1999

Touching the Edge: Dharma Devotions from the Hummingbird Sangha (essays) 1999

Plum Stones: Cartoons of No Heaven (poetry) 2002

---

* Includes the plays *The Pansy*, *The Meatball*, and *Spider Rabbit*.

† Includes the plays *Spider Rabbit*, *The Meatball*, *The Shell*, *Apple Glove*, *The Authentic Radio Life of Bruce Conner and Snoutburbler*, and *The Feather*.

PRIMARY SOURCES

MICHAEL MCCLURE (POEM DATE 1959)

SOURCE: McClure, Michael. "Point Lobos: Animism." In *Hymns for St. Geryon and Other Poems*, pp. 4-5. San Francisco, Calif.: Auerhahn Press, 1959.

This poem, from McClure's first collection, is representative of his interest in nature, a theme which pervades much of his work.

"POINT LOBOS: ANIMISM"

It is possible my friend
If I have had a fat belly
That the wolf lives on fat
Gnawing slowly
Through a visceral night of rancor.

It is possible that the absense of pain
May be so great
That the possibility of care
May be impossible.
Perhaps to know pain.
Anxiety, rather than the fear
Of the fear of anxiety.
This talk of miracles!
Of Animism:
I have been in a spot so full of spirits
That even the most joyful animist
Brooded
When all in sight was less to be cared about
Than death
And there was no noise in the ears
That mattered.
(I knelt in the shade
By a cold salt pool
And felt the entrance of hate
On many legs,
The soul like a clambering
Water vascular system.
No scuttling could matter
Yet I formed in my mind
The most beautiful
Of maxims.
How could I care
For your illness or mine?)
This talk of bodies!
It is impossible to speak
Of lupine or tulips
When one may read
His name
Spelled by the mold on the stumps
When the forest moves about one.
Heel. Nostril.
Light. Light! Light!
This is the bird's song
You may tell it
to your children.

MICHAEL MCCLURE (ESSAY DATE 1982)

SOURCE: McClure, Michael. "A Mammal Gallery." In *Scratching the Beat Surface*, pp. 149-60. Berkeley, Calif.: North Point Press, 1982.

This stream-of-consciousness piece first appeared in McClure's 1982 collection of essays.

THE GIANT PANDA, huge mammal, furred in black and white, basks and lolls in the shadiness of the bamboo grove. T'he panda sometimes sits like a man, on his rump with legs outspread, on an earthy mound covered with moss. Perhaps he looks at his beloved and family. He is surrounded by his nutriment, by the tips of bamboo plants that reach many times his height from the surface of the earth towards the sun. Perhaps strange, thoughtless philosophies drift across the platens of his sensorium and create and recreate themselves in his limbs and organs. All of his being is an accumulation of his plasm and the activities of his body. He sprang from the matter of the earth as it was energied by the nearby star that he sees through the sparse places in the glade. The bamboos about the panda are air creatures. They draw nitrates, some material substance, and water from the earth through the pores of their searching motile root tips. But much of the substance of the bamboo is drawn from thin air, from the gasses of the atmosphere, which are changed by a chemical cycle and the sun's rays into solid substance. Gasses become the BODY of the panda via the bamboo. The bamboos are threads that reach from the planet toward the star that energies them.

AN INVISIBLE WATCHER is in a room with a man and woman who are arguing—they are a lover and beloved, a man and wife. They are quarreling about the payment on a car, or about the loss of a laundry ticket. The argument becomes too intensive for so minor an issue. It appears that the man and woman are enacting a rite. If the invisible observer closes his ears to the meanings of the words and listens only to the vocalization as sounds, a thought occurs to him:

He is listening to two mammals. It might be two snow leopards, two bison, two wolves. It is a mammal conversation. The man and woman are growling, hissing, whimpering, cooing, pleading, cajoling, and threatening. The specific rite and biomelodic patterning of meat conversation rises and falls in volume. It makes variations, it repeats itself, it begins again, it grows, diminishes. There is a hiss and counterhiss. There is a reply and new outburst. The game that the man and woman are enacting, and the ritual, is as old as their plasm. It is capable of extremes of nervous modulation because of their neuronic complexity but it is more than ancient—it is an Ur-rite.

If the man and woman are lucky, and if their intelligences are open, then one of them will HEAR that it is a rite—that they are growling and hissing. Then he, or she, will laugh at the comedy and the ridiculousness of the pretext. The other partner will laugh in response, intuiting the same perception. Most likely it is a sexual ritual. They are hungry for contact with each other. Their intellective and emotional processes have been frozen into simulations of indifference by pressures of the surroundings and events. If they are lucky enough, one of them will raise a hand to the other, and touch or stroke, recognizing the other as the universe, the counterpart of a star, a galaxy, a planet, a bacterium, a virus, a leopard. Then they have enacted and completed a tantra of Shiva and Shakti. They have become mammals and gods and goddesses.

A MAN IS SITTING CROSS-LEGGED in bright afternoon sunlight. He opens a book of reproductions of Egyptian art. Clear light gleams off the paper. The alto relievo statuary is uncanny. The lazy intellectual mind scans the opposite page and finds text describing the statuary in a foreign language. It says, apparently, that this is a Pharaoh and two goddesses. The man's attention returns to the reproduction—passing perception takes the shape of a fragmentary poem:

> THE MESSENGER (RNA)
> slides to the ribosome
> (to the Constellation).
> The beads move.
> The Pharaoh, Chacal, & Hathor are glabrous
> perfectly
> balanced
> arm in arm. The weight
> of the Man-God
> is on one foot / or the other.
> They create the gleam
> of this dimension,
> of this single process,
> of perfection.
> But who is who? and WHAT?

The words mime the balance of the figures as they stand—Goddess, Pharaoh, Goddess—side by side, touching one another. Their weight is immaculately balanced. The sculptor of the archaic figures had a knowledge difficult to regain, though easy to reperceive thousands of years later. The sculptor sensed that man-mammal is created from the inside outward. That man begins at the interior of his cells and from their perfect balance the body is created.

((Within the human body the RNA slides through the walls of the cell's nucleus, through infinitesimal tubes in the structure, and finds the pear-like ribosome bodies in the cytoplasm. The bodies MOVE across the long threadlike molecules of RNA and create the substances of the cell.))

The three figures show muscular development that is excellent, generalized, not excessive. The bodies rest naturally in mammal fashion. A wolf can be seen standing in relaxation, peering with interest, involved and yet disinvolved. The carved stone reproduces muscle tone that is healthy and without contradictory strains. The faces of the Pharaoh and goddesses are as interesting, or as uninteresting, as the faces of snow leopards. Their bodies are erect, with the pelvis slightly forward to balance the weight of the head. The Pharaoh stands with one foot a little forward—it is impossible to tell which foot bears his weight, or if both feet do. The goddesses stand in variations of this posture.

I STAND IN FRONT of the cyclone wire cage containing the female snow leopard. My friend has a tape recorder. We have been taping sounds of animals before the zoo opens. I step over the guardrail where the snow leopardess is watching us. She is indifferent to humans when they keep at a distance. Her task is to fight the physical psychosis of encagement and madness. Most of her waking is spent pacing the constricted outlines of her cage. But now it is early morning and she is resting. When I step over the guard rail she growls in anger without moving—except her head, which swivels to watch me.

No part of her can reach through the mesh of the cyclone wire. I put my face almost to the wire and nearly to her face. There are only a few inches between her mouth and my face. She is enraged, and her face, which seems divine in such proximity, twists into feline lines of rage. The anger and rage are clearer than the conflicting human expressions on the daily streets. She knows the uselessness of pawing or clawing at me.

She puts her face within an inch of the wire and SPEAKS to me. The growl begins instantly and almost without musical attack. It begins gutturally. It grows in volume and it expands till I can feel the interior of her body from whence the energy of the growl extends itself as it gains full volume of fury. It extends itself, vibrating and looping. Then, still with the full capacity of untapped energy, the growl drops in volume and changes in pitch to a hiss. The flecks of her saliva spatter my face. I feel not smirched but cleansed. Her eyes are fixed on me. The growl, without a freshly drawn breath, begins again. It is a language that I understand more clearly than any other. I hear rage, anger, anguish, warning, pain, even humor, fury all bound into one statement.

I am surrounded by the physicality of her speech. It is a real thing in the air. It absorbs me and I can hear and feel and see nothing else. Her face and features disappear, becoming one entity with her speech. The speech is the purest, most perfect music I have ever heard, and I know that I am touched by the divine, on my cheeks, and on my brow, and on the tympanums of my ears, and the vibrations on my chest, and on the inner organs of perception.

It is music-speech. It is like the music one hears when he places his head on the stomach of his beloved. The gurglings, the drips, the rumblings, the heart, and the pulsebeats in the interior of the body are perfect music. It is the meat speaking and moving—as the testicles move and twist and writhe within the sac making their own motility and pursuing their ends. I am overcome with the universality of the experience. I hope that the drops of leopard saliva will never dry on my face.

We play back the several minutes of this growl and it is more beautiful than any composition of Mozart. Three-quarters of the way into the tape is the clear piercing crow of a bantam rooster making his reply to the mise-en-scène about him—to the calls of his ladies, to the sparrows, to the sounds of traffic, to the growling of the leopardess, to the morning sun, to the needs of his own being to vocally establish his territory. The crow of the tiny rooster is smaller but no less perfect or monumental or meaningful than the statement of the leopardess—they make a gestalt. The tape is a work of art as we listen. But we have no desire to add it to the universe of media and plastic artifacts. We see, hear, feel through the veil. WE are translated.

TRAVELING ON A SMALL SHIP to the Farallon Islands near the San Francisco coast, I spoke with a virologist who had just returned from Australia. He was traveling to the Farallons to study the rabbits there. A lighthouse keeper's son had a pair of rabbits that escaped on the island. The rabbits and their progeny devastated the island of every leaf of plant life. The island was left bare rock, without any vestige of higher plant life. The virologist believed that the rabbits—still populous on the island—ate the desiccated corpses of gulls and seabirds. His idea was that only one type of rabbit had the capability of surviving under these conditions.

I wandered on the island—seeing a rabbit and traces of rabbits—but not a blade of grass or a bush. The island is rocky, craggy, like a miniature, eroding crest of the Alps. After climbing the tiny peak, I descended to the beach, which was scattered with boulderlike rocks. I found myself looking down onto a herd of sea lions, the closest no more than thirty feet away. They were drowsing and lolling in the sun. Seeing something comic in the scene, I raised my hand and began speaking as if I were delivering a sermon. The astonished sea lions dived into the ocean. The ones in the ocean swung about to see me. They began a chorus of YOWPS, and huge angered MEAT CRIES, dense in volume and range. I continued my performance and they carried on their yowping. Perhaps thirty or forty of the animals were yowling at one time. They were FURIOUS, ENRAGED, ASTONISHED. Like the leopardess, their voices were driven by hundreds of pounds of meat force

and energy. I was frightened, worried that they might change about, clamber out, and pursue me. They remained in the water cursing me in a clear ancient language that left little doubt about meaning.

AND THEN I knew that not only were the monster shapes of meat enraged, they were PLEASED. THEY WERE SMILING AS WELL AS ENRAGED! They were overjoyed to be stimulated to anger by a novel—and clearly harmless—intruder. Undoubtedly they enjoyed my astonishment and fear as well as the physical pleasure of their rage. Perhaps they relished my physical reaction to their blitzkrieg of sound. They began to yowp not only at me but to each other.

My ears could not take it any longer and I began walking up the beach. I walked halfway around the island. Five members of the tribe followed in the waves. They watched, taunted, encouraged, scolded, and enjoyed me to the fullest. I have not been in finer company.

GENERAL COMMENTARY

MICHAEL MCCLURE, DAVID MELTZER, AND JACK SHOEMAKER (INTERVIEW DATE 1969)

SOURCE: McClure, Michael, David Meltzer, and Jack Shoemaker. "Michael McClure I (1969)." In *San Francisco Beat: Talking with the Poets,* edited by David Meltzer, pp. 150-76. San Francisco, Calif.: City Lights Books, 2001.

In the following excerpt from an interview conducted in 1969, Meltzer and Shoemaker discuss with McClure the early influences on his art—including Blake, Yeats, Milton, and Robert Duncan—and briefly consider his plays.

Fall 1969: Walked up a long wooden staircase into the light-filled living room, of the McClure's house in the Haight-Ashbury hills. We set up the clunky Sony reel-to-reel portable tape recorder on a coffee table in the living room, whose windows looked down into a backyard filled with trees. Paintings by Bruce Conner, Jean Conner, Jess, and McClure on the walls. Here's where memory mangles history: at least two other people were present, friends and/or visitors of McClure who shared his ecopoetic mission, but whose names and faces I can't recall. McClure's an archetypal Romantic in the full-blown heroic sense that Goethe was: naturalist, dramatist, poet, essayist, novelist. A serious, playful, complex trickster and sage; a smoothly amiable and disarming presence. After reassuring small talk and gossip, the machine's turned on, and the interview begins.—DM

1

[McClure]: I came to San Francisco for two reasons: (1) I was pursuing Joanna, and (2) I came here to take classes from Mark Rothko and Clifford Still. When I arrived I found out that they had left the year before.

The mystique of abstract expressionism fascinated me. I would have painted had I taken classes from them, but I never really thought of myself as a painter. It was that I was experiencing what the painters were experiencing at that time.

[*Meltzer*]: *This was your fourth year of college?*

Yes. I graduated from San Francisco State. The year before I spent at the University of Arizona. All that I took there that I can remember was German and the Short Story. Oh, I also took an advanced painting class and some advanced anthropology. Both classes were very interesting to me.

When did you discover the work of William Blake?

Very early. I was writing poems in the style of Blake when I was seventeen. After high school I finished writing the pictographic poems I told you about—although they became less and less pictographic and more and more formal vers libre. Then I discovered Blake.

I bought the collected poems of Blake and Donne because somebody had recommended Donne to me. I couldn't read Donne, but I discovered those unbelievable poems of Blake. In the process of that I also discovered Milton. And between Blake, Yeats, and Milton I felt challenged to teach myself metric, to teach myself stanzaic patterns and shapes of poetry, like the sonnet and the villanelle.

I wrote very little in college and not much of it did I care for. I suppose it was a hermetic period. It was like a very long silent meditation on forms.

I also idealized what Dylan Thomas was doing. And I was terrifically impressed with Roethke.

I was writing poems in the manner of Blake. A cross between Blake and Baudelaire, and at the same time learning forms like the Petrarchan sonnet, the ballad, the villanelle, the sestina.

It was very hard for me to write a sonnet. I might spend several weeks on a sonnet and then wait several weeks before I wrote another poem. I was very intent on having the meter correct, following the voice.

As for Blake, I used to dream I was Blake!

So there was Blake, Yeats, and Milton?

Yes, all about the same time.

What a rich panoply of teachers!

Yes. And I wasn't alone in this. There were five or six of us waiting, and we fed each other intellectively.

During the first couple of years of college, I ran with what were then called "beboppers," with jazz musicians, in the middle fifties.

Did you enjoy music?

No, I didn't. I got very little out of music. It wasn't until later that I was able to get it. I listened to a lot of classical music and enjoyed it. I like Beethoven and Mozart most.

I ran with the beboppers, going to all their jam sessions and nightclub engagements, and not really hearing their music until I had been listening to it for more than a year. I was doing it for the drugs and excitement and because you stayed up all night and slept all day. Then, one day, somebody was playing a record by Thelonious Monk. And I heard that. Then I heard Bud Powell, and then I could hear it all. By that time, I was headed somewhere else.

What did you hear in Thelonious Monk?

A very exotic, highly structured, mysterious, emotional occasion. Elegance. Elegance of the intellect and the body moving in tune with the elements. Because you have to, you have to move. Move your hands around.

I found Monk and then, I think, I found Powell and then Gerry Mulligan—and who was the young trumpet player with Mulligan . . . ?

Chet Baker.

Chet Baker, Anita O'Day, Charlie Parker. I went through all of those: Gillespie, Parker, "Salt Peanuts," "A Night in Tunisia," "Ornithology," "How High the Moon" . . . and a whole host of people I've almost forgotten. I listened to the music for a year before touching it. Before it even got through my skin.

When did you get to San Francisco?

Nineteen fifty-four. I took Robert Duncan's poetry workshop, and I was handing in sonnets to Robert. Robert was astounded that a person who was so interested in poetry would hand in sonnets and villanelles. He kept trying to get me to write free verse, and I wasn't mature enough to explain to him that I had already been through it. Yet what I was doing interested him.

I think at first we were amazed with each other. I was amazed by his clarity of perception and his ability to express himself and to be concise. I had been through free verse, completely through free verse, and was experimenting with the very traditional forms like the sestina, the classical Petrarchan sonnet, and so on. Robert couldn't figure out why I was doing this, because he thought this kind of thing was a dead horse. For me, it was the final grounding in what I wanted to know before I split those forms completely.

We wrote poems every week, and Robert would be slightly dismayed at my sonnets. It was a very interesting confluence. Then I became personal friends with Robert and with Jess. They offered an opening to the possibilities that I was searching for.

Was he a good teacher?

Fantastic. It was one of the most brilliant things that ever happened in my life. To have Robert stand at the blackboard and speak for two or three hours about a line of poetry or a word or a poem or whatever came into his mind in relationship to his own work, or to the work that other people were bringing in. I believe in the cliché that poetry or painting can't be taught, but I was also present at the exception to the rule which makes the rule, which was Robert's class.

When did you start publishing?

The next thing that happened was that I met Jonathan Williams, and he offered to do my first book, *Passage.* It started out as a great stack of poems, but I kept editing them down. There was no size restriction. I imposed that restriction on myself.

I knew when I wrote those two villanelles for Roethke that meter and genre held no more interest for me. I had satisfied the desire to handle genre.

In looking at a sonnet you have to realize that you have an idea, a resolution of the idea, and a couplet to cap it. It makes you aware of the intellective process in writing the poem. Besides merely saying: I have a girl; it's spring; I got fucked; I didn't get fucked; the water is great; look, there's an animal . . . I mean, it makes you realize that you have relationships other than those, and you are forced to look at the structure of ideas behind a poem. A poem can't interest me very much unless it is both intellective and emotional.

All that was going through my head. It was like what was happening with the abstract expressionists at that time. They were learning to write their biographies in the movements of their body

on a canvas. Whether this painting is looked at in 200 or 300 years was not of interest to me. What was of interest to me, although I couldn't formulate it until years later, was the fact that it was a spiritual occasion that I could believe in. And it was alive and brilliant while I looked at it. I was very much taken with that concept, and that's influenced me enormously. I still see things in those terms. I see rock and roll as a spiritual occasion. I saw the assemblage movement as being a spiritual occasion. I see the new earthwork sculpture as being a spiritual occasion. I saw Ginsberg as a spiritual occasion. The Beat Generation thing as being a spiritual occasion, the San Francisco Renaissance as being a spiritual occasion. I feel as if I am a string and these spiritual occasions are beads or pearls that pass over me in much the same way that a complex molecule, RNA, slides across the ribosome to create protein. It's as if I am a string that the pearls, or ribosomes, of events pass over and from this I form the protein of my being around it.

If we are, in a sense, genetically indestructible until we are brought to our termination, I think it's reasonable that, rather than starting with a predisposed philosophy or cosmology, we allow it to form itself around us. I also have the feeling that everything grows. My relationships to things grow. Oh, there are dead spaces. There are the knots on a necklace between the pearls. I also look forward to the knots.

I think a lot of us tend to exist in static situations—very much to our loss. Some can exist statically because of drugs. They can exist statically because of the situation dealt to them. By luck, you fall upon certain concepts. You can also form a feedback of intellectivity or emotionality or physical being and throw it out and bring back more with it.

Your many references to chemical procedures come from what revelation?

In the last year I read a book called *The Anatomy of the Cell,* by Björn Afzelius. He is a Swedish electromicroscopist. Although I had read quite a bit about genetic structure, it wasn't until I read this book that I totally changed my relationship to the material that we are made of—to our protoplasm. I realized that my picture of it was highly simplified. Even with a layman's understanding of contemporary microbiology, I still didn't have a picture of the complexity of the events that we are. I was still buying the idea we were given in high school that the cell is a kind of bag. I realized the complex structure within the bag, but I didn't realize that the structure within the bag *creates* the bag. Topologically, the inside of the cell is as complex a structure as we can conceive of. Any given cell. There are three trillion cells in each of us.

I think your idea of, what did you say, rearranging the skin web is probably exactly where it's at.

I think that's what it is. It has to do with facing a series of crises of self-image, self-perception, realizing the depth of the selfless forms.

It happened when I wrote **Fleas.**

Some of which were in **Caterpillar** *8/9?*

Yes. Those were the first nine. There are 250 of them. They are spontaneous and unrewritten. They're all in rhyme and average about twenty lines each. They are childhood memories. They are an obsession, like Billy the Kid and Jean Harlow were obsessions. The idea of doing **Fleas** became an obsession, and when I finished them and reread them, I found that I had awakened many of the more complex responses.

In other words, when I look at that chair I remember the chairs I've seen in my childhood, which were out of mind before.

I became interested in the topology of how our mind works, and about two-thirds of the way through writing, I discovered how information is stored hologramistically in the brain. In other words, in multitudinous sources, overlapping, instead of one, and it was precisely what was going on in me.

Everything overlaps everything else and lights it up. It isn't stored according to our ideas of rationality. It's stored on an organic basis, and everything overlaps everything, and as one memory is lit, it lights the corner of another memory. If you light up another memory near it, it will light up a memory that was unsuspected. Then that lights the corner of another memory, and you light up another one near it, and it lights up the one in between.

The new sciences of microbiology have a very small relationship to the sciences that precede them. Boehme said that the universe we live in is the result of the friction of the celestial-bliss universe rubbing against the black fires—which I find as believable as atoms and molecules.

I think we have to believe everything that's reasonable to us. Boehme's concept of our existence is as spiritually true, or truer, than atoms and molecules.

In John Lilly's book, *The Mind of the Dolphin,* he goes to great length about how little we know. And how much of mental health is accepting the things that come from beyond limitations. Just accepting them. I think that the more that happens to me that I can take per se, the happier I am. When you're young and specters appear before you, you learn very quickly either not to see specters anymore or to accept the fact that specters appear. I accept.

We often deny what we may be afraid of. The unknown is often a fearful connation and becomes an obstacle. . . . There are aspects of the unknown that provoke fear, and we can face fear a lot of times by rejecting it.

Byron was afraid he would never die.

So much of it is coming to accept whatever happens, being able to cope with it without much expectation.

I think the most exciting thing that's happened to me is the ability to think. When I say "think," it's nothing so heavy. It's just that I will imagine I'm at a Mexican temple in the year 1450 when it's being inaugurated. Forty thousand people are being sacrificed. Then I'll envision the scene, and I'll skip from there to another thought to another thought to another thought, so that I can't . . . it's very difficult for me to be bored anymore.

I saw Kerouac the day after he died.

You did?

Yes. I woke up in the morning, and he was flying through blackness, and it was great. And I yelled at him: "Hey, hey!"

And what did he say?

He didn't say anything. I wrote a poem in my mind. I didn't have my pen, but I wrote down what I could remember.

Kerouac was important to you, wasn't he?

Yes, absolutely. I think with Kerouac the most important thing was that I don't agree with Kerouac about very much. Yet I loved his writing. He is so graphic and concrete that I experience what he experienced—even though it is totally foreign to me. And it knocks me out to know what he felt and what he saw. So that, in a sense, he is like a real paragon. If there were 500 men like this that you could follow, you would really be in great shape. If you could see out of 500 sets of eyes besides your own and smell through 500 noses . . . I am willing to do it, if anybody will present it for me. I just read a book called *The Way of All*

ON THE SUBJECT OF...

Flesh, by Samuel Butler. It was of equal importance to me as the book on microbiology. I mean, to see into Victorian society and to see into the interior of the cell are two really great sights.

2

When did you start writing plays?

Nineteen fifty-nine. I finished the first one then. The first one was called **The Raptors.** Then I did a play called **The Blossom. The Feast** was next, a play in beast language.

Could you explain the formulation of beast language?

There was no evolution. The idea of **The Feast** sprang into my head, went off light a light bulb over my head—like in the cartoons. Flash, flash, flash! And I saw the whole play, and I started to write it down in beast language with thirteen characters drinking black wine and eating loaves of French bread. Then I said, this is ridiculous! And I started writing what I imagined I should do. I wrote a great deal but had to throw it all away and go back to what I originally saw, what first flashed over my head. That was the only beast language I wrote until three or four years later when I felt a ball of silence within myself—and inside of that ball was beast language. It was a source of pleasure, entertainment, and amusement and a great deal of concentration not to lose it. I knew there would be a hundred poems to write down as I heard them.

We were talking earlier about the form, the contour of your work.

I see what I'm doing as pulling out possibilities within myself. As a possibility opens itself, I create it. It isn't anything that wasn't already there. I can see the possibilities now.

All these events hinge upon a moment, the available perception, your disposal toward the moment. As a spectator to your work, as the audience, I can sense from your work a kind of pattern of development.

A lot of that has to do with my editing. A lot of it is self-acceptance. Like in **Hymns to St. Geryon,** I decided I should be what is represented there. In **The New Book/A Book of Torture,** I decided I should be what is represented there. Each one is like a very narrow vibration of what I am doing at a given time—what I felt was the most appropriate vibration.

There will be a lot of poems in my book that Grove is publishing right now, the book called **Star,** that are very much like the unpublished poems I was writing in 1955, 1956, and 1957, but I couldn't accept them then. [. . .]

MICHAEL MCCLURE AND HARALD MESCH (INTERVIEW DATE 1983-84)

SOURCE: McClure, Michael, and Harald Mesch. "Writing One's Body: Interview with Michael McClure." *Amerikastudien/American Studies* 32, no. 3 (1987): 357-69.

In the following interview, originally conducted in 1983 and 1984, Mesch and McClure discuss the poet's political perspective as it coincides with his position as an artist. McClure explains that he writes to make himself "conscious" and to inspire others to consciousness as well.

The following interview is the outcome of two meetings: On April 28, 1983, I interviewed Michael McClure in the living room of his house in San Francisco; almost a year later, on April 2, 1984, while McClure was touring Europe, we met for a second session in a hotel-room in Munich.

*[Mesch]: In your book **Scratching the Beat Surface** you speak of the interrelatedness of poetry and environmental consciousness. Could you trace the history of your relationship as a poet to the environmental movement?*

[McClure]: From early childhood I wanted to be a naturalist, then came an interest in archeology and anthropology, followed by a love of painting. When I arrived in San Francisco, as a young man, in 1954, I was involved primarily in painting and in poetry. Soon I met a naturalist, Sterling Bunnel, a man of my own age who began introducing me to areas of California that I had not had the opportunity to see. With him I was able to watch coyotes and foxes and weasels and deer, and walk through savannah country, hike through the foothills, go over mountains, and to the seashore and look into tide pools. But, earlier, in 1955 we "Beats" gave our first reading at the Six Gallery in San Francisco. At that reading Allen Ginsberg read "Howl," which has as its basis—in my thinking—consciousness itself. At the same reading Gary Snyder read his "A Berry Feast"-poem, which is a celebration of nature, especially as seen through American Indian rites. And I read my poems almost all of which were inclined toward nature.

I was fascinated by your statement that the Beat movement is part of a larger and deeper environmental movement because in such a perspective the Beat movement appears in a completely new light. How did you gain that perspective?

That first became clear at the United Nations Environmental Conference in Stockholm in 1972, when I looked around and saw that in fact a great many of my friends were there. Gary Snyder was there, Peter Berg, the bioregionalist, was present, I was there, my wife was there, Joan McIntyre was there with project Jonah, Steward Brand was there with *Whole Earth Catalogue*, friends of mine in the biological and botanical fields, like Richard Felger, were there. We were speaking for the diversity of the environment; speaking for the whales, speaking for the preservation of diversity of human culture: for the American Indians, for the Laplanders.

I looked back and saw the connection between what we had started in 1955 and where we were 1972. In our first poetry reading in 1955 there was an interest in mind as consciousness, in nature, and in biology. That impulse has been picked up and amplified in the rock-music that we influenced (in the basically organismic approach of the Beatles), in the return to dance by young people which is a direct expression of the bodies as opposed to the more intellectual, abstracted pattern dancing and as contrasted to a more intellectual pattern music that preceded rock-music. Remember the Beatles began calling themselves the b-e-a-t, the Beat, Beatles. They had originally called themselves the "Silver Beetles." When they became more organismic, when they felt themselves alive with a kind of surge, with what was happening in the physiological sense, they became the Beatles as we know them today. At about that time books on the environment, on environmental subjects and on conservational subjects were beginning to pour out. They were beginning to quote the poets, and there was a great sense of oneness that was occurring.

What I'm saying is overlooked because of the newspaper image that was formed of beat-niks wearing berets, sandals and playing bongo drums. There was a lot of that, but those beat-nik poets who were in places like North Beach and the lower east side in New York City were a temporary phenomenon. They've disappeared. They were there for the newspapers to photograph, and we weren't close to them. Those of us who survived continued our work.

It is within the fence posts of the Beat-environmental movement that you have been carrying on a dialogue with Lawrence Ferlinghetti. And it is here that your differentiation between "revolution" and "revolt" seems to be central. Refusing to define the movement as a revolution, you seem to deny its political relevance. You seem to be saying that it is non-political. On the other hand you are saying: "There is but one politics and that is biology."

Yes, you're right, I read that poem last year, the poem **"Listen Lawrence,"** at the University of California along with a reading by Denise Levertov. We were reading for the nuclear freeze movement. I read the lines "capitalism will not help, socialism will not help, communism will not help," and some people in the audience who were at Berkeley, liberal political types, hissed, which was interesting—ugly, but interesting. A week later, I was giving a reading with a fellow poet to raise money to give to the Salvadorian guerillas for medical supplies. So, I don't believe that because one takes a deeper approach to the reality that one can avoid politics. I go on making political gestures that I believe are necessary, that are important. I don't back away from them. I do not exist in an ivory tower because I believe that biology is the only meaningful area of change. I go ahead and make the changes that I can make politically, at least those that I can align myself with spiritually. And I can align myself spiritually with the guerillas in El Salvador, and with raising money for them. But I don't believe that helping them is going to make any kind of permanent change in Central America—which is going to be in a permanent state of revolution and in a permanent state of disarray until something can be done about the overpopulation problems there as well as the problems of colonization. The only thing that's going to make anything better for them is to find a biological solution to the problems. Some solutions to their need for basic resources and agriculture and some solution for their overpopulation. Those are both biological problems.

So you tend to think in longer terms, because biological solutions are not short-term solutions.

I think that short-term solutions are not solutions. Short-term solutions are necessary simply to stave off pain and criminality and disastrous chaos. But there are no simple solutions. And people are going to have to start determining what the problems are, and they are going to have to start thinking in unity, they're going to have to start thinking together about what the possibilities of solutions may be. I don't believe that people have even begun to envision what the *problems* are. The problems are not the wars and the starvation and the chaos that's going on. The problems are what's causing the wars and the starvations and the chaos. Those are biological. I do whatever I can, as I can do it, to align myself with causes, to confront and to alleviate war, pain, starvation. But I don't think that I'm doing anything except helping put on a surgical dressing. I'm glad to put a band-aid on whenever I can. Ferlinghetti, on the other hand, believes that if we had a socialist world, we wouldn't have any problems. But we would have the same problems we would have with a capitalist world; they just might be a slightly different color. We'd have the same problems we'd have with a communist world; they just might have a slightly different odor. Problems are very, very deep, and the problems are permanent until we look at the complex of them and determine to do something which is very long-range. We're talking about generations. We're talking about a generation or two just to determine what the problems are and then we're talking about whatever generations are necessary, whatever decades are necessary, to work out the determinations in a flexible manner.

In one of your poems you say: "In turn we give flesh to the revolution / like Che, Darwin, and Francis Crick / creating visions not solutions."

That's right. I don't really think that there are solutions in the sense that people speak of solution. And I've been using "solution" in what I've said before this, but I think I really mean something else. I don't mean a solution, it's a new path.

Would you see your poetry moving toward a new path or would you see your poetry as making the problems conscious?

My poetry is to make myself conscious. And my poetry is to illuminate a reader, if he or she is interested, with what I've been able to do with my consciousness, which may be of use to them on their own. Perhaps my poetry is to broaden my sensorium, and hopefully it will broaden the sensoriums of other individuals who read it. In other words, the function of poetry, as I see it, is to create a myriad-mindedness.

I see myself wholly as an artist, as a poet. I am not a utopian. I'm not a socio-biological thinker. But I do align myself with a movement or a thread or a stream or a surge of individuals who are interested in the liberation of the body, in the liberation of the imagination and the liberation of consciousness. In that sense, we may be of help to those who begin to deal with the situations that need to be dealt with. I constantly ask biologists, botanists, or bio-philosophers what we may do, what we may think about, what the situation is. That's reflected in my poetry. I'm an artist.

There's a general saying that "poetry won't help." In other words, poetry is in an ivory tower.

I think most poetry won't help and most poetry is in an ivory tower, speaking of what's generally accepted as poetry. If you look in the *New York Times'* book review section, what they review as poetry won't help and it is in an ivory tower. If you look in the *London Times' Literary Supplement*, what they speak of won't help and it is in an ivory tower. So, what does one say to that? I'm speaking about people such as myself, Robert Creeley, Robert Duncan, Philip Whalen, Amiri Baraka, Diane di Prima.

At Martin Luther King Junior High School (Berkeley) a month or two ago, there was a reading by Gary Snyder, Robert Creeley, and a Vietnamese monk poet. More than a thousand individuals from Berkeley came to that reading and listened to the exercise of consciousness that the deconstruction of event and autobiography presents in Creeley's work. This could only give individuals a new stance toward their own lives if they listened to what Creeley was saying, and I'm sure they did listen. Those individuals present were also listening to Gary Snyder's consciousness-deepening stance toward nature as represented in his poems. A thousand people at an event like that have widespreading possibilities. For a thousand people to have an experience that intense and that meaningful makes waves and surges of consciousness with a potential to spread throughout a much larger community. I suppose bourgeois poetry is essentially aesthetic entertainment—well within the contains and bounds of the universe of discourse. But the other, the Creeley/Snyder reading is an event which is a revolt against the status quo, and it is a profound experience. It is like comparing a film of the Sierras with a trip to the Sierras. A film of the Sierras will only have the function of entertainment; a trip to the Sierras is liable to change somebody's world view.

To me it seems to be a fundamental requirement that our understanding of language is being transformed. For unless this understanding is transformed our stance toward reality won't change. And if our stance toward reality won't change we will not be able to act adequately in the critical ecological situation in which we find ourselves.

I agree with you completely. If those thousand people are given the example of the use of language in both Creeley's way and Snyder's way, both of which are revolutionary ways to use language, they're bound to absorb some of those values and will, I believe, in many instances make changes in their own use of language, which is equivalent to their own feelings and their own intellectivity. Then we can see changes. I do think Shelley was right that poets are the unacknowledged legislators of the earth. I don't think that they're the only unacknowledged legislators of the earth, but they are *some* of the unacknowledged legislators of the earth. Again, I'm not talking about the ones who are reviewed in the *New York Times'* Sunday literary section, but certain of those who are *not*. You see the new poetry that I'm speaking of is no longer new, the poetry that I'm speaking of is a poetry about experience, it's a poetry about consciousness, it's a poetry about the senses.

Language is used in a way which is in revolt against a previous use of language, and it is in mutational divergence from the previous common use of language. It's in this change that we open the possibilities for a new ground upon which people may think and act. That's our duty as artists. We are not eco-politicians. We are not eco-philosophers. We are not eco-metaphysicians. We're *artists.*

Ferlinghetti, in the introduction to your **Meat Science Essays**, *speaks about you as the cat that is "willfully incapable" of understanding Camus. Camus himself may be regarded as one of the staunch defenders of the humanistic tradition in the sense of an anthropocentric position. From that position you*

might be accused of consistent desublimation, even of regression, of anti-intellectualism. What would you say to that?

There's not anything very difficult to understand about anything that Camus says. Sartre is more challenging intellectually than Camus, and I think that what both Sartre and Camus did in founding existentialism is extremely important to my work and to the work of my friends and to the work of many of those whom I admire. The primary thing that existentialism does is to deny that there is a secret beneath the surface of things. Sartre makes evident that that which you see is that which is. He calls it the confrontation with the absurd. He does not pretend that there is a mysterious poem lurking beneath the eyelids of stones, which makes charming symbolist art, but is a cultural mystification. However, neither Sartre nor Camus, when they speak of the universe, or even the universe of the absurd are speaking of anything *beyond* the human universe. Both men are wholly bound within the social level, they have no experience *outside* the social level. Their work was done at the time when important discoveries were just *beginning* to be made in the biological sciences and they did not comprehend their value or meaning. But Sartre and Camus are certainly our direct forebears intellectually. As much as Emerson is a direct forebear. And we owe much to Camus.

In regard to anti-intellectualism, I would as soon be an anti-intellectual as not. However I am pro intellective. I believe in the use of the intellective powers. Intellectualism means that one assumes values with insufficient questioning of the culture of which he or she is a part. Intellectualism is equivalent to one-dimensionality as far as I'm concerned. *Intellectivity,* however, means that one has a vivid and athletic intellect.

"Intellectivity" and "intellectualism." How do you differentiate between these notions?

"Intellectivity" is the willingness to use one's perceptual integrative high level mental capacities; "intellectual" means plugging into an already established program or grammar of those activities. So one can be an intellective giant and not have been to college. I mean you could have a man who is a lumberjack who is an intellective wizard, and you can have somebody who is a great intellectual but is not intellective at all. In fact most intellectuals are not.

One-dimensionality, as you speak of it, would mean the exclusion of what you call the mystery out of the "social bubble"?

No. One-dimensionality, according to Marcuse, who uses the term best to my way of thinking, means that the individual in contemporary society has so little interior, individuated self remaining that the introjection of the values of society hardly phase his consciousness. They *are* his consciousness. There is only one dimension. Marcuse believes that the individual in today's society has so accepted the outer values of society that they can hardly be introjected into the personality. They are already *one*. There is only one dimension. There is not an interior and an exterior dimension.

Your return to the body—I would describe your poetry as such—would implicitly mean that your poetry is moving in the direction of re-discovering the biological self?

It's moving in the direction of recovering the biological self. I don't know if there's a re-discovery. I think perhaps each of us has to recover our biological selves. There is always a blockade of our process of discovery of the biological self which is a blockade of each individual's normal, personal discovery of the biological self.

Again, from a humanistic, anthropocentric position you might be accused of narcissism. That is, the return to the body as a narcissistic move. What would you reply to that?

"Narcissism" is used to identify a pathological state. I've known a few narcissists who probably have some degree of pathology. But I must say that not only did I not dislike them, I rather liked them. The problem with pathological, or semi-pathological narcissists is that they're not dependable. However, they're enjoyable to be around because they honor themselves, they enjoy themselves, they treat themselves well, which is something that many people do not do. On the other hand, the use of the term "narcissism" as it was used in the 60s and 70s as a pejorative is something like the pejorative use of the term "elitist." I have the distinct feeling that narcissism is used as a pejorative by those who, in some sense, feel inferior about themselves. They believe that if they use that term against individuals, that others will sheepishly gather behind them and join in the stoning of those who are called that particular name. I see nothing narcissistic about the experience of one's self. I see a great lack of the experience of oneself in present society. Probably in all cultures there's a lack of experience of oneself, except the social self. If one experiences oneself in senses other than the social self, as long as it is

adherent to relatively healthful, mammalian processes, I think it's wholly to be admired. That is, provided it doesn't cause blindness to the needs of others or interfere with the normal functioning of one's friends, relatives, and associates.

S. P. R. Charter, the ecologist, you may know him, speaks about the necessity that we recognize and accept both self and "beyond self." Would you see that move in the direction of "beyond self" as a discovery of the biological self?

The more one discovers one's *bio-self* as opposed to one's *social self*, the more one is moving out, but one has to move *in* to move *out*. The more you discover your biological person and your biological functions, the more you find your biological self, and the more you discover your biological self, the more value you can be to yourself. The more value you can be to yourself, the more value you can be to those around you. People fear such acts because they believe that their biological self is a monster. That is certainly not the case. I mean, we're social primates, and we have distinct social patterns. The more we find those deeper patterns and the less we are robotized by cultural patterns, the better we'll be. If so-called narcissism is an escape from the robotism of the culture, I'm all for it.

Your first experience of stepping, so to speak, out of time, "changing time itself into space," was this experience helped by drugs?

Everything that I feel today has, in part, for a source the use of psychedelic drugs. But then everything that I feel today has in part for its source the fact that my grandfather was a doctor who loved nature. Everything that I feel today has in part for its source the fact that I found Robert Creeley's poetry when I was a young man. I don't feel that as a poet I stepped whole from Athena's brow and had no progenitors and sources.

As one begins to become aware of oneself as an organism, as a body, as a body consciousness, one says, this body consciousness is not wholly mine. Yes, I think psychedelic drugs are important, but I also embrace observations and perceptions of my fellow poets, of my wife, of my child, of my grandfather, of Jackson Pollock, of Arp, of Artaud, of Lorca and Shelley.

Your statement in **Scratching the Beat Surface** *that we must "change time itself into space through an alchemic act. Then we may move in it and step outside of the disaster that we have wreaked upon the environment and upon our phylogenetic selves"* *seems to me to be central both in the context of your poetry and of the contemporary fundamental environmental concerns.*

What I'm speaking of, in part, is the Taoist notion that the universe that we perceive is an *uncarved block*, that all time/space occurrences that have happened in the past, present, and future are one giant sculpture of which we're a part. It's not as if something is going to exist in the future or that something has happened in the past, but that it's all going on at once. And we're in it. If we're aware of that, there's a *proportion-lessness* that is a liberating state or condition. If we understand that we're not of a particular size, of a particular diminution, or of a particular "be-hemothness," then we sense that we are without scale. We're without measurement in the same way that we're without time. When we have that experience, there's a peace and an understanding that can come over us. We can make better judgements and more positive actions.

I am an artist. I observe moments of propor-tionlessness. I observe moments of bio-alchemy. As I become more practiced, or sometimes when I become more liberated through the exercise of my art, I seem to be able to call on meaningful moments more and more. But they're not some-thing to be utilized. They're something that oc-curs if we exercise for them, if we create our art for them, if we pursue our discipline for them, then we notice those moments happening more and more. I'm not sure that we actually bring them about. But we can partake of them more and more if we're clear, more and more if we're less and less robotized, if we're less and less one-dimensional and more myriad.

Would you see that alchemic act of "changing time itself into space" as coming close to what Charles Olson might speak of as the stepping out of the "universe of discourse"?

When we step out of the universe of discourse, we are in a more primal, more phylogenetic state, a more primal, more phylogenetic condition. I would imagine that the exterior world is more coordinate with the *Umwelt* when we step out of the universe of discourse. In other words, I believe that when we step from the social sphere (that's lifted itself from the earth like a bubble away from the substrate) back into our biological selves, that we feel a proportionlessness. The descriptions of the "Uncarved Block" of the Taoists are much like that state. It's an inherent, organismic condition. If, on the other hand, we step out of the universe

of discourse into a tribal condition which is another kind of one-dimensionality, that is, into a tribal sociology, it's of no advantage whatsoever. We must fuse our intellectivity and our emotional force and the feedback loops of our sensorium and our perceptions to step back into our bodies. When we step back into our bodies, we are more liable to find a condition of timelessness, of pro-portionlessness, or a timefulness which is rich with the meanings of our evolution, and which is rich with the meanings of our possibilities and our extensions.

I'm not for moving out of the one-dimensionality of the universe of discourse into a tribal condition which I feel is an equally, and possibly more, limited condition. A tribal condi-tion is probably more limiting to the intellective capacities and the emotional capacities than the urban life of one-dimensionality, though of course it is rich in other ways.

As far as I can see, stepping back into what you describe as tribal would be a regressive move.

Cultures have certain things in common. It seems to be a common teaching of all of them that we are not animals, that we are minds. That is wrong. Not to confuse the term "monism" with "monism" as it's used in philosophy: There was a German biologist who called himself both a disciple of Goethe and a disciple of Darwin, a man named Ernst Haeckel. He described himself as a monist because he believed that the universe itself, or all existence, is a single, great organism or a single, great "critter" with organismic characteris-tics. Whitehead carries that a step further, he believes that any point in the universe is a novel point of "prehension," i.e., a point of the universe experiencing itself. We are all, at any time, every one of us, every thing, the universe experiencing itself. Our sensoriums are spirit mechanisms that light up the cave around them for the experience.

That's beautiful. That certainly connects—for me at least—with Charles Olson's essay "Proprioception."

The mystic philosopher Jakob Böhme says that the world that we inhabit is created by the universe of celestial bliss rubbing against the universe of black fire. In other words, the strata that we inhabit is the friction between the uni-verse of celestial bliss and the universe of black fire.

In a way Olson's "Proprioception" is the rub-bing of Charles' desire to experience against his internal capacities, and then the projection of that which he might experience. It's as if Charles becomes alight with an idea, as if he's inspired by the outer universe to an idea which he internalizes, and that internalization calls upon itself to create a kind of rampaging bull within himself that tramples around in the inner residences of his sensorium to create ideas about that which he desired to have ideas. Then he projects them outward and examines the ideas. Then, he re-internalizes the ideas and the wild bull of his consciousness tramples around again in the sensorium of what he's experienced and creates another idea which is projected outward which comes to a field which is then perceived and internalized again. You see, Charles' "system" is definitely a systemless system and that's the most attractive thing about it. Charles' proprioceptive essay is inspiring not for saying anything, because I don't believe that it says much, it's inspiring because it's an energy construct that recommends to us that we proceed in our lives with the same energy. In other words, it's like a painting by Clyfford Still. It's not like a direct mimesis of nature.

It occurs to me that one might describe it, in your own words, again as "not a solution but a vision."

It's a vision. It is definitely no solution. It has no answer except to return to the inside and trample around some more.

What was your relation to Charles Olson? In what ways did he help you in developing you[r] own language, your own poetics?

When I found Charles' essay on "Projective Verse," I found one of the bases for my own poetics. My own poetics has several distinct substrata and one of them is traditional English prosodic poetry, such as Blake or Keats or Yeats or Shelley. Another is the modernist tradition of Pound and Williams, and particularly the poetics of Olson since I come of a later generation.

The poetics of Pound and Williams was not wholly appropriate for me since their poetics preceded the important recent discoveries made in biology and physics. I had to create a poetics of the 50s and the later period that I could speak with. I do not imply a superior poetics but a poetics appropriate for my field, my wave. Olson's recognition that the mind is a construct of the heart, of the nervous system, and his interest in the energy charge that we derive from the subject, whether in the mind or in the world, as the motivating force, was a help. Also his recognition that the syllable is the unit of measurement rather than the foot or the word. That gave me a cue.

You have an argument with Olson in your manifesto "The Rose Flush, Straight Speech, Exclamation and the Drift (1958)"—the kernel of the argument being about the anagogic and the pre-anagogic. Could you comment on that?

It was my feeling that Olson was still contained within the humanistic world of history and traditional disciplines. As much as he was forcing himself against the very wall of it, I felt that he was still contained within it. As much as he was proposing for all of us to go beyond the traditional, I felt that he was still constrained by the viewpoint that history had a greater significance than biology.

Could you specify the difference between what you in the manifesto called the "anagogic" and what you called the "pre-anagogic"?

I wrote the poem thinking of that:

AND COLD TIRED EMPTY TO BE SO SPREAD IN
    AIR
            is Hell too.
The predator's world is space. Time the instant
            (taken) in the strike.
But to be spread to strike at (so many) unwanted
        half-desires. Is Hell too. To be so
        self-flung in so many ways. To leap
        at so many half-loves. To fall back
            and find that part of you
        still hangs (there) so many times.
HELL PAIN BEWILDERED EMPTINESS
        the part left smolders.
Does not burn clear and drifts too
            upon the air. Hot Hell
                is freedom.

So, it's like a hot hell, the burning of our bodies, whether it's in the mitochondrian furnace or whether it's in the aspirations of our macrophysiology as the basis for our poetry, as the basis for what we feel rather than history. Charles' field began as history. It's as he moves into the *Maximus Poems* that he discovers his body. If you look at the first twenty or thirty sections of the *Maximus Poems,* you'll find that he's trying to deal with history. He does crash through in the same way Creeley crashes through the same problem. By the time he writes *Pieces* Creeley is no longer making poems about the traditional concerns, but is *writing his body.* By the time Charles gets to the last volume of the *Maximus Poems,* what he's talking about is coming directly out of his own sensorium. He no longer feels that he has to have the pretext of history—names and dates. He uses them, but doesn't need them as a pretext. They've become part of his experience. It's a noble thing that Charles did, because he's the only person— the only poet—I know of who internalized history. It was a great struggle for him to internalize it and make it part of his physiology. So when I had a disagreement with Charles, it's at a point where the disagreement is entirely fair. I had that disagreement with Charles in 1958. By 1962 or 63 Charles was in an entirely different stance in his long poem.

The concept of the "field" is central for Olson's poetics. In Scratching the Beat Surface *you also speak about the "felt," the "veldt," i.e., the field. How does that lock in with Olson's "field"?*

I'm taking Duncan's poem "The Opening of the Field" to mean the feeled, or the felt. With Duncan it's the field of the threshers and the dance. With Olson it's a field similar to the one that Pollock has in his painting—the area that he paints upon. For me, it's the cave that I see lit up by our senses, that which is felt is that which is alighted by our senses.

The Beard's *central image seems to be the "velvet eternity." Does that image relate in any way with the "veldt"?*

It's a field of velvet. "Velvet eternity" is the eternity that we touch with our fingertips, that we smell with our nose, that we feel with the seats of our ass when we sit on a chair, when we hear the sounds of someone else who's speaking. Those are the parts of the universe that are available to our prehension, those are the parts of the universe that we light up around us when we are the universe prehending itself. The universe seems to have an unending appetition for itself, an unending appetite for itself. And it certainly would be true narcissism if we felt we were anything more than points in the universe experiencing itself, or if we had any more proportionlessness than any other point that was prehending itself.

So realizing ourselves as being in a seamless web means that we experience not ourselves but the universe? And in that way we escape narcissism?

I don't even know that we need to escape it. As I said earlier, some of the interesting people I know are narcissists. I admire them in some ways, though I find them undependable. I do find it a great pleasure to watch them admiring themselves in the mirror. I tend to fall into admiring them also when I see them doing it.

By the way, since we mentioned The Beard: *what is the history of its title?*

"Beard" is Elizabethan slang, and it means to quarrel with someone; it means to pull their beard when you beard someone. As a matter of fact there

is an old Spanish saying. The Elizabethans could have taken it from the Spanish because the Elizabethans had a great deal of contact with the Spanish. The Spanish saying was "pluck not the beard of the sleeping lion," and the Elizabethans used the term "beard" as to quarrel with someone, to beard someone.

In Scratching the Beat Surface *you speak at one point about the invisible observer who closes his ears to the meanings of words and listens only to the vocalization as sounds. And you suggest further on that if the intelligence is open and is able to follow the sounds it will hear something. What is actually the direction in which this hearing might be moving?*

There I'm talking about the split between what we say we're talking about and what we're speaking of. I think what I spoke of there was a man and a woman arguing about the laundry tickets. But if you listen to the language, if you listen to the sounds coming out of the body, you realize that what's being spoken of is not really the laundry ticket. It's probably about their sex lives, or about their children that they're conversing, because one does not truly speak of laundry tickets with that emotional passion, or that intensity.

In other words, we use very limited vocabularies to describe our true emotional states. And that is what I'm suggesting that one listen for. It's not a statement about language, it's a statement about, well, about sociology and language in that particular instance. However, I was thinking about something in my poems today. One of the reasons for the shapes of my poems is to give body language to the poem itself. In other words, we do judge by body language. We judge by shifted position or cock of head or posture or eye squint or the way the body is turned with what's being spoken. There are a lot of cues that can be given in terms of body language in the shape of a poem.

By giving a sharpness, by giving a width to a passage of speech versus a narrowness of a passage of speech, one can follow the thrust of two things. One, that is true in speech, and not mimesis. But second, there can be hidden cues as to the subject that's being spoken of as well as to the intention of the musicality of what's being said.

So what is to be heard, what should be listened to is also the sound, the rhythm?

Oh, rhythm, volume, intensity, timbre.

In that connection I am interested in the principle of repetition in your poetry. At one point, in Scratch-

ing the Beat Surface, *you compare a poem by Philip Whalen to a Sung Dynasty landscape painting with the proper number of strokes, not too many and not too few. How does that relate to the principle of repetition the working of which is observable in your own poetry? Doesn't repetition imply redundancy?*

Well, I don't think of my poetry as having any resemblance to a Sung Dynasty landscape painting, although I would be pleased if it did. I don't work that way. That's a comparison I made to Philip's work, particularly to that poem.

The principles, the intentions, underlying the repetition are much more organic. It is our nature to repeat. As it is another part of our nature to delicately inscribe superb, small, correctly numbered strokes to represent something. It is equally as natural for us to repeat. For instance music repeats, dance repeats. Much of painting repeats, particularly today's repetitious minimalist painting, or pop art. They're very natural ways of expression.

If you begin a poem with the words, "the gesture," repeated nine times, fifteen times, the first time you hear "the gesture," the second time you hear "the gesture" and so forth, then the meaning does crumble. As a matter of fact the meaning disappears. Then the meaning becomes ritual. Then the meaning becomes meaning again. Then the meaning becomes something else. Then the meaning becomes a metric. Then the meaning becomes a sound pattern, it no longer has justifiable significance. Then it returns to significance. In the process of repetition of words you're playing not with one or two processes—you're playing with a number of processes. You must operate intuitively. One uses everything from deconstruction to ritualization to prosodization all in a very short space. This is possible because words do have such powerful meanings and significance.

How do you feel about the observation that there is a structural similarity between **The Adept, Rare Angel,** *and your play* **VKTMS:** *the structural similarity being the repeated return to a scene, a horrible scene, a climactic scene? How would you comment on that?*

I think that's simply true. I was troubled about something last night and I kept thinking about it and returning to thinking about it, and thinking about something else and returning to thinking about it, I had a hard time going to sleep. I mean that's one of our ways of thinking. We have other ways of thinking that are expansive, where we go

from one delightful imagining to another. It's one of our processes of thinking: It is to move away from a scene, to come back to the scene, to move away from it in another direction, to come back to it. We are creating an expanding field around the scene, and that gives the scene other resonances, other connections, other possibilities.

I would describe the essence of the scene in all the instances I've mentioned as the "felt" or the "veldt." Would you agree with that?

Well, I think the field or the "felt" or the "veldt" is what's created by moving away from the scene, coming back to the scene, moving away from it in a different direction, coming back to it, moving away from it in a different direction. That's what makes the moderation that allows us to live with primal scenes of horror.

It's a very moving scene in **The Adept** *when he kills unwillingly. Olson's words perhaps paraphrase it very well: "We do what we know, before we know what we do." I see the killing in this sense as an event, as a "field" in which you are included and you really don't know what you are doing, you just do it. Which is horrible because you realize that your body does what you don't know that you're doing. At the same time it's beautiful because you're completely inside what's happening.*

That's kind of a description of the "Uncarved Block" that you just made. . . .

In my understanding there is therefore a connection between the "field" and the "Uncarved Block." You don't see it that way?

In the way you said, one could, certainly.

There are two central notions or concepts that seem to be fulcrums in your poetry. They're "flesh" and "meat." Could you comment on the difference between and also on the mutual relatedness of these terms?

I don't know that I've ever opposed the idea of flesh and meat. What I propose is that we say meat when we're speaking about flesh, since flesh seems to be a euphemism for meat. In other words, the Victorians spoke about the limb of a chair rather than saying a leg of a chair because they wanted to avoid reference to the body. "Flesh," in the English language, is a way of avoiding the fact that the reference is a chopped-up piece of an animal—which is meat. Next, we avoid the reality that we are comprised of this same meat. It seems appropriate, if I am going to speak about real things, to speak about the real thing which is meat. It's not such a critical distinction anymore, in some part because of my work. I found myself titling a new lecture "Being Flesh" rather than "Being Meat." At one time I felt compelled to say **Meat Science Essays,** so that people would understand that I was really speaking about meat. I think that's clear enough now, certainly in my own work.

You have mentioned quite a few forces or sources which have been formative for your poetry. But you have mentioned him only in passing though he is definitely a source—Artaud. Could you comment on the fact that on the one hand you speak about Artaud as the anti-physical mystic poet, and on the other hand he in fact seems to have led you toward a "physicality of thought."

Artaud's anti-physicality and the stance that he takes against the body requires me, as a brother—and I felt like a younger brother of Artaud—requires me to take a position in regard to that anti-physicality. I must either agree with Artaud or decide how I feel. So in that way he's instrumental in helping me make the decisions I made. The intensity and the beauty and the perception of his gnostic anti-physicality requires that I accept it or that I disagree with it. And if I disagree with it, then I must have some understanding of why I disagree. Therefore it gives me a field upon which to work, or shows me that I need a field upon which to work. I choose my physicality. So, Artaud has been a major source for me. In the same way, when one reads D. H. Lawrence, one must say, I feel that this man is right or I do not feel that this man is right. And if I do not feel that this man is right, why is he not right? Thus I agree with much that Lawrence speaks about. I admire Lawrence's use of the preceptions as I admire Kerouac's extraordinary sensorium. So in the case of Kerouac and Lawrence I'm given the gift of their sensorium. In the case of Artaud I'm given the gift of his nervous system.

Speaking about the Beat movement you point out that there is a change going on, a change of the understanding of the nature of consciousness. And one may see your poetry as forcing that change in the sense of changing the traditional hierarchy of the senses, in changing the place of consciousness, in moving it closer from the locus of thinking—in the sense of Descartes' cogito—to the locus of the sensorium.

Rimbaud wanted an arranged derangement of the senses. We have an established hierarchy of the senses in Western civilization, with the eye being the one on top and I suppose the ear is second, and so forth. And I've done a lot of experi-

ments which sometimes clearly look at mind like organism, in them I arrangedly derange the traditional values of the senses. In doing so I place as much emphasis on the imagery of hearing as on the imagery of sight, as on the imagery of smell.

The effect sometimes is what appears to be a freeing up of an established stance towards experience. In other words, in the creation of spontaneous images, in **Rare Angel,** or in **Organism,** I have often deliberately, although spontaneously, written out *synesthesia* imaging processes that cause a startling effect upon traditional modalities of perception. The intention of the work is to give myself a view that I haven't had before. Hopefully, when someone reads an exercise, they can take a view that they haven't seen before. In other words, our traditional ways of seeing things are only *our* traditional ways of seeing things. They may also be our *biologically* traditional ways of seeing things, but we can deliberately arrange or derange them. And it can be constructive. It need not be frightening.

Let me quote a few verses from **Little Odes** *and* **Star:** *". . . the Blackness, the Blackness . . ." "I move in the deep pool of the black Lily / of Space. Like a worm without Head . . . mindlessly scenting the perfumes . . . ," "I Am Lost O, in the Lily / without eyes . . . ," "Life is not thought, not Intellect, / But Perfect Creations . . . ," "Light or intellect (or soul) / is no perfection . . ." There seems to exist a relation between intellect and sight and light opposed to a positive blackness and blindness. I wonder whether that points to a shift in the spectrum of the sensorium.*

Let me just comment from an entirely different direction: I've always since the mid-Fifties been interested in *agnosia,* in the kind of vision proposed by the progenitors of Meister Eckhart, like Dionysius the Areopagite or like Hildegard von Bingen. I've always been interested in that idea that *one sees with blackness,* one sees through poverty of knowledge. It's only through the poverty of knowledge that we acknowledge our own blackness so that perceptions can happen. When we think we know something, when we intellectually believe we know something, there is no black field upon which perceptions may happen. Hildegard von Bingen is saying that, Dionysius the Areopagite is saying that, I think Meister Eckhart is saying that, I think Jakob Böhme is saying that, and I think that it is even more common but stated in another way in Eastern thought.

I thought "agnosia" was something you got from the East.

No. From the Western mystic tradition. Although one can say that agnosia is what takes place in forms of Eastern meditation. I mean one is attempting to clear the reticular formation, to make it blank, so that perception passes over. One observes the naturalness and ordinariness . . .

*In **Rare Angel** there seems to be a significant interplay between the—as far as I can see—synonymous term: "curb," "edge," and "on the precipice." Did you intend any relation among them?*

I was completely unaware of it. But there probably is.

You couldn't comment on that?

The whole poem is about being on the edge.

What do you understand by "being on the edge"?

Being on the edge of the explosion.

Of the ecological catastrophe?

It's happening right now. We all thought that the world is going to blow up, and it is, we didn't realize how slowly it was going to blow up. It's blowing up *now* in slow motion.

*In **"Stanzas Composed in Turmoil"** you speak of the danger, of the "brink" or of the "edge" we are on. At the same time you're saying that we're in love with this danger. Since we love it, we obviously look for it, provoke it. We obviously enlarge and enhance that danger—isn't that a contradiction?*

I don't know that it is a contradiction. I want people to be aware, though, that it is our primate nature to enjoy what we're doing.

Even if we are burning up gas and polluting the biosphere, even if we are exploding the substrata of our being?

Yes, and if we realize how much we enjoy it and why we enjoy it and what a great thrill it is and what enormous machinery . . .

But it might be stupid, too.

Clearly. Clearly. But it is too easy to say it is stupid. We can't self-righteously tell other people who are enjoying it, when we are in the process of enjoying it ourselves, that it is simply stupid, that they are fools. So, one thing that we can do is make people understand how beautiful it is and that it is our nature to do those things and that they are beautiful *and* that they are stupid at this time for us and for the future.

It's not necessarily our nature, is it? I mean the Indians wouldn't do it.

The Indians were enormously destructive, nearly as destructive as Westerners. I'm talking about the Plains Indians now, I'm not talking about the Hopis and I'm not talking about the Indians on the West coast but the American Plains Indians—or take the Eskimo. This is why I talk about Paul Martin's idea that it was the ancestors of these Indians who wiped out twenty-six genera of mega-fauna, the entire upper tier of the Pleistocene mega-fauna in the New World when they entered it from the mastodons to the giant ground sloth. And if we see that, then we say: Oh, that's what we love to do, that's what we like to do, we like to do that. We love to kill big animals. Then we say: But if we like to do that, if we go any further, we are not going to have any brethren left at all. But first of all, you can't righteously take a stance that this is wrong, this is evil, this is not human. This is entirely human, this *is* our nature. Then we say: Ah, but our nature has *other* possibilities. If we acknowledge that this is our nature, what *other* possibilities does our nature have? What else could we do that is natural? That's the critical aspect that I see. Yes, I think it has to be stopped right away, but I think it has to be stopped by saying: Oh, *that's* who we are. Oooooh, I get it! I see! I understand. That's me!

You are saying: "Politics is dead—Biology is here . . ." Biology, i.e., the revolt of our bodies, or with our bodies? How would you describe that revolt as it may take place in everyday life?

There is a wonderful young man in California. He was concerned about a river that was about to be dammed, a wild river which would be dammed for the sheer fucking purpose of sending water to Southern California, water that they didn't need. The young man announced to the newspapers and to all the media that he was going to chain himself to a rock in the bottom of the canyon that would be filled up if they dammed the river. And he went down and chained himself to a rock where no one could find him and they didn't dam the river.

I fully agree with such acts.

That's biology.

ROD PHILLIPS (ESSAY DATE 2000)

SOURCE: Phillips, Rod. "'Let Us Throw out the Word *Man*': Michael McClure's Mammalian Poetics." In *"Forest Beatniks" and "Urban Thoreaus": Gary Snyder, Jack Kerouac, Lew Welch, and Michael McClure*, pp. 103-24. New York: Peter Lang, 2000.

In the following excerpt, Phillips considers McClure's work and career in terms of his environmental discourse.

"If there shall be love and content between the
    father
and the son and if the greatness of the son is the
    exuding
of the greatness of the father there shall be love
    between
the poet and the man of demonstrable science.
    In the
beauty of poems are the tuft and final applause
    of science."
    Walt Whitman, introduction to *Leaves of Grass*
                             (1855)
"Science walks in beauty."
    Gary Snyder, "Towards Climax," *Turtle Island*
                             (1974)

Beat writers of the 1950's and 60's took a variety of approaches in their attempts to reconnect with the natural world, among them Gary Snyder's emphasis on the physical body and its place in the world, Jack Kerouac's romantic rucksack quest for truth and solace in nature, and Lew Welch's anti-urban withdrawal into the wilderness. Often, these approaches utilized older models—what Snyder has referred to as "the old ways"—as vehicles in this reconnection: Buddhism and other forms of ancient Eastern thought, American Indian religion and myth, as well as the Romantic traditions of eighteenth and nineteenth century English and American literature.

Poet, playwright, essayist, and novelist Michael McClure shares these interests in "the old ways" with several other members of the Beat circle, often relying on them as both source and background for his own literary efforts. More often, however, the primary vehicle in McClure's nature poetry is not seventh century Buddhism or nineteenth century Romanticism, but instead the twentieth century scientific disciplines of biology and ecology. More than any other writer within Beat Movement, McClure relies on the scientific disciplines of the present as a means of discussing environmental issues and forging his own reconnection with the natural world.[1] Despite the many modern scientific sources of his poetry however, McClure's journey as a writer has taken him even further back into history than those of his colleagues within the Beat circle; his is a journey whose ultimate goal is the "recovery" of what he has referred to as "the biological self" (Mesch 5) and "the frightening and joyous" acknowledgment of a visceral "undersoul" which unites all of nature (*Surface* [*Scratching the Beat Surface*.] 26). "My interest in biology," McClure notes, "has remained a constant thread through my searching" (*Surface* 11).

The author of more than forty volumes of poetry, fiction, essays, and plays, Michael McClure is one of the most prolific and enduring figures to

emerge from the Beat Movement. He shares a long and rich history with Allen Ginsberg, Jack Kerouac, Lawrence Ferlinghetti, Gary Snyder, Philip Lamantia, Robert Creeley, and many other writers of San Francisco's Beat period. As one of the youngest members of the Beat circle, McClure played an important role as a bridge between writers and artists of the Beat Movement and the region's youth counterculture during of 1960's, and has been a close friend and collaborator with figures such as Richard Brautigan, Bob Dylan, and Janis Joplin.[2] For more than four decades, what Lawrence Ferlinghetti once called "McClure's lush green ideas" have been a highly visible and controversial topic of both American literary and environmental discourse.[3]

"The Fields of Kansas"

Born in 1932 in Marysville, Kansas, Michael McClure divided his early childhood years between the farmlands of Kansas and the Pacific rain forests of Seattle, Washington, where his interest in nature was heightened by time spent with his maternal grandfather, physician and naturalist Ellis Johnston. Poems such as his "**MEMORIES FROM CHILDHOOD**" (from his 1983 collection, *Fragments of Perseus*), recall the writer's formative years, and an early awareness of a clash between the human and non-human worlds:

    I REMEMBER THE FIELDS
      of Kansas and the laws

        that made
        them flat and bare

I know when and where
the field mouse died.

I watched the rivers tried
for treason,

then laid straight,
and the cottonwood and opossum

placed upon the grate
of petroleum civilization!

(43)

Educated first at the Universities of Witchita and Arizona, McClure gravitated westward towards San Francisco during his senior year. Following his marriage to Joanna Kinnison, he enrolled at San Francisco State College in 1954. It was here that McClure's long-standing interest in poetry was sparked by a writing course with a poet who would be a mentor to many of the Bay Area's new voices, Robert Duncan. Despite his new teacher's efforts to introduce him to free verse, McClure's early poems display a rigid formal structure which is absent in much of his later work—the result, perhaps, of his intensive study of Milton, Blake, and Yeats during his undergraduate education. His earliest published poems, which appeared in the prestigious journal *Poetry* when McClure was only 23, are two villanelles dedicated to Theodore Roethke, a fellow Midwesterner also much enamored with the natural world. Even in these early formal poems, there is evidenced a strong desire on the poet's part to experience the world not as a "civilized "human, but on a more instinctual level, as other life forms must. The first of the villanelles, **"Premonition,"** speaks of the poet's desire to see life as a bird views it, and his frustration at finding himself bound to Earth; the final stanza reads:

The skin and wingless skull I wear grow tight.
The echoes from the sky are never clear.
My bones ascend by arsenics of sight.
Beginning in the heart, I work towards light.

(218)[4]

As he matured as a writer, the form, as well as the subject, of McClure's poetry from the mid 1950's onward became reflective of his growing interest in biology and nature. The stiff, imposed structures evidenced in the iambic measures of early poems, such as the villanelles for Theodore Roethke, gave way to innovative free-verse poems which were centered on the page, a form which has become a recognizable trademark of McClure's verse, and one which, according to the poet, "gave the poems the lengthwise symmetry found in higher animals" (**Rebel Lions** vii).

The Six Gallery and Hymns for St. Geryon: Unveiling the "Undersoul"

McClure's friendship with Duncan quickly led to associations with others in the rapidly emerging San Francisco poetry community, including Kenneth Rexroth and the mystic surrealist poet Philip Lamantia (King 383-84). In early 1955, he met Allen Ginsberg at a party given in honor of visiting poet W.H. Auden, where Ginsberg told him of his intentions to organize a poetry reading featuring himself and several other young poets from the area—the event which later become known as the Six Gallery Reading. Here, McClure, along with Philip Lamantia, Gary Snyder, Philip Whalen, and Allen Ginsberg, helped to launch the Beat Movement, and his presence at the event helped to instill in the fledgling movement his life-long fascination with the natural world. The poems which McClure selected to read at this, his very first public reading, are indicative of his early environmental concerns. They include **"For The Death of 100 Whales,"** a powerful poem which condemns the slaughter of a pod of Icelandic killer whales by the United States military (and in doing so, predates by more than a decade the many calls for protection of marine mammals which would emerge in the late 1960's), and **"Point Lobos: Animism,"** a poem which provides an early glimpse of what the poet would later refer to as the visceral "undersoul" through which all of nature is united. The poem's final stanzas read:

(I knelt in the shade
By a cold salt pool
And felt the entrance of hate
On many legs,
The soul like a clambering
Water vascular system.

No scuttling could matter
Yet I formed in my mind
The most beautiful
Of maxims.
How could I care
For your illness or mine?)
This talk of bodies!

It is impossible to speak
Of lupine or tulips
When one may read
His name
Spelled by the mold on the stumps
When the forest moves about one.

Heel. Nostril.
Light. Light! Light!
This is the bird's song
You may tell it
to your children.
(Hymns [Hymns to St. Geyron and Other Poems]
4-5)

In his 1982 essay **"Scratching the Beat Surface,"** an essay in which McClure argues that nature and ecology were a central theme to many of the poems read at the Six Gallery as well as to many other Beat texts, he recalls his visit to Point Lobos, and his motivation in writing the poem:

> I wanted to tell of my feelings of hunger, of emptiness, and of epiphany. I hoped to state the sharpness of a demonic joy that I found in a place of incredible beauty on the coast of Northern California. I wanted to say how I was overwhelmed by the sense of animism—and how everything (breath, spot, rock, ripple in the tidepool, cloud, and stone) was alive and spirited. It was a frightening and joyous awareness of my undersoul. I say *undersoul* because I did not want to join Nature by my mind but by my viscera—my belly. The German language has two words, *Geist* for the soul of man and *Odem* for the spirit of beasts. Odem is the undersoul. I was becoming sharply aware of it.
>
> (26)[5]

Although couched in the philosophical terminology of animism, the ancient notion which holds that all natural phenomena and objects—whether animate or inanimate—possess an innate soul, McClure's early intuitive attempts to "join Nature" seem to draw more from science than from philosophy. McClure has written of "the important, yet little known reaching out from science to poetry and from poetry to science that was part of the Beat movement" (**Surface** 11).[6] Clearly, such a "reaching out" to science has manifested itself in both the sources and subjects of McClure's own work. Although the majority of his associates during the 1950's in San Francisco were mainly other poets and painters, his closest friend during the period was Sterling Bunnell, a scientist whom McClure terms "a visionary naturalist" (**Surface** 11). Bunnell shared McClure's interest in both nature and consciousness (he would later work in conjunction with Dr. Timothy Leary), and the poet credits him as being the person responsible for his first close look into the biological wealth which Northern California offered: "With him," McClure recalls, "I was able to watch coyotes and foxes and weasels and deer, and walk through savannah country, hike through foothills, go over the mountains, and to the seashore and look into tidepools" (**Lighting** [*Lighting the Corners: On Art, Nature, and the Visionary*] 3).

McClure's first collection of poems, **Hymns for St. Geryon,** published by his friend Dave Haselwood's Auerhahn Press in 1959, and which contains both **"For the Death of 100 Whales,"** and **"Point Lobos: Animism,"** exemplifies the writer's early application of biology to poetry. As William R. King has noted, "Geryon was Dante's beast of falsehood, a fair face atop a dragon's body. For McClure, St. Geryon was the apotheosized conflict between the social facade and instinctual desires" (387). **Hymns for St. Geryon** attempts to bridge this gap between the social facade (i.e. the cerebral trappings of all human culture) and instinctual desires (the body, and what McClure would later refer to as aspects of the "biological self"), and in doing so, the poems make readers aware of the possibility of unifying both aspects of their beings. As McClure notes in the title poem, "Even Geryon (as Geryon) is beautiful but not if you look / only at the head or body" (**Selected Poems** 7). Often, this task is accomplished by means of a microbiological perspective which forces us to view ourselves in close relation to "lower" forms of life, as in the poem entitled **"Canticle":**

> We who do not make way for creatures
> OUR CREATURE
> Warm blooded we move in a cold sea denying-
>
> -our guts cousins filling the cracks of the earth,
> sleeping at the bottom.
> Amphioxus, rotifers, arrow-worms hunting their
> prey,[7]
> predators in bodies
> of translucence and color, formed
> by the element they move about them
> AND
> hunger!!!!!!
>
> I put off my feelings today let the language
> move me tomorrow. A lie
>
> I say! The thing comes out moved
> by the man inside me who is a creature sprung
> from the chain. Let me regain it.
>
> (24-25)

The "thing" to be regained is the poet's own biological identity—an acknowledgment of his role as fellow "creature" and "cousin" to the microscopic organisms the poem describes. Like many of the poems in **Hymns to St. Geryon,** "Canticle" yearns for a biological wholeness, or what McClure has called "the monism of nature," exemplified by both the ancient Taoist view of the universe as a single uncarved block, and by modern scientific theories of ecology. Under such a view, the "amphioxus, rotifers" and "arrow-worms" are not "lower" forms of life, but are, instead, valuable and even "divine" expressions of a common life force. McClure explains:

> Ernst Haekel and Alfred North Whitehead believed that the universe is a single organism—that the whole thing is alive and that its existence is its sacredness and its breathing. If all is divine and

alive—and if everything is the Uncarved Block of the Taoists—then all of it and any part is beauteous (or possibly hideous) and of enormous value. It is beyond proportion. One cannot say that a virus is less special or less divine than a wolf or a butterfly or a rose blossom. One cannot say that a star or cluster of galaxies is more important—has more proportion—than a chipmunk or a floorboard. This recognition is always with us.

(*Surface* 27).

Meat Science

McClure's poetry can often be difficult, and the poet has at times adopted the abstract expressionist painter Clyfford Still's dictum that "Demands for communication [in art] are presumptuous and irrelevant" (*Surface* 26).[8] Although always present (yet not always easily decipherable) in his early poetry, McClure's biological and ecological notions are first clearly described in his 1961 collection, *Meat Science Essays*. The eight essays contained in this slim volume cover a diverse range of subjects—from detailed and vivid descriptions of the author's early experiments with mind-altering drugs, to essays in response to the French surrealist writer Antonin Artaud and the existentialist philosopher Albert Camus. But a common thread which finds its way into each of the essays, as the book's title indicates, is the notion of a shared biological connection among all creatures, human and non-human: "that all," as McClure notes, "are finally creatures of Meat and Spirit" (44).

The *Meat Science Essays* mark for McClure a turning point, as he begins to move from the vision of universal interconnectedness (i.e. the "uncarved block" of Tao) first posited in the *St. Geryon* poems, to a refined and somewhat more narrow view of his role as "mammal." While he in no way abandons his earlier monistic view of nature (and would, in fact, occasionally return to it throughout his career), as McClure notes in his essay "**Reflections After a Poem**," the complex differences between humans and creatures vastly different from ourselves prevent humans from fully knowing or understanding them. After first pointing out "our kinship with all creatures," he reserves his true feelings of empathy for species more closely related to humans:

> We feel close to all living creatures here . . . but we feel the most close and the most joined with the warm blooded. We cannot know the universal and philosophical consciousness of deep seas animals. We fill the universe in our sympathy for all being, but moments of extreme vision and beauty swell us out so that we feel immediately more related to a larger group than Man. We become Mammals as we once were Men. . . . Or-

nette Coleman[9] is a mammal, the snow leopard is a mammal, Schubert is a mammal.

(*Meat Science* [*Meat Science Essays*] 79-80)

Asking enthusiastically "What greater thing is there than to fill out the fullness of being a mammal?" (82), McClure admonishes his readers to reconsider their place in the world, and their relationship to the rest of nature. "LET US THROW OUT THE WORD *MAN*!," he urges, and seek in place of this limited role the "mammalian possibility" of "a larger place" (79-80)—a taxonomic broadening from the single species *Homo sapiens* to full membership among the more than 15,000 species of the class *Mammalia*.

Experimentation with hallucinogenic substances was an important source for McClure's evolving view of nature, as it was for other Beat era writers and artists.[10] The *Meat Science Essays* contain several pieces detailing McClure's use of peyote, heroin, cocaine, and the hallucinogenic psilocybin mushroom. Although the author has in recent times cited drugs as being merely one source among many other influences on his thought and writing, McClure's essay, *Drug Notes*, provides an insight into the central importance which his drug experimentation played in shaping his view of nature. McClure himself seems to acknowledge the centrality of his drug experimentation by describing making his first use of peyote the topic of the opening sentence of *Scratching the Beat Surface*, the book in which he explores the connection between his work and nature: "In 1958 I ate the American Indian drug peyote for the first time" (5).[11]

The "adventure of consciousness" (6) which McClure entered into with his first taste of peyote, may well be at the root of the poet's mammalian vision. In the section on peyote in "**Drug Notes**," after noting that "We have learned to see by a code first invented by Michelangelo and Da Vinci," McClure writes that to experience the world through the drug's effects "is to know that you've lived denying and dimly sensing reality through a haze" (26). When the aesthetic "code" imposed by human culture drops away, the author finds in its place a universe in which all are "animals":

> All things beam inner light and color like a pearl or shell. All men are strange beast-animals with their mysterious histories upon their faces and they stare outward from the walls of their skin— their hair is fur—secretly far beneath all they are animals and know it. Far underneath the actions they make, their animal actions are still being performed as they walk and smile . . .

(26)

McClure's essay, "**The Mushroom**," from the same volume, describes another drug experiment into what the author calls the "Olympian universe" into which hallucinogenic substances can offer a window (15). Although he notes that when using psilocybin mushrooms, one feels "utterly human and humane," McClure finds here too, a bridge to the non-human world, and an acknowledgment of the "beastliness of mankind" (15). The essay describes a long, mundane afternoon's simple activities—lunch, a drive, a trip to an art museum—turned into a dazzling and illuminating psychedelic adventure through the use of the mushroom. As he did under the influence of peyote, the poet experiences a vision of the human body apart from the aesthetics of "Michelangelo and Da Vinci," but rather than viewing them as "animals," as he did in the earlier peyote vision, he now views humans as far simpler creatures:

> All of our notions of the human body's shape are wrong. We think it is a head joined on a torso and sprouting arms and legs and genitals and breasts, but we're wrong. It is more unified than that. It's all one total unity of protoplasm and our ideas of its appearance are too much a matter of habit.
>
> (19)

As McClure and his companion enter a vacant church, the essay ends with one of the poet's first experiments with what he calls "Beast Language," a guttural, growling form of poetic "speech" divorced from human meaning and designed to further bridge the gap between species. Standing at the church lectern, still high from the effects of the mushrooms, McClure recalls, "I began to speak in the language of beasts" (21). The essay ends with a poem describing the event, and exemplifying the poet's use of "Beast Language":

> By the stained glass windows
> of dream hills and landscapes—I raised back my
>   head
>   AND SANG
> into the Olympian world, growling with the
>   worshipping
>   and directing voice of Man-Beasts!
> GROOOHOOOOR GROOOOOOOR SHARAKTAR
>   GRAHR GROOOOOOR GREEEER
> SHROOOOOOOLOWVEEEEEEEEEE.
>   The white flecks of my spittle
> floated like clumps of alyssum in the dimness
> of the here, now, eternal, beauteous peace and
>   reality.
>
> (21-22)[12]

No doubt because of his life-long preoccupation with the natural world, nature seems at the center of all of McClure's early drug experiments—even his experiments with drugs which have not been traditionally seen as hallucinogenic or mystical. His recollections concerning his first use of cocaine, for example, contained in his essay "**Drug Notes**," begin with a description of a late night ritual which would seem to preclude any topic except nature from entering into the author's altered consciousness:

> I had come from Walden Pond to New York City. In my hand was a new book pressing an oak leaf from Thoreau's hearth. In the dim apartment a friend poured water out of a bronze vial onto my head. The water was from the Ganges. . . . I was very joyful, it was 3:00 in the morning, hot July, in New York City. Perhaps the river water and Thoreau *alone* could have made me divinely high.
>
> (39)

The changes in perception which follow McClure's first cocaine experiment in some ways parallel those which he had undergone while using peyote and psilocybin mushrooms. What the poet now perceives as a facade of social construct falls away, leaving in its absence a new vision, which in this case involves a view of wild nature hidden beneath Manhattan:

> All, all was reality. In the dark of morning by the East River I saw nature made anew—as in any redwood forest of the West. The city becomes nature. The streets of the lower East Side are pastoral and simple fields of summer haze. . . . I saw through the rat's eyes. Grimy barges and ancient factories leaned into eternity. If it shall be our nature to live this way we must know that Nature is here in a strange garment.
>
> (40)

While much of McClure's early writing concerning nature seems to stem from an intuitive, often Romantic, sense of empathy towards the natural world (an empathy which was forcefully heightened by a series of intense drug experiences), his interest in biology provided his imagination, and apparently his hallucinations, with a solid mooring. McClure's essay, "**Revolt**," first published in *Journal for the Protection of All Beings* (a journal which he co-edited along with Lawrence Ferlinghetti and David Meltzer) and later collected in **Meat Science Essays**, exemplifies the writer's use of biological imagery to discuss philosophical, and even political issues facing humans. In the essay, McClure uses the planarian worm[13] as a biological "example of revolt" (57) living in "a smaller universe of clearer beauty and simpler Good and Bad" (61). The author finds, in these small worms, a "basic relevant meaning of revolt to us as many-celled meat-creatures," since the planaria has the ability to "revolt" through asexual reproduction by dividing its head from its body and forming two new beings. Humans, unable to simply split in half when the head (or mind) and body are in discord, must choose other methods of revolt to maintain the equilibrium between the high powered forces of the human intellect and the often ignored and under-developed "subspirits" of the body (61). Too often in humans, McClure notes, "The Head is Chief and the Body follows" (59). But, like Geryon in McClure's earlier poem, the human form can only be seen as complete when viewed as a whole composed of both head and body, and the "revolt" of the physical side of one's nature (the biological self) in opposition to the powerful forces of the mind (the social self) is an on-going part of this quest for this equilibrium:

> At all times revolt is the search for health and naturality. Revolt is a desire to experience normal physiological processes that give pleasure of full-ness and expansion
>
> (59).

"Politics is Dead and Biology is Here!"

The mid-1960's marked a period of McClure's career in which he placed more emphasis on drama than poetry. His most famous and most controversial play, *The Beard*, was penned and first performed in 1965. The obscenity trials result-ing from the production would occupy much of the writer's time and energy for the next three years.

During this same period, McClure released a small but fascinating poetry chapbook entitled *Poisoned Wheat*. Written as a protest against American involvement in the war in Vietnam, the book's title refers to the wartime practice of poisoning grain fields in Cambodia. The poet mailed over 500 of the pamphlets to journalists and politicians whom he felt might have some influence on American policy in Southeast Asia (King 394). While in retrospect this seems a relatively futile act, McClure's small book was not without its impact; the real importance, however, of *Poisoned Wheat* was not its small stab at the American war machine, but in its radical merging of biology and politics.

In a poetic manifesto which would fore-shadow much of the poet's writing for the next three decades, McClure's *Poisoned Wheat* at-tempts to look for solutions to the world's cata-strophic problems outside the normal channels of politics and ideology. Although the long poem deals ostensibly with the war in Southeast Asia, the war quickly becomes just one symbolic symp-tom of a much larger malaise resulting from a cor-rupt society which clings to political dogma rather than biological realities. McClure's response is to divorce himself from the war and the misguided and cruel society which wages it:

> I AM NOT RESPONSIBLE
> FOR THOSE WHO HAVE CREATED
> AND / OR CAPTURED the CONTROL DEVICES
> OF THE SOCIETY THAT SURROUNDS ME!
> I despise Society that creates
> bundles of cruelties
> and presses them en masse
> against the helpless.
>
> (4)

McClure's staunch anti-war stance was a radi-cal one in 1965, a time when opposition to the Vietnam War was still largely smothered beneath Cold War rhetoric of the Iron Curtain, the Domino Theory, and the rapidly accelerating arms race. But far more radical is his insistence that we look beyond political rhetoric to the realization that the Vietnam War was not about a political struggle between Communism and Democracy, but was instead symptomatic of a much larger problem to which neither side possesses a solution. McClure's poem attacks each of the world's prevailing politi-cal systems—capitalism, communism and fas-cism—for their failure to effectively address the problems of life on the planet.

> COMMUNISM WILL NOT WORK!
> Communism will not create food in quantities
> necessary for man's survival.
> CAPITALISM IS FAILURE!
> It creates overpopulation, slavery,
> and starvation.
>
> (4-5)

Stating that "I have escaped politics," and that the "meanings of Marxism and Laissez faire are extinct" (6), the poet rejects the political and social systems which have been artificially im-posed upon the biological realities of life. Just as he suggested in his earlier essay "Revolt," as well as in the *St. Geryon* poems, the social and intel-lectual forces of the mind (in this case, the abstract notions of "politics" and "government") have repressed the biological aspects of human life, often resulting in disastrous consequences.

In place of political issues, McClure points to the stark biological realities facing the Earth—realities that have gone unaddressed by both Capitalism and Communism:

> The population of the United States will double
> by the year 2000. Certain South American
> nations double each eighteen and twenty years.
> There is no answer
> but a multiplicity of answers created by men.
> A large proportion of men are on the verge
> OF STARVATION!
> When density of creature to creature reaches

a certain degree
the ultra-crowded condition is a
biological sink.

(6)

The results of the "biological sink" which Mc-Clure describes are starvation, exploitation of world resources, and an increasingly repressive and war-like society that has already fallen victim to its own suicide. The poem continues:

WESTERN SOCIETY HAS ALREADY DESTROYED
ITSELF!
The culture is extinct! The last sentry
at the gate has pressed the muzzle to his
Forehead and pulled the trigger!
The new civilization will not be communism!
POLITICS ARE AS DEAD AS THE CULTURE
they supported!

(8)

In place of a culture governed by political theory, McClure offers what Allen Van Newkirk has called a "bioculture" (22). In his brief 1975 analysis of McClure's work as it relates to new frontiers of ecological thought, "The Protein Grail," Newkirk describes the tenets of the biocul-turist worldview:

. . . [B]iocultural thought . . . is distinguished by its emphasis on the wild realities of the landscape as a field for discourse and action. Bioculturists assert a biological interpretation of history; that the human situation is mammalian, that the human mammal has over-domesticated itself and the landscape it utilizes, and that wild nature contains economic and sensate possibilities overlooked by the inherited civilization construct.

(22)

With the poet's emphatic line, near the end of *Poison Wheat*, declaring that "NEW SOCIETY WILL BE BIOLOGICAL!" (9), and further, that "POLITICS IS DEAD AND BIOLOGY IS HERE!," McClure demands nothing short of a total reorga-nization of society along these biocultural lines. Tellingly, the long poem ends, as it began, with an utterance of McClure's trademark beast lan-guage, a "Grahhr" symbolizing humanity's mam-malian past—and its mammalian future.

The Early Seventies: "The Shape of Energy"

In the late 1960's and early 70's, McClure spent a good deal of his time and effort on prose works as well as drama. During this period, the content of McClure's writing became much more thoroughly anchored in biology, as his psychedelic experiences and his early intuitive feelings of an interconnectedness with nature were bolstered by his reading of several biological and ecological

thinkers. "In the early seventies," he recalls in his essay **"The Shape of Energy,"** "the thinking of H. T. Odum, of Harold Morowitz in biophysics, and of [Ramon] Margalef in ecological systems did much to clarify my unorganized perceptions of the fifties and sixties" (**Surface** 95).[14] Feeling more certain than ever "that it was no longer appropri-ate to continue the Descartian division of mind and physiology" (**Surface** 88), McClure turned to science for support for his intuitions.

It was during this period that the poet began to view poetry as an "extension of physiology" and further, to consider the possibility "that a poem could even become a living bio-alchemical organism" (89):

The mind is inseparable from the body and too much energy has been spent looking at the mind (whether shapely or not)[15] of poetry, and not enough at the body. Similarly, the structure of poetry had often been looked at (though not clearly), but such structure had never been looked at as an extension of physiology.

(**Surface** 89)

If the Cartesian split between mind and body can be unified, McClure argues, then similarly, why couldn't a poem be seen as "an extension" of this unified "Bulk" of the poet's mind and body: "extensions of myself as much as my hand or arm are extensions of me" (**Surface** 89). Further, Mc-Clure began to envision a poem "that like a wolf or salmon . . . could turn its head from side to side to test the elements and seek for breath. I wanted to write a poem that could come to life and be a living Organism" (**Surface** 89).

As a way of understanding this "bio-alchemical" transfer of energy between poet and poem, McClure began to investigate the writings of Ramon Margalef, particularly his 1968 work *Perspectives in Ecological Theory*. Margalef's section entitled "The Ecosystem as a Cybernetic System" became especially important as "one of the well-springs of exuberance" in the poet's thought; Mar-galef's work became, for McClure, a way "to see energy in action in the bundles and bodies that contain it" (**Surface** 92-3). Out of his reading of Margalef, McClure began to view his own poems—and those of his colleagues in the Beat circle—as biological extensions born of an "organic process" in which one life form (the poet) transfers energy from "a powerful, complex, informed—ultimately stable substrate" (the poet's life experience) to cre-ate yet another life form (the poem) (96). In Mc-Clure's view, poets such as "Olson, Snyder, Cree-ley, Duncan, Kerouac, Ginsberg, [and] Whalen" (as well as, we are to presume, McClure himself)

. . . "develop the containment of complex energy as they mature. They feed from the energy of the substrate around them as it informs their senses. It is an organic process" (96). As McClure puts it in his essay, **"The Shape of Energy,"** in *Scratching the Beat Surface,* poetry thus becomes "an image of the universe" in which:

> Densified areas of greater organization [the poet] react with nebulous matter in space [i.e. experience, ideas, inspiration] and are informed by it. There is further densification [i.e. the creative process]. It reaches climax. It explodes [the poem is created]—the material retains certain pieces of information and gains more organization [the poem's content and structure] in the explosion—and so forth.
>
> (94)[16]

Another key scientific influence on McClure's work during the early seventies was Howard T. Odum's study *Environment, Power and Society* (1971), a work which shares Margalef's interest in the manner which energy functions in nature, and more importantly, one which sparked the poet's interest in the notion of biological diversity. In Odum's scientific text, McClure found ample justification for his earlier feelings of interconnectedness with nature, since Odum's work often focused on the diverse and inscrutable "species networks" which combine to form a healthy and stable eco-system. In his section entitled "Complex and Beautiful Systems," in *Environment, Power and Society,* Odum writes: "Nature reaches its most appealing manifestations of beauty, intricacy, and mystery in the very complex systems: the tropical coral reef, the tropical rain forest, the benthos-dominated marine systems on the west coasts of continents of temperate zones, the bottom of the sea, and some ancient lakes of Africa" (quoted in *Surface* 83).

In the mysterious and interwoven fabric of such "complex and beautiful systems" as Odum describes, McClure found the scientific support for the intuitive feelings of species interconnectedness which he had been struggling with for more than twenty years. Here was the "uncarved block" of Tao dressed in the garb of Western science—a scientific truth as beautiful, all-encompassing, and terrifying as any peyote vision of the undersoul. All *is* connected, Odum posited, but the message also carried with it a further caution, all *must be* connected in order to ensure a healthy and stable environment.

McClure's poetry of the period bristles with a renewed intensity. No longer was it simply enough to acknowledge humanity's kinship with nature's other life-forms, as the poems in *Hymns to Saint Geryon* did. Odum's models of ecological systems made it clear to McClure that not only were species interrelated, but also strongly interdependent; the survival of one species—and indeed the entire eco-system—could very well hinge on maintaining the diversity of other species within the system. Poems such as **"Listen Lawrence"** from *Fragments of Perseus* (a piece aimed at converting poet Lawrence Ferlinghetti from a Socialist to a biological world-view), approach the themes of ecological interconnectedness and the need for a biocentric worldview with a reformer's zeal, as he tells his friend:

> OUR REAL BODIES ARE NOT DIVISABLE
> from the bulks of our
> brother and sister beings!
> We're alarmed by the simultaneous extinction
> and overcrowding of creatures
>
> (39)

The poem revisits the idea of a familial relationship between species first posited in **"Canticle"** twenty years before—although the "cousins" of other species described in the earlier poem have been brought closer into the family fold, and are now tellingly referred to as "brother and sister beings." Just as **"Poisoned Wheat"** had done a decade earlier, **"Listen Lawrence"** places the ultimate blame for the Earth's rapidly dwindling biological diversity squarely on the shoulders of the world's political systems. What is needed to fend off the loss of the planet's species, McClure argues, is not the Socialist reform which Ferlinghetti favors, but a wholesale rejection of all politics: "ANY, ANY, ANY / POLITICS / is the POLITICS OF EXTINCTION!" (41):

> We live near the shadow
> AT THE NEAR EDGE OF THE SHADOW
> ((TOO NEAR!!))
> of the extermination
> of the diversity
> of living beings. No need
> to list their names
> (Mountain Gorilla, Grizzly, Dune Tansy)
> for it
> is a too terrible
> elegy to do so!
>
> COMMUNISM,
> CAPITALISM
> SOCIALISM,
> will do
> NOTHING,
> NOTHING
> to save the surge
> of life—the ten thousand
> to the ten-thousandth, vast
> Da Vincian molecule of which
> ALL LIFE,
> ALL LIFE
> is a particle!
>
> (40)

The Eighties and Nineties: "Rebel Lions"

McClure's demand that his friend Ferlinghetti—and all humanity—"come out of the closet—/ OUT OF THE CLOSET OF POLITICS / and into the light of their flesh and bodies!" (*Fragments* [*Fragments of Perseus*] 42) remains a constant in his message as the poet enters his sixties. For McClure, the only means of survival is the rejection of political solutions, and the embrace of a new, biologically informed, world-view. In his most recent collection of poems, *Rebel Lions* (1991), McClure returns to the vision he has held since the Six Gallery reading now nearly forty years ago. In a poem entitled "**Mammal Life**," the poet again discusses the importance of this reconnection to what he has called the "biological self":

> The real mammal life
>   with its clear sensorium
> and the wisdom of the gut
>   and the meat in the blackness
>   that stretches back in time
>   to the stars
> through the bodies of strange
>   forefather beasts
> is the powerful NEGATIVITY,
>   powerful negativity,
>   THAT WE USE FOR OUR REVOLT.
> Mammal life is deep and luminous as the belly
>   of a shark
>   or the white fungi on cedar trunks
> in the cool rainforest[17]
> AND
>   it
>   is
>   me
>
>   (109)

Acknowledging the "biological self," embracing humankind's mammalian "wisdom of the gut," and envisioning the universal "undersoul" are the means of McClure's revolt against the political forces he sees as leading to ecological catastrophe—and also his means of reconnecting to the natural world. As he said in a recent interview, his is not a poetry that provides the answers to the problems plaguing the environment; instead, he sees his role as a visionary, aimed at providing "a new path" away from politics and towards biology (*Lighting* 6). In his poem entitled "**Villanelle for Gary Snyder**," from his 1975 collection *Jaguar Skies*, McClure aligns himself (and supposedly, Snyder) with others who he identifies as revolutionary visionaries:

> IN TURN WE GIVE FLESH TO THE REVOLU-
>   TION
>   like Che,[18] Darwin, and Francis Crick
>   creating visions not solution.
>
>   (68)

Not surprisingly, McClure finds two of his intellectual compatriots among scientific visionaries Charles Darwin and Francis Crick—the theorist who developed the concept of species evolution, and the Nobel Prize winning scientist who first shed light on the double helix structure of the DNA molecule. For above all, McClure is a poet concerned with science, a poet whose knowledge and interest in biological and ecological issues provide him with a rich scientific "substrate" which allows him to write in what his friend Gary Snyder calls "a specific biological / wild / unconscious / fairytale / new / scientific / imagination form."[19]

McClure's admiration of visionary scientists like Francis Crick is not unrequited. Crick has been an admirer and close reader of McClure's poetry since the mid 1950's, when he first discovered a copy of "**Peyote Poem**" in a San Francisco book shop, and he has paid tribute to the poet's treatment of scientific issues in his essay "The Poetry of Michael McClure: A Scientist's View." Unlike many other poets writing today who "are rather ignorant of science" and even hostile to it, Crick notes that: "Michael McClure is so at home in the fantastic world that science has conjured out of ourselves and our surroundings . . . that he takes it all in stride" (23). Crick closes his homage to McClure and his scientifically based poetry with a final tribute which can leave little doubt that he is indeed a poet of science:

> The worlds in which I myself live, the private world of personal reactions, the biological world (animals and plants and even bacteria chase each other through the poems), the world of the atom and molecule, the stars and the galaxies, are all there; and in between, above and below, stands man, the howling mammal, contrived out of "meat" by chance and necessity. If I were a poet I would write like Michael McClure—if only I had his talent.
>
>   (24)

Notes

1. Although the Beats have often been wrongly labeled as anti-intellectual and, at times, anti-scientific, McClure is not alone, among Beat poets, in his use of scientific sources; his friend Gary Snyder has also made extensive use of the scientific disciplines of biology, ecology, and anthropology. See James I. McClintock's excellent discussion of Snyder's scientific sources in "Gary Snyder: Posthumanist," collected in *Nature's Kindred Spirits: Aldo Leopold, Joseph Wood Krutch, Edward Abbey, Annie Dillard, and Gary Snyder.* (Madison: University of Wisconsin Press, 1994) 109-28. Also, see John Elder's discussion of Snyder's use of science in *Imagining the Earth: Poetry and the Vision of Nature* (Urbana: University of Illinois Press, 1985) 185-206.

2. Among his many and diverse publication credits, McClure proudly lists "Mercedes Benz," a humorous

critique of America's quest for material goods, which he co-wrote with Joplin, and which Joplin later recorded and made popular.

3. Ferlinghetti's remarks are contained in his introduction to McClure's first book of essays: *Meat Science Essays* (1963): 3.

4. McClure's poem may have been intended as a response, or a compliment, to Theodore Roethke's poem of the same name (included in his 1941 collection *Open House*). Both poems utilize images of bone as a means of depicting human limitations and mortality. See: *The Collected Poems of Theodore Roethke*. New York: Anchor Press, 6.

5. The contrast with Emerson's notion of the transcendental "Over-Soul," which he refers to as "the universal beauty, to which every part and particle is equally related: the eternal ONE," is implicit in this passage, yet McClure makes no direct mention of it until his 1985 collection of journal musings, *Specks*. See McClure's *Lighting the Corners*: 108, and "The Over-Soul," in *Ralph Waldo Emerson: Essays and Lectures*. New York: Library of America, 1983. 383-400.

6. As evidence of this "reaching out from science to poetry," McClure notes that Nobel laureate Francis Crick, one of the scientists who first shed light on the double helix structure of the DNA molecule, quoted from McClure's early "Peyote Poem" in his 1958 study, *Of Molecules and Men*:

> THIS IS THE POWERFUL KNOWLEDGE
> we smile with it
>
> *(Hymns* 42)

See Crick's tribute to McClure in "The Poetry of Michael McClure: A Scientist's View." *Margins* 18 (1975): 23-24.

7. "Amphioxus": a primitive chordate organism, also known as the lancet. "Rotifer": a minute, multicellular aquatic organism of the phylum *Rotifera*, possessing a wheellike ring of cilia—also known as "wheel animalcule." "Arrow-worms": small, slender marine worms of the phylum *Chaetognatha*, having prehensile bristles on each side of the mouth.

8. Poet Ed Dorn, commenting on the difficulty of making meaning from McClure's poetry, has noted that readers must approach the work using biology as a key: ". . . contact, if it is ever made," Dorn writes, "is made with all the biological circuits plugged in" (*Views* 88).

9. Ornette Coleman: (b. 1930) alto saxophone player and key member of the "Free Jazz" school of the early 1960's.

10. See Allen Ginsberg's poem "Wales Visitation," a meditation on nature inspired by one of the poet's many experiences with LSD, contained in *Planet News: 1961-1967*. See also Clayton Eshleman's "Imagination's Body and Comradely Display," in *Gary Snyder: Dimensions of a Life*, for an account of an LSD vision which provided the poet "an interchange between inner and outer worlds" (241). The most complete discussion of the use of hallucinogens among Beat writers can be found in Jay Stevens's *Storming Heaven: LSD and the American Dream*: 100-120. LSD advocate Timothy Leary also recalls his early hallucinogenic drug experiments with Ginsberg, Kerouac, Neal

Cassidy, and Peter Orlovsky in his 1983 autobiography, *Flashbacks: A Personal and Cultural History of an Era*: 45-70.

11. Always the consummate naturalist, McClure's second sentence is "Peyote is, of course, the cactus *Lophophora williamsii*—a small, spineless, flat-topped plant found mainly in the vicinity of Laredo and Northern Sonora" (*Surface* 5).

12. In the years to come, McClure would continue to make extensive use of "beast language" in his work, including his first play entitled "*!The Feast!*" (1960) written and performed entirely in this invented idiom. A 1960 stage production of the play at San Francisco's Batman Gallery featured a cast which included, among others, Robert LaVigne, Ron Loewinsohn, David Meltzer, Philip Whalen, Joanna McClure and Kirby Doyle (King 389). McClure's 1964 collection, *Ghost Tantras*, includes ninety-nine poems written in beast language.

13. A species, according to McClure, of "small flat black worms with triangular heads that live in icy streams." Since they possess simple nervous systems, as well as eyes, and utilize a simple process of digestion, McClure calls them "our farthest close-cousins" (*Meat Science Essays* 57).

14. Gary Snyder has also acknowledged the influence which H. T. Odum and Margalef had on his developing work.

15. Probably a comment on Allen Ginsberg's dictum "Mind is shapely, art is shapely."

16. Others within the Beat circle also seemed in tune with McClure's view of poetry as energy transfer. Gary Snyder calls a sequence of short poems in *Left Out in the Rain* "Tiny Energies," a phrase taken from H. T. Odum's *Environment, Power and Society*. McClure's good friend Richard Brautigan took a less scientific and more whimsical approach to the question of poetry as an organic process of energy transfer with his *Please Plant This Book*, a collection of poetry broadsides printed on packets of vegetable seeds.

17. McClure notes that the "cool rainforest" he refers to here is Oregon's Olympic Peninsula. *Rebel Lions* 115.

18. Che Guevara: 1928-67. Cuban revolutionary who was killed in South America while taking part in a popular revolt there.

19. Snyder's remarks come in an interview with Peter Chowka in *The Real Work: Interviews & Talks 1964-79*: 124. Snyder mentions McClure as one of a handful of American poets whom he reads with interest.

Works Cited

WORKS BY MICHAEL MCCLURE

McClure, Michael. *Fragments of Perseus*. New York: New Direction, 1983.

———. *Hymns to St. Geyron and Other Poems*. San Francisco: The Auerhahn Press, 1959.

———. *Lighting the Corners: On Art, Nature, and the Visionary*. Albuquerque: University of New Mexico College of Arts and Sciences, 1993.

———. *Meat Science Essays*. San Francisco: City Lights Books, 1966.

——. *Scratching the Beat Surface.* San Francisco: North Point Press, 1982.

——. *Rebel Lions.* New York: New Directions, 1991.

——. "2 for theodare roethke." *Poetry* 4 (1956): 218-19.

WORKS BY OTHERS

Crick, Francis. "The Poetry of Michael McClure: A Scientist's View." *Margins* 18 (1975): 23-24.

Dorn, Edward. *Views.* San Francisco: Four Seasons Foundation, 1980.

Emerson, Ralph Waldo. *Ralph Waldo Emerson: Essays and Lectures.* New York: Library of America, 1983.

Ginsberg, Allen. *Planet News.* San Francisco: City Lights, 1990.

King, William R. "Michael McClure." *The Beats: Literary Bohemians in Postward America.* Ed. Ann Charters. 2 vols. Detroit: Bruccoli Clark Books, 1983.

McClintock, James I. *Nature's Kindred Spirits: Aldo Leopold, Joseph Wood Krutch, Edward Abbey, Annie Dillard, and Gary Snyder.* Madison: University of Wisconsin Press, 1994.

Mesch, Harald. "Writing One's Body: An Interview with Michael McClure." *Poetry Flash* 209 (August 1990): 1, 4-6, 18-19.

Newkirk, Allen Van. "The Protein Grail." *Margins* 18 (1975): 21-23.

Stevens, Jay. *Storming Heaven: LSD and the American Dream.* New York: Harper & Row, 1988.

FURTHER READING

Criticism

Bartlett, Lee. "Review of *Scratching the Beat Surface.*" *Western American Literature* 18, no. 1 (spring 1983): 57-9.

Review of McClure's retrospective anthology and poetry Scratching the Beat Surface, *briefly considering the author's meat poetics.*

——. "Meat Science to Wolf Net: Michael McClure's Poetics of Revolt." In *The Sun Is but a Morning Star: Studies in West Coast Poetry and Poetics,* pp. 107-23. Albuquerque: University of New Mexico Press, 1989.

Examines McClure's Scratching the Beat Surface *as demonstrating that the author is above all a poet of revolt.*

Brakhage, Stan. "Review." *Chicago Review* 47-48, nos. 4-1 (winter 2001): 38-41.

Examines how McClure's aesthetic evolution gives the reader insight through language into the biological thoughts of the body.

Cherkovski, Neeli. "Lyrical Light: Michael McClure." In *Whitman's Wild Children: Portraits of Twelve Poets,* pp. 89-111. South Royalton, Vermont: Steerforth Press, 1999.

Originally published in 1988, this essay includes personal recollections of McClure and a comparison of the poet and Walt Whitman.

Davidson, Michael. "The Darkness Surrounds Us." In *The San Francisco Renaissance: Poetics and Community at Mid-Century,* pp. 85-94. Cambridge: Cambridge University Press, 1989.

Explores McClure's beast language poetry and mammalian poetics for their biological consideration of the nature of existence.

Holden, Jonathan. "A Prompt Book." *American Book Review* 9-10 (1987-1989): 19.

Review of McClure's 1986 Selected Poems.

Kherdian, David. "Michael McClure." In *Six Poets of the San Francisco Renaissance: Portraits and Checklists,* pp. 109-12. Fresno, Calif.: The Giligia Press, 1965.

Brief examination of McClure's literary traits followed by a personal account of the author.

Lauridsen, Inger Thorup, and Per Dalgard. "Interview with Michael McClure." In *The Beat Generation and the Russian New Wave,* pp. 115-22. Ann Arbor, Mich.: Ardis, 1990.

Interview examining McClure's relationship to the Beat movement and its Russian counterpart, the New Wave movement.

McAllister, Mick, and Michael McClure. "The Beat Journey: An Interview." In *Lighting the Corners: On Art, Nature, and the Visionary Essays and Interviews,* pp. 128-39. Albuquerque: University of New Mexico College of Arts and Sciences, 1993.

Interview between McClure and Mick McAllister considering the author's poetics and his works Fleas *and* Rare Angel.

Stephenson, Gregory. "From the Substrate: Notes on the Work of Michael McClure." In *The Daybreak Boys: Essays on the Literature of the Beat Generation,* pp. 105-30. Carbondale: Southern Illinois University Press, 1990.

Provides a comprehensive exploration of the direction McClure's poetry, prose, and plays take in his search for personal liberation and his creation of his "bio-alchemical" artistic vision, with careful consideration of several of the author's works.

Thurley, Geoffrey. "The Development of the New Language: Wieners, Jones, McClure, Whalen, Corso." In *The American Moment: American Poetry in the Mid-Century,* pp. 187-209. London: Edward Arnold, 1977.

Explores the work of McClure and others in the context of the New Language School.

OTHER SOURCES FROM GALE:

Additional coverage of McClure's life and career is contained in the following sources published by the Gale Group: *Contemporary American Dramatists; Contemporary Authors,* Vols. 21-24R; *Contemporary Authors New Revision Series,* Vols. 17, 46, 77; *Contemporary Dramatists,* Ed. 5; *Contemporary Literary Criticism,* Vols. 6, 10; *Contemporary Poets,* Ed. 7; *Dictionary of Literary Biography,* Vol. 16; *Literature Resource Center;* and *World Poets.*

KENNETH PATCHEN

(1911 - 1972)

American novelist, poet, and playwright.

An archetypal rebel poet, Patchen wrote angry, uncompromising, anti-war poetry, experimented with the form of the novel, attempted to merge poetry with graphics and jazz, and even disparaged the Beat movement, which sought to embrace him. As an elder statesman of the American avant-garde and author of a large body of work reaching back to the 1930s, Patchen was an inspiration and groundbreaker for numerous Beat poets emerging in the 1950s. In his most celebrated work, the anti-war novel (some call this work an "anti-novel") *The Journal of Albion Moonlight* (1941), he portrays the world as a hell, its inhabitants mad with heartless capitalism and the urge to kill. In this and many other works, Patchen used a free-form, stream-of-consciousness style that confounded attempts at classification and sharply divided critics of his works into two camps—admirers and detractors. Although his maverick work was championed by the Beat poets and their followers, Patchen adamantly denied any affiliation with the Beat and San Francisco poetry movements and condemned their fondness for drugs, loveless sex, and self-promotion.

BIOGRAPHICAL INFORMATION

Patchen was born in Niles, Ohio, on December 13, 1911, the third of five children of Wayne and Eva Patchen. His father was a steel mill worker, as were some of his relatives. Patchen began writing at age twelve, and wrote for the school newspaper at Warren G. Harding High School where he played football and ran track, graduating in 1928. After a summer working in a steel mill, he took part in Alexander Meikeljohn's Experimental College, followed by a semester at the Commonwealth College in Mena, Arkansas, in 1930. During the Great Depression Patchen could not afford to stay in school and took various jobs as a farm laborer, gardener, janitor, and factory worker. His professional debut as a writer occurred in 1932 in the *New York Times,* which published his sonnet "Permanence," written in 1929. In 1934 he married Miriam Oikemus, whom he met at a Christmas party the previous year. They moved to Greenwich Village in New York, where Patchen wrote book reviews for the *New Republic.* In 1936 his first collection of poetry was published, *Before the Brave,* and he was awarded a Guggenheim Fellowship. The couple moved to Phoenix, then to Santa Fe, New Mexico, and then to Los Angeles in 1937, where Patchen worked on film scripts. While in Los Angeles, Patchen injured his back while trying to separate two automobiles with locked bumpers—suffering the first of many injuries that would plague him for the rest of his life. In 1939 the Patchens returned to Connecticut and began working for the New Directions publishing house; Miriam served as an accountant and Patchen as a member of the shipping staff.

New Directions published his second volume of poetry, *First Will & Testament* (1939). In 1940 they moved back to Greenwich Village and became friends with Robert Duncan, Anäis Nin, and Henry Miller. Despite almost constant back pain, which had been misdiagnosed as arthritis, Patchen produced numerous works in the 1940s. In 1950, after the first of several spinal fusion operations, Patchen experienced some temporary relief from pain, and he and Miriam moved to San Francisco, where they thrived in its anarchist and libertarian environment. In 1954 Patchen became friends with Lawrence Ferlinghetti, who published Patchen's *Poems of Humor & Protest* in that year through his City Lights book store as part of its Pocket Poets series. In 1957 Patchen created a new genre, poetry-jazz, by reading his poems with the instrumental backing of jazz musicians. In the next few years he took his act to assorted universities, appeared on the radio, and made recordings of his poetry accompanied by jazz music. His success was abruptly halted in 1959 when, during the course of his third spinal-fusion surgery, he fell to the floor from the operating table and suffered severe spinal damage. For the majority of his remaining years he was in extreme pain and mostly bedridden. He died of a heart attack January 8, 1972.

MAJOR WORKS

Patchen published numerous volumes which combine poetry with illustration, possibly inspired by the books of William Blake, whom Patchen greatly admired. These poem-paintings demonstrate Patchen's dissatisfaction with the limitations of conventional forms, an aversion also made clear by his pioneering work in the poetry-jazz movement where he read poems in clubs, coffee houses, and made sound recordings to the accompaniment of musicians. *Before the Brave* consists of proletarian poems urging revolution. *First Will & Testament* also champions the proletariat, but is more encompassing in defining the image of the worker, far more diverse, and displays Patchen's mature style. *The Journal of Albion Moonlight* is generally considered his master work; although it was specifically written in reaction to World War II, it is equally applicable to other wars. The hero, Moonlight, suffers from insanity; and as his disease worsens, it is reflected in the writing itself which becomes more and more difficult to decipher. *The Dark Kingdom* (1942) defies categorization as a true novel—in it Patchen posits his own mystical world and rages against proponents of evil. *The Memoirs of a Shy Pornographer: An*

Amusement (1945), also loosely considered a novel, is a more optimistic work, and features a private detective as its hero. The book emphasizes the need to love and understand all things, and the importance of speaking the truth. *See You in the Morning* (1948) is Patchen's only standard novel and was admittedly written strictly for financial profit to help recoup large losses suffered after a previous effort. In spite of a limited reading audience causing Patchen to exist on the brink of poverty for most of his career, he maintained an impressive schedule of releasing volumes of poetry. *Hurrah for Anything: Poems and Drawings* (1957) focuses on chaos and death, albeit with frequent touches of humor, and also contains experimental poems meant to be recited with a jazz accompaniment and expressionistic illustrations. In *Poemscapes* (1958), Patchen continued to push the poetic form, writing prose poems each a page long. *Hallelujah Anyway* (1966) collects previously written and illustrated poem-paintings. A collection of his most well-regarded poetry was published in 1968 as *The Collected Poems of Kenneth Patchen*.

CRITICAL RECEPTION

Patchen never garnered an exceptionally wide reading audience, and it has been surmised that more people have read Henry Miller's profile, "Patchen: Man of Anger and Light," than have read Patchen's own works. Miller called Patchen a "fizzing human bomb ever threatening to explode in our midst," and lauded his prose, maintaining that "every page contains some new marvel." Miller used Patchen's writings, and their lack of critical attention, as an example of society's neglect of artists. Miller further asserted that Patchen's works "defy classification"—an assessment generally held by many reviewers. Commenting on Patchen's dislike of formal poetic style, James Dickey wrote: "To evoke the usual standards of formal art in Patchen's case is worse than meaningless. He cannot give anything through the traditional forms." Although Dickey called him "the best poet that American literary expressionism can show," he also characterized much of Patchen's work as tasteless and derided Patchen for treating language with "indifference and contempt." Reviewer Larry R. Smith characterized Patchen's work as "an ongoing search for an irrational path to meaning." Smith held that because Patchen's work is radically different from that of other writers, it "demands a radically new criticism." Smith additionally contended that it is necessary to understand Patchen's worldview before attempting to interpret the form and function of his work, which is ultimately aimed at "saving mankind from itself." In his review of *The Journal of Albion Moonlight*, William Carlos Williams noted weaknesses in the book and declared the novel's purpose as an endeavor to find a cure for man's madness. Carolyn See examined Patchen's controversial attempt to merge poetry and jazz; while she lauded his work, she expressed concern that some of the language is "purposely vague and nonliterate," creating a potential for a breakdown in communication with those outside the specialized world of jazz. Many critics have defined Patchen's work as exclusively mystical, but Raymond Nelson deems such a characterization as too narrow. While Nelson generally accepts the classification of mysticism, he offers alternatives for interpreting Patchen's works. Carroll F. Terrell traced the history of criticism concerning Patchen's work, noting the consistent division between supporters and detractors, and lamenting the fact that Patchen has not received more serious attention. Terrell offers explanations for the literary establishment's disregard of Patchen during and after the early years of his career, but has noted evidence that this general neglect may be ending.

PRINCIPAL WORKS

Before the Brave (poetry) 1936

First Will & Testament (poetry) 1939

The Journal of Albion Moonlight (novel) 1941

The Dark Kingdom (novel) 1942

Cloth of the Tempest (poetry and illustrations) 1943

The Memoirs of a Shy Pornographer: An Amusement (novel) 1945

Panels for the Walls of Heaven (poetry and drawings) 1946

Sleepers Awake (novel) 1946

They Keep Riding Down All the Time (prose) 1946

See You in the Morning (novel) 1948

Red Wine & Yellow Hair (poetry) 1949

Fables and Other Little Tales (poetry) 1953

Poems of Humor & Protest (poetry) 1954

Hurrah for Anything: Poems and Drawings (poetry and drawings) 1957

When We Were Here Together (poetry) 1957

Poemscapes (poetry) 1958

Hallelujah Anyway (poetry and drawings) 1966

The Collected Poems of Kenneth Patchen (poetry) 1968

Wonderings (poetry) 1971

Patchen's Lost Plays (plays) 1977

PRIMARY SOURCES

KENNETH PATCHEN (NOVEL DATE 1941)

SOURCE: Patchen, Kenneth. "The Artist's Duty." In *The Journal of Albion Moonlight*, pp. 253-56. New York: New Directions, 1961.

"The Artist's Duty" has been viewed as a precursor to the Buddhist-influenced work of the Beats, and Patchen's vision is widely considered to be succinctly stated in this excerpt from his novel, which was originally published in 1941.

Editor's Note: The format of the text below is a close approximation of the original four-column-wide layout, which could not be replicated exactly due to page design restrictions.

"The Artist's Duty"

So it is the duty of the artist to discourage all
    traces of shame
To extend all boundaries   *I hit*
To fog them in right over   *the undertaker*
    the plate
To kill only what is ridiculous   *in the eye*
To establish problems   *with a wet*
To ignore solutions   *snowball*
To listen to no one   *Ha. Ha. You*
To omit nothing   *are frightened*
To contradict everything   *and you no*
To generate the free brain   *longer want*
To bear no cross   *me to get*
To take part in no crucifixion   *into bed*
To tinkle a warning when man-   *with you.*
    kind strays
To explode upon all parties
To wound deeper than the soldier
To heal this poor obstinate monkey once and
    for all
To have kids with pretty angels
To display his dancing seed   *My soul*
To sail only in polar seas   *and I*
To laugh at every situation   *both*
To besiege all their cities   *wish*
To exhaust the primitive   *you*
To follow every false track   *a good mark*
To verify the irrational   *in God's*
To exaggerate all things   *little school.*
To inhabit everyone   *Our weeping*

To lubricate each proportion   *is for*
To experience only experience   *everybody*
To deviate at every point   *but*
SO   To offer no   *especially*
SMALL . . .   examples
SO   To dismiss all   *for you.*
WEAK . . .   support
THIS   To make one   *I feel*
BLOODY   monster at least
SWEAT OF   To go under-   *your hand*
   ground immediately
LOVING   To smell the   *on my arm. . .*
   shark's ass
To multiply all opinions
To work only in the distance
To extend all shapes
To acquire a sublime reputation
To consort forever with the runaway
To sport the glacial eye   *I am the love.*
To direct all smouldering   *I am the hate.*
   ambitions
To frequent only the   *I am the pain.*
   exterminating planets
To kidnap the phantom's   *I am the tears.*
   first-born
To forego no succulent filth
To masquerade as the author of every platitude
To overwhelm the mariner   *I . . .*
   with improper charts
To expose himself to   *I . . .*
   every ridicule
To ambush their blownose   *I . . . help me!*
   Providence
To set a flame in the   *I am*
   high air
To exclaim at the   *afraid . . .*
   commonplace alone
To cause the unseen eyes   *Please! !*
   to open
To advance with the majesty of the praying
   serpent
I MUST   To contrive always to be
   caught with his pants down
CONFESS   To sprinkle mule-milk on
I AM   the lifted brows of virgins
A CANNIBAL   To attach no importance
   whatever to his activity
To admire only the absurd
To be concerned with every profession save his
   own
To raise a fortuitous stink on the boulevards of
   truth and beauty
To desire an electrifiable intercourse with a
   female alligator
To lift the flesh above the suffering
To forgive the beautiful its disconsolate deceit
To send the world away to crawl under his
   discarded pedestals
To have the cunning of the imperilled wave
To hide his lamentations in the shredded lungs
   of the tempest
To recommend stone eyelashes for all candid
   lookers
To attribute every magnificence to himself
To maintain that the earth is neither round nor
   flat but a scomaphoid
To flash his vengeful badge at every abyss

To be revolted by only the sacred cow which
   piddles at the toes of the swamp
To kneel with the blind and the drunk brigands
   and learn their songs
To *happen*
To embrace the intemperate hermaphrodite of
   memory
It is the artist's duty to be alive
To drag people into glittering occupations
To return always to the renewing stranger
To observe only the funereal spectator
To assume the ecstasy in all conceivable attitudes
To follow the plundering whirlpool to its source
To cry out nervously with every knock
To stock his shelves with plaintive confessions
   and pernicious desires
To outflow the volcano   **GREEN GLINT**
   in semen and phlegm
To be treacherous when   **OF**
nothing is to be gained
To enrich   *I have no*   **CHILDREN'S**
himself at   *desire*
the expense
of everyone
To reel in   *to be*   **VOICES AS**
an exquisite   *intelligent*
sobriety
To blush perpetually   **THEY PICK**
   in gaping innocence
To drift happily through   **FLOWERS**
   the ruined race-intelligence
To burrow beneath the subconscious
To defend the unreal at the cost of   *I have*
   his reason
To obey each outrageous impulse   *no money*
To commit his company to all   *whatever.*
   enchantments
To rage against the sacrificing   *I can't*
   shepherds
To return to a place remote from   *make a*
   his native land
To pursue the languid executioner   *living*
   to his hall bedroom
To torment the spirit-lice   *at all*
To cover the mud with distinguished
   vegetation
To regain the emporer's chair   *I am*
To pass from one world to   *hungry*
   another in carefree devotion
To withdraw only when all   *and cold*
   have been profaned
To contract every battering   *. . . tired.*
   disease
To peel off all substances from the face of
   horror
AND SO I WOO   To glue himself to every
   lascivious breast
THE WANTON   To hurl his vigorous cone
   into every trough
WOLF WHICH   To unroll the hide from that
   repugnant rhinoceros Time
HOWLS AT   To refrain from no ownership
THE DEATH   To crowd the squat-rumped
   centuries into his own
   special residence
OF MY WORLD   To plunge beyond their
   smoking armpits

GENERAL COMMENTARY

HENRY MILLER (ESSAY DATE 1946)

SOURCE: Miller, Henry. "Patchen: Man of Anger and Light." In *Kenneth Patchen: A Collection of Essays*, edited by Richard G. Morgan, pp. 33-42. New York: AMS Press Inc., 1977.

In the following essay, originally published in 1946, Miller offers a character sketch of Patchen, describing the poet variously as "monstrous," "gentle," "merciless," and "sensitive," and discusses the status of the starving artist in society.

The first thing one would remark on meeting Kenneth Patchen is that he is the living symbol of protest. I remember distinctly my first impression of him when we met in New York: it was that of a powerful, sensitive being who moved on velvet pads. A sort of sincere assassin, I thought to myself, as we shook hands. This impression has never left me. True or not, I feel that it would give him supreme joy to destroy with his own hands all the tyrants and sadists of this earth together with the art, the institutions and all the machinery of everyday life which sustain and glorify them. He is a fizzing human bomb ever threatening to explode in our midst. Tender and ruthless at the same time, he has the faculty of estranging the very ones who wish to help him. He is inexorable: he has no manners, no tact, no grace. He gives no quarter. Like the gangster, he follows a code of his own. He gives you the chance to put up your hands before shooting you down. Most people however, are too terrified to throw up their hands. They get mowed down.

This is the monstrous side of him, which makes him appear ruthless and rapacious. Within the snorting dragon, however, there is a gentle prince who suffers at the mention of the slightest cruelty or injustice. A tender soul, who soon learned to envelope himself in a mantle of fire in order to protect his sensitive skin. No American poet is as merciless in his invective as Patchen. There is almost an insanity to his fury and rebellion.

Like Gorky, Patchen began his career in the university of life early. The hours he sacrificed in the steel mills of Ohio, where he was born, served to fan his hatred for a society in which inequality, injustice and intolerance form the foundation of life. His years as a wanderer, during which he scattered his manuscripts like seed, corroborated the impressions gained at home, school and mill. Today he is practically an invalid, thanks to the system which puts the life of a machine above that of a human being. Suffering from arthritis of the spine, he is confined to bed most of the time. He lies on a huge bed in a doll's house near the river named after Henry Hudson, a sick giant consumed by the poisonous indifference of a world which has more use for mousetraps than for poets. He writes book after book, prose as well as poetry, never certain when "they" will come and dump him (with the bed) into the street. This has been going on now for over seven years, if I am not mistaken. If Patchen were to become well, able to use his hands and feet freely, it is just possible that he would celebrate the occasion by pulling the house down about the ears of some unsuspecting victim of his scorn and contempt. He would do it slowly, deliberately, thoroughly. And in utter silence.

That is another quality of Patchen's which inspires dread on first meeting—his awesome silence. It seems to spring from his flesh, as though he had silenced the flesh. It is uncanny. Here is a man with the gift of tongues and he speaks not. Here is a man who drips words but he refuses to open his mouth. Here is a man dying to communicate, but instead of conversing with you he hands you a book or a manuscript to read. The silence which emanates from him is black. He puts one on tenterhooks. It breeds hysteria. Of course he is shy. And no matter how long he lives he will never become urbane. He is American through and through, and Americans, despite their talkiness, are fundamentally silent creatures. They talk in order to conceal their innate reticence. It is only in moments of deep intimacy that they break loose. Patchen is typical. When finally he does open his mouth it is to release a hot flood of words. His emotion tears loose in clots.

A voracious reader, he exposes himself to every influence, even the worst. Like Picasso, he makes use of everything. The innovator and initiator are strong in him. Rather than accept the collaboration of a second-rate artist, he will do the covers for a book himself, a different one for each copy. And how beautiful and original are these individual cover designs[1] from the hand of a writer who makes no pretense of being a painter or illustrator! How interesting, too, are the typographical arrangements which he dictates for his books! How competent he can be when he has to be his own publisher! (See *The Journal of Albion Moonlight*.) From a sickbed the poet defies and surmounts all obstacles. He has only to pick up the telephone to throw an editorial staff into a panic. He has the will of a tyrant, the persistence of a bull. "This is the way I want it done!" he bellows. And by God it gets done that way.

Let me quote a few passages from his answers to certain questions of mine:

> The pain is almost a natural part of me now—only the fits of depression, common to this disease, really sap my energies and distort my native spirit. I could speak quite morbidly in this last connection. The sickness of the world probably didn't cause mine, but it certainly conditions my handling of it. Actually, the worst part is that I feel that I would be something else if I weren't rigid inside with the constant pressure of illness; I would be purer, less inclined to write, say, for the sake of being able to show my sick part that it can never become all powerful; I could experience more in other artists if I didn't have to be concerned so closely with happenings inside myself; I would have less need to be pure in the presence of the things I love, and therefore, probably, would have a more personal view of myself. . . . I think the more articulate an artist becomes the less he will know about himself to say, for usually one's greatest sense of love is inseparable from a sense of creature foreboding . . . it is hard to imagine why God should "think," yet this "thinking" is the material of the greatest art . . . we don't wish to know ourselves, we wish to be lost in knowing, as a seed in a gust of wind.

> I think that if I ever got near an assured income I'd write books along the order of great canvases, including everything in them—huge symphonies that would handle poetry and prose as they present themselves from day to day and from one aspect of my life and interests to another. But that's all over, I think. They're going to blow everything up next time—and I don't believe we have long. Always men have talked about THE END OF THE WORLD—it's nearly here. A few more straws in the wall . . . a loose brick or two replaced . . . then no stone left standing on another—and the long silence; really forever. What is there to struggle against? Nobody can put the stars back together again. There isn't much time at all. I can't say it doesn't matter; it matters more than anything—but we are helpless to stop it now.

> It's very hard for me to answer your questions. Some were Rebels out of choice; I had none—I wish they'd give me just one speck of proof that this "world of theirs" couldn't have been set up and handled better by a half-dozen drugged idiots bound hand and foot at the bottom of a ten-mile well. It's always because we love that we are rebellious; it takes a great deal of love to give a damn one way or another what happens from now on: I still do. The situation for human beings is hopeless. For the while that's left, though, we can remember the Great and the gods.

The mixture of hope and despair, of love and resignation, of courage and the sense of futility, which emanates from these excerpts is revelatory. Setting himself apart from the world, as poet, as man of vision, Patchen nevertheless identifies himself with the world in the malady which has become universal. He has the humility to acknowledge that his genius, that all genius, springs from the divine source. He is also innocent enough to think that the creature world should recognize God's voice and give it its due. He has the clarity to realize that his suffering is not important, that it distorts his native spirit, as he puts it, but does he admit to himself, can he admit to himself, that the suffering of the world also distorts the world's true spirit? If he could believe in his own cure might he not believe in a universal cure? "The situation for human beings is hopeless," he says. But he is a human being himself, and he is not at all convinced that his case is hopeless. With a bit of security he imagines that he will be able to give profounder expression to his powers. The whole world now cries for security. It cries for peace, too, but makes no real effort to stop the forces which are working for war. In his agony each sincere soul doubtless refers to the world as "their world." No one in his senses wishes to admit being a voluntary part of this world, so thoroughly inhuman, so intolerable has it become. We are all, whether we admit it or not, waiting for the end of the world, as though it were not a world of our own making but a hell into which we had been thrust by a malevolent fate.

Patchen uses the language of revolt. There is no other language left to use. There is no time, when you are holding up a bank, to explain to the directors the sinister injustice of the present economic system. Explanations have been given time and again; warnings have been posted everywhere. They have gone unheeded. Time to act. "Stick up your hands! Deliver the goods!"

It is in his prose works that Patchen uses this language most effectively. With **The Journal of Albion Moonlight**, Patchen opened up a vein unique in English literature. These prose works, of which the latest to appear is **Sleepers Awake**, defy classification. Like the Wonder Books of old, every page contains some new marvel. Behind the surface chaos and madness one quickly detects the logic and the will of a daring creator. One thinks of Blake, of Lautréamont, of Picasso—and of Jakob Boehme. Strange predecessors! But one thinks also of Savonarola, of Grünewald, of John of Patmos, of Hieronymous Bosch—and of times, events and scenes recognizable only in the waiting room of sleep. Each new volume is an increasingly astonishing feat of legerdemain, not only in the protean variety of the text but in design, composition and format. One is no longer looking at a dead, printed book but at something alive and breathing, something which looks back at you with equal astonishment. Novelty is employed not as seduction but like the stern fist of the Zen master—to awaken and arouse the consciousness of the reader. THE WAY MEN LIVE IS A LIE!—that is the reality which screams from the pages of these books. Once again we have the revolt of the angels.

This is not the place to discuss the merits or defects of the author's work. What concerns me at the moment is the fact that, despite everything, he is a poet. I am vitally interested in the man who today has the misfortune of being an artist and a human being. By the same token I am as much interested in the maneuvers of the gangster as I am in those of the financier or the military man. They are all part and parcel of society; some are lauded for their efforts, some reviled, some persecuted and hunted like beasts. In our society the artist is not encouraged, not lauded, not rewarded, unless he makes use of a weapon more powerful than those employed by his adversaries. Such a weapon is not to be found in shops or arsenals: it has to be forged by the artist himself out of his own tissue. When he releases it he also destroys himself. It is the only method he has found to preserve his own kind. From the outset his life is mortgaged. He is a martyr whether he chooses to be or not. He no longer seeks to generate warmth, he seeks for a virus with which society must allow itself to be injected or perish. It does not matter whether he preaches love or hate, freedom or slavery; he must create room to be heard, ears that will hear. He must create, by the sacrifice of his own being, the awareness of a value and a dignity which the word *human* once connoted. This is not the time to analyze and criticize works of art. This is not the time to select the flowers of genius, differentiate between them, label and categorize. This is the time to accept what is offered and be thankful that something other than mass intolerance, mass suicide, can preoccupy the human intellect.

If through indifference and inertia we can create human as well as atomic bombs, then it seems to me that the poet has the right to explode in his own fashion at his own appointed time. If all is hopelessly given over to destruction, why should the poet not lead the way? Why should he remain amid the ruins like a crazed beast? If we deny our Maker, why should we preserve the maker of words and images? Are the forms and symbols he spins to be put above Creation itself?

When men deliberately create instruments of destruction to be used against the innocent as well as the guilty, against babes in arms as well as against the aged, the sick, the halt, the maimed, the blind, the insane, when their targets embrace whole populations, when they are immune to every appeal, then we know that the heart and the imagination of man are no longer capable of being stirred. If the powerful ones of this earth are in the grip of fear and trembling, what hope is there for the weaker ones? What does it matter to those monsters now in control what becomes of the poet, the sculptor, the musician?

In the richest and the most powerful country in the world there is no means of insuring an invalid poet such as Kenneth Patchen against starvation or eviction. Neither is there a band of loyal fellow artists who will unite to defend him against the unnecessary attacks of shallow, spiteful critics. Every day ushers in some fresh blow, some fresh insults, some fresh punishment. In spite of it all he continues to create. He works on two or three books at once. He labors in a state of almost unremitting pain. He lives in a room just about big enough to hold his carcass, a rented coffin you might call it, and a most insecure one at that. Would he not be better off dead? What is there for him to look forward to—as a man, as an artist, as a member of society?

I am writing these lines for an English and a French edition of his work. It is hardly the orthodox preface to a man's work. But my hope is that in these distant countries Patchen (and other now unknown American writers) will find friends, find support and encouragement to go on living and working. America is immune to all appeals. Her people do not understand the language of the poet. They do not wish to recognize suffering—it is too embarrassing. They do not greet Beauty with open arms—her presence is disturbing to heartless automatons. Their fear of violence drives them to commit insane cruelties. They have no reverence for form or image: they are bent on destroying whatever does not conform to their pattern, which is chaos. They are not even concerned with their own disintegration, because they are already putrescent. A vast congeries of rotting sepulchres, America holds for yet a little while, awaiting the opportune moment to blow itself to smithereens.

The one thing which Patchen cannot understand, will not tolerate, indeed, is the refusal to act. In this he is adamant. Confronted with excuses and explanations, he becomes a raging lion.

It is the well-off who especially draw his ire. Now and then he is thrown a bone. Instead of quieting him, he growls more ferociously. We know, of course, what patronage means. Usually it is hush money. "What is one to do with a man like that?" exclaim the poor rich. Yes, a man like Patchen puts them in a dilemma. Either he increases his demands or he uses what is given to voice his scorn and contempt. He needs money for food and rent, money for the doctor, money for operations, money for medicines—yet he goes on turning out beautiful books. Books of violence clothed in outward elegance. The man has uncommon taste, no gainsaying it. But what right has he to a cultivated appetite? Tomorrow he will be asking for a seaside cottage perhaps, or for a Rouault, whose work he reveres. Perhaps for a Capehart, since he loves music. How can one satisfy a monster such as that?

That is the way rich people think about the starving artist. Poor people too, sometimes. Why doesn't he get himself a job? Why doesn't he make his wife support him? Does he have to live in a house with two rooms? Must he have all those books and records? When the man happens also to be an invalid, they become even more resentful, more malicious. They will accuse him of permitting his illness to distort his vision. "The work of a sick man," they say, shrugging their shoulders. If he bellows, then it is "the work of an impotent man." If he begs and entreats, then "he has lost all sense of dignity." But if he roars? Then he is hopelessly insane. No matter what attitude he adopts he is condemned beforehand. When he is buried they praise him as another "*poète maudit.*" What beautiful crocodile tears are shed over our dead and accursed poets! What a galaxy of them we have already in the short span of our history!

In 1909 Charles Péguy penned a *morceau* for his *Cahiers de la Quinzaine* which described the then imminent debacle of the modern world. "We are defeated," it begins. "We are defeated to such an extent, so completely, that I doubt whether history will ever have to record an instance of defeat such as the one we furnish. . . . To be defeated, that is nothing. It would be nothing. On the contrary, it can be a great thing. It can be all: the final consummation. To be defeated is nothing: [but] we have been beaten. We have even been given a good drubbing. In a few years society, this modern society, before we have even had the time to sketch the critique of it, has fallen into a state of decomposition, into a dissolution, such, that I believe, that I am assured history had never seen anything comparable. . . . That great historical decomposition, that great dissolution, that great precedent which in a literary manner we call

the decay of the Roman decadence, the dissolution of the Roman Empire, and which it suffices to call, with Sorel, the ruin of the ancient world, was nothing by comparison with the dissolution of present society, by comparison with the dissolution and degradation of this society, of the present modern society. Doubtless, at that time there were far more crimes and still more vice[s]. But there were also infinitely more resources. This putrefaction was full of seeds. People at that time did not have this sort of promise of sterility which we have today, if one may say so, if these two words can be used together."[2]

After two annihilating wars, in one of which Péguy gave his life, this "promise of sterility" appears anything but empty. The condition of society which was then manifest to the poet and thinker, and of course more so today (even the man in the street is aware of it), Péguy described as "a real disorder of impotence and sterility." It is well to remember these words when the hired critics of the press (both of the right and the left) direct their fulminations against the poets of the day. It is precisely the artists with the vital spark whom they set out to attack most viciously. It is the creative individual (*sic*) whom they accuse of undermining the social structure. A persecutory mania manifests itself the moment an honest word is spoken. The atmosphere of the whole modern world, from Communist Russia to capitalist America, is heavy with guilt. We are in the Time of the Assassins. The order of the day is: liquidate! The enemy, the archenemy, is the man who speaks the truth. Every realm of society is permeated with falsity and falsification. What survives, what is upheld, what is defended to the last ditch, is the lie.

"It is perhaps this condition of confusion and distress," wrote Péguy, "which, more imperiously than ever, makes it our duty not to surrender. One must never surrender. All the less since the position is so important and so isolated and so menaced, and that precisely the country is in the hands of the enemy."

Those who know Kenneth Patchen will realize that I am identifying his stand with Péguy's. Perhaps there could not be two individuals more different one from another. Perhaps there is nothing at all in common between them except this refusal to swallow the lie, this refusal to surrender even in the blackest hour. I know of no American who has as vigorously insisted that the enemy is within. If he refuses to play the game it is not because he has been defeated; it is because he has never recognized those phantoms created out of fear and confusion which men call "the enemy." He knows that the enemy of man is man. He rebels out of love, not out of hate. Given his temperament, his love of honesty, his adherence to truth, is he not justified in saying that "he had no choice" but to rebel? Do we find him aligned with those rebels who wish merely to depose those on top, in order that they may hold the whip hand? No, we find him alone, in a tiny garret, riveted to a sickbed, turning frantically from side to side as if imprisoned in an iron cage. And it is a very real cage indeed. He has only to open his eyes each day to be aware of his helplessness. He could not surrender even if he wished to: there is no one to surrender to except death. He lies on the edge of the precipice with eyes wide open. The world which condemns him to imprisonment is fast asleep. He is furiously aware that his release does not depend on acceptance by the multitude but on the dissolution of the world which is strangling him.

"The situation for human beings is hopeless," did he say? In **Albion Moonlight** this desperation is expressed artistically: "I want to be a carpet in a cat-house." Thus, to use the title from one of his own poems, **"The Furious Crown Conceals Its Throne."** Thus, to paraphrase Miró, persons magnetized by the stars may walk in comfort on the music of a furrowed landscape. Thus we take leave of our atavistic friend, the poet, doomed to inhabit a world that never was, never will be, the world of "flowers born in shining wombs." For flowers will always be born and wombs will always be radiant, particularly when the poet is accursed. For him the beast is always number, the landscape stars, the time and the place of creation now and here. He moves in a "circle of apparent fates," ruler of the dark kingdom, maligned, persecuted and forsaken in the light of the day.

Once again the night approaches. And once again "the dark kingdom" will reveal to us its splendors. In the middle of this twentieth century we have all of us, none excepted, crossed a river made of human tears. We have no fathers, no mothers, no brothers, no sisters. We are returned to the creature state.

"I have put language to sleep," said Joyce. Aye, and now conscience too is being put to sleep.

Notes

1. So far Patchen has done paintings for limited editions of *The Dark Kingdom* and *Sleepers Awake,* one hundred and fifty covers in all. To date he has turned a deaf ear to suggestions that these remarkable productions be exhibited—I, for one, hope he changes his mind. It would be a feather in the hat of any gallery to show these wonderful paintings!

2. See *Men and Saints,* Charles Péguy, Pantheon Books, New York.

JAMES DICKEY (ESSAY DATE 1958)

SOURCE: Dickey, James. "Kenneth Patchen." In *Babel to Byzantium: Poets and Poetry Now,* pp. 71-2. New York: Farrar, Straus and Giroux, 1968.

In the following essay, originally published in 1958, Dickey offers an analysis of Patchen's poetry, contending that conventional standards of art are not applicable to Patchen's work.

Often at night, when I see that, indeed, the sky is a "deep throw of stars," I think of a poet named Kenneth Patchen, who once told me that it is. Because of this and a few other passages I remember years after first reading them, I have tried to keep track of Patchen, and have gone through most of his books (all, in fact, except *Sleepers Awake,* which I abandoned in despair). I have heard recently that he has joined the "San Francisco School," but in reality he was its only permanent member twenty years before the group was ever conceived in the impatient mind of Kenneth Rexroth, and is still, despite having produced a genuinely impassable mountain of tiresome, obvious, self-important, sprawling, sentimental, witless, preachy, tasteless, useless poems and books, the best poet that American literary expressionism can show. Occasionally, in fragments and odds and ends nobody wants to seek out any more, he is a writer of superb daring and invention, the author of a few passages which are, so far as I can tell, comparable to the most intuitively beautiful writing ever done. He is a poet not so much in form as in essence, a condition of which we should all be envious, and with which we should never be satisfied. To evoke the usual standards of formal art in Patchen's case is worse than meaningless. He cannot give anything through the traditional forms (those who suggest that he ought at least to try should take a look at some of the rhymed poems in *Before the Brave*). I do not like to read most of Patchen's work, for it seems to me a cruel waste, but he somehow manages to make continuing claims on my attention that other more consistent poets do not. If there is such a thing as pure or crude imagination, Patchen has it, or has had it. With it he has made twenty-five years of Notes, in the form of scrappy, unsatisfactory, fragmentarily brilliant poems, for a single, unwritten cosmic Work, which bears, at

ABOUT THE AUTHOR

REXROTH ON PATCHEN

Patchen is the only widely published poet of my generation in the United States who has not abandoned the international idiom of twentieth-century verse. He is the only one we have . . . to compare with Henri Michaux or Paul Éluard. Twenty-five ago no one would have prophesied such a comeuppance for what we then thought, and I still think, was the only significant tendency in American literature. What happened to the Revolution of the Word? Why is Patchen still there? Why did everybody else "sell out" or sink, like Louis Zukofsky, Parker Tyler, Walter Lowenfels, into undeserved obscurity? Why did American poetry, a part of world literature in 1920, become a pale, provincial imitation of British verse in 1957? We are back, two generations behind Australia.

Rexroth, Kenneth. An excerpt from "Kenneth Patchen, Naturalist of the Public Nightmare." In his *Bird in the Bush: Obvious Essays.* New York: New Directions, 1959.

least in some of its parts, analogies to the prophetic books of Blake. Yet the words, the phrases, and the lines that are supposed to make up the individual pieces almost never coalesce, themselves, into wholes, because Patchen looks upon language as patently unworthy of the Vision, and treats it with corresponding indifference and contempt. This is the reason he is not a good writer, or a good prophet, either: this, and the fact that his alternately raging and super-sentimental view of things is too violent, centerless, convulsive, and one-dimensional to be entirely convincing. But he has made and peopled a place that would never have had existence without him: the realm of the "Dark Kingdom," where "all who have opposed in secret, are . . . provided with green crowns," and where the vague, powerful figures of fantasmagoric limbo, the dream people, and, above all, the mythic animals that only he sees, are sometimes as inconsolably troubling as the hallucinations of the madman or the alcoholic, and are occasionally, as if by accident,

rendered in language that accords them the only kind of value possible to this kind of writing: makes them obsessive, unpardonable, and magnificent. It is wrong of us to wish that Patchen would "pull himself together." He has never been together. He cannot write poems, as the present book [**When We Were Here Together**] heartlessly demonstrates. But his authentic and terrible hallucinations infrequently come to great good among the words which they must use. We should leave it at that, and take what we can from him.

LARRY R. SMITH (ESSAY DATE 1978)

SOURCE: Smith, Larry R. "A Vision of Life and Art." In *Kenneth Patchen*, pp. 33-48. Boston: Twayne Publishers, 1978.

In the following essay, Smith describes Patchen's artistic vision, contends that he uses art pragmatically in a fight against the base and absurd elements of society, and discusses assorted approaches critics have taken in reviewing his works.

Characterized by its abundance, its social relevance, its extreme individuality, and its formal innovations, Kenneth Patchen's art demands a radically new criticism. While academic critics have contented themselves with either avoiding Patchen's work or forcing it into distorting categorical classification, this study is based on the premise that Patchen's radical independence as an artist requires an individual approach. An understanding of the form and function of Patchen's work can only be gained through a recognition of his personal vision of life and art.

Though Patchen is a visionary and not a philosopher, three pervading and felt principles underlying his world view and controlling his art can be identified: 1) "man's madness"—the estrangement of man from his true life through the corruptions of violence, state, and materialistic controls, the inhumanity of man, and an insane conditioning by society; 2) "engagement"—commitment to life through love, brotherhood, and a belief in the unity of life; 3) "wonder"—an innocent, free, and imaginative response to the world's beauty as the ideal approach to life. Within this desperate yet vital view of life, Patchen's theory of art is "functional." His art is designed to both reform and form man by forcing a recognition and consequent rejection of "man's madness" and by demanding an "engagement" in the true life of "wonder." Following William Blake's vision of the poet as prophet and priest, Patchen creates an art whose chief function is the saving of mankind from itself. Combining a realistic appraisal of existence with Romantic ideals of life, he ideally becomes the prophet and forgotten conscience of mankind and a creator, through his art, of a radically new human consciousness. A description of Patchen's vision as a critical launching place is thus imperative for an understanding of his art.

Following related ideals of the master creator "total artist" whose life and art are one, and the independently controlled and created "total book," Patchen incorporates a mixture of media within his art, seeks to perform his art upon his audience, and works for an expanded and rejuvenated view of art based on its affective results. As a poet of the will, he is a model of the contemporary engaged artist. His pragmatic aesthetics, based as they are upon the affective results generated within the audience, thus lead to the creation of his protean experimental forms.

In defining an artist's vision, one risks distortion if he denies it development. Patchen's own vital concern for growth is reflected in his world vision, which develops according to a pattern of shifted emphasis within his tripartite and consistent view of madness, engagement, and wonder. Raymond J. Nelson's study of "American Mysticism: The Example of Kenneth Patchen" parallels Patchen's development with the mystical path, progressing from the Illumination to the Purgation to the Union.[1] In reality, the developmental pattern in Patchen's world view is not this linear and clearcut, but is a series of shifting interrelationships. These relationships broaden in meaning and shift in importance: first, "man's madness" immediately broadens in meaning from the controlling insanity of institutions and power to the irrationality underlying all of man's societal behavior; second, "engagement" shifts in emphasis from an involvement in social reform (viewed now as futile) to a commitment to personal reform and salvation; third, the concept of "wonder" remains consistent in meaning but receives primary emphasis in later works, emerging as Patchen's central theme. Recognizing that any assessment of a philosophical development oversimplifies, it is provident to acknowledge here the complex pattern of interrelatedness that does appear. Patchen's overall image of the world, however, remains clear; it is man's pathway within that world that changes. Believing that man's madness is all too apparent and that engagement in mass social reform leads to corruption and ultimate futility, Patchen turns in his late writings to man's potential for wonder as his best and only alternative.

Playfully employing the titles of poems, often satirically, obliquely, or even with disdain for audience comprehension, Patchen's use of titles for his books is another case entirely. These are given the significance of overall statements of the book's message, and thus they can immediately suggest Patchen's shifting world vision. His initial work, *Before the Brave* (1936), sounded a proletarian challenge to the workers against those in power, but it is followed by the broader and more human issues of *First Will and Testament* (1939). The chronicle of man's destruction is recorded in *The Journal of Albion Moonlight* (1941). By 1946 his concern had become that of a desperate forewarning to all of mankind, viewed now as *Sleepers Awake on the Precipice* and lamented as *They Keep Riding Down All the Time*. By the 1950's he had shifted completely from organized social reform to a realization of personal imaginative wonder, which he celebrates in titles *Hurrah for Anything* (1957), *Because It Is* (1961), *Hallelujah Anyway* (1966), *But Even So* (1968), and ultimately a book of *Wonderings* (1971). These titles, indicative of free celebration, also acknowledge the world's chaos and the necessity of turning from it. They are celebrations of life despite the gaping abyss man has dug for himself. Such an overview of Patchen's art must be completed with a close analysis of his vision and the experimental art created to fulfill it.

I An Individual Art

Whether it was by virtue of his proletarian roots, his underground artistic associations, or his unceasing and uncompromising quest for radically new forms, Patchen's art received relatively little critical attention. Another contributing factor was the literary scholar's reluctance earlier in the century to deal seriously with defiant and radical experimentalists. This position of the avant-garde artist against the academic world and thus against critical scholarship is something Patchen himself encouraged. Literary critics and liberal intellectuals often appear in his works as villainous do nothings, as people apart from the concerns of real life. His parody of the educated critic, Mr. Brill, in *Memoirs of a Shy Pornographer*, reveals his own estimation of his relationship with critics. The scene is a cocktail party, and Patchen discloses his tone by entitling this chapter, "The Last Party I Ever Went To":

"And Patchen?" she asked, pencil poised.

"Oh, Patchen—nobody takes him seriously," one of them said. "He's just a rough-neck who never grew up."

"He's just a boring child—a lot of noise about nothing," another said.

"Patchen missed the boat," Mr. Brill said.[2]

His attacks could, of course, be more direct, and under his fiery cursing also came the aloof critic, the poet who listened to critics, the money oriented publishers, and a simple minded and obedient public. In **Sleepers Awake** he protests:

> I think the moaning outsounds the tinkle
> of fat sticky little bards
> who twang their navels in the orderly and
> empty drawingrooms of "Our Literature"—
>   I am so full of rage!
>   I am so full of contempt for these smug lice!
>   I tell them to stay away from my books!
>   I want to stand outside their blood-
> drenched "culture"![3]

Patchen's defiance of critical aloofness was encouraged by the reviews of fellow poet experimentalists and friends. Rexroth has protested the treatment of Patchen's work as "A conspiracy of silence of the whole of literary America."[4] Jonathan Williams terms it "A collective turning of the backs and shifting of the asses. Nothing very organized, simply the unionized apathy, jealous disinterest, and niggardly behavior of literary drones."[5] Though the existing lack of critical response to Patchen's work does lend some credence to these accusations, it is well to remember that the radical nature of his theme and form impeded scholarly treatment of his work. He certainly runs antithetic to the New Critics of that time. The point, however, to be recognized is that Patchen has suffered from this long critical rivalry. Willing to be a martyr for any cause he believed in, he may have martyred his art to years of undeserved obscurity.

A second problem in approaching Patchen's works is the distorting oversimplification fostered by criticism bent on "placing" him in a literary movement. Labels such as proletarian, surrealist, beat, and mystic belie his true range and motive.

As early as 1940, when American criticism was awakening to the curious phenomenon of the proletarian writer, Patchen was hailed by Amos N. Wilder as "the American proletarian poet."[6] Comparing him with Muriel Rukeyser, Charles I. Glicksberg labeled him "a fullfledged proletarian poet for whom revolt is a spiritual necessity."[7] Though proletarian themes run strongest in Patchen's early books, even there they are only one element of his art, as an examination of the richly complex **First Will and Testament** readily reveals. Henry Miller's 1946 study, *Patchen: Man of*

Anger and Light, though heavily laced with biographical impressionism, added a recognition of the dualistic character of Patchen's art, seeing him as capable of great tenderness as well as blistering social protest.[8]

By the 1950's the surrealistic aspects of Patchen's works were so prominent that Glicksberg reappraised him as a surrealist, or, more accurately, as a failed surrealist. This 1952 summary of his work forced Patchen into the surrealist mold and then found his writing "Surrealism run amok."[9] Though Glicksberg is a revealing critic, he distorts one aspect of Patchen's writing for a general characteristic. Similar dadaist comparisons are best seen as just that—analogous descriptions.

Perhaps the most detrimental label placed upon Patchen has been that of "Beat." Linked by geography, associations, and influence with the San Francisco Renaissance of the late fifties and sixties, Patchen, like Lawrence Ferlinghetti and Gary Snyder, had to spend much time and temper disclaiming the Beat label. In the early misunderstanding of the Beat movement, anthologizers tended to stereotype anyone who read poetry to jazz as Beat. Although Patchen partially sympathized with the Beat poets' rejection of academia and of a materialistic and violent society, he opposed "hipster" nihilism, and naturally resented the restriction of his twenty years of writing to an inappropriate label. His antagonism grew until he struck out at the hypocrisy in the movement, calling them "A Freakshow worth every Madison Ave. penny of the three-dollar-bill admission."[10]

Most recently, Raymond J. Nelson has attempted to follow a Whitmanesque strain in Patchen's work.[11] His study places Patchen at the heart of an American mysticism movement, but here too the categorical labeling of "mystic" mars the insights of this scholarly treatment.

Certainly, revealing insights have been made into Patchen's methods, among them Frederick Eckman's assessment of the essential Blaken character of Patchen's vision and William Carlos Williams's startling analysis of **The Journal of Albion Moonlight**.[12] It was Kenneth Rexroth, however, who directed new attention to other aspects of Patchen's writing: his love poetry, his anti-war writing, his drawings and poems, and his fables.[13] Aligning Patchen's art with international counterparts in Paul Eluard, Henri Michaux, and Wyndham Lewis, Rexroth offered valuable insights into the anti-literature methods, particularly the methods of madness which Patchen used functionally as a curative mirror of social insanity. However, the criticism stands generally as slanted, scattered, and sparse.

To a unique degree, Patchen, as man and artist, provides the truest source to his art. His conjoined view of life and art reveals the form and function of his works. Harvey Breit's early analysis of "Kenneth Patchen and the Critical Blind Alley" first recognized the inescapable sense of Patchen's personal and individual manness that so controls his art: "Kenneth Patchen's poetry is a last testing of the critic's seriousness. In Patchen the poem's tension is not in the quantities and measurements where the critic is safest, but in what is human: in hate and love, in what men remember and in what men dream, in what they must get. . . . The critic is pretty much by himself, thrust out into an intensified and heightened, but very real, world. He must say something—as a critic and, more, as a responsible man."[14] The critic is forced to abandon literary clichés and go to the heart of the work—Patchen's bold and vital view of life and art.

William Carlos Williams explains the source and authority by which Patchen creates: "There is no authority evidenced in this but the man himself. If there are others like him, if we are not all somewhat as he is, provided he write truthfully and out of a gifted mind, he has a right to speak and needs no other authority."[15] Not literary polish, but the capturing of personal and universal truth is the authority for Patchen's art. James Dickey cautions us on this requisite expanded view for Patchen: "He is a poet not so much in form as in essence, a condition of which we should all be envious, and with which we should never be satisfied. To evoke the usual standards of formal art in Patchen's case is worse than meaningless."[16] It is clear that Patchen's vital view of life and his functional view of art are at once his poetic "essence," and the critical key to understanding his works. The critic Breit advocates this approach to Patchen:

> What is required for an understanding of Patchen's poetry is an understanding into the creative process itself. And by this process is meant, too, what it feeds upon, that is the multitude of sources, the values and beliefs, the time, the pastness in it, the credible things and the outmoded things, above all, the sums of these which . . . the poet must create for himself. If for no other reason, Kenneth Patchen's poetry is of significance for us because it reveals more sensitively, more truthfully, the poet's function.[17]

It is precisely this interrelated vision of his role as man and poet, as the poet-prophet for his age, that offers the critical pathway to illuminating Patchen's works.

II Patchen as Poet-Prophet

"I am a poet of life,"[18] declares Patchen's narrator-hero-persona in **Albion Moonlight.** Not an uncommon claim for any artist, Patchen elaborates on the extreme degree to which his view of life will affect his art: "You will be told that what I write is confused, without order—and I tell you that my book is not concerned with the problems of art, but with the problems of this world, with the problems of life itself—yes, of *life itself*" (**Albion,** 200). The desperate needs of this life—where Patchen saw man's violence and insane greed precluding a life of love and wonder and advancing man to the threshold of destruction—control his art. The role of the forgotten, insistent, and prophetic conscience of mankind is the task he takes on, and voices in "**The Hunted City**":

> My Poem will be building in the blood of young
> men
> and I shall remember what they have been
> forced to forget.
> There is a desperate task here.
> (*C.P.,* [*The Collected Poems of Kenneth
> Patchen,*] 163)

As poet-prophet to man, Patchen offers a message, nevertheless, directed and founded in the reality of the *now*. If it is a forgotten conscience, our recognition of it makes it more emphatically our own. His *Panels for the Walls of Heaven* contains his prayer to poets descriptive of the state of the world and the artist's new function within it:

> O my poor lost brothers if any of you has poems to write write them now O if any of you has anything to add to the long tall dignity of human creation please add it now O if any of you has a pure heart let that heart beat in praise of God for O my brothers the world is dying and we will not let it die.
> (*C.P.* 348)

The artist must meet the world's dying with his belief in the divinity of human life, and through the action of his committed art restore vitality to that life:

> TO FORGIVE IS TO UNDERSTAND
> ART IS GIVING
> THE SAVED MUST SAVE THE REST![19]

It is just this sense of imperative action and spiritual mission which dictate Patchen's func-

Charles Mingus plays bass while Kenneth Patchen (far right) reads poetry during a 1959 performance at the Living Theatre in Greenwich Village. Copyright © by Fred W. McDarrah.

tional aesthetics and his concern for redefining the artist's role in society. His long surrealist drama-poem **"THE OLD LEAN OVER THE TOMBSTONES"** closes with his impassioned self-image of the poet-prophet: "I sing for the flame and against the ever-grinning darkness" (*C.P.* 95).

In an art so dedicated to the visionary function of presenting the world as it is and as it should be, it becomes essential to delineate Patchen's perception of the present world. What are the characteristics of his world view that will shape his art? We must recognize at the start that Patchen is not a "philosopher," that he is not concerned with presenting a complex system of thought, but with portraying accurately his felt reaction to the world. His world view is not theorized; it is beheld. We admire, not its intricate complexity of thought, but its searing frankness and consistent moral stand. Kenneth Patchen's vision of life is surprisingly simple and constant. Underlying all his work, it frequently rises to the surface as a desperate appeal expressed in a radical

form, and, at other times, issues forth as an open attempt to communicate.

Man is the center of Patchen's world, and therein lies all the hope and all the blame. In *The Journal of Albion Moonlight,* Patchen has his narrator state simply, "Our message was this: we live, we love you. Our religion was life" (*Albion,* 17). In one of the poem prefaces to *The Dark Kingdom* he states metaphorically the same theme, "Life's end is life. . . . Your native zone is silence; everything you want is within you. Do not seek the ungranting fire; man himself is the flame" (*C.P.* 247). Such idealism concerning man's potential was conditioned by the reality which Patchen saw around him, yet he refused to accept things as they were or to blame them on an Absurd existence. It is a man centered theism that he preaches in **"Red Wine and Yellow Hair"**:

Come cry come in wrath of love and be not
    comforted
Until the grave that is this world is torn asunder
For human the lock and human the key

O everything that lives is holy!
And Man and God are one in that mystery.

(*C.P.* 404)

Patchen's consistent reference to God, puzzling to many readers, is best understood as directed to the divinity he found in man, and not to the traditional Christian concept. His **"A Letter To God,"** first published in 1946, leads to this conclusion: "Believe in man. Belief in man is God."[20] Glicksberg summarizes well Patchen's compelling human theology: "Patchen cries: *'We must learn to live for the first time.'* That is his categorical imperative: Man as God must learn to worship himself and the murder in his heart must be torn out by the roots."[21]

Patchen's ironic sense of the social absurdity which man has created despite his divine potential leads to the "Anger and Light" dualism which Henry Miller observes in Patchen's works. "I know of no American who has as vigorously insisted that the enemy is within. . . . He knows that the enemy of man is man. He rebels out of love, not out of hate."[22] Such a compassionate rebellion is confirmed in a letter which Patchen wrote to Miller, "It's always because we love that we are rebellious; it takes a great deal of love to give a damn one way or another what happens from now on: I still do."[23] A man centered world where God is in man, a universe of unimaginable potential and an absurdly futile reality, characterize Patchen's vision of life. "A hundred thousand no ones / With just themselves to blame, not God."[24]

To attribute an existential or Absurdist outlook to Patchen is a mistake, for the absurdity he finds is in the insane waste man has brought into the world, not in an insane or absurd existence. Viewing himself as a voice in man's irrational wilderness, Patchen is best approached as one who holds before man the mirror of his wrongs. Like Molière and the true Camus, he is a "moralist" of his times. His concern for the larger circle of mankind is expounded in *Albion*: "Let me explain: we all of us live in many worlds, worlds made up of the color of our skins, the size of our noses, the amount of our incomes, the condition of our teeth, our capacity for joy, pain, fear and reverence, the way we walk, the sound of our voices; and there is above these little worlds another world which is common to all men: the world of what is everywhere on earth" (*Albion,* 305).

In this larger universal world Patchen recognizes the mad and wrongful influences of man. He once observed to Henry Miller, "I wish they'd give me just one speck of proof that this 'world of theirs' couldn't have been set up and handled better by a half-dozen drugged idiots bound hand and foot at the bottom of a ten-mile well."[25] This perception of the world molds his art into a prophetic warning. Of the irrational method of systematizing mankind he alerts us in **"Sure There Is Food"**:

> There is eating one's self . . .
> The way you've got it made
> Everybody is mad after while
> Then you can come up with a world
> Where madness is the normal thing . . .
>
> This world's the best example I know.

(*C.P.* 343)

In his prose Patchen's indictment of social insanity often takes the form of direct statement: "It's crazy to believe, is it? Let me tell you that it exceeds the wildest insanity to accept some of the things which the world takes for granted—" (*Memoirs,* 176-177). Thus "man's madness" is an essential element in Patchen's vision; basically he believes that "There is no danger from the world; all that is dangerous lives in us" (*Albion,* 83). As poet-prophet Patchen must confront us with this madness in his art, forcing us to recognize and reject it.

Against this dark vision of the world as it is rests Patchen's pervasive idealism concerning human potential—the world as it should be. He concludes **Albion Moonlight** with the assurance that "There is no darkness anywhere. There are only sick little men who have turned away from the light" (313). Ingredients in the "light" he speaks of include the key visionary components of "engagement" and "wonder." They encompass a belief in love (including the sexual); a belief in brotherhood, which embraces an everyman concept based on the unity of life; a belief in faith as essential to life; and a belief in an open and freely imaginative response to the world's beauty.

Patchen uses a platform speaker in *Memoirs* to preach the basis of his belief: "To love all things is to understand all things; and that which is understood by any of us becomes a knowledge embedded in all of us. . . . To recognize truth it is only necessary to recognize each other" (87). Love and brotherhood are put in the larger perspective of that common world which we all share, the unity of all life. A little further on he explains, "One who speaks the truth shall eventually and inevitably outsound the world; and one who lives the truth shall have a life in everyman forever" (*Memoirs,* 89). This belief in speaking the truth for the universal everyman is thus the basic motive of Patchen's visionary art. The seeming paradox of Patchen's being a poet of both protest and love, which he shares with E. E. Cummings, resolves itself when his love of mankind is seen as the motive for his protest over the needless sacrifice of human values. In his only conventional novel, *See You in the Morning,* the idealism of his vision is openly expressed: "Clouds. Trees. Grass. These are beautiful things. The wonder of life is in them. Life's holiness. . . . In Brotherhood, live—or, blind and without faith, we shall all go down into darkness together."[26] In the Romantic tradition of Wordsworth, Emerson, Thoreau, and Whitman, "wonder" is affirmed as a transcendent force pervading all existence. One does not analyze the world; one beholds it with open childlike wonder. This engaged response to life Patchen characterizes as "Humbly—but without caution (in unbridled vigor of faith: acceptful of joy for whatever reason, for no reason—humbly I believe!) . . . In the serene and beautiful prevailation of life, from causes beyond understanding, I believe!" (*C.P.* 459).

Against this suggested background of a man centered theism, Patchen, aware of man's irrationality and committed to restoring his lost ideals, presents his prophetic message. His art is a testament to the ultimate reformability of each man. As Miller accurately observes, "Setting himself apart from the world, as poet, as man of vision, Patchen nevertheless identifies himself with the world in the malady which has become universal."[27] Before considering how Patchen's art directly fulfills his tripartite world view, it is necessary to understand his individual and functional aesthetics. Just as his art is devoted to restoring meaning to life, Patchen's continuing concern for redefining the role of the poet today is deeply embedded in his writing.

III A Functional Art

As part of the desperate means to deal with a desperate world, art is used by Patchen as a functional tool. It therefore must be dissociated from traditional views of art that would limit it to its asocial aesthetic value alone. Because Patchen views art as a pragmatic tool in an era of spiritual emptiness, he shows little concern for writing about "Art" for art's sake. One rare exception is the brief introductory declaration in "**The Hunted City**" printed in the 1939 *First Will and Testament* and later reprinted in the *Naked Poetry* anthology of 1969, as if to say this is all I have to say about craft.[28] This scarcity is indicative of his

disdain for those who idly indulged in art worship, and suggests the anti-art, anti-literature, direction of his works. "How much better the world would be without 'Art'" (*Albion,* 19), his narrator concludes, the quotation marks and capitalization of "Art" are significant. He would write *art,* and it would be a tool used to save mankind, not a glorified tradition. Patchen's aesthetics and poetics must, therefore, occur within his writings as functional observations or as demands and directions toward redefining art and reestablishing the artist's role. Like the Surrealists and Dadaists, and like Henry Miller, Patchen debunks traditional "Art" in favor of a more vital "art."

Returning to John Dryden's classic *An Essay on Dramatic Poesy,* quoted in "A Note on '**The Hunted City,**'" Patchen explains the need for new and more living forms. Dryden speaks against the stagnation of traditional "Art" forms: "There is scarce an humor, a character, or any kind of plot, which they have not used. All comes sullied or wasted to us: and were they to entertain this age, they could not now make so plenteous treatments out of such decayed fortunes. This therefore will be a good argument to us, either not to write at all, or to attempt some other way."[29] Using Dryden as an established tool against "Art" and in justification of avant-garde innovation, Patchen is declaring his own artistic mission to "attempt some other way." He expresses Dryden's sentiment with more color when he proclaims through Albion, "Our images are fat with the grease of old caves where madmen sit thinking out new horrors—our art, religion, society . . . where is the sunlight!" (*Albion,* 27). Like Blake, Patchen believes that man has been corrupted by the language of images and symbols of the past. The false and limited icons of "art, religion, and society" must be thrown off. "I am telling the truth. Man has been corrupted by his symbols. Language has killed his animal" (*Albion,* 15) is the complaint of *Albion Moonlight,* Patchen's most profound book on art and society. As the long list of his experimental forms testifies, there is in Patchen a driving compulsion to 'make it new,' to advance the guard of art into striking forms and broadened relevance.

A second characteristic of Patchen's functional aesthetics is his compulsion to go beyond "Art" by openly confronting the reader with direct communication. Glicksberg describes it as Patchen's breaking "into the prophetic, ejaculatory strain, as if his heart can no longer contain itself and leaps beyond the confines of art."[30] This drive toward direct confrontation Glicksberg correctly attributes to the fierce urgency of the message: "This explains the nature of his creative purpose, his religious motive. He is trying to make light shine in the universal darkness. He would do without the protective and distorting garments of Art."[31] Patchen's methods are necessarily severe; as Henry Miller explains, "Patchen uses the language of revolt. There is no other language left to use. There is no time."[32]

In *Albion Moonlight,* a chronicle of the allegorical pilgrimage of a band of individuals in a world gone mad with violence, Patchen employs the perceptual double exposure as the reader watches a novelist writing about a novelist writing. This technique operates functionally to explore the nature of the artist's stance toward his art and toward the pragmatic and insistent demands of life. His narrator-self breaks into open expression of narrative consciousness within the personal atmosphere of journal writing: "They will not really listen because at times I became afraid and tried to clothe my spirit in Art; but I was a fool to think this—they can *feel* me coming out at them" (**Albion,** 23). Not only must the artist make it new, he must use any means necessary, regardless of conventional "Art" standards, to affect and engage his audience. "In art there is ever the demand for the distorted, for an indefinable thing termed 'magic.' But for the artist, there can be only one distortion: that which is not art. To say it another way, the world is in a mess precisely because a bunch of stuffy fools insist that there be no mess" (**Albion,** 120). It is well to remember here and elsewhere that Patchen's own definition of "art" and the "mess" provide the truest understanding of his works. It is the "stuffy fools" defining "Art" who refuse "art" and ironically perpetuate the world's "mess." The Dadaist parallels are striking.

Patchen's art is at once functional and creative, for he seeks to generate new forms to create a new world. "The great writer will take a heroic stand against literature: *by changing the nature of what is to be done*" (**Albion,** 308), and for Patchen no less than a world resurrection dictates the change required. In curing this sickness of the world, Patchen requires that the artist maintain personal integrity and avoid political propaganda: "It is my belief that in a troubled age like ours the poet can be of service only if he permit no half-truths indigenous to political maneuvering to obscure his own deepest convictions and instincts. Poetry is inimical to the lie—whether it be a 'good' lie or a 'bad' lie."[33] Besides his independence and

honesty, the artist is viewed here in "service" to a "troubled age." This is the position Patchen adopts for himself and for all true artists. As poet-prophet for this age he declares, "I speak for a generation born in one war and doomed to die in another."[34]

Patchen's answer to what the artist should do is, of course, revealed in the art he made; however, it is also the subject of a long and important statement on the artist's duty outlined in *Albion Moonlight.* Printed on the page with two other messages in the juxtaposed and simultaneous printed form characteristic of Patchen, it nevertheless can be isolated and revealed as Patchen's manifesto as an artist. He begins by describing the artist's stance toward life and his audience:

So it is the duty of the artist to discourage all
   traces of shame
To extend all boundaries . . .
To establish problems
To ignore solutions
To listen to no one
To omit nothing
To contradict everything
To generate the free brain . . .
To tinkle a warning when mankind strays
To explode upon all parties
To wound deeper than the soldier
To heal this poor monkey once and for all.
                                        (**Albion,** 253)

Using the action form of the infinitive, Patchen suggests the kind of engaged involvement required of the artist today as he moves from daring individualism to acts of generating, exploding, wounding, and finally the overall metaphor of healing. The action of wounding is the immediate precedent to that of healing, suggestive of Patchen's method of attacking his audience so that he might cure them. He clarifies the artist's world involvement:

To inhabit everyone
To lubricate each proportion
To experience only experience . . .
To extend all shapes . . .
To exclaim at the commonplace alone
To cause the unseen eye to open . . .
To raise a fortuitous stink on the boulevards of
   truth and beauty . . .
To lift the flesh above the suffering
To forgive the beautiful its disconsolate
   deceit . . .
To flash a vengeful badge at every abyss.
                                     (**Albion,** 253-255)

Revealed as a universal presence, the artist is involved in the "commonplace" of life, and in awakening the "unseen eyes" of the world. The "fortuitous stink on the boulevards of truth and beauty" directly suggests the provocative but necessary anti-art which he must make. His art then becomes the "vengeful badge" flashed at the lying abyss of nihilism and despair.

A final look at this song of the artist reveals a sharp focus on the artist's own personal involvement:

To *happen* . . .
It is the artist's duty to be alive
To drag people into glittering occupations . . .
To assume the ecstasy in all conceivable
    attitudes . . .
To blush perpetually in gaping innocence
To drift happily through the ruined race-
    intelligence
To burrow beneath the subconscious
To defend the unreal at the cost of his reason
To obey each outrageous impulse
To commit his company to all enchantments.

                        (**Albion**, 255)

One ultimately arrives at the path of wonder that Patchen so perpetually followed. Forcing his readers to realize the "glittering occupations" of imaginative joy through wonder, he drifts happily in the "gaping innocence" of ideal childhood. To achieve this state Patchen suggests burrowing into the repressed "subconscious" and obeying "each outrageous impulse." His dualistic mission is suggested in his leading to a positive world of "all enchantments" while also requiring the artist "To peel off all substances from the face of horror" (**Albion**, 256). Though laced with deliberate ambiguity and presented in the outraged chaos of the simultaneous poem form to tone down its didactic directness, this poetic statement of the artist's duty in a troubled age stands as a clear guide to Patchen's art and world vision.

The interrelationship of Patchen's view of life and art are thus contained in his image of the poet-prophet's role. In a direct address interjected in **Albion Moonlight** he defines Albion's and his own artistic role: "The reader will remember that A. Moonlight is not a reformer, nor an informer, an outformer, an underformer nor an overformer; he is a *former*—savvy?" (**Albion**, 143). Respecting no insular customs in his attempt to awaken mankind, the artist begins by forming an art which in turn will leave his audience "formed" as well. His involvement in life is not on the level of an instructor (an "informer") but on that of a poet-prophet who would rejuvenate the reader and thus the world through his art. In a glimpse at the artist's ultimate function Patchen sums up much of the misunderstanding of his own artistic mission: "The function of the artist is to express love. What most people fail to understand is not the artist's work, but his essential unworldliness in wanting to give love."[35]

Notes

1. Raymond J. Nelson, "American Mysticism: The Example of Kenneth Patchen," Diss. Stanford 1970,p. 84.

2. Kenneth Patchen, *Memoirs of a Shy Pornographer* (New York, 1945),p. 98. All future references to this book, designated as *Memoirs,* will be given in parentheses in the text.

3. Kenneth Patchen, *Sleepers Awake,* 2nd ed. (1946; rpt. New York, 1969),p. 291. All future references to this book, designated as *Sleepers,* will be given in parentheses in the text.

4. Kenneth Rexroth, "Kenneth Patchen, Naturalist of the Public Nightmare," *Bird in the Bush: Obvious Essays* (New York, 1959),p. 100.

5. Jonathan Williams, "How Fables Trapped Along Sunken Corridors," *Aflame and Afun of Walking Faces* (New York, 1970),p. 87.

6. Amos N. Wilder, *The Spiritual Aspects of the New Poetry* (New York, 1940),p. 181.

7. Charles I. Glicksberg, "Proletarian Poetry in the United States," *Fantasy,* 10, No. 26 (1942),p. 29.

8. Henry Miller, *Patchen: Man of Anger and Light,* in *Stand Still Like a Hummingbird: Collected Essays* (New York, 1967).

9. Charles I. Glicksberg, "The World of Kenneth Patchen," *Arizona Quarterly,* 7 (1951),p. 266.

10. Kenneth Patchen, quoted in "Alan Neil's Account of the Session," *Kenneth Patchen Reads with Jazz in Canada* (New York, 1959),p. 3.

11. Nelson, "American Mysticism."

12. Frederick Eckman, "The Comic Apocalypse of Kenneth Patchen," *Poetry,* 92 (1958), pp. 389-392. William Carlos Williams, "A Counsel of Madness," *Fantasy,* 10, No. 26 (1942), pp. 102-107.

13. Rexroth, "Naturalist," pp. 94-105.

14. Harvey Breit, "Kenneth Patchen and the Critical Blind Alley," *Fantasy,* 6, No. 4 (1940), pp. 21-25.

15. William Carlos Williams, "A Counsel,"p. 103.

16. James Dickey, "Kenneth Patchen," *Babel to Byzantium* (New York, 1968),p. 71.

17. Breit,p. 25.

18. Kenneth Patchen, *The Journal of Albion Moonlight* (1941; rpt. New York, 1961),p. 206. All future references to this book, designated as *Albion,* will be given in parentheses in the text.

19. Kenneth Patchen, "Blake," introduction to *The Book of Job* by William Blake (New York, 1947).

20. Kenneth Patchen, "A Letter to God," in *Doubleheader* (1946; rpt. New York, 1965),p. 47.

21. Glicksberg, "The World,"p. 268.

22. Miller,p. 36.

23. Patchen, quoted in Miller,p. 30.

24. Kenneth Patchen, "O quietly the SUN-MAN sits," *Wonderings* (New York, 1971), #45; unpaged.

25. Patchen, quoted in Miller, p. 30.

26. Kenneth Patchen, *See You in the Morning* (New York, 1947), p. 155.

27. Miller, p. 30.

28. Kenneth Patchen, "A Note on 'The Hunted City,'" *First Will and Testament* (Norfolk, Conn., 1939), pp. 167-168. Reprinted in *Naked Poetry: Recent Poetry in Open Forms*, eds. Steven Berg and Robert Mezey (New York, 1969), p. 69.

29. John Dryden, quoted in Patchen, "A Note," *First*, p. 168.

30. Glicksberg, "The World," p. 265.

31. Glicksberg, "The World," p. 275.

32. Miller, p. 31.

33. Patchen, "A Note," *First*, p. 167.

34. Kenneth Patchen, quoted in Rexroth, p. 100.

35. Kenneth Patchen, *They Keep Riding Down All the Time* (New York, 1946), reprinted in *In Quest of Candlelighters*, p. 124.

RAYMOND NELSON (ESSAY DATE 1984)

SOURCE: Nelson, Raymond. "Patchen: A Mystical Writer's Career." In *Kenneth Patchen and American Mysticism*, pp. 24-43. Chapel Hill: University of North Carolina Press, 1984.

In the following essay, Nelson identifies three phases in Patchen's literary output roughly analogous to the stages of Christian mysticism and illustrates his thesis with examples from various periods in Patchen's career.

"And Patchen?" she asked, pencil poised.

"Oh, Patchen—nobody takes him seriously," one of them said. "He's just a rough-neck who never grew up."

"He's just a boring child—a lot of noise about nothing," another said.

"Patchen missed the boat," Mr. Brill said. "He made the mistake of thinking a poem was a sort of garbage pail you could throw anything into and a lot of the time he certainly went beyond the pale altogether."

—Patchen, *Memoirs of a Shy Pornographer*

I am no pioneer in my approach to Kenneth Patchen. Nearly all of the critics and reviewers of the work he published for some thirty-five years eased their problems of definition and judgment by calling him a mystic. On the one hand, that body of common opinion validates and encourages my enterprise; on the other, it represents the gravest of critical dangers. Nothing seems more likely to discourage the reader of nonsectarian books about mysticism than the vagueness of reference the concept has attracted, and Patchen has been hurt by it. The attribution of mysticism has been as often derogatory as affirmative, has as often dismissed as identified Patchen's work. It is an example of the loosely metaphorical and invocatory usage about the mystical life that annoyed Thomas Merton, who complained in *The Ascent to Truth*, his study of Saint John of the Cross, that: "Since the Romantic Revival the term mysticism has been usurped by literary critics and historians and applied to anyone who has sought to liberate the emotional and affective life of man from the restraint of conventional or reactionary norms of thought. In fact, any political or artistic dreamer who could bring tears to your eyes or smother you with sensations of unutterable *Weltschmerz* was considered a 'mystic.'"[1]

Merton's own definition of mysticism was, for good reason, rigorously exclusive, and he would have resisted suggestions that he think in mystical terms about Patchen, even though he admired Patchen's work and heard in it echoes of Saint John of the Cross.[2] However, it may be that my predecessors were often right for the wrong reasons, and I may be able to justify their vocabulary, if not always their insightfulness, in part by looking at the shape of Patchen's career. Such an inquiry must rely upon implication and indirection, because Patchen's testimony about mystical experience is lacking. Although he often tantalizes us with hints of personal narrative, they are but sparkles from the wheel. Patchen is never explicitly autobiographical, nor does he write veiled autobiography in any extensive way. Rather, he makes himself known to us according to the qualities of imagination and perception we feel in his writing, which in overview assume a suggestive pattern.

Patchen's literary output falls naturally into three distinct phases, which require the exercise of only modest ingenuity to be compared to the three stages of mystical development identified by patristic Christianity—the sequence of illumination (or conversion), purgation, and union.[3] The traditional theological language may seem incongruous, but, when secularized, the three stages define accurately Patchen's progression as a writer and thinker. His mystical impulse is expressed not in religious terms, but in his idea of the artist, his attitude toward the self, his very diction and syntax. At one level, he develops from the political revolutionary, determined to reform familiar institutions, to the visionary who has seen and re-created a transcendent world with its own geography, laws, and citizenship.

The particular terms of Patchen's development may be represented by the way he regrouped the opening and closing selections in his *Collected Poems* (1968). He had opened his first book, *Before the Brave* (1936), with "when in the course of human events," a poem that invokes egalitarian revolution, pronounces judgment on the past, and announces the new order ("Turn out the lights around the statues. . . . Their time is up. The curtain's down. We take power"). For *Collected Poems*, however, Patchen chose to begin closer to his subsequent thematic interest. The lines that now introduce his life's work are: "Let us have madness openly, O men / Of my generation." A similar selectivity is at work at the end of *Collected Poems.* The last volume collected is *When We Were Here Together* (1957), which ended with its title poem, a fine cry of anguish against the corrupting influence of society. Patchen replaced it with a short lyric that restates by implication many of his important themes, and is explicitly a celebration of what he called elsewhere "the architecture of our innocence." The *Collected Poems,*[4] then, begins with insanity and ends in triumph in the calm world of a poem which one commentator characterized as "almost saintly":[5]

> Wide, wide in the rose's side
> Sleeps a child without sin,
> And any man who loves in this world
> Stands here on guard over him.
>
> (487)

In the first traditional mystical stage the soul glimpses the primordial goal and is converted to the difficult search for the absolute ground of being. The joy of discovery and excited optimism that usually characterize this experience are paralleled in the first period of Patchen's career, when he published *Before the Brave* and *First Will & Testament* (1939), and defined the terms of his revolution. *Before the Brave* can stand among literary expressions of Patchen's mysticism for the dissociation—both of language and emotion—from which he starts. It is an emotionally powerful book with a few fine poems, but the personality and technique of its author are still immature (Patchen was just twenty-five when it was published). Most reviewers, while acknowledging the power and originality of *Before the Brave*, noticed that Patchen's thought was elliptical and his syntax so strained that he was occasionally incomprehensible. Lines like those opening **"Prayer to Go to Paradise with the Asses,"**[6] with their too-well disguised exploitation of Christian myth:

> Marshal the quaint barren fogbeats in harbors
> left by wings of those whose mansioned lonely
> powers rode a hermit's riderless hurricane
> into
> the dark-fretted eyes of the Golden City
>
> (32)

are clearly ill-suited to a revolutionary audience and out of keeping with the direct social statement about history's defeat or perversion of old idealisms toward which the poem seems to move. Such language attempts (voluntarily or involuntarily) to mate radical themes with visionary perspectives. It tends to break down boundaries rather than make use of categories for analysis.[7] In 1936, Patchen could not unify his transcendent language and his social protest, and he had yet to discover the peculiar voice that is immediately recognizable in his later work.

Still, *Before the Brave* has much to recommend it. At times Patchen defeats his standoff between manner and matter, and breaks into a dense but probing language, which transforms the proletarian theme into an expression of individual and cosmic as well as social process. Those breakthroughs occur most often in single lines, in which Patchen discovers the aphoristic ability that will characterize his subsequent work. But he also occasionally manages a sustained eloquence, as in the only slightly obscure stanza that concludes the book:

> Who were the property of every dunce and
>   prophet,
> Of every gust of wind, of every goutish giant on
>   earth,
> Are come now to claim ourselves and the profit
> Of an ownership which has been our own since
>   birth.
> We are not cool: our hate has made us wise, not
>   clever.
> Beloved, listen, the stirring of life from the
>   grave—
> The heart breaks with the groan and the grind of
>   a lever
> Which lifts a world whose very sun retreats
>   before the brave.
>
> (130-31)

Before the Brave is also interesting for its subdued introduction of Patchen's mystical attitudes. Although far from the center of interest, they are strong enough to have encouraged Amos N. Wilder to devote a chapter to Patchen in his *Spiritual Aspects of the New Poetry* (1940), in which he argued that Patchen belonged to a Marxist church militant.[8] That was a standard explanation for the passion of leftist intellectuals then, and, although it certainly could be made pertinent to

Patchen, it led Wilder slightly astray. His misemphasis, however, is probably observable only in retrospect, because Patchen's incipient mysticism can be genuinely confusing. When a typical poem introduces "Comrades" to the fiery "Red Woman" with "Kremlin lamps" in her eyes, and the usual proletarian rhetoric is aimed at specific capitalists and German and Italian fascism, it is startling to come across the definitive statement by which **"Fields of Earth"** is concluded: "our country is the careless star in man" (78). Not only does the image anticipate Patchen's later emphasis on the indwelling divine, but it may not be entirely an overreading to relate the unexpected adjective "careless" to the "nonchalance" of Walt Whitman's exemplary democrats.

Patchen anticipates another subsequent emphasis in his use of insanity in **Before the Brave.** The imperative "Let us have madness openly" calls upon members of his generation to abandon all contemporary standards, so that as psychological and political outcasts they may dare the insanity of searching for love and light in this "slaughtered age." The association of mystical knowledge with what society calls madness is common enough in literary and philosophical thought to be respectable. "We have agreed that sanity consists in sharing the hallucinations of our neighbours," Evelyn Underhill wrote,[9] and Wallace Fowlie explained the authority of the metaphor of insanity in an essay specifically about poetry and mysticism. "Madness," he argued, "become sanity and the way of life in freedom, could therefore be a simplified definition of a state or experience of those who deliberately set themselves off from the world and thus are better able to understand it."[10]

The heterodox Marxism of **Before the Brave** and the orthodox Catholicism which had influenced Patchen's youth were symbolically shed in a story called **"Bury Them in God,"** which was published in the New Directions annual for 1939.[11] Like many contemporaneous intellectuals, Patchen had been disillusioned by the Stalinist purges of the late thirties, and he responded in part by abandoning the search for an external system, even while he continued to think of himself as a revolutionary. He had never really developed the proper socialist personality anyway, and his recognition of the individualism of the moral life was a major step toward his artistic identity. His new distrust of orthodoxies and refusal to subordinate immediate moral problems to "larger issues" were expressed in one of his uncompromising poems of the period:

Those smug saints, whether of church or Stalin,
Can get off the back of my people, and stay off.
Somebody is supposed to be fighting for
  somebody . . .
And Lenin is terribly silent, terribly silent and
  dead.

"The Hangman's Great Hands," from which these angry lines are taken, was published in **First Will & Testament,** the first book in Patchen's mature style. It contained a remarkable range of poems: protest pieces of the kind familiar from **Before the Brave,** but without the obscure, sometimes turgid language of the earlier book; love poems, often of striking originality and delicacy; fantastic narratives and landscapes; brief dadaist dramas; and social satires. In addition, **First Will & Testament** was characterized by a strong comic element, which had been missing in **Before the Brave.** Although Patchen made no attempt to develop an overall thematic unity, his book in general recorded the experience of a universalized "I" who found his only value in a naturally innocent love which broke down the distinction of human identities, and who lived in a world which betrayed such love, often violently. The development of this "I" linked Patchen with the Whitmanian tradition of American mysticism, and established his conversion, as it were, to his own mystical enterprise.

The association of Patchen and Whitman is, I suppose, open to challenge. Perhaps because the comparison had been frequently made[12] and he wished to resist it, Patchen wrote with some hostility about Whitman's gregariousness and messianism. He mentioned Whitman with distaste in **"Bury Them in God,"** and gave him an unflattering walk-on role as Walter Snowbeard Whitman in one of the dadaist dramas of **First Will & Testament.** Later, however, Whitman became a more ambiguous figure. In **The Journal of Albion Moonlight,** for instance, he was used both as a victim of a failure in our emotional life and as an eloquent spokesman against the horrors of war. Like anyone who was truly informed, directly or indirectly, by Whitman's rowdy spirit, Patchen was well anticipated by the master's statement of revolutionary succession: "He most honors my style who learns under it to destroy the teacher."

Patchen's explicit comments aside, the validity of the comparison with Whitman rests largely on the quality of that "I" on which **First Will & Testament** is built. It is much more accommodating and compassionate than the authorial voice of **Before the Brave**; it is not limited by class or economic position, and is able to identify with even those brutalized by the world. The first poem introduces this "I" in language reminiscent of Whitman's:

> I am standing open.
> You must not lower your eyes.
>
> I want them all to know me.
> I want my breath to go over them.
> They should withhold nothing from me.
> I am a respecter of dirt.

Like Whitman's "self," Patchen's "I" is free. It floats, accepting identities and exposing secrets, sharing the torments of flesh and years as well as transfiguring moments of love. Like Whitman's self also, it is able to probe beneath even a placid exterior in order to share pain. **"Peter's Diary in Goodentown"** is the first of Patchen's remarkable portraits of gentle individuals who live at the threshold between the natural and supernatural worlds and experience the terrors of both.

Patchen's poetic self is also related to Whitman's in its prophetic and visionary function; it is the spokesman for the human spirit and the umpire of the moral life. Whitman's optimism and Patchen's bitter rage originate in the same idealizing vision of America and human capability, and each man assumes at times the point of view that characterizes the other. The potential harshness of judgment Whitman brought to his nation is established in a relatively ignored passage from *Democratic Vistas*. "I say of all this tremendous and dominant play of solely materialistic bearings upon current life in the United States," as Whitman discussed the relationship between material and spiritual progress, "that they must either be confronted and met by at least an equally subtle and tremendous force-infusion for purposes of spiritualization . . . or else our modern civilization, with all its improvements, is in vain, and we are on the road to a destiny, a status, equivalent, in its real world, to that of the fabled damned."[13] Whitman, of course, assumed that the spiritualization would be realized, but many of the twentieth-century writers who have succeeded him have emphasized the consequence of his condition. Patchen, especially, has lived among the fabled damned for all of his adult life, and has recorded their viciousness, smugness, and hypocrisy.

The new mystical attitude is reflected as well in other qualities of *First Will & Testament*. In **"The Fox"**:

> Because she can't afford to die
> Killing the young in her belly

> I don't know what to say of a soldier's dying
> Because there are no proportions in death.
>
> (19)

and in other poems which stress the unity of life, Patchen moves closer to an explicit monism. **"The Black Panther and the Little Boy"** expresses an almost Buddhistic compassion for the demands of nature, whether gentle or fierce. The tantricism that is to be expected in a poetry stressing unity also surfaces in such poems as **"And What with the Blunders,"** in which sexual lovers leave their physical bodies and journey toward immortality. Finally, Patchen's mysticism begins here to influence his diction, which often becomes paradoxical ("Dying, he turned his face from death") and sometimes names things according to the sounds and meanings of an unfamiliar realm (the Bya Deena of "Peter's Diary in Gooden-town"). Language that has significance only if one can assume Patchen's context is relatively unusual in *First Will & Testament*, but becomes important later.

After his conversion to mystical writing, Patchen's career resembles the life of the prototypical mystic even more suggestively. The second period of the traditional mystical way is one of self-torture and near despair. In theological terms purgation is the process by which the old worldly self, the prideful and perverse will, is destroyed in order that the divine or cosmic identity may be apprehended. Psychologically, it is a period of self-mistrust, when one torments himself for his inadequacy before the absolute standard he has sensed and feels irrevocably cut off from the divine. This period in Patchen's career corresponds to the duration of World War II, which becomes in his work the agency of destruction for that suffering humanity which is the identity accepted by the mystical poet.

Patchen introduced the themes of war and the death of the self in *The Journal of Albion Moonlight* (1941), a hallucinatory narrative of pilgrimage. Here he gives his first vigorous expression to what D. H. Lawrence claimed to be the archetypal theme of American literature: the sloughing off of the decadent self which is rooted in history and sin and the emergence of a new self with a new relationship to others.[14] Albion Moonlight, the author-narrator-hero who is explicitly an Everyman, journeys increasingly deeply into the forbidden areas of his own identity, shedding protective layers of self, until a series of deaths that leave the actual act of dying obscure frees him from the perceptual limitations of the human condition, so that he recognizes identity and causality. The war that is the setting for the narrative (the *Journal* is about the "plague summer" of 1940, but the war it describes is all war and is everywhere) represents the failure of history and the alienation of humanity from its own nature. This dissociation (between man and "his animal," as Patchen put it) is one of the many failures of wholeness in the early work. The nature that has been betrayed is the innocence and holiness of perception that Patchen insists is the essential human condition.

Reason has been betrayed too. In this violently deranged book, Patchen continues to use insanity as a key metaphor for mystical insight, and analyzes extensively the relative sanity and insanity of the human community. "There is a new plague," Albion writes near the end of his *Journal.* "There is a plague from which there is no escape for anyone. *The great grey plague*—the plague of universal madness" (305). In the world of the *Journal* consciousness has been so distorted by the institutionalization of everything antithetical to human nature (war, economic competition, hatred) that people have accepted as real the fables of original sin and the fallen world. Behavior according to that misunderstanding is insane, and in a world of total insanity there is no reference for sanity—that is, sanity ("sharing the hallucinations of our neighbors") is itself insane. Only the poet-mystic, who perceives the reality beyond that defined by the defeated institutional consciousness, and who consequently is considered mad by his neighbors, is truly sane. As a social being, Albion is insane because he is forced to think with communal concepts, but as a mystic and visionary, who is capable finally of innocent perception, he achieves absolute sanity. The madness of the world forces him to write a raving book in order to be sane.

The *Journal* reflects another of society's challenges to Patchen the man in its theme of the alienation of the artist from his art. Because artistic forms and language itself are part of the institutionalized insanity against which he struggles, the artist must in a sense abandon art. He must recognize a distinction between human and traditionally artistic values—"as an artist I could have wished that there had been more structure and design to it [the *Journal*]—as a man, that there had been less of the kind there was" (305). Having no art to replace what the world calls "art," but being an artist in need of expression, Albion (or Patchen) resorts to antiart, which uses conventions by inverting or destroying them. The formal pattern of *The Journal of Albion Moon-*

light, then, is one of disintegration. The book opens in familiar literary forms (the journal, the romance, the novel) by which we are able to follow the action easily and are kept aware of the relationships within the narrative; but as Albion moves increasingly out of his diseased self the familiar forms break down, and it becomes increasingly difficult to discover what is "really" happening. By the time Albion is free of his old identity, formal categories have collapsed altogether. The *Journal* reads at its ending like a collection of the scraps found in the rubble of an exploded library. In subsequent books the search for an art to replace what he was forced to destroy occupies much of Patchen's attention and becomes one sustained pattern of healing integration.

The Journal of Albion Moonlight was followed by *The Teeth of the Lion* (1942), a small collection of poems notable chiefly for its shrill anger and the hostility of the few reviews it received. *The Dark Kingdom,* also published in 1942, is a superior book, both in literary quality and as an expression of Patchen's mysticism. Here Patchen for the first time attempted to create his own world, with its own laws, according to his own vision. The full title is a page-long prose-poem, which reads in part: "The Dark Kingdom stands above the waters as a sentinel warning man of danger from his own kind. On its altars the deeds of blood are not offered; . . . What has been common and tarnished in these poor wombs, here partakes of immortality. . . . All who have opposed in secret are here provided with green crowns. . . . Here all who sorrow and are weary under strange burdens—fearing death, are seen to enter the white throne room of God." The darkness of the title is, of course, the darkness of Saint John of the Cross's *Dark Night of the Soul,* and Patchen respects the ambiguity of the image. Although his kingdom is a place of great distress and evil, often ragingly violent and animalistic, it is also a place of promise.

Evil in *The Dark Kingdom* provokes Patchen to an almost uncontrollable anger, because it is in a sense absolute. Patchen acknowledges no Emersonian compensation by which evil becomes a subordinate element in a cosmic pattern that is actively working toward good. Emerson, Whitman, even Henry Miller, are perhaps more typical mystics, because they are willing to step momentarily outside human affairs and view the whole with dispassionate imagination—to see that evil is illusory, or that it is that part of human nature still in the process of evolution. But Patchen does not understand evil—that is, he recognizes its existence, but not its necessity. To him, evil is un-natural. Humanity is by nature innocent, kind, loving, full of wonder; evil is a disease caused by human failure to respect that nature. Because Patchen does not accept compensation or related ideas about a compensatory afterlife, he feels that no evil act can ever be redressed. The existence of an original innocent world does not justify the failures of the immediate human world. The impending apocalypse cannot restore what the evils leading to it have destroyed. Evil is simply a violation. Evil must incessantly be resisted.

The Dark Kingdom is not only evil, however. Here, humanity has descended so far into itself that it is able to face, and perhaps overcome, the ultimate horror. In some of the poems we recognize that Patchen's world is frightening only because it is strange. Many of the weird beings and rituals he invokes are gentle and wonderful, and we misunderstand when we project our secret fears upon them. Although the book is haunted by a tone of preternatural terror, that terror rises from self-knowledge and a purgation of self that can lead the brave spirit to both human and divine fulfillment.

The mysticism of **The Dark Kingdom** is at heart like that of the earlier books. It exploits the same prophetic "I" as **First Will & Testament** and **The Journal of Albion Moonlight,** makes use of the same vantage point of insanity, and celebrates the same tantricism. It differs chiefly in its greater reliance on the special language Patchen first used in **First Will & Testament.** Here we are introduced to people named Ad and Cuu, who live in towns like Lenada, Criha, and Mega, along the Cumber road. In one sense, these are private names for private experience, but in another sense they are part of a remarkably evocative public language which takes its imagery and diction from that racial memory Carl Jung called the collective unconscious. Unlike the prophecies of William Blake, to which it has been compared, **The Dark Kingdom** does not ask the reader to discover an allegorical or anagrammatical significance in its strange terminology. The words are their own meaning, and when we are introduced, for instance, to "Tegos, who is the Bishop / of Black Church—near Tarn," we should not feel compelled to go rummaging through the scholarship of the various historical Black Churches, but should recognize the indisputable need for an established Black Church in a Dark Kingdom.

After **The Dark Kingdom** Patchen published **Cloth of the Tempest** (1943), a discussion of which can stand for **The Teeth of the Lion** and

other books like it from the same period, for example, **An Astonished Eye Looks out of the Air** (1945) and **Pictures of Life and of Death** (1946). These are uneven collections of poems without any deliberate thematic unity, and, although each contains excellent work, they are not particularly good books. In elaborating his themes of cosmic terror and moral outrage, Patchen is often repetitious, his prophetic voice is sometimes nothing more than raw anger, and he is at times liable to the artistic deterioration that had been a thematic concern in **The Journal of Albion Moonlight. Cloth of the Tempest,** however, includes in its philosophical poems about Confucius, Lao Tzu, Mohammed, and Buddha the first expressions of Patchen's interest in Eastern mysticisms. These poems display considerable familiarity with Eastern philosophies and are directed sympathetically at central philosophical problems. "Lao Tsze," for instance, considers the troublesome Taoist attitude that regards attempts to share enlightenment as weak or foolish.

Cloth of the Tempest also developed the visual element in the integration of mysticism and art that Patchen had first used in **The Journal of Albion Moonlight.** In these early books it is rarely anything more than inspired doodling, but it becomes fundamental in later years. Although **Cloth of the Tempest** contains a number of rather complex visual compositions, its pictorial element generally takes the form of crude stick figures, and at its best it contributes to an epigrammatic wit—as in the poem which consists of concentric squares, surrounded by footprints, and enclosing the text: "The Impatient / Explorer / invents / a box in which / all journeys / may be kept." Many of the poems in these books are also typographically experimental. Patchen's inventiveness may be demonstrated by his discovery (or at least anticipation) here of the concrete poetry which would become an important mode more than a decade later.[15]

Patchen continued to integrate verbal and visual effects in **Panels for the Walls of Heaven** and **Sleepers Awake** (both 1946). **Sleepers Awake** is a long, typographically eccentric prose narrative, which extends many of the concerns of **The Journal of Albion Moonlight,** but with even less of a sustained story. Although more uneven than **Sleepers Awake, Panels for the Walls of Heaven** culminates the second, or purgative, stage of Patchen's career, and consequently is more interesting for immediate purposes. Its forty-four panels are either verbal or visual (or, infrequently, both) expressions of extreme rage, frustration, and fear. They range in quality from some of Patchen's most successful single pieces to expressionistic outbursts which are at best inarticulate, and which may represent the final appearance of the artist as inspired madman.

The terror and despair of this strange book are all but unrelieved. Opening with a lament for a lost clean world, it moves to a final rejection of hope and an invitation to death. While Patchen continues to recommend his old remedies, love and art are powerless here as they had never been previously. Love is simply a moment's escape from terror; art is an almost gratuitous bleat against the apocalyptic thunder. Overwhelmingly, *Panels for the Walls of Heaven* is about the triumph of death, both individual and collective, and in death is found neither hope nor rest. Death is rather the fundamental terror, and its characteristic description is as a sickening, involuntary removal to a nightmarish country, a ground of blood and filth. One almost inevitably sees in *Panels for the Walls of Heaven* a correspondence to the despair and loss of personal will which in mystical autobiography precedes illumination. It is Patchen's most unrelievedly grim and humorless book.

The point of transition to the unitive third phase is difficult to locate because of the cluster of books Patchen published in 1945 and 1946. His state of mind, and consequently the tone of his work, was unsettled during these years of psychological reaction and counterreaction, when he shifted back and forth between bleak pessimism and geniality.[16] A relaxed hilarity not found in his earlier humor informs his prose romance, *Memoirs of a Shy Pornographer* (1945), which was published before several of the titles I have assigned to the second period. The structure of *Memoirs* can be analyzed according to an influential model of the mystical way and for the first time Patchen permits himself something resembling a traditional happy ending—in a comic-strip heaven, which is made up largely of primitivistic and alchemical paintings, and which represents the power of the artistic imagination to create its own salvation. As an ultimate goal, however, the afterlife of *Memoirs* is too significantly fictive. That another world is needed to enjoy a normal family life with all of its jealous squabbles—which is what the heaven of *Memoirs* provides—is clearly a radical irony in Patchen's thoughts about salvation.

However the ambiguities of *Memoirs* are finally to be interpreted, the pessimism of Patchen's early career is distinctly eased with the publication in 1946 of *They Keep Riding Down All the Time*, a short prose narrative set in a house by the sea, where the protagonist and his lover are admittedly "leading impossible lives in an impossible world." Although Patchen has not abandoned moral indignation, the tone of this little book is calm, reflective—wise, one is tempted to say. Its imperturbability is explained by the title sentence: "O they keep riding down all the time. Nobody can ever stop them. Some from the light and some from the darkness—O see with what stern tenderness they keep riding down on this world!" (13). The "they" of the passage is not particularly paraphrasable, but refers to something like "the messengers of death," and the emphasis on time and motion in the title indicates that Patchen has come to understand death as process rather than the ugly end of process it had been earlier. His description of the organic universe of mysticism helps to justify his sense of resolution and confidence:

> Sometimes I think that every man's life has a meaning in a greater life which is being lived by a single creature whose nerves and cells and tissues we are. Just as there is no star, but stars; no tree, but trees; no brook or hill or sea which exists alone from all others of its kind; no road, but roads whose direction is everywhere; just as there is no pain or joy or fear which has not been felt by all of us; so must there forever be no man, but men whose lives cross and recross in a majestic pattern, unknowing, unstained, and beautiful, therefore, beyond comprehension. We are, to put it another way, cells in the brain of God.
>
> (17)

The theme of fulfillment even in the teeth of destruction is simplified in *See You in the Morning* (1947), the story of two lovers whose faith overcomes the emotional weight of war and death. *See You in the Morning* was Patchen's only novel and his only compromise with the marketplace. He wrote it in the best imitation of a popular style he could muster in an attempt to recover for his publisher some of the large sums that had been lost in the publication of *Sleepers Awake*.[17] It is embarrassingly sentimental, and its traces of the mystical theme are left undeveloped.

Patchen returned to his serious work in *Red Wine & Yellow Hair* (1949), a collection of poems in which quiet wisdom continues to control the rage of the early work. Although still preoccupied with death, horror, and failure, Patchen no longer seems personally threatened by them, and he is frequently as whimsical as he is bitter. He writes now with compassion rather than anxiety about human suffering, and his ability to share pain fulfills one condition of the Whitmanian technique he developed in *First Will & Testament.* The triumphs of *Red Wine & Yellow Hair* are the compassionate portraits—"**The Lute in the Attic,**" "**A Plate of Steaming Fish,**" "**Old Man,**" and "**Poor Gorrel**"—in which the humanity of even the crooked, failed, and ugly is made accessible and celebrated.

Orchards, Thrones & Caravans, a collection later incorporated into *When We Were Here Together,* was published in 1952, and *Fables and Other Little Tales,* the first of Patchen's books to be written wholly out of the special culture of union, appeared the following year. *Fables* can best be described as a series of anecdotes about people who live in a genial version of the Dark Kingdom. Its chief forms are variations on the allegorical story (Patchen's allegories often seem exact, but elude paraphrase) and the explanatory animal fable, complete with moral application. Patchen's explanations are always thorough in this very fabulous book, and they often become exercise in extending his outrageous ingenuity beyond decent limits—as in "**The Evolution of the Hippopotamus,**" which involves a horse, a bathing suit, and a swimming race, among other improbable details.

Like the later *Because It Is* (1960), which differs chiefly by being written in verse, and for which the present discussion can stand, *Fables* has often been compared to the nonsense of Edward Lear. The comparison is apt, although Lear's reputation as a children's writer may be misleading. Children might enjoy many of these *Fables* because their unstated theme has to do with the joys of discovery and the virtues of play, and certainly we must recover at least something of the imaginative world of childhood to read them to our own profit. But in another sense, Patchen's work is not for children at all. In spite of his high spirits, he exposes greed and brutality in his humorous world, and frequently he drops into a sudden spasm of pain. It would be foolhardy to attempt to paraphrase the book, but the first and last fables—the first with its poignant metaphors of process, and the last with its mythological models of both celebration and destiny—appear to introduce and complete a body of thematically related work. The themes are youth and age, love, birth and death, and change.

More pertinent to our concern with the unitive state, *Fables* and *Because It Is* are written in the special language for which Patchen had been building the vocabulary since *First Will & Testament.* It is the spiritual creole of a far country where the usual categories have been defeated and things as well as sentient creatures share a common life. Like the languages of all mysticisms it is heavily paradoxical, and it is more particularly Patchen's in its punning and its slippery allusiveness. Patchen incessantly uses cliches, but always twists them in order to salvage some significance. "**Tat for Two,**" "**The Business, as Usual,**" and "**Because Sometimes the Handwriting Eats Away the Wall**" are titles that exploit the garbled cliche or allusion in obvious ways. More often, we are tantalized, but not satisfied, by the apparent familiarity of a phrase to which Patchen has refused to return the old meaning. The closeness of his language to English permits us to share the landscape of his imagination, but his slight strangeness of syntax and his portmanteau vocabulary keep us from lapsing into our native tongue. In this way Patchen eases the tension that troubled his experiments with integral language in *The Dark Kingdom,* where the strange vocabulary often became intrusive by appearing to invite translation into some traditional allegory.

Something of the formal experimentation of *Fables* (which one notice helplessly labeled "semi-prose") was continued in *The Famous Boating Party and Other Poems in Prose* (1954), notable chiefly for a few good poems in a genre which Patchen had earlier used only rarely and with indifferent success. He attained a more significant stage in his development in 1955-56 with the publication of *Glory Never Guesses* and *A Surprise for the Bagpipe Player,* two packets of silk-screened "poem-paintings" which he later collected in a limited edition entitled *The Moment* (1960). These large, bright, inventive artifacts fully integrate into his poetry the visual element of such earlier books as *Cloth of the Tempest* and *Sleepers Awake.* Patchen's marriage of painter and poet had also been expressed in his series of "painted books," in which he decorated the boards by hand. Such efforts had only limited success; visual artistry never became integrally related to the text. The silk-screened poems, however, merged the two ways of art fully into one another. The poem is not broken into lines or stanzas, but takes its shape from the space of the painting, and usually is organically part of the picture. In the best of the silk screens, the visual element, paradoxically oblique language, and epigrammatic wit combine to produce a tersely suggestive work of art—as in a composition of red and white rectangles, arranged so as to give the illusion of great perspective, in which the text—"With one tiny stick / To arrange the air over the eating-shed / And the evil part of the earth around it / So that at last / Not even the stick is left"—is set at varying distances into the geometrical structure.[18]

In 1957 Patchen published his first collection of miscellaneous verse since 1949, **When We Were Here Together,** and **Hurrah for Anything,** a book of illustrated comic poems in a form related to the limerick. **When We Were Here Together** also includes comic poems, as well as contemporary nursery rhymes, love lyrics, poems of horror and protest, mythologies, and psychological portraits. Many of these poems are written in a new form based on word and line count, which Frederick Eckman considered clearly a "sonnet variation."[19] Whether or not Eckman was correct, Patchen's ability to use this tight form for extremes of expression is impressive, as is a similar dexterity in **Hurrah for Anything,** and in general all of his formal experimentation during the 1950s.

After **Hurrah for Anything,** Patchen brought out **Poemscapes** (1958), another book in a new form: page-long prose-poems, with regular spatial divisions within them. The formal discoveries of this book continue the patterns of integration after 1946, but the speaker of **Poemscapes** is more immediately striking than its form. Whoever he is, he is wise and free, like some absurdist Montaigne, and he has gained a perspective by which he understands both the world's rhythms and conflicts. He is the transcendent Whitmanian poet-hero, turning his world over on his page, naming its realities, creating its values. Although he shares the anger about injustice and hypocrisy that marked the career of Kenneth Patchen, he is beyond the power of such things to hurt him. He answers, finally, the request Patchen had made in his first book, more than twenty years before:

> O give us words that shrug
> Giant shoulders at the false display of poetry
> That does not show the pilgrim far before the
> brave.
>
> (25)

Patchen next turned his hand to playwriting. **Don't Look Now** was produced in Palo Alto in 1959 and off Broadway a few years later (as **Now You See It**). **Because It Is** followed in 1960, and after it Patchen did not publish another book until **Hallelujah Anyway** and **But Even So** in 1966 and 1968 respectively. Both were collections of the poem-paintings which had become increasingly less accessible to literary analysis, and, with the passing of time, more steeped in calm wisdom. Patchen had never been very much at home in the world, and he seemed to grow cheerful and confident as he prepared to leave it. Although he was a semiinvalid during these years, his work showed no diminution of the feistiness of the old days ("This room, this battlefield" is the motto of one of the poems in **But Even So**), but it does show a kind of exemplary mystical nonattachment, a refusal to define oneself according to the results of battle, even while continuing to fight lustily.

In these books also the poetic and visual lines have become inseparably integrated. The arrangement of words is balanced in the area between space and grammar, and the strange protoplasmic figures with which Patchen peoples his visionary world create an emptiness around them which is nicely filled by his calligraphy. In the portentous context established by the mixed form, Patchen's talent for epigrammatic wit and syntactical balance is particularly fortunate. A lifetime of emotional, technical, and thematic concern is gathered into the best of these picture-poems—in, for instance, a compact text from **Hallelujah Anyway**: "Man is not / a / town / where things / live / but a / worry & / a weeping / of unused wings."

As a vehicle by which Patchen coordinated his creative energies, the poem-painting identifies one culmination of his career and one of the resolutions he reached for his personal perturbations. His rediscovery of the lore and suggestiveness of mysticism coincided with his creation of new forms of perception, and so he returns us to the timelessness of art and its sources in human experience.

Notes

1. Merton, *The Ascent to Truth,* pp. 61-62. Bonnie Bowman Thurston reminded me of the existence of this useful passage.

2. Merton, *The Sign of Jonas,* p. 244.

3. See, for instance, Andreach, *Studies in Structure,* pp. 6-7. Andreach also describes the five-fold way first identified by Evelyn Underhill, with which Patchen has displayed his familiarity. Either system might have been applied to Patchen, but the tripartite has the virtue of requiring less ingenuity of application and less attention to explaining the system itself.

4. Page references to the volumes under discussion will be included in parentheses in the text.

5. Eckman, "The Comic Apocalypse of Kenneth Patchen," pp. 389-92.

6. In *Collected Poems* Patchen retitled this piece "Prayer *Not* to Go to Paradise with the Asses" (my emphasis). I am not sure I know why.

7. For a socialist critique of *Before the Brave* see Lozar, "Before the Brave," pp. 193-207.

8. Wilder, *Spiritual Aspects of the New Poetry,* pp. 178-95.

9. Underhill, *Mysticism,* p. 10.

10. Fowlie, *Clowns and Angels,* p. 182.

11. Patchen, "Bury Them in God," pp. 128-44.

12. One good comparison between Whitman and Patchen appears in Taylor, "Puck in the Gardens of the Sun," pp. 269-74.

13. Whitman, *Prose Works 1892,* 2:424.

14. Lawrence, *Studies in Classic American Literature.* See especially the essays on James Fenimore Cooper and Edgar Allan Poe.

15. For a discussion of Patchen's concrete poetry, see Smith, *Kenneth Patchen,* pp. 113-24.

16. According to Miriam Patchen (letter to author, June 1969), the books of this transitional time were composed in the following order: *Pictures of Life and of Death* and *They Keep Riding Down All the Time* (about simultaneously), *Panels for the Walls of Heaven, Memoirs of a Shy Pornographer, Sleepers Awake,* and *See You in the Morning.*

17. Miriam Patchen to author, 23 December 1966.

18. This poem-painting is reproduced in color in Patchen, *The Argument of Innocence,* p. 50. There is a murky black and white reproduction in Patchen, *Wonderings,* an unpaged volume.

19. Eckman, "Comic Apocalypse," pp. 390-91.

Works Cited

I have generally preferred to cite the most readily accessible editions of all authors except Patchen, whose works are listed in their original versions. During the 1960s and 1970s New Directions reissued most of the collections, pamphlets, and fugitive pieces Patchen had earlier published with Padell and other small houses, but the reissues are often typographically so different from the originals that they are in effect different texts.

Andreach, Robert J. *Studies in Structure.* New York: Fordham University Press, 1964.

Astro, Richard. *John Steinbeck and Edward F. Ricketts: The Shaping of A Novelist.* Minneapolis: University of Minnesota Press, 1973.

———. "Steinbeck and Ricketts: The Morphology of a Metaphysic." *University of Windsor Review* 8 (1973): 24-33.

Bittner, William. *The Novels of Waldo Frank.* Philadelphia: University of Pennsylvania Press, 1958.

Blyth, Robert H. *Zen in English Literature and Oriental Classics.* Tokyo: Hokuseido Press, 1942.

Breit, Harvey. "On a Bronze Horse." *Poetry* 40 (1942): 160-63.

Bridges, Leonard Hal. *American Mysticism from William James to Zen.* New York: Harper and Row, 1970.

Brooks, Van Wyck. *America's Coming-of-Age.* New York: B. W. Huebsch, 1915.

———. *The Malady of the Ideal.* Philadelphia: University of Pennsylvania Press, 1947.

Bucke, Richard M. *Cosmic Consciousness.* 5th edition. New York: Dutton, 1926.

Carlisle, E. Fred. *The Uncertain Self: Whitman's Drama of Identity.* N.p.: Michigan State University Press, 1973.

Chaplin, Ralph. *Wobbly: The Rough-and-Tumble Story of an American Radical.* Chicago: University of Chicago Press, 1948.

Chari, V. K. *Whitman in the Light of Vedantic Mysticism.* Lincoln: University of Nebraska Press, 1964.

Chase, Richard. *Walt Whitman Reconsidered.* New York: William Sloane, 1955.

Childs, Barney. "Articulation in Sound Structure: Some Notes toward an Analytic." *Texas Studies in Literature and Language* 8 (1967): 423-45.

Christy, Arthur. *The Orient in American Transcendentalism.* New York: Columbia University Press, 1932.

Cowley, Malcolm. Introduction to *Leaves of Grass: The First (1855) Edition.* New York: Viking, 1959.

Crastre, Victor. *Poesie et Mystique.* Newchatel: La Baconniere, 1966.

Detro, Gene. "Patchen Interviewed." In *Kenneth Patchen: A Collection of Essays,* edited by Richard Morgan, pp. 68-78. New York: AMS Press, 1977.

Eckman, Frederick. "The Comic Apocalypse of Kenneth Patchen." *Poetry* 92 (1958): 389-92.

Edwards, Jonathan. "Personal Narrative." In *Jonathan Edwards,* edited by Clarence H. Faust and Thomas H. Johnson, pp. 57-72. New York: Hill and Wang, 1962.

Eliot, T. S. *The Use of Poetry and the Use of Criticism.* Cambridge: Harvard University Press, 1933.

Emerson, Ralph Waldo. *Works.* Edited by Edward W. Emerson. 12 vols. Boston: Houghton Mifflin Company, 1903-4.

Ewer, Mary Anita. *A Survey of Mystical Symbolism.* New York: Macmillan, 1933.

Fiedler, Leslie, ed. *Whitman.* New York: Dell, 1959.

Fowlie, Wallace. *Clowns and Angels.* New York: Sheed and Ward, 1943.

Frank, Waldo. *Our America.* New York: Boni and Liveright, 1919.

———. *The Re-Discovery of America.* New York: Scribner's, 1929.

Gascoyne, David. Introduction to *Outlaw of the Lowest Planet* by Kenneth Patchen. London: Grey Walls Press, 1946.

Ghose, Sisirkumar. *Mystics and Society: A Point of View.* Bombay: Asia Publishing House, 1968.

Ginger, Ray. *The Bending Cross: A Biography of Eugene Victor Debs.* New Brunswick: Rutgers University Press, 1949.

Ginsberg, Allen. *Howl and Other Poems.* San Francisco: City Lights, 1956.

———. *Kaddish and Other Poems.* San Francisco: City Lights, 1961.

Glicksberg, Charles I. "Mysticism in Contemporary Poetry." *Antioch Review* 3 (1943): 233-45.

Goetzmann, William H. *The American Hegelians: An Intellectual Episode in the History of Western America.* New York: Knopf, 1973.

Govinda, Anagarika. *Foundations of Tibetan Mysticism.* London: Rider and Company, 1969.

Hack, Richard. "Memorial Poetry Reading for Kenneth Patchen." In *Kenneth Patchen: A Collection of Essays,* edited by Richard Morgan, pp. 87-97. New York: AMS Press, 1977.

Happold, F. C. *Mysticism: A Study and An Anthology.* Baltimore: Penguin, 1970.

Hartman, Charles O. *Free Verse: An Essay on Prosody.* Princeton: Princeton University Press, 1980.

Hill, Joe [Joseph Hillstrom]. *The Letters of Joe Hill.* Edited by Philip S. Foner. New York: Oak Publications, 1965.

Holland, E. G. *Essays and a Drama.* Boston: Phillips, Sampson, and Company, 1852.

Inge, W. R. *Christian Mysticism.* New York: Scribner's, 1899.

Jacoby, John E. *Le Mysticisme dans le Penseé Américaine.* Paris: Les Universitaires de France, 1931.

James, William. *The Varieties of Religious Experience.* New York: Longmans, Green and Company, 1902.

Jones, Rufus. *Some Exponents of Mystical Religion.* New York: Abingdon Press, 1930.

Katz, Steven T. "Language, Epistemology, and Mysticism." In *Mysticism and Philosophical Analysis,* edited by Steven T. Katz, pp. 22-74. New York: Oxford University Press, 1978.

Kennedy, Leo. Review of *Cloth of the Tempest,* by Kenneth Patchen. Chicago *Sun Book Week,* 7 November 1943.

Lawrence, D. H. *Studies in Classic American Literature.* New York: Thomas Seltzer, 1923.

Lazarus, H. P. Review of *Cloth of the Tempest,* by Kenneth Patchen. *The Nation* 158 (15 January 1944): 80.

Legge, James, trans. *The Texts of Taoism.* 2 vols. New York: Dover, 1962.

Le Maître, Georges. *From Cubism to Surrealism in French Literature.* Cambridge: Harvard University Press, 1941.

Leuba, James H. *The Psychology of Religious Mysticism.* New York: Harcourt Brace, 1925.

Levertov, Denise. "Some Notes on Organic Form." In *Naked Poetry,* edited by Stephen Berg and Robert Mezey, pp. 141-45. Indianapolis: Bobbs-Merrill, 1969.

Lozar, Tom. "*Before the Brave*: Portrait of Man as a Young Artist." In *Kenneth Patchen: A Collection of Essays,* edited by Richard Morgan, pp. 193-207. New York: AMS Press, 1977.

Maclear, J. F. "'Heart of New England Rent': The Mystical Element in Early Puritan History." *Mississippi Valley Historical Review* 42 (1956): 621-52.

McGovern, Hugh. "Kenneth Patchen's Prose Works." *New Mexico Quarterly* 21 (1951): 189-97.

Merton, Thomas. *The Ascent to Truth.* New York: Harcourt Brace, 1951.

———. *The Sign of Jonas.* New York: Harcourt Brace, 1953.

Miller, Henry. *The Air-Conditioned Nightmare.* New York: New Directions, 1945.

———. *The Books in My Life.* New York: New Directions, 1952.

———. *The Colossus of Maroussi.* New York: New Directions, 1958.

———. *Patchen: Man of Anger and Light.* New York: Padell, 1947.

———. *Remember to Remember.* New York: New Directions, 1947.

———. *Stand Still Like the Hummingbird.* New York: New Directions, 1962.

———. *Tropic of Capricorn.* New York: Grove Press, 1961.

———. *The Wisdom of the Heart.* Norfolk, Conn.: New Directions, 1941.

Miller, James E., Jr. *A Critical Guide to Leaves of Grass.* Chicago: University of Chicago Press, 1966.

Miller, J. Hillis. *Poets of Reality.* Cambridge: Harvard University Press, 1965.

Miller, Perry. *Errand into the Wilderness.* Cambridge: Harvard University Press, 1956.

Moore, Peter. "Mystical Experience, Mystical Doctrine, Mystical Technique." In *Mysticism and Philosophical Analysis,* edited by Steven T. Katz, pp. 101-31. New York: Oxford University Press, 1978.

Morgan, Richard. "*The Journal of Albion Moonlight*: Its Form and Meaning." In *Kenneth Patchen: A Collection of Essays,* edited by Richard Morgan, pp. 152-80. New York: AMS Press, 1977.

Morris, Charles W. "Mysticism and Its Language." In *Language: An Enquiry into Its Meaning and Function,* edited by Ruth N. Anshen, pp. 179-87. New York: Harper and Brothers, 1957.

Mumford, Lewis. *The Conduct of Life.* New York: Harcourt Brace, 1951.

Nelson, Cary. *Our Last First Poets.* Urbana: University of Illinois Press, 1981.

Nelson, Raymond. "Mysticism and the Problems of Mystical Literature." *Rocky Mountain Review of Language and Literature* 30 (1976): 1-26.

———. *Van Wyck Brooks: A Writer's Life.* New York: Dutton, 1981.

Neumann, Eric. "Mystical Man." In *The Mystic Vision: Papers from the Eranos Yearbooks,* vol. 4, edited by Joseph Campbell, pp. 375-415. Bollingen Series 30. Princeton: Princeton University Press, 1968.

Organ, Troy. "The Language of Mysticism." *The Monist* 47 (1963): 417-43.

Patchen, Kenneth. *The Argument of Innocence: A Selection from the Arts of Kenneth Patchen,* text by Peter Veres. Oakland: Scrimshaw Press, 1976.

———. *An Astonished Eye Looks out of the Air.* Waldport, Oreg.: Untide Press, 1945.

———. *Because It Is.* New York: New Directions, 1960.

———. *Before the Brave.* New York: Random House, 1936.

———. "Blake" in *Job: Invented & Engraved by William Blake.* New York: United Book Guild, 1947.

———. "Bury Them in God." In *New Directions in Prose and Poetry,* no. 4, edited by James Laughlin, pp. 128-44. Norfolk, Conn.: New Directions, 1939.

———. *But Even So.* New York: New Directions, 1968.

———. *Cloth of the Tempest.* New York: Harper and Brothers, 1943.

———. *Collected Poems.* New York: New Directions, 1968.

———. *The Dark Kingdom.* New York: Harriss & Givens, 1942.

———. *Don't Look Now* [*Now You See It*]. In *Patchen's Lost Plays*, edited by Richard G. Morgan, pp. 13-67. Santa Barbara: Capra Press, 1977.

———. *Fables and Other Little Tales.* Karlsruhe/Baden: Jonathan Williams, 1953.

———. *The Famous Boating Party and Other Poems in Prose.* New York: New Directions, 1954.

———. *First Will & Testament.* Norfolk, Conn.: New Directions, 1939.

———. "from 'A Note on *The Hunted City.*'" In *Naked Poetry*, edited by Stephen Berg and Robert Mezey,p. 69. Indianapolis: Bobbs-Merrill, 1969.

———. *Hallelujah Anyway.* New York: New Directions, 1966.

———. *Hurrah for Anything.* Highlands, N.C.: Jonathan Williams, 1957.

———. *The Journal of Albion Moonlight.* Mount Vernon, N.Y.: privately printed, 1941.

———. *Love & War Poems, whisper & shout* 1 (special Patchen issue). Derby, England: Whisper and Shout, 1968.

———. *The Love Poems of Kenneth Patchen.* San Francisco: City Lights, 1960.

———. *Memoirs of a Shy Pornographer.* New York: New Directions, 1945.

———. "A Mercy-Filled & Defiant Xmas To All Still Worthy To Be Called Men." *Mano-Mano* 2 (1971): 63-64.

———. *The Moment.* Alhambra, Calif.: privately printed, 1960.

———. *Orchards, Thrones & Caravans.* N.p.: The Print Workshop, 1952.

———. *Outlaw of the Lowest Planet.* Edited by David Gascoyne. London: Grey Walls Press, 1946.

———. *Panels for the Walls of Heaven.* Berkeley, Calif.: Bern Porter, 1946.

———. *Pictures of Life and of Death.* New York: Padell, 1946.

———. *Poemscapes.* Highlands, N.C.: Jonathan Williams, 1957.

———. *Red Wine & Yellow Hair.* New York: New Directions, 1949.

———. *See You in the Morning.* New York: Padell, 1947.

———. *Sleepers Awake.* New York: Padell, 1946.

———. *The Teeth of the Lion.* Norfolk, Conn.: New Directions, 1942.

———. *Tell You That I Love You.* Kansas City, Mo.: Hallmark, 1971.

———. *There's Love All Day.* Kansas City, Mo.: Hallmark, 1970.

———. *They Keep Riding Down All the Time.* New York: Padell, 1946.

———. *To Say If You Love Someone.* Prairie City, Ill.: The Decker Press, 1948.

———. *When We Were Here Together.* New York: New Directions, 1957.

———. *Wonderings.* New York: New Directions, 1971.

Rauch, Frederick A. *Psychology: or, A View of the Human Soul.* New York: M. W. Dodd, 1840.

Reps, Paul. *Zen Flesh, Zen Bones.* Rutland, Vt.: C. E. Tuttle, 1957.

Rexroth, Kenneth. *Bird in the Bush.* New York: New Directions, 1958.

Royce, Josiah. *The World and the Individual.* New York: Dover, 1959.

Saint John of the Cross [Juan de Yepes]. *Complete Works.* Edited by E. Allison Peers. 3 vols. Westminister, Md.: Newman Bookshop, 1946.

Sanders, Jo. "Zen Buddhism and the Japanese Haiku." In *Anagogic Qualities of Literature.* Yearbook of Comparative Literature, vol. 4, edited by Joseph P. Strelka, pp. 211-17. University Park: Pennsylvania State University Press, 1971.

Scharfstein, Ben-ami. *Mystical Experience.* Oxford and Baltimore: Blackwell, 1973.

Schwartz, Delmore. "'I Feel Drunk All the Time.'" *Nation* 164 (22 February 1947): 220, 222.

Smith, Larry R. *Kenneth Patchen.* Boston: Twayne, 1978.

Staal, Fritz. *Exploring Mysticism.* Berkeley: University of California Press, 1975.

Stace, W. T. *Mysticism and Philosophy.* Philadelphia and New York: Lippincott, 1960.

Steinbeck, John. *The Log from The Sea of Cortez.* New York: Viking, 1962.

Stevens, Wallace. "William Carlos Williams." In *William Carlos Williams*, edited by J. Hillis Miller, pp. 62-65. Englewood Cliffs, N.J.: Prentice-Hall, 1966.

Stovall, Floyd. *The Foreground of Leaves of Grass.* Charlottesville: University of Virginia Press, 1974.

Taylor, Frajam. "Puck in the Gardens of the Sun." *Poetry* 70 (1947): 269-74.

Trismosin, Solomon. *Splendor Solis.* London: Kegan Paul, Trench, Trubner and Company, n.d.

Trueblood, D. Elton. "The fullness of the Godhead dwelt in every blade of grass." In *The Quaker Reader*, edited by Jessamyn West, pp. 332-34. New York: Viking, 1962.

Underhill, Evelyn. *Mysticism.* New York: World, 1955.

Untermeyer, Jean Starr. "Problem of Patchen." *Saturday Review of Literature* 30 (22 March 1947): 15-16.

The Upanishads. Translated by Swami Prabhavananda and Frederick Manchester. New York: New American Library, 1957.

Walton, E. L. Review of *First Will & Testament*, by Kenneth Patchen. *New York Times Book Review*, 21 January 1940.

Warren, Robert Penn. Review of *The Dark Kingdom,* by Kenneth Patchen. *The Nation* 155 (4 July 1942): 220, 222.

Watts, Alan W. *The Spirit of Zen.* New York: Grove Press, 1960.

——. *The Way of Zen.* New York: New American Library, 1959.

Whitman, Walt. *Leaves of Grass: The First (1855) Edition.* Edited by Malcolm Cowley. New York: Viking, 1959.

——. *Leaves of Grass.* 3d edition. Boston: Thayer & Eldridge, 1860.

——. *Leaves of Grass.* Comprehensive Reader's Edition. Edited by Harold W. Blodgett and Sculley Bradley. New York: New York University Press, 1965.

——. *Prose Works 1892.* Edited by Floyd Stovall. 2 vols. New York: New York University Press, 1964.

Wilder, Amos N. *The Spiritual Aspects of the New Poetry.* New York: Harper and Brothers, 1940.

Williams, William Carlos. "America, Whitman, and the Art of Poetry." *The Poetry Journal* 8 (November 1917): 27-36.

——. *The Autobiography of William Carlos Williams.* New York: Random House, 1951.

——. *The Collected Earlier Poems.* New York: New Directions, 1951.

——. *In the American Grain.* New York: New Directions, 1956.

——. Introduction to *Howl and Other Poems* by Allen Ginsberg. San Francisco: City Lights, 1956.

——. *I Wanted to Write a Poem.* Edited by Edith Heal. Boston: Beacon Press, 1958.

——. *Paterson.* New York: New Directions, 1963.

——. *The Selected Letters of William Carlos Williams.* New York: McDowell Obolensky, 1957.

——. *Spring and All.* In *Imaginations,* edited by Webster Schott, pp. 83-151. New York: New Directions, n.d.

Wilson, Edmund. *The Shores of Light.* New York: Farrar, Straus and Giroux, 1952.

Winters, Yvor. *In Defense of Reason.* Denver: Alan Swallow, 1947.

Zaehner, R. C. *Mysticism Sacred and Profane.* Oxford: Clarendon Press, 1957.

TITLE COMMENTARY

The Journal of Albion Moonlight

WILLIAM CARLOS WILLIAMS (ESSAY DATE 1942)

SOURCE: Williams, William Carlos. "A Counsel of Madness: A Review of *The Journal of Albion Moonlight.*" In *Kenneth Patchen: A Collection of Essays,* edited by Richard G. Morgan, pp. 3-9. New York: AMS Press Inc., 1977.

In the following essay, originally published in 1942, Williams discusses The Journal of Albion Moonlight *and*

considers that, in spite of its flaws, it is a book of desperate discovery that needed to be written.

White moonlight, penetrating, distorting the mind is a symbol of madness. It denotes, negatively, also an absence of the sun. The sun does not touch the pages of Kenneth Patchen's **The Journal of Albion Moonlight.** So that what virtues are to be found here may be taken for madness. Could we interpret them we should know the cure. That is, I think, Patchen's intention, so, in reverse, to make the cure not only apparent but, by the horror of his picture, imperative.

By such exhibitions the paterfamilias of fifty years or more ago, showing the horrible effects of syphilis, would seek to drive his sons to chastity. The age is syphilitic, cancerous, even leprous in Patchen's opinion—show it then, in itself and in its effects, upon the body and upon the mind—that we may know ourselves and be made whole thereby. And of it all, says Patchen, perhaps the only really normal and good thing remaining is the sexual kiss of two bodies, full fledged.

In criticising such a book one should pay Patchen at least the compliment of being as low down as he is himself—and as outspoken. If he has attempted drastic strictures upon his age may we not demand of him by what authority he does so? Is his picture a true one? And does he prove himself sufficiently powerful as a writer to portray it? To scream violently against vile practices does not dispose of them. Furthermore, though this book is full of violent statement, is it violent, really? Violence overthrows. Does this succeed in overthrowing anything at all or is it not, lacking full ability, no more than a sign of the author's and our own defeat, hiding itself in noise? Shall not one say, finally, that this book is erotically and pornographically sound; if it lives at all it will be for no more than its lewdity that it does so? That is the danger.

Everything depends upon the writing, a dangerous genre: either to the minds of those who read it it will work toward the light or burrow in the mud. It can't be half good. It can't do both.

For myself I ask for no authorities, so likely to be gutted of any worth in our day, if not positively rotten. There is no authority evidenced in this but the man himself. If there are others like him, if we are not all somewhat as he is, provided he write truthfully and out of a gifted mind, he has a right to speak and needs no other authority. But if he belies himself and us, overpreens himself and makes use of devices that are shopworn and cheap, that's a different matter. We owe Patchen nothing as Patchen. But if he's a man and we feel a great fellowship with him, a deep sympathy, then we can tolerate his vagaries, his stupidities even, even his screaming. But if he shows that he enjoys that more than the cure. That would be bad.

For what we're after is a cure. That at its best is what the book's about. A man terribly bitten and seeking a cure, a cure for the bedeviled spirit of his day. Nor are we interested in a Punch and Judy morality with a lily-white soul wrapped in a sheet—or a fog, it doesn't matter which. We are ready and willing to accept a low down human spirit which if it didn't have a hip-joint we'd never be in a position to speak of it at all. We know and can feel for that raving reality, bedeviled by erotic dreams, which often enough is ourselves. This book is from the gutter.

The story is that oldest of all themes, the journey, evangelical in purpose, that is to say, with a purpose to save the world from impending doom. A message must be got through to Roivas, read the name backward.

May 2. It starts under a sky of stone, from the region about New York City, in a countryside where an angel lies in a "little thicket." "It couldn't have hurt much when they slit its throat."

There is a simple statement of faith at the beginning:

> He was the Word that spake it;
> He took the bread and brake it;
> And what the Word did make it,
> I do believe and take it.

He must get through a message to the people such as they are who have lost hope in the world.

It gets up to August 27. And that is all. It ends. It ends because it has never succeeded in starting. There is—after a hundred thousand words—nothing to be said.

Albion's heart is broken by the war in Europe. Surely his message has to do with that. That is the message. But it is not advice to go in or to stay out. It is order lost. For the war has been caused by humanity, thwarted not by lack of order but by too much. Murder is the desperate theme. Murder out of despair.

The chief defect of such a book lies in the very plan and method of it, one is locked up with the other.

Patchen slams his vivid impressions on the page and lets them go at that. He is investigating the deformities of truth which he perceives in and about him. Not idly. He is seeking, the book is seeking, if I am correct, a new order among the debris of a mind conditioned by old and persistent wreckage. Patchen is seeking a way through among the debris and, as he goes, seeks also to reveal his meaning by truthful statement—under conditions of white moonlight. From that to reorder the universe.

There can be no checks, taboos or revisions permitted to such a plan since the only chance it has of laying down positive values comes from first impressions, and they distorted. What else, in the writing, could a man do or say other than to put down the moonlight delineaments of the landscape he is witnessing? Could any traveller through a jungle do more? Or less? All that we demand of him is that he do not see and put down what is not there. Also that he do not fail to put down what is there. It is, in fact, one mind, his tortured own, that Patchen is travelling through and attempting to reveal to us by its observed attributes. In treating of that there can be no deleting, no pruning no matter how the initiative may wander.

Where does the journey take place did I say? In America? Why not? One place is like another. In the mind? How? What is the mind? You can't separate it from the body or the land any more than you can separate America from the world. We are all one, we are all guilty. No accusation is here permitted—Moonlight himself must, is forced to, take part in the murder no matter how he would escape it. All he can do is take part *willingly*.

The journey does traverse the mind. Therefore it gets to Chicago, Arizona, Galen. The dream which is more solid than the earth. And out of the cauldron of thought the earth itself is reborn and we walk on it into the small towns of Texas and Missouri.

There can be no graph except the map you pick up at a gas station—but as we hold it the graph becomes vertical also and takes us up into the tips of the mountains of Galen. People expand and shrink to the varying proportions of those in *Alice in Wonderland,* and every day but—desperately. We are at war, we are insane.

Reality? Do we think that America is not reality or that human beings are excluded from it? Death Valley appears. It is the mind itself, where Jackeen lies murdered. By Moonlight himself. It rots and stinks and is arrested and hung up—while one foot drops off on the gallows and a geranium sprouts from its left ear with roots in the heart of that corpse. Who is doing the hanging? It is again—Moonlight. Moonlight. He himself must be identified with the foulest crimes he imagines. He must. He cannot separate himself and be alone. Such is his journey.

Naturally everything observed will not be significant or new and it is the business of the writer to be careful of that. Yet, I shouldn't wish to advise him—at the edge of the thicket may lie a discovery, no matter how small it will seem at the time, which holds that quality of coming out of foulness faultlessly clean, a new order of thought shucking off the old which may justify a thousand redundancies. That's the chance taken by such a method. Tortured and perverted as we may think it, the book represents the same outlook over the world as did the Vita Nuova—reversed.

It is a book come of desperation, the desperation of the thwarted and the young. Write and discover. Go, move, waggle your legs in more terrible jungles than any primitive continent could ever afford, the present day shambles of the Mind. Tortured as you may be, seek cleanliness, seek vigor, unafraid. Seek love! Such is the New Life dimly perceivable through the mediaeval horrors of Patchen's hell. This is the order he is seeking.

Oh, we had a call to "order" some years ago, dead now or nearly dead now, fortunately. Its warts, like the hair of corpses, continue a separate existence, in the academies, and breed others of the sort from year to year; but the body has hygienically rotted away. This is not what Patchen is thinking of. Such an "order" consisted mainly in amputating all the extravagances, all the unimaginable off-shoots of the living thing to make it conform to—those very restrictions from which, at its best, the present day is an almost miraculous escape. What they attempted was like that Nazi "order" now familiar in Europe which already in order to maintain itself has found it necessary to commit three hundred and fifty thousand murders among the civilian population.

Whether or not this book is a good one (let's not talk prematurely of genius) I believe it to be a right one, a well directed one and a hopeful one. It is the sort of book that must be attempted from time to time, a book to violate all the taboos, a racial necessity as it is a paradisiacal one, a purge in the best sense—suggesting a return to health and to the craft itself after the little word-and-thought pansies have got through their nibbling.

I don't say it's the best *sort* of book, as the world goes, but it is the sort of book some one should write in every generation, some one writer—let himself go! and drop it for at least twenty years thereafter.

Patchen lets himself go. Such a book will rest heavily on the character, ability and learning of the man who writes it. If it is a failure, not clear or powerful enough to deserve the concept of it I am suggesting, that is his hard luck. But the book should be written, a book that had better perhaps have been postponed to a maturer period of the man's career—but which had after all to be written *now*.

That's precisely it. Even though it acknowledge itself to be a foregone failure—the book must still have been made as it is, the work of a young man, a new man—finding himself unprepared, though vocal, in the world. He voices the world of the young—as he finds it, screaming against what we, older, have given him. This precisely is the book's prime validity.

Though Patchen is still young, still not ready, shall he be silent for that? That is the significance and reason for all his passion, that he is young, the seriousness and poignancy of it. And it does, whatever its failings, find a crack in the armament of the killing suppression which is driving the world to the only relief it knows, murder! today. It is itself evidence, as a thing in itself, of our perversity and failure.

We destroy because we cannot escape. Because we are confined. There is no opening for us from the desperate womb of our times. We cannot get out. Everywhere we turn, to Christ himself, we are met by a wall of "order," a murderous cross fire which is offered us by "learning" and the frightened conformists of our world.

For once a writer insists on the maddening facts of our plight in plain terms; we grow afraid, we dare not pretend that we know or can know anything, straight out, in our own right. We have to be "correctly" educated first. But here and there, confronting Christ with Hitler—you won't believe it can be done—there are passages in this book where the mind threatens to open and a vivid reality of the spirit to burst forth and bloom in terrifying destructfulness—the destroying of all that we think we know in our time. It threatens to break out through the writing into a fact of the spirit even though it may not often be quite powerful enough to do so. I cannot specify these knots of understanding, of candor that—are the book's high places. The feeling that is experienced at those best moments is of an impending purity that might be. This is the order that I speak of.

What might it not do to the world if ONCE a universal truth, order, of the sort glimpsed here could be made free. It is as if it were too bright and that that is the reason no one has yet glimpsed it. Too bright! Van Gogh went mad staring at the sun and the stars.

I say all this in approbation—but writing is also a craft and we have to look well at that in this book. Florid and uncontrolled as Patchen's imagination may be, his images foetid, the passions of his Honeys and Claras funnelled into the socket of sex, compressed as a bomb to explode in colored lights—the writing must not be florid in any loose sense. And I should say, tangential as the thought may be, the writing is, in general well muscled, the word often brilliantly clear.

Many devices are used at times successfully, but not always so. There are lapses, disheartening lapses, and though I have said that in this sort of writing a man cannot stop for corrections yet, as readers, we have a right to object.

However we face it, one must still hold to the writing. Writing is not an instrument. The best writing happens on the page. It is the proof, with that stamp of the man upon it signifying it alive to live on independent of him, a thing in itself. The Word. We are responsible finally to that.

The book's defects are glaring, conjoined, as I have said, inextricably with its virtues. It must have been written haphazard to unearth the good. Whether or not there is enough good to carry off the method will remain the question. Many will doubt it, find the book to be no more a journey than that taken by a dog trying to catch his own tail.

One of the chief weaknesses of the book is its total lack of humor. Certainly the style is green and needs seasoning—but having said that, one has begged the entire question—nevertheless it must be said. The book would benefit by revisions and rather severe cutting. Sometimes the effect is fat and soft, even spotted, when Patchen confuses his subject matter with the workmanship to bad effect. These things make it at times difficult for the reader to plow ahead. But if, in spite of that, he is willing to face and cross these sapless spaces he will come to patches of really astonishing observation, profound feeling and a strongly imaginative and just use of the word which, to me, give the book a highly distinctive character.

FURTHER READING

Bibliography

Morgan, Richard. *Kenneth Patchen: An Annotated, Descriptive Bibliography.* Mamaroneck, N.Y.: Paul Appel, 1978, 174p.

Bibliographic study of Patchen's complex publishing history; foreword by Lawrence Ferlinghetti.

Biographies

Smith, Larry. *Kenneth Patchen: Rebel Poet in America.* Huron, Oh.: Bottom Dog Press, 2000, 279p.

Authorized biography explores how Patchen's political influences and health problems are manifested in his work.

Wilder, Amos N. "A Poet in the Depression: Letters of Kenneth Patchen, 1934-1941." *Sagetrieb* 5, no. 3 (winter 1986): 111-26.

Features many letters to Wilder concerning Patchen's prospects for getting his works published and his desperate financial situation.

Criticism

Blocker, Jane. "The Bed Took up Most of the Room." In *The Ends of Performance,* edited by Peggy Phelan and Jill Lane, pp. 262-81. New York: New York University Press, 1998.

Discusses some of the picture-poems Patchen created while bedridden.

Clodd, Alan, editor. *Tribute to Kenneth Patchen.* London: Enitharmon Press, 1977, 61p.

Includes brief essays and elegies by thirteen contributors.

Eckman, Frederick. "The Comic Apocalypse of Kenneth Patchen." *Poetry* 92, no. 6 (September 1958): 389-92.

Reviews of Selected Poems, When We Were Here Together, *and* Poemscapes.

Lozar, Tomaz. "The Little Journal of Kenneth Patchen." *Acta Neophilologica* 11 (1978): 47-56.

Contends that, through the completion of The Journal of Albion Moonlight, *Patchen freed himself from the limitations of a poet.*

McGovern, Hugh. "Kenneth Patchen's Prose Works." *New Mexico Quarterly* 21, no. 2 (summer 1951): 181-97.

Argues that Patchen is at his best when eschewing, or completely destroying, conventional forms.

Morgan, Richard G., editor. Introduction to *Patchen's Lost Plays: "Don't Look Now" and "The City Wears a Slouch Hat,"* by Kenneth Patchen, pp. 7-10. Santa Barbara, Calif.: Capra Press, 1977.

Supplies a brief background for the two plays Don't Look Now *and* The City Wears a Slouch Hat.

Pichaske, David. "Kenneth Patchen, Norbert Blei: The Literary Text as Graphic Form." In *Crossing Borders: American Literature and Other Artistic Media,* edited by Maszewska Jadwiga, pp. 79-89. Warsaw: Wydawnictwo Naukowe, 1992.

Examines the illustrations of some of Patchen's picture-poems.

Robitaille, Stephen J. "Vulcan Revisited: Kenneth Patchen's *Journal of Albion Moonlight*." In *Forms of the Fantastic: Selected Essays from the Third International Conference on the Fantastic in Literature and Film,* edited by Jan Hokenson and Howard Pearce, pp. 109-17. New York: Greenwood Press, 1986.

Attempts to apply a deconstructive literary interpretation to The Journal of Albion Moonlight.

See, Carolyn. "The Jazz Musician as Patchen's Hero." In *Kenneth Patchen: A Collection of Essays,* edited by Richard G. Morgan, pp. 218-28. New York: AMS Press Inc., 1977.

Essay was first published in 1961, and examines the imagery and stylistic devices Patchen uses in his jazz poetry.

Smith, Larry. "The Poetry-and-Jazz Movement of the United States." *Itinerary,* no. 7 (fall 1977): 89-104.

Outlines the development of the poetry-and-jazz movement and explains why modern jazz worked well with Patchen's work.

OTHER SOURCES FROM GALE:

Additional coverage of Patchen's life and career is contained in the following sources published by the Gale Group: *Contemporary Authors,* Vols. 1-4R; *Contemporary Authors New Revision Series,* Vols. 3, 35; *Contemporary Literary Criticism,* Vols. 1, 2, 18; *Dictionary of Literary Biography,* Vols. 16, 48; *DISCovering Authors Modules: Poets; Literature Resource Center; Major 20th-Century Writers,* Ed. 1; and *Reference Guide to American Literature,* Ed. 4.

KENNETH REXROTH

(1905 - 1982)

(Full name Kenneth Charles Marion Rexroth) American poet, translator, critic, biographer, and novelist.

Although he disavowed the title, Rexroth is known as the father of the Beat Generation by writers who contend that his works foreshadowed many of the characteristics associated with the literary movement. Among these qualities are the rejection of American social conventions and a preoccupation with spiritual development. Along with Kenneth Patchen and Lawrence Ferlinghetti, Rexroth was also at the forefront of experimenting with recitation of poetry to jazz music.

BIOGRAPHICAL INFORMATION

Rexroth was born in South Bend, Indiana, the only son of Charles, a pharmaceuticals salesman, and Delia Rexroth. As a child, Rexroth was instructed at home, where his mother instilled in him her love of literature and the arts. After Delia's death when Rexroth was ten years old, he went to live with an aunt in Toledo, Ohio. There, Rexroth joined a youth gang, participated in a major labor strike, and learned of socialism. In 1918 he was taken in by an aunt who lived in Chicago, where he attended Englewood High School. Although he dropped out of high school,

he studied at the Chicago Art Institute and audited classes at the University of Chicago. Aided by a photographic memory, Rexroth immersed himself in the flourishing artistic and intellectual scene of the city and began teaching himself Chinese. By age sixteen he had become an accomplished painter, poet, actor, director, and journalist. At the home of Jacob Loeb, Rexroth took part in a salon which at various times included Clarence Darrow, Sherwood Anderson, Frank Lloyd Wright, and Carl Sandburg. Upon teaching himself Greek, he began translating the poetry of Sappho in addition to Asian poetry. After serving a brief jail sentence relating to his presence in a brothel, Rexroth fell in love with his assigned social worker, Lesley Smith, who served as partial inspiration for his first important work, the long poem *The Homestead Called Damascus*. This four-part, philosophical work was written between 1920 and 1925 but not published in book form until 1963. Around 1925 Rexroth followed Smith to New York, where he worked as a journalist for radical leftist publications and gained an interview with Italian anarchists Nicola Sacco and Bartolomeo Vanzetti shortly before their executions. After Rexroth's love affair with Smith ended, he hitchhiked to the west coast and there worked as a mess on a ship for passage to Europe and Buenos Aires; he also traveled widely in Mexico. In 1927 Rexroth married Andrée Deutcher, a painter and active communist, and moved to San Francisco.

Rexroth's first published poems appeared in 1929 in a small literary magazine called *Blues*, but he did not receive much recognition until his Cubism-influenced poem "Prolegomena to a Theodicy" appeared in Louis Zukofsky's *An Objectivist's Anthology* in 1932. Throughout the 1930s Rexroth continued to aid leftist causes, wrote for labor newspapers, and painted. He did not publish his first book of poetry, *In What Hour,* until 1940, the same year his wife died from a hereditary brain disease. During World War II, Rexroth, a conscientious objector, served as a psychiatric orderly in a ward in San Francisco. In 1944 he released the poetry collection *The Phoenix and the Tortoise,* which interspersed philosophical narrative with sensual imagery. In the late 1940s Rexroth established a Friday-evening salon and a Wednesday-night philosophy club to discuss theories of politics and poetry; among those who attended were Robert Duncan, William Everson, Richard Eberhart, Philip Lamantia, and later, Allen Ginsberg, Gary Snyder, and Ferlinghetti. The year 1948 saw the end of Rexroth's relationship with his second wife, Marie Kass, and afterward he devoted his time to working at the Poetry Center at San Francisco State University and contributing to the *New York Times, The Nation,* and the *Saturday Review,* among other publications. After receiving funds from a Guggenheim fellowship, he traveled in Europe, where he met Marthe Larsen. They were married in France in 1949, but the union was not legal because Rexroth and his previous wife were not divorced until 1955. (He legally married Larsen in 1958, but they too were divorced in 1961.) During the 1950s, Rexroth hosted a weekly radio show popular with the Beats, and in 1957 he was an important witness in the censorship trial of Ginsberg's *Howl and Other Poems* (1956). In 1964 Rexroth received a National Institute of Arts and Letters grant and subsequently taught at San Francisco State, the University of Wisconsin in Milwaukee, and the University of California at Santa Barbara. In 1967 he received a Rockefeller grant, and used it to travel to Europe and Japan. He married Carol Tinker, his live-in secretary, in 1974. Rexroth died of a stroke at his home in 1982.

MAJOR WORKS

In What Hour collects many of Rexroth's poems from the 1930s. These works include poetic memorials for Sacco and Venzetti, responses to the Sino-Japanese and Spanish Civil Wars, and nature poetry. His next book, *The Phoenix and the Tortoise,* was more focused in its subject matter than the first, which had been criticized for being disjointed. *The Phoenix and the Tortoise* contains poems on one of Rexroth's most characteristic and enduring themes: the attainment of spiritual transcendence in the sexual union of two lovers. In the same volume, he also rages against the power of the state, declaring it the source of the evil instincts of humanity. The simple, spare lyrics of Rexroth's next collection, *The Signature of All Things: Poems, Songs, Elegies, Translations, and Epigrams* (1950), reveal the influence of the eighth-century Chinese poet Tu Fu. Rexroth's affinity for Asian aesthetics, which emphasize subtlety and restraint rather than overt expression, is also found in *Beyond the Mountains* (1951), a tetralogy of verse dramas that combines elements of classical Greek tragedy with features of Noh drama, a highly stylized form of Japanese theater. *In Defense of the Earth* (1956) is a diverse collection that includes Japanese translations, epigrams, and highly charged erotic poetry. This volume also contains one of Rexroth's best known poems: "Thou Shalt Not Kill," a commemoration of the death of Dylan Thomas in which Rexroth bitterly indicts everyone in contemporary America who gives in to conformist pressures and conventional morality. *The Homestead Called Damascus* relates an introspective quest for spiritual meaning told through the dialogue and metaphysical speculation of two brothers and an omniscient narrator who ponders with skepticism the received wisdom of the ages. *An Autobiographical Novel* (1966) covers, somewhat fancifully, the first twenty-two years of Rexroth's life. His well-informed interest in Asian literature and Eastern religions can be seen in his volumes of Chinese and Japanese verse translations, as well as in *The Heart's Garden, the Garden's Heart* (1967), whose title poem describes a visionary journey. Many of Rexroth's most respected essays are found in *Bird in the Bush: Obvious Essays* (1959), *Assays* (1961), *Classics Revisited* (1968), and *American Poetry in the Twentieth Century* (1971).

CRITICAL RECEPTION

While Rexroth has received high praise for his body of work—Lee Bartlett states that for "over forty years Rexroth wrote some of the most moving and durable American verse of our century"—his work has not received the degree of attention accorded to many of his contemporaries. That he is not more recognized is partially due to the fact that during his lifetime many critics responded to his contempt for the literary establishment by dismissing or ignoring him and also because his aesthetics encompassed too many diverse elements to fit in neatly with the Beat Generation or any other single artistic movement or category. In addition, as Morgan Gibson observes, Rexroth's personal life and aesthetic practice did not include the drug use, casual sex, or scandalizing language that gained both popular and critical attention for many Beat writers. In his examination of Rexroth's work of the 1950s, Gibson cites these and other qualities that distinguish Rexroth from the Beats in order to account for his break with this younger generation of writers. In his examination of Rexroth's poems, George Woodcock focuses on their political ideology, particularly in the poet's expression of anarchist views. Kenneth Knabb and John P. O'Grady focus on the nature of Rexroth's spirituality, the latter critic finding that for Rexroth spiritual transcendence functions alongside "a compelling moral vision" and a love for nature. While many reviewers disparage Rexroth, poet William Carlos Williams praises his work, particularly his translations. "As a translator of the Chinese lyrics of Tu Fu his ear is finer than that of anyone I have ever encountered," Williams writes, adding that *One Hundred Poems from the Chinese* (1955) is "one of the most brilliantly sensitive books of poems in the American idiom it has ever been my good fortune to read." In his analysis of Rexroth's poetic style, Gordon K. Grigsby illustrates how Rexroth pulled himself "out of artifice and the overcooked" to achieve a clarity and depth rarely found in modern poetry.

PRINCIPAL WORKS

In What Hour (poetry) 1940

The Phoenix and the Tortoise (poetry) 1944

The Signature of All Things: Poems, Songs, Elegies, Translations, and Epigrams (poetry) 1950

Beyond the Mountains (poetry) 1951

The Dragon and the Unicorn (poetry) 1952

A Bestiary for My Daughters Mary and Katherine (poetry) 1955

One Hundred Poems from the Japanese [translator] (poetry) 1955

Thou Shalt Not Kill: A Memorial for Dylan Thomas (poetry) 1955

In Defense of the Earth [translator] (poetry and epigrams) 1956

One Hundred Poems from the Chinese [translator] (poetry) 1956

Bird in the Bush: Obvious Essays (essays) 1959

Assays (essays) 1961

The Homestead Called Damascus (poetry) 1963

Natural Numbers: New and Selected Poetry (poetry) 1963

An Autobiographical Novel (novel) 1966

The Collected Shorter Poems (poetry) 1966

The Heart's Garden, the Garden's Heart (poetry) 1967

Classics Revisited (essays) 1968

The Collected Longer Poems of Kenneth Rexroth (poetry) 1968

Pierre Reverdy Selected Poems [author of preface] (poetry) 1969

The Alternative Society (essays) 1970

American Poetry in the Twentieth Century (essays) 1971

The Morning Star (poetry) 1974

New Poems (poems) 1974

New and Selected Poems (poetry) 1979

Selected Poems (poetry) 1984

Sacramental Acts: The Love Poems of Kenneth Rexroth (poetry) 1987

Thirty-Six Poems by Tu Fu [translator] (poetry) 1987

PRIMARY SOURCES

KENNETH REXROTH (POEM DATE 1956)

SOURCE: Rexroth, Kenneth. "Thou Shalt Not Kill." In *In Defense of the Earth*, pp. 52-9. New York: New Directions, 1956.

The following poem, subtitled "A Memorial for Dylan Thomas," is often cited as Rexroth's best known Beat poem. The author would often read this work to the accompaniment of a jazz band.

"THOU SHALT NOT KILL"

I

They are murdering all the young men.
For half a century now, every day,
They have hunted them down and killed them.
They are killing them now.

At this minute, all over the world,
They are killing the young men.
They know ten thousand ways to kill them.
Every year they invent new ones.
In the jungles of Africa,
In the marshes of Asia,
In the deserts of Asia,
In the slave pens of Siberia,
In the slums of Europe,
In the nightclubs of America,
The murderers are at work.

They are stoning Stephen,
They are casting him forth from every city in the
    world.
Under the Welcome sign,
Under the Rotary emblem,
On the highway in the suburbs,
His body lies under the hurling stones.
He was full of faith and power.
He did great wonders among the people.
They could not stand against his wisdom.
They could not bear the spirit with which he
    spoke.
He cried out in the name
Of the tabernacle of witness in the wilderness.
They were cut to the heart.
They gnashed against him with their teeth.
They cried out with a loud voice.
They stopped their ears.
They ran on him with one accord.
They cast him out of the city and stoned him.
The witnesses laid down their clothes
At the feet of a man whose name was your
    name—
You.

You are the murderer.
You are killing the young men.
You are broiling Lawrence on his gridiron.
When you demanded he divulge
The hidden treasures of the spirit,
He showed you the poor.
You set your heart against him.
You seized him and bound him with rage.
You roasted him on a slow fire.
His fat dripped and spurted in the flame.
The smell was sweet to your nose.
He cried out,
"I am cooked on this side,
Turn me over and eat,
You
Eat of my flesh."

You are murdering the young men.
You are shooting Sebastian with arrows.
He kept the faithful steadfast under persecution.
First you shot him with arrows.
Then you beat him with rods.
Then you threw him in a sewer.
You fear nothing more than courage.
You who turn away your eyes
At the bravery of the young men.

You,
The hyena with polished face and bow tie,
In the office of a billion dollar

Corporation devoted to service;
The vulture dripping with carrion,
Carefully and carelessly robed in imported
    tweeds,
Lecturing on the Age of Abundance;
The jackal in double-breasted gabardine,
Barking by remote control,
In the United Nations;
The vampire bat seated at the couch head,
Notebook in hand, toying with his decerebrator;
The autonomous, ambulatory cancer,
The Superego in a thousand uniforms;
You, the finger man of behemoth,
The murderer of the young men.

II

What happened to Robinson,
Who used to stagger down Eighth Street,
Dizzy with solitary gin?
Where is Masters, who crouched in
His law office for ruinous decades?
Where is Leonard who thought he was
A locomotive? And Lindsay,
Wise as a dove, innocent
As a serpent, where is he?
    Timor mortis conturbat me.

What became of Jim Oppenheim?
Lola Ridge alone in an
Icy furnished room? Orrick Johns,
Hopping into the surf on his
One leg? Elinor Wylie
Who leaped like Kierkegaard?
Sara Teasdale, where is she?
    Timor mortis conturbat me.

Where is George Sterling, that tame fawn?
Phelps Putnam who stole away?
Jack Wheelwright who couldn't cross the bridge?
Donald Evans with his cane and
Monocle, where is he?
    Timor mortis conturbat me.

John Gould Fletcher who could not
Unbreak his powerful heart?
Bodenheim butchered in stinking
Squalor? Edna Millay who took
Her last straight whiskey? Genevieve
Who loved so much; where is she?
    Timor mortis conturbat me.

Harry who didn't care at all?
Hart who went back to the sea?
    Timor mortis conturbat me.

Where is Sol Funaroff?
What happened to Potamkin?
Isidor Schneider? Claude McKay?
Countee Cullen? Clarence Weinstock?
Who animates their corpses today?
    Timor mortis conturbat me.

Where is Ezra, that noisy man?
Where is Larsson whose poems were prayers?
Where is Charles Snider, that gentle
Bitter boy? Carnevali,

What became of him?
Carol who was so beautiful, where is she?
  Timor mortis conturbat me.

III

Was their end noble and tragic,
Like the mask of a tyrant?
Like Agamemnon's secret golden face?
Indeed it was not. Up all night
In the fo'c'sle, bemused and beaten,
Bleeding at the rectum, in his
Pocket a review by the one
Colleague he respected, "If he
Really means what these poems
Pretend to say, he has only
One way out—." Into the
Hot acrid Caribbean sun,
Into the acrid, transparent,
Smoky sea. Or another, lice in his
Armpits and crotch, garbage littered
On the floor, gray greasy rags on
The bed. "I killed them because they
Were dirty, stinking Communists.
I should get a medal." Again,
Another, Simenon foretold
His end at a glance. "I dare you
To pull the trigger." She shut her eyes
And spilled gin over her dress.
The pistol wobbled in his hand.
It took them hours to die.
Another threw herself downstairs,
And broke her back. It took her years.
Two put their heads under water
In the bath and filled their lungs.
Another threw himself under
The traffic of a crowded bridge.
Another, drunk, jumped from a
Balcony and broke her neck.
Another soaked herself in
Gasoline and ran blazing
Into the street and lived on
In custody. One made love
Only once with a beggar woman.
He died years later of syphilis
Of the brain and spine. Fifteen
Years of pain and poverty,
While his mind leaked away.
One tried three times in twenty years
To drown himself. The last time
He succeeded. One turned on the gas
When she had no more food, no more
Money, and only half a lung.
One went up to Harlem, took on
Thirty men, came home and
Cut her throat. One sat up all night
Talking to H.L. Mencken and
Drowned himself in the morning.
How many stopped writing at thirty?
How many went to work for *Time*?
How many died of prefrontal
Lobotomies in the Communist Party?
How many are lost in the back wards
Of provincial madhouses?
How many on the advice of
Their psychoanalysts, decided
A business career was best after all?

How many are hopeless alcoholics?
René Crevel!
Jacques Rigaud!
Antonin Artaud!
Mayakofsky!
Essenin!
Robert Desnos!
Saint Pol Roux!
Max Jacob!
All over the world
The same disembodied hand
Strikes us down.
Here is a mountain of death.
A hill of heads like the Khans piled up.
The first-born of a century
Slaughtered by Herod.
Three generations of infants
Stuffed down the maw of Moloch.

IV

He is dead.
The bird of Rhiannon.
He is dead.
In the winter of the heart.
He is Dead.
In the canyons of death,
They found him dumb at last,
In the blizzard of lies.
He never spoke again.
He died.
He is dead.
In their antiseptic hands,
He is dead.
The little spellbinder of Cader Idris.
He is dead.
The sparrow of Cardiff.
He is dead.
The canary of Swansea.
Who killed him?
Who killed the bright-headed bird?
You did, you son of a bitch.
You drowned him in your cocktail brain.
He fell down and died in your synthetic heart.
You killed him,
Oppenheimer the Million-Killer,
You killed him,
Einstein the Gray Eminence.
You killed him,
Havanahavana, with your Nobel Prize.
You killed him, General,
Through the proper channels.
You strangled him, Le Mouton,
With your *mains étendues*.
He confessed in open court to a pince-nezed
    skull.
You shot him in the back of the head
As he stumbled in the last cellar.
You killed him,
Benign Lady on the postage stamp.
He was found dead at a Liberal Weekly
    luncheon.
He was found dead on the cutting room floor.
He was found dead at a *Time* policy conference.
Henry Luce killed him with a telegram to the
    Pope.

Mademoiselle strangled him with a padded bras-
siere.
Old Possum sprinkled him with a tea ball.
After the wolves were done, the vaticides
Crawled off with his bowels to their classrooms
and quarterlies.
When the news came over the radio
You personally rose up shouting, "Give us Barab-
bas!"
In your lonely crowd you swept over him.
Your custom-built brogans and your ballet slip-
pers
Pummeled him to death in the gritty street.
You hit him with an album of Hindemith.
You stabbed him with stainless steel by Isamu
Noguchi,
He is dead.
He is Dead.
Like Ignacio the bullfighter,
At four o'clock in the afternoon.
At precisely four o'clock.
I too do not want to hear it.
I too do not want to know it.
I want to run into the street,
Shouting, "Remember Vanzetti!"
I want to pour gasoline down your chimneys.
I want to blow up your galleries.
I want to bum down your editorial offices.
I want to slit the bellies of your frigid women.
I want to sink your sailboats and launches.
I want to strangle your children at their finger
paintings.
I want to poison your Afghans and poodles.
He is dead, the little drunken cherub.
He is dead,
The effulgent tub thumper.
He is Dead.
The ever living birds are not singing
To the head of Bran.
The sea birds are still
Over Bardsey of Ten Thousand Saints.
The underground men are not singing
On their way to work.
There is a smell of blood
In the smell of the turf smoke.
They have struck him down,
The son of David ap Gwilym.
They have murdered him,
The Baby of Taliessin.
There he lies dead,
By the Iceberg of the United Nations.
There he lies sandbagged,
At the foot of the Statue of Liberty.
The Gulf Stream smells of blood
As it breaks on the sand of Iona
And the blue rocks of Canarvon.
And all the birds of the deep sea rise up
Over the luxury liners and scream,
"You killed him! You killed him.
In your God damned Brooks Brothers suit,
You son of a bitch."

KENNETH REXROTH (LETTER DATE 1962)

SOURCE: Rexroth, Kenneth. "Beat Generation Dead as Davy Crockett Caps, Says Rexroth, Passing Through." In *The Village Voice Reader*, edited by Daniel Wolf and Edwin Fancher, pp. 337-9. New York: Doubleday, 1962.

In the following letter to the editors of the Village Voice, *Rexroth expounds on several topics, including the death of the Beat Generation.*

Pursuant, as they say, to our conversation, the Village hasn't changed much. I grew up in high chairs at the Brevoort and Lafayette. There's more of it, and it's sharper. I don't think there's much doubt, for instance, that The Voice is a more civilized organ than Bruno's Weekly. The place is full of uptowners; it always was. It is expensive; it was in 1920. As a way of life, it goes on un-changed, amongst the call girls, customers' men, aboriginal Italians and Irish. But where one girl wore colored stockings in 1905, thousands wear them today. Where Floyd Dell read Nietzsche, untold numbers read Beckett in the dim light of cold-water walk-ups.

As for the Beat Generation. Let's all stop. Right now. This has turned into a Madison Avenue gim-mick. When the fall book lists come out, it will be as dead as Davy Crockett caps. It is a pity that as fine an artist as Jack Kerouac got hooked by this label. Of course it happened because of Jack's naivete—the innocence of heart which is his special virtue. I am sure he is as sick of it as I am. I for one never belonged to it. I am neither beati-fied nor pummelled. I'm getting on, but I've man-aged to dodge the gimmick generations as they went past; I was never Lost nor Proletarian nor Reactionary. This stuff is strictly for the customers.

As for Jack himself. Yes, I threw him out. He was frightening the children. He doesn't frighten me, though when he gets excessively beatified he bores me slightly. I think he is one of the finest prose writers now writing prose. He is a naive writer, like Restif de la Bretonne or Henry Miller, who accurately reflects a world without under-standing it very well in the rational sense. For that, Clellan Holmes is far better on the same scene, shrewd and objective; but, as I am pretty sure he himself would be the first to admit, not the artist Jack is, and lacking, because of his very objectiv-ity, Jack's poignancy and terror. One thing about Jack and Allen Ginsberg, who, I might remind you, are Villagers, and only were temporarily on loan to San Francisco: I had to come back to New York to realize how good they are. They have sure as hell made just the right enemies.

Now about jazz poetry. Let anybody who wants to have started it go right ahead and have started it. I'm pretty sure I didn't. But Lawrence Ferlinghetti and I did first start it off as public entertainment before concert and club audiences. For better or worse, I guess we started the craze. It is a lot more than a craze as far as I am concerned. I am not interested in a freak gig. I think the art of poetry in America is in a bad way. It is largely the business of seminars, conducted by aging poets for five or six budding poets.

Jazz poetry gets poetry out of the classrooms and into contact with large audiences who have not read any verse since grammar school. They listen, they like it, they come back for more. It demands of poetry, however deep and complex, something of a public surface, like the plays of Shakespeare that had stuff for everybody, the commonalty, the middle class, the nobility, the intellectuals.

Jazz gives poetry, too, the rhythms of itself, so expressive of the world we live in, and it gives it the inspiration of the jazz world, with its hard simple morality and its direct honesty—especially its erotic honesty. Fish or cut bait. Poetry gives modern jazz a verbal content infinitely superior to the silly falsities of the typical Tin Pan Alley lyric. It provides people who do not understand music technically something to hook onto—something to lead them into the complex world of modern jazz—as serious and as artistically important as any music being produced today. And then, the reciting, rather than singing voice, if properly managed, *swings* more than an awful lot of vocalists. As you may know, most jazz men like two singers—Frankie and Ella. With a poet who understands what is going on, they are not at the mercy of a vocalist who wants just to vocalize and who looks on the band as a necessary evil at best. Too, the emotional complexity of good poetry provides the musician with continuous creative stimulus, but at the same time gives him the widest possible creative freedom.

All this requires skill. Like if you just want to blow a lot of crazy words, man, if you think jazz is jungle music while the missionary soup comes to a boil, if you believe in the jazz myth of the hipster, you are going to fall on your face. Charlie Parker, or many younger men, are just as sophisticated artists as T. S. Eliot, and in some cases better, and have a lot more kinship with Couperin than with the King of the Cannibal Isles. And the combination of jazz and poetry requires good poetry, competent recitation, everybody in the group really digging what everybody else is doing,

and, of course, real tasty music. Then it's great, and everybody loves it, specially you, baby.

KENNETH REXROTH AND DAVID MELTZER (INTERVIEW DATE 1971)

SOURCE: Rexroth, Kenneth, and David Meltzer. Excerpts from "Kenneth Rexroth (1971)." In *The San Francisco Poets,* by David Meltzer, pp. 42-44. New York: Ballantine, 1971.

In the following excerpts from an interview, Rexroth discusses the genesis of mixing jazz elements with poetry, the evolution of the American jazz scene, and how the practice of mixing jazz and poetry came to define Beat writings.

[Meltzer]: Would it be possible to talk about the poetry and jazz? For instance, when did you actually begin experimenting with it?

[Rexroth]: When I was a young kid in my teens. I ran a place in Chicago, with a couple of girls, called the Green Mask. We used to have poetry readings there all the time. The girls were a couple of carny and show-business women, and the Green Mask was a hangout for show-business people. One of those old-time places where everybody goes after the show, where people get up and sing. Maxwell Bodenheim (who couldn't write for sour owlshit) and Langston Hughes and myself used to do poetry and jazz with a Chicago group, the Austin High Gang.

Dave Tough was the youngest member of the group and was himself a poet. Dave Tough was just about the first hipster. He was a head, and most of the time lived with gay women, and he wrote poetry—real far-out poetry. There was another drummer, whose name I forget, who lives in Florida now, who has Dave's poetry. I have tried to get at it. I turned Barney Rosset on to it, but I don't know what happened. It wasn't amateur illiterate stuff. Dave Tough was, of course, the greatest organic drummer . . . the only musician, except Mary Lou Williams, who went from the old-time jazz to the new-time jazz. Nobody else did.

I remember hearing Pee Wee Russell playing "Blue Monk" recently . . .

Yeah, but played in that strange Pee Wee way. I mean, the thing about Dave Tough is that he moved from Chicago jazz into modern jazz. He was in the first Herd with Woody Herman, for instance, and through it all became a thoroughly modern drummer. He was certainly as interesting as Roach or even Elvin Jones.

Later, in the John Reed Club we used to do a certain amount of revolutionary verse. I did a thing with Louis Aragon's "Red Front" . . . and then it all sorta died. Jazz died. There was very little action in jazz for years.

See, the great problem, is that to do a thing really well in the first place, the poet has to know a great deal about music, either play an instrument or be able to write music or both. He should have some idea about what is happening. Then the band has to rehearse. You don't just get up and blow. And if you lived in San Francisco, the better bands were not available because they were on tour. The musicians were moving around all the time. That's why we started in The Cellar, because the owners were the band. The piano player (Bill Weisjahn) and the drummer (Sonny Wayne) were the owners. And Bruce Lippincott on tenor . . . they were the house band. Other musicians came and went and played with the band. (Mingus and I did something a long time ago in The Black Cat during the war, just for fun one night.) As soon as Ferlinghetti did it, then Patchen brought out his record with a highly trained group. Mingus and Langston Hughes played the Five Spot in New York after I did, and I understand it was very successful.

Two things happened during the Beat Generation time. The hucksters couldn't understand it at all. I remember having a conference with a record company, with Laughlin and the New Directions people, about marketing Patchen's record. The executives of the company didn't know what they had at all. They didn't know how to sell it. The only thing that was selling at all was this Ken Nordine record . . . which was to us what Rod McKuen is to Ginsberg. A strictly commercial scene.

Steve Allen got that same idea. I don't know how he formed his friendship with Kerouac. I was booked into the Village Vanguard, and Kerouac recruited the gig. They throw you out of the Musicians' Union for doing something like that, but he went to Max Gordon and recruited the gig. He said it would help build up my show. Well, he was pissy-ass drunk every night, vomited on the piano, and made a general ass of himself, and Max said to me, "Look, I'll buy your contract." Steve was very upset. I said no to Max (Max started out in life as an anarchist poet; very few people know that.) Well, this started a thing so that in every Greenwich Village coffee shop and bar for about two years, all kinds of bums with pawnshop saxophones put together with scotch tape, and some other guy with something called poetry, were, like, you know, blowing poetry, man, dig? And it was absolutely unmitigated crap. It killed the whole thing. It had a terribly bad effect. There

wasn't anything like it in San Francisco because we had done the thing in San Francisco . . . People knew it, people knew all about it, even though there was an awful lot of trash at the Coffee Gallery, but by and large the music was better and the poetry was better too. But the stuff in New York was ridiculous, and of course it's that whole New York commercial scene. That was all it was for. To make the tourist go to Greenwich Village. You went down there where the first miniskirts were worn, and the miniskirted chicks were waitresses, and you got yourself a free grope, and you listened to free jazz and poetry done by a couple of stumblebums who weren't being paid anything, and it killed the whole thing. Then Lipton in Southern California staged the first big show. It was very successful, Shorty Rogers heading one group with me and Freddy Katz heading the other. Lipton, Stu Perkoff, and some others. This was quite a show. And it ran for weeks and drew all kinds of people and made all kinds of bread. The musicians were top musicians.

I was always luckier than anybody else because I knew more about what I was doing. I got top musicians. The people I had working with me at the Five Spot were part of the Blakey organization: Bobby Timmons, Doug Watkins, and the star of those days, Donald Byrd, and Elvin Jones on drums, and then Pepper Adams on baritone. The same in Chicago. The band I worked with up and down the coast was built around Brew Moore, who was a Lester Young-type tenor. He was very good for Kansas City soul. An awful lot of work went into this, long rehearsals. I always worked with head-arrangements. Patchen worked with stuff that was all written down.

But you discover that jazz audiences don't know shit from wild honey . . . and that includes a lot of the musicians. One of the things that I did, and still do, is done against Eric Satie's "Gymnopédie No. 1." It is called "This Night Only." People always think it is a George Shearing number. I used to do a thing with a Neruda poem to a 12/8 which was the essence of Jimmy Yancey, of boogie-woogie. Yet they didn't know it was Latin music. Dig? They were jazz habitués. In the Five Spot at least one night a week. That's one of the things that's heartbreaking about jazz.

Today, you have a highly trained audience which has grown up listening to, you name it, Judy Collins, Joan Baez, Pete Seeger. They have good taste in rock, which is why they put down most rock now because it has been debauched. You have a trained audience, which you did not have in the day of bop.

People still say the most absurd things. "You know, that Charlie Parker is polyrhythmic and atonal." Oh, my ass! I mean, there isn't anything in Charlie Parker that isn't in Beethoven!

WILLIAM EVERSON (ESSAY DATE 1980)

Everson, William. "Rexroth: Shaker and Maker." In *For Rexroth*, edited by Geoffrey Gardner, pp. 23-6. New York: Ark, 1980.

In the following essay, Everson lauds Rexroth, offering his personal recollection of the author's life and works.

I first heard of Kenneth Rexroth in the late Thirties when friends in Fresno told me about this radical poet on the picket lines in San Francisco. I didn't meet him, however, till World War II, when I headed up an arts program in a conscientious objector's camp at Waldport, Oregon. He wrote praising what we were doing and invited me to visit when next I came south. I found him a very winning personality and instantly fell under his spell. For his part he presented my work to James Laughlin of New Directions which led to my first national publication. Though I was neither the first nor the last to benefit by his discernment, it goes without saying that it was for me the most telling instance of what I would naturally come to recognize as a remarkable nose for talent!

After the War I moved to the Bay Area when Kenneth was welding together the nucleus of the movement that would surface ten years later as the San Francisco Renaissance, ushering in the Beat Generation which would itself usher in the Sixties, decade of confrontations and revolt, and change the lifestyle of American youth as radically as it changed the practice of contemporary poetry.

This movement did not take at its inception because the country was too preoccupied with post war problems: the cold war was freezing down and the McCarthy era was warming up. Though we did gain some national notoriety from a blast in *Harper's* called "The New Cult of Sex and Anarchy," there was no real recognition, and the movement dissolved before it could jell. It would take the passing of world crisis and the arrival of the bland Eisenhower years to provide the complacency for its revolt to be effective. It would also take the arrival in San Francisco of East Coast voices like Ginsberg and Kerouac to deepen the combustibility and extend the range. Then the media, always on the lookout for the sensational, would finally take notice. The Beat Generation was picked up by *Time* and *Life* magazines and as-

siduously promulgated. *Life*'s feature on the Beats was called "The Only Rebellion Around," as if its editors were praying for some sign, any sign, of youthful dissent. The Sixties were the answer to that prayer, and with an awesome vengeance. People had scoffed when Rexroth called *Howl* "the confession of faith of a generation," but ten years later they were not scoffing anymore, and their prayers were choking in their throats.

All this was the product of an intense group dynamic, but it could never have happened but for the presence of a single man. That honor is usually accorded to William Carlos Williams, who is the ranking poet of open form in this country, whereas Rexroth has never received his due as a poet. But there are many reasons why Williams could not have engineered the revolt that Rexroth did, though Williams sought it, at least in literature, every bit as long.

For Williams was too exclusively literary. True, he was a professional physician who identified with his caste, simply not having the time for extracurricular activity except for his own writing. But his instincts were essentially apolitical, where Rexroth's were gut-level political. Rexroth was a radical from his youth and had earned his spurs on the picket lines of San Francisco, which brings up another important difference. Williams' region, Rutherford and the Passaic, lacks the charisma of San Francisco and Big Sur: it is too urbanized to evoke the inceptive environmental passion. Also Rexroth is a profoundly religious man while Williams was doggedly agnostic. Rexroth caught the awakening religious vibration and espoused it—the first time I ever heard the name of Martin Buber was from Kenneth's lips. Also San Francisco is the gateway to the Orient and Rexroth extolled Pacific Basin culture, translating Chinese and Japanese poetry into the vital American verse idiom. Moreover, Rexroth is erotic in a way Williams never was. His graphic imagination was on the wavelength of the future sexual liberation. Then too his pacifism and anarchism prefigured the anti-war and anti-establishment Sixties, and helped bring them into being. This summation shows that no one standing on the threshold as elder statesman sums up in his person so much of what was approaching as Rexroth did. He needed only to express it with sufficient force to initiate the wave of the future.

And the gifts of expression were not lacking in him. He is a powerful spokesman for any cause he espouses. A born journalist, he has a flair for vigorous public speech and the guts to speak out in unequivocal terms. He has fantastic intellectual and moral courage, taking on the establishment and throwing it on the defensive through the sheer force of his invective. His rhetoric is savage, sometimes shockingly so, but it is never ineffectual.

Consequently, his career has been stormy. His faults are the excesses of his virtues and he quarrels with his friends as readily as he clobbers his enemies. He demands unwavering loyalty and, poets being what they are, that is not always forthcoming. He tends to drop the movement he has fostered as soon as it shows signs of fragmenting. His precipitate departure for Europe in 1949 insured the eclipse of the first wave of the Renaissance, and it is well known how he turned against the Beat Generation when he returned from his second sojourn in Europe a decade later, enabling Charles Olson of the Black Mountain group to capture the new literary incentive with a questionable dialectic.

But his constitutional restlessness could not jeopardize the work he actually accomplished. He touched the nerve of the future and more than any other voice in the movement called it into being. Though others picked up his mantle and received the plaudits, it remains true that today

we enjoy the freedom of expression and lifestyle we actually possess largely because he convinced us that it was not only desirable but possible, and inspired us to make it be.

GENERAL COMMENTARY

WILLIAM CARLOS WILLIAMS (REVIEW DATE APRIL 1957)

SOURCE: Williams, William Carlos. "Two New Books by Kenneth Rexroth." *Poetry* 90, no. 1 (April 1957): 180-90.

In the following excerpted review, Williams praises Rexroth's In Defense of the Earth.

The technical problem of what to do with the modern poetic line has been solved by Kenneth Rexroth by internal combustion! Whether that can be said to be activated by atomic fission or otherwise is immaterial. The line, in Rexroth's opinion, is to be kept intact no matter if it may be true, as the painters have shown, that any part of a poem (or painting) may stand for the poem if it is well made; therefore if anything at all is done with it, keeping it intact, it must give at the seams, it must spread its confinements to make more room for the thought. We have been beaten about the ears by all the loose talk about "free verse" until Rexroth has grown tired of it.

But the problem still remains. If you are intent on getting rid of conventional verse what are you going to accept in its place? It is purely a matter of how you are going to handle the meter. Forget for a moment the meaning of the poems in this book, *In Defense of the Earth,* which is not, I think, a good title, the poet has ignored all formal line divisions save by the use of an axe.

The first ten or fifteen poems trespass perilously close upon sentimentality, they can be passed over at once as of mere personal interest to the poet himself, no matter how deeply experienced, having to do with individuals of his family. With **"A Living Pearl,"** the general interest may be said to begin, the technical and ideational interest that is inherent in the poems (there is not room enough in the pages of *Poetry* to quote the poem in full):

"A LIVING PEARL"

At sixteen I came West, riding
Freights on the Chicago, Milwaukee
And St. Paul, the Great Northern,

The Northern Pacific.
A job as helper to a man

. . . . .

Tonight,
Thirty years later, I walk
Out of the deserted miner's
Cabin in Mono Pass, under
The full moon and the few large stars.

And so it goes for about seventy-five lines. It is written as verse, the initial letter of every line is capitalized as in Marlow or Lope de Vega or Edna St. Vincent Millay. But there the similarity to any verse form with which I am familiar ceases. It is a sequence we are more familiar with in prose: the words are direct, without any circumlocution, no figure of speech is permitted to intervene between the meaning of the words and the sense in which they are to be understood.

There is no inversion of the phrase. The diction is correct to the idiom in which the poet speaks, a language "which cats and dogs can read." But it is a language unfamiliar to the ordinary poetry reader. Poems are just not written in those words.

More serious is the question as to whether or not, since poems are universally thought to be musical, Rexroth has any ear for music. And if so what constitutes his music.

Can the lines be counted—forget for the moment the prosy diction? It may have been put down purposely to subvert any poetic implication in the lines that it is associated with the lies of the ordinary poem in the usual facilely lilting measures. This American author is dedicated to the truth. To hell with tuneful cadences in the manner, let us say, of Robert Burns or T. S. Eliot or Rimbaud at least while the world is being cheated and starved and befouled.

Rexroth is a moralist with his hand at the trigger ready to fire at the turn of a hair. But he's a poet, and a good one, for all that. So as to the music of his lines let us not be too hasty. As a translator of the Chinese lyrics of Tu Fu his ear is finer than that of anyone I have ever encountered. It has been conclusively proved to my ear, at least, that if he does not give himself to our contemporary building of the line he doesn't want to soil himself as all others are doing.

Toward the end of this book of eighty-odd pages, after that fine poem, "A Living Pearl," with its unfamiliar turns of phrase, there are some shorter pieces or longer ones broken into shorter subsections (like the one to Dylan Thomas) which are arresting by the directness of their speech: by the way, when I attempt to measure the stresses in one of his typical lines, which are short, I find that there are for the most part three. The pace is uniformly iambic, using a variable foot according to the American idiom.

The poems themselves are the importance. Their moral tone is stressed, except in the translations from the Japanese at the end. The book's seriousness, sting, and satiric punch dominate these pages. A miscellany of bitter stabs masquerading as, and meant to be, nursery rhymes, Mother Goose, a-b-c's and other accounts, scathing denunciations of our society which would have done credit to a Daumier or a Goya: "A Bestiary, For My Daughters Mary and Katharine"; "Murder Poem No. 74321"; "Portrait of the Author as a Young Anarchist"—a grieving memorial to Vanzetti and others; and another, "Thou Shalt Not Kill," a memorial to Dylan Thomas.

The latter half of the book is a diatribe of the most comprehensive virulence. It should be posted in the clubrooms of all universities so that it could never be forgotten. For the poem is the focal point for all activity among the intellectuals of the world from New York, Paris and Helsinki. Rexroth puts down many of their names here—a lunatic fringe it may be:

They are murdering all the young men.
For half a century now, every day,

. . . . .

Stephen, Lawrence ("on his gridiron"), Robinson, Masters ("who crouched in / His law office for ruinous decades"), Lola Ridge, Jim Oppenheim, Orrick Johns, Elinor Wylie, Sara Teasdale, George Sterling, Phelps Putnam, Jack Wheelright, Donald Evans, John Gould Fletcher, Edna Millay, Bodenheim ("butchered in stinking / Squalor"), Sol Funaroff, Isidor Schneider, Claude McKay, Countee Cullen, Ezra, "that noisy man," Carnevali, etc. etc.

He may sometimes be mistaken in his choice of those to remember but that is a mere choice among individuals: his sympathies are amply justified.

He is dead,
The bird of Rhiannon.
He is dead.

You killed him, General,
Through the proper channels.
You strangled him, Le Mouton,
With your *mains étendus.*

The gulf stream smells of blood
As it breaks on the sands of Iona

And the blue rocks of Canarvon.
And all the birds of the deep sea rise up
Over the luxury liners and scream,
"You killed him! You killed him.
In your God damned Brooks Brothers suit,
You son of a bitch."

There is another memorable passage showing the sardonic temper with which the poems have been salted down. This occurs toward the end of the **"Mother Goose"** (for his daughters), and note that he treats his children with the same respect as though they had been adults at whose throats their murderous weapons are addressed. Addressing his countrymen in general he tells them:

Hide the white stone
in the left fist.
Hide the white stone
In the right fist.
I am your secret brother.
Where is the white stone?
You have swallowed it.

It may not be welcome in a review of this kind to stress an author's pointed reference to an unlovely fact. But in this case when in the text reference has been made to Martial's satyrs whose whole mood of violent attack on the corruption of his own age has been invoked by Rexroth in his own revolt and revulsion, nothing could be more appropriate to this than the following anecdote:

There were two classes of kids, and they
Had nothing in common: the rich kids
Who worked as caddies, and the poor kids
Who snitched golf balls. I belonged to the
Saving group of exceptionalists
Who, after dark, and on rainy days,
Stole out and shit in the golf holes.

Kenneth Rexroth has been an avid reader in universal literature. He is familiar with a variety of foreign languages, ancient and modern. He is familiar with the capitals of Europe, has read extensively of philosophy and the history of the social sciences. I think, as men go, there is no better read person in America. You should see his library! all his books, and most of his collected magazine articles, filed in orderly fashion for twenty or thirty years back for ready reference.

He is an authority on his subject of modern poetry. As a lecturer he is respected (and feared) throughout the academic world.

The present book, *In Defense of the Earth*, has been dedicated *To Marthe, Mary, Katharine*; his wife and daughters whom he speaks of extensively in the first part. . . .

GORDON K. GRIGSBY (ESSAY DATE FALL 1971)

SOURCE: Grigsby, Gordon K. "The Presence of Reality: The Poetry of Kenneth Rexroth." *Antioch Review* 31, no. 3 (fall 1971): 405-22.

In the following essay, Grigsby examines the style and themes of Rexroth's poems and commends them for their directness and their images, which "draw us into depths of feelings."

One of the poems in *The Phoenix and the Tortoise* (1944) is a brief elegy for Rexroth's first wife, Andree:

Now once more grey mottled buckeye branches
Explode their emerald stars,
And alders smoulder in a rosy smoke
Of innumerable buds.
I know that spring again is splendid
As ever, the hidden thrush
As sweetly tongued, the sun as vital—
But these are the forest trails we walked together,
These paths, ten years together.
We thought the years would last forever,
They are all gone now, the days
We thought would not come for us are here.
Bright trout poised in the current—
The raccoon's track at the water's edge—
A bittern booming in the distance—
Your ashes scattered on this mountain—
Moving seaward on this stream.

In its unpretentiousness, directness, clarity, in the resonance of its apparently simple natural images, in the surface casualness which at the same time evokes a rich pattern of underlying relationships—the alders smouldering, the buckeyes exploding with life against the fire-destroyed body of the young wife—the fish, animal and water-bird finding life in the water, the remembering mind seeing death there—in all these ways this poem seems to me a comparatively rare achievement in modern poetry. But you won't find it mentioned anywhere. There are quite a few others as good or better in *Natural Numbers: New and Selected Poems,* first published as a New Directions paperback in 1963, a modest selection from more that thirty years' work in a little over 100 pages. And there are scores of fine poems in *The Collected Shorter Poems* (1967), which contains all of Rexroth's poetry to date except the long poems (recently published in a companion volume) and the plays. All of this is largely unacknowledged—not by readers, but by critics. It is true that this situation is at least to some extent the result of Rexroth's deliberate choice. He writes in a recent letter:

I now make about $200 a month, slightly more, from poetry books alone. I am not in "the quarterlies" for the simple reason I have never submitted anything to any of them. I am not written up in them because I have consistently referred to them as the "pillowcase headdress school"—or in the case of *PR*—"the, as Comrade Koba so aptly put it, Left Social Fascists." I refuse permission for anthologization except for one old friend once. Me, Winters and Laura Riding, are not in anthologies by our own choice.

Such a choice must be respected, yet Rexroth has by now published a sizable body of work that presses for attention. The quality of that work deserves, I think, both a larger audience and an attentive criticism.[1]

What appears to have excluded Rexroth from serious attention and criticism between the 1940s and 1960s was not only his intransigent independence, his making a career outside groups and universities, but the unfashionableness of his style. His mature personal style, achieved in *In What Hour* (1940) and *The Phoenix and the Tortoise* is not, in his own phrase, "corn belt metaphysical." It is not much indebted to Rimbaud or Laforgue, Whitman or Eliot, Auden or Stevens. It is not even much indebted to Williams, a poet for whom Rexroth has great admiration. In an age of paradox, complexity, allusiveness, obliquity, his is a clear and natural voice.

Such a style was not easily come by. One of the interests of *The Collected Shorter Poems* is the evidence it gives that the form and language of Rexroth's mature poetry, which seems so natural, so artless, was the result of a long process of growth and self-discipline. It was not something given but something achieved. It was not the result of insulation from or complacent rejection of the qualities praised in modernist poetics. On the contrary, it was the result of an initial acceptance of almost all that was fashionable and a gradual working *through* the modish toward clarity, honesty, a personal idiom. The process is, I think, exemplary for our especially Alexandrian age.[2]

Reading through *An Autobiographical Novel,* which covers only the first twenty-two years of his life, one may be surprised by the fact that Rexroth's talent survived at all: not only was he artily precocious as both a painter and a poet, but he grew up in a hothouse intellectual-radical bohemian world, the *avant garde* world of Chicago and New York in the 1920s. In some ways, of course, this is the best environment for an adolescent who knows he's going to be an artist (as Rexroth says he knew at least as early as age 11)—open, free, knowing, racially mixed and fraternal,

cosmopolitan and, especially in politics, international, at once proletarian and elite (so Rexroth never absorbed Midwestern middle class prejudices nor had to revolt against Midwestern rawness and lack of "culture" as Pound and Eliot did). But in other ways, it is the worst—ideological and fad-ridden in everything, art, politics, philosophy, religion. It is a wonder that he didn't simply disappear—as most of his acquaintances did—into some obscure Anarcho-Syndicalist sect, into the rites of the Plumed Serpent or Anglo-Catholicism, into Dada or Theosophy. That he didn't is evidence of a certain tough reasonableness in his character, an eye for sham whether Right or Left ("the lunatic fringe of radical Chicago in those days"), an integrity that prevented him from believing easily:

> The radical disbelief which has been characteristic of all my contemporaries I shared from the beginning, but I was never led by it to embrace any of the extraordinary follies which were to become fashionable in intellectual circles in the next thirty or forty years.

His first book, however, *The Art of Worldly Wisdom* (dated 1922 in *Natural Numbers* and 1920-30 in *CSP* [*The Collected Shorter Poems*]), reveals almost all the fashionable influences a precocious artist-intellectual was exposed to in those days: the bookish abstruse diction of Eliot, Crane and the Metaphysicals ("**The Place**"); the ornate vocabulary of early Stevens ("**Phronesis**" and much of a long poem written at this time, *The Homestead Called Damascus*); the heavy sarcasm of Poundian satire ("**Into the Shandy Wilderness**"); Poundian archaisms ("**Okeanos**"); the unpunctuated dissociation and weird metaphors of Dada and Surrealism ("**Phronesis**" and "**Fundamental Disagreement with Two Contemporaries**," the latter imitating while disagreeing with Tristan Tzara and Andre Breton); the historical and mythological allusiveness of *The Waste Land* (**Homestead** [*The Homestead Called Damascus*]); the imagist sequence of spare scenes and concrete unexplained details ("**The Thin Edge of Your Pride**").

It was the last, as it turned out, combined with an early interest in Chinese, Latin and Greek translation, that pointed the way out of all this literariness. As Rexroth himself implicitly acknowledged when he made the selections for *Natural Numbers,* the only really successful poems in this first youthful volume are the simplest, most direct, most honest ones: out of some fifty pages of *The Art of Wordly Wisdom,* he selected only 21 lines, less than one page, all 21 from "**The Thin Edge of Your Pride.**" I don't mean to say that there are not lines and passages in the rest of this early work which succeed and might bear study. The point is that these poems persistently call up the response best expressed by James Dickey in *The Suspect in Poetry*:

> At one time or another, and perhaps at most times, the long-term reader of poetry must marvel at the hundreds and hundreds of lines, stanzas, themes, and whole poems which seem to be sheer effrontery to his sense of what the truth of their subjects must be or could possibly be . . . a truly remarkable amount of utter humbug, absolutely and uselessly far-fetched and complex manipulation of language.

It is a point Rexroth was to make himself in a poem written some twenty-five years after his first volume, a "**Codicil**" to *In Defense of the Earth* (1956):

> Most of the world's poetry
> Is artifice, construction.
> No one reads it but scholars.
> After a generation
> It has grown so overcooked,
> It cannot be digested.
> There is little I haven't
> Read, and dreary stuff it was.
> Lamartine—Gower—Tasso—
> Or the metaphysicals
> Of Cambridge, ancient or modern,
> And their American apes.

On the basis of the pattern revealed by *The Collected Shorter Poems,* we can conjecture about what pulled Rexroth out of artifice and the overcooked. One influence was the Spanish Civil War: several poems in his second volume, *In What Hour,* including the opening poem, deal with Spain. The effect was, I think, put simply: such material demanded humility. Its substance was so important, so humanly significant that only fidelity would serve. Instead of constantly calling attention to itself, and to the cleverness of its author, the language of these poems begins to attend to experience. Another influence—perhaps *the* influence—was life in the western mountains, the Cascades, the Rockies, the Sierra Nevada. Rexroth left Chicago for good in 1927, at the age of 22, and has lived ever since in or around San Francisco, only a few hours from mountains, wilderness and silence. No one, it seems to me, has presented the experience of those mountains with such clarity, poignancy and symbolic depth. *In What Hour* contains the first poems on this subject and among them are the finest ones in the book. One in particular, a four-page poem called

"**Toward an Organic Philosophy,**" marks the first major achievement in Rexroth's mature style.

That style, like life in the mountains, has analogues with the Chinese poets Rexroth loves. It gives form to his experience, while being faithful to "what *is*," and provides him, as it provided Tu Fu, with a valuable perspective on the violence, waste and beauty of nature and of history. Asked once to describe his style, Rexroth said:

> I've never understood why I'm a member of the *avant garde*. I write more or less like Allen Tate thinks he writes—like the great Greeks and Romans and the Chinese. . . . I try to say, as simply as I can, the simplest and most profound experiences of my life, which I think will be of significance to others on a similar level—that is, which will touch them in significant regions of their experience. And, I suppose that my whole attitude toward poetry—toward my own poetry—is to keep always before myself an objective of clarity and depth, and hope that out of this you'll get exaltation.

Clarity and depth, communication and construction, simplicity and intensity—these are, in their difficult fusion, Rexroth's overriding concerns. They are expressed in a slightly different way in the title of the selected poems, *Natural Numbers,* with its emphasis on both naturalness and form. He has long been interested in the relations between mathematics and the natural universe, "the forms Pythagoras / Sought, the organic relations / Of stone and cloud and flower / And moving planet and falling / Water." He has found, for his own art, the best expression of these organic relations, the best wedding of naturalness and form, in an unrhymed but measured verse, frequently though not always syllabic. Believing that poetry is both a construction and a communication, something "made" and something "spoken," Rexroth achieves a style that is direct, sometimes quite prosaic and plain, almost always immediate in impact, and, at the same time, formally controlled. The emphasis on construction distinguishes him from (in Pound's phrases) the "rhetorical din" and "luxurious riot" of most of what is considered *avant garde*; the emphasis on communication distinguishes him from the academic modernists who write poems for each other in the Quarterlies. The result is an unfashionable style all around, neither obscure and over-intellectual, nor wild and bombastic. The nearest comparisons among modern poets are, I suppose, Williams at his clearest, Jeffers at his least rhetorical (especially in the short poems), and Lawrence, whose *Selected Poems* Rexroth edited and introduced in 1947. Here are the opening stanzas of Lawrence's "On the Balcony:"

In front of the sombre mountains, a faint, lost
    ribbon of rainbow;
And between us and it, the thunder;
And down below in the green wheat, the labor-
    ers
Stand like dark stumps, still in the green wheat.

You are near to me, and your naked feet in their
    sandals,
And through the scent of the balcony's naked
    timber
I distinguish the scent of your hair: so now the
    limber
Lightning falls from heaven.

And here is Rexroth on a similar theme, the second section of a love poem with a mathematical title, "**Inversely as the Square of Their Distances Apart . . .**":

It is warm tonight and very still.
The stars are hazy and the river—
Vague and monstrous under the fireflies—
Is hardly audible, resonant
And profound at the edge of hearing.
I can just see your eyes and wet lips.
Invisible, solemn, and fragrant,
Your flesh opens to me in secret.
We shall know no further enigma.
After all the years there is nothing
Stranger than this. We who know ourselves
As one doubled thing, and move our limbs
As deft implements of one fused lust,
Are mysteries in each other's arms.

The poem develops as a rich pattern of imagery fusing the natural and the human (as the title suggests), yet permits, through simple language, the concrete details to reveal their own depths. The medium Rexroth has achieved is almost transparent. It resembles clear water through which we see his world as he sees laurel leaves sink in a mountain pool in the opening lines of one of his finest poems, "**The Signature of All Things**":

My head and shoulders, and my book
In the cool shade, and my body
Stretched bathing in the sun, I lie
Reading beside the waterfall—
Boehme's "Signature of all Things."
Through the deep July day the leaves
Of the laurel, all the colors
Of gold, spin down through the moving
Deep laurel shade all day. They float
On the mirrored sky and forest
For a while, and then, still slowly
Spinning, sink through the crystal deep
Of the pool to its leaf gold floor.

This is precise syllabic verse, eight syllables to the line, and in its ease, clarity and beauty, represents the kind of art that conceals its art, thereby achieving qualities frequently lost in modern poetry. Some of these qualities are classi-cal; some are Oriental. It seems to me true to say that Rexroth is the first considerable poet in English to have really absorbed and made his own the dominant qualities of Chinese poetry, its tone and spirit. Pound, who helped to make this possible, wanted to make the techniques his own without absorbing the Chinese tone and attitude toward experience: he Westernized—or American-ized—everything he touched. Rexroth is less imperial, and his ability to learn from the East by yielding to it contributes to his achieving—after comprehending, absorbing "modernism"—both naturalness and form, "clarity and depth," out of which sometimes comes "exaltation."

When I dragged the rotten log
From the bottom of the pool,
It seemed heavy as stone.
I let it lie in the sun
For a month; and then chopped it
Into sections, and split them
For kindling, and spread them out
To dry some more. Late that night
After reading for hours,
While moths rattled at the lamp—
The saints and philosophers
On the destiny of man—
I went out on my cabin porch,
And looked up through the black forest
At the swaying islands of stars.
Suddenly I saw at my feet,
Spread on the floor of night, ingots
Of quivering phosphorescence,
And all about were scattered chips
Of pale cold light that was alive.

This is a poetry of reality, a poetry of the world that exists beyond metaphor and opinion, beyond—ultimately—all poetry and all language. It is one measure of Rexroth's style that, within the limits of language, it brings us frequently into the presence of the real.

Although this poetry speaks clearly for itself and usually carries its learning lightly, the simplicity often has complex meanings, the learning is there, and the poems as a whole develop "more or less systematically," in Rexroth's own phrase, "a definite point of view." Publication of *The Collected Shorter Poems* provides the opportunity not only for a consideration of the development of the style, but also for a comprehensive view of the substance of Rexroth's poetry—central themes, their interrelationships, their significance. The volume contains, first, twenty pages of new poems, previously unpublished, under the title "**Gödel's Proof**" (1965); then, all of the shorter poems (except some translations which are now available in other books) from six of Rexroth's seven published books of Poetry, arranged in chronological order: *The Art of Worldly Wisdom* (1920-30), *In What Hour* (1940), *The Phoenix and the Tortoise* (1944), *The Signature of All Things* (1949), *In Defense of the Earth* (1956), and *Natural Numbers* (1963). It also includes excerpts from the seventh book, a long poem entitled *The Dragon and the Unicorn* (1952)—nine poems which can stand alone and were first published separately in *Natural Numbers*. A comparison of *The Collected Shorter Poems* with its sources reveals that there has been no revision of language or of lines, but considerable revision of titles and some rearrangement of the order of poems in each volume.[3]

Rexroth is not a poet of the academic scene but neither is he a poet of tormented confession, family agony, drugged visions, insanity, or existential *angst*. He is not a poet of hallucination, real or synthetic, private or public. This does not mean, however, that he is simply impervious to modern confusion, suffering and despair. As a political radical he is acutely aware of these realities, but as a scholar and artist he knows they are not peculiarly modern. That knowledge, that long view of nature and history, combined with an acceptance of the simplest and most profound emotions, gives him not hope, not faith, but a rare kind of intellectual courage. In the preface to *The Phoenix and the Tortoise,* he notes that his classical translations and paraphrases, "mostly from Hellenistic, Byzantine and Late Roman sources," express "a sense of desperation and abandon in the face of a collapsing system of cultural values." This desperation is the background for his own work: he sees clearly the disorder and contradictions of Western civilization in the twentieth century which found expression in *The Waste Land,* "The Second Coming," the "tragedy and evil farce" of Kafka, Beckett, Ionesco, Genet. But he is also aware that, barring total holocaust, men have survived such collapses, or endured them with dignity and a clear-eyed confrontation of death. He is aware that in the midst of desperation and abandon, it is a characteristic of wisdom, as Thoreau said, not to do desperate things.

Thoreau also said, "Let nothing come between you and the light." No doubt an impossible demand. But in the ethos of that demand we come closest, I think, to Rexroth's own point of view. Writing about the poems of *In Defense of the Earth,* he said:

Many of these poems deal with similar locations and events, seeking over and over again for the changing forms of an unchanging significance in stars, insects, mountains, daughters. They do not

of course try to answer, "Why am I here?" "Why is it out there?"—but *to snare the fact that is the only answer,* the only meaning of present or presence. (emphasis added)

The emphasis here is not only on the concrete, but on disciplined perception, a poetry of fact or, more accurately, the vision of fact: the ordinary world seen with compelling clarity. Rexroth has called such sight the most "supernatural" of all visions and, in an essay on the poetry of D. H. Lawrence, has defined it in purely aesthetic terms: "Bad poetry always suffers from the same defects: synthetic hallucination and artifice. Invention is not poetry. Invention is defense, the projection of pseudopods out of the ego to ward off the 'other.' Poetry is vision, the pure act of sensual communion and contemplation."

I have said that one of Rexroth's great virtues as a poet and as an example for our age is his fusion in a personal style of qualities from both East and West. These are qualities not only of language but of mind and spirit. In his own words, "the lyric poets of Greece . . . and the Chinese have shaped me for better or worse as a poet, and they have given me whatever philosophy of life I have." One of the essentials of that philosophy, and one of the ways in which his work differs from almost all Western poetry since the Greeks, including most modern poetry, is its full acceptance of time, mortality, the flowing world. Like the *Tao te Ching*, Rexroth accepts, in his own words, "the movement of the universe—not from Infinity to Eternity, but just endless." A poetry of fact must reflect the most ineluctable of all facts: "everything flows." Everything. There is no still point of the turning world or, more precisely, there is no metaphysical still point, only psychological stillnesses, moments not of transcendence—though they seem transcendent—but of immanence, which Rexroth describes as "fleeting eternities." This does not mean that he denies that nostalgia for the Absolute, that intransigent longing for the timeless which is so characteristic of Western culture from Plato to Yeats, Eliot, Pound, Auden, Muir; but he understands that it is wishful. Here is "**Another Spring.**"

The seasons revolve and the years change
With no assistance or supervision.
The moon, without taking thought,
Moves in its cycle, full, crescent, and full.

The white moon enters the heart of the river;
The air is drugged with azalea blossoms;
Deep in the night a pine cone falls;
Our campfire dies out in the empty mountains.

The sharp stars flicker in the tremulous branches;
The lake is black, bottomless in the crystalline
     night;
High in the sky the Northern Crown
Is cut in half by the dim summit of a snow peak.

O heart, heart, so singularly
Intransigent and corruptible,
Here we lie entranced by the starlit water,
And moments that should each last forever
Slide unconsciously by us like water.

Nature is time: its Being is its Becoming; its Becoming is its Being. It moves without supervision, without an overseeing Mind, Logos, God, or Soul. In Chinese terms, the Tao is "of itself so," spontaneous, effortless as the moonlight entering the heart of the river. Like the Mahayana Buddhist "Void," the term Tao is a conventional sign, a word for what is beyond words: the endlessly creating, conserving, destroying "way" of the universe. In this poem the human heart, so singularly subject to change and death because so conscious of them, is unreconciled. But Rexroth emphasizes both the wishfulness and the ambiguity of its longing. He sees, with Stevens, that in fact "death is the mother of beauty." In a phrase borrowed from Blake for the title of one of his finest and most significant poems, **Time Is the Mercy of Eternity.** For Rexroth, the temporal, relative world, with all its various levels of being, is the *only* world, its very relativity a kind of blessing and, if we accept it, the only kind of "salvation."

Far away the writhing city
Burns in a fire of transcendence
And commodities. The bowels
Of men are wrung between the poles
Of meaningless antithesis.
The holiness of the real
Is always there, accessible
In total immanence.
                    —"Time Is the Mercy"

By a waterfall in the Sierra Nevada in early spring, "the high passes closed with snow," "Alone there / In the midst of a hundred mountains," Rexroth experiences for a time the holiness of the real and drinks the water of the flowing world:

The moon lifts into
The cleft of the mountains and a
Cloud of light pours around me like
Blazing perfume. When the moon has
Passed on and the owls are loud in
My ears again, I kneel and drink
The cold, sweet, twisting water.

It is in the purity and completeness of his acceptance of change, and his concomitant rejection of all the tiresome clichés expressing fear of

time and death which are the primary stock in trade of Western poetry, the inventions by which the imagination tries to deny the plain facts—it is here that Rexroth achieves a poetry which is especially fresh and valuable. He also achieves, as compared with the "writhing city," a particular kind of serenity. Its source, I think, is his awareness that acceptance of the flux as reality is not surrender to mere chaos. He understands that the alternatives posed by Western thought—either absolute order or complete incoherence, either "Law" or anarchy, either God or chance—are not the only ones, do not exhaust the real, are in fact nothing but reifications and thus "poles / Of meaningless antithesis." As Western science has discovered in this century, not only in genetics and the biological sciences but also in particle physics and in mathematics itself (Gödel's proof), once the sanctum of the Absolute, none of the "laws" of nature is absolute; all are abstractions of statistical probability. We are gradually admitting that we live in a world of relative not Euclidian order, that the space-time continuum, like the Tao, reveals patterns, rhythms, organic relations, but all are imperfect, geometrically speaking, and all are impermanent. None is *exactly* repeatable. The processes of nature unite (but even that suggests a prior separation)—*are a unity of* freedom and form, sameness and difference, order and . . . but our language is hopelessly polar and simplistic, an instrument, as Bergson, Nagarjuna and the Zen masters have said, for manipulating rather than for understanding the world. This concept of relative order, of form in nature which is recognized as form yet is not symmetrical, resembles the concept of *li* (literally, the pattern of grain in jade), the basic concept of form in the Chinese philosophy of nature. As Joseph Needham in *Science and Civilization in China* (a book Rexroth once reviewed), F. S. C. Northrop and L. L. Whyte have shown, this concept of form is now congruent with the growing edge of Western thought.

Rexroth sees, then, that "the annual and diurnal patterns hold" (**We Come Back**), and repeatedly emphasizes their concrete manifestations: sun, seasons, moon, earth, the lives of men, insects, beasts, daughters, stars. In his remarkable nature poems—**Toward an Organic Philosophy,**" "**The Signature of All Things,**" "**Hojoki,**" "**Time Spirals,**" "**Elegy on Encountering the Trouble of the World,**" "**Time Is the Mercy of Eternity,**" to name a few of the best—he sees nature without "invention," without forcing significance upon it, without falsifying its "Thereness," and he places man in the rhythmic flow of life and time. He snares "the fact that is the only meaning of present or presence." And this is the source of the haunting serenity we feel in these poems, for Rexroth confronts the fact without fear and without extravagant hopes: man is mortal but both he and "his virtues are a part of the universe, like falling water and standing stone and drifting mist."

There is a crucial passage for our understanding of this whole point of view in Rexroth's long, sympathetic but finally unsubmissive essay on Martin Buber:

> As a poem, *I and Thou* is very beautiful. But it is [its] metaphysical greed which removes it from the category of the highest art. There is amongst men no absolute need. The realization of this is what makes Homer and the Greek tragedians so much sounder a Bible than the Old or New Testaments. Love does not last forever, friends betray each other, beauty fades, the mighty stumble in blood and their cities burn. The ultimate values are love and friendship and courage and magnanimity and grace, but it is a narrow ultimate, and lasts only a little while, contingent on the instability of men and the whims of Nature. . . . Like life, it is Helen's tragedy that gives her her beauty or gives Achilles and Agamemnon their nobility. Any art which has a happy ending in reserve in Infinity is, just to that degree, cheating. It is, I think, this pursuit of the absolute . . . which vitiates most Western art.

Courage and magnanimity and grace, "song and dance, the mutual love of the community—these are the values; they are beautiful precisely because they are not absolute." For Rexroth, man is no more an alien and outcast in the universe ("abandoned" in existentialist terminology) than he is its lord and master. These supposed opposites are actually two faces of the same thing, the loss of a fantasy lordship producing an equally fantastic self-debasement. Human values are only human but they are not created *ex nihil*. They have natural sources in the will to live and can unite man in a spiritual way with the vast creative process of the universe.

These are the themes of the love poems, the political poems, the poems of historical awareness and the imagination of disaster. From his autobiography and from the poems of the late '30s and early '40s, it appears that Rexroth's political commitment to radicalism came second only to his commitment to art in the pattern of his intellectual development. This radicalism, which Rexroth calls "only a development of that idealist anarchism which has been characteristic of American thought since its beginnings" (presumably in Paine, Jefferson, Thoreau, Whitman), and which

was during the last part of the nineteenth and first part of the twentieth centuries an international movement, is expressed implicitly in almost everything Rexroth has written and explicitly in poems on the Spanish Civil War, Sacco and Vanzetti, Emma Goldman, Alexander Berkman. Such anarchism has not fared well in the political arena during the past half century, the decades of Rexroth's maturity, unable, apparently, to compete with Marxist authoritarianism as a revolutionary movement on one hand or with the authoritarian centralized bourgeois state on the other. Aware of Bakunin's prophetic criticism of Marx, this radicalism finds little to choose between State Socialism and State Capitalism. Rexroth therefore takes the Russian Revolution as a fatal event for the anarchist revolutionary movement, with the execution of Sacco and Vanzetti in 1927 and the defeat of the Anarcho-Syndicalists in Barcelona during the Spanish Civil War as successive marks of its disintegration. In the face of these events, anarchism has seemed politically irrelevant. With what looks like "historical inevitability," the community disappears into the State all over the world, and any combination of Thoreau's individualism with Whitman's fraternity and Bakunin's social justice has seemed as quixotic as the Luddite's attack on machinery.

But Rexroth did not recant. He did not accommodate to *Realpolitik* of whatever kind; he did not become an apologist for *any* police State. He continued to fight what he called more than a decade ago, and perhaps prophetically, a "guerrilla war" against the domination of man by men. In a poem entitled "**The Bad Old Days**," published in 1956, he recalls his first visit in 1918 to the slums around the stockyards in Chicago, where he walked through the squalid streets "looking shyly" into the people's exhausted, starved and broken faces. Out of his misery and anger, he took a vow. Today, the poem concludes, "the evil is clean" but it is everywhere, and "the misery, and the / Anger, and the vow are the same." Like Orwell's, such radicalism resists the temptation of abstraction and absolutism and retains the virtues—so important for the artist—of humaneness, freedom and openness to experience. It also endures. Since it is not sanctioned by theology, metaphysics or historical determinism, it is not discredited by historical "failure." It is only human, only a moral ideal, true inheritor as Bakunin knew of the cause of liberty, equality and fraternity, but an ideal grounded in flesh and blood, the love of individuals. In these days of student revolt, communes, attempts toward an alternate culture, this ideal seems more relevant than ever.

Rexroth's political view cannot be separated from the other themes of his work. The love of individuals rather than abstractions is central to the love poems and the theme of sacramental marriage, influenced by D. H. Lawrence, Martin Buber, and Albert Schweitzer. In **The Phoenix and the Tortoise**, where this theme first explicitly appears, Rexroth remarks that he found in sacramental marriage a source of values in the midst of the disintegration of traditional culture. The aim, he says, is to show how from full love of one other person the self can develop a reverence for all life. "The process as I see it goes something like this: from abandon to erotic mysticism, from erotic mysticism to the ethical mysticism of universal responsibility—from the Dual to the Other. These poems might well be dedicated to D. H. Lawrence." He notes, in regard to "ethical mysticism," that the long title poem of the volume "might well be dedicated to Albert Schweitzer," whose phrase "reverence for life" Rexroth has called "the only kind of religion likely to outlast this century." In addition, the poems make the basic emphasis of Buber's *I and Thou*—the relationship of person to person rather than person to thing—but without Buber's effort to transcendentalize the person. Rexroth's love poems are of the earth and flesh. Their mysticism is natural, not supernatural. They focus on the erotic relationship in all its physical beauty and contingency and the best of them—**"When We with Sappho," "Floating," "Inversely as the Square of Their Distances Apart," "Incarnation," "Between Myself and Death"**—achieve a fine, frank sensuality without constantly calling attention to their frankness. Direct, natural if sometimes a bit formal in phrasing, without either idealizing or debasing the woman, they are among those comparatively rare love poems that actually communicate pleasure and joy.

> As I undress you, your pupils are black, wet,
> Immense, and your skin ivory and humid.
> Move softly, move hardly at all, part your thighs,
> Take me slowly while our gnawing lips
> Fumble against the humming blood in our
>   throats.
> Move softly, do not move at all, but hold me,
> Deep, still, deep within you, while time slides
>   away,
> As this river slides beyond this lily bed,
> And the thieving moments fuse and disappear
> In our mortal, timeless flesh.
>
> —"Floating"

Such love leads to an identification of the self with what Rexroth calls "the tragic unity of creative process"—tragic because love and death, creation and destruction, light and dark are inseparable phases of the whole process of the world. But it cannot lead beyond that process; it cannot lead us out of the world. Love is "essentially a relationship," and though it can be made the most important value in "the shifting and flowing of contingency," it cannot be made absolute. Just as mortality gives life its value, so relativity gives love its meaning and its pathos:

> It seems to me that the fullest realization of the self comes in the acceptance of the limits of contingency. It is harder, but more ennobling, to love a wife as another human being, fugitive as oneself, than it is to carry on imaginary conversations with an imaginary Absolute. The demand to be loved totally, irrevocably, destroys first the love and then the lover. It is a kind of depersonalization—the opposite pole, but exactly like prostitution.

Not an absolute, then, but a way of living fully, deeply, in the flowing world, the I-Thou relationship is, for Rexroth, the basis of true community. "The community emerges out of the I-Thou relationship, not conversely," a point which gets to the heart of Rexroth's mature radicalism and indicates the ground of his rejection of both crude individualism (in practice the power of the few) and collectivism (in theory the power of the many). In this regard, he quotes Buber with approval: "Individualism understands only a part of man, collectivism understands man only as a part; neither advances to the wholeness of man." The emphasis in the political poems—for example, **"Requiem for the Spanish Dead," "Light upon Waldheim," "Climbing Milestone Mountain," "Autumn in California," "For Eli Jacobson"**—is therefore on the I-Thou relationship among those committed to the radical cause. Though the cause seems to have failed, the community of men and women brought together by the cause has value in itself. This is why Rexroth can say at the end of his poem to Eli Jacobson,

> If the good days never come,
> We will not know. We will not care.
> Our lives were the best. We were the
> Happiest men alive in our day.

The means, then, justify the end, not conversely. For the end may never be achieved. Indeed, Rexroth is acutely aware that except perhaps in scattered enclaves, the goal seems farther off than ever, the true community more remote, the ideal lost in the violence, bloodshed and dehumanization of the twentieth century. In a 1963 poem he comes down from the Rockies into Ogden, Utah, and finds

> Harvest hands and gandy dancers
> With broken hands and broken
> Faces sleeping off cheap wine drunks
> In the scorching heat, while tired
> Savage-eyed whores paraded the street.
> —**"Fish Peddler and Cobbler"**

But in the midst of violence, in the midst of nuclear terror, there remains an affirmation of life in simple emotions, in the beautiful patterns of the world, in persistent political idealism, and in moments of union with the holiness of the real. "The blackbird / Sings and the baby laughs, midway / In the century of horror." Among the most rich and moving of these poems compounded of joy and disaster, nature and history, almost all of them from the 1950s and 60s, are **"Golden Section," "Empty Mirror"** the sequence of seven poems called **"The Lights in the Sky are Stars,"** the poems from Aix-en-Provence, and **"Venice—May Day."** Some of these express a kind of tragic beauty, a calm, clear-eyed confrontation of the darkness with, at the same time, an undestroyed spiritual grace, which is uncommon in any age, and especially so in ours. In early summer, "like an opal, in Venice," sitting with his little daughter in San Giorgio Maggiore, listening to the monks sing vespers, Rexroth remembers that six years ago, on another May Day, in another place, bombers were practicing overhead. "They are still there." Now, above the music of the *Magnificat,* "one / Of them breaks the sound barrier / With a shuddering belch of hate," and he thinks of the endless, fraudulent conferences on disarmament going on across the Alps. The well-dressed delegates, the Ministers of State, the Secretaries of Defense, the Presidents, the Premiers, the Party Chairmen—"the men whose names are great"—are

> pushing all this pretty
> Planet, Venice, and Palladio,
> And you and me, and the golden
> Sun, nearer and nearer to
> Total death. Nothing can stop them.
> Soon it will be over. But
> This music, and the incense,
> And the solemn columned thought,
> And the poem of a virgin,
> And you and me, and Venice
> In the May Day evening on the
> Fiery waters, we have our own
> Eternity, so fleeting that they
> Can never touch it, or even
> Know that it has passed them by.

With the kind of art that conceals art, Rexroth's best poems yield a complex pleasure. In

their directness, they give the pleasure of communication, recognition, of a man speaking to be understood. At the same time their images, whether natural or human or both—the mountains, the temple at Paestum, naked lovers, Venice "in the May Day evening on the / Fiery waters"—draw us into depths of feeling. For their clarity, beauty and humanity, they make, together, one of the significant poetic achievements of our time.

Notes

1. Such criticism has scarcely begun. There are some interesting reviews, the best by two poets, William Carlos Williams, Poetry (June 1957) and William Stafford, Poetry (December 1967); but only three articles of any length, two by Lawrence Lipton, "The Poetry of Kenneth Rexroth," Poetry (June 1957) and "Notes toward an Understanding of Kenneth Rexroth with Special Attention to *The Homestead Called Damascus,*" Quarterly Review of Literature (December 1957), and one—by far the best—by Richard Foster, "The Voice of a Poet," Minnesota Review (Spring 1962). None of these exceeds nine pages.

2. I should note that Rexroth partly disagrees with this view: "I see no important difference between the different kinds of poetry I write," he said in a letter to Per Se, "—just syntax and objective. . . . I still write in all the styles I did in the twenties and thirties." The latter point is quite true, as his most recent work, *Gödel's Proof,* makes clear. My argument is that there is a difference and that almost all of his best work is in what came to be his dominant idiom.

3. Unfortunately, there is no Table of Contents, an annoying omission, only an Index of titles and first lines, therefore no easy way to determine textual facts, see the interrelationships among poems, or get a simple overview of the poet's career.

GEORGE WOODCOCK (ESSAY DATE WINTER 1983)

SOURCE: Woodcock, George. "Rage and Serenity: The Poetic Politics of Kenneth Rexroth." *Sagetrieb* 2, no. 3 (winter 1983): 73-83.

In the following essay, Woodcock discusses Rexroth's early association with anarchism, his rejection of the movement, and his ultimate reconciliation with certain aspects of its philosophy, particularly concerning ecology.

My own relationship with Kenneth Rexroth, like that of many other people, was so largely within a context of the politics of the unpolitical that when I began this article I did not realize how largely implicit, in his poetry at least, I would find the expression of his political stance. Rexroth's attitude—an idiosyncratic but completely authentic kind of anarchism—was publicly stated and well known, yet not so much written of as spoken and lived. After publishing **An Autobiographical Novel**—that strange and inventive memoir largely of the America before the great wars—in 1966,

Rexroth seemed to sustain no further interest in writing about his own life, so that there is little available in narrative form about his activities after 1927, the year in which Sacco and Vanzetti were executed. Their execution happened just after Rexroth had moved to San Francisco, which from this time would be the center of his world:

> A great cleaver cut through all the intellectual life of America. The world in which Andrée and I had grown up came forever to an end.[1]

Rexroth was then twenty-two, and he followed the above sentences, and ended *An Autobiographical Novel* by remarking, "One book of my life was closed and it was time to begin another." That second book was lived and never written, though in many ways it was the more interesting and certainly the more fulfilled part of his life, the time when he wrote the best and the most of his poetry, the time of stormy friendships and devoted fatherhood, the time when he became a literary presence in San Francisco, on the picket lines as well as in the emergent west coast literary world, the time when, as William Everson said, "his pacifism and anarchism prefigured the anti-war and anti-establishment Sixties, and helped bring them into being."[2]

Everson first encountered Rexroth during World War II. Everson was a conscientious objector, publishing a poetry magazine and little books of verse (one of mine among them) from the camp at Waldport where he had been sent to work, and Rexroth wrote to praise what he was doing, a way of expressing solidarity with his pacifism as well as his poetry. At the same time I was involved actively in the anarchist movement in Britain. I was one of the editors of *War Commentary*, the anarchist paper that preceded *Freedom*, and of the Freedom Press, which published books and pamphlets by Herbert Read, Alex Comfort and other libertarian writers of the time, and was editing my own libertarian literary magazine, *NOW*. Rexroth wrote to me also. He had assembled an anarchist circle in San Francisco, consisting of young Californian poets and artists and of older Italian and Jewish militants who were veterans of the struggles of Emma Goldman's and Carlo Tresca's days. Judging from the quantities of literature Rexroth ordered, it must for a few years have been quite a large group, and I think it was devoted more to talk than to direct action. At least, when I arrived in San Francisco for the first time in 1951, I heard no reports of any activity other than the evenings of debate in which the older Italian comrades would often be scandalized by the statements of the younger poets, who would present defences of homosexuality and even—in those early days—of dope.

By this time Rexroth had abandoned the group, though it still continued, dominated, so he asserted, by young anarchists from New York who had moved in and were now running the show. He regarded them as in some way theoretically marred by the metropolis, lacking the kind of great expansive instinct for freedom that his beloved Wobblies had evolved in the western mountains and forests. He did not attend the meetings any longer, though his influence still hovered over them in their sometimes incongruous combination of the literary and the quasi-political, nor did he even turn up at the big, noisy socials being held that summer, with lots of music and wine and pasta, in the arbors of the vineyards which so many of the old anarchists now owned.

At that time, indeed, Rexroth was undergoing a revulsion from anarchists if not from anarchism. He went to Europe and wrote bitterly in that scurrilous and often beautiful verse travelogue, *The Dragon and the Unicorn*, of Italian theoreticians who could not see the poverty and exploitation on their own pavements, and of the comrades he encountered in London:

> The London Anarchist Group
> Like a debating club at an
> Exclusive Kansas private school.
> Emma Goldman said, years ago,
> 'You're not British anarchists,
> You're just British . . .'[3]

I have never identified the quotation from Emma, and in any case Rexroth was being—as he sometimes would—unfair, since the leading members of the anarchist group in London at that time had gone to prison for their beliefs during the last war, whereas the leading members of his own group, including Kenneth himself, had not.

At the same time there was indeed a doctrinaire aridity about anarchism in the later 1940s that made it almost qualify as one of George Orwell's "smelly little orthodoxies." The old movement of Kropotkin and Malatesta was virtually moribund, and the new movement of the late 1960s had not yet risen from the cooling ashes. The atmosphere of petty intolerance drove me out of the movement, and I suspect this was what repelled Rexroth—this and an absence of passion, which had breathed out of the British movement when Marie Louise Berneri died in 1949.

At the same time, during this period and far into the 1960s, Rexroth was manifesting a kind of generalized nostalgia that in *An Autobiographi-*

cal Novel made him portray the pre-1927 world in threnodic terms, so that it is haunted not only by the ghosts of slaughtered Sacco and Vanzetti, but also by the shades of a childhood and youth in which the vitality and even brutality of life were accompanied by a strange innocence. About the same period he said in one of his poems, thinking of the effects of two successive wars:

It is a terrible thing to see a world die twice,
'The first time as tragedy,
The second as evil farce.'[4]

The same elegiac feeling appears typically in the 1952 poem **"For Eli Jacobsen,"** which is an offering of friendship but also a lament for the withering of a good old cause.

There are so few of us now, soon
There will be none. We were comrades
Together, we believed we
Would see with our own eyes the new
World where man was no longer
Wolf to man, but men and women
Were all brothers and lovers
Together. We will not see it.
We will not see it, none of us.
It is farther off than we thought . . .
(*CSP* [*Collected Shorter Poems*], p. 244).

Yet the political poems and other poems with clear political allusions appear consistently through this period, scattered in the collections from **In What Hour** (1940) onwards.

Rexroth began his **Collected Shorter Poems** (1967) with the epigraph: "A self-contained system is a contradiction of terms. QED." This warning against trying to seek too consistent an order of thought, political or otherwise, is reinforced by the statement regarding political attitudes in the Introduction to the **Collected Longer Poems** (1968) which obfuscates the issue perhaps more than it clarifies.

The political stance of the poems never changes—the only Absolute is the Community of Love with which Time ends. Time is the nisus towards the Community of Love. One passage is a statement in philosophical terms of the I. W. W. Preamble, another of the cash nexus passage in *The Communist Manifesto*. "The State is the organization of the evil instincts of mankind." "Liberty is the mother, not the daughter, of order." "Property is robbery." And similar quotations from Tertullian, St. Clement, Origen, St. Augustine. It is easy to overcome alienations—the net of the cash nexus can simply be stepped out of, but only by the self actualizing man. But everyone is self actualizing and can realize it by the simplest act—the self unselfing itself, the only act that is actual act. I have tried to embody in verse the belief that the only valid conservation of value lies in the assumption of unlimited liability, the supernatural identification of the self with the tragic unity of creative process. I hope I have made it clear that the self does not do this by an act of will, by sheer assertion. He who would save his life must lose it.

In prose, as in verse, Rexroth is never at his best when he speaks in abstractions, and for this reason, even as we examine the explicit political statements in his poems, we cannot ignore the deeper connotations that may lie in more concrete and less direct suggestions offered elsewhere in the *forêt de symboles* that his poetry often becomes.

Turning to the poems themselves, one finds already in the early works written in the 1930s and published in **In What Hour** (1940) the peculiar counterpointing of the individual and the general, symbolized in the affairs of men and the affairs of mountains, that runs through Rexroth's work from beginning to end, so that one might almost say a man in the mountains is his crucial image of human enlightenment. In a simple way one finds it in a poem called **"Hiking on the Coast Range."** Walking, the poet remembers that it is the anniversary of the killing of two pickets in the San Francisco general strike, "Their Blood Spilled on the Pavement / of the Embarcadero." His attention turns back to the present, where

The skirl of the kingfisher was never
More clear than now, nor the scream of the jay,
As the deer shifts her covert at a footfall;
Nor the butterfly tulip ever brighter
In the white spent wheat; nor the pain
Of a wasp stab ever an omen more sure;
The blood alternately dark and brilliant
On the blue and white bandana pattern.

And he sees "This minimal prince rupert's drop of blood," the blood that flows in the veins of all living things as it flowed out of the veins of the slaughtered strikers, as "the source of valuation. . . ."

The measure of time, the measure of space,
The measure of achievement.
                                                 There is no
Other source than this
                                                 [*CSP*, p. 84].

In this way the mythology of revolt is subsumed in the wider reality of nature.

There are other poems of **In What Hour** where the approach to revolt is more direct, but still seen in a heroic and elegiac way, and sometimes leading on to the naively golden vision of hope that always irradiated the sense of doom which clouded the outlook of the Thirties, as in "**From the Paris Commune to the Kronstadt Rebellion**":

> They shall rise up heroes, there will be many,
> None shall prevail against them at last.
> They go saying each: "I am one of many";
> Their hands empty save for history.
> They die at bridges, bridge gates, and
>   drawbridges.
> Remember now there were others before;
> The sepulchres are full at ford and bridgehead.
> There will be children with flowers there,
> And lambs and golden-eyed lions there,
> And people remembering in the future
>   [*CSP*, pp. 81-82].

This kind of easy vision does not occur often even in the early poems of *In What Hour*. More typical, and certainly more characteristically Rexrothian is "**Autumn in California**," that "mild / And anonymous season," when Rexroth, idling, calls "the heart to order and the stiff brain / To passion," and thinks of what at this moment is happening in Nanking ravaged by Japanese planes and Madrid besieged by Franco's troops. His vision holds two young men talking in a room in Madrid of all the pleasure of a world they have left for war and perhaps for ever:

> The candlelight reddens, blue bars appear
> In the cracks of the shutters, the bombardment
> Begins again as though it had never stopped,
> The morning wind is cold and dusty,
> Their furloughs are over. They are shock troop-
>   ers,
> They may not meet again. The dead light holds
> In impersonal focus the patched uniforms,
> The dog-eared copy of Lenin's Imperialism,
> The heavy cartridge belt, holster and black
>   revolver butt.

There is no hope in this vision: only the commitment to the extreme situation, the existential pride, and beyond it, as in the writings of Camus, the benign indifference of the universe, manifested again in mountains:

> The moon rises late over Mt. Diablo,
> Huge, gibbous, warm; the wind goes out,
> Brown fog spreads over the bay from the
>   marshes,
> And overhead the cry of birds is suddenly
> Loud, wiry, and tremulous
>   [*CSP*, pp. 93-95].

And finally, in that grand long pessimistic poem of *In What Hour*, "**Ice Shall Cover Nineveh**," the fate of mountains and the fate of men are one:

> The glaciers are senile and covered with dust but the
>   mountain crack
>   The orange-red granite breaks and the long black slivers
>   fall

> Fine ice in the air and the stone blades falling and the opening
>   vault
> The high milk-blue lake tipping over its edge in a mile-long
>   wavering waterfall
>   And for these weapons in what forge and from what
>   steel
>   And for this wheat what winnowing floor what flail
>   [*CSP*, p. 136].

Moving out of the Thirties, *The Phoenix and the Tortoise* (1944) contains a long and loping speculative poem that bears the volume's title and a series of accompanying shorter pieces. "**The Phoenix and the Tortoise**" presents the poet sleeping out of doors, by the seashore this time, though the mountains impinge on his musings, and reflections on history, fragments of political theory, speculations on the human condition mingle with his half-waking perceptions of the immediate world. The urgency, the activity of the preceding volume are diminished. The disillusionment, the sense of the futility of militancy in the present time that, as we have seen, characterize the later *Dragon and the Unicorn*, have set in. As the poem nears its end what it emphasizes is "history's / Cruel irresponsibility" and the human condition as "tragic loss of value into / Barren novelty." Yet this, in the spirit of losing one's life to save it, becomes paradoxically the "condition of salvation." The poet sees what has happened to the world as

> my fault, the horrible term
> Of weakness, evasion, indulgence,
> The total of my petty fault—
> No other man's.

And he asks

> And out of this
> Shall I reclaim beauty, peace of soul,
> The perfect gift of self-sacrifice,
> Myself as act, as immortal person?

And the answer seems to come as he walks out on the sandspit and his wife comes swimming in through the breakers.

> The sun crosses
> The hills and fills her hair, as it lights
> The moon and glorifies the sea
> And deep in the empty mountains melts
> The snow of Winter and the glaciers
> Of ten thousand years
>   (*CLP* [*The Collected Longer Poems of Kenneth
>   Rexroth*], pp. 90-91).

The salvation seems to lie in intimate human communion and a life in harmony with nature, represented, always, by the mountains.

Yet the sense of the revolutionary tradition and all that at its best it represents in integrity and self-abnegation survives here and there in the shorter poems of **The Phoenix and the Tortoise.** "**Again at Waldheim,**" in keeping with the generally elegiac tone of the poetry in this period, is set in the Waldheim cemetery in Chicago where so many celebrated American anarchists were buried, and the poet asks, in this time of war and horror,

> What memory lasts, Emma, of you,
> Or of the intrepid comrades of your grave,
> Of Piotr, of 'mutual aid,'
> Against the iron clad flame throwing
> Course of time?

And what he answers means that even if the memory may fade, the gesture, the stance, is its own justification, perhaps even its own eternity.

> You knew that nothing could ever be
> More desperate than truth; and when every
>   voice
> Was cowed, you spoke against the coalitions
> For the duration of the emergency—
> In the permanent emergency
> You spoke for the irrefutable
> Coalition of the blood of men
>
> [CSP, p. 155].

We are back with the Spanish storm troopers of "**Autumn in California**" who "may not meet again."

The rather sour disillusionment of **The Dragon and the Unicorn** was the prelude to a shifting into a more generalized rebellion—social and cultural as well as political—which emerges in **In Defence of the Earth** (1956), a volume whose very title seems to anticipate the environmentalist movement of the next decade, for which Rexroth was a pioneer. Perhaps the most striking feature of this volume is the outpouring of anger and denunciation against the contemporary world and its materialist culture in the long poem, "**Thou Shalt Not Kill,**" a passionate, almost hysterical lament for the death of Dylan Thomas which bears some remarkable resemblances to Allen Ginsberg's *Howl*, a poem whose first reading Rexroth sponsored, calling it "the confession of faith of a generation." **In Defence of the Earth** and *Howl* were published in the same year, but I suspect that if there was any derivation it was on Ginsberg's part, since he showed me *Howl* in manuscript when he visited me in Vancouver early in 1955, while the immediacy of anger in Rexroth's poem suggests he wrote it shortly after Thomas' death in 1953:

> Who killed him?
> Who killed the bright-headed bird?
> You did, you son of a bitch,

> You drowned him in your cocktail brain,
> He fell down and died in your synthetic heart.
> You killed him,
> Oppenheimer the Million-Killer,
> You killed him,
> Einstein the Gray Eminence.
> You killed him,
> Havanahavana, with your Nobel Prize.
> You killed him, General,
> Through the proper channels.
> You strangled him, Le Mouton,
> With your *mains étendues.*
> He confessed in open court to a pince-nezed
>   skull.
> You shot him in the back of the head
> As he stumbled in the last cellar.
> You killed him,
> Benign Lady on the postage stamp.
> He was found dead at a Liberal Weekly
>   luncheon.
> He was found dead on the cutting room floor.
> He was found dead at a *Time* policy conference.
> Henry Luce killed him with a telegram to the
>   Pope.
> *Mademoiselle* strangled him with a padded bras-
>   siere.
> Old Possum sprinkled him with a tea ball
>
> [CSP, p. 273].

In such a piece Rexroth's link with the Beat poets becomes quite evident, though it is ironical that their much inferior poetry became better known than his. But this did not prevent Rexroth from sharing the sudden sense of hope we all experienced in the later 1960s, when anarchism seemed to be created anew by the young. The acrimony towards fellow radicals and the generally elagiac mood of his political poetry during the 1940s and 1950s seemed both to vanish as Rexroth turned largely to prose and began to celebrate, in collections of essays like **The Alternative Society** (1970), the renewal of poetic and political vigor:

> Today there is growing up throughout the world
> an entirely new pattern of life. For several years I
> have called it the subculture of secession but this
> is no more—it is a competing civilization, "a new
> society within the shell of the old."[5]

Rexroth goes on here to talk in enthusiastic terms of "a time of wholesale overturn, a transvaluation of values at least comparable with the revolutionary years around 1848. . . ." But there is another side of him that pulls up short to question whether the outcome will necessarily be good. The dark forces, also, are more powerful than they ever were before:

> Man has lost control. What is accelerating is not
> the breakdown of civilization, but the breakdown
> of the species as such. Unless the processes now
> operating are reversed, and when reversed, are still

able to win out, man is a failure. The species has failed. . . . Man has not just been crowded out of his ecological niche; he has destroyed everybody's ecology. The changes that have taken place already in this generation are greater than those postulated to account for the extinction of the dinosaurs

(*AS* [*The Alternative Society*], pp. 184-185).

In such passages as these we see how Rexroth's thought accords with the general anarchist tradition which rejected nineteenth century socialism's uncritically optimistic acceptance of open-ended material progress as a viable goal and substituted what one can describe as critical pessimism, which is by no means the resignation that accepts the worst as inevitable, but a positive state of mind that sees the worst as a threatening option and therefore assesses realistically the chances of evading it. Such a view, in Rexroth as in his comrades in the tradition, does not regard the future as necessarily better than the past; indeed, he looks back in the verse plays contained in *Beyond the Mountains* to Greek antiquity and in the fine translations of his later years to certain ages in China when men seemed to live fuller and more harmonious lives than we do. The good life, in the present or in the past, is not to be based on affluence, less on luxury; both Pierre-Joseph Proudhon and Paul Goodman among the anarchists have praised the life of dignified poverty. A rough cabin in the mountains, as Rexroth's Cordillera poems demonstrate so eloquently, a modest apartment in the city as his life declared, can be the center of experiential wealth if one is prepared for it. And, continuing with the factors that differentiate the anarchist from the socialist tradition, one recognizes, as Kropotkin did and Rexroth afterwards, the presence *here and now,* in every society, of elements of mutual aid, of networks of voluntary institutions, of potentials for freedom and responsibility, that are waiting to be uncovered if we are prepared to challenge the values of a society based on the twin myths of progress and authority. And the challenge can take many forms; in our time, as Rexroth remarked, all the important works of art "have rejected all the distinguishing marks of the civilization that produced it."

Such a view of man's role in society is not merely a complete "politics of the unpolitical," to use Herbert Read's fitting phrase; it also implies a fellowship with the environment and it accords with Rexroth's poetry about man in his relation to nature, so splendidly exemplified in his mountain poems and linked to a sense not only of the unity of all living beings but also of their symbiosis

with the inanimate forces of nature, a symbiosis that can be broken only at grave peril.

I always come back, when I consider Rexroth's political views in relation to his poetry and his sensitivity to the environment, to the first verse of his I ever read, about forty years ago, the little suite of mountain poems, "**Towards an Organic Philosophy**," that appears in *In What Hour.* I quote the beautiful concluding lines of the suite:

It is storming in the White Mountains,
On the arid fourteen-thousand-foot peaks;
Rain is falling on the narrow grey ranges
And the dark sedge meadows and white salt flats
   of Nevada.
Just before moonset a small dense cumulus
   cloud,
Gleaming like a grape cluster of metal,
Moves over the Sierra crest and grows down the
   westward slope.
Frost, the color and quality of the cloud,
Lies over the marsh below my campsite.
The wiry clumps of dwarfed whitebark pines
Are smoky and indistinct in the moonlight,
Only their shadows are really visible.
The lake is immobile and holds the stars
And the peaks deep in itself without a quiver.
In the shallows the geometrical tendrils of ice
Spread their wonderful mathematics in silence.
All night the eyes of deer shine for an instant
As they cross the radius of my firelight.
In the morning the trail will look like a sheep
   driveway,
All the tracks will point down to the lower
   canyon.
"Thus," says Tyndall, "the concerns of this little
   place
Are changed and fashioned by the obliquity of
   the earth's axis.
The chain of dependence which runs through
   creation,
And links the roll of a planet alike with the
   interests
Of marmots and of men"

[*CSP,* pp. 103-104].

It seems to me that all we need to know of Rexroth's thought is here encapsulated: Tyndall's central concept of the interdependence of all aspects of the universe and Kropotkin's of the mutual aid which among living beings exemplifies that unity; the core of the ecological theories that the anarchists and their allies like Patrick Geddes and Aldous Huxley so significantly anticipated; but also, visibly present, the poet's concrete world of the mountains and the life they shelter, and the world of thoght beyond, for which nature offers the silent and "wonderful mathematics" of its imagery. It is in the constant reconstruction of such harmonies as are here presented that the purpose of rebellion lies, and the rage and the

ON THE SUBJECT OF...

PHILIP LAMANTIA

Philip Lamantia was one of the first American poets of his generation to fully embrace surrealism. Lamantia's work diverged from the dominant poetic expressions of realism and positivism; while his contemporaries were influenced by Walt Whitman or Ezra Pound, Lamantia took inspiration from the darkest works of Edgar Allan Poe and H. P. Lovecraft. Rather than seeking perfection of form or accuracy of detail, his work is motivated by a pure expression of the imagination, viewing poetry as a means of attaining objects of desire. Compared with many of his Beat peers, Lamantia's published verse is sparse: some of his poems have been lost, and he has periodically destroyed many others to mark new creative cycles. Lamantia has not garnered substantial critical or popular attention, though he has long been acclaimed by a small but devoted following—notably other poets—for his passionate intensity, metaphoric daring, and imaginative power. In these circles, Lamantia is seen as a key link between French surrealism and the counterculture of the 1960s. Among his collections of poetry are *Ekstasis* (1959) and *Selected Poems 1943-1966* (1967).

serenity that at one and the same time characterized Rexroth are reconciled.

Notes

1. Kenneth Rexroth, *An Autobiographical Novel* (New York: New Directions, 1969),p. 367.

2. William Everson, "Rexroth: Shaker and Maker," in *For Rexroth: ARK 14*, ed. Geoffrey Gardner (New York: The Ark, 1980),p. 26.

3. Kenneth Rexroth, *The Collected Longer Poems* (New York: New Directions, 1968),p. 118.

4. Kenneth Rexroth, *The Collected Shorter Poems* (New York: New Directions, 1967),p. 159. Hereafter cited in the text as *CSP.*

5. Kenneth Rexroth, *The Alternative Society* (New York: Herder and Herder, 1970),p. 110. Hereafter cited in the text as *AS.*

WILLIAM J. LOCKWOOD (ESSAY DATE WINTER 1983)

SOURCE: Lockwood, William J. "Toward a Reappraisal of Kenneth Rexroth: The Poems of his Middle and Late Periods." *Sagetrieb* 2, no. 3 (winter 1983): 113-32.

In the following essay, Lockwood examines numerous lesser-known Rexroth poems, dating from the middle to late stages of the writer's career, and contends that they constitute an enactment of "a life-time's journeying toward self-realization."

. . . Nearly twenty years ago I felt dreadful about American poetry, certainly my own and certainly most of what I was reading in magazines. It seemed to me then that I was dead, or else the world was dead, and that we might as well lie down in our graves and shut up. Of course, the world of the learned and vital imagination was and is enormously alive, both in the poems and essays and translations of Kenneth Rexroth and in that immortal and truly (as distinguished from academically) traditional world which, almost alone among contemporary poets, he knows and can speak about. Over the years I have learned that I am far from being alone in being so grateful to Rexroth, and I believe he has saved many poets from imaginative death. His essays and translations are by turns exalted, learned, instructive, and very funny. But I believe it is his love poetry that matters most in the end. He is a great love poet in the most loveless time imaginable.[1]

To his grateful declaration concerning Kenneth's greatness as a love poet, the late James Wright thus attached two more general and worldwide issues: namely, the tenuous survival of "the world of the learned and vital imagination," and the degraded condition of the present age he characterized as "the most loveless time imaginable." Although the fundamental truthfulness of that outright declaration remains to be demonstrated, and the rationale for Wright's attaching to it those arguably related issues needs specifying and elaborating, that meditative line of thought deserves attention and reflection. Indeed, it supplies a reference point for the reassessing overview I propose to begin with here; though to undertake such a reassessment is to encounter immediate difficulties. The life-work is diverse, for better and for worse, both in the rather eclectic range of its poetic forms and in the extremities of its style, whether arcanely learned or aggressively blunt. Then, there is the more difficult, distracting fact that his achievement, especially in late career and especially in the United States, has been considerably blurred by Rexroth's cranky stance as the self-appointed, opposition-party man of letters, speaking from a vantage place he'd carved out for himself, decades ago, on the West Coast. Thus the reference point Wright supplies is useful, but one still wants a relatively unbiased mode of approaching the whole canon, and one needs an adequate working hypothesis.

The approach I here propose involves an equivalence of the geographer's mental outlook as it operates "in the field." I propose that, equipped with the geographer's phenomenologically-oriented attentiveness, we take a fresh look at several of Rexroth's poems—poems not generally anthologized and hence relatively unknown—viewing them as "naively-given sections of reality."[2] Next, I want to propose a working hypothesis: that, insofar as we can gauge it from the narrowed field of those middle-to-late career poems gathered in the **Collected Shorter Poems,** Rexroth's poetry enacts a life-time's journeying toward self-realization. Such a self-realizing impulse (expressed in actual as well as imaginative journeys, as we shall find) is not, certainly, unique to Rexroth's poetry; and yet his insistence that self-realization should serve as an act of responsible resistance to authority and, more particularly, to the mid-century culture's reduction of personal relationships to commodity relationships *is* distinctive. To re-state the latter point, our hypothesis requires the corollary that the thrust of Rexroth's life-long poetic journeying has been underlaid by the declaration he made in his essay on the "**Hasidism of Martin Buber**": that "the fullest realization of the self comes in the acceptance of the limits of contingency."[3] In that case personal desires are not simply personal but become enmeshed in and refined by prevailing public circumstances.

I.

Let us begin by pausing over three poems which span Rexroth's mid-career years between 1944 and 1952. The first of these, appearing midway through the **Collected Shorter Poems** and first published in 1944, is titled "**When We With Sappho.**" Written in five stanzas, with each stanza containing between 25 and 30 lines, it appears to be a poem of memory originating in a rural western Massachusetts locale. The second is a concise lyric, published in 1949, titled "**Blues.**" It recreates the speaker's reverie at the summit of one of the Sierra Nevada mountains—though, as we shall see, it also interpolates an image drawn from another memory of Massachusetts. My third example is a later set of verses excerpted from a long poem. Published in 1952 and titled "**Golden Section,**" it records a moment during a journey through Italy.

"**When We With Sappho**" opens by evoking both the luminous, sense-drenched world of lovers and the grave, ruinous orchard in which they lie:

> We lie here in the bee filled, ruinous
> Orchard of a decayed New England farm,
> Summer in our hair, and the smell
> Of summer in our twined bodies,
> Summer in our mouths, and summer
> In the luminous, fragmentary words
> Of this dead Greek woman.
> Stop reading. Lean back. Give me your mouth.
> Your grace is as beautiful as sleep.
> You move against me like a wave
> That moves in sleep.
> Your body spreads across my brain
> Like a bird filled summer;
> Not like a body, not like a separate thing,
> But like a nimbus that hovers
> Over every other thing in all the world.
> Lean back. You are beautiful,
> As beautiful as the folding
> Of your hands in sleep.[4]

The orchard of this decayed New England farm, so attentively placed in region and dated in time (historical, seasonal, and diurnal), inhabits the lovers' world as a real, living presence. It grounds the poem, becomes "our orchard" in stanza 2, for its aging images the lovers' own sense of transience, their own inclination toward slumber. The closing words of the poem's four-line epigraph-translation from Sappho—"Slumber pours down"—have implicitly triggered this falling sensation, for the lovers begin to feel themselves growing as old as Sappho herself, turned now to "gleaming dust" (in a distant sea) and "Flash[ing] in the wave crest / Or stain[ing] the murex shell" (**CSP** [*The Collected Shorter Poems*], p. 139). It is this imaged association of brightness and coloration with dust that allows a rich interplay of luminousness and gravity here. It brings into easy accord the delight of erotic love and the sense of life's decline into death beyond this high summer noon: "All about us the old farm subsides / Into the honey bearing chaos of high summer" [**CSP**, p. 139].

The lovers' orchard, metamorphosed into a landscape of the mind, recalls Robert Duncan's ideal "made-up" Meadow, that cherished place charged with resonances of intimacy ("Often I am Permitted to Return to a Meadow"), and that dwelling place of the soul H.D. spoke of when she declared "I go where I love and am loved."[5] The mysterious conjunction of Eros and ruinous orchard in the lovers' day-dreaming vision recalls, as well, Ezra Pound's vision of Aphrodite—she from whose grace flowed the astonishingly clear and sustaining revelation that "What thou lovest well shall not be reft from thee." And yet it needs to be emphasized that Rexroth's vision originates in a palpable, flesh and blood woman with a taste for Sapphic love poems, and not in a goddess invoked out of ancient myth. Relatedly, we should note that Rexroth's method of proceeding in this sequence of stanzas is to elaborate discovered correspondences between the real and ideal, between ordinary immediate presences and more extraordinary, remote ones. Thus the correspondence between this sense-drenched, high-summer-noon orchard and the orchards that once surrounded the ancient island temples in Sappho's native place becomes central to the poem's evolution in the third of the temporally-arranged sequence of five stanzas. The orchards of Sappho's place, pictured in the speaker's mind as overgrown with sea-grass, exist now only as faint traces; and yet, by virtue of that perceived correspondence, the very presence of Sappho passes into the lovers' lips, breasts and thighs. She comes to them, to their sacred place.

The writer of these verses has not been content to establish a purely Arcadian, "made-up" scene; the earthy tonality of the verse insists that vision must be anchored in this given, western Massachusetts locale in the North American continent. Indeed, by an extraordinary attentiveness to the "weather" peculiar to this mid-summer New England day, Rexroth artfully sustains in the poem's succeeding stanzas the lovers' moment of ecstasy. The moment is sustained because it becomes incorporated into the inclusive totality of the given occasion: domes of cumulous clouds lifting and thunder breaking far off over the Adirondacks enclose both "summer honeyed flesh" and the "acrid herbage / Of midsummer" [*CSP*, p. 140]; the stillness that ensues after the storm's veering off on the horizon enforces the lovers' sense of isolation in their orchard "hidden from fact and history" [*CSP*, p. 141]; and, the sun's declination (creating "amber / Long lights on the shattered / Boles of the ancient maple trees") brings the mortal lovers to "the verge of sleep." Such an achieved totality authenticates the speaker's earlier sense of vital, all-sufficient dwelling here, "as though I held / In my arms the bird filled / Evening sky of summer" [*CSP*, p. 142].

"**Blues**" originates in another locale, itself the terminus of another act of physical and imaginative journeying in Rexroth's lifetime, the summit of one of the Sierra mountains. Only here grows the blue flower adumbrated in the title. The voice we hear speaking in this meditative lyric speaks in the voice of an *amateur*, of one who loves the world of traditional and vital learning as much as he loves the starkly beautiful natural world he has sought out here. He uses the botanical name of this blue flower, peculiar to the highest elevations of the Sierras, as one who has familiarized himself with such knowledge and has done so for the pleasure of it. Similarly, he alludes to the fate of Endymion not as though he had ransacked Greek mythology for materials, but naturally, as one who recognized in Endymion's story a kindred inclination to become one with a like object of fully sensual and utterly inscrutable beauty.

His learned imagination expresses itself here, moreover, in a classical, i.e., insistently measuring and clarifying, structure. The courage of the mortal Endymion visited by Artemis, the courage of D. H. Lawrence day-dreaming his last imminent journey through death ("**Blue Gentians**"), the courage of Vanzetti in his Massachusetts jail cell finding composure in a vase of tall blue flowers gathered from a New England garden—by that deliberate sequence of images the verse presents not a random set of blue / beautiful associations, but rather an ordering of beautiful persons. Recalled to mind by the speaker's elegaic sense of what their loss means to the world of the vital imagination, they are here celebrated in song, a memorializing "blues" song. Begun with an extraordinary attentiveness to the unique and vital phenomena of the mountain summit, that song proceeds through the rehearsal of a life-time's storehouse of memories, affinities, and loyalties in order that it might finally affirm the identity of beauty and courage:

"BLUES"

The tops of the higher peaks
Of the Sierra Nevada
Of California are
Drenched in the perfume of
A flower which grows only there—
The blue *Polemonium*
Confertum eximium,
Soft, profound blue, like the eyes
Of impregnable innocence;
The perfume is heavy and
Clings thickly to the granite
Peaks, even in violent wind;
The leaves are clustered,
Fine, dull green, sticky, and musky.
I imagine that the scent
Of the body of Artemis
That put Endymion to sleep
Was like this and her eyes had the
Same inscrutable color.
Lawrence was lit into death
By the blue gentians of Kore.
Vanzetti had in his cell

A bowl of tall blue flowers
From a New England garden.
I hope that when I need it
My mind can always call back
This flower to its hidden senses

[*CSP*, p. 183].

This wedding of beauty and courage—it brings to mind the "excellently bright" conception of Diana in Ben Jonson's "Hymn to Diana"—issues in a kind of moral clarity rare in contemporary poetry. The correspondent imagery found in the opening and in the penultimate sections expresses in vivid visual form that feeling of camaraderie which joins the man who day-dreams on the West Coast and the man whose dreams of social justice stayed alive in his Massachusetts prison.[6] The bowl of tall blue flowers, gathered from a New England garden (from a region in which he ought to have been able to hope that tall men would come to his defense), not only sets down an image of a man's composure before death, but also brightly memorializes the immigrant Vanzetti's New World dream and hands it on as a legacy.

In retrospect, the comprehensive and sympathetic vantage point achieved in **"Blues"** seems to be made possible by the poet's self-realizing, hard-earned sense of finding himself at home satisfactorily in Northern California. In the image of the blue polemonium (it first appeared in an earlier, longer, and more emphatically political poem titled **"Climbing Milestone Mountain"**) Rexroth's own ability to hand on and to carve out of his adopted locale what Amerigo Castro speaks of as a *morada vital*, or vital dwelling place, lies implicit. The phrase signifies an area in which problems of pure subsistence have begun to be successfully resolved and man has shifted attention to qualitative matters. In **"Golden Section"** we are carried to another such place, not our own and yet one we may claim as part of our cultural inheritance. Hiking in our own locale or travelling by train through another continent, with visits to its uniquely sacred places, equally involve the journeying impulse toward self-realization, whether our day-dreaming be imaged in the Sierras' deep-blue brightness or in Italy's ancient goldenness.

Rexroth's journeying to Paestum is, however, shadowed by his sense of history's going awry, by his thoughts of modern man's loveless and homeless condition, and in this way it recalls Melville's visit a hundred years earlier, to the site of the Acropolis:

Not magnitude, not lavishness,
But Form—the Site;

Not innovating wilfulness,
But reverence for the Archetype.[7]

A shock of recognition mixed with awe thus ran through Melville, as he witnessed a reconciliation of man's making and of the natural landscape at that site. As Vincent Scully observes, it seems paradoxical that he "who saw more profoundly than anyone else into the depths and flux of the sea, should also have been able to state so succinctly the counter principles of clarity and permanence in a fixed and sacred landscape." That characteristically American sense of feeling adrift in the world had been momentarily displaced by a feeling of harmony that spoke of the local gods satisfactorily appeased.[8] A comparable response appears here in **"Golden Section"** although Rexroth is more resourceful and better practised in the art of carving out a satisfactory home for himself against the odds. And so we find him dilating upon the scene, elaborating his line of thought to make the celebrative occasion usefully accessible to the rest of us who, consciously or not, have grown weary of our drifting condition in a fragmented, loveless time:

Paestum of the twice blooming
Roses, the sea god's honey
Colored stone still strong against
The folly of the long decline
Of man. The snail climbs the Doric
Line, and the empty snail shell
Lies by the wild cyclamen.
The sandstone of the Roman
Road is marked with sun wrinkles
Of prehistoric beaches,
But no time at all has touched
The deep constant melodies
Of space as the columns swing
To the moving eye. The sea
Breathes like a drowsy woman.
The sun moves like a drowsy hand.
Poseidon's pillars have endured
All tempers of the sea and sun

[*CSP*, p. 218].

What is strong against folly, what is constant in time, what endures—such is the character of the palpable daydreams that furnish this gravely beautiful and sustained reflection on the cultural and natural landscape of Paestum. No static description here, no picturesqueness; rather, all things "swing to the moving eye," which prompts the tongue to utterance. It declares man's sense of his own limits alongside his transient right to claim, through love, a kinship here:

This is the order of the spheres,
The curve of the unwinding fern,
And the purple shell in the sea;
These are the spaces of the notes
Of every kind of music.

The world is made of number
And moved in order by love.
Mankind has risen to this point
And can only fall away,
As we can only turn homeward
Up Italy, through France, to life
Always pivoted on this place

[*CSP,* p. 218].

The poet's refusal to impose upon this scene his mind's preconceptions underlies the understated metrical patterning. A regular alternation between seven- and eight-syllable lines keeps out falsity and yet allows that variation of stressed syllables which enables an appropriate weight to fall upon what the scene essentially gives (stíll stróng . . . nó tíme at aĺl . . . deép coństant . . . endúred aĺl teḿpers). Such a quiet measuring avoids monotonality, moreover, by its incorporating the syntactic power of the speaker's voice as it rises toward declaration ("This is the order . . . The world is made . . . Mankind . . . We can only turn homeward").

"Homeward," as the subsequent three framing stanzas tell, means moving by train up Italy, through France, back to the north. That journey—like history's course—can only now proceed as a falling away. And yet the aliveness of Paestum is sustained en route to Naples by the presence of the laughing and singing girls heading back home from the fish canneries, lace factories, and farm fields to the south. Those "broad bottomed, / Deep bosomed angels, wet with sweat" [*CSP,*p. 219] appear here as an earthy equivalent of "the scent / of the body of Artemis / That put Endymion to sleep." Rexroth's sensuality is thus remarkably firm, is neither attenuated by an underlying Puritan self-consciousness nor hardened by cynicism; it simply opposes itself to any authoritarian denial of the fundamental human need to be nourished by love. Endymion's Artemis, these Italian working girls, the woman he made love to in the decayed New England orchard, all are celebrated, in this compendium of vital occasions cutting against the grain of ruinous history. They are celebrated without archness or bourgeois sentimentality as homely and earth-centered, lovely and life-radiating persons in their own right. The poet's self-realizing impulse, informed by his acceptance of the limiting contingencies of his time, thus generates a kind of liberating energy out of ordinary matter. It fills the void left by "the folly of the long decline of man"—fills that void with love.

II.

As one moves through the later *Collected Shorter Poems,* those published between 1956 and 1965, one is initially struck by an increased diversity in the kinds of poems, and, as well, by what appears to be a personal anxiety underlying them. To understand these changes in Rexroth's poetry, our angle of approach must begin to open out, then, to include a wider "field." Beyond the naively-given section of reality represented by those relatively unfamiliar texts which have thus far commanded attention, we must now seek to include a more comprehensive "section of reality," one that locates the texts in the context of Rexroth's life, a life increasingly taking shape around Rexroth's role as a man of letters. The multiple dimensions in so inclusive a field complicate the subject of Rexroth's journeying. And yet we find them conveniently crystallized in a single, significant occasion: Rexroth's journey to Provence, for a year's stay, in 1960.

The significance of that journey is mirrored in the introductory words Rexroth wrote for the 1966 edition of Ford Madox Ford's *Buckshee,* a long out-of-print volume Rexroth co-edited with Robert Lowell. In his portion of that introduction Rexroth celebrated Ford's achievement as a refreshingly courageous and honest poet of middle-aged love. Courageous and honest because, against adversity, Ford managed to live and write out of the ordinary circumstances of his life as an English writer exiled in Provence:

> They are possibly the most remarkable poems of middle-aged love in the language. Ford grown old, although he wasn't really all that old, in his *mas* on a hill in Provence, looking out over that old, worn out sea, with his young wife painting under the fig tree, is haunted by marriage come so late that it comes as a ghostly presence. . . . It is typical of Ford that when poets like Pound and Eliot were writing self-conscious philosophical reveries full of indigestible learning, and strictly avoiding the slightest hint of self-revelation . . . Ford should have sat himself down . . . and written . . . what was before his eyes and about himself.[9]

Rexroth's praise here calls to mind (perhaps echoes) William Carlos Williams' "To Ford Madox Ford in Heaven," that elegiac memorial in which Williams shrewdly perceived that Ford's extravagant day-dreaming derived from his need to transubstantiate the "narrowness . . . of a man that is homeless here on earth."[10] Williams' title itself alludes to Ford's "On Heaven," the narrative poem centered in an account of an exiled Englishman meeting his beloved after a period of painful separation. Having just arrived from England—where she, like him, had grown inured to that country's censorious and self-denying climate—she finds it strange to be transposed to a world that smiles on love and makes lovers feel at home. For Rexroth, as for Ford, Provence seems to offer a place of refuge from "narrowness" and self-denial.

Two aspects of Rexroth's praise, as voiced in his "Introduction," call for brief, elaborating comment here. First, in light of the fact that Rexroth was divorced from Marthe following his return from Provence to San Francisco in 1961, it would appear that Rexroth's journey to Provence was, like Ford's, accompanied by feelings of lovelessness and homelessness, and that it was undertaken out of his personal need to heal himself. Next, alongside his troubled marriage, it is also evident that he had begun to feel himself exiled in that place where, in the fifties, he had stood at the center of the so-called San Francisco Renaissance. The unhappy story is too complicated to rehearse here, but it may be thus briefly summarized: declaring himself squarely opposed to the nihilistic tendencies of those Beat movement poets whom he had, earlier, generously encouraged, Rexroth had begun to find himself isolated and exiled in his own Northern California area.

Our context for the late career poems and our reassessment of them begins with Provence, then, a landscape of the mind and heart, and a place Rexroth identified also with the well-springs of lyric verse in the Western tradition. The latter includes Rexroth's own reassessment of the imagist tradition in modern verse, awarding Ford (and, implicitly, William Carlos Williams as well) a new place of prominence among modernist poets while taking Pound and Eliot to task for their "self-conscious philosophical reveries full of indigestible learning and [for] strictly avoiding the slightest hint of self-revelation." Chiefly, however, we find in the Provence year another stage in Rexroth's imaginative journeying (itself a prelude to his journeying to Japan and to China). We may begin then with the "Provence poems" gathered in the two, fairly short volumes of poems published in 1964 and 1965. It is that pair of volumes with which Rexroth framed the *Collected Shorter Poems, Gödel's Proof: New Poems* (1965) being placed at the beginning of the collection, and *Natural Numbers* (1964) placed at the end. Among those poems evidently written *in* Provence and those arguably written *under the influence of* Provence (following his return to Northern

California), the following claim particular attention: three sections from a sequence of seven poems collectively titled "Aix en Provence"; a poem titled "High Provence"; and, from the "Air and Angels" sequence, a pair of poems titled "Coming" and "Pacific Beach."

The "Aix en Provence" sequence re-creates the Provencal landscape as a still vital dwelling place, still speaking the language "of the dwellers in the center of the earth." Each constitutes a lucid day-dream, its lucidity gained by Rexroth's effort to strip away illusions (including all bits of indigestible learning) and to be attentive to ordinary things right before his eyes. Lucidity seems here to arise out of imaginative retrieval, out of Rexroth's day-dreaming sense of that primary and nourishing warmth he once experienced as a child. That image of a cultivated place—an orchard or garden—which had appeared intermittently through Rexroth's earlier work returns here as an enclosed place. It protects the dreamer, clarifies his dreams, and begins to compensate for losses incurred in middle age. Simply, rain, falling on an autumn night in Provence, becomes here an occasion for celebration:

> The children have colds and snore
> In the night. The rain falls on
> All autumn Provence, the gold
> And orange and green and purple
> Hidden in rustling darkness.
>   . . . . .
> The wind is shifting, the pines
> On the opposite hill have
> Begun to murmur like water.
> Here it is still except for
> The slow sweep of massive rain.
> Heavy rain soaked gold leaves drop
> From the plane trees through the dark
>   [*CSP,* pp. 321-322].

Healing begins with such a grateful acceptance of what the procession of the turning seasons gives. And yet, for Rexroth, man must also save himself by cleansing himself, by curbing his nostalgic inclination to seek consoling elements in nature. In "Spring" (the third poem in the "Aix" sequence) it is precisely his refusal to clothe the night sky or the budding almond tree in the language of metaphor that makes possible Rexroth's intuitive grasp of the "lines of force" staging the spring night. For they are the same lines of force, he observes, that produce a summer night, an autumn night, or a winter night: they are

> Relationships rather than
> Images. Shifting darkness,

Strains of feeling, lines of force,
Webs of thought, no images,
Only night and time aging
The night in its darkness, just
Motion in space in the dark

[*CSP*, p. 323].

If such lucid day-dreaming teaches, it teaches a man to begin to view his existence in the local cosmos reductively—to perceive the elemental motions by which that life continues. Shifting attention to the almond tree standing under the same night sky as himself, Rexroth's speaker does, in subsequent lines, conceive of an earth-kinship; but he can not claim that life is self-renewing. His own life may or may not bloom again. For the moment the almond tree blooms and "it isn't an image of something else":

It is just an
Almond tree, in the night, by
The House, in the woods . . .
. . . in Provence, in the
Beginning of another Spring

[*CSP*, p. 324].

At the center of the Provence experience enacted in these poems—further inward from those necessary philosophical (and dialectical) margins—lies Rexroth's expressed affection for the people of Provence and for their cultivation of "Civic / calm, the contemplative heart" [*CSP*,p. 325]. That phrase, offered in praise of the Aixois (from **"On the Eve of the Plebiscite"**) celebrates strengths derived from the continuous history of a people who had managed to sustain nourishing contact with the life of their native land. It was such an affection as, in his **"Letter from San Francisco"** (published only two years earlier), Rexroth expressed when he declared San Francisco to be the best of all worlds within the country of his birth, a place of "Mediterranean ease," not settled overland by the "Puritan tradition, or by the . . . fake-cavalier tradition of the South." And if it ever lost that quality, he added, he would head straight for Provence.[11]

And so he did. In **"High Provence"** he celebrates that enviable calm of the Aixois, understood as an achieved harmony between man and locale. And he celebrates it alongside a personal sense of gratitude for the twined satisfaction of feeling at home and in love (love "come so late that it comes as a ghostly presence"):

Every evening at seven o'clock
We met under the soaring swallows
In the dense shade of the ancient plane trees
At the same café table
On a little square of golden limestone houses
Dry grass and gravel

Where a fountain spoke softly
The language of the dwellers
In the center of the earth

[*CSP*, p. 9].

I propose that in his Provence year Rexroth's middle-aged, self-exiled wanderer recovered and revived his own enabling resourcefulness, his life-long capacity for cleansing, healing, and forgiving himself.

In the years following Rexroth's return to California and preceding the first of his journeys to Japan, in 1966, that resourcefulness persisted in a number of characteristically luminous and grave poems. They are fewer, more spare, and simpler in language than those written at mid-career—an observation that also suggests a diminishing capacity for the kind of lyric poetry the youthful Rexroth had commanded—but, as evident notably in the **"Air and Angels"** sequence, they lodge in the memory as rich and clarifying utterances. The "whereness" of two of these love poems, **"Coming"** and **"Pacific Beach,"** is made explicit: the stretch of coastal highway lying between San Francisco and Los Angeles. The geographical direction signals a return and a retrieval: a return to that Southern California area (around Santa Monica) in which Rexroth had located on his first arrival in California forty years earlier, and a retrieval of love, sensuous and bright. **"Coming"** opens memorably by virtue of the vigorous language appropriate to the directly revealed dramatic situation ("tonight," "last night," "now"); and it closes memorably by virtue of its precisely splendid image ("Rushing . . . / To your curving lips and your / Ivory thighs"). Again, James Wright's declaration that Rexroth is a great love poet returns to mind:

You are driving to the airport
Along the glittering highway
Through the warm night,
Humming to yourself.
The yellow rose buds that stood
On the commode faded and fell
Two days ago. Last night the
Petals dropped from the tulips
On the dresser. The signs of
Your presence are leaving the
House one by one. Being without
You was almost more than I
Could bear. Now the work is squared
Away. All the arrangements
Have been made. All the delays
Are past and I am thirty
Thousand feet in the air over
A dark lustrous sea, under
A low half moon that makes the wings
Gleam like fish under water—
Rushing south four hundred miles

Down the California coast
To your curving lips and your
Ivory thighs

[*CSP*, p. 340].

"Pacific Beach," placed alongside "Coming" in the "Air and Angels" sequence, seems, at first sight, to re-create that journey. Only, because the speaker in this articulate occasion drives the coast highway instead of flying thirty-thousand feet over it, his attentiveness to the hissing surf along the shortline here induces a more meditative consciousness (more meditative and more elegaic in the manner of "Golden Section"). It begins by evoking a peaceful quietude enclosing the speaker's exhilarating eighty-mile-an-hour drive down the late-night, deserted and moonlit highway:

This is the sea called peaceful,
And tonight it is quiet
As sleeping flesh under
The October waning moon.
Late night, not a moving car
On all the moonlit Coast Highway.
No sound but the offshore bells
And the long, recurrent hiss
Of windless surf. "Sophocles
Long ago heard it by the
Aegean." I drive eighty
Miles an hour through the still,
Moonfilled air

[*CSP*, pp. 340-341].

Hissing surf, that sound pleasingly familiar to other late-night coastal California dwellers, recalls to this speaker's at once expectant and memorizing consciousness the voices of the lovers who spoke in Arnold's "Dover Beach":

The surf withdraws,
Returns, and brings into my
Mind the turgid ebb and flow
Of human loyalty—
The myriad ruined voices
That have said, "Ah, love, let us
Be true to one another."
The moon lured voyagers sleep
In all the voiceless city

[*CSP*, p. 341].

Still, it is the closing image—weighted by the speaker's willingness, again, to seek self-realization through acknowledging the limits of contingency—that catches in the reader's mind and that remains luminescent in his memory. It has metamorphosed the speaker's melancholy into the implicit affirmation that this is, finally, the place one is given to live and to love and to survive in:

Far out on the horizon
The lights of the albacore
Fleet gleam like a golden town
In another country

[*CSP*, p. 341].

III.

The final stage of Rexroth's journeying, marked in 1966 by the first of four extended stays in Kyoto, at the edge of the mountains, lies beyond the *Collected Shorter Poems* and most of it, devoted chiefly to translations, especially of Japanese and Chinese poets—as well as to essays, and to an *Autobiographical Novel*—lies outside the form of original poetry. And yet, I suggest, the work of these years, 1967 through 1982, carries forward the thrust of Rexroth's earlier poetic career, indeed carries it on with a new sense of urgency. Which is to argue that Rexroth's personal sense of responsibility for civic concerns issues in a new, deepened sense of a cultural impasse in Western thought and in Western modes of expression.

In retrospect, the journey to Provence seems to have involved a "Farewell to Provence." It signifies a determination to assert the imagist tradition of modernist verse against the vacuity of a narcissistic poetics of pure presence; but it also sought to defend that tradition against the tendency of Pound and Eliot to so weight it with historical and philosophical superstructures as to remove it from the difficult business of staying alive in the ordinary, given world. Rexroth's early-professed admiration of D. H. Lawrence and William Carlos Williams had always been underlain by an effort to articulate a passionate utterance in the idiom of common speech ("Who speaks? Who listens?").[12] But it was underlain, too, by what he perceived as a need to search for modes of thought and expression enriched by still-vital value systems, forms capable of re-articulating the ordering power of human love. It was that need, viewed in light of the perceived cultural impasse (particularly in the Western European, American, and Russian nations), that seems to have prompted Rexroth's translations from "third-world" nations, especially Japan and China.

It was as a mediator of saving values, in the role of a humane American man of letters working against his sense of history's drifting into unreality and ruin, then, that Rexroth acted in the last fifteen years of his life. One of his last set of notes, in the form of a concise introduction to one of Poland's leading writers, the exiled Czeslaw Milosz, characterizes Milosz's achievement in terms that I think fitly characterize Rexroth's own, as poet and as man of letters at a perilous moment in world history:

He . . . has been tireless, both as a translator and promoter of contemporary Polish poetry. . . . His translations, . . . are without exception considerable poetic achievements in their own right. His own poetry has a subtlety and a profundity that come from an intensely humane literary sensibility, a remarkable understanding of the complexity of the human mind and its speech and a breadth of experience unusual in contemporary writers. He had evolved as his personal idiom a literary humanism true to the traditions of his native language and culture without abandoning any of the revolutionary explorations which have taken place since Baudelaire and which have established the international idiom of modern poetry.[13]

That in his late career Rexroth remained a Poet in Emerson's sense of that word and that his peculiar greatness lay in his love poems I would here advance even though adequate demonstration lies beyond the intended confines of this call for reappraisal. I would, however, point to two works which seem to me major achievements, fully consistent with Rexroth's commitment to enlarging the possibilities of individual self-realization on this planet. They are *The Heart's Garden, the Garden's Heart* (1967) and *The Complete Poems of Li Chi'ng Chao* (1979).

A long, ten-sectioned poem written out of Rexroth's initial stay at a Kyoto monastery, *The Heart's Garden* weaves its meditative themes in the manner of Eliot's *Four Quartets*. They arise out of Rexroth's grounding of particular moments from the turning seasons in the ritual life of that monastic community. The closing section of the poem, summarizing Rexroth's intention to enact a retrieval and transmission of values—to fill the void with energy—ends by incorporating the language of all those courageous wanderers and lovers who have yearned to come home again to a satisfactory, healing sense of wholeness:

> The great hawk went down the river
> In the twilight. The belling owl
> Went up the river in the
> Moonlight. He returns to
> Penelope, the wanderer
> Of many devices, to
> The final woman who weaves,
> And unweaves, and weaves again.[14]

The hawk and the owl, the poet-wanderer of many devices, and the woman who is, elsewhere in the poem, heard incessantly weaving at her loom—these are all concrete local references. And yet the wider net of reference employed here—incorporating the active and suffering principles signified in hawk and owl, in the image of the heroic wanderer and in the elaborated image of Penelope—defines that sense of participation in the wider community which may bind the planet's living inhabitants into a new economy of being.

Rexroth's last great achievement, his versions of Li Chi'ng Chao's *tzu* lyrics, celebrate the extraordinary beauty of ordinary things attentively viewed. The wide range of topics under which the poems are grouped—Youth, Loneliness, Exile, His Death, Politics, Mysticism and Old Age—reflect Li's own resourceful and self-realizing response to the rich multi-dimensionality of her life. That response sought in the person who undertook to translate them a like resourcefulness, including a kindred devotion to the world of the vital and learned imagination, a capacity for cultivating a happy married life, the nerve to address political subjects, and the courage to endure exile, loneliness and old age without losing compassion for others who suffer more deeply. The closing twelve lines of a twenty-two line song, speaking of Li's love for her absent husband, are among the most memorable of those graceful, astonishingly rich and clarifying poems:

> Flowers, after their kind, flutter
> And scatter. Water after
> Its nature, when spilt, at last
> Gathers again in one place.
> Creatures of the same species
> Long for each other. But we
> Are far apart and I have
> Grown learned in sorrow.
> Nothing can make it dissolve
> And go away. One moment,
> It is on my eyebrows.
> The next, it weighs on my heart.[15]

This preliminary reassessment of Rexroth's poetry began with an equivalence of the geographer's deliberately-focussed angle of approach to the field under investigation because the prolific and varied nature of the life's work has tended to resist clear assessment and, also, because Rexroth's adoption of the cosmopolitan, controversial, often cranky role of the West Coast man of letters has had the effect of blurring the reading public's sense of it. Because the middle-to-late career poems have been especially varied and especially susceptible to such a blurring, we have begun with them. The poems of the late fifties and early sixties, in particular, I think, got overshadowed by Rexroth's individualistic and idealistic declarations (confusing in the aggregate) on such various matters as sacramental love, the nihilism of the Beats, the cultural dangers of homosexuality, the virtues of erotic expression, the wisdom of Oriental thought and the ignorance of some of its recent converts, and so on. Relatedly, attention to his poetry got distracted by Rexroth's turning in the late years toward meditative, polemical, or autobiographical prose writings and toward the work of translation. The need, therefore, has been to attempt a de-mystification of the mid-to-late career, beginning with a close attention to texts, then moving toward an examination of the texts in the wider context of Rexroth's life, that life viewed as a sustained and essentially continuous act of imaginative journeying.

One of the matters that has come clear in the process concerns the ring of authenticity in Rexroth's work. Among Rexroth's readers, Geoffrey Thurley and Eric Mottram have been particularly attentive to that quality. They have benefited, perhaps, by their trans-oceanic vantage points, Australia on the one hand and England on the other. Rexroth writes, Thurley acutely observed, without the need to prove himself or to vindicate his poetic vocation:

> He seems to have written poetry in fact much as he seems to read, steadily avid, or as he might fill buckets with water or chop firewood in camp—something meaningful in itself which nevertheless does not throw into meaningless shadow the rest of the daily round of which life is composed. . . . In his finest pages, this deep sanity rides over and through the sometimes quirky erudition.[16]

Similarly, Mottram commented on the sureness of Rexroth's stance and on the authentic quality of the poems derived from it. He found it implicit in the tonality of the best poems, so expressive of Rexroth's sense of who he is, of where he stands and of what he loves. He noted that it is that clear sense of himself that has allowed Rexroth to move comfortably and usefully through the country of his native birth. And it has made possible that wide and comprehensive view derived from Rexroth's self-created identity as "the poet in San Francisco, looking toward the Pacific and Asia to Russia and Europe, and imagining the living present of revolutionary writers as he moves within his own community of love."[17]

The reference point supplied by James Wright's initially-given declaration of gratitude—for Rexroth's defense of the vital and learned imagination and for the saving power of his great love poetry—seems thus authenticated, after all, by Thurley's and Mottram's observations, and those observations themselves seem verified by our own, partial, investigation of Rexroth's poetic career. If Rexroth is a great poet of love, it is because his poetry is so firmly and so resourcefully grounded in the real world of ordinary human longings, failings and occasional successes. "Blues," a poem not ostensibly *about* love, accordingly ends by achieving the status of a great love poem, one firmly anchored in the poet's full awareness of the constraints upon love in the world he is given. Not "Blues" singly, but most of the poems in *The Signature of All Things* (1949)—and notably the luminous, deservedly well-known title poem—achieve that status. Indeed, it is with that volume, and with the two volumes of poems which preceded it in the forties (*The Phoenix and the Tortoise* and *In What Hour*), that an attentive reassessment of Rexroth's whole achievement needs to continue. And it should continue, I suggest, with the following modification of Wright's remarkably useful declaration: Rexroth is a great poet of love and of home in the most loveless and homeless age imaginable.

Notes

1. In *For Kenneth Rexroth* (*The Ark 14*, ed. Geoffrey Gardner, New York, 1980), p. 101.

2. Preston James, "The Blackstone Valley: A Study in Chorology in Southern New England," *Annals of the Association of American Geographers*, XIX, No. 2 (June, 1929), 67-108.

3. The essay from *Bird in the Bush* (New York: New Directions, 1959) as reprinted in Eric Mottram, ed. *The Rexroth Reader* (London: Jonathan Cape, 1972), pp. 149-172.

4. This and all other poems quoted here are taken, unless otherwise noted, from *The Collected Shorter Poems* (New York: New Directions, 1966), p. 139. Hereafter this title will be abbreviated *CSP*, and all citations of this volume will be incorporated into the text.

5. As quoted in Robert Creeley's "I'm Given to Write Poems" in *The Poetics of New American Poetry*, ed. Donald Allen and Warren Tallman (New York: Grove Press, 1973), pp. 264-265.

6. Begun as a celebration of the bright and steadfast qualities of the *polemonium* and then shifted toward a memorialization of human courage in shadowed circumstances, "Blues" ends by creating what Rexroth spoke of in his earlier "August 22, 1939" as "an anastomosis"—as, literally, a network of canals or bloodlines, and, figuratively (in that poem's context), as a network bonded by love among comrades.

7. "Greek Architecture," in *Selected Poems of Herman Melville*, ed. Hennig Cohen (Carbondale: Southern Illinois University Press, 1964), p. 155.

8. Vincent Scully, *The Earth, The Temple, and The Gods* (New York: Praeger, 1969), p. 7.

9. Robert Lowell and Kenneth Rexroth, eds., *Ford Madox Ford: Buckshee* (Cambridge: Pym Randall Press, 1966), p. 3.

10. William Carlos Williams, *Collected Later Poems* (New York: New Directions, 1950), p. 60.

11. *Evergreen Review* I, No. 2 (1957), 5-14.

12. "Written in American" [a review of Richard Hugo and John Haines], *New York Times Book Review*, Aug. 27, 1965.

13. *Czeslaw Milosz: Selected Poems* (New York: Continuum, 1981), p. 11.

14. Kenneth Rexroth, *Collected Longer Poems* (New York: New Directions, 1968),p. 303.

15. *Li Chi'ng-Chao: Complete Poems*, trans. and ed. by Kenneth Rexroth and Ling Chung (New York: New Directions, 1979),p. 27.

16. Geoffrey Thurley, *The American Moment: American Poetry in the Mid-Century* (New York: St. Martin's, 1977),p. 161.

17. *The Rexroth Reader,*p. 20.

KENNETH KNABB (ESSAY DATE 1997)

SOURCE: Knabb, Kenneth. "The Relevance of Rexroth: Magnanimity and Mysticism." In *Public Secrets*. Berkeley, Calif.: Bureau of Public Secrets, (online source), www.bopsecrets.org/PS/rexroth2.htm (1997).

In the following essay, Knabb explores Rexroth's criticism of writers he considered self-indulgent and examines his views on spiritual awareness and transcendence.

HOFUKU: (pointing at mountains) "Is not this Reality?"
CHOKEI: "It is, but it's a pity to say so."[1]

If I had to pick out a single text to exemplify what I like about Rexroth it would probably be his essay on the classic Chinese novels. In this passage he is characterizing the virtues of those vast, marvelous books:

What are these virtues? First, an absolute mastery of pure narrative. Second, humanity. Third, as the synthesis of virtues one and two, a whole group of qualities that should have some one name— reticence, artistic humility, maturity, objectivity, total sympathy, the ability to reveal the macrocosm in the microcosm, the moral universe in the physical act, the depths of psychological insight in the trivia of happenstance, without ever saying anything about it, or them—the "big" things, that is. This is a quality of style. It is the fundamental quality of the greatest style. It does have a name, although it is not a term we usually think of as part of the jargon of literary criticism. The word is magnanimity. The antonym, I guess, is self-indulgence.[2]

He goes on to deplore the self-indulgence in one form or another of virtually all twentieth-century writers, from Proust and Henry James to Kerouac and on down. Then he singles out one notable exception, Ford Madox Ford's *Parade's End*, the only "completely adult major novel of my time":

Ford didn't label his thesis; he probably didn't know he had one in that sense. His characters didn't philosophize about it. He didn't snoop around in their minds with a lot of jargon. Nobody's consciousness streamed. It all just happened, like it does, and you were left with that— the brutal and the silly and the beautiful facts. It is so easy to be artistic. It is so hard to be mature.[3]

Variations on this theme recur throughout Rexroth's writings. In great drama, he says, "psychological and moral depth must be there, but there only to be discovered by those in the audience who themselves have such depth. These qualities cannot be written on the surface or they destroy the integrity of the action."[4] Whereas he agrees with Ford that "Dostoievsky was guilty of the worst possible taste in making his characters discuss the profundity of the very novel in which they were taking part."[5] "The troubled souls of Dostoievsky's novels are not grown men. They talk endlessly about things that adults learn it is better to keep quiet about. Tragedy ceases to be impressive when it is so garrulously articulate, and at last even to be believable."[6] Rexroth has a special fondness for certain writers who embody a quiet, modest, unselfconscious wisdom—the biographer-fisherman Izaak Walton, the amateur naturalist Gilbert White, the antislavery Quaker John Woolman—while he detests the vanity of artists who glory in their supposedly special role:

Michelangelo was surely
A noisy man, and terribly
Conceited. After all, nothing
Ever happened to him that
Doesn't happen to all of us.
If you have a tragedy to
Portray, you should be humble
About it, you are serving
The bread of communion.[7]

In his essay on Julius Caesar's writings he says: "Masterfully concealed in *The Gallic War* and *The Civil War* is a philosophy of human relationships that only maturity can comprehend or even recognize. The masterful concealment, of course, is an essential part of the maturity."[8] The same thing might be said of Rexroth's own writings. For my purposes in this book I have tended to cite his most explicit pronouncements, but if you read him through you will see that he usually deals with the "big things" with a light touch, and often leaves them implicit, to be discerned between the lines.

But if ever he does reveal his life philosophy, and even sum up its central themes in a single word, it is in that essay on the Chinese novels. Which continues:

During the Second World War I knew a little Quaker from a farm in Indiana who traveled around the country at his own expense and got up in First Day meetings to recite Webster's definition of magnanimity. He had "come with this concern to thee, because thee might find it helpful." This is the definition:

"magnanimity, n.; pl. ties. (F. *magnanimité,* L. *magnanimitas.*) 1. Quality of being magnanimous;

that quality or combination of qualities in character enabling one to encounter danger and trouble with tranquility and firmness, to disdain injustice, meanness, and revenge, and to act and sacrifice for noble objects. 2. A deed or a disposition characterized by magnanimity. 3. Grandiose temperament; extravagance of soul. Rare."

Having said that the little old Quaker sat down and next week appeared at another meeting. It certainly did help me, probably more than any other words in those hideous years.

No artist belongs in the very first rank who is the victim of his creations. Only this special kind of nobility guaranteed the independence of the primary creators. Homer has it, but Dante does not. It is a kind of courage, like Johnson's famous "Courage, Sir, is the first of virtues, because without it, it is sometimes difficult to exercise the others."[9]

It is the courage to endure the inevitable "ruin of all bright things," to face the fact that "love does not last forever, friends betray each other, beauty fades, the mighty stumble in blood and their cities burn."[10] The "message" of Homer, as Rexroth approvingly paraphrases it, is that the universe has no inherent meaning, everything is ephemeral, the only values are those that people create in relation with each other. "The thing that endures, that gives value to life, is comradeship, loyalty, bravery, magnanimity, love, the relations of men in direct communication with each other. From this comes the beauty of life, its tragedy and its meaning, and from nowhere else."[11]

This may sound rather "existential," but nothing is more foreign to Rexroth than what he calls the *"angst* for *angst*'s sake" of the "paralyzed rabbit metaphysics of existentialism." "I do not respond to the 'existentialist dilemma' at all. Its inventor, Søren Kierkegaard, has always seemed to me a sick man who treated his girl friend wretchedly. A man 'badly in need of help' as the headshrinkers say. . . . I do not look on my Being every hour as a dreadful meeting with reality. I like it."[12]

If Rexroth often evokes the "tragic sense of life," at other times his works reveal a more mystical consciousness. These two attitudes would seem to contradict each other, but he appears to treat them as complementary, equally valid perspectives—sometimes contrasting them, as in the dialectic of his philosophical reveries, sometimes combining them, as in his plays, which have tragic Greek themes but which, like Japanese Nô plays, culminate not in a dramatic climax but in a transcendent resolution of karmic entanglements.[13]

He describes his point of view as "a religious anarchism" or an "ethical mysticism," and in one place, in lieu of elaborating, he refers the reader to some of his major influences: "For better statements, I refer you to the work of Martin Buber, Albert Schweitzer, D.H. Lawrence, Boehme, D.T. Suzuki, Piotr Kropotkin, or, for that matter, to the Gospels and the sayings of Buddha, or to Lao Tze and Chuang Tze."[14] This may seem a rather eclectic list, but it does give a good idea of the different facets of his "religious" philosophy. Which might be summed up in his lines:

> What is taken in
> In contemplation is poured out
> In love.[15]

In his autobiography Rexroth describes an experience he had when he was four or five years old, sitting on the curb in front of his house in early summer:

> An awareness, not a feeling, of timeless, spaceless, total bliss occupied me or I occupied it completely. I do not want to use terms like "overwhelmed me" or "I was rapt away" or any other that would imply the possession of myself by anything external, much less abnormal. On the contrary, this seemed to me to be my normal and natural life which was going on all the time and my sudden acute consciousness of it only a matter of attention.[16]

In their deepest and most enduring form such "mystical" experiences are often associated with meditation and spiritual discipline; but Rexroth implies that the same awareness comes to all of us at moments, though we may scarcely know what is happening, and it is strangely easy to forget as we once again become caught up in the compulsive turmoil of the world.

> The peace which comes from the habit of contemplation . . . is not rare nor hard to find. It offers itself at moments to everyone, from early childhood on, although less and less often if it is not welcomed. It can be seized and trained and cultivated until it becomes a constant habit in the background of daily life. Without it life is only turbulence, from which eventually meaning and even all intensity of feeling die out in tedium and disorder.[17]

"At the core of life," he says in his essay on the *Tao Te Ching,* "is a tiny, steady flame of contemplation."[18] Even without knowing anything about it, people instinctively return to this "quiet center." It is always there, even amid the most turbulent situations; but some scenes are especially conducive.

> Whoever wrote the little psalms of the *Tao Te Ching* believed that the long calm regard of moving water was one of the highest forms of prayer. . . .

Many sports are actually forms of contemplative activity. Fishing in quiet waters is especially so. Countless men who would burst out laughing if presented with a popular vulgarization of Zen Buddhism, and who would certainly find it utterly incomprehensible, practice the contemplative life by flowing water, rod in hand, at least for a few days each year. As the great mystics have said, they too know it is the illumination of these few days that gives meaning to the rest of their lives.[19]

Rexroth's nature poems are full of such experiences. In this one he is lying under the stars:

> My body is asleep. Only
> My eyes and brain are awake.
> The stars stand around me
> Like gold eyes. I can no longer
> Tell where I begin and leave off.
> The faint breeze in the dark pines,
> And the invisible grass,
> The tipping earth, the swarming stars
> Have an eye that sees itself.[20]

Sometimes, as above, the experiences are described more or less explicitly. More often they are simply hinted at:

> When I dragged the rotten log
> From the bottom of the pool,
> It seemed heavy as stone.
> I let it lie in the sun
> For a month; and then chopped it
> Into sections, and split them
> For kindling, and spread them out
> To dry some more. . . .

Late that night, as he steps out of his cabin to look at the stars—

> Suddenly I saw at my feet,
> Spread on the floor of night, ingots
> Of quivering phosphorescence,
> And all about were scattered chips
> Of pale cold light that was alive.[21]

This was no doubt a real sequence of events, but at the same time it seems to suggest a parallel inner settling and illumination—and it does this in a manner truer to the "unselfing" character of the process than if he had said *I had* such and such experiences. As in many of the great Chinese and Japanese poems, a state of mind is conveyed through the lucidity of what at first appears as merely an objective nature scene. The outer landscape corresponds to the inner one, the macrocosm to the microcosm.

In a manner almost reminiscent of Whitman, Rexroth evokes the vastest connections and reflections—

> The immense stellar phenomenon
> Of dawn focuses in the egret
> And flows out, and focuses in me

> And flows infinitely away
> To touch the last galactic dust. . . .
> My wife has been swimming in the breakers,
> She comes up the beach to meet me, nude,
> Sparkling with water, singing high and clear
> Against the surf. The sun crosses
> The hills and fills her hair, as it lights
> The moon and glorifies the sea
> And deep in the empty mountains melts
> The snow of Winter and the glaciers
> Of ten thousand thousand years.[22]

In his last poems, mainly written in Japan, these moments of "cosmic consciousness" are expressed in increasingly Buddhist terms—above all in terms of the ultimate vision of the Avatamsaka (Flower Wreath) Sutra:

> the Net of Indra,
> The compound infinities of infinities,
> The Flower Wreath,
> Each universe reflecting
> Every other, reflecting
> Itself from every other . . .[23]

Rexroth's work seems to reflect a significant Zen influence, but actually he was quite critical of many aspects of Zen and professed a greater affinity with other forms of Buddhism. He lambasted popularized Western Zen as an irresponsible, pretentious fad, but he also criticized traditional Japanese Zen for its complicity with military regimes, from the samurai to World War II, and he seems to have had little taste for the cultism and guru worship too often found in Zen as well as in other Oriental religious disciplines. He would no doubt have granted that Zen meditation is one of the most effective ways to cultivate the peace of contemplation "until it becomes a constant habit in the background of daily life." But he seemed to feel that too urgent a striving for enlightenment may miss the point. Buddha's last words are said to have been: "The combinations of the world are unstable by nature. Monks, strive without ceasing." Rexroth, in a more Taoist frame of mind, advises:

> The combinations
> Of the world are unstable
> By nature. Take it easy.[24]

The truest illumination, he says, arises as a side-effect of a way of life, not as an experience sought for its own sake.

> I believe that an ever-increasing capacity for recollection and transcendence is developed by a kind of life rather than by manipulation. Buddhism is certainly pure religious empiricism. It has no beliefs, only the simply and purely defined religious experience which becomes for the experiencers an always accessible and ever-abiding present reality. The foundation for this is neither

nervous-system gymnastics nor theological notions. It is in the Noble Eightfold Path, whose culmination is the "unruffledness"—Nirvana—which underlies reality.[25]

He didn't think much of the idea of using psychedelics as a short cut to mystical vision—at most he conceded that they had given many young people their first hint of the "interiority" repressed by middle-class American culture. In this context he often quoted St. John of the Cross: "Visions are symptoms of the defect of vision." For Rexroth the transcendent religious experience is not a vision of some different, supernatural world, but a reawakened awareness of this one.

> The real objects are their own transcendental meaning. . . . The holy is in the heap of dust—it is the heap of dust. . . . True illumination is habitude. We are unaware that we live in the light of lights because it casts no shadow. When we become aware of it we know it as birds know air and fish know water.[26]

People tend to describe such moments of awareness in terms of their own diverse religious beliefs, but the actual experiences seem to be pretty much the same, and are also found among nonreligious people. Though beyond rational conceptualization, they do not necessarily imply anything supernatural. Rexroth is quite clear about this distinction. He is refreshingly free of New Age gush and too perceptive to be taken in by the superstitions and pseudosciences so widely believed in even today. Recalling the otherwise intelligent people of his own generation who swallowed astrology or Reichian orgone boxes, he observes: "Anyone who had taken a course in high school physics would have known that this stuff was arrant nonsense but the trouble was that these people had lost belief in high school physics along with their belief in capitalism or religion. It was all one fraud to them."[27]

He is almost equally skeptical about the scientific pretensions of modern psychology and psychoanalysis. In his amusing article **"My Head Gets Tooken Apart"** he describes a time when he was paid by an Institute of Personality Assessment and Research to participate in a three-day investigation of "the creative personality." After a hilarious account of the battery of tests, interviews and questionnaires he is put through, he concludes:

> What did it all mean? Nothing. . . . This unvarnished hokum with which our society intimidates itself is far less effective—far less scientific—than the varnished hokum of other days and peoples. Any Sioux medicine man, any kind and attentive priest, any properly aged grandmother, any Chinese herbalist, could have found out more in a half hour than these people did in three days. . . . I for one would, if I had my rathers, far rather trust myself to the boys in horns and bearskins who painted the Altamira cave.[28]

Some of the traditional practices, he implies, may at least possess a kernel of intuitive insight into the basic human situations. Hokum or not, people are instinctively drawn to whatever seems to express the psychological or spiritual archetypes, the perennial inner conflicts and relations and aspirations. "What is sought in Alchemy or the Hermetic Books or the Memphite Theology, or irrational fads like flying saucers, is the basic pattern of the human mind in symbolic garb."[29] And that basic pattern is found there because it came from other basically similar minds:

> What the Gnostics projected onto the screen of their profound ignorance as a picture of the universe was in reality a picture of their own minds. Its mythology is a symbolic portrayal, almost a deliberate one, of the forces which operate in the structuring and evolution of the human personality . . . an institutionalized panorama of what Jung has called the Collective Unconscious. . . . (This notion, as Jung has pointed out, does not involve any mysterious undersoul shared by all men—it is a collective picture because all men respond to life in much the same way, because they all have the same physiological endowment.) We can operate upon our minds by the manipulation of symbols if not on the cosmos.[30]

For Rexroth there is no question of believing in the objective validity of any occult or religious system; what he is interested in is the "interiority," the "values that cannot be reduced to quantities,"[31] which may find expression in such forms. Insofar as religion is an attempted explanation of objective reality, it is progressively outmoded by advances in mankind's knowledge; but it may, he says, have a continued relevance to inner, subjective realities:

> Ideally, religion is what would be left after man *knew* everything. . . . As the speculative constructions of religion fall away as explanations of "reality" they assume the character of symbolic masks of states of the soul. If they persist in the practices of a cult, we say they have been etherialized. It is precisely their irrationality which keeps dogma and ritual alive. If they can be reduced to "common-sense" explanations or denials they die away. Only the mysteries survive, because they correspond to the processes of man's internal life, outward visible signs of inner spiritual realities.[32]

Rexroth liked to say, "Religion is something you do, not something you believe." He had a fond interest in traditional folk-religious rituals and festivals of all sorts, to the point of extolling even their most threadbare modern vestiges. "I don't care if it takes Daddy a year to pay off the bills for the First Communion Party or the Bar Mitzvah or the wedding. For a moment there has been at least a token acknowledgment that even the poorest and most humdrum life is of transcendent importance, that no individual human being is insignificant."[33] In this spirit he himself participated in various religious communions—Buddhist, Vedantist, Quaker, and even Catholic.

> What attracted me [to Catholicism] was not its Christianity, but its paganism. . . . The liturgical life of the Church moved me because it echoes the most ancient responses to the turning of the year and the changing seasons, and the rhythms of animal and human life. For me the Sacraments transfigured the rites of passage. . . . In the rites of passage—the fundamental activities and relationships of life—birth, death, sexual intercourse, eating, drinking, choosing a vocation, adolescence, mortal illness—life at its important moments is ennobled by the ceremonious introduction of transcendence; the universe is focused on the event in a Mass or ceremony that is itself a kind of dance and a work of art.[34]

Needless to say, he was opposed to practically everything about the Catholic Church except its traditional rituals; but like many people he seems to have taken part in those religious practices that appealed to him and simply ignored the aspects that didn't. "Today we have large sections of our most literate population voluntarily adopting the religious behavior and beliefs of more primitive communities for purely pragmatic, psychologistic, personal reasons."[35] His Catholicizing was mostly within Anglo-Catholic communions, which offer the rituals while rejecting the central dogmatic authority of the Roman Church.

However that may be, it has always puzzled me how someone like Rexroth could have anything to do with any Christian church. It is one thing to practice some type of meditation or take part in some ritual or festival that everyone understands is simply an arbitrary form to focus one's life or celebrate communion; it is another to seem to lend credibility to repugnant institutions and to sick dogmas that are still widely believed. As Rexroth himself says in a different mood:

> For thousands of years men of good will have been trying to make Judaism and Christianity morally palatable to sane and civilized men. No other religions have ever required such efforts at etherialization. . . . Why do people bother? If they must have a religion, the basic texts of Taoism, Buddhism, Confucianism need no such reworking. It may be necessary, particularly of the Bud-

dhist documents, to trim off the exotic rhetoric, but it is not necessary to make them mean exactly the opposite of what they say.[36]

Whatever his personal taste in rituals, Rexroth's writings on religion are usually lucid enough. As always he is seeking what might be relevant, suggestive, exemplary. In his study of the nineteenth-century radical Catholic Lamennais, for example, it is Lamennais's "spiritual sensibility" that interests him, "not the details of his changing theology and philosophy." "His doctrines changed, his life did not, and so it is his life and the literary, one might say, poetic, expression of that life consistency which is important."[37]

One thing for sure, there's nothing puritanical or unworldly about Rexroth's mysticism. He says that the theme of his poems in *The Phoenix and the Tortoise* is

> the discovery of a basis for the recreation of a system of values in sacramental marriage. The process as I see it goes something like this: from abandon to erotic mysticism, from erotic mysticism to the ethical mysticism of sacramental marriage, thence to the realization of the ethical mysticism of universal responsibility—from the Dual to the Other. These poems might well be dedicated to D. H. Lawrence, who died in the attempt to refound a spiritual family.[38]

Like he said, there is a lot of bullshit in Lawrence—mushy rhetoric, corny primitivism, dated sexual polemics, even vaguely fascistic tendencies. What remains important is his struggle to get back to the primal realities, to restore the vital, organic connections; beginning with the most intimate one. Writing of Lawrence's love and nature poems, Rexroth says: "Reality streams through the body of Frieda, through everything she touches, every place she steps . . . everything stands out lit by a light not of this earth and at the same time completely of this earth. . . . Beyond Holy Matrimony lies the newly valued world of birds, beasts, and flowers—a sacramentalized, objective world. 'Look, we have come through'—to a transformed world, with a glory around it everywhere like ground lightning." And of his death poems: "Lawrence did not try to mislead himself with false promises, imaginary guarantees. Death is the absolute, unbreakable mystery. Communion and oblivion, sex and death, the mystery can be revealed—but it can be revealed only as totally inexplicable."[39]

Rexroth's own love poems manifest a Lawrencian reverence for sex as an ultimate, unfathomable mystery:

> Invisible, solemn, and fragrant,

Your flesh opens to me in secret.
We shall know no further enigma.
After all the years there is nothing
Stranger than this. We who know ourselves
As one doubled thing, and move our limbs
As deft implements of one fused lust,
Are mysteries in each other's arms.[40]

Ever so delicately he evokes the fleeting time-lessness of the communion of lovers:

The future is long gone by
And the past will never happen
We have only this
Our one forever
So small so infinite
So brief so vast
Immortal as our hands that touch
Deathless as the firelit wine we drink
Almighty as this single kiss
That has no beginning
That will never
Never
End[41]

Kabbalism or Tantrism or the *Song of Songs,* he likes to invoke the mysticisms that play on the connection or parallel between human and divine love, that see sex as a sacramental communion, or even as a mode of contemplation:

Love is the subjective
Aspect of contemplation.
Sexual love is one of
The most perfect forms of
Contemplation, as far as it
Is without ignorance, grasping,
And appetite.[42]

This is what he means by "from the Dual to the Other":

For the undeveloped heart,
The news or even the sight
Of the destruction of thousands
Of other human beings
May assume only the form
Of a distant cry. . . .
However, as the dual,
The beloved, is known and
Loved more and more fully, all
The universe of persons
Grows steadily more and more real.[43]

One of Rexroth's deepest influences was Martin Buber, the Jewish "philosopher of dialogue." Buber, he says, is "practically the only religious writer a non-religious person could take seriously today."[44] Religious he certainly is, but in a special way that has led his philosophy jokingly but not altogether inaccurately to be called "Zen Judaism." After an early occasion when he felt that his preoccupation with a special "religious experience" had led him to fail to respond fully to someone who had come to him for help, Buber wrote:

Since then I have given up the "religious" which is nothing but the exception, extraction, exaltation, ecstasy; or it has given me up. I possess nothing but the everyday out of which I am never taken. The mystery is no longer disclosed, it has escaped or it has made its dwelling here where everything happens as it happens. I know no fulness but each mortal hour's fulness of claim and responsibility. . . . If that is religion then it is just *everything,* simply all that is lived in its possibility of dialogue.[45]

Buber sees the most fundamental reality neither in subjective experience nor in the objective world, but in the "realm of the between." "In the beginning is relation." "All real living is meeting." In his great *I and Thou* he distinguishes two basic types of relation: I-It and I-Thou. I-It is a subject-object relation of using or experiencing; the It (or He or She) is only a "thing among things," susceptible to comparison and categorization. The I-Thou relation is unique, mutual, total, and inevitably temporary. "Egos appear by setting themselves apart from other egos. Persons appear by entering into relation to other persons."[46]

Rexroth stresses that Buber's view is not a sentimental preaching of "sharing" or "togetherness" ("our current Togetherness is simply the massing of frightened cyphers"), nor an advocacy of collectivism as opposed to individualism. "Individualism understands only a part of man, collectivism understands man only as a part."[47] Both Buber and Rexroth sharply distinguish collectivity (a collection of units) from genuine community (an ensemble of persons in direct living relations with each other).

Rexroth criticizes Buber on three main points: when he becomes an apologist for Zionism (although Buber's Zionism at least was never belligerent: he worked arduously for a genuine rapprochement between Jews and Arabs); when he concludes his study of libertarian communalist currents (*Paths in Utopia*) with too much wishful thinking as to the promise of the early Israeli kibbutzim; and when, in the last part of *I and Thou,* he arrives at the notion of God as the "eternal Thou." Rexroth objects to the repugnant aspects of Buber's biblical God; but more generally he distrusts any sort of "metaphysical greed" for some absolute relation. "Any art which has a happy ending in reserve in Infinity is, just to that degree, cheating. . . . It seems to me that the fullest realization of the self comes in the acceptance of the limits of contingency. It is harder, but more ennobling, to love a wife as another human being, fugitive as oneself, than it is to carry on imaginary conversations with an imaginary Absolute."[48] More fundamentally, however, acceptance of ephemeral, contingent relations is the very essence of Buber's standpoint; the notion of an "eternal Thou" is not really a necessary implication of his philosophy. "However Martin Buber might disagree doctrinally, take away his God and nothing important in his philosophy has changed. It remains a philosophy of joy, lived in a world full of others."[49]

A vital part of Buber's work is his presentation of Hasidism, a popular mystical movement that arose in the Jewish communities of eastern Europe in the eighteenth century. Rexroth discusses at length the history and nature of Hasidism, and how it differs in some ways from Buber's sophisticated reinterpretation of it; but what stands out regardless is a "holy good humor" and an affirmation of community all too rare in religious movements. Buber's *Tales of the Hasidim* somewhat resemble Zen or Taoist or Sufi anecdotes, but they have a more communal and ethical character. Like the latter, they often reveal a decisive event in a person's life, but this is generally not so much an experience of enlightenment as a moment of inner moral "turning." There is no definitive spiritual attainment; each new situation, each new encounter, calls for one's whole being. The Hasidic tales take place in the context of a quite orthodox traditional Judaism, full of superstitions, antiquated social relations and unappealing religious forms; yet in spite of all this,

> what comes through most is joy and wonder, love and quiet, in the face of the continuously vanishing world. It is called God's Will, but the movement of the universe . . . is accepted on very similar terms to those of the *Tao Te Ching*. Song and dance, the mutual love of the community—these are the values; they are beautiful precisely because they are not absolute. And on this foundation of modesty and love and joy is raised a moral structure which heals and illuminates as hardly any other Western European religious expression does.[50]

Rexroth is always enthusiastic about these ethical or "world-affirming" mysticisms, always quick to praise and encourage any tendencies toward joining contemplation and community, toward integrating religious life with ordinary life in the world. Mysticism has, of course, more often been used to provide a justification for ignoring ethical responsibilities and social realities. The experience of transcendent unity has been taken to imply that all the suffering and turmoil in the world is only illusory and need not concern us. The paradoxical statements of mysticism (transcendence of duality, "All is one," etc.) may

be appropriate figures of speech to hint at an indescribable experience, they may even be true in a certain sense, but it is confusing different levels of reality to conclude that they are also true in the ordinary sense. The simplest refutation of this sort of transcendental sophistry is to note that even those who preach it take some aspects of worldly life quite seriously (notably the money they charge).

Rexroth never falls for it. Whenever it appears he is quick to denounce it. "The real reason for the popularity of the Occult Ancient East was pointed out long ago by Kipling: 'Ship me somewhere East of Suez . . . where there ain't no ten commandments.' If your religion is just exotic enough, you don't need to bother about responsibility. You can get away with anything."[51] Nor does Rexroth buy the notion that one must first "heal oneself" before acting in the world. As he often noted, the great mystics of the past are virtually unanimous in insisting that the two go together. "The Catholic contemplative, the Sufi, the Buddhist monk, follow counsels of perfection—illumination comes as the crown of a life of intense ethical activism, of honesty, loyalty, poverty, chastity, and above all charity, positive, out-going love of all creatures. The good life creates the ambience into which spiritual illumination flows like a sourceless, totally diffused light."[52] A classic statement of priorities by one of the greatest Western mystics: "If a person were in such a rapturous state as St. Paul once entered, and he knew of a sick man who wanted a cup of soup, it would be far better to withdraw from the rapture for love's sake and serve him who is in need" (Meister Eckhart).[53] The same is implied, but with a significant additional nuance that Rexroth especially appreciates, in the Mahayana ideal of the bodhisattva:

> A bodhisattva, in case you don't know, is one who, at the brink of absorption into Nirvana, turns away with the vow that he shall not enter final peace until he can bring all other beings with him. He does this, says the most advanced Buddhist thought, "indifferently" because he knows that there is neither being nor not-being, neither peace nor illusion, neither saved nor saviors, neither truth nor consequence. This is the reason for that benign, world-weary expression on the faces in Far Eastern religious art.[54]

But a farseeing compassion ultimately implies opposing the social system that prevents it from being fulfilled. Rexroth adds a modern supplement to the bodhisattva vow:

> While there is a lower class,
> I am in it. While there is

A criminal element,
I am of it. Where there is
A soul in jail, I am not free.[55]

Notes

1. Quoted in R. H. Blyth's *Zen in English Literature and Oriental Classics* (Hokuseido, 1942), pp. 79-80.

2. "The Chinese Classic Novel in Translation: The Art of Magnanimity," BB 215. [In case you're interested, what are generally considered the five greatest Chinese novels are now each available in both abridged and complete translations: *The Dream of the Red Chamber* (a.k.a. *The Story of the Stone*), a wonderful novel of manners with Taoist undertones; *Outlaws of the Marsh* (*The Water Margin* or *All Men Are Brothers*), a larger-than-life series of picaresque adventures; *Monkey* (*The Journey to the West*), a satirical Buddhist fantasy; *Three Kingdoms* (*The Romance of the Three Kingdoms*), a historical novel full of military strategy and political intrigue; and the erotic *Chin P'ing Mei* (*The Golden Lotus* or *The Plum in the Golden Vase*).]

3. *Ibid.*, BB 216

4. SFE, 10 July 1960.

5. "Ford Madox Ford, *Parade's End*," MCR 139-140/ER 127.

6. "Dostoievsky, *The Brothers Karamazov*," CR 184.

7. "The Dragon and the Unicorn," CLP 185-186/SP 64. See CR and MCR/ER for essays on Walton, White and Woolman.

8. "Julius Caesar, *The War in Gaul*," CR 67.

9. "The Chinese Classic Novel in Translation," BB 216-217.

10. "The Hasidism of Martin Buber," BB 139/SE 99.

11. "Unacknowledged Legislators and *Art pour Art*," BB 18.

12. SFE, 20 November 1960.

13. Rexroth's four plays are collected in *Beyond the Mountains* (New Directions, 1951).

14. Introduction to *The Signature of All Things* (New Directions, 1950).

15. "The Dragon and the Unicorn," CLP 157.

16. AN 338.

17. SFE, 13 September 1965.

18. "Lao Tzu, *Tao Te Ching*," MCR 7/ER 10.

19. "Izaak Walton, *The Compleat Angler*," CR 143-144.

20. "The Lights in the Sky Are Stars," CSP 238.

21. "The Signature of All Things," CSP 178-179/SP 44.

22. "The Phoenix and the Tortoise," CLP 90-91/SP 23-25.

23. "On Flower Wreath Hill," MS 45.

24. *Ibid.*, MS 41.

25. AN 338. Rexroth's most extensive discussion of Buddhism is in his Introduction to *The Buddhist Writings of Lafcadio Hearn* (Ross-Erikson, 1977), reprinted in SE 303-319.

26. Introduction to CLP.

27. AN 119.

28. "My Head Gets Tooken Apart," BB 71-72.

29. "The Holy Kabbalah," A 43.

30. "Gnosticism," A 141-142/SE 141-142.

31. "The Bollingen Series," WEE 203.

32. "The Holy Kabbalah," A 42-43.

33. SFE, 25 December 1960.

34. AN 335, 252.

35. "The Hasidism of Martin Buber," BB 109/SE 79.

36. *Ibid.*, BB 136-137/SE 97-98.

37. "Lamennais," ER 186-187.

38. Introduction to *The Phoenix and the Tortoise* (New Directions, 1944).

39. Introduction to Lawrence's *Selected Poems* (New Directions, 1947; Viking, 1959), pp. 11, 14, 23; reprinted in BB 189, 192, 203/SE 16, 18, 25. Compare the later, more critical essay "D.H. Lawrence: The Other Face of the Coin" (WEE 34-39).

40. "Inversely, as the Square of Their Distances Apart," CSP 148/SP 32.

41. "This Night Only" (to Satie's *Gymnopédie #1*), CSP 338.

42. "The Dragon and the Unicorn," CLP 268.

43. *Ibid.*, CLP 178.

44. "The Hasidism of Martin Buber," BB 106/SE 77.

45. Martin Buber, *Between Man and Man*, translated by Ronald Gregor Smith (Macmillan, 1965),p. 14.

46. Martin Buber, *I and Thou*, translated by Walter Kaufmann (Scribner's, 1970),p. 112. The other two quotations are from the earlier translation by Ronald Gregor Smith (Scribner's, 1958), pp. 18, 11.

47. "The Hasidism of Martin Buber," BB 130-131/SE 93-94.

48. *Ibid.*, BB 139-140/SE 99-100.

49. *Ibid.*, BB 112/SE 81.

50. *Ibid.*, BB 141-142/SE 101.

51. *Ibid.*, BB 110-111/SE 80.

52. SFE, 30 August 1964.

53. Raymond Blakney, *Meister Eckhart: A Modern Translation* (Harper, 1941),p. 14.

54. "The World of the Shining Prince," ER 143.

55. "The Dragon and the Unicorn," CLP 233 (adapted from Eugene Debs).

JOHN P. O'GRADY (ESSAY DATE 1997)

SOURCE: O'Grady, John P. "Kenneth Rexroth." In *Updating the Literary West*, sponsored by the Western Literature Association, pp. 321-8. Fort Worth: Texas Christian University Press, 1997.

In the following essay, O'Grady provides an overview of Rexroth's life and works.

FROM THE AUTHOR

COMMERCE AND THE BEAT GENERATION

The Beat Generation may once have been human beings—today they are simply comical bogies conjured up by the Luce publications. Their leading spokesmen are just "Engine Charley" Wilson and Dr. Oppenheimer dressed up in scraggly beards and dirty socks. For this reason I have omitted from this collection all those articles which discussed the revolt or emotional suicide of young American writers, published back in the days when Madison Avenue and its outposts in the Quarterlies were all insisting that everything was conformity, peace, and professorships.

Success, alas, as it almost always does, led to the worst kind of emotional suicide. Those to whom that kind of success was a temptation have become the trained monkeys, the clowning helots of the Enemy. They came to us late, from the slums of Greenwich Village, and they departed early, for the salons of millionairesses.

Rexroth, Kenneth. Excerpt from the introduction to *Bird in the Bush: Obvious Essays*. New York: New Directions, 1959.

Poet, painter, essayist, mountain climber, translator, philosophical anarchist, cultural critic, raconteur extraordinaire, autodidact, and literary curmudgeon, Kenneth Rexroth (1905-1982) is one of the West Coast's most significant writers. He is certainly its greatest religious poet. Indeed, the best of Rexroth's poems actually were written in monasteries, hermitages, or the wild mountains of the Pacific Slope. The sensibility that emerges in his poetry is eclectic and wide ranging, drawing with ease from the mystical traditions in Christianity, Judaism, ancient Greece, Taoism, and Buddhism. "Poetry is vision, the pure act of sensual contemplation" (***Bird in the Bush*** 189). Kenneth Rexroth was an intellectual and poetic shaman.

Important as mystical experience may have been to him, Rexroth's work has a useful beauty. He cherished the poem's ability to communicate directly all manner of experience. "A love poem is

an act of communication of love, like a kiss. The poem of contempt and satire is like a punch in the nose" (***Bird in the Bush*** 12). Unlike the High Modernists, led by Ezra Pound, T. S. Eliot and poet-proponents of the New Criticism such as John Crowe Ransom, Rexroth embraced an aesthetic of clarity while rejecting technical emphases on form and rhetorical ingenuity. In the **"Art of Literature"** entry he originally wrote for the fifteenth edition of the *Encyclopedia Britannica*, Rexroth recorded: "Form simply refers to organization, and critics who attack form do not seem always to remember that a writer organizes more than words. He organizes experience. Thus, his organization stretches far back in his mental process. Form is the other face of content, the outward, visible sign of inner spiritual reality" (**World Outside the Window** 290).

At the core of all this is yet another distinguishing feature of his poetry: a compelling moral vision. In one of his most important essays, **"Unacknowledged Legislators and *Art Pour Art*,"** he presents the centerpiece of his poetics: "Poetry increases and guides our awareness to immediate experience. It organizes sensibility so that it is not wasted" (***Bird in the Bush*** 6). Martin Buber's *I-Thou*, says Rexroth, was "one of the determinative books of my life" (***Bird in the Bush*** 107). A reader can spot this at once in Rexroth's personal, pragmatic, and experiential approach to writing poetry. "The arts presume to speak directly from person to person, each polarity, the person at each end of the communication fully realized" (12). His poetry demonstrates a social awareness and engagement that made him an anathema to those readers (such as the New Critics) who insisted that art must stand autonomously or it cannot be considered art. Wrote William Carlos Williams in a review of **In Defense of the Earth** and **One Hundred Poems from the Chinese**: "Rexroth is a moralist with his hand at the trigger ready to fire at the turn of an hair" (Williams 182).

By all accounts Rexroth had a brilliant mind and a photographic memory. A high school dropout, he spent the last of his many creative years as a professor of poetry at the University of California, Santa Barbara. Despite this intellectual brilliance, he pursued in both his life and work a non-intellectualized individualism, a California literary tradition already well established by writers like Jack London, Frank Norris, Mary Austin, and Robinson Jeffers. "This is San Francisco speaking," he writes of Norris' *McTeague* but just as well could have been referring to his own work, "a city mercifully spared the westward radiation of the great light from Plymouth Rock" (**With Eye and Ear** 32). Rexroth cultivated a profound antipathy to Calvinism and the New England literary tradition (probably a reaction to the New Critics, who in the course of Rexroth's lifetime succeeded in canonizing writers such as Emerson, Thoreau, Hawthorne, and Melville), and he turned instead to Europe and especially Asia for his literary inspiration, citing the classical Chinese poet Tu Fu as "the major influence" on his work: "In some ways he is a better poet than either Shakespeare or Homer. At least he is more natural and intimate" (**Autobiographical Novel** 319). Rexroth in fact became one of the most important translators of Chinese and Japanese poetry into English. His deep and abiding interest in Buddhism rippled down in the form of influence upon younger generations of West Coast writers, most significant among them Gary Snyder.

In his day, Rexroth enjoyed a substantial literary reputation, especially in the Bay Area, where during the fifties and into the sixties he gave a weekly Sunday evening radio broadcast on literary and cultural matters that made him if not a purveyor of taste certainly one of the liveliest and best-known figures in the region. He was also known to a national audience through his regular contributions to *The Nation* and other widely circulated magazines but he never gained acceptance among the New York literary establishment, most likely because of his relentless attacks on them in his literary journalism. He loathed the New Critics, who in those days dominated American colleges and universities, and ridiculed to no end the "professor-poets." Perhaps Rexroth's most egregious violation of American writing-industry decorum was to thumb his nose at the New York literary establishment and instead make California his lifelong home, pledging his allegiance to its mountains and waters rather than to the vanity of publishers, editors, and reviewers who make and break literary reputations at Manhattan cocktail parties. No wonder Morgan Gibson in 1967 called him "America's greatest underground poet." The same might still be said.

In surveying today's anthologies, one quickly realizes that Rexroth's work has yet to surface in the academic canon. In a significant way, this critical neglect is one result of the posturing Rexroth engaged in from the start of his literary career. In a lecture delivered in November 1936 to the Conference of Western Writers in San Francisco, he took up the cudgels he never laid down: "I believe that to a certain extent always, but in modern times especially, the poet, by the very nature of his art, has been an enemy of society, that is, of the privileged and the powerful. He has sometimes been an ally of the unprivileged and weak, where such groups were articulate and organized, otherwise he has waged an individual and unaided war" (**World Outside The Window** 1).

Ironically enough, for all his blustering against the New England Transcendentalists, Rexroth very much seems a latter-day Emerson or, especially, Thoreau, staking out the high moral and spiritual ground on the western edge of North America. Whereas his reputation in the academy may have suffered for his bilious hauteur, his poetry did not—and his readers became the beneficiaries of his courage. His influence on fellow writers has been immense, the short list including Snyder, Lawrence Ferlinghetti, and Allen Ginsberg, all of whom do appear in the anthologies. Rexroth was at the center of the literary historical moment known as The San Francisco Renaissance. Much to his chagrin, he also acquired the moniker of "father of the Beat Generation," largely due to his having served as master of ceremonies at the famous Six Gallery poetry reading in San Francisco in October of 1955, and he was an early defender of and publicist for younger writers, including Jack Kerouac.

The details of Rexroth's life are abundant, colorful, and often contradictory. He loved to tell stories and embellish upon the facts, including those of his life, a tendency that forced his publisher to insist Rexroth title his autobiography **An Autobiographical Novel**. Midwesterner by birth and rearing, he did not embark upon a life in the West until advised by an unlikely spiritual benefactor, the anarchist Alexander Berkman, whom Rexroth had encountered in one of the Lost Generation cafes in Paris. "Go West," Berkman counseled the twenty-year-old aspiring artist. "There is more for you in the Far West than there is here. You can probably become famous here but you'll just be another one" (342). As if to repay the debt, Rexroth years later wrote an introduction to a new edition of Berkman's *Prison Memoirs of an Anarchist*. In 1927 Rexroth and his first wife, the painter Andree Dutcher, did indeed go West, settling in San Francisco. Although she died of epilepsy in 1940, he spent the next four decades in the City by the Bay, then moved south to Santa Barbara, where he was on the university faculty until his death in 1982.

Although Berkman might have been responsible for pointing Rexroth toward the West, it was the beauty of its mountains that held the poet in thrall for the rest of his life. He had an awakening to his life's purpose as he gazed upon the slopes of Glacier Peak, one of Washington's most prominent volcanoes: "To the southwest the great mountain rose up covered with walls of ice. There was no one near me for many miles in any direction. I realized then with complete certainty that this was the place for me. This was the kind of life I liked best. I resolved to live it as much as I could from then on. By and large I've kept that resolve and from that day much of my time and for some years most of my time was spent in the Western mountains" (282). During the thirties, Rexroth wrote a manuscript he called "**Camping in the Western Mountains**," one of the most eccentric books in all mountaineering literature. Part how-to manual, part anarchist philosophy, and part cranky opinion, the manuscript was never published, yet it stands as a record of the profound influence the western landscape played in Rexroth's creative life. "The mountains and glaciers, the forests and streams of America are a heritage shared equally by all the people, and they are not simply 'recreation areas,' but training grounds for group living and group sharing. . . . Each group that hikes or rides along the trail by day contented and alert, and makes camp at night 'decently and in good order' is a sort of test tube or kindergarten of the good life. So don't forget, when it's your turn to wash the dishes, the centuries are watching you."

Rexroth spent a great deal of his time in the outdoors. During his younger days in the summers, he would head to the backcountry of the Sierra Nevada for two months at a stretch, sometimes with companions and sometimes alone, adrift among the unpeopled ranges of the Kaweahs and the Great Western Divide, Clarence King country. He would often ascend those high and difficult mountains, but not as a mere "peak bagger"; mountaineering was for Rexroth—as it was for Petrarch, John Bunyan's Christian, and René Daumal—a form of spiritual practice. A reader encounters this in a poem like "**Climbing Milestone Mountain, August 22, 1937**," which fuses mountaineering, contemplation, and politics into a beautiful, accessible whole. The best of his mountain poems, though, are those that conjoin spiritual and erotic rapture to yield exquisite passion—"**Incarnation**" being representative, a poem that concludes in lines best described as Tantric in their revelatory power:

> Your thigh's exact curve, the fine gauze
> Slipping through my hands, and you
> Tense on the verge of abandon;

> Your breasts' very touch and smell;
> The sweet secret odor of sex.
> Forever the thought of you,
> And the splendor of the iris,
> The crinkled iris petal,
> The gold hairs powdered with pollen,
> And the obscure cantata
> Of the tangled water, and the
> Burning, impassive snow peaks,
> Are knotted together here.
> This moment of fact and vision
> Seizes immortality,
> Becomes the person of this place.
> The responsibility
> Of love realized and beauty
> Seen burns in a burning angel
> Real beyond flower or stone.
> (*Collected Shorter Poems* 162)

As counterpoise to this eroticism are the numerous poems of "withdrawal" that seem to come out of a monastic tradition of verse. During the thirties and forties Rexroth maintained a hermitage (actually an old sheepherder's shack) deep in one of the aromatic redwood and laurel canyons just north of San Francisco, and here he composed some of his finest work, including "**The Signature of All Things**," "**Hojoki**" (Japanese for "Account of My Hut," the title of a famous work in the Buddhist literature by Kamo no Chomei), and "**Time Spirals**." In his last years—during which he wrote the poems most clearly influenced by Buddhism—he remarked that he had lost interest in politics entirely, and now was "only interested in mystical experience."

Rexroth's experiences in the natural world had a profound effect on his sensibility as a poet, instilling in him an awareness of the immanence that put him at odds with the majority of his contemporaries. Whereas most modernist and post-modernist poetry seems preoccupied with directing attention to the poem itself, Rexroth's is a poetry of transmission. "A poem," he explained in a 1968 interview, "is an efficient vehicle for focusing attention, for giving direct experience" (Pondrom 320). This pragmatic approach to the poem invites comparison to the old Zen metaphor of the finger pointing to the moon: one would certainly be foolish to confuse the finger for the moon. A poetry—or a criticism—too caught up in its own language does indeed confuse the finger for the moon; it erects its own prison. Rexroth's nature poetry is among the best in American literature, and indeed provides a spiritual anodyne to the bleak vision of a critically acclaimed poet such as Robert Frost.

Central to Rexroth's poetics is his notion of "sacramental relationship." For him, poetry is a form of deep interpersonal communication. In this sense, poetry actually takes its place among those rituals that serve to establish and maintain community. Rather than privilege poetry as a "special" or "superior" activity, Rexroth restores it to its original religious context where it once again may be put to use. His radical practice reminds us that the origin of our word "poetry" is to be found in the ancient Greek verb *poein*, "to make." Thus poetry, like religion, is not something you believe but something you do. "In the arts—and ideally in much other communication—the relationship is not only active, it is the highest form of activity" (**Bird in the Bush** 13). Perhaps Rexroth's most considerable achievement was his effort to reinvigorate his culture's understanding of the poem, aligning it with other rites of passage, since all "the fundamental activities and relationships of life—birth, death, sexual intercourse, eating, drinking, choosing a vocation, adolescence, mortal illness—life at its important moments is ennobled by the ceremonious introduction of transcendence; the universe is focused on the event in a Mass or ceremony that is itself a kind of dance and work of art. This is the significance of religion" (**Autobiographical Novel** 252).

Selected Bibliography

PRIMARY SOURCES
The Alternative Society: Essays from the Other World. New York: Herder and Herder, 1970.

American Poetry in the Twentieth Century. New York: Herder and Herder, 1971.

An Autobiographical Novel. New York: Doubleday, 1966.

Beyond the Mountains. New York: New Directions, 1951.

Bird in the Bush. New York: New Directions, 1959.

The Burning Heart: Women Poets of Japan. With Ikuko Atsumi. New York: Seabury, 1977.

"Camping in the Western Mountains." Unpublished ms. c. 1936. Special Collections, Doheny Library, University of Southern California.

Classics Revisited. Chicago: Quadrangle Books, 1968.

The Collected Longer Poems. New York: New Directions, 1968.

The Collected Shorter Poems. New York: New Directions, 1966.

Communalism: From its Origins to the Twentieth Century. New York: Seabury, 1974.

The Elastic Retort: Essays in Literature and Ideas. New York: Seabury, 1973.

Li Ch'ing Chou: Complete Poems. With Ling Chung. New York: New Directions, 1979.

Love in the Turning Year: One Hundred More Poems from the Chinese. New York: New Directions, 1970.

The Morning Star. New York: New Directions, 1979.

One Hundred More Poems from the Japanese. New York: New Directions, 1974.

One Hundred Poems from the Chinese. New York: New Directions, 1956.

One Hundred Poems from the Japanese. New York: New Directions, 1955.

The Orchid Boat: Women Poets of China. With Ling Chung. New York: Herder and Herder, McGraw-Hill, 1972.

Pierre Reverdy: Selected Poems. New York: New Directions, 1969.

Poems from the Greek Anthology. Ann Arbor: University of Michigan Press, 1962.

Selected Poems. Bradford Morrow, ed and introduction. New York: New Directions, 1984.

Thirty Spanish Poems of Love and Exile. San Francisco: City Lights, 1956.

With Eye and Ear. New York: Herder and Herder, 1970.

World Outside the Window: The Selected Essays of Kenneth Rexroth. Edited with a preface by Bradford Morrow. New York: New Directions, 1987.

SECONDARY SOURCES
Bartlett, Lee. *Kenneth Rexroth.* Boise: Boise State University Western Writers Series, 1988.

———. *Kenneth Rexroth and James Laughlin: Selected Letters.* New York: Norton, 1991.

Gardner, Geoffrey, ed. *For Rexroth.* New York: The Ark, 1980.

Gibson, Morgan. *Revolutionary Rexroth: Poet of East-West Wisdom.* Hamden, Connecticut: Archon Books, 1986.

Gutierrez, Donald. "Natural Supernaturalism: The Nature Poetry of Kenneth Rexroth." *Literary Review,* 26 (Spring 1983): 405-422.

Hamalian, Linda. *A Life of Kenneth Rexroth.* New York: Norton, 1991.

Hass, Robert. *Twentieth Century Pleasures: Prose on Poetry.* New York: Ecco Press, 1984. Pp. 223-234.

Hatlen, Burton and Carroll F. Terrell, eds. *Sagetrieb: Special Issue Kenneth Rexroth,* 2 (Winter 1983).

Knabb, Ken. *The Relevance of Rexroth.* Berkeley: Bureau of Public Secrets, 1990.

Lipton, Lawrence. "The Poetry of Kenneth Rexroth," *Poetry,* 40:3 (June 1957): 168-180.

Meltzer, David. "Kenneth Rexroth." In *The San Francisco Poets.* New York: Ballantine, 1971. Pp. 9-55. (Interview.)

Parkinson, Thomas. "Kenneth Rexroth, Poet." *Ohio Review* (Winter 1976): 54-67.

Pondrom, Cyrena N. "Interview with Kenneth Rexroth." *Contemporary Literature,* 10 (Summer 1969): 313-330.

Richards, Janet. *Common Soldiers.* San Francisco: Archer, 1979.

Robertson, David. "Kenneth Rexroth in Devil's Gulch." *American Poetry,* 8 (1990): 116-127.

Williams, William Carlos. "Two New Books by Kenneth Rexroth." *Poetry,* 90 (June 1957): 180-190.

FURTHER READING

Bibliography

Hartzell, James, and Richard Zumwinkle. *Kenneth Rexroth: A Checklist of His Published Writings.* Los Angeles: Friends of the UCLA Library, University of California, 1967, 67p.

Primary bibliography of collected and uncollected works by Rexroth.

Biographies

Barlett, Lee, editor. Introduction to *Kenneth Rexroth and James Laughlin: Selected Letters*, pp. xi-xxiii. New York: W.W. Norton & Company, 1991.

Outlines relationship between Rexroth and New Directions publisher Laughlin.

Gibson, Morgan. *Revolutionary Rexroth: Poet of East-West Wisdom.* Hamden, Conn.: Archon Books, 1986, 153p.

Acclaimed biography by longtime friend of Rextroth.

Hamalian, Linda. *A Life of Kenneth Rexroth.* New York: W. W. Norton & Company, 1991, 444p.

Thorough portrait is often unflattering, especially concerning his relationships with women.

Watson, Steven. "Kenneth Rexroth." In *The Birth of the Beat Generation: Visionaries, Rebels, and Hipsters, 1944-1960*, pp. 197-200. New York: Pantheon Books, 1995.

Biographical sketch focusing on Rexroth's contributions to the Beat movement.

Woodcock, George. "Elegy for an Anarchist." *London Review of Books* 6, no. 1 (19 January-1 February 1984): 20, 22.

Remembrance of Rexroth.

Criticism

Garren, Samuel B. "Recreating Visionary Experience in Kenneth Rexroth's 'The Signature of All Things.'" *Studia Mystica* 9, no. 4 (winter 1986): 33-9.

Close reading of Rexroth's poem.

Gibson, Morgan. "Polemics and Elegies of the Atomic Age." In *Kenneth Rexroth*, pp. 92-109. New York: Twayne Publishers, 1972.

Surveys and critiques Rexroth's work from the mid 1950s through the early 1960s.

Gibson, Morgan. "'Poetry is Vision'—'Vision is Love': Kenneth Rexroth's Philosophy of Literature." *Sagetrieb* 2, no. 3 (winter 1983): 85-99.

Considers the multiple meanings "vision" possesses for Rexroth.

——. "Reviewing Rexroth." *American Poetry* 7, no. 1 (fall 1989): 88-95.

Morgan's defense against criticism of his work on Rexroth; discusses reasons why many academics disliked Rexroth.

Gutierrez, Donald. "Love Sacred and Profane: The Erotic Lyrics of Kenneth Rexroth." *Sagetrieb* 2, no. 3 (winter 1983): 101-12.

Praises Rexroth's erotic poetry for its variety, articulation, and control.

——. "Keeping an Eye on Nature: Kenneth Rexroth's 'Falling Leaves and Early Snow.'" *American Poetry* 1, no. 2 (winter 1984): 60-4.

Praises Rexroth's poem for its subtlety.

——. "Musing with Sappho: Kenneth Rexroth's Love Poem 'When We With Sappho' as Reverie." *American Poetry* 4, no. 1 (fall 1986): 54-63.

Explores Sappho's influence on Rexroth's poetics.

——. "The Holiness of the Ordinary: The Literary-Social Journalism of Kenneth Rexroth." *Northwest Review* 32, no. 2 (1994): 109-27.

Describes the extraordinary breadth of Rexroth's reading and evaluates him as critic.

——. "The West and Western Mountains in the Poetry of Kenneth Rexroth." *North Dakota Quarterly* 62, no. 3 (summer 1994-1995): 121-39.

Contends that Rexroth's Western verse transcends regionality.

——. "Rexroth's Incarnation." *Explicator* 53, no. 4 (1995): 236-8.

Review of "Incarnation" that notes sexual imagery in Rexroth's nature verse.

——. "'The Age of Gold versus the Age of Iron': Kenneth Rexroth's *The Dragon and the Unicorn*." *North Dakota Quarterly* 63, no. 2 (spring 1996): 189-205.

Study of Rexroth's book-length travel poem.

——. *"The Holiness of the Real": The Short Verse of Kenneth Rexroth.* Madison, N.J.: Fairleigh Dickinson University Press, 1996, 276p.

Explores the influence of Asian thought on Rexroth's philosophy and his place in American literary culture

Hamalian, Leo. "Scanning the Self: The Influence of Emerson on Kenneth Rexroth." *South Dakota Review* 27, no. 2 (summer 1989): 3-14.

Focuses on ideas of freedom and individualism Rexroth shared with Ralph Waldo Emerson.

Hamill, Sam. "Lyric, Miserable Lyric (Or: Whose Dog Are You?)." *American Poetry Review* 16, no. 5 (September-October 1987): 31-2.

Review of Rexroth's essay collection World Outside the Window.

Hamill, Sam, and Elaine Laura Kleiner. "*Sacramental Acts: The Love Poems of Kenneth Rexroth.*" *American Poetry Review* 26, no. 6 (November-December 1997): 17-18.

Praises Rexroth's erotic poetry and discusses his marriages.

Hart, George. "The Discursive Mode: Kenneth Rexroth, The California State Guide, and Nature Poetry in the 1930s." *Western American Literature* 37, no. 1 (spring 2002): 5-25.

Traces Rexroth's shift from Cubist verse to a style embracing wilderness, Christianity, and Buddhism.

Junkins, Donald. "Creeley and Rexroth: No Simple Poets." *Massachusetts Review* 9 (summer 1968): 598-603.

Review of The Heart's Garden, the Garden's Heart.

Kahn, Paul. "Kenneth Rexroth's Tu Fu." *Yearbook of Comparative and General Literature* 37 (1988): 79-97.

Analyzes Rexroth's translations of Tu Fu.

Kodama, Sanehide. "Kenneth Rexroth." In *American Poetry and Japanese Culture*, pp. 121-53. Hamden, Conn.: Archon Books, 1984.

Critiques, among other works, The Phoenix and the Tortoise, Beyond the Mountains, *and* The Dragon and the Unicorn.

Lefevere, André. "Translation as the Creation of Images or 'Excuse Me, Is This the Same Poem?'." In *Essays and Studies 1997: Translating Literature*, edited by Susan Bassnett, pp. 64-79. Cambridge, England: D. S. Brewer, 1997.

Compares Rexroth's approach to translation to that of other translators.

Morrow, Bradford, editor. Introduction to *Selected Poems*, by Kenneth Rexroth, pp. ix-xxii. New York: New Direction Books, 1984.

Describes Rexroth's education and literary principles.

Smith, Richard Cándida. "After the War or Before? Kenneth Rexroth Confronts History." In *Utopia and Dissent: Art, Poetry, and Politics in California*, pp. 32-66. Berkeley: University of California Press, 1995.

Chronicles Rexroth's political radicalism and poetry.

Woodcock, George. "Realms Beyond the Mountains: Notes on Kenneth Rexroth." *Ontario Review,* no. 6 (spring-summer 1977): 39-48.

Appreciation of Rexroth and his "ability to absorb and adapt" non-English poetry.

Zaller, Robert. "Jeffers, Rexroth, and the Trope of Hellenism." *Western American Literature* 36, no. 2 (summer 2001): 153-69.

Examines Rexroth's treatment of Greek drama and compares it to that of Robinson Jeffers.

OTHER SOURCES FROM GALE:

Additional coverage of Rexroth's life and career is contained in the following sources published by the Gale Group: *Concise Dictionary of American Literary Biography, 1941-1968; Contemporary Authors,* Vols. 5-8R; *Contemporary Authors New Revision Series,* Vols. 14, 34, 63; *Contemporary Literary Criticism,* Vols. 1, 2, 6, 11, 22, 49, 112; *Dictionary of Literary Biography,* Vols. 16, 48, 165, 212; *Dictionary of Literary Biography Yearbook, 1982; DISCovering Authors Modules: Poets; Literature Resource Center; Major 20th-Century Writers,* Eds. 1, 2; *Poetry Criticism,* Vol. 20; and *Reference Guide to American Literature,* Ed. 4.

ED SANDERS

(1939 -)

(Full name James Edward Sanders) American poet, novelist, essayist, playwright, nonfiction writer, short story writer, and songwriter.

Widely known as an activist, writer, and musician, Sanders gained recognition with his poetry magazine *Fuck You: A Magazine of the Arts*, which published works from a variety of major Beat authors including Allen Ginsberg and William Burroughs. He also is known for his nonfiction work *The Family: The Story of Charles Manson's Dune Buggy Attack Battalion* (1971), an account of serial murderer Charles Manson and his followers, as well as for founding the folk-rock band the Fugs. Combining a militant radicalism with a satirical disregard for the restrictions placed upon cultural expression, Sanders's works denounce conventional morality and government repression while celebrating physical and spiritual liberation and altered states of consciousness. Compared by some critics to such poets as William Blake, Walt Whitman, and Charles Olson, Sanders blends slang, profanity, and neologisisms with archaic diction and ancient hieroglyphs to create verse rich in satire and social commentary.

BIOGRAPHICAL INFORMATION

Sanders was born on August 17, 1939, in Kansas City, Missouri, to Lyle and Mollie Sanders.

Sanders studied engineering at the University of Missouri and then moved to New York City in the late 1950s, becoming an active figure in the local literary and political scene. He enrolled in New York University and earned a bachelor of arts degree in Greek. In keeping with his newfound activism, Sanders marched in a Walk for Peace in 1961. He was arrested during a peace vigil at a Polaris submarine base and served time in Montville State Jail, where he wrote his first work, *Poem from Jail* (1963). Following his release from prison, Sanders sought a forum for his radical political and literary ambitions, and in 1962 he founded *Fuck You: A Magazine of the Arts*. The journal attacked conventional cultural and social values, particularly censorship laws. In late 1964 Sanders expanded his activities by opening Peace Eye Bookstore on New York City's Lower East Side, which became a gathering place for the city's Beat culture. The store specialized in poetry books and magazines and also served as the offices for *Fuck You*. In 1965 the New York City police department raided Peace Eye and seized all copies of *Fuck You* as well as other materials, arresting Sanders on obscenity charges. With the help of the American Civil Liberties Union, Sanders successfully defended himself against the charges, but few of the confiscated materials were returned. At Peace Eye, Sanders met poet Tuli Kupferberg, and they later formed the musical group, the Fugs. After playing approximately nine-hundred shows in New York City, the Fugs toured the United States and Europe.

Sanders is remains politically and socially active, and serves as chairman of a committee to create environmentally-sensitive zoning ordinances for the town of Woodstock, New York, where he currently resides.

MAJOR WORKS

In such early volumes as *Poem from Jail, King Lord/Queen Freak* (1964), *The Toe Queen: Poems* (1964), and *Peace Eye* (1965), Sanders employs ancient and contemporary language, vulgar diction, myth, and commentary on current events to express his disillusionment with the world. Despite his pessimism, Sanders conveys his belief that salvation is possible through communal living and harmonious co-existence with nature. In *20,000 A.D.* (1976) Sanders reveals his fascination with ancient Egyptian culture through translations of hieroglyphics while also emphasizing his interest in the antiwar movement. *Investigative Poetry* (1981) and *The Z-D Generation* (1981) are poetic manifestos in which Sanders demands that writers describe instances of government corruption in their work. He has published eighteen volumes of poetry, including *Chekhov* (1995) and *The Poetry and Life of Allen Ginsberg: A Narrative Poem* (2000)—both biographies in verse—and three book-length histories in verse, *1968: A History in Verse* (1997) and *America: A History in Verse, Volumes I and II* (2000).

In his best-known work, *The Family,* Sanders documents the events leading up to the murder of Sharon Tate and six others in 1969 by Charles Manson and his group of disciples. Sanders conducted hundreds of interviews, attended the trial, read transcripts, and visited Manson's camp and the crime scenes in an attempt to explain how the California youth culture that supposedly championed peace and love could produce a "family" of mass murderers. In his fiction, Sanders often lampoons the New York bohemian milieu in which he lives. *Shards of God: A Novel of the Yippies* (1970) is a mock-epic tale detailing the political, social, and religious events that culminated in the formation of the Youth International Party during the 1968 Democratic National Convention. *Tales of Beatnik Glory* (1975) consists of satirical vignettes of the hedonistic Greenwich Village Beat culture of the late 1950s and early 1960s. The book focuses on Sam, an autobiographical character, who describes his rural childhood and his involvement in radical literary and political groups. *Fame and Love in New York* (1980) is an intricately plotted novel set in the near future that burlesques the greed of the New York art community.

CRITICAL RECEPTION

Sanders has been praised for his unbiased portrayals of the Beat era and the 1960s in his poetry and prose as well as for his often controversial subject material. Critics have lauded his continuing commitment to political issues and his unique skill with satirizing social conventions. Carl Solomon commented that "[Sanders] has always had a unique personal idiom and style occasionally reminiscent of satirists of the past but always recognizably Ed Sanders." Some reviewers have faulted Sanders's prose as often unfocused and repetitious. While *The Family* received some positive critical attention and was popular with readers, a number of reviewers have contended that Sanders concentrated too heavily on the minutiae of the case without examining the motivation behind the killings.

PRINCIPAL WORKS

Poem from Jail (poetry) 1963

King Lord/Queen Freak (poetry) 1964

The Toe Queen: Poems (poetry) 1964

Peace Eye (poetry) 1965; enlarged edition, 1967

Shards of God: A Novel of the Yippies (novel) 1970

The Family: The Story of Charles Manson's Dune Buggy Attack Battalion (nonfiction) 1971; revised as *The Family: The Manson Group and Its Aftermath,* 1990

Vote! [with Abbie Hoffman and Jerry Rubin] (nonfiction) 1972

Egyptian Hieroglyphs (poetry) 1973

Tales of Beatnik Glory (short stories) 1975; expanded edition, 1990

Investigative Poetry (essays) 1976

20,000 A.D. (poetry) 1976

The Karen Silkwood Cantata (play) 1979

Fame and Love in New York (novel) 1980

The Cutting Prow (poetry) 1981

The Z-D Generation (poetry) 1981

Hymn to Maple Syrup and Other Poems (poetry) 1985

Star Peace (play) 1986

Poems for Robin (poetry) 1987

Thirsting for Peace in a Raging Century: Selected Poems 1961-1985 (poetry) 1987

Cassandra (play) 1992

Hymn to the Rebel Cafe (short stories) 1993

Cracks of Grace (short stories) 1994

Chekhov (poetry) 1995

Der Sommer der Liebe (short stories) 1997

1968: A History in Verse (poetry) 1997

America: A History in Verse, Volume I, 1900-1939 (poetry) 2000

America: A History in Verse, Volume II, 1940-1961 (poetry) 2000

The Poetry and Life of Allen Ginsberg: A Narrative Poem (poetry) 2000

GENERAL COMMENTARY

ED SANDERS AND TANDY STURGEON (INTERVIEW DATE 1986 AND 1988)

SOURCE: Sanders, Ed, and Tandy Sturgeon. "An Interview with Edward Sanders." *Contemporary Literature* 31, no. 3 (fall 1990): 263-80.

In the following interview, which was conducted in 1986 and 1988, Sanders discusses his early childhood, the development of his love for poetry, his education, his move to New York, his founding of Fuck You *and the legal problems surrounding the publication of the magazine.*

Born in Kansas City on August 17, 1939, Ed Sanders migrated to New York's Greenwich Village as a young man. From this point on, as voracious reader and tireless literary *artiste*, he became a full-fledged writer (of poetry, fiction, and investigative journalism), editor, Peace Eye Bookstore owner, musician (founding member of the Fugs), and antiwar activist. The appearance of **Poem from Jail** from City Lights Books in 1963 was followed by a steady stream of poetry collections, many of which are excerpted in Sanders's collected poems, **Thirsting for Peace in a Raging Century** (Coffee House Press, 1987). Sanders's work, despite its variety of intonations, has always remained committed to the idea promulgated by his **Investigative Poetry** (City Lights Books, 1975):

"that poetry should again assume responsibility for the description of history."

As Charles Olson once noted, Sanders's work "advances in a direction of production which probably isn't even guessed at." In the 1975 edition of *Contemporary Poets*, Don Byrd remarked that in Sanders's poetry "the raw energy of a 1960s-style peace march, a rock concert, and an orgy impels a fine intelligence. Many of his poems can be read as political protest; some may be read, by a reader intent upon it, as pornography." This last possibility may explain why Sanders's work, soundly planted in his enthusiastic, scholarly study of the classics, Egyptology, political philosophy, and the English romantics, is not as widely circulated as it should be.

In 1979, in an essay introducing John Clarke's *The End of This Side*, "**The Clarke-Boat, the O-Boat, and the Bard-Boat**," Sanders described the modern poet's role as a perpetuation of Noah's task. He argues that "the establishment of mythic poetry and National Epic, in the 'God-is-Dead' mythless bureaucratic era of money-grubbers operating mines in the asteroid belt, will be difficult." Despite this difficulty, Sanders sails on, as exemplified by a recent project, a touring opera production entitled **Star Peace**.

This interview began in June 1986 at Sanders's home in Woodstock, New York, where he lives with his wife, Miriam, and his daughter, Deirdre. It was completed in April 1988 during a visit by Sanders to the Woodland Pattern Book Center in Milwaukee.

[*Sturgeon*]: *Can you tell me a little bit about your young adulthood?*

[Sanders]: I was raised a regular American by Stevensonian Democrats in the Midwest. I come from a family of engineers. My grandfather was an engineer, my brothers are both engineers. But in the roots of the family we're agricultural. My father's family were farmers for a number of generations in Kentucky, Tennessee, Alabama, Missouri. My maternal grandfather was very creative, an inventor. He invented a machine to automatically lay down ballast and straighten railroad tracks. He was a mad inventor. My mother was also very creative. She would do things like buy a piano and take it apart all over the floor and put it back, or she would fix her own sewing machine. She was very intelligent and extremely gifted in art and restoration and using her hands. I was raised a regular American. I was in the Boy Scouts, and I was president of my high school student council.

I played football and basketball, went on overnight hikes, and was a regular American kid, but I discovered poetry when I was fifteen and was encouraged by a high school English teacher who, although being of very puritanical, perfect American stock, could tolerate a wild, confused-and-trembling kid of fifteen, who wrote poetry that did not jibe entirely with the life of Plymouth Rock.

What kind of poetry were you reading?

My main heroes were, of course, those to whom I was supposed to be exposed. They were all from the middle of the nineteenth century. Hawthorne, Poe, Melville, maybe a little bit of William Cullen Bryant, and perhaps Robert Frost—all the ones in the pantheon of the golden age of American literature.

So it was all American. They didn't give you any Keats or Shelley?

No Shelley, nothing. Just America was where it was at. Manifest Destiny applied to writing also. You were forced to read in *Endymion* or maybe a little bit of "To a Skylark" for a little "furrin" vice. The main thing was Poe and a little Whitman, but not much. Mainly Poe—and John Greenleaf Whittier, who was thought of highly in the Midwest in my generation.

Yes. You can find dozens of editions of Whittier in any used bookstore today.

Right! So I was raised on that, and then I began writing my own poetry. And although I was a regular American guy, I would walk around high school with my clipboard full of poetry. I had really no one, no soulmate other than my schoolteacher with whom to share this poetry. The next person I could share it with would be three years later when I met my future wife Miriam in Greek class at NYU.

How did you get from Missouri to NYU?

I was a kid in the Midwest in a suburb of Kansas City and going to Blue Springs High School. Then, in the spring of '57, the worst thing that could befall a young man happened: my mother died suddenly, causing a lot of family turmoil—you know, here we go rebellious-teenage-boy-not-getting-along-with-his-parents, and one of them dies tragically and way before her time—that was the worst thing. I figured nothing could be worse than that. It just tore my mind apart. It's reflected in the poem **"Cemetery Hill"** [***Thirsting for Peace***, 29-36]. That was March 1957; I graduated from high school shortly thereafter, and I went for a year to Missouri University. My family demanded that I become an engineer, or a chemist, or a biologist. I thought I might want to be a physicist, because at that time I was interested in the space program that was beginning the following year—the Mercury program. I thought I might become one of these macho guys with a Ph.D. that actually get to go into orbit.

So you took classes in physics.

I studied physics and I studied a lot of math. I took a few semesters of calculus and functions and complex variables and differential equations.

Tell me about your transformation into a poet.

I was at Missouri University for a year and I did not like it. I was nobody—there was no literary scene that I felt I could cooperate with, nor were their simpatico brothers and sisters with whom I could share my interest in literature, so I got out of there. I hitchhiked to New York in the summer of 1958 with thirty-five dollars and got into Manhattan and went immediately to the Gotham Book Mart which I had been reading about a lot. I had in my knapsack my Dylan Thomas, my Ezra Pound, my William Carlos Williams, early issues of *Evergreen Review* (which I had purchased at the University of Missouri Bookstore), and Ginsberg's *Howl*. I had my little packet of sacred books. You know, I had *Waiting for Godot*, etcetera.

*D. H. Lawrence maybe? In **Tales of Beatnik Glory** the central character is carrying Lawrence's poems in a backpack.*

Kenneth Rexroth wrote a tremendous essay, as a preface to D. H. Lawrence's *Selected Poems*, that set me on Lawrence for all time.

You also had the Cantos *in your Book Boat, didn't you?*

I had my Book Boat. I had all that stuff. As I said, I had *Howl*, I had *Being and Nothingness* by Sartre. . . . I don't know. I think I must have had a New Directions William Carlos Williams, one of them.

I used to go out with these drinking buddies from my high school when I'd go home weekends from the University of Missouri, and the mode of operation was to circle around the county courthouse drinking beer and throw the cans into the Methodist Church front yard, and I had *Howl* memorized, and I would recite it to these guys. It's an embarrassing thing, like being Monk in a jazz club or something and having everybody talk while you play.

I was memorizing a lot of poetry. I went to New York City, spent all my money in the Gotham Book Mart, and decided to stay. I went to NYU, and out of deference to my mother who had just died—she had said that a gentleman always knows Greek or Latin—I decided to pick up Latin again and also to take Greek. I wandered into room 901 in the main building at NYU in the fall of '58, and there were about nine other people, and I met Miriam there, who was also taking Greek because she, at that time, intended to be an archaeologist. She was someone with whom I felt confident enough to show my poetry.

What was the New York literary scene like at that time?

I was too shy to meet many people. We would go out and go to all the bookstores and the poetry readings. I actually heard Jack Kerouac read in the Gaslight, and also Edward Dahlberg and Corso. I went to the Living Theatre and met Paul Goodman, who became a friend, and heard Frank O'Hara and Allen Ginsberg. I was just a guy on the edge of learning what was going on. At the same time I became intensely interested in languages. I was reading as much as I could, traveling around being a beatnik, hitchhiking in the summer across the country.

Once I dropped out to go on a peacewalk across America. After that I went to jail. The first little book, the one Ferlinghetti printed, was the result of a peace demonstration where I tried to board a Polaris Submarine at New London, Connecticut; we kept swimming out and trying to get on these submarines. I finally got arrested and spent a couple of weeks in jail. That was in August of '61, and I wrote a little book-length poem, a thirty-pager, which I thought was state of the art. I thought I had finally written something that was equal in quality to what was going on.

Is that **Poem from Jail***?*

Yes. I wrote **Poem from Jail** on toilet paper in my jail cell in specific Greek meters. I had taken a course at New York University in Greek lyric poetry, and I had memorized, and still do have memorized, all the little Greek meters, *ionic a minore, a majore,* etcetera. I'd elucidate a meter, like *ionic a minore,* say, which is two shorts followed by two longs, *di-di, da, da,* or I would think of a specific meter and then think of a line. All of the lines, basically, are written in little Greek paradigms. I don't think I ever told anybody that; it's not obvious. I wrote this in my jail cell and smuggled it out in my shoe and read it, along with Ginsberg's *Kaddish* and parts of Homer I had

memorized, to the people at the peace camp. I was the mad poet who would shriek out Ginsberg's *Kaddish* and other poems. I'd have all these trapped pacifists in their sleeping bags around the campfire and I would cry, "oh mother what have I left out, oh mother what have I forgotten, farewell with your torn black. . . ." Then the final thing: "Caw caw caw crow shriek in the white sun over the gravestones in Long Island Lord Lord." I sent a copy of the poem to Lawrence Ferlinghetti, and to my lasting gratitude, he wrote a very enthusiastic letter back, liked it, agreed to publish it. I was ecstatic. But it became one of those horrible situations for a person just beginning a career, where a reputable publisher says, I'm going to do the book, and you go out like an ape, beating your chest, blowing smoke in coffee houses, saying, Well, my book is going to be good, and I'm very important, you know. But then umpteen years go by, and it's, Sure, Ed, where's your book?

Did years go by?

Yeah. Finally I stopped telling people, and by the time the book came out, I no longer cared.

That was in 1963?

Yeah. Two years went by. But the fact is, this all led to *Fuck You* magazine. I had an apartment at 509 East Eleventh. I describe it in the editorial conference in **Tales of Beatnik Glory**. And that's where I formed *Fuck You: A Magazine of the Arts.* I was drinking all the time. I was hanging out at the Catholic Worker. I wasn't a Catholic, but I was very sympathetic to their peace cause. A number of the people at Polaris Action and in the various peace rallies were hard living Catholics. They were young people who felt very sympathetic to the Catholic vision as interpreted by Dorothy Day: voluntary poverty, helping others, antiwar.

Had you met the poet Jean Morton then? She's in your first issue in 1962.

Jean Morton was a friend of mine. She had been in the Air Force and then dropped out, and I met her at the soup kitchen at the Catholic Worker. I'd go get my clothing there; I'd go get a free lunch. I was totally broke. I had no money—zilch, nothing. They helped me, and later, when I first put out *Fuck You*, they let me type my stencils on the second floor. I used their paper, that green, grainy-textured, Catholic Worker protest-leaflet paper. When Dorothy Day found out about that, she went totally crazy. But I could understand her position. Even though I never imposed my beliefs on anyone there, they were given the choice: either sever connections with me or leave the

Catholic Worker. A number of people associated with the Worker left out of protest; others stayed.

So were people generally sympathetic to Fuck You?

Sure, because I was totally in the pacifist, direct-action, nonviolent, peace-walk group of people. One night in February of '62 I said, "I'm gonna start a magazine called *Fuck You: A Magazine of the Arts,* and I need some poetry." And everybody said, "Sure." I collected poetry and I added a lot of my own poetry—featured myself in the first issue, in fact. But I had Jean Morton's stuff, and I sucked some various verses out of people. There were some things about the magazine that I now regret emphasizing, such as heroin and some male chauvinism, but at the time I felt like it was free and good and pure and that I was doing something that was wonderful. I was having such a great time giving out these values, giving the magazine away for free; through all its faults, I thought I was promulgating something that made sense: pacifism and disarmament.

Did anybody help you with the magazine?

No. I did it all, and I gave it away free except I was making up little book catalogues to earn money. I did sell it to university libraries such as the one in Madison, Wisconsin, and other places, but I mostly gave it all away. I'd walk around the Lower East Side and just give this stuff away, and I got kind of instantly famous. From friends I developed a mailing list of people I wanted to send *Fuck You: A Magazine of the Arts* to. I sent it to Pablo Picasso, I sent it to Samuel Beckett at Ussy sur Marne.

Did he ever answer?

He didn't, but I heard he read it. I heard rumors. I'd know people that he gave copies to. I also sent it to Fidel Castro, Allen Ginsberg in India, Gary Snyder, Philip Whalen, and Marianne Moore. I sent it to Ferlinghetti, of course. Allen sent poems and so did Charles Olson. I started a fairly extensive correspondence with Olson that lasted until he died—we must have exchanged fifty or sixty letters.

Tell me about this connection to Olson.

He and I intersected on Hesiod. One of the first things I sent him, after reading "Maximus from Dogtown 1," was a copy of Hesiod in the original Greek. He knew enough Greek that he could get into it a little bit. I had a lot of Hesiod's *Theogony* memorized—it's the only thing I like of his. **Poem from Jail** comes out of Hesiod. All the myth is from Hesiod and from certain Egyptian myths, and Olson loved that. We exchanged letters, and I visited him in Boston, saw him here and there. But the first time I sent him something I couldn't write directly—I just sent him a copy of *Fuck You.*

So you did the magazine alone. Would you do it all in one run, all night long?

I would work—I've always been a workaholic, and I worked real hard. I just never slept, I guess. I had a terrific amount of energy, and I would stay up all night drinking and smoking pot and turning it out.

You never had any collators?

I don't know if I have ever written about the yoga of doing this. I developed a system of sitting in lotus posture on my black floor surrounded by concentric semicircles of pages, and I have long arms like a gibbon and could reach about six feet out from a lotus posture and suck up these concentric semicircles of pagination. Later on when the issues got real thick, Peter Orlovsky, who was in his manic amphetamine phase, and his brother Julius, who was a little slower but could function, used to help me collate, sometimes. Like the "God" issue—the one with the Tibetan Martian Mantra cover [5:7, Sept. 1964]. That was the cover that Robert Levine did. That was a giant issue and those two helped, but mainly I did it myself.

And you drew the covers?

Yes. Except for—well, Warhol did a cover [5:8, Feb. 1965] and Robert Levine did the one I just mentioned. Most of them were done by me. I didn't have any electricity in my apartment, so I became quite skilled at drawing with a thin stylus and engraver's tools on stencils. All those *Fuck Yous* except for the very last few issues were hand drawn on stencils, and it took me forever because I'd use a flashlight—no lights on, so I'd have to have a flashlight shining up through the back of the stencil. I remember late at night drawing those fairly complicated drawings. It was like a Sumi painting—make a mistake with a stencil and you've got to do it again.

And then you used a stapler to bind it.

Right. I'd stack and staple it. I loved the physical labor of stapling and squashing with the heel of my hand on a good stapler. It became a healthy, holistic thing to do. What wasn't healthy and holistic were the ink cutters, the benzine. I discovered after trial and error that benzine was great at cleaning off ink. Then to my horror I learned—after having bathed my knuckles in this damned substance for five years in the sixties and breathing it—that it's leukogenic. It's a carcinogen.

Tell me about the erotic Auden poem you published in Fuck You *[5:8, Feb. 1965], "Platonic Blow." That must have caused something of a furor. Where did you obtain the manuscript?*

I got the poem from two sources. One was a friend of mine, a poet who had a relationship with this librarian at the Morgan Library. The other source was another acquaintance, another poet, who somehow had his own copy and sent it to me from the islands, Trinidad or St. Thomas. The poem describes the male oral experience. I've never had a homosexual experience, but I'm very sympathetic to gays. It was a good poem, and it didn't seem to me to be out of bounds to have been written by Auden, whom everybody knew was gay. And I'd heard that there are other erotic poems of Auden's out there. So I went ahead and printed it—all by itself to begin with, and later in *Fuck You.* Ted Berrigan helped me with the first version, and we made a couple hundred dollars, enough to pay rent and expenses, and of course gave a lot of them away, too.

You had met Berrigan around that time?

Yes, I met him at the mimeograph machine in Bob Wilson's Phoenix Bookshop. I was printing *Fuck You* and he was doing *C* magazine. He and I really hit it off. We had unique language systems. Together, our verbal styles created a kind of universe—people would copy the way we spoke. Berrigan was one of those wall-to-wall poets. He was the guy who made up the dictum that there are no weekends for poets. Anyway, we distributed the Auden booklet together.

And the reaction?

Well, I remember having the third anniversary party for *Fuck You: A Magazine of the Arts* in February 1965 at my bookstore. Burroughs and Warhol were there; Warhol had put up big banners for the party. Jason Epstein and James Michener and some other friends of Auden came in, and they were really bent out of shape. They felt that the author of "The Age of Anxiety" could never have written "The Platonic Blow," but it seemed to me the same verse line, for one thing. Somebody told me that whoever's done the bibliography on Auden has accepted it as a legitimate Auden poem. So I don't feel bad about it.

That was 1965, and you mention your Peace Eye Bookstore. When did you start that?

The bookstore began in late '64. I had been putting out book catalogues to help put myself

through college, and I'd get telegrams from university libraries fighting for this material. I'd go around to parties and collect things and get people to sign them. I'd sell Allen Ginsberg's cold cream jar but also books and pamphlets.

Allen didn't care?

Allen couldn't find his cold cream. I'd go over to his house and get his cold cream. All that stuff was getting snuffed right up, and I was making money, so I figured, why not open a bookstore rather than go to graduate school? I found an old kosher meat market, left up the Hebrew sign, "strictly kosher," cleaned all the chicken feathers and rendered fat off the floor, painted it, and opened it up. It went on for approximately four and a half years, and it was something of a gold mine; people would rush in from all over the country to go to Peace Eye. I stopped it in early 1970. Miriam and I flew out to L.A., and I began the Manson book a week later [**The Family,** Dutton 1971]. I just opened the doors and said, Who wants this stuff? Boy, they came and got it.

During the bookstore period, you were arrested for publishing your "lewd" magazine. Can you tell me about that?

I guess I'll never know precisely what was going on. Since I have an FBI file, I guess the government became aware of me somehow. I was getting the ink. I was getting some articles written so I was getting a fair amount of renown, and, beginning with late '65, it looks [according to my FBI files] like they're trying to figure out what to do. I had formed the Fugs. We had gone on a cross-country caravan against the Vietnam War. We had records out. Somebody was writing to the FBI in the fall of '65 about this scurrilous, creepy group named the Fugs and please do something about them. Right at the time the Justice Department actually did mount an investigation. That's in my FBI files. It made me proud to be an American when I read in the FBI document that we weren't indictable. We were using the freedoms of expression found in the Constitution.

Go on.

Anyway, strange things were happening. We gave a Fugs show in 1966 in New York, on New Year's night, and late that night a junkie apparently broke into my bookstore, smashed the window and stole stuff. Tuli Kupferberg came to my house at four in the morning, waking Miriam and me. He said, "Ed, these police are in your store, and there's this guy in there really upset." So I took a cab down, and there was a sergeant there named Fetta who was so upset by *Fuck You* that he was trembling. He said, "Did you do this, is this yours?" I said, "Yeah." They were boxing up my stuff—the *Fuck You* press, including **The Toe Queen: Poems** [Fuck You Press, 1964], and the poem I printed of Auden's, and all my copies of *Fuck You*. In fact, for years, they kept a box of *Fuck You*s at the ninth precinct to show to visiting dignitaries—local smut, definitely "actionable" smut, even though I later won the case.

I was arrested and taken to the ninth precinct. There was one cover of *Fuck You* [5:4, Fall 1963] with a picture of a boy with a lizard on his leg and an Egyptian hawk with a phallus in its claw. So Fetta is coming up to me, saying, "What about this bird with this penis? It's going to attack this boy, right?" And I said, "No, it's just a lizard spurting things out of its mouth." I told him I copied the boy off a Danish tobacco pouch, and the hawk represents a sound in ancient Egyptian and not to get bent out of shape about it, it's satirical, don't worry about it. Later, while I'm waiting with one of the arresting officers, who's pecking out my name and social security number on an old Underwood typewriter, Fetta rushes in. He's totally upset. He says, "Do you have any tattoos?" I said no. Then I see he's clutching a copy of *Fuck You* magazine, and he says, "You said you had no tattoos. Go in the other room and take off your clothes." Well, it turns out that in my editorial notes I had said, "Ed Sanders has the first twenty-five hieroglyphs of Akhenaton's 'Hymn to the Sun Disk' tattooed on his genitals."

This Fetta was one of your most careful readers!

Yeah. So I go in this little room and I take off my clothes and I've got these two heads of these two cops down, you know, they don't want to touch, they couldn't lift up my balls and look. They're in there like a couple of boys about three feet from my naked body, looking at me. I said, "Hey, take a look. It was a joke!" Anyway, I went before the judge the first time after being all night in the wino tank with all the puke and drunks.

How long did you actually spend in jail?

About a day, but you see the idea was to keep me coming to court to humiliate me. I think I went seventeen times before I finally won the case, and I'd have to go in at nine o'clock in the morning, feeling like a criminal. Especially that first morning—I felt like mucus. I didn't have any sleep. I had just given a concert. But I knew my Bill of Rights, and I told Fetta as we were waiting to go in to court, "Someday I'm going to win this case because I'm in the right and I represent

freedom and I'm not doing anything wrong. And I'm going to invite you to the party."

I'm a night person, and in those days I'd go to bed at five in the morning and get up at three. But I could never tell when the trial would happen and it just went on and on. I got a lot of support from the ACLU and letters from Frank O'Hara, John Ashbery, Ed Dorn. Stephanie Harrington wrote a nice article in the *Village Voice*. Meanwhile I'm on the cover of *Life*—I'm getting terribly famous for a young guy from the Midwest. I tour, I play off Broadway for nine hundred performances. I've got Peter O'Toole and Richard Burton coming backstage, yet I have to trudge down regularly every month or so to this courtroom.

One day I showed up totally dressed in white—white suit, white tie, white shoes; I'm in my Beau Brummell phase of fluff, of post-beatnik foppery. Then at the next court date I come dressed in red, everything red—red tie, red scarf, red shoes, red socks, red pants, red sweater, red coat. And the judge said, "Young man, this is not a ski lodge. I want you to come to my court dressed properly." I'm brought to this point—I'm playing games. It was that very same judge who got me off, when the case finally went to trial a year and a half after the arrest, in 1967. That was Judge Ringel, and I'm forever in his debt because he realized that what I was doing was protected by the Constitution.

So I'm planning the party and I turn around to find Sergeant Fetta and he's gone, because he knows I'm going to invite him to the party. I have a party and the prosecutor comes to the party. It's really weird.

Sergeant Fetta didn't come?

Fetta didn't show. I had a great party. I polished my bookstore up and had champagne, and I had all the court exhibits all over the wall, my jail photos—I had the whole thing. I was so happy and proud of my country. I was thinking, by that time, gee, I can do the magazine again, but I couldn't pick it up again. I was too busy.

So actually Sergeant Fetta and his tribe only managed to stop the magazine by default. As far as the trial's outcome—one can't help but think of D. H. Lawrence, of Joyce, and of course Burroughs's and Ginsberg's pornography trials. In all of those instances, society needed to be taught a lesson regarding the definition of literature. The kernel of knowledge you seem to have imparted, as a result of this experience, has to do with the fact that much of what was on trial was not the product of a single author. As a small magazine, Fuck You *was a time capsule, as you might call it, containing various "literatures."*

That's very true, especially since I was preparing a prose issue on poetics when I was arrested. I had some really interesting stuff from Olson that I had received, some from Gary Snyder and others. I could detect that there wasn't a lot of poetics being discussed in free form. I was trained in classical Greek and Latin and knew Egyptian and Mycenaean and some other languages, as well as being trained as a mathematician and a scientist, so I had a really cold, analytical mind, despite my being a space cadet. I felt I could get a really interesting discussion going on poetics that utilized my anarchic-pacifist perspective—I thought I would surprise my audience a little. I guess it all ended up in the part of my archives that I've turned over to the University of Connecticut [Storrs]—that included my correspondence with Olson as well. Anyway, the ACLU, specifically Rosenberg, my lawyer, who's now Judge Rosenberg, convinced me not to run any more issues.

Why?

They felt that it would just add more fuel, or that the judges could interpret it that way. Basically, it probably was just to make their time easier. Anyway, when you're young and hot and you drop something, you tend not to pick it up again.

So the magazine went the way of the bookstore by the end of the sixties.

Right.

Yet Fuck You *is a repository of early, often first appearances of so many writers. I went through its thirteen-issue run, 1962 to 1965, and found all these names . . . Tuli Kupferberg, Carol Berge, John Weiners, Michael McClure, Jackson MacLow, Ray Bremser, Robert Duncan, Robert Creeley, William Burroughs, Joel Oppenheimer, Barbara Moraff, Charles Olson, Paul Blackburn, Lenore Kandel, Rochelle Owens, Diane Wakoski, Ted Berrigan, Frank O'Hara, Allen Ginsberg—*

All these stars—and more! You might call it my pre-saturation phase. Olson said if you want to prepare yourself as a historian or a writer who uses history or real events you need one giant saturation job. He said it doesn't matter whether you study pemmican or whatever. The idea is that you immerse yourself in it.

The Family was my first big saturation job. That prepared me as a novice. People think I did too good a job. I've got a giant map of every bloodstain in that house that I questioned all the defendants with; I sent them lists of questions asking how they killed these people. I got a lot of inside information. But if I had to do the book over again, I probably wouldn't have described the murder so well. I would be a little less intense in that murder description, and I think I would have been—the criticism that I got was that the book was not analytical or sociological enough. Because the information that's in there was known by everybody at the time. But a few years go by and people forget or a new generation comes up and so it *becomes* more sociological because the information is not fresh and known. I did my best. I worked hard for eighteen months and haven't read it in many years. I haven't looked at it in a long time.

You explain in the introduction that you took on a persona to secure data: "I posed as a Satanic guru-maniac and dope-trapped psychopath."

If you're talking to people to whom killing doesn't matter, you also have to act like it doesn't matter. That's probably a bit overstated; I never engaged in any weird activity. But if you're talking to people who would kill you for a candy bar, you have to talk their language. It's like any reporting on the beat: if you're covering the CIA, you've got to talk that lingo, if you're covering the State Department, you talk their lingo, if you're covering the street crimes in the Bronx, you're talking street language. Whatever you're covering, you've got to have an exchange of minds. You've got to be able to talk to them in order to get more information. That's what I meant by that.

The Family *has been touted as the story of the other side of the sixties, a dream about the idea of a commune of gentle hippies whose wills combine in such a way that it turns into something quite other than what might have been intended. So isn't* **The Family** *a critique of a certain time as well as of specific people?*

No. It doesn't have *my* politics and beliefs in it. I was a little too old to be a hippie, but I was sympathetic to them. I used to go out to California during the sixties all the time to perform, give poetry readings, hang out, goof off, so I was very sympathetic to the communal movement. But the problem was that there were no institutions set up to support that world view. If you have a world view that's shared by a lot of people, you have to set up institutions that support that world view. And the hippies, of course—and they're not to be judged for it—could not easily set up hippiedom.

There's the question of who cooks while everybody's dancing and making love or playing the tambourine. That surfaced as the woman's movement. There are other questions that surfaced that grew out of that time. How do you have non-rat-race, free-time oriented society where you still have dental care? What do you do about cancer? All the issues that were latent are still working themselves through. The institutions to solve these many problems are still growing.

I sense that you're expressing a lack of interest in this part of your career, that you've turned in other directions.

Basically I've worked through the necessary interest I once had in the Manson case. Eventually you come to a determination about evil—that you can't do anything about it. What you can do something about is the overt, public aspects of evil. Now I'd rather work for cleaning up the environment than cleaning up cults. For example, my poetic manifesto **The Z-D Generation** [Station Hill, 1981] is a call for new reform of the secret side of the American military apparatus.

*Yes. It's a realization of the quotation you use in its epigraph, as well as in **Investigative Poetry**, Olson's "know the new facts early." Your work has a very broad range, and I was wondering whether you think of it as being divided into poetry and prose, or along some other lines. Do you have a particular division in mind?*

I don't know. I don't really think of it like that. Most of my writing nobody knows about. Obviously it's a simple division—poetry and prose. Most things I write are done in poetic lines, including my book on the Manson family. Almost everything I do has a version in poetry. **The Z-D Generation** is prose, but it's broken up. It's a manifesto—it's the kind of prose that has line breaks that's still prose, not poetry, and why not?

*Yes, and that's a form you've already established in **Investigative Poetry**. There you make your claims like this:*

> when practicing
> writing up Morality Lists or data-grids
> you will feel
> the lines break—
> you will automatically break
> your data torrent on
> the lines.

Is that the sort of thing you're talking about?

I do that naturally because I think prose is trapped in the Gutenberg Bible. The guy who printed the Gutenberg Bible in two columns locked everybody forever into that concept. It's convenient. Your eye moves back and forth and picks up the page as a gestalt so you're really reading the whole page while you're reading each line. It can be useful, but there's no reason theoretically that one couldn't—especially now that everybody's going digital—make line breaks for prose at will.

There are two or three guiding lights for this kind of thinking. There's Olson's metaphor of a high energy grid in which one line instantly leads to another. That's from *Projective Verse*. There's an "energy warp" going on between the page and the mind, and your eyes are drawn down the page by the energy of the poem. The Pound metaphor is "distillation." There you have data clusters. He was really good at line arrangement. He would distill, out of his information, all these lyrics that would appear in his *Cantos*, these little four or five lines and all of a sudden bring out the essence, or part of the essence—and they're found all through the *Cantos*.

And then there's Blackburn, the guy who was always bending down putting reel-to-reel tape on the spool at poetry readings. He was an inspiration and a proto-archivist. What made the biggest impression on me was watching him read. The guy was the first besides Ginsberg who really knew what he was doing with cadence. At the end of a line he would drop a tone—it wasn't a quarter tone, but an eighth of a tone drop—so his lines were like layers of bluestone because each one was separate, and he was great. He knew how to end a line so beautifully and how to use his voice as an instrument.

What attracts you, then, is the idea of having some lyric passages set in a "grid"?

Right. The problem is that things change so much that you can't be guaranteed that the basic information that supplies the poem will be understood ten years from now. So the poet has an obligation. It's like a court record. You can assume facts, not evidence. You can't be overly didactic.

One of your attributes is that you have a mania for facts and information, and yet I'm puzzled at a paradox in your work. It's that you record so much factually, and at the same time there's this whole other you, this sort of Irish songbird quality. Do you find any kind of contradiction in that?

I'm a poet! I'm supposed to be a difficult individual and full of contradictions. Seriously, though, a poet is a person who has poetic skills. But not all poets partake equally of all poetic skills.

I have certain skills that I know to a moral certainty are good, and so therefore I array those poetic skills on a page. I have a gift for telling a story, for nature poetry, for certain types of image structures. I have an ear, a sense of sequence of vowels which carry the melody and consonants which are the guts of things. I have, through long practice and probably through inherited genetics, the gift of the skill to present these vowels and consonants in interesting patterns, and then I have a further skill of observation.

The thing about this is that you work very hard and that you isolate your poetic skills. Know what you can do and try to do that. Also there are more than nine muses. There are maybe a couple hundred, and you have to know from which of those couple hundred muses your skills are derived.

Do you have names for any of these muses?

Yes. I would say one is Retentia—the use of the retained image, so that in an age of data retention poets use more typesetting and graphic images. I use her in my long ghost poem **"Sappho on East 7th"** [*Thirsting for Peace*, 169-96]. A good example is Robert Duncan—or Charles Olson. One could think of, if one really wanted to, linking two parts of the brain. For instance, the muse of intense visual images might be in your hippocampus, which is where your primal fear/ nonfear image-sorting system is. You could go to modern brain taxonomy and isolate all kinds of muses. There are many different skills.

*You've definitely got the lyric skill. Could you tell me how you came to write your ode about the "pondic lun' flash" (**"The Plane,"** Thirsting for Peace 218)?*

I did that one while flying back from reading at the Chicago Art Institute in 1984. I was flying to Albany at night, during the full moon, and I went over these little lakes. They're not the Finger Lakes. They're smaller. They're just gouged-out-of-gravel glacial lakes. They're very beautiful. "Pond 'pon pond." That's a twenty thousand dollar line. It's a transmission poem, a shamanistic transmission poem, as I wrote it. In the instant—two minutes, three minutes, five minutes—just before the terror: Are we going to crash? The plane's getting a lot lower. Landing in Albany is always iffy. Before the final terror-tremor, you go over these lakes, and the moon's out, and you actually see— it's a quick thing. And I'm saying, Wait, that's fun. Let's have more of that.

So you've practiced many trades, yet maintain you're basically a poet. Do you see yourself as a policy maker, artistically as well as politically?

Yeah. I'm in the left wing of the Democratic party, believing that anything's possible.

You mean you're really democratic with a small d?

Demos, "people," *kratos,* "rule"—people ruling. People ruling people. It requires a kind of faith that human nature may be capable of, after all.

ED SANDERS AND KEVIN RING (INTERVIEW DATE AUTUMN 1993)

SOURCE: Sanders, Ed, and Kevin Ring. "Thirsting for Peace: An Interview with Ed Sanders." *Beat Scene* 17 (autumn 1993).

In the following interview, Sanders discusses his play Cassandra, *his home in Woodstock, New York, the other members of his musical group, the Fugs, and his teaching at Naropa in Colorado.*

He's one of America's bravest and most outspoken writers. He crosses into so many areas of living it's hard to keep pace. Environmental concerns, Charles Manson, investigative journalism, classic poetry, raging novels and also the life of a musician in The Fugs. A direct descendant of the Beats, he teaches at Naropa in Colorado and continues the same hectic pace as ever. A new book of poems and the reissuing of those outrageous Fugs albums on compact disc has brought Ed Sanders out from the seclusion of rural life in New York state. Through the post, where he wrote answers at Gary Snyder's home in Northern California, and on the phone, Ed Sanders spoke to *Beat Scene* recently.

[Sanders]: Did you get my letter? I did it at Gary Snyder's. Is that where I sent it from? I finally had a moment, it was right in the middle of eighty acres of forest, it was really beautiful to sit there on a rainy day. Me and my wife had just spent three days with Carol and Gary at their house, it was quite beautiful. It's outside of Nevada City. There's a big environmental fight there over a huge goldmine they're trying to revive from a hundred years ago, where they're trying to scoop a million gallons of water a day to blast this gold out of the ground. They're fighting it. Otherwise it's a beautiful Ponderosa Pine and Black Oak forest. Manzanita bushes, dark, wine coloured bush. Very beautiful, just paradise. He makes his electricity with solar panels, quite rural. He's been there about twenty years. It's a whole complex, outbuildings, he's got an old barn. He and his wife use it as their studio. They have a beautiful rounded house with all the accoutrements of modern civilization. All solar powered. And then various outbuildings, pond, wash house. It's quite lovely. Nevada City, it's northwest of Sacramento San Francisco couple of hundred miles. Gold country, nuggets washed down in the creek beds, stuff like that. But there's the spirit of greed there, that's always a problem. You're supposed to leave the gold in Mother Gaia.

[Ring]: Apparently there's no phone there?

Yeah, he has a phone. He has a phone, fax, modems. He's high tech. He's got a Macintosh computer. He's got all the accoutrements. I'm sure you can reach him automatically, because he's quite internationally renowned, as you know. In order to write and be part of your, what you call your bioregion, or your drainage area, you need to have solitude in order to be there with it. But he's in good spirits. He's sharp as ever, witty and full of life. It's always a thrill to be around him.

You've been friends for a long time?

Oh Yes. Since around the Berkeley Poetry Festival in 1965. We've corresponded, I guess, since the early sixties. I used to print stuff of his, poems. He was always a friend. He sent me, from Japan, very early in the sixties, an Egyptian eye, carved in one of those Japanese stamps. He's been a friend a long time.

Apparently you're working on a screenplay?

No, a play. I was working this spring right up until when we left for California, every day for ten hours a day, on *Cassandra,* which is a musical drama I wrote, tracing the life of the Trojan prophetess and princess Cassandra, from ancient sources—so I was working very hard all year getting that ready. There's a full professional production. The other thing is there's a movie of *Tales of Beatnik Glory,* which is supposed to start filming this month, in New York City. I don't have anything to do with it. I did not write the screenplay. Philip Hartman and Mark Jacobsen wrote the screenplay. I guess I'm not allowed to say who's in it. Quite a prestigious lineup of people apparently in the film. I have nothing to do with it. I hope they'll let me on the set, I think they will. But they often don't let the author of the book on the set, so they don't go jumping up and down.

I heard a rumour that Willem Defoe is in it.

I have no idea, that's a rumour I heard too. Defoe has got a . . . he'll be in Europe in August. He may be in it. It's what the producer told me,

that Defoe was gonna be in it. I have no idea. I'm only relying on what I'm told from the producer and the director.

What are your feelings on this?

I'm honoured. I never thought a book of mine would be made into a movie. I think it's perfectly adaptable to a film, *Tales of Beatnik Glory.* They used stories from volume one and volume two. They've woven together a very interesting storyline, it combines some of the women characters and other characters . . . which is alright. So I think they came up with a good storyline, they use the kid, On the Road Mulligan . . . a character. They use various stories. I think the weave is pretty good.

Are you optimistic they'll do a reasonable version?

I don't know. Yes, of course I am. I'm optimistic and I'm sure it'll be an interesting film. I think some of it has to do with the kind of music they put together for it. I think they're gonna kind of put together a kind of all-star neo beatnik band maybe for the music, which would be a smart move. I think it'll get general release, I have no idea. I don't know how much that I know is secret or how much I can say. Basically they have a good distribution deal with it, fairly large distributor. I expect it to be released. I'd like to go over to Cannes and hang out there and drink coffee at dawn. (Laughs)

The play is being put on by the Woodstock Guild. Tell us a little about that.

Yes. Cassandra was the daughter of the King and Queen of Troy. It's set at the time of the Trojan War, which is around 1184 BC. I take material from Eurypedes, from *Trojan Women* and from *The Odyssey,* books ten and eleven. That's the major amount of ancient material on Cassandra. There's also material on Cassandra in Virgil and Ovid (mentions other ancient sources here). So I take all this information and I stitched it all together in a kind of rhapsody storyline and left some of the Greek choruses from Eurypedes and Homer, not much, but a little bit. Then wrote a kind of poetic treatment to her life. No one has ever done it. It's a kind of modern thing. It's as old as the Bosnian Croatian Serbian battle, or the Trojan battle. The ancient struggle between Asia Minor and Greece is reflected forward into the Greek/Turkish struggles now, or the Bosnian situation. It's very ancient, this idea of cyclical violence, multi-generational vengeance. Multi-century ire and anger is a continuing problem. It's also about the plight of women in ancient times, as reflected in the modern era. Cassandra nowadays would be a woman who is very intelligent, has a lot of energy, a certain amount of aggression. Demanding to have her place in society. So I interpret Cassandra as being a Princess of a royal family, privy to state secrets, always demanding to know things, pushy, aggressive and very witty. She's fluent with words and she gets into trouble. That's her psychological situation. In the spiritual or religious areas she offends the god Apollo. A kind of schizophrenic god. Apollo, the god of mathematics, beauty, statues, pleasing paintings, order, form, healing—but he's also the god of male rage, of violence, of violence of men. He's the god of plagues, tuberculosis and AIDS. He has a down side to him. He offers her a deal, that if she will make love with him he will give her the gift of prophecy and she takes the gift of prophecy and tells him to come back later for the love and when he comes . . . she . . . like many a young girl . . . changes her mind, and he curses her. That's the spiritual side of it. So when she wants her parents not to let the Trojan horse into Troy they laugh at her. Or when she wants her country to send Helen back to the Greeks . . . You see this Trojan War thing, it's as if Boris Yeltsin ran off with Margaret Thatcher when Margaret Thatcher was head of England. Then the English would bomb Moscow and send over cruise missiles or whatever, nuclear weapons. It was that level of conflict. Cassandra warned against it. Her tragedy is that she's the woman to whom no one will listen. So basically that's the whole plotline. It traces it from ancient sources and then she's murdered by Clytemnestra. Cassandra is also raped in the fall of Troy by a surly Greek soldier named Ajax, which is a modern paradigm for all the rape and plunder which goes on during any war. So we have that in there. So I think it's an interesting story. Little bit of a modern twist at the ending. I have Cassandra and Hades join forces with Persephone. I add a little Sanders fillip at the end.

Does Tolstoy know about this, it sounds like one heck of a play?

Maybe on the astral plane. It tells a good story. It has thirty-one musical sections. The Cassandra role is very demanding, it's a soprano role, the songs are fairly demanding. We have a very good Cassandra named Amy Fraden, she's quite skilled. Leslie Ritter sings the play of Persephone. Those two voices are just terrific, very beautiful voices and they sing very well together. So it's going to be real good.

What sort of place is Woodstock?

It's 6,000 people when it's ten below zero and in the summertime it swells up to 20,000 people. It's beautiful. The mountains are up to thirty-eight hundred feet, it's very hilly and quite beautiful. We keep it quite rural, we don't let McDonalds in there, don't let malls in and we keep it pretty. We had a production last summer which sold out, there were huge waiting lines. We feel that probably, though you never know, it will do well. Our goal is to take it to Broadway if we can. Or to make a movie out of it, that's my real goal. If there are any readers of your magazine want to produce a movie of Cassandra I'm in the Woodstock telephone directory. Woodstock is extremely beautiful in August! We don't want to see a house every three feet in Woodstock, the animals have a right to live there too. These deer and these chipmunks, raccoons and groundhogs have been here millions of years, they have a right to live here too. There's a whole group of jazz musicians and experimental composers, a whole variety of different . . . Carla Bley lives here, Jack Dejohnette lives there, lots of musicians. I've been there since '74. We moved up there to get clean air. A woman can walk in the streets in the middle of the night in Woodstock and nothing will happen. There's never been a woman attacked in twenty years, that I know of. Safety, that's good. A woman has a right, if she wants to go walk out and look at the moon at three in the morning. She should be allowed. There's that kind of safety and that's good.

We moved to Woodstock in 1974, in part to escape the geeky, confusion rife, quasi-violent world of 1970s New York leftist factionalism. Plus there was more and more street hostility from muggers. Miriam was held up by a young addict brandishing a butcher's knife, so we "headed for the hills" 100 mile north of NYC. Living in the country is not that much less hectic. "There are no weekends for poets." It's the era of faxes at midnight, crickets at dawn.

What's happened to the other guys in The Fugs?

Well, Tuli Kupferberg and I founded the band, we continue the legacy. We own the mastertapes and we are making arrangements to have them put out. We have hundreds of hours of performances and stuff. Tuli's OK, he lives in New York. He's doing quite well, he has a son that has just graduated from Harvard, which is unusual for an anarcho-syndicalist! He raised a couple of wonderful children, he and his wife Sylvia. Ken Weaver is in Tucson, I talked to him a couple of weeks ago, he's OK. Steve Weber, he's in Portland. Quite a folk hero and still having fun I heard, playing music. Peter Stampfel, I met a couple of weeks ago at a Poets Cafe down on the Lower East Side, I went down there for a reading. He's doing quite well. I think he does gigs, still writing his razor sharp witty tunes I believe. Jake Jacobs, he's OK and doing a record I understand. Danny Kootch, is of course Don Henley's co-songwriter and plays in Don Henley's band. Charlie Larkie, I dunno, he married Carol King. Carol King came to a Fugs concert and squirreled off our bass player! He left the band soon thereafter. Should never have gone to L.A. I guess! I don't know, they trickle on. There's one or two Fugs, I think, are dead. Lee Crabtree died in the early 70s and I believe Pete Carney, who was on our second record may be dead. John Anderson, who played bass on our first two albums, is now a lawyer in Portland, Oregon. He's done quite well, he went to Harvard Law School I guess. He lives on an Island off Portland. Bob Mason, one of our drummers, was out in Venice, California. I think he's a session man. I know where they are. All that is from basically keeping in touch. Not close, but enough to cover a certain amount of cordiality. Certainly with Tuli, Tuli's my brother. We work very close together. We're gonna do one more rock and roll record by the way. We're gonna do our final rock album. It's our last one. Tuli's 69 and we decided to do one more and then fade it. One more rock record. That's no sentimental throb tunes, no ballads, just rock. We'll do that this fall. Then cap our career. I wanted to do a career that lasted a little. Actually, a career should be like fifty years. Our career, beginning with our first jumping up and down and screaming studio thing in '65 will now have its final moments twenty-eight years later in a high tech environment. We'll use the latest recording techniques, do it on a big Mac with a 5,000 meg hard disc. We're there.

You've lasted longer than The Beatles, The Who . . .

That's right! I wouldn't call us The Who or The Beatles! We're The Fugs. We're bards. We're in the tradition of Coleridge singing "Christabel" to Wordsworth. William Blake intoning and singing from *The Songs of Experience* or the tradition of Walt Whitman singsonging "When Lilacs Last in the Dooryard Bloomed" to a large crowd in New York City after the Civil War. Or in the tradition of Sappho on a Greek island singing to her students. We're in that tradition, singing poets. Not singers who use poetry.

Besides all the noise The Fugs made, you are obviously people who are concerned. Do you feel your generation and the prevailing spirit of the '60s has been allowed to slip, as regards the environment and a generally better society?

I think there's a lot more work now on the environment. Nobody really knew . . . We didn't ask questions. Where does our water come from? Where does our waste go? Everybody I know now looks into that, even casually. So I think things are a little better in the environment. There's more personal freedom now. I think some battles have been won, there's a better deal for women. So I think it's a little better for that struggle. It's true, you gotta try and reach every young generation and get them to pay attention to some of the good things of the past. Don't just totally ignore the past. Some good things that we did then and the young people now should be made aware of, so that they can use some of those things and do their own things. They have to mix a little bit of the past with a lot of the present. That's exactly what my generation did, we mixed in some stuff we learned when we were kids with a sense of newness, That's what this generation has to do. I'm sure it'll do OK.

Your early years . . . you talk about your literary influences, your parents.

Oh yeah. My dad making up spontaneous poem songs. My mother read us Charles Dickens for bedside reading. There was a certain exposure to literature. I had a good school, English teacher, who encouraged me to write poetry. Her name was Mrs. Hall, she encouraged me to write anything I wanted. In the Midwest I was allowed to write weird Poelike threnodies and she didn't try to censor them. This was in Missouri, Blue Springs High School. She's still alive. She uses some of my early religious poetry for her Sunday School classes. She sort of ignores some of my more randy . . .

How do you know this?

I always go visit her. I go clip the hedges on my parents' grave every summer, when I go to Naropa. I often stop off and tidy up my parents' grave. My English teacher lives about a mile away, so I always stop by and say hello to her. So she forgives me for some of my weird books. She has them all. I send her all my books, she just glides over some of the more randy sections!

I received a "regular" high school education in poetry, the romantics, a dash of Shakespeare,

Poe, Tennyson, Longfellow, Sandburg, Frost, and as a teenager in the '50s discovered by chance Dylan Thomas, Ezra Pound, Sappho, Charles Olson, the Beats—it wasn't easy. I had to travel hundreds of miles sometimes to encounter in the Midwest "Howl" and William Carlos Williams. It was studying Greek, Latin and languages that truly opened the world of poetry for me. My mother and father helped. My mother by reading to us at night.

You teach at Naropa?

Often. Every year I teach there, I'm on the guest faculty. It's a wonderful place. It brings a confluence of American poetics into the same place. It's not just beatnik stuff, it's a wide variety of poets and thinkers who go there. Of course Colorado is extremely beautiful in July, it's when all the Rocky Mountain flowers are out. You can drive up to about ten thousand feet above sea level, see ten miles off columbines and Indian paintbrushes, Colorado flowers up to the glaciers. Beautiful visually, the air is very nice. It has a kind of sense of the ancient academy. All the poets and students are housed in these complexes with courtyards, it encourages communication. Then there's always a lot of partying. So there's partying, teaching, intermingling of faculty and students, in a way that allows for direct transmission of mind, It's pretty good, They're not parochial, in the sense they don't . . . the type of poetry that's taught . . . they bring in every kind of American and international strain of verse, from performance poetry to rhymed poetry, to story poetry, to beatnik poetry, to language school poetry, to Black Mountain poetry, to the tradition of George Oppen and Chinese and Japanese poetry, French poetry. Many different streams that run together in one nice tributary there.

Do you still feel the same way about things you had strong convictions about in the 1960s?

There were many good things about the 1960s and some bad. I liked the twin paths of partying, aimless frenzy, good times and wildness, mixed with the demand for a more sharing world. There was too much male chauvinism and we did not factor in enough . . . the impact of jealousy, envy, greed, obsession, fanaticism, lying. All in all the era was good to me.

What are you doing now?

My career's over baby! (Laughs). We're gonna do one more rock album. I've got a television show called *The Sanders Report*. I'm going to experiment in song and chanted news stories, using the latest musical equipment. Singing news

stories. I've done two, one with Gary Snyder in California and I just did one from Sweden. Analysing the Swedish methods of supporting artists and the arts. Just overwhelmingly amazing.

Where do they broadcast?

In Woodstock and stations in California I'm sending them out to. I just began, this is my fifth show. In the fall I'll begin the song and chanted news shows. I have a book I've been working on for about three and a half years on organized crime, or the Mafia and illegal waste dumping in New York State. I've been working on that for three or four years.

Does that worry you?

Nah . . . after Manson. Once you've been threatened by Manson everything else seems pretty easy to take. And I'm very happy with my new book **Hymn to the Rebel Cafe** that Black Sparrow has just put out. I've been out on the road doing book parties around California and the East Coast. It represents about all my most complete statement, my social and economic philosophies mixed in with my storytelling ability, my researches into ancient civilizations and my environmental concerns. It contains the best poems I had written from 1986 through 1991, following **Thirsting for Peace in a Raging Century: Poems 1961-1985,** which came out in '87. **Hymn** has my work in site specific nature poetry and environmental concerns ("**Some Poems from Mead's Mountain Road,**" "**At Century's End,**" and "**For the Waterworkers,**" politics and economics; plus a long humorous poem in the tradition of Cowper's "John Gilpin" called "**An East Village Hippie in King Arthur's Court.**"

How did Black Sparrow come to publish the book?

Black Sparrow is one of America's premier publishers and the poet Tom Clark facilitated the placing of the manuscript of **Hymn to the Rebel Cafe** in the hands of John Martin, who, to my gratitude wanted to publish it.

You've always been recognised as a writer who has shown ecological and political concern and expressed that in your writing, where does this spring from?

I was very much part of the "rising tide of expectation" in the late 1950s and 1960s into the 1970s, when we wanted a sharing, war free society that promoted freedom and at the same time restructured the banking and money system to banish poverty. I grew up feeling close to the wilderness of the American outdoors. Some of the perfect haunts of my youth, ice skating ponds,

FROM THE AUTHOR

SANDERS ON THE FUGS

It was the era of happenings. You could fill up a bathtub with cherry Jell-O, get a strobe light and some paintings and have a happening in a gallery. We played all these galleries. We sang and shouted our songs but we had good timing. If you listen to those early tapes, one thing about them was that they weren't tuned perfectly to a tuning fork but the timing is good. Tuli, Weaver, and I and the others had good time. We sang together, you could hear the words, and they were quite clear. Our tunes seems to have some literary merit because they keep reissuing CDs of this stuff 30-35 years later.

Sanders, Ed and Billy Bob Hargus. "Interview." *Perfect Sound Forever* (website) <http://www.furious.com/perfect/sanders.html> (June 1997).

meadows, farmland, river banks, have long been seized by malls, tract housing and the bulldozer. So I have vowed to "go out in a blaze of leaflets" and to my last breath speak up for Gaia's wild ways and a democratic socialist economy.

Your writing has crossed from poetry, to journalism, investigative journalism, political writing, fiction, novels, a very broad span. Do you think this stops you reaching a wider audience?

If you write in one field you tend to be able to focus on others. I don't believe that working in a number of fields limits the results, but it might in some cases limit public renown, but so what? The examples of William Blake, Yeats and others are too strong not to be indifferent to the same wave of renown and fame-lack.

DAVID HERD (ESSAY DATE SPRING 1999)

SOURCE: Herd, David. "'After All, What Else Is There to Say': Ed Sanders and the Beat Aesthetic." *Review of Contemporary Fiction* 19, no. 1 (spring 1999): 122-37.

In the following essay, Herd considers Sanders work in general and how, in particular, it was influenced by Allen Ginsberg's Howl.

Among the more telling stories in the first volume of Ed Sanders's *Tales of Beatnik Glory* is "A Book of Verse." The story opens with a sharp image of provincial life in the tranquilized fifties. It is 1957 and a "carload" of "graduating seniors"—among them the unnamed young man from whose perspective events are narrated—drive from their small town on the Missouri-Kansas border for a fraternity weekend at the state university. Dressed for the occasion, "he," the central character, "wore his forty-five dollar R. H. Macy flannel suit with the pink and blue flecks he and his mother had bought for the homecoming dance in 1956." Unextravagant, off-the-peg, conventionally distinctive, the suit bespeaks a conformist sensibility. As does the weekend that consisted of an "afternoon beer and barbecue party" and "was otherwise uneventful except that he threw up into the waterfall of a local fancy restaurant when drunk," an act of socially acceptable rebellion that "guaranteed him an invitation to pledge the fraternity" (*Tales* 280-84).

While at the University, the young man buys a copy of "Howl," distantly aware that the title poem has caused controversy. Its impact is explosive.

> *Howl* ripped into his mind like the tornado that had uprooted the cherry tree in his backyard when he was a child. He began to cry. . . . He walked down the stairs in the middle of the night to wake his parents and read it to them. His mother threatened to call the state police. . . . Over and over he "howled" the poem, till much of it was held in his mind and he'd close his eyes and grab the book, almost tearing it, and shriek passages, stamping the ground. "God! God!" he yelled, "God!" . . .
>
> Gone were the days of shoe polish, clean shirts, and paste-on smiles. He began to spend almost all of his time writing poetry. . . . For days he worked on a howling masterpiece. He typed various versions and gradually the poem evolved into the rageful shape he desired.
>
> (*Tales* 280-81, 284)

The purpose of "A Book of Verse" is to measure the impact of "Howl" on a young mind—Sanders's—conditioned by a small American town in the 1950s. The story thus serves two functions. It testifies to the poem's importance in twentieth-century poetic history. It also poses a problem. Sanders, so the story goes, became a poet because he read Ginsberg's poem. The problem arising is thus one of influence. How does the poet react to such a transformative early reading experience? Or more specifically, how does the poet whose way of seeing has been fundamentally revised by

"Howl" proceed to write without reproducing Ginsberg's point of view?

The question can be more instructively, if more obliquely formulated, if one considers Sanders's poetic manifesto *Investigative Poetry*, published in 1976. The heart of the manifesto is Sanders's exhortation to fellow poets "to describe every aspect . . . of the historical present . . . for this is the era of the description of the All" (1). In so exhorting, Sanders has recourse to a familiar rhetoric: the rhetoric of inclusion. "Inclusion," it would seem fair to say, had been the watchword of every significantly innovative body of American poetry produced since the 1940s, so much so that by 1976, the notion of "inclusion" had solidified into the official idiom of experimental postmodern poetry. How else could Sanders write of "the era of the description of the All"? And not least among the significantly innovative American poets who had emphasized the value of poetic inclusion was Sanders's dedicatee, Allen Ginsberg, "who sets for all time the example that rebel poets not allow themselves to be driven into isolation." Ginsberg, indeed, had been feeling out the implications of this rhetoric of inclusion since early 1949. Witness "After All, What Else Is There to Say?"

> When I sit before a paper
>   writing my mind turns
> in a kind of feminine
>   madness of chatter;
> but to think to see, outside,
> in a tenement the walls
>   of the universe itself
> I wait: wait till the sky
>   appears as it is,
> wait for a moment when
>   the poem itself
> is my way of speaking out, not
> declaiming of celebrating, yet,
>   but telling the truth.
>
> (29)

Clearly Ginsberg had not "yet" managed (as John Ashbery puts it) to "put it all down" (*Three Poems* 3). The intention, however, is there. Ginsberg is prepared to "wait till the sky / appears as it is." After all, what else is worth telling if not the truth? And what is truth, after all, if not all there is to say?

In 1949, one imagines, Ginsberg's title would have read like a challenge: challenging the poet to a sublime response. Had Sanders reread Ginsberg's poem in 1976 as he prepared *Investigative Poetry*, its title could, or should, have read much more like a problem. Thus, in the first place, it is possible that Ginsberg has already said all that Sanders himself might want to say. What can Sanders add after Ginsberg, by whom he is so impressed, has commented on the historical present of which they are both a part? This is a serious but not a devastating difficulty. Sanders can evade the obsolescence the problem implies if he can eke out areas of his own experience for which Ginsberg, for all his capaciousness, has not accounted. A second, much more serious possibility is that the very rhetoric of "All" has itself, by 1976, some twenty-seven years after Ginsberg began to feel for its contours, become hollow. Arguably, that is, the poet who speaks of the "era of the description of the All" is no longer, in any real sense, issuing a sublime challenge but is settling instead into a kind of shorthand (a catchall if you will) that serves no longer to sharpen but actually to dull the attention. Glossed in this way, Ginsberg's question, echoing ironically down the years, comes to seem ominous indeed: "After All, What Else Is There to Say?"

The purpose of this essay is to answer that question. I want to consider what else Sanders has found to say, consider how he has advanced an aesthetic (the Beat aesthetic) that he finds so deeply compelling. To do this, I must start with Ginsberg and in particular with an appreciation of how he came to write with the impact he did. The nature of Ginsberg's poetic achievement, I will suggest, predicts the nature of Sanders's.

For all its characteristic spontaneity, "Howl," as James Breslin has observed, was a long time in the making (77-109). Ginsberg himself claimed he first had an inkling that he might write a poem in that style when, while reading Blake, he had a hallucinatory vision in which the poet spoke to him (Breslin 79-83). More prosaically, one can perhaps identify three phases in Ginsberg's early poetry, each constituting a stage in development of the aesthetic that finally found utterance in "Howl." These phases can be characterized, following John Muckle, in terms of the act of naming.

Consider the closing lines of "In Society," the first poem in Ginsberg's *Collected Poems*. The narrator is at a cocktail party (in the society of the "In Society"):

> She glared at me and
> said immediately: "I don't like you,"
> turned her head away, and refused
> to be introduced. I said, "What!"
> in outrage. "Why you shit-faced fool!"
> This got everybody's attention.
> "Why you narcissistic bitch! How
> can you decide when you don't even

know me," I continued in a violent
and messianic voice, inspired at
last, dominating the whole room.

(3)

Early as it is, and for all its crudeness, this passage contains many of the elements from which Ginsberg would come to fuse his Beat aesthetic. Its angle of vision is telling. Whereas Prufrock was happy to observe the comings and goings of society women from outside and so to accept both his own exclusion and the principle of exclusion, Ginsberg's narrator blunders in uninvited, determined to become involved. Indeed, one can already see his rhetoric beginning to congeal around the principle of exclusion: the woman's refusal to be "introduced" stimulating the narrator's "outrage." And as he negotiates the ins and outs of polite society, one can hear Ginsberg feeling toward a name for his attitude to that society and toward a theme through which to examine it. Thus, in the woman's refusal to speak to the narrator, one glimpses Ginsberg's reciprocal refusal of the values she articulates, his subsequent social status as a refusenik, and his Baudelairean fascination with the garbage (the refuse) of American society. In "In Society," then, Ginsberg can be observed struggling to name elements that will become crucial to his mature style.[1]

The second phase of Ginsberg's early career finds the poet moving beyond the nomination of a general category and beginning to identify those elements in American culture that are refused: that which America has made abject. The shift is entirely self-conscious. "Stanzas: Written at Night in Radio City" urges,

No more of this too pretty talk,
Dead glimpses of apocalypse:
The child pissing off the rock,
Or woman withered in the lips,
Contemplate the unseen Cock
That crows all beasts to ecstasy. . . .

(28)

The word *apocalypse* is carefully chosen. Ginsberg is declaring an intention to devastate American society by revealing that which it would choose to conceal: "child pissing," "woman withered," "unseen Cock." Advances in Ginsberg's aesthetic are thus increasingly marked by a naming of things conventionally unspeakable. "Paterson," written in 1949, is exemplary. Refusing "rooms papered with visions of money," Ginsberg wonders what will happen

If I put new heels on my shoes,
bathe my body reeking of masturbation and
sweat, layer upon layer of excrement

dried in employment bureaus, magazine
hallways, statistical cubicles, factory
stairways. . . .

Instead of settling for the "dumbbells of the ego with money and power," Ginsberg would

rather jar my body down the road, crying by a
diner in the Western sun;
rather crawl on my naked belly over the tincans
of Cincinnati;
rather drag a rotten railroad tie to a Golgotha in
the Rockies. . . .

(40)

"Paterson" is the first poem in which Ginsberg begins to find a truly distinctive measure for contemporary America. In certain respects, of course, that measure is familiar. The long, inclusive lines are Whitman's, and the journey west is the stuff of national mythology. But without attempting to obscure either inheritance, Ginsberg twists form and content into contemporary shape. Instead of loafing along Whitman lines, Ginsberg crawls, and where the journey west signaled progress and the new Jerusalem, now it implies Golgotha. With "a mouthful of shit, and the hair raising on my scalp," "Paterson" finds a new set of terms through which to interpret the American way, a set of terms novel and powerful enough to require a name.

The third phase of Ginsberg's early career is a search for that name, and it is with "Sakyamuni Coming out from the Mountain," written in 1952, that he begins to define his vision:

He drags his bare feet
out of a cave
under a tree,
eyebrows
grown long with weeping
and hooknosed woe,
in ragged soft robes
wearing a fine beard,
unhappy hands
clasped to his naked breast—
humility is beatness
humility is beatness—

(90)

Bearded, barefoot, clothed only in "ragged soft robes," Ginsberg cuts a recognizable figure here. He has begun to find a form of self-definition, through his researches into Buddhism, with which he can feel comfortable. And with self-definition comes aesthetic definition, the mantra—"humility is beatness"—formulating an attitude that had been evolving in his poetry for some years, but with a simplicity that has hitherto exceeded his grasp. It is with "Malest Cornifici Tuo Catullo," however, one of the last poems written before

"Howl," that Ginsberg finally achieved an aesthetic formulation strong enough to underpin an influential work of art:

> Ah don't think I'm sickening.
> You're angry at me. For all my lovers?
> It's hard to eat shit, without having visions;
> when they have eyes for me it's like Heaven.
>
> (123)

"Howl" is an exploration of the contention that "It's hard to eat shit, without having visions." Following a memorably simple structure, the poem first presents the refuseniks, then that which they refuse, then envisions a new world, the keystone of which, as the refrain "I'm with you in Rockland" makes clear, is solidarity. Crucially, the poem is not a straightforward celebration of Beat values but rather a measure of the cost of refusing. The Beats refuse, are refused, and so are left among the garbage. Better, the poem proposes, to be among the garbage hallucinating angels than sacrificing the next generation to Moloch. Better still, however, to be in Rockland, "where we hug and kiss the United States" (133). This sense of the cost of Beatnik choice is crucial to Ginsberg. To be Beat is not simply to drop out (as Timothy Leary's later, weaker definition suggested). Rather, it is to make a sacrifice, Ginsberg himself having seen the best minds of his generation sacrifice themselves to a refusal of the values incorporated by Moloch. "Howl" names the cost of this sacrifice. It names, that is, the cost of living in contemporary America. That poem proved a defining moment in American literary history, and that it redefined otherwise nonliterary lives in the way Sanders's story shows, testifies to a simplicity of vision born of Ginsberg's ongoing effort to name all that he saw.

In "A Book of Verse" Sanders described how "Howl" "ripped into his mind like the tornado that had uprooted the cherry tree in his backyard when he was a child" (*Tales* 281). The question, arising from this order of influence was, how does the poet for whom Ginsberg proves such a transformative early reading experience proceed to write without simply reproducing Ginsberg's point of view? John Muckle has indicated one way out of the impasse this question would seem to imply. In his essay "The Names: Allen Ginsberg's Writings," Muckle notes that Gertrude Stein "speaks of poetry as naming, prose as telling how the names became names. From an original unity of these functions in epic, poetry and narrative have developed a cleavage in which one names and the other tells" (14). For Muckle, therefore, Ginsberg is an important poet because, like Whit-

man before him, he shows an awareness of "America's need for new nomenclatures" (14). Following this imaginative application of Stein's formulation to the context of Beat writing, one can usefully conceive of Sanders as a poet caught between functions. If the force, and so the impact, of Ginsberg's writing lies very largely in its willingness to dare a new nomenclature, then it should not be surprising to find Sanders, on occasion, also engaged in the act of naming, in the Adamic act of carrying the Beat idiom into new areas of experience. Yet precisely because that idiom precedes him, Sanders is aware that the need to name is less pressing than it was. Accordingly, and prudently one might think, Sanders chooses to contribute to the Beat aesthetic in large part by "telling how the names became the names." This might explain the narrative drift in Sanders's poetic manifesto: "Investigative Poetry: that poetry should again assume responsibility for the description of history" (*Investigative Poetry* 3). It might also explain the characteristic poem: narrative in form; prosy in texture; concerned, invariably, to tell the story of the emergence of the Beat sensibility. Sanders, then, can be understood as a poet poised between the compulsion to name and the obligation to narrate. To understand what it means to be so poised, I will explore his relation to the Beat aesthetic through three categories central to his writing: controls, histories, and journeys.

"Poem from Jail," the first work in Sanders's *Selected Poems*, was written during his imprisonment (for seventy-five days) following his participation in the protest against the commissioning of the Polaris nuclear submarine *Ethan Allen* (*Thirsting* 238-41). This direct contact with a confining social institution proved foundational to Sanders's poetry, giving rise to a sustained (career-long) meditation on forms of social control. The experience of jail was, of course, Sanders's own.[2] Control, however, was a theme already much explored by Beat writing, "Howl" in particular, making it its business to name the mechanisms of social control (Moloch). It is in his variation on this theme that Sanders registers most clearly the difficulties of writing after Ginsberg.

This is not to deny that in certain respects Sanders extends and deepens the Beat analysis of control. His outstanding volume in this respect is *Egyptian Hieroglyphics* (1973). The volume is not without its measure of strain, casting as far back as "Ab-Mer: A Love Story of 1985 B.C." and as far forward as "A.D. 20,000" in an attempt to find new poetic territory. As these temporal extremes indicate, however, *Egyptian Hieroglyphics* is Sanders's most experimental volume, and through these experiments he advances the Beat appreciation of social control. In particular, he develops a nuanced idiom for the description of forms of surveillance.[3] Starting with **"The Singer"** and concluding with **"Report: Council of Eye-Forms Data Squad,"** Sanders devotes a series of poems to this question, the aim of which is to render what might be termed a post-Watergate sensibility, the outcome being a poetry derived from the idiom of the case report:

> Dimensional Adjustment Procedures enabled the
> Eye-Form Surveillance Team to observe the
> > Princess
> arriving in the first sections of the Underworld.
> > > (*Thirsting* 115)

Sanders's response, in turn, to the fact of surveillance is the rhetoric of "investigation." **"The Age"** opens with the declaration that

> This is the Age of Investigation, and every citizen
> > must
> > > investigate! For the pallid tracks of guilt
> and death,
> > > slight as they are, suffuse upon the retentive
> > > electromagnetic data-retrieval systems of
> our era.
> > > > (*Thirsting* 137)

Investigation is Sanders's big idea: witness his confident proclamation of it here and his extended exploration of its implications in his manifesto. And it is, in fact, a skillful development of Beat rhetoric. The effect of the term is to adjust the spirit of avant-garde inquiry to the demands of an environment in which state power is increasingly intrusive. *Investigative Poetry* is therefore an act of naming, Sanders endeavoring to name the aesthetic procedure by which poetry can usefully engage with modern forms of social control. With his rhetoric of investigation Sanders can confidently be thought to have achieved a way of writing after "Howl."

By the same token, it is hardly deniable that it is in his endeavor to advance the Beat inquiry into the thematics of control that Sanders demonstrates most clearly the difficulties of his position. His attempts, for instance, to continue the testing of taboos and his efforts to extend the language of excess invariably result in a form of poetic utterance that serves only to parody the Beat achievement. **"Elm-Fuck Poem"** is a case in point:

> The ba ba lanolin fur-ears
> > sex
> > > Trembling Lamb
> where I enter the

> matted meat
> of trembly sheep
> and the cunt warm
> > & woman sized
> offered by the lamb.
> > > (*Thirsting* 47)

No doubt the justification for such a poem has to do with organicism. It does not seem humorless to suggest, however, that poetry of this sort is much more likely to entrench gender oppression than it is to liberate its reader from sexual constraints. And if the desire to continue to test the limits of social control can find Sanders producing the kind of gratuitous poetry that gives Beat a bad name, so his analysis of the mechanisms of social control too often results in a distorted sense of the poet's role. Thus in *Investigative Poetry* Sanders urges the reader not to "forget for one microsecond that the government throughout history has tried to suppress, stamp down, hinder dissident or left-wing poets" (12). There is more than a whiff of paranoia here, and arguably that intense anxiety has as much to do with the compulsion to find ways of writing about control after "Howl" as it has to do with the post-Watergate climate in which the poem was written. Either way it is a paranoid vision that generates a dismayingly partial view of the poet's function. Thus Blake is observed to "back away from historical poetry and to retreat, if that is the word, into a poetry of symbols" (*Investigative Poetry* 12). As if symbolism had nothing to do with poetry—as if it had nothing to do with Beat.

To recall Stein's formulation, Sanders's efforts to develop the Beat nomenclature measure the difficulty of coming after. After all, what else is there to say? His investigation of the theme of control, though marked by a certain deepening, has tended to lead him down blind alleys, exploring corners of experience and writing that have gone unnamed precisely because they are of peripheral significance. His response to this difficulty, as Muckle's equation and Ginsberg's achievement predict, has been increasingly to tell the story, one way or another, of the emergence of the Beat sensibility, of how the names became the names. This should not be thought to represent a falling off. Sanders, as *Tales of Beatnik Glory* shows, tells a good story. He is also intimate, as his anxious relationship with Ginsberg makes clear, with the inner workings of the Beat aesthetic. Arguably, the story of the aesthetic is his proper subject. In telling that story, Sanders sometimes dwells directly, as in his *Tales*, on his part in the history of the Beat period. The poem **"Ramamir,"** for instance, relates a late-fifties love affair, whereas "**Sappho on East Seventh**" recalls the visions of an ambitious young poet. Invariably, though, his more ambitious intention is to contextualize the Beat way of being. What such contextualizing amounts to is an ongoing study of historical subcultures and bohemian milieus. These studies start with "**Egyptian Hieroglyphics**," which, as Sanders observes, were "inspired by researchers into possible artistic rebellion in the rather totalitarian milieu of ancient Egypt. I was looking for Lost Generations, for sistra-shaking Dadaists in tent towns on the edge of half-finished pyramids, for cubists in basalt, for free-speech movements on papyrus" (**Thirsting** 244). He was looking, that is, for a genealogy of dissent, for a historical angle of vision that shows the Beat project to be not a momentary aberration but a further eruption of a vibrant radical tradition. "**Yiddish-Speaking Socialists of the Lower East Side**" traces that genealogy closer to home, telling how the arrival of East European émigrés in the first decade of the century radicalized the quarter the Beats would later make their own. More recently, *Chekhov,* Sanders's extended verse biography of the Russian writer, amounts to a study of dissent in czarist Russia. With the names already named, the second generation of Beat writers was allocated the more prosaic task of telling how the names became the names. Sanders's histories of poetic dissent constitute an effective strategy for writing after Ginsberg.

It is, however, in his development of the trope of the journey that Sanders has dealt most effectively with his particular anxieties of influence. The journey is, of course, pivotal to the rhetoric of Beat inquiry, affording an opportunity both to critique and to revitalize the American experience. In both *On the Road* and *Naked Lunch* progress west is displaced by an itinerant, unsettled lifestyle, whereas the idea of the frontier is transformed from a colonial limit to a pragmatic encounter with the new. For Ginsberg in particular, the journey thus carries religious overtones, Beat becoming a pilgrimage by which the revelation is perpetually earned. In "The Green Automobile" the car proves a form not just of transportation but of transport, in which

> we'd batter up the cloudy highway
> where the angels of anxiety
> careen through the trees
> and scream out of the engine.
>
> (Ginsberg 83)

Broadly speaking, then, Sanders's poetic journeying locates his writing in the Beat tradition. There is a more precise sense, however, in which the idea of the journey comes to enable Sanders to explore his relation to the Beat aesthetic. The journey affords his poetry a structure, but one which is loose enough not to restrict inquiry. Formally speaking, it enables the poet both to relate a story (of how one traveled from a to b) and to digress into areas of his own experience. It permits him, in other words, to mediate the differing functions of narrating and naming. Accordingly, it is through the trope of the journey that Sanders is most able to negotiate his relation to his immediate predecessors, is most able to sustain the momentum of the Beat movement while arriving at observations distinctively his own.

In the note to "**Poem from Jail**" Sanders observes that "It was my first work, after years of search, that I felt fit in with the best of my generation" (**Thirsting** 241). Sanders's reflection betrays an anxiety. The poem is a product of both years of search (so by implication the desire to find something differentiating to say) and a desire to fit in with the best of his generation. The anxiety of influence that results from these competing compulsions is apparent in the rhetorical texture of "**Poem from Jail**." A passage from the first part of the poem recalls how

> we have seen denied
> Mao's creation,
> And we have denied
> van Gogh's crow
> shrieking on the
>   horizon,
> and Rouault's Jesus.
> Chant Chant
>   O American!
> lift up the Stele
>   anti bomb.
>
> (**Thirsting** 5)

Despite the "shrieking" and chanting, one would not mistake this for a passage from Ginsberg. The collage of sources is Ginsberg-like, but the sources themselves are not. Yet if this is not Ginsberg's rhetoric, one could not confidently say that it was Sanders's either. The passage is characterized not by an identity of its own but by a determination not to be subsumed by another's identity. This explains the wilfully eclectic range of sources: Mao, van Gogh, Rouault. It also explains the fact that those sources do not combine to generate anything one could reasonably call a style.

That Sanders should be so determined for the surface of his poem to mark an evasion of Ginsberg's influence comes, I would suggest, from his nagging awareness that at a structural level "**Poem from Jail**" is heavily indebted. The poem takes its form from the opposition between two forms of journey, undertaken by two kinds of traveler. The first is of mythic proportions, his journey being the wanderings of a visionary:

> O American
> O Traveller.
> The Sun boat
> enters the Vastness
> Anubis stomps
> with the sun shafts,
> & the man awaits,
> the sun, the
> eye of the
> Trembling Lamb.

In the second journey the road "twisted / like a knife / across the desert" while

> I crawled,
> onward,
> clutching guts
> and coughing blood,
> scrawling poems
> on rocks
> with a charred log.

The poem aims throughout for a resolution of these two forms of motion, achieving it, finally, at "**Goof City**" where the reward for the journeying is revelation:

> Bristling in the
> bat black,
> mind spews out to Nebulae;
> > balling the All;
> Darkness; swivelled
> > into the Mountain;
> Shriek it All!
> > Wand waved
> over the thigh!
> Sucked to the
> Vortex,
> Universal hole.

> (*Thirsting* 9, 24, 27)

All that this apocalyptic scene really reveals, however, is quite how conditioned Sanders is, at this early stage in his career, by Ginsberg's way of seeing. The howl has become a shriek, but as the poem is sucked into the "Vortex," the idiom reveals that Sanders's "All" is in fact Ginsberg's "All." The poem arrives at such a neo-Ginsberg scene because of its means of travel. The process whereby spiritual and destitute journeys—pilgrimage and crawl—come to terminate at Goof City so exactly reduces the passage through "shit" and "visions" that takes Ginsberg to "Rockland" (and which forms the structure of "Howl") that the outcome can hardly be different. For all its seeming mobility, then, "**Poem from Jail**" is, in fact, another static poem, caught, one might say, in the wheel ruts of another poet's "Green Automobile." It does represent, however, a breakthrough of sorts, as Sanders's annotation indicates, insofar

as it does at least identify the journey as a means of engaging the Beat aesthetic.

One measure of Sanders's subsequent poetic development is precisely the degree to which he has proved able to adjust the trope of the journey to his own perceptions. "**The Pilgrimage**," for instance, opens by tracing a route:

> There is nothing on the
> wet morning grass
> not even a mound
> to mark the grave.
> I have started in the
> shade of the walnut
> tree & walked
> up the hill
> to make my
> proskynesis at thy altar
> O daughter of Ra.

> (*Thirsting* 40)

This is an altogether less anxious piece of writing than anything to be found in "**Poem from Jail**." Thus, for all the echoes in the title, Sanders does not here reproduce a Ginsberg journey but uses his familiarity with Ginsberg's forms to appreciate his own experience. This is explicitly Sanders's pilgrimage, and he arrives at a voice much more his own, not out of the need to distinguish himself, but out of the need to detail the private significance of the visit he has made. The poem thus finds Sanders using Beat forms to get close to his own experience. And yet in a dialectical (rather than a contradictory) respect the poem also shows how deeply informed Sanders's thinking has become by the rhetoric of the journey. Intensely lyrical as it is, the graveside contemplation is a potentially static experience. Sanders's imagination, however, has been mobilized by his encounter with the Beat aesthetic. The journey (if only from the walnut tree to the hill) has become the form of his experience.

"**A Flower from Robert Kennedy's Grave**" marks a further development in Sanders's handling of the trope of the journey. Addressing the occasion of Nixon's second inauguration (20 January 1973), the poem observes both how "Richard Nixon / oozed down Pennsylvania Avenue / flashing V's from a limousine" and how the poet, after having demonstrated against the proceedings, walked

> past the guardhouse
> circling circling
> around the Catholic henge
>
> coming finally to pick
>
> > a yellow petal
>
> from thy grave
> > Mr. Robert Kennedy.

> (*Thirsting* 80-81)

Here again the poem follows Ginsberg in its formal dependence on the idea of the pilgrimage. But here more than ever Sanders's confident handling of that idea signifies an independent poetic intelligence. By visiting Bobby Kennedy's grave, Sanders crosses the line that divides private feelings from civic protest, signaling an intimacy with a public figure that shows in turn that politics is a matter not of distant institutions but of individual lives. And if Sanders shows here that he has succeeded in adapting a Ginsberg motif to his own purposes, the confidence this gesture signifies is perhaps measured by his self-conscious allusion to "When Lilacs Last in the Dooryard Bloom'd." So far has his engagement with Ginsberg developed, that he is now willing to risk comparison with Whitman.

It is Sanders's long narrative poem "**The V.F.W. Crawling Contest,**" however, that most marks the development, through the trope of the journey, of his engagement with the Beat aesthetic. Describing the poem's history, Sanders notes how "For years I had wanted to write this poem of the long, groaning road. It was sort of a secular version of the more mystic crawl at the end of '**Poem from Jail**'" (*Thirsting* 243). Ginsberg, it will be recalled, was crawling long before Sanders—on his "naked belly over the tincans of Cincinnati." But if the crawling in "**Poem from Jail**" showed the tentativeness of imitated behavior, Sanders in "**The V.F.W. Crawling Contest**" makes so bold with the central metaphor as to sever any connection to Ginsberg. The poem narrates a journey, made on hands and knees, through the United States. If its commentary on contemporary American ways recalls any Beat predecessor, it is probably Burroughs. Comparison seems inappropriate, however, because the sustained tone of wry disgust this poem manages is more than ever Sanders's own:

> As I approached the
> drive-in restaurant
>
> saliva began to drip from
> my crust-cambered lips
>
>> No automobiles parked
>> silently full of potato-eating
>> families
>>> did leave the lot
>>> as I rounded
>>> the bend
>>> out of a clump
>>> of ditch weeds
>
> "a hot dog
>> & baked beans please
>>> just drop it in the tar."
>>>> (*Thirsting* 68)

With "**The V.F.W. Crawling Contest**" Sanders arrives at a genuinely persuasive way of writing after "Howl." In dealing ironically with the same abjection that fueled Ginsberg's rage, he finds a way of referring again to aspects of American life the older poet has already named. It might be argued that such a recourse to the doubleness of irony marks a falling off from the grace of Ginsberg's original, beatific vision. Possibly also, however, it provides a means of continuing the Beat journey beyond the point at which pure outrage is spent.

Notes

1. The result is damagingly unrefined. Seeking rather than commanding attention, Ginsberg draws on the language of misogyny to make his presence felt, an act of self-contradictory idiomatic exclusion that is compounded by his unreflective willingness to dominate the whole room. Ginsberg's misogynist rhetoric is not, of course, merely a function of his youthfulness, Beat writing generally being marked by masculinities of one sort or another. Sanders, as I indicate below, provides no exception.

2. This experience is vividly represented in Sanders's Chekhovian story "The AEC Sit-In" (*Tales* 223-34).

3. Sanders's task here is perhaps to advance Burroughs's insights rather than Ginsberg's, *Naked Lunch* being a handbook of observational techniques of all kinds.

Works Cited

Ashbery, John. *Three Poems*. New York: Ecco, 1972.

Breslin, James. *From Modern to Contemporary: American Poetry, 1945-1965*. Chicago: Univ. of Chicago Press, 1984.

Ginsberg, Allen. *Collected Poems 1947-1980*. New York: Harper, 1984.

Muckle, John. "The Names: Allen Ginsberg's Writings." *The Beat Generation Writers*. Ed. A. Robert Lee. London: Pluto, 1996. 10-36.

Sanders, Ed. *Investigative Poetry*. San Francisco: City Lights, 1976.

———. *Tales of Beatnik Glory*. 2 vols. New York: Citadel-Carol, 1990.

———. *Thirsting for Peace in a Raging Century: Selected Poems 1961-1985*. Minneapolis: Coffee House, 1987.

TITLE COMMENTARY

Fame and Love in New York

CARL SOLOMON (ESSAY DATE MAY-JUNE 1981)

SOURCE: Solomon, Carl. "A Review of *Fame and Love in New York*." *American Book Review* 3, no. 4 (May-June 1981): 14.

In the following review, Solomon examines Sander's novel Fame and Love in New York, *focusing on Sander's skill as a satirist.*

[With *Fame and Love in New York,* Ed Sanders] has written a Strangelovian novel about farce and terror in the New York art world. From Soho to Brooklyn-ho to Queens-ho to Bronx-ho to Staten Island-ho and from their to Ho-ho, Burroughsian and Queneau-like characters (Ione Appleton the poetess, Milton Rose the artist, J'Accuse the rock band members) scuffle for bread, pleasure, and integrity while terror in the form of Hunk Forbes, the para-military right-wing nut, lurks in the wings preparing for a sudden apocalyptic appearance. Traditionally in America, the Jack London Iron Heel vision of a right-wing hell has complemented the Orwellian vision of a left-wing hell. In Sanders, these two hells overlap. He has a complex, screwball, Rube Goldberg-like grasp of the technology of the future and fills out his satire with drawings, charts, lists and other devices hilarious at first impact but unfortunately growing a bit tedious with repetition before the novel ends.

Sanders has been a first-rate satirist since at least the mid-sixties when he was the leader of the Fugs and has always had a unique personal idiom and style occasionally reminiscent of satirists of the past but always recognizably Ed Sanders. In his novel, he introduces some of his past experience (like references to William Szabo—an old poet pal—the Fugs, and idiosyncratic verbal constructions redolent of, say, his Toe-Queen poems). Who can deny a man his personal idiom? It's the way he speaks. His dissection of Ione Appleton, poetess, founder of the Balzac Study Group, committer of "public fornication," and an individual determined to make it by hook or by crook, ranks with the best of early Waugh.

However, Sanders does have a few shortcomings. Chief among them is an inability to edit himself and a tendency toward repetition. *Fame and Love in New York* is undoubtedly too long, far longer than his subject matter warrants. Waugh seldom bored and his books had greater entertainment value than *Fame and Love* for that reason. Sanders indulges himself too greatly at the readers' expense. This book is not a satirical classic but is nevertheless head and shoulders above most current fiction. It would be an injustice to Ed Sanders to deny or to fail to mention that his enormous erudition (not as commonplace a commodity these days as one might think) shines through on every page. His prose blossoms everywhere with recondite words and information in a manner rivalling William Buckley or Anatole Broyard.

The barbs he directs at his avant-garde rebels are as sharp as those he hurls at the culture in general. Ione becomes, for a while, the epitome of the irksome female aesthete everybody remembers from his English classes. The rebels reach a peak of absurdity when they consider substituting a poem by Allen Ginsberg for "The Star-Spangled Banner" as our national anthem. Soho and Tribeca are stripped of their in-group glamour and become less intimidating to the uptown layman as a result of Sanders' debunking satire. . . .

His overall weakness seems to be a unidimensionality of subject matter and technique. All comics have a few special identifying routines and Sanders' greatest and most typical comes when he discusses crass aspects of his exaggerated culture boom, like the sale of Proust-brand cork-lined rooms. He is best when he reveals the commercial exploitation of culture generally—for the sake of "mon" and to avoid "pov"—and the madness of selling and collecting memorabilia of great and long-gone cultural names; when he reveals the shallow Darwinian survival bent behind our superficial idealism. . . .

Fame and Love in New York should be read by everybody who loves art, enjoys genuine intelligent humanism and likes good, normal, gritty wit.

1968: A History in Verse

M. L. LIEBLER (ESSAY DATE SPRING 1999)

SOURCE: Liebler, M. L. "A Terrible Beauty Is Born: Edward Sanders, the Techniques of Investigative Writing, and 1968." *Review of Contemporary Fiction* 19, no. 1 (spring 1999): 112-21.

In the following essay, Liebler offers a practical look at Sanders's process of investigative writing in 1968: A History in Verse.

Being certain that they and I
But lived where motley is worn:
All changed, changed utterly:
A terrible beauty is born.
　　　　　　—W. B. Yeats, "Easter 1916"

My intention is to offer readers a practical approach to Edward Sanders's process of investigative writing and to his 1997 book *1968: A History in Verse.* I offer this essay as primer and overview. For those readers expecting another stuffy academic meandering on the state of American literature in the late twentieth century, be warned from the start: there's far too much of that crap already. Ed Sanders's creative work as a poet, fiction writer, musician, and political activist has always been about getting closer to the truth, even if the end result should be "a terrible beauty." Because Ed has always approached his art as a search for truth and justice, which may seem quite quirky in the weird business of contemporary American letters and postmodern theory, this essay will be straightforward rather than encoded garble meant to stump rather than lead. In order properly to inform the reader about Ed Sanders's investigative process and its application in this book, I will first need to provide some basic background: Ed's discovery of this unique process, the process itself, the debt owed to the great American bard Charles Olson, and the birth of investigative poetry.

In 1970 Edward Sanders published the very first book (**The Family**) dealing with Charles Manson, his Family, and their horrific murders of Sharon Tate and the LaBiancas in Los Angeles, California, in 1969. These murders and the Manson Family confirmed for older Americans everything they believed to be evil and terrible about the youth culture of sixties America. Charles Manson's vision was that a race war was coming down in America (aka "Helter Skelter") and that the Beatles' *White Album* contained the prophetic message of the evil gloom doom about to settle upon the American teenage wasteland already cluttered with Vietnam, drugs, student protests, rock'n' roll, civil rights, and a seeming disdain for the older generation. Ed Sanders, with his intense interest in history and literature, along with his belief in Charles Olson's concept of composition by field, gained press credentials through the *Los Angeles Free Press,* and he thus began to collect data through interviews, research, and a well-planned, thorough investigation. In his research he discovered the terrible reality of cult behavior in general and of youth cults in particular in sixties America. While these revelations were as startling to Ed as they were to the public at large, the investigative process drew him deeper into exploring and working exclusively with what he later called investigative poetry. During a radio interview on Detroit's WXYT in the summer of 1997, I asked Ed if, perhaps, **The Family** was the beginning of his interest and work in what would later become known as investigative poetry. He paused, carefully thought a minute, and then responded that yes, he now believed that his interest in and experience with the process was indeed spawned during those difficult and strange times. But the whole story of Ed's interest in this unique

concept of writing and research goes back a bit further than 1969 and Charlie Manson.

In 1950 humdrum, straight-laced, post-World-War-II America, Charles Olson, controversial American poet and critic from Gloucester, Maine, wrote perhaps one of the most famous and challenging essays on contemporary American poetics, entitled "Projective Verse." This mind-expanding essay has moments of great insight and clarity, and these moments wholly inspired a young Midwestern boy, who had been raised in suburban Kansas City, to delve more deeply into the essay's meaning and to bring further focus to its application. Olson believed at the time that if poetry and poetics were to change, advance, and remain vital in American culture and art, then each area (poetry and poetics) must "catch up and put into itself certain laws and possibilities of the breath, of the breathing of the man who writes as well as of his listenings (The revolution of the ear . . .)" (Olson 15). Olson then advocated that contemporary poets consider working "OPEN, or what can also be called COMPOSITION BY FIELD, as opposed to inherited line, stanza, overall form, what is the 'old' base of the non-projective" (Olson 16). Olson stated that there were three important aspects of this new style of writing:

- The Kinetics: "A poem is energy transferred from where the poet got it . . . by way of the poem itself to . . . the reader."

- The Principle: "Form is never more than an extension of content."

- The Process: "One perception must immediately and directly lead to a further perception."

Olson then concluded this section of his essay by stating, "So there we are, fast, there's the dogma. And its excuse, its usableness, in practice. Which gets us, it ought to get us, inside the machinery, now, 1950, of how projective verse is made" (Olson 17). For Charles Olson, it was all that easy and that difficult, but it is this basic concept and its subsequent theory that attracted the attention of young Ed Sanders, who then began his journey on the road to furthering Olson's theory and, eventually, to creating his own style of investigative writing.

At this point I think it important to mention a bit about the type of writer and artist Ed Sanders was and continues to be. After leaving Kansas City immediately upon graduation from high school, Ed split the Midwest for New York City, where he determined to become a poet. Ed had been inspired first by Allen Ginsberg's legendary poem

"Howl" and such Beat generation writers as Jack Kerouac, William Burroughs, and Gregory Corso in addition to Charles Olson. The brief overview of Sanders's history is that he attended New York University as a student of Greek and Latin, opened the now historically famous Lower East Side Peace Eye bookstore, started up and edited *Fuck You / A Magazine of the Arts,* and shortly thereafter formed, with New York City poet and artist Tuli Kupferberg, the art-rock group the Fugs in 1964. The Fugs took their name from a fornicatory euphemism in Norman Mailer's *The Naked and the Dead.* The Fugs became quite popular on the mid-sixties Greenwich Village cultural scene with their several-times-a-week performances of poetry, storytelling, and rock music at the Playhouse Theater on Astor Place. Word spread around Manhattan about this group's sold-out performances, and soon the Fugs were offered a major recording contract. This was the beginning of Ed's rock'n' roll career. The Fugs recorded some ten albums, and Ed later released two solo albums for Warner Brothers/Reprise.

During the same time as Fug-mania, Ed continued his other career as an established poet, known ever since his first book, *Poem from Jail* in 1963, as a serious writer who chronicled the rapidly changing political and social scenery of sixties America. He became an identified antiwar activist after his visible involvement with Abbie Hoffman, Jerry Rubin, David Dellinger, the Berrigan brothers, Dorothy Day and the Catholic Worker Movement, and others in the 1967 March on the Pentagon and because of his many social democratic musings in prose and poetry. Eventually, he used the Fugs' music to spotlight and encourage political action and social change in America. The Fugs played many antiwar rallies. They often performed with Janis Joplin, Jimi Hendrix, the Doors, and Frank Zappa and the Mothers of Invention, and they toured Europe with Fleetwood Mac. The Fugs became to rock'n' roll of the late sixties what Lenny Bruce was to comedy in the fifties. They were known for their outrageous political, social, cultural performances that made the older generation extremely nervous and uncertain about America's future.

With all of this history behind the writer/musician/bookstore owner/songwriter, it isn't too difficult to see where Ed was heading in carving his own unique niche in American literature and art. Ed became famous for inventing everything from new words for the changing American lexicon to new electronic instruments made from

ties, gloves, etc. All of these interests boded well for the beginning of his search for an original process of writing.

In July 1975 Ed Sanders was asked to deliver a lecture on some aspect of contemporary poetics for the Visiting Spontaneous Poetics Academy at Naropa Institute's Summer Program. Sanders then prepared what has now become his landmark lecture, published by Lawrence Ferlinghetti's City Lights as *Investigative Poetry,* to articulate the belief "that poetry should again assume responsibility for the description of history" (3):

> move over Herodotus
> move over Thuc'
> move over Arthur Schlesinger
> move over logographers and chroniclers
> and compulsive investigators
> for the poets are
> marching again
> upon the hills
> of history.
>
> *(Investigative Poetry* 5)

In his City Lights booklet Ed clearly sets forth his theory: "My statement is this: that poetry, to go forward, in my view, has to begin a voyage into the description of *historical reality*" (7). Here the reader will notice how closely Sanders is following in Charles Olson's footsteps. Both poets are stating that some kind of change is imperative for their times if poetry is to move forward. Hence, projective verse; hence, investigative poetry.

Sanders argues in his new poetics that poets are responsible for "mak[ing] reality" and therefore for making freedom. He believes that dealing with reality through history and investigation can and does lead to a profound sense of freedom and a lucid understanding of reality. In his manifesto about investigative poetry he elaborates on how this form of poetry can best further an understanding of our world and ourselves. He writes,

> Investigative poesy is freed from capitalism, churchism, and other totalitarianisms; free from racisms, free from allegiance to napalm-dropping military police states—a poetry adequate to discharge from its verse-grids the undefiled high energy purely-distilled verse-frags, using *every* bardic skill and meter and method of the last 5 or 6 generations, in order to describe *every* aspect (no more secret governments!) of the historical present, while aiding the future, even placing bard-babble once again into a role as shaper of the future.
>
> (11)

While I realize this is a mouthful (it is even written in Charles Olson's style of comma-laden explanations), I also think this paragraph best sums up for the reader the essence of the process of investigative poetry. It seems rather easy to understand and to be as enthused as the bard himself when he first learned of Olson's liberating concept. We, too, the poets of the world, are liberated, excited, and filled with the freedom of the Sanders mantra, "move over . . . for the poets are marching again upon the hills of history" (5). Now, poets everywhere can raise their voices in a grace-giving chant to take control of our history, our future, and, most important, ourselves.

Through Holy Bards like Sanders and Olson, we are freed to create, to open case files, to investigate the investigators, to ask the forbidden questions of those in power, of those craving absolute power, of those striving for a modicum of power in the strained world gap of selfishness and lost love. Sanders's contention is that poets must never again be pushed like Pushkin in the Petrograds of the painful bygone years, left to die as stifled poets writing little. Sanders describes this state as "a right-winger's vision of paradise for a poet" (*Investigative Poetry* 18). We are free to assert ourselves and to shout out "NEVER AGAIN!" Poets must strive to see a new day where they can open case files, collect data, and engage in the unstoppable, fearless pursuit of the data clusters that will reveal reality and truth. However, with poets now cheered, it is only fair to warn that this new freedom-oriented pursuit of knowledge is not going to be taken well by those who hoard authority and power. Investigative poetry can be a dangerous business: consider Sanders's *The Family*, his detailed investigation of the mob's waste dumping in upstate New York ("Death by Water," a project in progress), even his initial investigative project involving the poetry war between W. S. Merwin, Allen Ginsberg (his own hero), and the Buddhists at Naropa Institute in the late seventies, well-documented in *The Party* (co-authored by Sanders and his Naropa students) and in Tom Clark's *The Great Naropa Poetry Wars*. Now, upon reconsidering *The Party*, I think that it might be more dangerous to investigate poets than dictators and evil empires à la Pushkin, but I digress. All in all, I have found *Investigative Poetry* inspirational for my own writing and for countless advanced students of poetry. Whatever its occasional flaws (pulling off an investigation is usually not the tidy process Sanders describes), investigative poetry is a genuine liberation for writers, teaching them that it is OK to write whatever they want to write in whatever way or style they want. Ah! Richie Haven at Woodstock, 1969: "Freedom! Freedom!!"

All of this preliminary set-up now leads to the point of this article—Ed Sanders's use of the investigative technique in *1968: A History in Verse.*

Sanders has always stated that the investigative process must involve honesty, a serious confrontation of the facts, and a fearless pursuit of data, even if the consequences result in discomfort to the investigator. He clearly states in the City Lights booklet, "Therefore, NEVER HESITATE TO OPEN / UP A CASE FILE / EVEN UPON THE BLOODIEST OF BEASTS OR PLOTS" (23). Later, he adds, "And do not hesitate / to open up a case file / on anything or anybody! / When in doubt, / interrogate . . ." (26). Thus Sanders states on the very first page of *1968*,

> I will not pretend
> that I was a very big part
>   of '68
>
> I surged through the year on my own little mis-
>   sions . . .
>
> daring to be part
>   of the history
>   of the era.
>
>   (5)

I find these lines to be true to Charles Olson's original concept, when Olson stated, as quoted by Sanders, "If a man or woman does not live / in the thought that he or she / is a history, he or she / is not capable of / himself or herself" (*Investigative Poetry* 26). With this said and with Olson's admonishment in mind, Sanders begins to take his readers on a chronological journey from New Year's Eve 1967 to New Year's Eve 1968, moving month by month through one of the most traumatic, unbelievable, and essential years in contemporary American history.

Not since the Civil War had America been so torn and at odds with itself. These are the chaotic times that Sanders chronicles in a sensitive, poetic, serious, and, at appropriate times, light-hearted way. He realizes that on the way to the birth of a terrible beauty, many incredible events must take place that can forever change the poet himself and the people of his country. Sanders's book is part history and part autobiography—autobiography because the poet played a bigger role in sixties America than he often gives himself credit for. He founded and led one of the most successful political/social rock bands of recent times; he was there at the planning and events that surrounded the 1968 Democratic Convention/Police Riot in Chicago; he performed with some of the now-legendary musicians of rock music; he worked for

Robert F. Kennedy's campaign and supported Martin Luther King's civil rights movement. So all in all, Ed Sanders has a history to tell, and unlike most historians, this writer puts all of his heart and soul into the telling of his story.

There are many times in the book when Sanders is brutally honest about himself and his contributions. For example, early on in the text he comes to realize that he cannot bring himself to chant, with the other protesters at the New York State University at Stony Brook "Pigasus for President Rally," "Off th' pi-ig!" in reference to police officers standing guard. He then writes that he thought it was a mistake to chant such statements, "just as I thought it was a mistake / for the Futurists / to call the Austrian gendarmes / 'walking pissoirs'" (*1968* 27). After the rally and concert, Sanders reflects in a very real and honest way that

> It was at the Stony Brook gig
> tired at dawn
> I began to feel the long, craving shame
>   for some of my work
> I didn't have the type
> of idealistic and topical repertoire
>   to inspire the streets
> & I didn't take the time to research & write them
>
> Instead I was working on tunes like
> "Johnny Pissoff Meets the Red Angel"
>   & "Ramses the II is Dead, My Love."
>   (27-28)

At this point in his history, Sanders says, essentially, that the Fugs continued to perform their basic repertoire, but he felt audiences were listening in a sleepy wakefulness. He decided that he had to change and become more aware and involved in his culture and history, so after the Stony Brook shows, he went back to New York City's Lower East Side and immediately signed a lease to reopen Peace Eye bookstore. Peace Eye was a place for intellectuals, bo-hos, politicos, and other hipsters to hang, discuss literature and revolution, and print broadsides, chapbooks, etc., dealing with everything and anything. This may actually be the point where Sanders realized the importance and perhaps necessity of research and of fearless approaches to history and reality through what later became investigative poetry, rather than just playing for time with a rock'n' roll group.

Increasingly, Sanders's story of 1968 turns to the politics of the time. Throughout the text, he chronicles such important events as Martin Luther King's plan for the Poor People's Campaign in Washington, DC, an event that Dr. King would not live to see. Sanders goes into a fair amount of creative research on Dr. King's alleged assassin, James Earl Ray. He does the same thing later with Robert Kennedy's alleged assassin, Sirhan Sirhan. Sanders also writes of My Lai. Sanders noticed two things about the massacre at My Lai. First, the incident occurred on the very same morning that Robert Kennedy announced his candidacy for president, and, second, the incident itself was a "thread of evil / that led forever to" a labyrinth (indicated in the book by a line drawing) (48). At almost every key moment of American history in 1968, like Edward R. Murrow, Sanders was there.

On page after page, Sanders informs us about the controversial events of 1968 that forever changed America. He goes into detail surrounding the Black Power salute controversy during the 1968 Mexico City Olympics and even notices Denny McLain's thirty-one wins as a pitcher for the Detroit Tigers. Sanders is able to pull the entire year together. As he says in a later portion of the book dealing with the Chicago Democratic Convention,

> That is, those crazy youth and not-so-youth
> their hasty signs, their hasty props, their
>   hasty yells
> were transformed in the
>   Chicago injustice
>   so that
> *A terrible beauty was born.*
>
>   (203)

It is this "terrible beauty" that has haunted Ed Sanders well into the nineties.

Sanders is still a poet, writer, musician, and political activist of intense dedication and sincerity. Although he could have easily hibernated in the Catskills with his many accomplishments (American Book Award, NEA and Guggenheim Fellowships, record industry awards, and numerous publications and recordings), he continues to build for the future, to investigate the abyss, to challenge those in authority, to hold everyone responsible for his or her actions and decisions. He continues to produce poetry, fiction, nonfiction, his weekly newspaper, the *Woodstock Journal*, and his weekly *Sanders Report* television show. In doing so, Sanders relearns every day what his experiences of previous years had already taught him: that although there is a mighty high price to be paid for beauty and truth, the battle is worth the energy and time invested, the research and experiences endured.

Finally, the purpose of this essay is to pay homage to the uniqueness of this great American bard who has served as my mentor in my social/

political and cultural art. It is my hope that this essay will at least crack open the door of understanding just enough to let the light of Sanders's insights and good humor, his honesty and compassion and love, shine through.

Ed ends his history on the Lower East Side of Manhattan in his neighborhood bar on New Year's Eve, 1968, where he and his wife toasted the past year:

> We whistled, we shouted
>   we stamped on the sawdust floor
> while in my soul
>   a year-long carillon of bells was
>   tolling. . . .
>
> All your inky fury is gone, o year—
> but the struggle
>   for freedom
>   & a just, sharing world
>   where no one is hungry or cold
>   is always in the air
>
> No police state
>   Cointelpro or Chaos
>   no teargas truck no battle-maddened mind
>   no urge to control & enslave
>   can stop that struggle
>   or erase it
> Farewell, o '68.
>
>   (245-46)

And fare thee well, O Holy Bard of honest spirit and willing quest for truth and justice. Thanks for your truthful and sincere horn of history. We are grateful for your poetic language that has shaken the establishments of bureaucratic lies to their very foundations, and in their place you have helped to birth a terrible beauty that we all can understand and cherish in the populist universe of art and culture. You have taught us the meaning of Bob Dylan's "To live outside the law you must be honest."

When tear gas and the smog of hate hung in the skies of 1968, where Allen Ginsberg cried to the heavens that "Chicago [and America] has no government. . . . It's just anarchy maintained by pistol" (*1968* 203), it was there that one found Edward Sanders and the investigative poets of the past and future marching up the steep hill of history to report the terrible beauty hidden beneath the mountainous bedrock of shameful power and injustice.

Works Cited

Dylan, Bob. "Absolutely Sweet Marie." *Writings and Drawings*. New York: Knopf, 1973. 217.

Olson, Charles. *Selected Writings*. Ed. Robert Creeley. New York: New Directions, 1966.

Sanders, Edward. *Investigative Poetry*. San Francisco: City Lights, 1975.

———. *1968: A History in Verse*. Santa Rosa: Black Sparrow Press, 1997.

FURTHER READING

Bibliography

Horvath, Brooke. "An Ed Sanders Checklist." *Review of Contemporary Fiction* 19, no. 1 (spring 1999): 138-43.

Primary and secondary bibliography of Sanders's work, including a discography of his recordings.

Criticism

Berman, Paul. Review of *The Z-D Generation*, by Ed Sanders. *Village Voice* 27, no. 16 (20 April 1982): 41.

Compliments the satirical edge of Sanders's poetic "manifesto" The Z-D Generation.

Boddy, Kasia. "Shards of God: An Epinician to the Heroes of the Peaceswarm." *Review of Contemporary Fiction* 19, no. 1 (spring 1999): 61-80.

Considers the manner in which Sanders's work was influenced by 1960s culture, especially the 1968 Democratic Convention and the writings of Allen Ginsberg and Norman Mailer.

Christgau, Robert. "Lumpenhippies and their Games." *New York Times Book Review* (31 October 1971): 2, 24-5.

Praises Sanders's examination of Charles Manson in The Family, calling the book "terrifying."

Clark, Tom. "Ed Sanders and Black Sparrow Press." *Review of Contemporary Fiction* 19, no. 1 (spring 1999): 55-6.

Discusses Sanders's association with Black Sparrow Press, the publisher of several of his works.

Dewey, Joseph. "Helter Shelter: Strategic Interment in *Tales of Beatnik Glory*." *Review of Contemporary Fiction* 19, no. 1 (spring 1999): 101-11.

Considers Sanders's book Tales of Beatnik Glory and its treatment of the issues and concerns of the Beat Generation.

Duerden, Richard. "Eyes and 'I.'" *Poetry* 108, no. 2 (May 1966): 125-30.

Discusses Sanders's use of colloquial language in King Lord/Queen Freak.

Horvath, Brooke. "Ed Sanders and His Fiction: An Interview." *Review of Contemporary Fiction* 19, no. 1 (spring 1999): 23-30.

Discusses Sanders's fiction, including Tales of Beatnik Glory and Shards of God.

Leonard, John. Review of *Fame and Love in New York*, by Ed Sanders. *New York Times* (17 December 1980): C33.

Calls Fame and Love in New York, "a very funny mess," noting that Sanders's prose is reminiscent of Kurt Vonnegut and Joseph Heller.

Miles, Barry. "An Interview with Ed Sanders—1 October 1968." *Review of Contemporary Fiction* 19, no. 1 (spring 1999): 14-22.

Discusses topics such as Scientology, how the United States is viewed in Europe, and Sanders's theatrical work.

Tracy, Phil. "'Sleazo Inputs' and Psychedelic Madness." *Commonweal* 95, no. 18 (4 February 1972): 428.

Argues that, despite his compelling prose, Sanders fails to connect the data in The Family *"into some discernible pattern."*

Wallenstein, Barry. "Mr. Ed Sanders." *Review of Contemporary Fiction* 19, no. 1 (spring 1999): 50-4.

Examines Sanders's influence on New York's cultural life during the 1960s.

OTHER SOURCES FROM GALE:

Additional coverage of Sanders's life and career is contained in the following sources published by the Gale Group: *Contemporary Authors,* Vols. 13-16R; *Contemporary Authors Autobiography Series,* Vol. 21; *Contemporary Authors New Revision Series,* Vols. 13, 44, 78; *Contemporary Literary Criticism,* Vol. 53; *Contemporary Poets,* Ed. 7; *Dictionary of Literary Biography,* Vols. 16, 244; *DISCovering Authors Modules: Poets;* and *Literature Resource Center.*

GARY SNYDER

(1930 -)

(Full name Gary Sherman Snyder) American poet, translator, autobiographer, travel writer, and essayist.

Snyder's stature as both a counterculture figure and an innovative mainstream poet places him in an uncommon position in contemporary literature. Although only briefly involved with the San Francisco Beat movement of the 1950s, Snyder's influence on the Beats was nevertheless significant and he is often linked with them. However, unlike many Beat writers, Snyder has also received extensive scholarly attention. The literary influences of Walt Whitman, Ezra Pound, and Ralph Waldo Emerson have been noted in Snyder's works. He is the recipient of several literary honors and awards, including a Pulitzer Prize for his collection *Turtle Island* (1974) and an American Book Award for *Axe Handles* (1983).

BIOGRAPHICAL INFORMATION

Snyder, the son of Harold Alton and Lois Wilkie Snyder, was born on May 8, 1930, in San Francisco, California. Snyder was raised on small farms, first in Washington and later in Oregon, and held jobs as a logger, seaman, fire lookout, and United States Forest Service trail crew worker. His interest in American Indian culture led him to acquire degrees in literature and anthropology at

Reed College. It was here that Snyder met Lew Welch and Philip Whalen, a trio that would later become known as the Reed College poets. Snyder began graduate work in linguistics at Indiana University, and then transferred to the University of California at Berkeley, where he pursued his interest in Asian thought and culture by studying Oriental languages.

Snyder's years at Berkeley coincide with the era of the San Francisco Poetry Renaissance, when the Beats of New York—Jack Kerouac and Allen Ginsberg, in particular—met up with the bohemians of the west: Kenneth Rexroth, Lawrence Ferlinghetti, Michael McClure, and the Reed College poets, among others. Rexroth arranged the meeting of Ginsberg and Snyder, sending Ginsberg out to Berkeley to meet Snyder and invite him to take part in a poetry reading. Thus Snyder was one of the poets performing at the legendary Six Gallery reading of 1955. By 1956, Beat writing was widely read and debated, and Ginsberg and Kerouac were nationally known figures. Snyder, however, had left the country for Kyoto, Japan, to study Zen Buddhism and meditation. By the time his earliest books of poetry were published—*Riprap* in 1959 and *Myths and Texts* in 1960—Snyder was primarily known as the fictional character Japhy Ryder of Kerouac's novel *The Dharma Bums* (1958). Snyder's time in Japan was occasionally interrupted by odd jobs—in 1957 he worked for eight months on an oil tanker, and in 1964 he taught for one semester in the English department at Berkeley. During this period he also met and married Joanne Kyger; they remained together from 1960 to 1964.

Widespread recognition of Snyder's poetry did not occur until 1965, with the re-release of *Riprap*, which included Snyder's translations of Japanese poetry. That same year he was awarded a Bollingen Foundation grant to fund his study of Zen in Japan for another year, and in 1966 he was a National Institute of Arts and Letters poetry award winner. Returning to the United States, Snyder became a part of the burgeoning hippie movement in San Francisco, presiding with Ginsberg over the Great Human Be-In of 1967. Later that year he married Masa Uehara in Japan; their son Kai was born in 1968 in Kyoto, and their son Gen was born in San Francisco in 1969. Those years were also a time of prolific writing for Snyder, leading to the publication of *The Back Country* (1967), *The Blue Sky* (1969), *Earth House Hold: Technical Notes and Queries for Fellow Dharma Revolutionaries* (1969), and *Regarding Wave* (1969). He built a home and working farm for his family in the Sierra Nevada, called Kitkitdizze, moving a Buddhist temple over from Japan in 1973 to add to the property.

Snyder became active in ecological issues, speaking in public forums including the 1972 United National Conference on the Human Environment in Stockholm, Sweden, and the 1983 E. F. Schumacher lecture in England. These interests are reflected in later collections of his writing, such as *Turtle Island*, *The Old Ways: Six Essays* (1977), *Axe Handles*, *The Practice of the Wild* (1990), and *A Place in Space: Ethics, Aesthetics, and Watersheds* (1995). In 1996 Snyder completed a project that he had worked on for nearly forty years. *Mountains and Rivers without End* had been published in smaller sections, starting with *Six Sections from Mountains and Rivers without End* in 1965, then *Six Sections from Mountains and Rivers without End Plus One* in 1970, and again in *North Pacific Lands & Waters: A Further Six Sections* (1993). The completed book-length poem had been long anticipated by critics and readers as a potential companion to his mentor William Carlos Williams's *Patterson* or Ezra Pound's *Cantos* in the canon of modern poetry. Snyder divorced his third wife, Masa Uehara, and married Carole Koda in 1991; he continues to live at his self-built home in the Sierra Nevada.

MAJOR WORKS

The themes of Snyder's poetry and prose have remained consistent: his interests in Asian cultures, Buddhism, and the environment are present in all of his works. The poems in his first collection, *Riprap*, remain some of his most frequently read and include "Mid-August at Sourdough Mountain Lookout," "Piute Creek," "Above Pate Valley," "Water," and "Milton by Firelight." These are primarily shorter poems that capture details of Snyder's daily life and work. The poems are quiet and measured—not recognizably "Beat" in the strictest terms, but sharing the Beat engagement with the seemingly mundane aspects of life. The poems of *Myths and Texts* were written at roughly the same time, demonstrating Snyder's ability to work in a variety of forms. A collection of forty-eight poems, the volume is best read as a single unified work in three parts, a long work pointing toward the magnum opus of *Mountains and Rivers without End*.

The Back Country treats similar themes from a highly personal perspective; several poems are intimate portraits of love and friendship, as in "Rolling In at Twilight" and "After Work." In *Regarding Wave* Snyder's personal reflections include his wife, children, and a thriving household—themes that dominate alternately erotic and sweet poems like "It Was When," "The Bed in the Sky," and "Not Leaving the House." The intimacy of Snyder's poetry remains closely connected to his environmental concerns, with the family providing an ideal model of the interconnections of all life on earth and a motive for preserving it. "The Bath," from Snyder's *Turtle Island*, further expresses these themes. Such issues are also the central concerns of *Mountains and Rivers without End*. Although Snyder's reputation rests primarily on his long career as a poet, he has published several significant prose collections. The first of these is *Earth House Hold*, a selection of journal writings and essays on poetry, meditation, and ecology. The growth of his prose has tended to follow the growth of his engagement in ecological issues, culminating in *The Practice of the Wild*.

CRITICAL RECEPTION

Though Snyder received crucial early encouragement from Williams and later Kenneth Rexroth, critics in general did not immediately respond favorably to his style. Snyder's short, imagistic poems were viewed as formless and vague, and though he was linked to the Beats, his poetry lacked the manic energy and rapid-fire wordplay Beat writers popularized. Among the earliest champions of Snyder's work was literary scholar and critic Thomas Parkinson, who assessed Snyder as a careful craftsman and a genuine moral authority. By the 1970s, Snyder's reputation as a Zen nature poet was established, and the themes of his work resonated with the cultural concerns of the day. Snyder's efforts at communal living and ecological activism were highly informative of his poetry and contributed greatly to others' interest in his poetry. Critics discussed Snyder as the poetic voice of a counterculture, and as a regional poet of a specific place. In particular, Snyder embodied for some the essence of the Western writer: rugged, good with his hands, traditionally masculine in every regard, but sensitive to women, children, and the land. As Thomas J. Lyon has suggested, Snyder presented a viable alternative to the Eastern intellectual writer, with an image and ethos unique to the American West. Later studies have focused on similar themes, looking back to mid-century America and seeing in Snyder a particularly American voice. Studies by such commentators as Tim Dean, Charles Molesworth, and Lars Nordstrom stress Snyder's unique ability to capture and express essentially American concerns and trends with a distinctly American voice. Despite the elements of Asian language and culture with which he infuses his works, critics have consistently found in Snyder a Western voice linked to the tradition of Whitman, Henry David Thoreau, and other American nature writers.

PRINCIPAL WORKS

Riprap (poetry) 1959; revised edition, 1965

Myths and Texts (poetry) 1960

Six Sections from Mountains and Rivers without End (poetry) 1965; revised editions published as *Six Sections from Mountains and Rivers without End Plus One*, 1970, and *North Pacific Lands and Waters: A Further Six Sections*, 1993

A Range of Poems (poetry and translations) 1966

The Back Country (poetry) 1967

The Blue Sky (poetry) 1969

Earth House Hold: Technical Notes and Queries to Fellow Dharma Revolutionaries (journal and essays) 1969

Regarding Wave (poetry) 1969; enlarged edition, 1970

Manzanita (poetry) 1971

The Fudo Trilogy (poetry) 1973

Turtle Island (poetry) 1974

The Old Ways: Six Essays (essays) 1977

On Bread and Poetry: A Panel Discussion with Gary Snyder, Lew Welch, and Philip Whalen (interviews) 1977

The Real Work: Interviews and Talks, 1964-1979 [edited by W. Scott McLean] (interviews and lectures) 1980

Axe Handles (poetry) 1983

Passage through India (autobiography and travel writing) 1983

Left out in the Rain: New Poems, 1947-1985 (poetry) 1986

The Practice of the Wild: Essays (essays) 1990

No Nature: New and Selected Poems (poetry) 1992

A Place in Space: Ethics, Aesthetics, and Watersheds (essays) 1995

Mountains and Rivers without End (poetry) 1996

The Gary Snyder Reader: Prose, Poetry, and Translations, 1952-1998 (poetry, prose, essays, letters, and translations) 1999

Look Out: A Selection of Writings (poetry and essays) 2002

PRIMARY SOURCES

GARY SNYDER (POEM DATE 1959)

SOURCE: Snyder, Gary. "Riprap." In *Riprap*, p. 36. Kyoto, Japan: Origin Press, 1959.

The following poem is representative of Snyder's poetic output, encouraging the preservation of the natural world.

"RIPRAP"

Lay down these words
Before your mind like rocks.
    placed solid, by hands
In choice of place, set
Before the body of the mind
    in space and time:
Solidity of bark, leaf or wall
    riprap of things:
Cobble of milky way,
    straying planets,
These poems, people,
    lost ponies with
Dragging saddles—
    and rocky sure-foot trails.
The worlds like an endless

four-dimensional
Game of *Go.*
ants and pebbles
In the thin loam, each rock a word
a creek-washed stone
Granite: ingrained
with torment of fire and weight
Crystal and sediment linked hot
all change, in thoughts,
As well as things.

GARY SNYDER (POEM DATE 1967)

SOURCE: Snyder, Gary. "Smokey the Bear Sutra." In *The Fudo Trilogy*, pp. 9-14. Berkeley, Calif.: Shaman Drum, 1973.

Originally written by Snyder in 1967, the following poem was distributed at the San Francisco Human Be-In as a call to promote ecological awareness. It was later collected in The Fudo Trilogy.

"THE SMOKEY THE BEAR SUTRA"

Once in the Jurassic about 150 million years ago, the Great Sun Buddha in this corner of the Infinite Void gave a Discourse to all the assembled elements and energies: to the standing beings, the walking beings, the flying beings, and the sitting beings—even grasses, to the number of thirteen billion, each one born from a seed, assembled there: a Discourse concerning Enlightenment on the planet Earth.

"In some future time, there will be a continent called America. It will have great centers of power called such as Pyramid Lake, Walden Pond, Mt. Rainier, Big Sur, Everglades, and so forth; and powerful nerves and channels such as Columbia River, Mississippi River, and Grand Canyon. The human race in that era will get into troubles all over its head, and practically wreck everything in spite of its own strong intelligent Buddha-nature."

"The twisting strata of the great mountains and the pulsings of volcanoes are my love burning deep in the earth. My obstinate compassion is schist and basalt and granite, to be mountains, to bring down the rain. In that future American Era I shall enter a new form; to cure the world of loveless knowledge that seeks with blind hunger, and mindless rage eating food that will not fill it."

And he showed himself in his true form of

SMOKEY THE BEAR.

A handsome smokey-colored brown bear standing on his hind legs, showing that he is aroused and watchful.

Bearing in his right paw the Shovel that digs to the truth beneath appearances; cuts the roots of useless attachments, and flings damp sand on the fires of greed and war;

His left paw in the Mudra of Comradely Display—indicating that all creatures have the full right to live to their limits and that deer, rabbits, chipmunks, snakes, dandelions, and lizards all grow in the realm of the Dharma;

Wearing the blue work overalls symbolic of slaves and laborers, the countless men oppressed by a civilization that claims to save but often destroys;

Wearing the broad-brimmed hat of the West, symbolic of the forces that guard the Wilderness, which is the Natural State of the Dharma and the True Path of man on earth: all true paths lead through mountains—

With a halo of smoke and flame behind, the forest fires of the kali-yuga, fires caused by the stupidity of those who think things can be gained and lost whereas in truth all is contained vast and free in the Blue Sky and Green Earth of One Mind;

Round-bellied to show his kind nature and that the great earth has food enough for everyone who loves her and trusts her;

Trampling underfoot wasteful freeways and needless suburbs; smashing the worms of capitalism and totalitarianism;

Indicating the Task: his followers, becoming free of cars, houses, canned foods, universities, and shoes, master the Three Mysteries of their own Body, Speech, and Mind; and fearlessly chop down the rotten trees and prune out the sick limbs of this country America and then burn the leftover trash.

Wrathful but Calm. Austere but Comic. Smokey the Bear will Illuminate those who would help him; but for those who would hinder or slander him,

HE WILL PUT THEM OUT.

Thus his great Mantra:

Namah samanta vajranam chanda maharoshana Sphataya hum traks ham mam

"I DEDICATE MYSELF TO THE UNIVERSAL DIAMOND
BE THIS RAGING FURY DESTROYED"

And he will protect those who love woods and rivers, Gods and animals, hobos and madmen, prisoners and sick people, musicians, playful women, and hopeful children;

And if anyone is threatened by advertising, air pollution, television, or the police, they should chant SMOKEY THE BEAR'S WAR SPELL:

DROWN THEIR BUTTS
CRUSH THEIR BUTTS
DROWN THEIR BUTTS
CRUSH THEIR BUTTS

And SMOKEY THE BEAR will surely appear to put the enemy out with his vajra-shovel.

Now those who recite this Sutra and then try to put it in practice will accumulate merit as countless as the sands of Arizona and Nevada.
Will help save the planet Earth from total oil slick.

Will enter the age of harmony of man and
   nature.
Will win the tender love and caresses of men,
   women, and beats
Will always have ripe blackberries to eat and a
   sunny spot under a pine tree to sit at.

AND IN THE END WILL WIN HIGHEST
PERFECT ENLIGHTENMENT

thus have we heard.

                (may be reproduced free forever)

GENERAL COMMENTARY

CRUNK (ESSAY DATE SPRING 1962)

SOURCE: Crunk. "The Work of Gary Snyder." *Sixties*,
no. 6 (spring 1962): 25-42.

*In the following essay, Crunk praises Snyder for the
compassion and strength of his poetry, arguing that in
his care for others Snyder distinguishes himself from other
Beat writers. Crunk also discusses Snyder's debt to Asian
literature and notes Snyder's engagement with Chinese
and Japanese culture.*

I

Gary Snyder is an original man. He has written a poetry which is quite unusual and very different from most poetry written in the last years.

The poems take place "In the Woods and at
sea." In the woods and at sea, Mr. Snyder has been
able to enjoy and praise the physical life. The
movements of all physical things are not abstract
or intellectualist, of course, and Mr. Snyder sees
that all growing, physical things are in a sense like
women, who have "a difficult dance to do, but
not in mind."

Mr. Snyder's first book was published in 1959
by Cid Corman, called *Riprap* (Origin Press, 1959,
$1.25). In an appendix to the Grove Press anthol-
ogy, Mr. Snyder made some remarks on *Riprap*:

I've recently come to realize that the rhythms of
my poems follow the rhythm of the physical work
I'm doing and the life I'm leading at any given
time—which makes the music in my head which
creates the line. Conditioned by the poetic tradition of the English language and whatever feeling
I have for the sound of poems I dig in other
languages. *Riprap* is really a class of poems I wrote
under the influence of the geology of the Sierra
Nevada and the daily trail-crew work of picking
up and placing granite stones in tight cobble patterns on hard slab. "What are you doing?" I asked
Roy Marchbanks. "Rip-rapping," he said. His selection of natural rocks was perfect—. . . I tried writing poems of touch, simple, short words, with the
complexity far beneath the surface texture. In part

FROM THE AUTHOR

the line was influenced by the five-and-seven-
character line Chinese poems I'd been reading,
which work like sharp blows on the mind.

The human voices and persons who sometimes rise in Mr. Snyder's poems are always
distinguished by this dignity. For example, in a
poem in *Riprap* called **"Hay for the Horses,"** we
see a man arrive at a barn with a load of hay. Suddenly, at lunch time, his voice breaks out with his
broodings:

"HAY FOR THE HORSES"

He had driven half the night
From far down San Joaquin
Through Mariposa, up the
Dangerous mountain roads,
And pulled in at eight a.m.
With his big truckload of hay
             behind the barn.
With winch and ropes and hooks
We stacked the bales up clean
To splintery redwood rafters
High in the dark, flecks of alfalfa
Whirling through shingle-cracks of light,
Itch of haydust in the
             sweaty shirt and shoes.
At lunchtime under Black oak
Out in the hot corral,
—The old mare nosing lunchpails,
Grasshoppers crackling in the weeds—
"I'm sixty-eight," he said,
"I first bucked hay when I was seventeen.

I thought, that day I started,
I sure would hate to do this all my life.
And dammit, that's just what
I've gone and done."

Snyder is not the man to make some complacent moralistic observation on the driver's words. This sense of worth in the lives of all human beings is not shared by very many recent American poets. But it recalls Whitman, with whom Mr. Snyder has other powers in common. For example, there is the presence of the poet himself as a living figure in nearly every poem. I mean here much more than the mere grammatical first person: I mean the pervading presence of the poet who simultaneously shares in the processes of life and reveals some of its meaning through his actions. Another power which Snyder shares with Whitman is his occasionally humorous awareness of himself in situations that challenge conventional pride. Give or take a few differences, Whitman might have written Mr. Snyder's poem "Cartagena":

Rain and thunder beat down and flooded the
    streets—
We danced with Indian girls in a bar water half-
    way to our knees,
The youngest one slipped down her dress and
    danced bare to the waist,
The big negro deckhand made out with his girl
    on his lap in a chair her dress over her eyes
Coca-Cola and rum, and rainwater all over the
    floor.
In the glittering light I got drunk and reeled
    through the rooms,
And cried, "Cartagena! swamp of unholy loves!"
And wept for the Indian whores who were
    younger than me, and I was eighteen,
And splashed after the crew down the streets
    wearing sandals bought at a stall
And got back to the ship, dawn came, We were
    far out at sea.

This poem, in its direct description of life in impolite society, might seem a Beat poem—up to a crucial point. Mr. Snyder's difference from the Beats (to which I shall return later) is apparent in a superior sensitivity. Like Whitman before him, he brings a sense of delicacy to bear upon his treatment of other people's lives. He also has a sense of privacy, even in the most raucous life, which appears in the several meditative poems in **Riprap**. The very first poem in the book is a short poem formed out of a moment in a forest look-out station. It is called **"Mid-August at Sourdough Mountain Lookout"**:

Down valley a smoke haze
Three days heat, after five days rain
Pitch glows on the fir-cones

Across rocks and meadows
Swarms of new flies.

I cannot remember things I once read
A few friends, but they are in cities.
Drinking cold snow-water from a tin cup
Looking down for miles
Through high still air.

This poem ends, like the previous poem, with an image of utter clarity, as of clear water—a promise of spiritual depth.

The meditative power and the privacy that characterize this brief, beautiful poem are powers which Mr. Snyder displays throughout his work. It is important to mention them, because they imply the presence behind the work of a man who has thought deeply about the body and value of existence conscious of itself. In short, I think that Mr. Snyder is a poet who might be called devout, or religious in the most elementary sense. He regards life with a seriousness so profound that he is able to experience and express the inner life without resorting to the worn-out abstractions which so often nullify the public discussions of spiritual matters.

The poems cited are from his first volume, **Riprap.** It is a beautiful book, and one of the two or three finest books of poetry of the last ten years.

Riprap was a simple collection of occasional poems, but Snyder's next book, **Myths and Texts,** is more carefully organized. It was published by LeRoi Jones with the Eighth Street Bookstore in 1960.

Myths and Texts is arranged in three sections: **"Logging,"** which describes Snyder's experience as a logger in Oregon, and also develops the theme of the destruction of the forests; **"Hunting,"** which describes with great delicacy the lives of animals; and **"Burning,"** which describes certain steps of spiritual life and labors of transformation from one level of life to another. The theme of the book as a whole is praise of physical life. There is a struggle to overcome what the poet calls the "ancient meaningless abstractions of the educated mind." "Get off my back, Confucius."

In the first section, Mr. Snyder is able to describe the violation of living creatures that takes place during a logging operation; he does so by leaping beyond the "meaningless abstractions." The following example is taken from Poem #8:

Each dawn is clear
Cold air bites the throat.
Thick frost on the pine bough
Leaps from the tree
        snapped by the diesel

Drifts and glitters in the
            horizontal sun.
In the frozen grass
        smoking boulders
          ground by steel tracks.
In the frozen grass
        wild horses stand
          beyond a row of pines.
The D8 tears through piss-fir,
Scrapes the seed-pine
                chipmunks flee,
A black ant carries an egg
Aimlessly from the battered ground.
Yellowjackets swarm and circle
Above the crushed dead-log, their home.
Pine oozes from barked
           trees still standing,
Mashed bushes make strange smells . . .

Although the poet seems most directly concerned, in this poem, with describing a process of destruction, it is interesting to note that his vision also includes a great number of living creatures, whose lives he watches carefully and tenderly. It is this very sense of detail in lives which, in the next group of poems, gathers into such intense focus as to see beyond the literal physical lives of the animals. That is, the group called **"Hunting"** moves beyond literal description into the beginnings of a spiritual evocativeness. At the end of the first poem in the section, the poet describes himself:

I sit without thoughts by the log-road
Hatching a new myth . . .

And it is true. Snyder is always "hatching a new myth," in the sense that he is always seeking for a way to embody his celebration of physical life in some form that will reveal its religious meanings. He never refers to the tired terms of classical mythology. They do not even seem to occur to him. He does use myths, however, not by referring to them but by recreating them in his own poems. He has several poems dedicated to animals; and he refers to "deer" and "bear" as the northwest Indians do—not simply as single living creatures but also as spiritual forces. The result is a poetry of authentic strangeness, where the spirituality of living creatures shines upon them in the darkness. The following is a passage from Poem #6:

The others had all gone down
From the blackberry brambles, but one girl
Spilled her basket, and was picking up her
Berries in the dark.
A tall man stood in the shadow, took her arm,
Led her to his home. He was a bear.
In a house under the mountain
She gave birth to sleek dark children

With sharp teeth, and lived in the hollow
Mountain many years.

It is in the third group of poems, **"Burning,"** that Mr. Snyder more frequently refers to the religious ideas of the Orient. What makes his religious meditations and descriptions in **"Burning"** so strong is his ability to present them in terms of the living plants and creatures which he has already described and celebrated in previous parts of his book. The following passages taken from Poem #6, Poem #16, and Poem #17 illustrate the tone of the third section:

"Forming the New Society
           Within the shell of the Old"
The motto in the Wobbly Hall
Some old Finns and Swedes playing cards
Fourth and Yesler in Seattle.
O you modest, retiring, virtuous young ladies
           pick the watercress, pluck the yar-
    row
"Kwan kwan" goes the crane in the field,
         I'll meet you tomorrow;
A million workers dressed in black and buried,
We make love in leafy shade.
              . . . . .
Earth! those beings living on your surface
none of them disappearing, will all be
    transformed.
When I have spoken to them
when they have spoken to me, from that mo-
    ment on,
their words and their bodies which they
usually use to move about with, will all change.
I will not have heard them. Signed

                      ( )
                     Coyote
            . . . . .
Rain falls for centuries
Soaking the loose rocks in space
Sweet rain, the fire's out
The black snag glistens in the rain
And the last wisp of smoke floats up
Into the absolute cold
Into the spiral whorls of fire
The storms of the Milky Way . . .
The sun is but a morning star.

The theme of the praise of physical life present everywhere in the book dominates Poem #16, **"Hunting,"** which deals with a birth:

How rare to be born a human being!
Wash him off with cedar-bark and milkweed
         send the damned doctors home.
Baby, baby, noble baby
Noble-hearted baby . . .

All the virtues of humor, delicacy, respect for living creatures, human and animal, patience and silence, are to be found in *Myths and Texts,* and in a more generally coherent and disciplined form than in *Riprap.* It is best to conclude this brief introduction to the second book by allowing Mr.

Snyder to speak for himself. His words are quoted in the Appendix to *The New American Poetry*:

> ***Myths and Texts*** grew between 1952 and 1956. Its several rhythms are based on long days of quiet in look-out cabins; settling chokers for the Warm Springs Lumber Co. (looping cables on logs and hooking them to 'D' Caterpillars—dragging and rumbling through the brush); and the songs and dances of Great Basin Indian tribes I used to hang around. The title comes from the happy collections of Sapir, Boas, Swanton, and others made of American Indian folktales early in this century; it also means the two sources of human knowledge—symbols and sense-impressions. I tried to make my life as a hobo and worker, the questions of history and philosophy in my head, and the glimpses of the roots of religion I'd seen through meditation, peyote, and "secret frantic rituals" into one whole thing.

II

I have three ideas about Snyder's work as a whole that I want to bring up. First, his is essentially a Western imagination. His poems are powerfully located—sown, rooted—in the landscape of the far Western states. He is a Western writer just as, for example, Delmore Schwartz, Anthony Hecht, and Howard Moss are Eastern writers. This is the same distinction one would have made earlier between Theodore Dreiser and John P. Marquand; or between Sherwood Anderson and Lionel Trilling. These two sets of writers deal with different geographical landscapes but the distinction is deeper and subtler than that. They differ in what might be called the landscape of the imagination—which each in his way tries to discover and explore.

The Western writer feels a need to approach his characters and incidents with an imagination totally, if temporarily, freed from all concern with abstract ideas. The Eastern writer, such as Mr. Schwartz or Mr. Trilling, does not. Mr. Trilling, thoroughly aware of the existence of the west and the mid-west and of the writers from these areas, still writes of them as a philosopher would write: his imagination, for better or for worse, is so saturated with abstract ideas that it would be difficult, if not impossible, for him to prevent their existence in the forefront of his mind. Existing there, they blot out many details of physical life. The poetry of Howard Moss, Anthony Hecht, and Delmore Schwartz is similarly saturated with abstract ideas.

Mark Twain is a Western writer: that is, his imagination is most powerfully moved when he is concerned with concrete details in the lives of non-intellectual people. Of course, he examines such lives with an intellect of great force and clarity. This is also true of early Hemingway. Similarly, Dreiser remains a Westerner even when he writes of New York or Boston. I think that one major sign of these writers' intellectual power is their ability to penetrate and explore the lives of people who are invisible to the academies—the "custodian" who comes in the afternoon and empties the professor's wastebasket; the timid young man who cleans out the rest rooms after ten o'clock at night; the frightened and ambitious textbook pitchman; the farmer who works in the field nearby; the idiot hired man. To force the fact of their mere existence into the consciousness of people whose whole lives are worries over social status is evidence of a strong intellect. With this power the grasp of the writers is permanently caught in sensuous details and imaginative images fresh in themselves. At any rate, the powerful mind that expresses its understanding of life in the forms of the imagination rather than in the forms of abstraction is the kind of American mind I have called Western. Most of its greatest representatives so far have been writers of fiction. One of the most interesting features of Gary Snyder's poetry is that in him we see this "western" imagination in a poet.

The point is worth examining further: it helps to identity Mr. Snyder's originality and it suggests a kind of American poetry that hasn't been very much explored—a kind of poetry which Mr. Snyder has been writing with freshness and dignity, which might be called a poetry of the Western imagination. The term itself doesn't matter much, except for the sake of convenience. It ought to suggest, however, certain features of poetry which are imaginative rather than rhetorical. In such poetry the forms of poems emerge from within the living growth of each particular poem and most definitely *not* in a set of conventions (such as the classical English iambic, with all its masterpieces of the past and its suffocating influence in the present). This new poetry is also marked by the presence of a powerful intelligence which does its thinking through the imagination itself, and not through repetition of the thoughts of established philosophical authorities or of classical myths which are degenerated through excessive or inaccurate use into obstructions rather than doorways to clear thought. Mr. Snyder does indeed embody certain myths in his poetry, but they are not classical myths, but "bear myths," and myths of the senses.

My second idea is that Mr. Snyder's poetry is very different from "Beat" poetry. Snyder has been associated primarily in magazines with the Black Mountain school and the Beats. His association with the latter (he is the hero of *Dharma Bums*) results from his friendship with Kerouac. Snyder's poetry is, however, immediately distinct both in imagination and in style from Beat work. A certain gentleness and care for civilization in Snyder is utterly absent in Ginsberg or Orlovsky, who are in favor, as they say, of "cat vommit." Ginsberg and Orlovsky make strong efforts to coarsen themselves, whereas Snyder does the very opposite. The Beat writers are opposed to civilization of all kinds: Snyder is not. Snyder's work everywhere reveals the grave mind of a man who is highly civilized and who, moreover, makes no pretense of denying his own intelligence.

Snyder's life is entirely different from the life of a Beat poet. Snyder took no part in the race for publicity among the Beats. Instead of merely talking about Zen, he went to Japan and entered a Buddhist monastery in Kyoto, where he still remains, learning Japanese, and undertaking serious study. The difference between his devotion to the Orient and the public exploitation of oriental religiosity by Jack Kerouac, among others, becomes immediately apparent. In order to read Chinese poets, Snyder learned ancient Chinese, a difficult language. He now makes his living translating from ancient Chinese and Japanese texts at a Zen institute in Kyoto, working in the institute in the afternoon and spending the morning at the monastery. His dedication to Chinese civilization is also shown in his translation of some ancient Chinese poems; here is his translation of a little poem by Po Chu-i:

> Tears soak her thin shawl
> dreams won't come
> —In the dark night, from the front palace,
> girls rehearsing songs.
> Still fresh and young,
> already put down,
> She leans across the brazier
> to wait the coming dawn.
> *From Floating World, 3*

My third idea is the reality of the oriental influence on Snyder. The influence of the orient on Snyder is interior: it is the desire to overcome vanity and ambition. This is an influence that is not necessarily available to collectors of oriental objects and books.

The great poets of Japan and, especially, of China, are almost invariably men who pride themselves on being men who devote their entire selves to the life of contemplation and imagination. In their poems they succeed in the struggle against vanity and the desire for power.

Another oriental influence concerns the method of construction of the poem. Chinese poems are formed out of images whose sensory force strikes the mind directly, not as an abstract substitute for an experience, but as an original experience in itself. Let me quote two short poems. The first is Chinese, the second one of Mr. Snyder's:

"SLEEPING A SPRING NIGHT IN THE PALACE ANNEXE"

The flowers hide palace walls sunk in shadow,
Birds chatter on their way to roost,
The stars shine and twinkle into the ten
thousand palace windows,
The nine terraces of heaven lie lulled in the
added brightness of the moon.
Unable to sleep, I listen for the turning of the
golden key in the lock.
Because of the wind I think I hear the jade ornaments tinkle.
Tomorrow morning I have to report to the
throne,
So I keep wondering how much of the night has
flown.
—Tu Fu, Translated by Soame Jenyns

"WATER"

Pressure of sun on the rockslide
Whirled me in dizzy hop-and-step descent,
Pool of pebbles buzzed in a Juniper shadow,
Tiny tongue of a this-year rattlesnake flicked,
I leaped, laughing for little boulder-color coil—
Pounded by heat raced down the slabs to the
creek
Deep tumbling under arching walls and stuck
Whole head and shoulders in the water:
Stretched full on cobble—ears roaring
Eyes open aching from the cold and faced a
trout.

Mr. Snyder's poem, above, contains no external reference to China or to Chinese poetry. Somebody once said that the prose of the young Ernest Hemingway resembled clean pebbles shining side by side at the bottom of a clear stream-channel; and that is the way Mr. Snyder has let the images of his poem arrange themselves into lines. There is no forcing of the imagination into external and conventional rhetorical patterns, such as have ruptured a good many poems during recent years in America. And yet Mr. Snyder's poem is not formless. It is exquisitely formed from the inside. It follows the clear rhythm of the poet's run down the hill in the hot sun, turns suddenly when he plunges his head in the cold water, and comes to a delightful close with the poet, his skin alive with the chill, gazing under the surface, face to face with a fish.

I began by noting Mr. Snyder's conscious debt to Chinese poets, and ended by admiring his ability to convey the astonishment of a fish. The two points suggest the importance of Mr. Snyder's study of Chinese. He has bypassed its biographical and historical externals, such as might be flaunted by someone who wanted to impress his readers, and has learned how to form his imagination into poems according to a tradition which is great and vital, and which is wholly distinct from the tradition of British poetry, very great in itself but somewhat inhibiting to American imaginative experience.

It is distressing to have to say it again, but few people in American literary discussion seem to take seriously the fact that what Walt Whitman accurately called "British literature" is not the only tradition from which American writers can be permitted to learn anything. It is one thing, of course, for scholars and critics to make plump careers of writing articles on, say, Pasternak, Quasimodo, Joyce, Yeats, Tagore, and even Mao Tsetung. But American poets, with a frequency that is dismal in proportion as it seems automatic—that is, conditioned—tend either to give up all hope of imaginative precision and delicacy altogether, as Ginsberg in his "Howl" or Freeman in his *Apollonian Poems,* or to regard all deviation from the iambic rhetoric of the British tradition as an absurdity when it fails or as a crime akin to parricide when it succeeds. Whitman patiently suggested the exploration of traditions beyond the British; but, as Hart Crane complained with terrible despair in one of his greatest letters, many people won't even read *Democratic Vistas.*

Perhaps the reading of such a work, endangering as it does the trite and completely false public image of Whitman which still persists in America despite the Beats' attempt to appropriate him, requires a courage which few men are willing to assume—a courage akin to Whitman's own. In any case, Gary Snyder has displayed a courage of similar kind, not in order to face Whitman's devastating and perhaps unsurpassed criticism of America's puritanical materialism; but in order to undertake one of the tasks of the imagination for which Whitman often felt poets in America should prove most capable: the exploration of living traditions which, shunning the British tradition, nonetheless display powers of poetry which equal and sometimes surpass that tradition; and to make this search for the purpose of claiming America itself—by which I mean literally our own lives and the people and places we live among day by day—for the imagination.

I have discussed the Chinese poets at some length in this essay because they mean so much to Mr. Snyder, and because they reveal in their own work the possibility of a further growth in American poetry which has scarcely been considered. My final impression of Mr. Snyder himself, however, does not depend on his debt to this or that writer.

What matters most to me is that Snyder has been able to live his daily life with the full power of his imagination awake to all the details of that life. A civilized and educated man, he is at his most sensitive and intelligent when he is writing about loggers, sailors, and animals. He has a poem which deals movingly with the moment when surveying the clutter of American life, he seems to decide to put off ambition and to be true to the imagination. The poem is called **"Nooksack Valley."** The poet has been sitting in a berry-picker's cabin, "at the end of a far trip north," and meditates on his American life so far, and on his possible future:

> . . . a week and I go back
> Down 99, through towns, to San Francisco and
> Japan.
> All America south and east,
> Twenty-five years in it brought to a trip-stop
> Mind-point, where I turn
> Caught more on this land—rock tree and man,
> Awake, than ever before, yet ready to leave.
> damned memories,
> Whole wasted theories, failures and worse success,
> Schools, girls, deals, try to get in
> To make this poem a froth, a pity,
> A dead fiddle for lost good jobs.
> the cedar walls
> Smell of our farm-house, half built in '35.
> Clouds sink down the hills
> Coffee is hot again. The dog
> Turns and turns about, stops and sleeps.

In this poem, as in so many others, the poet meditates alone. His recording of solitude in his poems is another striking feature of his work, one which makes it rather unusual in recent American poetry. American poets in recent years have tended to be like other Americans in shunning any experience which has to be undertaken alone.

Mr. Snyder has courage and an air of faithful patience. He keeps his voice low, not out of timidity but out of strength.

THOMAS J. LYON (ESSAY DATE FALL 1968)

SOURCE: Lyon, Thomas J. "Gary Snyder: A Western Poet." *Western American Literature* 3, no. 3 (fall 1968): 207-16.

In the following essay, Lyon uses the early poetry of Snyder to define his works as Western, as opposed to East

Coast American, poetry. Lyon cites Snyder's sense of place, the centrality of nature to his poetry and worldview, and his mythic consciousness as features of a Western school of poetry.

Probably the spirit of poetry works against such categorizing distinctions, but I would like to approach the problem of defining what a *Western* poet is as directly and particularly as possible by outlining a critical introduction to the 38-year-old Californian, Gary Snyder.

Snyder is a highly interesting man, a famous figure in the underground or sub-culture identified with San Francisco, the Beat Generation, and its present-day inheritors. Jack Kerouac made him practically a legendary guru as "Japhy Ryder" in the 1958 novel, *The Dharma Bums.* In that book, Japhy Ryder was a major influence on Ray Smith (Kerouac) in getting him into the mountains, teaching him how to backpack and climb, and pointing in the right direction (which is all you can do) in matters of Buddhism. As is typical in Kerouac's autobiographical "Duluoz Legend" books, the character was taken directly from life. Ryder was, at the time of his meeting with Smith, a graduate student in Oriental Languages at Berkeley, a supreme liver-off-the-land (including Safeway market throw-aways), and a contagiously free mountaineer spirit, the last most vague but most important. Besides Kerouac's, Snyder has Allen Ginsberg's admiration: Snyder (as a poet) is "very wise and very reliable,"[1] one of the few poets in this country capable of writing genuine Haiku. Berkeley professor Thomas Parkinson recently wrote, "Snyder is skilled in the use of his hands. If he were put down in the most remote wilderness with only a pocket knife, he would come cheerfully out of it within two weeks, full of fresh experience, and with no loss of weight. . . . If there has been a San Francisco renaissance, Snyder is its renaissance man: scholar, woodsman, guru, artist . . . accessible, open, and full of fun."[2] Perhaps the truest signal of Snyder's standing in the sub-culture is that last year he was invited to be the fourth member of a free-wheeling public symposium on the somewhat large topic of the future of world consciousness, along with Alan Watts, Allen Ginsberg, and Timothy Leary.[3] So in the great underground American night of the West, to paraphrase Kerouac weakly, Snyder is *in.* But what kind of *poet* is he? One more bit of background. When we hear "sub-culture," we think of "Tune in, turn on, drop out." But Snyder eschews this formulaic pronouncement: he writes, which means he's talking, communicating, contributing; he translates Japanese and Chinese poetry, the latter acceptably enough to have his

ON THE SUBJECT OF...

ALAN WATTS

Any discussion of the Beat connection to Zen Buddhism must take into account the part Alan Watts played in popularizing Taoist and Buddhist thought in America. As an expounder of Eastern philosophy for Westerners, Watts became a near cult figure in the 1950s and 1960s, and those who were attracted to Beat Generation values were likely to be interested in what he had to say about religion. Despite sharing similar ideologies, Watts was often critical of the Beats for appropriating Zen as their own, for embracing "this philosophy to justify a very self-defensive Bohemianism." In his important essay "Beat Zen, Square Zen, and Zen" (published in the summer 1958 issue of *Chicago Review*), he describes Zen as "above all the liberation of the mind from conventional thought." And this liberation, he was quick to assert, is quite different from "rebellion against convention, on the one hand, or adapting foreign conventions, on the other."

work included in a major anthology;[4] and most importantly, he brings to the sub-culture itself the bright clean air of the mountains, a deeply felt connection to the natural world that makes the city drug scene appear unbearably artificial, and which has been a factor, I am told, in the hippie move to the country which has the Nevadans so scared.

Snyder has five slim volumes of poems, only the last one published by a major firm. This is *The Back Country,* New Directions, 1968. Of the others, *Myths and Texts* and *Riprap* were printed by Totem Press and Origin Press, respectively, and *Six Sections from Mountains and Rivers without End* and *Riprap & Cold Mountain Poems* by the Four Seasons Foundation in San Francisco. So far, about 120 published poems.

Basically, Snyder is in the Blake-Whitman-Ginsberg tradition of Reality Poets; that is, he is interested in showing reality in its particulars, absolutely directly, through a clear and uninhibited sense perception. There is almost no abstract philosophizing in his work, no rationalistic or even intellectual formulations: just *things*. This follows William Carlos Williams' dictum: "No ideas but in things." But with the moving surface forms there is most certainly a coherent life-view; it, in fact, informs the selection of the particulars, and paces the peculiar Snyder rhythms and ellipses, of which more later. This life-view is deeply Oriental. Snyder spent several years in the Zen monastery at Kyoto, and has been a close student of the direct and economical and sense-oriented philosophy and poetry of Japan. But most of his poetry has American West subject matter, and a good deal of it is couched in familiar, colloquial idiom—talk of Northwest loggers or trail crews of Yosemite back country, or the strangely poetic cut-off sentences characteristic of the more laconic Beats.

Mentioning Whitman and Ginsberg as comparison figures suggests that Snyder is perhaps an incantatory singer of long, pulsing lines—a poet of drift rather than limit. Actually, the contrary is true, for Snyder's line is typically very short, and his method correspondingly selective and exclusive rather than expansive. This, I think, might be seen as the Haiku influence. Haiku is the most demanding poetry: the exact thing, that thing only and rendered in just *that* way, will do. Haiku is extremely formal, too. So there is a discipline here that is pointed in a different direction from that of the bardic or inclusive. And yet, in traditional Haiku, the finished poem cannot be seen as a *poem*, product of refinement and agonizing selection. It has to be effortless and perfectly natural. This discipline without effort corresponds exactly to the paradoxical Zen doctrine of "no-mind," meaning the easy swing of harmonious activity that comes to or is liberated from the mind when the straining rational or conceptual consciousness no longer tries to fight, to impose its will on the other centers of perception. The enormous sense of freedom that grows here is often found in Snyder's work.

There is another respect in which mention of Haiku may provide an illuminating parallel for Snyder's poetry. R. H. Blyth, the great Orientalist, once wrote, "Paradox is the life of haiku, for in each verse some particular thing is seen, and at the same time, without loss of its individuality and separateness, its distinctive difference from all other things, it is seen as a no-thing, as all things, as an all-thing."[5] This is what is going on, I think, in the following two haiku by Snyder:

They didn't hire him
      so he ate his lunch alone:
the noon whistle

"OVER THE MINDANAO DEEP":
Scrap brass
      dumpt off the fantail
falling six miles

Quoting, as everyone professes, is all that can be done with Haiku, but we *can* say that the easy directness of the genre seems to be the guiding principle of Snyder's poetics, whatever the length of the application. When properly handled, detail becomes a world. Let me give an example of this, from *The Back Country.* This is called "Rolling In At Twilight."

Rolling in at twilight—Newport Oregon—
    cool of september ocean air, I
saw Phil Whalen with a load of groceries
    walking through a dirt lot full
      of logging trucks, cats
        and skidders
    looking at the ground.
I yelld as the bus wheeld by
    but he kept looking down.
    ten minutes later with my books and pack
      knockt at his door
"Thought you might be on that bus"
    he said, and
showed me all the food.

Now this is obviously nothing effortfully philosophical, in the sense of calling up cosmic magnificences. But it is a marvelous evocation of Philip Whalen, the absorbed walker, and of the humble life of the bus-riding Pacific Coast poets who visit each other calmly and treat groceries with proper respect, not paying much attention to the machinery around them. The inverted elliptic phrasing of "cool of september ocean air" is worth noting for its full load. The bus window is open for us, too. This economy in suggesting a whole environment and lifestyle is typical of Snyder's work.

Looking back to Whitman again, sometimes Snyder matches the bard's great delight in things, cataloguing particular images line after line. This is Whitman's "Objects gross and the unseen soul are one," the Zen justification for the direct sensual perception of reality from "A Song For Occupations," in action. One of Snyder's best poems, "The Market," illustrates this very well. The Market in this poem, I believe, is the final nexus, in a sense oneness, of all diversified, particular reality. In a way, and again Oriental terminology is appropriate, the market is like the Tao which is (paradoxically, to the logical mind) both the One and the Many. Snyder portrays the nature of this equivalence with characteristically fresh imagery in this short selection:

> seventy-five feet hoed rows equals
> one hour explaining power steering
> equals two big crayfish =
> > all the buttermilk you can drink
> = twelve pounds cauliflower
> = five cartons greek olives = hitch-hiking
> > from Ogden Utah to Burns Oregon
> = aspirin, iodine, and bandages
> = a lay in Naples = beef
> = lamb ribs = Patna
> > long grain rice, eight pounds
> equals two kilogram soybeans   a boxwood
> > geisha comb.
> equals the whole family at the movies
> equals whipping dirty clothes on rocks
> > three days, some Indian river

Perhaps we should turn to *The Dharma Bums*, which Allen Ginsberg calls "actually a very scholarly, esoteric book,"[6] and let Japhy Ryder, instructing Ray Smith on a California camping trip, make this basic idea more explicit:

> "I keep thinking of my abandoned Crater Mountain Lookout house sitting up there with nobody but the conies down in their furry nests deep under boulders, and warm, eating seeds or whatever they eat. The closer you get to real matter, rock air fire and wood, boy, the more spiritual the world is. All these people thinking they're hardheaded materialistic practical types, they don't know shit about matter, their heads are full of dreamy ideas and notions." He raised his hand. "Listen to that quail calling."[7]

So far, then, we can see that Snyder's description of the world is fundamentally Buddhist. His joy in portraying experience probably compares well with the great wandering Haiku masters or with our own Whitman. His free and easy diction place him again as an inheritor of Whitman's, yet his discipline in selection and fondness for purposefully pregnant ellipses betray a careful student of Oriental poetry. But what, to return to the title of this paper, is *Western* about Snyder, outside the fact that, for instance, Crater Mountain is in Washington?

I am going to answer this tough question by linking Snyder to some other Western writers, in an attempt to create a definition by statistical preponderance. The writers are John Muir, Robinson Jeffers, and Frank Waters. These men, with Snyder, share a certain feeling for Western nature that shapes their ultimate philosophical view of reality and also, importantly, their value judgments on civilization, American technological civilization, to be more exact. Their starting point is nature: the mythic, direct, non-intellectualized

apprehension of the real that is poetic or mystic, being outside the bounds of the *rational* categories of epistemology. They feel into nature, they know it; expressed as a mountain, ocean, or desert perspective, it is their standard. I believe this is a significant theme, probably the most reliable indicator in fact, of truly Western American writing. Because here nature was first, and awesome. The takers, techno-progress dominators, reacted in terms of a power struggle. They got what they wanted—"The ticket that exploded," in William Burrough's memorable words. The creative receptors like the writers named see that the victory was empty, or even evil. They write from a standpoint outside the madness, like every great American writer of any region. John Muir is not simply a mountain rhapsodist, a safely dismissable "nature writer": he is a religiously powerful nay-sayer to the whole materialistic, destructive drift of the manipulative life. We are beginning to see that when he inveighs against the sheep, it isn't the "hooved locusts" that he blames, but rather a basic failing in American civilization.[8] I think that Jeffers' famous Inhumanism is simply the furthest logical extension of the naturalistic view outlined above; his Cassandra-like forecasts for our self-destruction are always balanced with the beauty that will remain. Likewise, Frank Waters's perspective on both ontological and social matters is natural and mythic, most closely identified with the Indian mind.

Gary Snyder slants off this religious, or "sacral" tradition as Max Westbrook has called it, somewhat with his Beat and Buddhist background and associations, but the linking is still fitting. Let me work for proof by way of poetry, with **"Marin-An"**:

> sun breaks over the eucalyptus
> grove below the wet pasture,
> water's about hot,
> I sit in the open window
> & roll a smoke.
> distant dogs bark, a pair of
> cawing crows; the twang
> of a pygmy nuthatch high in a pine—
> from behind the cypress windrow
> the mare moves up, grazing.
> a soft continuous roar
> comes out of the far valley
> of the six-lane highway—thousands
> and thousands of cars
> driving men to work.

This is perhaps more like Boone Caudill in the door of his teepee than Muir in his meadows or Jeffers on the cliffs, but the basic contrast is the same: the natural order is full of peace and harmony . . . sounds drift slowly, and a man has time to roll a smoke, consciously primitive technique, as his tea water comes to a boil. Down on U.S. 101, the cars are in control, fulfilling some fantastic abstract daily requirement in funneling men to San Francisco. It's muted—a "soft continuous roar"—but the critique is there, in the perfectly rendered audial images.

Is this too simple? Maybe so. A critical sophisticate might prefer the self-conscious, honest ambivalence of **"Nooksack Valley,"** an early reflection also set in a cabin removed from the mainstream society.

"FEBRUARY 1956"

At the far end of a trip north
In a berry-pickers cabin
At the edge of a wide muddy field
Stretching to the woods and cloudy mountains,
Feeding the stove all afternoon with cedar,
watching the dark sky darken, a heron flap by,
A huge setter pup nap on the dusty cot.
High rotten stumps in the second-growth woods
Flat scattered farms in the bend of the Nooksack
River. Steelhead run now
    a week and I go back
Down 99, through towns, to San Francisco
        and Japan.
All America south and east,
Twenty-five years in it brought to a trip-stop
Mind-point, where I turn
Caught more on this land—rock tree and man,
Awake, than ever before, yet ready to leave.
    damned memories,
Whole wasted theories, failures and worse suc-
    cess,
Schools, girls, deals, try to get in
To make this poem a forth, a pity,
A dead fiddle for lost good jobs.
        the cedar walls
Smell of our farm-house, half built in '35.
Clouds sink down the hills
Coffee is hot again. The dog
Turns and turns about, stops and sleeps.

There is plenty to praise here: the late-winter, Watteau mood of "Feeding the stove all afternoon with cedar, / Watching the dark sky darken, a heron flap by"; the pace of the lines and the significant lacunae, beautifully suggesting the hitchy, associative string of thoughts, from which finally a whole life emerges; the suggestive use of the dog and his turning as metaphors for the ultimate circles of birth and death we are all rooted in. The poet recognizes that this afternoon in the cabin is a crucial moment, a "trip-stop / Mind-point." He has already decided, literally speaking, to go to the Zen monastery at Kyoto, but what really matters, following the Oriental principles of synchronicity and complementarity, is his attitude toward the going; reflection on this

shows that he is both "caught" and "ready to leave"—honestly ambivalent—and this in turn leads to deeper retrospection, because the whole sum of deeds and thoughts past makes the personality now. The succinct answer to the karmic riddle is given in one immediate, mnemonic image: "the cedar walls / Smell of our farm-house, half built in '35." Just so. Can you go back past the age of 5? And what is more evocative than smell, for an image that creates at once the mystery of birth and death? Finally, there is nothing but to recognize the fact of being on the wheel. He does not say, "Oh, how did I get the way I am?" Just "The dog / Turns and turns about, stops and sleeps."

Recently, Snyder has become deeply interested in the American Indian. He thinks that our cultural task now is to establish a felt connection with our "Almost Ancestors," learn the spirit of the land and thereby know our past and ourselves as well. This is remarkably like the recommendations of Frank Waters, to name just one Western writer with a mythic consciousness. One might as well mention Frederick Manfred and Walter Van Tilburg Clark in this connection, both major Western writers who have seen that the Indian is a key.

In a 1965 television interview, Snyder spoke of this need to develop the mythic consciousness, what might be called the *natural* perspective. He seemed confident that there was a great groundswell movement going on: "We won't be white men a thousand years from now. We won't be white men *fifty* years from now. Our whole culture is going someplace else. The work of poetry is to capture those areas of the consciousness which belong to the American continent, the non-white world . . . ultimately getting in contact with the natural world, which we've been out of contact with so long we've almost destroyed the planet."[9]

But poetry has to both instruct and delight. Most of the time, Gary Snyder handles the dual task beautifully. Let me quote one more poem to support that contention, and then conclude with a judgment from Louis Simpson. First, **"Milton By Firelight"**:

Piute Creek, August 1955
"O hell, what do mine eyes
    with grief behold?"
Working with an old
Singlejack miner, who can sense
The vein and cleavage
In the very guts of rock, can
Blast granite, build
Switchbacks that last for years
Under the beat of snow, thaw, mule-hooves.

What use, Milton, a silly story
Of our lost general parents,
      eaters of fruit?
The Indian, the chainsaw boy,
And a string of six mules
Came riding down to camp
Hungry for tomatoes and green apples.
Sleeping in saddle-blankets
Under a bright night-sky
Han River slantwise by morning.
Jays squall
Coffee boils
In ten thousand years the Sierras
Will be dry and dead, home of the scorpion.
Ice-scratched slabs and bent trees.
No paradise, no fall,
Only the weathering land
The wheeling sky,
Man, with his Satan
Scouring the chaos of the mind.
Oh Hell!
Fire down
Too dark to read, miles from a road
The bell-mare clangs in the meadow
That packed dirt for a fill-in
Scrambling through loose rocks
On an old trail
All of a summer's day.

Louis Simpson was one of several poets asked questions by John Milton in a South Dakota Review symposium last year, and his concluding remarks seem to be to make an apt finish for this paper:

> Last, you ask about "new experimentation." I think that the work of every true poet is a continuing experiment, and quite unlike the work of any other. I think these are true poets: Gary Snyder, James Wright, Robert Bly, Robert Creeley, Allen Ginsberg, Denise Levertov. . . . These poets have an inner life that they express in original images and rhythms. To discover what they are doing there is really no other way than to read their poems, and I cheerfully recommend this.[10]

Notes

1. Thomas Clark, "Allen Ginsberg," in *Writers At Work: The Paris Review Interviews, Third Series* (New York: Viking Press, 1967),p. 319.

2. Thomas Parkinson, "After the Beat Generation," *Colorado Quarterly* XVII (Summer, 1968),p. 46.

3. The text of this symposium is in *The City of San Francisco Oracle*, Vol. I, No. 7 (February, 1967).

4. Cyril Birch, ed. *Anthology of Chinese Literature*, Vol. 1 (New York: Grove Press, 1966).

5. R. H. Blyth, *Haiku* (Vol. 1, *Eastern Culture*) (Tokyo: Hokuseido, 1949),p. 211.

6. Quoted in Jane Kramer, "Paterfamilias," *New Yorker* (August 17, 1968),p. 60.

7. Jack Kerouac, *The Dharma Bums* (New York: Signet Books, 1958),p. 162.

8. Herbert Smith's *John Muir* (New York: Twayne Publishers, 1965), shows Muir's ideas in something like their true depth.

9. "Philip Whalen and Gary Snyder," *Poetry U.S.A.* (Bloomington, Indiana: National Educational Television, 1965).

10. John Milton (ed.), "A Symposium of Poets," *South Dakota Review* V (Autumn, 1967),p. 18.

GARY SNYDER, INGER THORUP LAURIDSEN, AND PER DALGARD (INTERVIEW DATE 1990)

SOURCE: Snyder, Gary, Inger Thorup Lauridsen, and Per Dalgard. "Interview with Gary Snyder." In *The Beat Generation and the Russian New Wave*, pp. 67-78. Ann Arbor, Mich.: Ardis, 1990.

In the following interview, Snyder discusses his sympathies and differences with the Beat Generation, the sources and influences on his poetry, and political philosophy. Snyder makes connections between his poetry, other Beat writing, and international writers from Europe, Russia, and China.

Mr. Snyder, do you consider yourself part of the Beat Generation?

Well, it depends on what you mean by the Beat Generation. There are two or three phenomena enclosed within that, depending on how wide your scope or definition is. There is what is sometimes called the San Francisco poetry renaissance which is a literary movement—a literary and political movement—centered in San Francisco, that started early in the fifties and became really apparent in the mid-fifties, and it is characterized by its independence from East Coast and European poetic thinking, its independence from what we call neo-Formalism, its freedom from the problems and contradictions experienced by American intellectuals of that period, in the American left, who had gone from Stalinism to complete rejection of all left-wing thought. The characteristic political thought of the West Coast and of San Francisco was never Stalinist really, but was anarchist, and I don't mean that metaphorically. There was a very strong anti-war spirit on the West Coast, a number of writers like Bill Everson and Robert Duncan refused to participate in the Second World War. In addition a sense of the West as a rare landscape, and an interest in the evolving Pacific Basin culture. Kenneth Rexroth and Robinson Jeffers are very important to that background. So I'm definitely part of the San Francisco poetry renaissance, the West Coast poetry renaissance. In the Bay area, that movement, because of the poetry readings that we were giving, generated a much larger sphere of interest and excitement very quickly, and our anarchist revolt was rapidly translated into a large social sphere of revolt which became the San Francisco Beat movement. Now, the name Beat was given it by the *San Francisco Chronicle* newspaper columnist Herb Caen about 1956, probably, although the original use of the term Beat Generation was in a short story by Jack Kerouac published in 1953 or 54. So then in turn, when Kerouac's *On the Road* came out and the publicity and controversy surrounding "Howl" came out, similar phenomena rapidly erupted in Denver, Chicago, New York, following the lead of the San Francisco poetry's road. And they started having poetry readings in large numbers and the whole phenomenon was called the Beat Generation. So, if you talk about poetry, it should be described that way; if you talk about the overall social phenomenon, you can use the term Beat for the latter part of the fifties. As a poet I belong to the San Francisco renaissance, but I'm not a Beat poet and I've never been called a Beat poet.

But you are always mentioned . . .

Oh, as part of the social phenomenon. The esthetic phenomenon identified with Beat is poetry of the sort that Gregory Corso and Allen Ginsberg write, which is very expansive and very Whitmanesque. My poetry is not of that sort and I didn't contribute anything to that poetry, only to the social and political aspect of the phenomenon.

So, what you are saying is that what unites the Beat Generation is really not esthetic or literary?

It's social and political.

Do you see the Beat Generation as part of an international phenomenon?

In hindsight it seems part of the struggle to transcend the pre-World War II over-simplified dualistic confrontation of monolithic capitalism and monolithic communism, and it's an attempt in various ways to find a third way. So that is where an anarchist point of view, or a Buddhist point of view, or a simple communitarian point of view, all those points of views are based within that post-World War II phenomenon of minds trying to break out of saying: I'm either a socialist-communist or a capitalist, which is the way it was right before the war.

But then some poets, like Ferlinghetti, have become increasingly left-wing, some in a rather traditional way.

True. Some have joined this or that socialist party.

What has become of the Beat Generation?

I was going to ask you!—In a sense it was a worldwide nascent stirring of establishing an independence from the simple-mindedness of the socialist-capitalist dialogue. Much has happened since then, the women's movement has emerged into politics; and what happened to the Beat Generation was that it transformed into the hippie-generation and continued. . . .

Into the grassroot movements?

And then it reaches out and connects with the peace movement, the civil rights movement, ultimately with the ecology movement.

You mentioned the women's movement just now—do you think the Beat writers were a bunch of male chauvinist pigs?

Oh sure. But there were woman writers too, and they were probably male chauvinists too as all women were at that time, with some few exceptions.

Do you see any connection between the Beat Generation and the British Angry Young Men?

It seemed to be very close at that time, I read some of that stuff then and it seemed to reflect that same international phenomenon, post-World War II phenomenon. That phenomenon did not happen in Japan till much later, and the post-war literary generation in Japan called itself the "Waste Land" Generation and they went on for about ten years in a kind of austere, realistic spirit, and were more interested in, for instance, Existentialism for a long time after the war. In fact, I think that the spirit of the Beat Generation, that type of spirit is only now beginning to come into Japan. If there is anything that carries through from the Beat Generation right up till now—one of the threads that is very consistent—it is the interest in nature and in the environment that is from the beginning in our poetry and our protests. The peace movement, the civil rights movement, this and that, may not pick up on it, but it is still like the main thread that comes through. That interest is now beginning to rise in Russia and in Japan and in China. That's a contribution that some of us made to world poetical and political culture. Now, I got into that discussion with some Chinese writers just last year at a conference in L.A. where they said: "Our task as writers is to serve the people, we feel that we serve the people." And I said: "What do you mean by the people?" and they said: "Well, we mean the people." And I said: "My poetry is to serve people too, but it doesn't include just human people, but animal people and fish people and bird people and tree people, we must serve all these people." It blew their minds! They loved it! It really caught them, just like that. So they've been writing about that in China.

But not in Russia.

No, the Chinese aren't the Russians.

Do you know any of your contemporaries among Russian writers?

I talked to Voznesensky on the two-way radio once, and I met Evtushenko in San Francisco. He said to me: "You look like a Pirate." He looked like a tennis star. He had all these bouquets of flowers and champagne and pretty girls.

Have you read them?

Yeah. I can see the influence of Whitman. Whitman was a very large influence in Europe and in Russia, and you can see it come through in those guys—Mayakovsky too was probably touched by Whitman. The importance of Whitman is not to be overlooked; he is very important to Allen Ginsberg and his poetry, and very important to me, although my poetics do not reflect Whitman as a strategy of writing, I'm very much indebted to Whitman for inspiration. There is no other American poet but Whitman, really, in the nineteenth century who sets out the vision of what America is. That vision of America touched everybody in the world.

What does your poetics reflect?

I think it would be a combination of Walt Whitman, Ezra Pound, Chinese poetry, oral literature, American Indian songs, in the original languages and in translations, ballads, traditional Irish, Scotch and English ballads, and the Greek tradition. I was a close student of Ezra Pound's poetics. Pound is very important to this century, you know. Whitman to the nineteenth century, and Pound to the twentieth century. But for the West Coast we have a very special ancestor, Robinson Jeffers. He is very special to us. The rest of the U.S. can't stand him. He remains very special to California.

In connection with the Beat Generation there is often talk about spontaneous creation, spontaneity, as a means of making contact with the unconscious. . . .

That's not me! Spontaneity is really not a good way to get in touch with the unconscious. Spontaneity takes you down about two centimeters, then you are writing about what is just below the surface. But to work with the deep unconscious you have to be more deliberate.

Meditation?

Meditation, thoughtfulness, time silence, deliberate writing and deliberate thinking, that is how you work with that.

Is this why you live out here in the middle of nowhere?

No. I was raised in the country and so I would live in the country no matter what—I don't need any reasons to live in the country.

Whom do you feel you're addressing when you write? Is it necessarily somebody who knows American Indian myths and Buddhism and so on?

Well, if they don't, they'll learn, you see. It's education.

Have you ever thought of writing commentaries to your works?

No, I leave that to the scholars. They're doing it too. My book **Myths and Texts**, which was written in 1958, is now finally being understood. The times have caught up with it, and people have worked on it enough. It's like Pound's work—in the process of reading the work you get yourself an extra education.

You seem to write about what you see. Do you think it's necessary to know your surroundings, this area, to understand your poetry?

Actually my poetry refers to a territory which is from the Mexican border to Alaska, on the West Coast, and then goes around the Northern Pacific and includes Japan—that's my territory of natural reference.

Are you translatable?

There are already translations of my poetry in fifteen languages.

Do they work though?

You have to realize that my poetry is very broad and I don't just write about raccoons. Because my poetry actually is quite broad, there are many poems that have a universal frame of reference, there are poems that translate into Serbo-Croatian, Chinese, Polish, Norwegian, Swedish. And the books seem to be doing OK in those countries.

Does your poetry come about as sound?

It's all those things. It may be a preverbal image, pictures, rhythmic beat, a rhythmic pattern, even a melodic line, and out of that preverbal set of perceptions, internal perceptions, out of that would come the actual verbalization of it.

Your use of verse line, which is quite characteristic, is that an expression of this preverbal perception?

No, these things come about as one writes with a particular rhythm, yeah, that's my rhythm, but it's also the way I hear the genius of the English language. It reflects, probably, some of the sense I have of and the pleasure I take in the way Chinese poetry sounds in Chinese. And it's part of an esthetics of spareness. The genius of the English language is in its monosyllabism, which is going to the Anglo-Saxon rather than the Norman side of English; in the crispness that's possible in English—that's a real virtue.

So you never feel that the grammatical requirements of the language get in the way?

I'm the one who decides what the grammatical requirements of the language are, I'm the poet. The poet determines the grammar and syntax, not the teacher. Syntactical and grammatical errors that I have made, so to speak, will be enshrined as proper grammar two hundred years from now. That's the power of the writer, to redefine what correctness is. So the writer hears the genius of the language and determines from intuition what sounds right, and that's actually one contribution that literature makes to formal grammar. The lead poem in my new book has a syntactic error in it, a deliberate error. I knew right away when I wrote it. I said "That's not syntactically right," but it is right, so I kept it.

Have you done any experimenting with synthesizing different art forms?

I've done some of that and I continue to do it. I'm working sometimes with music and sometimes with dance—my wife is a dancer. I'm very aware of the intimate connections between music and poetry and poetry and dance. I would be inclined to work closely with original models. One of my models for the proper use of poetry, music and drama is in the Japanese No drama which is really a beautiful synthesis. On one side it is very primitive, it has the most archaic forms of poetic and drama events, on the other side it is extremely refined and has passed through a highly deliberate esthetic process.

Do you read mostly poetry yourself?

No I don't read very much poetry. I read science, biology, anthropology, history, politics, economics, and Ivan Ilych, and a little bit of poetry.

Is there a large body of Western literature—the literature of alienation—that means nothing to you?

You have to understand that my intellectual perspective is, for lack of a better word, anthropological. My perspective is from the larger framework of human culture, human history in which I look for the norm of human culture. I'm always looking for the norm, for the models, rather than the anomalies. Literature of alienation is an anomaly. It belongs only to the last two centuries and does not reflect the overall function or use of literature in culture, which is to go with the culture, not against the culture, which is to serve larger purposes of human sanity rather than to demonstrate craziness. So in a larger perspective I'm interested in the poetry of sanity rather than the poetry of alienation in literature. Although I understand literature of alienation as politically useful, that poets and writers who have to be alienated are like soldiers you sacrifice in the battlefield. It's a pity that they have to go that way. I have had too many friends commit suicide or die of alcoholism or die of drug overdoses because they thought that was part of being a writer. And that's not interesting to me. I don't think the writer's purpose is to kill himself. You have too much of that kind in Europe, more than here. There's more deaths by overdose in Germany and perhaps in Holland, than any place in the world right now, not only by poets, but young people, by everybody.

In the U.S. drugs seem to have become integrated into society. . . .

In such a way that it doesn't kill us. I don't give any romance to that, you know. There's nothing new, nothing romantic and nothing admirable in dying of an overdose.

Another concept often connected with the Beats is a certain anti-intellectualism?

That's the largest social phenomenon of the Beat Generation and the one I like the least.

Still, you have written poems about how Milton became meaningless to you when you were logging in the mountains.

That's not anti-intellectualism. Anti-intellectualism is an American problem. It's not just anti-intellectualism per se, but it's understanding how to deal with information and with the cultivation of the intellect, understanding what the right balance is.

The Japanese are too respectful of intellectualism and information and of learning, so that there is not enough free creative imaginative play territory left in Japanese education, and it produces an enormous group of highly trained technicians.

But creativity in technology, the sciences, the arts and humanities, is won personally at great psychic sacrifice in Japanese culture. You have to make yourself a little bit crazy. To some extent, you win your role as a creative person by accepting alienation or craziness, and making that part of your life and leading a short life often, as a result, with many broken marriages and many miserable children. So that's a function of over-attachment to intellectualism. The main stream of American culture is what we call red-neck. It's a term for very playful, very relaxed, anti-intellectual, racist, good-natured, physical people who drink a lot, drive pick-up trucks, have a good time, are really good friends, if they are friends, and who have a certain kind of limited perspective and who are in a sense natural anarchists. They are not particularly alienated, and they don't have that many problems. America doesn't have that many problems.

We stopped at Reno on the way here—it's kind of depressing. . . .

I love Reno. I mean it. It's a tremendous little world of its own.

Nobody seemed to be having fun there.

There are lots of people having lots of fun there. It's just that variety of fun that wants to stake everything on a hope. In a sense it is capitalism personified, but not quite, because capitalism is really deliberate and ordered, whereas gambling is simply a transcendentalizing of greed. Anyway, having a place like Reno or Las Vegas is a true function of a pluralistic society. In a true democracy you're allowed to suffer from your vices. Which I think is an interesting position. It would be the case in an anarchist society too. Neither the Russians nor the Chinese are about to allow people to suffer from their vices. So it's very paternalistic. America is not paternalistic, and in some ways I like that. There are things to be learned about that for a possible future society. Like, there should be an allowance for crime, an allowance for vice. Not alienated crime or vice but just that which you do.

What forces or movements in society today can you identify with, where do you think your country is going?

Where do I think my country is going! Well I think the whole world is going to hell in a hand basket, as we say, but we have to make some really fine distinctions about what that means. I remain politically and socially an anarchist, an anthropological anarchist, which is to say that I

can present a very coherent critique of civilization and of the state, that is, without flaw. The state is unnecessary and civilization is highly overvalued and progress is the religion of the twentieth century. And it is shared by the socialist block and the capitalist block alike.

Sounds like Tolstoy and Thoreau.

It sounds like it, but it is more sophisticated, intellectually more developed, and it is backed by a larger array of accurate information. The thinker that I most admire in this area is Ivan Ilych. He is a leading post-Marxist, that is to say, he has digested Marxism and has gone beyond it. He has written a dozen books in English which are really acute critiques of the ways the various aspects of the national state have disenfranchised us all. And talking about alienation, people walking around in the city talking about alienation don't know what alienation is.

A final question: What do you think of Kerouac's portrait of you in The Dharma Bums?

Well, it's a fiction piece, it's a novel, and so it's a portrait of me which obviously reflects some things that I can recognize. Some of it is his own way of seeing me. So seeing yourself through someone else's eyes is always to see differently. Even when you look at yourself in a mirror it looks different from what you think you are, and when you see yourself in a novel, it is quite a bit different. And some of the things in the book reflect real events and some are invented. It's mixed together.

TITLE COMMENTARY

Earth House Hold: Technical Notes and Queries to Fellow Dharma Revolutionaries

THOMAS PARKINSON (ESSAY DATE 1971-1972)

SOURCE: Parkinson, Thomas. "Theory and Practice of Gary Snyder." *Journal of Modern Literature* 2, no. 3 (1971-1972): 448-52.

In the following essay, Parkinson analyzes Earth House Hold *and* Regarding Wave, *suggesting that in these works Snyder sharply defines his identity as a thinker and writer. Parkinson maintains that the two works demonstrate two modes of Snyder's writing: quick and witty in the journals and essays, and contemplative and direct in his poems.*

Earth House Hold includes selections from Snyder's journals, as early as 1953, book reviews, notes on social and religious movements, and essays that define his sense of poetic mission. Although the initial impact of the book is miscellaneous, a sequence of prose unified only by his sensibility, that sensibility is so integral a cultural complex that the book has essential singleness of motive. If it does nothing else, it demonstrates in precept and example the base of his verse. Along with his most recent collection of poetry, *Regarding Wave,* it shows the continuity and development of his remarkable enterprise.

The world in *Earth House Hold* is the same world treated with the deepened intensity of poetry in *A Range of Poems* and *The Back Country.* The primary stress is on the forests of the western states and their seashore, Japan, India. In more ordered times China would play a large role. The interests are familiar: wilderness, work, poetry, Amerindian lore, Buddhism, political radicalism. They form a complex of concerns that mesh into an attractive whole. Snyder is no amateur in any of these areas. Some of the essays are review articles for professional anthropological journals. Some of them are the product of his disciplined proficiency in Oriental studies, both religious and linguistic, his life in Japanese Zen monasteries, his scholarly detailed knowledge of the several varieties of Buddhism. Underlying all these or rather interpenetrating them is his quest for the poetic measure that will release the major forms of experience in all their implication.

The random chronological form is misleading. The several segments of the book connect and culminate in the crystallizing form of the essay on "Poetry and the Primitive." The primitive and poetry—Snyder's meditations on the subject are revealing about his own work, but they also suggest certain speculations about current psychology. He cites Lévi-Strauss's analogy between the status of art and the status of a national park as permitted wilderness. The analogy fits, but it seems to me that in Snyder's arguments he tends to understress the basic difference: if one leaves alone and refuses to interfere with nature, it can regain (within limits) the status of wilderness. But leaving the human psyche alone does only that, leaves it without any reference except to the depleted and debilitating environment that has effectively denied psychic fullness. Hence the primitive that Snyder admires can be attained only by disciplined exclusion and distortion, a gardening operation rather than a matter of drawing boundaries. A massive gardening operation is

what we should call an enabling act that creates a national park or seashore or wilderness area.

The same process occurs in establishing the lines of a poem and of a poetic vision. The difficulty for current writers is that they are deluged with phenomena that are not accountable. This does not mean that the world is chaotic in any final sense, but that the disorders of mind and history have reached so great a volume that they menace any kind of order, natural, social, aesthetic, or personal. If one reads twenty or thirty books of new poetry a month (and that is only a sketchy survey) the most troubling thing is not the simplicity of much poetry but its messy repetitive complexity, its all unconscious reflecting of external and internal disorder. A purifying process is required previous to the poem. The process of stripping and cleansing is a personal undertaking as complex in its way as an enabling act of a legislature. It requires a sophistication that may eventually be left behind, and from such sophistication, such intellectual and imaginative exploration, true simplicity *may* emerge. Simplicity in the medieval sense: the elemental, irreducible.

If one takes Snyder's poetry as exemplary in this respect, one can also discriminate his work from that of many of his contemporaries. *Earth House Hold* is essentially the record of the intellectual and religious disciplines that underlay and preceded the poetry. Snyder is, however, not the purist that Yeats was, who wrote *A Vision* primarily to keep certain elements out of his poetry. He is not so inclusive as Robert Duncan, who attempts to take the reader through the process of poetic discovery. He is not so absorbed with his own inner tensions as Robert Lowell. There are poetic dimensions and vocabularies and obsessions that by will or temperament Snyder ignores or excludes.

Snyder is not an ideologue, but it is still true that among distinguished contemporary writers, he is one whose attitudes are his subjects. Insofar as the poetry involves struggle and tension—and it does so very infrequently—it is the struggle to create a mind purified of the lusts and greeds of history. This restoration of the primitive being would permit the inclusion of ritual that gives ratio to the ecstatic, the passionate, the physical. This is its positive direction, but in the prose and verse it is frequently defined as *non*: non-Western, non-Christian, non-white, non-capitalist, non-national, non-military, non-civilization. When the facility of negative definition is followed, these negations become prejudices growing from justified revulsion against the abominations of immediate life that can rightly be laid at the door of militarism, unbridled capitalist exploiting, debased Christianity, and white chauvinism. This is Snyder's main argument, in social terms, and his spiritual vocation is to offer measure that can be taken by the soul to create a world that "matters" and has texture and specific gravity and joy.

Underlying all this, as **Earth House Hold** bears witness, is a discipline of senses and of intelligence. The result in the realm of poetics is a theory curiously Miltonic (simple, sensuous, passionate) and even neo-classical. Without that discipline, the Snyder optique brings in a wave of stereotypes that are associated with romanticism, granted—Snyder mentions Rousseau approvingly—but there is something more rigorous at work. Ten years ago he wrote a note on the religious tendencies of the Beat movement. This note is excluded from **Earth House Hold**, probably on the ground that he has gone past that point. It seems worth recalling:

> *Discipline, aesthetics, and tradition.* This was going on well before the beat generation got into print. It differs from the 'All is one' stance in that its practitioners settle on one traditional religion, try to absorb the feel of its art and history and carry out whatever ascesis is required. One could become an Aimu bear-dancer or a Yurok shaman as well as a Trappist monk, if he put himself to it.

In the preceding sections of the note, he cites "Quakers, Shinshu Buddhism, Sufism" and Whitman as equivalents in spiritual power.

Now his attitudes seem more exclusive, to narrow on what has come to satisfy his needs, a limited religious and legendary matter, an almost stubborn closure. When he cites Lynn White's description of Christianity's role in creating the current ecological crisis, he does not mention White's description of the Franciscan alternative to the first chapter of Genesis. The *I Fiori* of St. Francis are close to Snyder's rendering of the "Record and life of the Ch'an Master Po-Chang Huai-Hai." Even St. Augustine's *City of God* advocates a custodial rather than exploitative relation between man and nature. Equal time for St. Francis? Hardly, and I don't expect Snyder to master Franciscan theology any more than he expects to master Zen. It may be ascribable to Snyder's maturing, but there is a drift toward orthodoxy in his thought, toward exclusion and limitation. The poetry then becomes subsidiary, only one of a set of instruments in a spiritual quest.

This is not only inevitable but in a serious sense right. Identity is limitation; to function, it is necessary to exclude. Snyder's distortions and omissions are no worse, are in fact considerably better, than the notorious selectivity of most modern artists. They grant his insights: the identification of the wilderness with the subconscious; the Oriental and European garden as product of guilty fear of threatening and at last destroyed nature; the proper stress on the interconnected mutual dependence of body, voice, and mind.

Revolutionary and counter-revolutionary minds produce neo-classical theories, the one projecting fixed values into an existent structure, the other creating an imagined and hence by definition fixed structure. Articulate modern neo-classicism from Hulme on has tended to be reactionary politically, and that blurs matters. When a poet is more concerned with what can be done through words than with the surface of his art, he tends toward the neo-classical, and that is where Snyder's poetry rests. Such a poetic action is in the most profound sense conservative; dependent upon a belief in some common sense of things that endures through fashion and historic changes. It does not imply the use of inherited forms but an obsession with traditional matter, so that the work of the poem is to vivify what would otherwise be lost.

To many people terms like neo-classicism and romanticism are pejorative or honorific. I intend them as descriptive, as a way of getting at the qualities of Snyder's verse, especially in **Regarding Wave,** and perhaps explaining problems that his verse raises.

One of the most annoying arguments against Snyder's verse is that it does not develop. This is part of the romantic prejudice, exacerbated by the rate of change in fad and fashion in the 20th century. Why should his poetry develop, other than in the sense that it comes to explore and include more life as he remains receptive to fresh perception? Limitation and exclusion are necessary parts of any poetic enterprise, and so long as Snyder's style answers to his vision of experience, then it would be frivolous of him to change for the sake of change. What should alter style is the revelation of subject matters that shatter the form hitherto adequate; or through the imposition of fresh technical demands by some other medium, like drama.

These poems in **Regarding Wave** provide no surprises because they impose no disturbing new subject matter and are contemplative presentative lyrics that make no fresh technical impositions. Snyder has become the most observed of all observers, and it doesn't seem to do much good.

For one thing, it compels him to repeated publication, and if there is legitimate objection to *Regarding Wave* it comes from the fact that much of the material in the final sections of the book seems more appropriate to the notebook sections of *Earth House Hold.* Snyder's mind works at two distinct levels. One is fluent, wise, witty, meditative and hortatory; the other is measured, dramatic, definite (to avoid that cliché *concrete*) in design, formal, and contemplative. The second mode is the one that produces his best poetry; the first is essentially pre-poetic. When he is taken up, effectively carried by a subject, each poem gives momentum to the succeeding one. When he is accepting random notation, the poems are sketches toward a poetics, interesting but not any more interesting than the notes and explorations of *Earth House Hold.*

His choice of *Regarding Wave* for title is effectively explained in his essay on poetry and the primitive. The Muse is a woman, and the voice comes from a goddess. The Goddess Vāk is ". . . the lover of Brahma and his actual creative energy . . . the Divine in the aspect of wisdom and learning . . ."

> As Vāk is wife to Brahma ('wife' means 'wave' means 'vibrator' in Indo-European etymology) so the voice, in everyone, is a mirror of his own deepest self.

So the book is regarding—concerning, observing—this principle as manifest in Snyder's wife. At least the first three sections are.

And it is there that the book maintains its momentum, the poems blending to a steady harmony. These poems are classic in the best sense, as in **"Not Leaving the House,"** presentation of a common moment that changes all being:

"NOT LEAVING THE HOUSE"

When Kai is born
I quit going out
Hang around the kitchen—make cornbread
Let nobody in.
Mail is flat.
    Masa lies on her side, Kai sighs,
    Non washes and sweeps
We sit and watch
    Masa nurse, and drink green tea.
Navajo turquoise beads over the bed
A peacock tail feather at the head
A badger pelt from Nagano-ken
For a mattress; under the sheet;
A pot of yogurt setting
Under the blankets, at his feet.
Masa, Kai,
And Non, our friend

In the green garden light reflected in
Not leaving the house.
From dawn til late at night
    making a new world of ourselves
    around this life.

Charm. In itself, the poem is full of charm and of magical charms, not least the child with such careful provisions. The child culminates the sequence—the final poem following it paraphrases freshly the relation between Vāk (voice) and Brahma, extending and rendering symbolic what was individual and domestic. And above all *common.*

In spite of the overtly contemporary poetics in *Regarding Wave,* Snyder stands to one side of the current poetic question. His appeal to a common sense of life has had a momentary echo in the conventions of the current young, who would certainly approve of what seems to be the quietism of this poem. It is all OK, organic, the helping friend, the nursing mother, the charms from Amerindia and Japan, the green garden light. A desirable life. The first thirty-five pages of *Regarding Wave* make that notation through the series of twenty-five poems that form the title section. Like his earlier *Myths and Texts, Regarding Wave* is an informing work exploring basic principles.

The remaining two sections, **"Long Hair"** and **"Target Practice"** are miscellaneous and relaxed. Snyder has made so attractive a complex of being—as opposed to an individual optique or style—that he finds himself compelled to publishing books that contain matter interesting enough but not working toward a cumulative effect. These two sections are notes of a witty intelligent man on experience. They lack the compressed intensity of art.

Earth House Hold and *Regarding Wave* certify Snyder's directions and involvements. His concern with the primitive is not romanticism but an effort to find basic common human elements, principles rather than subjects that he can undergo and explore. Sometimes he is concerned with keeping up a habit of perception, and the notation becomes relaxed and humorous and didactic. When he is in the grip of a major principle, something else occurs. He becomes the agent of a voice, that of common experience, and the personal and superficially exotic change to the general and present. In an age of multiple options he holds firmly to his vision of the classically humane. The superficial aspects are easy to imitate or ridicule, but what is fundamental has a life well beyond the particular.

Left out in the Rain

JACK HICKS (ESSAY DATE 1991)

SOURCE: Hicks, Jack. "Poetic Composting in Gary Snyder's *Left out in the Rain*." In *Critical Essays on Gary Snyder*, edited by Patrick D. Murphy, pp. 247-57. Boston, Mass.: G. K. Hall, 1991.

In the following essay, Hicks surveys Snyder's poetic development in Left out in the Rain, *his collection of selected works spanning the years 1947 through 1985. Hicks views the volume as a poetic autobiography, revealing Snyder's maturation and his involvement in the Beat Generation, Zen, and ecology.*

In a 1977 interview, Gary Snyder distinguishes between poets "who have fed on a certain kind of destructiveness for their creative glow," and those closer to his own energies (like Wendell Berry and Robert Duncan) "who have 'composted' themselves and turned part of themselves back in on themselves to become richer and stronger . . ."[1] *Left Out in the Rain: New Poems 1947-1985,* Snyder's most recent collection, is, in the richest sense, an extended instance of poetic composting, a mingled cycle of 154 poems, some more than forty years old, some freshly harvested, serving as a personal, cultural, and poetic recapitulation, offering glimpses of new turns on the trail.[2]

It is a risky book: one danger—of which Snyder and his North Point publishers had to be aware—was that it would be seen as merely a collection of juvenilia, ephemera, and poetic turnings swept up from the workshop floor. And some of the poems do fall into those categories.

But read properly, it is an intriguing collection: it is a corrective volume, restoring some of the dimensions of the man and the mature poet, revealing him first as apprentice working through influences, experimenting with verse forms and techniques. In the later poems, Snyder finds in the process of working with his first work—indeed, in the poems themselves—this principle of poetic composting, a source of poetic energy. He sets a dialogue with his own past in motion, a shuttling that invigorates the recent work and promises to energize that of the future.

"I wanted to finish publishing all my shorter poems—those worth seeing print—to date," he says in a recent interview. He picks up the metaphor: "Having accomplished this digestion, the *composting* of the material, I didn't have to work on it anymore. The cycle is complete."[3]

Appropriately, both the title of this volume and the physical text are recycled. The title derives

from no poem herein, reaching back to *Myths & Texts* (1960). Near the end of the opening "Logging" section, as the poet and a fellow logger eat fresh oysters at the American rim of the Pacific, "looking off toward China and Japan," the friend wisecracks, silenic: "If you're gonna work these woods / Don't want nothing / That can't be left out in the rain—".[4]

The early manuscript itself was packed in orange crates and stored with friends (Bob and Jean Greensfelder) in Marin County when Snyder left for Japan in 1956. In 1969, having returned with wife Masa Uehara Snyder and son Kai a year earlier, building what would become Kitkitdizze, he moved the crates in a pickup truck to the rugged site north of Nevada City, California. Busy raising a house, he stashed them "outdoors under some oak trees, covered with black plastic. Literally left out in the rain—and the snow and the sun and the wind, too."[5]

In winter, 1971, Kitkitdizze well-established, he uncovered his cache to find his early work had become a home. "Woodrats had eaten into the boxes," he laughs. "They nested, chewed up some manuscripts, shit in there, generally made themselves a little home in my poetry."[6]

Repacked, the files went to the loft of the main house, where they remained until 1982. Working through his papers (they were deposited later as the Snyder Collection at the University of California, Davis), he rediscovered the early poems and moved them to his office in a nearby wood. After *Axe Handles,* Snyder had planned to return to *Mountains and Rivers without End,* hoping to complete that cycle. And he planned as well to work on a prose book on nature in China and Japan, a project that is taking shape slowly as *The Great Clod.*[7] But the pre-Kyoto poems lingered in his mind (about forty poems survive in *Left Out in the Rain*) and took precedence.

The last five years have been distinctly transitional for Gary Snyder's life and writing. After a long, healthy suspicion of formal American institutions and academies, he joined the English/Creative Writing faculty at the University of California, Davis, a choice providing a base for his intellectual life. At Kitkitdizze, his dream of a Zen community in the Sierra foothills—a grafting of East and West—has come to flower with the building of the Ring of Bone Zendo (named in honor of poet Lew Welch, who vanished nearby) and the growth of that community. And after a time of family and "reinhabitation" in a region ravaged by hydraulic gold mining in the 1870s, he set off on two major turns. The first is his separation from his former mate of twenty years, Masa Ue-hara Snyder, who continues her life in the community. The second is a series of voyages in apparently diametric landscapes: in once-hostile cityscapes like New York City (the basis for his recent **"Walking the New York Bedrock: Alive in the Sea of Information"**) and in Beijing, in which **"The Persimmons"** is rooted.[8]

In the same period, he has traveled extensively in Alaska and the northern wilderness, to see through "an invigorating window into the essential nature of planetary normal, the diversity and richness of wildlife and terrain and people as it ought to be—and was, up until recently."[9]

Five Alaskan treks to date percolate through his work, a body of poems that constitute "a mind of tumbling water," as it is termed in **"Raven's Beak River at the End,"** a projected sequence for *Mountains and Rivers without End.*[10] The poems are new, but they recycle through familiar figures, as in **"The Sweat,"** which echoes **"The Bath"** (*Turtle Island*) two decades later.[11] And some archetypes are rediscovered, as in **"The Bear Mother"**:

> She veils herself
>   to speak of eating salmon
> Teases me with
>   "what do you know of my ways"
> and kisses me through the mountain
>
> Through and under its layers, its
>   gullies, its folds;
> Her mouth full of blackberries,
> We share.[12]

But deeper, the urban and wild are not opposing: the "composting" of *Left Out in the Rain* turns him back on himself, to see the wild in New York. It is a mind, an ecosystem, that is alive, especially with predators and scavengers. A "—Peregrine sails past the window / . . . and stoops in a blur on a pigeon." And street people are "bottom feeders."[13] And he finds worldly in the wild, as on remote Baranoff Island (Alaska), in which the women of **"The Sweat"** are fully in the 1980s, talking of returns to college, running businesses, careers, "science, writing, values, spirit, politics, poems—".[14]

The work begun in organizing *Left Out in the Rain,* then, and expressed in the later poems, has invigorated his sense of interpenetration, set him on a course which "is attempting to deconstruct the dichotomy between nature and human culture."[15]

As his vision matures, Snyder has become less rigidly "anti-" and more "alternative-," embracing apparent contradiction and paradox—not unlike Coyote who shows up as a cosmic gunfighter to end gunfights in **"Coyote Man, Mr. President, & the Gunfighters"** (206-209). In Snyder's imagination by metamorphosis and transformation, city and wilderness each become a system charged with the same energy, as filled with life as a single drop of water from the Bering Sea.

He views the forthcoming *Mountains and Rivers without End* as "a highly intuitive and unpredictable exercise."[16] But the composition is powered by the poet's walking the doab between wilderness and the city, imaging the weave between natural weft and urban or cultural warp—and looking at the vast hieroglyphics of those two places on earth, watching for clues to the state of the single and social spirit, the buried structure of mind.

So *Left Out in the Rain* is part of a series of demarcations, the decision to compile and publish the book marking "a period of fresh directions . . . a real turn in my strategies . . . like recomposting—turning the soil over one more time."[17] What began in the earliest manuscripts grew to a larger undertaking, and Snyder finally saw a six-part chronological cycle that would reveal all early work worthy of publication, adding recent major poetry, appending two sections of jeux d'esprit, **"Tiny Energies 1970-1984"** (155-178) and **"Satires, Inventions & Diversions 1951-1980"** (181-209).

His intent was to bring the early poems into print faithful to the original texts, with little revision. Only a few were reworked—most notably, **"Longitude 170° West, Latitude 35° North"** (59-61). Revision strengthened this night-sea meditation, a series of the poet's suspensions between worlds: East and West, sky and water, waking and dreaming, past and future, illusion and the Void.

Some poems he had simply lost track of. Eight or ten had been overlooked, especially **"Crash"** (97), an etched narrative speaking to the dangers of inattention, alive even in the practice of concentration in Kyoto. The search also led him back to his voluminous journals and notebooks. He retrieved **"Straits of Malacca 24 October 1957"** (76), an excellent study of the move from perception to poem (by selective excision and compression) from a notebook. And **"First Landfall on Turtle Island"** (115) was a whole-cloth journal "finding" depicting his first glimpse of America on returning from Japan in 1968.

As the concept grew, Snyder also pruned, working the folders through which his writing sifts, disposing of many poems, setting aside sixty to seventy others he will hold but not publish. What results lengthens the span of his poetic career at each end. **"Elk Trails"** (5-7) was written at age seventeen, **"The Persimmons"** (159-61) at fifty-three, and they give us a richer sense of the origins and dimensions of the corpus.[18]

This is Gary Snyder's most directly autobiographical volume, chronicling key moments in the life of a poet and a generation. As one of the nation's most closely attended literary figures, he has learned to steward carefully aspects of his private life and those of his friends, choosing when and how to yield his pith. Thus some of the poems in *Left Out in the Rain* were withheld previously because they were too personal, too autobiographical, or depicted the living too graphically. **"Ballad of Rolling Heads"** (192-94) gave him greatest pause. It is a winey reminiscence drafted at Shokoku-ji temple, "the Shavehead Roshis put to bed / Like babies simple in the head" (192). The poet recalls a last Beat Generation debauch in which names are named (Kerouac, Whalen, Ginsberg, Orlovsky, Cassady, lesser lights), "the whole wild tribe on the vag" (193).

He acknowledges the "hot and cool" strains of the Beats, warning last that "squares and fools will be revealed / By Whalen's calm and classic dance, / Allen Ginsberg's naked dance" (194).

Similarly, **"On Vulture Peak"** (170-73) is primarily of cultural, historical interest, recording in rhymed couplets the poet and his confreres, some drunk, some hung over, roistering at McClure Beach. Kerouac and Snyder feast on fresh mussels, squat naked in the sand, "a pair of drunk Siwash starting a shellmound" (70).

"Alabaster" (116), composed in 1970, a celebration of the women carpenters who helped build Kitkitdizze, working bare-chested in the summer heat, was also held back out of respect to individual privacies. Prior to publication here, Snyder sought and received permission from each of the five women depicted.[19]

The early **"Atthis"** sequence (20-31)—inspired by Ezra Pound's figure in *Personae* and trimmed to ten from an original eighteen or twenty poems—was also withheld because Snyder felt it "too personal, too close to the people involved."[20] The published sequence is a good corrective to the flattening of Snyder's personae, and here we see the young poet groping painfully through a lost love,

ending nine years later on a sailor's hornpipe, but one more melancholy than rollicking:

> Now if we'd stayed together,
> There's much we'd never've known
> But dreary books and weary lands
> Weigh on me like a stone.
>
>   **("Seaman's Ditty,"** 31)

Held back, as well, were the **"Three Poems for Joanne"** (91-93), limning the growth and death of the marriage between Snyder and poet Joanne Kyger. The poems move from a Western celebration outdoors "in loving words" of two poets who also love words, to bitter lees in a cold Japanese bed, "fights and the frown / at dawn" (93). This harshness flares even brighter in the "tiny energy" of domestic hell, where "some lovers wake one day" (160).

So, too, was **"Versions of Anacreon"** in Part VIII, **"Satires, Inventions, & Diversions 1951-1980"** (197-99), which is not merely an exercise in anacreontics, but offers, as well, a more explicit glimpse of the poet as sexual figure than he wished earlier in his life.

This energy burns most intensely in **"April"** (55), a fevered glimpse of "brief, doomed love" between the poet and an unnamed woman, pregnant with her husband's third child. The poem is charged with dangerous solar and human heat, and it serves a corrective function, as does the whole body of sensual, sexual, erotic, and bawdy poems in *Left Out in the Rain,* restoring to us the yang of the passionate, appetitive man of, say, **"The Song of the Taste."**[21] Too often, his readers—followers and detractors—reduce him, imagine him a pristine Zen priest of fish and blossom. Such sexual poems counter this reading.

Based on work I have seen recently, I suspect this tapping of the range from the sensual through the erotic and bawdy (see **"Fear Not,"** 142)—poems Snyder terms "in the line of delight in the flower of the body. More to follow."—will surface strongly in *Mountains and Rivers without End* and coming work.[22]

Other poems were withheld for broad aesthetic reasons. Through *Axe Handles,* Snyder has composed collections not merely to offer his strongest individual works, but with an eye to defining "a path," at once a poetic aesthetic and a way of living in the world. "Once I had established my aesthetic clearly," he explains, "a good *track,* then I could play around the edges by bringing this book out."[23]

"Playing at the edges" is often a corrective impulse in *Left Out in the Rain.* Snyder's personae assert their sexuality and eroticism, and they restore other dimensions to our readings. The voice of the youth in **"Elk Trails"** (5-7) is stern, sapwood adolescent, and that of the young man in **"Atthis"** (20-31) embraces the pain of rejection and lost love. A sequence of poems in IV and V enriches our sense of the Kyoto period, one his readers tend to see through a romanticized haze of plum blossom and delicate kimonos. Being a foreigner and a seeker via templed discipline entails periods of drudgery and complex doubt, and **"Dullness in February: Japan"** (64-65), **"Riding the hot electric train"** (100), and **"In Tokyo: At Loose Ends"** ("me on my feet through the town. / liking it, / ready to leave," 104) all suggest this.

Grant, then, the sterner energies here, but note also the sense of play, a tone of relaxed, bemused acceptance that grows as poet and poetry mature. "Lots of play / in the way things work" (**"Lots of play,"** 17), he advises, and one face of play here is pleasure in baring early sources and influences, a willingness to offer poems that show the apprentice at work as well as those of the mature craftsman.

Gary Snyder's Eastern and American Indian influences and his assimilation of their spiritual and poetic modes have been well-established, but in *Left Out in the Rain* he demonstrates his debts to Western traditions and individual talents. His approach to influence and the "anxiety of influence" is direct: "Harold Bloom's position is very patriarchal, very Occidental, and very Jewish. The Chinese have been happy poetically for millennia to refer, adopt whole lines, to nourish their poetry with the speech of others. And they certainly don't have any anxiety about that. My feeling is that the artist is a shameless thief. You know, the raven flies over and anything left out gets picked up. It's not a problem for me."[24]

Snyder has acknowledged the poetic influences of European and American Modernists in earlier interviews ("Stevens, Eliot, Pound, Williams and Yeats"), and the poems in this collection clearly show such "picking-up."[25]

"Elk Trails" (5-7), his earliest published verse, establishes a figure ripening in his work more than forty years later, but it originates in the poet's reading Robinson Jeffers.[26] There is a flinty disdain of modern life and mind ("man-made trails, / Precise-cut babies of the mountain / Ignorant of the fine, high-soaring ridges," 6). Jeffers courses through the poem, in sound, diction, line, and metaphor, but mainly by the rocky, antihuman vision, fiercely adolescent, that conjures the spirits of the Elk *trails* (*not* the Elk), an "ancient, coarse-haired, / Thin-flanked God" who laughs "at man, and all his trails" (7).

The shade of William Butler Yeats also looms large in the apprentice poetry, in what Snyder terms "his special sense of symbol and imagery."[27] The **"Atthis"** sequence (20-31) opens with an Eliotic invocation far too obvious to miss, but the vision and craft of Yeats—in image, line, sound, and rhythm—is remarkable in poems three and four, as it is elsewhere in the roughly contemporaneous **"Message from Outside"** (15).

More surprising is the influence of Alexander Pope, shown in Snyder's satiric imitation, **"The Elusiad, or Culture Still Uncaught"** (183-84), and elsewhere in the final two sections. "I've always had a funny, closet fondness for eighteenth century verse, especially Pope and Swift," he admits.[28] And his playing with Pope (one serious work of the apprentice) is evident. Composed in his early twenties, the poem was submitted as a graduate paper for a course in "Anthropology and Culture" at the University of Indiana in 1952. The imitation traces, in rhyme, meter, image, and ironic vision, Pope's influence, as "*Culture's* net unseen" tangles "man in folly all his days" (183).[29]

Snyder's sense that one real work of the poet originates in play expresses itself in several other ways. If we see a "trying on" of earlier poets, we also see an interest in formal structures; echoing and imitation are tools of the apprenticeship. *Left Out in the Rain* offers us heroic satires (**"The Elusiad,"** 183-84), sestinas (**"Sestina of the End of the Kalpa,"** 187), villanelles (**"Villanelle of the Wandering Lapps,"** 181), and a wide range of exercises with couplet, quatrain, and metered rhyme.

If the poet's work is often serious play, play is also fun, funny, even frivolous. Snyder's most recent collection mirrors this sense of the shuttle at work, in one sense by a recurrent interest in trickster figures, shape-shifters, transformers, and metamorphosers. Coyote—merely invoked in the early **"Message from Outside"** (15) but comically potent in the closing **"Coyote Man, Mr. President, & the Gunfighters"** (206-209)—is the clearest instance, and "the ugly infant" and "Greasy Boy" of **"The Professor as Transformer"** (182) and "Fox-girls" who "switch from / humans to fox-form / right during the party!" (**"Fear Not,"** 142) are also metamorphosers. Such figures insist that the serious can be silly in an instant.

Most basically, they manifest Snyder's sense of the illusion of a dualistic universe. Han-Shan was first a crazy, wandering drunk, the Yamabushi deity Fudō Myō-ō is a "punk or street-Buddha," a marauder who "forcibly rescues folks from hell whether they want it or not."[30] All of these shape-shifters and transformers feed on apparent contradiction and paradox. Good and evil, the pure light and drunken folly, moments of sexual heat and bad practical jokes—all are convenient dualistic separations to be dissolved.

Thus play is at once "serious" work and "frivolous," which conclusion led Snyder to append the final two sections of **Left Out in the Rain.** His intent, once again, was corrective: "I had questions about them. They'd previously been too frivolous to publish. Then, I thought, why not let frivolity show? Show the 'goofy' side as well— what I'm really like at times. And one power of such figures 'at play' is that we cannot easily contain them."[31]

Such thinking is undeniably seductive, and readers do tend to overlook the comic strain in the poetry, the delight in language, puns, word-play, arcane echoes, but taken to the extreme, it yields such ephemera as "**Smog**" (204), an instance of concrete verse which is surely the nadir of this collection and probably of Snyder's entire poetic career.

Finally, the metaphor of composting implies that the past is alive and feeding the present and future, that Gary Snyder derived impetus from the process of retrieving and publishing his earliest poetry, used it as an energy source, a fuel for his most recent work. The structure of the poem **Left Out in the Rain** (Snyder's collections are carefully arranged extended poems) is one of a series of arcs, starting with "**Elk Trails**" (5-7) and "**Out of the soil and rock**" (8), brought to close in "**At the White River Roadhouse in the Yukon**" (148) and "**The Persimmons**" (149-51). Thus opening and closing sets of poems are end-pieces, framing a series of arcs that bend outward from Pacific Coast wilderness, to California and Beat life, to Asia, back to home and family, back to the Northwest (Alaska), finally striking a series of complex balances in "**The Persimmons**" (149-51), one of Snyder's most resonant poems in many years.

These arcs—seen as oppositions to, movements away from—are set off in the persona of "**Elk Trails**" and "**Out of the soil and rock**," a young, stern, solitary seeker of exotic bedrock. He burns on a summer eve for the destruction of cities, disdains all forms of human civilization and culture. Gazing first at Mt. St. Helens and Spirit Lake and then New York, he is Western youth and egoism personified.[32] Abstract and strained in language and image, seeing mainly death in the elements of life before him, he is unable to engage the present, yearning, instead, for the ancient wisdom of an unknown memory that may offer a radically transformed future.

The texts suggest that Snyder writes in response to this earliest poetic self in "**At White River Roadhouse . . .**" and "**The Persimmons**," turns back in on himself to conduct an implied dialogue. He composts from that stern, dichotomized, arcing self, transforming to the mature, mellowed persona who gathers arcs into cycles. For this second self, the past is alive, and the future is charged with potential, yet he stands fully realized in the present, no longer stranded, redeemed in the concrete moment of ripe fruit. The boy abstractly imagines the steel and cement of New York ephemeral; the man responds in his own specific vision, a dream in which a ringing bell links him to both the solitary and the social, a Buddhist temple and wayfarers on an Alaskan highway. He radiates into "**The Persimmons**," first a traveler in winter Alaska, then voyager in October China, and he dissolves, heals the arcs spoken and implied in the mind of the earliest poems, to balances, cycles: God and men, the ancient wild and the city of the 1980s, harsh spirit and failing matter, the freedom of the single self and the prisons of family, culture and history, life and death. These are all connected in the mind of the poem.

And so the mature "I" of "**The Persimmons**" composts himself from "**Elk Trails**," turns back in on himself for new energy, just as he recycles the energy of the universe in the simple act of eating a persimmon ("each orb some life left from summer," 149). He recalls an afternoon walk on The Great Wall and a descent into a deep Ming tomb, in which he saw a ripe Tamopan persimmon on a plaited tray. And now, on an adjacent Beijing street filled with travelers and other persimmon vendors, he gathers the arcs set off in his young persona's mind. He composts from it with a simple, delighted gesture, the purchase of a fruit from an old man, a balance that entitles him, as well, to join "the people and the trees that prevail" (151). Doing so, the mature man rises from life in the boy (his poetic father), composts him in a cycle, "richer and stronger."[33] From physical text to title to conceptual evolution to the emergence of the mature persona from the chrysalis of his past, **Left Out in the Rain** speaks of the transformation of poetic composting.

Notes

1. Gary Snyder, "The *East West* Interview," interview by Peter Barry Chowka, in *The Real Work: Interviews and Talks 1964-1979*, ed. William Scott McLean (New York: New Directions, 1980), 123.

2. Gary Snyder, *Left Out in the Rain: New Poems 1947-1985* (Berkeley, Calif.: North Point Press, 1986). Subsequent references to poems in this collection appear parenthetically in the text.

3. Gary Snyder, interview by Jack Hicks, tape recording, Davis, California, 23 August 1987.

4. Gary Snyder, *Myths and Texts* (New York: New Directions, 1978), 14.

5. Snyder-Hicks interview.

6. Snyder-Hicks interview.

7. Three chapters of *The Great Clod* are complete to date. A subsequent prose book, *Practice of the Wild*, of which six chapters have been privately circulated, is approximately three-fourths complete.

8. Gary Snyder, "Walking the New York Bedrock: Alive in the Sea of Information," in *The Best American Poetry 1988*, ed. John Ashbery (New York: Collier Books, 1988), 175-80.

9. Snyder-Hicks interview.

10. Gary Snyder, "Raven's Beak River at the End," *Sulfur* 22 (Spring 1988): 118-19.

11. Gary Snyder, "The Sweat," privately circulated, June 1987. See also "The Bath," *Turtle Island* (New York: New Directions, 1974), 12-14.

12. Gary Snyder, "The Bear Mother," *Sulfur* 22 (Spring 1988): 115.

13. Snyder, "Walking the New York Bedrock," 179-80.

14. Snyder, "The Sweat," 2.

15. Snyder-Hicks interview.

16. Snyder-Hicks interview.

17. Snyder-Hicks interview.

18. Snyder-Hicks interview.

19. Snyder-Hicks interview.

20. Snyder-Hicks interview. See also Ezra Pound, "Atthis," in *Personae* (New York: New Directions, 1926), 112.

21. Gary Snyder, "Song of the Taste," *Regarding Wave* (New York: New Directions, 1972), 17.

22. Gary Snyder, letter to Jack Hicks, 20 October 1987.

23. Snyder-Hicks interview.

24. Snyder-Hicks interview.

25. See Gary Snyder, "The Real Work," interview by Paul Geneson, in *The Real Work*, 57-58.

26. Snyder makes a major distinction between "path" and "trail" in "On the Path and Off the Trail," *Practice of the Wild*, privately circulated, September 1988. Here *trail* is a utilitarian concept, implying destination, quantification, and mastery over the wild. To be on the *path* is to have a spiritual "way."

27. Snyder, *The Real Work*, 58.

28. Snyder-Hicks interview.

29. Snyder-Hicks interview.

30. Gary Snyder, *Riprap & Cold Mountain Poems* (San Francisco: Four Seasons Foundation, 1965), 33-60. Fudō Myō-ō is described at length in the fourteen-page catalog, *Contributions to the Ring of Bone Zendo Dharma Art Exhibit*, privately circulated, September 1987.

31. Snyder-Hicks interview.

32. "Elk Trails" was composed during the summer of 1947; the New York poem, in the summer of 1948.

33. Gary Snyder, *The Real Work*, 123.

FURTHER READING

Bibliography

Lavazzi, Tom. "Gary Snyder: An International Checklist of Criticism." *Sagetrieb* 12, no. 1 (spring 1993): 97-128.

Lists critical studies, interviews, and earlier bibliographies; includes sources in languages other than English.

Biographies

Kherdian, David. "Gary Snyder." In *Six Poets of the San Francisco Renaissance*, pp. 47-70. Fresno, Calif.: Giligia Press, 1967.

Focuses on Snyder's work for the forest service and on an oil tanker as significant sources for his work; includes a short bibliography.

Steuding, Bob. *Gary Snyder*. Boston: G. K. Hall & Co., 1976, 175p.

Examination of Snyder and his poetry, providing an in-depth view of his major writing.

Watson, Steven. "Gary Snyder." In *The Birth of the Beat Generation*, pp. 212-5. New York: Pantheon Books, 1995.

Briefly details Snyder's early life and student years up through his meeting with Ginsberg and Kerouac and the events that inspired The Dharma Bums.

Criticism

Bartlett, Lee. "Gary Snyder's *Myths and Texts* and the Monomyth." *Western American Literature: Quarterly Journal of the Western Literature Association* 17, no. 2 (summer 1982): 137-48.

Reveals how Myths and Texts *mirrors the basic structure of the classic model of the monomyth: separation, initiation, and return.*

———. "'The Sun is but a Morning Star': Notes on Gary Snyder." In *The Sun is but a Morning Star: Studies in West Coast Poetry and Poetics*, pp. 77-106. Albuquerque: University of New Mexico Press, 1989.

Links Snyder's translation work to his poetry, also discussing Myths and Texts *in terms of the heroic tradition.*

Boyers, Robert. "Mixed Bag." *Partisan Review* 36, no. 2 (1969): 306-15.

> Reviews The Back Country *harshly, calling it monotonous and superficial and dismisses Snyder's worldview as uninformed and self-righteous.*

Carpenter, David A. "Gary Snyder's Inhumanism, from *Riprap*, to *Axehandles*." *South Dakota Review* 26, no. 1 (spring 1988): 110-38.

> Claims Snyder follows Robinson Jeffers in a tradition that does not see humanity as central to existence.

Davidson, Michael. "'Spotting That Design': Incarnation and Interpretation in Gary Snyder and Philip Whalen." In *The San Francisco Renaissance: Poetics and Community at Mid-Century*, pp. 95-124. Cambridge: Cambridge University Press, 1989.

> Compares the treatment of Buddhism in the work of Snyder and Whalen; suggests that Snyder's poetry merges nature and spirituality in a more transcendent, less personal way than that of Whalen.

Dean, Tim. *Gary Snyder and the American Unconscious.* London: MacMillan Press, 1991, 240p.

> Describes Snyder's work as an example of postmodern poetics, placing it in the context of cultural narratives and stereotypes about the American West.

Fraser, G. S. "The Magicians." *Partisan Review* 38, no. 4 (winter 1971-72): 469-78.

> Reviews Regarding Wave *briefly, calling Snyder repetitive and simplistic, with images too vague to be successfully imagistic.*

Holaday, Woon-Ping Chin. "Formlessness and Form in Gary Snyder's *Mountains and Rivers without End*." *Sagetrieb* 5, no. 1 (spring 1986): 41-51.

> Examines Mountains and Rivers without End *from the vantage point of an environmentalist and reaches a conclusion far different from most critical opinions of this work.*

Hunt, Anthony. "Singing the Dyads: The Chinese Landscape Scroll and Gary Snyder's *Mountains and Rivers without End*." *Journal of Modern Literature* 23, no. 1 (1999): 7-34.

> Emphasizes the importance of Chinese landscape painting to the development of Snyder's Mountains and Rivers without End; *explores the movement in the poem through space and non-space.*

Kern, Robert. "Clearing the Ground: Gary Snyder and the Modernist Imperative." In *The Beats: Essays in Criticism*, pp. 147-64. Jefferson, N.C.: McFarland, 1981.

> Proposes that Snyder's work is better understood as Modernist rather than postmodern, focusing on his early poetry and his development of a modern poetics.

Lavazzi, Tom. "Pattern of Flux: Sex, Buddhism, and Ecology in Gary Snyder's Poetry." *Sagetrieb* 8, nos. 1-2 (spring and fall 1989): 41-68.

> Purports that Snyder's desire in all of his poetry is to institute a change of perceptions and worldview, not to overthrow social-political institutions.

Leed, Jacob. "Gary Snyder, Han Shan, and Jack Kerouac." *Journal of Modern Literature* 11, no. 1 (1984): 185-93.

> Discusses Snyder's revision process in translating the Han Shan poems, using Kerouac's Dharma Bums *as one piece of evidence. Leed finds Snyder's translation more immediate than earlier versions.*

Molesworth, Charles. *Gary Snyder's Vision: Poetry and the Real Work.* Columbia: University of Missouri Press, 1983, 128p.

> Considers Snyder's work both as modernist and as a response to multinational capitalist culture, observing that Snyder's Western ethos comes out of the American expansionist tradition.

Murphy, Patrick D., editor. *A Place for Wayfaring: The Poetry and Prose of Gary Snyder.* Corvallis: Oregon State University Press, 2000, 256p.

> Traces the development of the central themes of Snyder's poetry and prose, especially work and nature, from Riprap to Mountains and Rivers without End.

Murphy, Patrick D., editor. *Critical Essays on Gary Snyder.* Boston: G. K. Hall, 1991, 267p.

> Collects essays from the 1960s through the 1980s; primarily a scholarly approach to Snyder's work.

———. *Understanding Gary Snyder.* Columbia, S.C.: University of South Carolina Press, 1992, 186p.

> Provides an intensive critique of all of Snyder's work from his first piece to his most recent publications.

Nordstrom, Lars. *Theodore Roethke, William Stafford, and Gary Snyder: The Ecological Metaphor as Transformed Regionalism.* Stockholm: Uppsala, 1989, 197p.

> Distinguishes Snyder from other regional poets of the Northwest due to his interest in ecological ethics. Nordstrom also compares Snyder's work to that of Native-American poets.

Parkinson, Thomas. "After the Beat Generation." *Colorado Quarterly* 17, no. 1 (summer 1968): 45-56.

> As one of the earliest academic supporters of Snyder and other Beat poets, Parkinson suggests that Beat writers and 1960s counterculture reflect many social concerns of American youth.

———. "Poetry of Gary Snyder." *Southern Review* 4, no. 3 (1968): 616-32.

> Heralds Snyder as the voice of a new poetic culture, suggesting that the young poet needs to develop force and focus.

Phillips, Rod. "'This is Our Body': Gary Snyder's Erotic Universe." In *'Forest Beatniks' and 'Urban Thoreaus': Gary Snyder, Jack Kerouac, Lew Welch, and Michael McClure*, pp. 71-102. New York: Peter Lang, 2000.

> Connects Snyder's sensual and erotic writings to his interest in nature, suggesting that Snyder's attention to the body represents common ground between him and other Beat authors.

Robertson, David. "Gary Snyder Ripprapping in Yosemite, 1955." *American Poetry* 2, no. 1 (fall 1984): 52-9.

> Discusses the importance of Snyder's time spent working for the forest service in Yosemite to his poetry.

———. "Real Matter, Spiritual Mountain: Gary Snyder and Jack Kerouac on Mt. Tamalpais." *Western American Literature* 27, no. 3 (November 1992): 209-26.

> Combines traditional criticism with photojournalism and personal meditations from Robertson's own hikes on Mt. Tamalpais, with a focus on spirituality.

Paul, Sherman. "From Lookout to Ashram: The Way of Gary Snyder, Part One." *Iowa Review* 1, no. 3 (summer 1970): 76-91.

Traces the development of ecological themes in Snyder's early writings, observing a movement from the individual to a social communal consciousness.

Smith, M. Bennett. "Snyder's 'The Call of the Wild.'" *Explicator* 60, no. 1 (fall 2001): 47-9.

Analyzes a poem from Turtle Island *with emphasis on the coyote as a metaphor for life and a creative relationship with the land.*

Smith, Richard Cándida. "Gary Snyder on the Responsibilities of Utopia: Expanding the Boundaries of Domesticity." *Utopia and Dissent: Art, Poetry, and Politics in California*, pp. 372-99. Berkeley: University of California Press, 1995.

Addresses Snyder's political philosophy and his efforts to create a utopia on a personal level, noting several failings in Snyder's utopian vision.

Snyder, Gary. *On Bread and Poetry: A Panel Discussion with Gary Snyder, Lew Welch, and Philip Whalen*, edited by Donald Allen. Bolinas, Calif.: Grey Fox Press, 1977, 47 p.

Presents Snyder's ideas on poetry and culture in an extended interview with the other Reed College poets.

———. "'Notes on the Beat Generation' and 'The New Wind.'" *American Poetry* 2, no. 1 (fall 1984): 44-51.

Recalls Snyder's first meeting with Ginsberg and the development of the Beat movement as a significant part of American culture; originally written to introduce Beat poetry and philosophy to the Japanese.

Whalen-Bridge, John. "Spirit of Place and Wild Politics in Two Recent Snyder Poems." *Northwest Review* 29, no. 3 (1991): 123-31.

Considers Snyder's embrace of urban environments in "Walking the New York Bedrock" and "Buildings."

OTHER SOURCES FROM GALE:

Additional coverage of Snyder's life and career is contained in the following sources published by the Gale Group: *American Nature Writers; American Writers Supplement; Contemporary Authors*, Vols. 17-20; *Contemporary Authors New Revision Series*, Vols. 30, 60; *Contemporary Literary Criticism*, Vols. 1, 2, 5, 9, 32, 120; *Contemporary Poets*, Ed. 7; *Dictionary of Literary Biography*, Vols. 5, 16, 165, 212, 237, 275; *DISCovering Authors Modules: Poetry; DISCovering Authors 3.0; Literature Resource Center; Major 20th-Century Writers*, Ed. 2; *Poetry Criticism*, Vol. 21; *Poetry for Students*, Vol. 9; *Reference Guide to American Literature*, Ed. 4; and *World Poets*.

JACK SPICER

(1925 - 1965)

American poet, novelist, and essayist.

Spicer was associated with the Beat Generation primarily because of his social activities and attitudes, his friendships with Bay-area poets, and his involvement with several small presses and magazines developed by counterculture writers as an alternative means of publishing their works. Although Spicer and the Beats espoused similar ideals and sensibilities, he repeatedly accused financially successful Beat writers such as Jack Kerouac and Allen Ginsberg of "selling out" to what he termed the "English department" establishment of commercial publishing. In addition, Spicer disputed the Beats' belief that poetry is primarily a means of personal expression; instead, he asserted his theory that writing poetry is a form of dictation in which the poet derived mysterious codes or messages from an external source. According to Spicer, the poet's role was similar to that of a radio, receiving and transmitting signals with minimal interference.

BIOGRAPHICAL INFORMATION

Spicer was born in 1925 in Los Angeles, California. He attended the University of Redlands in 1943 and the following year transferred to the University of California at Berkeley, where he received his bachelor's degree in 1947 and his master's degree in 1950. While at Berkeley, Spicer established strong friendships with poets Robert Duncan and Robin Blaser, and together they envisioned forming a literary circle which, in emulation of the *Georgekreis* ("George Circle") of the twentieth-century German poet Stefan George, would inspire a poetic revival. This ambition ended when Spicer was forced to leave Berkeley after refusing to sign a loyalty oath that was required of all faculty.

Spicer spent the next seven years teaching, studying, and working in academic institutions in various states. In 1957 he returned to California to live in the San Francisco Bay area and founded his Magic Workshop at the San Francisco State College Poetry Center. Ostensibly a poetry workshop, the sessions held there were experiments in which participants would occupy themselves in such activities as writing blasphemies and dramatizing roles from *The Wizard of Oz*. Through his workshop Spicer met many of San Francisco's poets, including Helen Adam, George Stanley, Ebbe Borregaard, Joe Duncan, and Jack Gilbert. The workshop was later held informally at various North Beach bars, where Spicer presided over activities such as "Blabbermouth Night," in which poets would utter nonsense words, spontaneous chatter, and noises in a manner that resembled Spicer's poetic theory of dictation. Because Spicer refused to publish in well-known literary periodicals or through established publishers, his works remained virtually unknown outside the Bay area. Most of Spicer's books were published surreptitiously in mimeographed editions by Joe Dunn, who worked in a Greyhound bus printing office that later became known as the office of White Rabbit Press, and individual poems were published in obscure local magazines such as *Open Space,* or Spicer's own short-lived journal, *J.* In addition to writing poetry, Spicer worked from 1958 until his death on a linguistic atlas of the Pacific Coast. He died in 1965 from complications resulting from alcoholism.

MAJOR WORKS

Spicer wrote relatively conventional poetry from 1946 to 1956, but he is primarily known for works written after he conceived his method of dictation. He employed dictation in his first book of poems, *After Lorca* (1957), in which he "communicates" with the Spanish poet Federico García Lorca, who was murdered in 1936. The book is a mixture of poetry and prose; through the technique of dictation Lorca is presented as the author of the introduction to the volume, and in the process of translating Lorca's poetry Spicer alters words and lines, adds original poems, and composes an exchange of letters between himself and the deceased Spanish poet. Spicer's 1962 work, *The Heads of the Town up to the Aether,* is written in a three-part structure that also combines poetry and prose. In the third section of the book, "A Textbook of Poetry," Spicer compares communication between poet and reader to that of a radio and a listener, wherein the reader might misinterpret a poem due to "faulty reception" or choose not to "listen" by not reading the poem. Spicer's final works reflect his concern with what it means to be a human. *The Holy Grail* (1964) is a collection of seven poems, each named after an Arthurian hero, and serves as a modern interpretation of humanity's search for meaning. The volume *Language* (1965) reveals Spicer's increased sense of isolation as a poet from society: "being a poet / a disyllable in a world of monosyllables." Spicer's last work, *Book of Magazine Verse* (1966), discusses humanity's relationship to God, whose existence Spicer never completely acknowledges or denies. Spicer's contempt for the literary establishment is epitomized by the cover of *Book of Magazine Verse,* which mocks the design of *Poetry* magazine, and in the final poem of the collection, which is an attack on Ginsberg: "At least we both know how shitty the world is / You / wearing a beard and a mask to disguise it. I / wearing my tired / smile. I don't see how you do it. One hundred thousand university students marching with you. / Toward / A necessity which is not love but is a name. / King of the May . . ." After his death in 1965, Spicer's friends and publishers released a number of posthumous works, including *Some Things from Jack* (1972), *The Collected Books of Jack Spicer* (1975), *One Night Stand and Other Poems* (1980), *The House That Jack Built: The Collected Lectures of Jack Spicer* (1998), and *Golem* (1999). Spicer's only work of prose, *The Tower of Babel* (1994), an unfinished detective novel set during the San Francisco Renaissance of the 1950s and 1960s, was also published after his death.

CRITICAL RECEPTION

Due to the efforts of his friends and colleagues, Spicer's body of work has received increasing critical recognition since his death. After the posthumous publication of *The Collected Books of Jack Spicer,* various academic journals devoted issues to the study of Spicer's works. Michael Davidson, for example, examined Spicer's unique theories regarding the role of poetry as a form of spiritual dictation and how Spicer influenced and was influenced by other San Francisco Renaissance artists. Davidson commented that, "[I]f we were to concentrate solely on the act of writing, Spicer's theory of diction would not seem so different from Ginsberg's ideas of spontaneity or Kerouac's sketching. What is different about Spicer is what might be called his negative theology, his rejection of immanent or essentialist ideologies in favor of an utter dualism of subject and object, word and thing, human and God."

PRINCIPAL WORKS

Homage to Creeley (poetry) 1952

*After Lorca (poetry) 1957

Billy the Kid (poetry) 1959

The Heads of the Town up to the Aether (poetry) 1962

Lament for the Makers (poetry) 1962

The Holy Grail (poetry) 1964

The Spicer/Ferlinghetti Correspondence: Dear Jack [with Lawrence Ferlinghetti] (letters) 1964

Language (poetry) 1965

Book of Magazine Verse (poetry) 1966

The Day Five Thousand Fish Died in the Charles
   River (poetry) 1967

The Red Wheelbarrow (poetry) 1968

Book of Music (poetry) 1969

Some Things from Jack (poetry) 1972

Admonitions (poetry) 1974

15 False Propositions about God (poetry) 1974

A Lost Poem (poetry) 1974

An Ode and Arcadia [with Robert Duncan] (poetry)
   1974

The Collected Books of Jack Spicer [edited by Robin
   Blaser] (poetry, essays, lectures, and letters)
   1975

One Night Stand and Other Poems [edited by
   Donald Allen] (poetry) 1980

The Tower of Babel: Detective Novel (unfinished
   novel) 1994

The House That Jack Built: The Collected Lectures
   of Jack Spicer [edited by Peter Gizzi] (lectures)
   1998

Golem (poetry) 1999

* This volume includes translations of poetry by Federico
   García Lorca as well as original material by Spicer.

PRIMARY SOURCES

JACK SPICER (POEM DATE 1954)

SOURCE: Spicer, Jack. "A Postscript to the Berkeley
Renaissance." In One Night Stand and Other Poems,
edited by Donald Allen, pp. 43-4. San Francisco, Calif.:
Grey Fox Press, 1980.

Written in 1954, this poem was collected in One Night
Stand and Other Poems.

"A POSTSCRIPT TO THE BERKELEY
RENAISSANCE"

What have I lost? When shall I start to sing
A loud and idiotic song that makes
The heart rise frightened into poetry
Like birds disturbed?

I was a singer once. I sang that song.
I saw the thousands of bewildered birds
Breaking their cover into poetry
Up from the heart.

What have I lost? We lived in forests then,
Naked as jaybirds in the ever-real,

Eating our toasted buns and catching flies,
And sometimes angels, with our hooting
   tongues.

I was a singer once. In distant trees
We made the forests ring with sacred noise
Of gods and bears and swans and sodomy,
And no one but a bird could hear our voice.

What have I lost? The trees were full of birds.
We sat there drinking at the sour wine
In gallon bottles. Shouting song
Until the hunters came.

I was a singer once, bird-ignorant.
Time with a gun said, "Stop,
Find other forests. Teach the innocent."
God got another and a third
Birdlimed in Eloquence.

What have I lost? At night my hooting tongue,
Naked of feathers and of softening years,
Sings through the mirror at me like a whippoor-
   will
And then I cannot sleep.

"I was a singer once," it sings.
"I sing the song that every captured tongue
Sang once when free and wants again to sing.
But I can sing no song I have not sung."

What have I lost? Spook singer, hold your
   tongue.
I sing a newer song no ghost-bird sings.
My tongue is sharpened on the iron's edge.
Canaries need no trees. They have their cage.

JACK SPICER (POEM DATE 1964)

SOURCE: Spicer, Jack. "Sporting Life." In The Collected
Books of Jack Spicer, edited by Robin Blaser, p. 218. Los
Angeles, Calif.: Black Sparrow Press, 1975.

Written in 1964, the following poem depicts Spicer's
theory of poetic inspiration, comparing a poet with a
radio.

"SPORTING LIFE"

The trouble with comparing a poet with a radio
   is that radios don't develop scar-tissue. The
   tubes burn out, or with a transistor, which
   most souls are, the battery or diagram burns
   out replacable or not replacable, but not like
   that punchdrunk fighter in a bar. The poet

Takes too many messages. The right to the ear
   that floored him in New Jersey. The right to
   say that he stood six rounds with a
   champion.

Then they sell beer or go on sporting commis-
   sions, or, if the scar tissue is too heavy,
   demonstrate in a bar where the invisible
   champions might not have hit him. Too
   many of them.

The poet is a radio. The poet is a liar. The poet is
a counterpunching radio.

And those messages (God would not damn
them) do not even know they are
champions.

GENERAL COMMENTARY

MICHAEL DAVIDSON (ESSAY DATE 1989)

SOURCE: Davidson, Michael. "'The City Redefined:'
Community and Dialogue in Jack Spicer." In *The San
Francisco Renaissance: Poetics and Community at Mid-
century,* pp. 150-9. Cambridge: Cambridge University
Press, 1989.

*In the following excerpt, Davidson considers Spicer's
resentment and rejection of Beat poetics and examines
the poet's theories as they informed his poetry and
influenced other San Francisco Renaissance poets.*

"Both of Us Were Object"

One of the outrageous events of North Beach
life during the 1950s was Blabbermouth Night, a
weekly feature at one of Grant Avenue's best-
known literary bars, The Place. Using a kind of
spontaneous and unrehearsed glossolalia, poets
would babble into the mike, the best babbler winning a free drink. One function of Blabbermouth
Night was to "bug the squares" pouring into
North Beach in search of Beatniks, but another,
more important function was to reinforce the
sense of community that had arisen within the
North Beach bar scene. For this community,
poetry was a public event, something performed
on stage in front of an audience. Blabbermouth
Night extended this public dimension, introducing an element of competition—complete with
hecklers, claques, and door prizes. Jack Spicer was
one of the event's strongest supporters, helping to
organize the participants and sometimes presenting the victor's prize. To some extent Blabbermouth Night was the perfect embodiment of Spicer's poetics: a public gospel in which the Logos
speaks through the spontaneous jabberwocky of
poets.[1]

Jack Spicer's position in the North Beach
poetry scene was central, and at the same time,
eccentric. His table at The Place was the focus of a
circle of poets who remained fiercely loyal to him
and to the spirit of play and competition that he
encouraged through events like Blabbermouth
Night. The Spicer circle maintained an uneasy
truce with the more recognizable North Beach
bohemians and used them as foils for a good deal

of barbed wit and occasional grumbling. Spicer
certainly shared with the Beats their sense of
linguistic freedom and iconoclasm, and he ap-
proved of their public mode of address, but he
deeply distrusted the hipster persona, its projection of cool detachment and mindlessness. He
satirizes these qualities in **"Ferlinghetti,"** a short
poem from *Heads of the Town up to the Aether.*

> Be bop de beep
> They are asleep
> There where were they like us
> It goes
> From nose to nose
> From stop to stop
> Violations are rare
> And the air is fair
> It is spring
> On the thing
> We sing.
> Beep bop de beep
> They are all asleep
> They're all asleep.[2]

Spicer's leaden endrhymes, his use of passive
verbal forms, and his repetitious phrasing suggest
that the "bebop" poem induces a kind of torpor
in which "Violations are rare." In the "explanatory note" attached to this poem, he indicates that
"Ferlinghetti is a nonsense syllable invented by
the Poet."

Behind Spicer's resentment of the Beats as a
social phenomenon lies a more complicated rejection of their visionary, expressivist poetics. He
regards the poem not as originating within the
individual but as a foreign agent that invades the
poet's language and expresses what "it" wants to
say. The poet must clear away the intrusive authorial will and allow entrance to an alien and ghost-
like language. Nor does poetry find its source in
the natural landscape, where acts of sympathetic
identification connect the poet to numinous
qualities latent in all living things. For Spicer, the
poet is a medium through whom a disinterested
message must penetrate, often at some cost to the
receiver. As he says in the Vancouver Lectures, "I
don't think the messages are for the poet . . .
anymore than a radio program is for the radio
set."[3]

If we were to concentrate solely on the act of
writing, Spicer's theory of diction would not seem
so different from Ginsberg's ideas of spontaneity
or Kerouac's sketching. What is different about
Spicer is what might be called his negative theology, his rejection of immanent or essentialist
ideologies in favor of an utter dualism of subject
and object, word and thing, human and God. This
view, radically Protestant in impulse, emphasizes

learning through opposition and confrontation. James Herndon tells how Spicer "refuted child psychology" by encouraging Herndon's young son Jay to say "Chicken-ship" in his nursery school: "Jack figured that if Jay said Chicken-ship enough times to the nursery-school teacher, she would in the end get mad and forbid Chicken-ship and betray herself as a tyrant, and then Jay would learn Where It Was At."[4] According to Spicer's somewhat perverse pedagogy, the truth value of any act cannot be tested by reference to qualities inherent in the act itself; it must be subjected to the world, and the world is not a friendly place. For the poet as well as for the three-year-old Jay Herndon, words "Turn mysteriously against those who use them." That is, words often subvert the purposes to which they are put:

> Dante would have blamed Beatrice
> If she turned up alive in a local bordello
> Or Newton gravity
> If apples fell upward
> What I mean is words
> Turn mysteriously against those who use them
> Hello says the apple
> Both of us were object.[5]

Spicer adapted this Protestant poetics to his personal relations as well. I have already spoken of the insularity of Spicer's North Beach bar scene, and this quality was formalized in his "Poetry as Magic" workshop at the San Francisco Public Library in 1957. Participants included many of the most active poets on the scene—Ebbe Borregaard, Jack Gilbert, George Stanley, Helen Adam, Joe Dunn, Robert Duncan—and, as Robin Blaser points out, the curriculum was hardly that of the conventional creative writing workshop: "For all the magical interest of the workshop, magic, it became clear, was a matter of disturbance, entrance and passion, rather than abracadabra. Jack once commented that there was no good source from which to learn magic; it was something we did among ourselves" (*CB*, [*The Collected Books of Jack Spicer,*] 353). Spicer heightened the "secret society" quality of the workshop by seating everyone at a round table with himself facing west. Assignments involved tasks like writing blasphemies, impersonating characters from the Oz books, and creating a universe. Participation in the workshop was restricted to poets willing to fill out a questionnaire that asked, "What political group, slogan, or idea in the world today has the most to do with Magic," "What card of the ordinary playing-card deck . . . represents the absolute of your desires?" and "What animal do you most resemble?" These rituals were designed less for the purpose of evaluating students than

FROM THE AUTHOR

COMMUNICATING THROUGH POETRY
But the things don't come through very fast, and it's quite true that you don't get messages like, "arrive tomorrow at 7:30, plane so-and-so" and so forth and so on. It doesn't come like that, obviously. But they do come as messages nonetheless. And not just for having pleasure . . . that pleasure [is] the thing about poetry. It isn't. It has to do with messages. But they come through awfully unclear and you don't really know when you're even delivering them whether the person you send the telegram to is going to sock you in the eye or give you a quarter tip.

Spicer, Jack. Excerpt from "Vancouver Lecture 3 (17 June 1965)." In *The House That Jack Built: The Collected Lectures of Jack Spicer,* edited with an afterword by Peter Gizzi. Hanover, N.H.: University Press of New England, 1998.

for reinforcing bonds among members already within the magic circle. Each test was designed to place the student in a state of vulnerability and risk, conditions Spicer felt were essential to poetry.

Though Spicer's effect on poets within his own circle was substantial, he was relatively unknown outside the Bay Area. One of the reasons for this is that he refused to participate in any traditional sort of literary self-promotion. He did not publish through established literary channels (if, in fact, his work would have been accepted by them in the first place), and he avoided copyrighting his books. When Duncan published *The Opening of the Field* with Grove Press, Spicer admonished him publicly by reprinting the copyright page of that book, including its list of publication acknowledgments, as the frontispiece to his own *Lament for the Makers.* In Duncan's version of the incident, publication of his book "had been sold to the papists or the heathen or it had been sold out to the grownups world."[6]

Spicer's output was limited to a series of twelve small poetic sequences, or "serial poems" as he called them. All of these were published by small presses in limited editions. Spicer made access to his work difficult by demanding a geographical limit to its distribution, not to extend beyond the San Francisco Bay Area—a deliberate (or half-playful) attempt to ignore the East Coast literary scene. And, as if this were not enough, Spicer and his friends often wrote fake poems of other local poets, aping the styles of those currently held in disrepute. These poems were then published in local magazines under the name of the poet being imitated.

This oppositional stance was more than a series of schoolboy pranks. It reflected Spicer's view that poetry is a world, and in it are warring camps, traitors, loyal subjects, secret codes, and internecine conflicts. The enemy is the academic establishment, presided over by the New Critical ideology and supported by a hegemonic publishing network. On the other side was the small group of poets who met with Spicer in various North Beach bars for whom he served as teacher, critic, and goad. Spicer's almost medieval sense of poetic trothes and fealties emerged early in his career, during the Berkeley period that I have described in earlier chapters. And throughout Spicer's life such circles became increasingly important as a public forum in which poetry could be debated and argued into existence. The Magic Workshop, Sunday poetry readings, favorite bars like The Place and Gino Carlos, group magazines like *J* and *Open Space* were the major venues for the Spicer group, each held together by pledges of loyalty and claims of territoriality. However insular such a community might have been, it created an audience that could set itself against a heathen world that had failed to listen.[7]

"The City That We Create in Our Bartalk"

For Spicer, listening is everything. In a 1949 symposium sponsored by the University of California literary magazine *Occident,* he introduces a theme that will preoccupy him throughout his career:

> Here we are, holding a ghostly symposium—five poets holding forth on their peculiar problems. One will say magic: one will say God: one will say form. When my turn comes I can only ask an embarrassing question—"Why is nobody here? Who is listening to us?"[8]

This question was to reappear many years later in the first poem of *Language*:

> This ocean, humiliating in its disguises
> Tougher than anything.
> No one listens to poetry. The ocean
> Does not mean to be listened to.
>
> (CB 217)

We could regard such remarks as typical of any poet's worries about audience, but in the case of Spicer the question of who is listening implies something quite different. The fact that no one listens to poetry means two things: No one listens to the poetry that "we" write but, also, poets consistently fail to listen to the poetry that reaches their ears all the time. The first proposition pertains to the creation of community—those persons joined by a common willingness to listen to one another; the second pertains to the particular dispensation such a community makes toward communication. The two areas are inextricably linked. Spicer's poetics is based on the premise that the audience for poetry will, of necessity, be limited, and therein lies its virtue.

In the *Occident* symposium of 1949, Spicer complains that the New Critics have "taken poetry (already removed from its main source of interest—the human voice) and have completed the job of denuding it of any remaining connection with person, place and time."[9] What Spicer wanted returned to poetry was a kind of vaudeville Orphism in which theatrical gestures, props, and pratfalls could defuse any expectations of high seriousness. When he said, as he did in the *Occident* symposium, that poets "must become singers, become entertainers,"[10] he was reacting against the more reflective and meditative tone of the then-popular metaphysical lyric and was, at the same time, anticipating the poetry-reading revolution of the 1950s. But unlike Charles Olson or Allen Ginsberg, for whom the voice is the outward sign of a unitary, emotive subject, voice for Spicer is a dimension of public, interactive experiences. Poetry is created in dialogue and argumentation, whether it takes place between poet and friend or between poet and God. If that dialogue is contentious (and it almost always is in Spicer's world) so much the better, since it means that language is being tested (to adapt a line from Frank O'Hara) between persons instead of between pages.[11]

The role of community and dialogue in Spicer's poetics is important to stress, since much of what little commentary on him exists has tended to see his work in service to a metaphysical ideal of the "outside."[12] Spicer contributed to this view by using certain theological and metaphysical models to explain his poetics. As I said earlier, Spicer regards poetry as something dictated from an endistanced "Other" through the poet, who, through a process of self-emptying, serves as a medium. His primary image of the poem is that of the radio in Cocteau's *Orphée,* which is tuned by the receptive poet to receive cryptic messages from Hell. The idea of poetic dictation coming from the outside is set against what Spicer called the "big lie of the personal," in which objects are subsumed by intention, in which lemons, oceans, and seagulls "become things to be traded for a smile or the sound of conversation" (*CB*, 48). Spicer, in going beyond an expressivist poetics, reaches in the other direction—to surrealism, fantasy, nonsense rhymes, games, and cartoons—to find discursive models that circumvent lyrical subjectivity. In so doing he appears to privilege another kind of aestheticism, based on a disinterested poetic source outside or beyond. In other words, he creates a metaphysics. I would like to qualify this metaphysical view of his poetics in order to see Spicer's dictation as being more dialogical and social. That is, I would like to propose that the "outside" has its base in human intercourse within a community and that its reception takes the form of a conversation or, in Spicer's words, "an argument between the dead and the living" (*CB*, 171).

Cocteau's radio metaphor has tended to obscure the degree to which Spicer's outside is a world of voices, contending and arguing like those in the bar world of North Beach or in the linguistic playfulness of the Magic Workshop. The voices that intrude into poems like **The Imaginary Elegies**" or "**Homage to Creeley**" may be ghosts, but they speak a very human rhetoric. "It is as if we conjure the dead and they speak only / Through our own damned trumpets, through our damned medium" (*CB*, 333). Spicer himself seems to have become dissatisfied with his radio motif toward the end of his life and in **Language** qualifies the metaphor: "The trouble with comparing a poet with a radio is that radios don't develope scartissue" (*CB*, 218). He then goes on to amend Cocteau's formulation: "The poet is a radio. The poet is a liar. The poet is a counterpunching radio." The metaphor has become too static, leaving little room for the possibility of response.

It is out of this spirit of verbal sparring and contention that Spicer's poetics merges with his politics. That politics is based on anarchist principles of private refusal and mutual aid.[13] Spicer believed that power relations are acted out in language, and language is subject to contextual transformations with each new utterance. Things like electoral politics, bureaucracies, and social programs only sediment power in intransigent discursive modes like contracts and legal briefs. For Spicer, real power is created in dialogue:[14]

> The city redefined becomes a church. A movement of poetry. Not merely a system of belief but their beliefs and their hearts living together.
>
> But the city that we create in our bartalk or in our fuss and fury about each other is in an utterly mixed and mirrored way an image of the city. A return from exile.
>
> (*CB*, 176)

Spicer's model here is Dante, who, exiled from Florence, creates a divine comedy out of historical contingency and in the process turns his local city into a system of belief. In Spicer's imagination, San Francisco could be such a city, "redefined" through its poetry movement and acted out in its "bartalk."[15] It is little wonder that Spicer placed such faith in the poetry wars of North Beach since they became, in his imagination, latter-day versions of the Albigensian Crusade.

An interesting portrait of the dynamics of Spicer's bar community can be seen in a chapter from his unpublished detective novel. In this chapter, an East Coast college professor named J. J. Ralston comes into a Grant Avenue Bar called the Birdcage (modeled on The Place) to "dig the San Francisco Renaissance." He has published his poems in the *Partisan Review* and *Hudson Review*, and his book has been reviewed by no less than Randall Jarrell in the *New York Times Book Review*. For the group of scraggly poets who patronize the bar he is a perfect foil. He represents the "outside" in every sense: East Coast academic, liberal humanist, established writer, literary critic. Ralston's strategy for dealing with the strange characters he encounters is to pigeonhole them as various bohemian types, all the while pigeonholing himself as an uptight square (at one point, in a gesture of self-mockery, he begins calling himself W. H. Auden). After some uncomfortable banter, one of the young poets does the unspeakable thing: he rips Ralston's copy of the *Paritsan Review* in half. Infuriated, Ralston leaves the table to drink his ale in solitude, but the offending poet brings him an odd peace token: a live fish in whose mouth is a folded piece of paper:

> Ralston unfolded the wedge of paper. It was, he could see, two pages of poetry written in large childish handwriting. Without allowing himself to read so much as a word of what was written, he folded over the pages once and then methodically began to tear the paper to shreds.
>
> "See," Ralston said, "I can tear paper too." The boy watched the pieces of paper flutter down to the floor. He looked as if he were going to cry. "It was a poem," he said softly. "You bastard. Oh, you bastard." Almost as a single movement he grabbed

the fish in his hand and ran out of the door. Ralston waited for a moment then stumbled out of the bar himself, in what he hoped was the other direction.

(*CAT*, [*Caterpillar* magazine,] 161)

We recognize Spicer in the "large childish handwriting" sending, through a young Orpheus, a cryptic message to a poet who will not recognize the gesture and in a vehicle very much the opposite of the *Partisan Review*. The poem does not exist solely on the piece of paper but in the complicated social interaction between alien and denizen.

These dramas of "inside" and "outside," of private language and public gesture are social versions of the same arguments that occur in Spicer's poems themselves. From *After Lorca* on, the poetry develops more and more strategies for engaging dialogue, whether it is between living poet and dead poet (*After Lorca*), between poet and friends (*Admonitions*), between text and commentary ("**Homage to Creeley**"), or between pronouns (*Language*). Comments from conversations are embedded in the poems, often without address and in many cases without quotation marks. And the serial poem itself, as described in *Admonitions*, offers its own kind of dialogue, each poem within the book engaged in a dialogue with others: "Poems should echo and reecho against each other. They should create resonances. They cannot live alone any more than we can" (*CB*, 61).

Nowhere are the full implications of this dialogism more prevalent than in *Language*, where the outside is given a linguistic frame. In its original edition, the book's cover reproduces the July-September 1952 cover of *Language: The Journal of the Linguistic Society of America*, in which Spicer's first and only professional publication appeared.[16] The essay, "**Correlation Methods of Comparing Idiolects in a Transition Area**," was coauthored with David Reed and represents a summary of research the two linguists were doing on California dialects, research that was to take the form of a comprehensive linguistic atlas. The essay is worth considering in relation to Spicer's poetry, if only because it indicates that as a linguist and as a poet, Spicer was concerned with language as a body of objective data, whose meanings were directly affected by specific geographical locales and small communities. In terms of the linguistic atlas that Spicer helped to compile, this language was dictated from a native informant to a participant-observer and then to Spicer, who, in turn, translated it into phonetic equivalents.

Although Spicer's daily professional work was largely empirical, he endorsed the theoretical position of American structural linguistics as formulated by Sapir and Whorf, who, in a series of articles, speculated on the close relationship between social behavior and language. Their well-known thesis is that what we call knowledge is the direct result of inherited linguistic structures. What we know and how we act are a function of acceptable ways of stating such knowledge. Though Spicer's *Language* is by no means a systematic working-out of the Sapir-Whorf thesis, it does speculate on the linguistic basis of cognition and the social structures that accrue thereby. Consider "**Transformations II**":

> "In Scarlet Town where I was born
> There was a fair maid dwelling."
> We make up a different language for poetry
> And for the heart—ungrammatical.
> It is not that the name of the town changes
> (Scarlet becomes Charlotte or even in Gold City I
>   once heard a good Western singer make it
>   Tonapah. We don't have towns here)
> (That sort of thing would please the Jungian
>   astronauts)
> But that the syntax changes. This is older than
>   towns.
> Troy was a baby when Greek sentence structure
>   emerged. This was the real Trojan Horse.
> The order changes. The Trojans
> Having no idea of true or false syntax and hav-
>   ing no recorded language
> Never knew what hit them.

(*CB*, 233)

Spicer suggests that at the source of culture is the structure of its syntax. In a tone half playful and half serious, he implies that the fall of Troy owes less to any relative weakness of its arms or troops than to its weak sentence structure. The fact that we have only the Greek side's version of this war reinforces Spicer's point: that what we call "history" is, to a large extent, the function of what narratives survive. The endurance of culture depends upon the ability of any individual to translate the "ungrammatical" language of the heart into the "language of poetry." The fact that a folk tradition may change the names of proper nouns to accommodate a specific locale is less significant than the fact that "syntax changes" and, with it, the development of culture. Hence Spicer moves from the local tradition with its specific folk songs to the larger oral epics, mocking the Jungian tendency to universalize and emphasizing instead the power of local variants.

The Trojan War, in this sense, is no different than the minor internecine conflicts within poetry communities. In the "**Transformation**" that precedes this poem, Spicer takes on the warfare within his own poetry circle:

> They say "he need (present) enemy (plural)"
> I am not them. This is the first transformation.
> They say "we need (present) no enemy
>   (singular)" No enemy in the universe is
>   theirs worth having. We is an intimate
>   pronoun which shifts its context almost as
>   the I blinks at it.
>   Those
> Swans we saw in the garden coming out of the
>   water we hated them. "Out of place," you
>   said in passing. Those swans and I (a blink
>   in context), all out of place we hated you.
> He need (present) enemy (plural) and now it is
>   the swans and me against you
> Everything out of place
> (And now another blink of moment) the last
>   swan back in place. We
> Hated them.
>
> (CB 232)

Spicer had been accused by Robert Duncan and George Stanley of needing enemies in order to create poetry.[17] Using the descriptive procedures of transformational linguistics as formulated by Chomsky, Spicer takes the basic kernel, "he needs enemies," and subjects it to various permutations. The shifting of pronouns throughout the passage undercuts the thrust of the attack, turning it upon itself until "he" and "they" switch places. In so doing he denudes the phrase of its ontological status by establishing its deixis, its relation to an audience. All claims to truth in the phrase "he needs enemies" are called into question by the framing phrase "They say." Once "they" becomes the governing basis for an accusation, "they" too must be seen as contributing to the creation of enemies.

These examples indicate that, for Spicer, the outside is language—not a symbolist language purified of all contingency, but a social language used by individuals to celebrate their local villages in song or to argue with others. It is dialogic in the sense that it is always addressed to an other, one presumably with whom one cares to argue. And this dialogism occurs within a closed community. For a homosexual poet, living in Cold War America during the 1950s and 1960s, such community was especially vital. Spicer's cultivation of insularity (what Duncan calls Tom Sawyer's gang) may have been a necessary strategy in gaining speech at all. The McCarthy trials, HUAC hearings, and civil rights clashes were providing plenty of models of the "outside" (Communists, blacks, eggheads, ethnics, and queers) against which average white citizens should defend themselves. Spicer, rather than rejecting such exclusionary rhetoric, inverted it to his own uses.

Unfortunately, Spicer's cultivation of group affiliations and cult loyalties tended to exacerbate the poet's own xenophobia, misogyny, and anti-Semitism.[18] Rather than opt for "safe" political positions (the Democratic Party, the Sierra Club, Marxism-Leninism), Spicer chose the considerably more dangerous route of cadre and cell with their attendant restrictions and prejudices. It would be wrong to justify Spicer's problematic attitudes toward women or even toward homosexuals by seeing them strictly in aesthetic terms, but it is important to note how cultural conditions of the country at large were being acted out at the local level. "The enemy," Spicer says in **The Holy Grail**, "is in your own country" and not in some far-distant jungle or State Department office. And if the audience for poetry is limited, at least you know everyone in the audience by name.

Notes

1. On Blabbermouth Night and the Spicer circle in general, the best sources are a series of interviews conducted by Lew Ellingham and published in the following magazines: *Jimmy and Lucy's House of 'K,'* 4 (June 1985), pp. 61-8; *Acts* 3 (1984), n.p.; *No Apologies* 3 (Fall, 1984), pp. 74-88; *No Apologies* 4 (n.d.), pp. 6-20; *Soup* 4 (1985), pp. 101-7; *Ironwood* 28 (Fall 1986), pp. 152-64; *Line* 9 (Spring 1987), pp. 59-69. See also *Manroot* 10 (Fall 1974-Winter 1975): Robert Duncan, Introduction to Jack Spicer, *One Night Stand*, ed. Donald Allen (San Francisco: Grey Fox Press, 1980); James Herndon, *Everything as Expected* (San Francisco: n.p., 1973). Robert Duncan conducted an extensive interview with Eloyde Tovey on the San Francisco writing scene with particular emphasis on the Spicer circle, which is available at the Bancroft Library, University of California, Berkeley. Jack Spicer discusses Blabbermouth Night in "The Vancouver Lectures [no. 1]," *Caterpillar* 12 (July 1970), pp. 181-2.

2. Jack Spicer, *The Collected Books of Jack Spicer*, ed. Robin Blaser (Los Angeles: Black Sparrow Press, 1975), p. 133; hereafter cited as *CB*. Abbreviations of other Spicer publications will be as follows: *Caterpillar* magazine, 12 (July 1970), *CAT*; *One Night Stand and Other Poems*, ed. Donald Allen (San Francisco: Grey Fox Press, 1980), *ONS*.

3. *CAT*, 184. A lengthy excerpt from the "Vancouver Lectures" appears in *The Poetics of the New American Poetry*, ed. Donald Allen (New York: Grove, 1973), pp. 227-34.

4. James Herndon, "Thus Jack Spicer Refuted Child Psychology," *Manroot* 10 (Fall 1974-Winter 1975), p. 56.

5. *CB*, 125. The "explanatory note" to this poem indicates that the laws of physics as well as of love are determined by the language in which they are expressed: "What Beatrice did did not become her own business. Dante saw to that. Sawed away the last plank anyone he loved could stand on."

6. Robert Duncan, "The Underside," unpublished manuscript in the Poetry/Rare Books Collections, University Libraries, State University of New York, Buffalo, p. 5.

7. Duncan regards this side of Spicer as a cultivation of a permanent boyhood ethos whose origins can be found in Tom Sawyer or the stories of Penrod and Sam. Duncan relates this spirit of boyhood to Spicer's early poetry community in Berkeley: "We were—Robin Blaser and I—in 1946-1950, for him, members of his secret boys' club, hero-friends and teammates in this new game of poetry. Playing poetry. He wanted to keep us true to the game. That was always what the public meant to him—the public a game has, the public of poetry like the public of baseball or football." Ibid.,p. 3.

8. *University of California Occident* (Fall 1949),p. 43. Republished in *ONS*, pp. 90-2.

9. *Occident*,p. 44; *ONS*, 91.

10. Ibid.,p. 45; *ONS*, 92.

11. Frank O'Hara, "Personism," in *Poetics of the New American Poetry*,p. 355.

12. This is the general thrust of Robin Blaser's afterword to *The Collected Books of Jack Spicer*, entitled "The Practice of Outside," as it is in the essays included in the special issue of *boundary 2* devoted to Jack Spicer's work (*boundary 2* 6, no. 1 [1977]), including my own essay in that volume. Although the present chapter makes use of portions of that earlier essay I have revised its treatment of Spicer's theological terms to account for the issue of community.

13. On Spicer's anarchist politics, James Herndon remembers "the appearance of Jack at pompous, highly-organized politics meetings in VFW hall at Berkeley; only students representing organizations could speak and vote—Jack's appearance causing an uproar among both Wallacites and Socialists etc. big argument about his credentials and Jack announced he represented the 'Committee for Anarchist Unity'—an organization which he then admitted consisted only of himself, since there could 'By definition be no unity among more than one anarchist'" (*CB*, 376).

14. I am adapting terms developed by Mikhail Bakhtin, who uses "dialogic" in terms of the novel but whose remarks could as easily refer to much postmodern poetry. See "Discourse in the Novel," in *The Dialogic Imagination,* ed. Michael Holquist (Austin: University of Texas Press, 1981),p. 276. I have developed the possibilities of Bakhtin's work for poetics in "Discourse in Poetry: Bakhtin and Extensions of the Dialogical," *Code of Signals: Recent Writings in Poetics (Io 30)*, ed. Michael Palmer (1983), pp. 141-50.

15. Spicer's remarks on the City of God and its relation to community are spelled out in his first Vancouver lecture, published in *CAT*,p. 202.

16. Jack Spicer, *Language* (San Francisco: White Rabbit Press, 1965). The essay was Spicer's only "professional" publication as a linguist. Spicer did publish a review of the Johnson edition of Emily Dickinson's *Complete Poems*: John L. Spicer, "The Poems of Emily Dickinson," *Boston Public Library Quarterly* (July 1956), pp. 135-43; partially reprinted in *Ironwood* 28 (Fall 1986), p. 207.

17. Colin Christopher Stuart and John Scoggan, "The Orientation of the Parasols: Saussure, Derrida, and Spicer," *boundary 2* 6, no. 1 (1977),p. 228. See also Robin Blaser in *CB*,p. 318.

18. See Bruce Boone, "For Jack Spicer—and a Truth Element," *Social Text* (Spring-Summer, 1983) pp. 120-6.

MARIA DAMON (ESSAY DATE SPRING 1992)

SOURCE: Damon, Maria. "Jack Spicer's Ghost Forms." *New Orleans Review* 19, no. 1 (spring 1992): 10-16.

In the following essay, Damon examines how ghosts and apparitions are used in Spicer's writing to bring meaning out of emptiness; she also discusses issues of homosexuality in Spicer's poetry.

. . . there is buried in the structurality of any structure the ghostly origin of that structure, because the origin will be structurally determined as a ghost, a palpably absent origin, by virtue of the very structurality it fathers. Every structure must begin with such an effacing, retroactive revaluation of its beginning, with such a murder of its diacritical source.
    —Joel Fineman, "The Structure of Allegorical Desire"

What I am . . . is by degrees a ghost.
    —Jack Spicer

My intention to present Jack Spicer's intertextual poetics and politics on an MLA panel whose original title was "Vestigial Forms in Contemporary Poetry" seemed both appropriate and mildly transgressive. Since I intend to investigate the politics of vestigial form, and to explore why, in a particular instance, one poet with an embattled position *vis à vis* his historical circumstance used the themes, lines, and forms of older poets and poetic traditions, my project is slightly transgressive in that I will not be executing a formal analysis in which I trace the presence of a particular traditional Western poetic form in Spicer's work, though I will look closely at one poem. However, it is appropriate in the wider senses of the phrase "Vestigial Form." Spicer's preoccupation with ghostliness as a trope lends itself to the notion of vestige, whose derivation from *vestigium*—footprint—implies a negative space which asserts, an absent presence, something or someone who has come and gone, leaving a trace of writing. The second word of the phrase, "form," exacerbates and overdetermines this intimation of haunting—form< shape< shade< ghost. Form is both materiality—the rock-bottom, palpable "real"—and simulacrum, the term "vestigial form" already perhaps a redundancy. It's here and it's not. It's matter and it's spirit. It's an apparition disrupting the present with news of the past. It's a hollowed out shell whose negativity tells us how to read absence, loss, nostalgia, dislocation all the more painful for retaining a trace of propriety, of location, orientation, right trajectory. "It"—the ghost, vestigial form, the evidence that has been dragged off the scene leaving its tracks and lines in the surface dirt of cultural history—is the poet, the poet's body, the poem, the generation of the poem (what we call "process"), and especially significant for a discussion of Jack Spicer in historical context, it is the body of already available poetry on which any poet's work feeds—that is, it is The Tradition or Traditions—which both exist and do not.

More than two decades after his death from alcoholism in 1965, Jack Spicer continues to be something of a cult poet shadowing the modernist canon. I propose to examine this shadowing, this spying on and blackmailing, this negative dis/embodiment of the Western poetic tradition, and to place it in the cultural context of a gay man's ambivalent attack on the homosociality of the "heads of the town," as Spicer referred to the elite club of the literary canon. His hermeneutics, an ichnology of poetry, investigates and reinscribes fossilized footprints—the tracings of dead poets. The posthumously published *Collected Books of Jack Spicer* (1977) is a compendium of campy attacks on his literary forebears and contemporaries, his oppressors, rivals, friends, and idols.[1] To give just a few specifics, the refrain of the poem "**Ferlinghetti**" reads "be bop de beep / they are all asleep," and the "explanatory note" as follows: "Ferlinghetti is a nonsense syllable invented by the poet" (*HT*, [*Heads of the Town up to the Aether*,] 133). *The Book of Magazine Verse*, a series of satires on typical magazine poems, addresses the Beats (among others) even more sharply; in "**Ten Poems for Downbeat**," the self-promoting philosophy of love touted by crossover figure Allen Ginsberg comes under fire (the "100,000 students" refers to the Czech May Day celebration in which Ginsberg was crowned King of the May):

> At least we both know how s——ty the world
>   is. You wearing a beard as mask to
>   disguise it. I wearing my tired smile . . . I
>   don't see how you do it. . . .
>
>   . . . If (the police had) attacked
> The kind of love (not sex but love) you gave
>   the one hundred thousand students I'd
>   have been very glad. And loved the
>   policemen . . .
>
> (*BMV*, [*Book of Magazine Verse*,] 267)

In this instance, it's Ginsberg's sidestepping of the social pain of his own sexuality in the name of some self-designated mythic higher love that incurs Spicer's disdain—the diffusion of a specifically gay sexuality and culture into a smarmy, vague, romanticized a- or pan-sexual oppositionality leads to the vulgarianism of which the members of the self-consciously gay "Berkeley Renaissance" accused the mostly straight Beats.

Lament for the Makers (1961) charges certain poets, his friend Robert Duncan among them, with selling out to "the English Department in (the) skull" (110). *Heads of the Town up to the Aether* (1961) presents poems accompanied by "explanatory notes"; one subsection is called "**Homage to Creeley**"; and there are swipes at Emerson (he glosses his own "**Concord Hymn**" with the note "'Conquered Him' is the name of a poem by Emerson" [*HT* 120]); Dickinson (the token female in the American canon is acknowledged by the title "**Dash**" [*HT* 146]); Ginsberg again (in a poem called "**Drugs**," Spicer writes, "angel-talk howls / at the edge of our beds / and all of us now / are going to hell" [*HT* 139]); Yeats (Spicer's "**Prayer for my Daughter**" [*HT* 142] is a minimalist deconstruction of the Lord's Prayer); Pound, whose signature poem from his imagist period is turned into eerie masturbatory emptiness, a vestigial form of itself:

> Ghosts drip
> And then they leap
> The boy sang, and the singing that I heard:
> Wet shadows on a stick.
>
> (*HT* 131)

However, *The Collected Books* is also a vicious self-parody in which language always has the upper hand over the struggling poet. At the same time as Spicer disembowels the fossilized literary canon, he also hollows himself out as well, so that the illusory opposition Spicer v. Canon cedes to the parasitic devourings of language itself, that virus from outer space, or, to make William Burrough's formulation more specifically Spicerian, from "Mars." (Spicer believed that he took poetic dictation from Mars.) "What I am . . . is by degrees a ghost," Spicer writes in one of a series of letters that, like Keats', constitute the most explicit articulation of his bleak poetics (*HT* 182). This poetics, which insists that the poet obliterate himself in order to make room for the messages that prey upon him in the process of dictation, is an extreme, agonistic take on the concept of negative capability, and, in the bitterness of the poet's self-denial, an explicit end-product of Eliot's closet-epistemologically-founded "objective correlative." "Loneliness is necessary for pure poetry" (*AL*, [*After Lorca*,] 48), Spicer the aspiring dead man wrote to Lorca the dead man, his gay Andalusian forebear, and he told his admiring coterie of younger poets that "the emotions of the poem are not the emotions of the poet." Spicer's double-voiced discourse, desirous and reviling, participatory and transgressive, transforms the weighty matter of the grand canon into its negative correlative, a Grand Canyon of emptied-out space-text into which ghostly messages swarm to inhabit parasitically, as they do the poet's own body. Thus, with regard to the passage from Joel Fineman which opened this discussion, the double origin of the structure which comprises Jack Spicer's poetry is the homosexual (gay) body of Jack Spicer and the homosocial body of Western poetry; both must be killed off in a writing process which simultaneously invokes and murders them, calls them into absent presence.[2]

The particular language that ravaged Spicer and also served as his weapon against the canon was the language of camping, the gay vernacular whose wealth lies in a rich deployment of puns, double entendres, sexual innuendo, gender parody, and that peculiar histrionic redundancy he campily characterizes as "Negros [sic] in blackface." In his prose piece, **"Excerpts from Oliver Charming's Diary,"** Spicer identifies camping as an ethnic style, a vernacular, a minority discourse:

> "We homosexuals are the only minority group that completely lacks any vestige of a separate cultural heritage. We have no songs, no folklore, even our customs are borrowed from our upper-middleclass mothers," he [S.] said.
>
> "What about camping?" I [Oliver Charming] asked. "Isn't that a cultural pattern worthy at least of Ruth Benedict's cunt?"
>
> "What about camping?" he asked rhetorically. "A perpetual Jewish vaudeville joke—or at the very best, a minstrel show impeccably played by Negros [sic] in blackface."
>
> The trouble with S. is that he doesn't understand Martian . . .
>
> (*Collected Books* 344)

While this exchange is by no means an unambiguous endorsement of the vernacular, the debate, cast in the witty repartee that characterizes its subject, acknowledges the post-war gay male community as a burgeoning presence which might do well to define itself as an identifiable culture with specific interests. Furthermore, it suggests that camp is synonymous or at least coextensive with poetry (through Martian, the third element of the equation), thus affirming poetry as the voice of the typically silenced, though, again through the mediation of the Martian trope, agency is displaced from political human subjects to disembodied extraplanetary energy. Since Spicer's period of mature poetic productivity coincided with the years in which his home, San Francisco—a major military base where ex-soldiers could meet and fraternize—emerged as the center of gay men's culture and of alternative, anti-academic literary activity, and yet predated by

several years the era of self-conscious gay activism (he died a year before the first gay community center in the country opened—in, of course, his native San Francisco), his work bears the stamp of manifesto in spite of its concerted effort at dematerialization. In fact, Stan Persky, one of the younger members of the Berkeley Renaissance coterie after it had migrated across the Bay, has described Spicer, Duncan, and Robin Blaser as having a conscious missionary sense of lineage:

> (they) "not only kept alive a public homosexual presence in their own work, but kept alive a tradition, teaching us about Rimbaud, Crane and Lorca. . . . They carried into the contemporary culture the tradition of homosexual art and were sensitive to the work of European homosexual contemporaries. There was a conscious searching out, in fraternity, of homosexual writers. Thus, in my 'training' as a poet, homoerotic novels would be recommended to me. . . . This was at a time when the English departments of the country told us that Walt Whitman wasn't gay." Because of their local stature, the three men helped to create "a social milieu in which it was possible to be gay."[3]

Camping is the primary mode of Spicer's poetry; ideally suited to his project in that it manifests through parody and negativity, its hyperreality mocks dominant cultural claims on the real. To draw the analogy to another marginalized culture, camp is the gay version of African-American signifying, exemplary of what Renato Rosaldo has termed "wit as a weapon in subaltern social analysis":

> Precisely because of their oppression, subordinate people often avoid unambiguous literal speech. They take up more oblique modes of address laced with double meanings, metaphor, irony and humor. They often hone their skills through repartee and . . . taunting banter. . . . The subversive potential and the sheer fun of speech play go hand in hand. Wit and figurative language enable not only the articulation of grievances and aspirations under repressive conditions but also the analysis of conflicts and ironies produced by differences of class, race, gender, and sexual orientation.[4]

Rosaldo's mention of the "biting self-mockery" as a common feature of the subaltern's humorous social commentary bears relevance to camping and to Spicer's entire aesthetic as well. Supremely expressive in its indirection, irony, and humor, camping, which Fredric Jameson has termed the "hysterical sublime," is a style (not only verbal, but primarily verbal for my purposes) both modern and postmodern in that its structure both necessarily acknowledges and denies any antecedent emotional referent, nodding to its dominant cultural prototypes only in terms of the most violent deconstruction through exaggeration.[5] But violence implies emotion—the outrage of abandonment and betrayal, and is born of nostalgia and piety—the double bind of Spicer's debt to the Western tradition. The relationship of homosexuality to homosociality is not only one of uneasy and ambiguous proximity but of downright trauma. Camping up the canon is the primary strategy of Spicer's intertextual offensive, his weapon of revenge against a tradition that has betrayed him. In wielding it, he remakes the language.

Thus, paradoxically, Spicer's poetry not only *dis*embodies the great and apparently straight tradition, and also himself as an individual gay man; its very negativity positively asserts and actively *embodies* a gay community through its language; furthermore, it documents the gay subculture of the 1950s and '60s as a minority group. This positive constitution of one community/structure over another implies that this community can be read as a text allegorically commenting on its oppressive and/or closeted parent cultures; the ghostly origin buried within, and allegorically glossed, is both the straight community—the homosocial dominant culture—and also the older homoerotic poets and cultures retroactively understood as comprising a "gay tradition"—and that both of these parental figures, the straight father and the gay father—need to be ghosted—killed and ghostwritten into the service of some new poetics of community and of sexuality. I'd like to turn to one poem, "Car Song," from *Heads of the Town up to the Aether,* which nods to and rewrites (ghostwrites) an earlier sexual rebel. The poem articulates a vexed commentary upon the parent poem; the parent poem in turn is a vestigial form imprinted on the new poem, emptying it out Here is "Car Song":

> Away we go with no moon at all
> Actually we are going to hell.
> We pin our puns to our backs and cross in a car
> The intersection where lovers are.
> The wheel and the road turn into a stair
> The pun at our backs is a yellow star.
> We pinned our puns on the windshield like
> We crossed each crossing in hell's despite.

One of the notes meant to clarify this text reads: "'I like it better in L.A. because there're more men and they're prettier,' someone said in the Handlebar tonight" (*HT* 119).

The multiple puns (moon, p/buns, cross/cruise, star/stair/stare) in this spare incantation, as well as the focus on p/buns as indices of differ-ence, point complicatedly toward a coextension of language, physical/erotic body parts, sacredness and cursedness. These puns, reified in the poem, refer to the vernacular ("vernacular": the language of the homeborn slave—the argot of the other within the state's boundaries); its elaborate wit, word-play on sexual imagery and/or reversals or exaggerations of stereotypical sex roles, broadcasts itself, like the yellow star, as insignia of otherness.[6] The yellow star is also the "buns," or "moon," the flaunting of erotic and erogenous body parts through costume and physical mannerism, which subject the wearer to the objectifying gaze, or "stare," of potential partners and also judgmental members of the dominant culture. The emphasis on "crossing" suggests the martyrdom and oppression of a gay person coming from Spicer's strict Calvinist background, but more importantly indicates gay culture as a "crossover" or liminal culture—"crossdressing," "gender-benders," crossing/cruising between two worlds—"intersections where lovers are." The act of love is a meeting of worlds, here, an intersection—a marriage—of heaven and hell. The vestigial form invoked here is the ghost of William Blake. Spicer's poem, drenched with the loneliness of life on the borderline, finds precedence in the marginality of Blake's self-consciously childish and spiritual belief in the free expression of physical love. The ambiguous ending of "Car Song," with its Blakean phrase, "in hell's despite," as well as the rhythm of Spicer's poem echoes "The Clod and the Pebble," one of the *Songs of Experience,* which unlike other poems in the series has no complement in the *Songs of Innocence*:

> "Love seeketh not Itself to please,
> Nor for itself hath any care;
> But for another gives its ease,
> And builds a Heaven in Hell's despair."
>
> So sang a little Clod of Clay
> Trodden with the cattle's feet
> But a Pebble of the brook,
> Warbled out these metres meet:
>
> "Love seeketh only Self to please,
> To bind another to its delight;
> Joys in another's loss of ease,
> And build a Hell in Heaven's despite."[7]

These dialectically juxtaposed ways of understanding what is called love articulate exactly the ambivalence Spicer envinced not only toward the dominant heterosexist culture, but also toward his own gay community, with the self-seeking of its individual members vying with an acknowledged need for bonding and friendship if that community is to survive at all. The note also ambiguously holds the line between vapid bartalk and campily positive assertion of cultural values. L.A., of course, is Los Angeles, the city of angels: Heaven, or the Pebble's provocatively hellish rejoinder to the assertion of star-crossed love in the verse part of Spicer's poem. It is at least another reference to mixing worlds, since angels like ghosts are crossover figures who inhabit both invisible and visible worlds, who have bodies only at will, and who mediate between heaven and earth.

What is compelling about Spicer's use of Blake as the vestigial parent of a cruising poem is the simultaneous sardonic and nostalgic allegorizing of Blake's Romanticism. As the Romantic poet most occupied with spiritual realms and otherwordly prophesying. Blake espoused a "poetics of outside" similar to Spicer's—not only should the poet live outside the dominant culture and embody values in direct opposition to it, but poetry itself comes from outside the poet's willed creative power—through dictation. Blake's preoccupation with the denizens of heaven—angels—gets rewritten into Spicer's preoccupation with the tropes of Mars as the site for poetic production, and of angels as gay men ("angel" was in fact a gay vernacular term for gay man, and a frequently recurring figure in gay literature).[8] "'I like it better in the city of angels because there're more men and they're prettier,' someone said in the Handlebar tonight." In another poem, **"Orpheus in Hell,"** hell is a bar with a "jukebox groaning of the damned"—if the Handlebar (its name an ironic pun given the reality of police raids on bars at which gay men were subject to arrest for touching each other) is hell, the speaker is "building a Heaven in Hell's despair" by invoking L.A. and its angels, although in fact the statement smacks of an illusory, grass-is-greener desire to believe in a less oppressive environment.[9] The oppositions that Blake constructs—clod/pebble, selfless/selfish as well as self/other, soft/hard, land/water—become in Spicer's poem a dizzying series of metamorphoses—wheel and road become a stair, round and straight become spiral, horizontal becomes vertical, front becomes back. One could extend this—male and female, active and passive, nature and culture, appearance and truth, top and bottom, Heaven and Hell become relative terms insofar as they have meaning at all; they become simply indices of difference and self-difference, constant change in which they turn into something different even from their own opposites. Blake's neat rhythm becomes skewed, and rhyme becomes off-rhyme: all/hell, stair/star, like/despite.

All this to suggest that the love of clod and pebble, both passive and motionless in their respective settings, takes on a series of twists and deviations—movement, random and frantic, snatches life from the jaws of hell.

Spicer's specifically homoeroticized revision of "The Clod and the Pebble" blows the cover off the Romantic canon's dissimulation and/or displacement of such homoerotic content. In a roundabout way it touches on one of Spicer's favorite themes—Beat-baiting and, in particular, Ginsberg-baiting. Ginsberg has widely publicized his felt connection to Blake as a guiding inspiration: well-known is his anecdote of hearing the voice of Blake reciting "Ah Sunflower" when, as an undergraduate at Columbia, he lay on his dorm-room bed disconsolate. The story has the power and narrative structure of a conversion experience, a metaphysical rescue. For Ginsberg, Blake represented a vast prophetic consciousness that gave mystical meaning to his sexual loneliness and suffering—poetry dignified the taboo, spiritualized the dregs of social life. Naming otherwise unnameable "sordid realities" in religious terms redeemed them. "Howl," for instance, owes its most obvious debts to Blake and Whitman, with its longline paeans to "angel-headed hipsters searching the neon streets at dawn, burning for that ancient heavenly connection."[10] This rhapsodic cry of pain is Ginsberg's Blake, the sacralizer of the debased. Although "Howl" makes several specific references to homoerotic activity, these are enumerating along with and disappear inside a catalogue of scenarios of social outsiderhood, each of which is given equal weight: drug use, mental illness, the physical hardship of homelessness, visionary alcoholism transfigured into terms that suggest the search for enlightenment conducted by Ginsberg himself and his group of ambiguously straight cameradoes. Ginsberg celebrates an outlaw homosociality which includes homosexuality as an almost furtive subset.

By appropriating Ginsberg's prime Romantic legitimator and turning one of his verses into a cruising song, Spicer is localizing the grand sweep of Ginsberg's mystical claims. A **"Car Song"** is considerably more specific, modest, disciplined, high-tech, and culturally specific than a "howl," a bestial, indeterminate, preverbal burst of emotion. Impatient with what he considers Ginsberg's disingenuously innocent primitivism, Spicer positions Blake in his own camp of jaded and restless experience, intersection and mobility ranging over a two-dimensional post-modern surface—the intersection where lovers are—rather than the archeological metaphorizing of Ginsberg's "ancient heavenly connection." Spicer's phrase "crossed each crossing in Hell's despite" is also an oblique swipe at the Beats' most valued image— the car full of men traversing the country in search of visions. The Beat men on the road cling to their heterosexuality with such fervor that it is immediately questionable. Spicer goes for the jugular, claiming greater honesty by exposing his "puns," his yellow star.

What is the purpose of Spicer's picking on Ginsberg, a fellow-rebel in the fight for visibility against the complacently vicious 1950s and the academic canon, a fellow gay man trying to survive an historical transition from total invisibility to recognition, with all the violent backlash attendant on such a change? One affirmative answer is that a necessarily oppositional culture really comes into its own when internal differences can be acknowledged at a public level— cultural integrity is as much about difference as it is about solidarity. However, I think this question also touches on one of the uncomfortable subtexts of this discussion: given that Spicer's work is a gay commentary on a tradition that dissimulates its own homoeroticism, and given that he is writing in an historical moment in which gay men were beginning to be perceived and to perceive themselves as a community with a culture and with political interests—but as yet had no political voice and were subject to the most degrading legal and social harassment—given this acute and poignant positioning in social and literary history, one must consider how the double-consciousness which any oppressed persons experiences operates in this instance. Writing the gay community, Spicer simultaneously undermines the potential spectrum of its variety. He writes himself into and out of existence. The vestigial forms appear in his work as encomia and as bitter revilements. In charging Ginsberg with "not doing it right," Spicer articulates an internalized, pebblish homophobia, casting Ginsberg, that loveable, popular, paradigmatically cloddish would-be fool of God, as a *shande fur die goyim*: a disgrace before the straight dominant culture, a sellout to the macho Beat boys. With respect to the emergent gay culture or any self-consciously marginal culture, the pebble/clod difference parallels that of segregation v. integration. The fight against the fathers gets displaced, according to their parental designs, onto a fight against one's siblings. We see this again and again as the dominant culture plays non-dominant groups off against each other. The

ghosts still rule from their other world, their burial ground within the structure of Spicer's poetry, calling the shots from between the lines that would master them. I feel the need to come out from behind the vague term "ambivalence" and use the words "internalized self-hatred" because I find that much commentary on Spicer takes him at his word when he advocates pure loneliness, "outside," self-ghostifying, violent self-abnegation in the service of language. This tendency paradoxically feeds the construction of a personality cult, which is an interesting phenomenon but could stand some critique, and also encourages a belief that it is noble or even possible to escape into the freedom of pure language. This is problematic and ahistorical. Contorted, brilliant, electrifying, Spicer's camping instantiates clod and pebble, empowered by community and embarrassed to be taking up space. No human being should have to be a lightning rod.

Notes

1. *The Collected Books of Jack Spicer,* ed. Robin Blaser (Santa Barbara: Black Sparrow Press, 1977). Henceforth references to the books within this book will appear in the text using the following codes: *After Lorca (AL); Admonitions (A); Lament for the Makers (LM); Heads of the Town up to the Aether (HT); Book of Magazine Verse (BMV).*

2. The term "homosocial," as well as the concept of the "homosocial/homosexual" continuum, is developed by Eve Sedgewick in *Between Men* (New York: Columbia Univ. Press, 1985). See esp. the introductory chapter.

3. John D'Emilio quotes Persky in *Sexual Politics, Sexual Communities: The Making of a Homosexual Minority in the United States 1940-70* (Chicago: Univ. of Chicago Press, 1983) 180.

4. Renato Rosaldo, *Culture and Truth* (Boston: Beacon Press, 1989) 190-93.

5. Fredric Jameson, "Baudelaire as Modernist and Postmodernist," *Lyric Poetry: Beyond New Criticism,* eds. Chaviva Hosek and Patricia Parker (Ithaca: Cornell, 1986) 262.

6. See Houston A. Baker, *Blues, Ideology, and Afro-American Literature* (Chicago: Univ. of Chicago Press, 1984) xii.

7. William Blake, "The Clod and the Pebble," *Songs of Innocence and of Experience,* ed. Geoffrey Keynes (New York: Orion Press, 1967) pl. 32.

8. See "angel" in Bruce Rodgers' *The Queen's Vernacular: A Gay Lexicon* (San Francisco: Straight Arrow, 1972).

9. Spicer, *One Night Stand & Other Poems* (Bolinas: Grey Fox Press, 1980).

10. Allen Ginsberg, "Howl," *Howl and Other Poems* (San Francisco: City Lights, 1956).

TITLE COMMENTARY

The Collected Books of Jack Spicer

ROBIN BLASER (ESSAY DATE 1975)

SOURCE: Blaser, Robin. "The Practice of Outside." In *The Collected Books of Jack Spicer*, by Jack Spicer, edited by Robin Blaser, pp. 271-88. Los Angeles: Black Sparrow Press, 1975.

In the following excerpt, Blaser considers Spicer's Collected Books, *examining his philosophy that poetry is necessary for understanding the real and that poetry, not the poet, carries the truth, placing the poet outside the poetic act.*

> With fifteen cents and that I could get a
>   subway ride in New York. My heart
> Is completely broken. Only an enemy
> Could pick up the pieces.
> "Fragments of what," the man asked, "what?"
> A disordered devotion towards the real
> A death note. With fifteen cents and real
> Estate I could ride a subway in New York. No
> Poet starved. They died of it.
>
>   (from a Spicer notebook, late, 1964)

At first this essay was short and simple—about Jack. But that became a reduction which every twist and turn of the work denied—a biography without the world the poet earned or a split between the man and the work which drank him up and left him behind. I fell into the experience of another poet's request: *until you understand a writer's ignorance, presume yourself ignorant of his understanding.*[1] It is difficult, out of friendship and care, to find details disappearing into details rather than into meanings. My essay then became watchful of the context of the poetry and of the composing "real" that is Jack's concern. His ignorance is not one of lack of assurance. He knew the good and size of his work and he had assurance to give away to others. His ignorance seems to have been of the cost of this venture which he turned into a narrative. It is part of his notion that poetry is necessary to the composition or knowledge of the "real" and this drew him into a combat for the context of poetry—that it was an act or event of the real, rather than a discourse true only to itself. He had said early on in conversation with a young poet that one had first to learn to use the I and then to lose it. This becomes an attack on the "subjective aim" and assurance of a whole culture. And it cuts the ground from under a poetry that ceaselessly returns to wrap itself around a personality. It was especially costly to a poet who refused those resolving images of the writer as victim or hero. In the face of this work, both hero and victim are humanisms which do not measure up. In an extreme move to gain what he variously called a dictation, the unknown, an outside, Jack's work contradicts them as resolutions or explanations of anything. They become names rather than acts, as in the last poem he wrote at the end of the *Book of Magazine Verse.* In an earlier poem on heroes, he laughs at them and at the same time puts them back into a mystery.

> Heros eat soup like anyone else. Sometimes
>   the kitchen is so far away
> That there is no soup. No kitchen. An open
>   space of ground recovered by
> The sky.
> Heros eat soup like anyone else. False
>   ground.
> Soup
> Of the evening
> Beautifull soup.
> And the sky stays there not an image
> And the heros
> Like the image of an image
> (What is made of soup from)
> Zooms.
>
>   (*Language*)

In *The Collected Books*, it is as if the reader and the poet had to begin again—not with a false ground—perhaps with a ground that is simultaneously true and false—where a composition begins again. In *Admonitions* he took it up in a poem for himself, "For Jack":

> Tell everyone to have guts
> Do it yourself
> Have guts until the guts
> Come through the margins
> Clear and pure
> Like love is.

And in "A Postscript for Charles Olson" at the end of the same book:

> If nothing happens it is possible
> To make things happen.
> Human history shows this
> And an ape
> Is likely (presently) to be an Angel.

Simply and almost childishly expressed, this opens into the ranging care of his work and into its extremity, where the poems carry "messages" and the poet tends to disappear from his work. There may be, in this sense, an "angel of the work."

The poetry of *The Collected Books* begins in 1957, when that composing factor—the dictation, the unknown, or the outside—enters the work, and Jack began to construct a poetry that was not lyric but narrative. This narrative, he came—"jokingly," he said—to call "the serial poem." It had to hold on to a motivation that was not strictly his own. [. . .]

Jack's lively and storied language pushes us into a polarity and experienced dialectic with something other than ourselves. It involves a reversal of language into experience, which is not a dialexis between ourselves or a discourse true only to itself, but a broken and reforming language which composes a "real." The doubleness of a man and a world are recovered to operate in the language. Where, so to speak, a public language has closed itself in order to hold a meaning, it becomes less than the composition of meaning. It stops and relegates both the language and its hold on the "real" to the past. The place of language in the social, as a performance of the "real," is displaced to a transparency and becomes an imposition rather than a disclosure. In Jack's work, a fundamental quarrel with a discourse that does not hold a present or a future possibility is apparent from the visibility and invisibility of *After Lorca*, through the logos and low-ghost of *Heads of the Town up to the Aether* and the dissonant noisy voices of *The Holy Grail* to a culminating argument in the pieces of language in the book *Language*. The last poems of the *Book of Magazine Verse* turn repeatedly from an anger and rage to a simple love that flows from and composes out of the real. A *reopened language* lets the unknown, the Other, the outside in again as a voice in the language. Thus, the reversal is not a reduction, but an openness. The safety of a closed language is gone and its tendency to reduce thought to a reasonableness and definiteness is disturbed. Poetry has always kept the unreasonable voice but it is said to be true only in a poetic discourse and, of course, peripheral to the reason our lives are referred to. Here in the insistence of Jack's outside, an other than the reasonable is said to enter the real. The real doubles in the experience and in the language. The voice arguing the necessity of an outside may strike a reader as odd since the outside, in whatever sense one takes it, is usually assumed. It belongs then to a discourse or to a science. Its placement here as a composing factor in the poem disturbs our sense of a settled relation to language. It does, as I hope the ensuing argument makes clear, insist that language is not so simply relational, but rather a knowing, an event in men's lives, as words are important to hold on to whatever it is that composes us.

From *After Lorca* on, Jack works in a poetry that is a "compound of the visible and the invisible." These words are not so difficult once one realized that the visibility of men in speech opens on an invisibility he has not spoken or thought. This fundamental polarity extends into a space that is not recognized. The movement of Jack's work is to retie language and experience as they are composed in the exchange of visibility and invisibility. Perhaps, it was his knowledge as a professional linguist that brought him to this point in an understanding of a composing "real,"—as a "sense" seems visible and a "non-sense" seems fallen out of the visible or about to enter it.

Following a lecture on his own work, he was accused of being more interested in truth than in poetry and he replied, "Well, I'm interested in being a conveyor of messages." (Vancouver Lecture II) This insistence upon an outside becomes an intricate argument for a transcendence—both a distance and a verticality. This verticality—and the looseness of any discourse we have at hand to hold on to it—is caught exactly in the rope trick of "A Textbook of Poetry":

> The Indian rope trick. And a little Indian boy climbs up it. And the Jungians and the Freudians and the Social Reformers all leave satisfied. Knowing how the trick was played. There is nothing to stop the top of the rope though.

Jack was not much given to explaining his work, for it seemed to him that was the reader's job as much as his own, but one of his observations draws attention here. "A Textbook of Poetry," he says, takes the divine in relation to the human and *The Holy Grail* turns this around to take the human in relation to the divine. (Vancouver Lecture II) As I note here in the essay, the word divine is among the ruins of a discourse, broken in thought and experience into belief and disbelief. In Jack's work, the divine is resituated in a composition where belief and disbelief are composing elements of its meaning. The dictation of the outside brings us up against a number of words that float in and out of a meaning. It is not, for Jack, any ordinary supernaturalism, but literal to a condition that may be called a "polar logic" of experience. A meaning is constantly playing within the poetry because the poetry in its openness is more than a meaning and in the composition less than a meaning. Unfixed. A meaning in the poems is also constantly doubling back to meet the manhood and the ghostly, silver voices of it ("A Textbook"), where death is an interrogation close to the world because it is not ourselves. Death and ghostliness in this work must be seen, not as a choice against life or even a helplessness within it, but as a literal pole, where life is present to a point and then suddenly absent from an articulation. The curious thing about language and experience, which haunts Jack's work, is that they are so immediately reversible. And as a friend said, discussing this essay with me, if you don't have knowledge of that reversal, then you don't have the heart of it. This goes for translation, as in *After Lorca,* and for all directnesses of language. Suddenly, in the contemporary experience, the formal, public language does not hold and our language in the midst of a recomposition has to account for what is stopped, lost, loose and silent. I am reminded of Merleau-Ponty's "wild-meaning" and "wild-logos" which include an experience of a "birth of meaning."

It was for this reason Jack refused to accept a language for poetry that is a poetic discourse true only to itself and as such, simply another discourse patterned on the language system we have lived in, and though it is heightened, it has remained equally peripheral, an addition to the real. The "infinitely, small vocabulary," the purity and pointing of *After Lorca* comes into a literal condition, where the meaning plays and composes before our eyes. This comes to be an essential aspect of the narration or serial poem. According to Jack, "you have to go into a serial poem not knowing what the hell you're doing." "You have to be tricked into it, it has to be some path that you've never seen on a map before. . . ." It has to be a renewed language and information that becomes a kind of map. Ideally, Jack worked in that long form without looking back and without thought of the previous poem, so that the poet could be led by what was composing. The serial poem is often like a series of rooms where the lights go on and off. It is also a sequence of energies which burn out, and it may, by the path it takes, include the constellated. There is further a special analogy with serial music: the voice or tongue, the tone, of the poem sounds individually, as alone and small as the poet is (the cleft palate of Jack's example), but sounded in series, it enters a field.[2] In this way the dictation and the serial form join to bring the poet, his voice, tone and stance into a dimension where he is either lost or found. A "necessary world" is composed in the serial poem.

For this occasion, which is Jack's, I have chosen to follow this polarity through. Our words for it may lead to confusion: a dualism, a dialectic, a contrarium. The point is to take the doubleness out of statement and return the process to experience where the language composes. This man, now silent, leaves us to face his work. The darkness, the torn shapes and ghosts of Jack's poems are an admission and they are also an openness, where thought and feeling begin again. They shadow the laughter, the jokes and the naturalness of his language. Such polarity is not reductive to a simple-minded authenticity or to a signature that is only one's self. The "only-feeling" of so much bad and helpless verse. Where I have found the public language removed from a real, or only, by an irony Jack's ghosts laugh at, an expression of ourselves, I have also found Jack's work returning the language to us. It brings us close to "what must be thought" and to what has been under or outside our discourse (Foucault). Merleau-Ponty again comes to mind in his remarks on dialectic become statement, "embalmed dialectic," and the edge we have reached where we must "recommence perception" and a "thinking speech."[3] Such speech will account for the other that opens before us. It amazes me that Jack Spicer's work moves us to this point, which contemporary philosophers, especially Foucault and Merleau-Ponty, have argued. Though they inform my essay in the effort I am making to say that this is a fundamental poetic concern, Jack did not know their work or care. He moved from the necessity. His fascination with the "unknown" including the complex experience of the contents of an invisibility led him to emphasize the silence around and between poems. This renewed speech, in another man's words, "teaches us a necessity that is not logical but ontological":

> Thus we were to understand that speech is between two silences: it gives expression to an experience that is mute and ignorant of its own meaning, but only in order to make that experience appear in its purity; it does not break our contact with the things, but it draws us from our state of confusion with all things in order to awaken us to the truth of their presence and to render palpable their relief and the tie that binds us to them. At least such is the speech that speaks in conformity with its essence and . . . does not cede to the vertigo of eloquence, does not wish to suffice to itself or close in upon itself and upon its sense, but opens upon and leads to the outside.[4]

To trace this is difficult. I begin with Jack's visibility and invisibility in *After Lorca,* with the life and death of one poet flowing into another. But I wish to give this a context in a more than personal challenge to the visibility we understand ourselves to be speaking in our language. Or, I wish to take it back to the composition, the ontology, the beginning of a language that is full of the world. It is within language that the world speaks to us with a voice that is not our own. This is, I believe, a first and fundamental experience of dictation and correspondence—the dead speaking to us in language is only one level of the outside that ceaselessly invades our thought. In this way, I mean to suggest Jack's effort to trace the vectors of a composing real in his "disordered devotion." In his books, we begin in an exchange of life and death, visibility and invisibility, known and unknown, human and divine. In the reversal of language into experience, these fold into one another and unfold, composing as voices in our language. They are elemental and also ultimate at either end of a narration. To understand the "outside," that curiously naive-sounding insistence of this work, it will not do to take off on those supernaturalisms which precondition and explain the experience. The dictation remains persistently of the world and as it is unknown, it moves into the language as the imageless moves into image. Jack's discipline of emptying himself in order to allow his language to receive an other than himself may be traced back to his tradition and sources, but he works there independently and fiercely. The discipline is intended to reopen the discourse. (Here I could place him among his direct peers—Poe, Mallarmé, Artaud and Duchamp in their emphasis upon loss of meaning turning into necessity of meaning.) There is a dangerous factor in such work, for it removes the manhood or the image of it, which the settled discourse gathered and held together in a stoppage or finitude that spoke only of himself. My companions in this thought, which Jack's work forces me to articulate, will help clarify this openness later. Just now, I need only say that Jack's "outside" implies a world and a cosmology without an image. It is unknown and entering the time of language again.

If, along with my sources, I am right that a discourse, a language system, has ended in a "transparency" of descriptions and relations (Foucault), which set the imaginative apart from the real and give it up to the ideal or by a twist, dump the whole business into a sadly limited personality, then I may take seriously the profound consequences of the strangeness and estrangement that enter Jack's work. That "transparency" leaves entire realms unacknowledged. They become unknown, unimaged and unthought. Such "transparency" reverses itself into a lie. And the unknown comes forward without visibility— outside oneself and outside one's language, but it begins to compose itself within language. This brings us to a "recommencement of perception" that has barely begun, and within it, we re-enter a composition of the real.

> Strange, I had words for dinner
> Stranger, I had words for dinner
> Stranger, strange, do you believe me?

Honestly, I had your heart for supper
Honesty has had your heart for supper
Honesty honestly are your pain

I burned the bones of it
And the letters of it
And the numbers of it
That go 1, 2, 3, 4, 5, 6, 7
And so far.

Stranger, I had bones for dinner
Stranger, I had bones for dinner
Stranger, stranger, strange, did you believe me?
                    (["Magic" in] *Heads of the Town*)

In this poem, the movement from words to bones is an exact expression of a condition. The words disappear into the bones and even those are eaten by the strange voice of the poem. The Orphic explanatory note to the poem makes it clear that in the telling, the voice of the poem is a ghostly other and outside of meaning.

> Orpheus was never really threatened by the
>   Underworld during his visits there. In this
>   poem they present him with a diplomatic
>   note.
> Honesty does not occur again in the poem.
> The numbers do.

The poem and the note both return us to time, a running of the numbers and a traversal. This poem is from the first section of the book *Heads of the Town up to the Aether,* a hell of meaning, a playing out of sense and nonsense, which precedes the concern for paradise in the final section.

The entrance of a strangeness to the work takes many forms—most obviously in the ghosts, who are "not the same as the dead" (Vancouver Lecture III), but who are voices and shadows that enter life. This haunted meaning wanders in and out of the poems. And it is a proposal of the wildness of meaning—a lost and found, a going and coming. It is harsh and beautiful—and, as Jack would say, "scary." It takes the question—who is speaking in a poem?—and changes it into a question of where he is speaking—from what place—in what order—in what composition—a shadowy participant in a folding with something outside himself. I may attach this to traditional motifs and to common experience—the sense of a "cosmic crypt," Spengler's dread, gnostic dualism, and so forth, but Jack's work does not stop in fear. It summons. It brings again into the present a beginning of a man and a world.[5]

The largest, most difficult proposal of this work is then to be found in the stake of Jack's poetics. The outside as it becomes technical to our experience reposes a tense discourse, which interrogates the humanism and anthropomorphism of what is usually thought to be the poem's expression. The guide here is not the poet of a limited biographical occasion because he is guided toward the disclosure of a tied and retied heart, a manhood entangled with the world. This disclosure must not be reduced to psyche, however much we find it in a time of one man or in the disfigurations of our own time. It is more likely that the limited, psychic man, pushed in this direction, will find another, still unfigured manhood. For this reason, Jack would remove himself, as that which is expressed, from his language in order to reopen the worldliness of language. An old story comes to mind that once when Pythagoras was asked what Chronos is, he answered that it is the psyche of the universe. His answer implies a differently posed intelligence. As for the disclosure of the retied heart, that veiled thing that is so mixed with thought, I am reminded of Pound's lovely Latin citation in Canto XC: *the human soul is not love, but from it love proceeds, and therefore, the soul does not delight in itself, but in the love which proceeds from it.* I know these are difficult elements that bring us into a love composed within a commotion of belief and disbelief, but I am after the public love in these poems and the magic of disturbance Jack used among his friends, as if nothing could rest, not even friendship. The love tends to manifest itself as a folding and unfolding of a real which composes out of North Beach and Berkeley and then leads to an outward of contents which are unspoken, unthought and unknown, like the possible diamond in **Book of Magazine Verse.** Why there is this flowing kind of genesis that one either dams up, forgets and gives up to a dead discourse or participates in, is difficult to put into words because it is process and names pop out of it and are never up to date. It may be recognized as elemental. The genesis changes the lyric question, who is speaking, into a double voice. This double voice, as it accounts for the "dictation" opens into speech and begins a redefinition of the heart. I put it back, so to speak, in an ancient sense into the thought that it is participant in intelligence. By way of the poetics, the constant elemental aspect of poetic thought, we "recommence the perception." As perceptions are veils of the heart, at the edge of them there folds an other than oneself. We reach, especially in Jack's work, the poem's real business, an "exhibition of world" (Heidegger). I have, I think, said enough to foreground this extravagant outside, its presence and absence, the edge of its necessity. To be

without a discourse, or rather to be within "a disappearance of discourse" (Foucault), as this essay argues, is something like being in a space ship. The outside invades and doubles over us.

A poetry that composes that meeting is tied to the event in the language. One is, to Jack's sporting language, batting or pitching or catching one's life. This is the terrible meaning of

> God is a big white baseball that has nothing to
>   do but go in a curve or a straight line. I
>   studied geometry in highschool and know
>   that this is true.

> Given these facts the pitcher, the batter, and the
>   catcher all look pretty silly.
>   (*Book of Magazine Verse*)

To live in a discourse, to use a discourse, which does not hold on to this composition is, as Jack says in **Language,** to "have the ground cut from under us." In such circumstances the language of the real appears to belong to an imposed order rather than to a disclosed order that is performed in public speech. Just here, poetry may become a necessary function of the real, not something added to it. It can best handle thought that is a disclosure. In his last years, Jack talked about "the fix." He meant by that both a political and an economic fix that stops us. He also meant the language of it—a fix of the language that is not true to its own structure and that tends to stop the real in something one can only refer to. This brings forward in Jack's work both an explanation and a performance of all that poetry talking about itself, which has haunted contemporary poetry and annoyed a lot of readers. It does confuse when it is only a young man's desire to be a poet that is being expressed or an older one's failure to get through. In Jack's work, it is a renewal of language and an interrogation of it in terms of our inward and outward life—dangerous because the manhood in the language comes close to a disappearance. I think of Mallarmé's "master" who disappears from the "ceremony of his book" (Foucault).

Jack's oppositions and contrariness look destructive, even despairing, but they tend to bring forward a language that holds. We may read this as an aspect of his sure-footed Americanness—a Puritanism, a Calvinism at the heart of his experience. And certainly, his life-long interest in Hawthorne comes to mind. Such a reading could be useful, but it would, I think, lead to a misreading. Here, it is the holding power and what I have called the commotion of his work that I wish to describe. His last work, **Book of Magazine Verse,** is an example of this. The idea behind the title is an old one with Jack and it is meant to challenge the public place of poetry. The poems were written in order to prove that the magazines for which he wrote them would not publish them. It is a setup, of course, but that does not spoil the point he is making. Some of them are for magazines which cannot be expected to publish poetry, though Jack's point is that poetry belongs to the real of them, whether that real is of sports, jazz or politics. The only poems he actually submitted were for *The Nation* and they were predictably rejected. Jack commented that it would have spoiled everything if they'd been accepted. He seemed to want the bitter laughter I heard when the space where his poetry belonged turned out not to be there. The **Book of Magazine Verse** is an unfair interrogation of the public place of poetry. The poems of it combine an anger and an affirmation that unravels the real the magazines talk about:

> I can't stand to see them shimmering
>   in the impossible music of the Star
>   Spangled Banner. No
> One accepts this system better than poets
>   Their hearts healed for a few dollars.
> Hunt
> The right animals. I can't. The poetry
> Of the absurd comes through San Francisco
>   television. Directly connected
>   with moon-rockets.
> If this is dictation, it is driving
> Me wild.

The poem is dedicated to a young poet, Huntz, and in the poem, his name is changed into the act and event of the "Hunt" as a directive. The hunt for the right animals takes place in an absurd of the shimmering astronauts landing on the moon. The rage at the center of the poem is caught in this lifting of the Star Spangled Banner into space, a shimmering there as false as it is here. It is not, so to speak, a real landing on the moon, a movement beyond the walls, but an extension of the same discourse and its resulting social form. The landing on the moon would perhaps be real if it were not an extension into space of the same conditions. We have landed ourselves on the moon. As the work moves in those last poems from the imagination of a city on a "baseball diamond high / In the Runcible Mountain wilderness" (**Poems for the Vancouver Festival**, 1) toward a departure, "Things desert him" (**Poems for Down Beat**, 6), the shimmer is not true. The shimmering image of the astronauts suggests a beauty one would like to hold just there, but the words, "I can't stand to see them," turn that beauty back to what it covers. In a stunning refusal, Jack reverses language into experience, where it must begin again. The moon in the poem

disappears or is returned to what we will make of it. And the wildness of the poem is a loosened meaning. If one follows the contents of the serial narrative in this book and looks back on the field of its composition, the city on a diamond stands there on a Lewis Carroll mountain—a nonsense fundamental to the sense. This duplicity or commotion is remarkable in his thought and it was both terrible and joyous in his life, as a long list of friends, poets, and enemies may testify. He was so alive in the commotion he made around him. The condition of that beginning again in language and meaning is between our manhood, the anthropology of our thought, and everything outside its orders. It is, at times, almost a *divestment* of the memory of words. Undressed words. Jack shares the profound issue of this divestment in modern poetics, in its lack of wisdom and in its thought and feeling at the edge of a disclosure, with Mallarmé and Artaud.

In the movement of the whole of Jack's work toward the imagination of that city, which remains where he left it, only a possibility, there is also an *investment* of words. An installation. This is the "spiritual discipline" he says a poem must be—out of the dictation. For this Jack used an Orphic methodology, as if the cosmos or love had fallen into hell. The experience is tropic—in the turn, hell is discovered and the true and the false begin to play. And, unfortunately, as Jack says, the dictation will be true and false (tape, Vancouver Lecture III), because as a proposition of an ultimate duplicity in the real itself, the dictation will be wild and playful, a disappearance and an appearance, an invisibility and a visibility exchanging their powers in the heart. The looking into something as it composes in the poem, especially as it is of our own time, is to see what is on the other side, but not separate from this side or its terror. One can't see without meaning and this is the momentary interruption of the "I can't" in the poem for Huntz. As these last poems move to an open end,

> The poem begins to mirror itself.
>   The identity of the poet gets more obvious.
>   (*Poems for Down Beat*, 6)

The poems reflect this reversal of language into experience. This is a costly recovery of an "operative language" (Merleau-Ponty's phrase),

> which possesses meaning less than it is possessed by it, does not speak of it, but speaks *it*, or speaks *according to it*, or lets it speak and be spoken within us, breaks through our present.[6]

This language is then "open upon." In the last poems, the "identity of the poet" returns almost nakedly, driven by the wildness, just at the point where the poet is to disappear from his work. This insistence of the dictation that an outside, an other than ourselves, speaks to us notices first a disappearance or emptying out of a manhood from his language, and then watchfully approaches "a field" including the other and a "topography" that is a folding and unfolding of a real that contains us.[7] Such language may disclose a new manhood and a new visibility along with another courage.

The poet is in the field of his work. He becomes a voice sounded in series that is also another voice, a doubling in the heart of an intelligence. Jack's voice remained to the end outside the paradise or city of its concern because such a city is outside our time or at the edge of it. As his language is open upon an outside, whose meaning disturbs and changes, his poetry becomes a profound interrogation, an operation of language, because it is a meeting.

> You flicker,
> If I move my finger through a
>   candleflame, I know that there
>   is nothing there. But if I hold my
>   finger there a few minutes longer,
> It blisters.
> This is an act of will and the flame is
>   is not really there for the candle, I
> Am writing my own will
> Or does the flame cast shadows?
>   At Hiroshima, I hear, the shadows
>   of the victims were as if photographed
>   into concrete building blocks.
> Or does it flicker? Or are we both
>   candles and fingers?
> Or do they both point us to the
>   grapheme on the concrete wall—
> The space between it
> Where the shadow and the flame are one?
>   (Graphemics 6, *Language*)

Morphemics, Phonemics, Graphemics, as his book *Language* follows them through, will be "words" and "loves" in a composing real.

This is an extraordinary poetry for us to take on. It was, of course, for the most part not taken on at all, though it opened language again and again to the young who drifted across the country to meet Jack at his table in the bar. San Francisco became a loved habit of friends, bars, streets, the Broadway Tunnel, and Aquatic Park. His hours were pretty much set. If it became too quiet, Jack would disturb it and "make things happen." San Francisco is an odd place. With all the beauty and comfort of its landscape, it is the end of the land. It seems to be at the edge of something, a gated place, an end which opens again. And so one finds it in Jack's poems where the imagery of the sea carries an openness, strangeness and endlessness. This edge becomes a literal quality of his work.

It is this edginess which leads me to speak of Jack's poetic argument. It involves the place and context of poetry in a composition of the real, which I have already touched upon and now wish to tie down. This argumentativeness about poetics, as it is widely reflected in contemporary poetry, has been dismissed by the criticism as the weakness of poetry talking about itself. The helplessness of poetry mirroring itself. On the contrary, it is indicative of a new consciousness of the power and violence of language, and in Jack's work, it becomes an insistent argument for the performance of the real by way of poetry. I am reminded of Vico's far away argument that all thought and experience begin in poetry and of Heidegger's that we end there too. I do not wish to be long-winded, slap-dash or pretentious here at the end of a distinguished work, but it is in this issue of the context of poetry that I find a way to tell you the cost of what Jack tried to do.

Wherever I go I hear the question—what killed Jack Spicer? Some offer the comfortable explanation that it was booze. But most who knew him well say poetry. This is the hidden issue of what I wish to say. It's interesting that the question always takes the same form, as in a detective story, except they ask what rather than who. Jack collapsed in an elevator. Two days later I found him in a hospital. No one had been notified. His body had given way and his speech become a garble—just the other side of what he meant to say. Listening to him, I thought of Artaud's special language, another language that seems to begin again. And I thought of the "Martian" Jack sometimes spoke with his friends—full of laughter, catching us in what he was doing. One day I leaned over his bed and asked him to repeat the words or phrases he wanted to say because I would, I said, figure the pattern of the nonsense. The garble of his speech was the shadow of his sense and equally real. With extreme physical effort, he somehow retied his head and his speech to speak clearly. What he said, I've relegated to the end of this essay where I think it will be understood—just as I have had so much trouble understanding it. In between what I have already written and his last words, I wish to take on the context of the poetry. This is my way of explaining what he meant when he said language is "the furniture in the room" through which the world speaks. He was not in the final poetics speaking only of himself. The "disordered devotion towards the real" of the poem with which I opened is no naive realism, and what it leads to requires some meditation. Here, I return to the ignorance I spoke of. Jack did not, it seems, know how far he had to go. In that emptying out in order to free the language, which is part of his care, he found a discipline which suggests that we are free to think again.

Notes

1. Coleridge, *Biographia Literaria*, XII.

2. The possibility of this analogy was drawn to my attention in A. Lingis's preface to Merleau-Ponty's *The Visible and the Invisible* (Northwestern, 1968), pp. xlix-l: "serial music, Merleau-Ponty points out . . . , discovers the ability of any tone in a series to function as an individual sounded in a field and as the dominant, the field tone, the level at which the melody plays."

3. M. Merleau-Ponty, *The Visible and the Invisible,* p. 175.

4. C. Lefort in his "Foreword" to Merleau-Ponty's *The Visible and the Invisible*, pp. xxviii-xxix.

5. Here, I am informed by Henry Corbin's discussion of the stranger and the guide in *Avicenna and the Visionary Recital* (Pantheon, 1960), p. 16 ff.

6. Lingus, op. cit., p. liii.

7. See Merleau-Ponty's sense of visibility as it is discussed by Lingus, op. cit., p. 1 ff.

FURTHER READING

Biography

Charters, Ann. "Jack Spicer." In *Beat Down to Your Soul: What Was the Beat Generation?*, pp. 533-7. New York: Penguin Books, 2001.

Brief sketch of the author's life with some selections of his poetry.

Ellingham, Lewis, and Kevin Killian. *Poet Be Like God: Jack Spicer and the San Francisco Renaissance,* Hanover: University Press of New England, 1998, 425p.

Full-length biography on Jack Spicer's life and works.

Foster, Edward Halsey. *Jack Spicer.* Boisie, Idaho: Boise State University, 1991, 47p.

Brief biographical consideration of Jack Spicer's life and works.

Criticism

Chamberlain, Lori. "Ghostwriting the Text: Translation and the Poetics of Jack Spicer." *Contemporary Literature* 26, no. 4 (winter 1985): 426-42.

Examines Spicer's translations in After Lorca *as prefiguring his poetics of dictation and characteristic of postmodern poetics of translation, and considers the original Spicer poems included among the Lorca translations.*

Clarkson, Ross. "Jack Spicer's Ghosts and the Immemorial Community." *Mosaic* 34, no. 4 (December 2001): 199-211.

Examines Spicer's work After Lorca, *focusing on the poet's relationship to the deceased poet Garcia Lorca and demonstrating Spicer's central interest in community and its relationship to and communication with its dead.*

Davidson, Michael. "Incarnations of Jack Spicer: *Heads of the Town up to the Aether.*" *boundary 2* 6, no. 1 (fall 1977): 103-34.

Examines Spicer's philosophy of antinomianism, which encouraged learning through confrontation and opposition, and the space that exists between God and the poet as demonstrated in his work Heads of the Town up to the Aether.

Ellingham, Lewis. "The Death of Jack Spicer." *Ironwood* 28 (1986): 152-64.

Examines Spicer's alcoholism, his mindset during his final days, and the circumstances surrounding his death.

Ellingham, Lewis, and Kevin Killian. "Ducks for Grownups: Jack Spicer, Larry Kearney, Jamie MacInnis 1964." *Chicago Review* 43, no. 4 (fall 1997): 45-61.

Considers the troubled relationship between Beat figures Spicer, Larry Kearney, and Jaime MacInnis and recounts their activities in San Francisco in 1964.

Eshleman, Clayton. "The Lorca Working." *boundary 2* 6, no. 1 (fall 1977): 31-49.

Looks at After Lorca *and* Billy the Kid *as the pinnacles of the first half of Spicer's career, and considers how the poetry of* After Lorca *demonstrates a connection between the two works.*

Feld, Ross. "The Apostle's Grudge at the Persistence of Poetry." *Ironwood* 28 (1986): 188-94.

Considers Spicer's notion of poet as medium between poetry and God, with the poet and poetry both being ultimately meaningless in the presence of that communication.

Finkelstein, Norman M. "Jack Spicer's Ghosts and the Gnosis of History." *boundary 2* 9, no. 2 (winter 1981): 81-100.

Considers Spicer's poetic discourse, shaped by both Romantic and Modern influences, for its symbolic reliance on ghosts to synthesize those influences.

——. "The New Arcady." In *The Utopian Moment in Contemporary American Poetry*, pp. 68-101. London: Associated University Presses, 1993.

Looks at Spicer and Robert Duncan's differing uses of Romantic and Modern themes as resulting in complementary views of poetry.

FitzGerald, Dora. "Jack as Coyote." *Ironwood* 28 (1986): 147-50.

Offers personal reminiscences of Spicer as teacher and poet.

Gizzi, Peter. "The House That Jack Built: Preface to the Collected Lectures of Jack Spicer." *American Poetry Review* (January-February 1998): 26-7.

Considers Spicer's four lectures given in Vancouver in 1965 shortly before his death as the only authoritative account of his poetics beyond his poetry and letters.

Granger, John. "The Loss of the Bride in *Heads of the Town* and the Reclamation of the Text." *boundary 2* 6, no. 1 (fall 1977): 145-61.

Examines Spicer's three books in Heads of the Town up to the Aether *as presenting the poet's conditions of language, which is not centered around any time, place, or space.*

———. "The Idea of the Alien in the Four Dictated Books." *Ironwood* 28 (1986): 165-86.

Looks at Spicer's four dictated books as containing poetry at war with God and considers the distanced voices as "alien" and "other."

Hatlen, Burton. "Crawling into Bed with Sorrow: Jack Spicer's *After Lorca.*" *Ironwood* 28 (1986): 118-35.

Focuses on Spicer's language for its openness and examines After Lorca *for its relativistic individualism to uncover a grammar and rhetoric of "the other."*

Judy, Stephanie A. "'The Grand Concord of What': Preliminary Thoughts on Musical Composition in Poetry." *boundary 2* 6, no. 1 (fall 1977): 267-85.

Examines Poe's and Spicer's poetry for its creative musical language as it presents a "dynamism of thought and experience."

Liddy, James. "A Problem with Sparrows: Spicer's Last Stance." *boundary 2* 6, no. 1 (fall 1977): 259-66.

Examines Spicer's Book of Magazine Verse *and provides a sequence of notes on individual poems.*

McClure, Michael. "An Empire of Signs: Jack Spicer." In *Lighting the Corners: On Art, Nature, and the Visionary: Essays and Interviews,* pp. 113-27. Albuquerque: University of New Mexico College of Arts and Sciences, 1993.

Discusses Jack Spicer, including his relationship with other San Francisco Renaissance artists, and the art and theater scenes, and considers the nature of Spicer's work.

Rasula, Jed. "Spicer's Orpheus and the Emancipation of Pronouns." *boundary 2* 6, no. 1 (fall 1977): 51-102.

Looks at Spicer's work through the lens of Saussure's economic model of language to understand the dictation poetry as it brought about self-knowledge.

Riley, Peter. "The Narratives of *The Holy Grail.*" *boundary 2* 6, no. 1 (fall 1977): 163-90.

Examines Spicer's serial poem The Holy Grail *as it demonstrates the author's exploration of perception-as-love.*

Sadler, Frank. "The Frontier in Jack Spicer's *Billy the Kid.*" *Concerning Poetry* 9, no. 2 (fall 1976): 15-21.

Silliman, Ron. "Spicer's Language." In *Writing/Talks,* edited by Bob Perelman, pp. 167-91. Carbondale, Illinois: Southern Illinois University Press, 1985.

Considers the merit in Spicer's work outside the mythos that has grown up around his persona and reads the poetry of Language *and* Book of Magazine Verse *as dissimilar in style and intent.*

Stanley, George. "Diamond and Heart: The Transition in Jack Spicer's Poetry." *Ironwood* 28 (1986): 136-46.

Considers the poetic events that occur in Spicer's work during the transition between "For Billy" and "Apollo Sends Seven Nursery Rhymes to James Alexander I."

OTHER SOURCES FROM GALE:

Additional coverage of Spicer's life and career is contained in the following sources published by the Gale Group: *Contemporary Authors,* Vols. 85-88; *Contemporary Literary Criticism,* Vols. 8, 18, 72; *Dictionary of Literary Biography,* Vols. 5, 16, 193; *DISCovering Authors Modules: Poetry; Gay and Lesbian Literature,* Ed. 1; *Literature Resource Center;* and *World Poets.*

ANNE WALDMAN

(1945 -)

(Full name Anne Lesley Waldman) American poet, performance artist, and editor.

Anne Waldman is best known as a dynamic, performing poet who actively seeks to increase the popularity of poetry readings among the general public. A professor at the Naropa Institute in Boulder, Colorado, since 1974, Waldman has also toured as a performer in North America, Europe, and South America. According to Ann Charters, Waldman's "poetry exhibits the open-form aesthetic often found in Beat writing, since she uses the literary methods and practices of spontaneous composition, collage, cut-up, and dream and journal investigations in her own work. Waldman is, however, more often characterized as a member of the community of younger East Side New York City poets than she is called a Beat writer."

BIOGRAPHICAL INFORMATION

Waldman was born in Millville, New Jersey, in 1945 and raised on McDougal Street in New York's Greenwich Village. Both of her parents were involved with literature, teaching and translating poetry and writing magazine articles. Waldman became fond of poetry at an early age and was drawn to the Beat Generation poets she encoun-tered on the streets of New York City. She attended Bennington College in Vermont, where she studied with Howard Nemerov, Bernard Malamud, and Stanley Edgar Hyman; during the summer of 1965, Waldman attended the Berkeley Poetry Conference and subsequently determined that she wished to become a poet. Waldman completed her Bachelor of Arts degree in 1966 and returned to New York City, where she became assistant director of the Poetry Project at St. Mark's Church-in-the-Bowery. By 1968, Waldman was running the Poetry Project, and became acquainted with a wide variety of poets and essayists of both her own and previous generations. Waldman began to read her poetry at the Poetry Project, and was encouraged by such writers as Ted Berrigan, Allen Ginsberg, Barbara Guest, Diane di Prima, and Kenneth Koch. By the early 1980s Waldman had presented her unique blend of poetry and theatre on radio, television, and in a music video with a poem called "Uh-oh Plutonium!" She cofounded the Jack Kerouac School of Disembodied Poetics at the Naropa Institute in Boulder with Allen Ginsberg, with whom she shared a close friendship. Ginsberg served as both a literary and spiritual mentor for Waldman, augmenting her studies of Buddhism and other innovative methods for expanding her mind to generate fresh ideas for and approaches to her poetry. Waldman has continued her association with the Poetry Project. Ann Charters has observed that "with her talent for organizing readings, little magazines, and fundraising events, along with her many appearances reading her own poetry and encouraging poetry students, . . . Waldman has worked hard for the cause of poetry in America." Waldman's work as a performance poet has been credited with influencing such artists as David Byrne and Laurie Anderson.

MAJOR WORKS

Waldman began publishing her poetry in the late 1960s with small presses such as her own New York City-based Angel Hair Press and Joe Brainard's Boke Press, moving to Bobbs-Merrill in 1970 with the collection *Baby Breakdown*. *Giant Night* was also published in 1970, followed by *No Hassles* in 1971 and *Life Notes* in 1973. Much of Waldman's early work is informed by an oral, incantatory tradition; she began to earn a considerable reputation for her exciting, unique readings of these early works. With the publication of *Fast Speaking Woman* in 1975, written after a trip to South America and inspired by a recording of a chanting Mazatec Indian shamaness, Waldman garnered considerable recognition as a unique literary and theatrical talent. "Fast Speaking Woman" is a poem intended for performance. Waldman wrote of this work: "Reading it aloud as intended, I can be more playful improvising new words and sounds, thus expanding the territory I'm in." Waldman's later works include *Troubairitz* (1993) and *Kill or Cure* (1994). Ken Tucker has described the former work as a "song of a female troubadour" asserting that "[its] dreamy urgency occasionally drifts into a kind of willed incoherence." *Kill or Cure* includes a long journal poem called "Shaman Hisses You Slide Back into the Night," which Waldman wrote while on tour with Bob Dylan. Waldman's collection *Marriage: A Sentence* (2000) explores close associations that bring two individuals into psychic union. The poems in this volume are written in haibun, a traditional form combining prose and lyric poetry, and demonstrate, according to Stephen Whited, "Waldman's attention to what Ezra Pound called 'melopoeia'—that is, the music of language that supports the images and the words."

CRITICAL RECEPTION

Commentary on Waldman's work is often comprised of discussions about whether her poetry is better suited to live performance or the written page. The audience's experience of Waldman's poetry, critics contend, is greatly affected by the medium in which it is communicated. Susan Braudy has called Waldman's poems "a sort of instant autobiography" displaying "her natural ear for language and her keen eye for deploying words on a page." Aram Saroyan has written that "Waldman's poems are a kind of high-energy shorthand, elliptical brain movies of her life and times, . . . repetitive, chant-like 'songs,' which bring to mind tribal shaman ceremonies." Claudia Ricci maintained that what Waldman "is attempting to do on the page is to give readers not 'a refined gist' or 'an extrapolation' of feeling, thought, and emotion, but an actual 'experience' of a 'high moment.' In effect, Waldman is attempting to bring to poetry on the page the same kind of immediacy and sense of immersion that she brings to her poetry, in public performance."

PRINCIPAL WORKS

O My Life (poetry) 1969

Baby Breakdown (poetry) 1970

Giant Night (poetry) 1970

No Hassles (poetry) 1971

Life Notes (poetry) 1973

Memorial Day [with Ted Berrigan] (poetry) 1974

Fast Speaking Woman (poetry) 1975

Sun the Blond Out (poetry) 1975

Journals and Dreams: Poems (poetry) 1976

Four Travels (poetry) 1979

Countries: Poems (poetry) 1980

First Baby Poems (poetry) 1982

Makeup on Empty Space: Poems (poetry) 1983

Invention (poetry) 1985

Skin Meat Bones: Poems (poetry) 1985

The Romance Thing: Travel Sketches (poetry) 1987

Helping the Dreamer: New and Selected Poems, 1966-1988 (poetry) 1989

Iovis: All Is Full of Jove (poetry) 1993

Troubairitz (poetry) 1993

Kill or Cure (poetry) 1994

Marriage: A Sentence (poetry) 2000

ANNE WALDMAN (POEM DATE 1988)

SOURCE: Waldman, Anne. "Our Past." In *Blue Mosque*, pp. 56-8. United Artists, 1988.

In the following poem, Waldman recounts a journey she took with several other poets.

"OUR PAST"

You said my life was meant to run from yours as
    streams from the river.
You are the ocean I won't run to you
We were standing on Arapahoe in front of the
    Silver Saddle Motel
They had no rooms for us
I wore the high red huaraches of Mexico & a
    long skirt of patches
You had traveled back from Utah
I thought of the Salt Lakes, seeing them once
    from a plane they were like blank patches in
    the mind or bandaged places of the heart
I felt chilly
I had just ridden down the mountain with a car
    full of poets, one terrified of the shifting
    heights, the dark, the mountains, he said,
    closing in
I said Wait for me, but I have to go here first, or,
    it's too complicated, some kind of stalling
    because I wanted you
You were direct, you were traveling light, your
    feet were light, your hair was light, you were
    attentive
Were you rushing me?
We walked by the stream, you held me, I said I
    have to get back soon because he's waiting,
    maybe he's suffering
I think the moon was waning
You walked me back along 9th Street under dark
    trees
The night we'd met, June 6, we'd come out of
    the New York Church to observe a
    performer jumping over signposts
I was with my friend, a mentor, much older
You were introduced to him, to me
You said you'd followed me out from that night
    to where the continent divides, where my
    heart divided
I wrote poems to you in Santa Fe
You followed me all the way to Kitkitdizze
I waited for you, when you came I was away
I drove miles to speak with you on the telephone
I met you in Nevada City after nearly turning
    back to put out a fire
We went to Alta, the lake of your childhood
I wanted to stay forever in the big room with all
    the little white beds, like a nursery
You were like first love
All the impossibilities were upon us
We never had enough time
In Palo Alto where they name the streets after
    poets I admired your mother's pretty
    oriental things
In San Francisco we ate hurriedly at the joint
    near the opera house

I lied about going to Chicago for your birthday
    in New York
I lied about spending Christmas with you in
    Cherry Valley
I will never forget the dance you did to the pipes
    of Finbar Furey on New Year's day. You kept
    your torso bent to protect your heart
Then I moved to Colorado
We met and sat in the yard of a friend's brother's
    house in Missoula, Montana
It's wonderful the way this city turns serenely
    into country with no fuss, the city is shed,
    or is it the other way around, the country
    falls off into the city?
It was how I wanted us to shed our other lives at
    least when we were together
In that yard you made me feel our situation was
    intolerable
We seemed to be in constant pain
When we parted at the small airport early that
    morning my heart finally ripped
In the spring back in New York, things got darker
I was sick, my head was swollen
I remember reading to you about the Abidharma
    on a mattress
I had trouble speaking
I behaved badly and embarrassed you at the
    uptown party
A part of you had left me for good
You'd given your loft over to weekly parties
You were having a public life. I felt you were
    turning into me
I wanted our private romance
Was I being straight with you, I wondered?
I let you think things of me that weren't true.
    You thought I was wise & couldn't be hurt
    Then I had the person I lived with and what
    could be said about that?
That summer you visited my hotel in Boulder.
    We slept on separate mattresses. I felt I was
    trying to imprison you and after you left I
    couldn't go back there for days. When I did
    I found a dead bird had gotten entrapped,
    struggled fiercely to get out
The following winter I waited for you in sub zero
    cold, wearing black. I was told you'd come
    & gone. You didn't return. We spoke on the
    phone a long time.
I said I was going home and falling in love with
    someone else. You said It sounds like you
    want to
My mother heard me crying and came to me in
    the bathtub and said O don't, it breaks my
    heart! I told her I was going to the hell for a
    while I'd often made for others, karma
    works that way. Bosh karma she said
We've met briefly in Portland, Oregon and New
    York
We've corresponded all this time, following the
    details of each other's lives and work
Your father has recently died
My baby son grows stronger
The last time I saw you you were standing on
    my street corner
As I came toward you you said What a youthful
    gait you have

GENERAL COMMENTARY

SUSAN BRAUDY (ESSAY DATE 22 NOVEMBER 1971)

SOURCE: Braudy, Susan. "Queen Anne." *Newsweek* (22 November 1971): 128, 130.

In the following essay, Braudy offers an overview of Waldman's life, as well as her literary influences and accomplishments.

At 26, Anne Waldman has the face of a Christmas-tree angel, the intense energy of an actress and the soul of a poet. Her three books, *Giant Night, Baby Breakdown* and *No Hassles,* are perfect examples of the kind of personal, wide-open writing that is coming out of the youngest generation of poets, a generation that has passed beyond the critical battles of the last 50 years and that has made the rhythms of their personalities and their daily lives the style and substance of their poetry. "For me poetry is living," says Miss Waldman. And in one of her poems she writes: "Just give me a chance to explain myself . . . / it may take all of me / until I die."

Besides having written her books, edited two anthologies and won several prizes including the Dylan Thomas Memorial Award, she is also the reigning queen of the downtown poetry scene in New York, where she directs the Poetry Project at St. Mark's Church in-the-Bowery. Anne has been the energetic whirlwind behind the weekly poetry readings, classes and mimeographed magazines that have established St. Mark's as the communal center for leading younger poets like Aram Saroyan, Ted Berrigan and Ron Padgett.

Moods

Growing up in Greenwich Village, Anne Waldman was a true child of poetry. Her father, an English professor, and her mother, a translator, both encouraged her to write a family newssheet in which Anne would record, often in verse, the events of the day. At the age of 11 she awoke in the middle of the night with a fully composed poem which began: "Tell me your secrets O success." In high school, she wrote more formal poetry. "From reading poetry then," she says, "I had the idea that poetry is a certain kind of language. When you sat down to write it, you were supposed to turn off your daily life and start thinking in these lofty higher terms. The more and more poetry I read, I realized that you could write about anything—just getting up in the morning, going outside and taking a walk, looking at street signs. When you're young and sensi-

tive you get into this tragic mood about people or life—this happens when you're full of other people's poems. But poetry is just language—that's what it's all about, using language that's alive."

Waldman's poems are a sort of instant autobiography. Most are deceptively literal and casually associative. They are part of a current "pop" mood that she and her poetry peers are experimenting with. She catches the heartbeat of a real person—living in New York, sitting at her typewriter, smoking dope, making love, trying to catch the mortal music of her ups and downs. Several of her poems are in the simple form of lists; **"Sexy Things"** is literally a 23-item list starting with "eyes / tall dark and skinny men / certain blond boys / The Rolling Stones / little titties" and ending with "wrists / my lover's back / pussycats / certain works by Andy Warhol / Italy." "I don't make big or solemn claims for my poetry," says Anne, "but no matter how rough the poems seem, they're me, out of my own head, and the product of my work."

Ear

For Waldman and her group, poetry often begins by just sitting down at the typewriter and letting it happen. She works in collaboration with other poets, while the television news is droning, or even during a party. Her poetry displays her natural ear for language and her keen eye for deploying words on a page, and reflects the influence of rock music on her generation. In the title poem of **"Baby Breakdown,"** Waldman juxtaposes a "ha" she has just heard on a record, her own clapping along and the confused syllables of a badly transmitted telephone conversation with Ted Berrigan. Anne created the poem by dictating it into a tape recorder. With her tense, golden energy (she still acts in plays and her friends' films) she characteristically performs it as a mini-drama, complete with singing and clapping, when reading it before an audience.

Anne's poetic stance has devastated many members of the poetry establishment. **"Baby Breakdown"** was attacked in The New York Review of Books as the work of a "self-indulgent spoiled brat," but the scholarly Partisan Review praised the same book as "a simple joy." Says Ted Berrigan, "Anne is brave. She is experimenting, and I think she is the most exciting poet of her generation."

Anne is no cardboard anarchist who dismisses the past. "Every time I read Keats's 'Ode to a Nightingale' it sends chills through me," she says. "My God, it's as high as you can go." Her intense subjectivity is the opposite of egotism; it is her way of trying to get a true grip on reality, a true relationship between the human scale of one's natural concerns and appetites, and the big, crushingly abstract events of a time of perpetual crisis. Her best poems are moving evocations of this struggle toward balance, toward a personal honor that fuses an urge to love with a clear-eyed vision of the way things are. Here is her poem **"Mother Country"**:

> What is around me is
> this huge shape I can't visualize
> from here, sitting here quietly
> nights go by the same way
> noisy people outside on the block
> I want to move from
> so I can understand it better
>
> Not all streets are like this one
> bursting with so much energy
> you can't keep still
> with cops watching over every second
> nothing gets out of hand out there
> but does deep inside you somewhere
> down in your American soul
>
> It's hard to kill, harder still to love
> where you come from when it hurts you
> but you know you do, you do

CLAUDIA RICCI (ESSAY DATE FALL 1996)

SOURCE: Ricci, Claudia. "Anne Waldman: A Profile." *Writers Online* 1, no. 2 (online magazine), <http:// www.albany. edu/writers-inst/olv1n2.html> (fall 1996).

In the following essay, Ricci comments on Waldman's literary career and discusses her book-length poem Iovis.

In the history of modern performance poetry, Anne Waldman's contributions would fill the introduction and at least the first three chapters.

Thirty years ago, Waldman began arranging poetry readings in Manhattan at St. Mark's Church in-the-Bowery. Over the next dozen years, she brought hundreds and hundreds of poets from all over the world to New York to read and perform at the church.

> Ms. Waldman presided over the St. Mark's scene as some combination of oracle, siren and den mother, The New York Times noted in 1993. Besides feeding and promoting the public's growing appetite for poetry, the St. Mark's program also served as an important historical bridge between the New York beat poetry scene of the 1950s and movements that followed. Among Waldman's regular early readers at St. Mark's were beat poets Allen Ginsberg, William Burroughs and Gregory Corso. But 70's punk poets Patti Smith

and Lou Reed have also read, as have members of the new generation of poets writing in what the Times calls "punk-intensive, form-splattering verbal styles.

The St. Mark's program went far to help revive the notion that poetry is an oral—and a public—art. To be fully appreciated, a poem must lift off the page and enter the public arena as theatrical event and/or public ritual.

"Of all the poets of my generation, none has done more than Anne Waldman to bring poetry before the public at large," concluded poet Aram Saroyan, writing of Waldman and her poetry in the *New York Times* in 1976.

At the same time she was promoting the work of other poets, Waldman herself emerged in the 1970s as a reader-performer of her own poetry. She quickly gained a reputation for wildly spirited readings.

"Waldman's poems are a kind of high-energy shorthand, elliptical brain-movies of her life and times," Saroyan noted. Speaking of her performance piece **Fast-Speaking Woman,** Saroyan said that Waldman's hypnotically repetitive chants "bring to mind tribal shaman ceremonies."

Over the years, Waldman has worked her magic on audiences throughout the United States and around the world, giving poetry readings in Germany, England, Italy, Scotland, Czechoslovakia, Norway, The Netherlands, Bali, India, Nicaragua and Canada. She has frequently appeared with Allen Ginsberg and has read with Gary Snyder, Diane di Prima, William Burroughs, Kenneth Koch and Clark Coolidge, among other poets. Waldman has also worked and performed with a number of well-known musicians, composers and dancers. More recently, she has collaborated with many visual artists.

In 1978, when Waldman left her position as director of the Poetry Project at St. Mark's, she joined forces with Allen Ginsberg to found the Jack Kerouac School of Disembodied Poetics at the Naropa Institute in Boulder, Colorado. She now directs the MFA writing and poetics program there.

Her list of publications is voluminous. She has written more than 42 books, most recently **Kill or Cure** (Penguin Poets) and her book-length poem, **Iovis** (Coffee House Press). She is now working on Book II of **Iovis**.

With the publication of **Iovis**, Waldman has been acknowledged as a major—and a mature—voice in American poetry. In the 336-page epic,

Anne Waldman reads a poem in tribute to the late Allen Ginsberg at the Wadsworth Theater in Los Angeles, California.

Waldman delves deeply into the masculine soul and its sources of energy. Her goal: to speak against, about, around and through the all-pervasive forces of Western patriarchy and its many manifestations. Waldman invokes a myriad of male voices in the poem, including those of her grandfather, her son, and male deities from other cultures. Throughout the poem, Waldman is trying to come to terms with her own male energy and impulses.

"There are many references to war and weaponry in the poem's weave," Waldman noted in an interview last year. "The act of the poem helped me make sense of—or clarify—my own outrage at aggression or my own aggression. Everything happening seemed to be grist for the poem."

In part to demonstrate the all-pervasive force of patriarchy worldwide, Waldman includes numerous languages in the poem. Besides English, she writes in Greek, Spanish, French, Italian, German, Balinese, Indonesian, Mayan, Czech, Sanskrit and Gaelic.

"I wish there were even more languages in it," Waldman says. "I have them in my ear when I'm traveling . . . when I travel in Germany, there are these sounds that I don't understand, but there's a

deep male gruffness and intellectual superiority that I want to capture, and maybe in the next book I'll play with that a little more, have longer text in some other languages. I'm working on a section in *Iovis II* called 'Lacrimare, Lacrimatus' with Latin phrases."

In the end, Waldman takes an antagonistic position toward the male energy she explores in *Iovis.* But that antagonism is complex, noted a Gary Allen in *The Bloomsbury Review.* Waldman's take on feminism avoids a simple "good girl/bad guy" point of view. Hers, instead, is a many-layered "tantric approach derived from the poet's Buddhist perspectives," said Allen. "Rather than reject the [male] energy out of hand, one invites it in and experiences it in as undiluted a fashion as possible, desiring thereby to liberate it from the artificial constructs placed on it by egotism.

"Her strategy, instead of seeking to empower the female side by dwelling on women or calling down goddesses, is to explore the masculine in every conceivable manifestation, piling up innumerable correspondences and oblique angles into a large, male energy mandala which the poet then inhabits, struggles with, surrenders to, etc."

She has, in *Iovis,* managed to produce, according to the *New York Times,* "an engrossing poem in which ideological axes do not grind in the background. She's the fastest, wisest woman to run with the wolves in some time."

In earlier work, Waldman explores the joys of motherhood. Her *First Baby Poems* include a brisk "**Number Song,**" a play on the numbers game that generates and accompanies the procreative act:

> I've multiplied, I'm 2.
> He was part of me
> he came out of me,
> he took a part of me
> He took me apart.
> I'm 2, he's my art,
> no, he's separate.
> He art one. I'm not
> done & I'm still one.
> I sing of my son. I've
> multiplied. My heart's
> in 2, half to him & half
> to you,
> who are also a part
> of him, & you & he
> & I make trio of
> kind congruity.

Reaching into the voice of an infant, Waldman attempts to record in "**Baby's Pantoum**" the kind of moment-by-moment, "always changing" consciousness that closely observes the small detail of life:

I lie in my crib midday this is
unusual I don't sleep really
Mamma's sweeping or else boiling water for tea
Other Sounds are creak of chair & floor, water
dripping on heater from laundry, cat licking
        itself

In her newest long poem, *Iovis II*, Waldman says she is continuing the exploration she began in *Iovis*. Now, however, she has shifted gears; that is, she is writing to explore not male, but female energy. In so doing, the widest possible set of themes has opened up for her, all of which center on the confusion of roles that confront a woman poet in the final years of the twentieth century.

"The opening section is entitled '**So Help Me Sappho**,'" Waldman says. "[It is] an invocation of sorts. There's absolute chaos in my own mind, much of the time, and I continue to write this poem to make sense of the chaos, without achieving any particular goal. The chaos of patriarchy, of being daughter, mother, lover, rainbow-skinned Tantric deity, of being passionately in love with the dazzling violent phones and phonemes of, speech, of mind into language, which is why the poem is in the shape of a spiral."

Waldman's goal for her poetry is simple, and yet anything but simple to achieve. She says, in effect, that what she is attempting to do on the page is to give readers not "a refined gist" or "an extrapolation" of feeling, thought and emotion, but an actual "experience" of "a high moment." In effect, Waldman is attempting to bring to poetry on the page the same kind of immediacy and sense of immersion that she brings to her poetry, in public performance.

"I want [my poetry] to *be* the experience . . . a sustained experience, a voyage, a magnificent dream, something that would take you in myriad directions simultaneously, and you could draw on all of these other voices and you could pay homage to ancestors and other languages—a poem that would include everything and yet dwell in the interstices of imagination and action."

BRENDA KNIGHT (ESSAY DATE 1996)

SOURCE: Knight, Brenda. "Anne Waldman: Fast Speaking Woman." In *Women of the Beat Generation: The Writers, Artists, and Muses at the Heart of a Revolution*, pp. 287-90. Berkeley, Calif.: Conari Press, 1996.

In the following essay, Knight discusses Waldman's early influences, her development as a second-generation Beat, and her experiences as a woman artist in a male-dominated literary arena.

"Anne Waldman is a poet orator, her body is an instrument for vocalization, her voice a trembling flame rising out of a strong body, her texts the accurate energetic fine notations of words with spoken music latent in mindful arrangement on the page."

—Allen Ginsberg

Born in 1945, Anne Waldman is a relative latecomer to the Beat scene, but her influence on the poetry world has been significant. A prolific writer, powerful reader of her own work, an editor of numerous magazines and anthologies over the years, and director of both the Seminal Poetry Project in New York and the Jack Kerouac School of Disembodied Poetics at the Naropa Institute in Boulder, she has been instrumental in creating renewed interest in poetry.

Anne Waldman's youth was anything but conventional. The family lived in Greenwich Village, the heart of the New York alternative artistic scene. Her father, a soldier during the Second World War, was, in Anne's own words, a "sensitive, literate, former bohemian piano player and a frustrated novelist." Her mother, formerly married to the son of the Greek poet Anghelos Sikelianos (whom she translated), had lived in Greece where she knew Isadora Duncan, among other "exile" artists. Both her parents and the bohemian/artistic setting in which Anne was raised were profound influences on her development as a woman and a poet. Close to the end of her life, Anne's mother was playing the role of the Spirit of Heroin in an off-off-Broadway production of William Burroughs' *Naked Lunch*.

At age six, Anne joined the Greenwich Village Children's Theatre, performing regularly until she was fourteen. As an adolescent in the fifties roaming the Village's bohemian-charged streets, she recalls seeing Gregory Corso, who then seemed to epitomize the *poet maudit*, a romantic figure of her early imagination. At sixteen, while working with the American Shakespeare Festival, she met composer and jazz musician David Amram, and a year later was introduced to Diane di Prima, who was studying Buddhism and occult religions while writing poems and plays and raising her first child.

Thus began a steady stream of friendships—with Allen Ginsberg (she lived on his farm in Cherry Valley for a time in the seventies), Joanne Kyger, Lew Welch, Philip Whalen, Michael McClure, Brenda Frazer, and later, Robert Duncan. She also was very involved with the so-called New York School of Poets and met Frank O'Hara before his death. In 1967, she met Gary Snyder and in 1968, William Burroughs. She became part of what she terms "a unique creative generation, a second generation Beat."

FROM THE AUTHOR

WALDMAN'S FIRST EXPERIENCE WITH LSD

At the core of the trip was a very elaborate panoramic vision which inhabits and informs my genetic makeup still, a vision I return to in Buddhist practice and in dreams, which provides a kind of mental fortitude against the icy, sterile void. I visualized, witnessed, and encountered every person I'd ever known, even some with whom I'd had only remote contact, in a sort of rainbow gathering or holy convocation that brought the various strands of my own personal world together. I was the thread through which these folk gathered, which, in turn, conjured great responsibility for me, of care, attendance and witness. I felt a duty to these sentient beings I'd been touched by or touched. The vision was not just a tableau, but interactive. When I looked at all these creatures, they returned the gaze and communicated in a new way to me.

Waldman, Anne. "Point and click: Icons in the window to the ancestral manse" *Psychedelic Adventures* (website) <http://www.psychedelic adventures.com/AnneWaldman.htm> (7 January 2003).

Beyond her own early writing, which was developing along "expansive chant-like structures" influenced by jazz, Anne's serious interest in Buddhism and subsequent travels in Asia also established a solid link to her Beat elders. (At age eighteen she had met the Mongolian lama Geshe Wangyal and later was to spend time in Nepal with Tibetan lama Chatral Sangye Dorje Rinpoche.) She identified strongly with "the expansive visionary thrust of Ginsberg as poet-ambassador" and started to see herself clearly defined as "key player/persona in a hybrid outrider tradition influenced by the so-called New York School, the San Francisco Renaissance, Black Mountain," and ethnopoetics—lineages "that combined to foster a generation that would continue many of the experiments and thinking of its forebears . . . a continuation of those magnificent epiphanies."

Anne credits the "freedoms espoused by the Beat Movement" as important spring-boards for the women's movement, noting, "I certainly felt empowered by the early shifts of consciousness that were taking place in the '60s as a result of the freedoms and explorations espoused by the Beats and others."

As a student at Bennington College, Waldman also came under the influence of Howard Nemerov, Stanley Edgar Hyman, Bernard Malamud, and Barbara Hernstein Smith. It was during this period that she first traveled abroad, to Greece and Egypt, a vivid journey that "ignited a life-long fascination with studying and traveling within other cultures." After attending the Berkeley Poetry Festival in 1965, where she heard the works of Charles Olson, Ed Dorn, Ted Berrigan, Lenore Kandel, and others, she returned to New York, where she produced poetry and plays for Riverside Radio, saw herself published in *City Magazine*, co-founded *Angel Hair* magazine (and, later, *The World*) and went to work for The Poetry Project at St. Marks Church-in-the-Bowery, becoming its director in 1968.

Her own books soon started to appear, including **Giant Night, Baby Breakdown,** and **No Hassles.** In 1974, she was invited along with Allen Ginsberg to help found what became the Jack Kerouac School of Disembodied Poetics at the experimental, Buddhist-inspired Naropa Institute in Boulder, Colorado. That same year Lawrence Ferlinghetti published **Fast Speaking Woman,** subsequent books have included **Makeup on Empty Space, Skin Meat Bones, Kill or Cure,** and the ongoing epic **Iovis Books I** and **II,** her "all encompassing exploratory collage / argument with male energy."

On being a woman writer she has this to say:

I pushed myself hard and fought for having a life and career as a writer in a field that was blatantly (at first) dominated by men. You make sacrifices. Relationships suffer because men were/are not used to strong women with purpose and discipline. There's a subtle psychological discrimination that goes on. It is an added pressure for women because they are often not taken seriously and have to push against a certain bias. I think I became an over-achiever for this reason.

[However,] I came later into the beat nexus (1970s) and did not experience the same frustrations as some of the maverick women did. . . . The '50s were a conservative time and it was difficult for artistic 'bohemian' women to live outside the norm. Often they were incarcerated by their families, or were driven to suicide. Many talented women perished. But male writers of this literary generation were not entirely to blame, it was the ignorance of a whole culture.

Anne, who has consistently sought "a hermaphroditic literature, a transvestite literature, and finally a poetics of transformation beyond gender," has always found encouragement, support, and inspiration from her male mentors and contemporaries:

> I was treated extremely well by male literary "elders." I have studied and absorbed and benefited by the wisdom of their own writing and activity in the world. This friendship and support has been a real blessing. I hung out with them, worked with them, travelled with them with equal billing as a poet, and have never felt an ounce of condescension.

TITLE COMMENTARY

Life Notes and No Hassles

ALICIA OSTRIKER (ESSAY DATE FALL-WINTER 1974)

SOURCE: Ostriker, Alicia. "Girls, Ladies, and Women." *Parnassus* 3, no. 1 (fall-winter 1974): 185-91.

In the following excerpt, Ostriker comments on Waldman's poetry in her collections Life Notes *and* No Hassles.

From another part of New York's soul, less refined and more zealous, comes Anne Waldman. Head of the Poetry Project at St. Mark's, and editor of *The World* and Angel Hair Books, Waldman is a child of the idealistic '60's. She is sexy, peaceful, open, funny, pretty fond of herself (and giving lessons in how to do this through good times and ill), and prepared to write about any damn thing in any damn style, but inclined toward the gloriously vulgar vernacular. We can see the worst of this, I think, in *No Hassles,* which succumbs to in-group temptations of cuteness and simple narcissism. We can see the best of it in *Life Notes.* Most of this book was written for oral performance, and "Pressure"—a catalogue of "no way out"—was the show-stopper at a huge East Village poetry rally back in 1972 when the War was still on. But *Life Notes* reads well in the hand also, perhaps because graphic alternations of small tight poems with poems spaced all over the page, with occasional near-empty pages and occasional fits of drawing or handwriting, may direct the tempo of the eye as a live performance directs that of the ear. But that sounds academic; fact is, I adored

this book. To suggest the range, let me cite a bit of imagism transformed, called "**Color Photo**":

> The sky was azure
>   & Peking basked in the golden
> sunshine
> Chairman Mao, the never-setting red sun, was
>   taking a nap
> All the Wisdom of China, a big white dog, lay
>   sleeping at his feet.

A bit of rapping from the title poem:

> well it's too damn bad
> well it's a horrible shame
> well it's well well well
> we'll have to well well well
>
> (a song of defeat)
>
> but indefatigable ME say
> hey, it's ME ME ME
>
> even the fish agree
> when it comes to SURVIVAL
>   . . . . .
>
> survival of the wittiest
> that's what we'd like

A bit of cameo social portraiture from the volume's West Indies section, this one called "**Young Black Girls Splashing**":

> Young black girls splashing by the edge of
> the sea tell me they are on their *vacances*
> from Guadeloupe a month, staying in the
> yellow pastel school in Marigot. They say
> the nuns cross themselves all the time,
> and speak happily of their own beautiful
> island. And their names are Georgette,
> Marie-France, Lucette & Petite Georgette.

Waldman's work is the more serious as it does not pretend to seriousness; *playing* with words, rhythms and ideas is its sign of life; the lady wants life, liberty and the pursuit of happiness for herself and us, and *play* means the energy it takes to keep this project buoyant, against the downward pulls, from within and without, of despair.

Makeup on Empty Space: Poems

PATRICIA HAMPL (REVIEW DATE 25 NOVEMBER 1984)

SOURCE: Hampl, Patricia. "Women Who Say What They Mean." *New York Times Book Review* (25 November 1984): 36.

In the following excerpt, Hampl provides a laudatory assessment of Makeup on Empty Space: Poems.

"Incantation," Anne Waldman's superb long final poem in *Makeup on Empty Space*, is well worth the trouble it takes to read it. The famous "difficulty" of contemporary poetry is here, the surface angularity that confines poetry to a skimpy audience. Miss Waldman seems to feel reading is a participant, not a spectator, sport. It's a workout, but the poem delivers and has a right to make its demands.

The angularity of **"Incantation"** is a result of its accuracy, of Miss Waldman's commitment to immediacy. The way she sees her job: "transmute rawness of your time and feel alert." And it is a commitment; she even uses the religious word: "your vows, that vow to contact experience with all wakefulness."

"Incantation" is a passionate reflection on the poet's craft and role, on the contemporary meaning and purpose of expression itself. Miss Waldman understands that the poet, to be a representative figure, must claim not to be a specially entitled person but a dedicated one.

She sustains the poem's personal urgency without a slump and takes care of autobiography in less than a stanza:

> I was in one mind of being a student, I
> was in another mind of your lover, I was becom-
>   ing
> organized, I was the actress & diplomat, I was a
>   reporter,
> ambassador, hostess, traveller, singing for my
>   supper.

It is the snappy résumé of a careerist, the fast track of ambition and exhausting effort. This is a poem of mid-passage, however, about a profound change of spirit—though blessedly without self-praise or self-blame. It is written from "self-imposed isolation" in Colorado, explicitly "not literary convention." The beauty and "largesse of oxygen" of the mountains are "a grasp of territory arriving like shock troops" that startle her. This assault of the physical world, its violent beauty, is evoked in repeated quick turns to the Colorado landscape.

The air, especially, becomes a figure of transformation—both the fine air of the mountains and the focused breathing of meditation which creates a balance between self and world: "We are breathing special air, growing more radial, more plant-like."

This poem of "reciprocity between the woman and her mind" has its best moments in its recognition of the planet's vulnerability in the face of greed and weapons technology. "I can only offer the Symphony Number 103 in E Flat major to this current problem and," she adds, "the beauty of the state I live in." The modesty of this peace plan, in the context of the poem, suggests neither passivity nor hermetic espheticism. That the spiritual and political urgencies of the poem are naturally, inevitably related is its finest triumph.

Miss Waldman succeeds in locating the power of the individual in the vast threat of annihilation:

> O vision of hell of fire of destruction of resurrec-
>   tion
> of human being writing it down of dragon head.
>   We run
>   to
> caves in this artistic sieve, is there circuit to your
> heart to your eye is it moving you toward your
>   own
> version of world.

The imagination becomes politically and personally necessary, for each of us must create that "version of world" needed to *un*imagine the vision of hell that otherwise will engulf us. It's an impressive, heartening achievement.

Some of the shorter poems, apparently intended for public performance (**"Matriarchly,"** **"Anti-Nuclear Warheads Chant,"** and the book's title poem) are more dogged and insistent, repetitious rather than rhythmic. And sometimes the elliptical lines, meant to be immediate and telegraphic, seem stylized, a hip shorthand.

But there are fine shorter poems too, especially those about poetry, and two dialogue poems, one between the soul and the self, the other between "He" and "She."

If, as the publisher of this beautifully produced book says, Anne Waldman has made her way most forcefully thus far as a performance poet, maybe she has a new role ahead. For these poems are most moving not when they perform, but when they ponder and reflect. Then their difficulty resolves itself into light, the pure transparency of the soul given speech as it breathes in and out.

Iovis: All Is Full of Jove

CHRISTA BUSCHENDORF (ESSAY DATE 1998)

SOURCE: Buschendorf, Christa. "Gods and Heroes Revised: Mythological Concepts of Masculinity in Contemporary Women's Poetry." *Amerikastudien/ American Studies* 43, no. 4 (1998): 599-617.

In the following excerpt, Buschendorf analyzes three long poems by contemporary women poets, including Waldman's Iovis, *focusing on how the various writers approach mythical concepts of masculinity.*

A major writing strategy of twentieth-century women poets is the reinterpretation of classical myths. According to Hans Blumenberg, "work on myth" is by nature revisionary, for "[m]yth has always already passed over into the process of reception."[1] A woman poet who chooses myth as her subject generally aims at a particular act of revision. She attempts to challenge and correct traditional gender roles embodied in myth. As Adrienne Rich puts it: "Re-vision, the act of looking back, of seeing with fresh eyes, of entering an old text from a new critical direction, is for women more than a chapter in cultural history: it is an act of survival." And she adds: "We need to know the writing of the past . . . not to pass on a tradition but to break its hold over us."[2] In this process, as defined by Alicia Ostriker, "the poet simultaneously deconstructs a prior 'myth' . . . and constructs a new one which includes, instead of excluding, herself."[3] Ostriker's definition, with its emphasis on the de-marginalization of the female poet and/or heroine, is a particularly apt description of the type of revisionary mythmaking H. D. attempts in *Helen in Egypt.* In this long poem, written in the 1950s, published shortly before her death in 1961, H. D. rewrites the story of Helen of Troy. She turns the quintessential woman-as-erotic-object into a heroine engaged in an intense process of self-discovery.[4] One of the milestones of the genre, *Helen in Egypt* has exerted a great influence on the ever-increasing amount of revisionary myth poetry. Consequently, I will first discuss *Helen in Egypt.* In a second step, I will examine concepts of masculinity as presented in the mythopoesis of two contemporary poets, Anne Waldman and Diane Wakoski. And finally, I will ask to what extent these myth revisions offer a valid contribution to the contemporary debate on cultural constructions of masculinity.

I

Eros? Eris?

H. D., *Helen in Egypt*

Helena's quest in *Helen in Egypt*[5] is a journey of the soul, whose stages are marked by episodic encounters with the men in her life. These men represent the different male roles and types of masculinity Helena questions and tries to come to terms with. There is her seductive, youthful lover Paris, called "Eros-Adonis" (160), who proves himself to be incapable of developing a relation-

ship beyond the sexual. And there is, on the other hand, the wise father-lover Theseus to whom Helena turns for advice: ". . . together they will forget and together they will remember" (153). Theseus, then, is yet another "tribute to Freud," whom H. D. had consulted in 1933 and 1934.[6]

Above all, there is Achilles, H. D.'s "paradigmatic patriarchal male . . . . Heroic, male-centered, immortality-seeking,"[7] he embodies the one-sided male who represses and rejects the feminine principle within him. In their first encounter, Helena recognizes "in his eyes / the sea-echantment" (14), connected with his mother, the sea-goddess Thetis. Yet, in the beginning, Achilles's anger, a "latent hostility" (18), the "fixed stare of Achilles," "the metallic glitter" in his eyes (35) prove stronger than the sea-enchantment. It is suggested, though, that Achilles's love for Helena softens his anger and turns his unfeelingness into love and understanding. Helena, for her part, discovers her "heroic voice" and accepts the element of aggression and conflict in her: "do I love War? / is this Helena?" (177). Helena and Achilles represent femininity and masculinity as interdependent poles. The ideal is a whole being, a kind of hermaphrodite in spirit, in whom the opposing forces are balanced. A perfect balance does not just presuppose two equal and opposite poles. Rather, it is the result of a dialectical process, in which each of them, femininity and masculinity, adopts characteristics of the other in order to converge.

H. D. draws a clear parallel between Achilles, the ruthless leader of a group of elect warriors dedicated to discipline and control, and fascism. By historicizing the hero of Greek myth, she relates him to contemporary socio-historical conditions. And by changing the "hero-god" (9) Achilles into "the new Mortal, / shedding his glory" (10), H. D. expresses her conviction that the male role of the violent aggressor is a cultural construction susceptible to change. The question of how the desired cultural change could become possible is not answered on the plot level of *Helen in Egypt.* In accordance with the mythic law of metamorphosis, Achilles's memory of his mother's heritage, "the magic / of little things" (286), i. e., the acceptance of the "sea-enchantment" within him, comes about miraculously: "he had followed the lure of war, / and there was never a braver, / a better among the heroes, / but he stared and stared / through the smoke and the glowing embers, and wondered why he forgot / and why he just now remembered" (287).

By means of literary technique, however, H. D. indicates the possibility of change. The basic structural pattern of the smallest unit of *Helen in Egypt* is an alternation between prose and verse: each chapter consists of an introductory prose section, which provides a guideline through the ensuing poem—triplets in varying numbers—and their maze of images.[8] The alternation is also one between third-person narrative and first-person narrative, mostly Helena's voice, between an outside and an inside point of view; between distance and emotional involvement; between discursive and metaphorical language. And yet, the two voices are remarkably similar so that we may even come to think of them as of "a single mind having an urgent dialogue with itself, probing, questioning . . . and persisting despite confusion."[9] The two voices, while differing from each other, also depend on each other. Whether they confirm, contradict, revise or repeat each other, it is always the two of them forming a whole: the chapter. The dialogical structure of the book can also be seen as a model of the relationship between the sexes: Whether they love, fight, doubt, or believe each other, they depend on each other—not because they want or need each other, but because they cannot define themselves without reference to the other. If, on the one hand, the interdependence of the sexes implies lack of freedom, there is, on the other hand, unrestricted freedom in the shaping of their mutual exchange. Or again, in terms of the protagonists of the text: Helena's effort toward feminine self-definition relies on her coming to terms with her male "soulmate"; within this given frame, however, the power relation between her and Achilles is constantly shifting, allowing for a great variety of gender configurations. The extremes of their exchange—fight to the death and love-embrace—are both enacted in their first meeting in Egypt. When the shipwrecked Achilles sees Helena, he believes her to be a phantom, a witch, and he tries to throttle her. But Love triumphs over Strife: "*O Thetis, O sea-mother, / I prayed, as he clutched my throat / with his fingers' remorseless steel, / let me go out, let me forget, / let me be lost. . . . / O Thetis, O sea-mother, I prayed under his cloak, / let me remember, let me remember, / forever, this Star in the night*" (17). The encounter illustrates that war and peace, hate and love, or in terms of the text, Eris and Eros (115), or La Mort and L'Amour (271), just like the two sexes, are complimentary sides of an ideal whole, each containing the other.[10] The dialogical structure indicates the dialectical process

of communication between the sexes. It changes them by allowing for their convergence.

The most conspicuous rhetorical device of H. D.'s "semidramatic lyrical narrative"[11] is the question. There is hardly a chapter without one, and there are several chapters consisting of a series of questions. For Helena, reconstructing her life means, above all, questioning the various versions of the Helena myth: "I am not, nor mean to be / the Daemon they made of me" (109). The subsequent section not only poses a number of questions but thematizes their importance for the telling of the tale, which, indeed, seems "to inspire us with endless, / intricate questioning":

> Was Troy lost for a kiss
> or a run of notes on a lyre?
> was the lyre-frame stronger
>
> than the bowman's arc,
> the chord tauter?
> was it a challenge to Death,
>
> to all song forever?
> was it a question asked
> to which there was no answer?
>
> was it Paris? was it Apollo?
> was it a game played over and over
> with numbers or counters?
>
> who set the scene?
> who lured the players from home
> or imprisoned them in the Walls,
>
> to inspire us with endless,
> intricate questioning?
> why did they fight at all?
>
> was Helen a daemon or goddess?
> how did they scale the Walls?
> was the iron-horse an ancient symbol
>
> or a new battering-ram?
> was Helen another symbol,
> a star, a ship or a temple?
>
> how will the story end?
> was Paris more skillful than Teucer?
> Achilles than Hector?
>
> (230-31)

These questions are not posed to be answered. The beginning of the story is uncertain, its end is open, and the meanings of its characters and events, far from being clear, require interpretation.[12] In short, contrary to the epic tradition, the narrator does not claim authority. Consequently, answers are to be found in the very process of remembering and questioning the past, of reconstructing and deconstructing the myths. Instead of simply listening to a tale, we as readers are deeply involved in this process. The first words of the text ("We all know the story of Helen of Troy but few of us have followed her to Egypt. How did she get there?") involves us in the act of contemplation, and from the first question on the first page to the last threefold question on the last page ("But what could Paris know of the sea, / . . . what does Paris know of the hill and the hollow / . . . what could he know of the ships / . . . ?") we are made to share its intimacy and its intensity.

II

dear shape-shifter, dear Iovis
who are you?

Waldman, *Iovis*

These few remarks on *Helen in Egypt* cannot possibly do justice to its complexity, to its intricate interweaving of Greek myths, Egyptian hermeticism, and psychoanalytic symbolism.[13] But they may suffice to demonstrate its influence on a contemporary long poem, Anne Waldman's *Iovis*.[14] Even if Waldman did not mention in her introduction that she writes "with the narrative of H. D.'s *Helen in Egypt* in mind, and her play with 'argument'" (3), we cannot but notice a striking similarity in structure.

Each chapter or section of *Iovis* begins with a prose passage set in italics. Its function is the same as in H. D.'s text: "Narrative tags at the beginning of each section track the poet's steps as they thread through a maze" (3). As in *Helen in Egypt,* the alternation is between two different viewpoints. The prose summary is written in a neutral, third-person voice; and the second part of each section, or the section proper, is in the first person. Yet in contrast to *Helen in Egypt,* where the first-person voice in general is that of the protagonist Helena, Waldman's first-person speaker is not an assumed mythological mask but the persona of the poet herself. Both the third-person and the first-person voices represent different aspects of the poet's persona, and again, as in *Helen in Egypt,* the alternation is one between an outside and an inside point of view: between distance and involvement, between discursive and metaphorical language. What in analogy to *Helen in Egypt* would have to be called the verse section is, however, far more complex in structure. Waldman makes use of a large-scale technique, designing "fields," as she calls these extensive structures in allusion to Charles Olson. Incorporated "in the web of '*Iovis,*' which is a long collage anyway,"[15] are prose genres such as letters, journal entries, dream records as well as overheard conversations, quotations from ancient texts, news clips. Even a

few drawings are interspersed among long sequences of 'free verse' greatly varying in form. The heterogeneity of the multi-faceted structure of the text is enforced by the use of multiple male voices. Appropriately, the title of the book is not 'Jove' or 'Zeus,' which would unequivocally refer to the single figure of the highest male deity of the Graeco-Roman pantheon, but instead "Iovis." As the poet explains, it is taken from a verse by Vergil: "Iovis omnia plena," "all is full of Jove." In this phrase, "Iovis, literally *of Jove,* is the possessive case, *owned by Jove.* As well as about him, a weave. . . . I wanted that sense of filling up: 'plerosis.' How that is both a celebration and a danger. And how complex is the relationship of this poet to the energy principle that does that" (2). Rather than an effort toward feminine self-definition, *Iovis* is an effort toward a feminine definition of masculinity. And, more than that, it is an attempt to explore a creative energy beyond gender.[16]

Just as each of the twenty-three sections of the book starts with an introductory prose passage supposed to facilitate the reader's orientation, there is an introduction mapping out, as it were, the whole book. The title of the introduction—**"both both"**—reveals the poet's main principle of approach: asked to take her choice of any 'either/ or,' she will always prefer inclusion to exclusion and emphatically insist on "both both." This dominant principle is also expressed in the fact that there is a second introductory chapter. Its title **"Manggala,"** which means 'invocation,' prepares us for the inclusion of Eastern thought. In an interview conducted at the time she was working on *Iovis,* Waldman spoke about India as "a frequent ground for dreams, musings, the 'other' landscape in my life and work."[17] And, indeed, we find references to Buddhism throughout the book. In **"Manggala,"** however, the poet invokes not an Eastern deity, but "the familiar Judeo-Christian patriarch" (4), thus again stating her principle of "both both."

"Both both" expresses her desire for encompassing both the phenomenal world as well as the "holy," the body as well as the mind. It also expresses the poet's wish to let herself be infused by all the male energy available in order then to turn it into a creative energy of her own: "I feel myself always an open system (woman) available to any words or sounds I'm informed by" (1), "& wherever the energy is, / seize it! / grabbing the power from the male deities / she lives inside them / they haunt her / eclipse her / . . . / a kind of bondage / & then she transmutes their form /

. . . / to her own" (165). Inclusion implies extension, and consequently, the poet declares: "I want & need the long poem" (3). And in an interview she explains: "The epic is a way to parallel the instability and potent energy of our world. My epic takes on both the nightmare and the nirvana of male energy."[18] Yet another reason for the need for extension is the protean nature of male energy. Taking hold of it means to grasp the innumerable masks of its appearance. "[D]ear shape-shifter, dear Iovis / who are you?" (157) the poet asks, and states: "You contradict your many selves" (19); or, as she puts it elsewhere: "One searches / in vain for the mask that will describe all you / represent, all you mention in your ravings" (144).

The formular **"both both"** also implies the poet's ability to sustain contrariety: "She wants an oppositional poetics" (298). "Why dream of Hegel? Attempt, perhaps, to bring an all-embracing male mind into situation (thesis) to evoke its antithesis. Poem, yes, is synthesis" (63).[19] Connected with the antithetical feature is the poet's ambivalence toward male energy: "How that is both a celebration and a danger" (2). And accordingly she calls her "[p]oint of view: both accommodation and scorn" (3), or, with the motto of chapter 10, taken from a poem by Catullus, "Odi et amo"—I love and hate. Male energy itself consists of two interrelated elements: derived from 'Iovis' there is "that sense of filling up"; likewise we have to think of "the masculine energy principle" as a "skillfull means," derived from Sanskrit "Upaya" (205). Considering both Western and Eastern concepts, masculinity is both force and skill, force and accuracy.

It goes without saying that "both both" also refers to the essential male-female opposition. Yet, this opposition is not thought of as necessarily excluding the opposites. Rather, the aim is to fuse the alternatives: "Take your pick. Both, both" (2). It is by way of mimesis that the Other is to be appropriated. Conceived of as a magical practice, the act of imitation allows for the partaking of the power of the Other: "She moves through the lives of particular men as a kind of sympathetic magic to catch experience. She wants the men to do the same: change into women" (34). As Waldman affirms in the introduction: "It is a *body poetics*" (2).

"Both both," then, is also the formula of the ideal of the hermaphrodite: "*Pondering this, she continues to honor the hermaphrodite as the ultimate mental state, . . .*" (34). Yet while H. D. illustrated the ideal of the hermaphrodite in the union of just one female and male mythological mask, Helena and Achilles, Waldman evokes a broad range of gods, heroes, men. "For this poem I summoned male images, 'voices,' & histories as deities out of throat, heart, gut, correspondence & mind" (3). Among the "voices" she uses, there are, for example, a series of letters by her grandfather to his wife, letters by her father concerning his experiences in World War II, tales by male friends about their first sexual experience, conversations with her son, and reactions of her students to her poetry. Then there are statements of the poet herself directed to various men, for example, among many others, to Jove, to President Reagan, as well as to her colleagues Jack Kerouac, Frank O'Hara, and Robert Creeley, or to John Cage, "*quintessential artist of this century, likely the most innovative*" (309). The voices and echoes of these individual men are at the same time representative of male roles and types. Apart from the common family roles of lover, husband, father, son, there is the warrior, the politician, the inventor, the creator/poet. With few exceptions, such as Cage's "*'passivity,' if you could call it that, both gentle & active*" (309), she endows most of them with traits that in Western cultures are traditionally attributed to men (aggression, domination, protectiveness). Waldman's incorporation of Eastern thought reveals the cultural dependence of concepts of masculinity. Traveling in Indonesia, the poet becomes aware of a different idea of masculinity: "*The 'male' here is more dormant deity, integrated into a transcendent yet powerful hermaphrodite consciousness & the dust of her pencil*" (154).

The multitude of male voices is answered on the poet's side by multiple shifts of identity. "*She'll travel in her head and shift identity*" (143). She wears the mask of several goddesses: she is Athena born of Zeus's head; she is Diana and can be Venus as well; she is also a witch, signing her letters with "Anne Grasping-the-Broom-Tighter," and she "*takes on the persona of aged hag who has stuck by her patriarchal male companion, following him to the ends of the earth*" (143). In accordance with her intention to include Eastern mythology in her masquerade, the poet imagines to be "*a pamurtian—a gigantic supernatural being with thousands of heads & arms brandishing weapons. Weapons like articulate speech & poetry, beauty. This is her basic image of herself*" (154).

Basic, however, seems to her yet another role to which she reverts repeatedly and tries to come to terms with, namely, her part as a daughter. The structure of the book reveals that the poet deals with the father-daughter relationship in especially prominent places. The book has twenty-three chapters, at first sight an inconspicuous number, which, however, allows for a meaningful division: there is one chapter in the middle, the twelfth, framed by two sections of eleven chapters, each of which, in turn, has a middle chapter. And, in fact, all three "middle" chapters, the sixth, the twelfth, and the eighteenth, prove to be truly central.

The title of the sixth chapter is "**Leir**," which, though differing in spelling from Shakespeare's tragedy, clearly refers to it. "Call me Cordelia" (93), the poet says, and speaks about the "*vulnerability of father to daughters and how it goes the other way too*" (92).[20] L-e-i-r is just a variant spelling of L-e-a-r, both meaning "learning," "knowledge gained through instruction."[21] The unfamiliar spelling, through which we become aware of the meaning of the word, alludes to the father-daughter relationship in spirit and thus foreshadows the structurally corresponding chapter, chapter 18, around which the second part of the book revolves. Its title is "**I Am the Guard**," a line repeated in the text and attributed to Jack Kerouac. "Father, I call him, / captain Kerouac / or husband / needing him most / by his words" (275). As daughter-in-spirit, she addresses and quotes other "masters" as well. She acknowledges "a debt & challenge of epic masters Williams, Pound, Zukofsky & Olson" (2). "*The challenge of the elder poet-men*," she writes, "*is their emotional pitch she wants to set her own higher than*" (270).

Although her role as daughter in body and in spirit is pivotal, it may not come as a surprise that in the center of the book she dons a male mask, not that of a man, however, but of a boy. "**Puer Speaks**" is the title of the twelfth chapter, in which the "*poet can finally resemble the boy in herself*" (177): "Somewhere the boy rises up in me. And the words become chants of mock battle or curiosity. For curiosity is the boy's guest-song" (177). In the process of her performative act, her body changes in order for her mind to expand:

> I am boyant. . . . My muscles grow. I study the forms of other men and their words. Soon I can swear with the best of them. I write for my comrades as Dante did. I show them how the quest in me is to reach them through words, to make words dance out of a body without breasts and womb, or to take that body and establish the will of a man coming to life, just coming to life. Male poet on the brink of his/her fortune. . . .
>
> (178)

In this central chapter, the poet sets off single words or a cluster of words against each other by enclosing them within rectangles, thus creating "boxes," or "windows," on which she comments in the introductory prose section of chapter 12 as

follows: "*Thus poet becomes name of a boy for the time being. And takes on implications of Muse ('mouth-forming words') & then puts those new mixes into boxes, assured now of a place on the page. Windows are two-ways and may be locked*" (177). Windows, mediators between inside and outside, display the joint verbal efforts of the young male and the ancient (traditionally female) Muse. The remark that "windows may be locked" seems to be a fitting reference to the isolated position of chapter 12. It is 'locked' in the sense that unlike the others it is lacking a corresponding chapter.

Another look at the structure of the book reveals its twofold nature. As mentioned before, the book can be divided into two parts, eleven chapters before and eleven chapters after chapter 12, which forms the center of the text. It seems that not only do the two chapters "**Leir**" (chap. 6) and "**I Am the Guard**" (chap. 18), which share the distance to the central chapter, mirror each other,[22] but in fact they can be imagined as folded up around the central chapter. We may, therefore, conceive of the two times eleven chapters as eleven corresponding or mirroring pairs. This structural aspect reflects the principle of "both both," i. e., the juxtaposition of opposing elements.

In addition, there is a circular structure: "*She moves in circles, not lines*" (154), the poet maintains, referring to the technique of constantly turning back to certain subjects or persons. Moving in circles also reflects the central position of several chapters, around which the other chapters, as it were, revolve.[23] Moving forward in circles could also be said to be Helena's way of advancing in H. D.'s *Helen in Egypt*. Yet while Helena returns to a few crucial events in her life, ever and again trying to interpret them, as one might do in a psychotherapeutical process, Waldman's persona in turning back always adds new material, thus acting in compliance with the principle of plerosis. The field technique is Waldman's appropriation of the Jovian "sense of filling up," and it is this spreading of energy in which she most conspicuously differs from H. D. While both poets share the ideal of the hermaphrodite, the combination of the male and the female in one figure, Waldman, in accordance with postmodern concepts of the self, wants to overcome the limitations of gender boundaries altogether by going beyond the thought in binary oppositions. In any essay entitled "**Feminafesto**," Waldman summarizes her concept of a poetics beyond gender, of transsexual writing and living, as follows:

I'd like here to declare an enlightened poetics, an androgynist poetics, a poetics defined by your primal energy not by a heterosexist world that must measure every word, act against itself. Not by a norm that assumes a dominant note subordinating, mistreating, excluding any other possibility. . . . I propose a utopian creative field where we are defined by our *energy,* not by gender. I propose a transsexual literature, a hermaphroditic literature, a transvestite literature, and finally a poetics of transformation beyond gender. That just sings its wisdom. That the body be an extension of energy, that we are not defined by our sexual positions as men or women in bed or on the page. . . . That masculine and feminine energies be perhaps comprehended in the Buddhist sense of *Prajna* and *Upaya,* wisdom and skillful means, which exist in *all* sentient beings. That these energies co-exist and are essential one to the other. That poetry is perceived as a kind of *siddhi* or magical accomplishment that understands these fundamental energies.[24]

What then can we take to be the accomplishment of Waldman's concept in regard to the conceptualization of masculinity? Like H. D., Waldman insists on the interrelatedness of the opposing principles. Yet Waldman's position is far more radical than that of her forerunner's. H. D. still thinks of the male and the female as, so to speak, entities, substances, and she believes that humanity can be improved if these substances are brought together in a dialogical process of learning, ultimately united in the ideal of the hermaphrodite. Waldman, however, on the basis of plerosis, i. e., on the principle of plenitude, fullness, has given up the concept of gender as substance, and consequently, has given up the difference between femininity and masculinity altogether. In her understanding of gender, the concept of substance is replaced by the concept of function or construction. The world, being full of Jove, basically contains infinite possibilities and combinations of singular traits. Of these innumerable possibilities, only a finite number are realized. Due to a process of selection and combination, which depends on historical and cultural conditions, certain types of gender roles are formed, and certain gender stereotypes come into being and are handed on. *Iovis,* then, is an attempt to recreate the state of fullness. The poem demonstrates the possibility of overcoming the one-sidedness of gender-role realizations. Waldman achieves this by departing from the concept of character or self, confronting us instead with aspects of partial selves.[25] The permanent shift of perspectives, masks, and performative acts in combination with the poet's insistence on the principle of "both both," i. e., the inclusion of opposites, not only makes us aware of the complexity of the phenom-

enon of male energy but, by revealing its cultural construction, forces us to rethink the concept of masculinity altogether.

Notes

1. Hans Blumenberg, *Work on Myth,* trans. Robert M. Wallace (Cambridge, MA: MIT Press, 1990) 270.

2. Adrienne Rich, "When We Dead Awaken: Writing as Re-Vision," *On Lies, Secrets, and Silence: Selected Prose 1966-1978* (London: Virago, 1980) 33-49; 35; first published in *College English* 34 (1972).

3. Alicia Suskin Ostriker, *Stealing the Language: The Emergence of Women's Poetry in America* (Boston: Beacon Press, 1986) 212. For a "roughly chronological list of some myth-poems by poets prior to 1960" and a list of "representative post-1960 myth-poems" see notes 13 and 14 of chapter 6: "Thieves of Language: Women Poets and Revisionist Mythology" (Ostriker 284-88). For further recent myth-poems, see Annis Pratt, *Dancing With Goddesses: Archetypes, Poetry, and Empowerment* (Bloomington: Indiana UP, 1994).

4. See Ostriker 222-28. Cf. Rachel Blau DuPlessis's definition of this strategy as "narrative displacement," which "can occur whenever a well-known story is accepted but told from some noncanonical perspective": "By putting the female eye, ego, and voice at the center of the tale, displacement asks the kind of questions that certain feminist historians have, in parallel ways, put forth: How do events, selves, and grids for understanding look when viewed by a female subject evaluated in ways she chooses?" ("'Perceiving the other-side of everything': Tactics of Revisionary Mythopoesis," *Writing Beyond the Ending: Narrative Strategies of Twentieth-Century Women Writers* [Bloomington: Indiana UP, 1985] 105-22; 109). For a comprehensive discussion of *Helen in Egypt* see, e.g., Susan Stanford Friedman's essay "Creating a Women's Mythology: H. D.'s *Helen in Egypt*" (1977), *Signets: Reading H. D.,* ed. Susan Stanford Friedman and Rachel Blau DuPlessis (Madison: U of Wisconsin P, 1990) 373-405.

5. As H. D. explains, she takes up a variant myth brought forth by Stesichorus and developed by Euripides, which acquits Helena of guilt. According to Stesichorus's *Pallinode,* "Helen was never in Troy. She had been transposed or translated from Greece into Egypt. Helen of Troy was a phantom, substituted for the real Helen, by jealous deities. The Greeks and the Trojans alike fought for an illusion" (H. D., *Helen in Egypt* [1961; New York: New Directions, 1974] 1); all subsequent quotations are taken from this edition. H. D.'s "Pallinode" of Helena goes beyond such trickery, finally claiming "that it is only from the perspective of the man's world that she is the source of evil" (Friedman 379): "I am not nor mean to be / the Daemon they made of me" (109).

6. See H. D., *Tribute to Freud* (1956; New York: New Directions, 1974).

7. Nor do I claim to have done justice to the steadily growing amount of criticism on *Helen in Egypt.* For an interesting discussion of the "transition from liberal-feminist to post-structuralist-feminist readings," see Edmunds 3-4.

8. Anne Waldman, *Iovis: All Is Full of Jove* (Minneapolis: Coffee House Press, 1993). In 1997, too late to be

considered in this article, Waldman published the second volume of her long poem, in which the "poet continues a long meditation on the nature of male energy & its attendant strife & delight" (*Iovis: All is Full of Jove. Book II* [Minneapolis: Coffee House Press, 1997] 11).

9. Waldman in Randy Roarck, "Vow to Poetry: Anne Waldman Interview," *Disembodied Poetics: Annals of the Jack Kerouac School,* ed. Anne Waldman and Andrew Schelling (Albuquerque: U of New Mexico P, 1994) 33-67; 48. Cf. H. D.'s "various montage strategies," as related by Edmunds to the film aesthetic of Sergei Eisenstein; see Edmunds *passim.*

10. Accordingly, the cover of *Iovis* does not present an image of Jove, but an ancient wall painting from a Villa at Boscoreale, showing a "Lady Playing the Cithara," an image of the woman poet. Her expression is one of concentration and meditation; her eyes are fixed on an object at a distance. Her companion standing behind her is looking at us, drawing us into the scene of contemplation. A snake on the floor, a phallic symbol of old, and, moreover, clearly resembling a lightning flash, reminds us of the object of the song. In the words of the poet who, having explained the use and meaning of the possessive case, changes to the nominative: "Dear Iovis: / Thinking about you: others in you & the way / You are the sprawling male world today" (18).

11. Waldman in Roarck, "Vow to Poetry" 36.

12. Waldman in Roarck, "Vow to Poetry" 40. Cf. Ostriker on the gender-related significance of the epic mode: "If male poets write large, thoughtful poems while women poets write petite, emotional poems, the existence of book-length mythological poems by women on a literary landscape signifies trespass. To be great in our culture usually requires being big" (Ostriker 223).

13. Cf. Waldman quoting Andrew Schelling: "A poem is a mind that holds contraries" (Waldman in Roarck, "Vow to Poetry" 56).

14. Like H. D., Waldman here refers to Freud: "*Freud, her favorite of the doctors enters here to make a few comments*" (92).

15. *OED;* cf. also *OED* s. v. "lear-father": "a master in learning."

16. The two chapters next to the center, 11 and 13, for example, both deal with traveling, 11 mostly with travels in Indonesia, 13 with travels in Europe. Likewise, the second and the second-to-last chapters are interrelated by the subject of "*her own animal nature*" (21); "*His [Cage's] work gives permission to speak of the animals inside her*" (309).

17. Just as chapter 12 is central to the whole text, chapter 6 is the central chapter of the first eleven chapters, which again may be divided into two parts, of which chapter 3 is the center of the first part (chapters 1-4), and chapter 9 the center of the second part (chapters 7-11), etc.

18. Anne Waldman, *Kill or Cure* (New York: Penguin, 1994) 145.

19. Waldman is aware of the paradoxical notion of "self": "There is no 'self,' which is a very heretical notion. When you go to look for a solid self, a soul, something made of DNA, recognizable, this big 'me' that will carry your identity for ever and ever, you can't find it. And yet you are colorful, individual, only you will write that particular poem, only you manifest a very wonderful and particular vivid energy. . . . Only you suffer what you suffer" (Waldman in Roarck, "Vow to Poetry" 54).

FURTHER READING

Criticism

Allen, Frank. Review of *Iovis: All Is Full of Jove,* by Anne Waldman. *Library Journal* 118, no. 4 (1 March 1993): 82.

Concludes that Iovis *would be better heard in performance than read on the page.*

Foster, Edward. "An Interview with Anne Waldman." *Talisman* 13 (fall-winter 1994-95): 62-78.

Interview focusing on Waldman's poetry.

Kaufman, Ellen. Review of *Kill or Cure,* by Anne Waldman. *Library Journal* 119, no. 13 (August 1994): 92.

Comments that a number of the poems in Kill or Cure *may annoy readers more interested in conventional poetry than in stream-of-consciousness narrative.*

Notley, Alice. "Iovis Omnia Plena." *Chicago Review* 44, no. 1 (1998): 117-29.

Provides a glowing assessment and analysis of Iovis.

Review of *Marriage: A Sentence,* by Anne Waldman. *Publisher's Weekly* 247, no. 10 (6 March 2000): 106.

Views Marriage: A Sentence *to be an interesting depiction of its subject.*

Saroyan, Aram. Review of *Journals & Dreams: Poems,* by Anne Waldman. *New York Times Book Review* (25 April 1976): 18.

Offers a mixed assessment of Journals & Dreams: Poems.

Whited, Stephen. Review of *Marriage: A Sentence,* by Anne Waldman. *Book* (March 2001): 84.

Finds Waldman's book an entertaining celebration of the ways people live in relationships.

OTHER SOURCES FROM GALE:

Additional coverage of Waldman's life and career is contained in the following sources published by the Gale Group: *Contemporary Authors,* Vols. 37-40R; *Contemporary Authors Autobiography Series,* Vol. 17; *Contemporary Authors New Revision Series,* Vols. 34, 69; *Contemporary Literary Criticism,* Vol. 7; *Contemporary Poets,* Ed. 7; *Contemporary Women Poets; Dictionary of Literary Biography,* Vol. 16; and *Literature Resource Center.*

LEW WELCH

(1926 - 1971)

(Born Lewis Barrett Welch Jr.) American poet.

While Welch was never among the most celebrated figures of the Beat Generation, in the years since his death his work has gained recognition as the product of a particularly talented and tragic writer. As Samuel Charters has observed, Welch shared the Beat reverence for nature and the mysteries of life, and he "expressed all of this . . . with an intensity and bitter rage that left him hollowed out and too worn to live at age forty-four but that also left a group of poems that are among the purest and the most precise of all the Beat creations."

BIOGRAPHICAL INFORMATION

Welch was born in 1926 in Phoenix, Arizona, the son of Lewis Barrett and Dorothy Welch. Welch's mother belonged to a wealthy family; his father was a man of limited financial means who turned to embezzling from his wife's family's bank, where he had been given a job. Lewis and Dorothy Welch separated in 1929, at which time Welch moved with his mother and his sister to California, and then relocated within the state frequently over the course of the next fifteen years. In 1945, after graduating from high school, Welch enlisted in the U.S. Air Force. After return-

ing to civilian life following the end of World War II, he enrolled in Stockton Junior College. There, he read extensively and was especially influenced by Gertrude Stein's *Three Lives* (1909), which he later cited as inspiring him to pursue a literary career. After two years at Stockton, Welch entered Reed College, a school known for its arts curriculum. At Reed, he met the celebrated poet William Carlos Williams who was visiting the school to perform a reading. Welch quickly established a rapport with the older poet, who expressed particular praise for Welch's thesis on Gertrude Stein. Responding to an invitation from Williams, Welch traveled east, eventually settling in New York City and devoting himself to a writing career. Soon thereafter, Williams suffered a stroke and was inaccessible to the younger poet, who became increasingly depressed over his failure to publish his poems or his Stein thesis. Welch entered the University of Chicago in 1951 and majored in English; however, his approach to literature was at odds with the more conventional, academic approach of the university's English department. Welch experienced another bout of despair and eventually a mental breakdown.

Through psychoanalysis, Welch sufficiently recovered his mental and emotional stability and was able to find work in the advertising department of the Montgomery Ward company in 1953. Although Welch married during this period of his life, the marriage soon dissolved, and he began drinking to excess. For the next few years, Welch remained in Chicago and continued to study at the university and work at Montgomery Ward. In 1957, he began writing poetry again and renewed his friendship with two other Beat writers of the period, Gary Snyder and Philip Whalen. Hoping to join his friends in San Francisco, Welch obtained a transfer to Montgomery Ward's office in nearby Oakland. After relocating to California, he soon found himself involved in the hectic literary scene centered in San Francisco. He entered graduate school at San Francisco State University and began a pivotal period in his life. Under the increasing influence of the Beats, who expressed disdain for conventional dress and conduct, Welch soon came to show an increasing disregard for the wishes of his employers, and was consequently fired. Despite his excessive drinking and unemployment, Welch continued to write poetry and began to earn some measure of recognition as a writer. In 1960, Welch published *Wobbly Rock,* a long autobiographical poem written in a simple, prose-like style. In the following years, Welch produced several other volumes of poetry such as *On Out* (1965), *At Times We're Almost Able to See* (1965), *Courses* (1968), *The Song Mt. Tamalpais Sings* (1969), and *Redwood Haiku and Other Poems* (1972). He also obtained a teaching position at Colorado State University. To address his drinking problem, Welch eventually resorted to Antabuse, a drug that induces sickness when combined with alcohol. He periodically ceased taking Antabuse and returned to drinking. His alcoholism, together with his periodic use of Antabuse—which can produce extreme depression—are believed to have contributed to his final phase of personal despair. In the spring of 1971, after appointing a literary executor and settling his financial affairs, Welch armed himself and wandered into a forest, where he is presumed to have committed suicide.

MAJOR WORKS

Following the publication of *Wobbly Rock,* Welch's earlier work was collected as *On Out;* later poems were published in the volumes *Hermit Poems* (1965) and *At Times We're Almost Able to See.* These works further established Welch's reputation as a Beat poet. The volume *Selected Poems,* with a preface by Snyder, was published in 1976; while this collection sparked new interest in Welch and new appreciation for his work, he remains largely unknown outside of Beat literature circles. A prose collection entitled *How I Work as a Poet,* was published in 1977, and the two-volume

I Remain: The Letters of Lew Welch with the Correspondence of His Friends followed in 1980. *How I Read Gertrude Stein* was published in 1996.

CRITICAL RECEPTION

In the years since Welch's death, the majority of commentary has focused on the biographical details of his life, rather than on his literary output. In particular, the tragic nature of Welch's life, and the mysterious circumstances surrounding his death have garnered far more attention than his works. David Meltzer indicates in the opening of his 1969 interview with Welch that the poet was dismayed that his work had not been given the critical attention many of his Beat contemporaries' works had received. In this interview, Welch candidly discusses his troubled life and the effect it had on his work, as well as reflecting on his education as a poet. "Learning the art of poetry," he stated, "becomes learning the art of hearing. Ear training and voice training, just as surely as a musician does it. . . ." Critic Rod Phillips examines several of Welch's writings and notes that "more often than not, these creations dealt with nature and humanity's place in it, for Welch was a writer who struggled with, and reveled in, this theme for much of his career."

PRINCIPAL WORKS

Wobbly Rock (poetry) 1960

At Times We're Almost Able to See (poetry) 1965

Hermit Poems (poetry) 1965

On Out (poetry) 1965

The Basic Con (poetry) 1967

Courses (poetry) 1968

The Song Mt. Tamalpais Sings (poetry) 1969

Redwood Haiku and Other Poems (poetry) 1972

Ring of Bone (poetry) 1973

Trip Trap: Haiku along the Road from San Francisco to New York, 1959 [with Jack Kerouac and Albert Saijo] (poetry) 1973

Selected Poems (poetry) 1976

How I Work as a Poet (essays) 1977

I, Leo: An Unfinished Novel (novel) 1977

I Remain: The Letters of Lew Welch and the Correspondence of His Friends. 2 vols. (letters) 1980

How I Read Gertrude Stein (criticism) 1996

Lew Welch. © by Fred W. McDarrah.

GENERAL COMMENTARY

LEW WELCH AND DAVID MELTZER (INTERVIEW DATE 1969)

SOURCE: Welch, Lew, and David Meltzer. "Lew Welch (1969)." In *San Francisco Beat: Talking with the Poets*, pp. 294-324. San Francisco: City Lights Books, 2001.

In the following interview, conducted in 1969, Welch discusses his life, poetry, favorite poets and their influence on his work, and meeting with William Carlos Williams.

Summer 1969: Jack Shoemaker and I drove up into the hills of Marin City to Lew and Magda's house. It was late in the afternoon, and Lew was waiting and anxious to begin. He was a tall, skinny, lantern-jawed redhead man who looked like a baseball pitcher. He said he'd been thinking about the interview for a week and knew what he wanted to say and where he wanted to go with it and that it was important to him to get it right. He'd been drinking and offered us some jug wine. Plugged in the Sony and began. As the interview intensified, it started getting dark outside. The green oscillator light on the tape recorder was our only light source as Lew reached an intensely emotional diatribe against his mother; in the darkness it seemed to gather volume and rage. When he was done, we fell silent, and he, suddenly aware of the darkness in the living room, turned

on a light and went to the record player to put on an LP of Charlie Parker. More wine, cigarettes. End of first interview. The second time we went to Marin City, it was to talk about Lew's poetics, which he did with that same singing precision in his poems. I was very pleased with this interview. Of all the poets in *The San Francisco Poets*, Welch was the least known and felt unjustly left out of the fast-breaking pantheon of Beat bards. As I've written earlier, my hope was that the mass-market paperback publication of *The San Francisco Poets* would enhance his visibility as a poet. Ironically, on May 23, 1971, just weeks before the book came out, Lew left a farewell note in the cabin he was living in on Gary Snyder's property in Grass Valley. He was never seen again, and his body was never found.

—[David Meltzer] . . .

1

[Welch]: My mother was the daughter of a very famous surgeon in Phoenix. And her friends were President Hoover, Alan Campbell, the Goldwaters. The father and mother of Barry Goldwater killed my grandfather. Quite accidentally and sorrowfully. They would liked to have had it be any other way.

The story is this: you have a proud-born only daughter of a family, the Brownfields. . . .

Six boys came from Ulster, Ireland, and it appeared that they had to come there because of some kind of political necessity. They were the Brownfields. They were peasants, and their names came from peasant stock, and somehow or other they had to come to America. And they did. And there were six of them, and they were all men, and the entire issue was my mother. Six men could have made a lot of children, but there was only one and that was my mother.

My mother married a man named Lew Welch, and he had one sister, and she died when she was forty-four, and he died when he was forty-seven. So you have in my life a thing very much like *Buddenbrooks,* where you have the end of a very strong line. My sister will never have a child. I have never had a child from my loins. (I have and enjoy having two stepsons, but have none of my own.) My mother had myself and my sister, and so it is over. The father is dead. The grandmothers on both sides are dead. There is nobody alive in my family, except my mother, me, and my sister. And we are both barren.

My father was called Speed Welch because he was very fast in high-school football. In Redfield, Kansas, he was a very good football player and ran very fast. And how he met my mother, I have no idea. He really was very handsome. He looked like Tyrone Power and Cary Grant. I can show a photo to prove it. My mother, naturally, fell terribly in love with him. She really loved my father. It was a good love match. My mother had all the money, however. He didn't have a nickel.

He was the kind of guy that would play in the high sixties and low seventies in golf and knew everybody and didn't have a nickel unless it came from my mother. And she held on to her money. . . .

My grandfather looks exactly like me. It's spooky. You look at the goddamn photo and it's weird. My mother's father. A man named Robert Roy Brownfield. He was a man of great parts. He invented, among other things, the way of pulling out tonsils instead of cutting them. He was the first man to invent a decent machine to test hearing ability. He was a very fine surgeon. And he was also a sort of John Wayne-type cat. Seriously, he was an unbelievable man.

Robert Roy Brownfield never weighed more than 168 and was the heavyweight champ of the state of Nebraska. He put himself through school and got to be a doctor, got his M.D. His father wanted him to be an engineer, and when he wanted to be a doctor, his father disowned him.

Bob Brownfield was a real gutty cat. He not only had to put himself through college, and did, but he became the amateur heavyweight champion of the state while doing it . . . *while* earning the money to get through school. A tough dude. I regret that I never met him.

He married a woman named Sims, Edith Sims, who came from a Pennsylvania Dutch family. They met in Nebraska, and their only issue was my mother. His brothers all were without issue, except one, and that issue, whoever he was, disappeared. There is nobody left. Six strong boys came over from Ireland, and six strong girls came out of Pennsylvania. And the whole thing produced only me and my sister.

My grandfather was probably the best surgeon in the West in 1920. Bob Brownfield knew more about the problems of cataracts than anyone. He operated on something like 4,000 cataracts in a year, and few had ever done forty in a whole lifetime. He would write papers about it, and they would get published. Here it is 1910 and he was the first cat to want to buy an airplane.

You know what happened? My grandfather, Bob Brownfield, and his wife, Edie, and the Goldwaters, the parents of Barry, went to a country-club dance. And Bob had an operation to do the next morning, and he didn't drink a drop. He said, "Please let me drive." And Mrs. Goldwater said, "I am all right, I'll drive." Bob Brownfield couldn't win the day and she drove. She made a mistake, rolled in a ditch, and he was dead at thirty-eight years old. His neck snapped.

And Mrs. Goldwater was so ashamed of herself. She was very lovely about it. The Goldwaters were very lovely. (Barry was my mother's schoolmate, about two years younger. He was a fat little Jewish boy that nobody liked. Spoiled rotten. The only Jew in Phoenix. The whole bit.) And Mrs. Goldwater would rather have died herself than to have killed Bob Brownfield. She loved him that much. He was a beautiful man. You could give him any musical instrument, and he could learn it in a half-hour and would sing on it and make up the lyrics. I have whole books by Bob Brownfield. Short stories he wrote. They are terrible. But he was in there working. And he was a goddamn good doctor.

2

My father, Lew Welch (I am a "junior"), was the son of a very simple Kansas farmer and his wife. Real good, straight, go-to-church-every-

Sunday American, Kansas people. I met them once when I was five. We spent a whole summer with them. And my grandfather had lost four fingers on his hand. He was a fuck-up. The Welches were fuck-ups. My grandfather was respected and loved by everybody in his county, but you wouldn't want to take him on a dangerous mission. That kind of thing.

You know what they finally did with Frank? (Frank Welch was my grandfather's name.) They finally made him a district judge because they respected him so much. They knew he could not make an immoral decision about anyone. He would be a great judge, even though he was stupid enough to cut all his fingers off on his right hand. And he always sold the land cheap when he should have sold it dear. And his cows always died. When he bought a bull it would always be sterile. Frank Welch had bad luck, they called it. But the community still loved this man so much they made him a judge and lived by his decisions. He lived the rest of his life, with his bum hand, as a judge. And no one ever pretended he ever read a book. He never did.

My father was so bad, you can't believe it. He was an embezzler against the family which gave him a job only because he married my mother. He was a teller in the bank. The reason he was a teller was because my mother got hot pants for him. This beautiful man who looks like Tyrone Power, who comes from Kansas, Speed Welch. Bam! He comes in and she can't believe it. And when the dance is through they are married. My grandfather is already dead. My grandfather would have seen this. That this man was a phony. But the kid came up to her, and he was very handsome and very sharp.

My mother had $100,000, American big ones, in 1922. She was rich. I mean superrich. And her friends were all superrich. Well, Lew Welch, my father, was a poor man who was very clever. And he really loved my mother, there is no question about that. This is a very interesting part of it. My mother really loved that man, and that man really loved my mother. And the stories that go to prove it are really intricate and probably not worth going into. Suffice it to say that I know I was not born into a wedlock of hate.

This should be put into this. It is very important. I went to the loony bin when I was fourteen months old.

[*Meltzer*]: *I don't understand.*

I know you don't. It is the world's record. Even among my Beat Generation friends. I have the world's record. I copped out, I went crazy, split, I said, "Forget it! No, I don't want it," when I was fourteen months old. I'll tell you why.

It's a very simple thing. I refused to eat. And I would have died unless I got really strict attention. My mother was a twenties flapper, pretty, and high-style, who had little breasts and probably taped *them* down. Anyway, there wasn't enough milk, and to this day, when I go into rages like I do, she'll say, "You used to look like that when you were a little baby. You used to pound on my chest and turn red and scream." She made feeding so awful, I cracked up.

When I was six, I remember her sticking enormous bowls of oatmeal in front of me. It was disgusting. She'd scream, "Eat! Eat!" I still have trouble eating. I'm a classic case of the alcoholic with an eating problem. To this day I suck on the tit of the bottle. I try to control it, but the scars are very deep.

It's awful to be born to a rich, selfish shiksa. It wasn't her fault, but whose bad habits of mind are purely their own? It's still awful. Growing up was something I'd sure never want to do, that way, ever again.

Let's get out to the positive part of it. All I have done correctly in literature, if I have done anything correctly, was done because I resisted a terrible mother who was the absolute form of Kali, death. Even her pets die inside of a year or two. And then you can see why I praise the planet so highly. Why I take other goddesses.

The thing is that my need for the woman, my mother, was very deep and frustrated. So I hated my mother very strongly for not being able to give it to me. Though she tried. God, did she try! But maybe because of this I admire all of the great feminine traits in the world, such as the mountains, or my present wife, Magda. I am especially sensitive to how beautiful it is when it comes.

So this is why if I sound like I am exaggerating about Mount Tamalpais, it is just that I have taken Mount Tamalpais as my goddess in a very real way, like a priest takes a vow. I mean it.

I ask her, Mount Tamalpais, about this, about that, and I listen to what she tells me. A lot of people think I am being goofy about it, you know, or being poetic about it, but I mean it. I really mean it, and the only way to say it is in the poetry. The praises. Prayers.

How did I get out of it? When I was eleven years old I wanted a pair of tennis shoes very badly. And this was a way out of it. My mother explained to me that I had very bad feet, because when I was in kindergarten, that was in Santa

Monica, she got in the grips of some idiot who made a steel-trap shoe that ruined my feet so bad . . . you know, if you put anything into a cast long enough it becomes atrophied. When I was in the seventh grade, my feet were atrophied because I had to wear high shoes. I insisted on tennis shoes, and there was a big scene, and luckily we were in a school where we had a good coach. I was very fast. And we would run barefooted. We didn't have any shoes and I won. I was the county champion at fifty yards in the sixth grade, and I was really a small tad then. I really ran faster than anybody else in the whole county and broke my arches doing it. Because my mother had put my feet in those iron shoes. But I won it, anyway. Because I took them off and did it. And when it got to be that way, when my feet were really broken and I couldn't walk, I had a confrontation with her and I won it. And the doctor did what was needed.

I had to walk backward for the entire time I was in the ninth grade. Backward, because I could not walk any other way, and I would not let my mother give me another crutch. And there were exercises to do, which I did, and my feet got fairly normal.

In Chicago, about 1954, I got a poem out of a dream I had. I often dream poems, and if everything is just right I can go back in there and dig the poem out by re-dreaming it. It is a poetic skill I'm proud of and on which I work very hard. I hope to be able to have a mind, finally, which has the thinking of sleep (which we call dreaming) and the thinking of waking (which we call thinking) be the same available thing.

I was dreaming, in Chicago, on a hot summer afternoon nap, that I was reading a book called *Expediencyitis*. Isn't that a great word? And the book was written by a German whose name I can't remember. The book was written as Cocteau writes, and as Wittgenstein, the form I feel is the finest form for the true mind transmission: the form is little paragraphs separated by dots, and the paragraphs have no obvious connection with one another, but the whole form finally comes through. You can see it in Cocteau's *Opium* and in Wittgenstein's *Philosophical Investigations* (originally his *Brown and Blue Books*) and in that book about Huang Po—*On the Transmission of Mind*. It's also in Stein's lectures and, I hope, somewhat there already, in this piece we're doing here.

Anyway, I am dreaming I'm reading this perfect book, *Expediencyitis*, which has this perfect form and is very wise, and I realize, while dreaming, that this is not written by any German but is

being dreamed by me, therefore written by me. I'm dreaming this thought about the dream. So it is so fascinating that, when I awake, I say to myself: "Let's go back in there and get some of that." And I rolled over and forced myself back into sleep and that dream, and came up with this:

> Through the years of her speech
> a persistent gong
> told us how grief had
> cracked the bell of her soul.

It was months before I realized this poem exactly said what I felt about my mother's agony and her language. When I wrote it down upon recovering the dream, I had no idea what it meant.

3

When you come into a new school, the first guy that comes up to talk to you is the guy that is suspicious. If he has to come up to you and you are the only new kid, then he can't be any good, can he? The second thing that happens is that there are games in the yard. And it turns out that I was gifted with very swift legs. I could always hang back, play very quiet. I have already rejected the first kid that came up to me, because you know he was no good because he had to come up to the new kid. He doesn't have any friends, so who the hell wants to know him, right? Then there gets to be this day, and I remember it with really great pleasure.

They had a game called "Pom-Pom Pull-Away." It was very simple. One guy is "it" and he stands in the middle of the football field, and everybody runs by him, and everybody he tags is also "it." And finally everybody is "it," and there are a few people who try to work through.

OK, I am the new kid. Nobody knows who I am, and we are playing Pom-Pom Pull-Away, and we have only an hour to do this. So there is a guy named "it," and everybody runs across the football field a couple of times, and then everybody is on the football field, and there are about fifteen of us, and I was one of them. And they say: "Who are you?" and I say: "I am Lew Welch."

And we ran through the next time, and nobody could catch me. And we went through the next time, and still nobody could catch me. I will never forget this triumph. This was a real triumph. Finally, the entire school was "it." And I was the only guy that wasn't, and nobody knew who I was. I made it three times through all of them, and the coach came up and said: "Do you want to come out for football?" And I said: "Yeah." That's a true story. And I did it, man.

There was a very beautiful man named Robert Rideout, who was a teacher in the seventh grade, and he had a very simple thing going. He said, "If you ever like a book, you will probably like another book by the man that wrote it." He would lay books on us.

I must say this in defense of my mother. One of the best things she said to me was, "You know, all the knowledge of the world is in the library, and I will show you how to use it." And she did. She took me to the library, and we walked in, and she showed me how the card catalog worked, and she introduced me to the lady who worked there, and I spent a very beautiful summer there and was very proud of it. Like, I could really go up to the card catalog, look up books, get authors, pull the books off the shelves, and so on. It was too much, man.

Did you teach yourself to read, or were you taught to read?

No, like most of us, the real readers, it all happened accidentally. My mother was a very good reader . . . this is in defense of my mother. She was very good about that. She would always read us stories when we were very young. I started reading when I was five or six, because she sat us on her lap as she read *Dr. Dolittle,* or whatever it was, and she would move her finger over the words, and I learned accidentally how to read. No, it wasn't accidentally. Not really. It was because of her good grace. She really loved books. So all blessings to her.

I am going to mention right out in my author's preface to my new book, ***Ring of Bone*** (Grove Press, 1971), you know, where it says: thank you. I don't even know where he is now, but Robert Rideout was a seventh-grade teacher in El Cajon, California, and he had this little thing about how books were to be used.

I am on a pirate kick, so he gets me *Falcon of France.* Nordhoff and Hall wrote *Mutiny on the Bounty.* Hall was really a World War I pilot. Rideout had the sense to see that if the kid liked pirates, he would certainly like this. So then, bang! I go into all the World War I airplane books.

Rideout said: "Every time you read a book, write it down. Write down the author and tell whether you liked it or not." He had a five-star system. One star for bad, two, etc. You know what I did? I read 160 books in one year under Rideout. Most of them were about pirates or airplanes. He was too much.

He got me into Ernest Thompson Seton. He got me into all the Lassie books, the dog and animal bit. But Ernest Thompson Seton was a re-

ally important writer, and Nordhoff and Hall were great. And, most of all, Will James.

When did you start reading poetry?

Ha! Right then! In the middle of all this reading, I read "Trees" by Joyce Kilmer. I ran into and out of the pirate thing. I ran into and out of the Ernest Thompson Seton thing. And suddenly I got into poetry, and believe it or not, it was Joyce Kilmer's "Trees" first, and more importantly, Robert Service. No kidding. This is true, man. That son of a bitch is a terribly good poet.

I got *Rhymes of a Red Cross Man* when I was about eleven years old. And when he talks about the man on the wire—I said: *"There!"* That was the great thing that drove me to poetry. Service never cheats. And his *On the Wire,* that man is festering on the wire and people are shooting at him and it is getting hot . . . whew! I got it! I got truth! So Robert Service is a super-American poet.

No doubt about it. He is incredible. He is tremendous to read aloud to people.

Right! When I was on my hermitage, and it really was a hermitage, we would sit and weep with bad sherry wine. Me and a bunch of bad-ass drunk Indians. And we would read a poem about a dog by Service and we would break up. It was relevant. It was truly relevant. I would like to have poetry be the kind of thing that a man can say with good friends in a mountain cabin. And Robert Service can do it.

How did you become interested in language? For instance, you talk about your speed, being able to move . . . when did you realize that language was a way of moving, too?

That's a well-put question.

When you say something right, "with your finger on the throttle and your foot upon the pedal of the clutch," you are doing something in language that becomes almost abstract to most minds, but to my mind this is the supreme act.

The difference between the ordinary kind of language that we use every day and the language that we call poetry is very slim when we have great poets working. Example. Take Burns's "Loch Lomond." You think that's language, and you can actually sing it. But you don't realize how complicatedly the man has bent language in order for it to be said that way.

I would like to be the kind of singer that is respected by his tribe in the way Bobby Burns is respected. I would much rather have that kind of a feeling from my people than anything else I can think of.

What I would really like to do . . . say, wouldn't it be wonderful to write a song or a story that anybody would say, "*That* is art," on any given evening just because he loved the way it went? And that is what I want to do. And that is what I think poetry is about. And I think at times that some of my poetry has done that.

Do you remember when you wrote your first poem. Can you remember what it was about?

"Skunk Cabbage" was my first poem.

I began to be a poet at Reed College, and one day I was walking around the pond they had there . . . a very lovely lake . . . and there is also a swamp behind it where you could get laid by your girl. I saw this thing, and it was really weird. It was a skunk cabbage. I believe this was my first poem.

> 1
> Slowly in the swamps unfold
> great yellow petals of a
> savage thing, a
> tropic thing—
>
> While no stilt-legged birds watch,
> no monkey screams,
> those great yellow petals
> unfold.
>
> 2
> Rank plant.

I really thought that then. I saw that then. That is when I started to be a poet.

The way I went to Reed College is a long story. I went to the war and got through it, and that's not interesting. World War II. No, I didn't fight. It was just a big bummer. I tried very hard to fight. I wanted to be Errol Flynn. Let's get back to that later. I want to tell you how I got to Reed College, and it takes about eight hours from one point to the other. I mean, like World War II was not interesting at all. A bummer. I want to tell you what I feel about poetry. I can do it easily with a poem of mine.

> I WANT THE WHOLE THING, the moment
>   when what we thought was rock, or
>   sea
>   became clear Mind, and
>
> what we thought was clearest Mind really
>   *was* that glancing girl, that
>   Swirl of birds . . .
>
>   (all of that)
>
> AND AT THE SAME TIME that very poem
>   pasted in the florist's window
>
>   (as Whalen's *I wanted to bring you this Jap Iris*
>   was)

> carefully re-typed and
> put right out there on Divisadero St.
>
>   just because the florist thought it
>   pretty,
>
>   that it might remind of love,
>   that it might sell flowers . . .

The line

Tangled in Samsara!

4

I want to get into that now. The thing about poetry that is usually wrong is that the people who tend to be writing it are not poets. They don't know what their tribe is speaking, and they don't have anything to talk about themselves.

I met William Carlos Williams in 1950. I had graduated in June and waited all summer, with a fine redheaded girl, to meet him in September. I remember I put all my poems together, I was only about twenty-four, and added great long explanations, so I'd be ready for him.

Whalen, Snyder, and I were asked by the school—Reed was really a groovy place then—to go meet him at the airport. After all, we were the poets of Reed, and the faculty was sort of embarrassed about it all. So we got him into his hotel and rapped with him, it was like meeting a saint, a really important man, and he came on like a Middle Western hick, really, shy and everything. I always think of him as looking like President Truman.

He was so sweet and humble, and we loved him so much. He had saved our lives. And when we told him how he had truly defeated T. S. Eliot, he was really touched. That young men, poets, would come to him and say he had won the battle of his life.

We took him to our pad, where Whalen and Snyder and I lived, and we played poetry games and talked, and we gave him our stuff. And when he gave his reading at Reed, he began by saying, "It's good to be in a place where they will give a degree for a thesis on Gertrude Stein." I was so overwhelmed, after nobody wanted me to do the Stein thesis, and then my hero said that! He was the first poet I had met. He asked me to visit him in Rutherford. Again, I was overwhelmed. But I did it. I went to see him at his home maybe three or four times. I was pure mind transmission. I really became a poet only because of Williams. Williams and Gertrude Stein.

One day we were waiting for the dinner, served as "supper" in New Jersey at two in the afternoon, and Williams invited me upstairs to wash up. On the way we stopped at a three-drawer file cabinet, and he said, "That's my autobiography in there." And then he took me into a large room with a big oak table in the middle of it, and on the table was a funky old typewriter. Very neat. No clutter at all. And he said, to me, the punk, "This is where I work."

I felt like I was somebody in the baby trade, that I had come to investigate a foster father, and that he was saying: "See, I am raising it with love." I could hardly eat.

Years later he wrote to me: "I knew you were cracking up in New York, but it's like a concentration camp, one look of recognition and you too are done in. Thanks for the book. Sometimes it's a long time coming."

I had sent him **Wobbly Rock,** and he was into his fourth or fifth stroke, dying, and I wanted to thank him for what he had done for me.

Maybe five meetings altogether, but the result is total mind transmission, when the man is that great, and I hope I carry it well.

You have to know what the tribe is speaking, and you have to have something to talk about yourself. This is a two-part argument. Let's take the first part.

You have to have a sense of what the tribe is speaking. This takes ear training. You have to go out into the street and listen to the way people talk. You have to really listen to the kind of things that people say. You have to listen to the birds that are in the air, the helicopters, the big rush of jets. . . . Listen to this, you can't even talk in my living room without the din of it. You have to have your ears open. You have to have your goddamn ears open or you are not going to be a poet. Or you are not going to be a writer of any importance whatsoever.

I am sick and tired of all these punk kids trying to tell me how sad they are every time they walk through a park. Come on. Step one.

We have two things . . . you have to hear what is. You have to hear how your mother talked. You have to hear how your mother talked in a way that is so straight that it will almost kill you. Not only what she said, but how the language moved in what she said. And how the language affected the people around her. Because that is what is going to affect you. And you have to know what the people in the town talk like. How it is said. You have to know it so perfectly that you can never ever make an error. Even Hemingway made errors, and we must not, if we are poets, ever make an error. It is a very precise art and a strong and a good one. I die behind it . . . its strength and its purpose.

I had the privilege of seeing a poem of mine pasted in the No Name Bar window. I was asked by the owner of that bar to partake in a small demonstration to protest against the misuse of the beautiful area that the city of Sausalito is. It's being badly misused. You have this gorgeous beach that is nothing but asphalt and parking meters. So we had this demonstration, and it was really touching to me, and a source of great gratification, to be asked by an innkeeper in one's own village to partake in such a thing because of the fact that I am a poet. He wanted me to write a prayer and speak it. And I did. And then he published it . . . it's just a little short poem. We published it by going to the public library and for a dime apiece Xeroxed it until we got forty copies, and we gave them to the press and gave them to the people in the crowd, and they could read behind me. And then it was pasted in the window of the bar for the people on the street to see.

"SAUSALITO TRASH PRAYER"

Sausalito,
　Little Willow,
Perfect Beach by the last Bay in the world,
　None more beautiful,

Today we kneel at thy feet
　And curse the men who have misused you.

I think that poetry should be at least as lively as Robert Burns is. Where it can be used by the tribe in moments of need. When the chips are down, it's the turn of the New Year, and you are drunk and you can't even move, but you still sing "Auld Lang Syne."

I remember, back a few years ago, you were involved with trying to organize a fund to feed the poets of America. . . . You were planning to put out a magazine called Bread that would contain material showing how hard it is to survive economically as a poet in America. . . .

A big organization called Bread, Inc. All I would have needed was $10 million, and then we would be able to support all the poets that would be in America, ever. I figured $10 million would be the capital. You would have a half-million a year, 500,000 bucks, and also a hospital fund so poets could have babies and fix their wives' teeth and the other things that we need. The rest would be doled out. . . .

See, the trouble with most grants is that the grants are either for a book that is going to be written, or not written, or it's for going to Italy and doing something. Nobody just gives you bread. I don't need any grants. I know what I am going to do next year. What I need is $4,000! Like maybe I'll just sit here and spend it all on bourbon, but that's my goddamn right. If I am a poet I need bread to go, just like a car. You have to put gas in it. So that was the idea behind Bread, Inc. The fortunes of life have gone in such a way that I now have a way to get bread by myself, but it's very time-consuming and it's a big drag. But at least I have it.

What work do you do now to earn a living?

I work on the docks as a longshoreman's clerk. And I also get fees for going around and reading poetry. I ask for $500 and I get about $350. I work for as cheap as $100, if it is close, like Davis. At American River I went for $100 because it is in Sacramento. In fact, in the last two years, I have covered every part of the U. of California except UCLA.

I want poetry to be as useful as singing "The Star Spangled Banner" at a baseball game. I want it to be right in there. It is really strange to see that's possible, even in a culture as vulgar as America. It has happened. Like Phil Whalen's poem was really pasted in that florist's window. I didn't make that up. And my poem was really stuck up in a bar window.

I got two free drinks from a guy in Riverside just a few weeks ago. Before the poetry reading there, I asked the guys that were driving me from the airport to the reading to stop at a bar and we would all have a drink together. And as we had a drink, I got all excited . . . I am getting ready for the reading and I happen to mention this to a very groovy bartender why I was in town, and would he like to have a book of mine. He said: "Why sure." And I said, "You can't have it unless I can read it out loud, right here." And he got very nervous because he expected some gloomy poem . . . "I-love-the-night" bunch of bullshit to come out of me. Here it was, eleven in the morning, and who was ready for poetry? Who was ready for poetry in a bar in Riverside at 11 A.M. in the morning?

And I read *Courses* to him from start to finish, and he broke up. He thought it was the funniest thing he had ever heard. So I laid the book on him and said, "See, I work. Like Bobby Burns worked. I am trying to get the poem back into the bar." And he said, "That's a good idea. You should hear most of the shit these people talk around here!"

It could easily follow from such a position that, therefore, poetry would be quite mundane, watered down, made popular. Pop art instead of great art. Now, I think that Bobby Burns wrote as fine a set of lyrics as any poet ever wrote. Or even more heavily, probably the greatest poet that ever lived was Milarepa, the great Tibetan Buddhist. All of his teachings are in the form of songs. They are poems that he sang out loud to his students, his disciples, the people in the town.

The poetry of Homer, after all, are simply the songs of a blind old man in a time when there weren't printed books. Men would go around and tell the kings what their history was. Chaucer is the same thing. Chaucer is the man who made poetry of the streets, just as Han Shan's poetry would be scribbled on shit-house walls. . . . People found them on the rocks. Han Shan wrote them on the rocks on the mountains. People would run down to town and say: "Han Shan's written a new poem!" They would write it on the walls.

Po Chü-i, the great Chinese bard . . . his poetry was memorized by all the harlots in China and was sung by all the whores and pimps. I am not talking about writing down something. I believe if a poem is really well made, it can be strong enough to stand inside the general din of the speaking world.

We do a lot of talking, don't we? And the best talking we call poetry.

If the poem is made right, it will sit well in any room. Now, I believe this is the starkest, most unmundane standard for a poet to set for himself and his work. The opposite is . . . you take a guy like Rod McKuen, he is not a poet at all. He is not doing anything that is even interesting. Contrast him to a real poet like Bob Dylan, whose poems are in every living room.

I remember when I read my taxicab poem in a pool hall I used to play in when I was a cabdriver. I got to know these guys very well. This is a problem in America because America is such a vulgar place. I mean vulgar in the real sense, like coarse. If you are a cabdriver and you have cab-driver friends and they finally get to know and like you and then you say: "I am a poet" . . . they instantly think you are a goddamn queer. It is very hard to be a virile man going about his life when the main part of your life is being a poet. The main part of my life, the part I hold closest to my sense of self, is Lew Welch, the poet. I am also a father and a lover and a husband and a worker and a good shot or whatever it is that I think about myself, but always riding over it is: I am really Lew Welch, poet. Now you find you have to say to your cabdriving, pool-playing buddies that you are a poet, sooner or later. You have to tell them, you have to let them in on it, you have to. Otherwise, you are cheating them of your friendship. And when you do, you get this: "Mm-mm, uh-uh, oh, yeah. . . ."

Anyway, I told them at this pool game. I said, "By the way, do you know that I am a poet? If you don't mind, I would like to read you one." And I read them **"After Anacreon."** And they stopped chalking their cues, and they stopped playing, and they really started listening. And when I finished, they said: "Goddamn, Lewie, I don't know whether or not that is a poem, but that is the way it *is* to drive a cab."

I said, "Thanks, I am just testing it."

Now, Po Chü-i used to do that, too. He was a very great poet that used to have a peasant lady who was illiterate yet very, very smart. She was a peasant lady who ran a good garden down the road, and he would go and engage her in conversation. And then he would dump the poem on her, and if she didn't recognize that he had just said a poem, he figured that he had written it right. If she had a little "huh?" about it or something, if it seemed awkward to her or wrong, somehow ungraceful, then Po Chü-i would go back and fix it. At the same time, that very poem would have more literary references in it for the literate reader than we can imagine today. Po Chü-i is a real master at this, a super T. S. Eliot. He can put more echoes of old poems into four or five lines than any Chinese ever did before or after, and that is really something. He tested it against this lady who never read a poem in her life or wanted to. That's a standard, and that's the way I feel about that standard.

Let's get a little more technical about it. Talking about it like a poet talks to another poet.

You have a sense of language where language is held as a music, where that music is the sound of a taut soul singing. You have this kind of sense of language for some mysterious reason. It is a mystery. I don't understand it. There are people who write and sometimes make a poem. But then a weird thing happens to those of us who have this sense of language with this kind of intensity. It causes us to train ourselves as carefully as a flutist will. It is very, very close to music where you have to learn how to practice and practice. You have to learn how to shave the reed just right—you have to learn how to breathe just right. . . .

The poem should be able to be spoken so that the performance is just as much a part of it. . . . In other words, what you do when you write down a poem is that you are transcribing a voice.

You are not learning how to read the poem, you are learning how to write the song. For me, poetry is the sound of a man in words. And it partakes of song, of chanting, of prayer, of all the things we do when we really intensify language.

Learning the art of poetry also becomes learning the art of hearing. Ear training and voice training, just as surely as a musician does it.

I have always respected Rexroth's opinions on these matters. I have never found him to be incorrect. He put it this way once. He said he likes translating poetry when the muse isn't with him. He was going back to the old thing . . . that the muse wasn't there. You haven't got a poem of your own, and you are getting restless. You are saying, "My God, I am a poet and I have no poem. What will I do today?" You know how awful it is? Rexroth says, "Keep your hand in by making translations." He says, "More often than not, halfway through the translating, a poem comes out." The muse . . . that crazy little chick running around and rapping at a bunch of idiots who don't understand what she is saying . . . and she goes over and sees you are working very hard, and she says, "Sweet old Lewie," and goes over and says, "Bark," in your ear, and pretty soon, bang! you have a poem. And the translation falls by, or it comes out close enough to the guy so that you say **"After Anacreon"** or **"After William Blake."**

It's fun to translate English poets. For example, like Yeats has a poem that could be a very great poem, but he wrote it badly because he took the wrong meter. Yeats was really kind of meter-dumb. He is, I think, the greatest English-writing poet of the century, but he had a funny trick ear.

5

The art of poetry, in my mind, is connected with the art of music, because in my life it was. I sometimes ask myself: when did you start being a poet? I remember when I was four years old, running in to my mother: "You should have heard what Milton the gardener said," I said. "'I ain't got nothing.'" And I laughed because I thought that was the funniest thing I had ever heard. My mother had a very quick ear for language, up to a point, and she could see that that was a very unusual thing for a four-year-old boy to hear. To hear a funny word structure and to laugh at it. But my mother took it to mean that I was a natural scholar or that I knew right from wrong. I wasn't hearing "wrong," I was hearing what he said. Like, "can't hardly" always hits my ear with a very funny ring.

You see, the stuff of poetry insists that you have this kind of sense, somehow or other, and it is quite a mystery. It's just there or it isn't there. There is no way of teaching it. There is a way of honing it down, refining it, sharpening it up.

John Handy told me that after a few weeks he could play horn, alto sax; he already knew the clarinet, almost perfectly, not to his ear, but to everybody else's ear. He had to go into the hard work of it. Practicing scales over and over again. Long slow tones.

The second thing was that we had a jug, which I still have on my desk, to remind me of my sources. And on this jug is a little poem that I think was the start of it. It goes:

> Do the work that's nearest
> though it is dull at whiles,
> helping when you meet them
> lame dogs over stiles.

I found myself at twelve or thirteen reading that poem on the jug and thinking that those people needed some help. It's almost like a parody of Thelonious Monk. "Helping when you meet them" . . . what a funny meter! I'd see it every morning. The jug was on what my mother called a Welsh dresser, which is a piece of furniture that you put in the dining room and display all your pretty plates on.

Can you remember your first interest in music, specifically in jazz?

It was so early that I can't even figure it out. My mother reports once that I was about three or four and I was walking through a store in San Diego and I was singing something I had just heard on the phonograph or the radio. I had remarkable retention. And I could sing right in tune and with great pleasure.

I did play clarinet but never had the patience to learn an instrument. I've always been a very impatient person, and this business of embouchure, lingering, the little black notes, always stopped me. I started on clarinet, accordion, piano, bass, and now my music is entirely singing.

I used to call myself the best jug player in America, but I realized just yesterday that I wasn't. I was playing with an Okie chick that really knows that kind of music. Do you know Peter Coyote's old lady with a tattoo on her tit? She's the best Jew's-harp player in the whole world! God, she's good! I was playing with her, and she said, "You don't play jug, you play bottle." And it's true. Jug players play big three-quart ceramic instruments that have a tuba sound to them. But I play a glass bottle which has a high frequency and a high

resonance. The best general jug, believe it or not, is a quart Coca-Cola bottle. Something about the curves in it, I guess.

I remember that the only way my mother could make me wake up happy was to put on Cootie Williams. I just loved Cootie Williams! Do you know, he played a trumpet in such a way that you could *taste* the notes. Really chewy. Chu Berry I dug. He had that bite, that mouth thing going, like Hawkins did. So it was people like Cootie Williams, Hawkins, Prez, and of course, the real capper was Charlie Parker. Goddamn! That man astounds me to this day! When I listen to his records, I still can't believe it.

It's sad to note that only a small percentage of Parker's total record output is available in his country.

Is that so? I wouldn't doubt it. America is so vulgar! Americans just can't see heroes!

I had the great privilege of hearing that man "live" every single night for nearly two years. Because I went to the trouble to go hear him. The blessing was that he was there. I was also very grateful that somehow or other my hearing and my sense of the importance of this man was such that I availed myself of the opportunity.

I was at the U. of Chicago, in '51, '52, '53, and '54, and at that time Charles was damn near dead. I really enjoy calling him *Charles* Parker. There is something about "Charlie" that doesn't fit the man. He was Charles. He was dying, and none of us realized it.

He was working in a little joint on Sixty-Third Street in Chicago, and all of his side musicians were high-school kids. Just a thrown-together band: a piano, bass, drum, and Parker. That's all. The kids would be eighteen, nineteen, twenty, maybe twenty-one . . . if they weren't old enough, they would fake their age or something. But really nowhere. I mean the kind of group you would expect to find in an after-hours joint in San Francisco. Really dedicated, really young musicians who knew who the hell Parker was. Boy, did they know! They just played their asses off.

And he would come up after a set . . . oh, I remember him so well! He always wore double-breasted brown suits—God, or a brown double-breasted gabardine coat with blue pinstripe pants and bad shoes, just terrible. The cat just didn't give a fuck how he looked, he just didn't care at all. And his horn always hanging from his neck, and he had these funny walleyes . . . the one eye was high and to the outside. . . .

He would come after a set, you know, one of those fantastic tunes [*Lew scats "Scrapple from the*

Apple"], and the kids are trying to stay in there with him, and they are staying as best they can because they know who they are playing with. They know it. (I'd like to run into a couple of those kids now. I bet they are big guys now. Real heavy.) After the set was over—and here was everyone, a bunch of Okies in a Chicago bar giving you so much *crap*. No one was even listening, man . . . just nothing going on . . . there would be maybe eight people there: me and seven pimps and whores. Weird, man, because it was really a down Chicago bar scene. One of the places was called The Beehive. Charles Parker revolved around four joints within six blocks on Sixty-Third Street, which is a famous old jazz street. Apparently, he had a good contact for his heroin. That is the reason why he stayed there. Because he had a big name, Jesus, he could have made three or four thousand a week!

You know who he reminded me of? The only person I have ever met that reminded me of Charles Parker was Jack Spicer. They were the same man. They were just hell-bent on self-destruction. They were both six feet plus and heavy. They were big and strong. Jesus, Charles Parker had hands like a fucking farmer! Big hands. He had a working body, and it turned all into mind at a terrible price. They were very similar men, and they both had the same approach to their art.

Parker used to get up after a set and walk over to the piano player, and he would be so sweet . . . his horn hanging from his neck like a big necklace. He was big enough, he was really a strong man, his horn just hung and swung around. He didn't hold it like other guys do. And he leaned over and showed the kid how the chords should have gone. And the kid would sit there like: "Oh yeah, oh yeah . . . of course . . . B flat 7th . . . oh, B 9th minor . . . wow. . . ." And the next time Charles would say: "Let's do 'Salt Peanuts.'" And these tremendous tempos he would lay on these poor kids. Tremendous tempos that he would take with great ease and brilliance. . . .

The great breakthrough for me was of a structural nature. My ear began to hear things in terms of structure, not in terms of meaning. Almost as far back as I can remember, I was hearing structures. The big breakthrough came when I was freaking out as a twenty-year-old college student will freak out. I had this dear teacher who understood everything, I thought, and I had to see him.

I was really freaking out . . . I was on a $600-a-year track scholarship, wearing the saddle shoes, a fraternity boy at Stockton Junior College. And I have all that going for me . . . fraternity houses where I can't get laid . . . my head's breaking . . .

and I had to talk to this man who is named James Wilson and is now a teacher at San Francisco State . . . a very dedicated teacher, one of those rare men who regards teaching as an art. He really got through to me, and I had to talk to him. I don't know what I wanted to say to him . . . you know how it is when you are that young. I go into his office, and he is not there. His desk is very littered, and there are lots of books and most of them are open, and I decide I am going to sit there and wait until he comes back, no matter how long it takes.

I picked up a book called *Three Lives* by Gertrude Stein, and I read *Melanctha,* And I became a writer. It's the damnedest thing. It's like Malraux reports in *The Voices of Silence:* "We are brought to art by an artist. We are not brought to art by a natural wonder." I read *Melanctha,* and the impression was really wonderful. She is not so hard to understand. Everyone has been telling me that Gertrude Stein was "A rose is a rose is a rose. . . ."

You had been writing, hadn't you?

No, I was only twenty then. Oh, yes, I was sports editor for the paper. I did all the writing for the tribe. When they needed somebody, it was: "Lew, will you do this, Lew would you make a speech?" I always did it, but I thought of myself as a painter, a singer, and a track star. I was a voracious reader. I never read less than four books a week since I was about nine. And then in college I ran the 440 in 49.7 seconds.

Suddenly, reading *Melanctha* I felt as though I had been invited to a very distinguished party, a weekend party in the country, and at this party there were Shakespeare, Poe, Stein, Joyce, Dickens, Chaucer, all of the people that I had admired. And because of Stein's story *Melanctha,* it was like an invitation. "Why don't you come out to the country and spend a weekend with us?"

I came to that house, and I came with great humbleness. And I didn't say a word. I just listened. I listened for a long time, and it was a good long party. Now I am forty-three and I do most of the talking. After all, they are tired, but the same people are there. And that is who I am talking to, and it is wonderful to want to listen once in a while. I don't know how I see them. Do I see them as a monkey in a zoo with the visitors or what? But I must do my talking, my poetry, to them, the hosts of the party. That is my real audience.

Anyway, there was this moment in my life reading this one story, and I suddenly said: "Goddamn, writing is not only a good thing to do, it is very easy. The thing you have to do is to put your words down absolutely true like Gertrude Stein is doing here." It wasn't so much that I loved the story better than other stories or that I liked the writing more, it was a moment of revelation. A vision. The mystical part, the mystery of it, is contained in an experience like that.

That was my presence at the great garden party. I worked for them for nearly ten years to learn exactly what Gertrude Stein had going for her and why. And I still believe that Gertrude Stein is probably the best writer if you just want to take writing as a supreme exquisite art. Nobody ever did it as purely as Gertrude Stein, because everybody gets the story in the way somehow or other, or gets themselves in the way. She really went word, word, word, word, word. You know how musicians talk about Mozart? Well, that is the way Stein is as a writer, in my mind.

I know writers I prefer to read now, but I don't know of anybody who can write better than Gertrude Stein, ever. She is just a supreme master of this business of getting what is in your head out of your head and into words. Writing as opposed to storytelling. Making a *poem* instead of "making it up." Anderson I respect at the same level and Hemingway, too, but I really think that Gertrude was right, that Hemingway learned from Stein, not vice versa. She also said: "But I have a weakness for Hemingway." She saw that. She also said that, and she's right: "The first person that ever wrote an American sentence was Sherwood Anderson."

Sherwood Anderson is another very wrongly placed person in the literary fable. This man was a real giant, and you never hear anybody talking about him anymore. I think Gertrude was a little wrong about him being first, because the opening of Mark Twain's *Life on the Mississippi* has, for me, the first American sentences. One after the other. Hundreds of them, and they are all perfect and big.

What about Thoreau?

Thoreau, Melville, Hawthorne, Emerson, and Whitman . . . they are very great Americans and great writers, but they didn't write in this funny diction that has now become the major language of the Earth. But Twain did, and Stein did, and Sherwood Anderson did, and Hemingway did.

But Hemingway did it as if he had heard Sherwood Anderson and Stein do it so perfectly that he could not miss. No, he wasn't cheating any more than Shakespeare was cheating when he came onto his Elizabethan English because Marlowe and Sidney had done so much hard work that he could do it easily without thinking about it. He didn't cheat. In other words, it gave him the strength of confidence he needed in order to write it truly in the way that he spoke. I don't think Hemingway could have done it by himself. It was Stein, Twain, and Sherwood Anderson that rapped it in his ear and gave him the freedom to work with it.

You see, Marlowe made up the line that Shakespeare was free to use. This doesn't put Hemingway down to say it, at all. It just places him in another order of creativity.

I find myself in this role. There is a lot of hard work that I don't have to do because men like William Carlos Williams did it for me. Stein did it for me. Also Hemingway did it for me, and Sherwood Anderson did it for me. I find that when I read Whitman I feel I am reading a translation. . . .

You see, you have a tree, and you have the real limbs and leaves, and always you have the sports. Now, at times these sports are the most prized. They are really beautiful. I think Robert Duncan's work is very beautiful. But it is utterly useless and will not have any heirs. And it will not go anywhere, and it came from part of the trunk that I don't understand—but I respect it. It's really a strong piece of the tree. But it is a sport. It is a sucker that comes off the side. I don't know or care where it comes from.

T. S. Eliot would be in the same class. He had nothing to do with English literature, at all. He is a sport off the side of it. While T. S. Eliot is fumbling around with his imitations of seventeenth-century sermons, the real work is being done by Hart Crane, William Carlos Williams, Fitzgerald, e. e. cummings, Gertrude Stein, Hemingway. Emily Dickinson is right there in the heartwood of the tree; so are Rexroth and Patchen and Miller. But not Pound and certainly not Eliot.

The thing about the sucker, the sport, was that Eliot captured the imagination of so many people and made so many people look away from the real tree for so long. Eliot didn't say one thing pertinent to the twentieth century. He simply is a recording of the best of the seventeenth-century sermon writers. Where the hell is the twentieth century? His language is an absolute failure. Pound's language is even worse. I love Pound, but. . . .

Those who seek to find poetry in the library, as Duncan and Eliot do, are ultimately doomed to failure. Duncan's language at a cocktail party is very lively. He is wonderful, but why the hell can't he get it into his poetry? He doesn't get it in there, and therefore his poetry is dead.

Robin Blaser suffers from the same thing. Robin Blaser is one of the most erudite, witty, charming, good men that I have ever known, and I can't understand why he uses poetry like some kind of shield between himself and reality. He uses it like I use chess in my life. I play chess as well as Robin writes poetry. He writes exquisite things that don't matter at all. There is no matter in them.

I find myself very uncomfortable talking against Duncan because I don't want to talk against Duncan, you know what I mean? But it evolves into an example, because he is so strong. He is so strong in doing whatever he is doing. But whatever he is doing does not, finally, matter.

6

Let's get to the mystery. As I see it, it is like this. A vision is what you see with the mind's eye; which is to say, a vision is what you see. Of course, we see everything with the mind's eye, don't we? And the word "seer" is simply see-er. A person who sees.

We talked about how there are people who have an absurdly tense understanding of the way that language moves, and we call them poets. But then there are some people who have that gift and don't have anything to say. Like, W. H. Auden would be one. He is just impeccable in his ability to handle word problems, yet he hasn't ever said one interesting thing to us, nor has Eliot, where William Blake really did.

Now a vision is what you see with the mind's eye; which is to say, a vision is what you see. A seer is a man who can see things that others cannot see. He is Prometheus, a man who goes into the void, and brings back something and shows it to you, so that that kind of void is forever illuminated. After he has done that, anybody can look into that void, and they can see it because the man brought it back. He illuminates something that anyone *could* see, but they don't see it. He does it some way. He paints it, he dances it, he writes it down.

Blake put it his way: "I do not distrust my corporal or vegetative eye any more than I would distrust a window for its sight. I look through it, not with it." That is the source of vision. That is a man who *sees*. A vision is what you see with the mind's eye; which is to say, a vision is what you see.

In my life I have never found a need to wonder about whether or not there is a God, let alone believe in it. The whole idea of another power has always seemed to me the most outrageously unnecessary and dangerous human idea that ever was. Yet I have always worshipped this planet, which is, of course, another power.

There is something that is not us, right? Now for me, it is this earth that I stand on, these trees, this sweet air, the lovely water I drink, the fish that swim in it . . . all of this is a source of endless wonder. But it is the see-er in us who, as Stein put it, can "know themselves knowing it." We are the poets. When I was six years old, I used to take my bicycle to the ocean because my household was filled with very nervous women and I had to get out of there and my friends were nowhere, just kick-the-can bullshit friends . . . so I would go to the ocean and sit on an ocean rock and sit for hours and get all the sound of that ocean and pick those mussels and eat them raw—knowing that they are going to "poison you . . . impossible to eat them, you better not eat them . . ."— fuck it! And I taught myself how to swim in it and rub sand on my arms, and I figured out how to catch minnows with a little orange-juice strainer, which I did because I was that patient. I didn't get very many, but I got them. And I saw an octopus as big as a coffee cup, a real octopus, and I got him and I put him in the tub and I looked at him and I said: "Shit, I am not going to take you home, baby." And I put him back, but I got him. That was my God, and still is my God, and I really deeply believe that if it can be that simple a God for everybody, then all the troubles we have would go away.

When you start talking to me about trinities and Christs and virgin births and saints and Buddhas, like, forget it, man. That's all words. That's all shit, shit. That's trash. That's mind trash. Because it is right there under your feet, see? And it is not only your feet and your eyes that let you "know yourself knowing it." It's God.

Those are visions. They are things that you can see. You can see them. They are not special states of mind, although when I see them at times, the ecstasies get to the point that it is physically painful. I actually writhe like I am in a fit and I weep and I bellow. And that is the source of my poems. And I don't write from any other source, because the rest of it is just shit, trash. Mind trash.

You read poems by people who are always crying about how their girl left them or some kind of crap. I got a poem the other day from a student. A very nice poem about the moon. He had some good things in it.

It looked like he really looked at it a little. A little bit. Then he looked inside his own squirmy gut and he said: "Oh, it is sad!" He puts it in Spanish that the moon is sad. What a goddamn cop-out lie! The moon is not sad! When I look at that moon, I get so high, I blow my mind. Now don't tell me the moon is sad, because it isn't sad. Even Shelley wasn't that bad!

These ecstasies that I suffer have been suffered by every real poet that ever lived. And if you can't know them, you probably don't have a source strong enough to write a poem from.

You know my poem called **"Ring of Bone"**? I will let you in on a little secret. Here's what really happened.

I had to leave Lenore Kandel because she was corny, and our life was not getting on together because of that. I have an exquisite kind of fineness to my life that she could not meet. She could not meet the other stuff that I needed desperately with perfection. She was a perfect helpmate. A goddamn good wife. But I didn't need it. I needed some other goddamn thing.

By this time I am thirty-eight, I am no punk, anymore. It is really hurting. And how can you give up the most beautiful girl in San Francisco, who you need? But I had to go. I had to split, and I remember the split. It was really wild. She is weeping at the top of the stairs, and I am weeping at the bottom of the stairs, and like there are no words left. And we are both poets. And she knows I've got to leave, yet she really doesn't know why.

Ferlinghetti loaned me his cabin in Big Sur. I went to him and said: "Look, man, it's really freak-city time. Can I borrow your cabin?"

He's beautiful that way. Sure. And bang, here's the key. OK, so down I go. I take enough groceries to last about two weeks and a typewriter and a lot of paper, and I just thrashed around in it. And one day, I got it.

I woke up after a wine drunk—I had brought a lot of red wine with me—I woke up about three in the afternoon and I saw it.

> I saw myself
> a ring of bone
> in the clear stream
> of all of it
>
> and vowed
> always to be open to it
> that all of it
> might flow through
>
> and then heard
> "ring of bone" where
> ring is what a
>
> bell does

And in the middle of it I got an erection and put my dick out the open window, and I came without even touching it. And that's the kind of ecstasies I am talking about. It's like that old joke, you know, a girl has a cunt that is too big, and you say it is like sticking your prick out the window and fucking the world. That was it. I stuck my prick out and I fucked the world.

And I freaked out. And I knew I am not kidding now. I didn't make this up. I had to recover that experience, and I made this neat tight little poem, out of it. If I didn't have the chops now after twenty years of hard work getting the chops down, I couldn't capture it. People read that poem, and they see and sense a strange power. And they can't figure out why.

Now you heard the vision, and now you have heard the poem. Now these two things are terribly important. Without the practice I could not have captured it. I would have said: "I sure had a bad freak-out in Big Sur, David. I think I had better go to Langley Porter."

But if you are a poet, you can snag it, put it down, and then you look at the poem, and then you look at your wet prick, and you look at the earth you just came on, and you say, "Goddamn, it is all right, isn't it?" You get a big up out of it. And I am *that* crazy.

It's the vision brought back. And it is not the vision, either. The poem is not the vision. The vision is the source of the poem. The poem is the chops, but the real chops are being able to go across that river and come back with something that is readable.

The ecstasies get to a point where they are usually unbearable. That one was on wine and despair. *Wobbly Rock* was done on despair. Period. And rain. We are in a drug era now. Everybody asks you, "Like, what did you do it on?" Well, you do it cold sometimes. When ecstasies hit me, they hit me so hard sometimes that I wouldn't even entertain the idea of taking so much as a drink of wine, if it would mess with it.

The danger is that you begin to like them very much. The ecstasies. You require that every day you have one. This is, of course, a drag. No one could survive it. It is really debilitating. As Saints Teresa and John pointed out, as Huang Po does. All the big mystics have pointed out that ecstasies are dangerous. They really are. I mean they are all right, and it is certainly wrong to deny yourself ecstasies if you happen to be available to them. Apparently, some people are not available to ecstasies. . . .

ROD PHILLIPS (ESSAY DATE 2000)

SOURCE: Phillips, Rod. "'The Journal of Strategic Withdrawal': Nature and the Poetry of Lew Welch." In *"Forest Beatniks" and "Urban Thoreaus": Gary Snyder,*

Jack Kerouac, Lew Welch, and Michael McClure, pp. 71-102. New York: Peter Lang, 2000.

In the following essay, Phillips provides a brief biography of Welch and explores the dominant themes of his work.

> ". . . when the cities lie at the
> monster's feet there are left the mountains."
> Robinson Jeffers "Shine, Perishing Republic"
> (1925)

"I am a poet," wrote Lew Welch in 1964:

> My job is writing poems, reading them out loud, getting them printed, studying, learning how to become the kind of man who has something of worth to say. It's a great job. Naturally I'm starving to death.
> **(How I Work [How I Work as a Poet]** 3)

A poetic career which spanned two decades earned Lew Welch little fame and almost no income. His collected poems, **Ring of Bone,** remained unpublished until two years after his death in 1971. Aside from Aram Saroyan's slim, loosely structured biography, *Genesis Angels: The Saga of Lew Welch and the Beat Generation,* almost no serious study of the poet and his work has yet been undertaken.

This is unfortunate, since in the poet's brief forty-four years, he was able to produce a finely crafted and innovative body of work which Samuel Charters has rightfully called "a group of poems that are among the purest and most precise of all the Beat creations" (539). Welch wrote in a variety of forms—poems, songs, fiction, one act plays—on topics which reflected his varied life experiences as he strived to subsidize his art: ad man, commercial fisherman, cab driver, dock worker, teacher. But more often than not, these creations dealt with nature and humanity's place in it, for Welch was a writer who struggled with, and reveled in, this theme for much of his career. As his friend Gary Snyder noted in his introduction to Welch's posthumously published **Selected Poems** (1973):

> Ultimately, Lew's poems are devotional songs to the Goddess Gaia: Planet Earth's Biosphere: and he is truly one of the few who have Gone Beyond, in grasping the beauty of that ecstatic Mutual Offering called the Food Chain.
> (ii)

Indeed, much of Welch's work can be seen as a reflection of a life-long discomfort with modern, urban America, and a yearning to find his place as what he referred to as "a Native of a World" (**Ring** [**Ring of Bone**] 108). In the preface to his collected poems, **Ring of Bone,** Welch pointed to the tension between life in the urban, human-centered world and the world dominated by nature as a central point of balance in his writing:

ON THE SUBJECT OF...

KIRBY DOYLE

A West Coast Beat, Kirby Doyle emerged from the San Francisco Poetry Renaissance of the late 1950s. Like his friend and mentor Lew Welch, Doyle possessed a passion for the wilderness of California and the Pacific Northwest. True to the Beat aesthetic, Doyle rejected the more formal, often self-important verse of the literary establishment. Like his peers, he sought to free his poetry from the excessive refinement that he felt burdened American academic verse. The San Francisco poets believed that poetry could retain a nonconformist, idiomatic expression, while remaining passionate and meaningful in its expression—a lesson learned through their study of the Zen poets of Asia. Among Doyle's published work are the collections *Angels Faint* (1967) and *Happiness Bastard* (1968).

> The shape of **Ring of Bone** is circular, or back and forth. Naturally such a form never ends. The principle characters are The Mountain, The City, and The Man who attempts to understand and live with them. The Man changes more than The Mountain and The City, and it appears he will always need both.
> (3)

Although this balance between Man and Mountain, city and wilderness, is a constant in Welch's writing, there can be little doubt which side of the scale the poet favored; as he wrote to James Wilson: "Enlightenment, as I see it, is a process whereby a person gradually resigns from the world that is man, and thereby becomes a member of the world that is not man."[1]

Beginnings

Lewis Barrett Welch was born in Phoenix, Arizona on August 16, 1926, the son of a wealthy, highly intelligent mother, and an inattentive, often absent, father. His parents' marriage was short-lived, and in 1929 Welch's mother, Dorothy Brownfield, took him and his sister west, where they spent the next fifteen years in what the poet would recall as "dozens of little California towns, never in one place three years" (**IR** [**I Remain:**

The Letters of Lew Welch and the Correspondence of His Friends] II, 129). Welch rarely saw his father, Lew "Speed" Welch, again, but seems to have credited his brief relationship with his father with instilling in him an enduring love for hunting, fishing, and the outdoors. "This is the one thing Lew gave me," he wrote later in a letter to his mother:

> By the one thing Lew gave me I mean that when a boy knows his father is good at something that's male and easy to understand, and that everyone can admire, then, whether or not he does it with the guy, he has the built-in right to it. I came to guns not as a stranger. And, you know, in all fairness, a great many men get far less from their fathers.
>
> (*IR* I, 87)

During his school years, Welch's family continued to move often, never allowing him to spend more than two or three years attending the same school. One of the few constants in his early life was his love of reading, and here too, a developing fascination with nature can be noted. Ernest Thompson Seton, the turn of the century naturalist/author of works such *Lives of the Hunted* and *Wild Animals I Have Known* was among Welch's favorite writers in junior high school. When Welch began to read poetry during his early teens, the poet he was most drawn to was Robert Service, whose tales of the Alaskan wilderness, such as those captured in *The Spell of the Yukon*, earned him a permanent place in Welch's library (Meltzer 200).

After finishing high school in Palo Alto, Welch enlisted for a brief stint in the U.S. Air Force, but quickly rejoined civilian life a year later when the Second World War ended. He then attended Stockton Junior College, where his interests in literature and writing began in earnest. In 1948, Welch transferred to Reed College in Portland, Oregon as an English major (Samuel Charters 542). It was here that the writer would make some acquaintances who would change the course of his career.

In the spring of 1949 Welch rented a house near campus with a room-mate he deemed, in a letter home, "one of the finest people I've ever known," an undergraduate anthropology major named Gary Snyder (*IR* I, 1). In January of the following year, the two were joined by a third room-mate, an ex-G.I. undergraduate with an interest in literature and Oriental languages, Philip Whalen. The three were all aspiring writers, and a strong friendship based on this shared craft quickly developed—a friendship which would last as long as Welch lived.

By his senior year, Welch was already beginning to publish his first poems in *Janus*, the little magazine he co-edited with other Reed students. The first of these, a brief imagist poem entitled **"Skunk Cabbage,"** foreshadows the poet's life-long fascination with close observation of the natural world:

> Slowly in the swamps unfold
> great yellow petals of a
> savage thing, a
> tropic thing—
>
> While no stilt-legged birds watch,
> no monkey screams,
> those great yellow petals,
> unfold.
>
> Rank plant.
>
> (*Ring* 37)

Many of Welch's early poems, like this one, bear a strong resemblance to the work of William Carlos Williams: short powerful lines, an insistence on common language, and stark yet bold imagery. This is no coincidence; Welch knew and respected the poetry of Williams—especially the older poet's epic, *Paterson*.[2] During Welch's final semester at Reed College, Williams came to the college to read his work. When he arrived, he was met by Welch, Whalen and Snyder, who each brought with them drafts of their poems for his examination. In addition, Welch showed Williams his senior thesis on Gertrude Stein, which he read enthusiastically. Williams recommended that Welch try to revise and publish the manuscript, and offered to arrange for a reading of the text with an editor at Random House (*IR* I, 40-41).

The help and encouragement offered by Williams provided Welch with the needed impetus to think of himself as a writer; he jokingly signed a letter to his mother describing his meeting with Williams "Lew (the voice of the latter half of the 20th century)" (*IR* I, 42). Following his graduation, he set off to New York in order to visit Williams and to continue work on the Stein book. He rented an apartment on West 82nd Street, found a job as a clerk in a large department store, and spent his off hours researching and revising the Stein manuscript in the rare book room at the New York Library, but he abandoned the project after only a few months in the city. In April 1951 he wrote to his mother, in what would be the first of many statements concerning the claustrophobia he felt in large cities:

> New York I'm afraid is nothing more than a
>   noisy rock.
> I can't breathe in it even.

It whupped me.
Therefore leave.

(*IR* I, 52)

Chicago: In the Heart of the "Murcan Machine"

Abandoning, at least temporarily, his ambitions as a writer, in the Fall of 1951, Welch applied for admission to the University of Chicago's graduate school, majoring first in History of Philosophy, and then switching after a semester, to English. He found some of his courses stimulating, but as a whole, Welch found the experience—and the setting—difficult to endure. He wrote to Snyder, who was preparing to enter graduate school at Berkeley:

What are you goin' to do in that Western province. I ought to go with you. This place has me stifled already. And I tried. Honest. Three weeks in a literature course and not one (1) word have I heard about literature. . . . These people hate pomes [sic].

(*IR* I, 65)

After several semesters of graduate work at the University of Chicago, Welch left the school, but stayed on in the city, taking a job with Montgomery Ward's retail advertising department.[3] For a time, it seemed that Lew Welch could live happily within the city; a new marriage to native Chicagoan Mary Garber, and the promise of a high salary for his work as an advertising copy writer made Chicago seem, he wrote, "more bearable all the time" (*IR* I, 76). Weekend hunting trips into the countryside outside of Chicago even yielded occasional glimpses of beauty, although Welch clearly longed for his native West. In a 1957 letter to his mother, he notes:

But the farm country of Illinois is beautiful if you give it a chance. It's silly to keep expecting the land to look like the Rockies. All you accomplish is a blindness to the flat, gold, low-skied beauty that's all over the Midwest.

(*IR* I, 87)

But such observations became increasingly rare in the months that followed, as Welch's growing unhappiness and discontent with Chicago—and the modern city in general—again rose to the surface. What had a few years before appeared as a lucrative job as an ad writer now was seen by Welch as a prostitution of his talents. "It finally got through to me that this is humiliating. . . ." he wrote to Gary Snyder on April 22, 1957, "We are paid for pieces of pride" (*IR* I, 90). That same day, Welch wrote to Philip Whalen about his "intolerable daily life" in Chicago, advising him that he was "putting everything together into a poem about cities" (*IR* I, 91). Enclosed with the letter were five pages of poetry, some of which later became part of Welch's urban collage "**Din Poem.**" In it, the poet puts forth what would become a recurring image in his poems and essays—the modern city as an artificial construct imposed upon the landscape of the natural world:

I am on top of the Empire State Building leaning on the
railing which I have carefully examined to see if it's
strongly made. The sound of it comes all that way, up,
to me. A hum. Thousands of ventilators far away. Now
and then I hear an improbable clank. The air, even up
here, is warmed by it.

To the north a large green rectangle, Central Park, lies
flat, clean-edged, indented. A skin has been pulled off,
a bandage removed, and a small section of the Planet has
been allowed to grow.

I think, "They have chosen to do this in order to save
their lives." And then I think, "It is not really a section
of the Planet, it is a perfect imitation of a section of the Planet
(remembering the zoo). It is how they think it might look."
I am struck by their wisdom. Moved.

(*Ring* 107)

To Welch's discerning eye, even those areas within the modern city which have traditionally been seen as oases where nature is allowed to flourish—the parks—are themselves urban impositions on the natural terrain. "Flat, clean-edged," and "indented," Central Park represents for Welch not an effort aimed at preserving a "small section of the Planet," but instead at preserving the sanity of the city's human population by means of illusion and fantasy. The comment on the "wisdom" involved in such an arrangement in the final line of the section's third stanza is likely ironic.

By the summer of 1957, Welch had come to realize that life in Chicago had become unbearable for him. His drinking increased, as did his discomfort at life within the confines of what he called "this dangerous city" (*IR* I, 106). "This is how I live:" he angrily wrote to Philip Whalen:

The alarm clock starts me. I have a hangover. I am nauseated all morning. . . . I can't keep down orange juice, toast, and tea. I chew gum and go to my car dressed in a suit and a tie. I fight idiots who don't know how [to] drive on a highway where thousands of cars go too fast and all the signs, streetlights, and policemen are confused and wrong. . . . At the office I do the urgent, not the important. A friend describes it as "pissing on small fires." . . . All day long I am humiliated by inferior people who insist that I must do something in less time than it takes. . . . Then I come home. The same idiots that can't drive are now as furious as I am. We try to kill each other for 30 minutes. Then I am home. I have a cocktail. I have 5 more.

(*IR* I, 106)

Welch ended the letter with his plans to quit Chicago and return to graduate school, and ultimately, a college teaching job in his native West: "Back to health. Back to friends. Back to beautiful country" (107).

By the following October, Welch had realized part of this goal; Montgomery Ward granted him a transfer to their Oakland, California office, and he and his wife relocated there soon after. At long last Welch was back in his home region, and squarely in the middle of the San Francisco poetry renaissance he'd read so much about in the national press. His plan was to continue his advertising work for the firm long enough to pay off his bills and then, as he told Snyder, "kick the Business Habit" and devote his time to writing (*IR* I, 116). He vowed to Whalen also that he was through with the "Murcan [American][4] Machine," saying:

> . . . [T]here is nothing for me to do except get out of it and make it as well as possible and know finally and for all time that it's quite important not to help the damned thing . . .
>
> (*IR* I, 115)

If the path to enlightenment, for Lew Welch, meant gradually resigning "from the world that is man," then this decision to leave the financial security offered by corporate America marks an important step on that path; for the remainder of his life Welch struggled to feed and clothe himself by means of a variety of part-time occupations, but from this period forward he identified himself, and his occupation, as writer.

Welch's "**Chicago Poem**," perhaps his most famous and most frequently anthologized piece, is an eloquent statement in verse of the poet's mid-life change in direction away from urban, corporate America. First drafted in June 1957, near the end of the poet's residence in the Midwest, the poem begins with the first person narrator (presumably Welch)[5] recalling the gray, dismal landscape of mid-twentieth century Chicago:

> I lived here nearly 5 years before I could
> > meet the middle western day with
> > anything approaching
> Dignity. It's a place that lets you

understand why the Bible is the way it
> is:
Proud people cannot live here.

The land's too flat. Ugly sullen and big it
> pounds men down past humbleness.
> They
Stoop at 35 possibly cringing from the heavy
> and
> > terrible sky. In country like this there
Can be no God but Jahweh.

(*Ring* 10)

As an early San Francisco reviewer, Grover Sales, wrote in response to hearing Welch read the poem: "This is not the Chicago of Sandburg but the *Rome* of Juvenal and the *London* of William Blake" (*IR* II, 141). In place of Sandburg's 1916 vision of Chicago as "Stormy, husky, brawling, / City of the Big Shoulders," four decades later Welch portrays a hopeless urban atmosphere where men "Stoop at 35" under the horrible weight of their surroundings. And in place of Sandburg's romantic vision of a vital and expansive city "proud to be Hog Butcher, Tool Maker, Stacker of Wheat, Player with Railroads and Freight Handler to the Nation," Welch depicts a city fallen victim to its own industrial excesses:

> In the mills and refineries of its south side
> > Chicago
> > > passes its natural gas in flames
> Bouncing like bunsens from stacks a hundred
> > feet high.
> > > The stench stabs at your eyeballs.
> The whole sky green and yellow backdrop for
> > the skeleton
> > > steel of a bombed-out town.
>
> (10)

The speaker's only solace is not found within the city, but in nature. Where Sandburg had written of Chicago as being "cunning as a savage pitted against the wilderness," the narrator in Welch's poem finds his only moments of hope in the wild. After five years inside the city, an alternative arises which allows him to "recognize the ferocity" inherent in his urban existence: "Finally I found some quiet lakes / and a farm where they let me shoot pheasant" (10). Away from the city while pheasant hunting or fishing, he is able to differentiate between the manmade chaos of Chicago's south side, and what Welch might call "the world that is not man":

> All things considered, it's a gentle and
> > undemanding
> > > planet, even here. Far gentler
> Here than any of a dozen other places. The
> > trouble is
> > > always and only with what we build on
> top of it.
>
> (11)

As the speaker returns to Chicago after a day in the farmlands, he is determined to accept the modern city for what it is: a human creation which is no longer under human control—a violent and dangerous monster who now threatens those to whom it once offered shelter:

> Driving back I saw Chicago rising in its gasses
>   and I
>   knew again that never will the
> Man be made to stand against this pitiless,
>   unparalleled
>   monstrosity. It
> Snuffles on the beach of its Great Lake like a
>   blind, red, rhinoceros.
> It's already running us down.
>
> You can't fix it. You can't make it go away.
>   I don't know what you're going to do
>   about it,
> But I know what I'm going to do about it. I'm
>   just
>   going to walk away from it. Maybe
> A small part of it will die if I'm not around
>
>   feeding it anymore.
>   (11)

The solution, according to Welch's speaker, is total resignation from the "monstrosity" of urban, industrial, America: "I'm just / going to walk away from it." But the poem's final stanza presents more than just a statement of dejection and defeat. It is a radical act of individual civil disobedience which recalls Henry David Thoreau's statement in *Walden* that "I might have resisted forcibly with more or less effect, might have run 'amok' against society; but I preferred that society should run 'amok' against me, it being the desperate party" (155). In the mid-nineteenth century, Thoreau had urged Americans to let their lives be a "friction to stop the machine" of an unjust and cruel society (644); but a hundred years later, Welch seems to suggest, what he referred to as the "Murcan Machine" had become unstoppable: "You can't fix it. You can't make it go away." The best one could hope for is to not be used as fuel—to let your absence be a friction to stop the machine.

San Francisco: Meditation at Muir Beach

When Welch arrived in the West with his wife Mary in the fall of 1957, he found a California quite different from the one he had left more than a decade earlier. San Francisco, long a haven for America's Bohemian population, now hosted a burgeoning youth sub-culture: "Telegraph Hill with its children-type Bohemes was a real shock," he wrote to Whalen (*IR* I, 118). Welch found San Francisco a welcome change from life in Chicago, and enjoyed the thriving poetry and arts com-

munity which had sprung up in the Bay Area. He took in readings by Kenneth Rexroth, Kenneth Patchen, and Lawrence Ferlinghetti during his first few months in the city, as well as jazz performances by Dave Brubeck and others at clubs like the Blackhawk. "Everything is jumping here," he wrote to Snyder, who was at sea aboard a Pacific tanker, "or so it seems to be in contrast to the plain" (*IR* I, 120).

Despite Welch's appreciation for San Francisco's cultural life, however, there are signals in his letters from the period indicating a desire for an even deeper withdrawal from urban life than his move from Chicago offered. Just after Christmas 1957, in a letter to Whalen, he intimated his longing for a life uncluttered by all but the essentials: "There's plenty of time left over after meeting the very gentle needs of the planet, the bowels, the heart. The only overly demanding thing is all those people who try to fill their days with something that can't possibly demand that much. Then they try to get us to do it too. They stone us if we sit" (*IR* I, 126).

The events of 1958 moved Welch closer to the kind of life he described to his friend Whalen. In March he was fired from his job as an advertising writer with Montgomery Ward, and in July his marriage to Mary Garber dissolved. Like the world of commerce, the "American Homemaking Bit," as Welch referred to marriage, seemed to be just one more mystifying institution for the poet. He wrote Whalen that "for me it's all soap and machinery ritualized to a point beyond my understanding," adding that "I bungle around like a guy trying to play shortstop for the Giants while wearing the equipment for, and observing the rules of, badminton. I've sent myself to the showers, I'm sure to the relief of all concerned" (*IR* I, 146).

His marriage over, his career as an ad writer behind him, Welch moved deeper into the rapidly developing counterculture. He found work as a cab driver, and after a brief stay at Gary Snyder's Mill Valley cabin, moved into San Francisco's East-West House, one of the city's early experiments in communal living.[6] It was during this period that Welch first seriously examined Zen Buddhism, which was then enjoying an unprecedented popularity among American youth. In October he began a course of Zen practice (zazen) and meditation under the guidance of Gary Snyder at Snyder's Marin-an cabin in nearby Mill Valley. From the beginning, the poet appears to have been a sincere but at times skeptical adherent to Buddhist practice. Soon after beginning his Zen studies he described the routine to Whalen:

Mister Snyder has us sitting in his shack Japanese style all the while ringing bells and smacking blocks of wood together. Then we run around the woods in pitch darkness falling over fences and otherwise being foolish, return, sit, drink tea, sit, and go home.

(*IR* I, 149)

Although Welch would later renounce Buddhism—and indeed all religion—as "mind trash" (Meltzer 225), Zen practice does seem to lie at the root of a good deal of the poet's thought during the late fifties and early sixties. The poet's long introspective piece, **"Wobbly Rock,"** which was published as Welch's first small chapbook in 1960, exemplifies Welch's use of Buddhist sources in his writing during this period.[7] The poem begins with an epigraph which both dedicates the work to Snyder and quotes him: "for Gary Snyder / 'I think I'll be the Buddha of this place' / and sat himself / down" (*Ring* 54).

"Wobbly Rock" is a long poem, a meditation on nature in six sections, occasioned by an encounter Welch had with a balancing boulder along the sea-shore at Muir Beach, California. The poem's first section attempts to place the action of the poem, and the reader it directly addresses, squarely in the physical world: "It's a real rock":

   (believe this first)

Resting on actual sand at the surf's edge:
Muir Beach, California

   (like everything else I have
   somebody showed it to me and I found it
    myself)

Hard common stone
Size of a large haystack
It moves when hit by waves
Actually shudders

   (even a good gust of wind will do it
   if you sit real still and keep your mouth shut)

Notched to certain center it
Yields and then comes back to it:

Wobbly tons

      (54)

The poet's precise choice of adjectives—"real," "actual," "common," and "certain"—can leave little doubt that he intends the rock to be seen as genuine, a rock as real as words alone can make it, to serve as the starting point for the meditative stream of consciousness which follows throughout the remainder of the poem.[8] The poem's sections are loosely linked, leaping from one subject to the next, with only the ocean and the speaker's mind to contain them. In the second section, the focus

of attention is drawn away from the lone balancing boulder, where the poem's speaker is seated, to the surrounding sea-scape, which takes on the aura of a carefully constructed Japanese Zen garden as the speaker attempts to empty his mind in meditation:

Sitting here you look below to other rocks
Precisely placed as rocks of Ryoanji:
Foam like swept stones

   (the mind getting it all confused again:
   "snow like frosting on a cake"
   "rose so beautiful it don't look real")

Isn't there a clear example here—
Stone garden shown to me by
Berkeley painter I never met[9]
A thousand books and somebody else's boatride
   ROCKS

   (garden)

EYE

   (nearly empty despite this clutter-image all
   the opposites cancelling out a
   CIRCULAR process: *Frosting-snow*)

      (55)

The speaker's mind is a jumble of conflicting "clutter-image" as he strives to empty his mind in meditation. The stones visible from his vantage point suggest another meditation site on the other side of the Pacific—the stone gardens of Ryoanji. This thought, in turn, leads him to wonder at the authenticity of his own experience, having gained his knowledge of Ryoanji second hand after reading an article on them "by a Berkeley painter I never met." The inner life of the mind, experienced through "A thousand books and somebody else's boatride," is juxtaposed against the reality he experiences at the moment: "ROCKS."

In the next stanza, these "opposites" which the speaker holds in his mind (the sea-scape and the stone garden, "Frosting-snow") become reconciled, as the "CIRCULAR process" of the speaker's thought becomes complete, and he realizes that the Japanese stone garden is in fact an imitation of a natural sea-shore much like the one he occupies:

Or think of the monks who made it 4 hundred
   50 years ago
lugged the boulders from the sea
Swept to foam original gravelstone from the sea
      (55)

The final lines of this portion of the poem further blur the distinction between Ryoanji and Muir Beach, between nature and imitation. All that remain are rocks, "all rocks," and the spaces between them.

And now all rocks are different and
All the spaces in between

(which includes about everything)

The instant
After it is made

(55)

The poem's third section examines the role of nature in shaping and transforming the individual, as the speaker reflects on his own life-long—and eternal—connections to the sea. *"I have been in many shapes before I attained congenial form,"*[10] he begins, "All those years on the beach, lifetimes . . .":

When I was a boy I used to watch the Pelican:
It always seemed his wings broke
As he dropped, like scissors, in the sea . . .
Night fire flicking the shale cliff
Balls tight as a cat after the cold swim
Her young snatch sandy . . .

(56)

Here, the sea become an integral part of the poet's autobiography—the backdrop for earlier "lifetimes" on the beach as a child, the setting for a youthful sexual encounter, before the speaker separated himself from the ocean. The section's middle stanza speaks of a return: *"I have travelled / I have made a circuit / I have lived in 14 cities"* (56) The speaker's "circuit" is of course a reflection of Welch's own life: a youth spent on the California coast, the middle years spent removed from nature in Eastern cities, before finally returning to the "congenial form" we now see meditating again by the ocean. The section ends with a riddle, a koan, which asks: "Waves and the sea. If you / take away the sea / Tell me what it is" (56). Although the koan deals ostensibly with the unbreakable bond between wave and sea, coming as it does at the end of this autobiographical section of **"Wobbly Rock,"** it is also suggestive of another unbreakable bond, between the poet and the sea.

This question of one man's relationship to nature is broadened in the poem's fourth section, which begins to explore the theme which preoccupies much of the second half of Welch's **"Wobbly Rock"**: humankind's relation to the natural world. From his vantage point atop the rock, the speaker recalls the previous day's activity at the beach:

Yesterday the weather was nice there were lots of
people
Today it rains, the only other figure is far up the
beach

(by the curve of his body I know he
leans against the

tug of his fishingline: there is no
separation)

Yesterday they gathered and broke, gathered and
broke like
Feeding swallows dipped down to pick up
something ran back to
Show it
And a young girl with jeans rolled to mid-thigh
ran
Splashing in the rain creek

(57)

But the idyllic picture from the previous day of humans enjoying the beach as naturally as "feeding swallows" is short-lived, lasting only until something as trivial as a change in the weather again divorces them from the natural world. Only a lone fisherman remains in contact with the non-human world, a reminder that in reality "there is no separation" between man and nature.[11]

The long-distance perspective achieved by the speaker from his station on the faraway rock allows for a viewpoint which is both detached and at the same time very intimate. His focus shifts from a wide angle view of the mass actions of the crowd as "they gathered and broke" like a flock of birds, to a close-up of a single young girl "splashing in the rain creek." Yet throughout the section the observer's tone is decidedly isolated, as if he were viewing his fellow humans as strange creatures to be pitied—as detached from them as they are from the rest of nature. He asks them:

Did it mean nothing to you Animal that turns
this
Planet to a smoky rock?
Back among your quarrels
How can I remind you of your gentleness?

Jeans are washed
Shells all lost or broken
Driftwood sits in shadow boxes on a
tracthouse wall

Like swallows you were, gathering
Like people I wish for . . .

(57)

In Welch's view, the weekend visitors who flock to the beach in good weather, only to return to the "quarrels" of their human existence with their shells and driftwood, have flirted with a potential not apparent to them—the potential to realize their place in the natural world. "Like swallows you were, gathering," the speaker laments, "Like people I wish for . . ."

The poem's fifth section presents a view of humanity's role in nature quite different from that of the fair weather tourist, as Welch's speaker recalls a fishing trip with two companions, "3 of us in a boat the size of a bathtub" (58). His description of the life surrounding him as the boat enters a small cove is stratified, with each stanza coming to represent a different niche in the sea-side environment:

> Below us:
>   fronds of kelp
>   fish
>   crustaceans
>   eels
> Then us
>   then rocks at the cliff's base
>   starfish
>   (hundreds of them sunning themselves)
>   final starfish on the highest rock then
> Cliff
>   4 feet up the cliff a flower
>   grass
>   further up more grass
>   grass over the cliff's edge
>   branch of pine then
> Far up in the sky
>
>   a hawk
>
>   (58)

The passage is decidedly bio-centric, an ecological reworking of the medieval notion of a "great chain of being" which placed God at the top of the philosophical ladder, above angels, followed by man, and finally, the "lower" forms of animal life. Welch's depiction of the ocean ecosystem works consciously to overturn such hierarchies by placing the human figures inconspicuously afloat amidst eels, rocks, and starfish, with only the words "Then us" to quietly give away their position. This section of the poem seems to possess an ecological vision not unlike Aldo Leopold's notion of the "land ethic" presented in Leopold's *A Sand County Almanac* (1949). "The land ethic," in Leopold's words, "simply enlarges the boundaries of the community to include soils, waters, plants, and animals, or collectively: the land." Under such an ethic, man becomes not a ruler or "conqueror of the land-community," but instead, a "plain member and citizen of it" (204). Clearly, such a reworking of humanity's place in the environment is at work in Welch's portrayal of the Pacific eco-system.

The poem's fifth section ends with a view of the earth's biosphere which again calls into question traditional Western views of humanity's place in the vast and finally unknowable natural world:

> Clutching to our chip we are jittering in a
>   spectrum
> Hung in the film of this narrow band
> Green
>   to our eyes only
>
>   (58)

Again, the human role is portrayed as diminutive, creatures invisibly struggling "in the film of this narrow band" which makes up the Earth's surface. The final lines, "Green / to our eyes only," serves as a final reminder that there exist many perspectives from which life on Earth can be viewed—all but one of them non-human.

In the final section of "**Wobbly Rock**," the poet returns to the theme of ecological wholeness. He recalls an insight during an earlier moment of meditation which provided him with a vision of complete unity with the natural world:

> On a trail not far from here
> Walking in meditation
> We entered a dark grove
> And I lost all separation in step with the
> Eucalyptus as the trail walked back beneath me
>
>   (59)

The blurring of human and plant life, of the animate and the inanimate, in this stanza's final lines, is carried still further in the poem's climax, in which all boundaries which separate one form of matter or energy from another are erased: "Wind water / Wave rock / Sea sand / (there is no separation)" (59). "**Wobbly Rock**" ends, as it began, with an image of balance—an image made richer and more complex throughout each of the poem's six sections:

> Wind that wets my lips is salt
> Sea breaking within me balanced as the
> Sea that floods these rocks. Rock
> Returning to the sea, easily, as
> Sea once rose from it. It
> Is a sea rock
>
>   (easily)
>
> I am
> Rocked by the sea
>
>   (59)

"Step out onto the Planet"

Despite the publication of "**Wobbly Rock**" in 1960 at David Haselwood's Auerhahn Press, and the inclusion of his poems in Donald Allen's ground-breaking anthology, *The New American Poetry,* the year 1960 proved to be a traumatic one for Welch. Nearly a decade of heavy drinking and overwork ended in a physical and emotional breakdown and a bout with cirrhosis of the liver. The moment of crisis brought on by Welch's deteriorating health rekindled the poet's desire for refuge from modern urban life. In a letter he wrote to Jack Kerouac in April, he described a moment of "satori" experienced during his recovery: "It all seems so silly—punishing my poor ole liver just because I can't bear to see the absurd bastards tear this planet and each other apart. I'm just going to stand back and watch from now on" (*IR* I, 190). In July of the same year, he closed a long letter to Allen Ginsberg by saying: "I seem to be entering the years of hermitage, and I welcome them—almost long for it" (**IR** I, 222).

A letter Welch wrote to his old college professor James Wilson during this period clearly illustrates the poet's evolving determination to distance himself from what he saw as a corrupt and false society. Immediately after noting to Wilson that he had been "reading the works of John Muir," whom Welch terms an "incredible genius," he describes the rationale behind his withdrawal from human concerns:

> One way of dividing everything for purposes of thought is to separate the *world of man* from the *world that is not man*. Since this came through my mind, many things are now perfectly clear which used to be very confusing. . . . The world of man is entirely arbitrary (i.e. arbitration, law) and illusory. The world that is not man is chaos, void, discontinuous.
>
> (**IR** I, 195)

After establishing such a distinction, and noting that "most men spend all their time in the world of man," where their "feet only touch pavement," Welch reminds Wilson that although the majority of humans may not acknowledge it, they are also part of a larger, non-human world: "Now, of course, they are also in the world that is not man—all their gestures are about this, or with this—but they are asleep to this" (195).

The alternative to this societal slumber, in Welch's view, is a rejection of the forces which had imposed it, and the acceptance of, and the awakening to, the natural world. He tells Wilson: "Enlightenment, as I see it, is a process whereby a person gradually resigns from the world that is man, and thereby becomes a member of the world that is not man" (**IR** I, 196). But, the poet adds, becoming a member of the non-human community in no way provides a Rosetta Stone for understanding nature: "Understand," he writes, "world that is not man, though seen as larger, is not seen by me at all. It is unimaginable, inscrutable. I can only recognize timeless experiences 'with it'" (196).

Welch's poem from this period, **"Step out onto the Planet"** (later included in his **Hermit Poems** collection) is a challenge for his readers to awaken themselves to the wonders to their "unimaginable, inscrutable" surroundings. The poem was originally published as a broadside to publicize a reading done in conjunction with Snyder and Whalen in the early sixties. The leaflet featured a crude circle drawn in Chinese brush style with the text of the poem written in calligraphy beneath it:

> Step out onto the planet.
> Draw a circle a hundred feet round.

> Inside the circle are
> 300 things nobody understands, and, maybe
> nobody's ever really seen.
>
> How many can you find?
>
> (**Ring** 73)

The challenge offered in the poem—to face nature with a new and heightened sense of wonder, and to rejoice in the attempt to know the unknowable—was one which the poet took upon himself for much of the remainder of his life. By 1961, what he referred to as his "hypersensitivity to the senselessness of human interference upon each other's easy lives: the lead-pipe cinch made difficult," made even the relaxed, non-conformist routine of San Francisco's East-West House unbearable for Welch (**IR** II, 31). That spring, at the age of 35, he began what would be two years of the most meaningful work of his life, as a commercial fisherman.

Welch's writings from his days in San Francisco's salmon fleet indicate that what he most valued in the work was not the paycheck (although the money was at times good), but instead the closeness to natural forces. "The work," he wrote Snyder, "is connected with things I know are real: weather, animals, tides, fatigue, cranky tools" (**IR** II, 34). Describing the "state of near nirvana" he attained on the water, Welch told his mother: "You float, wheel, through a universe so real as to make the human world even more absurd & petty" (33).

In an essay he wrote later on his experiences aboard the Pacific salmon trollers, Welch extolled the virtues of what he referred to as "real work," a phrase which Gary Snyder would return to again and again in the decade to follow. For Welch, the term meant work which placed one in close contact with the production of useful goods. "Real work" describes the difficult, but often ecstatic experience of "how it is to go fishing, that is to catch fish for the people to eat," versus what Welch called "the oppressive vision" he had left behind in the world of corporate America, "what it is that a smart strong man might devote his entire life to Post Toasties or Prudential Life Insurance" (**IR** II, 44).

This first-hand experience with the rudimentary elements of the natural world had benefits for the writer as well, Welch believed. He told Snyder that "there is something very wrong with being a professional artist," who was a mere observer of natural events. To be fully accurate and truthful, he contended, the artist must also be an active participant:

> [I]t seems to me that even Whitman is out of focus because it isn't the same watching the wheat be-

ing harvested and actually getting the chaff in your collarband & Hemingway never hunted as an Eskimo does, for the work of it, the providing, & naturally he never hunted with the same depth & skill.

(*IR* II, 37)

For Welch then, the "real work" of salmon fishing allowed him to fulfill a useful and meaningful role in human commerce, as well as providing him with the kind of first-hand experience he valued as an artist; but more importantly, it also provided him a means of acknowledging his place in a much larger system. Embedded in his essay on salmon fishing, amongst the many colorful and exciting details of life on board a troller, is the following paragraph:

> I have lived all my life with people who will laugh at all of this, being too sophisticated to hear what I said except as "another plea to return to nature." But nature is larger than that, expressible in the word-game "Nature." It is all that goes on whether we look at it or not. All-that-goes-on-whether-we-look-at-it-or-not will always go on (though we almost never look at it) and we are in it, in this form, for a little while at least. There is nothing to join since we are as much a charter member as a jellyfish is, as the seasons are. The rest is what drives us mad. And we all know what the rest is.
>
> (*IR* II, 43)[12]

Like many of the endeavors in Lew Welch's life, his career as a commercial fisherman ended abruptly. Economic factors, combined with environmental deterioration, pushed Welch away from what he called "a dying industry," in "a dying sea" (*IR* II, 57). Only two years before, he had seen a promising future in life as a fisherman, but by July 1962, his vision of hope had turned to one of environmental ruin. He told Charles Olson: "It is all over. You know it and I know it. I can't, here, tell you all about West Coast fishing, the land which made me, as the coast you MADE, stand, has made you. It is over. All of it" (*IR* II, 57).

"The Journal of a Strategic Withdrawal": Hermit Poems

Following a severe breakdown in the summer of 1962, and the end of his two year relationship with the poet Lenore Kandel, Welch's attentions turned inland. He told Whalen of his plan to "go up to the Salmon River and live in a mining claim cabin & catch big steelhead and never see people," at the same time "writing all truth into imperishable pomes [sic]" (*IR* II, 59). By September he had made the plan a reality, taking over an abandoned Civilian Conservation Corps cabin in a remote area near Forks of Salmon, California.[13] After a

lifetime of transience, the simple cabin he dubbed "Rat Flat," seemed to the poet like his final destination; "I have finally taken to the woods," he wrote Charles Olson, "I hope forever" (*IR* II, 67). In November, he wrote to Donald Allen, then editor of *Evergreen Review,* telling him that he intended to write a prose work on his coming "home" to his mountain cabin entitled "**A Place to Put the Typewriter**"; its subtitle was to be "**The Journal of a Strategic Withdrawal**" (*IR* II, 86).

The writings emerging from Welch's withdrawal into the California wilderness comprise what Gary Snyder has called the "heart" of Welch's body of work, the poems which comprise his small collection *Hermit Poems* (1965), and another sequence entitled "**The Way Back**." Snyder notes in his introduction to Welch's *Selected Poems,* that in these works, "Lew really achieved the meeting of an ancient Asian sage-tradition, the 'shack simple'[14] post-frontier back country out-of-work workingman's style, and the rebel modernism of modern art" (ii). In addition, Welch's *Hermit Poems* and those in "**The Way Back**" fit also into a tradition of American letters spawned by Thoreau's *Walden* and carried into the late twentieth century by writers such as Edward Abbey (*Desert Solitaire,* 1968) and Annie Dillard (*Pilgrim at Tinker Creek,* 1974): that of the lone, isolated artist learning from and sharing what Abbey called "a season in the wilderness." Welch's work from the period resounds with Thoreau's stated purpose in *Walden* "to drive life into a corner, and reduce it to its lowest terms" (82):

> The hermit locks his door against the blizzard.
> He keeps the cabin warm.
>
> All winter long he sorts out all he has.
> What was well started shall be finished.
> What was not, should be thrown away.
>
> In spring he emerges with one garment
> and a single book.
>
> (*Ring* 76)

Later, in a poem from the "**Way Back**" series, "**He Thanks His Woodpile**," Welch places himself in the long lineage of writers who have chosen a life of lonely asceticism over the comforts offered by society:

> All winter long I make wood stews:
>
> Poem to stove to woodpile to stove to
> typewriter.   woodpile.   stove.
>
> and can't stop peeking at it!
> can't stop opening up the door!
> can't stop giggling at it
>
> "Shack Simple"
> crazy as Han Shan as

Wittgenstein in his German hut,[15]
all the others ever were and are

Ancient Order of the Fire Gigglers

who walked away from it, finally,
kicked the habit, finally, of Self, of
man-hooked Man

(which is not, at last, estrangement)

(***Ring*** 84)

Welch denies that the ascetic hermit's life is one of "estrangement," since for him the rejection of "man-hooked Man" makes possible the embrace of the non-human world. For while the majority of the poems Welch composed at his Forks of Salmon cabin have only one human subject—the poet himself—they are set amongst a world which is teeming with life and energy. In the poet's view, it is not he that has become estranged from humanity, but rather it is humanity who has become estranged from the non-human world. The opening stanzas for the preface to the ***Hermit Poems,*** a poem entitled "**The Bath**," describe a setting of tremendous beauty which has been abandoned as "obsolete" by its previous human inhabitants:

At last it is raining, the first sign of spring.
The Blue Jay gets all wet.

Frost-flowers, tiny bright and dry like
inch high crystal trees or sparkling silver mold,
acres of them, on heaps of placer boulders all
    around me,
are finally washing away. They were beautiful.
And the big trees rising, dark, behind them.

This canyon is so steep we didn't get sun since
    late November,
my "CC" shack and I. Obsolete. The two of us.
He for his de-funct agency.
I for this useless art?

(***Ring*** 67)

Welch refers to his shack as "he," with what might seem to be a personification of an inanimate object with which he himself identifies.[16] Given the other poems in the collection, however, it would be a mistake to view the reference to the shack as a personification. It could more accurately be seen as an animation—the acknowledgment of a common life force present in all matter. Rather than portraying the landscape and creatures of Rat Flat in human terms, Welch attempts to depict all beings, human and non-human, as sharing a common energy:

Apparently wasps
work all their only summer at the nest,
so that new wasps work
all their only summer at the nest,
et cetera.

All my green lizards lost their tails, mating.
Six snakes ate all my frogs.
Butterflies do very odd things with their tongues.

There seems to be no escaping it.
I planted nine tomato plants and water them.
I replace my rotten stoop with a
clean Fir block.

Twelve new poems in less than a week!

(***Ring*** 71)

Here, the actions of the human—tending a garden to feed himself, repairing his home, and even producing art—are viewed in terms of the supposedly instinctive actions of reptiles and insects engaged in similar tasks. While Welch's voice still harbors some anthropocentric features (i.e. the stewardship of "his" frogs and lizards, and the use of the judgmental word "odd"), there is in the poem a conscious effort to show the poet gradually coming to grips (i.e. "Apparently" and "There *seems* to be no escaping it") with a view of himself as one of many creatures from whom, as the speaker in "**Wobbly Rock**" stressed, "there is no separation."

"The Way Back"

Welch's stay at Forks of Salmon was not permanent, as he had predicted it would be early in 1962. By November, 1963, Welch decided to again pull up stakes and return to the San Francisco area, where he would live for the next seven years with Magda Cregg, the new love in his life. The poems in Welch's "**The Way Back**" sequence chronicle his final days at the remote cabin, and his eventual return to city life. Despite the sense of failure and even, impending doom, which Welch must have felt in his return to the city, there is, in these poems, a kind of missionary zeal, a desire to share the lessons of his hermitage with others. The first poem in the sequence, "**He Prepares to Take Leave of His Hut**," begins with the pilgrim's dutiful return to the city:

And They, The Blessed Ones, said to him,
"Beautiful trip, Avalokiteshvara.[17]
You never have to go back there again."

And he said, "Thank you very much, but I think
    I will.
Those people need all the help they can get."

(***Ring*** 81)

Although the poems in the "**Way Back**" sequence document what Welch calls "the Mystical Return" of "The Mountain Man" to the human world (***Ring*** 90-92), the focus of most of the poems is still squarely on nature. The centerpiece of the sequence is a long prose-poem entitled "**He Begins to Recount His Adventures,**" a work which encapsulates Welch's holistic view of nature in clear but eloquent language. It begins:

> I can't remember seeing it any other way but
>   whole, a big
> round rock wheeling about the heavens and
>   comin' on green to
> crack sidewalks, gentle and undemanding, as if I
>   saw it first,
> approaching it from somewhere else.
>
> Everything about it always seemed right. The
>   roundness is
> right. The way it spins.
>
> (***Ring*** 94)

The portrait of the planet Welch paints is one of exquisite balance and intricate beauty, one in which "Everything is right, clear down to the smallest parts of it" (95). The view of Earth as "a gentle and undemanding / planet" first posited in "**Chicago Poem,**" is merged with the poet's later ecological vision of the Earth as an inscrutable and mysterious network of systems—"subworlds living off / further subworlds"—which he had first alluded to in "**Step out onto the Planet.**" The poem has only one human inhabitant—the lone figure of John Muir:

> Or John Muir waking in a Sierra meadow, in
>   spring, and
> finding, inches from his waking eye, a wildflower
>   he, and nobody
> else, had ever seen. Rising, he found himself in a
>   field of delicate
> color so complicated he spent the whole day in
>   only ten square
> feet of it, classifying and drawing pictures of
>   hundreds of little
> plants for the first time in the world.[18]
>
> An average of a ton of insects for every acre of
>   a field like
> that. Deer hoof crushing a flower. Rodents at the
>   roots of it.
> Birds diving and pecking at it. Big trees crowding
>   it out with
> their shade. Mushrooms in the warm fall rains.
>
> (***Ring*** 95)

Welch's emphasis in the poem is on the "subworlds" which combine to make up what Muir experiences as "meadow"—subworlds invisible until enlightened humans like Muir can approach them with a "waking eye." While the term "ecology" is not present in any of Welch's published writings or letters of the period,[19] passages such as this one make clear that by the early 1960's the poet had come to view nature from an ecological perspective—as an infinite number of intricate and interconnecting systems.

"Final City"

The middle years of the 1960's marked for Welch the beginning of his public recognition as a writer. In 1964 several of the poems written at Forks of Salmon were accepted by *Poetry,* then the nation's premiere literary journal, and in conjunction with Gary Snyder and Philip Whalen, he took part in the very successful "Freeway Reading" of June 12 of that year. 1965 brought with it the publication of his second chapbook, ***Hermit Poems,*** and Welch began more often to read publicly the two decades of poetry he had stored in his notebooks.

With the publication, in 1965, of his third collection of poems, ***On Out,*** which included both "Chicago Poem" and "Wobbly Rock," Welch had become a well known—if not well paid—member of the San Francisco arts community. Although the poet was now earning a significant part of his living as a teacher of creative writing at the University of California Extension in San Francisco, and supplementing his income with fees from readings, he still had to support himself and his writing mainly by working as a dock worker and ship's clerk (Samuel Charters 552).

Despite his growing reputation as a writer within the San Francisco community, however, Welch again began to grow uneasy within the city. By 1967, the Bay Area counterculture in which he had placed so much hope was deteriorating rapidly, as the city was shaken by racial violence and elements of organized crime moved in to take over Haight-Ashbury's profitable drug trade. What had begun as a self-styled utopian experiment now had turned into a crowded scene of anger, violence and dangerously powerful and impure drugs (***IR*** II, 145).

In a leaflet distributed in the Haight in early 1967, "**A MOVING TARGET IS HARD TO HIT,**" Welch predicted the immanent destruction of the district and its counterculture by a repressive government afraid of the counterculture's mushrooming growth: "When 200,000 folks from places like lima ohio and cleveland and lompoc and visalia and amsterdam and london and moscow and lodz suddenly descend, as they will, on the haight-ashbury, the scene will be burnt down" (*How I Work* 6). Welch's advice to members of the Haight community was not "to stand there and take it, as the poles did, . . . with futile swords," but instead, to take refuge in the forests and mountains of California:

> Disperse. Gather into smaller tribes. Use the beautiful land your state and national governments have already set up for you, free. If you want to.

Most Indians are nomads. The haight-ashbury is not where it's at—it's in your head and hands. Take it anywhere.

(7)

This vision of nature as a refuge from cultural apocalypse was further developed in **"Final City / Tap City,"** a 1968 essay Welch contributed to the prominent underground publication, *The San Francisco Oracle*. In the essay, he contends that the ills associated with the modern city—pollution, over-crowding, and a dangerous alienation from nature—had created the youth counterculture: "a huge number of people who are Immigrants in their own native land" (**How I Work** 19). Warning that "We face great holocausts, terrible catastrophes, all American cities burned from within, and without," the poet envisioned a post-urban world in which America's countercultural "immigrants" will "slip away" until nature reclaims the ruined landscape:

> However, our beautiful Planet will germinate—underneath this thin skin of City, Green will come on to crack our sidewalks! Stinking air will blow away at last! The bays flow clean!
>
> (20)

Until this green revolution could take place, however, Welch urged America's youthful counterculture to remain patient and clear-headed, to return to wilderness and to what Gary Snyder would later refer to as "the old ways":[20]

> In the meantime, stay healthy. There are hundreds of miles to walk, and lots of work to be done. Keep your mind. We will need it. Stake out a retreat. Learn berries and nuts and fruit and small animals and all the plants. Learn water.
>
> For there must be good men and women in the mountains, on the beaches, in all the neglected and beautiful places, so that one day we come back to ghostly cities and try to set them right.
>
> (21)

By the end of the decade, Welch was ready to take his own advice. In February 1970, he wrote to Katharine George, an old neighbor from his days at Forks of Salmon, telling her of his life in San Francisco. In the letter, he marvels at his relative financial success as a writer and teacher, noting "I'll make $6,000 this year *as a poet*!" (**IR** II, 167). Yet, despite this long-sought financial reward, there is in the letter a longing to leave what he refers to as "this madhouse of a Bay Area," and return to the land:

> I'm sure (have checked it out) that the Bay Area is better than any urban area in the world, but it just may not be good enough for those, like us, who are blessed with the choice of moving away as a real possibility. I am still not bought.
>
> (166)

"Not the Bronze Casket but the Brazen Wing"

Despite the hard-won acceptance as an artist which Welch enjoyed in the late sixties, the poet's life entered a tail-spin during the first months of the new decade. In May 1970 Welch resigned his teaching position at San Francisco's Urban School, citing as a reason his feelings that he could better serve the anti-war and civil rights causes outside the classroom. His life-long drinking problem worsened, and in December 1970 Magda Cregg left him, ending the longest and most stable relationship of his life (**IR** II, 169-76).

In early 1971, Welch planned again to take to the woods. His friends Gary Snyder and Allen Ginsberg offered to let him build a cabin at Kitkit-dizze, a tract of land which they jointly owned near Nevada City, California. Sober for the first time in years, as a result of the prescription drug Antabuse, Welch selected a building site and began to formulate plans for the small cabin which would be his hermitage in the woods, a simple twelve by twenty foot structure with no electricity or running water (**IR** II, 186). It was a task which the poet was ill prepared for—both physically and financially—but one on which he placed the utmost importance. "I absolutely have to do this to survive," he wrote to Magda Cregg, "It's hard but it's real, at last, and I know it is the only way for me now" (**IR** II, 183).

The forest cabin Welch envisioned was never completed. Physically drained by years of hard drinking and the side effects of his Antabuse therapy, and depressed at the prospect of finding himself at 44, living on the kindness of his friends, on May 22, 1971 Lew Welch disappeared into the foothills of the Sierras, taking with him only a gun. He left behind a note reading:

> I never could make anything work out right and now I'm betraying my friends. I can't make anything out of it—never could. I had great visions but never could bring them together with reality. I used it all up. It's all gone. Don Allen is to be my literary executor—use MSS at Gary's and at Grove Press. I have $2000 in Nevada City Bank of America—use it to cover my affairs and debts. I don't owe Allen G. anything yet nor my Mother. I went Southwest. Goodbye. Lew Welch.
>
> (**IR** II, 187)

Despite extensive searching, Welch's body was never found, leading some to speculate, hopefully, that the poet's last note signaled not a suicide, but a planned disappearance—a twentieth century Huck Finn's plan to "light out for the Territory." Albert Saijo, Welch's neighbor from his days at

East-West House, eulogizes his friend by wistfully denying his death ever occurred:

> I sometimes believe you went into the mountains that last time and had a truly illuminating experience. That there in the pine-oak woodland or coniferous forest you reran your life and came out ahead of it. That then you crossed over the mountains and descended to the Great Basin where you still are. Your hair has gone completely white but you are younger in the face. You drink nothing but water. You eat wild weeds, comb honey, and the fat larvae of the brine fly that breeds in saline waters.
>
> (*Trip Trap* [*Trip Trap: Haiku along the Road from San Francisco to New York, 1959*] 1-2)

But such pleasant imaginings aside, the numerous references to suicide in Welch's letters, as well as his fragile emotional state at the time of his disappearance, can leave little doubt that the poet did take his own life. Welch's final collection of poems, a slim chapbook published in 1969 entitled *The Song Mt. Tamalpais Sings*, offers further evidence that this is the case. *The Song Mt. Tamalpais Sings* is a book which would serve as both a tribute to the California landscape and the poet's final epitaph. The opening line of the book's title poem—"*This is the last place. There is no place else to go*"—speaks to both the time-worn notion of civilization's westward progression as well as the westward path of the poet's own wanderings—including his final walk away from Kitkitdizze (*Ring* 121).

The eclectic volume contains a dozen small pieces in various forms—a haiku, two riddles which Welch refers to as "the first American Koans," a curse against ocean polluters in a brief poem called "**Sausalito Trash Prayer**"—but the book's centerpiece is the poem which serves as the writer's final statement: "**Song of the Turkey Buzzard.**" The poem is Welch's acceptance of the death of his human form, but more importantly, it is a joyful embrace of his next form, as he envisions himself devoured by—and thereby becoming—a buzzard.

"I bequeath myself to the dirt to grow from the grass I love, / If you want me again look for me under your bootsoles," wrote Walt Whitman at the end of "Song of Myself," in 1855 (88). Since this fearless acknowledgment of death as a part of the chain of life, numerous American writers had voiced similar sentiments. The most recent, and most local example of this tradition, for Welch, was his fellow Californian Robinson Jeffers. Jeffers's 1963 poem, "Vulture," features an encounter between the sleeping poet and a vulture who circles above him, eyeing him as a meal, only to be frightened away when the bird realizes his prey is not yet carrion. The poem ends with a reverie in which the poet imagines a different outcome, in which he is devoured by the bird and thus, become a part of him, "to share those / wings and those eyes."

> What a sublime end of one's body, what an enskyment:
>> What a life after death.
>>> (107)

In "**Song of the Turkey Buzzard**," Welch extends this fantasy of "enskyment" expressed by the earlier poet, and demands it as his own final reality. Where Jeffers views being consumed by a vulture as the "sublime end of one's body," a reworking of the traditional Christian afterlife in heaven, Welch sees the experience not as an end, but as what he calls a "continuance":

> The very opposite of
>> death
> Bird of re-birth
>> Buzzard)
> meat is rotten meat made
>> sweet again . . .
>>> (*Ring* 135)

The poem's final stanzas offer the poet's "last Will & Testament," the detailed orders Welch calls the "instructions / for my continuance" in his new form. They harbor not the slightest trace of sadness at the death of his own human form; on the contrary, the lines are emphatic with the poet's sense of wonder at the beauty and efficiency of the food chain he prepares to enter:

> *Let no one grieve.*
> *I shall have used it all up*
> *used up every bit of it.*
>
> *What an extravagance!*
> *What a relief!*
>> (*Ring* 136)

The stanzas which follow are the poem's darkest, an effect perhaps designed to make the biological transformation from man to bird which will follow all the more exuberant. The terminology is harsh and direct—the language of the slaughterhouse rather than the funeral parlor. "On a marked rock . . . ," Welch tells his attendants, "place my meat":

> *All care must be taken not to*
> *frighten the natives of this*
> *barbarous land, who*
> *will not let us die, even,*
> *as we wish.*
>
> With proper ceremony disembowel what I
> no longer need, that it might more quickly
> rot and tempt
>
> my new form
>> (*Ring* 136)

This macabre tone is quickly overturned in the poem's final section, as Welch rejects the traditional trappings of the Western burial ritual, and ecstatically embraces his "new form" and takes to the skies surrounding Mt. Tamalpais:

NOT THE BRONZE CASKET BUT THE BRAZEN
WING
SOARING FOREVER ABOVE THEE O PERFECT
O SWEETEST WATER O GLORIOUS
WHEELING

BIRD

(*Ring* 137)

The death outlined in **"Song of the Turkey Buzzard"**—if indeed the term "death" can be used at all in this case—is emblematic of Lew Welch's lifetime struggle to achieve enlightenment by leaving behind "the world that is man," and becoming "a member of the world that is not man" (**IR** I, 196). More than a decade after Welch's disappearance, Gary Snyder dedicated a poem to his old friend, "For/From Lew," in which he comes to terms with Welch's final decision:

> Lew Welch just turned up one day,
> live as you and me. "Damn, Lew" I said,
> "you didn't shoot yourself after all."
> "Yes I did" he said,
> and even then I felt the tingling down my back.
> "Yes you did, too" I said—"I can feel it now."
> "Yeah" he said,
> "There's a basic fear between your world and
> mine. I don't know why.
> What I came to say was,
> Teach the children about the cycles.
> The life cycles. All the other cycles.
> That's what it's all about, and it's all forgot."
>
> (*Axe Handles* 7)[21]

In Lew Welch's view, and in Gary Snyder's, the poet's final act on that day in 1971 when he walked off into the Sierra foothills may not have been to take his own life, but to give it, to what Snyder has called "that ecstatic Mutual Offering called the Food Chain" (Welch, **Selected Poems** ii).

Notes

1. *I Remain: The Letters of Lew Welch & The Correspondence of His Friends*. Ed. Donald Allen. 2 vols. Bolinas CA: Grey Fox Press, 1980.p. 196. Subsequent citations within the text and chapter notes will be abbreviated *IR*.

2. In a letter to William Carlos Williams dated 14 August, 1951, Welch told his mentor: "I read *Paterson IV*, and I tell you I was drunk with it" (*IR* I, 58).

3. Apparently not all of Welch's advertising copy took the same positive stance towards nature as his later writing. Aram Saroyan credits him as being the writer responsible for the pesticide slogan "Raid Kills Bugs Dead!" (*Genesis Angels* 109).

4. This substitution of the colloquial "Murcan" or "Murca" for American or America seems to have been a standard feature of the correspondence among Welch, Gary Snyder, and Philip Whalen.

5. Welch tells his readers in the preface to *Ring of Bone* that "The poems are autobiographical lyrics" (3). Although it would be incorrect to accept this as true for all of the poems contained in the collection, it is quite safe to say that in the majority, including "Chicago Poem," Welch himself is the speaker.

6. Also referred to at times as "Hyphen House."

7. In a letter dated 2 May 1960, Welch told James Wilson that "the whole poem meant to carry most of what I've learned from Zen, expressed in an American vocabulary" (*IR* I, 194).

8. A letter Welch wrote to Robert Duncan conclusively demonstrates that the poem's rock is intended as genuine. Complaining of those who found his poetry too difficult, he wrote: "And still to get ((from *Wobbly Rock*))!!!! the cry 'I don't understand it. Why don't you write so that everybody can understand it.?'

> It
> is
> a
> real
> rock
> My God!!!"
>
> (*IR* II, 53-54).

9. A letter dated 22 September 1960 from Welch to Will Petersen identifies him as the "Berkeley painter" (*IR* II, 9). Welch had seen Petersen's article on Ryoanji, "Stone Garden," in *Evergreen Review* 4, 1957.

10. Welch claims that this section's opening line is from *Taliesin*, an old Welsh epic. The borrowing is a subtle joke, says the poet, since "this is the history section of this poem, and it's Old Welch." See *How I Work as a Poet & Other Essays*, 82.

11. Welch was an enthusiastic fisherman for much of his life, so it seems only natural that he would select the figure of a fisherman to stand as a symbol of interconnectedness between man and nature.

12. Thirty years later, Welch's friend Gary Snyder would echo his views on "the word-game 'Nature'" in his explanation of the title of his 1992 volume of collected poems *No Nature*:

> *No Nature.* Human societies each have their own nutty fads, mass delusions, and enabling mythologies. Daily life still gets done. Wild nature is probably equally goofy, with a stunning variety of creatures somehow getting by in all these landscapes. Nature also means the physical universe, including the urban, industrial, and toxic. But we do not easily *know* nature, or even know ourselves. Whatever it actually is, it will not fulfil our conceptions and assumptions. . . . There is no single or set "nature" either as "the natural world" or "the nature of things." The greatest respect we can pay to nature is not to trap it, but to acknowledge that it eludes us and that our own nature is also fluid, open, and conditional.
>
> ("Preface" unpaginated)

13. A town Welch described as "only a Post Office and a gradually rotting Oldsmobile under a tree" (*IR* II, 87).

14. A Western term for those suffering from "cabin fever."

15. Han Shan: Chinese hermit poet of the seventh century whose "Cold Mountain Poems" Welch's friend Gary Snyder had translated. Ludwig Wittgenstein: (1889-1951) Austrian/British philosopher who, in the years following the First World War, dedicated himself to a life of strict asceticism. Welch had read his *Philosophical Investigations* (Meltzer 196).

16. As does Jack Kerouac's Ray Smith in *Dharma Bums*. See the novel's final paragraphs: 192.

17. Identified later by Welch as the "Buddha of Compassion" (*Ring* 82).

18. Welch may be referring here to a passage from John Muir's essay "The Bee-Pastures" (1894) in which he discusses sleeping amidst "countless forms of life thronging about me": "And what glorious botanical beds I had! Oftentimes on waking I would find several new species leaning over me and looking me full in the face, so that my studies would begin before rising" (*The Mountains of California* 260).

19. The term's first appearance in Welch's writings comes in a letter to Jim Koller dated 23 January 1971, about an oil tanker spill in San Francisco Bay: "Here there is the panic of those who realize it's all over, that all that ecology stuff was true . . . (*IR* II, 175).

20. See Gary Snyder's essay, "Re-inhabitation," in *The Old Ways: Six Essays*, 57-66.

21. More recently, in Gary Snyder's collection *No Nature: New and Selected Poems*, the poet again pays tribute to his old friend with the poem "For Lew Welch in a Snowfall" (380). Also, see Michael McClure's tribute to Welch, "A Spirit of Mount Tamalpais," in his 1974 collection *September Blackberries*: 107.

Works Cited

Charters, Samuel. "Lew Welch." *The Beats: Literary Bohemians in Postwar America*. Ed. Ann Charters. 2 vols. Detroit: Bruccoli Clark Books, 1983.

Jeffers, Robinson. *Selected Poems*. New York: Vintage, 1965.

Leopold, Aldo. *A Sand County Almanac and Sketches Here and There*. London: Oxford University Press, 1949.

Meltzer, David. *The San Francisco Poets*. New York: Ballantine Books, 1971.

Welch, Lew. *How I Work As a Pote & Other Essays*. San Francisco: Grey Fox Press, 1983.

———. *I Remain: The Letters of Lew Welch with Correspondence of His Friends*. Ed. Donald Allen. 2 vols. Bolinas, CA: Grey Fox Press, 1980.

———. *Ring of Bone: Collected Poems 1950–71*. San Francisco: Grey Fox Press, 1989.

———. *Selected Poems*. Bolinas, CA: Grey Fox Press, 1973.

FURTHER READING

Biography

Saroyan, Aram. *Genesis Angels: The Saga of Lew Welch and the Beat Generation*. New York: William Morrow, 1979, 128p.

Biography of Welch's life that considers the circumstances that may have led to his death in 1972.

Criticism

Allen, Donald, editor. *On Bread and Poetry: A Panel Discussion with Gary Snyder, Lew Welch, and Philip Whalen*. Bolinas, Calif.: Grey Fox Press, 1973, 47p.

Discussion among three of the Beat Generation's most significant poets, who ruminate on the life of a poet and their views on poetry.

Cregg, Magda, editor. *Hey Lew: Homage to Lew Welch*. Bolinas, Calif.: Grey Fox Press, 1997, 101p.

A tribute to Welch by his friends and associates.

OTHER SOURCES FROM GALE:

Additional coverage of Welch's life and career is contained in the following sources published by the Gale Group: *Contemporary Authors*, Vols. 113, 153; *Dictionary of Literary Biography*, Vol. 16; and *Literature Resource Center*.

PHILIP WHALEN

(1923 - 2002)

American poet, nonfiction writer, and novelist.

One of the leading figures of the San Francisco Renaissance, Whalen was an ally and confidant of many of the major figures of the Beat Generation. He is also known as one of the Reed College poets, a group that included Lew Welch and Gary Snyder. Although he is often labeled as a Beat poet, Whalen's poetry differs from much of the Beat writings. His preoccupation with the wilderness and Zen Buddhism, along with his witty and self-deprecating sense of humor, distinguish his work from the more political, sometimes more sordid writings of his Beat contemporaries.

BIOGRAPHICAL INFORMATION

Whalen grew up in a small town near Portland, Oregon. He began writing poetry while in high school, and hoped to follow in the footsteps of one of his poetic heroes, William Carlos Williams, by being both a doctor and a poet. However, his family could not afford the expense of a medical education, and Whalen worked at odd jobs after his graduation until he was drafted into the army in 1943. Although Whalen disliked serving in the Army, comparing it to jail, his military service later allowed him to attend college; his GI Bill paid his way to Reed College, in Portland,

Oregon. Whalen's move to Reed was fateful in several ways—he moved into a rooming house with Welch and Snyder, whose poetic careers would develop with his own; he met William Carlos Williams, who read and encouraged his work; and he studied poetry and calligraphy under Lloyd Reynolds, influencing his interest in the use of space within a poem. After graduating from Reed in 1951, Whalen again worked at odd jobs, wandering around San Francisco, Los Angeles, and the upper West Coast. In 1955 Whalen was invited to a poetry reading that featured the first public reading of Allen Ginsberg's "Howl." Known as the Six Gallery reading, the event included such poets as Snyder, Jack Kerouac, Kenneth Rexroth, Michael McClure and Philip Lamantia. All the poets involved in the reading became suddenly famous, and Whalen subsequently befriended Kerouac and Ginsberg. Whalen later credited his early contact with these Beat figures, particularly Ginsberg, for freeing him to write poetry that fell outside of academic dogma. For the next five years, Whalen worked and wrote with various companions, including Kerouac, Ginsberg, Jack Spicer, and Robert Duncan. In 1960 he published three collections of poetry, *Like I Say*, *Self-Portrait from Another Direction*, and *Memoirs of an Interglacial Age*. As the Beat Movement declined and a new counterculture began to emerge, Whalen, like Snyder and Ginsberg, further developed and changed his poetic voice. His writing became more personal, as reflected in the 1965 collection *Every Day.* By that time, Whalen was nationally recognized as a serious poet and was preparing to leave for Kyoto, Japan, with a grant from the National Academy of Arts and Letters, which Ginsberg had helped him acquire. Whalen moved back to the United States in 1971 and settled in Bolinas, California. Soon afterwards, a friend invited him to the San Francisco Zen Center, and within a year, Whalen was preparing for ordination as a Zen monk. By 1975 he was head monk at the Zen Mountain Center in Tassajara Springs, California. In later years Whalen also served as the head monk at the Hartford Street Zen Center, in the heart of the AIDS-stricken Castro district of San Francisco, and remained a Zen monk for the rest of his life. He released eight collections between 1976 and 1999—several of which addressed Buddhism and Buddhist themes—including *The Kindness of Strangers: Poems, 1969-1974* (1976), *Decompressions: Selected Poems* (1977), *Heavy Breathing: Poems, 1967-1980* (1983), *Canoeing Up Cabarga Creek: Buddhist Poems, 1955-1986* (1996), and *Overtime: Selected Poems* (1999). Whalen died on June 26, 2002.

MAJOR WORKS

Whalen's first book of poetry, *Like I Say,* introduced some of the major recurring themes in his work, including an interest in Buddhism, nature, and his quest for self-knowledge. One of the most recognized poems from this collection, "Sourdough Mountain Lookout," captures Whalen's humor and introspection, presenting the mountains as a place for spiritual exploration. *Like I Say* also reflects Whalen's connection with the Beat Movement, capturing its energy and freedom through his experiments with using verse that approximates everyday speech. *Memoirs of an Interglacial Age* also exhibits the ideals of the Beat era, most notably in the poem "On Which I Renounce the Notion of Social Responsibility." Most of the poems in this collection—including "Metaphysical Insomnia Jazz," "Self-Portrait, from another Direction," and "Complaint to the Muse"—display a subtle use of colloquial language and an emphasis on whimsical word- and memory-play. Despite the strong presence of East Coast writers within the Beat movement, Whalen's work asserts his West Coast heritage and portrays the poet as happily carefree rather than ensconced in a hedonistic lifestyle. His later collections became strongly influenced by his Buddhist beliefs, featuring poems that embraced the mundane details of day-to-day life. *On Bear's Head: Selected Poems* (1969), a collection that includes a heavy focus on free association, contains "Homage to Rodin," a long poem significant in Whalen's oeuvre as a mixture of the poet's emphasis on humor and his increasing spiritualism. *Severance Pay: Poems 1967-1969* (1970) was Whalen's last work published before his ordination, although the works published after he became a Zen monk are not radically different from much of his previous writing. In *The Kindness of Strangers: Poems, 1969-1974* many of Whalen's friends from the Beat movement appear as characters throughout the verse. His final poetry collection, *Overtime,* assembles poems from the 1950s through the 1980s, illustrating a continuum of thought and tone throughout Whalen's career. In addition to poetry, Whalen also wrote two novels: *Your Didn't Even Try* (1967), which relates the story of a maturing artist that in some ways parallels Whalen's own life, and *Imaginary Speeches for a Brazen Head* (1972), which follows a similar plot.

CRITICAL RECEPTION

Critical responses to Whalen's work have been fairly consistent throughout his career. Reviewers have routinely praised Whalen's gift for marrying the sacred and the profane in his verse, although his light touch with his subject material has been viewed as shallow by some critics. Many commentators have lauded Whalen's skill at creating approximations of spontaneous, conversational speech in his poems, but others have faulted Whalen's use of language as undisciplined and chaotic. Whalen's recurring exploration of issues pertaining to Zen Buddhism has received numerous accolades by critics, despite the assertion by some that his use of Oriental terminology is unnecessarily obscure. As a member of the Beat movement, Whalen has often been singled out by reviewers for his playful sense of humor and whimsy. Geoffrey Thurley noted that, "No poet illustrates the sophistication of Beat poetry more strikingly than Philip Whalen. Whalen's stock-in-trade is an attractive self-awareness, a wry, biting humor. . . ." While commenting on the poets of the San Francisco Renaissance, Michael Davidson concurred with this assessment, commenting that Whalen is "arguably the wittiest poet of the group, able to debunk the more transcendental claims of his peers without sacrificing Buddhist beliefs in numinous reality."

PRINCIPAL WORKS

Three Satires (poetry) 1951

Like I Say (poetry) 1960

Memoirs of an Interglacial Age (poetry) 1960

Self-Portrait from Another Direction (poetry) 1960

Monday in the Evening (poetry) 1964

Every Day (poetry) 1965

Highgrade: Doodles, Poems (poetry and nonfiction) 1966

T/O (poetry) 1967

You Didn't Even Try (novel) 1967

On Bear's Head: Selected Poems (poetry) 1969

Scenes of Life at the Capital (poetry) 1970; revised edition, 1971

Severance Pay: Poems 1967-1969 (poetry) 1970

Imaginary Speeches for a Brazen Head (novel) 1972

The Kindness of Strangers: Poems, 1969-1974 (poetry) 1976

Prolegomena to a Study of the Universe (poetry) 1976

Decompressions: Selected Poems (poetry) 1977

The Diamond Noodle (poetry) 1979

Enough Said: Fluctuat Nec Mergitur: Poems, 1974-1979 (poetry) 1980

Heavy Breathing: Poems, 1967-1980 (poetry) 1983

Two Novels (novels) 1985

Canoeing up Cabarga Creek: Buddhist Poems, 1955-1986 (poetry) 1996

Overtime: Selected Poems (poetry) 1999

* This volume reprints Whalen's novels *You Didn't Even Try* and *Imaginary Speeches for a Brazen Head*.

GENERAL COMMENTARY

PHILIP WHALEN AND ARAM SAROYAN (INTERVIEW DATE 1972)

SOURCE: Whalen, Philip and Aram Saroyan. "Interview with Aram Saroyan." In *Off the Wall: Interviews with Philip Whalen*, edited by Donald Allen, pp. 38-49. Bolinas, Calif.: Four Seasons Foundation, 1978.

In the following interview, originally published in 1972, Saroyan asks Whalen about his introduction to poetry and his early development as a writer.

This interview took place in July 1972, in Philip Whalen's room on the second floor of the Zen Center in San Francisco, a large redbrick building on the corner of a quiet residential street on a hill a few blocks above Market Street. The room's outstanding feature was a floor-to-ceiling bookcase filled from top to bottom with books on Eastern culture and volumes of poetry. It stood beside the room's single window, which overlooked a courtyard garden and faced windows on the other side of the Zen Center. In a corner of the room, running lengthwise against the wall opposite the window, was Whalen's bed, very low in the Japanese style, at the foot of which was a small writing desk. Whalen, who will be fifty next year, sat Indian-style on a rug by the window for the duration of the interview, holding and speaking into the microphone of the Uher I brought. I sat opposite him. His voice is soft and somewhat high, with a slight nasal quality, and he spoke with a steady, measured pace throughout. . . .

* * *

[Saroyan]: *Do you remember the first poem that you ever wrote?*

[Whalen]: Hmmm. I think the first one I wrote was one in a social-science class in high school. It was something about—oh, you know, it was a high-school-kid poem—something about birds, the stars, and tra-la-la, and so on. As I recall, it was an unrhymed one, it was so-called free verse. And I handed it to the girl who was sitting ahead of me—she was a girl I had gone to grade school with, and here we all were, we were still going to school, we were still in high school—and I handed it to her, and she liked it, she was delighted, wrote me a nice note back again. So I think that was about the first one that I ever manufactured. That's the earliest one I can remember, anyway. I was about sixteen, I guess.

When did you first begin to consider the possibility of being a poet as a way of life?

Well, I didn't think of it that way, actually. I started getting interested in writing right then, and there was a man called Albert Hingston, who was teaching English at that time—that was in The Dalles High School, public high school up there—and he had just been there a little while, and he was having all things happen around there. He organized a lot of interesting plays for the drama club to do, and he had a choral speaking group, and he got a magazine going to teach—teaching creative writing—and he was, you know, he was jumping all over the place. And so I took him on for my first teacher having anything to do with writing and thinking about writing as something to do or you could learn. And so he taught us, simply, all the usual forms, you know, like sonnets, and ballads, and various French forms like triolets, and so on. And it was a lot of fun to try to make stuff in these shapes. And then I also started writing stories. When I got out of high school, I sort of thought, well, I would do like Dr. Williams, I would become a doctor and write poems—because I thought at that time that I really wanted to be a doctor more than anything. But it turned out there wasn't enough money in the family to manufacture me into one. So I got a job. I was working as an office boy.

How old were you then?

Eighteen. And then the next year—well, I had two more office jobs, a job for a little while in an airplane factory, and a job in a shipyard, and then I got drafted—so I was in the Army for three years, in the Air Corps.

What was your feeling about having the jobs, how did you feel while you were working?

Oh, I didn't like it. Sometimes it was interesting, learning about office machinery, learning how to operate a telephone switchboard was fascinating. One of the jobs I had I worked for a real estate outfit, and they were into Title Insurance, and I would go down to the courthouse and look up title claims on a piece of property, where you find out that this piece of property was originally laid out by a certain man, and then he sold it to somebody else, or maybe he made a will and willed it to his children, and so you'd look up the will, and find out what the will said, and then the next thing that happened to the property is that it was mortgaged to the bank, and you'd look up and find out what the terms of the mortgage were, and who had it and who it was sold to next—and this is in order to prove that the person who is selling it to you really owns it, so that if you buy it some other guy isn't going to sue for replevin: "I'm going to sue you to get it back from you, for a lot of money." So that's why you have Title Insurance, if you buy a piece of property. Well, anyway, it's based on this funny kind of research, in these old records in the courthouse, and it all involves lots of funny names, and various kinds of law suits, things like some of the heirs being incompetent, being declared loony and locked up, and so there'd be a court proceeding about that, who is legal owner of this stuff but who can't do anything about it, so he has a guardian, or he is a ward of the court, or something like that.

This was all in Portland?

Yeah.

What was that like, relative to a place like San Francisco?

Oh well, to me at that time it was a large town, and interesting, because I had grown up in The Dalles, which was, you know, somewhere not more than about 5,000 people at that time, and of course, Portland to me seemed like a grand metropolis, with streetcars, and big movie houses and restaurants, and so forth—and it had a museum, an art museum—and all that was very exciting and interesting. Then I went into the Army.

Did you go to a lot of movies in those days?

Oh yeah. Yeah, I went to the movies all the time—but I got out of the habit. I got out of the habit after I got out of the Army, 'cause I was so broke all the time. I guess the last time that I went to the movies regularly was when I was still in the Army, about thirty years ago.

What was the Army like?

Well, it was like being in jail, kind of. I had a good job—all I had to do was teach radio operation and mechanics. But, you know, after a while, there was so much extra baloney, you had to stand inspections, and do all kinds of funny little extra nowhere work, kitchen duties of various kinds. And people yell at you, and try to scare you, and shove you around. So it's boring.

What rank were you?

I was a Private First Class. I got to be a Private First Class because the Congress said that anybody who was in a technical school should be raised in rank one degree. Well, that's all the further I ever got.

And then, what happened next when you got out of the Army?

I went back to Portland. And I thought, well, I have this GI Bill thing coming, and it would be nice to go to the University of California at Berkeley and do Chinese studies and mess around like that.

How did Chinese come into it?

Oh, I had read, before I ever got into the Army I had started reading translations of Chinese poetry, and Confucius and what not. I had found Lin Yutang's book, *My Country and My People*, in the town library, and got into it that way.

Were you in contact with any people at that time who shared your interests generally?

No. I only had one friend who was interested in writing, and he was a guy I had known in high school, and he had moved away to Portland. And then when I moved down there, I saw him again. He had started going to Reed by that time, Reed College. And then we were in the Army at the same time, but in different places. He went off to Europe. But, of course, we corresponded all through that time. It was in the Army I met a lot more guys who had either been writing or were interested in it, and who had read a lot more than I had, and told me what to read. And then, of course in college this friend of mine came back after the war, and so we were at Reed together.

Who is that?

His name was Paul Fetzer. He's dead now; he died when he was in graduate school. He developed throat cancer. But, anyway, at Reed there were a whole lot of people who were interested in writing, and who were producing a literary magazine. And then various new, sort of counter-official literary magazines came out. And so a whole bunch of us were all involved with that: Lewis Welch, and Gary Snyder, and Dell Himes, who is now in linguistics and anthropology, and what not, and Bill Dickey, who I think is still teaching out here at San Francisco State. William Hobart Dickey, as different from Uncle Jim from North Carolina, a different fellow. Well, anyway, at Reed, of course, there was a great teacher: Lloyd Reynolds, who taught creative writing, and eighteenth-century literature, and art history, and graphic arts, and he was the one that got us all into trying to improve our handwriting. We all learned Chancery Cursive handwriting from him, and all sorts of other kinds of lettering, and so forth.

You and Gary Snyder and Lew Welch all have that handwriting . . .

Ummm, no, not quite, 'cause Gary never actually took that course, and neither did Lew—out of the bunch, I was the only one that really worked with Lloyd, and I can't—I'm the only one whose handwriting doesn't look like anything [laughs]. Gary and Lew both have quite distinctive handwriting. Anyway, Lloyd, again, made Reed interesting—not much was happening there, and Portland is a very dull place.

Had you begun to write poems by this time?

Oh, I had started as I say in high school, and then I continued all through the time I was in the Army . . .

Oh, I didn't realize that with that first poem you were really starting to write . . .

Yeah . . .

Do you write in longhand?

Yeah.

And then you type it.

Yeah.

You never use the typewriter first?

Very, very seldom. I haven't for years and years now.

Any particular reason? Or just convenience?

Oh, I like to feel myself doing it. I like the feeling of writing on paper, making the pen go, or a pencil, or whatever. It's fun. And besides, a typewriter won't draw pictures [laughs]. I like to do something else on the side.

Can you write a poem on purpose?

Sometimes, but not often. I mean, like if we'd be—if some of us were sitting around together yakking and screeching and carrying on, somebody would—well, like one time Gregory [Corso] was hollering at us. Everybody was sitting around sort of half-zonked on wine, and pot, and what not, and Gregory was typing off in the corner. And he started screeching at us, saying, "Whyncha . . . You people are all poets, whyncha do something beautiful, like Shelley. Here ya are just all sitting around, whatsa matter with with you anyway? Whyncha do something beautiful?" And so everybody started trying to write a poem to try to calm Gregory down. And, of course, nobody turned up anything of any use. When I was at Reed though, one day Lew Welch and a girl called Kate Ward and I were talking about words, and Kate had this idea that there were some words you couldn't use in a poem, because they were just too ugly—I mean physically ugly, I don't mean that they meant something ugly, but they were intractable, lumpy words—and Lew and I were both saying, no, that isn't so, you could use any word if you wanted to, if it would work. And Kate said she didn't believe it, and she kept giving examples, and we kept telling her, well, you could say this, and that, and the other thing.

What kind of words?

Well, we would take, we would take . . .

"Gorgeous"?

Yeah, we'd take a word out of some book of prose. First of all, the first list we had, we used ten words out of a dictionary at random, and we came up with some very strange ones. But, in any case, we decided, well, all right, we'll take these words, and we'll each make a poem. And so, on that occasion, we did. And then we came up with these funny poems. Later on, we did this some more times, and we made up rules, finally, about how we would use a book of prose, any book of prose, and pick out five words, and you had to make a poem five lines long, and use each of those words in the poem. It didn't matter what form it was, or whether it rhymed, but you had to use those words. And so that was the Adelaide Crapsey [laughs]—that was the Adelaide Crapsey-Oswald Spengler Mutual Admiration and Poetaster Society.

Oh wow . . .

It grew a fairly large membership that would meet whenever a whole bunch of us were together and decided to do it. And it would be fun.

You said a while ago that you don't have any sense of yourself as specifically a poet, is that true?

Well, I only have a sense of me in my own history as an individual, and also connected to a whole lot of other history, and physically to the West Coast, and to all sorts of other things, a feeling for music . . .

You don't think you were "touched"?

Oh, yeah, but not about poetry. I'm just naturally batty in a whole lot of ways.

I didn't mean it in that sense—I just meant having to go in that particular direction as if somebody . . .

Well, no, I fell into that direction. I mean it's one of the manifestations of my character. But then, so is my interest in music, and in visionary experiences of various kinds, and in—being me. And, later on, people decided that what I was doing was called "poetry," but, to me, it's something—just one of the things I do, part of what I see, feel.

When you say visionary experiences of various kinds, what do you mean by that? I mean what particular kinds of visionary experience?

Well, one time, for example, I was working in the Forest Service up in Washington, and—Jack Kerouac has described this, has described the place in *Desolation Angels*, I guess—it was a big guard station that was built on a raft on Ross Lake, way up by the Canadian border. And we used horses to pack people into the lookouts from that raft, and one night all the horses were on a raft that was tied up next to ours, and in the middle of the night one of the horses fell off, with a great splash, because they had all been jumping around—I don't know what got at them, the moon or something—and the horses were all dancing and singing, and one of them got excited and went overboard. And so I got up out of bed, and some other guys got up, and we were all rushing around trying to find the horse that had fallen overboard. Well, I was the one that found her. She was a horse with one eye called Maybelle, and here she was in the water, so that people yelled at me, and I said, "I found it." And they said, "Well, hold up her chin, and we'll get a rope on her." And so, the packer brought the rope and wrapped it around the horse a little bit, around its throat sort of, kind of tied it up so I could hang onto it easier. And then he went off to get a boat, and I was kneeling over the edge of this raft in my underwear, and holding this horse under the chin, and the rope in the other hand, and the sense—you know, it was two o'clock in the morning, and it was a beautiful summer night, and the mountains were all around, and the lake, and this horse, and me—and I suddenly had a great, weird, kind of satori, a sort of feeling about the absolute connection between me, and the horse, and the mountains, and everything else. And—you can't describe it very well, the feeling, because the feeling is a feeling. But it was, you know, it was a big take of some kind . . .

A big "O.K."?

Yeah, you know, that kind of thing.

That's really interesting. Have you had . . .

But, you see, I don't think you can start out at age seventeen or something and say, "O.K., I'm a poet, and a poet is a guy who writes sonnets, and now I'll do some Miltonian sonnets, and some Petrarchian sonnets, and some Shakespearean sonnets, and now I'll do some in the manner of Dante"—until you learn how to write sonnets—and pretty soon you start publishing in the *New Yorker,* and you become rich and famous. I think you really have to be into some—or capable of some funny—what Timothy Leary or somebody calls "trans-personative" conditions or states—you have to get out of yourself, some way or another, to get in, to operate, as a poet, or a painter, or a musician. It's not just poetry—or, you could cop out like Cocteau did and call everything poetry, you know, poetry of the novel, poetry of the movies, poetry of the dance, or whatever.

When you talk about that, do you mean a sense of yourself as submitting to something, or a sense of tremendous humility that beckons this possibility?

No, I don't think so.

What do you mean, then, in terms of making poetry possible? I read something by John Wieners in which he said it was a state of "female apprehension" that he felt made a poem happen.

Well no, it's a state of freedom actually, of being untied from all of your usual paranoias, or loopiness, or whatever, that you can suddenly move, or decide, or see something, or hear something, or know something, that isn't where you're usually at when you're worrying about the rent, or about washing the dishes, or something else.

How can you tell whether a poem is good or not?

You mean one of my own or somebody else's?

One of your own. I mean in terms of your craft—I mean I guess you have an aesthetic that is clear to you . . .

Not terribly well, no. I don't know. A lot of things I do I don't like, and a lot of other ones that I don't know what's going on, but it's quite obvious to me that it isn't making it, and then another kind is one that I like O.K. but doesn't do too much, and there's another kind that seems to really work, and there's that, and sometimes people see that it does, and sometimes not. But I don't know, it's all pretty much a feeling-tone affair, and I don't rationalize it too much. There are a lot of things I like in writing, or reading.

Are you interested in your mind? I mean are you interested in the way the mind works as a subject for poetry?

Sometimes, yeah. I've said a lot about it, I know, in writing, but most of it is nonsense, I think [laughs]. Mostly, they're only approximations of all that. I think it's on the wrong track, actually. I think that I should probably—if I ever live to have a collected works, I'd cut out all that part in my work.

How do you feel about memory?

Well, I more and more believe what Blake and Gertrude Stein said—that memory doesn't have anything to do with creation. If you're making something, you're not remembering at that time. Like Gertrude Stein says, "I am not when I see." And Blake, on the other hand, says terrible things about memory, all about how it's this big vegetable and everything, it's all this big net of roots, and

tangles, and so forth, and that the imagination soars beyond all that, and that's where art and poetry and music ought to come out of: the imagination, the active imagination, and not the memory, which apparently both he and Stein thought of as static and dead.

Do you make a distinction, in that regard, between poetry and prose?

No, no, I don't think so.

Poetry is not necessarily a memory medium . . .

I don't think so, no, I hope not. Quite often even when I'm quoting something in a poem, I don't think it's the same thing as memory. Gertrude Stein said, you know, when she's talking about Shakespeare's sonnets and Shakespeare's plays and why they are different, and how the sonnets were written the way they are because he knew what he was going to write ahead of time, whereas when he was writing dialogue and writing the stuff that's in the plays he wrote it down immediately without knowing what he was going to do next—and so that's why the plays are more lively, why the writing is more interesting than it is in the sonnets. She says it was smooth, that knowing ahead of time what you're going to do makes it all polished and smooth and you're remembering, and so on, and that this is what makes the writing come off all polished, and so forth, and dead.

Do you revise?

Sometimes, to a certain extent, but not very much. It depends on the object I've got. If it's a short thing, sometimes I'll add words, or take out words, or what not. And other times, if it's a long thing, I'll cut out sections or add sections. I'll do really gross revising, and then do some final cutting. But, for me, most revision is cutting, and then very small alterations, it seems like. You know, when you're working, it doesn't seem like you're working, in the sense that people usually say, "Wow, you must have worked a long time to make that book." Well, you know that a book is done in about a half a second, actually.

Can you see any direct parallels between your work and any painter's work?

Well, only insofar as the best things I do, I think, come directly from the imagination, a combination of imagination and immediate experience. Sometimes it comes out of long pondering about something, and I think painting must, or music must or any kind of art has to come out of the funny combination of digesting a whole lot of stuff, and also flashes, and takes and fits and starts.

What painters do you like?

I can't think of anybody right this minute, nobody comes immediately to mind, because I haven't looked recently, I haven't had a chance to go to galleries, or what not, to see what's happening. See, I moved here, into the Zen Center, directly from Bolinas in February, and since I've been here, I've been on this loony schedule. So I can't go around very much, and my head is all bent [laughs].

What is your schedule?

Oh, I start out at—I sit, I do zazen from five to seven in the morning, and then we do chanting, and then we have breakfast. Then there's work. And then there's the afternoon. I sit another 40 minutes in the afternoon. Then there's more chanting and dinner.

What is zazen?

Well, to do zazen, you sit, that's all. You have to put your feet up in your lap—you sit on this little round cushion—and you try to think the unthinkable, like Suzuki Roshi said, or try to just sit there without letting the thoughts that you do have scare you, or drag you, or do anything more than just go by, sort of let them all go.

In other words, don't fix on anything?

Yeah, don't hang on—just sort of let it go—and try to sit straight, try to keep your back straight, and try to breathe smoothly, and try not to go to sleep.

Do you think that abstract expressionism as a movement in painting has any relationship to the work of the beat generation?

Well, I think Mike McClure thought so. He knew a great deal more about painting and painters than I ever did, and I don't really know. Anyway, it's a whole different medium. But we were all having the same kinds of problems, I suppose, at that time, working them out different ways. I liked the work that I saw at that time, and Mike told me what to look at, and then Creeley also knew a lot of the guys who were in that New York School and told me a lot about it. So I was able to learn and pick up and see that they were doing something exciting and interesting, and was able to get some good out of it.

I notice you have a poem you mention Frank O'Hara in. Did you have much contact with him?

Not really, no. I only met him a few times. One time Ginsberg took McClure and me over to his house to talk to him. And then I saw him also at some readings in New York during the couple of times I was there—1959 and '60—and that's all. No, I remember in one poem I just say Frank has Hart Crane's eyes, and he did.

Did you know Hart Crane?

No, I was thinking of that portrait and some photographs of him where you see those great big eyes, and Frank's eyes were very large and blue. But Frank also had the habit of shutting them, or drooping his lids down so that you couldn't see his eyes, like in the Siqueiros portrait of Crane, where you can scarcely see his eyes at all, he's looking down.

How do you feel about drugs now?

Fine [laughs]. I don't have anything against people taking drugs, if they want to. And if I felt like I wanted to get high, I would run around, and find somebody, and see if they had any, I suppose, see if I could bum some, or buy some.

Was there ever a time when you were getting high regularly?

Yeah, when we were all in Berkeley together. There was a great deal of grass around, and what not. And then in the last few years, say 1966 and '67 and '69 to '71—those years that I was in Japan—there was a great deal of goody to be had in Kyoto. And so I had many kinds of trips and it was very nice. Kyoto is the best place in the world to get loaded because it's so beautiful to see, just to look at, and walk around in.

GEOFFREY THURLEY (ESSAY DATE 1981)

SOURCE: Thurley, Geoffrey. "The Development of the New Language: Michael McClure, Philip Whalen, and Gregory Corso." In *The Beats: Essays in Criticism,* edited by Lee Bartlett, pp. 165-80. Jefferson, N.C.: McFarland, 1981.

In the following excerpt, Thurley considers Whalen among those poets who characterize later Beat poetry. Comparing Whalen to Michael McClure in particular, Thurley maintains that Whalen is more sophisticated and self-aware but that at times his wit becomes mere cleverness and lacks passion.

Even if we see Ginsberg as a wren who used the cover of Whitman's wingspan to fly higher than he could have flown unaided, the fact is that he *did* fly higher—higher than he could have flown had he not had the intelligence and the energy to exploit the various influences that lay in the background; higher than his older contemporaries, the liberal academics who were still cramped and twisted up with the self-consciousness endemic to the ironist tradition. He evaded the grip of the attitudes which were stifling the creative forces of American and English poets—the obligatory alienation, the by now stultifying isolationism, the cowardice of irony, the negativity which eventually congealed into the poetry of nervous breakdown. Ginsberg's breakthrough, such as it was, was a matter not so much of technique as of ideology. The cult of the nervous breakdown is, I have suggested, a phenomenon of affluence, like the extreme self-consciousness of modern America.[1] In this sense it seems relevant to describe the cult of the nervous breakdown in poets like Lowell, Berryman, Roethke, Sexton[2] as ideological symptoms; their varying academicism is only secondarily a technical matter. It is primarily a question of outlook, purpose and belief. If we turn to Allen Ginsberg's poetry or Kerouac's fiction we shall not need to look far for evidence of the spiritual suffering and nervous exhaustion which are part of life in an over-organized but chaotic society like America. The first line of *"Howl"* prepares us for the saga of sickness and pointless debauch we duly get; Kerouac's novels are the reverse of orgiastic: *Big Sur,* for instance, offers one of the most harrowing experiences available to the modern reader. Yet still, *"Howl"* is as different in purpose and impact from Berryman's *Dream Songs,* or a more recent work, like Galway Kinnell's *Book of Nightmares,* as *Big Sur* is from *Herzog.* Ideologically, Ginsberg and Kerouac are in a different age from Berryman and Bellow. And this difference is to be understood less through technical analysis than through an appreciation of a subtle, decisive shift in emphasis and direction. The nightmare is no longer hugged, as providing identity; the isolation no longer clutched, the alienation no longer cherished, the agony no longer needed.

[. . .]

The use so many Beat poets made of drugs clearly formed part of its basic orientation towards non-striving, passivity and feminity. The experimentation with different drugs carries on the long tradition of *avant garde* spiritual exploration. But the ideal of the narcotic mandarin is a passive world, in which people do nothing because there's nothing they want to do but turn on.[3] It's at this point that one usually starts talking about a new consciousness. It would be better to talk about a new orientation than a new consciousness. Consciousness does not alter: the psychedelic facts still have to be sorted somewhere in the human control-tower. An interesting confirmation of this is Michael McClure's first "Peyote Poem," written down the day after the experience:

> I KNOW EVERYTHING! I PASS INTO THE ROOM
> there is a golden bed radiating all light
> the air is full of silver hangings and sheathes
>   I smile to myself. I know
> all that there is to know. I see all there
>   is to feel. I am friendly with the ache
>   in my belly. The answer
>   to love is my voice. There is no Time!
> No answers. The answer to feeling is my feeling.

It is exhilarating and the moral authority assumed by the poet guarantees a consistent air of seriousness. It also brought McClure a following: he seemed in the mid-1960s the poet closest in intention to Timothy Leary. But this poem is really not typical of the sort of effusion it helped to encourage from so many other poets.

There is of course a sameness about all mystical and narcotic experience—or at least about the reports mystics and drug-users have given of it. Whether the experience is gained through a natural oddity of bodily chemistry, whether it is deliberately induced or involuntary, whether it is celebrated in awe or suffered in terror, whether it is mystical or schizophrenic—the experience of the world we are here concerned with has certain unvarying properties: we may be familiar with McClure's intense lighting effects, his sense of great significance and his feeling of being at the center of the universe from the works of Blake, De Quincey, Boehme, Swedenborg, Strindberg—or from a psychiatrist's casebook. Mysticism and extreme schizophrenia depend as much on the body's chemistry as the hallucinations of the drug-user. The important variable is the intellectual context in which they take place—the use, in other words, which the victim of these bodily states makes of them. This is not the place to discuss the implications of these ideas. Whether a poet uses hallucinogens or not, the only question that concerns the reader of what purports to be poetry is, is the poetry produced good, bad or indifferent? Nor need this inquiry stay academic. It may be more significant than at first appears likely, for instance, that Michael McClure's poetry is by no means always as good as its tone suggests it must be. Poetry—for Michael McClure as well as for F. R. Leavis—is important beyond the performance of certain linguistic skills. If, to put it bluntly, poetry fails certain acid-tests, the conclusion critic and reader are justified in drawing is that there is something more radically wrong with the utterance than some technical incompetence.

This is commonplace. But it needs re-stating here, I think: for Michael McClure, in the volumes that followed the poem quoted above, makes certain assumptions, certain claims, which, if justified, undercut a great deal of conventional intellectual and spiritual life: the poet, it is claimed, is able with the use of hallucinogens to penetrate to a layer of experience, of reality, which lies within or beneath "normal" vision, and is in some sense "more true," more real. So the normal version of the dogma runs. I have already indicated my opinion of the metaphysical bases of this dogman: hallucinogens cannot be said to make contact with reality, or truth. They simply change the body's chemistry and thereby its perception, which reverts, unless the equipment is damaged in the process, back to its former state (which we may therefore call "normal") upon the cessation of the narcotic effect. The most that could be claimed is that it is somehow morally better or healthier to perceive and experience hallucinogenically than in the ordinary way. Rimbaud's *Une Saison en Enfer*, the decline of Coleridge, and the testimony of William Burroughs suggest otherwise, but this is not, as I have said, the place to discuss that question. What is relevant here is the question, how do the aesthetic facts bear out the metaphysics? Why, and how, does McClure's verse fail? What are the moral implications of the aesthetic facts?

If McClure had been right, he ought to have hit a poetic gusher: there ought to be no difference between one poem and the next, whereas in fact there are enormous differences—of quality, tone, effect—even within one passage of one poem. Excellent as McClure's best drug poems are, there is little evidence of his having achieved the goal of every poetic mineralogist: the level of his verse fluctuates wildly, it moves from near-sublimity to near-bathos from one to the next. This is so in the peyote poem already quoted. This, for instance, is the note hit so monotonously by psychosis—"I KNOW EVERYTHING!" McClure's poetry, like Christopher Smart's, moves into and out of relevance, while itself apparently remaining convinced of its own oracular profundity. The nuttiness of "I KNOW EVERYTHING!" is familiar to many users of hallucinogens, to say nothing of alcohol. Everyone who has ever been drunk or high knows this feeling of *significance*: the things said in this state—afterwards recollected to have been quite trivial—seem at the time to be tremendously, ultimately, profound. Later, in the same poem, McClure tones it down and drops the block capitals—"I know all that I need to know"—ar-

rogant still perhaps, but not absurd. The second statement occurs after a passage of considerable beauty—

> The dark brown space behind the door is precious,
> intimate, silent, still. The birth-place
> of Brahms.
>
> [Peyote Poem]

That is an adjective sequence, we feel, which might have come into being without the peyote, though it's unlikely that the actual instigation—the space behind the door—would have caused it. Not so the Nerval-ish pretensions of "I read the meaning of scratched walls and cracked ceilings." This is surely private—an attestation only. Poetry comes into existence in the space between the poet and the world, between his experience and ours. McClure's over-use of upper-case type is a telltale sign of exasperation, an inability to communicate. But poetry, to say it another way, is not—much pseudo-symbolist claptrap to the contrary—concerned with the incommunicable, but with the *otherwise incommunicable*. Chairs are inexpressible, if you like, but our experience of them, or what this experience means to us, is not. In the same way, McClure's poetry succeeds when it is not trying to gesticulate towards the INEXPRESSIBLE, but precisely when it concerns itself with the frontierland between the experience of drugs and his own waking consciousness, between his extraordinary experience and our own more ordinary. It is, in other words, half-critical, half-comparative. It is blasphemous to seek to "say" God, to say what should be left unsaid. The true mystic's concern is what his experience teaches him and his readers about the whole meaning and conduct of life itself. Much of McClure's poetry invalidates itself in trying to declare the undeclarable. So, in the peyote poem under discussion, the interesting and comprehensible statement,

> Here in my Apartment I think tribal thoughts

(we think of Wise Indians smoking pipes of peace, of the wholeness the white man has lost), is followed by a straight line rules across the page, and then the single word "STOMACHE!!!" It is hard to know which is funnier, the upper-case type or the triple exclamation marks. Here, truly, is the absurd of drunkenness, the ludicrous conviction of *significance*. It is a phenomenon which could be illustrated at random from any of McClure's longer poems, those sprawling numinous extravaganzas. This is the sort of thing "poor Kit Smart" stumbled on in his madness: "STOMA-

CHE!" In this instance, McClure immediately goes on to fish out a genuinely fascinating emblem from the unconscious—

> I am visited by a man
> who is the god of foxes
> there is dirt under the nails of his paw
>   fresh from his den.
> We smile at one another in recognition.

The episode is strangely meaningful, though its significance is hard to define without talking in Jungian terms about archetypes and collective memories. Anyway, McClure's memory becomes ours here: the weirdly alarming beauty of childhood is skilfully conjured up. Almost at once—so drastic are McClure's transitions—the scene vanishes: the poet closes his eyes—"Closing my eyes there are flashes of light—My eyes won't focus but leap." The reporting here is interesting and to the point: the physiological facts are relevant at this juncture. We want to know what it feels like, what actually happens, and he tells us, with a frank courage which is an important part of McClure's make-up. It doesn't seem important in the same way to know that he then felt he had three feet. But the odd detail—"I see seven places at once"—has a factual authenticity which tells us something we ought to know about the trip. Throughout this passage, indeed, the reporting is absorbing and pointful, probably because it keeps the inner narrative closely related to the outside world. "Seeing the loose chaos of words on the page"—we all know that aspect of language. In the middle of the passage there is another hilarious interjection—"STOM? ACHE!"—which must, but can't, be ironical; then, after another line ruled across the page, McClure again tells us solemnly of his feelings about his belly[4]:

> My belly and I are two individuals
>   joined together
>   in life.

The conclusion of the poem, however, returns to the archetypal world to which it is McClure's peculiar gift and privilege to be able to penetrate:

> I stare into clouds seeing
>   their misty convolutions.
>
> The whirls of vapor
> I will small clouds out of existence.
>
> They become fish devouring each other.
> And change like Dante's holy spirits
>   becoming an osprey frozen skyhigh
>   to challenge me.
>   ["Peyote Poem"]

Those ospreys, like the fox-man earlier and the lion men in the beautiful short poem "The Child," come from an impersonal realm, a timeless symbol-bank, which sets all the rest of the hallucination in a meaningful context. All McClure's best verse connects his drug-experience with some deeper, broader metaphoric layer, and in just this connection lies the poetry:

> COLD COLD COLD COLD COLD COLD COLD
>   COLD
>   COLD AND FAR AWAY
> and we are not cold in our space and not cool
>   and not different. And I do
> not mean this as a metaphor or fact.
>   Even the strained act it is.
>
> Bending by the brook and filling cups.
>   ["Peyote Depression"]

The last line suddenly makes contact with Chinese religious thought; at the same time, it provides a metaphor for life itself which is at once ancient and original. The "fact-act" echo here reminds us again of McClure's verbal subtlety, subtlety evident more in a non-narcotic piece, like "Canoe: Explication" which reveals most strikingly McClure's provenance from Robert Duncan:

> it's the imagined song, the concept
>   of anarchy set to music
> Wavering, symmetrical, unsymmetrical
> Pointed and strange as a matchflame
>   Held in sunlight.

The almost invisible image (so much more apt than Olson's shot at the same thing) beautifully captures the elusiveness of the thought. The same delicacy is applied later to the motion of the canoe:

> A volta appears—the serene charged pause.
>   Thought alone wonders
>   At the connection
> And the duet begins again.

The simple yet subtle physical event—canoeing—has been "explicated" by the metaphor of music, just as the experience of hearing music has been enlarged by the physical analogy. The slightness of the theme produces a poetry of equal delicacy. McClure is a poet with or without drugs.

Whether he has realized his enormous potential is another matter. Since he came down from his narcotics plateau—a decade ago now—McClure has written a great deal of good poetry. Its sheer quantity indeed makes it impossible for this kind of survey to do it anything like justice. It is enough to say that at its best it achieves a poise and a sinewy delicacy rarely to be found in recent American writing. Its essence is a clarification and refinement of the archetypal symbolism which emerged so excitingly from the highs and lows of his peyote poems.

His best poems balance on a needle-point, yet are as sure as rock. What we might perhaps question is that power to engage our deepest human interest. Here is a more recent instance of this quasi-Blakean mode:

> EACH
> MAMMAL
> does
> a
> small perfect
> thing
> like
> to be himself
> or herself
> and to hold a new creation
> on a shining platter
> as he
> (or she)
> steps towards
> the waiting car.
>
> ["For Robert Creeley"]

A derivate of Duncan's pedestal pieces, this poem has the shape of a baroque fountain. But one wonders whether it doesn't also share that non-problematicness essential to Duncan's often rather bland celebrations. The central assertion of the poem—that each created mammal (especially, by implication, man) is in itself perfect and in need of celebration—is finely illustrated by the final clause—the step towards the waiting car. No matter how trivial or transient the act, the poem asserts, we are in ourselves at any point perfect. But little of that complexity of all good poetry is generated out of the combination of the two major elements of the poem: we look in vain for that tension of contraries that gives Blake's smallest poems such force. Beat poetry offered Blakean celebration as opposed to existentialist nihilism. But it also offered at its best—in McClure's best peyote poems, in "*Howl,*" in Corso's "Mutation of the Spirit"—an awareness of the foulness and complexity of the conditions against which the capacity for joy has to strive. I have noted above that Whitman himself shortcircuited exploration by the expedient of mass-acceptance—acceptance which really accepted nothing, since it did not *know* what it was claiming to accept. Much of Michael McClure's later poetry, like much of Duncan's, seems to me to limit itself by a desire to say "Yea," or, still worse, to tell the rest of us that *we* ought to say "Yea"—yet without admitting all the facts. There is a feeling that the affirmativeness has been too easily acquired.

That vital intelligence characteristic of the best Beat poetry of the 1960s has gradually gone under to an elegant and stylish blandness. The impression is reinforced rather than gainsaid by the obligatory abuse of easy targets—the Pentagon, the Man in the Grey Flannel Suit, and so on. But McClure is still—comparatively—young, and we have not seen his best.

No poet illustrates the sophistication of Beat poetry more strikingly than Philip Whalen. Whalen's stock-in-trade is an attractive self-awareness, a wry, biting humor, a negligent familiarity with the numinous that contrasts interestingly with Michael McClure's solemnity:

> The trouble with you is
> That sitting on a bench in the back yard
> You see an old plank in the fence become
> A jewelled honeycomb of golden wires
> Discoursing music, etc.
> [Whalen, "**Denunciation, Or, Unfrock'd Again**"]

The subject-matter of the poem is much the same as in McClure's verse; but the psychedelic experience, the mind-changing effect of the drug, is not dashed down in rapt awe. It becomes a source of self-mockery:

> The trouble is aggravated by the grass
> Flashing alternately green and invisible
> Green and non-existent
> While the piano in the house plays
> *The Stars and Stripes Forever*

The self-mockery is more fertile, more purposeful than we had been accustomed to expect in modern verse. There is no covert self-satisfaction in the self-unmasking:

> The trouble with you is you keep acting
> Like a genius: Now you're not a genius
> You're nothing but a prick . . . in fact you're
> Not even that, you're nothing but a son-of-a-
>   bitch
>   GET OUT OF MY HOUSE!

Whalen obviously does find himself absurd, yet remains quite confident of the significance of what he has experienced:

> What plant put out those
> Tall thin stiff green leaves? Lines
> Drawn from the tip of each one
> Would describe the surface of what
> Regular solid polyhedron?
> You don't dare invent a name.

So closely are Whalen's satiric wit and his intellectual insight related. Once again, we are reminded of the significance of the new release of humor and wit: here something like the wholeness of sensibility it was the design of intellectualist criticism to guarantee with irony? Behind Whalen, as behind Leroi Jones, is the complex efficiency of Black Mountain imagism, with its subtle sense of vegetable life:

Bud-clusters hang straight down from the
	sharply crooked
Geranium stem like strawberries, the wild
	mountain kind
These flowers almost as wild right here
Barbarous thick-jointed tangle, waist-high
Escaped once for all from the green-houses of the
	north
A weed, its heavy stalks jointing upwards and
	winding out
In all directions, too heavy to stand straight
The neighbors clipped some out of their yard
The stalks lay in the gutter and grew for days
In the rain water, flowering
Ignorant of their disconnection.

	["Soufflé—Take IX"]

The endless "takes" and jottings do, to some extent, betray a disorganized mind. Whalen has never produced the *magnum opus* he seems intellectually qualified to have written. Instead, there are the shorter ironic pieces ("**For C,**" "**Fond Farewell to the *Chicago Quarterly***") which are often perfect, and the longer, fragmented works which only occasionally achieve the moments of penetrating insight:

The wind increases as the sun goes down
The weight of that star pulling air after it
Naturally the prune trees blossom now
And some kind of bush with pink trumpet flow-
	ers
All the other trees except acacias have quit.

	["Soufflé—Take III"]

It seems to have been Whalen's destiny, his function perhaps, to accept a kind of failure. We may speculate once again on the influence of the feminization of the mind encouraged by Buddhism. It is unlikely that a forthright Christian ethic of duty, obligation and striving would have been able to give us the things Whalen has given. If we compare him with Roethke, for instance, whom he resembles in many ways (they write the tragicomedy of obesity), Roethke's labor and strain seem inadequate recompense for the loss of the humor and the play of mind Whalen's detachment affords him:

All day Christmas the sea whirled this tangle—
Spruce logs, redwood stumps, fishboxes and
	lightglobes—
A big eddy at the creek mouth
Carting back several tons of debris back and
	forth
		across a hundred feet of beach
In water maybe a foot and a half in depth.

	["**Letter to Mme E T S, 2.1.58**"]

Curiously, many of Whalen's most strange and powerful perceptions are, like this, entirely unmetaphoric. It is enough, he intimates, merely to observe. There is, in my opinion, nothing in Carlos Williams or Olson to match the eerie real-ity of these things in Whalen. "All that comparison ever does," Olson had observed,[5] "is set up a series of reference points: to compare is to take one thing and try to understand it by marking its similarities to or differences from another thing." Yet Olson's own verse swills around pointlessly, unless some metaphor creeps in.[6] It is to Whalen that we must turn for evidence of the power of annotated reality.

This is especially true of the earlier work. *Like I Say* (1950-58) still seems his best collection. The wryness is already there. But the intelligence about himself (what we have come to regard as intelligent behavior in a poet this century being largely a matter of laughing at himself) is displayed as much in the mental energy that vaults beyond itself in order to see itself as it is in the self-depreciation. Whalen notes his failure—his obesity, his never getting anything done—with an athletic intellectuality strangely inconsistent with it and with the image of himself that he otherwise projects in his verse. This intellectual energy was what made possible the notation of unadorned reality just noted as being so important in Whalen's verse: the logs swilling about in the tide, the cut-off flowers still growing—these things are comprehended by an act of the imagination, in Coleridge's understanding of the term, not copied by a prose-camera. In his best pieces Whalen sets these natural images in a sound-pattern of considerable subtlety and a very complex intellectual frame. "**Homage to Lucretius**" (written in 1952, printed in the *Evergreen Review* of 1956, included in **Monday in the Evening,** 1961) suggests a systematic scheme in the title which is belied in the characteristic throwaway manner:

It all depends on how fast you're going
Tending towards light, sound
Or the quiet of mere polarity

But the casual manner is supported here (or it supports) a very wide-ranging and economically presented argument. "We want crystals," he observes, but "can't easily imagine another world"—and the reason is that this one (we remember at this point the atoms of Lucretius) is itself "barely / Visible." Enough to say that this genuinely philosophical inquiry lacks altogether the portentousness of Robert Duncan's pronouncements, but also that it succeeds in giving the abstract speculation a natural expression: the root-experience, which, I imagine, gave rise to the poem in the first place, is now disclosed, to fill out and illustrate the Lucretian speculations which were in fact suggested by it:

We lined up and pissed in a snowbank
A slight thaw would expose
Three tubes of yellow ice. . . .
And so on. . . .

The last phrase is disarming, and—of course—charming: we are meant to be delighted by the performance, and we are. This seems to me to be close in many ways to William Empson's more successfully philosophical explorations. What is characteristic of Whalen is not just the colloquial casualness which he shares with Empson, but the ease with which he succeeds in giving the insights—the piss frozen into tubes yields an insight into "A world not entirely new, But realized . . ."—a greater context of meaning. And the point is this meaning, not the attractive casualness, which is merely instrumental.

At his best, Whalen succeeds in relating this order of intelligence to the random events of a life—wasted, according to the world's view, in meditations, reading, and staring out of the window—and in holding it all in one perspective. The best of these complex efforts to marshal everything is, in my opinion, "Sourdough Mountain Lookout" (1955-1956), which displays, in its moments of inertia and fatigue, as much as in its explosions of mental energy, a wholeness rare in contemporary writing:

Then I'm alone in a glass house on a ridge
Encircled by chiming mountains
With one sun roaring through the house all day
& the others crashing through the glass all night
Conscious even while sleeping. . . .

The poem exercises a fine virtuosity of feeling, moving from sharp imagist observation, instinct with life, to the inward world, the relations between which are Whalen's real theme. The intellectual vitality which holds together the details and the percepts is revealed also in the apparently random reading which structures the poem: Heraclitus, Byron, Empedocles, Buddha—the sources and influences file into and out of the poem according to a rhythm of walking, resting, climbing and reflection. When he is tired ("pooping out, exhausted"), the ironic awareness of himself comes to the surface ("Remember smart guy there's something / Bigger, something smarter than you"). And this wry self-ridicule—what a reader fresh to Whalen is most likely to take away from the experience—is a product of his intellectual vigor as much as the ability to "get round"—come round the back of—his wider intellectual interests. He concludes with a generalization that holds the whole of what has gone before easily within itself:

What we see of the world is the mind's
Invention and the mind
Though stained by it, becoming
Rivers, sun, mule-dung, flies—
Can shift instantly
A dirty bird in a square time. . . .
["**Sourdough Mountain Lookout**"]

Such reflections upon the relations between the mind and the outer world constitute Whalen's major theme. It is a slippery ramp to get on: it is easy to feel, in moving through *On Bear's Head*, that Whalen is too clever for his own good. He does not work up the excitement in the face of the world which we see in the best of McClure; he cannot, it could be, put all the bits together right. He finds it easier to negate what he has just said than to find reasons for moving from it onto something greater. Scepticism is his essence.

Notes

1. In an earlier chapter of his study, Thurley had written that in the poetry of Anne Sexton "it is even more difficult with her poetry than with that of Lowell and Berryman to resist the inference that its *raison d'être* was the nervous breakdown, and that the breakdown itself . . . provided structure not only for the individual poems and sequences, but for the *oeuvre* itself" (p. 86) [editor's note].

2. This list of names may suggest to some readers A. Alvarez's *The Savage God* (London, 1971). It was not meant to, and I should regard that book too as itself symptomatic. Sylvia Plath's apparent self-sacrifice to this cult is only a particularly fierce example of the feedback: nervous breakdown, the post-Freudian version of Romantic agony, becomes itself not a symptom but a cause of behavior. Mr. Alvarez fails to see the difference between the poetry of nervous breakdown and that of Ted Hughes.

3. See Aldous Huxley, *The Doors of Perception* (London, 1954).

4. Peyote characteristically produces intense stomach pains, which McClure has duly—but unpoetically—honored.

5. "Towards a human universe," 187.

6. Viz. "what blows about and blocks a hole where the wind was used to go?"

PAUL CHRISTENSEN (ESSAY DATE 1985)

SOURCE: Christensen, Paul. Introduction to *Two Novels*, by Philip Whalen, pp. vii-xiv. Somerville, Mass.: Zephyr Press, 1985.

In the following essay, Christensen examines the connections between Whalen's novels and his life, relationships, and poetry.

Every life has a few important seams in it, things or events that change destiny; one in Philip Whalen's life was meeting Gary Snyder and Lew

Welch while he was attending Reed College in Oregon. Here were a couple of young men with ambitions to become serious artists; with deep reserves of talent and discipline to draw upon, already they seemed well on their way to writing effectively. Like Whalen, both were caught up in the awakening of youth that rumbled like thunder across the nation in the post-war years. The three men lived in a boarding house together near the Reed campus, shared their convictions about writing and invented a dadaistic game for composing poetry. Choosing a difficult, "unpoetic" word at random from the dictionary, each would develop a poem around it, writing without calculation; few of these experiments were ever published. But when William Carlos Williams visited the campus on his western reading tour in 1950, he was impressed with the writing of all three men: "Good kids, all of them, doing solid work," he noted in his *Autobiography* (1951).

Whalen was older than Snyder and Welch by a few years and had served in the Army Air Corps (1943-46) before going to college on the new G.I. Bill. His own ambition had already taken root during the war years, when, as an instructor for radio operators in B-17 bombers, he had the leisure to try a novel in the manner of Thomas Wolfe. Like Jack Kerouac, who had written *The Town and the City* (1950) in the passionate, lyric style of Wolfe, Whalen was also trying to learn style from one of his generation's literary heroes. But he destroyed this effort and went on to try another novel when he lived with Snyder and Welch in 1950, a "dotty period" as he has called it, in which he wrote in obsessive nine-hour jags each day. That manuscript went up in smoke as well.

If Whalen's abortive novels were about friendships in the Army and at Reed which had educated him and precipitated changes in his life, they would hold with the pattern of his two published novels, for they are careful reconstructions of circles of friends and of the circumstances which precipitated new directions in his career. In a sense, Whalen's two novels are self-prophecies. In *You Didn't Even Try*, published originally by Coyote in 1967, we are treated to the elaborate social life of the Berkeley intelligentsia during the years Whalen lived there, on and off from 1959 to 1964. The novel's protagonist, Ken, is reminiscent of Whalen, with some discrepancies—Whalen has never married, for example. The friends are portraits and composites of actual figures. Ken is introduced to us as married to Helen, a petulant but beautiful woman with a keen mind whom Whalen describes with zest. At the novel's end,

FROM THE AUTHOR

WHALEN ON FINANCES, WRITING, AND MEDITATION
I thought that I'd write books and make money enough from them to travel abroad and to have a private life of reading and study and music. I developed a habit of writing and I've written a great deal, but I've got very little money for it.

With meditation I supposed that one could acquire magical powers. Then I learned that it would produce enlightenment. Much later, I found out that Dogen is somewhere on the right track when he tells us that the practice of zazen is the practice of enlightenment. Certainly there's no money in it. Now I have a meditation habit.

Whalen, Philip. "About Writing and Meditation." In *Beneath a Single Moon: Buddhism in Contemporary American Poetry*, edited by Kent Johnson and Craig Paulenich. Boston: Shambhala Press, 1991.

Ken is divorced and chased after, not only by Helen, but by two other women, each infatuated with his independence and whimsical nature. Instead of choosing a second wife, Ken promises to create a "work" which will bear the weight of his love and to "distribute it to the rest of the world"; he vows to be an artist.

Like the novels of Thomas Wolfe, *You Didn't Even Try* is about the making of an artist, beginning with the moment at which the hero is freed from domesticity and made to face life alone, when he chooses to follow a deep-seated though unnamed calling. After completing his final draft of this novel, Whalen received a grant from the National Academy of Arts and Letters (with the help of Allen Ginsberg) which paid for his move to Kyoto, Japan, in early 1965; there, he began writing his mature poetry. So in its own way, the novel parallels Whalen's life.

In *Imaginary Speeches for a Brazen Head*, written during Whalen's second sojourn in Kyoto (1969-71) and published in 1972 by Black Sparrow, the plot and its outcome are similar to those of *You Didn't Even Try*. The protagonist, Roy Aherne, another character reminiscent of Whalen, is a poet who has enjoyed wide reputation and awards for his writing, and he is welcomed into the same sort of intelligentsia which populates the earlier novel. As social life wearies Roy, he is slowly pulled away from his ties and commitments and made to choose a new path. In a parallel occurrence, shortly after completing work on the novel Whalen attended the Zen Center in San Francisco at the suggestion of his friend Dick Baker; a year later he requested ordination as an *Unsui,* or Zen monk. In 1975, Whalen was appointed *Shuso,* head monk, at the Zen Mountain Center in Tassajara Springs, California.

In one way, the two novels connect in their self-prophecies; the move to Kyoto in 1965 exposed Whalen to Gary Snyder's conversion to Buddhism, and may have started the psychological process that is completed in 1971 with his attendance at the San Francisco Zen Center. Both novels bring their protagonists wearily to an end of material pleasures, which have grown tediously repetitive; in both cases, a compelling alternative lies ahead. The novels break off just as Whalen's life takes the next step toward this alternative, and so might be viewed as imaginary rehearsals for the author's forthcoming decisions.

These are not novels strictly predicated on escape from conformity. Far from it, they make the society and terrain of Berkeley so inviting that only the most resolute quester could think of quitting it. But they are novels which spring from a literary tradition of flight from convention. Many male-authored novels about visionaries and artists—and there have been many in the mid-century—put up an easy foil to the dreamer longing for release. Dingy households where parents bitterly eke out a life, small-minded communities that scorn ambition or artistic goals—all that drabness could be easily left behind, as in Kerouac's first statement on the theme, *The Town and the City.* It was only what one was fleeing *to* that appealed to most of these authors: the urban landscape of bohemian life, where casual sex and serious conversation floated in the same night currents, as in Norman Mailer's *Barbary Shore* (1951), John Clellon Holmes's *Go* (1952), and Chandler Brossard's *Who Walk in Darkness* (1952). Each one takes off from Wolfe to invent a disaffected but gifted rebel.

The dim surroundings darken even more by the next round of escaping heroes, as in the grim absurdity of Yossarian's service in *Catch-22* (1961) and Ken Kesey's asylum captivity of Chief Bromden in *One Flew Over the Cuckoo's Nest* (1962),

and they turn completely mad in the novels of Barth, Vonnegut and Pynchon. A long hatred for domestic entrapment and dead-ended employment builds up the drear landscape from which the dreamer bolts in modern male-authored fiction. In Whalen's novels, the flight from home is already behind the protagonist; he has arrived at his urban destination, where he finds great pleasure and enrichment but discovers it is not the end of his quest. Something lies beyond the city to complete his fulfillment as an artist and he seeks it out.

Whalen's two portraits of Berkeley and San Francisco give us the minds, the glittering personalities, the eccentrics of human excellence in an otherwise drab America. These gems jut out at odd angles from the conforming silhouette of the average citizen. Ken, Whalen's first protagonist, and the poet Roy Aherne of *Imaginary Speeches* both trawl the waters of this society in constant curiosity of what might turn up from its depths. The women are brash, smart, and keenly witty, of an independence that tortures some of their husbands; they are stately, willowy people looked at almost with the longings of a voyeur, though Whalen gives to both his heroes strong charms that attract a variety of these heady females to their beds. The men are powerful, stubborn, aloof in their thoughts, of convoluted personality that often irks their wives, who stay with them through the thin years because of their cranky, gifted intellects and interesting lives. This is what cements Whalen's social microcosm: a love of intelligence, the freedom it brings, the sweetness it confers on daily life; without it, nothing.

This swirl of humanity is compressed within the municipal boundaries of the city of Berkeley, headquarters of the University of California's preeminent campus, a magnet for high achievers who are gathered together in a new culture that is by turns Viennese, Parisian, Oxonian—with a dash of American. Whalen lavishes attention on the high culture of the West Coast and on the beautiful landscapes too, especially Mt. Tamalpais, a haven from the madding crowd celebrated in both novels. But the most remarkable aspect of Whalen's two novels is this core of humanity gifted with sight, powered by a consciousness that will not permit of mere survival.

Whalen's portraits are complex, a social commentary on American life. Equated with elements found in postmodern poetics, the social interactions of his characters dramatize the dynamics that Charles Olson and Robert Creeley worked out as the dynamics of a poem. Whalen applies these heady notions from physics and poetics to his fictional characters, partly in jest, partly in earnest. At one point in **You Didn't Even Try,** Ken compares his friends to phenomena of a force field:

> . . . It was strange to spot them, rising above the fairly regular Riemann surface he looked out upon whenever he sat still and looked. There were these discontinuities in it, sudden multidimensional warpings that indicated the presence of a field of action or force which was operating autonomously.

The plot places such figures of power into a field of relations; they affect one another much the way perceptions affect the ongoing course of a poem, in which, Olson would say often, the awareness is being widened and enriched. The figures of intellectual power who move in Ken's orbit warp the field by their own dynamic influences. Indeed, their influence on Ken throughout the plot may be the catalytic agent delivering him to higher consciousness at the end, because of which he ironically more or less abandons them.

Ken remembers the best things said by his gifted friends, but no one collects them more assiduously than does the novelist Marilynn Marjoribanks. Her husband Travis

> rigged up a tape recorder so that it would pick up whatever came over the telephone as long as Marilynn kept her foot on the treadle-switch. She'd give the switch a kick whenever one of her callers got going on a particularly poignant or self-revelatory theme. Marilynn had a nice ear for turns of speech and colorful expression, a great sense for recognizing the dramatic, intriguing bits that people throw away in conversation.

Ken's friends are sources of open consciousness, the alert sensibility that is at the heart of postmodern poetics. Whalen gives to Marilynn Marjoribanks the methodology he himself uses as a poet; her treadle-switch phone is the equivalent of the many journals in which he has recorded the *bon mots, apercus,* brainstorms and other delights of daily consciousness. From them a poem is drafted, not in a sudden frenzy of lyric outburst, but carefully, built up as in mosaic, in which bits and pieces of the journals are juxtaposed into a single, high-velocity streak of perception that implodes years of rambling and digression.

Here is how Whalen expresses his poetic through Marilynn:

> She edited the tape at the end of the day, transcribing onto paper the phrases and anecdotes she believed she might use. For, very slowly, she was taking all these words and little homey incidents and breaking them down, boiling and smelting them into the fabric of an enormous novel. The final composition and editing of this vast collage were a little more than half done.

The friends are the natural phenomena of the field; the artist Marilynn is the concentrator of the perceptions and brilliant phrases that have been uttered and then forgotten. Like an alchemist, she compresses them into a frame; by "smelting" and laborious mixing, she comes up with something like gold, a filament of purity, a rarified instance of human consciousness at its fiery best. Only then, is the implicit argument, is an artistic work made. This view is expressed by the full range of the arts at mid-century, many of which are governed by a single goal: to reach for the center of human awareness, to find its molten core of understanding and to reproduce it in some medium where its original force is not lost.

In both of Whalen's novels, Berkeley is an intellectual Eden where a few good minds are able to have great perceptions and many others are able to live at a high altitude of talent and intelligence. The rest, of which few are noticed, are of that dull, even Riemann surface of the grid, the humble clerks and go-fers who also serve. Brooding over Berkeley's paradise are the forces which threaten to undermine it—government and big business, whose alluring contracts can easily seduce the freest spirits into drudgery and deceit. Work is not in and of itself redeeming in Whalen's cosmos, especially work by contract, by the clock, wherein many dull efforts accompany the one or two good things achieved.

The most admired members of Whalen's cast are those who have retained their intellectual independence. Travis is one of them:

> He was much consulted by the Government (for whom he declined to work), by other physicists, and by such vast invisible corporate beings as the General Dynamics organization. He could, if he chose, take a week off to work on the electronic organ which he was building at home, and nobody would complain to him or try to fire him from his job.

Stanford, where Travis is employed, pays him vast sums "to sit around discussing [why] the current theories were all wrong."

Clifford Barlow of **Imaginary Speeches** is another independent thinker. He too likes to play the organ, has a well-rounded, powerful intellect, but is the more artfully drawn of the two characters; he embodies a subtle freedom that permits him to contradict his own personality and still retain the preeminence and self-confidence of the true free spirit. He stays apart by living outside the country, and when he has to take employment, limits it to teaching for nine months. The distinction made in both characters is between an interest and a career, a capacity and an obligation to perform it routinely.

Both men are measures of achievement to their friends; they are like pinnacles thrust up out of the grid to remind everyone of the reach a human being is capable of making. They are each necessary to the others as an inspiration and, at times, a goad, but there is a significant shift of interest between the two portraits of genius. Travis, a speculative scientist, is a contentious, daring theorist willing to take a leap or risk in thought. Clifford is earthier, more interested in human beings and their cultural and anthropological unities; his gift for language allows him to decipher the underlying patterns that link ages and cultures. The portraits of Travis and Clifford in part parallel a change of interests in Whalen, from the grand program which Olson had set out for poets that Whalen early admired, to the concern for the small, the simple, the plain, a unifying principle of everyday life to be found in Snyder's poetry, and increasingly in Whalen's.

Much of the rollicking humor and complaint of the poems in **On Bear's Head** (1969)—a large selection of Whalen's best poems, in which he portrays himself a "laughing Buddha," an impractical but brilliant hanger-on in the social scene of San Francisco—are found in the character of Roy Aherne, popular poet and social boor. Alice Lammergeier complains to her husband in an early scene of **Imaginary Speeches** that "He talks too loud. He dominates the room. It's like having a sound truck in the house." But her husband Max defends Roy and even insinuates that his wife is attracted to him. Whalen is clearly amused by Roy and gives him sex appeal, enormous intellectual powers, and a flat-footed manner. Roy is a little too forthright with his student admirers, as in an opening scene at a bar, or too thoughtful and slow on the draw with the imposing figures of higher Berkeley society. But more than anything, Roy is a wanderer enjoying the drift of fate or folly.

In Roy's characterization, as in Whalen's persona as poet, is an old paradigm of the beggar poets, those mountain bards of India and China who taunted their fellow villagers with sly verses of seeming madness in exchange for a little food and drink. Whalen's dependence on friends (as noted in his book of poems, **The Kindness of Strangers** [1976], the title taken from Blanche

Dubois's famous line in *A Streetcar Named Desire*), is an inverted arrogance of sorts, wearing in time but charming and nevertheless potent. But below the smiling mask of the bards is an ideology intact from the start—the conviction that the artist must remain free to be good and should be paid tuppence for the pleasure of his company.

In certain ways, **Imaginary Speeches** is a better novel than **You Didn't Even Try.** The prose glistens with intelligence, is smooth, flexible, deft and precise, never prosaic or labored. It is obviously from the pen of a craftsman, a poet who has written verse for long years and who knows how to prevent the rhythm of a long passage from flagging. He can turn on a dime when attention seems to wander or interject wit that lifts up a long, perhaps flabby digression or deflate his own drift toward some abstraction not entirely intended. The point of the prose is pleasure first—in the sound of the word, the chemistry of sound in a phrase, the overlap and harmony of inner-rhyme, delicate nuance, shading. These all make entirely forgivable the sometimes soap opera plotting of the novel, for what powers the imbroglios and subplots is a pure, limpid language springing from a master.

The doctrines of postmodernism are present in subtle form; the ideas are ironed out, digested, placed in the exposition and characterization. The three-dot section break that marks off scenes is one manifestation of postmodernism, a subtle way of noting the discontinuity principle of the work, present in all of Whalen, present indeed through much of the art of the period. The rivulet of prose overcomes each of the seams, flows through and around its impediments, but the section break, like particles of a hexagram, floats there to remind us that nothing is seamless, everything is made up out of the vastness of things and chosen, juxtaposed, by hand.

The colors are vivid but less obvious in **Imaginary Speeches.** The Berkeley social world is muted, the extremes not so widely placed. Dorothy, a character similar to the first novel's Helen, dramatizes the new mean. She has been sharing the love of two good men, Roy and Clifford, and has known the agony and pleasure of their fine intellects. Only after having that experience can she willingly accept less in her new lover, Tom, and appreciate him more. In **You Didn't Even Try,** fame, notoriety, crowds of admirers may have intrigued Ken and might have precipitated a change of life, but in **Imaginary Speeches,** Roy grows weary of them. His drinking has become

BEAT GENERATION: A GALE CRITICAL COMPANION, VOL. 3

habitual and boring, his nights lost in a boozy haze. Whalen himself was the figure of much attention in the press, as were all the members of the San Francisco Renaissance. From the start, at the poetry reading at the Six Gallery in San Francisco, in 1955, when Ginsberg first read his poem "Howl" in public, the group was hounded by the media and a certain flamboyance of style was reinforced by the attention. Whalen looks on this celebrity with a jaundiced eye in his treatment of Roy as he steers him to the edge of the city. In one scene late in the novel, Roy wakes up in a stranger's apartment, repairs himself like a rag doll, and leaves wondering who has kept him for the night. It is the tattered end of one stage of a poet's life.

Roy's change of heart takes something of the form of Ken's in the way he expresses his new detachment from the Berkeley social whirl: "I don't really love them, I love their beauty. The trouble is that I don't love just one single person. If I really loved one, I wouldn't be interested in the judgments of all the others, nor would I be seeing all the others as judges." He is chafing to be let free; "We are all such fixtures here," he tells Dorothy. When he implies he wants to travel, Dorothy tells him to get a job. But for the first time he calls *writing* his job: "I haven't got time to work for anybody else." The story closes a little later, but it is obvious Roy must now find shelter someplace where his work comes first.

Soon after finishing this novel, Whalen visited the Zen Center and discerned in the religious order the possibility of a new life. There is no clue what Roy will do, of course, but for Whalen the Center was a kind of uncontaminated university of the spirit, without corporate sponsors or government interference, where one could contemplate the imagination, much as he had all along, and be secure in the fact that it was the duty expected of him. This was the one meaningful employment Whalen had searched for throughout his life. It was a place where mind was given its unfettered freedom. In **You Didn't Even Try** and **Imaginary Speeches for a Brazen Head,** Whalen gives us the progress of poets making their way to this spiritual and artistic fulfillment beyond the city of first dreams.

DAVIDSON, MICHAEL (ESSAY DATE 1989)

SOURCE: Davidson, Michael. "'Spotting That Design': Incarnation and Interpretation in Gary Snyder and Philip Whalen." In *The San Francisco Renaissance: Poet-*ics and Community at Mid-Century, pp. 94-124. Cambridge: Cambridge University Press, 1989.

In the following excerpt, Davidson emphasizes the role of Eastern spirituality in shaping Beat poetry, using Snyder and Whalen as examples.

Forms of Spiritual Practice

A popular misconception about the Beats is that they were dabblers in esoteric religion, turning to Zen, cabala, or activist versions of Catholicism in order to discover new spiritual highs. John Ciardi, writing in the *Saturday Review* in 1960, claims that the Beats have "raided from Zen whatever offered them an easy rationale for what they wanted to do in the first place,"[1] and Herbert Gold, writing in *Playboy*, says that "Zen Buddhism has spread like Asian flu. . . . Zen and other religions surely have their beauties, but the hipster dives through them like a side show acrobat through a paper hoop."[2] Though it is certainly true that poets turned to alternative religious systems and practices during the 1950s and 1960s, it is demonstrably *not* true that this interest was in any way casual.

Consider the facts: Gary Snyder left San Francisco in 1955 to live in Japan on and off for the next twelve years while engaged in formal Zen training. During this time, under the tutelage of Roshi Oda Sesso, he took formal vows as a Zen monk. Allen Ginsberg has spent much of his time during the past fifteen years as a follower of Tibetan Buddhism, traveling extensively in India and the East as part of his spiritual training. During this period he was a disciple of Chögyam Trungpa at the Naropa Institute, where Ginsberg helped direct the Jack Kerouac poetics program. Philip Whalen has, until recently, lived at the San Francisco Zen Center, where, in 1973, he was ordained Unsui (Zen Buddhist monk), and later, in 1975, became Shuso (head monk) of the Zen Mountain Center at Tassajara Springs, California. In 1949 William Everson converted to Catholicism and soon after (1951) entered the Dominican Order at St. Albert's College in Oakland, California. He adopted the name Brother Antoninus and served as a lay monk until he left the order in 1969. Kenneth Rexroth was Anglo-Catholic for most of his adult life and in his last years converted to Roman Catholicism.[3] He was active in the Catholic workers movement during the 1930s and has written extensively on Western and Eastern religions, devoting an entire book, *Communalism*, to a history of alternative religious and political practices.[4] Most of the poets we shall encounter in this book developed the terms for their poetics out of specific theological concerns (Robert Duncan's theosophy, Jack Spicer's Calvinism, Michael McClure's animism, David Meltzer and Diane DiPrima's cabalism) that provided both the problematic of belief and the rhetoric by which that belief could be translated into aesthetic terms. Such religious activism was based not on a casual glance into a primer on comparative religion but on sustained study and research.

Given this active involvement in both Eastern and Western religious traditions, it is difficult to see how anyone could dismiss it as "dabbling." In fact, it is hard to think of any modern literary movement in which writers so actively yoked their poetic vocation to specific spiritual practices. Of course, what critics usually implied by their deprecations was not that the Beats were not interested in religion but that they were not interested in the *right* religion. While a poet like Robert Lowell was trying to solve the thorny question of incarnation within the doctrinal framework of Catholicism, poets of the San Francisco Renaissance turned increasingly to Eastern religions (Buddhism, Hinduism) and to various forms of pantheism to deal with many of the same questions. For Lowell in the early 1950s the supreme task of poetry was to render the complex logic of God's word through metaphors that would, by their rhetorical complexity and rigor, manifest something of the inconceivable quality of Deity itself. The poem was the site of what John Crowe Ransom called a "miraculist fusion" of particulars with some universal, nondiscursive order, presenting at the level of local texture an equivalent "supernatural" force.[5] The tough metaphysical conceit, yoking diverse ideas together, stood as a concrete universal, giving form to that which has no form and voice to that which cannot speak. As Charles Altieri has characterized it, incarnation for the New Critics provided "a doctrinal basis by which an essentially symbolist poetic can assert the value of the mind's orders while insisting that universals are not mere fictions but contain the actual structure and meaning of particular experiences."[6]

For poets like Gary Snyder, William Everson, and Allen Ginsberg incarnation is a matter not of reconciliation but of activation and energy. God is manifest in terms of Lorca's "dark and quivering Duende" or as Lawrentian sexuality, a force emerging from the earth and from the unconscious. Lawrence, in his preface to the American edition of *New Poems*, equates this power with an emerging free verse. "The seething poetry of the incar-

nate Now," as he calls it, participates directly with natural forces and, as such, is distinct from metrical verse. In free verse,

> we look for the insurgent naked throb of the instant moment. To break the lovely form of metrical verse and to dish up the fragments of a new substance, called *vers libre*, this is what most of the free-versifiers accomplish. They do not know that free verse has its own *nature*, that it is neither star nor pearl, but instantaneous like plasm. . . . The utterance is like a spasm, naked contact with all influences at once.[7]

For Lawrence as well as for his latter-day adherents, the poem does not reconcile opposites by sustaining rhetorical tension but provides examples of oppositions living in harmony in the natural world. Many of Gary Snyder's and Philip Whalen's poems consist of catalogues or lists of disparate things existing side by side as part of a "vast jewelled net" of interconnected elements.[8] God is present as process, revealed in physical labor, sexual ecstasy, and moments of visionary insight. The Kantian or Coleridgean view of the creative imagination as a repetition of the "eternal act of creation in the infinite I AM" is replaced by Wordsworth's view of the artist as one who need only "look steadily at the subject."[9] Pound's "natural object" replaces the "miraculist" objective correlative as the poet seeks to find—not represent—the interknit modalities of God's presence. What for the New Critics involved the imposition of order on flux becomes, for the Beat writers, the rediscovery of the creative potentiality of flux itself.

Within this "poetics of numinous presence," as Altieri has called it, we find a separation between the poets described in Chapter 2 (Ginsberg, Kerouac, McClure) from their Northwest counterparts, Gary Snyder and Philip Whalen. Though both groups have a common frame of religious beliefs, based largely on Buddhist tenets, they differ in the nature of their spiritual practices. Using two concepts from Buddhism, we could divide the poets of the Beat movement into two camps: those who take the direction of *karuna* (compassion) and those who follow the way of *prajna* (wisdom). These are by no means incompatible concepts; both encourage the pursuit of enlightenment, but they suggest different emphases. In more familiar terms, this division could be seen as that between Emersonian idealism with its belief in an unmediated relationship between phenomenal reality and spiritual life, and a more solitary, speculative form of transcendentalism like that practiced by Thoreau.

For Ginsberg, Kerouac, and McClure, Buddhist compassion for all sentient things is expressed through forms of worship (and embodied in poems) that are essentially passive and receptive. The individual attempts to become an empty vehicle, free of all material desires, through whom what Emerson called the "currents of universal Being" may flow. Ginsberg's emphasis on mantric forms of poetry, on Hindu breathing exercises, and on communal chanting could be seen as gestures directed at achieving this emptiness by returning self to body and participating broadly in the creative powers of nature. His most formative experiences—his Blake visions of the late 1940s, his peyote and yage experiences of the 1950s, and his psychedelic trips of the 1960s— represent moments in which he literally *hears* "the voice of the Bard." He does not create a persona or mask through which a projected spiritual voice may speak, but directly transcribes the presence of that voice in his life. And in similar ways, Kerouac's and McClure's ideas of spontaneity, simplicity, and ecstatic testimony could be seen as alternative ways of transcending boundaries between temporal and spiritual realms, between secular vision and visionary potential.

For Gary Snyder and Philip Whalen, by contrast, the pursuit of enlightenment involves processes of intellection, discrimination, and observation that focus attention on the here and now. In describing why he chose the Rinzai sect of Zen Buddhism, Snyder quotes Yeats's lines, "The fascination of what's difficult / has dried the sap out of my veins . . . ," and elsewhere approves of the hard "Dharma combat" tied to Zen koan study.[10] Enlightenment is achieved not in a sudden flash of illumination but as a result of years of study and meditation.[11] Philip Whalen, though less inclined to celebrate the rigors of spiritual practice, tends toward the same intellectual position as Snyder. In his poetry, Whalen can usually be found negotiating the conflicting claims of ego identity and mindlessness. With a sardonic and often rueful humor he mocks his own self-consciousness while in pursuit of some unmediated, natural state.

When translated into poetics, these differences in spiritual practice can be seen in the opposition between a poetics of immediacy and improvisation, derived from Whitman or jazz, and a poetics of objectivist clarity and economy, as-sociated with Pound and Williams. Certainly Ginsberg wrote many of his early poems in imitation of Williams, but the bulk of his post-"Howl" poems are modeled on mantra and chant. Snyder and Whalen and their Reed College roommate, Lew Welch, developed their poetics out of readings in modernists like Pound, Williams, and Stein as well as the Chinese T'ang dynasty poets, whom they read in translations by Arthur Waley. The result is a considerably more clipped, terse syntax and a shorter line. In some sense the two groups that I am describing here represent two strands of Eastern influence on American writing in general: the Indian, Vedic tradition that nurtured the American romantics of the mid-nineteenth century and the Chinese lyric tradition, focused in the haiku, that became the model for much of modernist lyricism in the early part of the twentieth century. That both traditions were tied to specific religious and cultural ideologies should not be disregarded in considering any of these poets.

If Gary Snyder and Philip Whalen can be paired by their shared commitment to the "wisdom-oriented line"[12] of Zen or by their common northwestern background, they can be differentiated according to the way each poet treats his own voice in the poem. Snyder typically removes himself, allowing the particulars of a landscape or the events of a day to constellate realms of value. When the first-person pronoun enters the poem, it is not the expressive "I" of romantic subjectivity but rather the "I" as interpreter who establishes relationships between local and universal. Charles Altieri sees a conflict between Snyder's early poetry, in which this "I" is content to see without interpreting, and his later poetry, in which the "I" is fully invested with its prophetic role.[13] Though I would agree with Altieri's sense of the limitations of the later work, I would say that even early poems like "Milton by Firelight" and *Myths and Texts* evidence the same prophetic intent.

Philip Whalen's poems often have the same objectivist surface as Snyder's but with far more investment of the mediating ego and with a greater range of tonal variation in the poet's voice. Whalen is invariably the subject of his poems, asking questions, worrying about his relations to others, and worrying about worrying too much. But instead of producing the ironic circularity one associates with John Ashbery or James Merrill, this self-consciousness dramatizes the difficulty of uniting a belief in natural process with complex dramatic and perceptual frames that create their own demands:

> Suzuki Roshi said, "If I die, it's all right.
> If I should live, it's all right. Sun-face Buddha,
>   Moon-face Buddha."
> Why do I always fall for that old line?
>
> We don't treat each other any better. When will I
> Stop writing it down.[14]

These lines typify Whalen's meditational style: The Zen paradox must be tested within epistemological structures at the level of poem itself. "Why do I always fall for that old line?" is a recognition of the difficulties encountered in living *with* the difficulties posed by Suzuki Roshi's paradox, a resignation signaled in the poem's last line.

In a sense Gary Snyder and Philip Whalen represent two possible variations on the Buddhist notion of no-mind, the attempt to achieve an essentially egoless state necessary for illumination. In Western terms, we may see this impulse in terms of the romantics' desire for a state of "negative capability" or in Charles Olson's concern with avoiding the "lyrical interference of the ego." Certainly all of the Beats idealized various forms of mindlessness, whether enhanced by drugs and booze or by mantric chant and jazz. For Snyder and Whalen, however, the achievement of such a state is directly linked to a sense of community. Unlike their Beat colleagues who stress a kind of global inclusiveness or democratic ensemble, Snyder and Whalen advocate the tribe or family as models of social organization. The pursuit of personal enlightenment must be effected through the tribe, because spiritual activity is linked to other forms of group interaction. What Snyder calls the "communities of practice" are those tribal units that have existed since the Neolithic period within which work, prayer, childrearing and art are shared.[15] He feels that the tribe is still alive and well, even in urban America, and much of his writing has been devoted to celebrating its endurance.

In our attempt to differentiate the Beat writers, the idea of tribe as the synthesis of personal vision and social cohesion will become a major issue. Not only has it been a theme in Snyder's and Whalen's work; it became a reality during the 1960s as young people—often with Snyder as a model—turned increasingly away from state politics and official church religion to the commune and the collective. Snyder himself left for the foothills of the Sierras, where he lives in a semicommunal settlement, and Whalen spent fifteen years at the Zen Center. Their example is a logical outgrowth of that incarnationalist spirit I have already described, a desire to make spirit flesh not only in words but in social practice as well.

"A Walking Grove of Trees": Philip Whalen

Gary Snyder's name is usually linked with two other poets, Philip Whalen and Lew Welch, whom he met while an undergraduate at Reed College during the early 1950s. They became lifelong friends, sharing common interests in Eastern religion and philosophy, the poetry of William Carlos Williams and Kenneth Rexroth, and the mountains of the Pacific Northwest. One of the distinguishing marks of this triad is their rather elegant calligraphic script, modeled on a distinctive sixteenth-century hand called "Arrighi." Their instruction in calligraphy came to them by a teacher of graphic arts and English literature at Reed, Lloyd Reynolds, who exerted a profound influence on most students who came into contact with him—especially Philip Whalen.[16] In addition to his courses in calligraphy, Reynolds taught courses in eighteenth-century literature, and it was in these classes that Whalen first read the work of Pope, Swift, and Dr. Johnson, the last of whom became a kind of literary model:

> (Not that Johnson was right—nor that I am trying to inherit his mantle as literary dictator but only the title *Doctor, i.e., teacher*—who is constantly studying). I do not put down the academy but have assumed its function in my own person, and in the strictest sense of the word—*academy*: a walking grove of trees.[17]

Philip Whalen's poetry can be best approached through the two disciplines taught in Lloyd Reynolds's classes: writing as inscription performed by the hand and writing as a kind of peripatetic walking. What began with calligraphic exercises in Lloyd Reynolds's classes has become an important dimension of Whalen's poetry. He fills notebooks with lettering exercises, doodles, lists, drawings, quotations, and short poems that together produce a handsome and often witty verbal collage. Poetry, he has said, is a "graph of the mind's movements" (**On Bear's Head**, 93), and these notebooks are a vivid instance of this graphic intention.[18] Whalen loves the sensuous properties of letters, and he embellishes them on the page, turning words into elaborate designs. He loves the sensuous properties of thought as well, and many of his poems seem to be a desultory record of his mind at play just as his notebook page is a congeries of verbal doodles:

I look through the notebooks I've been doing and sometimes, . . . it seems like it's all completed but then other times there are just stray lines and if I look through it and see that some stray line connects it reminds me of some lines that are in another notebook and I look at that and it may all go together or it may not and the very longest poems that are in *Memoirs of an Interglacial Age* or the real long poems that are in *On Bear's Head* were done that way.

(*Off the Wall: Interviews with Philip Whalen,* 14)

This description is like the poems themselves, full of qualifications, second thoughts, and reversals, all held together with conjunctions.

Whalen's discursiveness seems the very opposite of Gary Snyder's hard, impersonal lyrics with their emphasis on economy and precision of statement. The poems feel leisurely, as though written during a long walk. And, indeed, many of them were written if not *on* then *about* a walk. Take, for example, "America inside & outside Bill Brown's House in Bolinas":

> Some kind of early waking take about bread (should be
> whole-grain flour & c.) cheese, wine, vegetables & fruits.
> I can leave the meat for whoever must have *that* responsibility
>   (a fit of enthusiastic praise here to all the horses,
>   cows, chickens, ducks, turkeys, geese, pheasants & c.
>   whose (bear, deer, elk, rabbit) generosity & benevolence
>   I have (whales, oysters, eels and sea urchins) so much
>   enjoyed; I guess I can leave them alone, now.)
>
> Shall I go past John Armstrong's house & wake him up
> with bells, but it might disturb Lynne and the baby so
> I write now good morning joy and beauty to John and Lynne
> and Angelina
>
> I do have to move around outside the house. The sun wasn't
> quite up—a great roaring pink and salmon commotion in the
> east flashes and glitters among eucalyptus trees— here are
> no fields where food is growing, no smell of night-soil,
> here's all this free and open country, a real luxury that
> we can afford this emptiness and the color of dawn
> radiating right out of the ground

> Flowers thick & various, fuchsias all over everything
> Houses all scattered, all different, unrelated to the ground
> or to each other except by road and waterpipe
> Each person isolated, carefully watching for some guy
> to make some funny move & then let him have it POW
> Right on the beezer
>
> Monday Indian eye in the roofbeams
> Drumhead flyrod curtain-ring cloud
> This is Tony's room. Sound of whistle-buoy as at Newport
> Roaring water for the suicide's bath.
>
>   Dumb dirty dog
>   Dirty dumb dog
>   Dumb dirty dog
>
> Dumb dirty dog, dirty dumb dog, dumb dirty dog.
> Black spayed Labrador bitch. Molly Brown.
>   4:XII:67 (*Heavy Breathing: Poems, 1967-1980,*
>   11-12)

The date that closes the poem emphasizes the fact that this poem is very much *about* a particular day, its diversity and distractions. In the opening lines the poet tries to remember food he is to buy that day, but is the midst of his shopping list he delivers a parenthetical ode to the various animals he has "so much / enjoyed." Then he speculates on where he will walk, a meditation that leads him to "John Armstrong's house," where he (at least hypothetically) leaves a message of greeting. He then reflects on the openness and freshness of the landscape of Bolinas at sunrise, the "luxury" of such "emptiness." But in the midst of this passage of celebration, he reflects on the houses of the neighborhood, "all scattered, all different, unrelated to the ground / or to each other except by road and waterpipe." The people who live in them are "isolated, carefully watching for some guy / to make some funny move & then let him have it POW / Right on the beezer." This observation is a casual aside like all the others, but it introduces a note of threat and uncertainty that qualifies the celebratory mood of the moment.

Soon, however, Whalen returns to his lists, noting the interior of "Tony's room" and the sound of water roaring into—and then out of— the "suicide's bath." Despite this ominous note, Whalen's reference to suicide is simply a form of self-mockery, as excessive in one direction as his celebration of animals is excessive in another. He ends his poem as he ends his bath with the sound of water rushing out the drain, rendered by the repeated phrase, "Dumb dirty dog." And even this phrase, chosen presumably for its onomatopoeia, leads to a final image: the literal "dirty dog" who lives at Bill Brown's house, Molly Brown.

In this poem we become so taken up with the welter of details and texture of sounds that we miss the title: This is a poem about "America," both inside and outside a specific house in a specific place. At another level it is about the America that lives inside and outside one citizen, a fact stressed by the poem's oscillation between descriptive and reflective passages. Whalen sees the glory and wonder of a landscape as well as the distrust and paranoia that lie behind the walls of "separate houses." He does not propose some panacea for joining the two landscapes but *shows* them as being part of the same world. And he does more: He walks, both physically and mentally among the houses, linking them together by praising, identifying, and noticing them. And he leaves notes to link persons by bonds of affection and care. Ultimately, he creates a poem that is its own kind of personal note to the world—as fragile as a notebook page or grocery list, but in its own way an enduring "fit of praise" for that which might be forgotten.

Whalen's poetry in general could be seen as providing such links between things; he sees an octopus as a "yummy and noble beast" or a spider web as "polygonal vacancies," but he notices himself noticing as well. It is in this quality of self-reflexiveness that he differs most radically from Gary Snyder. Whalen fully inhabits his poems, often relying on the ironic or melodramatic quality of his voice. Both poets reach toward the historic occasion, but for Whalen the occasion is always framed by an experiencing subject and a specific voice.

That voice is multiple in the range of its registers and personae, constantly shifting to accommodate a mood or heighten drama. Whalen can be alternately cranky, reflective, or pompous in the same poem. One of his characteristic voices is that of the philosopher manqué who ponders life's mysteries from a slightly pompous and ironic perspective. The titles of his poems read like chapter titles taken from treatises on art and aesthetics: **"The Art of Literature," "Philippic, Against Whitehead and a Friend," "20:vii:58, On Which I Renounce the Notion of Social Responsibility," "All About Art and Life," "Theophany," "Technicalities for Jack Spicer," "Homage to Lucretius."** These poems often interrogate a proposition by subjecting it to the author's immediate circumstances. Whalen at times resembles Wallace Stevens in his attempt to

provide reflective variations on a single perspective. Consider **"Absolute Realty Co.: Two Views"**:

1.

THE GREAT GLOBE ITSELF

I keep hearing the airplanes tell me
The world is tinier every minute
I begin believing them, getting scared.
I forget how the country looks when I'm flying:
Very small brown or green spots of cities on the
    edges
        of great oceans, forests, deserts

There's enough room. I can afford to be pleasant
    & cordial to you
        . . . at least for a while . . .
Remembering the Matto Grosso, Idaho,
    Montana, British Columbia,
New Hampshire, other waste places,
All the plains and mountains where I can get
    away from you
To remember you all the more fondly,
All your nobler virtues.

                                                7:v:64

2.
Vulture Peak

Although my room is very small
The ceiling is high.

Space enough for me and the 500 books I need
    most
The great pipe organ and Sebastian Bach in 46
    volumes
        (I really NEED the Bachgesellschaft
            Edition)
        will arrive soon, if I have any luck at all.

Plenty room for everybody:
Manjusri and 4700 bodhisattvas, arhats, pratyek-
    abuddhas,
        disciples, hearers, Devas, Gandharvas,
            Apsaras, kinnaras,
        gnomes, giants, nauch girls, great
            serpents, garudas,
        demons, men, and beings not human,
            flower ladies,
        water babies, beach boys, poets, angels,
            policemen, taxi
        drivers, gondoliers, fry cooks and the Five
Marx Brothers

All of us happy, drinking tea, eating *Linsertorte*,
Admiring my soft plum-colored rug
The view of Mt. Diablo.
                        11:v:64 (*On Bear's Head*, 276-7)

The "absolute" real is relative, a matter of perspective and point of view. From the air, the world seems large enough to dispel any worries about overpopulation. From the perspective of Whalen's room, the world is no less capacious. The title of the second section, "Vulture Peak," invokes the famous story of Śākyamuni, the historical Buddha who in a sermon to his disciples at the Mount of the Holy Vulture held up a bouquet of flowers without saying a word. No one in the congregation understood the significance of this gesture except Mahakasyapa, who simply smiled at his teacher. Śākyamuni responded, "I have the most precious treasure, spiritual and transcendental, which this moment I hand over to you, O venerable Mahakasyapa!" To some extent, Whalen is playing Śākyamuni by refusing to make reality "absolute" and offering, instead, a vision of infinite potentiality. Vulture Peak, the site of the sermon, is replaced in the poem by Mt. Diablo as Whalen focuses his final line on a specific place in the distance—a nice retrieval of that aerial view of the world initiated in the poem's first section. Whalen's cheerful, open-armed embrace of both "views" of reality dispenses with formal analysis and puts the burden of proof squarely on the shoulders of the perceiving individual.

This emphasis on the situational frame resembles the "personism" of New York poets like Frank O'Hara and Ted Berrigan, whose poetry insists on the temporary and contingent in art. Consider Whalen's "Hymnus ad Patrem Sinensis":

> I praise those ancient Chinamen
> Who left me a few words,
> Usually a pointless joke or a silly question
> A line of poetry drunkenly scrawled on the
>   margin of a quick
>   splashed picture—bug, leaf,
>   caricature of Teacher
>   on paper held together now by little
>   more than ink
>   & their own strength brushed
>   momentarily over it
> Their world & several others since
> Gone to hell in a handbasket, they knew it—
> Cheered as it whizzed by—
> & conked out among the busted spring rain
>   cherryblossom winejars
> Happy to have saved us all.
>   (*On Bear's Head,* 61-2)

As in many of O'Hara's "I do this I do that" poems, Whalen's rhetoric here performs and demonstrates the very immediacy he admires in "those ancient Chinamen." Phrases like "Gone to hell in a handbasket" or words like "whizzed," "conked," and "busted" have the same particularity and contingency of the Zen art described in the opening stanza. The ponderous Latin title is gradually debunked as his hymn of praise illustrates the endurance of the absolutely temporary.

Whalen has acknowledged the influence of William Carlos Williams on his development of these qualities of brevity and immediacy. One can see this influence in the short, single-image poems like "A Couple Blocks South of the Heian Shrine":

> She builds a fire of small clean square sticks
> balanced on top of a small white clay hibachi
> which stands on a sewing-machine set between
>   her
> house wall and the street where my taxi honks
>   past
>   (*Heavy Breathing: Poems, 1967-1980,* 10)

The four, evenly balanced lines steadily "build" the image of the woman until the last few words, when the camera swings around to reveal the observer driving by in his taxi. Whalen's other lyric mode comes from Japanese haiku, which, in his hands, becomes a considerably more self-conscious genre:

> 25:I:68
>
> Sadly unroll sleepingbag
> The missing lid for teapot!
>   (*Heavy Breathing: Poems, 1967-1980,* 12)
>
> Saturday 15:ix:62
>
> No help for it. I'm so funny—
>   looking that I can't see the trees.
>   (*On Bear's Head,* 175)

Such sudden, often whimsical observations form the basis for his longer poems—and Whalen is a writer of long, occasionally *very* long, poems. Works like "My Songs Induce Prophetic Dreams," "Minor Moralia," "Homage to Rodin," "The Best of It," "The Education Continues Along," and the book-length *Scenes of Life at the Capital* allow Whalen a broad canvas on which to trace the movements of his ruminative, speculative imagination. *Scenes of Life at the Capital* is a case in point. It was written while Whalen lived in Kyoto, Japan, during the years 1969-71. It was the period of the late expansionist stages of the Vietnam War, and in a sense the poem is about the war seen from the standpoint of Asia. The "capital" in the title is both Kyoto and Washington, although the latter makes an appearance only through its effects on the rest of the world. The many references to Western food, clothing, television, and literature suggest the enormous influence of American life on the East. But lest the reader expect a polemical jeremiad on the order of Robert Duncan's "Up-Rising" or Robert Bly's "The Teeth Mother, Naked at Last," *Scenes of Life* remains quietly meditative. The poem seems more a journal than an antiwar poem, but this is part of its strength: that it focuses its global theme on one Western individual trying to make sense of his cultural origins in an Eastern setting.

There is not enough space here to do justice to *Scenes of Life at the Capital,* but one can see how Whalen focuses global issues on the particular in a shorter poem like "**Homage to Rodin.**" Like so many others, it is a "walking" poem, a sort of docent tour of three pieces of sculpture in San Francisco: Rodin's *The Thinker* located at the Palace of the Legion of Honor, *The Shades* adjacent to the palace, and finally Rodin's small statue *Iris* at the De Young Museum.[19] These three pieces of sculpture serve as foci for Whalen's reflections on various subjects, the general theme of which is an ideal of muscular beauty embodied in the work of Rodin. The poem's three sections describe the poet lost in a series of gloomy reflections on the state of the world until he is able to relieve his depression by recognizing the possibility of human intercourse made palpable through art.

Whalen begins by interrogating Rodin's heroic nude, *The Thinker:*

> Rodin says: "ANIMAL WHO SITS DOWN
> which is one difference, apparently
> doing nothing
> TO CALCULATE, CEREBRATE"
> & that's of the first
> significance:
> Meat thinking and got hands to
> build you what he
> Means or throttle you if you get in
> the way, either action
> without too many qualms
> (*On Bear's Head,* 225)

Whalen answers those who dismiss Rodin's perpetuation of the heroic tradition:

> Old stuff, we say, "Oh, Ro-*dan.* . . .
> Rilke's employer . . . oh yes, Rodin, but after
> all—
> Archipenko, Arp, Brancusi, Henry Moore—
> Sculpture for our time . . ."
>   (they appear in Harpo's Bazzooo, modern,
>   chic,
>   seriously discussed in *Vogue*—
> Epstein and Lipchitz are OUT, the heroic
> tedious as Rodin)
> (*On Bear's Head,* 226)

Rodin's *Thinker* reinforces the outmoded idea that thinking is done by a physical being, "BODY: with head containing brains, / hands to grab with, build. . . ." The art of Rodin, unlike the more streamlined work of Brancusi or Arp, is Whitmanian, "Hulking Beefy Nude." The male figure,

subject of "old *New Yorker* cartoons," is valued all the more for its solidity and mass.

In the second section, Whalen frames his celebration of the heroic mode against the backdrop of contemporary dehumanization. He describes himself walking along the cliffs overlooking the Golden Gate straits, beginning at Playland at the Beach and ending at the Palace of the Legion of Honor. At Playland, he pauses to admire the merry-go-round and "2 old men" who watch it:

> No amount of sympathetic observation will do
>   any good
> Why not get older, fatter, poorer
> Fall apart in creaky amusement park and let the
>   world holler
> Softly shining pewter ocean
> Or let it quit, who cares?
> (*On Bear's Head,* 227)

What appears to be a fairly casual question, "who cares?", becomes the central issue of the poem: Who cares enough about the physical world to see it as a dimension of the human universe? Who cares enough about other humans to sympathize truly? Some answer would seem to be provided by the Palace of the Legion of Honor, which is dedicated to the war dead. But the monument seems as empty as the concrete bunkers left over from World War II that molder on the cliffs overlooking the straits. The "Formal building pillared propylon and stoa" devoted to the principles of "HONNEUR ET PATRIE" strikes a hollow note, even if it houses the work of Rodin.

Presiding over the entire vista is another Rodin statue, *The Shades,* three figures who stand "heads bent down, three arms pointing toward / The ground that covers them." But instead of honoring "the noble prospectless dead," they are "blanked, puzzled-looking." Their legacy seems only to be a quality of "loose hatefulness" that Whalen finds embodied in a conversation between a hysterical young kid and his equally hysterical father:

> Fat kid wants expensive camera Daddy to put two-bits into Cliff House binoculars his father screams in reply, furious insane, "Whaddaya wanna looka them rocks whaddaya gonna see in this fog?" "Come on!" the fat kid hollers, "Gimme twenty-five cents, put the twenny-fi'cents in, gimme tenficens I wanna see them! R O C K S! out there is COME ON! Gimme twenty-five cents!" and his father screaming back at him like he might tear the kid limb from limb but actually looking in another direction, quite relaxed.
> (*On Bear's Head,* 228)

Whalen juxtaposes to this incident a woman playing in the surf who, "Oblivious to her girl-friend hollering at her from the sand . . . plunges, laughing, through a wave." Her gesture stands in vivid contrast to the hysteria of the father and son and introduces, for the first time, an idea of independence and solitude that is an alternative to the personal malaise the poet observes every-where.

In the poem's third section, dedicated to the waterlilies growing in the reflection pool in front of the De Young Museum, Whalen becomes less gloomy and begins to contemplate forces of growth and life that exist near to hand. He finds solace in the sexual appearance of waterlilies, "No mystery, genes in every cell manifest themselves / Bulb of the earth showing itself here as lilies / The summer flowers, underwater globes of winter all the same." The flowers remind him of a former lover, whose memory is invoked by the manifest sexuality of the flowers:

> Since you'd gone I hadn't thought of other
>   women, only you
> Alive inside my head the rest of me
>   ghosted up and down the town alone
> Thinking how we were together
> You bright as I am dark, hidden
>
> Inside the Museum I see Rodin's IRIS
> Torso of a woman, some sort of dancer's exercise
> Left foot down, toes grasping the ground
> Right hand clutches right instep
> Right elbow dislocating
> Reveals the flower entirely open, purely itself
> Unconscious (all concentration's on the pose;
>   she has no head)
>
> Its light blasts all my foggy notions
> Snaps me back into the general flesh, an order
> Greater than my personal gloom
> Frees me, I let you go at last
> I can reach and touch again, summer flesh &
>   winter bronze
> Opposite seasons of a single earth.
>   (*On Bear's Head*, 229-30)

In these concluding lines, all of the previous descriptions and images are refocused. Whalen is "hidden" inside the museum and inside himself until he encounters a female counterpart to *The Thinker*, who "blasts" all of his "foggy notions" and provides a "light" to match his darkness. Rod-in's sculpture is not Keats's Grecian urn, freezing time in mythic stillness. It is a sensual object that returns the observer to the "general flesh, an order / Greater than my personal gloom." The poet has reconciled a series of dichotomies, "summer flesh & winter bronze," life and art, immediacy and

reflection, by releasing his focus from himself and looking outward. Rodin's *Thinker* had already proposed an ideal of solitude, but as the second section of the poem evidences, the ideal has not become identified with Whalen's own condition. It is only when Whalen is able to relate Rodin's sculpture to another person that he is able to get outside his "foggy notions" and "touch again."

Despite Whalen's numerous disparaging re-marks about the "mothball smell" (*Heavy Breath-ing: Poems, 1967-1980*, 60) emanating from English romantic poetry, **"Homage to Rodin"** resembles poems like "This Lime Tree Bower My Prison" or "Fears in Solitude," in which Coleridge broods on "Carnage and groans beneath this blessed sun" only to discover at the end of the poem "a livelier impulse and a dance of thought" inspired by his ability to project himself beyond his own self-consciousness. Whalen, like Col-eridge, comes to a similar understanding by first dramatizing the conflicting postures—righteous anger, self-mortification, reverence, self-delusion—that the ego provides as temporary hedges against solitude. Only after projecting these voices of self-identity can he see the world without grasping it:

> One of the most wonderful and magical actions
> We can perform: Let something alone.
>   (*Heavy Breathing: Poems, 1967-1980*, 85)

Philip Whalen's poetry is firmly rooted in the romantic anxiety that Geoffrey Hartman has characterized as "anti-self-consciousness."[20] The poet, seeking one kind of dissolution of the ego, despairs over his tendency toward extreme self-analysis, thereby raising self-concern to an even higher level. Whalen often wants to "Let some-thing alone" but must account, at the same time, for cognitive and ethical frames in which "some-thing" exists at all. His great advantage, unlike that of most other poets of the San Francisco Renaissance, lies in being able to manipulate a wide range of registers and voices. He is also argu-ably the wittiest poet of the group, able to debunk the more transcendental claims of his peers without sacrificing Buddhist beliefs in numinous reality.

"The Incarnate Now"

The title of this chapter is taken from a poem by Gary Snyder, "Vapor Trails":

> Twin streaks twice higher than cumulus,
> Precise plane icetracks in the vertical blue
> Cloud-flaked light-shot shadow-arcing
> Field of all future war, edging off to space.

Young expert U.S. pilots waiting
The day of criss-cross rockets
And white blossoming smoke of bomb,
The air world torn and staggered for these
Specks of brushy land and ant-hill towns—

　　I stumble on the cobble rockpath,
　　Passing through temples,
　　Watching for two-leaf pine
　　　—spotting that design.

　　　　　　　　　　(*The Back Country*, 37)

The final stanza could speak for both Snyder and Whalen in their attempt to identify connections between natural, social, and spiritual orders. In the case of "Vapor Trails," the design exists at two levels: those features that distinguish one plant from another and those that indicate American global adventurism. Both levels are readable by the poet as a "design," implying both structure and intent, and it is ever Snyder's purpose to articulate those correspondences in his capacities as ecological activist and as poet. Writing is a kind of hermeneutics in which, like his transcendentalist forebears, Snyder reads the signature of the divine etched in the great book of nature. These patterns do not translate into nonhuman, transmundane terms, but reflect, like the whorls of the redwood, the larger life of the planet.

Like Snyder, Whalen sees himself as a reader of larger designs in things, but in his case the man, Philip Whalen, is always part of the design—a large, sensual, often cranky, sometimes rhapsodic, and always curious historical individual who not only spots the design but suffers its effects. To adapt a remark by Frank O'Hara, he is "needed by things,"[21] not because things are valuable in themselves but because they provide him with occasions for reflection and observation. He is more willing than Snyder to find the design in the artifacts and intellectual traditions of western Europe or in the distinctly material world of the city. He admits to liking such decadent pleasures as linzertorte, Rodin, Edward Gibbon, Charles Baudelaire, ice cream, and Gabriel Fauré. He has a "taste for marble in a wooden age / a weakness for the epic that betrays / a twiddy mind." Whalen's openness to the multitude of things, natural and cultural, creates a certain vulnerability that allows him a wide variety of what I have called "voices." These voices allow him to dramatize the specific contours of the mind as it reads the world.

In my introduction to this chapter I spoke of the sacramental impulse among San Francisco poets—their attempt to participate with a numinous or spiritual presence found in nature and realized through a process of self-expiation. It may seem that, at least in speaking of Whalen, I have moved rather far from my topic. Whalen thrusts his ego directly in front of the reader and seems far more concerned with listing the attributes of birds and plants than he does with enlightenment. Such acts of naming and annotating are very much a part of Zen practice. As Whalen observes, there is

> the problem of right now: what are you doing right this minute and how do you get through that and how can you make it alive, vivid, solid? In Zen there is a great deal to understand—the long historical tradition, the connections with the various sutras and so forth—but the Zen experience cannot be explained, you have to be it, you have to practice it.
>
> (*Off the Wall: Interviews with Philip Whalen*, 60)

Poetry, like Zen practice, involves participating with the "right now," whether presented objectively in photographic images or filtered through the mind's eye. New Critical versions of sacramentalism tended to emphasize the parallel between metaphor and incarnation and the ability of the creative imagination to synthesize a concrete universal. For Snyder and Whalen there is no hierarchical relation between flesh and spirit, word and logos. Snyder holds that "the universe and all creatures in it are intrinsically in a state of complete wisdom, love and compassion; acting in natural response and mutual interdependence" (*Earth House Hold*, 90). The poet's task is to respond in kind, provide constant testimony to the "mutual interdependence" of all things. "I keep trying to live as if this world were heaven," Philip Whalen says (**On Bear's Head**, 346), and he and Gary Snyder have devoted their poetic careers to erasing the "as if."

Notes

1. John Ciardi, "Epitaph for the Dead Beats," *Saturday Review* (February 6, 1960),p. 11. Reprinted in *A Casebook on the Beat*, ed. Thomas Parkinson (New York: Crowell, 1961), pp. 257-65.

2. Herbert Gold, "The Beat Mystique," *Playboy* (February 1958),p. 85. Reprinted in *A Casebook on the Beat*.

3. Rexroth discusses his religious awakening in *An Autobiographical Novel* (Garden City, N.Y.: Doubleday, 1966), pp. 247-52, 332-9.

4. Kenneth Rexroth, *Communalism: From Its Origins to the Twentieth Century* (New York: Seabury, 1973).

5. John Crowe Ransom, "Poetry: A Note in Ontology," in *Critical Theory Since Plato*, ed. Hazard Adams (New York: Harcourt, Brace & World, 1971),p. 880.

6. Charles Altieri, *Enlarging the Temple: New Directions in American Poetry During the 1960's* (Lewisburg, Pa.: Bucknell University Press, 1979),p. 55.

7. D. H. Lawrence, "Preface to the American Edition of *New Poems,*" in *The Poetics of the New American Poetry,* ed. Donald Allen and Warren Tallman (New York: Grove, 1973),p. 71.

8. On catalogues and lists in Snyder see Robert Kern, "Recipes, Catalogues, Open-Form Poetics: Gary Snyder's Archetypal Voice," *Contemporary Literature* 18, no. 2 (1977), pp. 173-97.

9. It could be suggested that Wordsworth's imperative to "look steadily at the subject" might suggest a pictorialist aesthetic based on an entirely mimetic theory of language, but as Paul DeMan says, "This urge to keep the eye on the subject is only Wordsworth's starting point and . . . perhaps more than any poet, he appreciates the complexity of what happens when eye and object meet. The delicate interplay between perception and imagination could nowhere be more intricate than in the representation of a natural scene, transmuted and recollected in the ordering form of Wordsworth's poetic language." Paul DeMan, "Landscape in Wordsworth and Yeats," in *The Rhetoric of Romanticism* (New York: Columbia University Press, 1984),p. 126.

10. Gary Snyder, "The *East-West* Interview," in *The Real Work: Interviews and Talks, 1964-1979* (New York: New Directions, 1980),p. 98; hereafter cited in text as TRW. Subsequent references to Snyder's poetry in the text and the notes will appear as follows: *The Back Country* (New York: New Directions, 1968), BC; *Earth House Hold* (New York: New Directions, 1969), EHH; *Myths and Texts* (New York: New Directions, 1978), MT; *Regarding Wave* (New York: New Directions, 1970), RW; *Riprap and Cold Mountain Poems* (San Francisco: Four Seasons Foundation, 1966), R; *Turtle Island* (New York: New Directions, 1974), TI.

11. Snyder discusses the role of koan study in an interview with Dom Aelred Graham collected in *Conversations: Christian and Buddhist,* ed. Dom Aelred Graham (New York: Harcourt, Brace, & World, 1968),p. 65.

12. On the "wisdom-oriented line" of Mahayana Buddhism, see TRW,p. 94.

13. Altieri, *Enlarging the Temple,* pp. 128-50.

14. Philip Whalen, *Heavy Breathing: Poems, 1967-1980* (San Francisco: Four Seasons Foundation, 1983),p. 28; hereafter cited in text as HB. Other references to Whalen's work will be the following: *Off the Wall: Interviews with Philip Whalen* (San Francisco: Four Seasons Foundation, 1978), OW; *On Bear's Head* (New York: Harcourt, Brace, & World, 1969), OBH.

15. On "communities of practice," TRW, pp. 136-37.

16. On the influence of Lloyd Reynolds, see Philip Whalen, OW, pp. 12-13, 42.

17. Allen, *The New American Poetry,* p. 420.

18. Several of Whalen's notebooks have been published in facsimile, among them *Highgrade* (San Francisco: Coyote's Journal, 1966); *Intransit: The Philip Whalen Issue* (Eugene, Ore.: Toad Press, 1967); *The Invention of the Letter: A Beastly Morality* (copyright Philip Whalen, 1966).

19. The poet visits the sites described in the poem in a documentary made by National Educational Television in its "Poetry USA" series.

20. Geoffrey Hartman, "Romanticism and Anti-Self-Consciousness," in *Beyond Formalism: Literary Essays, 1958-1970* (New Haven, Conn.: Yale University Press, 1970), pp. 298-310.

21. Frank O'Hara, "Meditations in an Emergency," *The Collected Poems of Frank O'Hara,* ed. Donald Allen (New York: Knopf, 1971),p. 197.

FURTHER READING

Biographies

Allen, Donald, editor. *Off The Wall: Interviews with Philip Whalen.* Bolinas, Calif.: Four Seasons Foundation, 1978, 88p.

Collection of interviews with Whalen that explore his attraction to Zen, his relationships with other writers of the Beat Movement, and his ideas on poetic practice and theory.

Carpenter, Don. "Poetry at the Old Longshoreman's Hall." *Literary Kicks,* (online magazine) http://www.litkicks. com (27 July 2002).

Tells the story of the 1964 "Freeway Reading" involving Whalen, Lew Welch, and Gary Snyder.

Gach, Gary. "Phillip Whalen, 1923-2002." *National Obituary Archives,* (online magazine) http://arrangeonline. com (28 July 2002).

Provides highlights of Whalen's life during the Beat era.

Suiter, John. *Poets on the Peaks: Gary Snyder, Philip Whalen, and Jack Kerouac in the North Cascades.* Washington, D.C.: Counterpoint, 2002, 340p.

Examines the influence of the mountains on Whalen's work, and explores their relationship to specific poems.

Watson, Steven. *The Birth of the Beat Generation,* pp. 217-9. New York: Pantheon Books, 1995.

Recounts Whalen's involvement with more famous Beats such as Allen Ginsberg, Jack Kerouac, and William Burroughs.

Criticism

Clark, Tom. Review of *Overtime: Selected Poems,* by Philip Whalen. *Jacket* (online magazine) http://www.jacket. zip.com.au 7 (27 July 2002).

Observes the humor and interiority of Whalen's poetry, in contrast to other Beat authors whose work tended to be more extroverted.

French, Warren. "Upbeat and Offbeat: Philip Whalen." In *The San Francisco Poetry Renaissance, 1955-1960,* pp. 71-3. Boston: Twayne Publishers, 1991.

Describes Whalen as a reluctant Beat whose interest in spirituality seemed to contradict the other Beats' quest for excitement and the exotic.

Kheridan, David. "Philip Whalen." In *Six Poets of the San Francisco Renaissance: Portraits and Checklists,* pp. 73-4. Fresno, Calif.: Giligia Press: 1967.

Account of Whalen's early career, characterizing the poet as passive and self-absorbed.

Robertson, David. "The Circumambulation of Mt. Tamalpais." *Western American Literature* 30, no. 1 (1995): 3-28.

Includes memoirs of conversations and hiking trips with Gary Snyder and Whalen, as well as criticism of their poetry.

Snyder, Gary, Lew Welch, and Philip Whalen. *On Bread and Poetry,* edited by Donald Allen. Bolinas, Calif.: Grey Fox Press, 1977.

Analysis of the poetry of Gary Snyder, Lew Welch, and Whalen.

OTHER SOURCES FROM GALE:

Additional coverage of Whalen's life and career is contained in the following sources published by the Gale Group: *Contemporary Authors,* Vols. 9-12R; *Contemporary Authors New Revision Series,* Vols. 5, 39; *Contemporary Literary Criticism,* Vols. 6, 29; *Contemporary Poets,* Ed. 7; *Dictionary of Literary Biography,* Vol. 16; *Literature Resource Center;* and *World Poets.*

JOHN WIENERS

(1934 - 2002)

American poet and playwright.

While Wieners remains one of the lesser-known of the Beat poets, the innovative style and highly personal subject matter of his work place him among the defining figures of the movement. His poetry is noted for its slow and hermetic pacing, rejecting the flamboyant use of language found in other Beat poetry. A recurring theme in Wieners's verse is the imposing of order upon chaos. When asked for whom he wrote, Wieners replied, "For the poetical, the people. Not for myself merely. Or ever. Only for the better, warm, human loving, kind person. The guy on the street who might hold open a door for you, left the bumper on your car, stops to give you instructions, spares some change, lets you in his bookshop."

BIOGRAPHICAL INFORMATION

Wieners, who always considered himself "a Boston poet" regardless of the Beat generation's emphasis on New York and West Coast venues, was born on January 6, 1934, and reared in a middle-class Catholic household. He attended public schools and graduated from Boston College in 1954 with a degree in English. After working for a time in a library at Harvard University, Wien-

ers met poet Charles Olson—then a faculty member at Black Mountain College in North Carolina—at a poetry reading and, at Olson's urging, enrolled at Black Mountain in the spring of 1955. He finished at Black Mountain in 1956 and moved on to San Francisco, where he became part of the local literary scene that included such figures as Allen Ginsberg, Lawrence Ferlinghetti, David Meltzer, and Michael McClure. Wieners's first book of poetry, *The Hotel Wentley Poems*, was published in 1958, shortly after his arrival in San Francisco, and marked the beginning of a period of depression for the poet. In 1961 he moved to New York, where his plays *Still Life* (1961) and *In Hell's Despite* (1963) were produced. After moving back to Boston to live with his parents between 1963 and 1965, he returned to San Francisco in the fall of 1967, despondent and impoverished. This began a period of drinking, drug use, and eventual institutionalization in the spring of 1969. Upon his release in the fall of 1969, Wieners settled in Boston, holding poetry readings and publishing in local magazines. Wieners died in Boston on March 1, 2002.

MAJOR WORKS

Written in only six days, the eight poems in *The Hotel Wentley Poems* examine the dark underside of the lives of those who live in San Francisco's seedy red-light district. The collection was well received by both critics and Wieners's contemporaries in the Beat movement, earning high praise from Allen Ginsberg and LeRoi Jones. *Ace of Pentacles* (1964) marked a significant shift in poetic form for Wieners—away from the spare lines of *The Hotel Wentley Poems* and toward a fuller, denser versification. The poems use the traditional verse forms of couplet, sonnet, and ballad, but Wieners uses inverted word order and abrupt shifts in cadence to imbue the poems with a quality of artifice. The subject matter of the collection includes a variety of themes that frequently appeared in the works of Beat writers—madness, despair, drugs, and homosexual love. The poems in *Pressed Wafer* (1967) were written by Wieners while he was living in Buffalo, New York, between 1965 and 1967. At the time, he was serving as Charles Olson's teaching assistant at the State University of New York. As the title suggests—alluding to Christian communion wafers—the poems make extensive use of religious metaphors. Critics have noted the feminine aspects of *Pressed Wafer* as evidenced by Wieners's preoccupation with the problems of women. A collection of sixty poems written from 1966 to 1970, *Nerves* includes several poems written by Wieners during his confinement in a mental institution and is considered by many to be the poet's strongest work. *Behind the State Capitol, or Cincinnati Pike* (1975) is an eclectic collection of Wiener's work written between 1970 and 1975.

CRITICAL RECEPTION

Overall, critical reception of Wieners's works has been positive, with several critics acknowledging and praising the difficult and raw emotions that Wieners evokes in his poetry. In his overview of Wieners's poetry from *The Hotel Wentley Poems* to *Behind the State Capitol*, Neeli Cherkovski compliments the verbal precision that characterizes the poet's work, observing that, "[s]et deep within the texture of his writing are straightforward insights, wrapping images into tight, fiery orbs, flinging them outward to coverconsciousness, forever mocking the scalpels of literary critics absorbed in the intellectual life of poetry." Gilbert Sorrentino, in his review of *Selected Poems* (1972), argued that Wieners took the suffering he experienced in his life and turned it into "a powerful and singular poetry, a part of which is consti-

tuted of lyrics as beautiful as any written by an American poet in this century."

PRINCIPAL WORKS

The Hotel Wentley Poems (poetry) 1958

Still Life (poetry) 1961

In Hell's Despite (play) 1963

Ace of Pentacles (poetry) 1964

Chinoiserie (poetry) 1965

Gardenias (poetry) 1966

Hart Crane, Harry Crosby, I See You Going over the Edge (poetry) 1966

Jive Shoelaces and Anklesox (play) 1967

King Solomon's Magnetic Quiz (poetry) 1967

Pressed Wafer (poetry) 1967

Ring of Bone (poetry) 1967

A Letter to Charles Olson (poetry) 1968

Unhired (poetry) 1968

Asylum Poems (poetry) 1969

A Memory of Black Mountain College (poetry) 1969

Untitled Essay on Frank O'Hara (essay) 1969

Invitation (poetry) 1970

Larders (poetry) 1970

Nerves (poetry) 1970

Youth (poetry) 1970

The Lanterns along the Wall (poetry) 1972

Playboy (poetry) 1972

Selected Poems (poetry) 1972

We Were There! (poetry) 1972

Woman (poetry) 1972

Hotels (poetry) 1974

Behind the State Capitol, or Cincinnati Pike (poetry) 1975

Selected Poems, 1958-1984 (poetry) 1986

A Superficial Estimation (poetry) 1986

Conjugal Contraries and Quart (poetry) 1987

Cultural Affairs in Boston: Poetry and Prose, 1956-1985 (poetry and prose) 1988

The Journal of John Wieners Is to Be Called 707 Scott Street for Billie Holiday, 1959 (journal) 1996

GENERAL COMMENTARY

JOHN WIENERS AND ROBERT VON HALLBERG (INTERVIEW DATE 1974)

SOURCE: Wieners, John, and Robert von Hallberg. "A Talk with John Wieners." *Chicago Review* 26, no. 1 (1974): 112-7.

In the following interview, Wieners discusses his view of himself as a lyric poet, his experience at Black Mountain College, and his progression to less traditional metres in his poetry.

[von Hallberg]: In your statement on poetics for the Don Allen anthology in 1960, you said, "A poem does not have to be a major thing. Or a statement? I am allowed to ask many things because it has been given me the means to plunge into the depths and come up with answers? No. Poems, which are my salvation alone. The reader can do with them what he likes." I wonder if you still conceive of poetry as your salvation and yours alone. What do you think is now the role of the poet?

[Wieners]: The poet's role establishes distance from his address and distance from his audience. The audience is a sport of the author, and he must remember that. And as he ages, he relinquishes his former addresses which must hold great faith to their facts. I haven't made personal choices of poetic theories since the Allen anthology, because of the inadequacies of so doing. I hope that the Allen anthology is supplanted by a genuine criticism that centers on the "hit-or-miss" terms my words express.

You mention that the poet's past addresses should stay rooted in the facts of their address; you seem to have a firm sense of a poem's commitment to a moment in history. Do you feel that at a particular moment in history, specifically in the last few years, the pressure of political tensions may push the poet, even a lyric poet, toward a more public and rhetorical poetry? I'm thinking particularly of Denise Levertov's recent journal poem, To Stay Alive.

Yes, I do. Denise's knowledge comes from all over the earth: North Vietnam, New York, Germany. She sees her audience as does the writer of odes, of celebrations, celebrations of the condition.

So that if the condition is one of political tension, a lyric poet can celebrate that condition and still be true to himself or herself as a lyric poet.

Yes. Lyricism is still a quality of a political career.

Do you think of yourself as a lyric poet in these terms?

Sincerely. Until the right moment, I create from post-inhabited experiences, or vice versa. These topics arise only upon consideration. It follows generally, in the course of a day, sleeping, preparing food, hiking in town, and examining contemporary documents, that, with these occupations maintaining inherently their own law and order, a combination of the two, of poetry and politics, is deemed operable.

Olson says that the poem is a transfer of energy from the poet to the reader rather than simply an expression of the poet's own energies. Is there anything inherent in that conception of poetry which lends itself to a rhetorical poetry, a poetry that would, at the proper moment of history, accommodate political poetry, poetry addressed to an audience from whom it is hoped political change my come?

Yes, there is. And Charles' manner of address causes respect, respect even for the spoof that he releases both through his pen and through his oracular power.

Do you mean that the presence of the voice itself commands authority?

Yes, by enlightening.

Some of the Black Mountain poets, like Olson and Ed Dorn, write a poetry of statement. Others, like Creeley, do not. In the '50s did you feel closer to Creeley's poetry than to Olson's or Dorn's?

Before 1950 the poetry I chose as model was stanzaic. None of those poets seem to care for the division between expression and excessive actuality, something that has never been restricted, or has not been felt to be restricted. It is this excessive actuality that Edward and Charles convey which has been corrupted by obfuscation.

Are you thinking of imitators?

Yes. What might be considered sacrilegious interpositions between what has been spoken and what is affectation.

Creeley has said that he has felt embarrassed for a larger view. I wonder if you feel any affinity with such modesty.

Creeley deserves more encouragement, after having labored outside of Spain and outside of acclaim. He has been a terrific stimulus for honest material apart from the historical.

Yes, his poetry doesn't rely upon a large knowledge of history in the way that Pound's and Olson's often seem to. When you were at Black Mountain College, did you learn more about poetry from any one particular person?

I learned from sitting before labor, a labor of words, a labor of worth, a labor of wit.

I would like to return to your discussion of metrical and free verse. Do you find anything helpful in Olson's notion of breath? Or what principles, do you believe, govern your own rhythms?

The gauge is intellectual.

Do you mean that you use a line break to focus on the meaning of the words; that you break the words up into units of meaning rather than units of breath or sound, say?

Yes. The breath is so relative. Charles was a post-Einstein critic. The discipline of relativity had to be spoken out through successive experimentations; Charles had to suffer awful tribulations as a post-Einstein examiner.

Were Olson's statements useful to you in breaking out of regular metres and traditional stanzaic patterns?

Well, his own practice, his own verse, came from Washington dictation. He worked for the foreign nationalities in Washington. He left the nation's capital at the invitation of a man who had likewise suffered commercial neglect, Edward Dahlberg, who was neglected because of his work for the bottom dogs of our American contemporary society, and because of his examination of this state and its prime industries.

Was Olson at all bitter about leaving political activity behind to go to Black Mountain College?

He didn't plan to stay in North Carolina. He was from New England but could not find employment in the U.S. Postal Service. He had met Mr. Dahlberg and worked on 19th century literature while doing some doctoral research. He left Harvard, though, without, obtaining all of his credits. I think that the time at Black Mountain, being nested in the plantation, brought him peace. And when he closed the school in 1957, he left behind, in the archives of the state capital, an important contribution to education.

Paul Blackburn seemed to have felt that the poets at Black Mountain shared a concern for speech rhythms and an interest in composition by field. Did you think that Olson's theories were very important at the College when you were there?

No. The school was founded as a place for transcendental transpositions of scholarship. Olson's tactful care maintained the trust of the Corporation.

When you were there, then, there was still a lot of activity in arts other than poetry and in other disciplines.

Decidedly.

When you left Boston in 1955 to go to Black Mountain, did you feel that you were leaving behind a locale in which you had deep roots? Did you feel isolated at Black Mountain?

I did feel isolated by poverty. The salaries one could earn in the state of North Carolina were minimal. And at the College we had barely the revenue for all of the studies that were thought to occur.

Did you feel isolated as well from the mainstream of literary activity in America?

Yes.

In "Acts of Youth" you speak of the pain and suffering which is "the formula all great art is made from." You also say, "If one could just get out of the country. Some place / where he may eat the lotus in peace." Do you think that the desire to withdraw from history into art is a constant or a recent one?

I haven't gone over the United States as scrupulously as I have to, when I become more independent of impecuniousness. But I have learned, after going over some of the terrain and after encountering fifty- to seventy-thousand hard-working, long-houred wage-earners that poetry is a postulation of the gifted among our species.

Your own poetry comes so directly from an urban experience that it's hard to see how Olson or Creeley or Dorn could have offered much sympathy or direction for your work. Do you feel closer to other poets not associated with the projectivist movement—poets like Ginsberg or O'Hara?

I felt close to most writers in the 1950's due to my own youth. Any writer qualified for total embracing.

Your poetry is quietly accepting, even serene, where Ginsberg's is painfully discomforted. Do you think that difference is attributable to what Richard Howard describes as a religious sensibility behind the **Hotel Wentley Poems**? *Do you have a faith in an order that transcends the disarray of urban experience?*

I think my faith is in the humanity, the humanity which receives my specious attempts at edification.

Last night, at a poetry reading, you spoke of having had, when you were younger, a nineteenth century transcendentalist sensibility. But you are saying that now your faith is not so much in a transcendent order as in the people of this world.

Yes, and in the meditations of masters, of genius.

Pound and Williams are often placed behind the Black Mountain poets, and occasionally Hart Crane is mentioned in the same regard. I wonder if you felt Crane to be one of your own masters.

Yes, I've used him as a continuation of these principles: attention, reverence, and popularity.

Would you like to be a popular poet?

Yes.

For whom do you write?

For the poetical, the people. Not for myself, merely. Or ever. Only for the better, warm, human loving, kind person. The guy on the street who might hold open a door for you, left the bumper on your car, stops to give you instructions, spares some change, lets you in his bookshop. Friends I take for granted, like the future.

I would like to ask you one last question about Olson. In the last few years of his life, Olson was a great admirer of your poetry. Do you have a sense of just what it is about your work that really fired him in the late '60s?

I think be began to see the books for the future: we are different sides of a coin, reversed in spirits.

NEELI CHERKOVSKI (ESSAY DATE 1999)

SOURCE: Cherkovski, Neeli. "The Memory of Love: John Wieners." In *Whitman's Portraits of Twelve Poets: Wild Children*, pp. 41-66. South Royalton, Vt.: Steerforth Press, 1999.

In the following essay, Cherkovski weaves events from Wiener's life with commentary on several of his poems.

"The poem does not lie to us. We lie under its law," John Wieners wrote. Now his poetry lies bound in a volume that ranges over his entire poetic life, *Selected Poems* from Black Sparrow Press. *Selected Poems* opens with the complete version of *The Hotel Wentley Poems,* originally published in 1958 by Auerhahn Press; Wieners was twenty-four at the time and *Wentley* was his first published volume.

I received a copy of *Selected Poems* for review. Before that, I had been asked to write an appreciation of Wieners for *Mirage*, a literary journal published in San Francisco. Both tasks seemed easy. *Wentley* is an implosion, a spiritual journey into the body and mind, the opposite of the explosive, outward-flowing work of Wieners' contemporaries. There is an intimacy to his early poems, a young man looking inward, naming the aloneness he feels and cannot rid himself of while his signs are universal and his music exquisite. He cries, and the tears turn to revelation. The grim aesthetic beauty he shapes is reminiscent of Edgar Allan Poe, who was also born in Boston. Wieners is restless, even feverish in his barrage of human feelings and passion, a great architect of the poem, while the sureness of his language sustains him and gives range to the desolate memories and visions of the poet's sorrowful life. The lines are lean. There is no excess. Every word counts. He worries about self-indulgence even as his work bespeaks an enormous generosity of feeling. He searches for sustaining relationships. As his desperation grows, remaining with him through the years, so does his talent.

In reading through Wieners' poetry, I found myself going back to Whitman's "Calamus" poems where the yearning for love is so deep, where we find those "frailest leaves of me," and gain insight into the deep and sustaining sexual yearnings that Whitman felt so passionately. It is in "Calamus" that the desire for comrades is intensely celebrated. Reverberating from that poem is Whitman's private self, which is often hidden behind an onslaught of imagery ranging over the entire world. The leaves he turns over here are from a personal notebook of passion. It is that journey into the self, ribbed always with images of the land as in "**I Saw in Louisiana a Live-Oak Growing**," that Wieners continues in his work.

My attempts at writing the review failed. After ten tries at an appreciation of the poet for the magazine, I was defeated. Nothing seemed right. I called the patient editor and said, "Listen, I know you've waited for my piece. I just can't get it right. Whenever I read the poems I go into a deep depression. The words flood in. I look at some of those poems and see my face staring back. I'd be unfair to the work if I sent in anything now." I couldn't get beyond a sense of grief, of personal doom, in Wieners' work. I kept reading one line over and over again: "I burn in the memory of love." Everything I wrote appeared awkward and wrong in the face of that admission. And, as I read through the later poems, which are sometimes convoluted, I felt dragged down by a sense of loss. I let the book sit on my shelf. Once in awhile, I'd take it down and read. Finally I found myself reading every night, and then in the morning and at night. I began to see things I hadn't noticed before. John stood at the center of an entire universe of tone and texture. Vistas existed I had failed to see. Entire stanzas and poems came alive. I tried to imagine him in San Francisco during the Poetry Renaissance, 1957 to 1959, far from his Boston home, busted up with his lover, Dana, of whom he writes in **Wentley**. He loved many places in San Francisco, but lived in solitude, mostly, and with the memory of love, as in "a poem for the old man":

> Remove this desire
> from the man I love.
> Who has opened
> the savagery
> of the sea to me.
> See to it that
> his wants are filled
> on California street
> Bestow on him lar-
> gesse that allows him
> peace in his loins.

Shadows of the land and its solitary splendor crowd in on Wieners' writings. Like Hart Crane, the immense American earth becomes internalized in his own sufferings (as with Ginsberg in *Wichita Vortex Sutra*). Wieners gradually comes to a sharply defined understanding of his native land. This is seen mainly in poems from the mid-1960s, written long after he left San Francisco. He even looks farther from American soil, toward other lands. In **"With Meaning"** he writes:

> in the canyons of L.A.
> plus the journeys over oceans
> and islands, to metropolis
> spreadeagled the earth.
> Yes rise shining martyrs
>
> out of your graves, tell us
> what to do, read your poems
> under springtime moonlight.
> Rise and salvage our century.

Set deep within the texture of his writing are straightforward insights, wrapping images into tight, fiery orbs, flinging them outward to cover consciousness, forever mocking the scalpels of literary critics absorbed in the intellectual life of poetry, and tragically blind to the whole unbefuddling, totally trustworthy and, at root, intuitive

process. The poem **"Supplication"** illustrates the care Wieners takes with language:

> O poetry, visit this house often,
> imbue my life with success,
> leave me not alone,
> give me a wife and home.
>
> Take this curse off
> of early death and drugs,
> make me a friend among peers,
> lend me love, and timeliness.
>
> Return me to the men who teach
> and above all, cure the
> hurts of wanting the impossible
> through this suspended vacuum.

This caravan is laden with jewels of every shape and color and travels toward Byzantium with quiet visionary prowess. Wieners is gently oracular. He has Charles Olson's authority without the bombast, tempered not merely by his gentleness, but also by his refusal to wear the mantle of the poet as priest. "My new work which I presume / already lies scattered, lost and / in error prompts memories of / a dark address in Hell's Kitchen." John Wieners is committed to feeling through the development of his craft, as in the **Wentley** poems of his youth.

For Wieners, rules of prosody thrust themselves against his skull, and he works them into an intensely personal search, with an implicit understanding of how the process of composition reshapes our use of language. Olson, one of John's teachers at Black Mountain College, is seen throughout Wieners' work, not as an ocean or a mountain range but as himself: a man, a person, human flesh with joys and sorrows. A person. A dead man. And what Wieners did with language. How he held the lance and sat firmly in the saddle. Which is not to say that Wieners is on his way to Gloucester, but simply that what may seem incomprehensible in his work is, for me, very clear. His poetry is a public journal of private emotion. He wants to bring language home again. In his journey back to the body, Wieners creates a language sculpted entirely out of his own experience and sets it in a light that makes his meaning unmistakable. It is not a happy vision.

Born in 1934, Wieners was raised in a middle-class Catholic family in a Boston suburb. He attended school there and graduated from Boston College with a bachelor's degree in English in 1954. Following graduation he worked at the Lamont Library at Harvard University and was active in the Poet's Theater, where he acted in plays by Frank O'Hara and John Ashbery. O'Hara was immensely impressed by the young poet, then twenty years old, who regularly wore eye makeup and attended meetings of the Beacon Hill chapter of the Poetry Society of America, which consisted of five elegant, elderly ladies plus Wieners. He had already begun to write, but a chance event made poetry his life's vocation. As he recalled in Donald Allen's *New American Poetry* anthology, on September 11, 1954, he was walking past the Charles Street Meeting House and heard Charles Olson reciting poetry. Intrigued, he walked into the reading room where he was handed a copy of *The Black Mountain Review.*

In the spring of 1955 he enrolled at Black Mountain College in the rural hill country of North Carolina. Poet Robert Duncan recalls that he and Olson were impressed by the twenty-one-year-old's talent. They soon thought of him as an equal. Olson frequently referred to Wieners as "elemental—literally like an element." Recalling Olson, Wieners has said, "Charles' manner of address causes respect, respect even for the spoof that he releases both through his pen and through his oracular power . . . we are different sides of a coin, reversed in spirit."

After a semester at Black Mountain, Wieners returned to Boston where he edited *Measure,* a literary magazine that published the works of many of his friends from college. As Foye tells it, "When *Measure* hit the stands, John was fired from his job at the Lamont Library and drove across the country to San Francisco with his lover, Dana. There he would soon find himself at the center of an important literary scene."

In San Francisco, Wieners contacted Robert Duncan and was soon introduced to Allen Ginsberg, Kirby Doyle, Michael McClure, Philip Lamantia, David Meltzer, Bob Kaufman, and others who made-up the Bay Area literary scene. He sought out the company of painters, most notably Wallace Berman and Robert LaVigne and soon wrote **"A Poem for Painters."**

The **Hotel Wentley Poems** was written following Wieners' break up with Dana. The eight poems in the book were written in six days while he lived in the boardinghouse of that name in San Francisco's red-light district. Kirby Doyle once told me, "John's book had an immediate impact. We all felt compelled to read and study his work." Ginsberg wrote, "The whole book is the work of a naked flower, a tragic clown, doomed sensibility, absolutely *real*, no more self-pity." Thinking of Ginsberg's perception, I came across these lines from **"A Poem for Painters"**:

At last the game is over
　　　　　　　and the line lengthens.
Let us stay with what we know.

That love is my strength, that
I am overpowered by it:
　　　　　　　desire
　　　　　　　　　　that too

is on the face: gone stale.
When green was the bed my love
and I laid down upon.
Such it is, heart's complaint,
You hear upon a day in June.
And I see no end in view
when summer goes, as it will,
upon the roads, like singing
companions across the land.

Go with it man, if you must,
but leave us markers on your way.

I look at John and think of him at Black Mountain: focal point and oasis amid air-conditioning and presidential primaries. There they were: Charles Olson, Ed Dorn, Robert Duncan, Robert Creeley, and young, curly-haired John Wieners. Then, in San Francisco, far from his Boston home, Wieners explodes—not in a volcanic way, more like a bright red rose standing taller and brighter than the others, lifting petals upward toward the sun.

"John's reputation has in fact suffered from the great success of the **Wentley** poems," Raymond Foye told me. "It's one reason why he has always written of childhood stars. At a certain point he despaired of ever getting out from under that book. But in another sense, he hid behind the **Wentley** poems. They established him as a poet, and freed him to pursue a more experimental, unconforming path." The **Wentley** poems are more approachable to readers than much of the later work. There is the poem for painters, for fathers, for the wheat of Kansas, and for our generations of dissent and bewilderment. There is, in **Wentley,** so much given over to love and the need for it, and the outer boundaries of it, that I keep returning, renewing my sense of being. If I become unnerved by life, I go to those melancholic lines John Wieners created in his early poems.

I meet Wieners in New York, hoping he will join me at a reading in which Allen Ginsberg will dedicate several poems to the Boston poet, but that is not enough to entice him down into the subway. He wants to stay at the Ninth Street townhouse where he and I are both guests. I shake his hand. I think of the photograph of him standing under a poster with Philip Lamantia, Michael Mc-

Clure, and David Meltzer—how many centuries ago in San Francisco? Now, before me, stands a person who has been through intense pain. I see it. I feel it. He smiles and says how nice it is to meet me. I can't even understand my own words. I see a poem in his face. Knowing something of what he had gone through in the past two decades, I am not surprised. There are ruins and wounds there. His eyes speak more forcibly than he does. I think of a few lines from **"A Poem for Early Risers"**:

> It is not doors. It is
> the ground of my soul
> where dinosaurs left
> their marks. Their tracks
> are upon me. They
> walk flatfooted.

The words seemed to hang in the air of Ninth Street in Greenwich Village as I turned right at Balducci's market and walked toward the subway.

Ace of Pentacles was published in 1964 by James A. Carr and Robert Wilson in New York, when they discovered that Wieners had not had a book out for six years. The title refers to the card in the tarot deck that signifies the triumph of the human spirit over despair—an enduring symbol for the poet. Among the poems of this collection, Wieners placed traditional verse: sonnet, ballad, and couplet. The most ambitious poem here is **"The Acts of Youth."** The poem invokes "the middle of the night," much in the tradition of Edward Young's *Night Thoughts* and Francis Thompson's *City of Dreadful Night.* In **"A Series,"** Wieners takes a long journey into himself, dealing with the themes of pain and suffering found in his early poetry. Through all the self-wrenching, one finds:

> Dread night is gone,
> you see suspended in a bar against the blackness
> the mighty lord, who makes his way
> Love in his eyes as a bride might say
> To put away all fear.

Pressed Wafer, published in 1967, brought together poems written in Buffalo between 1965 and 1967, where Wieners had enrolled in graduate studies at the suggestion of Charles Olson, who was teaching there. Olson made him his personal teaching assistant but treated him more as a colleague.

The title of the book refers to the Eucharist, the symbol of the body of Christ. Putting Catholic imagery into his poetry was not new for Wieners, but here his relationship to his own Catholic childhood becomes intensified as he continues his search for solace through sensual love:

> There are holy orders in life.
> I was born to be a priest
> defrocked as Spender says,
> an Epiphany to make manifest
>   mysteries.

There is a sense of authority in these lines and an awareness of the serious and fully aware poet that he aspired to be. Wiener sees the burden of his muse clearly and accepts it. Yet there would be no refuge, despite the full flowering of talent evidenced in his development and despite his enduring friendship with Olson and Robert Creeley. Nothing—not the past, Catholicism, or the community of poets—could rescue Wieners from his emotional turmoil.

In 1969 Wieners spent a few months in a mental hospital. While confined he wrote *Asylum Poems,* published that same year, and when he came home to Boston he plunged into a lively poetry scene centered around Steve Jonas, Charles Shively, and others. Poetry readings and gay activism kept him busy as he worked on the poems for a new book.

Unlike the long, flowing lines in *Ace of Pentacles,* the *Asylum Poems* are compressed, the vision tautly drawn, almost constricted, yet filled with lyrical notes probing the natural world in poignant detail. **"Private Estate"** begins:

> Dancing dandelions
>   and buttercups in the grass
> remind me of other summer
> flowers, simple blossoms
>
> roses and tiger lilies by the wall
>   milk pod, sumac branches

Within Wieners, contained between inner landscape and the outer, an unlimited vision thrust up from poem to reader, live these floral gatherings, together with demons, angels, and the lost or elusive beloved. Does he choose happiness? It appears that he would like to, but in his own frantic search to be held he encounters a familiar aloneness and insensitivity. **"How to Cope with This?"** portrays the poet's sense of alienation:

> A mean, dark man
> was my lover
> in a mean dark room
> for an evening
>
> till dawn came
> we hugged and kissed
> ever since, first and last
> I have missed
>
> him, his mean, dark ways.

As my friends and I sat and listened to Allen Ginsberg in a high school auditorium, I thought of Wieners and about how the two poets differ. Allen gives of himself in the manner of a Whitmanic bard, even in his introspective poems and the meditations on the death of his father. I link Wieners to Rainer Maria Rilke. Both wrote poems of introspection, profoundly interiorized canvases that compel us to leave the world of sight and sound; we enter mind and spirit. How much of himself can John Wieners expunge? He tries to obliterate the lyric line, but fails. He wants to leave language behind, but cannot.

Despite brief periods spent in mental hospitals, the poet continued his association with Boston-area poets. He was important to them not only for his poetry and his powerful presence, but also as a gay person who had been publicly out of the closet since the age of sixteen. He moved into a small walk-up apartment that he continues to occupy on Boston's historic Beacon Hill, a neighborhood of narrow cobblestone streets. The walls of his rooms are covered with a collage of movie stars, religious figures, and pornography that is constantly being added to or altered in some other way, depending on his mood.

Ginsberg encounters himself; John Wieners finds demon or angel, fire and void. As Allen spoke to us at the reading John wouldn't attend, alluding from time to time to the missing poet, I returned to "A Poem for Painters." In the first lines, Wieners spells out his yearning:

Our age bereft of nobility
How can our faces show it?
I look for love.
My lips stand out
dry and cracked with want.

The timing of those lines, the placement of "I look for love" after longer, more graceful and less commonplace lines lead into the inferno that is John Wieners. His sensibility remains squarely on the dime of his own being: "I look for love" means "I look for myself."

The precocious insights of the **Wentley** poems, akin to what is encountered in Robert Creeley's early poetry, remain foremost in my mind. Personal in the extreme, there are pictures that stand out with striking clarity: "a poem for vipers" is steeped in dark, metropolitan imagery:

I sit in Lee's. At 11:40 PM with
Jimmy the pusher. He teaches me
Ju Ju. Hot on the table before us
shrimp foo yong, rice and mushroom
chow yuke. Up the street under the wheels
of a strange car is his stash—The ritual.
We make it. And have made it.

Despair, loss, desire, and an overwhelming sense of futility bind the Wentley cycle into a cohesiveness that is one sustained music.

Before leaving Ninth Street, I had asked John if he felt excited about the publication of **Selected Poems.** He shrugged his shoulders and nodded toward Raymond Foye, who feigned lack of interest. The editor simply smiled and said: "Come on, or we'll be late for Allen's reading." I wanted to stay and talk, but John seemed to be saying he had said it all in **Wentley** and in his later books, like **Nerves, Ace of Pentacles,** and **Behind the State Capitol and the Cincinnati Pike.** The latter, published in 1975 by Charles Shively and The Good Gay Poets in Boston, received many negative reactions from John's admirers, some claiming he had burned out as a poet. They expected a repeat performance of the earlier, more accessible poetry, not appreciating that the poet had moved on with the poem into a house of "**Understood Disbelief in Paganism, Lies and Heresy**":

Prick any literary dichotomy
sung unrent gibberish from maxim skulls
West Manchester cemetery

recidivist testimony damned
promulgated post-mortem Harry Ghouls
wills pleasant chicanery hulled

in opposition to queer honesty,
flying hapless good humours
Morphe erroneous untedious mystery

Reaching into himself to the sounding of words, to the language buried away with the pain of unfulfillment, Wieners begins to probe a complex set of meanings beyond the linear.

"I look for love," John Wieners writes in a world that he reminds us is bereft of nobility. Well, good luck, John. Keep on looking. I wrap his whole poetic outlook around those four words. John has not come to throw America back in Whitman's tender face. He has only to look in the mirror and see himself, his own sad eyes, his own face growing older, lonelier. Like Rainer Maria Rilke, he confronts the deep, evolving vision on the border of the real and gives meaning to what otherwise might remain terrifying. Thinking of Rilke's reality, however, I am reminded that the real, for John, may not exist, shaped as it is by such demanding internal struggles. It wasn't a toy chest Wieners opened up when he wrote **Wentley.** The world for Rilke was still largely ordered by a romantic vision, but John is forever surpassing the momentary visions of chaotic American reality.

Ginsberg showed me the Hotel Wentley one day as I drove him through San Francisco. I saw the bay-windowed, wooden building and thought of John awakening:

> For me now the new.
> The unturned tricks
> of the trade: the Place
> of the heart where man
> is afraid to go.

These lines from **"A Poem for Early Risers"** are made awesome by timing. Deftly, Wieners begins with a clipped statement, then one a little longer, and finally, a lengthy sweep that lays down the law.

In *The Duino Elegies* Rilke goes to that place Wieners writes of, for the sake of his hand and his heart, to bind them together. The *Elegies* are a new poetic order that Rilke contrasts to the old-world hierarchies binding men to culture and civilization. Wieners is also obsessed with new definitions, hoping to create a map of consciousness in a universe that always remains tentative.

A terrible angel arcs over Rilke's language, wings overshadowing the intellect and imperiling the spiritual center of man, what some call the soul. Rilke has language with which to fight his way to an intimate relationship with the ineffable. This relationship ultimately must be a movement toward the unobtainable, a goal never actually reached. The poet probes. His search takes on a sacred, mythic quality, obliterating time and space. Fascinated by myth, the poet creates his own, weaving many fabrics into one, taking disparate images and tossing them into the furnace, bringing them out with a soft, hot glow surrounding them, and they become, miraculously, a unified, vibrating whole.

Wieners' dissatisfaction increases as the unobtainable covers his world. Acutely aware of the decaying social order, Wieners retreats into himself, mirroring that decay. The poetic craft brings a sense of beauty and, paradoxically, a feeling of dread—"cheap insult's glare"—as he sees in the face of a desired young man his own predicament. John rises to affirm his craft in **"II Alone,"** procuring some personal salvation:

> Sustained by poetry, fed anew
> by its fire to return from madness,
> the void does not beckon as it used to.
>
> Littered with syllables, the road does not loom
> as a chasm

The poet realizes just what the act and art of writing can bring him to, where it may land him.

"You poets dream on / and find out where the path leads you," Wieners writes knowingly. He finds renewal amid chaos, even as "the lover, Oh lover" evaporates. Then, "to sleep alone" becomes an obsession again, and "to make alone / desire alone" the reality.

Wieners implores men toward Whitmanic camaraderie. He tells all of us to strip away the desolation. Ginsberg aims "Howl" right at the soul of the machine—controlled by Moloch—and the madhouse becomes the doorway to the continent. Ginsberg takes old Walt by the hand and they cross the Brooklyn Bridge together, weeping. There is humor in their eyes, and sadness as they rip away the delusions that blind the nation. Whitman had warned of what could happen if this compassionate camaraderie didn't replace repulsive, class-bred arrogance. He wanted to take the walls down, and not just in the literary and cultural world. Unlike the expansive Ginsberg, who remains sane despite the madness, Wieners would not be spared: In a **"Howl"** of his own, he begins:

> You took two years of my life away from me,
>   locking me behind bars,
> for no reason other than common dishonest
>   perpetrated malice,
> running me from one cheap, enclosed kitchen
>   bidet unto another,
> in drug-induced
> collaboration with Apollo and the Nine Muses;
> experimenting on me involuntarily
> out of statehood apprehension. . . .

Not a pretty picture, as the dark angels of the state swoop down on this victim of the state and lock poet and poem away in an asylum. Instead of Whitman's hoped-for society of enlightened citizens, apprehension and mental instability await us.

I wanted to see John the morning after Allen's reading, but he had gone home to Boston. So there it was—one brief encounter and the memory of having called him once to come read in San Francisco for a reunion with the poets of his Hotel Wentley days, which, as yet, has never happened. In my call, I asked: "Will you come and read, maybe with Lamantia and McClure?" "Oh yes, of course," he answered, "and we will fly to Coit Tower and kiss the old stones and melt into the ocean, all together."

In his introduction to Wieners' **Selected Poems**, Ginsberg writes: "As that youthful idealism of **The Hotel Wentley Poems** dissolves in **Ace of Pentacles**, we see his intelligence delve deeper and deeper into the hole, or void, created by his imagination of an impossible love." There it is! That is what happens—John comes to see what a nightmare exists out there, beyond himself. There is the poet to love, the creative process to embrace, the interior world to outline, to form, to shape and reshape, to meditate on. But what about another person, another heart, the arms of another? It is at this point Wieners embodies the desperation of everyman while refusing to remain quiet.

In **"The Ages of Youth,"** a cycle of poems from *Ace of Pentacles,* Wieners begins in the night: "And with great fear I inhabit the middle of the night / What wrecks of the mind await me, what drugs / to dull the senses, what little I have left, / what more can be taken away?" Unlike Rilke, anxiety lies right on the surface, nailed there, permanent. Rilke could soar above it and eulogize the act of rising over pain and suffering and the misery of the flesh. John transcends in another way, more hurtful perhaps by remaining grounded and dealing face to face with himself and a society hell-bent on cheapening poetic impulse. He moves between reality and the void. The cycle continues with a concentrated history of a man's horror and hope, a brief poem, **"Two Years Later,"** which tells us:

> The hollow eyes of shock remain
> Electric sockets burnt out in the
> skull.
>
> The beauty of men never disappears
> But drives a blue car through the
> stars.

In his later work, Wieners often perceives things the way we do in daily thinking, randomly and unconsciously splicing our thoughts into elements entirely apart from the preceding perception. Taken as a whole, **Behind the State Capitol** is a precise montage of this process. Because he is "radicalized beyond belief," his language has moved on from the **Wentley** poems.

"In the 1970s, Wieners began a gradual, but radical process of nonattachment," according to Raymond Foye. "Possessions, ambitions, fame, money, friends, it all went out the window. Only poetry remained." Between 1976 and 1983, Wieners, for the most part, wrote only one poem per year, for himself, on his birthday. When he reemerged in 1984 with a new manuscript, he had alienated whatever audience he had left by writing in a cryptic, private voice of obtuse, seemingly unrelated images. The reader is often left hanging, peering in at these hermetically sealed verses so radically different from those of his youth. Yet he could recapture the clarity of the earlier work:

> My pillow a rock of stone
> My bed a bench of board
> These the treasure trove I hoard
> Against the rolling morn
>
> My symphony a choir of birds
> Family the passing cars
> And for friends the stars
> And for company words.

In highly condensed language, Wieners sums up themes common to his poetry and rediscovers a directness that reaches out to the reader. I often feel that he deliberately pauses from his later experiments with words to offer a bittersweet, linear note, which has immediate and universal appeal. Here is a mixture of profound suffering with a calm vision of nature made poignant in contemporary terms. Wieners has said of his career, "I am living out the logical conclusions of my books," but that does not dissuade him from continuing to write his poetry.

John Wieners, sustained by poetry, looks longingly over my shoulder. I think he is restless to go back to Boston. Soon he'll receive a twenty-thousand-dollar grant from the National Endowment for the Arts and Humanities and twenty-five thousand dollars as a Guggenheim Fellow. Not bad for a lifetime of work in a rigged society. "The right of freedom means improving what you're doing," he wrote. No wonder they gave him an award. What a sweet man. What a sad-faced man in shabby clothing standing on the beautiful floor of the Ninth Street townhouse.

One day in San Francisco, Gregory Corso and I read Auden's poem on the death of William Butler Yeats. "You got it?" Corso asked. "Do you dig that each line is important? Look," he said, "something in every line, real meaning. That's a biggie for a poet to do." That's it. That is how I feel about Wieners.

Selected Poems is an adventure, from the focused lyrics of the **Wentley** poems, to a wider line, and then to a series of poems with a decisive political edge. **Behind the State Capitol** means just that. Wieners shows us that the work of the poet may reveal unseen injustice, the life behind the facade of our political structure. There is none of the rhetoric here that one associates with political poetry. Wieners is intimate and the injustices he speaks of come from his own experiences. He is even able to look at society from within the context of a mental hospital. Much of what he has to say is not far from the spirit of Whitman's prefaces to *Leaves of Grass* or the vision of America found in *Democratic Vistas,* and yet in **"Children**

of the Working Class," Wieners writes: "I am witness / not to Whitman's vision, but instead the / poor-houses, the mad city asylums and re- / lief worklines. Yes, I am witness not to / God's goodness, but his better or less scorn." That was written on May 1, 1972.

"That love is my strength, that / I am overpowered by it . . ." This ironic note remains the root of Wieners' unfolding poetic commitment. The idea of love, its fulfillment or lack of it, is a primary quest for the lyric poet. Often he merges with the land in this quest. For example, **"A Poem for Painters"** contains the following lines:

> This nation is so large, like
> our hands, our love it lives
> with no lover, looking only
> for the beloved, back home
> into the heart, New York,
> New England, Vermont green
> mountains, and Massachusetts
> my city, Boston and the sea.
> Again to smell what this calm
> ocean cannot tell us.

The poem becomes a paean for the enormity of America and shows a strong connection to home, Boston. In a later poem Wieners wrote:

> In Devotion these orders
> about poverty and deprivation
> climb past New York's skyscrapers
> hearkening against oceanic tides
> Of humanity . . .
> see you everywhere hiding
> under the rubber of state VEHicles . . .

Imagine. He winds up in the streets, enlivening every sidewalk with his song. From **"Sequel to a Poem for Painters"**:

> Cavernous echoes obeyed lines on
>   heartache, only hangover upper
>
>   GRANT's Ave. horizon shriners
>   C
>   E
>   ntral Park dawn moonshiners lent,
>
>   strech small Hoosiers baker scratched
>   N
>   I
>   ckel trays when Mary had a little
>   arnd. the corner Corp.

A real projective priest for language, protecting his native language by not limiting the power of words, even single letters. What a patriot for the Mother Tongue.

I think the proper words for describing John Wieners' power within language, his feeling for the poem, are "passion" and "composure." What I have written here concerns his passion, expressed

in longing, and his texture, a grasp of craft that is a matter of composure. It is what Williams, Pound, and Olson sought for and sublimely mastered, and what is evident in Wieners. For all the weaknesses Wieners seems heir to regarding love and the lack of love, he wears strong armor, or, as Ginsberg observed, "his stubborn resilient strain of New England genius." In his youth he is close to William Carlos Williams, lyrically, but later Pound and Olson loom large. Wieners is the most familiar of the three—his escapades are more familiar. Instead of tromping through a semi-mythic China or Italy, as Pound does in the *Cantos,* Wieners is at home in America:

> I can't put my head on the pillow
> but all kinds of fear ensue,
> doubts plague the morning
> what will I do
>
> watch for the mail man
> I feel like a jaded movie star
> who missed the big-time
> and ended up mopping floors
>
> on South Street.

The lover is forever there: "The song of life, soft syllables from God" is a love song. Wieners becomes worn out by it. He would look for solace in the poem and find himself delving deeper into intellectual things, asking that a meaning be applied to the lack of love. His unfulfillment is what we have to face and to feel. We feel it because his art is deep, and his heart is never hidden. History becomes the story of his "being-in-need," his act of naming human vulnerability. Forest, river, city, and "love . . . to put away all fear" are wrapped within the language of his poetry. "Yes I am alone now" is one way he communicates his feelings, saying the same thing in a myriad of ways, captive of his fascination with love and loss.

Wieners uses strict stanzaic forms to "order" himself, to provide space between units of thought, threading those thoughts on a rhythmic line:

> I am the poet of benzedrine, bus stations,
> jazz, and negro lovers. I am the poet—
>
> so many ambulances ride by, in this city
> the old are dying in the cold,
> can't get their welfare checks, surplus food.
> I am the poet of overpasses,
> railroad yards and all night cafeterias

This poem, **"First Poem after Silence since Thanksgiving,"** offers a harmony of line break and rhythm enhanced by the dramatic placing and repetition of "I am the poet." Dark, metropolitan imagery stands over all, yet Wieners remains the great affirmer, echoing Walt Whitman in the lines: "I am the poet that stands between / the lover and his wife." Wieners binds himself to us, ending the poem with: "I am the poet of your life."

His editor once approached the poet, asking, "Is there a poem you've left to write?"

Wieners answered: "I want to write a poem about an old person dying of loneliness. I want to write a poem about an old person, alone in a room, dying of hunger and loneliness. No one has ever written a poem about an old person dying in the cold, of hunger and loneliness. Except, of course, Ava Gardner, who is always our master."

TITLE COMMENTARY

Selected Poems

GILBERT SORRENTINO (REVIEW DATE 1973)

SOURCE: Sorrentino, Gilbert. "Emerald on the Beach." *Parnassus* 1, no. 2 (1973): 121-5.

In the following review of Selected Poems, *Sorrentino objects to the selection of poems included, stating that it does not represent Wieners's best work and offers some examples of the poems he feels should have been chosen instead.*

The poems in this book are drawn from John Wieners' previous collections, starting with *The Hotel Wentley Poems* and ending with the remarkably beautiful *Nerves*, published in 1970. It is a reasonably good book for those readers who don't at all know Wieners, but it has the curious deficiency of making the work of these dozen years appear as a graph of subtle yet progressive stasis. The opposite is the fact, yet from this selection one would never know that *Ace of Pentacles* and *Nerves* are in every way more accomplished and mature than the *Wentley* collection. The problem lies in the selecting, of which more later.

Wieners has taken his world of drugs, despair, seamy and loveless sex and myriad defeats and made from it a powerful and singular poetry, a part of which is constituted of lyrics as beautiful as any written by an American poet in this century. He draws on everything for his poetic vocabulary—slang, popular song, bar- and party-talk, fragments of other verse, etc. At the core of the poems is a fine-drawn and fixed hopelessness in which beauty, love, nature and art itself are in no

way expected to right wrongs or ameliorate anything. In an odd way, Wieners is a religious poet, not, certainly, as Herbert is, but with similarities to Baudelaire. None of your "free and loving" acceptance of the earth's good here: guilt is real, and God is neither inside one nor a pal.

The poem, for such writers as Wieners, is not a way of improving one's life or fortunes, but is a kind of supplication to God, an offering given since there is nothing else to give. Taking Wieners this way, it is hard to conceive of a poet more out of the current swim. We live, it is no secret, in an age in which the contemporary poem is thought of, with increasing frequency, as a sort of slate on which any doodle may be scratched: the poem as placebo, as key to wisdom, as testament, confession, holy mystery, as tool to open any can of metaphysical soup. Or, the poem as intermediary between "life" and "art." In this thinking, the poem is rarely thought of as a finished product, a result, but as a conductor of ideas more important (of course) than the poor thing that conducts them. "Life is more important than art"is the banal motto on the banners of the true believers who exhaust you with their verbal electricity. These poems, replete with love of nature and mystical baloney, ooze and spread odorous slabs of Liederkranz. Nowhere can they be grasped, fixed, made to hold still so that one may determine of them their failure or success. Of course, they are not *meant* to fail or succeed, "uptight" conceptions indeed, if I know my kitsch. Things melt into each other, words slop and slide together, those cute and "vivid" images that Lovers of Poesie delight in extracting from the general morass glimmer at you from the pages and pages of slogging lines in which nothing is real but the "integrity of one's statement," etc., etc. Mystical baloney, to be sure, and sliced thick. Or sex as truth. The poet is delighted, in his effete and precious way, with the wonders of everyday life: a charming vase, a daisy (a real daisy!), a fantastic orgasm, his woman's full breasts, and on and on, good, good! yum-yum! As if the world were put here to amuse the intelligent and aware.

Wieners, on the other hand, is that most disconcerting of sports. His poems succeed or fail, written as they are out of an artistic sensibility. If his poem has saved his life, he doesn't tell you so in line after line. Nor are the poems flashed around like tailor's shears, cutting dandy suits in which to clothe his sensitive nature. At the risk of boring you to tears, let me say that Wieners grasps the materials of his life and refines them into art, which latter is long famed for being aloof from the artist's intent. If the idea does not carry itself over into the construction, too bad. As they say, just another long foul. Strike two! The poem explains nothing but its words: your new wife, your garden in the rain, your gallant doom—none of it matters in the least if the ear be tin or the poem a classroom blackboard. Some hick whose name I have forgotten recently wrote that "metaphor is real." That's the kind of magic you buy at the A & P. Five will get you ten that this same lout of the muses thinks that *Finnegans Wake* is "artificial." This is all funnier than W. C. Fields. The next step in this endless seminar is that "everything" is art, and that"everyone" is an artist. Meantime, Wieners, for one, gets on with his forms. His words glint against each other.

All the **Wentley** poems are in this book, wondrously charged early work that came, in the late fifties, sharply to the attention. At the time they seemed good, merely good, dazzled as we all were by that budding excitement of discovering that not all poems had to be written in the manner of Roethke or Auden. Now we can see that they have more than held their own against writings contemporaneous with them. But more importantly, Wieners has refined the language of these early poems into something gemlike, trusting it, all the way, to carry and structure his emotion. When he falters or seizes upon some aberrant manipulation of his form, he fails utterly:

> If thou in me the full flush of love see
> Know it comes from the rose that magnifies
> To breathe in some corner of that sure sky,
> A coarser blossom than eternity
> Likewise perishing and lost from earth
> To bloom anew in realms beyond pain
> Where fleshly vision cruel time disdain.

In these lines from **"Mermaid's Song,"** the stilted and clumsy rhyme forces the poet into inverted sentences, tortured syntax and a heavy, uncharacteristic use of abstract nouns to carry his meaning, a meaning which is never clearly etched. In **"Ally,"** a poem that is almost there, we find enormous ambiguities, none of which I take to be consciously made, but which are, on the contrary, the fruits of hurried and inexact syntax:

> My father's black ashtray
> hollowed out of 1930 foes
> of woe and death
>
> . . . . .
>
>   it stands here still
> to fill the sad stuffed cigarettes
> of Philip Morris, Ltd.

Is the word "foes" meant to stand for "cigarettes"? I think so, yet how is the ashtray hollowed

out of the cigarettes? And at the end of the poem, is it the ashtray that fills the cigarettes? How can that be? I don't want to be precious and insist that poems must have the logic of the philosopher or scientist, since that is exactly the logic that art has no use for. But here I speak of the bones of the poem, the syntax itself. Wieners is not a surrealist, he is not distorting language for a particular aesthetic end. This poem, quite simply, fails. When the syntax is questioned, it has no reply.

But these and other failures are, as I have said, there to be seen. Each poem holds itself, a closed system. One may say that Wieners' poems yearn toward perfection, they are not shards of a continuing process, but are lyrics. I mean, they are *unashamed* lyrics, ingeniously made scarecrows in the fields of corn. The reader can pick out specific flaws in every Wieners failure, they are functions of language. When he is working well, he can give us **"With Meaning,"** a poem that builds with the careful intensity of a sonata, and ends with a snap like a door being locked.

> Rise, shining martyrs
> over the multitudes
> for the season of migration
> between earth and heaven
>
> Rise shining martyrs
> cut down in fire
> and darkness,
> speeding past light
> straight through imagination's park.

and this poem closes—

> Yes rise shining martyrs
>
> out of your graves, tell us
> what to do, read your poems
> under springtime moonlight.
> Rise and salvage our century.

There are no tricks in **"With Meaning,"** none at all. The poem, like all of Wieners' poems, unravels before the eye, and as it moves to the poet's imagination, his sense of time, his manipulation of images, so it completes itself as an entity. One has the sense, almost always, of the poet feeling his way through his poem: as his intuition is right, so will his poem be right. When his intuition fails, his poem fails with it.

As I said at the beginning of this review, the one problem with this book, and it is major in that one expects a "selected poems" to contain the poet's best work, is in the selections themselves. I have no idea who was responsible for this selection, but if it was the editor, then he has no idea of Wieners' strengths. If it was the poet himself, the editor was remiss in not urging him to consider inclusion of those poems from *Ace of Pentacles* and *Nerves* that are necessary to an understanding of the poet's great gifts and accomplishment. I would say that a selection of Wieners' work, to be at all representative of post-*Wentley* writings, would have to include at least "Long Nook," "My Mother," "Dream," "Two Years Later," "Looking for Women," and "Forthcoming."

Finally, to support my opinion that Wieners, at the top of his form, is among the finest American poets of this century, this daring and perfect poem from *Ace of Pentacles*.

> "LONG NOOK"
>
> There she took her lover to sea
> and laid herself in the sand.
> Go up and undress in the dark.
>
> He is fast, was down the dune
> with silk around his waist.
> Her scarf was small.
>
> She opened her clothes to the moon.
> Her underarms were shaved.
> The wind was a wall between them.
>
> Waves break over the tide,
> hands tied to her side with silk,
> their mind was lost in the night.
>
> The green light at Provincetown
> became an emerald on the beach,
> and like stars fell on Alabama.

There is not a line in this miraculous poem not charged with risk. Yet the poem sings as if it were fated to be so constructed. It has the nobility of the inevitable that only the best art can claim.

Selected Poems, 1958-1984

ALLEN GINSBERG (ESSAY DATE 1986)

SOURCE: Ginsberg, Allen. Foreword to *Selected Poems, 1958-1984* by John Wieners, pp. 15-8. Santa Barbara, Calif.: Black Sparrow Press, 1986.

In the following essay, Ginsberg offers an overview of Wieners's poetry, emphasizing his wit in writing about sad themes and praising his gift for pure poetry.

John Wieners Speaks with Keatsian eloquence, pathos, substantiality, the sound of Immortality in auto exhaust same as nightingale. He presents emotion on the spot—despair, nostalgia, bliss of love, dissatisfaction, flesh pressing on flesh. And

Glamor, coming from desire for *Glamour:* "Paris Vancouver Hyannis Avignon New York and the Antilles" ("**The Windows**").

It's thrilling to watch the drama develop! After *The Hotel Wentley*'s commitment to the moment of Love, of Street, of Drug, glamors of the Underworld, Wieners then gives us retrospect of "**The Acts of Youth**," his supreme tragic American poem in rhymeless quatrain form. According to mode & morale of 19th century gnostic idealism, it ends with "Infinite particles of the divine sun."

Practical realism in the midst of glamor: "as we lie abed waiting for the pills to take effect." And practical realism in art, in relation to the moment of composition, an imprint of eternal prescience: "And the hand trembles / at the next word to put down." The poet's love-or-drug-hallucinated eye stares on reality, space, this universe—after being up all night on speedy narcotics that leave him awake as sun rises to notice "The color of the grass on Boston Common at dawn" ("**A Series**").

As that youthful idealism of *The Hotel Wentley Poems* dissolves in *Ace of Pentacles,* we see his intelligence delve deeper and deeper into the hole, or void, created by his imagination of an impossible love. This is chronicled in *Pressed Wafer, Asylum Poems,* and *Nerves*—three magisterial books of poetry that stand among the few truthful monuments of the late 1960s era.

There is a disciplined effort of spontaneity wherein we can read his mind. He leaves evidence of it in the casual conscious breaks in the verse—the urgency to remember what is being thought, capture the flash of enchantment in the mind pictures that pass, leaving words behind, arranged on the page the way they came, as thoughts rose clear enough to indite; so move by move we see his awareness of the line, the helplessness of the line, the inevitability of the line, displayed. Naked line, raw line, vulnerable line, a line of pain so fine it cannot be altered by primping or rougeing (i.e., correcting); his thought already was there, and left its mark:

> There is a new cross in the wind, and it is our
>
> minds, imagination, will
>
> where the discovery is made
>
> of how to pass the night, how to share the gift
>
> of love, our bodies, which is true
>   illumination
>   of the present instant.
>   ("**The blind see only this world . . .**")

And the story's rumored, that may never be told, of his romance with the European lady of means; his idyll like Rilke in a stately castle; the conception of a child—and the intrusion of another reality, abortion of his seed, rejection by the unique feminine glamor girl that could attract his romantic devotion.

John Wieners explains his condition clearly & early: "Poetry is a trance / of make-believe." And "it's a condition of gradual loss / of reality until there's only left / this shattering of the world" ("**Concentration**"). What's unique is the precise analysis of his situation, a common one for all of us, not only poets. "The shattering of the world" is universal, not merely Wieners' condition. He suffered it acutely, early, and without relief, but he does express, with strength, youth & clarity, the experience of one's grandmother, or old uncle, adrift in home for the aged, where one's world's taken away, or "Sunday evening / when one's parents feel old" ("**Determination**"). And it is this "**Concentration**" and "**Determination**" to persist in poetry that makes him poet amid the ruin of his life, of all our lives.

John Wieners' glory is solitary, as pure poet—a man reduced to loneness in poetry, without worldly distractions—and a man become one with his poetry. A life in contrast to the fluff and ambition of Pulitzer, National Book Awardees, Poetry Medalists from the American Arts & Letters & Poetry Academies—harmless bureaucratic functionaries among themselves, until the holders of these titles deny the pure genius of poets like John Wieners, in favor of society-minded misfits who drink flatter fuck & get interviewed, sucking up the attention of the young, who are misled into the study of minor poetry—till such books as this emerge from obscurity of decades, to reveal the true light of genius in the poem. And if this curse falls on myself, so be it, that John Wieners' genius may shine forth and be proclaimed by the authority of my own fame deserved or not.

Amazing how, though clinging to an emotional abstraction, or fixation, that takes him away from "reality" or himself, still details of the real world in all its sordid sacred flash remain vivid: "in gray mid-Manhattan / in mid-morning mist / as taxis splash through rain" ("**Consolation**"). Yet he knows that the emotional strategy of clinging can't last: "mad truth of these trysts to lose / in time their hidden passion & meaning" ("**Deprivation**"). This is of course a prophecy of what'll happen in his own poetry. How counter that strategy?

This book tells the story, a novel-like development of the drama—as in Shakespeare's sonnets, of the growth and decay of his singular passion.

"**Feminine Soliloquy**" coherently explains his fix, and his behavior. In the pit of his hell, he analyzes the odd steps that left him bereft—development of fantasy onanistic love since he was 12. This is one of the great analytic confessions I know of in U.S. literature. Written circa 1969, it explains the course of tragedy since *Wentley Poems* classics 1958.

"**Love-Life**" tells the result of this hopeless love: "Though the gift has gone. / The handwriting changed./ And the mind broken in two. / By such aimless arrow."

Now, "**Reading in Bed**," in order "to write a poem" one has "to pore over one's past / recall ultimate orders one has since doubted / in despair." He's set up an impossible situation for himself. This leads to a nervous condition: "I have sat here so often / in nervous trembling / this might be found out, with / a thousand pills in my stomach" ("**On the Back to the Cover of *The Algeria Poems***").

Where to go from here? That's the drama of the book. What development possible in this familiar stasis? That's the plot up to the end of *Nerves*. Next, a new definition of poetry's function for him: "Poetry is some way / of keeping in touch, / something to do / against staring at the wall, blankly. / It's some way / of filling loneliness / without politics" ("**Determination**").

So, *Behind the State Capitol*, a difficult book of the shattered mind, inventing a thousand recombinations. A thousand pieces, a thousand personae, a thousand pictures floating over the world.

Then in mental hospital another breakthrough, to social realization, "**Children of the Working Class**": an attack on God's created reality, on the lot & fate of the mad—a sudden awareness of a whole class of sufferers like himself, by what divine or human reason, outcast and deformed in America.

Later we find further political statement, "**After Dinner on Pinckney Street**," "How can a poor person matter in this world?" And an analysis of family & communal poverty that makes us all poor.

Behind the State Capitol makes an ideogrammatic picture of his mind, with a widening of subjects, and dissociation as method, after Charles Olson's dictum "One perception must directly lead to another." We have magical use of language, flashes of the mind working to subvert order, any order, and are left where we began—with the mystery of inspiration, the enigma of the poem.

Parallel with *State Capitol* (circa 1972-5) a number of poems of complete loneliness emerge, with various definitions of poetic friendship, rejection of false fame, estimates of the condition of middle and old age occupied by solitary art (e.g. "To Sleep Alone," "For Ed Dorn," "After the Orgasm," "Here for the Night"). Then Wieners fell into eight years of relative silence, curtly telling his friends "Poetry is not on my calendar" and "I am living out the logical conclusion of my books." And these were out of print.

By 1983, with the intervention of the editor of this book, poet Wieners began a new deliberation. He restates his spiritual themes, this time more playfully, with in fact comic treatment of the dilemma, almost Chaplinesque, the poet arrived to his own state of maturity.

Wieners always has an oddly humorous aesthetic floating on the surface of his somber reverie, or New Yorker glamor daydream. The puns & doubleplay or words almost dreamlike themselves suggest a mortal tangle too true & deep to be recognized in the gossip columns, a world of meat, drink, gambling, rich hotels, transvestite fellatio, married aristocrats, shopping, masturbation, tormented Pilgrim spirits. Tremendous morbid wit, derived from his stubborn resilient strain of New England genius (Emily Dickinson to Robert Creeley), is evident in swerve & switch of verse line & subject, last line moral, afterthought, or poem title.

ABOUT THE AUTHOR

ROBERT CREELEY ON WIENERS'S STATUS AS A POET

If "Beat" is to cover poets at the time who had, as John, put themselves entirely on the line—"At last. I come to the last defense"— then he was certainly one. But I think better to see him as *The New American Poetry* locates him, singular and primary—not simply as a "Beat" poet, nor defined only by drug use, nor a regional poet, nor one of a "school." Because that begs all the particulars of John's writing, his immense articulation of the situation and feelings in a relationship with another—literally, love. It's not a question of gay or straight—it's how we, humanly, are attracted to and moved by one another, how we know another as being here too. There is no greater poet of this condition than John.

Creeley, Robert. Quoted in "The Hipster of Joy Street: An Introduction to the Life and Works of John Wieners" by Pamela Petro. *Boston College Magazine* (online) <http://www.bc.edu/publications/bcm/fall_2000/ft_wieners.html> (fall 2000).

Cultural Affairs in Boston: Poetry & Prose, 1956-1985

ROBERT CREELEY (ESSAY DATE 1988)

SOURCE: Creeley, Robert. Preface to *Cultural Affairs in Boston: Poetry and Prose, 1956-1985* by John Wieners, pp. 11-2. Santa Rosa, Calif.: Black Sparrow Press, 1988.

In the following essay, Creeley comments on Wieners's realism and his ability to accurately portray common feelings.

The poetry of John Wieners has an exceptionally human beauty—as if there ever were any other. There is in it such a commonness of phrase and term, such a substantial fact of a daily life transformed by the articulateness of his feelings and the intensity of the inexorable world that is

forever out there waiting for any one of us. Charles Olson spoke of it as "a poetry of affect," by which I took him to mean a poetry that is in the process of a life being lived, literally, as Keats' was, or Hart Crane's, or Olson's own. In other words, the art becomes the complex act of "making real" all that one is given to live, and whatever in them may be style or fashion, the poems are so otherwise committed, so intensely a gesture of primary need and recognition, that their survival becomes the singular value, and their immense beauty.

In the brutal outrage of the late 1950's, when one could pick up a Government bulletin on the home manufacture of a bomb shelter at the post office, Mr. Wieners' painful survival in words became our own: "At last. I come to the last defense." There was nothing else to shelter or protect him. Time and again during the 60's one wondered, worried, whether he could make it. How specious such simply charitable impulse looks in retrospect. He *was* there, he *stayed* there—as Charles Olson once said, "he's *elemen-*

tal." His writing of this time is various, often magnificent, ringing curious changes on Augustan patterns. But whatever one would hope so to qualify becomes unequivocally clear in **"The Acts of Youth,"** that great poem of life's implacable realities and the will committed to suffer them.

If poetry might be taken as a distance, some space from the action, relief from the crowd, or if its discretions, what it managed to leave out, avoid, get rid of, were its virtue, then all these poems would be in one way or another suspect. They are far closer to a purported Chinese apothegm I read years ago and continue to muse on: "How is it far if you think it?" I don't truly know. It doesn't seem to be far at all. Nor do these poems, any of them, seem ever some place else, or where they move apart from an agent, either feeling or thinking. They're here, as we are—certainly a hopeful convention in all respects, but where else to meet?

The present collection is, then, an intense respect of this fact, and the range of its materials—three decades of poetry and prose—makes manifest the complex place from which all John Wieners' work finally has come, and to which it, as he also, insistently returns: "my city, Boston . . ." He said once to an interviewer, "I am a Boston poet," and there is no one for whom that city, or any other, has proved so determining and generative an experience. The changing faces of its presence and persons become articulate here in this dear man's immaculate art. Against the casual waste of our usual lives, his has proved a cost and commitment so remarkable. He has given everything to our common world.

We read together years ago at the 92nd Street Y in New York, with its great velvet curtain, raised stage. John remembered hearing Auden read there and was moved that now we would. He was thrilled that one might so follow, and so we did. But now, in these times so bitterly without human presence, risk, care, response, he becomes the consummate artist of our common voice, and his battered, singular presence our own.

JOHN WIENERS AND RAYMOND FOYE (INTERVIEW DATE 1988)

SOURCE: Wieners, John and Raymond Foye. Introduction to *Cultural Affairs in Boston: Poetry and Prose, 1956-1985* by John Wieners, pp. 13-7. Santa Rosa, Calif.: Black Sparrow Press, 1988.

In the following interview, Foye (who edited several of Wieners's books) asks Wieners about his early work, the influences on his poetry, and his slowed production in later years.

Our interview took place over the Christmas holiday, 1984. Mr. Wieners' apartment on Joy Street in Boston was gaily decorated for the season, with styrofoam reindeer, Santa Clauses, twinkling candles, elves made from red and green felt, and a plastic nativity scene perched atop the portable T.V. set in a corner of the bedroom. This is the same suite of rooms the poet has occupied for twelve years, and he tells visitors that he derives great pleasure from this corner of historic Beacon Hill. His three rooms are sparsely furnished. There is a front sitting room, a back bedroom where he sleeps and writes, and a guest bedroom. There are several bookcases but they are all empty. Old movie magazines and 1950s detective pulps collect on his bedside table, next to a copy of *Beyond Beauty* by Arlene Dahl. On the coffeetable in the front room Mr. Wieners has placed a black folio containing all of his work from the past two years.

A delicate porcelain Chinese bowl also sits on the table, filled to the brim with aspirin tablets, "for the guests," he explains. But Mr. Wieners is a genial host, and offers the pick of a bountiful cheese and fruit basket his sister Marion has sent for the holidays. Throughout the interview he smoked incessantly, but spoke in a relaxed manner. He occasionally rose to pace the room, or stood gazing out the window at the snowfall that had begun to dust the gold dome of the state capitol building.

At one point the phone rang, and it was his good friend Charles Shively, extending a dinner invitation in Cambridge that evening, which he accepted for both of us. Shively remains one of the few friends Wieners stays in touch with, and he has been a valued secretary, editor and publisher since the early seventies.

Mr. Wieners was eager for news of New York, and hoped to make his yearly visit over the New Year's. He asked about the repairs being made on St. Mark's Church, and inquired about a recent Cy Twombly exhibition. As we settled down to this interview, he turned on the radio, fiddled briefly with the dial, and found Billie Holiday singing "The Man I Love." The transcript captures some of the quixotic nature of his conversation, some of his wry and pithy delivery, but remains only a scanty residuum of any encounter with this rare poet, where the best is always left unsaid.

[*Foye*]: *What made up your mind to attend Black Mountain College?*

[Wieners]: They sent me train fare.

Recently I was reading some of your juvenilia, poems written as a student at Black Mountain.

Those were not supposed to be published.

I was surprised to find you writing in a very long line—Whitmanesque. Because your first book, **The Hotel Wentley Poems,** *is exceedingly spare. What precipitated that shift?*

I was starving, so I wrote lean poems.

Were you living at the Hotel Wentley?

For a summer. And hanging out in Bob's room. [La Vigne—R F.]

Was he away?

No, he was there.

It seems to have been a productive period.

Not really, I was reading, mostly, and watching Bob paint. It's hard to remember the follies of one's youth.

Do you ever miss San Francisco?

Not a day goes by that I don't think of it.

I noticed some tiny maps on your bedroom wall, of San Francisco, of Buffalo . . .

It's funny how these cities die when we leave them.

Who are the early influences on your poetry?

Edna St. Vincent Millay was the first. Later it was Charles Olson.

And at the time of the **Wentley** *poems?*

Olson, until 1973.

And who since then?

The Virgin Mary.

There aren't many books here, but I notice you're reading Melville.

He must have been wonderful company in those wooden frame houses!

I also saw the memoirs of Blaze Starr . . .

. . . from which I'm borrowing heavily for my own autobiography.

In assembling your **Collected Poems,** *you've been reluctant to reprint much of your early work.*

They're old faces I don't care to see again.

You've always spoken to me quite highly of Robert Creeley's work.

Oh yes, I'm mad about obtuseness!

I once saw a photograph of you, walking in San Marco in Venice, between Olson and Ezra Pound. Rather exalted company.

To say the least.

What was Pound like?

Oh, he was a mama's boy.

You once recommended to me translation, as a valuable exercise for a poet.

In teaching contrapunctus.

Can we talk about writing poetry?

I'm just the co-pilot.

Do you have a theory of poetics?

I try to write the most embarrassing thing I can think of.

Have you ever been bored by your great technical facility?

Yes.

Have you a preferred working method?

Confusion, usually.

Until the age of thirty-five, you were quite prolific as a poet, but as time went on, you wrote less and less.

When I first wrote poetry it was out of a need for personal expression. But as one works it's inevitable that one becomes more self-conscious, and it's so easy to slip into self-indulgence. And then the spontaneity begins to depart.

In that case it's better to stop?

Yes.

It seems to me a major shift took place in your work, circa 1972. You abandoned the terse, lyric poems for a more hallucinative prose style—more extroverted, and decidedly political.

I felt I'd exhausted my subjects at that point.

When I showed you what I'd assembled for the forthcoming Black Sparrow book [**Selected Poems: 1958-1984**—ed.] *you were somewhat taken aback by the size of it.*

My next book is going to consist of one word: Doris.

May we consult the texts? **Selected Poems, 1972.** *A poem called "Jive."*

That's rather promiscuous.

Do you remember writing each of these?

Oh yes.

"Monday Sunrise."

That was written out of Bellevue. On the eighth floor. You get a marvelous view of Manhattan and the East River. Don't be afraid if you ever get sent there, it's beautiful inside.

You've written several poems to painters.

I found them better company.

Than your fellow poets?

Yes, they were always too vampyric.

This one is to Delaunay ("The Windows").

It was requested by Mr. Schuyler who then worked for *Art News*. The idea was to publish poems derived from paintings. At the Farnsworth Collection in the Lamont Library at Harvard I used to look at the art books. And I came across this painting, which had been given to a poet. And I thought this might tie in. I stayed for three days, trying to equate each color or gesture with a sound. It was an attempt at approximation, without reference to thought. So the poem was rejected.

It was a little tenuous for Art News?

I was not capable of coherence then.

Yesterday we were talking of Lacan and you seemed to take a dim view.

To render psychology in terms of rationality is an outrage.

Do you ever tire of the literary life?

It never fags me.

You live very much alone, here in Boston. Are you disillusioned?

Oh, no. It's not possible to be disillusioned. Not when one lives in the Holy Spirit.

Your new poems are . . .

. . . scarce.

Well, they're that too. I think we've typed up about thirty pages.

Thirty pages from a fifty-year-old in 1984 is quite a lot, I think. But I am not ready to write my last book yet. I will write it in my old age.

And until then?

I am living out the logical conclusion of my books.

Is there a poem you've yet to write?

I want to write a poem about an old person dying of loneliness. I want to write a poem about an old person, alone in a room, dying of hunger and loneliness. No one has ever written a poem about an old person dying in the cold, of hunger and loneliness. Except of course Ava Gardner, who is always our master.

FURTHER READING

Criticism

Corbett, William, Michael Grizzi, and Joseph Torra, editors. *The Blind See Only This World: Poems for John Wieners.* New York: Granary Books, 2000, 109p.

A collection of poetic tributes to Wieners and his work.

Hornick, Lita. *Night Flight.* New York: The Kulchur Foundation, 1982, 191p.

Includes a chapter on Wieners.

Howard, Richard. "John Wieners: 'Now Watch the Windows Open by Themselves.'" *Iowa Review* 1, no. 1 (1970): 101-7.

Examination of Wieners's poetry.

Messerli, Douglas. "John Wieners and a 'Post Modernist' Quandry." *Sun and Moon: A Quarterly of Literature and Art* 2 (1976): 86-104.

Considers Wieners's poetry in the context of the norms and values of literary Postmodernism.

OTHER SOURCES FROM GALE:

Additional coverage of Wieners's life and career is contained in the following sources published by the Gale Group: *Contemporary Authors*, Vols. 13-16R; *Contemporary Literary Criticism*, Vol. 7; *Contemporary Poets*, Ed. 7; *Dictionary of Literary Biography*, Vol. 16; *Literature Resource Center*; and *World Poets.*

INDEXES

The main reference

Kerouac, Jack 1922-1969 **1:** 2, 14-18, 20, 21-25, 34,
37-41, 43, 49-52, 106-9, 118-21, 133-34, 141-42,
157-59, 161, 163, 164, 169-71, 179-80, 196, 213-14,
240-46, 305-6, 357-58, 363-68, 398-411; **2:** 113, 123-24,
127-30, 141-50, 318, 379-80, 490; **3:** 4-7, 9-11, 63,
63-142, 207-8, 272, 471

*lists the featured author's entry in either volume 2
or 3 of The Beat Generation; it also lists commentary on the featured author in other author
entries and in volume 1, which includes topics associated with the Beat Generation. Page references
to substantial discussions of the author appear in
boldface.*

The cross-references

See also AAYA 25; AITN 1; AMWS 3; BPFB 2; CA 5-8R;
CANR 26, 54, 95; CDALB 1941-1968; CLC 1, 2, 3, 5,
14, 29, 61; CPW; DA; DAB; DAC; DAM MST, NOV,
POET, POP; DLB 2, 16, 237; DLBD 3; DLBY 1995; GLL
1; MTCW 1, 2; NFS 8; RGAL 4; TCLC 117; WLC; WP

*list entries on the author in the following Gale
biographical and literary sources:*

AAL: Asian American Literature

AAYA: Authors & Artists for Young Adults

AFAW: African American Writers

AFW: African Writers

AITN: Authors in the News

AMW: American Writers

AMWR: American Writers Retrospective Supplement

AMWS: American Writers Supplement

ANW: American Nature Writers

AW: Ancient Writers

BEST: Bestsellers (quarterly, citations appear as
Year: Issue number)

BLC: Black Literature Criticism

BLCS: Black Literature Criticism Supplement

BPFB: Beacham's Encyclopedia of Popular Fiction:
Biography and Resources

BRW: British Writers

BRWS: British Writers Supplement

BW: Black Writers

BYA: Beacham's Guide to Literature for Young
Adults

CA: Contemporary Authors

CAAS: Contemporary Authors Autobiography
Series

CABS: Contemporary Authors Bibliographical
Series

CAD: Contemporary American Dramatists

CANR: Contemporary Authors New Revision
Series

CAP: Contemporary Authors Permanent Series

CBD: Contemporary British Dramatists

CCA: Contemporary Canadian Authors

CD: Contemporary Dramatists

CDALB: Concise Dictionary of American Literary
Biography

CDALBS: Concise Dictionary of American Literary
Biography Supplement

CDBLB: Concise Dictionary of British Literary
Biography

CLC: Contemporary Literary Criticism

CLR: Children's Literature Review

CMLC: Classical and Medieval Literature Criticism

CMW: St. James Guide to Crime & Mystery Writers

CN: Contemporary Novelists

CP: Contemporary Poets

CPW: Contemporary Popular Writers

CSW: Contemporary Southern Writers

CWD: Contemporary Women Dramatists

CWP: Contemporary Women Poets

CWRI: St. James Guide to Children's Writers

CWW: Contemporary World Writers

DA: DISCovering Authors

DA3: DISCovering Authors 3.0

DAB: DISCovering Authors: British Edition

DAC: DISCovering Authors: Canadian Edition

DAM: DISCovering Authors: Modules

> *DRAM:* Dramatists Module; *MST:* Most-
> Studied Authors Module;

> *MULT:* Multicultural Authors Module; *NOV:*
> Novelists Module;

> *POET:* Poets Module; *POP:* Popular Fiction and
> Genre Authors Module

DC: Drama Criticism

DFS: Drama for Students

DLB: Dictionary of Literary Biography

DLBD: Dictionary of Literary Biography Documentary Series

DLBY: Dictionary of Literary Biography Yearbook

DNFS: Literature of Developing Nations for Students

EFS: Epics for Students

EXPN: Exploring Novels

EXPP: Exploring Poetry

The Title Index alphabetically lists the titles of works written by the authors featured in volumes 2 and 3 of The Beat Generation and provides page numbers or page ranges where commentary on these titles can be found. English translations of foreign titles and variations of titles are cross referenced to the title under which a work was originally published. Titles of novels, dramas, nonfiction books, and poetry, short story, or essay collections are printed in italics; individual poems, short stories, and essays are printed in body type within quotation marks.

TITLE INDEX

The Subject Index includes the authors and titles that appear in the Author Index and the Title Index as well as the names of other authors and figures that are discussed in the Beat Generation set. The Subject Index also lists titles and authors of the critical essays that appear in the set, as well as literary terms and topics covered in the criticism. The index provides page numbers or page ranges where subjects are discussed and is fully cross referenced. Page references to significant discussions of authors, titles, or subjects appear in bold-face; page references to illustrations appear in italic.

A

SUBJECT INDEX